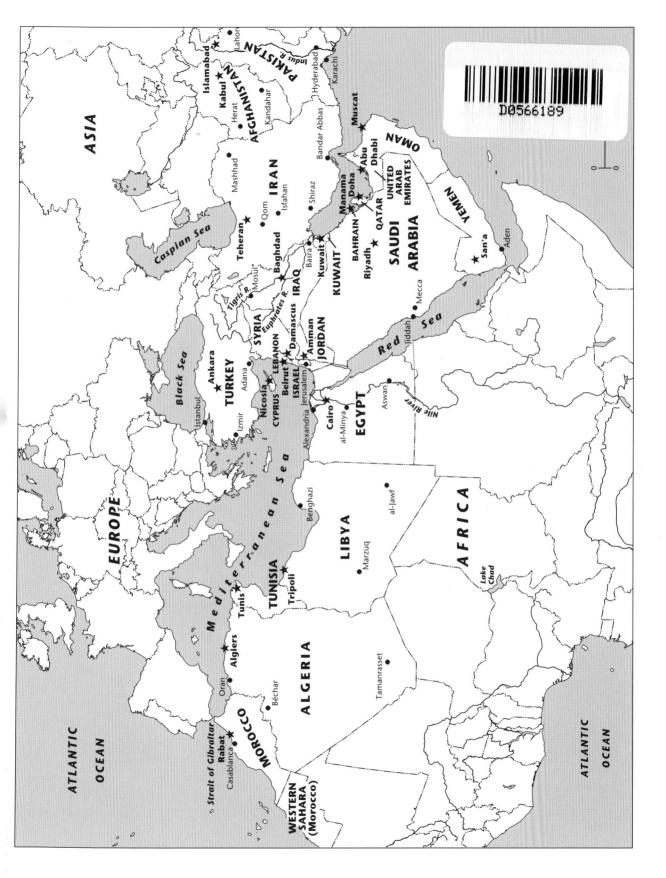

POLITICAL HANDBOOK
OF THE MIDDLE EAST
2006

INTERGOVERNMENTAL ORGANIZATION ABBREVIATIONS

Memberships in non-UN intergovernmental organizations are listed at the end of each country's section under Intergovernmental Representation. An asterisk in the list below indicates a nonofficial abbreviation. In the country profiles, associate memberships are in italics.

ADB	Asian Development Bank	ECO	Economic Cooperation Organization
*AfDB	African Development Bank		
*AFESD	Arab Fund for Economic and Social Development	EIB	European Investment Bank
		EU	European Union
AMF	Arab Monetary Fund	Eurocontrol	European Organization for the Safety of Air Navigation
AMU	Arab Maghreb Union		
AU	African Union	GCC	Gulf Cooperation Council
BADEA	Arab Bank for Economic Development in Africa	*IADB	Inter-American Development Bank
BDEAC	Central African States Development Bank	IDB	Islamic Development Bank
		IEA	International Energy Agency
BIS	Bank for International Settlements	Interpol	International Criminal Police Organization
BSEC	Organization of the Black Sea Economic Cooperation	IOM	International Organization for Migration
*CAEU	Council of Arab Economic Unity	IOR-ARC	Indian Ocean Rim Association for Regional Cooperation
CCC	Customs Cooperation Council		
*CEUR	Council of Europe	LAS	League of Arab States (Arab League)
Comesa	Common Market for Eastern and Southern Africa		
		*NAM	Nonaligned Movement
*CP	Colombo Plan for Cooperative Economic and Social Development in Asia and the Pacific	NATO	North Atlantic Treaty Organization
		OAPEC	Organization of Arab Petroleum Exporting Countries
*CWTH	Commonwealth	OECD	Organization for Economic Cooperation and Development
EBRD	European Bank for Reconstruction and Development		
		*OIC	Organization of the Islamic Conference

OIF	International Organization of the Francophonie	*PCA	Permanent Court of Arbitration
OPEC	Organization of the Petroleum Exporting Countries	SAARC	South Asian Association for Regional Cooperation
OSCE	Organization for Security and Cooperation in Europe	WEU	Western European Union
		WTO	World Trade Organization

PART ONE

INTRODUCTION

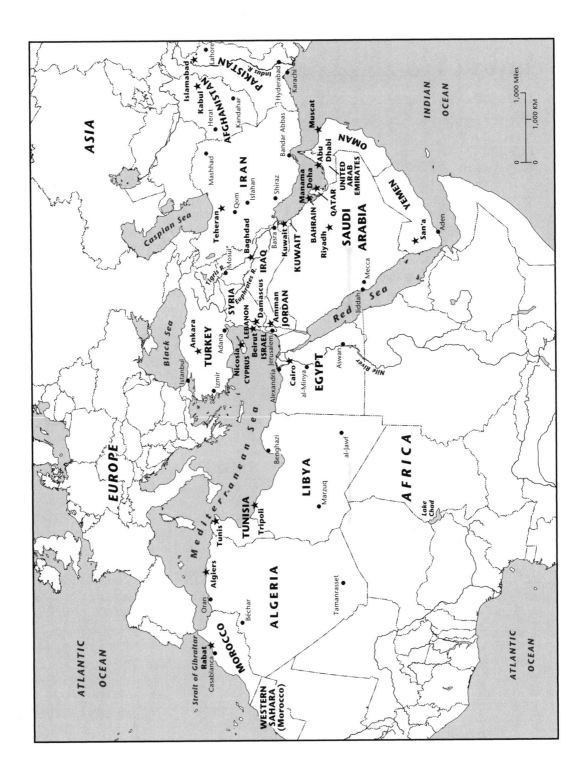

INTRODUCTION TO THE MIDDLE EAST

The geographical expanse of the Middle East consists mostly of arid countryside, although significant mountain ranges traverse landscapes in nearly all parts of the region. The Sahara, a natural demarcation between North Africa and sub-Saharan Africa, is the largest desert in the world, while the Empty Quarter (Rub al-Khali) in the Arabian Peninsula reigns as the largest sand expanse.

The stereotypical image of Middle Easterners as bedouin, or pastoralists, holds true in reality for a large but dwindling proportion of the population. At the same time, however, many of the region's inhabitants traditionally have been cultivators, fishermen, and traders. In the last century or so, economic development and the growth of industries and services have spurred the rise of cities, along with a large urban working class and a small but distinct middle class.

The Middle East is a well-recognized region of the world, but defining its limits can be problematic (see the map opposite). Under the most widely accepted definition, the Middle East includes the seventeen Arab countries plus the Palestinian territories and the non-Arab countries of Iran, Israel, and Turkey. Although Turkey, located mostly in Asia, is Muslim and shares a common history with its Middle Eastern neighbors, its aspirations to join the European Union sometimes lead to it being classified as a European country. (The US State Department includes it in its Bureau of European and Eurasian Affairs.) Predominantly Muslim Afghanistan and Pakistan, on the eastern side of the region, are also sometimes considered to be (non-Arab) Middle Eastern states because of cultural, historical, and political ties.

The Arab states can be divided into four groups based on their location. The Fertile Crescent—an arc stretching from the Mediterranean to the Persian Gulf and the site of some of the earliest known centers of civilization—includes Iraq, Jordan, Lebanon, and Syria. To its south lies the Arabian Peninsula, the site of seven states: Bahrain, Kuwait, Oman, Qatar, Saudi Arabia, the United Arab Emirates, and Yemen. In the Nile Valley, Egypt connects the region's Asian and North African territories. To the west lies the Maghreb—consisting of Algeria, Morocco, and Tunisia—with a Mediterranean coastline running to the Atlantic Ocean. Libya is sometimes included among the Maghreb countries.

Various criteria often serve to extend the boundaries of the Middle East. The Arab League, for example, counts among its members Eritrea, Mauritania, and Somalia although the inhabitants of these countries are neither ethnically Arab nor Arabic speakers. Because of cultural and historical ties, the countries of Central Asia are sometimes included in the region. The *Political Handbook of the Middle East* defines the Middle East as the seventeen Arab countries, in addition to Afghanistan, Iran, Israel, Pakistan, and Turkey.

The Middle East displays a great diversity in terms of ethnicity, culture, language, and religion. The majority of Middle Easterners are ethnically Arab, but the seventeen Arab states also contain significant populations of Azeris, Baluch, Berbers, Kurds, and black Africans. Azeris reside in the northwest Iranian region of Azerbaijan, and although of Persian origin, speak a Persianized Turkish language. Most Baluch, Sunni Muslims who speak Baluchi, live in southwestern Pakistan, but a sizeable number can be found across the border in Iran. Berbers are pre-Islamic inhabitants of North Africa and retain their own language. The Kurds, a distinct people speaking the Indo-European Kurdish language, are mostly Sunni Muslims who live in the mountainous area at the intersections of Iran, Iraq, Syria, and Turkey.

Most people in Turkey are ethnically Turkish, but large numbers of Kurds reside in the eastern region of the country; some Greeks live in the west. Israel was founded as a Jewish state, but many of its citizens are Arab. Iran, fundamentally a Persian state, contains sizeable minorities of Arabs, Azeris, Baluch, Kurds, and other groups. Arabic is spoken by more Middle Easterners than any other language, while Hebrew is the official language in Israel, Turkish in Turkey, and Persian in Iran.

Great diversity in religion also characterizes the Middle East. Muslims constitute the majority of the population by far. Most Muslims are Sunnis, adherents belonging to the mainstream, or "orthodox," branch of Islam. After the death of the Prophet Muhammad, to whom Allah revealed the Koran, the Islamic holy book, the community of Muslims elected his four immediate successors, or *caliphs*. Later, distant family members of Muhammad challenged for leadership of the Muslim community. Shi'ites, the largest variant sect among Muslims, broke away from the larger, Sunni community over this dispute, and the Islamic empire was never to again unite. In Shi'ite Islam, a line of hereditary *imams* (religious leaders) came to hold great sway and importance, providing leadership for the community. Today, there is no single leader of that community, and the same pertains for Sunni Muslims. Instead there exist numerous leaders with national or more local followers.

The Shi'ites further branched into various subsects. The largest group of Shi'ites believe that there were twelve imams and that the twelfth one will again return to lead his people. The great majority of Iranians are Twelver Shi'ites. Twelvers also form the majority in Iraq and Bahrain and are the largest confessional community in Lebanon.

They represent significant minorities in Kuwait and Saudi Arabia. More than one-third of Yemen's population belongs to a subsect of Shi'ites who believe in only five imams, and scattered throughout the region are small communities of yet another subsect who believe in seven imams.

In addition, Oman is home to Ibadis, an Islamic sect originating as part of the first community to split from the main branch of Islam and to elect imams chosen from the general population rather than based on Muhammad's lineage. Israel, Lebanon, and Syria are home to the Druze, a fiercely independent people who diverged from Islam in their belief in the divinity of several medieval Islamic rulers. The Alawites of Syria follow what is sometimes considered a separate religion derived originally from Shi'ite Islam. Their prominence far exceeds their numbers by virtue of their holding the top political positions in the country.

The region also contains many Christians and Jews. Most Christians belong to various Eastern rites, with the largest community being the Copts of Egypt. Other sects are found in Iraq, Lebanon, and Syria. Lebanon's Maronites are in communion with the Roman Catholic Church, while a number of Middle Eastern Christians have converted to Protestantism in the last century or so. Israel was created as a Jewish state, with its Jewish citizens immigrating in large numbers from elsewhere in the Middle East as well as from Europe and North America. Small Jewish communities remain in Egypt, Iran, Yemen, and the Maghreb.

The seventh-century emergence of Islam in Mecca, in western Saudi Arabia, transformed the Middle East and surrounding regions. In less than two centuries, Muslims had spread Islam to the extent that the Islamic world encompassed not just the Middle East, but much of Central Asia, northern India, the Iberian Peninsula, and present-day France. Islam expanded subsequently into Southeast Asia and sub-Saharan Africa. Although Arabs were the early leaders of the Islamic community, converts of other ethnicities soon rose to prominence in Islamic lands in politics, the military, religion, literature, and the sciences. The arrival of the Turks in the Middle East in the twelfth century helped shift the balance of power away from the Arabs. The Ottoman Empire, founded by Turks, more or less unified the Middle Eastern core of the Islamic world and extended its boundaries into southeastern Europe.

By the nineteenth century, the Ottoman state had become known as the "sick man of Europe," a decaying empire into which the European powers began to make inroads in the Middle East. In Egypt, Britain established a protectorate over the local ruler, who remained ostensibly a vassal of Istanbul, and in North Africa, France absorbed Algeria into metropolitan France. Istanbul's alliance with Germany during World War I provided France and Britain the opportunity, for which they had been waiting, to establish strongholds in the region. Using Indian troops, Britain invaded Mesopotamia (Iraq) and, after some setbacks, eventually wrested full control from its Ottoman defenders. In the Turkish-held areas of the Levant, Britain and France encouraged the so-called Arab Revolt and then sent an army to capture Jerusalem and Damascus. In addition, they launched a direct assault on Turkey at the battle of Gallipoli, which ended in disaster for the attackers.

By the end of World War I, the tattered Ottoman Empire had surrendered, and Kamal Mustafa, a Turkish army officer, took control of the Turkish heartland of the former empire. In a few short years, he had abolished the office of the caliph—the titular head of Islam and ruler of the empire—created the state of Turkey, and turned it toward secularism and Europe. The Arab lands fell under the subjugation of Britain and France. Although the two countries had promised the Arabs independence in return for their help in defeating the Ottomans, the secret Sykes-Picot Agreement of 1916 divided the Arab territories into European zones of influence. At the end of the war, these zones became mandates (protectorates) of the League of Nations under the control of these same European powers.

Britain took responsibility for Iraq (Mesopotamia), Palestine, Transjordan (the territory east of Palestine), and Egypt. France controlled Lebanon and Syria (both new states) and had already established protectorates over Tunisia and most of Morocco. Elsewhere in the region, Persia remained an independent though weak state, and Libya had become an Italian colony before the war. The new country of Saudi Arabia emerged in the Arabian Peninsula, while the small city-states of the Gulf were "protected" by Britain; Oman remained nominally independent though under British influence. North Yemen proclaimed its independence, but South Yemen became a British-protected area surrounding the colony of Aden.

As had happened in much of sub-Saharan Africa, in the Middle East new states rose as if from thin air, or more precisely, from lines drawn by colonial powers on maps. Lebanon represented a new creation, with boundaries drawn to ensure that the state contain a roughly equal number of Christians and Muslims. Syria similarly was cobbled together from various Ottoman districts. France, a republic, established republican forms of government in Lebanon and in Syria. The British Balfour Declaration of 1917 paved the way in Palestine for Jewish immigration, setting the scene for decades of Arab-Jewish confrontation.

Britain, a monarchy, established monarchies in its mandates. In Egypt, a royal line already existed, but Britain created two new states—Iraq and Jordan—with thrones for Hashemite kings. The Hashemi family traces its descent from the Prophet Muhammad, and its members served for centuries as the governors of Mecca. With the fall of the Ottoman Empire, the Hashemi family created an independent kingdom in al-Hijaz, the western part of the Arabian Peninsula that includes Mecca and Islam's second holiest city, al-Madinah (Medina). The kingdom was short-lived, however, as the Al Sa'ud family from central Arabia conquered al-Hijaz, incorporating it into what was to become the Kingdom of Saudi Arabia, stretching from the Persian Gulf to the Red Sea. To compensate the allied Hashemi family, Britain placed a Hashemite on the throne of Iraq, a unification of the formerly Ottoman regions of Baghdad, Basra, and Mosul. At the same time, the Europeans carved Transjordan out of the area east of the Jordan River to provide a throne for the other Hashemite king.

Although the imperial powers granted formal independence to their mandates in the 1920s and 1930s, they retained effective control over these states until well after World War II (apart from Italy, which lost Libya to British control during the war). Instability and conflict accompanied true independence. The founding of Israel in 1948 resulted in a prolonged war between the Jewish state and its Arab neighbors that settled little but the survival of Israel and the displacement of hundreds of thousands of Palestinians. Of the two Palestinian areas not absorbed by Israel, the West Bank was incorporated into Transjordan—which changed its name to Jordan—and the Gaza Strip along the Mediterranean fell under Egyptian administration.

A second Arab-Israeli war—the Suez War—took place in October and November 1956, when Israel, in collusion with Britain and France, invaded Egypt but was forced to withdraw under pressure from the United States. In June 1967, cross-border tensions escalated into a third war in which Israel overwhelmed its Arab opponents, capturing the Golan Heights from Syria, the West Bank and East Jerusalem from Jordan, and Gaza and the Sinai from Egypt. Six years later, in October 1973, the frontline Arab states of Syria and Egypt launched a surprise attack on Israel on the Jewish holy day of Yom Kippur (which was during the Muslim holy month of Ramadan) to regain territories lost in 1967. The attackers enjoyed initial success, but the war ended in a stalemate. Ultimately, however, the war would lead to the Egyptian-Israeli negotiations that culminated in the 1979 Camp David peace treaty between the two countries, permitting the return of Israeli-occupied territory to Egypt and the removal of Egypt from the ranks of the Arab "confrontation" states.

The most recent Arab-Israeli war occurred in 1982, when Israel invaded Lebanon in an attempt to destroy the Palestine Liberation Organization (PLO), which was based there and from whose territory the PLO launched attacks against Israel. Israeli forces eventually reached Beirut, forced the exile of the PLO leadership and evacuation of large numbers of fighters, and then withdrew to southern Lebanon, which it would occupy until 2000. During the course of the Israeli invasion, Syria—which had troops deployed in Lebanon ostensibly to help quell the civil war raging there—avoided engagement with the advancing Israelis, with whom its forces could not compete and win, and Jordan abstained from involvement.

Ideologies and Aspirations

The search for workable ideologies of political organization and socioeconomic development dominated the twentieth-century Middle East. Most of the ideologies embraced and then discarded were of European origin and leaned steadily toward the left. Their failure would leave political Islam seemingly in ascendance at the beginning of the twenty-first century.

Secular Ideologies

Long before the demise of the Ottoman Empire, the Arab nation had searched for an appropriate path for gaining independence and advancing its political and economic development. For a century, the favored paths consisted of secular ideologies. Not surprisingly, the first to appear, in the late nineteenth century, was that of nationalism. In the minds of Arab intellectuals and the educated, the Arab Revolt of World War I represented a step toward the creation of an independent state (or states), and for the first time in history, a specifically Arab state. Thus, the imposition of mandates came as a severe blow. Nevertheless, Arab elites continued to stress nationalism as a way of gaining independence for individual entities. With formal (or *de jure*) independence, these elites turned their attention to the European principles of liberalism, constitutionalism, and parliamentary democracy. The Egyptian Wafd, founded in 1919, became one of the first parties in this vein to organize. Its name translates as "the delegation," as its founders had sought unsuccessfully to plead their case before the conference drafting the Treaty of Versailles, which ended World War I. The liberal nationalists were, however, discredited, first by their willingness to cooperate with the mandate powers, then by the unbridgeable gap between new government structures and indigenous institutions, and finally by corruption and support only by elites.

The nationalists found their appeal superseded by other ideologies after World War II and the debacle of the Arab defeat in the first Arab-Israeli war of 1948–1950. In the postwar Middle East, Egyptian leader Gamal Abdel Nasser rose to typify the new breed of pan-Arab nationalist. Nasser seized power in 1952 in the name of the Free Officers, fellow young military officers disgusted by their government's corruption and unresponsiveness. This bloodless coup established a trend throughout much of the Arab world that would define the 1950s and 1960s. Nasserism was not a coherent, articulated ideology, but it embraced the themes of pan-Arab nationalism, anti-imperialism, state socialism, and the redress of social inequalities. The principles of the Baath Arab Socialist Party, founded in the 1940s, were similar to Nasserism in the emphasis on pan-Arab nationalism, state socialism, and the need for revolutionary action to reform Arab politics. Although Baathism arose as an intellectual movement, implementation of the ideology came about when military officers who seized power through coups and countercoups adopted it in Iraq and Syria. The battleground was thus set for an "Arab cold war" between the traditional monarchies and revolutionary and progressive regimes.

Revolutionary forces followed the Egyptian Free Officers' example in deposing the monarchies in Iraq in 1958, in Yemen in 1962, and in Libya in 1969. Some monarchies and more traditional republics proved more resilient than expected. Saudi Arabia and the smaller states of the Gulf persevered, because their political systems were extensions of traditional tribal and social institutions. The kings of Jordan and Morocco maintained their positions in part because of their religious appeal as descendants of the Prophet Muhammad as well as through astute leadership. The shah of Iran based his right to rule on a falsely claimed descent from 2,500 years of Persian kingship, but buttressed his position by encouraging modernists and repressing dissent.

Israel, by virtue of its history, was unique in the region although its founders based their ideology on the familiar notions of nationalism and socialism. Zionism had emerged in Europe as a form of Jewish nationalism, based on the creation of a Jewish state in Palestine to serve as a Jewish homeland. The push for statehood intensified before, during, and after World War II because of Nazi policies and atrocities against the Jews.

Disillusionment with pan-Arab socialism set in as Nasser held tight to power in Egypt, and military rulers in Syria and Iraq degraded Baathism in using it to serve their own political interests. Some intellectuals continued to espouse leftist ideologies, particularly proponents of the Arab nationalist movement and Marxism. Putting these ideologies into practice, however, proved impossible almost everywhere—the exception being in impoverished South Yemen—because of their limited appeal to only a few activists and intellectuals. Even in South Yemen, the quasi-Marxist experiment proved ill-suited to a largely rural, tribal society.

Arabs came increasingly to see the progression of secular ideologies as a series of wrong paths because of their inability to confront Israel militarily, measurably improve living standards, create better and more efficient government, unify the Arab nation, and engage the active support of the masses. Thus the march of revolution in the region, which seemed inevitable in the 1950s and 1960s, slowed and stalled as revolutionary regimes became more authoritarian and elitist. Meanwhile, traditional regimes continued to survive and prosper, aided in some states by oil revenues. Quite naturally these governments resisted political change although their citizenry increasingly sought it.

Islamist Ideologies

State corruption and disillusionment with secular ideologies led to renewed interest in political Islam in the Middle East. Islamic reformers began to emerge during the same period in the late nineteenth century that currents of nationalist and liberal thought began to circulate in the Middle East. Whereas the earliest of these reformers, typified by Jamal al-Din al-Afghani, espoused pan-Islamism and the combining of Islamic values with European science, later reformers held different ideas.

One branch, the "reformers," saw the decline of Islam as being due to the rigidity of political thought and sought to reform Islam with new institutions and skills to meet the demands of modern life. Another branch, the "rejectionists," argued that European thinking and technology had subjugated the Islamic world, because Muslims had lost the qualities that had made the Islamic world great in previous times; according to them, the proper strategy called for rejecting Western influences and returning completely to "pure" Islam. The rejectionist path attracted little support in the first half of the twentieth century. The more moderate reformist path became lost amid the attractions of secular ideologies, and the state attacked groups such as the Muslim Brotherhood in Egypt.

Despite the proliferation of secular regimes, Islam was never completely divorced from government and politics in the Middle East. Constitutions (apart from those of Israel and Lebanon) proclaimed the state to be Islamic, and states retained *shari'a* (Islamic law) in the areas of personal and family law. Many Muslims remained pious, and their culture identity continued to be clearly informed by Islam. Over time, an almost schizoid dichotomy developed, with these secular states governing Islamic societies, an occurrence somewhat paralleled in Israel in relations between Labor Party—led governments and ultra-religious Jews.

The Muslim Brotherhood, founded in Egypt in 1928, is one of the earliest and longest surviving Islamist groups. It advocates a return to the tenets of Islam (as it interprets them) to address the political, economic, and social issues of the modern age. The Brotherhood spread first among the lower classes and gradually assumed a more political role. Banned by the Egyptian government in 1948, the organization retaliated by assassinating Prime Minister Mahmud Nuqrashi later in the same year. It refused to recognize Nasser's

revolutionary government and was severely repressed after attempts on his life. Although forced underground, the Brotherhood still managed to establish branches in other countries. Some of its followers found jobs in Saudi Arabia, where they influenced a new generation of Wahhabis.

Wahhabism, the predominant form of Islam in Saudi Arabia, is based on the teachings of eighteenth-century religious reformer Muhammad Abd al-Wahhab. He denounced the corruption of Islam and, like other reformers, called for a return to "pure" Islam. The Wahhabis do not constitute a separate sect, but rather practice a very conservative form of Sunni Islam. They go further than other Sunnis in banning music, the mixing of the sexes in public, and the veneration of shrines and graves. Wahhabis also created a type of religious police to enforce conformity to Islamic requirements in public and to ensure that the population adheres to the tenet of prayers five times a day. The founding of the modern state of Saudi Arabia, with its oil-driven prosperity, development, and educational system, softened the edges of Wahhabi practices, but the influx of Muslim Brothers and other conservatives aided in the growth of an archconservative backlash. These radicalized Wahhabis burst onto the scene with a takeover of the Great Mosque in Mecca in 1979.

Islamists of varying kinds began to grow in numbers in other parts of the Middle East. In the 1960s and 1970s, Westerners popularly referred to this phenomenon as *Muslim fundamentalism,* based on the Christian experience of fundamentalism, though it has different connotations. The term *Islamist* is more appropriate in defining this "fundamentalism" among Muslims and its adherents. In general, it refers to those people who in turning away from the perceived "looseness" and indirection of modern society also become more religious. These Islamists want society and the state to adopt stricter Islamic practices, such as reinstituting the shari'a as the basis of all law, banning alcohol and pork, and enforcing modesty and conformity in dress for men and women. On another level, however, are Islamists compelled to move beyond the peaceful advocacy of stricter measures and into violent opposition to governments and secularist society. These radical Islamists, or Islamist extremists, made their presence felt first in Iraq, a heavily secularized state, in the 1950s and 1960s. In the 1970s in Egypt, they drew adherents away from the Muslim Brotherhood into more reactionary groups, such as al-Jihad, which assassinated President Anwar al-Sadat in 1981 and attacked foreign tourists. The largely Shi'ite radical Islamists in Iraq also influenced counterparts in Iran. Ayatollah Ruhollah Khomeini, the leader of 1979 Iranian Revolution, spent fifteen years in Iraq in the Shi'ite holy city of Najaf.

The Iranian Revolution undoubtedly catalyzed the reemergence of Islamist thought and the radical Islamist presence in today's Middle East. In one sweep, the movement deposed an authoritarian monarch (the shah), reversed the process of secularization, trumpeted justice for the working classes, and enforced the observance of a conservative view of Islam. It also initially espoused the spread of "Islamic revolution" to the rest of the region. Most important, the Iranian Revolution put conservative religious leaders, or *mullahs,* in charge of government as well as social conventions. In part, this new, elevated role for mullahs resulted from the emergence of Ayatollah Khomeini, a highly respected Islamic scholar, as the symbol of and most prominent figure of the revolution. It also represented a reestablishment of the clerical oversight of politics that had been a unique feature of the Twelver Shi'ite Islam prevalent in Iran.

In the region in general, as authoritarian and corrupt governments refused to or were unable to improve standards of living for the masses, Islamist movements grew in popularity, especially because they provided social services and financial assistance denied by government. Although the Iranian Revolution reverberated into the early 1980s, its lasting influence would largely be inspirational, rather than guiding, as traditional Arab-Persian and Sunni-Shi'ite antipathies came to the fore. The revolution encouraged the creation and growth of other Islamist movements throughout the Middle East and the Islamic world beyond. Some of the movements' adherents saw themselves as a "loyal opposition" to existing regimes, while others chose to work underground against governments they regarded as corrupt and illegitimate.

In Algeria, the Islamic Salvation Front (FIS) gained in popularity, and during elections held in 1992, many in Algeria and abroad feared that if the FIS won, it would change the constitution and eliminate the electoral process. The government, panicked after the FIS won large majorities in the preliminary round of voting, cancelled final elections. The government's action led to a long, brutal civil war between the FIS and more extremist groups on one side and the government and its supporters on the other. In Lebanon, the plight of the long-downtrodden Shi'ites led to the formation first of the group al-Amal to protect their political interests during the civil war that erupted in 1975–76 and then to the founding of Hezbollah, created and supported with Iranian backing with the purpose of carrying out a militant defense of the communities' interests against opposing Lebanese forces and Israeli troops occupying southern Lebanon. The failure of the PLO—founded in 1964 to oppose Israeli control of Palestine—to achieve an independent Palestinian state led to the founding and growth of Hamas and Islamic Jihad, Islamist organizations committed to providing services to impoverished and neglected Palestinian communities and to more forcefully challenging Israeli occupation. With the outbreak in 2000 of the al-Aqsa *intifada,* the second popular uprising against Israeli occupation, Hamas and Islamic Jihad became more widely known in the West for dispatching suicide bombers to carry out attacks against Israeli military targets and civilians.

Authoritarianism and Democratization

Political deficiencies throughout the Middle East provided the fertile ground for Islamists to nuture opposition to the status quo that earlier leftist secular ideologies had planted. Nearly half a century after the emergence of the Arab cold war, the Arab world remains divided between progressive republics and traditional monarchies. Although the phenomenon of army-led "revolving door" coups in countries such as Syria and Iraq has ceased, the civilian leaders of such republics continue to rely on authoritarian methods and showcase elections to maintain power. Several states are on the verge of becoming "hereditary republics," whereby leaders pass on their positions to their sons. This happened in Syria in 2000, when Bashar al-Assad succeeded his late father, Hafiz al-Assad, as president. Husni Mubarak in Egypt, Mu'ammar al-Qadhafi in Libya, and Ali 'Abdallah Salih in Yemen have all been grooming their sons for succession, as did Saddam Hussein in Iraq before the 2003 invasion and war overthrew his government.

In some ways, the balance in the struggle for supremacy has shifted from the republics to the monarchies. The last demise of a monarchy occurred in Libya in 1969. Undoubtedly the longevity of the monarchies in the Gulf has been aided by oil revenues used to create the most comprehensive systems of economic infrastructure and social welfare in the region. Like the republics, monarchical governments maintain tight control over their populations and either prohibit or limit political participation. The durability of monarchies has been aided as well by the emergence of new "reformist" leaders, among them Mohamed VI in Morocco, 'Abdallah II in Jordan, and 'Abdallah in Saudi Arabia.

The three non-Arab states differ politically from the Arab states as well as among themselves. Israel is by far the most democratic state in the region, with free elections to the Knesset (parliament) and for prime minister. Lively debate takes place among political parties espousing a wide range of ideologies, as reflected in the country's eclectic free press. At the same time, however, deep divisions exist between Israel's Jewish majority and its Arab citizens, who perceive themselves relegated to second-class status. Social and economic distinctions also are evident between Jews of European origin, who have dominated Israeli politics since its founding, and other Jews, primarily from Arab lands, who remain poorer. The right-wing Likud Party won the 1977 elections for the first time because of the defection from the left-wing Labor Party by Sephardic Jews (of African and Asian origin) after years of being ignored.

The most fundamental and festering political problem facing Israel, however, is its relations with the Palestinians. Israel occupies or through other means controls the West Bank, East Jerusalem, and Gaza, but it does not exercise sovereignty over the Palestinians, who remain in a decades-long limbo, impoverished, restricted in their relations with other Arabs, and increasingly banned from available jobs in Israel. A deepening cycle of violence appears to be the primary consequence of fundamental disagreement over the fine points of a peace plan: Israeli domination begets Palestinian resistance—such as attacks on Israeli settlers and soldiers in the occupied territories as well as targets in Israel—which begets overwhelming Israeli retaliation against the Palestinians.

Turkey has been a functioning democracy in theory since its founding nearly a century ago. Its democratic principles, however, have been tested by the usurpation of authority by the military—claiming to act as guardians of the state—on several occasions. The great majority of Turkey's people are Muslim, while the state has been avowedly secularist, largely opposed to a role for Islamists, and committed to seeking entry into the European Union. Its relations with its large Kurdish population in the east have been problematic and violent, and the post-2003 situation in Iraq—with the consolidation of a nearly independent and possibly expansionist Kurdish state in the north—has not helped the situation. Meanwhile in Iran, the state has held free elections for the Majlis (parliament) and for the presidency, although the mullahs have created a great deal of controversy and protest in denying some candidates access to the ballot.

All the predominantly Muslim countries of the Middle East have experienced a sustained debate in one form or another over the compatibility of democracy and Islam. At the two extremes of the debate are the modernists, who argue that the Islamic world must adapt to today's world and accept democratic principles as a fundamental human right, and the Islamists, who contend that there is no need for democracy in the Islamic world because Islam provides all the necessary answers, and a true Islamic state would govern according to divine, and therefore just, principles.

Terrorism

The roots of terrorism in the Middle East stem generally from the region's political instability, dissatisfaction with the domination of politics and economics by small elites, and perceptions of Western domination and interference. Much of the Middle East experienced European colonization, and many of its people believe that the West continues to exercise a kind of neocolonialism through political and military support of friendly regimes. Many people in the region regard Western culture as immoral and its intrusion as corrupting. Some view this cultural invasion as part of a broader strategy to increase Western control over the Middle East. In the minds of many Arabs and other Muslims, Israel is a Western creation with the aim of weakening the Arabs and the Islamic world.

Political violence has been an unfortunate feature of the region throughout the modern era. Revolutions in various states in the 1950s and 1960s often resulted in the widespread killing of enemies, and radical elements have often employed assassination to achieve their goals. Such is not, however, only an Islamic phenomenon. Jewish terror groups operated in Palestine before Israeli independence in 1948, and Christian groups engaged in terrorist activities during the Lebanese civil war of the 1970s and 1980s. In addition, certain states have also used assassination and terrorist activities against neighboring states and to maintain or enhance control internally.

Terrorism has for several reasons been on the rise in the Middle East in recent decades. Palestinian groups have carried out violent actions with the aim of regaining control of Palestine almost since Israel became independent. Such activity came to international attention in the late 1960s and early 1970s with operations by the Popular Front for the Liberation of Palestine (PFLP) and Black September, fringe secular groups, carried out to raise awareness of the Palestinian cause. The PFLP hijacked a number of civilian airliners bound to or from Israeli airports. Its hijacking of four airliners to remote airstrips in the Jordanian desert sparked a civil war between King Hussein's government and Palestinian forces in his country whose presence threatened to become a "state within a state," challenging the king's legitimacy. Events reached a head in September 1970, when the Jordanian military crushed the Palestinian forces, leading to their relocation to Lebanon. These hostilities, which became known as Black September, provided the inspiration for the shadowy Black September organization that gained notoriety in 1972 for taking Israeli athletes hostage during the Munich Olympics, resulting in the death of the hostages, some of the kidnappers, and a German policeman.

The United States has accused several Middle Eastern countries of "state-sponsored terrorism," a concern that has recently grown with efforts to acquire weapons of mass destruction (WMD). In January 1986, the United States banned trade with Libya and froze Libyan government assets in the country after Palestinian gunmen with ties to the Libyan government attacked Israeli El Al ticket counters at the Rome and Vienna airports. A few months later, in April, the United States carried out an air strike against Libya after determining that it had been involved in the bombing of a Berlin nightclub. In 1988, a Pan Am flight exploded over Lockerbie, Scotland, and in 1989 a French airplane blew up over Niger. In both cases, Western governments identified Libyan intelligence officials as having been involved. Libyan leader Mu'ammar al-Qadhafi's refusal to extradite the officials resulted in the adoption of economic sanctions by the UN Security Council. The deteriorating economic situation in Libya eventually forced the government to hand over the suspects in 1999 and compensate the victims' families. The United Nations lifted sanctions, and Libya normalized relations with most countries, with the exception of the United States.

The US government has been concerned about Iranian support for terrorist activities as well. Some government factions in postrevolutionary Iran had sought to export the revolution to neighboring countries and against perceived enemies. Arab and Western support for Iraq during the Iran-Iraq War, from 1980 to 1988, only heightened Iranian animosity. Bahrain accused Iran of supplying and assisting a number of Shi'ite dissidents arrested and charged in 1981 with plotting a coup. Iran was also suspected of aiding local Shi'ite activists who bombed several embassies in Kuwait in 1983.

Iranian-Saudi relations, troubled since the revolution, worsened during the Iran-Iraq War. In 1986 Iranian pilgrims making the *hajj,* the annual pilgrimage of Muslims from around the world to the holy city of Mecca in Saudi Arabia, attempted to smuggle in explosives. The following year, 400 people died in a clash between Iranian demonstrators and Saudi police during the pilgrimage. In 1989 Saudi Arabia executed sixteen Kuwaitis convicted of detonating bombs in Mecca, allegedly with Iranian assistance. In 1996 a truck bomb exploded at the US military barracks in al-Khobar, killing several dozen personnel. The United States accused Iran of working through Saudi Hezbollah—an offshoot of the Lebanese Hezbollah—to carry out the attack, but the connection was never proven, and suspicions later centered on al-Qaeda.

The United States points to Teheran's support for Hezbollah in Lebanon as evidence of Iranian involvement in terrorism. An offshoot of al-Amal, the principal Lebanese Shi'ite party, Hezbollah gained attention in the 1980s when it took part in the kidnapping of Westerners. The group later took the lead in resisting the Israeli occupation of southern Lebanon and is widely credited with making the cost of the occupation too high for Israel to sustain. It further bolstered its reputation by providing much-needed social services in Lebanese Shi'ite communities and later joined the Lebanese government. The United States placed Hezbollah on its list of terrorist organizations, but other Western countries did not follow its lead.

Western classification of terrorism and terrorist groups in the region has become a contentious issue. The Arab world has rejected the US designation of Hezbollah as a terrorist group, regarding it instead as a legitimate resistance group against Israeli occupation. Islamist Palestinian organizations, particularly Hamas and Islamic Jihad, gained in prominence while resisting the Israeli occupation of the West Bank, Gaza, and East Jerusalem during the second intifada. As with Hezbollah, their appeal in part derived from their provision of social services, in addition to opposition to corruption within the Palestinian Authority. Their popularity also rested, however, on their frequent attacks on Israeli soldiers and settlers and use of suicide bombers against civilian targets in Israel. The United States and Israel condemned Hamas and Islamic Jihad as terrorist organizations while much of the Arab world viewed their actions as legitimate forms of resistance. Their success inspired non-Islamist Palestinian groups—such as the al-Aqsa Martyrs' Brigade, a breakaway faction of Fatah, the largest and dominant group within the PLO—to adopt similar tactics.

In recent years, terrorism in the Middle East has been carried out largely by Islamist extremists. The most well known of these have belonged to or been associated with al-Qaeda, headed by Osama bin Laden, one of many sons of a successful Saudi contractor of Yemeni origin. Bin Laden counted himself among the thousands of "Afghan Arabs," Muslim volunteers who traveled to Afghanistan to fight the Soviet occupation from 1979 to 1989. Many of these fighters returned to their homelands radicalized by the experience and their conversion to an extremist worldview of an Islamic world under attack by nonbelievers. Upon his return to Saudi Arabia, bin Laden began organizing and gathering followers to fight back.

Bin Laden and Abd al-Aziz Azzam, a Palestinian religious theorist, had agreed that the organization they had established in Afghanistan should continue. This they developed into al-Qaeda (meaning "base," or "foundation"), whose goals would include creating a corps of Islamist volunteers to fight non-Muslims wherever they threatened Islamic lands and to overthrow Muslim-led governments perceived as being corrupt and anti-Islamic. After Azzam's assassination in 1989, bin Laden became the unquestioned leader of al-Qaeda, with prominent roles played by two Egyptians: blind cleric Omar Abdel Rahman (whose followers assassinated President Anwar al-Sadat in 1981 and attacked the World Trade Center in New York in 1993) and Ayman al-Zawahiri (who facilitated the Egyptian al-Jihad's merger into al-Qaeda).

As bin Laden's ideology grew more radical and he began recruiting followers, he relocated in 1991 to Sudan, then dominated by an Islamist movement. After international pressure forced the Sudanese to expel him, he found refuge in Afghanistan, where the extremist Taliban regime had taken power. The Taliban (meaning "the students"), educated at radical Islamic religious schools in nearby Pakistan, had seized power in Afghanistan with the goal of restoring their version of the pure Islamic state, free from outside influences. After taking up residence in Afghanistan, bin Laden established camps there to train al-Qaeda members in terrorism and guerrilla warfare.

In 1998 bin Laden and Zawahiri issued a *fatwa,* a religious declaration, declaring that because the United States had waged war on God and his messenger, Muhammad—by propping up corrupt regimes, supporting Israeli occupation of Muslim lands and holy sites, and carrying out attacks and sanctions on Iraq—Muslims were duty bound to carry out attacks on Americans everywhere. The first strike against a US target—the underground bombing of the World Trade Center in New York that killed six persons—had taken place previously, in 1993. In 1998 al-Qaeda carried out bombings against the US embassies in Kenya and Tanzania, killing several hundred people, mostly Africans. The organization was also implicated in the killing of US servicemen in Saudi Arabia and Somalia. In 2000 the group attacked the USS *Cole,* in the harbor of Aden, Yemen, killing 17 sailors.

The most brazen al-Qaeda operation thus far is the carefully planned attack launched on September 11, 2001. Preliminary steps began a year and a half before the event, when some of the participants enrolled in flight schools in the United States. Of the 19 hijackers involved, 15 were from Saudi Arabia, possibly in a deliberate attempt to damage US-Saudi relations. Early on the morning of September 11, four separate groups of hijackers boarded airplanes in Boston, Newark, and Washington, and after seizing control of the planes, flew two of them into the World Trade Center towers in New York and crashed one into the Pentagon outside Washington, D.C. The fourth planed crashed in Pennsylvania countryside after passengers challenged the hijackers. The death toll from the multiple attacks was 3,126.

When the Taliban ignored a US demand to shut down al-Qaeda's camps and hand over bin Laden, the United States launched a ground invasion of Afghanistan, capturing the country's main cities and driving the Taliban from power. Taliban leader Mullah Omar and al-Qaeda's leaders escaped and remained free as of late 2005. Believed to be hiding in the mountainous border region between Afghanistan and Pakistan, bin Laden and Zawahiri periodically issue videos and audio recordings threatening their enemies and exhorting their sympathizers to carry on the fight. Meanwhile, the United States helped establish a new government in Afghanistan, with Hamid Karzai appointed as president. A subsequent election in 2004 confirmed him in office.

Following the attacks on September 11, President George W. Bush declared that the United States would pursue a "global war on terror." His administration extended economic and other assistance to countries with radical Islamist insurgencies and those cooperating in the fight against terrorism. Bush and members of his administration cited the war on terror in part to justify invading Iraq in 2003. Links between Saddam Hussein's Iraqi regime and Islamist terrorists were never established, but attacks against US military targets, Iraqi civilians, and foreigners escalated in Iraq in the chaotic security situation after the fall of Hussein's government. Although Iraqi insurgents carried out many attacks, all those involving suicide bombers were the product of Islamist extremists. The supposed leader of the Islamists, Jordanian Abu Musab al-Zarqawi, declared his allegiance to bin Laden and claimed to lead the semi-independent organization al-Qaeda in Iraq.

The controversial treatment of prisoners taken during the wars in Afghanistan and Iraq and as part of the overall war on terror fueled suspicions about perceived US anti-Muslim attitudes. Although the status of the Guantanamo prisoners raised questions from the start, it gained added attention in the aftermath of the revelation in April 2004 that American soldiers had abused prisoners at the Abu Ghraib prison in Baghdad. Numerous non-Afghans were captured on suspicion of membership in or at least connections with al-Qaeda during the Afghan war. President Bush declared some 700 of these captives "enemy combatants," denying them prisoner-of-war status and transporting them to the US military base at Guantanamo Bay in Cuba or holding them at Bagram Air Base in Afghanistan and on Diego Garcia Island in the Indian Ocean. They were interrogated in secret, without access to attorneys, and confronted with the possibility of trial in special military tribunals. The United States "rendered," or transferred secretly, some of them to allied countries for further interrogation. By 2005, none had been convicted of any offense and a few had been released to their home countries, including Britain, France, Kuwait, and Saudi Arabia. It also came to light that some of the severe techniques used for interrogation in Iraq had earlier been practiced on prisoners at Guantanamo and in Afghanistan. Most of the prisoners at Abu Ghraib and Camp Bucca prisons in Iraq were suspected of criminal activity, not terrorism.

The Iraq War, Antecedents, and Aftermath

Political turmoil and international crises have troubled Iraq for most of the twentieth and early twenty-first centuries. Created as a British mandate after World War I, the country chafed under British control until the 1958 revolution toppled the monarchy and introduced a long period of military leadership. Civilian leaders eventually made their way to the top but retained their predecessors' Baathist ideology, using it to consolidate authoritarian control over the country. In 1979 Saddam Hussein rose to the presidency of Iraq, which he ruled with an iron fist and with the help of his two

sons, Udai and Qusai, as well as close relatives from his hometown of Tikrit.

Iraq had long clashed with Iran, its neighbor to the east, over issues Arab (Iraq) versus Persian (Iran), Iraq's progressive political system versus Iran's monarchical system, and contentious border issues, most prominently the struggle for control of the vital Shatt al-Arab waterway. When revolutionary Iran threatened to interfere in Iraqi politics, Hussein perceived an opportunity to take the upper hand and ordered an invasion of Iran's Khuzestan province in 1980. After initial military successes, the Iraqi military became bogged down, and Iran fought its way into Iraqi territory. The war teetered in an increasingly bloody stalemate until the countries negotiated an end to the fighting in 1988.

Despite having veered close to catastrophe, Hussein proclaimed victory in the war and set about rebuilding his military machine. Far from cowed, but financially sapped by eight years of war, Hussein set his sights on what appeared to be an easier opponent: Kuwait. Relations with Kuwait, to the south, had long been troubled. Baghdad had opposed Kuwaiti independence in 1961 because it claimed that Kuwait was properly an Iraqi province. In addition, Kuwait had demanded the repayment of massive loans extended to Iraq during the Iran-Iraq War. Hussein also accused Kuwait of stealing oil that belonged to Iraq from fields along their common border. In August 1990, Hussein ordered the invasion of his small, oil-rich and financially well-off neighbor. It took only a few short days to overrun the country. Iraq declared Kuwait a province, and the Kuwaiti ruling family fled to Saudi Arabia. Fearing that Iraq would invade the kingdom next, Saudi Arabia called for international assistance to defend itself and its smaller neighbors. The United States and dozens of other countries responded, deploying a massive coalition force along Saudi Arabia's borders with Kuwait and Iraq.

In January 1991, the coalition launched Operation Desert Storm with a 38-day aerial bombardment of the Iraqi capital and other military targets. Ground forces then surged across the frontiers: one prong, composed of US and Arab coalition forces, entered and liberated Kuwait, army. By the end of 2005, more than 2,100 American servicemen and women had died in Iraq, and an untold number of Iraqi civilians had been killed. In a December 2005 speech, Bush estimated the Iraqi death count at 30,000, but gave no specifics; other estimates cited more than 100,000 deaths.

Progress in rebuilding Iraq remained frustratingly slow. The United States initially created an Office of Reconstruction and Humanitarian Assistance (ORHA) to bridge the gap between the occupation and the establishment of a new sovereign state. A few weeks after Jay Garner, ORHA's head, had begun work, the United States replaced him with L. Paul Bremer III as President Bush's special envoy and head of the new Coalition Provisional Authority (CPA). The US Department of Defense oversaw both the ORHA and the CPA. In July 2003, the CPA established the Iraqi Governing Council (IGC) as an advisory body—with members drawn from the Kurdish, Sunni Arab, and Shi'ite communities—but factionalism soon hampered the IGC, and it attracted criticism for the prominent role that Iraqi exiles played in its operations.

In the meantime, several Shi'ite militias began to exercise power in key cities while opposing each other. The United States provoked armed opposition when it attempted to arrest Shi'ite firebrand Muqtada al-Sadr and had to launch an all-out assault on the city of Fallujah to dislodge insurgents there. The situation deteriorated further with a wave of kidnappings and killings of foreigners and bombings of Shi'ite mosques and centers. US credibility suffered when photographs surfaced of the mistreatment of Iraqi prisoners by American soldiers at the Abu Ghraib prison. Sabotage repeatedly disrupted oil pipelines, American military patrols suffered attacks with IEDs (improvised explosive devices), and problems persisted in sustaining simple infrastructural requirements, such as electricity.

In the midst of the turmoil, the United States sought to create the foundations of a new government in Iraq. The CPA and the IGC drafted a Transition Administrative Law in 2003 and 2004 as an interim constitution, and the CPA handed sovereignty to an interim government in June 2004. These steps prepared the way for elections in January 2005 of the National Assembly, which then appointed a Speaker, president, and prime minister (after months of factional wrangling). The assembly completed its principal task—the drafting of a new constitution—just before an August referendum on it. Although approval of the constitution received a solid majority, it failed in two Sunni Arab provinces and barely passed in a third, thus narrowly avoiding a Sunni Arab veto. This paved the way for the election in December 2005 of a permanent assembly. Initial reports indicated a high voter turnout, including among Sunni Arabs, who had largely boycotted the earlier elections, and pointed to, as expected, an overwhelming victory by Shi'ite Islamists.

Weapons of Mass Destruction

Since the start of the Cold War and Soviet acquisition of nuclear weapons, the international community has shared a concern over the proliferation of such weapons. Many states therefore joined in adopting a set of treaties, laws, and agreements creating a nuclear non-proliferation regime seeking to prevent the acquisition of nuclear weapons by militant groups as well as by states. Concern has also risen over the acquisition and use of capabilities for chemical and biological warfare, which along with nuclear weapons are commonly called weapons of mass destruction. Israel remains the only nuclear power in the Middle East. It has never admitted to possessing nuclear weapons, has not conducted a nuclear explosion, and steadfastly refuses to sign the Non-Proliferation Treaty (NPT). Its nuclear capability is often cited as a rationale for other countries in the region to acquire a similar capacity.

Countries on the fringes of the region have taken the most significant steps toward acquisition of nuclear capabilities. Longstanding enmity between Pakistan and India—punctuated by the three wars the two countries fought in 1947–48, 1965, and 1971, as well as their ongoing dispute over the Kashmir—drove both countries to establish nuclear research programs. In May 1998, India, under the while the other prong, spearheaded by US, British, and French troops, drove deep into Iraq. It took only 100 hours to crush the Iraqi armed forces, reputed to be the fourth largest in the world, and allow the coalition to declare a cease-fire.

Despite the collapse of the Iraqi military and his country's humiliation, a defiant Hussein remained at the helm and savagely crushed rebellions among the Shi'ites of southern Iraq and the Kurds in the north. As a consequence, the coalition members created and patrolled "no-fly" zones for the Iraqi air force over northern and southern Iraq. The United Nations imposed international sanctions that lasted for twelve years. It also authorized the United Nations Special Commission on Iraq (UNSCOM) to search for and destroy Iraqi weapons of mass destruction and ballistic missiles. Iraq cooperated only minimally for the first two years of the inspection regime. In 1993 President Bill Clinton ordered a missile strike on intelligence headquarters in Baghdad in retaliation for an alleged Iraqi plot to assassinate former president George H. W. Bush. Soon after, Iraq promised more cooperation, but in fact remained recalcitrant.

In 1996 the United Nations instituted an oil-for-food program, under which Iraq would be allowed to sell some of its oil and use the proceeds for humanitarian aid. Iraq, however, abused the program through surreptitious purchases of armaments and luxury items for the ruling elite. In 1998 frustration with Iraq's failure to cooperate with UN weapons inspectors provoked the United States and Britain to launch large-scale air and missile attacks on Iraqi military targets. Despite the attack, Iraq continued to defy cooperation with UN inspectors, and debate over the value of continuing the sanctions grew.

Although various quarters began to advocate regime change in Iraq after 1998, they mustered little support for launching a war to depose Hussein and his lieutenants. The new administration of George W. Bush, however, included advocates of aggressive action who successfully pushed for overthrowing Hussein in the wake of the September 11 attacks. The administration apparently made secret preparations to invade Iraq as the US military was uprooting the Taliban in Afghanistan. By early 2003, administration officials were stridently portraying Iraq as a danger to its neighbors and the world because it possessed weapons of mass destruction and supported terrorism.

The United States—despite its failure to gain a UN resolution authorizing military action—led an attack on Iraq in March 2003, supported by Britain and a number of smaller countries. Unlike the 1991 war, the Iraq War was carried out by simultaneous air strikes and ground attacks. Coalition troops massed in Saudi Arabia and Kuwait and quickly moved across the border, racing through the desert west of Iraq's major cities, confronting little opposition. Within a month, coalition forces had secured all of Iraq's major population centers and turned their attention to finding Hussein and his supporters. Udai and Qusai Hussein were killed in July 2003, and US forces captured their father that December.

Despite an overwhelming military victory, the Bush administration failed to achieve its goals in Iraq over the next several years. No weapons of mass destruction were found, and accusations of the deposed regime's ties to al-Qaeda and terrorism remained unproven. While Iraqis and outsiders alike applauded the end of the Hussein era, the declared American goal of bringing democracy to Iraq became mired in an escalating resistance—termed an "insurgency" by the United States—and infighting as well as actual fighting between Iraqi sectarian groups.

The "insurgents" appeared to include members of the old regime whose opposition was stoked in part by the US disbandment of the Iraqi armed forces and "de-Baathification" process, Sunni Arabs who had prospered under the old regime and feared growing Shi'ite strength, and growing numbers of Islamist extremists. Although a few of these extremists were Iraqi, most were Arabs who had infiltrated Iraq across the Saudi and Syrian borders, readily volunteering to serve as suicide bombers. Zarqawi rose to prominence in leading the extremists responsible for many of the suicide missions. As US military targets hardened, attacks increasingly focused on Iraqi civilians, particularly those who had or intended to join the Iraqi police and

BJP, a Hindu right-wing party, exploded a series of nuclear devices in the northwestern Rajasthan desert. Two weeks later, Pakistan responded with five nuclear explosions. International economic sanctions and condemnation from the United States followed among the immediate consequences.

Many Pakistanis and Muslims elsewhere in the region enthusiastically hailed the "Islamic bomb." It is doubtful, however, that any Middle Eastern government seriously expects that Pakistan would use its nuclear capability in their defense any more than Pakistan would be willing to use such weapons on their behalf. Some commentators noted the close security relationship between Saudi Arabia and Pakistan and opined that Saudi Arabia may have reached a secret deal or deals for a Pakistani nuclear umbrella or that Pakistan would assist Saudi Arabia in developing its own nuclear weapons. Thus far, no evidence exists to corroborate any such scenarios. Iran's reaction was tempered by the possibility of receiving Pakistani assistance for its own nuclear program and fear that Pakistan's nuclear capability might be a potential threat.

The international community also feared that Pakistan might be sharing knowledge and materials with other countries. In 2004 Abdul Qadeer Khan, the nuclear scientist who had headed Pakistan's program, admitted to secretly having sold technology and equipment to Iran, Libya, and North Korea. Western powers had long suspected Libyan efforts to achieve WMD capabilities and first focused on Tripoli's alleged use of chemical weapons during fighting with Chad in the 1980s and the building of several weapons plants in the 1990s. At the same time, Western powers accused Libyan leader Qadhafi of attempting to buy nuclear weapons from a number of countries. The Soviets built a small research reactor in Libya in 1981, but it was generally acknowledged that Libya's nuclear capabilities remained minimal. After years of negotiation with the United Kingdom and the United States, Libya announced in 2003 that it would abandon all its unconventional weapons programs. As a result, the remaining sanctions on aircraft and aircraft parts, air transportation, and access to Libyan assets in the United States (although not sanctions on the transferal of weapons) were lifted against it. Relations with the United States and the West improved markedly. Libya subsequently joined the Chemical Weapons Convention and signed the NPT.

The international community harbored more serious concerns about Iraq and its efforts at developing and improving its WMD capabilities. During the Iran-Iraq War, Iraq attacked the Kurdish village of Halabja in northeastern Iraq with chemical weapons following its capture by Iranian troops. As many as 5,000 people may have died in the attack. It was also alleged that Iraq had employed chemical warfare against Iranian military positions during the same war. The world had long suspected that Iraq possessed biological agents as well though it had never used any. Iraq finally admitted in 1995 that it had made anthrax, botulism, and germ warfare agents. Baghdad had been working to build a nuclear bomb since before the 1991 war through a covert scheme in tandem with its nuclear research and development program. Although a signatory to the NPT and accepting inspections of its nuclear facilities by the International Atomic Energy Agency (IAEA), Iraq managed to conceal its weapons program.

The countries contributing military resources to Operation Desert Storm to end Iraq's occupation of Kuwait in 1990 and 1991 expressed considerable concern that Iraq might use WMD against coalition troops or place chemical or biological warheads on Scud missiles capable of hitting Israel and Saudi Arabia. Fortunately, such events never unfolded. Forcing Iraq to renounce and relinquish its WMD was, however, a principal rationale behind the international sanctions imposed on it after the 1991 war. Part of UNSCOM's mission involved not only identifying and destroying Iraq's WMD and ballistic missiles, but also implementing a comprehensive monitoring system to prevent the development of programs in the future.

Iraq resisted cooperation with UNSCOM as much as possible until 1993, when coalition forces and the United States conducted air strikes against Baghdad targets. As a result, Iraq agreed to abide by the UN resolution requiring it to provide details of its WMD assets, and UNSCOM resumed its work. In the course of its inspections, UNSCOM discovered the evidence of a multibillion-dollar effort to build nuclear weapons and stocks of chemical and biological agents. Eventually, in 1994, UNSCOM reported the destruction of all of Iraq's known banned weapons, but it could not account for other WMD elements that Iraq was known to have at one time possessed.

Still, Iraq continued to resist inspections, leading to the extension of sanctions. This tense situation persisted until 1998, when Iraq expelled UNSCOM's inspectors and the United States and Britain, frustrated by Iraq's prevarications, carried out a bombing campaign dubbed Operation Desert Fox, the first major action against Iraq since the 1991 war. The United Nations Monitoring, Verification, and Inspection Commission (UNMOVIC) was created the following year to replace UNSCOM, but it too faced Iraqi intransigence.

The administration of George W. Bush came into office with a declared goal of regime change in Iraq, and following the 2001 attack by al-Qaeda, began to make preparations for an invasion of Iraq. As reasons for attacking Iraq, the United States advanced claims that Iraq still possessed WMD, was threatening to use them, and might hand them over to terrorists. Iraq denied that it still possessed any WMD, but UNMOVIC remained unconvinced. During and after the war launched in March 2003, US forces searched extensively but unsuccessfully for WMD in Iraq. The multinational Iraq Survey Group subsequently took charge of the hunt, and in 2004 issued its final report, which indicated that Iraq no longer possessed WMD.

Iran had begun a nuclear research and power generation program before the 1979 revolution that included the construction of a nuclear power plant begun in the 1970s at Bushehr on the Gulf with German assistance. The revolutionary government subsequently abandoned the plant, and later efforts to revive German interest failed. Russia, however, accepted an offer to work on completing the plant. Although Iran had signed the NPT and has allowed inspections of its nuclear program, suspicions remained that its civilian nuclear program served as a cover for developing a nuclear weapons capability.

Such suspicions about Iran had grown by late 2002, when the international community discovered that two facilities under construction at Natanz and Arak could be used for producing weapons-grade plutonium, unlike the reactor at Bushehr. A few months later, a statement by President Mohammad Khatami that Iran would produce its own uranium for the reactor and reprocess it—instead of buying it from Russia and returning it to Russia after its use—gave pause to many. The United States contended that such a plan would only make sense if it involved a weapons program.

During 2003, Mohamed ElBaradei, the head of the IAEA, conducted an investigation and met with Iranian officials. He noted in a November 2003 report that Iran had admitted to carrying out a uranium centrifuge enrichment program for 18 years and had failed numerous times to meet its obligations to the IAEA. Six months later, the agency's board condemned Iran's failure to cooperate and urged it to ratify additional IAEA protocols.

The United States has taken a hard-line view of Iran's activities and has sought action by the UN Security Council. In an attempt to bridge the gap, Britain, France, and Germany began negotiations with Iran through a European Union—sponsored effort and reached an agreement in November 2004 for Iran to suspend its enrichment and reprocessing activities. Russia subsequently assured the United States that it would supply the fuel for the Bushehr reactor and take back the spent fuel. After the June 2005 election of hard-liner Mahmoud Ahmadinejad as Iran's president, however, the situation deteriorated. Ahmadinejad soon announced that Iran would resume its uranium conversion, at which point the United States and the European Union threatened to take the issue to the Security Council for possible sanctions The fate of negotiations with the European countries was thrown into doubt.

Middle Eastern Oil

The Middle East controls by far the world's greatest concentration of oil. In 2004 countries in the region produced more than one-third of the world's total supply. Approximately 30 percent comes from the Persian Gulf alone. The United States is the world's biggest consumer, demanding about a quarter of the world's oil while producing only 7 to 8 percent of it. This level of consumption requires that the United States import the majority of the petroleum it uses, making it highly dependent on foreign supplies, especially from the Middle East.

The great oil fields of the Middle East were developed in the first half of the twentieth century by Western companies. The region provided the wealth, scope, and experience that spurred the emergence of the so-called Seven Sisters, the seven giant oil companies that once dominated the industry. By 1950 three of these companies—Exxon, BP (British Petroleum), and Shell—accounted for 70 percent of total world production. The Seven Sisters coordinated international oil prices by posting arbitrary selling prices, forcing recalcitrant producing countries into line by shifting production elsewhere, and, most important, implementing an extraordinary degree of vertical integration unlike most other industries. This vertical integration meant, in general, that the same company carried out exploration, production, transport, refining, distribution, and retailing of oil that it owned.

The Anglo-Persian Oil Company (later Anglo-Iranian and now BP) held the first of the "classical" concessions and recorded the region's first oil discovery and exploitation in Iran in 1908. Finds and production ensued in Iraq a few years later and then in Bahrain in the 1930s. Although oil had been discovered in Saudi Arabia before World War I, production did not begin until after the conflict. Subsequent strikes occurred in the 1950s and 1960s in Abu Dhabi, Algeria, Libya, Oman, and Qatar. In addition, Egypt, Syria, and Yemen became minor producers.

The Seven Sisters' domination of international oil and ownership of the major concessions enabled them to control production as well as prices. The countries in which the concessions were held initially received a flat-rate royalty on the oil produced in lieu of ownership and taxes. As inflation set in,

the producing countries demanded and negotiated better terms. Their strength increased with the appearance of the "independents," smaller, generally American, companies that offered better terms on new concessions, especially for offshore fields. The competition resulted first in higher royalties, then the imposition of income tax on the companies, and eventually profit-sharing. Most producing countries became extremely dependent on oil revenues, and the reduction of the posted price in the 1950s cut their total income by as much as 40 percent. The need for greater control to ensure stable oil prices for budgetary and development policy spurred a handful of producing countries to form the Organization of the Petroleum Exporting Countries (OPEC) in 1960.

OPEC and other producing countries had acquired a substantial amount of clout by the late 1960s because of increasing global demand and declining US production capacity. As a consequence, the Arab oil boycott of the United States and several other countries in response to the October 1973 Arab-Israeli war enabled OPEC to seize control of pricing. Within a few short months in 1973 and 1974, the price of oil shot up from $3 a barrel to more than $11. The abrupt, nearly four-fold, increase sparked a wave of shortages and the most severe worldwide recession since the 1930s. The income of oil-producing countries jumped by 400 percent. Lacking the absorptive capacity to use all of their current income for development, the phenomenon of "petrodollars" appeared, whereby oil producers used surplus funds to invest massively in Western companies and government bonds.

Oil prices remained relatively static in the years following, until the early stages of the revolution in Iran (1978–1979), which reduced production there. Inflationary pressure in the producing countries and increasing demand in the consuming nations also combined to push up prices. The upward spiral took another sharp rise in the early years of the Iran-Iraq War (1980–1988), peaking at $41 in 1981.

The restructuring of the international oil industry, brought about by a wave of nationalizations of oil companies in producing countries in the 1970s, also contributed to the oil price revolution. Changes in pricing made this development possible and were prompted or spurred by a belief in the producing countries' inherent right to ownership of their own natural resources. Beginning in the early 1970s, producing countries won agreements for participation in the concessions, that is, partial ownership. By the end of the decade, nearly all the major concessions had been nationalized: national oil companies were created to handle exploration, production, and export, while the Seven Sisters and the independents entered into agreements to buy the crude oil at preferential rates according to long-term contracts. Not surprisingly, national ownership of resources gave the OPEC states greater control over pricing, particularly as global demand rose and matched or outstripped supplies.

The price rises of the late 1970s and early 1980s were not, however, sustainable. They seemed to reflect concern about the uncertain political situation in the Middle East rather than stemming from a real imbalance of supply and demand. Prices began to drop precipitously. Most oil producers began working flat out to maintain the maximum volume of exports simply to offset the fall in income from lower prices per barrel. OPEC members widely flouted the cartel's efforts to set production quotas. By 1985, OPEC production had dropped by half, and a year later prices fell to nearly $10. Although prices subsequently recovered somewhat, the impact on producing countries' economies proved to be enormous. For example, Saudi Arabia—after years of having more income than it could absorb domestically—embarked on nearly two decades of persistent budget deficits; per capita income fell to one-quarter of its peak.

The situation came full circle in the early 2000s as prices again skyrocketed, resulting in part from political concerns about developments in the Gulf, in particular the war in Iraq and persistent questions about Iran's foreign policy and alleged development of a nuclear capability. Other factors played significant roles as well, among them heavy speculation in oil futures in 2003 and early 2004. Another was the legal action taken against Russian billionaire Mikhail Khodorkovsky that involved the Russian government forcing his business, Yukos,

one of Russia's largest oil companies, to cease production until the state could maneuver to take it from him. Strikes and other supply disruptions in Iraq, Nigeria, the United States, and Venezuela further contributed to spot shortages. The maintenance of high price levels owed much to demand pressures in the United States (particularly concerning gasoline because of tight refinery capacity) and growing demand in Brazil, China, India, and elsewhere. In autumn 2005, the international marker posted price (West Texas Intermediate) climbed above $70 for the first time (before subsequently declining $10 or more).

Many observers believed that a world of high oil prices would persist for years. By 2004 global spare capacity had become almost nonexistent. OPEC found itself producing at full capacity for the first time in a decade, and "NOPEC" (non-OPEC) producers, such as Mexico, Norway, Russia, and the United Kingdom, were also either at capacity or faced diminishing production levels. Some observers even postulated that growth in demand would be accompanied by the depletion of major fields, creating a nightmarish scenario just a decade or two down the line.

The existing giant oilfields are increasingly mature, and few new fields of comparable size have been found in decades. In the 1990s much attention focused on the promise of Caspian Sea petroleum in Azerbaijan, Kazakhstan, Russia, Turkmenistan, and Uzbekistan, with potential reserves equal to those of the United States or the North Sea. It, however, took a considerable amount of time to develop the long and politically insecure pipelines to the Black Sea, and maritime boundary disputes continue to plague the region. Even if the reserves prove to be as large as expected, they will constitute only about 2 percent of the world's total. Saudi reserves alone, at 25 percent of the total, dwarf this amount.

It is widely believed that global oil production will soon peak. Additions to reserves tend to be from smaller, more expensive fields producing less desirable oil. Furthermore, considerable debate continues over whether the reserves booked in Saudi Arabia and other countries with giant oilfields will ever be realized. Some observers even contend that aggressive drilling has damaged the Saudi fields (with similar results elsewhere), and that instead of being able to expand their capacity as planned, production will decline in the future as the mature fields fade.

Natural gas, long seen as a cleaner and cheaper energy alternative to crude oil, faces similar problems. Demand has increased markedly as the industrialized world relies more and more on natural gas for electricity generation. Domestic US gas production remains virtually unchanged although demand continues to grow, thus raising requirements for the import of liquefied natural gas (LNG). Much of this necessarily will come from the Middle East, which holds some 35 to 40 percent of the world's total reserves. Algeria, Egypt, and Oman are significant producers, while Iran and Yemen seek to join the market. Qatar alone holds 15 percent or more of the world's total reserves, and the tiny state's huge and extremely expensive LNG investments are now beginning to come to fruition.

Subregional Issues

A number of key developments in the Middle East are subregional in scope, involving only a few actors but demanding outside interest or involvement.

Israel and Palestine

Relations between Israel and the Arab world are the longest-running and most intractable political problem in the Middle East and perhaps the world. Britain assumed responsibility for Palestine under a League of Nations mandate after World War I, and the area witnessed a steady stream of immigration by Jews over the subsequent decades, in part due to agreement between Britain and Zionist leaders. After World War II, UN efforts failed to secure a partition plan for separate Arab and Jewish states, and upon British withdrawal in 1948, Zionists declared the state of Israel. Two years of war ensued between the new Jewish state and its Arab neighbors. When the fighting stopped, Israel

had acquired one-third more territory than the partition plan had envisioned, the Palestinian areas of the West Bank and East Jerusalem were incorporated into Jordan, and the Gaza Strip came under Egyptian administration.

The second Arab-Israeli war, the Suez War, took place in 1956, when Israel invaded the Sinai according to a plan devised with Britain and France to take control of the Suez Canal and occupy the peninsula. Israel, under pressure from the United States, soon withdrew from the territory it had captured. As a result of the June 1967 war, however, Israel recaptured the Sinai, along with the West Bank and East Jerusalem, Gaza, and the Golan Heights. The Palestinian territories and the Golan have since been under Israeli control. In 1973 Egypt and Syria launched a surprise attack against Israel to recover Arab territory, but the war essentially ended in a stalemate.

Divisions within Israeli society and disillusionment with the Labor Party establishment helped propel the Likud Party to power in elections held in 1977. Likud's victory marked a watershed in Israeli politics, as it bestowed on Likud the mantle of a respectable, mainstream party for the first time, and its leader, Menachem Begin, who had been a leader of an extremist Jewish organization prior to Israeli independence, became prime minister. Israel has been governed by the right wing more often than not since that time and generally has pursued a hard-line policy toward the Palestinians.

This policy was apparent in 1982, when Israeli forces invaded Lebanon in an attempt to crush the PLO. During the invasion, Israeli forces stood by as their right-wing Christian Lebanese allies massacred Palestinians in the Sabra and Shatila refugee camps in Beirut. The PLO leadership left Beirut for Tunis, and scores of its fighters dispersed. Although the Israelis soon withdrew from most of Lebanon, they continued to occupy territory along the southern border of the country until 2000, when Prime Minister Ehud Barak acted on a campaign promise to withdraw.

A partial breakthrough in the Arab-Israeli conflict had occurred in 1977, when President Anwar al-Sadat of Egypt made an unprecedented visit to

Israel. Eighteen months later, in 1979, US President Jimmy Carter brokered talks between Sadat and Begin at Camp David, Maryland, that produced a peace treaty between Egypt and Israel. Egypt's acceptance of a separate peace shattered the united Arab front against Israel and brought upon it the condemnation of most Arab states. All but two Arab governments severed diplomatic relations with Egypt, and the Arab League transferred its headquarters from Cairo to Tunis. Of great importance, with Egypt sidelined, the Arabs no longer had any hope of challenging Israel militarily. This weakness revealed itself early on during the 1982 Israeli invasion of Lebanon when Syria redeployed its troops in the country to avoid engaging the Israelis and the Jordanians sat out the war.

Few significant advances were made toward a resolution of the conflict in the following years. In some ways, the situation worsened. Many Egyptians became disillusioned with Sadat's policies well before Islamists assassinated him in 1981. Likud won elections held in 1981 despite Israel's deteriorating economic situation, but it failed to secure a clear majority and only managed to form a right-wing coalition. Later, although Likud obtained the largest number of votes of any party in the 1984 and 1988 elections, it was forced to form a coalition with Labor after both elections. At the same time, the Palestinians continued to chafe at the Israeli occupation and domination. By 1987 simmering unrest coalesced into the intifada, a coordinated uprising against the occupation. The Israeli government responded with brute force and other hard-line measures to Palestinians throwing stones at soldiers, and relations between the two peoples became even worse.

Only after the success of the 1991 war to drive Iraqi forces from Kuwait did the next breakthrough become possible. Having disposed of the Iraqi threat to Middle Eastern stability, the United States turned its attention to defusing the Israeli-Palestinian conflict. With Soviet co-sponsorship—and having used economic leverage to compel Israeli attendance—the United States convened an Arab-Israeli conference in Madrid in October 1991. Although the talks produced little of substantive agreement, they were significant in marking the first time that all the parties officially met, including Israeli and Palestinian representatives. In part, the stalemate helped ensure Labor's victory in the 1991 election.

The most significant breakthrough arrived in 1993, when Israel and the PLO reached an accord through secret negotiations held in Oslo. By the terms of the Oslo accords, the PLO agreed to recognize Israel's right to exist and to renounce violence, while Israel recognized the PLO as the legitimate representative of the Palestinian people. In addition, a plan was negotiated for eventual Israeli withdrawal from the West Bank and Gaza in favor of Palestinian self-rule. According to this timetable, negotiations were to begin in 1995 on a final solution to the conflict and an agreement was to take effect in 1999. In a further positive development, the Israeli-PLO accord paved the way for Israel and Jordan to enter into peace talks and sign a treaty in 1994.

Imprecisions in the terms of the Oslo accords prevented its implementation, so additional agreements became necessary before the creation of the Palestinian Authority (PA) to assume control over some areas of the occupied territories. Yasir 'Arafat and other Palestinian leaders returned to their homeland for the first time in a quarter-century, and the terms of Israel's withdrawal were made clearer.

Almost typically, the hope that these developments raised soon began to fade. Many people on both sides rejected the agreement. In 1996 a Jewish extremist assassinated Yitzhak Rabin, the Labor prime minister of Israel whose government had negotiated and signed the Oslo agreement. His successor, hard-line Likud leader Benjamin Netanyahu, rejected the accords and any compromise with the Palestinians. On the Palestinian side, the Islamist organization Hamas emerged to oppose compromise over the Palestinians' right to all of Palestine. Bitterness developed toward returning PLO members who were regarded as corrupt and out of touch with the local communities, having spent the intervening years in relative comfort abroad before assuming new positions of leadership in the Palestinian territories. In 1998 US President Bill Clinton managed to convince the two parties to accept the Wye River Memorandum, which called for Israeli withdrawals under the Oslo agreements to be carried out and for the Palestinian National Council to remove words regarding the liberation of all of Palestine from its charter.

The following years saw yet another return to stalemate as the two sides continued to bicker. After the election of Ehud Barak as Israel's prime minister in 1999, the two sides sat down and reached an agreement at Sharm el-Sheikh to implement their earlier accords. Even this agreement faltered, however. Of significance, 1999 marked the end of the period originally established for a final settlement to take effect. President Clinton persuaded Barak and 'Arafat to meet at Camp David in July 2000 in a last-ditch effort to achieve a solution. Barak presented what he contended was Israel's final and most generous offer. Israel would withdraw from most of the West Bank and swap land in the Negev Desert for the occupied lands it would retain. It would also cede part of East Jerusalem, and Palestinian refugees would be allowed to enter the West Bank and Gaza.

Despite pressure from Clinton, 'Arafat refused to accept the Israeli terms. His stance seemed to be based partly on an unwillingness to proceed without the explicit approval of the Palestinian establishment and on the grounds that the Israeli offer was not as generous as promoted: Israel would absorb too much of the West Bank; Israeli settlements throughout the West Bank and Gaza would remain in place and in the West Bank cut the territory into three noncontiguous areas; the Palestinians would not have control of their borders or airspace. Furthermore, the Palestinians felt that they could not accept less than full control over East Jerusalem, and the Palestinian right of return would not be recognized even symbolically. The Palestinians were unable or unwilling to make a counteroffer. Barak and Clinton left for home, angry and blaming 'Arafat for the meeting's failure.

Barak's inability to return with a final settlement damaged his chances for reelection. His rival, former defense minister Ariel Sharon, flexed his muscles in late September 2000 by leading a party of Likud legislators on a high-profile visit to East Jerusalem's Haram al-Sharif complex, the third holiest site in Islam and the Temple Mount to the Jews. Confrontations between Palestinians and Israeli security forces erupted almost immediately. Unlike the first intifada, the second uprising soon grew increasingly violent and more harshly repressed. Meanwhile, Israeli and Palestinian negotiators continued to hammer out their remaining differences, and the two sides came tantalizingly close to agreement in subsequent meetings, most notably at the Egyptian resort of Taba in January 2001. Many observers believed that, given more time, a settlement might have been reached. Barak, however, lost the elections held in February 2001 to Likud's Sharon, a hard-liner.

With the opportunity missed, the two sides have been barely on speaking terms since. Radical Palestinian groups—namely, Hamas and Islamic Jihad—began to challenge the authority of Fatah, the dominant group within the PLO. In addition to attacking Israeli military targets and settlers, these two groups began to carry out suicide missions against civilian targets in Israel. The al-Aqsa Martyrs' Brigade, a breakaway faction of Fatah, adopted the strategy as well. Sharon responded harshly, launching a major military incursion of the West Bank, largely closing Israel to Palestinian workers, establishing checkpoints throughout the West Bank to impede Palestinian movement, and permitting the creation of more settlements. He also confined 'Arafat to his West Bank headquarters in Ramallah and ordered assassinations—euphemistically called "targeted killings"—of suspected al-Aqsa, Hamas, and Islamic Jihad leaders.

After the attacks carried out by al-Qaeda on September 11, 2001, prompted the Bush administration to declare a "global war on terror," Sharon lost little time in convincing Bush that Israel's conflict with the Palestinians was one aspect of that campaign. The Bush administration, following Sharon's urgings, refused all contact with 'Arafat. As prospects for a settlement retreated farther into the distance, Palestinian attacks on Israelis became more frequent and the Israeli response more brutal.

Standards of living and nutrition in the Palestinian territories plummeted, and Sharon constantly accused 'Arafat of refusing to crack down on militant groups.

Israel eventually began to construct a wall primarily on and around the West Bank with the stated purpose of preventing Palestinian entry into Israel, but also resulting in the incorporation of West Bank lands into Israel. In populated areas, the fence consisted of a concrete barrier. The Palestinians protested the building of the fence on Palestinian land, rather than along the Green Line marking the border of Israel, and its deep detours into the West Bank to include Palestinian lands and Israeli settlements on the "Israeli side." The issues surrounding the barrier illustrate concretely the deepening divisions between the two societies—growing Israeli fear of and anger toward Palestinians in general and Palestinian anger at Israel's continued and heavy-handed occupation of their territory.

Isolated, 'Arafat bowed to US and Israeli pressure in 2003 and appointed a prime minister, Mahmoud Abbas, and committed himself to reigning in the militant groups. The violence abated somewhat after several cease-fires, but the calm did not last. 'Arafat's death in November 2004 and the succession of Abbas as PA president brought some improvement in official Israeli-PA relations, but serious discussions remained in abeyance. Sharon's decision to withdraw unilaterally from Gaza in 2005 appeared to be based more on the desire to cut Israeli losses, improve its security, and focus on control of the West Bank than any attempt to advance the peace process. In late 2005, however, Sharon abandoned the Likud Party to form the Kadima Party, to which he not only took many of his former Likud allies, but also enlisted former Labor head Shimon Peres. Kadima seemed to be positioning itself as a centrist party and thus better situated for working toward peace than was Likud. Netanyahu replaced Sharon as Likud Party leader.

External peacemaking efforts in recent years have focused at times on the so-called road map released in 2003 by the "Quartet"—the European Union, Russia, the United Nations, and the United States. The plan envisaged an immediate cease-fire, a freeze on Israeli settlements, and the establishment of a sovereign Palestinian state. By the end of 2005, however, little progress had been made in accomplishing even the goals considered most immediate at the time it was made public.

Syria and Lebanon

Syria experienced a procession of military coups following its independence after World War II. In 1963, another military-backed coup occurred in the name of the pan-Arab socialist Baath Party, and Syria has since remained a one-party state under Baathist leadership. In 1970 an army officer named Hafiz al-Assad emerged as the country's ruler, a position he would hold until his death in 2000. Over the years, Assad consolidated authoritarian control over the state through reliance on relatives and fellow members of his minority Alawite sect. He brooked no dissent, as graphically illustrated in his massacre of dissident Muslim Brotherhood members in the northern city of Hama in 1982.

In foreign affairs, Syria's confrontation with Israel led it to align with the Soviet Union in pursuit of financial assistance and military equipment. Defeat in the 1967 Arab-Israeli war meant the loss of the Golan Heights to Israel. Syria's insistence on the return of all this territory has been a consistent element over the years in serious negotiations between the two countries. The outbreak of civil war in neighboring Lebanon in 1976 raised Syrian concerns that the strife might make it vulnerable to attack by Israel through Lebanon's "soft underbelly." Thus Assad felt compelled to intervene in it.

Lebanon is an artificial state, created as a French mandate with boundaries purposefully drawn to include roughly equal numbers of Christians and Muslims. With independence, Lebanese politics emerged organized along confessional lines. The president must be a Maronite Christian, the prime minister a Sunni Muslim, and the Speaker of the parliament a Shi'ite. Each community came to be represented by one or more political parties, usually headed by strongmen, considered during the civil strife to be "warlords," who collectively comprised the political elite. The presence of hundreds of thousands of Palestinian refugees further complicated the situation, as did the use of southern Lebanon by Palestinian fighters as a platform for attacks on Israel.

A precarious balance between the sects held for decades, despite the higher growth rate of Muslims that made them the majority of the population, even if unacknowledged. In 1976 the equilibrium collapsed, and civil war ensued. Christian leaders wanted the Palestinians reined in while Muslim leaders called on the state to identify more closely with the Palestinian cause. Skirmishes erupted between the Maronite Phalange Party and Palestinian guerrillas in 1975, and fighting escalated the following year between Christian and Muslim factions. An abortive coup by Muslim military officers in early 1976 led to Syria deploying troops to protect the government. A few months later, the Arab League created the Arab Deterrent Force—in reality Syrian troops—to police a cease-fire.

The election of the right-wing Menachem Begin as prime minister of Israel in 1977 led to increased Israeli support for the right-wing Lebanese Maronites, who were fighting anti-Israeli Lebanese factions, and Israeli incursions into southern Lebanon to take on the PLO. This spurred greater conflict among the Lebanese factions; eventually each community boasted at least one private army. The country divided into Christian and Muslim enclaves, and prominent leaders from both sides were assassinated. In 1982 Israel invaded Lebanon in an attempt to stop attacks along its northern border and defeat the PLO. Its forces also swept to Beirut in part to lend assistance to their Christian allies, with whom Israel entered into a stillborn treaty of sorts.

The civil war ground on through the 1980s. International peacekeeping efforts in 1982 and "national reconciliation" talks in 1983 failed to produce anything of lasting value. Israel retaliated for attacks against its forces in southern Lebanon with the seizure of men from Shi'ite villages in the south. This accelerated the fragmentation of Shi'ite groups and rallied resistance to its occupation. As a result of the war, al-Amal emerged to

protect the interests of the Shi'ites, who sat by and large at the bottom of the Lebanese socioeconomic ladder. Militants within the party later broke away to form Hezbollah to carry out attacks on Israeli forces and their allies in southern Lebanon. Iran became a prominent supporter of Hezbollah.

A meeting of leading Lebanese politicians held at al-Taif, Saudi Arabia, in 1989 finally produced a compromise plan for peace. Although implementation would prove tortuous, the war in effect had ended by early 1991. In 1992, following the first parliamentary elections in 21 years, Rafiq Hariri, a prominent businessman who had made a fortune in Saudi Arabia, was appointed prime minister, formed a largely technocratic government, and began the process of reconstructing the country. The price for peace seemed to be the continued presence of Syrian troops in the country and Syria's domination of Lebanese politics.

Syria's policies during this period resulted in its increasing isolation. It had supported non-Arab Iran during the Iran-Iraq War because of the bitter rivalry between Damascus and Baghdad. Syria's enmity toward Iraq also prompted it to participate in the coalition that drove Iraqi forces from Kuwait in 1991. Border issues poisoned relations with Turkey to the north, and Jordan had been uneasy about Syrian intentions since 1970, when it threatened to intervene on the side of the Palestinians during the civil war. The collapse of the Soviet Union meant the loss of its major backer, and Syrian intransigence on Arab-Israeli matters alienated Washington.

President Assad's control over Syria seemed to weaken somewhat in the 1990s. No longer in good health, he faced challenges from his brother and other formerly close associates. His death in 2000 marked the end of a remarkable 30 years in power. He had groomed his eldest son to succeed him but, after the son was killed in a car accident, his second son, Bashar, was called home from London. Many observers doubted Bashar's ability to maintain a firm grip on the country, assuming that the older generation of his father's associates would dominate him or the Alawite stranglehold on power would be broken. During his first few years in office, Bashar proved himself capable, if not always adept, at sustaining many of the domestic and foreign policies of his father while posing as a reformist.

A turning point in the Syrian-Lebanese relationship arrived in February 2005, with the assassination of Rafiq Hariri in Beirut. Hariri had months earlier resigned as prime minister to protest Syrian interference in forcing the Lebanese parliament to accept an extra-constitutional extension of the term of the pro-Syrian president. Not surprisingly, many immediately suspected the hand of Damascus in Hariri's assassination. An outpouring of grief erupted over the genuinely respected Hariri, and mass demonstrations were organized against Syria's continued presence in Lebanon. Relations with the United States, already tense, got worse, with Washington accusing Syria of supporting terrorism through its patronage of Hezbollah. After the Iraq War, the United States also accused Syria of providing refuge for officials of the former Iraqi Baathist regime and not doing enough to prevent Islamist extremists from crossing its borders into Iraq. Even worse for Syrian, France and other countries joined the United States in condemning its presumed role in the assassination and its presence in Lebanon. Damascus finally bowed to international pressure and withdrew its troops from Lebanon in April 2005. A United Nations inquiry into the assassination threatened to implicate top Syrian officials.

Egypt and North Africa

Egypt has long been the most important Arab state in terms of history, politics, demography, and culture as well as other factors. The selection of Cairo for the headquarters of the League of Arab States at its founding in 1945 symbolizes Egypt's centrality in the Arab world. In the 1950s, the activist anti-imperialist stance of Egyptian President Gamal Abdel Nasser cemented the country's leadership of the Arab world, and Egypt's military strength made it the linchpin of the Arab confrontation states vis-à-vis Israel. Nasser's death in 1970 threatened to reduce Egypt's prominence

on the Arab and world stages, but his successor, Anwar al-Sadat, gained credibility in the West for making the historic visit to Jerusalem in 1977 that led to a separate peace treaty with Israel in 1979. Sadat also improved his standing in the West when he parted company with the Soviet Union in exchange for closer relations with the United States and introduced more liberal economic policies, though amid much dissension in Egypt. Since 1979 US aid to Egypt has averaged $2 billion a year, an arrangement reached as a result of the Camp David settlement with Israel.

Vice President Husni Mubarak assumed the presidency following Sadat's assassination by Islamist extremists in 1981. Mubarak was viewed initially as a weak interim choice, but he gradually strengthened his hold within the government by repressing dissent. He enhanced his regional standing by tolerating a "cold peace" with Israel and improving relations with other Arab countries. In addition, he bolstered his international posture by strengthening ties to the United States. Egypt also mediated between the Israelis and the Palestinians and contributed substantially to the 1991 coalition that ousted Iraq from Kuwait.

Nevertheless, Egypt's normally close relations with the United States have been strained at times. On the one hand, Egypt has coordinated closely with the United States on regional security matters and defense cooperation. In part because of its problems with Islamist extremism, Egypt has supported the US campaign against terrorism to the point of reportedly accepting prisoners rendered by the United States for harsh interrogation. On the other hand, however, Egypt refused to participate in the 2003 Iraq War, and along with other Arab countries, has steered clear of involvement in postwar Iraqi reconstruction.

US disappointment with Egypt also extends to the arena of human rights. Abuses by police are routine. Although the government has cracked down on Islamists, including executing some 60 alleged extremists since 1992, the state has done little to protect the large Coptic Christian minority. The government has made several high-profile arrests of human right activists and politicians. It only reluctantly reacts to outside pressures for greater democracy. Antigovernment demonstrations took place in early 2005, sparked in part by similar demonstrations in Lebanon after the assassination of former prime minister Rafiq Hariri in Beirut. The outlawed Muslim Brotherhood gained the most seats of any group outside the ruling party in relatively free parliamentary elections held in November 2005. It is widely believed that Mubarak has not appointed a vice president because he is preparing his son Gamal to succeed him, much as Hafiz al-Assad groomed his son to take the reins in Syria after his passing.

Egypt, although geographically part of Africa, lies at the center of the Middle East and Arab worlds. The North African countries bordering Egypt along the Mediterranean to the west are also Muslim, Arab, and members of the Arab League, but in some ways they are less Middle Eastern than other Arab states and form a distinct subregion. Although they participate in Middle Eastern politics and affairs, they also exhibit an African identity.

For the most part, recent political developments in North Africa have concerned the issues of democratization or liberalization and the influence of Islamists. Properly speaking, North Africa consists of the Maghreb—that is, the countries of Algeria, Morocco, and Tunisia—plus Libya. The Maghrebi states share a common experience of French colonization or mandates and the French language, which is still widely spoken throughout the area. Libya, a colony of Italy before World War I, fell under British protection until independence in 1951. Although the majority of the Maghrebi population is ethnically Arab, sizeable minorities of Berbers, the original pre-Islamic inhabitants, reside in the region, particularly in Algeria.

Algeria is the most populous of the North African states and faces the most severe internal problems. The National Liberation Front (FLN) led the independence struggle against the French from 1954 to 1962 and has controlled the government since. By the 1990s, its development strategy of using oil and gas revenues to build a heavy industrial base clearly had failed to achieve its objectives, and a rapidly exploding population lowered standards

of living and left increasing numbers of young people jobless—an experience shared by Morocco and Tunisia and many other countries in the Middle East.

As a consequence, Islamists began to attract support throughout the region in the 1980s and 1990s by offering social services to the needy, attacking corruption, and calling for social and economic justice. In Tunisia, the Islamic Tendency Movement, later al-Nahda, steadily intensified its criticism of the authoritarian government of Zine El-Abidine Ben Ali and suffered increasing persecution for it.

Algeria's experience proved to be far more deadly. The Islamic Salvation Front (FIS) won an overwhelming majority of the votes in the preliminary round of 1992 legislative elections—which were open to non-FLN parties for the first time—and threatened to repeat its success in the final round. The FIS, which had said that it would not maintain a "Western-style" democracy if it were to gain power, appeared to be on the verge of gaining the two-thirds of the parliamentary seats necessary to change the constitution. Panicked, the government cancelled the final round of elections. It then arrested FIS leaders, including moderates, which in turn sparked antigovernment demonstrations.

The government's decision to declare the FIS illegal and to intensify its campaign against Islamists provoked attacks on the military and police. The situation soon deteriorated into civil war. Extremist organizations, such as the Armed Islamic Group (GIA) and an offshoot named the Salifi Group for Preaching and Combat (GSPC), committed atrocities against government personnel and civilians. Counterattacks, launched by nebulous progovernment groups widely believed to be composed of security forces, often amounted to massacres of suspected Islamists and their supporters. The number of violent incidents declined sharply after the late 1990s, but by then the fighting had resulted in some 150,000 deaths. By 2005, the GIA appeared to be defunct, while the weakened GSPC announced its allegiance to al-Qaeda.

The Maghreb faced increased activity by Islamist extremists after the attacks of September 11, 2001, on the United States. A bombing of a synagogue on the Tunisian island of Djerba in 2002 killed more than 20 people. Although the unknown Islamic Army for the Liberation of Holy Places claimed responsibility, some observers suggested that al-Qaeda had at least inspired the operation, if not carried it out. The Western press has reported that as many as several thousand Algerians have trained in al-Qaeda camps in Afghanistan. Algerian members of the network have been arrested in London and in Canada.

Moroccans have exhibited the most extremist activity in the region. Suicide bombers with connections to al-Qaeda attacked Western and Jewish targets in Casablanca in 2003, killing 45 people, most of them Moroccans. Members of the same organization were blamed by the Spanish government for the 2004 train bombing in Madrid that killed some 200 commuters. In addition, US and German courts have convicted Europeans of Moroccan descent with intent to participate in the September 11 attacks, and a Dutch Moroccan murdered a Dutch filmmaker for making comments perceived as anti-Islamic in 2004.

All the North African regimes continue to demonstrate less-than-democratic tendencies. Although Algeria's FLN has loosened its hold on power and even fragmented in recent years, and multiparty elections have been institutionalized, the government continues to dominate politics and thwart true democratic processes. The leadership of Zine El-Abidine Ben Ali in Tunisia has failed to fulfill its early promise of liberalization. Libya remains politically mercurial with Qadhafi firmly in *de facto,* if not *de jure,* charge. Somewhat surprisingly, since King Mohamed VI ascended the throne in 1999, Morocco has opened up the most. The kingdom currently enjoys free multiparty elections and an improving human rights environment.

The millions of North Africans resident in Europe have raised concerns in governments there about increased involvement in extremist activities. French courts convicted a number of Algerians of placing bombs on railroad tracks. In France, attention turned to the poverty of ethnic Africans and their exclusion from French society in November 2005 after rioting erupted following the accidental electrocution of two young Frenchmen of North African descent who were being chased by police.

The Gulf

The Gulf—alternatively called the Persian Gulf or the Arabian Gulf—remains an area of particular interest to outsiders for at least two major reasons: (1) it contains nearly one-third of the world's oil reserves and (2) a succession of wars has threatened to disrupt oil supplies and harm the moderate monarchies that are friendly to the West. Contrary to widespread perceptions, the most serious threats to Gulf security flow only from its two northern littoral states, Iraq and Iran. The remaining Gulf states pose no threat to others.

Any potential menace to international order and neighboring states posed by Saddam Hussein's regime in Iraq appears to have ended with the successful prosecution of the Iraq War in 2003. The US-led invasion overthrew the Baathist regime, and the occupation authorities disbanded the Iraqi military. The regime apparently had no weapons of mass destruction. For the most part after the war, the initial impact of Iraq's problems—dealing with an insurgency organized by supporters of the former regime, restoring oil production and exports, rehabilitating the economy and infrastructure, and installing democratic institutions—seemed to be confined within its borders and of primary concern to the new regime's protecting power, the United States.

In time, however, two spillover factors became increasing problematic: the growing Islamist extremist element of the insurgency and the increasing strength and militancy of Iraq's Shi'ites. Most of the Islamists in Iraq and all of the suicide bombers that plague the country, killing mostly Iraqis, are infiltrators from outside Iraq (though some Iraqis seem to be involved). The majority of these extremists are Arab, many of them Saudis. They crossed into Iraq through Syria and to a lesser extent Saudi Arabia.

The situation resembles the phenomenon of the so-called Afghan Arabs, those Islamists who had fought in Afghanistan and returned home radical-ized. The continuing strength and even growth in the numbers of zealots attracted to Iraq portends a threat not only to Iraq, but also to the home countries of these men. Just as wartime experience in Afghanistan, and later training in al-Qaeda facilities, produced the first generation of extremists, the experience of Iraq threatens to unleash a new generation across borders. Ironically, there have been reports of Islamists trained in Iraq carrying out similar attacks in Afghanistan.

The Iraqi Shi'ites, long discriminated against even though they formed the majority of Iraq's population, proved to be well organized after the war. With a number of capable militias and political factions, there was some speculation that the Iraqi example could inspire similar activism among Shi'ite minorities in other Gulf states, notably Saudi Arabia, which is home to five million Shi'ites in the Eastern Province, and Bahrain, which has an already restive Shi'ite majority. Muqtada al-Sadr, a young firebrand with a large following among Iraq's urban Shi'ite poor and a formidable militia, provides a particularly unsettling example of what the Gulf's other rulers might face.

In some ways, post-2003 Iraq raised fears similar to those prompted by the success of the 1979 revolution in largely Shi'ite Iran. Although Iran's revolutionary regime presented itself as the defender of Shi'ites throughout the Islamic world (and apparently assisted Shi'ite dissidents in planning a 1981 coup attempt in Bahrain), it posed an even broader threat to neighboring states. The leaders and supporters of the revolution hoped that it would be seen as a model for all Muslims to follow in overthrowing corrupt regimes.

Teheran's aggressive position rattled the Arab Gulf states. Iraq responded by invading Iran in the belief that such an attack might cause Iran to collapse. Saddam Hussein badly miscalculated and nearly lost the eight-year war. The Gulf monarchies viewed Iraq as the lesser of two evils and provided Iraq massive loans in its war effort to blunt the perceived Iranian threat to all of them. Iran responded by attacking non-belligerent shipping in the Gulf and threatening to close the Strait of Hormuz, as

well as by infiltrating Saudi air space with a lone aircraft in 1984, attacking a Saudi offshore oil rig in 1987, and holding demonstrations during the 1987 hajj that turned violent. Kuwait was forced to ask the United States to escort and flag its oil tankers in 1987.

Postwar tensions eased somewhat as a result of the 1991 war against Iraq (notwithstanding the surprise in Teheran when Iraq had much of its air force and civilian aircraft flown to Iran for safekeeping). Cross-Gulf relations gradually improved throughout the 1990s, assisted by the more accommodating attitudes of Presidents Ali Akbar Hashemi Rafsanjani (1989–1997) and Mohammad Khatami (1997–2005). The unexpected election of ultra-conservative Mahmoud Ahmadinejad as president in 2005, however, threatened to derail normalized ties, and Ahmadinejad further injured Iran's international standing in December when he publicly expressed his hostility toward Israel and questioned the Holocaust.

Iran's revolutionary regime reversed the shah's policy of friendship with Israel and actively supported the Palestinians and Lebanon's Hezbollah Shi'ite militia fighting the Israeli occupation of southern Lebanon. This support fomented US antipathy toward Iran and prompted the classification of the Islamic republic as a supporter of terrorism. In addition to the still-palpable ill will over the holding of US diplomats as hostages in 1980, US allegations of Iran secretly attempting to acquire nuclear weapons also roiled US-Iranian relations. Iran denied having any intentions beyond a peaceful civilian use for its nuclear reactors, but even sympathetic observers doubted this assertion. They noted that the country's precarious position between American troops in neighboring Afghanistan to the east and in neighboring Iraq to the west might give Teheran pause about its security.

Meanwhile, the Gulf's southern littoral—comprising the six Arab monarchies of Bahrain, Kuwait, Oman, Qatar, Saudi Arabia, and the United Arab Emirates (UAE)—remained quiet on the domestic front and under US protection from regional threats. The Iran-Iraq War had sparked the creation of the Gulf Cooperation Council (GCC), the early objective of which was to coordinate and improve joint security. Little substantive progress was made on this front, in equal part because of the reluctance of the GCC's members to surrender control of their security forces and because even the combined defenses of the six could never be a match for the military machines of their neighbors. Fortunately, the council recorded relatively more success on the economic front, with the institution of a common tariff regime, agreement on the free movement of capital and labor, and movement toward a common currency.

From the mid-1980s to the early 2000s, the prolonged economic recession brought about by low oil prices preoccupied the GCC states (apart from a brief interlude during the 1990–1991 Iraqi occupation of Kuwait and subsequent war). Saudi Arabia, for example, recorded nearly two decades of budget deficits and incurred substantial international and domestic debts. The sharp rise in oil prices beginning in 2003 reversed the situation and subsequently fattened the oil-producing states' bank accounts. Old projects were dusted off, and the search ended for subsidies that could be cut without causing a political uproar. For Qatar and the UAE, higher oil prices represented nothing but bonus. For Bahrain, Oman, and Saudi Arabia, the bonanza could not have come at a better time, as their rapidly expanding populations had swelled the ranks of unemployed youth as desirable government jobs dried up.

By the mid-1990s, the monarchies faced a growing crisis of succession, as the incumbent generation of rulers grew old and infirm. Saudi Arabia's King Fahd suffered a stroke in 1995 and subsequently grew increasingly incapable of ruling the kingdom. The heir apparent, Prince 'Abdallah, took over day-to-day duties, but remained constrained in introducing significant new policies until he finally succeeded in 2005 following Fahd's death.

As the health of Kuwait's amir, Jabir, and heir apparent, Saad al-'Abdallah, deteriorated, the country seemed to enter a state of sclerosis. The older generation of the al-Sabah ruling family continued to thin, but it seemed as though little attention had been paid to who among the younger generation should rise to the top. Zayid Al Nuhayyan, the UAE's venerable president since 1971 (and ruler of Abu Dhabi since 1966) passed away in 2004. After the loss of the only president the country had ever known, succession passed quickly but rather uncertainly to Zayid's eldest son, Khalifah.

Bahrain and Qatar solved their succession problems in different ways. Qatari leader Hamad Al Thani deposed his father in 1995, when the latter went abroad, and immediately instituted a plethora of changes to open the country economically and politically. Qatar overcame a history of sometimes-strained relations with the United States to host major US military bases despite the irritant of the al-Jazeera satellite television network on its soil. Bahraini leader Hamad Al Khalifah succeeded on the death of his father in 1999 and quickly set about defusing a five-year dissident movement sustained mainly by the country's Shi'ites.

Oman's Sultan Qabus Al ibn Sa'id Al Sa'id straddles the Gulf rulers' generation gap. Born in 1940, he was younger than the Saudi and Kuwaiti rulers but significantly older than the two Hamads. By 2005, he had ruled Oman for 35 years and, worryingly, had no heir.

Democratization has made only slow and limited progress in the Gulf states. Surprisingly, Iran is undoubtedly the most democratic of all the littoral countries, having relatively free elections with universal suffrage for president and parliament. Constraints exist, however, in that the Council of Guardians, composed of religious notables, must approve all presidential candidates. Iraq's experiment with democracy, guided by the United States, took its first faltering steps in 2004 and 2005.

As might be expected, the six monarchies lagged behind more recently created states and governments in political change and liberalization. Still, significant liberalization has occurred since most of them received full independence in 1971. Kuwait's elected National Assembly has been in operation since 1962, albeit with a few suspensions. Bahrain's parliament, dismantled in 1973 after two fractious years of operation, returned in 2002, though with only half its members elected. Oman's consultative council expanded to full elections in 2003.

Qatar held its first municipal elections in 1997 and promised a partially elected parliament in 2006. Even Saudi Arabia permitted partial elections to municipal councils in 2005 amid indications that the experiment might be extended to the Consultative Council in the near future. As of 2005, only the UAE had no elected body, but the new president, Khalifah Al Nuhayyan, indicated at the end of the year that elections would be instituted shortly.

The GCC states currently face the specter of Islamist extremism. Saudi Arabia in particular has been targeted by a group known as al-Qaeda in the Arabian Peninsula. Attacks began in 2002 and escalated during the next two years. A cell from the group stormed three residential complexes in Riyadh in May 2003, killing 34 people. An attack on a second residential compound in Riyadh in November 2003 killed about 18, and a suicide attack on the general security headquarters in Riyadh killed 10 people in April 2004. Extremists also launched major attacks in Yanbu on the Red Sea and in al-Khobar on the Gulf coast in May 2004 and against the US consulate in Jiddah on the Red Sea in December 2004. Aggressive counteraction by Saudi security forces thinned the ranks of extremists through captures and killings; the remaining members appeared unable to launch additional large-scale attacks. Elsewhere in the Gulf, a suicide bomber in Qatar killed one expatriate in March 2005, and a limited number of attacks on civilian targets and US military vehicles were recorded in Kuwait after September 11.

Although the governments and ruling families of the GCC states have maintained and even intensified good relations with the United States, popular perceptions of the United States in these countries have grown increasingly negative. The regimes, however, concerned with security and survival, view a US relationship and umbrella as their best protection. Popular opinion has been inflamed, however, by a perceived US bias in favor of Israel and against the Palestinians, US policies vis-à-vis Iraq (ranging from enforcement of sanctions for 12 years that harmed the Iraqi people to invading a fellow Arab country), and revelations of American abuse of prisoners at Abu Ghraib prison in Iraq and Guantanamo Bay in Cuba.

Yemen, at the southern tip of the Arabian Peninsula, is not a Gulf state and is not a member of the GCC, though it wants to be. The problem for Yemen is that it mostly represents all that the GCC does not. A desperately poor country with a large and expanding population, Yemen's meager oil resources will likely play out in the short to medium term. The country has always suffered from weak government control of the hinterland as well as deep divisions between the formerly independent southern and northern halves caused by the 1994 civil war.

Yemen has endured Islamist extremists of a home-grown variety and al-Qaeda offshoots. A rash of kidnappings of foreigners in the 1990s turned into something far more deadly in 2001, when al-Qaeda members attacked the USS *Cole* anchored in the southern Yemeni port of Aden. Like the GCC states, Yemen has sought to portray itself as a partner of the United States in the war on terror and has received US assistance for improving internal security.

President Ali 'Abdallah Salih has ruled Yemen for 27 years much like his counterparts in other Arab republics—by restricting true political power to a small circle of supporters while maintaining the appearance of elections for president and the independence of parliament. The president is thought likely to adopt a strategy of the "hereditary republics" in having his son succeed him.

Turkey and the European Union

Modern Turkey rose from the wreckage of the Ottoman Empire, which expired almost mercifully as a result of World War I after centuries of decline. Mustafa Kemal Ataturk, the father of modern Turkey, maneuvered his fellow countrymen into embracing a secularist Turkey that looked to Europe for inspiration in political structure and socioeconomic development, bypassing traditional ties to the Middle East and the Islamic world. Ataturk also established a tradition of civilian government that several times was honored in the breach by the assumption of power by the military in the name of preserving the democratic process.

Turkey has long considered itself European and aspires to membership in the European Union (EU). In furtherance of its application, Turkey points to its Western-style democracy, its long and full membership in NATO, and the hundreds of thousands of Turks living in Western European countries, particularly in Germany. The EU formally recognized its candidacy for membership in 1999, but placed it in a class separate from other candidates because it had not met substantive requirements for membership. Among the outstanding issues were questions concerning the existence of stable institutions guaranteeing democracy and the rule of law, the functioning of a market economy ready to face increased competition, and adherence to the aims of political, economic, and monetary union.

Although Turkey has implemented many of the reforms necessary to fulfill the economic requirements for membership, serious doubts remain about the extent of its political reforms. These include the independence of the judiciary, the use of torture, and the extent of freedom of expression and assembly. In particular, the EU has demanded abolition of the death penalty and limitations on the role of the military in politics. Discriminatory treatment of the Kurdish minority poses another stumbling block. In other matters, the increasing popularity of Islamist parties, which has led to Islamists holding the post of prime minister—Necmettin Erbakan in 1996–1997 and Recep Tayyip Erdogan since 2003—threatens the secular nature of the Turkish state. Unease in Europe also exists about the possibility of dramatically increased Turkish emigration and Ankara's continuing support of the Turkish Republic of Northern Cyprus in defiance of Cyprus's admission to the EU.

In seeking to undertake some of the measures that the EU has demanded, Turkey restricted the death penalty to crimes against the state—though this did not completely satisfy EU expectations—and revised the penal code to bring it in line with European codes. The EU has, however, accused Ankara of backsliding on other reforms. It agreed to resume negotiations on entry in 2004, but imposed as conditions the understanding that talks did not guarantee eventual membership and that they could be suspended if the government failed to carry out reforms. Turkey's accession is viewed negatively by many Europeans for fear that an Islamic member in the EU might lead to greater problems with Islamist extremism.

Conclusion

The year 2005 brought pessimism as well as optimism to the outlook for the Middle East. The Israeli-Palestinian conflict continued unabated, but the level of violence lessened and signs appeared hinting that negotiations might resume. Despite a continuation of all manner of attacks in Iraq and the desperate situation of many Iraqis, the Bush administration insisted that matters were improving and pointed to parliamentary elections held in December as an encouraging sign. Outside Iraq, terrorism by Islamist extremists in the region decreased, but political reform still lagged. Beyond the headlines, the peoples of the Middle East continued to hope for lives lived in peace and for improvements to their standards of living and governance.

PART TWO

GOVERNMENTS

AFGHANISTAN

ISLAMIC STATE OF AFGHANISTAN

Note: On September 18, 2005, approximately 6.4 million Afghans cast ballots for the *Wolesi Jirga* (lower house of the National Assembly created by the 2004 constitution) in Afghanistan's first free, democratic elections for a parliament in more than 33 years. Close to 3,000 candidates contested the elections, with most running as independents rather than under party banners. The new National Assembly convened and its members were sworn in on December 19, 2005. Two days later, parliamentarians elected Yunos Qanuni, President Hamid Karzai's chief political rival, to chair the assembly.

The Country

Strategically located between the Middle East, Central Asia, and the Indian subcontinent, Afghanistan is a land marked by physical and social diversity. Physically, the landlocked country ranges from the high mountains of the Hindu Kush in the northeast to low-lying deserts along the western border. Pushtuns (alternatively Pashtuns or Pathans) constitute the largest of the population groups, followed by Tajiks, who speak Dari (an Afghan variant of Persian); others include Uzbeks, Hazaras, Baluchis, and Turkomans. Tribal distinctions (except among the Tajiks) may cut across ethnic cleavages, while religion is a major unifying factor: 90 percent of the people profess Islam (80 percent Sunni and the remainder Shiʻite [mostly from the Hazara population]). Prior to the Taliban takeover in 1996, women constituted a growing percentage of the paid work force in urban areas, particularly in health services and education, although female participation in government was minuscule; in the countryside the role of women has for a long time been heavily circumscribed by traditional Islamic fundamentalist strictures, which the Taliban movement also imposed on the urban population. The interim administration of December 2001, transitional government of June 2002, and permanent government of December 2004 all included women.

Economically, Afghanistan is one of the world's poorest countries, with a per capita GNP of less than $200 a year in 2004. Nearly 80 percent of the labor force is engaged in agriculture (largely at a subsistence level). The country's extensive mineral deposits are largely unexploited except for natural gas.

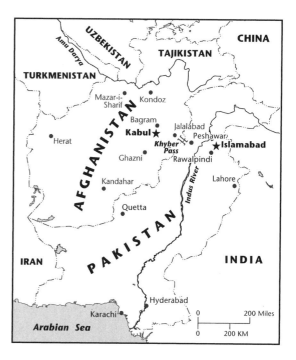

For many years the Soviet Union was Afghanistan's leading trade partner, while development aid from the West and from such international agencies as the Asian Development Bank was suspended as a result of the Soviet military intervention in late 1979. Thereafter, more than 20 years of civil war and subsequent turmoil left an estimated 2 million dead and much of the country in ruins. The Taliban government, which spent most of its energy following its partial takeover in 1996 in an attempt to secure complete control of the country, was described as having "no apparent economic program." The current major source of income reportedly is opium, as much as 40 percent of the world's heroin reportedly originating in Afghanistan. The rate of childhood death (mostly from preventable diseases) is among the highest in the world, and the illiteracy rate is estimated at 70 percent. Nearly all girls and two-thirds of boys reportedly did not attend school under the Taliban regime, the former in large part because of Taliban policy against education for women. (It was reported in 2005 that some 54 percent of school-aged children were now enrolled.) Life expectancy is only 45 years, an estimated 50 percent of the population lives in poverty, and 75 percent of the population lacks access to safe water. Economic development is hampered by the fact that much of the nation's wealth is concentrated in the hands of powerful warloads backed by private militias.

Western nations were eager in 1997 and early 1998 to see a resolution to the Afghan conflict so that progress could be made in laying oil and gas pipelines across the country from the huge and largely unexploited fields in Central Asia. However, alternate plans were subsequently adopted to run the pipelines through other countries as fighting continued in Afghanistan. Renewed Western interest in cross-Afghanistan pipelines returned following the overthrow of the Taliban in late 2001 and the subsequent installation of a transitional government of national unity. However, the most immediate concerns of the new administration were to start rebuilding the nation's infrastructure (experts estimated that as much as $15 billion in foreign aid would be needed over the next five years for that purpose), to facilitate the return of millions of refugees from neighboring countries, and to remove land mines (observers described Afghanistan as the most heavily mined country in the world).

The United States, which led the military campaign that had deposed the Taliban, was accused in some circles of losing its focus on Afghanistan in 2002–2003 as attention shifted to events involving Iraq. However, in 2004 the United States allocated $1.8 billion for reconstruction in Afghanistan and also increased the number of US troops dedicated to fighting Taliban and *al-Qaeda* remnants in Afghanistan. Overall, Western donors pledged $8.2 billion in new aid at a conference in April 2004 that also endorsed the Karzai administration's economic plans. However, private foreign investors remained leery of ongoing security problems and perceived deep-seated corruption at all levels of authority. In general, the transitional government received praise for its "crisis management" during 2002–2004, GDP growing by 29 percent in 2002, 16 percent in 2003, and 8 percent in 2004. Following its installation in late 2004, the new permanent administration pledged to pursue long-term stability and economic expansion through the promotion of free-market activity.

Government and Politics

Political Background

The history of Afghanistan reflects the interplay of a number of political forces, the most important of which traditionally were the monarchy, the army, religious and tribal leaders, and foreign powers. The existence of the country as a political entity is normally dated from 1747, when the Persians were overthrown and the foundations of an Afghan Empire were established by Ahmad Shah DURANI. Ahmad's successors, however, proved relatively ineffective in the face of dynastic and tribal conflicts coupled, in the 19th century, with increasingly frequent incursions by the Russians and British. The latter wielded decisive influence

Political Status: Republic established following military coup which overthrew traditional monarchy in July 1973; constitution of 1977 abolished following coup of April 27, 1978; successor regime, established following coup of December 27, 1979, effectively overthrown on April 16, 1992; successor regime effectively overthrown by the Taliban in late September 1996 but claimed to remain legitimate government; interim administration installed in December 2001 following overthrow of the Taliban; transitional government installed in June 2002; new constitution providing for multiparty democracy approved by a *Loya Jirga* (Grand National Council) on January 4, 2004; permanent government of the newly renamed Islamic Republic of Afghanistan established by inauguration of the president on December 7, 2004, and the cabinet on December 23.

Area: 249,999 sq. mi. (647,497 sq. km.).

Population: 13,051,358 (1979C), excluding an estimated 2.5 million nomads; 23,717,000 (2004E, including nomads). Nomads and refugees in western Pakistan and northern Iraq at one time totaled more than 5 million, many of whom have recently returned to Afghanistan.

Major Urban Centers (1988E): KABUL (urban area, 1,036,400), Kandahar (191,300), Herat (150,500), Mazar-i-Sharif (110,400). In the wake of the Taliban takeover, the population of Kabul was reported to have fallen to approximately 750,000; with the return of refugees after the Taliban defeat, some estimates were as high as 3 million.

Official Languages: Pushtu, Dari (Persian); in addition, the 2004 constitution authorized six minority languages (Baluchi, Nuristani, Pamiri, Pashai, Turkmen, and Uzbek) to serve as official third languages in the areas where the majority speaks them.

Monetary Unit: Afghani (market rate July 1, 2005: 42.79 afghanis = $1US). The afghani was "essentially worthless" during the Taliban regime (1996–2001). In late 2002 the transitional government introduced a "new afghani" to replace the old afghani at a rate of 1,000 old afghanis = 1 new afghani.

President: Hamid KARZAI (nonparty); appointed Chairman of the new Interim Administration at the UN-sponsored Bonn Conference on December 5, 2001, and inaugurated on December 22 for a six-month term (for a detailed description of the complicated issue of the leadership of Afghanistan prior to Karzai's inauguration, see the 2000–2002 *Handbook*); elected President of the new Transitional Government by an "emergency" *Loya Jirga* on June 13, 2002, and inaugurated on June 19 for a term that was scheduled not to exceed two years; elected by popular vote on October 9, 2004, and sworn in for a five-year term on December 7.

Vice Presidents: Karim KHALILI and Ahmad Zia MASOUD; elected on October 9, 2004, and inaugurated on December 7 for a term concurrent with that of the President. (For a detailed description of the prior vice-presidential situation, see the 2000–2002 *Handbook.*)

during the reign of ABDUR RAHMAN Khan and in 1898 imposed acceptance of the Durand line, which established the country's southern and eastern borders but which, by ignoring the geographic distribution of the Pushtun tribes, also laid the foundation for subsequent conflict over establishment of a Pushtunistan state. Emir AMANULLAH succeeded in forcing the British to relinquish control over Afghan foreign affairs in 1919 and attempted to implement such reforms as modern education, women's rights, and increased taxation before being forced to abdicate under pressure from traditional leaders.

The outbreak of World War II severely damaged the economy: markets were lost and access to imports and credit was cut off. Subsequently, dissent among intellectuals and failure to resolve the Pushtunistan issue led to a crisis of leadership. Prince Sardar Mohammad DAOUD, designated prime minister in 1953, succeeded in obtaining economic aid from both the United States and the Soviet Union, while modernization of the army helped to alleviate the threat posed by tribes hostile to the government. Politically, however, Daoud was quite conservative, ignoring the legislature, jailing his critics, and suppressing opposition publications. His dismissal in 1963 was followed by a series of moves toward a more modern political system, including the promulgation of a new constitution in 1964 and the holding of a parliamentary election in 1965. Nevertheless, problems encountered thereafter—recurrent famine; a worsening financial situation; increased restiveness on the part of the small, educated middle class; and a sense of impatience with civilian rule—led in 1973 to a military coup, the overthrow of the monarch (Mohammad ZAHIR SHAH) and the return of Daoud as president of a newly proclaimed republic.

On April 27, 1978, in the wake of unrest stemming from the assassination of a prominent opposition leader at Kabul, the Daoud regime was overthrown in a left-wing coup led by the deputy air force commander, Col. Abdul KHADIR. On April 30 a newly constituted Revolutionary Council designated Nur Mohammad TARAKI, secretary general of the formerly outlawed People's Democratic Party of Afghanistan (PDPA), as its president and announced the establishment of the Democratic Republic of Afghanistan, with Taraki as prime minister. Eleven months later, on March 27, 1979, Taraki yielded the office of prime minister to party hard-liner Hafizullah AMIN while remaining titular head of state by virtue of his presidency of the Revolutionary Council.

It was officially announced on September 16, 1979, that the PDPA Central Committee had unanimously elected Amin as its secretary general and, shortly thereafter, that the Revolutionary Council had designated him to succeed Taraki as president. While Kabul radio reported on October 9 that Taraki had died after "a severe and prolonged illness," it was generally assumed by foreign observers that the former president had succumbed on September 17 to wounds received three days earlier during an armed confrontation at the presidential palace. Subsequent reports suggested that a Soviet-backed effort by Taraki to remove the widely disliked Amin as part of a conciliatory policy toward rebel Muslim tribesmen had, in effect, backfired. Such suspicions heightened when Moscow, from December 25 to 26, airlifted some 4,000–5,000 troops to Kabul, which resulted in Amin's death and replacement on December 27 by his longtime PDPA rival Babrak KARMAL, theretofore living under Soviet protection in Czechoslovakia. Karmal proved scarcely more acceptable to the rebels than Amin, however, his regime being supported primarily by the continued presence of Soviet military personnel (estimated to number more than 110,000 by mid-1982). During the ensuing three years, the level of Soviet military involvement increased marginally because of continued resistance throughout the country by *mujaheddin* ("holy warrior") guerrillas, operating largely from rural bases and supplied from Pakistan, where more than 3 million Afghans had sought refuge. However, in 1985 a semblance of constitutional government was restored. A partially elected Grand National Council (*Loya Jirga*) was convened on April 23, for the first time in eight years; it promptly endorsed the Soviet presence, while elections for local village councils were held from August through October, despite disruptions attributable to *mujaheddin* activity.

On May 4, 1986, after a visit to the Soviet Union for what were described as medical reasons, Karmal stepped down as PDPA secretary general in favor of the former head of the state intelligence service, Mohammad NAJIBULLAH (Najib). On November 20 Karmal asked to be relieved of his remaining government and party posts, being succeeded as head of the Revolutionary Council by Haji Mohammad CHAMKANI, who was, however, designated only on an acting basis.

In December 1986 the PDPA Central Committee endorsed Najibullah's plan for "national reconciliation," calling for a cease-fire, political liberalization, and the formation of a coalition government. Although the seven-party *mujaheddin* alliance refused to negotiate and intense fighting continued, the government promoted its democratization campaign in 1987 by legalizing additional political parties, drafting a new constitution providing for an elected national legislature, and conducting local elections. However, in practical terms there was little challenge to Najibullah's consolidation of power: the Revolutionary Council on September 30, 1987, unanimously elected him as its president, and on November 30 the *Loya Jirga,* having approved the new constitution, named him as the first president of the Republic ("Democratic" having been deleted from the country's name).

On April 14, 1988, Afghanistan, Pakistan, the Soviet Union, and the United States concluded a series of agreements providing for a Soviet troop withdrawal within one year. Elections to the new National Assembly (*Meli Shura*) were held the same month, although the government was unable to convince the *mujaheddin* to participate. On May 26 the Revolutionary Council dissolved itself in deference to the Assembly, and, in a further effort by the government to reduce the appearance of PDPA dominance, Dr. Mohammad Hasan SHARQ, who was not a PDPA member, was appointed chairman of the Council of Ministers to replace Soltan Ali KESHTMAND.

The Soviet troop withdrawal was completed on February 15, 1989, precipitating significant political moves by both the government and *mujaheddin.* Najibullah, between February 18 and 19, dropped all non-PDPA members from the Council of Ministers; concurrently, a state of emergency was declared and a new 20-member Supreme Council for the Defense of the Homeland was created to serve, under Najibullah's leadership, as the "supreme military and political organ" for the duration of the emergency. On February 21 Keshtmand effectively resumed the duties of prime minister through his appointment as chairman of the Council of Ministers' Executive Committee.

For their part, the *mujaheddin* vowed to continue their resistance until an Islamic administration had been installed at Kabul. On February 24, 1989, the rebels proclaimed a "free Muslim state" under an Afghan Interim Government (AIG) headed by Imam Sibghatullah MOJADEDI as president and Abdul Rasul SAYAF as prime minister. However, the widespread belief that the rebels would quickly vanquish the Najibullah regime proved incorrect despite two reported coup plots in December and a nearly successful uprising led by the hard-line defense minister, Lt. Gen. Shahnawaz TANAY (in apparent collusion with rebel fundamentalist Gulbuddin HEKMATYAR) in March 1990.

On May 7, 1990, President Najibullah named Fazil Haq KHALIQYAR, a former minister-advisor in the Executive Council, to succeed Keshtmand as prime minister. Half of the members of the cabinet subsequently named by Khaliqyar were described as politically "neutral." From May 28 to 29 the *Loya Jirga* convened at Kabul to reiterate its commitment to private sector development and to ratify a number of reform-minded constitutional amendments.

On May 27, 1991, Najibullah announced that his government was prepared to observe a cease-fire with the *mujaheddin* to permit implementation of a peace plan advanced by UN Secretary General Javier Pérez de Cuéllar that would entail an end to external involvement in Afghan affairs and nationwide balloting to choose a new government. However, the offer was rejected by the AIG leadership. Two months later, at the conclusion of talks at Islamabad, Pakistan, the AIG reversed itself, stating that it "had recognized positive points" in the UN proposal. On September 1 the United States and the Soviet Union declared that they were halting arms supplies to the combatants, and trilateral discussions between US, USSR, and *mujaheddin* representatives were subsequently held on transfer of power to an interim regime that would oversee elections within two years. The fundamentalists, however, continued to call for Najibullah's immediate removal and the scheduling of an early poll.

On March 19, 1992, *mujaheddin* hard-liners rejected an offer by Najibullah to yield effective authority to an interim administration, reiterating their earlier demand that he resign. By early April, on the other hand, a pronounced shift in the balance of power had emerged in the strategic northern city of Mazar-i-Sharif, where local militias were forming alliances with moderate *mujaheddin* units. The realignment cut across both government and insurgent groupings, inaugurating a new cleavage between southern Pushtun fundamentalists led by Hekmatyar and non-Pushtun northerners under the command of Ahmed Shah MASOUD.

On April 16, 1992, Najibullah submitted his resignation and sought refuge in the Kabul UN office after four of his top generals had deserted to Masoud. Within a week the eastern city of Jalalabad became the last provincial capital to fall to joint *mujaheddin,* militia, and former government forces, who thereupon initiated a successful assault on Kabul. On April 24 the leaders of six rebel groups met at Peshawar, Pakistan, to announce the formation of a 51-member Islamic *Jihad* Council (IJC), headed by Imam Mojadedi, to assume power at the capital. After two months the IJC was to be replaced by an interim administration under Burhanuddin RABBANI (with Hekmatyar as prime minister and Masoud as defense minister), which would be succeeded four months later by a permanent government. However, Hekmatyar refused to participate, proceeding instead to launch an attack on his erstwhile allies. In three days of heavy fighting Hekmatyar's troops were unable to defeat the Masoud coalition, and on April 28 Mojadedi arrived to proclaim the formation of an Islamic republic. Meanwhile, Hekmatyar's forces continued to ring Kabul's southern and eastern outskirts, threatening to launch another offensive if Masoud did not break with the non-*mujaheddin* northerners (particularly with Gen. Abdul Rashid DOSTAM, an Uzbek, who had served under the former Communist regime). Subsequently, on May 25, Masoud and Hekmatyar held a seven-hour meeting, at the conclusion of which they agreed to halt hostilities and hold elections in six months. Even while they were talking, however, clashes were reported between units loyal to Hekmatyar and Dostam. In early June fighting also broke out between Iranian-backed

Hazara Shi'ites and Saudi Arabian–backed Sunni units loyal to Masoud. Reportedly the Shi'ites had demanded a minimum of eight ministerial posts in the Mojadedi government.

Although initially indicating that he wished to continue as acting president beyond his two-month mandate, Mojadedi stepped down on June 28, 1992, in favor of Rabbani. Concurrently, Hekmatyar agreed to the appointment of his deputy, Ustad FARID, as prime minister of an interim cabinet. Formally invested on July 6, Farid was forced from office a month later, after heavy fighting had erupted at Kabul between pro- and anti-Rabbani groups, including a massive artillery bombardment by Hekmatyar's forces that caused more than 1,800 deaths. On August 29 a cease-fire was announced, but it ended with a fresh outbreak of fighting on September 18.

On October 31, 1992, a Leadership Council, self-appointed five months earlier and chaired by Rabbani, extended the interim president's mandate beyond its four-month limit, permitting Rabbani to convene a Council of Resolution and Settlement in late December that elected him to a regular two-year term as head of state. Thereafter, Kabul was the scene of renewed fighting, culminating in a peace accord concluded by Rabbani and Hekmatyar at Islamabad, Pakistan, on March 7, 1993, that was endorsed by all but one of the major *mujaheddin* leaders. On March 8 Hekmatyar accepted appointment as prime minister, although differences immediately arose over the assignment of portfolios. On May 24, after further fighting at Kabul, a new cease-fire was announced, under which Masoud agreed to resign as defense minister and turn the ministry over to a tripartite commission. The principal obstacle having been overcome, a coalition cabinet was reportedly sworn in at an undisclosed location on June 17. However, the new administration was never effectively implemented in view of continued conflict between forces loyal to Rabbani and Hekmatyar, with General Dostam switching sides to join forces with Hekmatyar in fighting at Kabul and elsewhere in early 1994.

In late June 1994 Rabbani's troops succeeded in sweeping most Hekmatyar and Dostam units from the capital, and in mid-July the Organization of the Islamic Conference (OIC) reported that all parties had agreed to a peace process. Concurrently, however, there were reports that Pakistan's Inter-Services Intelligence (ISI) was supplying large quantities of arms and ammunition to Hekmatyar, who commenced a systematic bombardment of Kabul after the Supreme Court had extended Rabbani's presidential mandate for an additional six months without granting a similar extension of Hekmatyar's prime ministerial mandate.

On August 28, 1994, Maulawi Mohammad Nabi MOHAMMAD, of the moderate Islamic Revolutionary Movement, was named chairman of a *Loya Jirga* convening commission in preparation for national elections, and in mid-October representatives of Rabbani and Hekmatyar held proximity talks with UN special envoy Mahmoud Mestiri at Quetta, Pakistan. On November 6 Rabbani and his supporters accepted a modified version of a peace plan advanced by Mestiri, which called for a commission on which the principal *mujaheddin* units would have equal representation, with Rabbani subsequently announcing his willingness to step down as soon as "reliable mechanisms for a transfer of power" were in place.

Meanwhile the balance of power within Afghanistan was disrupted by an incursion of several thousand young Talibans (Islamic students) supported by Pakistan's fundamentalist *Jamiat-ul-Ulema-e-Islam* (Assembly of Islamic Clergy) and led by Maulana Fazlur RAHMAN. In November 1994 Taliban forces captured the city of Kandahar and initiated an anti-drug crusade throughout the opium-growing province of Helmand. The success of the new group appeared to reflect a major shift by Pakistan's ISI away from Hekmatyar and gave rise to speculation that the new element in Afghanistan's domestic turmoil might force a truce between Hekmatyar and Rabbani.

After winning control of a third of the country's provinces, the seemingly undefeatable Taliban by late February 1995 had driven Hekmatyar from his base at Charosyab, ten miles south of Kabul, and proceeded to advance on the capital. However, on March 11 the student militia suffered its first major defeat at the hands of Rabbani and Masoud and was subsequently forced to yield Charosyab to government forces. Routed in the east, the Taliban launched an offensive against the western city of Herat, which also failed after Masoud had dispatched a number of fighter bombers and some 2,000 troops to aid in the city's defense. Further Taliban defeats followed, while the anti-Rabbani *mujaheddin* front collapsed with Hekmatyar's withdrawal to the eastern city of Jalalabad and Dostam's unwillingness to commit his forces to battle.

On June 9, 1995, a truce was declared between government and Taliban forces. However, the latter mounted a major offensive in September that yielded the capture of Herat. On November 7 President Rabbani offered to resign if the Taliban agreed to a cease-fire and "foreign interference" (presumably by Pakistan in support of the students) were to end. Thereafter, fighting intensified in the vicinity of Kabul, followed by peace talks in which the government succeeded in reaching an accommodation with Hekmatyar (although not with his erstwhile *mujaheddin* allies) providing for joint military action against the Taliban and for governmental power-sharing. Under a peace accord signed on May 24, 1996, the supporters of Rabbani and Hekmatyar undertook to cooperate on the organization of new elections and to establish "genuine Islamic government," with Rabbani continuing as president and Hekmatyar being restored to the premiership. In accordance with the agreement, Hekmatyar was formally reappointed prime minister on June 26. Among the first actions of the restored prime minister were the closure of cinemas and the banning of music on radio and television on Sundays, on the ground that such activities were contrary to Islamic precepts. However, the potential for a new round of conflict was apparent in the reaction of Hekmatyar's former anti-Rabbani *mujaheddin* allies to the May agreement, which was to suspend Hekmatyar from membership of the coordination council established by the four main fundamentalist movements in 1994 under the chairmanship of former interim president Sibghatullah Mojadedi (leader of the National Liberation Front).

More ominously for the new government, the predominantly Sunni Taliban guerrillas, still strongly backed by Pakistan, continued to make military advances in July and August 1996, so that by early September they controlled 18 of the country's 30 provinces. The eastern city of Jalalabad, the country's second largest, was captured on September 11, whereupon Taliban forces pursued retreating government troops to Kabul and mounted a new onslaught on the capital. After some heavy fighting on the eastern side of the city, resistance crumbled and the government fled. By September 25 Taliban units were in complete control of Kabul, where on September 27 a six-member Provisional Council was installed under the chairmanship of Mullah Mohammad RABBANI (not related to the ousted president). Meanwhile, Mullah Mohammad OMAR (the spiritual leader of the Taliban) assumed the status of de facto head of state. Among the first acts of the new rulers was to seize ex-President Najibullah from the UN compound in which he had lived since April 1992 and to execute him in summary fashion, together with his brother Shahpur AHMADZAY (who had served as his security chief) and two aides. The executions were justified by Mullah Rabbani on the grounds that the former president had been "against Islam, a criminal and a Communist."

After a period of disorganization, the ousted government of Burhanuddin Rabbani relocated to northern Afghanistan, where a military alliance of the regrouped government troops under Masoud's command, the forces loyal to General Dostam, and Hazara fighters served to block the Taliban offensive. The military situation remained effectively stalemated until May 1997, when the Taliban troops were invited into the alliance's stronghold at Mazar-i-Sharif by Gen. Abdul Malik PAHLAWAN, who had apparently ousted General Dostam as leader of the National Front forces. However, just as the Taliban takeover of the entire country seemed imminent, Gen. Pahlawan's forces suddenly turned on the Taliban several days after the latter's arrival at Mazar-i-Sharif, killing, according to subsequent reports, some 2,000–3,000 Taliban fighters. Anti-Taliban groups, including,

significantly, Hekmatyar's Islamic Party, subsequently coalesced as the United National Islamic Front for the Salvation of Afghanistan (UNIFSA) and retained effective control of the north for the rest of the year. Collaterally, General Dostam, who had fled the country in June after Gen. Pahlawan's "coup," returned to Afghanistan in late October to wrest control of the Uzbek forces from Pahlawan, who apparently fled to Turkmenistan. Meanwhile, Mullah Omar was named emir of the Islamic Emirate of Afghanistan that was proclaimed by the Taliban on October 26, 1997.

In early 1998 the Taliban and UNIFSA appeared willing to consider a negotiated settlement, agreeing in principle to establish a joint council of religious scholars to assist in the process. However, the Taliban olive branch did not extend to the Hazara Shi'ite community in central Afghanistan, where the regime was enforcing an economic blockade that was said to be threatening famine. Consequently, despite UN, US, and OIC mediation efforts, the peace talks quickly broke down, and heavy fighting was renewed. The Taliban launched what its supporters hoped would be a final offensive to secure total control of the country in mid-July, and the key northern city of Mazar-i-Sharif fell out of UNIFSA hands in mid-August. However, as Taliban forces approached the northern borders, neighboring countries sent troops to defend their own territory from possible fundamentalist incursions and also provided assistance to the beleaguered UNIFSA fighters. In addition, Iran, angered over the killing of eight of its diplomats during the recent fighting and concerned over the threat to the Afghan Shi'ite community, amassed some 250,000 soldiers along its border with Afghanistan, raising fears of a full-blown regional war. Further complicating matters, on August 20 US cruise missiles struck camps in Afghanistan believed to be part of the alleged terrorist network run by Osama BIN LADEN. (The attack was ordered as retaliation for the bombing of US embassies in Kenya and Tanzania earlier in the month, in which Washington suspected bin Laden's followers to have been involved.) Bin Laden's presence in Afghanistan subsequently proved to be a barrier to Taliban attempts to gain additional international recognition. However, after the government rejected Western calls for bin Laden's extradition, an Afghan court in November ruled that the US had not produced evidence of his complicity in the embassy bombings and permitted him to remain in the country as long as he or his followers did not use it as a base for terrorist activity.

In July 1999 US President Clinton imposed economic sanctions on Afghanistan as the result of the Taliban's unwillingness to turn over bin Laden. Four months later, at Washington's urging, the UN Security Council directed UN members to freeze overseas assets of the Taliban government and to halt all flights to Afghanistan to pressure Kabul regarding bin Laden as well as to protest the perceived mistreatment of women and other human rights abuses and ongoing opium production. (One correspondent for the *Christian Science Monitor* described the Taliban as having achieved the "rare feat of provoking the hostility of all five permanent members of the Security Council." China, for example, reportedly expressed concern about Taliban influence on Islamic unrest within Chinese borders, while Russia went so far as to threaten to bomb Afghanistan if Kabul provided support to Chechnyan rebels or Islamist insurgents in neighboring Central Asian countries.) For their part, Taliban leaders appeared to remain preoccupied with attempting to secure control of the approximately 10 percent of the country in the northeast still in the hands of opposition forces. Major Taliban offenses were launched in the summers of 1999 and 2000, each being repulsed (after heavy fighting and large-scale civilian dislocation) by fighters, now referenced as the Northern Alliance, led by Ahmed Shah Masoud. Consequently, in September 2000 discussion was reported on yet another peace plan, under which Masoud would be given special administrative powers in an autonomous northeastern region.

Negotiations between the Northern Alliance and the Taliban continued for the rest of the year; however, they ultimately failed, and sporadic heavy fighting ensued in the first part of 2001. Meanwhile, tension intensified between the UN and the Taliban, the former rejecting a suggestion from the latter that bin Laden be tried in an Islamic country by Islamic religious leaders. Further complicating matters for the Taliban, Mullah Mohammad Rabbani, by then routinely referred to as chairman of the Taliban's "council of ministers," died on April 15 of natural causes. Although he had been the architect of many of the harsh strictures imposed on the population by the Taliban, Rabbani had been viewed by the international community as more approachable than most of the rest of the Taliban leadership. He was also generally well-respected within Afghanistan for the prominent role he had played while a member of *Hizb-i-Islami* in the *mujaheddin* war against the Soviets. Most of Rabbani's duties were assumed by the vice chairman of the ministerial council, Mohammed Hassan AKHUND, but no formal appointment to the chairmanship was announced.

The Taliban launched a major attack against the Northern Alliance in June 2001 and once again appeared dedicated to pursuit of a final, complete military victory. However, such hopes were irrevocably compromised by the terrorist attacks on September 11 in the United States, which the Bush administration quickly determined to be the work of *al-Qaeda*. Washington immediately demanded that bin Laden be turned over for prosecution or else military action would be initiated to remove him by force from Afghanistan. Intense debate was reported within the Taliban leadership on the issue, and efforts were made to forge a compromise under which, for example, bin Laden might be tried in a third country. However, President Bush declared the US terms to be "nonnegotiable," and Mullah Omar finally decided that the Taliban would take a stand in defense of its "guest." Consequently, after having secured broad "coalition" support for the action, the US, declaring it was acting in self-defense, launched "Operation Enduring Freedom" on October 7 against both *al-Qaeda* and Taliban targets. By that time, it was clear that the assault was intended not only to destroy *al-Qaeda* but also to produce a new regime in Afghanistan, Washington having concluded that *al-Qaeda* and the Taliban were now "one and the same."

Heavy bombing by US aircraft and cruise missiles quickly shattered the minimal infrastructure available to the Taliban military, while Omar's call on October 10 to the rest of the Muslim world for assistance in countering the US "invasion" elicited little response. The attention of the military campaign shifted later in the month to bombing *al-Qaeda* and Taliban troops in the north so as to support a ground assault by the Northern Alliance. After a disorganized start, the anti-Taliban forces, substantially rearmed and resupplied by the US and its allies, assumed an offensive posture at the end of October and drove toward the capital with few setbacks as many warlords previously aligned with the Taliban defected to the Northern Alliance. The first big prize, Mazar-i-Sharif, fell on November 9, and Kabul was surrounded by November 11. The swiftness of the Taliban collapse apparently surprised coalition military planners, and confusion reigned over how control of the capital would be achieved, US policy-makers being aware of the complica-ted political overtones involved in the establishment of a new Afghan government. Despite apparent US wishes to the contrary, the Northern Alliance moved into Kabul November 12–13, and the administration of Burhanuddin Rabbani announced it was reassuming authority, at least over the territory now controlled by the Northern Alliance.

Formal definition of the status of the Rabbani administration and governmental responsibility throughout the country overall remained ill-defined following the fall of Kabul pending the results of a UN-sponsored conference that convened at Bonn, Germany, on November 27, 2001, to negotiate a power-sharing post-Taliban government that would bridge the nation's myriad cleavages. In addition to UNIFSA/Northern Alliance officials, attendees at the conference included representatives from the so-called Rome Group (supporters of Afghanistan's former king, Mohammad Zahir Shah), the Peshawar Group (Afghan exiles who had been living in Pakistan), and a delegation of pro-Iranian refugees and exiles who had been centered at Cyprus. No Taliban officials were invited to participate.

Initial negotiations at the Bonn Conference proved difficult regarding the issues of proposed international peacekeepers for Afghanistan (opposed by the Northern Alliance) and the selection of the head of the planned interim government. A collapse of the talks appeared possible over the latter when it became apparent that the choice would not be Rabbani nor the 84-year-old ex-king. However, the Conference on December 3 agreed upon Hamid KARZAI, a relatively obscure former deputy minister with US backing. Karzai was formally appointed on December 5 as chairman of an Interim Administration which would eventually include a 29-member cabinet that had been carefully crafted to include as broad an ethnic base as possible. The Bonn Declaration which concluded the Conference on December 5 authorized the interim government for only six months, by which time an emergency *Loya Jirga* was to have established a new transitional government to prepare for free elections of a permanent government. The Conference participants also agreed that a UN peacekeeping force would be stationed at Kabul, although details on its mandate and size were left for further negotiation.

Meanwhile, as plans for the installation of the interim administration proceeded, the military campaign against the remaining Taliban and *al-Qaeda* forces continued unabated. After a sustained US bombing campaign, the Taliban surrendered its last remaining stronghold at Kandahar to the UNIFSA/Northern Alliance on December 7, although Mullah Omar and a number of Taliban ministers escaped capture, perhaps as part of controversial secret negotiations. The air assault subsequently focused on the cave complexes at Tora Bora southwest of Jalalabad, where it was estimated that as many as 1,700 *al-Qaeda* and Taliban fighters may have died before the complex was overrun. (The fate of bin Laden subsequently remained unclear.)

Karzai and his interim cabinet were inaugurated on December 22 in a ceremony at Kabul that featured a role for Rabbani as "outgoing president." Notable attendees included Gen. Dostam, who had threatened to boycott the proceedings because the Uzbek community was not sufficiently represented in the government. On December 26 Dostam accepted a post as vice chairman of the interim administration and deputy defense minister.

On January 10, 2002, final agreement was reached on the deployment of an International Security Assistance Force (ISAF), directed by the UN to assist in providing security at Kabul and surrounding areas but not to become involved outside that region. In May, the mandate of the ISAF (comprising some 4,500 troops from 19 countries at that point) was extended for another six months, some Western leaders reportedly pressing for its eventual extension to other areas of the country. Meanwhile, US ground forces (upwards of 7,000 strong) remained in Afghanistan to conduct mopping-up activities against remnants of the Taliban and *al-Qaeda*. No timetable was set for withdrawal of the American troops.

Former King Zahir Shah, who had returned to Afghanistan in April, was given the honor of opening the emergency *Loya Jirga* at Kabul on June 12, 2002. On June 13 Karzai received about 80 percent of the votes against two minor candidates in the balloting for the president for the new transitional government, all potentially major opponents (including Zahir Shah) having removed themselves from contention. On its final day (June 19) the *Loya Jirga* also endorsed, by a show of hands, the partial cabinet announced by Karzai. However, the *Loya Jirga* adjourned without having made a decision on the makeup of a proposed transitional legislature. The transitional government was authorized to hold power for up to two years, with a constitutional *Loya Jirga* to be convened in approximately 18 months to adopt a new constitution that would provide the framework for new elections by June 2004.

In April 2003 President Karzai appointed a 33-member constitutional commission that drafted new basic law in November that called for a multiparty system headed by a president with broad powers and a mostly elected bicameral legislature. The constitution, with modifications, was approved by a *Loya Jirga* on January 4, 2004 (see Constitution and government, below, for details). Although both presidential and legislative elections were initially scheduled for June 2004, they were postponed due to difficulties in completing voter registration and other electoral arrangements. Presidential balloting was finally held on October 9, with Karzai winning in the first round of balloting with 55.4 percent of the vote. Authority was formally transferred from the transitional administration upon Karzai's inauguration on December 7; a new "reconstruction" cabinet was appointed by Karzai on December 23.

Constitution and Government

The Afghan Interim Government (AIG) announced by the *mujaheddin* on February 24, 1989, resulted from a 400-member consultative assembly (*shura*) that convened on February 10 at the Pakistani city of Rawalpindi. In addition to the naming of a largely ceremonial president, nominal ministerial posts were distributed among the principal rebel factions on the basis of votes cast by the *shura* delegates. However, many of Afghanistan's northern and western provinces were unrepresented at the two-week conclave, and the shadow government contained no members of the country's Shi'ite Muslim minority.

A partial government announced on May 5, 1992, by Interim President Mojadedi stemmed not from the Rawalpindi conclave but from the Peshawar meeting of April 24. A substantial number of portfolios (including that of prime minister) remained unfilled (apparently because of the dispute with Hekmatyar), while many of the named appointees (Masoud, as defense minister, being a conspicuous exception) were relatively unknown.

At the Islamabad meeting of March 1993 the appointment of Burhanuddin Rabbani as president was confirmed for an 18-month (later a two-year) period from December 1992, while the accord of May 24 on tripartite control of the defense ministry paved the way for the nominal installation of an all-party cabinet in mid-June.

On January 28, 1995, the UN peace envoy, Mahmoud Mestiri, announced that plans were being finalized to transfer power to an interim council composed of two representatives from each of the country's 30 provinces, plus 15–20 individuals nominated by the UN. However, prior to

Hekmatyar's defeat by the Taliban, Rabbani insisted that the latter also be permitted to name council members. The suggestion was opposed by Mestiri on the ground that the students were "a different sort of force from the Afghan parties" and became moot after the Taliban's seizure of power in Kabul in September 1996. The Taliban quickly installed a six-member Provisional Council at Kabul which subsequently grew in stages into a full-fledged Council of Ministers. However, government decisionmaking authority appeared to remain in the hands of a small Taliban consultative council at Kandahar, the headquarters of the movement's spiritual leader (and emir of the Islamic Emirate of Afghanistan proclaimed in October 1997), Mullah Mohammad Omar, who served, among other things, as de facto head of state and commander in chief of the armed forces.

The constitution approved in January 2004 provided for a Western-style democracy with a strong central government headed by a popularly elected president (limited to two five-year terms) and a National Assembly (see Legislature, below, for details). The *Loya Jirga* (comprising the members of the Assembly and the chairpersons of the proposed elected provincial and district councils) was institutionalized as the "highest manifestation of the people of Afghanistan" and given full responsibility to amend the constitution, prosecute the president if necessary, and "make decisions relating to independence, national sovereignty, territorial integrity, and other supreme interests of the country." The new basic law enshrined Islam as the state religion but guaranteed freedom for other religions to be practiced. Equal rights were guaranteed for men and women, as were freedom of expression and of association (see Political Parties and Groups, below, for details). Provision was made for an independent human rights commission and an independent judiciary headed by a Supreme Court comprising presidential appointees subject to confirmation by the lower house of the Assembly.

The new constitution authorized the establishment of the Islamic Transitional State of Afghanistan pending what were expected to be simultaneous presidential and legislative elections. However, in view of the subsequent delay in holding Assembly balloting, the transitional state was declared to have concluded with the inauguration in December 2004 of President Karzai to head the administration of the newly renamed Islamic Republic of Afghanistan.

Foreign Relations

Afghan foreign policy historically reflected neutrality and nonalignment, but by the mid-1970s Soviet economic and military aid had become pronounced. After the April 1978 coup, the Taraki government, while formally committed to a posture of "positive nonalignment," solidified relations with what was increasingly identified as "our great northern neighbor." Following what was, for all practical purposes, Soviet occupation of the country in late 1979, the Karmal regime asserted that Soviet troops had been "invited" because of the "present aggressive actions of the enemies of Afghanistan" (apparently an allusion to the United States, China, Pakistan, and Iran, among others)—a statement which proved singularly unconvincing to most of the international community. On January 14, 1980, the UN General Assembly, meeting in special session, called by a vote of 104–18 (with 18 abstentions) for the immediate and unconditional withdrawal of the Soviet forces, while Afghanistan's membership in the OIC was suspended two weeks later. Subsequently, the General Assembly and other international bodies reiterated their condemnation, most nations refusing to recognize the Kabul regime; exceptions to the latter included India, which participated in a joint Indo-Afghan communiqué in early 1985 expressing concern about "the militarization of Pakistan."

In early 1986, following the accession to power of economy-conscious Mikhail Gorbachev, Moscow indicated a willingness to consider a timetable for withdrawal of Soviet troops, conditioned on withdrawal of international support for the *mujaheddin*. The signature of an Afghan-Pakistani agreement (guaranteed by the Soviet Union and the United States) called for mutual noninterference and nonintervention. Accompanying accords provided for the voluntary return of refugees and took note of a time frame established by Afghanistan and the Soviet Union for a "phased withdrawal of foreign troops" over a nine-month period commencing May 15. However, the agreements did not provide for a cease-fire, with both the United States and Pakistan reserving the right to provide additional military supplies to the Afghan guerrillas if Moscow continued to provide arms to Kabul.

In late 1990 the United States and the Soviet Union agreed on a policy of "negative symmetry," whereby both would cease supplying aid to their respective Afghan allies in expectation that the aid suspension would necessitate a cease-fire between the government and the rebels. Upon implementation of the mutual suspension in September 1991, even fundamentalist rebel leaders reportedly declared that they welcomed "the end of [foreign] interference." However, by early 1995 it was apparent that involvement by external powers had by no means ceased, although it was being conducted far less visibly than during the Najibullah era. The Taliban movement was launched by former students at Islamic seminaries in Pakistan, with one observer initially characterizing the seminarians as "cannon fodder" in a Pakistani effort to reopen vital highway shipping routes to Tajikistan and beyond. Countering Pakistan's support of the Taliban was Indian aid to Rabbani and Masoud, particularly the provision of military aircraft that were crucial to the defense of Herat. For his part, General Dostam, the northern Uzbek warlord, had long been backed by Russia and Uzbekistan.

Washington initially exhibited a somewhat surprisingly warm stance toward the Taliban takeover in late 1996, reportedly out of the hope that it offered Afghanistan a chance for "stability" after 17 years of civil war. However, the US posture cooled significantly during 1997 because of the Taliban human rights record and harsh religious strictures, US Secretary of State Madeleine Albright strongly criticizing the Taliban policies toward women. Meanwhile, Russia and members of the Commonwealth of Independent States (CIS), including Tajikistan and Uzbekistan, issued a stern warning to the Taliban in early 1997 not to attempt to spread militant fundamentalist influence beyond the Afghan borders. Collaterally, Iran displayed its support for the Shi'ite population in the Hazara region, which was aligned with the anti-Taliban forces.

Current Issues

Most of Afghanistan appeared in late 2001 to celebrate the collapse of the Taliban government, which had imposed a "joyless existence" on the population and fostered extreme international isolation. The festive mood was tempered, however, by the knowledge that many of the important components of the new interim government had been part of the disastrous *mujaheddin* regime in the first half of the 1990s that had created the opportunity for the Taliban to flourish in the first place. In addition, much of the country outside the capital remained under the control of warlords with very little inclination to acquiesce to a strong centralized government. The daunting task of maintaining stability under severe ongoing ethnic, regional, and religious strains fell to Hamid Karzai, whose emergence as the choice to head the interim administration had surprised most observers. Described as a "moderate" Muslim, Karzai had served as a deputy foreign minister in an early cabinet of Burhanuddin Rabbani's. Following the launching of Operation Enduring Freedom in October 2001, Karzai had returned to Afghanistan to rally the Pushtun community to the cause of the US-supported Northern Alliance (dominated by Tajiks and Uzbeks) and the eventual creation of a new broad-based national government. Western capitals widely praised the performance of Karzai and his interim administration in the first half of 2002 and were considered influential in assuring that he faced little serious challenge in the balloting for president of the two-year transitional government at the *Loya Jirga* in June. (After reported backroom debate, Zahir Shah had endorsed Karzai for the post; subsequently, Karzai declared Zahir Shah to be the nation's "ceremonial father," guaranteeing him an ongoing prominent public role.)

Western grants helped Afghanistan pay off its arrears to several international organizations in early 2003, but some officials reportedly worried in private that global attention had shifted away from Afghanistan and toward Iraq. In May US Defense Secretary Donald Rumsfeld declared that only "pockets of resistance" remained within Afghanistan and that reconstruction was the transitional administration's appropriate priority. However, a resurgence in the second half of the year of Taliban guerrilla attacks on US and government forces killed hundreds. President Karzai also had to contend with outbreaks of fighting between various warlord militias, many of whom were resisting the new UN/Afghani demobilization and disarmament campaign. Karzai appeared eager in mid-2004 to reach an agreement with the leaders of the private armies (particularly those in the north) in preparation for his presidential campaign. However, when Karzai dropped Vice President Mohammad Qasim FAHIM (a northern commander) as a running mate, many of the northern tribal leaders threw their support to Mohammad Yunos QANUNI, who finished second in the balloting with 16.3 percent of the vote. As a result, the election revealed a continued north/south divide that might still threaten national unity. On a more positive note, however, Taliban threats to disrupt the balloting proved mostly empty, and international observers accepted the results as accurately reflecting the popular will, despite a number of electoral irregularities.

At his inauguration in December 2004, President Karzai pledged to combat the "mortal threat" of drug production and trafficking, to fight systemic poverty, and to promote "governmental accountability." Toward those ends, his new cabinet appeared to rely more heavily on "technocrats" than his previous administration, although critics noted that most "power portfolios" remained in the hands of Pushtuns.

The frequency of rebel attacks remained relatively low for a number of months after the presidential poll, but the Taliban-led insurgency reintensified in the spring of 2005. In an apparently related vein, a special *Loya Jirga* endorsed Karzai's plan for a continued "strategic partnership" with the United States and NATO, although it was unclear if the final arrangements would include permanent US military bases in Afghanistan. Meanwhile, by that time US and NATO officials were reportedly considering a merger under a single command of the two main forces operating in Afghanistan. (The 8,400-strong ISAF, under NATO command since August 2003, was operating primarily as a peacekeeping and security mission in and around Kabul and in "stable" northern regions, while the US-led Combined Forces Command Afghanistan [about 17,000 US troops complemented by about 1,600 personnel from some 20 other nations] waged a higher-intensity campaign against Taliban and *al-Qaeda* fighters, mostly along the border with Pakistan.)

Political Parties and Groups

Based at Peshawar, Pakistan, the seven leading opponents of the Najibullah regime formed an Islamic Alliance of Afghan Holy Warriors (*Ittehad-i-Islami Afghan Mujaheddin*) in May 1985 to coordinate resistance to the Moscow-backed regime in Kabul, as well as to the Soviet expeditionary force that protected it until 1989. The alliance spearheaded the overthrow of President Najibullah in April 1992, but its fragile unity was quickly shattered by subsequent conflict within and between fundamentalist and moderate groups, amid a complex pattern of surrogate involvement by interested neighboring states such as Pakistan and Iran. A new factor from late 1994 was the rapid military success of the Pakistan-backed Taliban guerrillas, which culminated in their seizure of power in Kabul in September 1996.

Resistance to the Taliban was coordinated at first by a Supreme Defense Council formed in October 1996 by the Islamic Afghan Society, the National Front, and the Islamic Unity Front. The umbrella organization's name was changed to the United National Islamic Front for the Salvation of Afghanistan (UNIFSA) in mid-1997 to reflect the addition of new members (including the National Islamic Front) as well as expansion of the alliance's mandate to cover political as well as military initiatives. UNIFSA, with heavy US military and financial support, spearheaded the overthrow of the Taliban in late 2001.

The new constitution approved in January 2004 provides for freedom of association, political parties being authorized providing they have no military or paramilitary structures and that their platforms are not "contrary to the principles of Islam." Parties based on ethnicity, language, religious sects, or regions are also prohibited. Many small parties applied for legal status in 2004 and the first half of 2005, contributing to highly fluid and often confusing conditions in the run-up to the legislative balloting scheduled for September 2005.

National Understanding Front—NUF (*Jabha-i-Tafahon-i-Milli*). Launched in early 2005 by some 11 political parties, the NUF was described by one reporter as the "first attempt to forge a serious opposition" to the Karzai administration. NUF Chairman Mohammad Yunos Qanuni had finished second in the 2004 presidential poll after leaving his post as planning minister in the Karzai cabinet (see Current issues, above, for additional information). Qanuni's recently formed **New Afghanistan Party** (*Hizb-i-Afghanistan- i-Naween*) was among the NUF's core components, as were the Islamic Unity Party of the People of Afghanistan (*Hizb-i-Wahdat-i-Islami Mardom-i-Afghanistan*), a faction of the Islamic Unity Party that split off under the leadership of Mohammad Mohaqeq; the **Islamic Power Party** (*Hizb-i-Iqtedar-i-Islamic*), led by former resistance leader Ahmad Shah Ahmadzay; a faction of the **Islamic Movement Party** (*Hizb-i-Harakat-i-Islami*)led by Mohammad Ali Jawid; and a faction of the **Islamic Revolutionary Movement Party** (*Hizb-i-Harahat-i-Inqilah-i-Islami*) led by Ahmad NABI.

The leaders of the NUF announced that their first goal was to achieve parliamentary power in the National Assembly balloting scheduled for September 2005. They accused the Karzai administration of having failed to combat corruption in government, indicated opposition to the presence of foreign troops in Afghanistan, and called for the adoption of a proportional voting system in the Assembly. However, some observers described the Front as comprising "incongruous factions" that might lack sustained cohesion.

Leaders: Mohammad Yunos QANUNI (Chairman); Ahmad Shah AHMADZAY, Mohammad MOHAQEQ, Najia ZHARA (Deputy Chairmen); Mohammad Ali JAWID (Spokesman).

Islamic Afghan Society (*Jamaat-i-Islami Afghanistan*). The Afghan Society draws most of its support from Tajiks in the northern part of the country. It was long the most effective rebel force in the Panjsher Valley and engaged in heavy combat with Soviet forces in 1985, including sporadic invasions of Soviet Tajikistan. In July 1989 the *Jamaat* charged that a group of its leaders and fighters had been attacked and killed by guerrillas from the Islamic Party, subsequent retaliatory attacks leaving perhaps as many as 300 fighters dead.

Internal disagreement over relations with the Islamic Party threatened to splinter *Jamaat* in 1990, when military commander Ahmed Shah Masoud temporarily parted company with political leader Burhanuddin Rabbani in rejecting an appeal to aid the Islamic Party's offensive against Kabul. In October Masoud, long a leading military figure, gained additional prominence when he chaired a *shura* of Afghan military chiefs and then flew to Islamabad for the first time in more than a decade to confer with Pakistani President Khan. After the fall of Kabul in April 1992, Masoud was named defense minister in the Mojadedi government, continuing in that capacity during the Rabbani presidency.

Forces loyal to Rabbani fled from the Taliban offensive against Kabul in September 1996, subsequently coalescing under Masoud's command in the north, where, in conjunction with other anti-Taliban militias, they fought the Taliban to a stalemate. Masoud's forces, estimated to number 12,000–15,000, survived into the fall of 2001, having weathered heavy Taliban offensives during the summers of the past three years.

Masoud was killed in an attack by suicide bombers disguised as journalists on September 10,

2001. The assassination was widely attributed to *al-Qaeda* as a prelude to the terrorist attacks in the US the following day. Masoud was succeeded as military commander of the Northern Alliance by Mohammad Qasim FAHIM, who became one of the top leaders in the subsequent expulsion of the Taliban.

Rabbani, whose government had maintained the recognition of many countries throughout the Taliban regime, returned to Kabul in mid-November 2001 to resume the exercise of presidential authority. He reportedly hoped that the subsequent Bonn Conference would appoint him as president of the proposed new interim administration, and he only reluctantly accepted the appointment of Hamid Karzai after holding up the Conference for several days in apparent protest to being sidelined. Any remaining short-term political aspirations on Rabbani's part were also put on hold at the *Loya Jirga* in July 2002, where Rabbani endorsed Karzai's election as president of the new transitional government. Fahim, however, was named vice president and minister of defense, establishing himself as one of the administration's dominant figures. Rabbani supported Karzai in the 2004 presidential election even though Fahim was dropped from the Karzai ticket. *Jamaat* subsequently announced it would present candidates (including Rabbani) in the September 2005 legislative balloting.

Leader: Burhanuddin RABBANI (former President of the Islamic State), Munawar HASAN (Secretary General).

National Front (*Jumbish-i-Milli*). The *Jumbish-i-Milli* is an Uzbek grouping formed by Gen. Abdul Rashid Dostam, who had been a military commander under Najibullah before aligning himself with Ahmed Masoud in 1992. In early 1994 Dostam broke with Masoud to join forces with Hekmatyar's *Hizb-i-Islami* and Mazari's *Hizb-i-Wahdat* in an anti-Rabbani alliance. He did not, however, support his new colleagues in the decisive encounters of March 1995, thereby contributing to their defeat. Thereafter, the *Far Eastern Economic Review* reported that Rabbani

had attempted to "cut a deal" with Dostam, whose rejection of the terms contributed to the Rabbani government's subsequent readiness for an accommodation with Hekmatyar. Following the Taliban takeover of Kabul in 1996, General Dostam initially played an important role in the anti-Taliban alliance (see Political background, above). However, it was reported that he and his remaining forces had retreated to Uzbekistan following the Taliban offensive of the second half of 1998, and his influence had declined significantly by mid-2000.

Dostam returned to Afghanistan in March 2001 and rejoined the Northern Alliance. The general subsequently remained closely aligned with Rabbani during the overthrow of the Taliban and strongly objected to the selection at the Bonn Conference of Hamid Karzai over Rabbani as president of the new interim government in December. Initially, it appeared that Dostam's disgruntlement would prove a threat to stability, but he accepted positions as vice chairman of the interim administration and deputy minister of defense in late December, thereby calming the situation. General Dostam, burdened with a reputation for military ruthlessness and political shiftiness, was not included in the July 2002 cabinet.

Running as an independent, Dostam finished fourth in the 2004 presidential poll with 10 percent of the vote. In early 2005 Dostam registered a party called the **National Islamic Movement of Afghanistan** (*Jumbish-i-Milli-i-Islami Afghanistan*), but in April he resigned from that grouping and became the chief of staff of the high command of the armed forces in Karzai's administration.

Leader: Gen. Abdul Rashid DOSTAM, Azizullah KARQAR, Sayyed NUROLLAH, Faysollah ZAKI, Abdul Majid ROZI.

Islamic Unity Party (*Hizb-i-Wahdat-i-Islami*). The *Hizb-i-Wahdat* was launched in mid-1987 by the following Iran-based groups: the **Afghan Nasr Organization** (*Sazmane Nasr*); the **Da'wa Party of Islamic Unity of Afghanistan** (*Da'wa-i-Ittehad-i-Islami Afghanistan*); the **Guardians of**

the **Islamic Jihad of Afghanistan** (*Pasadaran-i-Jihhad-i-Afghanistan*); the **Islamic Force of Afghanistan** (*Nehzat-i-Afghanistan*); the **Islamic Movement of Afghanistan** (*Harakat-i-Islami Afghanistan*), led by Ayatollah Aseh MOHSENI; the **Islamic Struggle for Afghanistan** (*Narave Islami Afghanistan*), led by Zaidi MOHAZZIZI; the **Party of God** (*Hezbollah*), led by Qari AHMAD; and the **United Islamic Front of Afghanistan** (*Jabhe Muttahid-i-Afghanistan*). Also known as the "Teheran Eight," the group claimed at its inception to represent an estimated two million Shi'ite Afghan refugees in Iran. During 1992 and early 1993 it joined with Hekmatyar's *Hizb-i-Islami* in a number of clashes with Rabbani's *Jamaat-i-Islami* and the Saudi-backed *Ittihad-i-Islami*. Its principal leader, Abdul Ali MAZARI, was killed on March 13, 1995, reportedly in a helicopter crash south of Kabul after having been captured by the Taliban student militia.

Hizb-i-Wahdat was an important component of UNIFSA in that it represented the Hazara Shi'ite community in central Afghanistan. As of early 1998 the Hazara were reportedly exercising autonomous government control in the Hazarajat region while contributing substantially to the anti-Taliban military alliance in the north. However, Taliban forces pushed *Hizb-i-Wahdat* out of most of the populated areas in the region (including the important city of Bamiyan) in September 1998. In consonance with the ouster of the Taliban by the UNIFSA/Northern Alliance in late 2001, *Hizb-i-Wahdat* regained control of much of central Afghanistan, and party leader Karim Khalili was named as a vice president in the transitional government installed in June 2002.

Leaders: Karim KHALILI (Vice President of the Republic), Ayatollah FAZL.

National Islamic Front (*Mahaz-i-Milli-i-Islami*). The most left-leaning of the moderate groups, the National Islamic Front had refused to join the Supreme Council in 1981 because not all of the participants had agreed to the election of people's representatives to a provisional government.

In November 1990 party leader Pir Sayed Ahmad Gailani endorsed a reported US-USSR peace plan which would have left Najibullah in power after the two countries withdrew their support for the combatants. Thereafter, at a meeting at Geneva, Switzerland, Gailani allegedly turned down an offer by Najibullah to assume control of the government, suggesting instead the return of Mohammad Zahir Shah, the former monarch.

Gailani, the spiritual leader of the Sufi Muslims, served in the Rabbani cabinet 1992–1996, he and his supporters locating in Cyprus following the Taliban takeover. They subsequently served as the core component of the so-called "Cyprus Group" at the Bonn Conference in late 2001, where the Front continued to display a proroyalist orientation.

Leader: Pir Sayed Ahmad GAILANI.

Islamic Party (*Hizb-i-Islami*). Drawing most of its support from Pushtuns in the southeastern part of the country, the Islamic Party was one of the largest and most radical of the *mujaheddin* groups and often engaged in internecine clashes with former allies including, most notably, the *Jamaat-i-Islami*. Its principal leader, Gulbuddin Hekmatyar, was known to have ties to both Iran and Libya in the 1970s and early 1980s, although they subsequently were believed to have been reduced. In the second half of 1989 Hekmatyar announced a boycott of the interim government, of which he was the titular foreign minister, in the wake of clashes between his fighters and those of the Islamic Afghan Society; he also declared his opposition to the apparent willingness of some moderates to consider government peace offers.

Hekmatyar was named prime minister following the all-party accord of March 1993 but was at that stage deeply opposed to the Rabbani presidency; his appointment lapsed in mid-1994. Thereafter, he maintained a partial siege of Kabul until forced to withdraw after a decisive defeat in March 1995. This experience eventually impelled him to break ranks with other *mujaheddin* leaders by reaching his own accommodation with the government in May 1996, enabling him to resume the premiership from June until the overthrow of the government in September. Hekmatyar's decision to align his forces with those of Ahmed Masoud and General Dostam was considered an important factor in their subsequent ability to stall the Taliban offensive in the north in 1997. However, Hekmatyar and the Islamic Party were described in 1998 as only nominally associated with the UNIFSA and apparently not playing a major role in the remaining military opposition to the Taliban. Interviewed in Iran in mid-2000, Hekmatyar called on the Taliban to establish a provisional government including opposition representatives pending national elections, describing the civil war as benefiting only "foreign forces."

In the fall of 2001 Hekmatyar adopted a strongly anti-Northern Alliance stance and urged support for the Taliban against what he called a US "invasion." Hekmatyar returned to Afghanistan in early 2002 but remained noticeably outside the negotiations toward a government of national unity. Considered a threat to the stability of the interim administration, Hekmatyar was reportedly the target of an unsuccessful assassination attempt in May on the part of the US through the use of an unmanned "drone" bomber. Hekmatyar subsequently reportedly fled to Iran, but he was eventually expelled from that country. Having returned to Afghanistan, he was labeled a terrorist because of attacks on US and Afghani forces. In early 2005 it appeared that some Islamic Party adherents had begun peace negotiations with the Karzai administration, although Hekmatyar (who rejected an apparent amnesty offer) and others remained committed to *jihad* until US forces were removed from Afghanistan and an "Islamic System" was installed.

Leaders: Gulbuddin HEKMATYAR (former Prime Minister), Mohammad Yunos KHALES.

Islamic Unity (*Ittihad-i-Islami*). The *Ittihad-i-Islami* was a grouping of ultra-orthodox Sunni Muslims backed by Saudi Arabia. Like the other fundamentalist formations, it long opposed Westernizing influences in pursuing what it viewed largely as an Islamic holy war (*jihad*) against Soviet-backed forces. One of its leaders, Abdul Rasul Sayaf, headed the Alliance at its inception

in 1985. The party endorsed President Karzai in the 2004 presidential campaign.

Leader: Abdul Rasul SAYAF (former Prime Minister of Government-in-Exile).

National Liberation Front (*Jabh-i-Nijat-i-Milli*). The National Liberation Front is committed to Afghan self-determination and the establishment of a freely elected government. Its leader, Sibghatullah Mojadedi, was chairman of the moderate opposition bloc in the late 1980s. In November 1990 Mojadedi, along with Sayed Ahmad Gailani (National Islamic Front, above), reportedly met with President Najibullah at Geneva, Switzerland, in an abortive attempt to form a coalition government. Subsequently, Mojadedi served as Interim President from April to June 1992, before becoming a prominent opponent of the succeeding Rabbani government. In 1994 he became chairman of a coordination council linking his own movement with the Islamic Party, the Islamic Unity Party, and the National Front. Immediately following the Taliban takeover of Kabul in September 1996, it was reported that Mojadedi had announced his support for the new government. However, he was subsequently described as having moved to Egypt, from where he was "abstaining" from the conflict between the Taliban and its opponents. Mojadedi supported Hamid Karzai in the 2004 presidential campaign and was later named chairman of the fledgling national reconciliation commission.

Leaders: Imam Sibghatullah MOJADEDI (former President of Government-in-Exile and former Interim President of the Islamic State), Dr. Hashimatullah MOJADEDI.

Homeland Party (*Hizb-i-Watan*). Previously known as the People's Democratic Party of Afghanistan (PDPA), which dominated national political affairs during the late 1970s and most of the 1980s (see Political background, above), the Homeland Party adopted its new name at its second congress in June 1990. Although not formally dissolved following the fall of the pro-Soviet regime, the group's subsequent activity was limited to occasional contact at meetings of international communist organizations. It was reported in 2003 that the interim government had refused a request from the Homeland Party for legal status, and party adherents subsequently appeared to have launched several new groupings.

National Solidarity Movement of Afghanistan (*Nahzat-i Hambastagi-i Milli Afghanistan*). This party is led by Ishaq Gailani, who was a candidate for president in 2004 prior to withdrawing in support of Hamid Karzai.

Leader: Ishaq GAILANI.

Afghan Nation (*Afghan Mellat*). Established during the reign of King Zahir Shah in support of Pushtun nationalism, this grouping (also referenced as the Social Democratic Party of Afghanistan) has reportedly factionalized recently. One faction, which supported Hamid Karzai in the 2004 presidential campaign, is led by Anwar al-Haq Ahadi, who was named minister of finance in the December 2004 cabinet.

Leader: Anwar al-Haq AHADI.

National Congress Party of Afghanistan (*Hizb-i Kongra-i Milli-i Afghanistan*). This party was launched in April 2004 in support of the presidential candidacy of moderate Abdul Latif Pedram, who finished fifth in the October poll with 1.37 percent of the vote.

Leaders: Abdul Latif PEDRAM, Nasir OJABER.

Islamic Unity Party of the People of Afghanistan (*Hizb-i Wahdat-i Islami-i Mardum-i Afghanistan*). A splinter from the Islamic Unity Party, this grouping is led by Mohammad Mohaqeq (a representative of the Hazara ethnic group), who finished third as an independent candidate in the 2004 presidential balloting with 11.66 percent of the vote.

Leader: Mohammad MOHAQEQ.

National Movement of Afghanistan (*Hizb-i Nahzat-i Milli-i Afghanistan*). Primarily supported by Tajiks, *Nahzat* was launched by Ahmad Wali Masoud following the death of his brother, Ahmed Shah Masoud, the legendary *mujaheddin* military leader. The party was factionalized in 2004 when *Nahzat* member Yunos ran against Hamid Karzai in the 2004 presidential campaign, while another Masoud brother, Ahmad Zia Masoud, was one of Karzai's vice presidential running mates.

Leaders: Ahmad Wali MASOUD (Party Leader), Ahmad Zia MASOUD (Vice President of the Republic).

Other recently launched parties include the **National Unity Movement** (*Tabrik-i-Wahdat-i Milli*), led by Mahmud GHAZI; the **Afghanistan Independence Party** (*Hizb-i-Istiqlal-i Afghanistan*), led by Ghulam Faruq NEJRABI, who won 0.3 percent of the vote in the 2004 presidential poll; the **Freedom Party** (*Hizb-i Azadi*), led by Gen. Abdul MALEK, a former leader of the National Front; the **National Movement for Peace** (*Jumbish-i Milli-i Solk*), led by Shahnawaz TANAY, a former defense minister in the communist regime; the **People's Islamic Movement of Afghanistan** (*Harakat-i Islami-i Mardon-i Afghanistan*), led by Hosayn ANWARI, the minister of agriculture in the transitional government; the **National Party** (*Hizb-i Milli*), led by Abdul Rashid ARYAN, a former member of the PDPA and member of the cabinet during communist rule; and the **Republican Party** (*Hizb-i Jamhuri Khwahan*), led by Sebghatullah SANJAR, who supported Hamid Karzai in the 2004 presidential election.

Movement Formerly in Power

Taliban. Translated as "seekers" or "students," the Persian *taliban* was applied to a group of Islamic fundamentalist theology students from Pakistan who swept through southern Afghanistan during late 1994 in a campaign pledged to rid the country of its contending warlords and introduce "genuine" Islamic rule. The group captured the southeastern city of Kandahar on November 4 and pushed north, seizing one of the world's major drug producing regions. Its most dramatic success was the defeat of Gulbuddin Hekmatyar's *Hizb-i-Islami* on the outskirts of Kabul in mid-February 1995. The Taliban suffered a major defeat by forces loyal to President Burhanuddin Rabbani a month later but recovered to capture Herat in September and subsequently mounted a major offensive against Kabul.

In a statement issued in connection with US congressional hearings on Afghanistan in June 1996, the Taliban movement listed its basic demands as including the resignation of President Rabbani, the demilitarization of Kabul, the formation of a national security force, and the convening of an elected assembly of the Afghan people charged with forming "a national Islamic government." The group's seizure of power in Kabul three months later gave it the opportunity to implement this program. Previous assessment of the Taliban as espousing a less ferocious brand of fundamentalism than the ousted regime was speedily revised in light of its imposition of strict Islamic law (*shari'a*) and summary execution of opponents.

The Taliban militia launched several offensives in late 1996 and 1997 designed to win complete control of the country but was unable to defeat opposition forces in the north or maintain command of the Hazara region west of Kabul. In part, resistance to the Taliban was based on ethnicity or religion: in the north the opposition militias comprised Uzbeks and Tajiks who had long been wary of domination by Pushtuns (the core Taliban ethnic group), while the Hazara-Taliban split pitted Shi'ite versus Sunni Muslims. Despite heavy international criticism, the Taliban leaders in 1997 exhibited little moderation in their harsh interpretation of *shari'a,* described as "medieval" by some observers, particularly regarding strictures on women. Meanwhile, the Taliban's 38-year-old spiritual guide, Mullah Mohammad Omar, was described as a reclusive leader who rarely left Kandahar (where the movement was launched) and who, following Taliban interpretation of religious law, never permitted himself to be photographed. Omar reportedly was advised by a small consultative council located at Kandahar.

Although the Taliban nearly succeeded in the first half of 2001 in efforts to push opposition forces completely out of Afghanistan, the regime's fortunes reversed dramatically as the result of the terrorist attacks in the US in September. Washington quickly blamed the *al-Qaeda* network of Osama bin Laden (see below) for the hijackings and demanded that the Taliban turn their "guest" over for prosecution or face US military intervention. Although some Taliban leaders reportedly argued that the US demand should be met, Omar and other hard-liners refused and thereby sealed the movement's fate. Following the Taliban's final military defeat at the hands of the Northern Alliance in late December, Omar and a number of Taliban ministers were reported to have fled to Pakistan.

Although many observers predicted the total collapse of the Taliban in the wake of its fall from power, the movement subsequently regrouped and launched a series of deadly guerrilla attacks against US troops and the new Afghani army. Mullah Omar, now believed to be operating as the head of a ten-man Taliban leadership council, called for a *jihad* (holy war) against all foreign forces and vowed to "punish" Afghans who supported the Karzai administration. The Taliban failed in its announced plan to disrupt the October 2004 presidential election, but it intensified its attacks in mid-2005, apparently in an effort to complicate the upcoming legislative balloting. Although some former Taliban leaders by that time reportedly had entered into negotiations with the government toward a possible peace settlement, Mullah Omar maintained his hard line, rejecting an apparent amnesty offer from administration representatives. Some reports attributed the 2005 attacks to a "Neo-Taliban," while it was also clear that several Taliban splinter groups were operating, raising questions about the cohesiveness and precise leadership of the movement. Meanwhile, the United States, convinced of Mullah Omar's ties to *al-Qaeda,* continued to offer a $10 million reward for his capture.

Leaders: Mullah Mohammad OMAR (Spiritual Leader and former emir of the self-proclaimed Islamic Emirate of Afghanistan), Mullah OBAIDULLAH, Laftullah HAKIMI (self-proclaimed spokesman for the "Neo-Taliban").

Terrorist Group

Al-Qaeda (The Base). *Al-Qaeda* is the network established in the 1990s by Osama bin Laden in pursuit of his goal of getting US forces out of Saudi Arabia. Bin Laden, a member of one of the wealthiest Saudi families, had participated both personally and financially in the *mujaheddin* ("holy warrior") guerrilla campaign against Soviet forces in Afghanistan. Having returned to his native land following the Soviet withdrawal from Afghanistan in 1989, bin Laden subsequently focused his fundamentalist fervor on the buildup of US forces in Saudi Arabia in connection with the invasion of Kuwait by Iraqi forces and the subsequent Desert Storm counterattack. Bin Laden reportedly urged the Saudi royal family to reject the US forces and adopted an antimonarchical stance when his recommendations were rebuffed. In 1991 bin Laden moved his operations to Sudan, his attacks on the Saudi government becoming more scathing after he was stripped of his citizenship in 1995 for "irresponsible behavior," a reference to his having made large sums of money available to militant Islamic causes in a number of countries.

Under heavy pressure from the United States, the Sudanese government expelled bin Laden in 1996, and he established a base in Afghanistan, where he reportedly helped to finance the Taliban takeover. Bin Laden also declared war on the "occupying American enemy," which he blamed for the perceived repression and corruption on the part of the Saudi government.

In February 1998 *al-Qaeda* joined with several other regional militant organizations to form an International Islamic Front, which urged Arabs to kill "Americans and their allies" until US "hegemony" in the Gulf was dismantled. US officials subsequently accused bin Laden's "terrorist network" of masterminding the embassy bombings in Kenya and Tanzania on August 7, and American cruise missiles attacked suspected bin Laden camps in Afghanistan two weeks later. Several alleged supporters of bin Laden were arrested in the United States on conspiracy and terrorism charges later in the year, while bin Laden was indicted in absentia. An Afghan court ruled in November that Washington had failed to present credible evidence of bin Laden's guilt; he was therefore permitted to remain in Afghanistan, although the government

officially cautioned him against using his base there to coordinate terrorist activity in other countries.

In March 2000 Jordan announced the arrest of some 28 alleged bin Laden followers on charges of conspiring to conduct a terrorist campaign in the kingdom. Arrests were subsequently also made in the United Kingdom and Germany to combat what officials described as an international crackdown on groups affiliated with the alleged bin Laden network. The trial of four of his alleged associates charged in connection with the 1998 embassy bombings opened in New York in February 2001. Meanwhile, *al-Qaeda* was being considered a prime suspect in the bombing of the USS *Cole* in Yemen in October 2000 (see article on Yemen for details).

Immediately following the terrorist attacks in the US on September 11, 2001, Washington described bin Laden as the mastermind of the conspiracy that had left some 3,000 Americans dead. The US government unsuccessfully pressed the Taliban government to turn bin Laden and his associates over for prosecution before launching Operation Enduring Freedom in Afghanistan and its "War on Terrorism" throughout the world. A reward of $25 million was offered for bin Laden, US President Bush declaring the *al-Qaeda* leader would be brought to justice "dead or alive."

Al-Qaeda forces fought alongside the Taliban army against the Northern Alliance advances in October-December 2001, most analysts concluding that *al-Qaeda* had become the main financial backer of the Taliban and its strongest military component. Mohammed ATEF, an *al-Qaeda* military commander, was killed in a November 14 US air strike, and many *al-Qaeda* fighters died during heavy bombing of their cave complex at Tora Bora in the second half of December. Most analysts subsequently concluded that bin Laden had escaped to the "anarchic tribal areas" of western Pakistan along with a number of other *al-Qaeda* leaders, one of whom—Abu ZUBAYDAH—was captured in Pakistan in March 2002 and turned over to the US. Even though *al-Qaeda* had obviously suffered major losses at the hands of US forces, the international community remained extremely wary of the group's ongoing potential to conduct new terrorist activity. Underscoring the breadth of *al-Qaeda*'s appeal to a certain segment of the Muslim population, it was reported that the *al-Qaeda* prisoners being held by the US at the Guantanamo Bay naval base had come from more than 40 countries.

In early 2003 a purported audio tape from bin Laden called upon all Muslims to fight against any US-led action against Iraq, although the tape also described Iraqi President Saddam Hussein and his administration as "apostates." In March US officials announced that more than half of *al-Qaeda*'s "senior operatives" had been killed or captured, including Khalid Shaikh MOHAMMAD (considered one of the masterminds of the September 11, 2001, attacks on the United States), who was arrested in Pakistan. US forces continued their assault on *al-Qaeda* along the border with Pakistan in mid-2003, Pakistan having also sent soldiers to its side of the border to apply similar pressure. In response, in September Ayman al-Zawahiri (reportedly bin Laden's top lieutenant—see Holy War under Illegal Groups in the article on Egypt for additional information) urged Pakistanis to overthrow President Pervez Musharraf. Two assassination attempts against Musharraf were reported late in the year.

In April 2004 another bin Laden tape suggested that *al-Qaeda* would no longer support terrorist attacks in Europe if European governments agreed to remove their military forces from Iraq and Afghanistan. (Many observers had suggested a possible link between *al-Qaeda* and the train bombing in Madrid, Spain, the previous month.) The "offer" was immediately rejected by the European leaders, although political events in Spain were dramatically affected by the train attacks (see article on Spain).

Several leaders, including Abdelaziz Issa Abdul-Mohson al-MUQRIN, of a group calling itself "*Al-Qaeda* in the Arabian Peninsula" were killed by Saudi Arabian security forces in June 2004 in response to the killing of a kidnapped American. At the same time, many of the insurgent attacks against US and Iraqi targets in Iraq were reportedly being conducted by followers of Abu Musab al-Zarqawi, a Jordanian militant heading a group called *Tawhid*. Consequently, questions were raised concerning the extent to which bin Laden exercised control over *al-Qaeda* adherents in particular and militant Islamists in general. However, in October al-Zarqawi declared his allegiance to bin Laden, who subsequently endorsed al-Zarqawi as the *al-Qaeda* leader in Iraq. (See article on Iraq for further information on the campaign conducted in Iraq under al-Zarqawi's purported leadership.) As of mid-2005, *al-Qaeda* appeared to be attempting to intensify its campaign in Afghanistan, apparently in an effort to compromise the legislative balloting scheduled for September.

Leaders: Osama BIN LADEN, Ayman al-ZAWAHIRI, Abu Musab al-ZARQAWI.

Legislature

Following the overthrow of the Taliban in late 2001, an "emergency" *Loya Jirga* (Grand National Council) was held June 12–19, 2002, as authorized by the Bonn Conference of November–December 2001, to establish a transitional government. The *Loya Jirga* comprised more than 1,500 delegates, about two-thirds of whom were indirectly elected to represent various civic, business, academic, and religious organizations. The remaining delegates were selected by a special commission (appointed as part of the Bonn agreement) to represent minority groups and women.

A new *Loya Jirga* convened in December 2003 to consider a new proposed constitution drafted by a constitutional commission appointed by President Karzai in April. The *Loya Jirga* comprised 500 delegates—450 elected by representatives of the previous *Loya Jirga* and 50 appointed by the president. The constitution approved on January 4, 2004, provided for a bicameral **National Assembly.** The lower house (The **House of the People** [*Wolesi Jirga*]) was slated to include 249 representatives directly elected for a five-year term. The upper house (**House of Elders** [*Meshrana Jirga*]) was slated to include 102 members—34 (1 from each province) directly elected at the provincial level, 34 elected at the district level, and

Cabinet

As of June 1, 2005

President	Hamid Karzai (Pushtun)
Vice Presidents	Karim Khalili (Hazara)
	Ahmad Zia Masoud (Tajik)

Ministers

Adviser to the President on National Security	Zalmay Rasool
Agriculture and Food	Obaidullah Rameen
Border Affairs	Mohammed Karim Barahoye
Communications	Amir Zai Sangeen
Commerce	Hedavat Amin Arsala
Counter-Narcotics	Habibullah Qaderi
Defense	Gen. Abdurrahim Wardak
Economics	Mohammad Amin Farhang
Education	Noor Mohammad Qarqeen
Finance	Anwar al-Haq Ahadi
Foreign Affairs	Abdullah Abdullah
Haj and Islamic Affairs	Nematullah Shahrani
Higher Education	Amir Shah Hasanyar
Information and Culture	Syed Makhdoom Raheen
Interior	Ali Ahmad Jalali
Justice	Mohammad Sarwar Danish
Labor and Social Affairs	Ekramuddin Masoomi
Martyrs and Disabled	Sediqa Balkhi [f]
Mining and Industry	Mohammad Sediq
Public Health	Mohammad Amin Fatemi
Public Works	Suhrab Ali Safari
Refugee Affairs	Mohammad Azam Dadfar
Rural Development	Mohammad Hanif Atmar
Transportation	Enayatullah Qasemi
Urban Development	Mohammad Yousuf Pushtun
Water and Energy	Mohammad Ismael Khan
Women's Affairs	Masooda Jala [f]

[f] = female

34 appointed by the president. After several postponements, legislative elections were most recently scheduled for September 18, 2005. (Due to electoral difficulties, the balloting for the 34 upper house members to be elected in district polling was postponed until 2006. Pending that vote, the number of presidential appointments to the House of Elders was to be limited to 17.)

Communications

Press

Widespread civil war and other fighting in the 1980s and 1990s adversely affected the publication of many newspapers, some of which resumed publication following the overthrow of the Taliban government in 2001. Newspapers published at

Kabul that have been cited in recent reports include *Anis* (Friendship), a long-standing government-funded daily published in Dari; the *Kabul Times,* another state-owned daily (in English); *Erada,* an independent daily; *Arman-i Malli,* a daily; *Hewad* (Homeland); *Estah,* a state-owned daily; *Cheragh,* an independent daily; *Payam-i-Mujahid* (Holy Warrior's Message), an independent weekly; *Kilit* (Key, 13,000); and the *Kabul Weekly.*

News Agencies

The official domestic facility is the Bakhtar News Agency.

Broadcasting

Following the Taliban takeover, Radio Afghanistan was redesignated the *Voice of Shari'a,* while Kabul TV was shut down. Television service was resumed on a limited basis at the capital in 2001. TV Badakshan also broadcasts from Faizabad, although state-run Afghanistan Television resumed broadcasting following the overthrow of the Taliban in 2001. Several private stations have also been launched (including *Aina* and *Tolu*), as have a number of private radio stations. (A poll conducted by the *Financial Times* in 2004 found that some 60 percent of the Afghani population used radio as its primary source of news.) In May 2005 the Karzai administration, facing criticism for using the national radio and television stations for public relations purposes, announced plans to privatize the stations. Meanwhile, it was reported that the Taliban had resumed sporadic broadcasts of *Voice of Shari'a* from an undisclosed location.

Intergovernmental Representation

Ambassador to the US
Said Tayeb JAWAD

US Ambassador to Afghanistan
Zalmay KHALILZAD

Permanent Representative to the UN
Dr. Ravan A.G. FARHADI

IGO Memberships (Non-UN)
ADB, CCC, CP, ECO, IDB, Interpol, IOM, NAM, OIC

ALGERIA

DEMOCRATIC AND POPULAR REPUBLIC OF ALGERIA

al-Jumhuriyah al-Jaza'iriyah
al-Dimuqratiyah al-Sha'biyah

The Country

Located midway along the North African littoral and extending southward into the heart of the Sahara, Algeria is a Muslim country of Arab-Berber population, Islamic and French cultural traditions, and an economy in which the traditional importance of agriculture has been replaced by reliance on hydrocarbons, with petroleum and natural gas now accounting for more than 95 percent of exchange earnings. Women constitute only a small fraction of the paid labor force, concentrated in the service sector (particularly health care). The future role of women in government (and society as a whole) was one of the key issues separating the nation's Islamic fundamentalist movement from the dominant secularists in the 1990s.

For nearly two decades following independence Algeria was perceived by many as a model for Third World liberation movements: the socialist government attended to social welfare needs, while the economy grew rapidly as oil prices rose in the 1970s. Subsequently, declining oil revenues and poor economic management led to major setbacks. Once nearly self-sufficient in food, the country is now highly dependent on foreign imports. Other problems include 25 percent unemployment, high population growth (more than one-half of the population is under 20 years old), an external debt estimated at more than $26 billion, a severe shortage of adequate housing, a widespread perception of corruption among government officials, and a spreading black market. In the mid-1980s the government began to impose budget austerity while attempting to reduce state control of large industries and agricultural collectives, boost nonhydrocarbon production, and cultivate a free-market orientation. The pace of economic reform accelerated following an outbreak of domestic unrest in late 1988, which also precipitated the launching of what was initially considered one of the continent's "boldest democratic experiments." Although political liberalization was seriously compromised during the 1990s by confrontation with the fundamentalists, the government persevered with its new economic

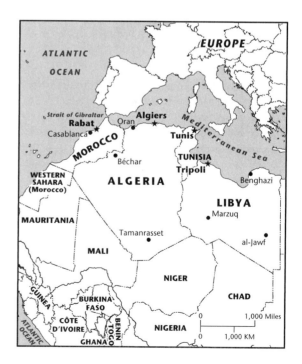

policies, thereby gaining partial rescheduling of the external debt and additional credits from the International Monetary Fund (IMF) and the World Bank. Meanwhile, as mandated by the IMF, privatization accelerated, the collateral loss of some 400,000 jobs in the public sector contributing to growing popular discontent with fiscal policy. Burgeoning terrorist activity in the second half of the 1990s impaired foreign investment in a number of sectors, but it did not affect activity in the oil and gas fields in the southern desert, where oil reserves were estimated at about 16 billion barrels. Foreign investors were described as exhibiting renewed interest as of mid-2000 in response to President Bouteflika's free-market orientation and efforts to negotiate a settlement with antigovernment militants.

GDP grew by 4.1 percent in 2002, 6.7 percent in 2003, and 5.5 percent in 2004, with inflation remaining manageable at slightly more than 2 percent annually. Growth has been fueled primarily by surging gas and oil prices, the government pledging to apply some of the additional revenue toward resolving the nation's many social problems.

Government and Politics

Political Background

Conquered by France in the 1830s and formally annexed by that country in 1842, Algeria achieved independence as the result of a nationalist guerrilla struggle that broke out in 1954 and yielded eventual French withdrawal on July 3, 1962. The eight-year war of liberation, led by the indigenous National Liberation Front (*Front de Libération Nationale*—FLN), caused the death of some 250,000 Algerians, the wounding of 500,000, and the uprooting of nearly 2 million others, as well as the emigration of some 1 million French settlers. The new Algerian regime was handicapped by deep divisions within the victorious FLN, particularly between commanders of the revolutionary army and a predominantly civilian political leadership headed by Ahmed BEN BELLA, who formed Algeria's first regular government and was elected to a five-year presidential term in September 1963. Despite his national popularity, Ben Bella exhibited an extravagant and flamboyant style that antagonized the army leadership, and he was deposed in June 1965 by a military coup under Col. Houari BOUMEDIENNE, who assumed power as president of the National Council of the Algerian Revolution.

During 1976 the Algerian people participated in three major referenda. The first, on June 27, yielded overwhelming approval of a National Charter that committed the nation to the building of a socialist society, designated Islam as the state religion, defined basic rights of citizenship, singled out the FLN as the "leading force in society," and stipulated that party and government cadres could not engage in "lucrative activities" other than those afforded by their primary employment. The second referendum, on November 17, approved a new constitution that, while recognizing the National Charter as "the fundamental source of the nation's policies and of its laws," assigned sweeping powers to the presidency. The third referendum, on December 10, reconfirmed Colonel Boumedienne as the nation's president by an official majority of 99.38 percent. Two months later, in the first legislative election since 1964, a unicameral National People's Assembly was established on the basis of a candidate list presented by the FLN.

President Boumedienne died on December 27, 1978, and he was immediately succeeded by Assembly president Rabah BITAT, who was legally ineligible to serve as chief executive for more than a 45-day period. Following a national election on February 7, 1979, Bitat yielded the office to Col. Chadli BENDJEDID, who had emerged in January as the FLN presidential designee during an unprecedented six-day meeting of a sharply divided party congress.

At a June 1980 FLN congress President Bendjedid was given authority to select members of the party's Political Bureau, and on July 15 he revived the military General Staff, which had been suppressed by his predecessor after a 1967 coup attempt by Col. Tahir ZBIRI. As a further indication that he had consolidated his control of

Political Status: Independent republic since July 3, 1962; one-party rule established by military coup July 5, 1965, and confirmed by constitution adopted November 19, 1976; multiparty system adopted through constitutional revision approved by national referendum on February 23, 1989; state of emergency declared for 12 months on February 9, 1992, by military-backed High Council of State and extended indefinitely on February 9, 1993; three-year transitional period declared by High Security Council effective January 31, 1994, as previously endorsed by National Dialogue Conference; constitutional amendments approved by national referendum on November 28, 1996, in advance of return to elected civilian government via multiparty local and national legislative elections in 1997.

Area: 919,590 sq. mi. (2,381,741 sq. km.).

Population: 29,100,867 (1998C); 31,543,000 (2004E), excluding nonresident nationals (estimated at upwards of 1 million in 1980).

Major Urban Centers (1998C): EL DJAZAIR (Algiers, 1,519,570), Wahran (Oran, 655,852), Qacentina (Constantine, 462,187). In May 1981 the government ordered the "Arabizing" of certain place names which did not conform to "Algerian translations." In 1988 the population of Algiers was reported to be 2.5 million and that of Oran, 900,000 (both figures including suburbs).

Official Language: Arabic (French and Berber are also widely spoken. However, in December 1996 the National Transitional Council adopted legislation banning the use of French in the public sector as of July 5, 1998, with the exception that universities were given until July 5, 2000, to switch to the use of Arabic only. In the wake of unrest in Berber areas, the government announced in October 2001 that the Berber language—Tamazight—would be elevated to a "national" language.)

Monetary Unit: Dinar (official rate July 1, 2005: 71.57 dinars = $1US).

President: Abdelaziz BOUTEFLIKA (National Liberation Front—FLN); declared winner of controversial election of April 15, 1999, and sworn in for a five-year term on April 27 to succeed Maj. Gen. (Ret.) Liamine ZEROUAL (nonparty), who in September 1998 had announced his intention to resign prior to the scheduled completion of his term in November 2000; reelected (due to internal FLN disputes, as the candidate of the National Democratic Rally and the Movement for a Peaceful Society) on April 8, 2004, and sworn in for a second five-year term on April 19.

Prime Minister: Ahmed OUYAHIA (National Democratic Rally); appointed by the President on May 5, 2003, to succeed Ali BENFLIS (National Liberation Front), who had been dismissed the same day.

---

state and party, Bendjedid on October 30 pardoned the exiled Zbiri and freed former president Ben Bella from house detention. (The latter had been released from 14 years' imprisonment in July 1979.)

Bendjedid was unopposed in his reelection bid of January 12, 1984, and on January 22 he appointed Abdelhamid BRAHIMI to succeed Col. Mohamed Ben Ahmed ABDELGHANI as prime minister. Thereafter, the regime was buffeted by deteriorating economic conditions, growing militancy among Islamic fundamentalists and students, and tension within the government, the FLN, and the army over proposed economic and political liberalization. The political infighting limited the effectiveness of reform efforts, critics charging that many of those entrenched in positions of power were reluctant to surrender economic and social privileges.

The pent-up discontent erupted into rioting at Algiers in early October 1988 and quickly spread to other cities, shattering Algeria's reputation as an "oasis of stability" in an otherwise turbulent region. Upwards of 500 persons died when the armed forces opened fire on demonstrators at the capital, while more than 3,000 were arrested. President Bendjedid thereupon adopted a conciliatory attitude, converting what could have been a challenge to his authority into a mandate for sweeping economic and political change. In a referendum on November 3 voters overwhelmingly approved a constitutional amendment reducing the FLN's political dominance by assigning greater responsibility to the prime minister and making him accountable to the Assembly. Two days later, Bendjedid appointed Kasdi MERBAH, described as a "determined" proponent of economic liberalization, as the new ministerial leader, and on November 9 Merbah announced a new cabinet from which a majority of the previous incumbents were excluded. Collaterally, the president instituted leadership changes in the military and the FLN, the latter agreeing late in the month to open future legislative elections to non-FLN candidates. On December 22 Bendjedid was reelected to a third five-year term, securing a reported 81 percent endorsement as the sole presidential candidate.

The FLN's status was eroded further by additional constitutional changes in February 1989 that provided, inter alia, for multiparty activity (see Constitution and government, below). Seven months later, arguing that economic reforms were not being implemented quickly enough, Bendjedid named Mouloud HAMROUCHE, a long-time political ally, to succeed Merbah as prime minister.

A multiparty format was introduced for the first time in elections for municipal and provincial councils on June 12, 1990. Contrary to expectations, the Islamic Salvation Front (*Front Islamique du Salut*—FIS), the country's leading Islamic fundamentalist organization, obtained 53 percent of the popular vote and a majority of the 15,000 seats being contested. Responding to demands from the FIS and other opposition parties, President Bendjedid announced in April 1991 that two-stage national legislative elections, originally scheduled for 1992, would be advanced to June 27 and July 18. However, the FIS called a general strike on May 25 to demand additional electoral law changes, the immediate application of *shari'a,* the resignation of Bendjedid, and scheduling of new presidential elections. Clashes at the capital between fundamentalists and police intensified in early June, leaving at least seven dead, and on June 5 Bendjedid declared a state of emergency, ordered the army to restore order, and postponed the legislative poll. He also called upon the foreign minister, Sid Ahmed GHOZALI, to form a new government.

On June 18, 1991, Ghozali, described as a "technocrat" committed to economic and political reform, announced his cabinet (the first since independence not to be dominated by FLN leaders) and pledged "free and clean" parliamentary elections by the end of the year. The schism between the government and the fundamentalists remained unbridged, however, and top FIS leaders and hundreds of their followers were arrested when new violence broke out in Algiers in early July.

Following a period of relative calm, the state of emergency was lifted on September 29, 1991, and two-round elections to a 430-seat Assembly were scheduled for December 26 and January 16, 1992. Again testifying to the remarkable surge in fundamentalist influence, FIS candidates won 188 seats outright in the first round (compared to 25 for the Berber-based Socialist Forces Front [*Front des Forces Socialistes*—FFS] and only 15 for the FLN). With the FIS poised to achieve a substantial majority (possibly even the two-thirds majority needed for constitutional revision), Bendjedid initiated talks with the fundamentalists regarding a power-sharing arrangement.

On January 11, 1992, Bendjedid, apparently under pressure from military leaders upset with his accommodation of the FIS, submitted his resignation. The High Security Council (HSC), composed of Ghozali and other top officials, including three senior military leaders, announced that it had assumed control to preserve public order and protect national security. (According to the constitution, the Assembly president was mandated to assume interim presidential duties, but the Assembly had been dissolved by a secret presidential decree on January 4. Although the president of the Constitutional Council was next in the line of temporary succession, the Council deferred to the HSC upon Bendjedid's resignation, reportedly ruling that "prevailing conditions" were not covered by the basic law.)

On January 12, 1992, the HSC canceled the second stage of the legislative election and nullified the results of the first. Two days later it announced that it had appointed a five-man High Council of State (HCS) to serve as an interim collegial presidency. Mohamed BOUDIAF, vice president of the country's wartime provisional government, was invited to return from 28 years of exile in Morocco to assume the chairmanship of the new body.

Following its "soft-gloved coup" in early 1992, the military launched what was described as an "all-out war" against the fundamentalist movement, arresting numerous FIS leaders, including moderates who had been counseling against violent confrontation, in addition to some 500 other FIS members. Bloody demonstrations throughout Algeria erupted shortly thereafter, and on February 9 the HCS declared a new 12-month state of emergency. With most constitutional rights effectively suspended by the declaration, the government intensified its anti-FIS campaign, while militant fundamentalists initiated guerrilla activity against police and security forces. The unrest continued following Ghozali's reappointment on February 23, even relatively moderate fundamentalists being driven underground by a March decision of the Algerian courts, acting on an HCS petition, to ban the FIS as a legal party. Meanwhile, the nonfundamentalist population appeared to accept the military intervention with relief, since it feared political, legal, and social constraints should the FIS come to power.

HCS Chairman Boudiaf was assassinated on June 29, 1992, while addressing a rally in the eastern city of Annaba. Official investigators subsequently concluded there was a broad conspiracy behind the attack without being able to identify those involved. Suspects ranged from militant fundamentalists to members of the "power elite" who may have felt threatened by Boudiaf's anticorruption efforts. (Only one person was arrested in connection with the incident—a member of the presidential guard who was convicted in June 1995 following a trial which shed little light on his motives or possi-

ble coconspirators.) On July 2 the HSC named Ali KAFI, the secretary general of the National Organization of Holy Warriors (a group of veterans from the war of independence) as Boudiaf's successor. Ghozali, blaming corrupt government officials and radical fundamentalists equally for the country's disorder, resigned on July 8. He was replaced on the same day by Belaid ABDESSELAM, longtime industry and energy minister under former president Boumedienne.

On February 9, 1993, the HCS extended the state of emergency indefinitely, declaring that steps toward restoration of an elected civilian government would be taken only after successful completion of the "antiterrorist" crackdown. Four months later it presented a blueprint for constitutional change, promising a democratic Muslim state and a free-market economy. In keeping with the new economic thrust, Prime Minister Abdesselam, viewed as strongly oriented towards state control of heavy industry, was replaced on August 21 by Redha MALEK, an advocate of privatization and other forms of liberalization geared to winning debt rescheduling from international creditors.

In October 1993 the HCS appointed an eight-member Committee for National Dialogue to negotiate an agreement among the legal political parties, labor organizations, and trade and professional groups on the nation's political future. However, talks were constrained by a mounting conviction among party leaders that full-scale civil war loomed unless the FIS was brought into the negotiations, a step the regime refused to accept. Consequently, the "National Dialogue Conference" held at Algiers on January 25–26, 1994, was boycotted by nearly all the political parties, and its influence was extremely limited. The Conference had been expected to name a president to succeed the HCS but failed to do so, reportedly because the military would not grant sufficient authority to a civilian leader. Therefore, on January 27 the HSC announced the appointment of Maj. Gen. (Ret.) Liamine ZEROUAL as president, his inauguration four days later coinciding with the dissolution of the HCS. Zeroual, who retained his former position as defense minister, was authorized to govern (in conjunction with the HSC) for a three-year transitional period, initial reports indicating he would seek a settlement with the FIS.

With debt rescheduling negotiations at a critical juncture, President Zeroual reappointed Prime Minister Malek on January 31, 1994, despite Malek's hard line regarding the FIS. Malek resigned on April 11, following the announcement of preliminary agreement with the IMF; he was replaced by Mokdad SIFI, who had held a number of ministerial posts recently. On April 15 Sifi announced the formation of a new government, described as comprised largely of "technocrats" who would concentrate on economic recovery while leaving political and security issues to the president and the HSC. One month later the military-dominated regime set up an appointive National Transitional Council to act in a quasi-legislative capacity prior to elections tentatively scheduled for 1997. However, most of the leading parties boycotted the body, severely undercutting its claim to legitimacy.

A number of groups (including, most significantly, the FIS, FLN, and FFS) drafted a proposed national reconciliation pact at Rome in late 1994 and early 1995. The plan called for a cessation of antigovernment violence, the release of fundamentalist detainees, recognition of the FIS, and the convening of a national conference to establish a transitional government pending new national elections. Despite strong international endorsement of the proposal, the government quickly rejected it on the ground that no "credible" truce could be achieved. Further illustrating the sway held by the military's hard-liners, security forces subsequently launched a massive campaign against the Armed Islamic Group (*Groupe Islamique Armée*—GIA) and other militant factions that had claimed responsibility for a series of bombings and assassinations. At the same time, the Zeroual administration reportedly continued negotiations with the FIS in the hope that the Front's supporters could be reintegrated into normal political processes. However, the talks collapsed in mid-1995, and the regime subsequently began to implement its own schedule for a gradual return to civilian government.

The first stage of the transition was a presidential election conducted on November 16, 1995, in which Zeroual, running as an independent but with the support of the military, was elected to a five-year term with 61 percent of the vote. His closest competitor, Sheikh Mahfoud NAHNAH of the moderate fundamentalist *Hamas* Party, secured 25 percent of the vote, followed by Saïd Saadi of the Berber Rally for Culture and Democracy (*Rassemblement pour la Culture et la Démocratie*—RCD), with 9 percent, and Noureddine BOUKROUH of the Algerian Renewal Party (*Parti pour le Renouveau de l'Algérie*—PRA), with 4 percent. President Zeroual's resounding first-round victory was initially seen as easing the "sense of crisis" somewhat, much of the electorate having apparently endorsed his continued hard line toward the militants. Zeroual, whose platform contained strong anticorruption language, was also reportedly perceived as a buffer, to a certain extent, against complete domination of political affairs by military leaders.

As anticipated, Prime Minister Sifi submitted his resignation following the successful completion of the election, and on December 31, 1995, President Zeroual appointed Ahmed OUYAHIA, former director of the president's office, to succeed Sifi. The government announced on January 5, 1996, included several members from *Hamas* and the PRA, seemingly in "reward" for their participation in the presidential poll, which had been boycotted by several major legal parties (including the FLN and the FFS) in protest over the lack of an agreement with the FIS.

In mid-1996 President Zeroual proposed a number of constitutional amendments granting sweeping new powers to the president and banning political parties based on religion (see Constitution and government, below). Between September 14 and 15 some 38 parties and organizations endorsed the proposals, although the absence of several major legal groupings (including the FFS and RCD) and, of course, the FIS (which would be precluded from any eventual legalization under the revisions) undercut the impact of the accord. The government subsequently reported that 85 percent of those voting in a national referendum on November 28 had supported the changes in the basic law, although opposition leaders and some international observers questioned those results and described the government's claim of an 80 percent vote turnout as vastly inflated.

A new wave of antiregime attacks broke out shortly after the constitutional referendum of November 1996 and reached an unprecedented scale July–August, despite (or perhaps because of) recent national legislative balloting and other progress toward full return to elected civilian government. Nevertheless, the administration proceeded with its timetable in 1997. Regulations for party registration were established in February, and new Assembly elections were held on June 5, the balloting being dominated by the recently established progovernment National Democratic Rally (*Rassemblement National et Démocratique*—RND), with 156 seats, followed by the Movement for a Peaceful Society (*Mouvement pour une Société Paisible*—MSP, as *Hamas* had been renamed) with 69 seats, and the FLN with 62. After several weeks of reportedly intense negotiations, the MSP and the FLN agreed to join a new RND-led coalition government, which was announced on June 25 under the continued direction of Prime Minister Ouyahia. The RND also secured most of the seats in municipal elections conducted on October 23, although some were allocated to other parties after a judicial review of allegations of widespread fraud made by a number of groups, including the MSP and the FLN. The political transition was completed on December 25, 1997, with indirect elections to the Council of Nations (the new upper house in the legislature), the RND winning 80 of the 96 contested seats. By that time, however, despite the progress on the institutional front, the wave of domestic violence had reached an unprecedented level.

As of early 1998 the government reported that about 26,000 people had died during the six-year insurgency, although other observers estimated the figure to be as high as 80,000. A special UN commission that visited Algeria at midyear placed the blame for the violence squarely on "Islamic terrorists" and argued that the Zeroual regime deserved international and domestic support. However, human rights organizations strongly criticized the UN

report for inadequately addressing the harsh retaliatory measures on the part of government security forces. In that context, it appeared that differences of opinion had emerged within the military and political elite over how to proceed vis-à-vis the fundamentalists. Hard-liners subsequently appeared to continue to dominate that debate, possibly contributing to the surprise announcement in September by Zeroual (seen as having come to favor a dialogue with moderate Islamist leaders) that he would leave office prior to the completion of his term.

New presidential elections were initially set for February 1999 and then rescheduled for April. Meanwhile, Prime Minister Ouyahia resigned on December 14, 1998, and the following day the president appointed Ismail HAMDANI, a senator and former ambassador, to serve as head of a caretaker government pending completion of the presidential balloting. Hamdani's cabinet, installed December 19, differed only slightly from his predecessor's.

The April 15, 1999, presidential election proved to be highly controversial, as six of the seven candidates quit the race shortly before the balloting out of conviction that the poll had been rigged in favor of the military's preferred candidate, Abdelaziz BOUTEFLIKA, who had served as foreign minister in the 1960s and 1970s but had been on the political sidelines for 20 years. Despite the opposition's demand for a postponement, the election proceeded as scheduled, Bouteflika being credited with 74 percent of the vote. (The names of the other candidates had remained on the ballot despite the boycott. Official results declared former foreign affairs minister Ahmed IBRAHIMI, who ran as an independent but enjoyed the informal support of the FIS, to be the runner-up with 13 percent of the vote. None of the other candidates received more than a 4 percent vote share.)

Following surprisingly long negotiations, President Bouteflika named Ahmed BENBITOUR, a former foreign minister who was described as a "close friend" of the president's, as prime minister on December 23, 1999. On the following day Benbitour formed a new government including seven parties, all of whom remained in the cabinet named by Ali BENFLIS after he replaced Benbitour in late August 2000. However, the RCD left the coalition in May 2001 as the result of unrest within the Berber community (see Current issues, below).

The FLN dominated the May 30, 2002, legislative balloting, securing 199 seats, while the RND declined to 47. Prime Minister Benflis was reappointed on June 1, and on June 17 he formed a new government comprising FLN, RND, and MSP ministers.

Further successes by the FLN in the October 2002 elections appeared to kindle presidential aspirations in Benflis, who was dismissed by President Bouteflika on May 5, 2003, Ahmed Ouyahia returning to the prime ministerial post he had held from 1995 to 1998. In September 2003 Bouteflika also dismissed several pro-Benflis cabinet ministers, exacerbating tensions that subsequently split the FLN into two camps (see FLN, below, for details). The FLN dispute resulted in confusing circumstances under which Bouteflika was reelected (with 85 percent of the vote) on April 8, 2004, as the candidate of the RND and MSP, while Benflis secured only 6.4 percent of the vote as the nominal FLN candidate.

Constitution and Government

The 1976 constitution established a single-party state with the FLN as its "vanguard force." Executive powers were concentrated in the president, who was designated president of the High Security Council (HSC) and of the Supreme Court, as well as commander in chief of the armed forces. He was empowered to appoint one or more vice presidents and, under a 1979 constitutional amendment that reduced his term of office from six to five years, was obligated to name a prime minister. He also named an 11-member High Islamic Council selected from among the country's "religious personalities." The 1976 document also stipulated that members of the National People's Assembly would be nominated by the FLN and established a judicial system headed by a Supreme Court, to which all lower magistrates were answerable.

In late 1983, as part of a decentralization move, the number of administrative departments

(*wilayaat*) was increased from 31 to 48, each continuing to be subdivided into districts (*da'iraat*) and communes. At both the *wilaya* and communal (town) levels there were provisions for popular assemblies, with an appointed governor (*wali*) assigned to each *wilaya*. The various administrative units were linked vertically to the minister of the interior, with party organization paralleling the administrative hierarchy.

On January 16, 1986, a referendum approved a new National Charter that, while maintaining allegiance to socialism and Islam, accorded President Bendjedid greater leeway in his approach to social and economic problems, particularly in regard to partial privatization of the "inefficient" public sector. Additional constitutional changes were approved by referendum on November 3, 1988. The revisions upgraded the prime minister's position, declaring him to be the "head of government" and making him directly responsible to the Assembly. In effect, the change transferred some of the power previously exercised by the FLN to the Assembly, particularly in light of a decision later in the month to permit non-FLN candidates in future elections. The role of the FLN was further attenuated by reference to the president as the "embodiment of the unity of the nation" rather than "of the unity of the party and the state."

Another national referendum on February 23, 1989, provided for even more drastic reform. It eliminated all mention of socialism, guaranteed the fundamental rights "of man and of the citizen" as opposed to the rights of "the people," excised reference to the military's political role, and imposed stricter separation of executive, legislative, and judicial powers. In addition, the FLN lost its "vanguard" status with the authorization of additional "associations of a political nature." Continuing the transfer to a multiparty system, the Assembly on July 2 established criteria for legal party status (see Political Parties and Groups, below) and on July 19 adopted a new electoral law governing political campaigns. The new code established multimember districts for local and national elections, with any party receiving more than 50 percent of the votes to be awarded all the seats in each. However, reacting to complaints from newly formed opposition parties, the government in March 1990 approved a system of proportional representation for the June municipal elections. After intense debate, the electoral law was further changed in 1991 to provide for two-round balloting in single-member districts in future Assembly elections.

In announcing a one-year state of emergency in February 1992, the newly formed High Council of State (HCS) suspended a number of key constitutional provisions, and over the next ten months it ordered the dissolution of nearly 800 municipal assemblies controlled by the FIS since the 1990 elections. In furtherance of its antifundamentalist campaign, the HCS in October also created three secret courts in which persons over 16 years of age charged with "subversion" or "terrorism" could be sentenced without the right of appeal. The state of emergency was extended indefinitely in February 1993, a transitional government being named a year later for a three-year period leading to proposed multiparty elections and a return to civilian leadership.

The electoral code was amended in 1995 to provide for multicandidate presidential elections, in two rounds if no candidate received an absolute majority in the first round. Potential candidates were required to obtain the signatures of 75,000 voters to be placed on the ballot, and anyone married to a foreigner was precluded from running.

In connection with the planned transition to civilian government, the Zeroual administration in the spring of 1996 proposed a number of constitutional amendments, which were approved by national referendum on November 28. Among other things, the amendments banned political parties from referencing religious or ethnic "identities," while codifying Islam as the state religion and Arabic as the official national language. The president was given authority to govern by decree in certain circumstances and to appoint one-third of the members of a new upper house in the Parliament—the Council of Nations. That second provision was viewed as one of the most significant aspects of the new charter since it gave the president effective blocking power on legislation. (New laws require the approval of three-quarters of the Council of Nations.) A Constitutional Council was established in April 1998, while a juridical State Council was installed two months later.

Foreign Relations

Algerian foreign relations have gone through a series of changes that date back to the preindependence period, formal contacts with many countries having been initiated by the provisional government created in September 1958. Foreign policy in the immediate postindependence period was dominated by President Ben Bella's anti-imperialist ideology. The period immediately following the 1965 coup was essentially an interregnum, with President Boumedienne concentrating his efforts on internal affairs. Following the Arab-Israeli War of 1967 Boumedienne became much more active in foreign policy, with a shift in interest from Africa and the Third World to a more concentrated focus on Arab affairs. After the 1973 war, the theme of "Third World liberation" reemerged, reflecting a conviction that Algeria should be in the forefront of the Nonaligned Movement. Subsequently, Algeria joined with Libya, Syria, the People's Democratic Republic of Yemen, and the Palestine Liberation Organization to form the so-called "Steadfastness Front" in opposition to Egyptian-Israeli rapprochement. However, in conjunction with a softening Arab posture toward Egypt, Algiers resumed full diplomatic relations with Cairo in November 1988.

A major controversy erupted following division of the former Spanish Sahara between Morocco and Mauritania in early 1976. In February the Algerian-supported Polisario Front (see under Morocco: Disputed Territory) announced the formation of a Saharan Arab Democratic Republic (SADR) in the Western Sahara that was formally recognized by Algeria on March 6; subsequently, a majority of other nonaligned states accorded the SADR similar recognition. However, the issue split the Organization of African Unity (OAU), with Morocco withdrawing from the grouping in 1984 in protest over the seating of an SADR delegation. Concurrently, relations between Algeria and Morocco deteriorated further, with President Bendjedid pledging full support for Mauritania's "territorial integrity" and Morocco referring to the Polisarios as "Algerian mercenaries." Relations improved significantly in late 1987, however, and in May 1988 Rabat and Algiers announced the restoration of formal ties, jointly expressing support for settlement of the Western Saharan problem through a self-determination referendum. Subsequent progress in Morocco-Polisario negotiations permitted Algiers to concentrate on a long-standing foreign policy goal: the promotion of economic, social, and political unity among Maghrebian states (see separate section on Arab Maghreb Union).

Relations with Libya worsened in response to Tripoli's "unification" Treaty of Oujda with Rabat in August 1984 (see entries under Libya and Morocco) and continued to plummet as a result of Libya's expulsion of Tunisian workers in the summer of 1985. Algiers felt obliged, however, to defend the Qadhafi regime in the events leading up to the US attacks on Tripoli and Benghazi in April 1986. During a January 28 meeting with Colonel Qadhafi, President Bendjedid deplored the "continuing conflict in the Western Sahara," while Libyan authorities subsequently called for "amalgamation" of the two countries. Although Algeria resisted federation with its eastern neighbor (preferring to concentrate on more inclusive Maghrebian unity), agreement was reached in July 1988 for the free movement of people between the two countries and the launching of bilateral economic projects.

Ties with France, Algeria's leading trade partner, were temporarily strained by legislation in July 1986 making visas mandatory for all North Africans seeking entry into the former metropole; however, swift action by French authorities against Algerian opposition activists later in the year led to an improvement in relations. Earlier, in April 1985, President Bendjedid became the first Algerian head of state since independence to visit Washington, utilizing the occasion to secure Algeria's removal from a list of countries prohibited from purchasing US weapons.

The victories of the Islamic fundamentalist movement in Algeria's 1990 and 1991 elections were characterized as generating "shock waves throughout northern Africa." The governments of Egypt, Libya, Morocco, and Tunisia (all struggling to contain fundamentalist influence) were reported to be greatly relieved by the military takeover in January 1992 and supportive of Algiers' anti-FIS campaign. The government/fundamentalist schism also led in March 1993 to the severing of ties with Iran, which the administration accused of supporting local terrorist activity. France, concerned over the possible influx of refugees should a fundamentalist government be established in Algiers, also supported the military regime, and a trial began at Paris in late 1998 of some 138 people accused of abetting recent violent antigovernment activity in Algeria.

President Bouteflika met with US President Bush in Washington in June 2001, their talks centering on "energy issues" rather than, as some reformists had hoped, democratization or good governance. Bouteflika returned to the US late in the year to pledge Algeria's support for Washington's recently launched war on terrorism. Among other things, the aftermath of 9/11 appeared to shine a more positive light, in the minds of many international observers, on the hard line adopted by the Algerian regime toward militant fundamentalism since 1992. In consonance with its renewed US ties, the Algerian government refused in 2003 to permit domestic protests against US actions in Iraq.

In March 2003 French President Jacques Chirac made the first formal state visit by a French leader to Algeria since the war of independence. The Algerian population warmly greeted Chirac, who pledged further "reconciliation" initiatives. Morocco also subsequently was reported to be seeking improved ties with Algeria, but the Algerian government remained committed to a self-determination referendum in the Western Sahara. Consequently, the border between Algeria and Morocco remained closed after more than a decade.

Current Issues

Facing an extremely difficult task in convincing the Algerian populace and the international community of the legitimacy of the April 1999 presidential poll, President Bouteflika moved quickly to establish his leadership credentials by, among other things, announcing plans for a "civil concord" which proposed amnesty for most fundamentalist militants in return for their permanent renunciation of violence and surrender of arms. The pact easily secured legislative approval in the summer and was endorsed by 98 percent of those voting in a national referendum on September 16. By the end of the cut-off date for the amnesty in mid-January 2000, upwards of 6,000 guerrillas had reportedly accepted the government's offer. However, most of them came from the FIS-affiliated Islamic Salvation Army, which had already been honoring a cease-fire since 1997. Significantly, the GIA rejected the peace plan, and deadly attacks and counterattacks continued on a nearly daily basis throughout the summer of 2000. By that time Bouteflika had also achieved only mixed results on the political front as well, as evidenced by the eight-month wait for the formation of a new government following the presidential election. Some analysts attributed the delay to efforts by Bouteflika to consolidate his authority, even, in some cases, at the expense of the military leaders who had propelled him to power. New Prime Minister Benbitour announced in December that economic reform would be his top priority, although a disagreement quickly developed with Bouteflika over the pace and process of privatization, leading to Benbitour's resignation in August 2000.

Despite the partial success of the civil concord, some 2,700 deaths were reported in 2000 from the ongoing conflict, and an upsurge of antigovernment violence was reported in December. In early 2001 President Bouteflika promised an "iron fist" in dealing with the remaining militants. However, the government faced a new crisis in April when riots broke out within the Berber population in the Kabylie region after a young man died under inadequately explained circumstances while in police custody. Government forces responded with a harsh crackdown, and some 1 million demonstrators reportedly participated in the antiregime protests that ensued in the Kabylie region and other areas, including Algiers. More than 60 people were killed and 2,000 injured in the clashes, which, fueled by economic malaise and long-standing concern over the authoritarian rule of what one journalist described as the "overwhelming power of an opaque military leadership," continued into 2002, prompting the leading Berber parties (the FFS and the RCD) to boycott the national legislative poll on May 30.

Deadly bomb attacks continued in 2003, mostly the work of the GIA offshoot called the Salafist Group for Preaching and Combat (*Groupe Salafiste pour la Prédiction et le Combat*—GSPC). However, the level of violence was greatly reduced from its height earlier in the decade (as one reporter put it, dozens killed per month rather than dozens per day). Most observers credited President Bouteflika's resounding reelection in April 2004 to popular appreciation of the improved security situation, along with recent economic advances and Algeria's renewed international status in connection with the US-led war on terrorism. For its part, the Algerian military appeared to step back from its previous level of background political involvement, possibly under the opinion that the "Islamist threat" had been for the most part overcome. Collaterally, the military and security forces as of early 2005 appeared likely to avoid any in-depth review of their actions during the "dirty war" with the militants. (Some 7,000 people had reportedly "disappeared" during government security operations, while 100,000–150,000 had died from all aspects of the war.) President Bouteflika called for a national referendum to be held on a proposed general amnesty that would cover both sides of the conflict. Improvement was also apparent in relations with the Berber community, a January 2005 accord calling for enhanced economic support from the government for Berber areas.

Political Parties and Groups

From independence until 1989 the National Liberation Front (FLN) was the only authorized political grouping, Algeria having been formally designated as a one-party state. Under constitutional changes approved in 1989, however, Algerians were permitted to form "associations of a political nature" as long as they did not "threaten the basic interests of the state" and were not "created exclusively on the basis of religion, language, region, sex, race, or profession." To operate legally, parties were also required to obtain government permits. The process of legalization began in August 1989, and multiparty activity was permitted for the first time at local elections in June 1990. By the end of 1991 there were nearly 60 legal parties. However, constitutional amendment of November 1996 and electoral law revision of February 1997 further restricted parties from referencing religion, ethnicity, or race, and a number of existing groups were deregistered for failure to adapt to the changes by the deadline of April 1997. In addition, a number of other parties were told to disband in May 1998, either for failing to have the minimum of 2,500 members or for violating other new regulations. Twenty-three parties participated in the 2002 legislative balloting.

Government Parties

National Liberation Front (*Front de Libération Nationale*–FLN). Founded in November 1954 and dedicated to socialism, nonalignment, and pan-Arabism, the FLN led the eight-year war of independence against France. Although weakened by factionalism and disagreement over the role of the army in politics, the Front subsequently assumed complete control of Algerian political and governmental affairs.

By the late 1980s a cleavage was apparent within the FLN between an "old guard," dedicated to the maintenance of strict socialist policies, and a group, led by President Bendjedid, favoring political and economic liberalization. The reformers having manifestly gained the ascendancy,

Mohamed Cherif MESSAADIA, the Front's leading socialist ideologue, was dismissed from the ruling Politburo in early November 1988. Subsequently, during the sixth party congress at Algiers November 27–28, the Politburo itself was abolished and the office of secretary general was dissociated from that of state president. (Bendjedid, however, was named to the newly created post of FLN president.) The delegates also voted to democratize the filling of FLN organs, approved the chief executive's proposals for economic reform, and nominated Bendjedid as sole candidate for a third presidential term. Although not specifically empowered by the congress to do so, the Central Committee in June 1989 endorsed the creation of a multiparty system, some continued opposition to Bendjedid's political and economic reforms notwithstanding.

Following the FLN's poor showing (about 34 percent of the popular vote) in the June 1990 municipal elections, a number of government officials were dismissed from the Politburo amid intense debate over how to check the rapid erosion of the Front's influence. In late June 1991 Bendjedid resigned as FLN president, and several other members of his administration relinquished their party posts as part of the government's effort to distance itself from FLN control. However, Abdelhamid MEHRI, Bendjedid's brother-in-law and close associate, was subsequently reelected FLN secretary-general.

Further illustrating the rapid decline in its electoral potency, the FLN won only 15 seats on the basis of a 24 percent vote share in the December 1991 first-round legislative poll. The party was subsequently reported to be divided over Bendjedid's resignation as president of the Republic and the assumption of power by the High Security Council. Mehri initially charged the army with having conducted a coup d'etat and suggested the FLN might join forces with other groups, including the FIS, to oppose the new regime. Subsequently, however, the FLN Central Committee announced it would support the High Council of State, assuming adherence to the Council's pledge to return the nation to a democratic process. Meanwhile, despite widespread popular resentment over long-standing official corruption, FLN members reportedly remained entrenched in many formal and informal positions of local and national influence.

By late 1994 the FLN was firmly in the opposition camp, its leaders joining with those of the FIS, FFS, and other parties in negotiating a proposed plan for a return to civilian government. At the urging of Secretary General Mehri, the FLN formally endorsed a boycott of the 1995 presidential election, although it appeared that many party members voted anyway, a large percentage of their support reportedly going to President Zeroual. Mehri was subsequently dismissed as secretary general in January 1996 by the FLN Central Committee, and his successor, Boualem BENHAMOUDA, quickly distanced the FLN from the FIS and other antiregime groupings.

The 1995 electoral boycott having been widely acknowledged as a mistake, the FLN participated full force in the three 1997 elections and accepted junior partner status in the RND-led coalition government formed in June. However, despite the solidly proadministration stance of the FLN leaders, it was reported that a "reformist" faction, led by former prime minister Mouloud Hamrouche, continued to promote, among other things, a negotiated settlement with the FIS.

The FLN held its first congress in nine years in March 1998, electing a 210-member Central Committee and reelecting Secretary General Benhamouda, thereby underline the party's return to a "conservative tendency." The FLN nominated military-backed Abdelaziz Bouteflika as its official candidate for the April 1999 presidential election, although a segment of the party supported Hamrouche, who ran as an independent and subsequently indicated his intention to form a new party. Benhamouda, viewed as a longstanding "rival" to Bouteflika, resigned as secretary general in September 2001; the post was later filled by Prime Minister Ali Benflis.

Following the resurgence of the FLN in the May 2002 Assembly balloting (199 seats [to lead all parties] on a 35 percent vote share) and the October 2002 municipal elections, Benflis was reelected as FLN secretary general at a July 2003 congress, which also installed a pro-Benflis Central Committee. By that time it was clear that Benflis (who had been dismissed as Prime Minister in April 2003) planned to run for president in 2004, thereby causing a rupture in the FLN between his supporters and those of President Bouteflika. The FLN convention in December 2003 selected Benflis as the party's standard-bearer, but an Algerian court (apparently under pressure from the Bouteflika administration) "annulled" that nomination and ordered FLN funds frozen. After Benflis secured only 8 percent of the vote in the April 2004 balloting, he resigned as FLN secretary general. At a party congress in February 2005, Bouteflika was named "honorary president" of the party, his supporters having clearly regained party control.

Leaders: Abdelaziz BOUTEFLIKA (President of the Republic), Ali BENFLIS (Former Prime Minister), Abdelaziz BELKHADEM (Secretary General).

National Democratic Rally (*Rassemblement National et Démocratique*—RND). Launched in February 1997 in support of the policies of President Zeroual, the RND dominated the subsequent Assembly, municipal, and Council of the Nation balloting, in part due to substantial financing and other assistance from sitting government officials, many of whom ran for office under the RND banner. Formally committed to pluralism, a "modern" economy (including emphasis on privatization), and "social justice," the RND was widely viewed primarily as a vehicle for entrenched authority to participate in an expanding democratic process without facing a genuine threat to its hold on power.

The first RND congress, held in April 1998, elected a National Committee and a 15-member National Bureau led by Secretary General Tahar BENBAIBECHE. However, a serious split subsequently developed in the party over whom to support in the April 1999 presidential balloting. Consequently, Benbaibeche, who had complained that military leaders had been inappropriately pressuring the RND to back Abdelaziz

Bouteflika, was dismissed as secretary general in January 1999 and replaced by Ahmed Ouyahia, who had recently resigned as prime minister. Ouyahia quickly announced that Bouteflika, the official candidate of the FLN, enjoyed the support of most of the RND.

By early 2002 the RND was described as having failed to attract as much popular support as originally expected, apparently because of the party's ongoing ties to the military. The RND's representation in the National People's Assembly fell from 156 to 47 in the 2002 balloting. Ouyahia returned to the prime ministership in April 2003, and the RND supported Bouteflika in the 2004 presidential poll.

Leaders: Ahmed OUYAHIA (Prime Minister and Secretary General), Abdelkader BENSALAH (Speaker of the Council of the Nation).

Movement for a Peaceful Society (*Mouvement pour une Société Paisible/Harakat Mujitamas al-Silm*–MSP/*Hamas*). Formerly known as the Movement for an Islamic Society (*Mouvement pour une Société Islamique*–MSI) or *Hamas* (an acronym from that grouping's name in Arabic), the MSP adopted its current rubric in 1997 in light of new national restrictions on party references to religion. The MSP is a moderate Islamic fundamentalist organization distinct from the more extreme Palestinian formation known as *Hamas*. It advocates "coexistence" with groups of opposing views in a democratic political structure and the introduction "by stages" of an Islamic state which would maintain "respect for individual liberties." Although it was reported in early 1992 that some *Hamas* members had been arrested in the sweeping antifundamentalist campaign, the government subsequently returned to its position that the grouping represented an acceptable moderate alternative to the FIS. Subsequently, Sheikh Mohamed BOUSLIMANI, a founder of *Hamas,* was killed in late 1993, while another leader, Aly AYEB, was assassinated in September 1994, the attacks being attributed to radicals opposed to *Hamas'* ongoing dialogue with the government.

Hamas leader Sheikh Mahfoud Nahnah, who had announced his support for the regime's "antiterrorist" campaign but had described the nation as stuck "in a political dead end" in view of the "lack of trust between people and authority," received 25 percent of the vote in the 1995 presidential election. Two members of the party were subsequently named to minor cabinet posts in the government formed in January 1996.

After finishing second in the June 1997 legislative balloting, the MSP joined the subsequent RND-led coalition government, a decision which was described as putting the party's "credibility on the line" vis-a-vis the more hard-line grouping, the MR (or *Nahda*), which was competing for Islamic support. The MSP subsequently continued to pursue a middle road, strongly criticizing perceived electoral fraud benefiting the RND in the October municipal elections while also demanding stricter security measures in early 1998 in the face of escalating terrorist attacks.

Nahnah attempted to run in the April 1999 presidential balloting, but his candidacy was disallowed, ostensibly on the ground that he had not provided proof he had participated in the country's "war of independence" as required of all presidential contenders under the 1996 constitutional revision. Nahnah died in July 2003 after a long illness.

The MSP, which had seen its Assembly representation fall from 69 to 38 in the 2002 balloting, supported President Bouteflika in the 2004 presidential campaign.

Leader: Abou Djerra SOLTANI (President).

Other Legislative Parties

Movement for National Reform (*Mouvement pour la Réforme Nationale*–MRN). The MRN, also known as *Islah* (Arabic for "reform"), was launched in early 1999 to promote the presidential campaign of Sheikh Abdallah Djaballah, who had recently split from *Nahda* (below). The MRN, supportive of eventual establishment of an "Islamic State," won 43 seats in the 2002 Assembly balloting, thereby becoming the largest opposition grouping. Djaballah won 4.9 percent of the vote in the 2004 presidential poll.

Leader: Sheikh Abdallah DJABALLAH (Party Leader and 2004 presidential candidate).

Workers' Party (*Parti des Travailleurs*–PT). The Trotskyist PT was one of the groups which signed the proposed national reconciliation pact in early 1995. It secured four seats in the June 1997 Assembly balloting and subsequently continued to urge the government to negotiate with the FIS. The PT improved dramatically to 21 seats in the 2002 Assembly balloting on a vote share of 4.8 percent. PT leader and women's rights activist Louisa Hannoun, described as the first woman to run for president in the Arab world, won 1.2 percent in the vote in the 2004 poll.
Leader: Louisa HANNOUN.

Algerian National Front (*Front National Algérien*–FNA/*Jabhah al-Wataniyah al-Jaza'i-riyah*). Organized in June 1999 in support of the "downtrodden," the FNA received official recognition the following November. It won eight seats in the 2002 legislative poll on a 3.2 percent vote share. However, Touati's proposed presidential bid in 2004 was rejected by the Constitutional Council.
Leader: Moussa TOUATI.

Renaissance Movement (*Mouvement de la Renaissance/Harakat al-Nahda*–MR/*Nahda*). Previously called the Islamic Renaissance Movement (*Mouvement de la Renaissance Islamique/Harakat al-Nahda al-Islamiyya*–MRI/*Nahda*), the party dropped the "Islamic" portion of its rubric in early 1997 to conform to new national regulations. Initially a small, moderate fundamentalist grouping, *Nahda* was promoted in the mid-1990s by the government as a legal alternative to the banned FIS. The grouping performed "surprisingly well" in the June 1997 legislative balloting, finishing fourth with 34 seats. By that time *Nahda* had adopted a tougher stance than the other main legal Islamic party (the MSP), and its leaders ultimately declined to participate in the new RND-led coalition government.

A *Nahda* congress in early 1998 reportedly directed that some authority previously exercised by

long-standing leader Sheikh Abdallah Djaballah be turned over to Secretary General Lahbib Adami. The apparent rivalry between the two came to a head late in the year when Adami announced that the party had agreed to support Abdelaziz Bouteflika, the military-backed FLN candidate, in the upcoming presidential balloting. Djaballah consequently left *Nahda* in January 1999 and formed the MRN (above), taking nearly half of the 34 *Nahda* Assembly representatives with him. *Nahda* fell to only one seat in the 2002 Assembly poll.
Leader: Lahbib ADAMI (Secretary General).

Algerian Renewal Party (*Parti pour le Renouveau de l'Algérie*–PRA). A moderate Islamic group which first surfaced during the October 1988 demonstrations, the PRA announced in 1989 that it would concentrate on economic issues, particularly a fight to end "state capitalism and interventionism." PRA leader Noureddine Boukrouh, described as a "liberal businessman," won 4 percent of the votes in the 1995 presidential election. Two PRA members were appointed to the January 1996 cabinet, but the party was not represented in the June 1997 government. The government disallowed Boukrouh's candidacy for the 1999 presidential election, citing insufficient signatures of support. Boukrouh subsequently joined the coalition government announced in December 1999. The PRA secured 2.2 percent of the vote in the 2002 Assembly balloting.
Leaders: Noureddine BOUKROUH, Yacine TORKMANE.

Movement of National Harmony (*Mouvement de l'Entente Nationale*–MEN). The MEN secured 1.9 percent of the vote in the 2002 Assembly balloting.
Leaders: Ali BOUKHAZNA, Amar LASSOUED.

Socialist Forces Front (*Front des Forces Socialistes*–FFS). Long a clandestine group, the predominantly Berber FFS was legalized in November 1989. Having earned the enmity of the government in 1985 when he briefly formed a "united front" with Ben Bella's MDS (below) to oppose the FLN, the FFS leader, revolutionary hero Hocine Aït-Ahmed, remained in Swiss exile until December 1989. The FFS boycotted the 1990 municipal elections but, after failing to create a multiparty coalition to "block" the FIS, presented over 300 candidates in the December 1991 legislative balloting on a platform that endorsed a "mixed economy," greater regional autonomy, and official recognition of the Berber language. The FFS won 25 seats (second to the FIS) on a 15 percent vote share in the first election round, Aït-Ahmed strongly criticizing cancellation of the second prior to returning to self-imposed exile in Switzerland. The FFS subsequently joined the FIS and the FLN as the leading proponents of the unsuccessful January 1995 peace plan and boycotted the 1995 presidential balloting. However, Aït-Ahmed then called for "conciliation" talks with the government in apparent recognition of the Zeroual regime's strengthened position following the election.

Aït-Ahmed, hitherto FFS general secretary, was elected to the newly created post of party president at the March 1996 FFS congress at Algiers. A ten-member secretariat and a 120-member national council were also installed. Dueling with the RCD for support within the Berber community, the FFS secured 20 seats in the June 1997 Assembly balloting but was not invited to participate in the new RND-led government because of the Front's insistence that negotiations should proceed with the goal of incorporating the FIS into the legal political process. A special congress in February 1999 nominated Aït-Ahmed as the FFS candidate for the upcoming presidential balloting, despite the reported poor health of the aging leader, who had recently returned from his self-imposed exile. A May 2000 congress reelected Aït-Ahmed as FFS chairman amid reports of deepening divisions within its party. In the wake of severe unrest in Berber areas, the FFS boycotted the 2002 Assembly balloting.

Leaders: Hocine AÏT-AHMED (President of the Party and 1999 presidential candidate), Samir BOUAKOUIR, Ahmed DJEDDAI (Secretary General).

Other Parties Competing in the 2002 Legislative Balloting

Ahd 54. A small, nationalist party, *Ahd 54* (*Ahd* is Arabic for "oath," reportedly a reference to principles espoused at the beginning of the war of independence) secured 0.9 percent of the vote in the 2002 Assembly balloting. Its leader, human rights activist Ali Fawzi Rebaine, won .7 percent of the vote in the 2004 presidential poll.

Leader: Ali Fawzi REBAINE, Toufik CHELLAL.

Patriotic Republican Rally (*Rassemblement Patriotique Républicain*–RPR). The RPR is a successor to the Algerian Movement for Justice and Development (*Mouvement Algérien pour la Justice et le Développement*–MAJD), a reformist group launched in November 1990 by former prime minister Kasdi Merbah, who had resigned in October from the FLN Central Committee. In March 1992 Merbah described the recently installed High Council of State as "unconstitutional" and called for lifting the state of emergency and creation of a "government of national welfare." Merbah, a staunch antifundamentalist, was assassinated in August 1993, the government accusing Islamic militants of the act. However, no group claimed responsibility for the killing, and observers pointed out that Merbah had a broad spectrum of enemies. In 1999 the government listed the RPR as the successor to the MAJD.

Leader: 'Abd al-Kader MERBAH (President).

National Party for Solidarity and Development (*Parti National pour la Solidarité et le Développement*–PNSD). The center-right PNSD won a reported 1.6 percent of the popular vote in the June 1990 municipal elections. The PNSD secured 1.8 percent of the vote in the 2002 Assembly poll.

Leader: Mohamed Cherif TALEB (President).

Other parties that competed unsuccessfully in the 2002 Assembly balloting included: the **Front of Algerian Democrats** (*Front des Algériens Démocrates*–FAD), led by Tayeb KABRI; the **National Constitutional Rally** (*Rassemblement*

National Constitutionnel–RNC), which in 2004 announced it had changed its name to the **Democratic National Front** (still under the leadership of Sassi MABROUK); the **National Movement of Algerian Youth** (*Mouvement National pour la Jeunesse Algérienne*–MNJA), led by Omar BOUACHA; the **National Movement of Hope** (*Mouvement National l'Espérance*–MNE), led by Mohamed HADEF; the **National Movement for Nature and Development** (*Mouvement National pour la Nature et le Développement*–MNND), led by Abderrahman AKIF; the **Progressive Republican Party** (*Parti Républicain et Progressiste*–PRP), which won three seats in the 1997 Assembly balloting under the leadership of Idriss KHADIR; the **Rally for Algeria** (*Rassemblement pour l'Algérie*–RPA), led by Mohamed HAMMOUMA; the **Rally for National Unity** (*Rassemblement pour l'Unité Nationale*–RUN), led by Yacine LEKHAL; and the **Union for Democracy and Liberties** (*Union pour la Démocratie et les Libertés*–UDL), which had won one seat in the 1997 Assembly election.

Other Parties

Republican National Alliance (*Alliance Nationale Républicaine*–ANR). The ANR was formed in early 1995 by several former government officials, including Redha Malek, prime minister in 1993–1994, and Ali Haroun, a member of the 1992–1994 collective presidency. Formally opposed to any compromise with the Islamic fundamentalist movement, the ANR was considered a vehicle for a presidential bid by Malek. However, Malek was prevented from contesting the 1995 election because he failed to obtain the required 75,000 signatures of support. Malek was reelected chairman of the party by the June 1996 ANR congress at Algiers, which also elected a new 145-member National Council.

Despite retaining a seat in the cabinet, the ANR in early 2002 was described as "steering clear" of the upcoming legislative poll.

Leaders: Redha MALEK (Chairman), Ali HAROUN.

Rally for Culture and Democracy (*Rassemblement pour la Culture et la Démocratie*–RCD). Formed in February 1989 to represent Berber interests, the RCD proclaimed its commitment to "economic centralism," linguistic pluralism, and separation of the state and Islamic religion. It won 2 percent of the votes in the June 1990 municipal balloting.

In early 1994 Mohamed Ouramadane TIGZIRI, the RCD's national secretary, was assassinated, apparently as part of the militant fundamentalist campaign against groups such as the RCD which advocate a secular, Western-style political system. The RCD's strongly antifundamentalist leader, Saïd Saadi, is also prominent in the Berber Cultural Movement, described by the *New York Times* as having evolved into an influential political group in its campaign to have the Berber language sanctioned for use in schools and other public forums. Saadi captured 9 percent of the votes in the 1995 presidential poll, having been assured of the lion's share of Berber votes because of the boycott by the FFS, the RCD's primary competitor for support within that ethnic group. The RCD secured 19 seats in the June 1997 Assembly elections but boycotted the December balloting for the new Council of the Nation. The RCD also announced in early 1999 that it was boycotting the upcoming presidential election. However, surprising many observers, the RCD subsequently joined the government coalition of December 1999, the party reportedly having become "increasingly closer" to President Bouteflika. The RCD left the coalition in May 2001 in the wake of severe government/Berber friction, and it boycotted the 2002 national and local elections. Saadi won 1.9 percent of the vote in the 2004 presidential poll.

Leader: Saïd SAADI (President).

Democratic and Social Movement (*Mouvement Démocratique et Social*–MDS). The MDS rubric reportedly was recently adopted by the grouping formerly known as Challenge (*Ettahaddi*). Dedicated to "the revolutionary transition of Algeria to modernity and progress," *Ettahaddi* had been launched in January 1993 as successor to the Socialist Vanguard Party (*Parti de l'Avant-Garde Socialist*–PAGS). The PAGS had emerged in 1966 as an illegal, but generally tolerated, heir to the Algerian Communist Party (*Parti Communiste Algérien*–PCA), which had been proscribed shortly after independence. Supportive of the Boumedienne government but less so of the Bendjedid administration, the PAGS reportedly applauded the 1988 unrest as helpful in its effort to "reestablish itself," particularly among labor unionists. It offered a limited number of candidates in the 1990 municipal elections, without success, and boycotted the 1991, 1997, and 2002 legislative elections as well as the 1999 presidential poll.

Leader: Hachemi CHERIF (Secretary General).

Fidelity (*Wafa*). Organized by former foreign affairs minister Ahmed Taleb Ibrahimi following his 1999 presidential campaign in the hope of coordinating nationalist and Islamist opposition groups, *Wafa* was subsequently denied recognition by the government on the grounds that it was essentially an FIS "clone." Ibrahimi was rejected by the Constitutional Council as a presidential candidate in 2004 and subsequently threw his support behind Ali Benflis.

Leaders: Ahmed Taleb IBRAHIMI, Mohammed SAID, Rashid LERARRI.

Democratic Front (*Front Démocratique*–FD). An anti-Bouteflika grouping, the FD elected former prime minister Sid Ahmed Ghozali as its chairman during the May 2000 inaugural congress. Ghozali was not permitted by the Constitutional Council to run in the 2004 presidential election, and he subsequently announced he was supporting Ali Benflis in that campaign.

Leader: Sid Ahmed GHOZALI (Chairman).

Socialist Workers Party (*Parti Socialist des Travailleurs*–PST). Legalized in early 1990, the Trotskyite PST supports "radical socialism," nonpayment of Algeria's external debt, and secular government. The PST boycotted the 2002 Assembly balloting.

Leader: Chawki SALHI.

Illegal Groups

Islamic Salvation Front (*Front Islamique du Salut*–FIS). The FIS was organized in early 1989 to represent the surging Islamic fundamentalist movement. Capitalizing upon strong antigovernment sentiment, it won control of a majority of town and departmental councils in the June 1990 municipal elections. Apparently to permit the broadest possible support for its effort to win national legislative control, the FIS leadership was subsequently reluctant to define its goals in specific terms. However, a significant proportion of the Front's supporters appeared committed to the adoption and enforcement of religious law (*shari'a*) throughout Algeria's theretofore relatively secular society and the imposition of measures such as the segregation of the sexes in schools and the workplace, a ban on alcohol consumption, and obligatory veils for women. FIS leaders also made it clear that a national fundamentalist government, even one which came to power through a multiparty election, would not feel bound to maintain a "Western-style" democracy.

In June 1991 FIS leader Dr. Abassi Madani, Ali Belhadj (his deputy), other members of the party's Constitutional Council, and hundreds of FIS followers were arrested on charges of fomenting an "armed conspiracy against the security of the state" in connection with violent demonstrations in Algiers and other cities. Although hard-line FIS factions reportedly called for continued protest and an election boycott unless the detainees were released, the FIS ultimately participated in the December 26 legislative balloting under the leadership of the moderate Abdelkader HACHANI.

After winning 188 seats in the first round of the 1991 Assembly poll, the FIS prepared to assume national political leadership, Hachani attempting to reassure the nonfundamentalist population that the FIS would "persuade, not oblige people into doing what we say." However, the party's plan to mount the world's first Islamic state via the ballot box was thwarted by the military takeover of the Algerian government in early January 1992. Nearly all of the remaining FIS national leaders, including Hachani, were subsequently arrested, as were hundreds of its local and provincial officials, with upwards of 30,000 FIS followers reportedly being placed in desert detention camps. In addition, Algerian courts in March formally banned the FIS as a political party upon petition of the High Council of State, which also ordered the dissolution of many municipal councils under FIS control and their replacement by appointed bodies. The Front was subsequently reported to be sharply divided between members remaining faithful to the group's official commitment to nonviolence and more radical adherents prepared to "move from words to rifles." It was generally believed that the latter were responsible for a number of attacks on Algerian security personnel during the rest of the year and for the subsequent emergence of armed groups such as the AIS and the GIA (below).

In July 1992 Madani and Belhadj were sentenced to 12 years in prison for conspiring against the authority of the state, five other leaders receiving shorter terms. However, the imprisoned FIS leaders reportedly met with Defense Minister Liamine Zeroual in December 1993 to discuss measures whereby the FIS could be reintegrated into the political mainstream. In the wake of Zeroual's appointment as president one month later, sporadic negotiations were reported between the government and the FIS, many reports suggesting that a breakthrough was imminent in mid-1995. However, the government finally declared the talks deadlocked, allegedly over the failure of the FIS leaders to renounce antiregime violence unequivocally. Consequently, no FIS participation was permitted in the 1995 presidential balloting, the Front calling upon supporters to boycott the election as a way of embarrassing the government. That strategy backfired, however, as heavy voter turnout and Zeroual's strong showing served to undercut the Front's insistence that it still held majority popular support. Postelection comments from some FIS leaders exhibited a conciliatory tone, observers suggesting that the Front would seek a compromise which would allow it to present candidates in the legislative elections planned for 1997. No such scenario developed in the first half of 1997,

but, perhaps with the prospect of renewed negotiations in mind, the government released Madani on July 15, 1997, one week after Hachani had been freed when a court found him guilty of "inciting rebellion" in 1992 but sentenced him to time served. However, the nature of subsequent FIS/government talks was unclear, and Madani was placed under house arrest in September after he had called for UN mediation of the Algerian political impasse. Not surprisingly, the FIS urged its supporters to boycott the October local elections. It was reported in early 1999 that the FIS had encouraged its supporters to vote for former foreign affairs minister Ibrahimi in the April 1999 presidential balloting.

FIS leaders expressed the hope that President Bouteflika's civil concord of the second half of 1999 would lead to legalization of the party (perhaps under a different name), but prospects in that regard remained dim. Meanwhile, the circumstances surrounding the assassination of Hachani in Algiers in November 1999 remained unclear, although the government had attributed the murder to the GIA.

FIS leaders Madani and Belhadj were released from house arrest and prison, respectively, in July 2003, the former subsequently settling in Qatar. Both men were barred from political activity, although in 2005 Madani was reported to have contacted President Bouteflika regarding Madani's possible participation in discussion about the proposed general amnesty.

Leaders: Dr. Abassi MADANI (in Qatar), Ali BELHADJ, Abdelkader BOUKHAMKHAM, Sheikh Abdelkader OMAR, Abdelkrim Ould ADDA (Foreign Spokesperson), Rabeh KEBIR (in Germany), and Anwar HADDAM (in the United States).

Islamic Salvation Army (*Armée Islamique du Salut*–AIS) The AIS, also previously referenced as the Armed Islamic Movement (*Mouvement Islamique Armée*–MIA), is an underground fundamentalist organization formed in response to the banning of the FIS in 1992. It is often described as the "military wing" of the FIS, although there have been reports of occasional policy differences between the leaders of the two groups.

Initially, the AIS was formally committed to antiregime military activity, although, unlike the GIA (below), it attacked only "official" military and police targets. (Shortly after the formation of the AIS, its fighters, estimated at about 10,000 strong, were reported to be operating under a unified command with GIA guerrillas, but extensive fighting, apparently emanating from disputes over tactics, broke out between the two groups in early 1994.) In early 1995 AIS leaders called for dialogue with the government, indicating that they would accept any "peace settlement" negotiated by the FIS. The AIS declared a "cease-fire" in antigovernment attacks as of October 1, 1997, apparently to disassociate itself from the shocking (even by recent Algerian standards) wave of violence gripping the country.

In June 1999 the AIS agreed to a permanent cease-fire in connection with President Bouteflika's plans for a civil concord including an amnesty for most AIS members and the restoration of their civil and political rights. In January 2000 AIS leader Madami MEZRAG signed documents formalizing the elements of the concord and announced the "dissolution" of the AIS, some 1,500 AIS members having reportedly been declared eligible for amnesty. Mezrag, by then reportedly working as a grocer, supported President Bouteflika's reelection bid in 2004.

Armed Islamic Group (*Groupe Islamique Armé*–GIA). The GIA is an outgrowth of antigovernment violence which first broke out in the mid-1980s around the city of Blida. In the 1990s the Group emerged as the most militant of the underground fundamentalist organizations, its targets including police, government officials, journalists, feminists, and, since 1994, foreigners. Vehemently anti-Western, the Group reportedly supported establishment of an Iranian-style "theocracy" in Algeria and firmly rejected dialogue with the military-backed Zeroual regime.

The GIA guerrilla force was once estimated at 2,500–10,000 fighters, some known as "Afghanis" in reference to their having fought with the *mujaheddin* in Afghanistan. In early 1994 the Group was reportedly in control of many rural areas and several urban districts. However, the government subsequently claimed that its intensive "antiterrorist" campaign had significantly weakened the GIA. Moreover, many GIA leaders have been killed by security forces or rival Islamists in recent years. In addition, one leader, Sheikh Abdel-Haq al-Ayadi, was arrested in Morocco in 1993 and extradited to Algeria, where he is currently under a death sentence following his conviction on terrorism charges.

In mid-1995 the GIA was placed on the US State Department's list of "terrorist" organizations. Although deemed by mid-1996 to be stronger militarily than the AIS, the GIA was believed to have lost much of whatever popular support it might once have commanded as the result of its assassination campaign and sometimes indiscriminate bomb attacks.

Friction within the GIA was also apparent following the kidnapping and eventual murder of seven French Trappist monks in Algeria in the spring of 1996. After the GIA claimed responsibility for the deaths, GIA leader Dhamel ZITOUNI (a.k.a. Abu Abderrahmane Amin) was reportedly ousted from the Group. He was subsequently reportedly killed by Algerian security forces. The GIA leadership mantle subsequently reportedly fell to Antar ZOUABI, while reports surfaced in late 1997 of another GIA leader—Slimane MAHERZI (a.k.a. Abu Djamil), a young guerrilla who had reportedly served the militant fundamentalist cause in Afghanistan and Bosnia and Herzegovina.

The GIA was broadly accused of the bulk of the terrorist incidents of 1997-2000, most of which occurred in central Algeria, where the Group's influence was considered the strongest. As the attacks grew more random and increasingly targeted civilians, some observers suggested that discipline had broken down within the GIA, a correspondent for the *New York Times* describing the Group as a "loose organization of roving bandits, including outlaws with little or no ideological commitment to Islam."

Ahmed Zaoui, described as a prominent external leader of the GIA following his disassociation with the FIS in 1997, was reportedly in Burkina Faso in late 1998, having been expelled from Switzerland. The GIA's Zouabi strongly rejected the government's amnesty offer included in President Bouteflika's civil concord of the second half of 1999, and most GIA fighters reportedly followed his lead, although some accepted the government's amnesty offer. Zouabi was reportedly killed by security forces in February 2002; Rachid Abou Tourab was subsequently reported to have been selected as the new GIA leader. Meanwhile, like the GSPC, the GIA was included on the list of "terrorist" organizations subject to asset seizure by the US as part of the war on terrorism announced after the September 11, 2001, attack.

Nourredine Boudiafi reportedly assumed leadership of the GIA in 2004; however, he was subsequently arrested, and the GIA mantle reportedly fell to Younes CHAABANE, who was killed during a security sweep in early 2005. By that time, the government was describing the GIA as "nearly extinct," jailed GIA founder Abdel-Haq al-Ayadi reportedly indicating a desire to discuss possible amnesty with the government.

Leaders: Sheikh Abdel-Haq al-AYADI (in prison), Nourredine BOUDIAFI (in prison), Mohammed SAID, Ahmed ZAOUI (in exile), Abdelmadjid DICHOU, Rachid Abou TOURAB.

Salafist Group for Preaching and Combat (*Groupe Salafiste pour la Prédication et le Combat*–GSPC). Also referenced as Appeal and Struggle, the GSPC was established in 1999 by members of the GIA opposed to the parent group's targeting of civilians but remaining committed to attacks on military sites and personnel. Although some reports suggested GSPC leaders had begun negotiations with the government in late 1999 regarding President Bouteflika's civil concord, that pact was ultimately rejected by the GSPC, which continued its guerrilla campaign. The GSPC was included on the list of proscribed organizations published by the US following the September 11, 2001, terrorist attacks. Several reports suggested that some GSPC fighters might have independently established ties with Osama bin Laden's *al-Qaeda* previously, although most observers doubted any formal connection between the two groups since the GSPC had never displayed any anti-US sentiment.

By 2003 the GSPC was one of the few Islamist groups "still fighting," hard-liner Nabil SAHRAOUI having supplanted GSPC founder Hassan HATAB as leader of the group. In October 2003 Sahraoui said that the GSPC supported bin Laden's *jihad* against "the American heretic," and the GSPC was held responsible for several attacks on Algerian forces in 2003–2004. However, Sahraoui was killed by the Algerian army in June 2004, analysts suggesting that GSPC forces had dwindled to 400–450 guerrillas by that time. Another GSPC leader, Amari SAIFI, was taken into custody in late 2004.

Defenders of the Salafi Call (*Dhanat Houmet Daawa Salafia*). One of the few Islamist militant groups active in Algeria as of 2005, this "Taliban-trained" grouping, another offshoot of the GIA, was reported to comprise about 150–250 fighters in Western Algeria. Like the GSPC, it has been declared a terrorist organization by the United States.

Leader: Mohammed BENSLIM.

Legislature

The 1996 constitution provided for a bicameral **Parliament** (*Barlaman*), consisting of a restructured National People's Assembly and a new upper house, the Council of the Nation. The former unicameral Assembly, consisting of 295 members serving five-year terms, had been most recently elected on February 26, 1987, deputies being selected from a list of 885 candidates (three for every seat) which had been drawn up by the National Liberation Front (FLN). The first round of multiparty balloting for a new 430-member Assembly was held December 26, 1991, with the Islamic Salvation Front (FIS) winning 188 seats, the Socialist Forces Front (FFS) 25, the FLN 15, and

Cabinet

As of May 1, 2005

Prime Minister	Ahmed Ouyahia (RND)

Ministers of State

Foreign Affairs	Mohamed Bedjaoui
Interior and Local Authorities	Nouredine Yazid Zerhouni (FLN)
Personal Representative of the Head of State	Abdelaziz Belkhadem (FLN)
Without Portfolio	Boudjerra Soltani

Ministers

Agriculture and Rural Development	Said Barkat
Commerce	El Hachemi Djaaboub (MSP)
Communication	(Vacant)
Culture	Khalida Toumi [f]
Employment and National Solidarity	Djamal Ould-Abbes
Energy and Mining	Chakib Khelil
Finance	Mourad Medelci
Fishing and Marine Resources	Smail Mimoune
Health, Population, and Hospital Reform	Amar Tou (FLN)
Higher Education and Scientific Research	Rachid Harraoubia (FLN)
Housing and Urban Affairs	Mohamed Nadir Hamimid
Industry	Mahmoud Khoudri
Justice, Keeper of the Seals	Tayeb Belaiz
Labor and Social Protection	Tayeb Louh (FLN)
National Education	Boubakeur Benbouzid (RND)
Posts and Information Technology	Boudjemaa Haichour (FLN)
Promotion of Investments	Abdelhamid Temmar
Public Works	Amar Ghoul (MSP)
Relations with Parliament	Abdelaziz Ziari (FLN)
Religious Affairs and Endowments	Bouabdallah Ghoulemallah (RND)
Small- and Medium-sized Enterprises and Crafts	Mustapha Benbada
Territorial Management and Environment	Cherif Rahmani
Tourism	Noureddine Moussa
Training and Professional Education	El Hadi Khaldi
Transportation	Mohamed Maghlaoui (RND)
War Veterans	Mohamed Cherif Abbas (RND)
Youth and Sports	Yahia Guiddoum

Ministers Delegate

Agriculture and Rural Development	Rachid Benaissa
Family and Women's Affairs	Nouara Saâdia Djaffar (RND) [f]
Finance	Karim Djoudi
Foreign Affairs	Abdelkader Messahel
Higher Education and Scientific Research	Souad Bendjaballah [f]
Interior and Local Communities	Daho Ould Kablia
National Defense	Abdelmalek Guenaizia
Territorial Management and Environment	Abderrachid Boukerzaza
Secretary General of the Government	Ahmed Noui (RND)

[f] = female

independents 3. A runoff round involving the top two vote-getters in the remaining districts was scheduled for January 16, 1992. However, the second poll was canceled on January 12 by the High Security Council, which also declared the results of the first round invalid. Subsequently, it was revealed that the former Assembly had been dissolved by a secret presidential decree on January 4.

In April 1992 the High Council of State announced the appointment of a 60-member National Consultative Council (*Majlis al-Shoura al-Watani*) to serve in an advisory capacity to the government pending new Assembly elections. The National Dialogue Conference of early 1994, in turn, authorized the appointment of a three-year National Transitional Council (NTC), which at its initial sitting in May encompassed 63 seats filled by parties, 85 by professional associations and trade unions, and 30 by government nominees, with 22 reserved for nonparticipating secular parties. The NTC was dissolved on May 18, 1997, in preparation for the elections to the bodies authorized by the new constitution.

Council of the Nation (*Majlis al-Umma/ Conseil de la Nation*). The upper house has 144 members, 96 (two from each *wilayaat*) elected in secret ballot by an electoral college of the members of local councils and communal and *wilayaat* assemblies and 48 appointed by the president. The term of office is six years, although one-half of the initial members (elected on December 25, 1997) served only three years to permit 50 percent replenishment of the Council every three years from that point. Following the balloting of December 30, 2003, the distribution of the elected seats was as follows: National Democratic Rally, 52; National Liberation Front, 31; Movement for a Peaceful Society, 10; Movement for National Reform, 2; Socialist Forces Front, 1.

Speaker: Abdulkader BENSALAH.

National People's Assembly (*Majlis Ech Chaabi al-Watani, Assemblée Popularie Nationale*). The lower house has 389 members, 381 representing the 48 *wilayaats* (each of which has at least 4 representatives) according to population,

and 8 (4 in Europe and 4 in other Arab nations) elected by Algerians living abroad. Members are elected for a five-year term on a proportional basis from lists presented by parties or independents. Following the election of May 30, 2002, the distribution of seats was as follows: National Liberation Front, 199; National Democratic Rally, 47; Movement for National Reform, 43; Movement for a Peaceful Society, 38; Workers' Party, 21; Algerian National Front, 8; Movement of National Harmony, 1; Renaissance Movement (*Nahda*), 1; Algerian Renewal Party; and independents, 30.

Speaker: Amar SAIDANI.

Communications

Press

After a long period of strict control of national and foreign press activities, the government introduced a new Information Code in mid-1989 which formally ended the state media monopoly and accorded journalists greater freedom of expression. It was succeeded in March 1990 by a more stringent Code which mandated imprisonment for journalists who "offended" Islam or any other religion and stipulated that all new periodicals be printed in Arabic. However, the new strictures were not rigorously implemented, and an information "explosion" subsequently took place in the increasingly independent press. By mid-1991 there were reportedly more than 110 daily, weekly, and monthly periodicals, many of them fostered by a government program under which journalists in state-owned enterprises were offered a sum equal to two years' salary to help establish private publications. Most of the new papers continued to be printed on government presses, which enabled the administration to suspend their issuance during the early phase of the 1991 state of emergency. Significant restrictions, largely directed at the Islamic fundamentalist press, were imposed following the declaration of a state of emergency in early 1992. A number of newspapers were also banned for a short time later in the year under a new decree permitting such action in cases of publications deemed to be operating "against public interest." In addition, journalists were permitted to report on "security matters" only with government authorization and only using information released by the state, stories on antigovernment activity consequently becoming quite limited. In part because they are often perceived as "apologists" for the government, journalists were subsequently targeted by fundamentalist radicals. New restrictions, including harsh penalties in a revised penal code, have been imposed on the press in recent years, prompting protests from both domestic and international journalism organizations. Among other things, opposition candidates complained in 2002 about the high level of control exercised by the administration of President Bouteflika over all aspects of the media.

The following are dailies published at El Djazair (Algiers) unless otherwise noted: *el-Moudjahid* (The Fighter, 440,000), former FLN organ in French; *Algérie Actualité* (255,000), government weekly in French; *Horizons* (200,000), in French; *al-Chaab* (The People, 150,000), former FLN information journal in Arabic; *al-Massa* (100,000), in Arabic. Other independent dailies include: *Le Soir de l'Algérie* (150,000), in French; *Al Khabar* (The News, 120,000), in Arabic; *El Watan* (The Nation, 80,000), in French; *Le Jeune Indépendant* (60,000), in French; *Al Djazair al-Joum* (54,000), in Arabic; *Al-Massa* (45,000), in Arabic; *Horizons* (35,000), in French; *Le Matin,* in French; *La Tribune,* in French; *al-Jumhuriyah* (The Republic, Wahran, 20,000), former FLN organ in Arabic; *Liberté* (20,000), in French;

Le Monde Aujourd'hui, in French; *Le Quotidien d'Oran* (Wahran), in French.

News Agencies

The domestic agency is the Algerian Press Service (*Wikalat al-Anba' al-Jaza'iriyah/Algérie Presse Service*–APS). A number of foreign agencies maintain offices at Algiers.

Broadcasting and Computing

The government decreased its control over broadcasting services in 2000, although it retained a supervisory role. The former state-controlled *Télévision Algérienne* continues to service about a dozen stations. There were approximately 3.8 million television receivers and 250,000 personal computers serving 380,000 Internet users in 2003.

Intergovernmental Representation

Ambassador to the US
Amine KHERBI

US Ambassador to Algeria
Richard W. ERDMAN

Permanent Representative to the UN
Abdallah BAALI

IGO Memberships (Non-UN)
AfDB, AFESD, AMF, AMU, AU, BADEA, BIS, CCC, IDB, Interpol, IOM, LAS, NAM, OAPEC, OIC, OPEC

BAHRAIN

KINGDOM OF BAHRAIN

al-Mamlakah al-Bahrayn

The Country

An archipelago of some 33 largely desert islands situated between the Qatar peninsula and Saudi Arabia, the Kingdom of Bahrain consists primarily of the main island of Bahrain plus the smaller islands of Muharraq, Sitra, and Umm-Nassan. Summer temperatures often exceed 100 degrees (F), and annual rainfall averages only about four inches; however, natural springs provide sufficient water. The predominantly Arab population is about two-thirds indigenous Bahraini, with small groups of Saudi Arabians, Omanis, Iranians, Asians, and Europeans. An estimated 65 percent consists of Shiʿite Muslims, while 30 percent, including the royal family, adheres to the Sunni sect.

Oil, produced commercially since 1936, and natural gas now account for some 65 percent of the government's income, although recoverable petroleum reserves may be exhausted in the first quarter of the twenty-first century. (As of 1998 Bahrain was producing 40,000 barrels per day, while its total reserves were estimated at about 210 million barrels.) Additional revenue is derived from operation of the Aluminum Bahrain smelter, which is one of the largest nonextractive enterprises in the Gulf area, and from one of the Middle East's largest oil refineries, devoted largely to processing crude (about 200,000 barrels per day) from Saudi Arabia. Bahrain has also been a prominent financial center for many years, its more than 50 offshore banks handling much of the region's oil-related wealth.

Aided by fiscal support from Saudi Arabia, Kuwait, and the United Arab Emirates, the government upon independence began to establish an extensive network of social services, including free education and medical care, and in 1982 mounted an ambitious program for infrastructure development and improvements in agriculture and education. An economic downturn in the mid-1980s, caused by declining foreign aid and marked by budget deficits and rising unemployment, appeared to have been reversed by the end of the decade; however, the Gulf crisis precipitated by the August 1990 Iraqi invasion of Kuwait generated additional economic problems for the emirate as

aid from Gulf neighbors was severely constrained and offshore banking activity fell sharply. In response, the government intensified its campaign to promote development of new small- and medium-scale industries, in large part by loosening restrictions on private foreign investment. The economy rebounded in the mid-1990s under the influence of steady oil revenue. Subsequently, falling oil prices in 1998 led to a 3-percent decline in GDP for the year and intensified concern over the government's budget deficit, observers suggesting that a growing segment of the population (particularly those under 27 years of age, who make up 70 percent of the total) was at risk of becoming economically disenfranchised. However, the economy rebounded strongly in 1999 as the result of the sharp turnaround in oil prices, foreign investors reportedly responding positively to that development. GDP growth subsequently remained strong, averaging more than 5 percent in 2000–2004, while inflation of only 1 percent was registered in 2004. The International Monetary Fund (IMF) described the economy as "one of the most advanced in the region," although unemployment remained a significant concern. However, despite the generally positive economic statistics, a number of observers warned that entrenched poverty (primarily within the Shi'ite population) still presented a threat to political and social stability.

Government and Politics

Political Background

Long ruled as a traditional monarchy, Bahrain became a British protectorate in 1861 when Britain concluded a treaty of friendship with the emir as part of a larger effort to secure communication lines with its Asian colonies. The treaty was modified in 1892, but little evolution in domestic politics occurred prior to the interwar period. In 1926 Sir Charles BELGRAVE was appointed adviser to the emir, providing guidance in reform of the administrative system—an especially important step in light of accelerated social change following the

discovery of oil in 1932. Belgrave continued to have a direct and personal effect on Bahraini policy until 1957, his departure coming as the result of Arab nationalist agitation that began in 1954 and reached a peak during the 1956 Anglo-French action in Egypt. Incipient nationalists also provoked disturbances in 1965 and in 1967, following the second Arab–Israeli conflict.

In 1968 Britain announced that it would withdraw most of its forces east of Suez by 1971, and steps were taken to prepare for the independence of all of the British-protected emirates on the Persian Gulf. Initially, a federation composed of Bahrain, Qatar, and the seven components of the present United Arab Emirates was envisaged. Bahrain, however, failed to secure what it considered an appropriate allocation of seats in the proposed federation's ruling body and declared separate independence on August 15, 1971.

Despite nominal efforts at modernization, such as the creation of an Administrative Council following the 1956 disturbances and a quasi-ministerial Council of State as its successor in 1970, virtually absolute power remained in the hands of the emir until the adoption in 1973 of the country's first constitution, which provided for a partially elected National Assembly. However, total control quickly returned to the royal family when the emir, describing the new legislative body as "obstructionist," ordered its dissolution in August 1975.

Although initially less intense than in other regional countries, rebellious sentiments among some of the majority Shi'ites, resentful of Sunni rule, precipitated conflict following the Iranian revolution of 1979 and the accompanying spread of Islamic fundamentalism. In December 1981 the government declared that it had thwarted a conspiracy involving the Iranian-backed Islamic Front for the Liberation of Bahrain (IFLB). That plot and the discovery in February 1984 of a rebel arms cache resulted in numerous arrests, the banning of a Shi'ite religious organization (the Islamic Enlightenment Society), and the issuance of compulsory identity cards to nationals and resident aliens.

The government subsequently maintained a tight rein on the activity of fundamentalists, a number of whom were arrested in 1992 for belonging to illegal organizations.

In January 1993, apparently in response to Western calls for political liberalization, the emir established a Consultative Council of 30 "elite and loyal men," including some former National Assembly members.

A wave of clashes with security forces erupted during the summit of the Gulf Cooperation Council (GCC) at Manama in December 1994, following the arrest of Sheikh 'Ali SALMAN, a religious leader who had demanded more jobs for Shi'ites. In January 1995 Salman and two followers were released, deported to Dubai, and thereafter granted temporary asylum in Britain. However, after the emir, in an implicit reference to Iran, had complained of "meddling by foreign countries in our internal affairs," further disturbances occurred in March in which a police officer was killed. In April two persons were killed and dozens injured during a raid on the home of another opposition cleric, Sheikh 'Abd al-Amir al-JAMRI, and on May 2 ten Shi'ites, including Jamri, were given jail terms for property damage resulting from the December and January outbreaks.

Sheikh Jamri was released on September 25, 1995, following the initiation of reconciliation talks between the government and the Shi'ite opposition. However, a new outbreak of violence in early 1996 prompted the rearrest of Jamri and seven followers. Additional arrests were made in February after a series of bombings at the capital, including a blast in the lobby of a luxury seafront hotel that wounded four people. Continued violence in March involved several bomb attacks on banks and other buildings.

Following further bombings in April–May 1996, the government announced on June 3 that it had foiled an allegedly Iranian-backed plot to seize power and that more than 80 of those involved had been arrested. Recalling its ambassador from Teheran, Bahrain claimed that the Iranian authorities had hatched the plot with a Bahraini

Political Status: Independent emirate proclaimed August 15, 1971; constitution adopted December 6, 1973; constitutional monarchy established on February 14, 2002, under constitutional amendment decreed by the emir in purported accordance with National Action Charter endorsed by national referendum on February 14–15, 2001.

Area: 258 sq. mi. (668 sq. km.).

Population: 651,604 (2001C); 701,000 (2004E). Both figures include non-nationals (approximately 264,000 in 1999).

Major Urban Centers (1997E): MANAMA (166,000); Muharraq (97,000).

Official Language: Arabic.

Monetary Unit: Dinar (official rate July 1, 2005: 1 dinar = $2.66US).

Sovereign: King Sheikh Hamad ibn 'Isa Al KHALIFA, descendant of a ruling dynasty which dates from 1782; succeeded to the throne as emir on March 6, 1999, upon the death of his father, Sheikh 'Isa ibn Salman Al KHALIFA; proclaimed himself king under constitutional amendment adopted on February 14, 2002.

Heir to the Throne: Crown Prince Sheikh Salman ibn Hamad Al KHALIFA.

Prime Minister: Sheikh Khalifa ibn Salman Al KHALIFA, uncle of the emir; appointed January 19, 1970, by his brother, then emir Sheikh 'Isa ibn Salman Al KHALIFA; continued in office upon independence.

branch of the Lebanon-based *Hezbollah* (Party of God), whose members had been trained in Iran and had been the principal instigators of the recent unrest among Bahraini Shi'ites. Denying the Bahraini charges, Iran responded by withdrawing its ambassador from Manama, while offering to mediate between the government and the Shi'ite opposition. Meanwhile, apparently responding to international pressure for political liberalization throughout the Gulf, the emir in September appointed an expanded

40-member Consultative Council, announcing that he expected it to assume additional responsibilities.

Sheikh 'Isa ibn Salman Al KHALIFA, the emir of Bahrain since 1961, died of a heart attack on March 6, 1999. He was immediately succeeded by his son and longtime heir apparent, Sheikh Hamad ibn 'Isa Al KHALIFA who was reportedly more reform-minded than his father. A new cabinet was appointed on May 31, although it comprised most members of the previous government, including Prime Minister Sheikh Khalifa ibn Salman Al KHALIFA. In November 2000 the emir appointed a 46-member Supreme National Committee to draft a National Action Charter that would serve as a blueprint for political development and democratization. Although some members reportedly resigned over alleged "interference" on the part of the emir, a draft charter was published in December and subjected on February 14–15, 2001, to a national referendum that endorsed the proposals by a reported 98.4-percent "yes" vote. One year later the emir decreed constitutional amendments that incorporated the charter's provisions, including the establishment of a constitutional monarchy in which authority was to be shared by a bicameral National Assembly and the former emir (now the king). As the first step in the progressive (by regional standards) democratization process, local elections were held in May, with a number of opposition political "associations" or "societies" participating in the balloting. However, several such groups boycotted the October balloting for the Chamber of Deputies to protest Hamad's decision that the Assembly's Consultative Council would not be elected but rather would be appointed by the king (see Current issues, below).

Constitution and Government

In December 1972 the emir convened a Constituent Council to consider a draft constitution that provided for a National Assembly composed of a cabinet (which had replaced the Council of State in 1971) and 30 members elected by popular vote. The constitution was approved in June 1973 and became effective December 6, 1973, an election being held the following day. However, the Assembly was dissolved in August 1975, with the emir suspending the constitutional provision for an elected legislative body. The Consultative Council named in January 1993 was established by the emir's decree, observers predicting it would operate on a "trial basis" before provision for it or some other such body was incorporated into the constitution. At the time of the appointment of the most recent Council in September 2000, the government announced plans to conduct elections in 2004 for the next Council. Meanwhile, the emir in April had decreed the establishment of a new Supreme Council for Economic Development, headed by the prime minister. (The chairmanship of the Council was later transferred to the Crown Prince.)

The constitutional amendments of February 2002 proclaimed the country a "constitutional monarchy" based on separation of powers, the rule of law, respect for human rights, and freedom of association. In addition, the changes in the basic law provided for formation of a bicameral legislature; women were empowered not only to vote, but also to run for office. However, critics accused King Hamad of reserving too much authority for himself. (The king was designated head of state and commander-in-chief of the armed forces and was given uncontested power to appoint cabinet ministers, judges, and members of the upper house in the new National Assembly.)

The legal system is based on *shari'a* (canonical Muslim law); the judiciary includes separate courts for members of the Sunni and Shi'ite sects. The constitutional amendments of February 2002 envisioned the formation of a constitutional court. The six main towns serve as bases of administrative divisions that are governed by municipal councils.

Foreign Relations

Since independence, Bahrain has closely followed Saudi Arabia's lead in foreign policy. However, it has been more moderate than most other Arab states in its support of the Palestine Liberation Organization and in condemning the Israeli–Egyptian peace treaty of 1979.

Generally regarded as the most vulnerable of the Gulf sheikhdoms, Bahrain was a target of Iranian agitation and territorial claims following the overthrow of the shah. Although Manama adopted a posture of noncommitment at the outbreak in 1980 of the Iran–Iraq war, it subsequently joined the other five members of the GCC, established in March 1981, in voicing support for Iraq. A security treaty with Saudi Arabia was concluded in December 1981, and in February 1982 the foreign ministers of the GCC states announced that they would actively oppose "Iranian sabotage acts aimed at wrecking the stability of the Gulf region." To this end, Bahrain joined with the other GCC states in annual joint military maneuvers. The spirit of cooperation was jolted in April 1986, however, by Bahrain's conflict with Qatar over a small uninhabited island, Fasht al-Dibal, that had been reclaimed from an underlying coral reef for use as a Bahraini coast guard station. Following a brief takeover by Qatari armed forces, an agreement was reached to return the site to its original condition. In January 1989 the two countries agreed to mediation by Saudi Arabia to resolve other territorial problems, including Bahrain's claim to Zubara, the ancestral home of the Al Khalifa family on the Qatari mainland. Nonetheless, in mid-1991 Qatar instituted a suit at the International Court of Justice (ICJ) claiming sovereignty not only over Fasht al-Dibal, but another reef, Qitat Jaradah, and the larger Hawar Island (see map). A period of naval posturing ensued, with Bahrain accusing Qatar of attempting to undercut the mediation effort and rejecting a ruling by the ICJ in February 1995 that it had jurisdiction in the dispute. (Bahrain later accepted the ICJ's jurisdiction.) Adding to the tension with Qatar was a report in early September that Bahrain had started construction of a tourist resort on Hawar. Relations deteriorated in 1996 to the point that some observers suggested that military conflict was possible before the GCC in 1997 mediated an apparent truce, albeit an uncomfortable and perhaps temporary one. Hope for a negotiated settlement grew in December 1999–January 2000 when the leaders of the two countries exchanged visits and agreed to establish a joint committee to try to settle their differences. However, the ICJ hearing on the matter proceeded as scheduled in June, and renewed friction between Manama and Doha was reported in the fall. Following the ICJ's March 2001 ruling on the dispute (wherein Zubara was awarded to Qatar and Fasht al-Dibal, Qitat Jaradah, and Hawar Island to Bahrain), relations between the two countries improved significantly.

Relations with Washington have long been cordial and in October 1991, following the UN action against Iraq, Bahrain and the United States signed a defense cooperation agreement, similar to one concluded between the United States and Kuwait, that provided for joint military exercises and authorized the storage of equipment and the use of port facilities by US forces. The Gulf crisis was seen as having provided the government with a powerful means of surmounting Sunni Arab fears that an ongoing US presence would promote unrest among the country's numerically predominant Shi'ite population, and in October 1995 Manama announced it had granted the United States permission to base 30 military aircraft in Bahrain. Meanwhile, the emirate and its GCC associates continued to seek regional security arrangements that would dilute domestic political pressure on individual members regarding military ties with the West. However, upon ascending to the throne in March 1999, Sheikh Hamad quickly pledged to maintain the close ties that his father had established with the Western powers. Subsequently, Bahrain signed a free trade agreement with the United States, whose naval base in Bahrain remained an important component of US military force in the Gulf. Anti-American sentiment (pronounced in many Arab states in recent years) has remained relatively low in Bahrain, although protests broke out in May 2004 against attacks by US forces on Shi'ite "holy cities" in Iraq.

Current Issues

Critics of Sheikh 'Isa's domestic policies (particularly the repression of dissent emanating from the Shi'ite population and secular liberals since the 1996 disturbances) expressed the hope in 1999 that the new emir, Sheikh Hamad, would prove more open to dialogue and compromise. Among other things, Shi'ite leaders called for the release of Sheikh Jamri, the popular cleric who had finally gone on trial in February 1999 after having been detained for three years in connection with the events of early 1996. Opposition groups also continued to lobby for restoration of an elected legislature, release of all political prisoners (arrests had continued throughout 1998), and the return of exiled dissidents–demands that attracted significant international support.

It was not immediately clear what the new emir's relationship would be with his uncle, Prime Minister Khalifa, who had been widely viewed as responsible for the anti-Shi'ite crackdown and with whom Sheikh Hamad was known to have a long-standing rivalry. However, the prime minister remained at the head of the slightly reshuffled cabinet announced at the end of May.

In July 1999 Sheikh Jamri was sentenced to ten years in jail on charges of inciting unrest and operating illegally on behalf of a foreign power. However, the emir pardoned the sheikh almost immediately, albeit not before coercing a "humiliating confession" from Jamri. Opposition groups welcomed the emir's decision in November to release a number of detainees, but they charged that numerous other political prisoners remained in jail. They were also only cautiously supportive of the government's decision to include women for the first time in the new Consultative Council appointed in September 2000 and its announcement that membership of the next Council would be determined through the ballot box. Skeptics argued that the measures were primarily aimed at mollifying international critics and would mean little domestically unless the Council was given true legislative authority. However, some of those concerns were alleviated by the referendum on the National Action Charter in February 2001. The emir also reduced tensions between his administration and its opponents by visiting Shi'ite-dominated areas, issuing a general amnesty for political detainees, permitting the return of prominent dissidents from exile, and repealing a number of hard-line security measures.

Although Sheikh Hamad promoted his constitutional amendments of February 2002 as moving Bahrain toward the status of a "modern democracy," complaints quickly arose within the opposition camp. Most importantly, opponents decried Hamad's decree that only the lower house of the National Assembly would be elected, with the presidentially appointed upper house having an effective veto over legislation. (Critics called that decision a violation of the intent of the 2001 National Action Charter.) King Hamad was also strongly attacked for a 2002 decree granting immunity to any security personnel or government officials accused of torture or other human rights violations prior to 2001. A number of public protests subsequently broke out, many of them among Shi'ites who continued to feel repressed by the royal family and Sunnis in general. In the wake of a boycott by several prominent political "societies" (see Political Groups, below), the turnout for the October 2002 balloting for the Chamber of Deputies was only 53 percent (down from more than 80 percent for the May municipal elections). International observers also began to question the government's enthusiasm for reform, particularly when Abd al-Hadi al-KHAWAJA (the executive director of the Bahrain Center for Human Rights [BCHR]) was arrested in late 2004 for criticizing Prime Minister Salman. (Khawaja was pardoned by the king following his conviction, but the BCHR remained closed.) Concerns were also raised about the new antiterrorism law proposed by the government in 2005, opponents describing the language in the bill as being so broad as to permit the detention of any government critic.

Political Groups

Political parties are proscribed in Bahrain. At the first National Assembly election in 1973, however, voters elected ten candidates of a loosely organized Popular Bloc of the Left, while such small clandestine groups as a Bahraini branch of the Popular Front for the Liberation of Oman and the Arabian Gulf (PFLOAG), apparently consisting mainly of leftist students, subsequently continued to engage in limited activity. During the 1994 disturbances, a Shi'ite opposition group, the Islamic Front for the Liberation of Bahrain (IFLB) insisted that security forces were arresting its followers "at random" and condemned deportations of regime opponents.

Reports in the first half of the 1990s concerning activity on behalf of Shi'ites focused on *Hezbollah*, based in Lebanon and believed to be financed by Iran. The government charged that a *Hezbollah*-Bahrain was formed in Iran in 1993 and contributed to anti-regime activity, including the alleged coup attempt of 1996. Meanwhile, the Bahrain Freedom Movement, based at London under the leadership of Mansur al-JAMRI (the son of popular Shi'ite leader Sheikh 'Abd al-Amir al-Jamri [see Political background and Current issues, above]), called for "passive resistance" on the part of the Bahraini populace to pressure the government into adopting "democratic reforms." A Committee for Popular Participation also lobbied for political liberalization under the leadership of Ali Qasem RABI.

Left-wing groups include the **National Liberation Front of Bahrain** (NLFB), a Marxist formation active mainly in exile since the mid-1950s, and the **Popular Front in Bahrain** (PFB). The NLF/B and the PFB reportedly initiated the formation of the **National Democratic Forum** as a "progressive front" in the late 1990s.

Although the constitutional amendment of February 2002 did not lift the ban on political parties, several "groups" and "societies" were subsequently legalized in line with the democratic reforms. Staffed largely by formerly exiled opposition figures who had returned to Bahrain following the amnesty issued by the king in February 2002, those groups and associations "unofficially" endorsed candidates in local elections in May. In addition to the groups listed below, other recognized associations included: the Sunni **Islamic National Forum** (INF); the pan-Arab nationalist **Islamic Arab Democratic Society** (IADS); the **Nationalist Democratic Rally** (NDR); and the **Association for Islamic National Reconciliation** (AINR).

Islamic National Accord Society (INAS). Referenced as "*al-Wifaq*," ("accord"), this Shi'ite grouping is led by youthful cleric Sheikh Ali Salman, a former prominent member of the Bahrain Freedom Movement. *Al-Wifaq* was credited with winning upwards of 70 percent of the seats in the municipal elections of May 2002. However, the INAS boycotted the October 2002 national balloting to protest some of the constitutional amendments decreed earlier in the year by King Hamad that *al-Wifaq* leaders considered inimical to genuine power-sharing (see Current issues, above). In 2004 it was reported that a number of INAS members had participated in a new **Justice and Development Society** that pledged to participate in the 2006 national poll.

Leaders: Sheikh Ali SALMAN, Husayn MU-SHAYMA.

Progressive Democratic Forum (PDF). Launched by former members of the NLFB upon their return to Bahrain in 2002, the PDF reportedly supported three successful candidates in the October balloting for the Chamber of Deputies.

Leaders: Ahmad al-THAWADI, Hassan MA-DANI.

Bahrain Freedom Movement (BFM). Some members of the London-based BFM returned to Bahrain in 2002, including former BFM leader Majid al-AWALI, who was named to the new cabinet in November. However, other BFM members remained in exile at London, criticizing King Hamad for orchestrating a "constitutional putsch."

Other groupings that boycotted the October 2002 balloting for the Chamber of Deputies were the leftist **National Democratic Action Society,** led by Abdul Rahman al-NUAIMI; the **Islamic Action Society,** a grouping of followers of Shi'ite religious scholar Muhammad Mahdi al-SHIRAZI, led by Sheikh Muhammad Ali MAHFUZ, a former leader of the IFLB; and the **National Society of Baathist Groups.**

Legislature

The first election to fill 30 nonnominated seats in the **National Assembly** was held December 7,

Cabinet

As of June 1, 2005

Prime Minister	Sheikh Khalifa ibn Salman Al Khalifa
Deputy Prime Ministers	Sheikh Abdullah ibn Khalid Al Khalifa
	Sheikh Muhammad ibn Mubarak Al Khalifa

Ministers

Cabinet Affairs	Muhammad ibn Ibrahim al-Mutawa
Commerce and Industry	Hassan ibn Abdullah Fakhro
Defense	Maj. Gen. Sheikh Khalifa ibn Ahmad Al Khalifa
Education	Majid ibn Ali al-Nuaimi
Electricity and Water	Sheikh Abdullah ibn Salman Al Khalifa
Finance	Sheikh Ahmed ibn Muhammad Al Khalifa
Foreign Affairs	Sheikh Muhammad ibn Mubarak Al Khalifa
Health	Dr. Nada Haffadh [f]
Housing and Public Works	Fahmi ibn Ali al-Jawder
Information	Muhammad ibn Abdulghaffar
Interior	Sheikh Rashid ibn Abdullah ibn Ahmad Al Khalifa
Islamic Affairs	Sheikh Abdallah ibn Khalid Al Khalifa
Justice	Muhammad ibn Ali Sheikh Mansur al-Sitri
Labor	Majid ibn Mushin al-Alawi
Municipalities and Agricultural Affairs	Ali ibn Salih al-Salih
Oil	Sheikh Isa ibn Ali Al Khalifa
Prime Minister's Court Minister	Sheikh Khalid ibn Abdullah Al Khalifa
Social Affairs	Fatima al-Balushi [f]
Transportation	Sheikh 'Ali ibn Khalifa Al Khalifa
Works	Fahmi Ali al-Juder

Ministers of State

Cabinet Affairs	Abdulhussain ibn Ali Mirza
Chamber of Deputies and Consultative Council Affairs	Brig. Gen. Abdulaziz al-Fadhil
Foreign Affairs	Muhammad ibn Abdulghaffar
Municipalities and Environmental Affairs	Jawad Salim al-Urayid
Without Portfolio	Muhammad Hassan Kamalidin

[f] = female

1973. In addition to the elected members, who were to serve four-year terms, the Assembly contained 14 cabinet members (including 2 ministers of state). The Assembly was dissolved on August 26, 1975, on the grounds that it had indulged in debates "dominated by ideas alien to the society and values of Bahrain."

In January 1993 the emir appointed a 30-member Consultative Council to contribute "advice and opinion" on legislation proposed by the cabinet and, in certain cases, suggest new laws on its own. In accordance with reforms announced in April 1996, the emir appointed new 40-member Councils on September 28, 1996, and September

27, 2000. (The Council appointed in 2000 included women for the first time.)

The king dissolved the Consultative Council on February 14, 2002, in anticipation of the establishment of the new bicameral National Assembly (*Majlis al-Watani*) provided for in the constitutional revision of the same day.

Consultative Council (*Majlis al-Shura*). The upper house comprises 40 members appointed by the king for a four-year term. The first appointments, including six women as well as representatives of the Christian and Jewish communities, were made by King Hamad on November 16, 2002.
Speaker: Dr. Faisal Radhi al-MUSAWI.

Chamber of Deputies (*Majlis al-Nuwwab*). The lower house comprises 40 members directly elected on a majoritarian basis for a four-year term. The first elections were held on October 24, 2002, with runoff balloting on October 31. Nineteen (12 Sunni and 7 Shi'ite) of the seats were reportedly won by candidates supported by moderate Islamist "societies." (Four major opposition organizations boycotted the balloting.) Of the remaining seats, 18 were reportedly won by independent "secularists" and 3 by "liberals.") No female candidates were successful. The next election was scheduled for October 2006.
Speaker: Khalifa al-DHAHRANI.

Communications

Press

Until recently, the ruling family strongly censored all media, the Bahraini press having been described by a correspondent for the *Financial Times* as "fawning." Some progress towards media freedom has been noted since early 2001 in line with recent democratic reforms, although "draconian" regulations remained formally in place. The following newspapers are published at Manama unless otherwise noted: *Akhbar al-Khalij* (Gulf News, 30,000), first Arabic daily, founded 1976; *al-Ayam* (The Days, 21,400), daily in Arabic; *al-Adhwaa* (Lights, 16,000), Arab weekly; *Bahrain Tribune* (12,500), sister paper to *al-Ayam* in English; *Gulf Daily News* (11,000), daily in English; *Sada al-Usbu* (Weekly Echo, 5,000), Arabic weekly; *al-Bahrain al-Yawm* (Bahrain Today, 5,000), Arabic weekly, published by the Ministry of Information; and *al-Wasat* (described as the "first truly independent" paper in Bahrain).

News Agencies

The official national facility is the Bahrain News Agency; *Agence France-Presse,* the Associated Press, the Gulf News Agency, and Reuters maintain offices at Manama.

Broadcasting and Computing

The Bahrain Broadcasting Service (*Idha'at al-Bahrayn*), a government facility that transmits in Arabic and English, and Radio Bahrain (*Radiyu al-Bahrayn*), an English-language commercial station, are the principal sources of radio programs and were received by approximately 355,000 sets in 1999. The government-operated Bahrain Television (*Tilifiziyun al-Bahrayn*), which has provided commercial programming in Arabic since 1973, added an English-language channel in 1981. In 2003, approximately 280,000 television sets were in use, while some 110,000 personal computers served 200,000 Internet users.

Intergovernmental Representation

Ambassador to the US
(Vacant)

US Ambassador to Bahrain
William T. MONROE

Permanent Representative to the UN
Tawfiq Ahmad ALMANSUR

IGO Memberships (Non-UN)
AFESD, AMF, BADEA, CCC, GCC, IDB, Interpol, LAS, NAM, OAPEC, OIC, WTO

CYPRUS

REPUBLIC OF CYPRUS

Kypriaki Dimokratia (Greek)
Kıbrıs Cumhuriyeti (Turkish)

The Country

Settled by Greeks in antiquity, conquered by the Ottoman Empire in 1571, placed under British administration in 1878, and annexed by Britain in 1914, Cyprus has been independent since 1960 (although effectively partitioned since 1974). The largest island in the eastern Mediterranean, it supports diverse and often antagonistic ethnic groups and traditions. More than 75 percent of the population speaks Greek and belongs to the Orthodox Church, while more than 20 percent is Turkish-speaking Muslim; adherents of other religions account for less than 2 percent.

Although Cyprus was historically an agricultural country, the Greek Cypriot rural sector presently employs only about 13 percent of the total labor force and contributes less than 6 percent of GDP (the corresponding Turkish Cypriot figures being 25 and 12 percent, respectively). Nonetheless, vegetables, fruits, nuts, and wine rank with clothing and footwear as leading exports. Following the de facto partition of the island into Greek and Turkish sectors in 1974, rebuilding in the south emphasized manufacturing of nondurable consumer goods, while the more severely damaged north has relied on its citrus groves, mines, and tourist facilities as well as on direct budgetary assistance from Turkey (estimated at around 20 percent of budgeted expenditure in recent years). Whereas 70 percent of predivision productive resources had been located in the north (including 80 percent of the island's citrus groves and 60 percent of tourist installations), the postdivision southern economy rapidly outdistanced that of the north, achieving consistently high annual growth rates and virtually full employment. In addition to developing tourism and agriculture, Greek Cyprus diversified into financial, shipping, and other services, becoming a major offshore banking center and suffering only a temporary downturn as a result of the 1990–1991 Gulf crisis.

The economy performed well in the first half of the 1990s, growth averaging more than 4 percent annually and unemployment remaining negligible. However, disturbances along the dividing line between the Greek Cypriot and Turkish Cypriot territories in 1996 led to a decline in tourism, the

Political Status: Independent republic established August 16, 1960; member of the Commonwealth since March 13, 1961; under ethnic Greek majority regime until coup led by Greek army officers and subsequent Turkish intervention on July 20, 1974; Turkish Federated State proclaimed February 13, 1975, in Turkish-controlled (northern) sector; permanent constitutional status under negotiation (currently suspended) despite proclamation of independent Turkish Republic of Northern Cyprus (TRNC) on November 15, 1983.

Area: 3,572 sq. mi. (9,251 sq. km.), embracing approximately 2,172 sq. mi. (5,625 sq. km.) in Greek-controlled (southern) sector and 1,400 sq. mi. (3,626 sq. km.) in Turkish-controlled (northern) sector.

Population: 913,000 (2001E, including Greek sector census figure of 703,529 and an estimate of 209,000 for the Turkish sector); a comparable overall estimate for 2004 would be 960,000, assuming accuracy of the 2001 TRNC figure, which includes settlers from Turkey (approximately 55 percent).

Major Urban Centers (Urban Areas, 1999E): NICOSIA/LEFKOSIA, (197,000, excluding Turkish sector), Limassol (156,000), Larnaca (69,000), Paphos (39,000). On February 16, 1995, the name of the capital was changed by the city's municipal government to Lefkosia as part of a campaign to standardize place-names in accordance with their Greek pronunciation; however, both names are accorded official status by the central government.

Official Languages: Greek, Turkish.

Monetary Unit: Cyprus Pound (market rate July 1, 2005: 1 pound = $2.14US). (Following its accession to the European Union in May 2004, Cyprus announced plans to adopt the euro "as soon as possible.")

President: Tassos PAPADOPOULOS (Democratic Party); elected in first-round popular balloting on February 16, 2003, and inaugurated for a five-year term on March 1, succeeding Glafcos CLERIDES (Democratic Rally).

Vice President: (Vacant). Rauf R. DENKTAŞ, then President of the Turkish Republic of Northern Cyprus (see Cyprus: Turkish Sector), was elected Vice President by vote of the Turkish Community in February 1973, but there has been no subsequent vice-presidential balloting.

collateral slowdown in economic growth being exacerbated by the effect of drought in 1996–1997 on agricultural production. Subsequently, the economic focus was on efforts to harmonize policies in areas such as taxation, customs, and government spending with those of the European Union (EU), with which Cyprus began conducting formal accession negotiations in 1998. With one of the strongest economies among the EU candidate states, Cyprus completed 24 out of 29 chapters in the EU accession process by late 2001. However, some economic slowdown was noted, mainly due to the global recession and declining tourism revenues.

GDP grew by 4.1 percent in 2001, 2.1 percent in 2000, and 1.9 percent in 2003. In order to join the EU, the government initiated broad reforms in the banking sector and agreed to raise taxes on its offshore financial companies. Accession to the EU on May 1, 2004, was seen as providing significant opportunities for economic growth, although the unresolved political division of the island continued to be a significant complication. In 2004 GDP grew by 3.5 percent, with inflation (2.5 percent) and unemployment (3.4 percent) remaining well below European averages. In addition, by that time per capita annual income had reportedly reached about 80 percent of EU norms. Current government priorities include deficit reduction (in part through pension reform and wage constraint for public sector workers) and overall labor market reform.

The northern economy (on which reliable figures are scarce) appears to have made only limited progress since 1974, being hard hit by the collapse in 1990 of the Polly Peck International fruit-packaging and tourism conglomerate (which had accounted for a third of the TRNC's GDP and 60 percent of its exports) and by external rulings banning imports from the TRNC as an unrecognized entity. The TRNC announced a five-year plan for economic development in 1997, although progress appeared to continue to depend on a resolution of the political statement on the island. Meanwhile, aid from Turkey remained the major support for the TRNC, which, by using the Turkish lira as its unit of currency, has been forced to deal with rapid inflation, unlike the Greek Cypriot sector.

The UN-controlled border between the TRNC and the south opened to some trade and travel in 2004, although the TRNC government charged that the Greek Cypriot government was limiting trade from the north through overly officious administrative requirements. The TRNC also objected to decisions by the Greek Cypriot government to block some EU assistance (see article on Cyprus: Turkish sector). However, in 2005 the TRNC reported that GDP per capita, previously only 20 percent of the Greek Cypriot figure, had risen to $7,000 in 2004, mostly because of a construction boom associated with the tourism sector.

Government and Politics

Political Background

The conflict between Greek and Turkish Cypriot aspirations shaped the political evolution of Cyprus both before and after the achievement of formal independence on August 16, 1960. Many Greek Cypriots had long agitated for *enosis*, or the union of Cyprus with Greece; most Turkish Cypriots, backed by the Turkish government, consistently rejected such demands, opposed the termination of British rule in 1960, and advocated division of the island into Greek- and Turkish-speaking sectors. Increased communal and anti-British violence after 1955 culminated in the Zürich and London compromise agreements of 1959, which provided for an independent Cyprus guaranteed by Greece, Turkey, and Britain, and instituted stringent constitutional safeguards for the protection of the Turkish minority. These agreements expressly prohibited either union with Greece or partition of the island between Greece and Turkey.

The government of Archbishop MAKARIOS proposed numerous constitutional changes in November 1963, including revision of articles considered inviolable by the Turkish Cypriots. The proposals led to a renewal of communal conflict, the withdrawal of Turkish Cypriots from the government, and, in 1964, the establishment of a United Nations peacekeeping force (UNFICYP), whose mandate was thereafter regularly extended for six-month periods by the Security Council (the cumulative cost of the operation being put at over $2 billion by 1996). Further conflict broke out in 1967, nearly precipitating war between Greece and Turkey.

Following the 1967 violence, Turkish Cypriots moved to implement an administration for their segment of the island. This organization, known as the Turkish Cypriot Provisional Administration, constituted de facto government in the Turkish communities. The Turkish Cypriot withdrawal also meant that from 1967 until the Turkish military intervention in July 1974 the prime conflicts were between the Makarios regime and radicals in the Greek community (led, until his death in January 1974, by Gen. George GRIVAS).

On July 15, 1974, the Greek Cypriot National Guard, commanded by Greek army officers, launched a coup against the Makarios government and installed a Greek Cypriot newspaper publisher and former terrorist, Nikos Giorgiades SAMPSON, as president following the archbishop's flight from the island. Five days later Turkish troops were dispatched to northern Cyprus, bringing some 1,400 square miles (39 percent of the total area) under their control before agreeing to a cease-fire. On July 23 the Sampson government resigned and the more moderate presiding officer of the Cypriot House of Representatives, Glafcos CLERIDES, was sworn in as acting president. On the same day the military government of Greece fell, and on July 25 representatives of Britain, Greece, and Turkey met at Geneva in an effort to resolve the Cyprus conflict. An agreement consolidating the cease-fire was concluded on July 30, but the broader issues were unresolved when the talks collapsed on August 14. Upon his return to Cyprus and resumption of the presidency on December 7, Makarios rejected Turkish demands for geographical partition of the island, although he had earlier indicated a willingness to give the Turks increased administrative responsibilities in their own communities.

On February 13, 1975, Turkish leaders in the occupied northern sector proclaimed a Turkish Federated State of Cyprus (see map) with Rauf DENKTAŞ, the nominal vice president of the Republic, as president. Although the action was immediately denounced by both President Makarios and Greek Prime Minister Caramanlis, the formation of a Turkish Cypriot Legislative Assembly was announced on February 24.

Extensive negotiations between Greek and Turkish representatives were held at Vienna in April 1977, following a meeting between Makarios and Denktaş in February. Although it was revealed that the more recent Greek proposals embraced the establishment of a bicommunal federal state, the Makarios government insisted that only 20 percent of the island's area be reserved for Turkish administration, while the Turks countered with demands that would entail judicial parity and a presidency to rotate between Greek and Turkish chief executives.

Archbishop Makarios died on August 3, 1977, and was succeeded, as acting president, by Spyros KYPRIANOU, who was elected on August 31 to fill the remaining six months of the Makarios term. Following the kidnapping of Kyprianou's son on December 14 by right-wing extremists, Clerides withdrew as a contender for the presidency, and Kyprianou became the only candidate at the close of nominations on January 26, 1978. As a result, the election scheduled for February 5 was canceled, Kyprianou being installed for a five-year term on

March 1. In April 1982 the two government parties, the Democratic Party (*Demokratiko Komma*—Deko) and the (Communist) Progressive Party of the Working People (*Anorthotiko Komma Ergazomenou Laou*—AKEL) agreed to support Kyprianou for reelection in February 1983.

In a three-way race that involved Clerides and Vassos LYSSARIDES, the leader of the United Democratic Union of Cyprus–Socialist Party (*Ethniki Demokratiki Enosi Kyprou–Socialistiko Komma*—EDEK–SK), who technically withdrew on January 4, Kyprianou won reelection on February 13, 1983, securing 57 percent of the vote. Nine months later, on November 15, the Turkish Cypriot Legislative Assembly unanimously approved the declaration of an independent "Turkish Republic of Northern Cyprus" (TRNC).

President Kyprianou and Turkish Cypriot leader Denktaş met at UN headquarters on January 17–20, 1985, for their first direct negotiations in five years. Prior to the meeting, the two had endorsed a draft proposal to establish a federal republic that entailed substantial territorial concessions by the Turkish Cypriots and the removal of foreign troops from the island. Although UN Secretary General Javier Pérez de Cuéllar declared that the gap had "never been so narrow" between the two sides, the talks collapsed after Kyprianou had reportedly characterized the plan as no more than an "agenda." Subsequently, the government's coalition partner, AKEL, joined with the opposition Democratic Rally (*Demokratikos Synagermos*—Desy) in blaming Kyprianou for the breakdown in the talks and calling for his resignation as president.

At the conclusion of a bitter debate on the president's negotiating posture, the House of Representatives voted unanimously on November 1, 1985, to dissolve itself, paving the way for an early legislative election. In the balloting on December 8, Kyprianou's Deko gained marginally (though remaining a minority grouping), while the opposition failed to secure the two-thirds majority necessary to enact a constitutional revision that would require the chief executive to conform to the wishes of the House.

Deprived of the backing of AKEL, Kyprianou placed third in first-round presidential balloting on February 14, 1988. In a runoff election one week later, George VASSILIOU, a millionaire businessman running with AKEL endorsement, defeated Clerides by securing a 51.5 percent majority.

On August 24, 1988, Presidents Vassiliou and Denktaş met at Geneva for the first summit talks between the two communities in over three years, with formal negotiations being resumed in September. By June 1989 deadlock had again been reached, an acceptance in principle by both sides of the UN-proposed concept of a bicommunal, bizonal federation under one sovereignty being negated by fundamental differences on implementation. More positively, a UNFICYP-supervised "deconfrontation" accord was implemented in May 1989 involving the withdrawal of both sides' forces from 24 military posts along the central Nicosia/Lefkosia sector of the "Attila Line" dividing the island.

A new round of UN-sponsored talks that opened in New York in February 1990 ended prematurely the following month when a demand by Denktaş for a "right of self-determination" was construed by Vassiliou as a demand for separate sovereignty. Relations were further exacerbated by the Greek Cypriot government's application in July for entry into the European Community (EC, subsequently the EU). Benefitting from association with Vassiliou's high negotiating profile, AKEL registered the biggest advance in legislative balloting on May 19, 1991, but Desy retained a narrow plurality as Deko representation plummeted.

US and UN diplomatic initiatives in 1991–1992 yielded further intercommunal talks, with the UN in mid-1992 suggesting a demarcation of Greek and Turkish sectors under a federal structure that would entail the transfer of about 25 percent of TRNC territory to Greek Cypriot administration. The UN plan was described as "totally unacceptable" by Denktaş, who warded off growing criticism from TRNC hard-liners by reiterating his self-determination/sovereignty demand for Turkish Cypriots. Also divided were the Greek Cypriots, with AKEL and Desy broadly supporting Vassiliou's acceptance of the UN plan, whereas Deko and the EDEK–SK complained that the president was accepting effective partition. Because of the continuing deadlock, the UN Security Council in November 1992 proposed that confidence-building measures (CBMs) should be implemented to lay the basis for an overall settlement, including reduction of troop levels, some small transfers of TRNC territory to UN administration, and the reopening of Nicosia international airport (closed since 1974). However, differences on the CBM proposal proved to be as intractable as those on the fundamental issues.

Veteran Desy leader Clerides emerged as the surprise victor in Greek Cypriot presidential balloting on February 7 and 14, 1993, when Vassiliou (again backed by AKEL) headed the first round with 44.2 percent but was narrowly defeated in the runoff contest (50.3–49.7 percent). During the campaign the Desy leader's previous support for the Vassiliou line had mutated into forceful criticism, this enabling Deko and the EDEK-SK (whose joint candidate was eliminated in the first round) to swing behind Clerides in the second round. A new government appointed by Clerides on February 25 contained six Desy and five Deko ministers.

Hopes that Clerides would break the deadlock in the Cyprus negotiations were quickly disappointed. On the other hand, because of continuing economic progress in Greek Cyprus, the administration went into legislative balloting on May 26, 1996, in a buoyant mood. Desy retained its narrow plurality of 20 seats, Deko lost 1 of its 11, and AKEL managed only a 1-seat advance, to 19; the remaining seats went to the EDEK–SK, 5; and the new Free Democrats Movement (*Kinima ton Eleftheron Demokraton*—KED), 2.

The Desy–Deko coalition headed by President Clerides collapsed when the Deko central committee decided to break from the government on November 4, 1997, after Clerides revealed his intention to seek reelection in the February 1998 elections. The five Deko cabinet members who consequently resigned were replaced by nonparty ministers. There were seven candidates in the

February 1998 presidential balloting: President Clerides; George IACOVOU, an independent backed by AKEL and Deko; George Vassiliou, former president and the leader of the KED; Nikos ROLANDIS, leader of the Liberal Party (KP); EDEK–SK President Vassos LYSSARIDES; Nicholaos KOUTSOU of New Horizons (NO); and independent candidate Alexis GALANOS, who had broken from Deko over its endorsement of Iacovou.

Iacovou led Clerides by a very slight margin in the first-round balloting (40.61 percent to 40.06 percent) on February 8, with Lyssarides finishing third with 10.59 percent. The EDEK–SK took no position regarding the runoff, but the other first-round contenders endorsed Clerides, who secured a 50.8–49.2 percent victory in the second round on February 15 at which a 94 percent turnout was reported. On February 28 Clerides announced a new "national unity" government comprising, in addition to Desy, the KP, EDEK–SK, United Democrats, and several Deko "rebels." Among other things, the multiparty cabinet was reportedly designed to present a unified stance regarding EU membership and proposed reunification talks. However, the EDEK–SK resigned from the government in late 1998 as the result of a dispute regarding the proposed deployment of Russian missiles on the island (see Current issues, below).

In legislative balloting on May 27, 2001, AKEL secured a plurality of 20 seats, followed by Desy with 19. In presidential elections on February 16, 2003, Tassos PAPADOPOULOS of Deko, campaigning on a hard-line platform regarding the proposed UN reunification plan, won a first-round election with 51.5 percent of the vote. His new coalition cabinet was sworn in on March 1, 2003.

On July 14, 2003, after the breakdown of negotiations between the Greek and Turkish Cypriots over reunification, the Greek Cypriot House of Representatives unanimously approved EU entry. Greek Cypriots rejected the UN-brokered peace plan on April 24, 2004, thereby ensuring that only the Greek areas of Cyprus joined the EU on May 1, 2004 (see Current issues, below).

Constitution and Government

The constitution of 1960, based on the Zürich and London agreements, provided for a carefully balanced system designed to protect both Greek Cypriot and Turkish Cypriot interests. A Greek president and a Turkish vice president, both elected for five-year terms, were to name a cabinet composed of representatives of both groups in specified proportions. Legislative authority was entrusted to a unicameral House of Representatives, with 35 Greek and 15 Turkish members to be elected by their respective communities. In addition, Greek and Turkish Communal Chambers were established to deal with internal community affairs. Collateral arrangements were made for judicial institutions, the army, and the police. Following the original outbreak of hostilities in 1963 and the consequent withdrawal of the Turkish Cypriots from the government, there were a number of changes, including merger of the police and gendarmerie, establishment of a National Guard, abolition of the Greek Communal Chamber, amendment of the electoral law, and modification of the judicial structure.

Subsequent to withdrawal, the Turkish community practiced a form of self-government under the Turkish Cypriot Provisional Administration, an extraconstitutional entity not recognized by the government. It formed a Turkish Cypriot Provisional Assembly composed of the 15 Turkish members of the national legislature and the 15 representatives to the Turkish Cypriot Communal Chamber. In early 1975 the Provisional Administration was reorganized as a Turkish Federated State in the northern sector of the island, followed by a unilateral declaration of independence in November 1983 (see Cyprus: Turkish Sector, below). From the December 1985 election the national membership of the House of Representatives was increased to 80 seats, although only the 56 Greek Cypriot seats were filled in that and subsequent contests.

Prior to the intervention by mainland Turkish forces, the island was divided into six administrative districts, each headed by an official appointed by the central government. Municipalities were governed by elected mayors.

Foreign Relations

Cyprus is a member of the United Nations and several other intergovernmental organizations. On a number of occasions Archbishop Makarios made diplomatic overtures toward Third World countries, although, even prior to the 1974 conflict, internal problems made it difficult for him to follow up on such initiatives.

As a result of the events of 1974, the domestic situation became in large measure a function of relations with Greece and Turkey, two uneasy NATO partners whose range of disagreement has by no means been confined to Cyprus. Britain, because of its treaty responsibilities in the area, has long played a major role in attempting to mediate the Cyprus dispute, while the United States, prior to the George H. W. Bush presidency, played a less active role. The intercommunal talks, held intermittently since 1975, were initiated at the request of the UN Security Council, which has assumed the principal responsibility for truce supervision through the UNFICYP.

In October 1987 the government concluded an agreement with the EC to establish a full customs union over a 15-year period commencing January 1, 1988; in July 1990 it submitted a formal application for full membership. In October 1993 the Council of Ministers of the EU called on the Brussels Commission to begin "substantive discussions" with Cyprus to prepare for accession negotiations. The result was agreement by the EU's Corfu summit in June 1994 that Cyprus would be included in the next round of enlargement negotiations due to begin in 1996 or 1997. Uncertainties remained, however, as to linkage between EU accession and resolution of the basic Cyprus question, especially in light of vehement opposition by both the TRNC and Turkey to the Greek Cypriots' unilateral pursuit of membership. (Formal negotiations regarding the accession of Cyprus to the EU were launched in March 1998, and substantial progress was reported

over the next year in bringing Cyprus's economic policies in line with EU requirements, the eventual membership of Cyprus being widely described as "inevitable." Collaterally, Cyprus has also applied for membership in the Western European Union.)

Turkish Cypriot hostility to Greek Cypriot EU aspirations was compounded when the European Court of Justice ruled on July 5, 1994, that all EU imports from Cyprus would require authorization from the Greek Cypriot government, thus in effect banning direct trade between the EU and the Turkish sector. President Denktaş informed the UN Security Council on July 26 that resumption of the peace talks was contingent on cancellation of the Court's ruling, while TRNC Assembly resolutions of late August called for defense and foreign policy coordination with Turkey and rejected a federal Cyprus solution as required by the United Nations, urging instead "political equality and sovereignty" for the Turkish sector.

Pursuant to an agreement of November 16, 1993, placing Cyprus within "the Greek defense area," joint Greek/Greek Cypriot military exercises were held for the first time in October 1994. Seven months later, President Clerides headed a visit to Athens by the Greek Cypriot National Council (consisting of the main party leaders) for a "unity" meeting with Greek government ministers. Concurrently, closer relations were established between the Greek Cypriot government and Russia, which in March 1995 informed Turkey of its firm commitment to a federal solution to the Cyprus problem in accordance with UN resolutions. Following the November 2002 elections in Turkey, the new government of Recep Tayyip Erdoğan began to increase pressure on the TRNC to accept UN efforts at a peace settlement in order to improve Turkey's chance of EU membership.

Current Issues

Amid persistent deadlock in intercommunal negotiations, the Greek Cypriot side took some comfort from the specific condemnations of Turkish

Cypriot intractability which issued regularly from the UN secretary general and Security Council beginning in 1992. President Clerides subsequently adopted a tougher stance by categorically ruling out any formal talks on a "confederation" and insisting that further discussions be based on the UN-endorsed concept of a bicommunal federation preserving a single sovereignty.

While continuing to attach importance to American and British mediation, the Greek Cypriot government gave increasing priority to the "EU route" to a settlement, believing that its application for full EU membership could yield a breakthrough in the intercommunal deadlock. Under this scenario, the Turkish Cypriot side would perceive the potential benefits of EU membership to the beleaguered northern economy, and would accordingly be brought to accept a federal "one sovereignty" settlement as the Greek Cypriot application progressed. However, hopes of a speedy breakthrough were dashed in August 1996 when Greek Cypriot anti-partition demonstrators clashed with Turkish soldiers and civilians after penetrating the UN buffer zone. An international mediation effort to ease the tension between the two communities was subsequently launched by France, Germany, and the UK.

The UN negotiator for Cyprus, Diego Cordovez, presented President Clerides and President Denktaş with a draft agreement for the establishment of a federal Cyprus in 1997. However, President Denktaş restated his demand that Cyprus suspend its application for EU membership before talks proceeded. The prospects for any future rapprochement remained slim, as Denktaş met with the Turkish minister of Foreign Affairs, İsmail Cem, and announced that a joint committee would be formed to implement "partial integration" between TRNC and Turkey.

In December 1997 the EU summit at Luxembourg included Cyprus among the six countries for whom formal membership negotiations would be launched in the spring of 1998 (Turkey being pointedly excluded from the list), and the TRNC subsequently suspended all bicommunal activities.

The Greek Cypriot government invited the TRNC to appoint representatives to the Cypriot team being established to negotiate with the EU; however, the Denktaş administration rejected the overture, reportedly out of concern (in part, at least) that it would be in a "subservient" position under such arrangements.

Tension between the Greek Cypriot government and the TRNC escalated sharply in late December 1998 when Clerides announced the impending deployment of Russian missiles on Greek Cypriot soil. Turkey quickly threatened possible military intervention, and the EU said it would suspend accession talks with Cyprus if the plan was pursued. Consequently, Clerides agreed to have the missiles deployed instead on the Greek island of Crete, with Greece maintaining "operational control" of the weapons. Subsequently, the administration called upon the international community to bring greater pressure on Ankara and the TRNC to return to the bargaining table. However, although both Washington and the UN pledged to intensify their mediation efforts, little hope for compromise had appeared by May 1999, nationalists having achieved significant gains in April 1999 balloting in Turkey and no sentiment for a "unitary state" having surfaced in the TRNC.

In August 2000 Cyprus came under pressure from the Organization for Economic Cooperation and Development (OECD) to change its image as an "international tax haven." The *Financial Times* reported that over 40,000 offshore companies were registered but only about 1,200 had a physical presence on the island.

Apparently in consonance with Greek-Turkish rapprochement (see articles on Turkey and Greece), the tension between Greek and Turkish Cypriots eased considerably after a major earthquake hit western Turkey in mid-August 1999, the Cypriot government sending monetary and humanitarian aid to Turkey. However, the improved relations failed to produce any breakthrough in a series of UN proximity talks conducted through 2000. In what some saw as a compromise step, Denktaş in 2001 backed away from his insistence of Cypriot recognition of the TRNC as a precondition to resuming talks and proposed in December a "partnership republic" instead of confederation.

For most of 2002 the Greek and Turkish sides conducted periodic negotiations that failed to produce tangible results. However, a report published in October by the European Commission announced that Cyprus, among others, had fulfilled the political criteria for admission to the EU and was expected to have fulfilled the economic and other criteria in time to sign an accession treaty in the spring of 2003 in anticipation of membership in 2004. Consequently, international pressure intensified for resolution of the Turkish/Cypriot dispute. (Although the EU made it clear that Cyprus's accession was not contingent on a political settlement and that the EU was prepared, if necessary, to admit only the "Greek" part of Cyprus, it was clear that the preference was strong for the island's entry as a "unified entity.") In an effort to solve the deadlock, UN Secretary General Kofi Annan launched a comprehensive plan in early November in which he proposed a "Swiss-model" for reunification in which the two component states would have equal status and substantial autonomy.

Central to Annan's plan was the return of property from the Turkish Cypriots to the Greek Cypriots and compensation for property losses in both communities. Annan's proposal envisioned a reduction of the TRNC from 36 percent of the island to 28.5 percent. The plan would displace 42,000 Turkish Cypriots and allow 85,000 Greek Cypriots to return to their former homes.

Tensions between the two communities increased with the February 2003 presidential election of Tassos Papadopoulos, who demanded that all Greek refugees have their property restored as part of any reunification. Despite apparent concessions from Denktaş regarding partial reopening of the border and some proposed land return, little progress was achieved in subsequent talks as Papadopoulos retained his hard-line stance. In early 2004 Papadopoulos agreed to present the revised UN reunification plan to a national referendum, although he campaigned against the plan, demanding more concessions from the TRNC, particularly

in regard to property reparations. Consequently, the plan was defeated by Greek Cypriots by a three-to-one margin on April 24, and, as a result only the Greek Cypriot sector joined the EU on May 1. (Voters in the TRNC handily supported the plan.) Although bitterness continued on both sides, new reunification talks were launched in mid-2005, Papadopoulos arguing that the island was "too small" to remain divided. (See article on TRNC, below, for additional information on the reunification issue.)

Political Parties

Throughout the 14 years preceding the Turkish intervention, the Cypriot party system was divided along communal lines. As a result of population transfers, the Greek parties now function exclusively in the south, while the Turkish parties function in the north. All are headquartered within the divided city of Nicosia. The Greek parties are listed below, while the Turkish parties are listed in the next section (Cyprus: Turkish Sector).

Government Parties

Democratic Party (*Demokratiko Komma–Deko*). The Democratic Party is a center-right grouping organized in 1976 as the Democratic Front to support President Makarios' policy of "long-term struggle" against the Turkish occupation of northern Cyprus. The leading component of the government alliance in the House of Representatives after the 1976 election, at which it won 21 seats, its representation fell to 8 seats in 1981. In December 1985 it obtained 16 seats (28 percent) in an enlarged House of 56 members, after its former coalition partner, AKEL (below), had supported a censure motion against (then) President Kyprianou. Deko absorbed the Center Union (*Enosi Kentrou–EK*), a minor formation led by former chief intercommunal negotiator Tassos Papadopoulos, in February 1989. It won 11 legislative seats in 1991 and endorsed Clerides for the presidency in 1993, then slipped to ten seats (on a 16.5 percent vote share) in May 1996.

The run-up to the February 1998 presidential election produced a serious split in Deko, whose leadership formally endorsed (along with AKEL) the candidacy of independent George Iacovou. Many Deko members reportedly objected to that endorsement, and Deko Vice President Alexis GALANOS presented himself as a candidate, securing 4 percent of the vote in the first round of balloting. Galanos (and, apparently, many of his backers) supported Clerides in the second round, and several Deko "rebels" were appointed as independents to the new coalition government, with Galanos being named a presidential advisor. Galanos, a former president of the House of Representatives, was subsequently identified as the leader of a new **Eurodemocratic Renewal Party.**

Deko's vote share fell to 14.8 in the May 2001 balloting and the party's legislative representation slipped to nine seats.

Kyprianou, former president of the Republic and a founder of Deko, stepped down as president of the party in 2000 due to ill health; he died in March 2002.

Kyprianou was replaced by Tassos Papadopoulos, who adroitly gained the support of AKEL and the Social Democrats' Movement (Kisos) in the February 2003 presidential election with a campaign that emphasized the need for more concessions from the TRNC in negotiations for a permanent peace plan. He won the election with 51.5 percent of the vote.

Leaders: Tassos PAPADOPOULOS (President of the Republic and Party President), Vassilis PALMAS (Secretary General).

Progressive Party of the Working People (*Anorthotiko Komma Ergazomenou Laou*–AKEL). Organized in 1941 as the Communist Party of Cyprus, AKEL dominates the Greek Cypriot labor movement and claims a membership of about 15,000. Its support of President Kyprianou, withdrawn for a period in 1980 because of the latter's handling of "the national issue," was renewed in September when the government agreed to a renewal of intercommunal talks; it was again withdrawn as a result of the breakdown in talks at

UN headquarters in January 1985. The Party won 12 legislative seats in 1981 and 15 in 1985; it endorsed the candidacy of George Vassiliou in 1988.

In January 1990 a number of dissidents, including 4 of the Politburo's 15 members, were dismissed or resigned in a controversy over democratic reforms that led to the creation of Adesok (see below, under the EDE) by five of the party's (then) 15 parliamentarians. None was reelected in May 1991 balloting, in which AKEL representation increased to 18 seats. A further advance, to 19 seats (and 33 percent of the vote), was registered in May 1996. AKEL supported independent George Iacovou in the February 1998 presidential poll. The party got a surprising victory in the May 2001 balloting with 34.7 percent of the vote and became the largest party in the legislature with 20 seats. AKEL supported Deko candidate Papadopoulos in the 2003 presidential elections, and the party received four posts in the new Council of Ministers.

Leaders: Andreas CHRISTOU (Parliamentary Spokesman), Dimitris CHRISTOFIAS (Secretary General and the President of the House of Representatives).

Social Democrats' Movement (*Kinima Sosial-dimokraton*–Kisos). This grouping was formerly known as the Unified Democratic Union of Cyprus–Socialist Party (*Ethniki Demokratiki Enosi Kyprou–Sosialistiko Komma*–EDEK–SK), a moderately left-of-center grouping which supported a unified and independent Cyprus. The EDEK-SK had concluded an electoral alliance with the Democratic Front and AKEL in 1976 but campaigned separately in 1981, its three representatives refusing to support the government after the new House convened. Its chairman, Dr. Vassos Lyssarides, campaigned for the presidency in 1983 as leader of a National Salvation Front; although announcing his withdrawal prior to the actual balloting as a means of reducing "polarization" within the Greek Cypriot community, he was nonetheless credited with obtaining a third-place 9.5 percent vote share. The party obtained six legislative seats in 1985. Lyssarides ran fourth in the first round of the 1988 presidential poll, after which EDEK–SK threw its support to George Vassiliou. The party improved to seven seats in the 1991 House election but fell back to five in May 1996 (on a 10 percent vote share). Lyssarides secured 10.6 percent of the votes in the first round of the February 1998 presidential balloting. Although the EDEK–SK did not endorse President Clerides in the second round (encouraging members to vote for the candidate of their choice), the party was given the defense and education portfolios in the subsequent coalition government. However, the EDEK–SK withdrew from the government following Clerides' decision to cancel the proposed deployment of Russian missiles on the island in December.

After adopting its current name in 1999, the party fell to 6.5 percent of the vote in the 2001 legislative balloting. Kisos supported Deko candidate Tassos Papadopoulos in the 2003 presidential elections and received two posts in the new coalition government.

Leaders: Dr. Vassos LYSSARIDES (President), Takis HADJIDEMETRIOU (Vice President), Yiannakis OMIROU (Secretary General).

Opposition Parties

Democratic Rally (*Demokratikos Synagermos*–Desy). The Democratic Rally was organized in May 1976 by Glafcos Clerides following his resignation as negotiator for the Greek Cypriots in the intercommunal talks at Vienna. The Rally has long favored a strongly pro-Western orientation as a means of maintaining sufficient pressure on the Turks to resolve the communal dispute. It secured 24.1 percent of the vote in 1976 but won no legislative seats. Its fortunes were dramatically reversed in the 1981 balloting, at which it obtained twelve seats with seven more being added in 1985. The party absorbed the small New Democratic Alignment (*Nea Demokratiki Parataxi*–Nedipa), led by Alekos MIHAILIDES, prior to the 1988 presidential balloting, at which

Clerides was defeated in the second round. The party won a plurality of 19 seats at the legislative election of May 1991, with an additional seat going to its coalition partner, the Liberal Party (*Komma Phileleftheron*–KP). Glafcos Clerides withdrew from the party presidency upon being elected president of the Republic in February 1993, following which he appointed a government of Desy and the Democratic Party (above). A Desy-Liberal alliance won 20 seats in the May 1996 election, with a vote share of 34 percent, all seats going to Desy candidates. In February 1998 the KP officially merged with the Desy. The KP had been organized in 1986 by Nikos ROLANDIS (formerly a close associate of President Kyprianou), who supported George Vassiliou in 1988. It secured one legislative seat as an electoral partner of Desy in 1991 but failed to retain it in 1996. Rolandis won less than 1 percent of the vote in the first round of the 1998 presidential balloting and, after throwing his support behind President Clerides in the second round, was subsequently named to the February 1998 cabinet as minister of commerce, industry, and tourism. In the first round of the February 2003 presidential elections, Clerides received 38.8 percent of the vote.

Leaders: Glafcos CLERIDES (Former President of the Republic and former President of the Party), Nicos ANASTASIADES (President), Eleni VRAHIMI (Secretary General).

United Democrats (*Enomeni Demokrates*–EDE). The leftist EDE was formed in 1996 by members of the Free Democrats Movement (*Kinima ton Eleftheron Demokraton*–KED) and the Democratic Socialist Reform Movement (*Ananeotiko Demokratico Socialistiko Kinema*–Adesok). The center-left KED had been launched in April 1993 by former President George Vassiliou following his unexpected failure to win a second term in February. He pledged that the new group would "contribute to the . . . struggle of our people in solving our national problem" and "promote the admission of Cyprus into Europe." The party won two seats on a 3.6 percent vote share in the May 1996 election.

The Adesok had been launched in early 1990 by a number of AKEL dissidents (including five House deputies), favoring settlement of the Cyprus issue on the basis of UN resolutions. It failed to retain legislative representation in the 1991 and 1996 elections, securing only 1.45 percent of the vote in the latter.

Vassiliou won 3 percent of the vote in the first round of the February 1998 presidential balloting and supported President Clerides in the second round. Vassiliou was subsequently named as the government's chief EU negotiator, while the EDE was also given the ministry for agriculture, natural resources, and the environment in Clerides' new coalition government. The EDE won a single seat in May 2001 with 2.5 percent of the vote.

Leaders: George VASSILIOU (former President of the Republic, President of the Party, and 1998 presidential candidate), Mikhalis PAPA-PETROU (Acting President), Kostas THEMISTO-CLEUS (Secretary General).

New Horizons (*Neoi Orizontes*–NO). NO was launched in early 1996 as a right-of-center party backed by the church and advocating that Cyprus should be a unitary rather than a federal state. It failed to win representation in the May 1996 election. Party leader Nicos Koutsou won less than 1 percent of the votes in the first round of the 1998 presidential balloting. The NO was described as supportive of the government sworn in on February 28, 1998, although it apparently did not receive a cabinet post. The party received 3 percent of the vote in the May 2001 balloting and won a single seat. In the 2003 presidential election, Koutsou received 2.1 percent of the vote.

Leaders: Nicos KOUTSOU (Chairman and 1998 presidential candidate), Stelios AMERI-KANOS (Secretary General).

Ecological Environmental Movement–Cyprus Green Party (*Kinima Oikologoi Perivallontistoi*). The Cyprus Green Party was established as a political party in February 1996

but failed to make much impact in the May 1996 election, winning only 1 percent of the vote. The party managed to gain legislative representation for the first time in the May 2001 balloting. It received 1.98 percent of the vote and won a single seat.

Leaders: Savvas PHILIPPOU (General Coordinator), George PERDIKIS (Deputy General Coordinator).

Fighting Democratic Movement (*Agonistiko Dimokratiko Kinima*–ADIK). The ADIK is a center-right breakaway formation from Deko which was launched in 1999. It won a single seat with 2.16 percent of the vote in the May 2001 balloting.

Leader: Dinos MICHAILADES (President), Yiannis PAPADOPOULIS (Secretary General).

Legislature

The Cypriot **House of Representatives** (*Vouli Antiprosópon/Temsilciler Meclisi*) is a unicameral body formerly encompassing 35 Greek and 15 Turkish members, although Turkish participation ceased in December 1963. By contrast, the balloting of December 8, 1985, was for an enlarged House of 56 Greek members. At the most recent election of May 27, 2001, the Progressive Party of the Working People won 20 seats; the Democratic Rally, 19; the Democratic Party, 9; the Social Democrats' Movement, 4; New Horizons, 1; the United Democrats, 1; the Fighting Democratic Movement, 1; the Ecological Environmental Movement-Cyprus Green Party, 1. There are also 24 seats nominally reserved for Turkish Cypriots.

President: Dimitris CHRISTOFIAS (AKEL).

Communications

The material that follows encompasses Greek-sector media only; for Turkish media see Cyprus: Turkish Sector, below.

Cabinet

As of July 1, 2005

President	Tassos Papadopoulos (Deko)
Deputy Minister to the President	Khristodhoulos Pasiardhis (ind.)

Ministers

Agriculture, Natural Resources, and Environment	Timmy A. Efthimiou (ind.)
Commerce, Industry, and Tourism	Yiorgos Lillikas (AKEL)
Communications and Works	Haris Thrasou (AKEL)
Defense	Kyriakos Mavronikolas (Kisos)
Education and Culture	Pefkios Georgiades (Deko)
Finance	Iacovos Keravnos (Deko)
Foreign Affairs	George Iacovou (ind.)
Government Spokesman	Kypros Chrysostomides (ind.)
Health	Andreas Gavrielides
Interior	Andreas Christou (AKEL)
Justice and Public Order	Doros Theodorou (Kisos)
Labor and Social Insurance	Christos Taliadoros (Deko)

Press

The following newspapers are published daily at Nicosia in Greek, unless otherwise noted (circulation figures are daily averages for 2002): *Phileleftheros* (Liberal, 26,000), independent; *Simerini* (Today, 9,000), right-wing; *Apogevmatini* (Afternoon, 8,000), independent; *Haravghi* (Dawn, 9,000), AKEL organ; *Alithia* (Truth, 11,000), right-wing; *Agon* (Struggle, 5,000), right-wing; *Cyprus Mail* (4,000), independent, in English; *Machi* (Battle, 3,000), right-wing.

News Agencies

A Greek-sector Cyprus News Agency (*Kypriakon Praktoreion Eidiseon*–KPE) was established in 1976; numerous foreign bureaus maintain offices at Nicosia.

Broadcasting and Computing

Prior to the 1974 conflict, broadcasting was controlled by the semigovernmental Cyprus Broadcasting Corporation (*Radiofonikon Idryma Kyprou*–RIK) and the government-owned *Radyo Bayrak* and *Radyo Bayrak Televizyon.* At present, radio service in the Greek sector is provided by the RIK, in addition to three private island-wide and 24 local stations. The RIK maintains television service from its station at Mount Olympus, while the RB and the RBT stations broadcast from the Turkish sector. The Greek channel ET-1 is rebroadcast on Cyprus, while radio service is also provided by the BBC East Mediterranean Relay and by the British Forces Broadcasting Service, Cyprus. There were approximately 363,000 television receivers and 200,000 personal computers serving 779,000 Internet users in the Greek sector in 2003.

Intergovernmental Representation

Ambassador to the US
Euripides L. EVRIVIADES

US Ambassador to Cyprus
Michael KLOSSON

Permanent Representative to the UN
Andreas D. MAVROYIANNIS

IGO Memberships (Non-UN)
CEUR, CWTH, EIB, EU, Eurocontrol, Interpol, IOM, OSCE, PCA, WTO

CYPRUS: TURKISH SECTOR

TURKISH REPUBLIC OF NORTHERN CYPRUS

Kuzey Kıbrıs Türk Cumhuriyeti

Government and Politics

Political Background

The Turkish Cypriots withdrew from participation in the government of the Republic of Cyprus in January 1964, in the wake of communal violence precipitated by Archbishop MAKARIOS' announcement of proposed constitutional changes in November 1963. In 1967 a Turkish Cypriot Provisional Administration was established to provide governmental services in the Turkish areas, its representatives subsequently engaging in sporadic constitutional discussions with members of the Greek Cypriot administration. Meanwhile, an uneasy peace between the two communities was maintained by a UN peacekeeping force that had been dispatched in 1964. The constitutional talks, which ran until 1974, failed to bridge the gulf between Greek insistence on a unitary form of government and Turkish demands for a bicommunal federation.

A Turkish Federated State of Cyprus was established on February 13, 1975, following the Greek army coup of July 15, 1974, and the subsequent Turkish occupation of northern Cyprus. Rauf DENKTAŞ, nominal vice president of the Republic of Cyprus and leader of the National Unity Party (*Ulusal Birlik Partisi*–UBP), was designated president of the Federated State, retaining the office as the result of a presidential election on June 20, 1976, in which he defeated the Republican Turkish Party (*Cumhuriyetçi Türk Partisi*–CTP) nominee,

Ahmet Mithat BERBEROĞLU, by a majority of nearly four to one. He was reelected for a five-year term in June 1981, remaining in office upon proclamation of the Turkish Republic of Northern Cyprus in November 1983.

Intercommunal discussions prior to the death of Archbishop Makarios on August 3, 1977, yielded apparent Greek abandonment of its long insistence on unitary government but left the two sides far apart on other issues, including Greek efforts to secure a reduction of approximately 50 percent in the size of the Turkish sector, and Turkish demands for virtual parity in such federal institutions as the presidency (to be effected on the basis of communal rotation) and the higher judiciary.

Prior to the breakdown in discussions between Denktaş and Greek Cypriot leader Spyros KYPRIANOU at UN headquarters in January 1985, the Turks had made substantial concessions, particularly in regard to power sharing and territorial demarcation of the projected federal units. Specifically, they had abandoned their earlier demand (revived in 1991) for presidential rotation and had agreed on a reduction of the area to be placed under Turkish local administration to approximately 29 percent of the island total. However, the two sides were unable to agree on a specific timetable for Turkish troop withdrawal, the identification of Turkish-held areas to be returned to Greek control, or a mechanism for external guarantees that the pact would be observed. In announcing on January 25 that presidential and legislative elections would be held in June, President Denktaş insisted that neither the balloting nor the adoption of the TRNC constitution should be construed as efforts to "close the door to a federal solution."

The constitution was approved by 70 percent of those participating in a referendum on May 5, 1985, with the leftist CTP actively campaigning for a "no" vote. At the presidential poll on June 9, Denktaş was accorded a like margin, while the UBP fell two seats short of a majority at the legislative balloting of June 23. On July 30 a coalition government involving the UBP and the Communal Liberation Party (*Toplumcu Kurtuluş Partisi–* TKP), with Derviş EROĞLU as prime minister, was confirmed by the Assembly.

The Eroğlu government fell on August 11, 1986, after the TKP had refused to endorse a proposal to expand the scope of trade and investment in the sector. However, the prime minister was able to form a new administration on September 2 that included the center-right New Dawn Party (*Yeni Doğuş Partisi–*YDP) as the UBP's coalition partner.

President Denktaş drew 67.5 percent of the vote in securing reelection to his fourth five-year term on April 22, 1990. Subsequently, a rift developed between Denktaş and Eroğlu over the conduct of negotiations with the south, the prime minister advocating a harder line on concessions to the Greek Cypriots than the president. As a result, a group of dissidents withdrew from the UBP in July 1992 to form the Democratic Party (*Demokrat Parti–*DP) to which Denktaş transferred his allegiance in late October, thereby provoking a power struggle with UBP leader Eroğlu, who became highly critical of the president's "unacceptable concessions" in negotiations with the Greek Cypriots.

Denktaş eventually gained the upper hand by calling an early Assembly election on December 12, 1993, in which the UBP, although retaining a narrow plurality, lost ground, while the DP and the CTP both registered gains. The outcome was the formation on January 1, 1994, of a center-left DP-CTP coalition headed by DP leader Hakki ATUN, which supported the Denktaş line in the intercommunal talks.

Political Status: Autonomous federal state proclaimed February 13, 1975; independent republic (thus far recognized only by Turkey) declared November 15, 1983; TRNC constitution approved by referendum of May 6, 1985.

Area: Approximately 1,400 sq. mi. (3,626 sq. km.).

Population: 200,587 (1996C); 218,000 (2004E), on the basis of Turkish Cypriot claims, which include nonindigenous settlers (more than half of the total); see also population note under Republic of Cyprus.

Major Urban Centers (1996C): LEFKOŞA (Turkish-occupied portion of Nicosia, 39,973), Gazi Mağusa (Famagusta, 27,742).

Principal Language: Turkish.

Monetary Unit: Turkish New Lira (market rate July 1, 2005: 1.34 liras = $1US). Use of the Cyprus pound as an alternative unit of exchange was terminated on May 16, 1983.

President: Mehmet Ali TALAT (Republican Turkish Party); elected in first round of popular balloting on April 17, 2005, and inaugurated April 24 for a five-year term in succession to Rauf R. DENKTAŞ (nonparty).

Prime Minister: Ferdi Sabit SOYER (Republican Turkish Party); asked on April 25, 2005, to form a government by Mehmet Ali Talat, who had resigned as prime minister on April 20 following his election as President; formed new coalition government on April 28, 2005, following the approval of President Talat and the Assembly of the Republic.

In the run-up to the 1995 presidential balloting, Atun resigned as prime minister on February 24 after the CTP had opposed President Denktaş's preelection offer to distribute to TRNC citizens the title deeds of Greek Cypriot property in the north. In the presidential contest on April 15 and 22, Denktaş for the first time failed to win an outright majority in the first round (taking only 40.4 percent of the vote), although he scored a comfortable 62.5 to 37.5 percent victory over Eroğlu in the second. Protracted interparty negotiations were needed to produce, on June 3, a new DP–CTP administration headed by Atun. The coalition again collapsed in November, following the resignation of the CTP deputy premier, Ösker ÖZGÜR, but was reestablished the following month with Mehmet Ali TALAT of the CTP as Atun's deputy. The DP–CTP coalition government resigned on July 4, 1996, and the UBP's Eroğlu was again given, on August 1, 1996, the job of forming a new government. A UBP-DP coalition cabinet headed by Eroğlu was approved by the president on August 16, 1996.

In the legislative balloting of December 6, 1998, the UBP improved from 17 to 24 seats. On December 30 President Denktaş approved Eroğlu to head a new UBP-TKP coalition government, the DP having fallen into dispute with the UBP over economic policies and cabinet representation. The legislature approved the new cabinet on January 12, 1999, by a strict party-line vote of 31–18. Denktaş kept his post as president after the election on April 15, 2000. He won 43.6 percent of the vote in the first round, while UBP candidate Eroğlu received 30.1 percent; the TKP's Mustafa AKINCI, 11.7 percent; the CTP's Mehmet Ali Talat 10 percent; and Arif Hasan TAHSIN of the Patriotic Unity Movement (*Yurtsever Birlik Hareketi*–YBH), 2.6 percent. Three other minor candidates each got less than 1 percent of the vote. The second round of balloting, scheduled for April 22, was canceled when Eroğlu withdrew on April 19 after the TKP decided to back neither of the candidates for the second round. Denktaş was sworn in on April 24.

After a series of disagreements between the coalition partners (mainly regarding the direction to be taken in foreign relations), the UBP-TKP government resigned on May 25, 2001. President Denktaş asked Eroğlu to form a new government, and a UBP-DP coalition was appointed on June 7.

The CTP returned to a plurality (19 seats) in the December 14, 2003, Assembly balloting, and Talat formed a CTP–DP coalition government on January 13, 2004. However, only two days after the TRNC population had endorsed a UN plan for reunification (see Current issues, below), the coalition became a minority government when two DP legislators quit the party to protest the administration's pro-unification stance. After numerous attempts by Talat and the UBP's Eroğlu to form coalition governments failed, new Assembly elections were held on February 20, 2005. The CTP increased its seat total to 24, and Talat was able to form a more secure CTP–DP coalition cabinet on March 16.

Talat secured 55.6 percent of the vote in the first round of presidential balloting on April 17, 2005, with Eroğlu finishing second with 22.7 percent. Talat resigned as prime minister on April 20 and was inaugurated as president on April 24. The following day, Ferdi Sabit SOYER, a close ally of Talat and CTP stalwart, formed another CTP-DP coalition government.

Constitution and Government

The constitution of the TRNC provides for a presidential-parliamentary system headed by a popularly elected chief executive, who cannot lead a party or be subject to its decisions. The president appoints a prime minister, who (unlike other ministers) must be a member of the legislature and whose government is subject to legislative recall. Like the president, the 50-member Assembly of the Republic is elected for a five-year term (subject to dissolution) and its presiding officer, who is chosen at the beginning of the first and fourth year of each term, becomes acting head of state in the event of presidential death, incapacity, or resignation. The Supreme Court, composed of a president and seven additional judges, also sits as a Constitutional Court (five members) and as a Court of Appeal and High Administrative Court (three members each). Lesser courts and local administrative units are established by legislative action.

Current Issues

The European Council meeting held in late 1997 decided that Cyprus would be included in the first group of applicants to join the expanded EU, while determining that "political and economic conditions" required for the membership of Turkey were not satisfied. The EU also expressed a wish "to see activated the Cyprus government's wish to include the Turkish Cypriots in the negotiating delegation." However, President Denktaş of the TRNC indicated his unwillingness to proceed with negotiations unless further international recognition of the TRNC was forthcoming, and new discussions were not launched as expected. In August Denktaş attempted to counter the UN push for reunification by formally proposing a confederation of "equal states," with the UN continuing to patrol the border. That proposal was quickly rejected by most of the international community, despite Denktaş' assessment that "Turks and Greece on Cyprus are like oil and water. They can no longer be mixed."

Tension between the government and the opposition parties and groups became more severe with Denktaş' decision to withdraw from the talks with the Greek Cypriot side in late 2000. However, observers noted some easing after Denktaş decided to resume dialogue in 2002 after the EU indicated that Cyprus had fulfilled the necessary criteria to begin accession negotiations in 2003 with the goal of membership in 2004, with or without resolution of the dispute with the TRNC. Denktaş reportedly made several unilateral offers regarding land return and the reopening of the border, but talks were described as deadlocked by March 2003. Attention subsequently focused almost exclusively on the plan forwarded by UN Secretary General Kofi Annan under which the island would be reunified in a loose confederation with the Greek Cypriot and Turkish Cypriot sectors retaining broad autonomy in most domestic areas. (For complete details on the Annan plan, see Current issues in article on Cyprus.)

With the encouragement of new Prime Minister Talat of the CTP (which had led all parties in the December 2003 Assembly balloting), the voters in the TRNC endorsed the reunification plan by a 65 percent yes vote in a national referendum on April 24, 2004. Unfortunately for the TRNC, however, the plan was rejected by a three-to-one margin by the Greek Cypriot community. Consequently, the TRNC was "left out in the cold" when Cyprus acceded to the EU with nine other new members on May 1. (Many Turkish Cypriots reportedly blamed President Denktaş' relatively hard line on the issue

for the negativity of the Greek Cypriots.) The EU immediately pledged substantial economic assistance to the TRNC as a reward for the yes vote regarding reunification. However, the stark reality of the situation became clear in October when Cyprus vetoed an EU plan to establish trade relations with the TRNC. The government of Cyprus indicated that too much assistance to the TRNC might embolden Turkish Cypriots still hoping for additional recognition for the TRNC.

The early legislative elections of February 2005 in the TRNC were widely viewed as a strong endorsement of reunification, the Turkish Cypriots clearly having suffered political and economic isolation since Cyprus's accession to the EU. Following Talat's election in April to succeed hawkish President Denktaş (who, at 81 years old, had decided to retire), prounification forces again saw reason for hope. Negotiations, again centered on the Annan plan, subsequently resumed in an atmosphere that led one observer to conclude nearly "everyone seems to want reunification." Included on that list were Russia (which had been unconvinced in early 2004), the United States (which sent economic development missions to the TRNC), Greece, and Turkey (for whom the stakes may have been higher than for any of the others). Turkey, scheduled to begin its own EU accession process in October 2005, keenly desired an end to the island's split in view of the fact that either Greece or Cyprus could block its entry. In July Turkey signed a protocol extending its long-term customs union with the EU to the ten new EU members, including Cyprus. However, Turkey, which still maintained some 30,000–40,000 troops in the TRNC, insisted its decision did not constitute recognition of the Greek Cypriot government. (Turkey was the only country to recognize the TRNC government and the only European country yet to recognize the Greek Cypriot government.)

Political Parties

Most of the Turkish Cypriot parties share a common outlook regarding the present division of the island. Differences have surfaced, however, as to the degree of firmness to be displayed in negotiations with the Greek community.

Government Parties

Republican Turkish Party (*Cumhuriyetçi Türk Partisi*–CTP). A Marxist formation at the time, the CTP campaigned against the 1985 constitution because of its alleged repressive and militaristic content. For the 1990 election (at which it lost five of twelve seats won in 1985) the CTP joined with the TKP and YDP (below) in a coalition styled the Democratic Struggle Party (*Demokratik Mücadele Partisi*–DMP). It made a comeback to 13 seats in the 1993 balloting, entering a coalition with the DP that effectively collapsed in February 1995 on the issue of Greek Cypriot property rights but was reconstituted in May. Two further coalition collapses and reconstitutions in 1995 led to the ouster of Östker ÖZGÜR as CTP leader in January 1996. A DP–CTP coalition government under the leadership of Hakki ATUN resigned on July 4, 1996, and the CTP became the main opposition party. However, it was supplanted in that regard by the DP following the 1998 legislative balloting, at which CTP representation fell from 13 to 6 seats on a vote share of 13.4 percent. In part, the electoral decline was attributed to the CTP's stance that negotiations should be resumed with Greek Cypriot officials regarding a settlement of the political stalemate on the island. Chairman Mehmet Ali Talat ran as the party's presidential candidate on April 15, 2000, and received 10 percent of the vote.

In the December 2003 legislative elections, the CTP received a plurality of 19 seats on a vote share of 35 percent. Talat subsequently formed a coalition government with the DP, which continued in office following the February 2005 Assembly balloting in which the CTP's vote share grew to 44 percent.

Leaders: Mehmet Ali TALAT (President of the TRNC), Ferdi Sabit SOYER (Prime Minister of the TRNC and Acting Chairman of the Party).

Democratic Party (*Demokrat Parti*–DP). The DP was formed in 1992 by a group of pro-Denktaş UBP dissidents who advocated a more concilia-

tory posture in the intercommunal talks than did the party mainstream. It was runner-up in the 1993 legislative balloting, thereupon entering into a majority coalition with the CTP (above). In 1993 the DP accepted the **New Dawn Party** (*Yeni Doğuş Partisi*–YDP), led by Ali Özkan ALTINIŞIK, into its ranks. The DP–CTP coalition government ended on July 4, 1996 and the UBP's Derviş EROĞLU formed a new coalition government with the DP as a partner, on August 16, 1996. In March 1998 Prime Minister Eroğlu dismissed the DP's Ali Özkan ALTINIŞIK from his post as minister of labor and housing after Altinişik became the focus of a corruption investigation. DP chairman Serdar Denktaş, son of President Denktaş, subsequently threatened to pull the party out of the government coalition but ultimately accepted Eroğlu's action. However, the DP moved into opposition status following the December legislative poll, at which it secured 22.6 percent of the vote. Meanwhile, in September 1998 the DP had reportedly accepted the Free Democratic Party (*Hür Demokrat Parti*–HDP) into its ranks. The HDP, led by İsmet KOTAK and Özel TAHSİN, was one of several parties launched following the 1990 election. Prior to the 1993 election, the HDP had joined with two smaller groups, the Homeland Party (*Anavatan Partisi*–AP) and the Nationalist Justice Party (*Milliyetçi Adalet Partisi*–MAP), led by Zorlu TÖRE, in a coalition styled the National Struggle Party (*Milli Mücadele Partisi*–MMP). The DP extended support to Rauf Denktaş in the 2000 presidential election. The DP became the junior partner in the new coalition government announced with the UBP in June 2001. Following the December 2003 balloting, the DP joined an unsteady CTP-led coalition. Two of the seven DP legislators resigned from the party in April 2004 to protest the government's prounification stance, forcing early elections in February 2005, at which the DP gained 6 seats on a 13.5 percent vote share. Mustafa Arabacioğlu won 13.2 percent of the vote in the first round of the April 2005 presidential poll.

Leaders: Serdar DENKTAŞ (Chairman and Deputy Prime Minister), Mustafa ARABACIOĞLU (2005 presidential candidate).

Opposition Parties

National Unity Party (*Ulusal Birlik Partisi*–UBP). The right-wing UBP was established in 1975 as an outgrowth of the former National Solidarity (*Ulusal Dayanışma*) movement. Originally committed to the establishment of a bicommunal federal state, it captured three-quarters of the seats in the Turkish Cypriot Legislative Assembly at the 1976 election but was reduced to a plurality of 18 seats in 1981 and survived a confidence vote in the Assembly on September 11 only because the motion failed to obtain an absolute majority. The UBP's former leader, Rauf Denktaş, was precluded by the constitution from serving as president of the party or from submitting to party discipline while president of the Republic; nevertheless, he was instrumental in launching the breakaway DP in 1992 after clashing with party leader Derviş Eroğlu, who moved to an increasingly propartition stance. The UBP retained its plurality in the 1993 balloting, but remained in opposition. Eroğlu took Denktaş to the second round in the 1995 presidential election, winning 37.5 percent of the vote. Staying in the opposition until a DP–CTP coalition government came to an end on July 4, 1996, the UBP rose to power as a member of a coalition government with the DP on August 16, 1996. The UBP increased its vote share to over 40 percent in the 1998 legislative balloting, Eroğlu subsequently forming a coalition with the TKP. Eroğlu ran as presidential candidate for the UBP on April 15, 2000, and won 30.1 percent of the vote at the first round. He withdrew from the race on April 19 prior to the scheduled second round between himself and Denktaş. The UBP–TKP coalition broke down in May 2001, and Eroğlu formed a new government with the DP in June. However, he was obliged to resign the prime ministership following the December 2003 legislative balloting, in which the UBP was outpolled by the CTP 35 percent to 33 percent. The UBP secured 19 seats on a vote share of 31.7 percent in the February 2005 Assembly balloting, while Eroğlu finished second in the first round of presidential balloting in April with 22.7 percent of the vote.

Leaders: Dr. Derviş EROĞLU (former Prime Minister, Chairman of the Party and 2005 presidential candidate), Vehbi Zeki SERTER (Secretary General).

Peace and Democracy Movement (*Bariş ve Demokrasi Hareketi*–BDH). The BDH is a coalition of leftist parties that joined together to improve their electoral opportunities prior to the 2003 legislative elections. The grouping was formed under the leadership of Mustafa Akıncı, formerly the party leader of TKP, which provided the core of the BDH. The BDH won six seats in the 2003 Assembly balloting but only one in the 2005 poll (on a 5.8 percent vote share).

Leader: Mustafa AKINCI.

Communal Liberation Party (*Toplumcu Kurtuluş Partisi*–TKP). Also known as the Socialist Salvation Party, the TKP is a left-of-center grouping organized in 1976. The six Assembly seats won by the party in 1976 were doubled in 1981, two of which (for an enlarged chamber) were lost in 1985. The TKP joined the Eroğlu government in July 1985, but withdrew in August 1986.

In 1989 the TKP absorbed the Progressive People's Party (*Atılımcı Halk Partisi*–AHP), which itself had resulted from the merger in early 1986 of the Democratic People's Party (*Demokratik Halk Partisi*–DHP) and the Communal Endeavor Party (*Toplumsal Atılım Partisi*–TAP). The DHP, which advocated the establishment of an independent, nonaligned, and biregional Cypriot state, was organized in 1979 by former prime ministers Nejat KONUK and Osman ÖREK, both of whom had left the UBP because of dissension within the party. The TAP was a centrist party formed in 1984. The TKP's legislative representation fell from ten seats to seven in 1990 and to five in 1993. It rebounded to seven seats (on a vote share of 15.4 percent) in December 1998 and became the junior partner in the subsequent coalition government with the UBP. Chairman Akıncı ran as the TKP's presidential candidate on April 15, 2000, and received 11.7 percent of the vote. The TKP subsequently decided to encourage its voters to vote for their candidate of choice for the second round, a move that caused the UBP's Eroğlu to withdraw from the race. Following the breakdown of the coalition government with the UBP in May 2001, the TKP joined the opposition. Chairman Akıncı subsequently stepped down as the party leader, and the post was assumed by the former secretary general, Hüseyin Angolemli.

Leaders: Hüseyin ANGOLEMLİ (Chairman), Güngör GÜNKAN.

Other Parties That Competed in the 2003 Legislative Elections

Nationalist Peace Party (*Milliyetçi Bariş Partisi*–MBP). The MBP was formed as the result of a merger between the MAP and the center-right, **Renewal Progress Party** (*Yenilikci Atilim Partisi*–YAP). In the 2003 legislative elections, the MBP received 3.23 percent of the vote. Its co-chairmen are Ali Riza GORGUN and former UBP member and former president of the legislature, Ertuğrul HASIPOĞLU.

Nationalist Justice Party (*Milliyetçi Adalet Partisi*–MAP). The far-right-wing MAP supports unification with Turkey and extension of Turkish citizenship to northern Cypriots. The party gained one seat in the Assembly after a former DP parliamentarian, Kenan AKIN, defected to the MAP in December 2000. In 1993 the party had joined with the HDP and AP to form MMP (see above, under DP). The MAP backed President Denktaş in the 2000 presidential election.

Leader: Zorlu TÖRE (Chairman).

Solution and EU Party (*Çözüm ye AB Partisi*–ÇABP). Established as a prounification grouping in 2003, the ÇABP secured 2 percent of the vote in the December 2003 legislative poll.

Leader: Ali EREL.

Other Parties

Patriotic Unity Movement (*Yurtsever Birlik Hareketi*–YBH). The left-wing YBH was formed in result of a merger of the New Cyprus Party

(*Yeni Kıbrıs Partisi*–YKP) and some former members of the CTP (above) in 1998. The YKP had been founded in 1989 by Alpay Durduran, the TKP/AHP 1985 presidential candidate. In 1998 Durduran urged Turkish Cypriot leaders to return to the bargaining table with their Greek Cypriot counterparts.

The YBH favors the unification of the island and equal treatment for all Cypriots, including Greek Cypriots. In 2003, the YBH filed suit with the European Court of Human Rights to challenge the electoral process of the TRNC. The party presented Arif Hasan TAHSİN as its candidate in the first round of presidential balloting in 1999.

Leaders: Alpay DURDURAN (Chairman), Ösker ÖZGÜR.

National Revival Party (*Ulusal Diriliş Partisi*–UDP). The UDP was founded on November 18, 1997, under the leadership of Enver Emin. A precursor of the UDP had been founded in 1994 as the National Birth Party (*Ulusal Doğuş Partisi*). As of November 1995, it had one seat in the Assembly. The National Birth Party then merged with the DP and ceased its legal existence. The UDP secured 4.6 percent of the vote and no seats in the December 1998 legislative balloting. The UDP backed President Denktaş in the presidential election on April 15, 2000.

Leaders: Enver EMİN (Chairman), Mustafa ERBİLEN (Secretary General).

Reports on the 1998 legislative balloting indicated that a **National Resistance Party** (*Ulusal Direnis Partisi*–UDİP) had received 4.5 percent of the vote, and the recently formed **Our Party** (*Bizim Parti*–BP), led by Okyay SADIKOĞLU), had received 1.2 percent. The BP, described in 1998 as the first Islamist grouping to participate in a TRNC election, supported President Denktaş in his reelection bid.

On August 25, 2000, Arif Salih KIRDAĞ formed the **Freedom and Justice Party** (*Özgürlük ve Adaleţ Partisi*–ÖAP) to "safeguard bank victims' rights" (see Current issues, above). In December a new centrist formation, the **New Democracy Party** (*Yeni Demokrasi Partisi*–YDP), was founded

Cabinet

As of August 1, 2005

Prime Minister	Ferdi Sabit Soyer (CTP)
Deputy Prime Minister	Serdar Denktaş (DP)

Ministers

Agriculture and Forestry	Hüseyin Öztoprak (DP)
Economy and Tourism	Dervis Kemal Deniz (DP)
Education and Culture	Canan Öztoprak (CTP)
Finance	Ahmet Uzun (CTP)
Foreign Affairs	Serdar Denktaş (DP)
Health and Social Assistance	Esref Vaiz (CTP)
Interior	Özkan Murat (CTP)
Labor and Social Security	Sonay Adem (CTP)
Public Works and Housing	Salih Usar (CTP)
Youth and Sports	Özkan Yorgancioğlu (CTP)

by Eşref DÜSENKALKAR. In January 2001 the **Liberal Party** (*Liberal Parti*–LP) was launched by Kemal BOLAYIR and Ünal Aki AKİF. In November 2002 the **Socialist Party of Cyprus** (*Kıbrıs Sosyalist Partisi*–KSP) was launched by Mehmet SÜLEYMANOĞLU. In 2004 the *Free Thought Party* was reportedly launched under the leadership of Salih COSAR; the party's initial membership reportedly included two defecting DP legislators, although one subsequently returned to the DP fold.

Legislature

A Turkish Cypriot Legislative Assembly, formerly the Legislative Assembly of the Autonomous Turkish Cypriot Administration, was organized in February 1975. Styled the **Assembly of the Republic** (*Cumhuriyet Meclisi*) under the 1985 constitution, it currently contains 50 members, who are elected for five-year terms on a proportional basis in which parties must surpass a 5 percent threshold to gain representation. Following the election of December 14, 2003, the Republican Turkish Party (CTP) held 19 seats; the National Unity Party (UBP), 18; the Democratic Party (DP), 7; and the Peace and Democracy Movement (BDH), 6.

Defections from the DP in late April 2004 cost the CTP-DP coalition government its legislative majority. Consequently, early elections were held on February 20, 2005, with the CTP winning 24 seats; the UBP, 19, the DP, 6; and the BDH, 1.

President: Fatma EKENOĞLU.

Communications

Press

Freedom of the press is guaranteed under the 1985 constitution, save for legislative restrictions intended to safeguard public order, national security, public morals, or the proper functioning of the judiciary. The following are published at Nicosia in Turkish: *Kıbrıs* (Cyprus), "populist" monthly; *Birlik* (Unity), center-right daily (affiliated with the UBP); *Halkın Sesi* (Voice of the People), daily; *Avrupa* (Europe), independent leftist; *Yeni Düzen* (New Order), CTP organ; *Ortam* (Situation), TKP organ; *Yeni Demokrat* (New Democrat), DP organ; and *Vatan* (Homeland). In addition, a number of mainland Turkish papers circulate, of which the leaders are *Sabah* (Morning), *Milliyet* (Nationality), and *Hürriyet* (Liberty).

News Agency

The Turkish-sector facilities are Turkish Agency Cyprus (*Türk Ajansı Kıbrıs*–TAK) and the Northern Cyprus News Agency (*Kuzey Kıbrıs Haber Ajansı*).

Broadcasting

Broadcasting in the Turkish sector is controlled by *Radyo Bayrak* and *Bayrak Radyo Televizyon* (BRT). There were approximately 306,000 radio and 77,400 television receivers in the sector in 1999. In addition to *Radio Bayrak* and the BRT, there are two private radio stations, *First FM* and *Kıbrıs FM,* and two private TV channels.

Intergovernmental Representation

The Turkish Federated State did not seek general international recognition and maintained no missions abroad, except for a representative at New York who was recognized by the United Nations as official spokesman for the Turkish Cypriot community; it did, however, participate in an Islamic Conference meeting on economic cooperation at Ankara, Turkey, November 4-6, 1980. The present Turkish Republic of Northern Cyprus has proclaimed itself independent, but has been recognized as such only by Turkey, with whom it exchanged ambassadors on April 17, 1985.

IGO Memberships (Non-UN)
ECO, OIC

EGYPT

ARAB REPUBLIC OF EGYPT

Jumhuriyat Misr al-'Arabiyah

Note: On September 7, 2005, Husni Mubarak won a fifth consecutive six-year term, officially securing 88.6 percent of the vote in Egypt's first multicandidate presidential election. Parliamentary balloting for the 444 elected seats of the *Majlis al-Sha'ab*, or People's Assembly, were held in three stages, on November 9 and 20 and December 1, 2005, with runoffs after each stage on November 15 and 26 and December 7. In the wake of strong returns for candidates affiliated with the banned Muslim Brotherhood in the first two rounds, Egyptian police used barricades and tear gas to block voters from reaching the polls in the third round in districts where the group had rallied strong support. According to news reports, at least 12 people died in clashes with police. Preliminary results showed the National Democratic Party (NDP) and its allies having secured as many as 335 seats (the NDP won 311 seats), independent candidates affiliated with the Muslim Brotherhood having won 88 seats, and other opposition parties taking control of 9 seats. Twelve undecided seats were to be determined by runoff. Voter turnout was 26 percent.

The Country

Situated in the northeast corner of Africa at its juncture with Asia, Egypt occupies a quadrangle of desert made habitable only by the waters of the Nile, which bisects the country from south to north. Although the greater part of the national territory has traditionally been regarded as wasteland, Egypt is the most populous country in the Arab world: 90 percent of the people are concentrated in 4 percent of the land area, with population densities in parts of the Nile Valley reaching 6,000 per square mile. (An ambitious project was inaugurated in 1997 whereby the government plans to build a 150-mile canal northwest into the desert from Lake Nasser [formed by the Aswan High Dam] in the south. It is hoped that the $2 billion irrigation project will permit significant agricultural expansion and population relocation. Another massive irrigation canal is under construction eastward from the Nile along the northern coast into the Sinai Peninsula.) Arabic is universally spoken, and more than 80 percent of the ethnically homogeneous people adhere to the Sunni sect of Islam, much of the remainder being Coptic Christian. Women were listed as 29 percent of the paid labor force in 1996, with the majority of rural women engaged in unpaid

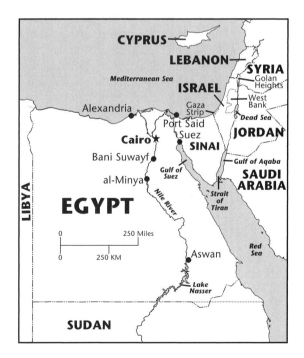

agricultural labor; urban employed women tend to be concentrated in lower levels of health care and education.

Completion of the Aswan High Dam in 1971 permitted the expansion of tillable acreage and of multiple cropping, while the use of fertilizers and mechanization also increased production of such crops as cotton, wheat, rice, sugarcane, and corn, although Egypt still imports more than 50 percent of its food. Much of the population continues to live near the subsistence level, high rural-to-urban migration having increased the number of urban unemployed. A growing industrial sector, which employs 30 percent of the labor force, has been centered on textiles and agriprocessing, although the return by Israel of Sinai oil fields in 1975 permitted Egypt to become a net exporter of petroleum. Other natural resources include gas, iron ore, phosphates, manganese, zinc, gypsum, and talc.

The reopening of the Suez Canal (closed from the 1967 war until 1975) helped stimulate the gross domestic product, which displayed average annual real growth of 9 percent from mid-1979 to mid-1983. By 1985 economic conditions had sharply deteriorated as the decline in world oil prices not only depressed export income but severely curtailed remittances from Egyptians employed in other oil-producing states; in addition, tourism, another important source of revenue, declined because of regional terrorism and domestic insecurity. Currently compounding the difficulties are rapid population growth (an increase of approximately one million every nine months), an illiteracy rate estimated at nearly 50 percent, a high external debt, and an inefficient, bloated, and often corrupt bureaucracy of some six million civil servants.

In the early 1990s the government pledged to privatize state-run enterprises, reduce tariffs and price subsidies, devalue the Egyptian pound, and pursue further economic liberalization. Progress has been slow, despite the appointment of Prime Minister Ahmed NAZIF, a younger and more technologically savvy presence in the government. Indications were that he would be more willing to move ahead on economic reform, but the populace

has repeatedly demonstrated its frustration over the slow pace of significant change. Finance Minister Yussef BOUTROS-GHALI announced a package of economic reforms in September 2004, including a reduction on import tariffs. Moderate growth has occurred since mid-2003, with real GDP growth of 4.8 percent in mid 2004–2005 and inflation cut by half, to 7 percent. Privatization, especially of banks, has been slow, but the government indicates it is responding to IMF recommendations to make monetary policies its highest priority. Tourism reached record levels in 2004, bringing in some $6 billion dollars in revenue.

Government and Politics

Political Background

The modern phase of Egypt's long history began in 1882 with the occupation of what was then an Ottoman province by a British military force, only token authority being retained by the local ruler (khedive). After establishing a protectorate in 1914, the United Kingdom granted formal independence to the government of King FU'AD I in 1922 but continued to exercise gradually dwindling control, which ended with its evacuation of the Suez Canal Zone in 1956. The rule of Fu'ad's successor, King FAROUK (FARUK) I, was abruptly terminated as the result of a military coup on July 23, 1952. A group of young officers (the "Free Officers"), nominally headed by Maj. Gen. Muhammad NAGIB, secured Farouk's abdication on June 18, 1953, and went on to establish a republic under Nagib's presidency. Col. Gamal Abdel NASSER (Jamal 'Abd al-NASIR), who had largely guided these events, replaced Nagib as prime minister and head of state in 1954, becoming president on June 23, 1956.

The institution of military rule signaled the commencement of an internal social and economic revolution, growing pressure for the termination of British and other external influences, and a drive toward greater Arab unity against Israel under Egyptian leadership. Failing to secure Western arms on satisfactory terms, Egypt accepted Soviet military assistance in 1955. In July 1956, following

Political Status: Nominally independent in 1922; republic established in 1953; joined with Syria as the United Arab Republic in 1958 and retained the name after Syria withdrew in 1961; present name adopted September 2, 1971; under limited multiparty system formally adopted by constitutional amendment approved in referendum of May 22, 1980.

Area: 386,659 sq. mi. (1,001,449 sq. km.).

Population: 61,452,382 (1996C); 72,318,000 (2004E), including Egyptian nationals living abroad.

Major Urban Centers (1996C) AL-QAHIRA (Cairo, 6,789,479), al-Giza (4,779,865), al-Iskandariyah (Alexandria, 3,328,196), Bur Sa'id (Port Said, 469,533), Es-Suweis (Suez, 417,610).

Official Language: Arabic.

Monetary Unit: Egyptian Pound (market rate July 1, 2005: 5.79 pounds = $1US).

President: (*See headnote.*) Muhammad Husni MUBARAK (National Democratic Party); appointed Vice President on April 15, 1975; succeeded to the presidency upon the assassination of Muhammad Ahmad Anwar al-SADAT on October 6, 1981; confirmed by national referendum of October 13 and sworn in for a six-year term on October 14; served additionally as Prime Minister from October 14, 1981, to January 2, 1982; sworn in for a second presidential term on October 13, 1987, for a third term on October 13, 1993, and for a fourth term on October 5, 1999, following unanimous nomination by the People's Assembly on June 2 and confirmation in national referendum of September 26.

Prime Minister: Ahmed NAZIF; appointed by the President on July 9, 2004, to succeed Atef Muhammad OBEID, who resigned. Obeid had served since October 5, 1999. A new cabinet was announced on July 14, 2004.

the withdrawal of a Western offer to help finance the High Dam at Aswan, Egypt nationalized the Suez Canal Company and took possession of its properties. Foreign retaliation resulted in the "Suez War" of October–November 1956, in which Israeli, British, and French forces invaded Egyptian territory but subsequently withdrew under pressure from the United States, the Soviet Union, and the United Nations.

On February 1, 1958, Egypt joined with Syria to form the United Arab Republic under Nasser's presidency. Although Syria reasserted its independence in September 1961, Egypt retained the UAR designation until 1971, when it adopted the name Arab Republic of Egypt. (A less formal linkage with North Yemen, the United Arab States, was also established in 1958 but dissolved in 1961.)

Egypt incurred heavy losses in the six-day Arab-Israeli War of June 1967, which resulted in the closing of the Suez Canal, the occupation by Israel of the Sinai Peninsula, and an increase in Egypt's military and economic dependence on the USSR.

Popular discontent resulting from the defeat was instrumental in bringing about a subsequent overhaul of the state machinery and a far-reaching reconstruction of the Arab Socialist Union (ASU), then the nation's only authorized political party.

A major turning point in Egypt's modern history occurred with the death of President Nasser on September 28, 1970, power subsequently being transferred to Vice President Anwar al-SADAT. The new president successfully weathered a government crisis in 1971 that included the dismissal of Vice President 'Ali SABRI and other political figures accused of plotting his overthrow. A thorough shake-up of the party and government followed, with Sadat's control being affirmed at a July ASU congress and, two months later, by voter approval of a new national constitution as well as a constitution for a projected Federation of Arab Republics involving Egypt, Libya, and Syria. At the same time, the pro-Soviet leanings of some of those involved in the Sabri plot, combined with Moscow's increasing reluctance to comply with Egyptian demands for armaments, generated increasing tension in Soviet-Egyptian relations. These factors, coupled with Sadat's desire to acquire US support in effecting a return of Israeli-held territory, culminated in the expulsion of some 17,000 Soviet personnel in mid-1972.

The apparent unwillingness of US President Nixon in 1972 to engage in diplomatic initiatives during an election year forced Sadat to return to the Soviet fold to prepare for another war with Israel, which broke out in October 1973. After 18 days of fighting a cease-fire was concluded under UN auspices, with US Secretary of State Henry Kissinger ultimately arranging for peace talks that resulted in the disengagement of Egyptian and Israeli forces east of the Suez Canal. Under an agreement signed on September 4, 1975, Israel withdrew to the Gidi and Mitla passes in the western Sinai and returned the Ras Sudar oil field to Egypt after securing political commitments from Egypt and a pledge of major economic and military support from the United States.

Although he had intimated earlier that he might step down from the presidency in 1976, Sadat accepted designation to a second six-year term on September 16. On October 26, in the first relatively free balloting since the early 1950s, the nation elected a new People's Assembly from candidates presented by three groups within the ASU. Two weeks later, the president declared that the new groups could be termed political parties but indicated that they would remain under the overall supervision of the ASU. The role of the ASU was further reduced in June 1977 by promulgation of a law that permitted the formation of additional parties under carefully circumscribed circumstances, while its vestigial status as an "umbrella" organization was terminated a year later.

On October 2, 1978, Sadat named Mustafa KHALIL to head a new "peace" cabinet that on March 15, 1979, unanimously approved a draft peace treaty with Israel. The People's Assembly ratified the document on April 10 by a 328–15 vote, while in a referendum held nine days later a reported 99.95 percent of those casting ballots voiced approval. At the same time, a series of political and constitutional reforms received overwhelming support from voters. As a result, President Sadat dissolved the Assembly two years ahead of schedule and called for a two-stage legislative election on June 7 and 14. Sadat's National Democratic Party (NDP) easily won the multiparty contest–the first such election since the overthrow of the monarchy in 1953–and on June 21 Prime Minister Khalil and a substantially unchanged cabinet were sworn in. On May 12, 1980, however, Khalil resigned, with President Sadat assuming the prime ministership two days later.

By 1981 Egypt was increasingly dependent on the United States for military and foreign policy support, while growing domestic unrest threatened the fragile political liberalization initiated in 1980. In an unprecedented move in early September, the government imprisoned over a thousand opposition leaders, ranging from Islamic fundamentalists to journalists and Nasserites.

On October 6, 1981, while attending a military review at Cairo, President Sadat was assassinated by a group of Muslim militants affiliated with *al-Jihad* ("Holy War"). The Assembly's nomination of Vice President Muhammad Husni MUBARAK as his successor was confirmed by a national referendum on October 13, the new president naming a cabinet headed by himself as prime minister two days later. On January 2, 1982, Mubarak yielded the latter office to First Deputy Prime Minister Ahmad Fu'ad MUHI al-DIN.

The NDP retained overwhelming control of the Assembly at the March 1984 election, the right-wing New Wafd Party being the only other group to surpass the 8 percent vote share needed to gain direct representation. However, popular discontent erupted later in the year over measures to combat economic deterioration and numerous opposition leaders, accused of "fomenting unrest," were arrested. Meanwhile, Islamic fundamentalists continued a campaign for the institution of full *shari'a* law that provoked a new wave of arrests in mid-1985.

At his death in June 1984 Muhi al-Din was succeeded as prime minister by Gen. Kamal Hasan 'ALI. 'Ali was replaced in September 1985 by

Dr. 'Ali Mahmud LUTFI, who, in turn, yielded office on November 12, 1986, to Dr. 'Atif Muhammad SIDQI, a lawyer and economist whose appointment appeared to signal a willingness to institute drastic reform measures sought by the IMF and World Bank. Anticipating a resurgence of opposition and facing court challenges to the legality of an Assembly that excluded independent members, the president confounded his critics by mounting a referendum in February 1987 on the question of legislative dissolution. The subsequent election of April 6 reconfirmed the NDP's control, and on October 5 Mubarak received public endorsement for a second term.

President Mubarak's swift response to the Iraqi invasion of Kuwait in August 1990 received widespread domestic support, and, at balloting on November 29 to replenish the Assembly (whose 1987 election had been declared illegal in May 1990), the ruling NDP won an increased majority. The landslide victory was tarnished, however, by low voter turnout and an election boycott by three leading opposition parties and the proscribed, but prominent, Muslim Brotherhood. On December 13 Dr. Ahmad Fathi SURUR was elected Assembly President, assuming the responsibilities left vacant by the assassination of the previous speaker, Dr. Rifa'at al-MAHGOUB, on October 12.

Following a May 1991 cabinet reshuffle, Mubarak indicated that measures would be considered to reduced the NDP stranglehold on government activity. However, the state of emergency in effect since 1981 was extended for three more years, Mubarak citing ongoing "subversion" by fundamentalist militants as justification. Subsequently, international human rights organizations charged that the administration was continuing to torture and otherwise abuse its opponents, particularly the fundamentalists, with whom a state of "all-out war" was said to exist by 1992. For their part, the militants, vowing to topple the "corrupt" Mubarak government and establish an Islamic state, intensified their guerrilla campaign against police, soldiers, government officials, and tourists.

On July 21, 1993, the Assembly nominated Mubarak for a third term by a vote of 439–7,

and the president received a reported 95 percent "yes" vote in the national referendum of October 4, opposition leaders strongly questioning the accuracy of the tally. Although President Mubarak had promised an infusion of "new blood" into his administration, many of the previous cabinet members were reappointed in the reshuffle announced on October 14 by Prime Minister Sidqi. In addition, no discernible results were achieved by the National Dialogue General Congress convened by the president in mid-1994 in response to demands from legal opposition parties for sweeping political reform.

On June 26, 1995, Mubarak narrowly escaped assassination when a group of alleged fundamentalists opened fire on his motorcade after his arrival in Addis Ababa, Ethiopia, for a summit of the Organization of African Unity (OAU). It was the third attempt on his life in 22 months. In September 1996, three defendants were sentenced to death by an Ethiopian court for their role in the 1995 attack, which President Mubarak blamed on the militant Islamic Group (see Illegal Groups under Political Parties, below).

Despite the regime's rhetorical commitment to broadening the governmental role of lesser parties, the NDP again completely dominated the legislative elections of late 1995, opposition leaders claiming they had been hamstrung by new press restrictions and the ongoing ban (under the longstanding state of emergency) on political demonstrations. On the other hand, the appointment of Dr. Kamal Ahmed al-GANZOURI as prime minister on January 3, 1996, launched what was widely perceived as significant economic liberalization.

The level of violence between the government and fundamentalist militants peaked in 1995 when more than 400 were killed from a combination of terrorist attacks and government reprisals against militant strongholds. International human rights organizations criticized the mass detention of political prisoners and "grossly unfair" trials leading, in many cases, to executions.

Sporadic incidents occurred throughout 1996 and into early 1997. In view of continued conflict with fundamentalist militants, the state of emergency in early 1997 was extended (and remained in effect as of mid-2005) permitting the government to continue to detain "terrorists" without formal charges for lengthy periods and to try defendants in special courts. Meanwhile, local elections in April again failed to reveal any hint of a political challenge to NDP control, nearly half of the ruling party's candidates running unopposed.

In mid-1997 imprisoned fundamentalist leaders reportedly called for a "cease-fire," and Egypt's vital tourist industry continued to revive. However, the government, apparently unconvinced that a truce had been achieved, proceeded with several mass trials and imposed harsh sentences on a number of defendants. Subsequently, militants massacred some 70 tourists at an ancient temple at Luxor in November, again bringing the conflict to the forefront of world attention. By that time, most observers agreed that a split had developed in the militant camp and that the faction committed to violence comprised possibly only several hundred guerrillas. It was also widely believed that there was little popular support for the militants, and only a few serious incidents were reported in 1998. By early 1999 the government had released an estimated 5,000 of the 20,000 people detained since the crackdown had begun, and in March the Islamic Group renounced violent methods. Meanwhile, domestic criticism of the regime, centered on the government's plan to limit the rights of human rights groups and other nongovernmental organizations as well as recent curbs placed on the media.

All political parties having been distinctly "marginalized," President Mubarak faced no challenge to his nomination in June 1999 by the People's Assembly for a fourth term, duly confirmed by an official "yes" vote of 94 percent in a national referendum on September 26. Upon his inauguration, Mubarak announced the appointment of Atef Muhammad OBEID as the new prime minister. Subsequently, the NDP ultimately again won unchallenged control of the Assembly in 2002 (see Current issues and Legislature, below). Some 70 percent of the NDP candidates also ran unopposed in the April 2002 municipal elections.

In June 2004, for the first time in Egypt's history, a member of the opposition leftist National Progressive Unionist Party (NPUP) won a seat in the Shura Council, and in October 2004, a third political party was allowed to form (see Constitution and government, below). Prime Minister Obeid resigned in 2004 and was succeeded by Ahmed Nazif, former minister of communications and information technology, who at age 52 was considerably younger than other government leaders. The next presidential elections were slated for September 2005. People's Assembly elections were to be held in October 2005. (See Constitution and government, below.)

Constitution and Government

Under the 1971 constitution, executive power is vested in the president, who is nominated by the People's Assembly and elected for a six-year term by popular referendum. The president may appoint vice presidents in addition to government ministers and may rule by decree when granted emergency powers by the 454-member Assembly, which functions primarily as a policy-approving rather than a policy-initiating body. (Since assuming the presidency in 1981, Mubarak has chosen to rule without a vice president.) In May 1990 the Supreme Constitutional Court invalidated the 1987 Assembly elections, claiming that the electoral system discriminated against opposition and independent contenders. Consequently, the government abolished electoral laws limiting the number of independent candidates, rejected the "party list" balloting system, and enlarged the number of constituencies.

For only the third time since forming in 1977, Egypt's Political Parties Committee allowed the creation of a new political party, Tomorrow (*al-Ghad*), in February 2005. On June 9, 2005, the Assembly approved a draft law to elect the president by direct, secret balloting, replacing the referendum system. This followed adoption of a constitutional amendment in May 2005 to allow Egypt's first multicandidate presidential election. The amendment was approved in a public referendum, albeit marked by huge public demonstrations over what is perceived as too much government control over potential candidates.

A Consultative Council (*Majlis al-Shura*), formerly the Central Committee of the ASU, is composed of 140 elected and 70 appointed members. It serves in an advisory capacity as an "upper house" of the Assembly. In addition to the Supreme Constitutional Court, the judicial system includes the Court of Cassation, geographically organized Courts of Appeal, Tribunals of First Instance, and District Tribunals. A Supreme Judicial Council is designed to guarantee the independence of the judiciary. Emergency laws, in effect since 1981, provide the government with broad arrest and detention powers. In addition, special military courts were established in late 1992 for the prosecution of persons charged with "terrorist acts" in connection with the conflict between the government and militant Islamic fundamentalists.

For administrative purposes Egypt is divided into 26 governorates, each with a governor appointed by the president, while most functions are shared with regional, town, and village officials. In April 1994 the People's Assembly approved legislation whereby previously elected village mayors would thenceforth be appointed by the Interior Ministry.

Constitutional amendments passed by the Assembly on April 30, 1980, and approved by referendum on May 22 included the following: designation of the country as "socialist democratic," rather than "democratic socialist," and designation of the Islamic legal code (*shari'a*) as "the" rather than "a" principal source of law.

Foreign Relations

As the most populous and most highly industrialized of the Arab states, Egypt has consistently aspired to a leading role in Arab, Islamic, Middle Eastern, African, and world affairs and has been an active participant in the UN, the Arab League, and the Organization of African Unity. For a number of years, its claim to a position of primacy in the Arab world made for somewhat unstable relations with other Arab governments, particularly the conservative regimes of Jordan and Saudi Arabia, although relations with those governments improved as a result of the 1967 and 1973 wars with Israel. Relations with the more radical regimes of Libya and Syria subsequently became strained, largely because of their displeasure with the terms of the US-brokered disengagement. Thus a January 1972 agreement by the three states to establish a loose Federation of Arab Republics was never implemented.

Formally nonaligned, Egypt has gone through a number of distinct phases, including the Western orientation of the colonial period and the monarchy, the anti-Western and increasingly pro-Soviet period initiated in 1955, a period of flexibility dating from the expulsion of Soviet personnel in 1972, and a renewed reliance on the West–particularly the United States–following widespread condemnation of Egyptian-Israeli rapprochement by most Communist and Arab governments.

On November 19, 1977, President Sadat began a precedent-shattering three-day trip to Jerusalem, the highlight of which was an address to the Israeli *Knesset*. While he offered no significant concessions in regard to the occupied territories, was unequivocal in his support of a Palestinian state, and declared that he did not intend to conclude a separate peace with Israel, the trip was hailed as a "historic breakthrough" in Arab-Israeli relations and was followed by an invitation to the principals in the Middle Eastern dispute and their great-power patrons to a December meeting in Egypt to prepare for a resumption of the Geneva peace conference. Israeli Prime Minister Begin responded affirmatively, but all of the Arab invitees declined. Consequently, on December 5 Egypt broke relations with five of its more radical neighbors (Algeria, Iraq, Libya, Syria, and South Yemen).

Little in the way of further progress toward an overall settlement was registered prior to a dramatic ten-day "summit" convened by US President Carter at Camp David, Maryland, in September 1978. The meeting yielded two documents–a "Framework for Peace in the Middle East" and a "Framework for a Peace Treaty between Israel and Egypt"–that were signed by President Sadat and Prime Minister Begin at the White House on September 17. By mid-November details of a peace treaty and three annexes had been agreed upon by Egyptian and Israeli representatives. Signing, however, was deferred beyond the target date of December 17 primarily because of Egyptian insistence on a specific timetable for Israeli withdrawal from the West Bank and Gaza, in addition to last-minute reservations regarding Article 6, which gave the document precedence over treaty commitments to other states. Thus, on March 8, US President Carter flew to the Middle East for talks with leaders of both countries, and within six days compromise proposals had been accepted. The completed treaty was signed by Begin and Sadat at Washington on March 26, and on April 25 the 31-year state of war between Egypt and Israel officially came to an end with the exchange of ratification documents at the US surveillance post at Um-Khashiba in the Sinai. On May 25 the first Israeli troops withdrew from the Sinai under the terms of the treaty and negotiations on autonomy for the West Bank and Gaza opened at Beersheba, Israel.

The Arab League responded to the Egyptian-Israeli rapprochement by calling for the diplomatic and economic isolation of Egypt. By midyear all League members but Oman, Somalia, and Sudan had severed relations with the Sadat regime, and Cairo's membership had been suspended from a number of Arab groupings, including the League, the Arab Monetary Fund, and the Organization of Arab Petroleum Exporting Countries. Egypt succeeded in weathering the hard-line Arab reaction largely because of increased economic aid from Western countries, including France, West Germany, Japan, and the United States, which alone committed itself to more aid on a real per capita basis than had been extended to Europe under the post–World War II Marshall Plan.

Although Egypt and Israel formally exchanged ambassadors on February 26, 1980, a month after opening their border at El Arish in the Sinai to land traffic, negotiations on the question of Palestinian autonomy were subsequently impeded by continued Jewish settlement on the West Bank,

the Israeli annexation of East Jerusalem in July 1980, and the invasion of Lebanon in June 1982. Following the massacre of Palestinian refugees at Sabra and Chatila in September 1982, Cairo recalled its ambassador from Tel Aviv. (Relations at the ambassadorial level were ultimately reestablished in September 1986, despite tension over Israel's bombing of the PLO headquarters at Tunis in October 1985.)

The Soviet intervention in Afghanistan in December 1979 generated concern in Egypt, with the government ordering Moscow in February 1980 to reduce its diplomatic staff at Cairo to seven, while offering military assistance to the Afghan rebels. In 1981, accusing the remaining Soviet embassy staff of aiding Islamic fundamentalist unrest, Cairo broke diplomatic relations and expelled the Soviet ambassador. Relations were resumed in September 1984, as the Mubarak government departed from the aggressively pro-US policy of the later Sadat years, while a three-year trade accord was signed by the two governments in late 1987.

Relations with most of the Arab world also changed during President Mubarak's first term, Egypt's stature among moderate neighbors being enhanced by a virtual freeze in dealings with Israel after the 1982 Lebanon invasion. Although relations with radical Arab states, particularly Libya, remained strained, Egypt's reemergence from the status of Arab pariah allowed it to act as a "silent partner" in negotiations between Jordan and the PLO that generated a 1985 peace plan (see entries on Jordan and the PLO). However, the subsequent collapse of the plan left the Mubarak administration in an uncomfortable middle position between its "good friend" King Hussein and the PLO, whose Cairo offices were closed in May 1987 after the passage of an "anti-Egyptian" resolution by the Palestine National Council.

During an Arab League summit at 'Amman, Jordan, in November 1987, the prohibition against diplomatic ties with Egypt was officially lifted, although the suspension of League membership remained in effect. It was widely believed that the threat of Iranian hegemony in the Gulf was the principal factor in Cairo's rehabilitation. Egypt, which had severed relations with Iran in May 1987 upon discovery of a fundamentalist Muslim network allegedly financed by Teheran, possessed the largest and best-equipped armed force in the region. Following the 'Amman summit, Egypt authorized reopening of the PLO facility, instituted joint military maneuvers with Jordan, increased the number of military advisors sent to Iraq, and arranged for military cooperation with Kuwait, Saudi Arabia, and the United Arab Emirates.

By January 1989 only three Arab League countries–Libya, Lebanon, and Syria–had not renewed diplomatic relations with Cairo, and Egypt returned to full participation in the organization at its Casablanca, Morocco, summit in May. Meanwhile, a dispute that had marred relations with Israel since the latter's 1982 withdrawal from the bulk of the Sinai was resolved on February 26, when the two countries agreed to reaffirm Egyptian sovereignty over Taba, a beach resort on the northern tip of the Gulf of Aqaba (see Israel map, p. 564).

Lebanon and Syria restored diplomatic relations with Cairo in 1989, and relations with Libya also improved as President Mubarak journeyed to Libya in October to meet with Colonel Qadhafi, the first such visit by an Egyptian president since 1972. Meanwhile, Cairo increased pressure on Jerusalem to begin negotiations with the Palestinians in the West Bank and Gaza Strip, forwarding a ten-point plan to speed the onset of elections and lobbying the United States to exercise its diplomatic influence over Israel.

Egyptian-Iraqi relations were rocked in June 1989 by Baghdad's imposition of remittance restrictions on foreign workers, leading to the repatriation of 1 million Egyptians, many of whom complained about Iraqi mistreatment. In what was clearly his boldest foreign relations move, President Mubarak spearheaded the Arab response to Iraq's incursion into Kuwait in August 1990. At an Arab League summit at Cairo on August 10 the Egyptian leader successfully argued for a declaration condemning the invasion and approving Saudi Arabia's request for non-Arab troops to help it defend its borders. Subsequent Egyptian efforts to facilitate an Iraqi withdrawal were rebuffed by Baghdad (in January 1991 Mubarak claimed to have made 26 personal appeals to Saddam Hussein). Overall, more than 45,000 Egyptian troops were deployed to Saudi Arabia, elements of which played a conspicuous role in the liberation of Kuwait.

In the wake of Iraq's defeat in 1991, policy differences arose between Egypt and its allies. Cairo had long urged that postwar regional security be entrusted to an all-Arab force. By contrast, Gulf Cooperation Council (GCC) members indicated that they looked with favor on a continued US presence in the area. Particularly irksome was a Saudi statement that the monarchy did not welcome the permanent stationing of Egyptian forces on its soil, Cairo subsequently withdrawing all its troops by the end of August. A corollary to the dispute over military policy was increased uncertainty as to the level of economic aid that Egypt could expect from its oil-rich neighbors. For their part, Western creditors quickly rewarded Cairo for its support during the Desert Shield and Desert Storm campaigns. Shortly after the defeat of Iraqi forces, the United States and Gulf Arab states forgave about $14 billion of Egypt's $50 billion external debt, and Paris Club members subsequently agreed to gradually write off another $11 billion. Globally, its prestige was enhanced by the selection of its leading diplomat, former deputy prime minister Boutros BOUTROS-GHALI, as the secretary general of the United Nations effective January 1, 1992.

Egyptian officials reportedly played an important advisory role in the secret talks that led up to the accord between Israel and the PLO in September 1993. In addition, Egypt won the backing of other North African governments for its hard-line antifundamentalist posture. Cairo's relations with 'Amman improved after a three-year rift caused by Jordan's pro-Iraqi stand during the Gulf crisis. In early February 1995 President Mubarak hosted Jordan's King Hussein, Israeli Prime Minister Yitzhak Rabin, and PLO Chairman Yasir 'Arafat in a regional summit designed to revitalize prospects for implementation of the Israel/PLO peace accord. The summit also reportedly addressed growing tension between Egypt and Israel regarding nuclear weapons. (Cairo had threatened to reject proposed extension of the Treaty on the Non-Proliferation of Nuclear Weapons [see the International Atomic Energy Agency, under UN: Related Organizations, for details] unless Israel agreed to discuss termination of its "secret" nuclear weapons program.)

By mid-1995 tension with Egypt's southern neighbor, Sudan, had intensified because of an intimation by Mubarak that Sudanese officials had played a role in the June 26 assassination attempt in Ethiopia. In June Sudan accused Egypt of provoking a clash in the disputed border region of Halaib, with Mubarak declaring his support for exiled opponents of the fundamentalist Khartoum regime. In 2004, Egypt reluctantly agreed to send military officers as observers to Sudan, but stopped short of getting involved in attempting to resolve the Sudanese civil war.

On March 13, 1996, Egypt hosted the so-called "terrorism summit" of some 27 heads of state and government in the wake of suicide bomb attacks in Israel earlier in the month that appeared to threaten the Middle East peace process. Following the election of Benjamin Netanyahu as Israel's new prime minister in May, President Mubarak became more critical of him over the next six months in the face of what he described as Netanyahu's "lack of action" in implementing the Israeli/PLO peace accord. The Egyptian president intensified his attacks on Netanyahu's policies in 1997, particularly in regard to the expansion of Jewish settlements in the West Bank. In early 1998 Mubarak strongly objected to US plans to take military action against Iraq after Baghdad blocked the activities of UN weapons inspectors. Meanwhile, by that time significant improvement had been registered in relations between Egypt and Sudan, the two countries having apparently agreed to address each other's "security" concerns, i.e., Sudanese support for fundamentalist militants in Egypt and Egyptian support for antiregime activity in Sudan, particularly on the part of southern rebels. Full diplomatic relations were restored between Sudan and Egypt in December 1999, following a visit by

Sudan's President Bashir to Cairo. Relations with Iran were also reported to have improved later in 1998, but in 2005 they were again strained after a security court convicted an Egyptian of plotting to assassinate the president and of spying for Iran.

President Mubarak welcomed the election of Ehud Barak as prime minister of Israel in May 1999 as a "hopeful sign" regarding a peace settlement between Israel and the Palestinians, and Egypt was a prominent mediator in negotiations through mid-2000. However, Egypt recalled its ambassador to Israel in November 2000 in response to the Israeli bombing of the Gaza Strip. Egyptian/Israeli relations cooled even further following the election of hard-liner Ariel Sharon as prime minister of Israel in February 2001. By 2004, however, after Sharon had unveiled his unilateral disengagement plan for the Gaza Strip, in consultation with Egypt and the United States, relations between Egypt and Israel had begun to thaw. Egypt's role in security arrangements in Gaza are vital to the process and widely seen as enhancing Egypt's role as a power broker in the region. Relations with Israel hit a low point in the fall of 2004 after an Israeli tank opened fire on Egyptian police at the Gaza border. In December 2004, Egypt and Israel conducted their first prisoner exchange, marking a shift in relations and paving the way for a December 12, 2004, pact between the two countries on exports. In February 2005, Mubarak again helped mediate between Israel and the Palestinians, adopting a high-profile diplomatic role.

Current Issues

Under increasing pressure from prodemocracy activists, as well as from the United States, President Mubarak in February 2005 called for a constitutional amendment to allow multicandidate elections. Unprecedented public demonstrations and calls for Mubarak to step down preceded his historic announcement. The amendment was approved in a referendum in May 2005, but the government still faced vehement criticism for the restrictive conditions it placed on potential candidates; for example, leaders of the recognized parties can run, but independent candidates must get the backing of 250 members of the Assembly and local councils. Four opposition parties immediately announced a boycott of the presidential elections scheduled for September 2005. Egyptian authorities had attempted to ban referendum-day protests, but large demonstrations took place nonetheless. The government also arrested members of the opposition Muslim Brotherhood. The ongoing crackdown against Islamists and other opposition groups sparked bold, massive protests, leading to further arrests. The leftist Tomorrow (*al-Ghad*), the one new party granted a permit, saw its leader Ayman NUR jailed for six weeks on charges of forging signatures on his political party application. His trial opened on June 28, 2005, but was shortly thereafter postponed until after presidential elections.

Even with obvious moves toward reform, the emergency law decreed in 1981 remains in effect, and human rights organizations report ongoing abuse by security services around the country. On April 11, 2005, the state-created National Council for Human Rights (NCHR) released its first report, addressing key issues of torture and other abuses and calling for the lifting of the emergency law. It is seen as part of the growing opposition movement and calls for reform. The government seemed to be responding somewhat by changing laws and appointing younger ministers, but the disenchanted regardless increasingly asserted themselves through highly visible demonstrations. Meanwhile, a jailed member of the banned Muslim Brotherhood announced his intent to challenge Mubarak in the 2005 presidential elections. An Islamist convicted in the assassination of Sadat announced his candidacy, as did four members of opposition parties.

Following *al-Qaeda*'s attacks on the United States in September 2001, the government, reportedly feeling vindicated in regard to its hardline tactics of recent years, intensified its anti-fundamentalist campaign in late 2001 and early 2002 and readily endorsed the US-led "war on terrorism." Nonmilitant opponents also continued to feel the government's weight, most notably Saad Eddin IBRAHIM, a prominent social activist with US and Egyptian citizenship who was sentenced in mid-2002 to seven years in prison for a variety of charges, including illegally receiving funds from overseas and "slandering Egypt." The EU, the source of some of the funds received by Ibrahim, strongly condemned the verdict, which was also criticized by Washington. (The Bush administration pointedly refused an Egyptian request for additional aid in view of the controversial court action.)

Political Parties and Groups

Egypt's old political parties were swept away with the destruction of the monarchy in 1953. Efforts by the Nasser regime centered on the creation of a single mass organization to support the government and its policies. Following unsuccessful experiments with two such organizations, the National Liberation Rally and the National Union, the Arab Socialist Union–ASU (*al-Ittihad al-Ishtiraki al-'Arabi*) was established as the country's sole political party in December 1962.

Prior to the legislative election of October 1976 President Sadat authorized the establishment of three "groups" within the ASU–the leftist National Progressive Unionist Assembly (NPUA), the centrist Egyptian Arab Socialist Organization (EASO), and the rightist Free Socialist Organization (FSO)–which presented separate lists of Assembly candidates. Following the election, Sadat indicated that it would be appropriate to refer to the groups as distinct parties, though the ASU would "stand above" the new organizations. A law adopted on June 27, 1977, authorized the establishment of additional parties under three conditions: (1) that they be sanctioned by the ASU; (2) that, except for those established in 1976, they include at least 20 members of the People's Assembly; and (3) that they not have been in existence prior to 1953.

On February 4, 1978, the ASU Central Committee modified the impact of the 1977 legislation by permitting the *Wafd,* the majority party under the monarchy, to reenter politics as the New Wafd Party (NWP). Less than four months later, however, representatives of the NWP voted unanimously to disband the party to protest the passage of a sweeping internal security law on June 1. Subsequently, President Sadat announced the formal abolition of the ASU, the conversion of its Central Committee into a Consultative Council (*Majlis al-Shura*) to meet annually on the anniversary of the 1952 revolution, and the establishment of a new centrist group which, on August 15, was named the National Democratic Party (NDP). In an April 1979 political referendum, the voters overwhelmingly approved removal of the first two conditions of the 1977 law, thus clearing the way for the formation of additional parties. In May 1980 a constitutional amendment, also approved by referendum, removed reference to the defunct ASU as the sole source of political activity, thus formally legitimizing the limited multiparty system. In July 1983 the Assembly approved a requirement that parties obtain 8 percent of the vote to gain parliamentary representation. One month later, the NWP announced that it was "resuming public activity," a government attempt to force the group to reregister as a new party being overturned by the State Administrative Court the following October.

At the 1984 election only the NDP and the NWP won elective seats, the former outdistancing the latter by a near 6-1 margin. In 1987 the NDP obtained a slightly reduced majority of 77.2 percent, the remaining seats being captured by the NWP and a coalition composed of the Socialist Labor Party (SLP), the Liberal Socialist Party (LSP), and "Islamists" representing the Muslim Brotherhood (see below). Following a Supreme Court decision in May 1990 that overturned the results of the 1987 balloting, the government enacted a number of electoral changes, including reversal of the 8 percent requirement.

In 2002 the administration introduced controversial new regulations that precluded political activity on the part of any group receiving money from overseas that had not been approved by and channeled through the government. Opponents of the regime decried the measure as an attempt to throttle parties who might be funded by foreign prodemocracy organizations. In 2004, eight parties formed an alliance to promote reforms (see Other Legislative Parties, below). Still other parties are summarily banned, while one new party was allowed to form in 2004 (see Other Legal Parties, below).

Government Party

National Democratic Party –NDP (*al-Hizb al-Watani al-Dimuqrati*). The NDP was organized by President Sadat in July 1978 as the principal government party, its name being derived from that of the historic National Party formed at the turn of the century by Mustapha Kamel. In late August it was reported that 275 deputies in the People's Assembly had joined the new group, all but 11 having been members of the Egyptian Arab Socialist Party–EASP (*Hizb Misr al-'Arabi al-Ishtiraki*), which, as an outgrowth of the EASO, had inherited many of the political functions earlier performed by the ASU. The EASP formally merged with the NDP in October 1978. President Mubarak, who had served as deputy chairman under President Sadat, was named NDP chairman at a party congress on January 26, 1982.

Two months after his pro forma reelection in October 1993, President Mubarak announced the composition of the new NDP political bureau, most leadership posts being retained by incumbents despite the president's campaign pledge to revitalize both the NDP and the national administration. In November 1998 the NDP nominated Mubarak as its candidate for the 1999 presidential election. Official NDP candidates reportedly won only 27 percent of the seats in the 2000 Assembly balloting, although many successful independent candidates joined (or rejoined) the party to give it 388 out of 442 elected seats. Analysts attributed the poor performance of the official NDP candidates to public perception that the party lacked an ideological foundation and existed only to rubber-stamp the administration's agenda.

President Mubarak was reelected as chairman of the NDP at the September 2002 congress, while his son, Gamal MUBARAK, who has been mentioned as a possible successor to his father, was elevated to a new post of head of the NDP's policy board.

Leaders: Muhammad Husni MUBARAK (President of the Republic and Chairman of the Party), Muhammad Safwat al-SHERIF (General Secretary), Kamal al-SHAZLY (Assistant General Secretary).

Other Legislative Parties

Consensus of National Forces for Reform (*Tawafuq al-Qiwa al-Wataniyah lil-Islah*). On September 9, 2004, eight opposition parties formed a group seeking to represent professional and civil organizations, but notably excluding the outlawed Muslim Brotherhood. The alliance includes the Democratic Generation, Egypt 2000, Nasserist Arab Democratic Party, National Party, National Progressive Unionist Party, Socialist Labor Party, National Consensus, and the Wafd. In early 2005, the group was trying to arrange a dialogue with the NDP to present a list of political reforms, including election reforms.

Leader: Dr. Rif'at al-SA'ID.

New Wafd Party–NWP (*Hizb al-Wafd al-Gadid*). Formed in February 1978 as a revival of the most powerful party in Egypt prior to 1952, the NWP formally disbanded the following June but reformed in August. In 1980 a "new generation of *Wafd* activists" instigated demonstrations in several cities, prompting the detention of its leader, Fuad SERAGEDDIN, until November 1981. In alliance with a number of Islamic groups, most importantly the proscribed Muslim Brotherhood (below), the *Wafd* won 15 percent of the vote in May 1984, thus becoming the only opposition party with parliamentary representation. In 1987 the NWP won 35 seats (23 less than in 1984), the Brotherhood having entered into a de facto coalition with the SLP and the LSP (below). The NWP boycotted the *Shura* poll in 1989, complaining that electoral procedures remained exclusionary; it also boycotted the 1990 Assembly elections, although party members running as independents retained at least 14 seats.

Following the 1995 national balloting, NWP leaders charged that electoral fraud had been the "worst in history." The NWP also boycotted the April 1997 local elections. However, although the NWP had urged a boycott of the 1993 presidential poll, it urged a "yes" vote for President Mubarak in 1999. Serageddin died in August 2000 and was succeeded as party leader by Numan Gomaa.

Leaders: Numan GOMAA, El Sayed BADAWI (Secretary General).

Liberal Socialist Party (*Hizb al-Ahrar al-Ishtiraki*). The Liberal Socialist Party, which was formed in 1976 from the right wing of the ASU, focuses on securing a greater role for private enterprise within the Egyptian economy while protecting the rights of workers and farmers. The party's Assembly representation fell from 12 to 3 seats in June 1979 and was eliminated entirely at the 1984 balloting, on the basis of a vote share of less than 1 percent. It obtained three elective seats in 1987 as a member of a Socialist Labor Party–led coalition. It subsequently discontinued its alliance with the SLP and Muslim Brotherhood. It boycotted the November 1990 poll, although one of its members reportedly won a seat as an independent. The party won one seat in the 2000 Assembly elections.

Leader: Hilmi SALIM.

National Progressive Unionist Party –NPUP (*Hizb al-Tajammu 'al-Watani al-Taqaddumi al-Wahdawi*). Although it received formal endorsement as the party of the Left in 1976, the NPUP temporarily ceased activity in 1978 following the enactment of restrictive internal security legislation. It contested the June 1979 Assembly election on a platform that, alone among those of the four sanctioned parties, opposed the Egyptian-Israeli peace treaty, and it failed to retain its two parliamentary seats. In both 1979 and 1984 the party leadership charged the government with fraud and harassment, although on the latter occasion, President Mubarak included a NPUP member among his Assembly nominees. In November 1990 the NPUP resisted opposition appeals for an electoral boycott and captured six Assembly seats; meanwhile, the party led opposition criticism against US military involvement in the Gulf. The NPUP urged a no vote against Mubarak in the 1993 presidential referendum and called for a boycott of the 1999 poll.

Leaders: Qabbari 'ABDALLAH, Abu al-'Izz al-HARIRI.

Nasserist Arab Democratic Party (NADP). Also referenced simply as the Nasserist Party, the NADP, formed in 1992, won one seat in the 1995 Assembly balloting and three in the 2000 poll. Its platform called for the government to retain a dominant role in directing the economy and to increase the provision of social services.

Leader: Diaeddin DAOUD.

Other Legal Parties

Tomorrow Party (*al-Ghad*). Officially recognized by the government in October 2004, this leftist party became only the third new party allowed since 1977. Tomorrow seeks constitutional reform to reduce the power of the presidency and an end to the country's emergency law. Espousing a commitment to social justice, the party is made up largely of dissidents from the Wafd Party. Its leader, jailed for six weeks in 2005 (see Current issues, above), ran for president that year.

Leader: Ayman NUR (Chairman), Muna Makram UBAYD [f] (Secretary General)

National Party (*Hizb al-'Umma*). A small Muslim organization, the National Party has ties to the supporters of Dr. Sadiq al-MAHDI, former prime minister of Sudan. It participated unsuccessfully in the 2000 Assembly balloting on a platform that called for the strengthening of the "democratic process."

Leader: Ahmad al-SABAHI Awadallah (Chairman).

Green Party (*Hizb al-Khudr*). The Green Party, recognized by the Political Parties Tribunal in April 1990, was reported to have emerged in response to a 1986 newspaper column by (then) Vice President Abdel Salam DAOUD which criticized his countrymen's lack of interest in environmental issues. The formation claimed 3,000 members and, while professing no interest in gaining political power, participated unsuccessfully in the 1990 legislative campaign.

Leader: Abdul Moneim al-AASAR (Chairman).

The other legal parties as of mid-2005 were **Arab Dignity** (*Karama al-Arabiya*), led by Essam al-ISLAMBOULI; the **Democratic Unionist Party,** led by Muhammad 'Abd al-Munim TURK; the **Egyptian Arab Socialist Party,** led by Gamal Eldin RABIE Youssef; **Enough** (*Kifaya*), a coalition; the **Generation Party** (*al-Gayl*), led by Naji al-SHAHABI; the **National Accord Party,** formed in March 2000; **New Center** (*Wasat al-Jadid*), led by Abul ELAMAADI; the **Social Justice Party,** formed in 1993 and led by Mohammad Abdul AAL; and **Solidarity** (*al-Takaful*), a socialist grouping led by Usama Mohammad SHALTOUT.

Illegal Groups

Muslim Brotherhood (*al-Ikhwan al-Muslimin*). Established in 1928 to promote creation of a pan-Arab Islamic state, the Brotherhood was declared to be an illegal organization in 1954 when the government accused its leaders, many of whom were executed or imprisoned, of plotting a coup attempt. However, for many years the Mubarak government tolerated some activity on the part of the Brotherhood since it claimed to eschew violence, as a means of undercutting the militant fundamentalist movement. With much of its support coming from the northern middle class, the Brotherhood retains the largest following and greatest financial resources among Egypt's Islamic organizations despite the emergence of more radical groups. It dominates many Egyptian professional associations, collaterally providing a wide range of charitable services in sharp contrast to inefficient government programs.

The Brotherhood secured indirect Assembly representation in 1984 and 1987. Although the Brotherhood boycotted the 1990 Assembly balloting, joint SLP/Brotherhood candidates contested a number of seats in November 1992 municipal elections. Many Brotherhood adherents were removed from local and national appointive positions in 1992–1993 as a side effect of the government's antifundamentalist campaign. Friction with the government intensified further in early 1995 when a group of Brotherhood members were charged with having links to the militant Islamic Group (below). The government arrested more than 50 members of the group in July on charges of belonging to an illegal organization. Sentences of up to five years in prison were handed down against most of the defendants in early November, essentially precluding effective Brotherhood participation in the legislative balloting later than month. (It was subsequently reported that only one successful Assembly candidate could be identified as a Brotherhood adherent.) The Brotherhood urged a boycott of the April 1997 local elections, claiming that many of its supporters and preferred candidates had been subjected to government "intimidation."

In January 1996 a number of former Brotherhood members reportedly launched a **Center Party** (*Hizb al-Wasat*) along with representatives of the Coptic community in an avowed effort to "heal the breaches" within the Egyptian populace. However, the government denied the party's request for recognition and arrested some 13 of its founders with purported Brotherhood ties. In August seven of the defendants were convicted of antigovernment activity by a military court and sentenced to three years in prison. *Al-Wasat* was again denied legal status in May 1998, the government describing it as insufficiently different from other parties to warrant recognition.

A number of the officially independent candidates in the 2000 Assembly balloting were clearly identifiable as belonging to the Brotherhood, and

17 of them were elected, permitting the return of the Brotherhood to the Assembly after a ten-year absence. However, even though Brotherhood leaders subsequently again denied any connection to militant groups, a number of Brotherhood members were arrested in the government crackdown on Islamists in late 2001 and early 2002.

The death of 83-year-old leader Mamoun al-HODAIBI on January 9, 2004, was seen as an opportunity to attract the younger generation, but on January 14 the party selected an "old guard" successor: Muhammad Mahdi Akef, 74. He maintained that the Brotherhood would not change its approach. Akef had been convicted in 1954 of the attempted assassination of President Nasser and served 20 years in prison.

While Akef called for dialogue with the government, in May 2004 security forces arrested 54 members of the Brotherhood and for the first time targeted the organization's funding sources, closing various businesses and the group's Web site. In March 2005, some 84 members were arrested in police raids in the midst of massive demonstrations, said to be the largest in Cairo's history. One of the jailed leaders of the Brotherhood announced in May 2005 that he will challenge Mubarak in September 2005 presidential elections.

Leaders: Muhammad Mahdi AKEF.

Holy War (*al-Jihad*). A secret organization of militant Muslims who had reportedly split from the Muslim Brotherhood in the second half of the 1970s because of the latter's objection to the use of violence, *al-Jihad* was blamed for attacks against Copts in 1979 and the assassination of President Sadat in 1981. In the first half of the 1980s it appeared to be linked to the Islamic Group (below), but the two organizations emerged with more distinct identities during the mid-1980s. Although some observers described *al-Jihad* as continuing to seek recruits, particularly in the military, its influence appeared to have diminished in the late 1980s as the result of government infiltration of its ranks and growing support for the Islamic Group. However, security officials charged that a revival of the group was attempted in the first half of the 1990s in conjunction with the increasingly violent fundamentalist/government conflict. A number of reported *al-Jihad* supporters were imprisoned in mid-1993 on charges of plotting the overthrow of the government, while, according to authorities, about 30 members were arrested in an April 1994 security sweep. Meanwhile, members of an apparent splinter, variously referenced as New *Jihad* or the Vanguards of Conquest (*Tala'i al-Fath*), were subsequently given death sentences for complicity in assassination plots against top government officials. Some reports linked that activity to Ayman al-ZAWAHIRI, a former Cairo surgeon who had been imprisoned (and reportedly subjected to extreme torture) for three years following the assassination of President Sadat. Zawahiri was also reportedly linked to the bombing of the Egyptian embassy in Pakistan in 1995.

In 1998, in the wake of the Luxor attack of 1997, Zawahiri and his brother, Mohammad al-ZAWAHIRI, were described as attempting to "reorganize" *al-Jihad* from Afghanistan, where they had reportedly established ties with the *al-Qaeda* network of Osama bin Laden. (Ayman al-Zawahiri had not been seen in Egypt since 1986.) Among other things, Ayman al-Zawahiri endorsed bin Laden's 1998 call for attacks on "Jews and Crusaders" (the latter a reference to Americans and their allies). At that point it appeared that a portion of *al-Jihad,* having been effectively suppressed in Egypt, had shifted away from a goal of overthrowing the Egyptian government to a global anti-Western campaign in concert with *al-Qaeda* (for information on *al-Qaeda,* see article on Afghanistan). However, some members of *al-Jihad* reportedly objected to that new focus and split from Zawahiri.

A number of alleged *al-Jihad* adherents received long prison terms in early 1999, while nine were sentenced to death in absentia, including Ayman al-Zawahiri and Yasser al-SIRRI, a London-based leader. Zawahiri was also indicted in absentia in 1999 in the United States for his alleged role in the planning of the bombings of the US embassies in Kenya and Pakistan in 1998. Following

the attacks on the United States in September 2001 that were quickly attributed to *al-Qaeda,* Zawahiri, noted for his organizational skills, was described as the number two leader, after bin Laden, in that network. As of mid-2005, he continued to elude US authorities.

Islamic Group (*Gamaat i-Islami*). The Islamic Group surfaced in the late 1970s as the student wing of the Muslim Brotherhood, subsequently breaking from that organization and aligning (until the mid-1980s) with *al-Jihad* in seeking overthrow of the government. Having gained adherents among the poor in the Cairo slums and the villages in southern Egypt, it served as a loosely knit, but highly militant, umbrella organization for as many as three dozen smaller organizations. The government accused the Group of spearheading attacks on security forces, government officials, and tourists beginning in 1992, and hanged a number of its members who had been convicted of terrorist activity.

Egyptian authorities in the mid-1990s asked the United States to extradite Sheikh Omar ABDEL RAHMAN, the blind theologian who is reputed to be the spiritual leader of the Islamic Group and had been in self-imposed exile in the New York City area since 1990. In April 1994 Sheikh Abdel Rahman was sentenced in absentia by an Egyptian security court to seven years in prison for inciting his followers to violence in 1989. In addition, 25 codefendants received jail terms of various lengths. In January 1996 Sheikh Abdel Rahman was sentenced to life in prison in the United States following his conviction of charges of conspiring to commit a series of bombings in the New York City area. Eight codefendants were given prison terms of 25 years to life. Meanwhile, Safwat 'Abd al-Ghani, viewed as the political leader of the Group, was confined to prison in Egypt on a charge of illegal weapons possession. Ghani and other Islamic Group defendants had initially been charged with murder in the 1990 assassination of Assembly President Rifa'at al-Mahgoub; however, the charges were dismissed in 1993 following a court ruling that confessions had been extracted from them by torture.

Talaat Yassin HAMMAN, described by Egyptian authorities as the "military commander" of the Islamic Group, was killed by security forces in April 1994. His "intended successor," Ahmad Hassan 'Abd al-GALIL, also died in a shoot-out with police the following November. It was subsequently reported that Group military activities were being conducted under the leadership of Mustapha HAMZA and Rifai TAHA, apparently based in Afghanistan.

Two members of the Group were executed in February 1995 after being convicted of a bomb attack in which a German tourist had been killed, while two others were executed in late March for the attempted killing of Nobel laureate Naguig MAHFOUZ in October 1994. The Egyptian government also accused the Group (and Hamza in particular) of being behind a June 1995 attempt on the life of President Mubarak in Ethiopia.

In mid-1996 reports surfaced that a faction of the Islamic Group had signaled an interest in negotiations with the government. However, that possibility was apparently rejected by the Mubarak administration. Factionalization within the Group was also apparent in 1997, particularly in regard to a "cease-fire" ordered by its imprisoned leaders at midyear. Although the militants responsible for the attack at Luxor in November appeared linked to the Group, longstanding Group leaders disavowed responsibility, suggesting they were no longer in control of at least some "rogue" guerrilla cells. Subsequently, spokesmen for the Group emphasized that it had reached "political maturity" and had renounced violence in favor of attempting to establish an Islamic state in Egypt through the political process. Sheikh Abdel Rahman appeared to endorse that shift in late 1998 when he called on his followers to pursue "peaceful means," and the Islamic Group announced in March 1999 that a unilateral cease-fire was in effect. That cease-fire remained in effect through mid-2005. Islamic Group members still committed to violence reportedly subsequently joined the *al-Qaeda* network of Osama bin Laden. In September 2003, it was reported that Egyptian authorities had released some 900 members of the organization.

Leaders: Safwat 'Abd al-GHANI, Salah HASHEM, Talaat Fuad QASIM (Spokesman in Europe).

Islamic Liberation Party (*Hizb al-Tahrir al-Islami*). This radical political movement wants to create an Islamic society in Egypt and is on the United States' list of foreign terrorist organizations.

In September 2002 some 51 defendants were given jail sentences in connection with the alleged activity of a clandestine organization known as *al-Wa'ad* (The Pledge). First arrested on charges of belonging to an illegal organization, the defendants were also subsequently accused of planning violent acts in pursuit of the establishment of an Islamic state in Egypt.

Also subject to government crackdowns have been the Islamic fundamentalist **Survivors from Hell** (*al-Najoun Min al-Nar*), charged in 1988 with the attempted murder of two anti-Muslim former government ministers, and **Denouncement and Holy Flight** (*Takfir wa al-Hijra*). (Some 245 members of the latter were reportedly arrested in April 1996.) An obscure Islamic group, Brigades of Pride, claimed responsibility for a bombing in the heart of Cairo in April 2005.

Clandestine left-wing formations against which the government has moved energetically in the past included, most prominently, the **Egyptian Communist Party** (*al-Hizb al-Shuyu'i al-Misri*). Founded in 1921, the party subsequently experienced numerous cleavages that yielded, among others, the **Egyptian Communist Labor Party** and the Maoist **Revolutionary Current.** In 1990 another splinter, the **People's Socialist Party,** was launched under the leadership of veteran Communist Michel KAMEL, who later died in exile in France.

Two Islamist groupings–the **Reform (Islah) Party,** formed in 1997 under the leadership of Gamal SULTAN; and the **Islamic Law (Shari'a) Party**–sought permission to participate in the 2000 Assembly elections, but their applications were emphatically rejected by the government.

Cabinet

As of July 14, 2005

Prime Minister	Ahmed Mahmoud Muhammad Nazif
Deputy Prime Minister	Yussef Amin Wali

Ministers

Agriculture and Land Reclamation	Ahmed 'Abd al-Munim al-Laythi
Civil Aviation	Lt. Gen. Ahmad Shafiq
Communications and Information Technology	Tariq Muhammad Kamal
Culture	Faruq 'Abd al-Aziz Husni
Defense and Military Production	Fld. Mar. Muhammad Hussein Tantawi Sulayman
Education	Ahmad Gamal al-Din 'Abd al-Fattah Musa
Electricity and Energy	Hassan Ahmed Younes
Finance	Yussef Boutros-Ghali
Foreign Affairs	Ahmed Ali Abu al-Ghayt
Foreign Trade and Industry	Rashid Muhammad Rashid
Health and Population	Muhammad Awad Taj al-Din
Higher Education	Amr Azet Salama
Housing, Utilities, and Urban Communities	Muhammed Ibrahim Sulieman
Information	Mamdouh al-Beltagi
Insurance and Social Affairs	Amina Hamza Muhammad al-Guindi [f]
Interior	Gen. Habib al-Adli
International Cooperation	Fayza Abu-al-Naga [f]
Investment	Mahmoud Muhiy al-Din
Irrigation and Water Resources	Mahmoud 'Abd al-Halim Abu Zayd
Justice	Mahmoud Abu Lail Rashid
Local Development	'Abd al-Rahim Shahata
Manpower and Immigration	Ahmed Ahmed al-Amawi
Petroleum	Amin Sameh Samir Fahmi
Planning	Othman Muhammad Othman
Religious Trusts	Mahmoud Hamdi Zakzuk
Supply	Hassan Ali Kheder
Tourism	Ahmed al-Maghrabi
Transport	Isam 'Abd al-Aziz Sharaf
Youth	Anas Ahmed al-Fiqy

Ministers of State

Administrative Development	Ahmed Mahmoud Darwish
Consultative Council Affairs	Mufid Mahmoud Shihab
Environmental Affairs	Majid George Ghattas
Military Production	Sayed Abdou Moustafa Mesh'al
People's Assembly	Kamal Muhammad al Shazli
Scientific Research Affairs	Amr Azet Salama

[f] = female

Legislature

The **People's Assembly** (*Majlis al-Sha'ab*) is a unicameral legislature elected in two-round balloting for a five-year term. As sanctioned by a popular referendum, President Sadat dissolved the existing Assembly (which had two years remaining in its term) on April 21, 1979, and announced expansion of the body from 350 to 392 members, in part to accommodate representatives from the Sinai. Prior to the election of May 27, 1984, the Assembly was further expanded to 458 members, including 10 appointed by the president.

On May 19, 1990, the Supreme Constitutional Court voided the results of an Assembly poll of April 6, 1987, because of improper restrictions on opposition and independent candidates, and an October 11 referendum approved formal dissolution of the body. A new election, boycotted by most of the leading opposition formations, was held November 29 and December 6, 1990, the Assembly having been reduced to 454 members, including the 10 presidential appointees.

Elections to the current Assembly were held in three segments (October 18 and 25, October 29 and November 5, and November 8 and 15, 2000) to accommodate a ruling from the Constitutional Court that the judiciary needed to monitor every polling station. (There were not enough judges available to conduct simultaneous nationwide balloting.) Many of the successful candidates initially ran as independents but joined (or rejoined) the governing National Democratic Party (NDP) prior to second-round balloting or soon after winning a seat. Consequently, according to officials results issued following the completion of those arrangements, the distribution of elected seats was as follows: the NDP, 388; the New Wafd Party, 7; the National Progressive Unionist Party, 6; the Nasserist Arab Democratic Party, 3; the Liberal Socialist Party, 1; independents, 37 (17 of whom had been identified as members of the Muslim Brotherhood); and vacant, 2. The next elections were scheduled for October 2005. Elections for the Shura Council, often referred to as the "upper house," were held in March 2004 for six-year terms, with one member of the leftist NPUP winning one seat. This marked the first time an opposition party took a seat on the council.

President: Dr. Ahmad Fathi SURUR.

Communications

The Supreme Press Council, established under a constitutional amendment in May 1980, oversees newspaper and magazine activity while government boards also direct the state information service, radio, and television. The government retains 51 percent ownership (exercised through the *Shura*) of many major newspapers and consequently exercises substantial editorial control. Although the development of an active and often highly critical opposition press was permitted in the 1980s, significant censorship has been imposed in recent years in conjunction with the conflict between the government and Islamic fundamentalist militants. A new press law was adopted in May 1995 providing for prison sentences and heavy fines for, among other things, "insulting" public officials or state institutions. However, in June 1996 some of the harshest elements of the new code were rescinded after the government was strongly criticized by domestic and international journalists for attempting to "muzzle" the press.

In February 2005, the president announced an end to imprisonment for various publication offenses, yet three months later, three journalists from an independent daily were found guilty of libeling the housing minister and sentenced to a year in jail.

Press

The following are Cairo dailies published in Arabic, unless otherwise noted: *al-Ahram* (1,000,000 daily, 1,200,000 Friday), semiofficial with *al-Ahram al-Massa'i* as an evening daily; *al-Akhbar* (800,000), Saturday edition published as *Akhbar al-Yawm* (1,100,000); *al-Jumhuriyah* (650,000), semi-official; *al-Misaa; Le Journal d'Egypte* (72,000), in French; *Egyptian Gazette* (36,000), in English; *Le Progrès Egyptien* (22,000), in French; *al-Hayat.* Among other newspapers are *al-Destour,* independent weekly; *al-Usbu,* independent "nationalist" weekly; and *al-Masr al-Yawm.* The party organs include the Socialist Labor Party's bi-weekly *al-Shaab* (50,000), which was closed in April 2005; the Socialist Liberal weekly *al-Ahrar;* the National Progressive Unionist weekly *al-Ahali;* The New Wafd's daily *al-Wafd;* the NDP's weekly *Shabab Beladi;* the Nasserist Arab Democratic Party's *al-Arabi*; the National Party's weekly *al-Umma*; and the Green Party's weekly *al-Khudr.*

News Agencies

The domestic agency is the Middle East News Agency–MENA (*Wakalat al-Anba' al-Sharq al-Awsat*). In addition, numerous foreign bureaus maintain offices at Cairo.

Broadcasting and Computing

The Egyptian Radio and Television Union (ERTU) operates numerous radio stations broadcasting in Arabic and other languages, and some three dozen television stations transmitting in two programs. Commercial radio service is offered by Middle East Radio (*Idha'at al-Sharq al-Awsat*). There were approximately 18.7 million television receivers and 1.5 million personal computers serving 2.7 million Internet users in 2003.

The first Egyptian communications satellite was launched by the European Space Agency in 1998; some 80 channels were expected to be broadcast regionally by the satellite, known as "Nilesat," under the control of the ERTU.

Intergovernmental Representation

Ambassador to the US
Nabil FAHMY

US Ambassador to Egypt
(Vacant)

Permanent Representative to the UN
Maged Abdelfattah ABDELAZIZ

IGO Memberships (Non-UN)
AfDB, AFESD, AMF, AU, BADEA, CAEU, CCC, Comesa, IDB, Interpol, IOM, LAS, NAM, OAPEC, OIC, OIF, PCA, WTO

IRAN

ISLAMIC REPUBLIC OF IRAN

Jomhori-e Islami-e Irân

Note: Shortly after taking office in August 2005, President Mahmoud Ahmadinejad appeared ready to return Iran to its revolutionary days of harsh rhetoric and international isolation after several years of reformist-led rule. During the campaign, Ahmadinejad promised a return to ultraconservative principles and a redistribution of Iran's vast oil wealth, but he quickly faced setbacks in implementing his domestic program. The parliament rejected three of his nominees to head the crucial Petroleum Ministry, citing their lack of experience, before finally approving Ahmadinejad's fourth choice. Iran elicited growing international concern over the purpose of its nuclear power program, which Teheran claims is only to produce energy but others suspect is being pursued to develop nuclear weapons. At the end of 2005, little progress had been made in negotiations with the United States and Europe to halt the country's conversion of uranium. Meanwhile, Ahmadinejad shocked the international community by calling for Israel to be "wiped off the map" and describing the Holocaust as a "myth."

The Country

A land of elevated plains, mountains, and deserts that is semiarid except for a fertile area on the Caspian coast, Iran is celebrated both for the richness of its cultural heritage and for the oil resources that have made it a center of world attention. Persians make up about one-half of the population, while the principal minority groups are Turks and Kurds, who speak their own languages and dialects. English and French are widely spoken in the cities. More than 90 percent of the people belong to the Shi'ite sect of Islam, the official religion. Prior to the 1979 Islamic revolution, women constituted approximately 10 percent of the paid labor force, with substantial representation in government and the professions. Since 1979, female participation in most areas of government has been limited, and many working women still serve as unpaid agricultural laborers on family landholdings. On the other hand, the government of President Ali Akbar Hashemi RAFSANJANI was less willing than its predecessor to enforce Islamic social codes, and at parliamentary balloting in 1992 and

1996 a number of women were top vote-getters in Teheran and outlying cities. Eleven female candidates were successful in the 2000 legislative elections. Educational and professional restrictions on women are less stringent, notwithstanding

widespread Western belief to the contrary, than in a number of nearby Arab states, although public socializing between the sexes is limited and most women cover their hair and limbs in public settings.

Despite a steady increase in petroleum production, both the economy and the society remained basically agricultural until the early 1960s, when a massive development program was launched. During the next decade and a half, the proportion of gross domestic product (exclusive of oil revenue) contributed by agriculture dropped by nearly 30 percent, Iran becoming a net importer of food in the course of a major population shift to urban areas. Under a 1973–1978 five-year plan, agriculture was slated to expand along with industry and oil and gas production; however, for a variety of reasons, including severe inflation and a substantial outflow of capital, these goals were not realized.

Conditions deteriorated further during the 1980–1988 war with Iraq, as heavy infrastructure damage contributed to a sharp reduction in petroleum exports. The government subsequently relaxed the tight economic controls imposed during the war, its new free-market posture emphasizing (at least rhetorically) the privatization of state-run enterprises, curtailment of agricultural subsidies, and efforts to attract foreign investment. However, although the long-term potential remained strong (Iran's oil reserves were estimated at upwards of 100 billion barrels), the economy was stressed through the mid-1990s by high inflation (exacerbated by cuts in state subsidies), rising unemployment, a fast-growing population, widespread corruption, a growing external debt burden, and food and housing shortages that sparked sporadic antigovernment demonstrations.

GDP grew by 4 percent in 1997, but growth slipped to 1 percent in 1998, primarily as the result of a dramatic drop in oil prices. By the end of 1998 unemployment was estimated at over 30 percent, with inflation running at more than 35 percent annually. The Khatami administration subsequently made overtures to the West in the hope of attracting investment, while pledging to revise domestic tax structures, simplify business regulations, and otherwise reform what has been described as an "impenetrable" and "dysfunctional" bureaucracy. However, reformists continued to face opposition from an "entrenched network" of merchants and conservative clerics, who, among other things, control the *bonyards*, foundations established following the 1979 revolution ostensibly to oversee the transfer of the assets of the shah's family to the underprivileged but which now exercise control over much of the financial sector and many public enterprises and services.

Real GDP growth rose to 3.6 percent in the 1999–2000 fiscal year and 5.7 percent in 2000–2001, mostly as the result of higher oil prices. The non-oil economic sector expanded by 6 percent in 2001–2002, contributing to total GDP growth of 4.8 percent despite a downward revision of oil production quotas by the Organization of the Petroleum Exporting Countries (OPEC). Also contributing to recent economic advances were liberalization measures, such as privatization, tax incentives for corporations, and loosening of trade regulations. Additional reform in 2002 included the licensing of the first private bank, approval of new foreign investment legislation, and adoption of a unified exchange rate. Nevertheless, substantial economic challenges remained, such as high unemployment (16 percent) within an increasingly youthful population (65 percent below the age of 25), poverty affecting an estimated 40 percent of the population, the ongoing drain on government resources by inefficient state-owned businesses, and a high number of refugees, especially from Afghanistan. The government has applied for membership in the World Trade Organization, but that request remained blocked as of 2005 by the United States, which objects to what it perceives as Iranian support for groups deemed to be responsible for terrorist activity (see Foreign relations and Current issues, below, for details). The United States and Israel have also criticized the World Bank's decision in 2000 to resume lending to Iran.

Political Status: Former monarchy; Islamic Republic proclaimed April 1–2, 1979, on basis of referendum of March 30–31; present constitution adopted at referendum of December 2–3, 1979.

Area: 636,293 sq. mi. (1,648,000 sq. km.).

Population: 60,055,488 (1996C, excluding adjustment for underenumeration); 67,431,000 (2004E).

Major Urban Centers (1999E): TEHERAN (6,935,000), Mashhad (1,968,000), Isfahan (1,357,000), Tabriz (1,257,000).

Official Language: Persian (Farsi).

Monetary Unit: Rial (official rate July 1, 2005: 8,980 rials = $1US). Until recently, a dual exchange rate was maintained—one (approximately 1,750 rials = $1US) for state imports of many basic goods and another, much higher, for all other transactions. To eliminate the economic distortions from that system–state enterprises were able to sell imports domestically at a much higher price than they had paid for them–a unified exchange

rate, established on a managed float basis, was adopted on March 21, 2002.

Supreme Religious Leader: Ayatollah Seyed Ali KHAMENEI; elected President October 2, 1981, and sworn in October 13, following the assassination of Mohammad Ali RAJAI on August 30; reelected August 16, 1985, and sworn in for a second four-year term on October 10; named Supreme Religious Leader by the Assembly of Experts on June 4, 1989, following the death of Ayatollah Ruhollah Musavi KHOMEINI on June 3.

President: Mahmoud AHMADINEJAD; elected in a runoff on June 24, 2005; confirmed on August 3 by the Supreme Religious Leader and sworn in before the legislature for a four-year term on August 6, succeeding Mohammad KHATAMI.

First Vice President: Mohamed Reza AREF; appointed by the President on August 25, 2001, to succeed Hasan Ebrahim HABIBI, who had announced his resignation on August 20.

Government and Politics

Political Background

Modern Iranian history began with nationalist uprisings against foreign economic intrusions in the late 19th century. In 1906 a coalition of clergy, merchants, and intellectuals forced the shah to grant a limited constitution. A second revolutionary movement, also directed largely against foreign influence, was initiated in 1921 by REZA Khan, an army officer who, four years after seizing power, ousted the Qajar family and established the Pahlavi dynasty. Although Reza Shah initiated forced modernization of the country with Kemalist Turkey as his model, his flirtation with the Nazis led to the occupation of Iran by Soviet and British forces in 1941 and his subsequent abdication in favor of his son, Mohammad Reza PAHLAVI. The end of World War II witnessed the formation of

separatist Azerbaijani and Kurdish regimes under Soviet patronage; however, these crumbled in 1946 because of pressure exerted by the United States and the United Nations. A subsequent upsurge of Iranian nationalism resulted in expropriation of the British-owned oil industry in 1951, during the two-year premiership of Mohammad MOSSADEQ.

In the wake of an abortive coup in August 1953, Mossadeq was arrested by loyalist army forces with assistance from the American Central Intelligence Agency. The period following his downfall was marked by the shah's assumption of a more active role, culminating in systematic efforts at political, economic, and social development that were hailed by the monarchy as a "White Revolution." However, the priorities established by the monarch, which included major outlays for sophisticated military weapon systems and a number of "showcase" projects (such as a subway system for the city of

Teheran), coupled with a vast influx of foreign workers and evidence of official corruption, led to criticism by traditional religious leaders, university students, labor unions, and elements within the business community.

In March 1975 the shah announced dissolution of the existing two-party system (both government and opposition parties having been controlled by the throne) and decreed the formation of a new National Resurgence Party to serve as the country's sole political group. In the face of mounting unrest and a number of public-service breakdowns in overcrowded Teheran, Emir Abbas HOVEYDA, who had served as prime minister since 1965, was dismissed in August 1977 and replaced by the National Resurgence secretary general, Jamshid AMOUZEGAR.

By late 1977 both political and religious opposition to the shah had further intensified. On December 11 a Union of National Front Forces was formed under Karim SANJABI, a former Mossadeq minister, to promote a return to the constitution, the nationalization of major industries, and the adoption of policies that would be "neither communist nor capitalist, but strictly nationalist." Conservative Muslim sentiment, on the other hand, centered on the senior mullah, Ayatollah Ruhollah KHOMEINI, who had lived in exile since mounting a series of street demonstrations against the "White Revolution" in 1963, and the more moderate Ayatollah Seyed Kazem SHARIATMADARI, based in the religious center of Qom. Both leaders were supported politically by the long-established Liberation Movement of Iran, led by Mehdi BAZARGAN.

By mid-1978 demonstrations against the regime had become increasingly violent, and Prime Minister Amouzegar was replaced on August 27 by the Senate president, Ja'afar SHARIF-EMAMI, whose parliamentary background and known regard for the country's religious leadership made him somewhat unique within the monarch's inner circle of advisers. Unable to arrest appeals for the shah's abdication, Sharif-Emami was forced to yield office on November 6 to a military government headed by the chief of staff of the armed forces, Gen. Gholam Reza AZHARI. The level of violence nonetheless continued to mount; numerous Kurds in northwest Iran joined the chorus of opposition, and the oil fields and major banks were shut down by strikes, bringing the economy to the verge of collapse. Thus, after an effort by Golam-Hossein SADIQI to form a new civilian government had failed, the shah on December 29 named a prominent National Front leader, Shahpur BAKHTIAR, as prime minister designate.

Ten days after Bakhtiar's formal investiture on January 6, 1979, the shah left the country on what was termed an extended "vacation." On February 1, amid widespread popular acclaim, Ayatollah Khomeini returned from exile, and a week later he announced the formation of a provisional government under a Revolutionary Council, which was subsequently reported to be chaired by Ayatollah Morteza MOTAHARI. On February 11 Prime Minister Bakhtiar resigned, with Bazargan being invested as his successor by the National Consultative Assembly immediately prior to the issuance of requests for dissolution by both the Assembly and the Senate.

Despite a series of clashes with ethnic minority groups, a referendum on March 30–31, 1979, approved the proclamation of an Islamic Republic by a reported 97 percent majority. A rising tide of political assassinations and other disruptions failed to delay the election on August 3 of a constituent assembly (formally called the Assembly of Experts) delegated to review a draft constitution that had been published in mid-June. The result of the council's work was subsequently approved in a national referendum on December 2–3 (see Constitution and government, below).

The most dramatic event of 1979 was the November 4 occupation of the US embassy at Teheran and the seizure of 66 hostages (13 of whom—5 white women and 8 black men—were released on November 17, while another was freed for health reasons in early July 1980), apparently in an effort to secure the return of the shah for trial; he had been admitted to a New York hospital for medical treatment. The action, undertaken by militant students, was not disavowed by the Revolutionary

Council, although the government appeared not to have been consulted. Prime Minister Bazargan felt obliged to tender his resignation the following day, without a successor being named. On December 4 the UN Security Council unanimously condemned the action and called for release of the hostages, while the International Court of Justice (ICJ) handed down a unanimous decision to the same effect on December 15. Both judgments were repudiated by Iranian leaders.

Notwithstanding the death of the shah in Egypt on July 27, 1980, and the outbreak of war with Iraq in late September (see Foreign relations, below), no resolution of the hostage issue occurred in 1980. American frustration at the lengthy impasse was partially evidenced by an abortive helicopter rescue effort undertaken by the US Air Force on April 24, and it was not until November 2 that Teheran agreed to formal negotiations with Washington, proposing the Algerian government as mediator. The remaining 52 hostages were ultimately freed after 444 days of captivity on January 20, 1981, coincident with the inauguration of Ronald Reagan as US president. In return for their freedom, Washington agreed (1) to abstain from interference in internal Iranian affairs; (2) to freeze the property and assets of the late shah's family pending resolution of lawsuits brought by the Islamic Republic; (3) to "bar and preclude" pending and future suits against Iran as a result of the 1979 revolution or the hostage seizure, with an Iran-United States Claims Tribunal to be established at The Hague, Netherlands; (4) to end trade sanctions against Teheran; and (5) to unfreeze some $7.97 billion in Iranian assets, including $2.87 billion to be transferred outright, $3.7 billion to be used as repayments for US bank loans, and $1.4 billion to be held in escrow to meet other commitments.

Internal developments in 1980 were highlighted by the election of the relatively moderate Abol Hasan BANI-SADR, a former advisor to Ayatollah Khomeini, as president on January 25 and the convening of a unicameral assembly, the *Majlis-e Shoura-e Islami*, on May 28, following two-stage balloting on March 14 and May 9. On August 9 Bani-Sadr reluctantly agreed to nominate Mohammad Ali RAJAI, an Islamic fundamentalist, as prime minister after three months of negotiations had failed to yield parliamentary support for a more centrist candidate.

Despite the support of secular nationalists, political moderates, much of the armed forces, and many Islamic leftists, Bani-Sadr was increasingly beleaguered by the powerful fundamentalist clergy centered around the Islamic Republican Party (IRP) and its (then) secretary general, Chief Justice of the Supreme Court Ayatollah Mohammad Hossein BEHESHTI. The IRP had emerged from the 1980 legislative balloting in firm control of the *Majlis,* enabling the clergy, ultimately with the support of Ayatollah Khomeini, to undermine presidential prerogatives during the first half of 1981. Moreover, on June 1 an arbitration committee, which had been established in the wake of violent clashes on March 5 between fundamentalists and Bani-Sadr supporters, declared that the president had not only incited unrest but had also violated the constitution by failing to sign into law bills passed by the *Majlis.* Nine days later, Khomeini removed Bani-Sadr as commander in chief, and on June 22, following a two-day impeachment debate in the assembly that culminated in a 177-1 vote declaring him incompetent, the chief executive was dismissed.

On June 28, 1981, a bomb ripped apart IRP headquarters at Teheran, killing Ayatollah Beheshti, 4 government ministers, 6 deputy ministers, 27 *Majlis* deputies, and 34 others. Prosecutor General Ayatollah Abdolkarim Musavi ARDEBILI was immediately appointed chief justice, while on July 24 Prime Minister Rajai, with more than 90 percent of the vote, was elected president. Having been confirmed by Ayatollah Khomeini on August 2, Rajai named Hojatolislam Mohammad Javad BAHONAR (Beheshti's successor as leader of the IRP) as prime minister, the *Majlis* endorsing the appointment three days later. Meanwhile, in late July deposed president Bani-Sadr, accompanied by Massoud RAJAVI of the *Mujaheddin-e Khalq* (see Political Parties and Groups, below), had fled to Paris, where he announced the formation of an exile National Resistance Council.

On August 30, 1981, President Rajai and Prime Minister Bahonar were assassinated by an explosion at the latter's offices, and on September 1 the minister of the interior, Hojatolislam Mohammad Reza MAHDAVI-KANI, was named interim prime minister. On October 2 Hojatolislam Seyed Ali KHAMENEI, Bahonar's replacement as secretary general of the IRP and a close associate of Khomeini, was elected president with 95 percent of the vote. Sworn in on October 13, he accepted the resignation of Mahdavi-Kani on October 15, with Mir Hosein MUSAVI, the foreign minister, being named the Islamic Republic's fifth prime minister on October 31, following confirmation by the *Majlis.* President Khamenei was elected to a second four-year term on August 16, 1985, defeating two IRP challengers. On October 13, following nomination by the president, Musavi was reconfirmed as prime minister.

At *Majlis* elections on April 8 and May 13, 1988, reformists won a clear majority. The elections, which were boycotted by the sole recognized opposition party, the Liberation Movement of Iran, also highlighted the increasing power of *Majlis* speaker Hojatolislam Ali Akbar Hashemi Rafsanjani, who on June 2 was named acting commander in chief of the armed forces. On June 6 Rafsanjani was renamed to his parliamentary post, despite the reported efforts of Ayatollah Hussein Ali MONTAZERI, Khomeini's officially designated successor, to force him to concentrate exclusively on his military responsibilities.

On March 27, 1989, following a meeting of the Presidium of the Assembly of Experts at which the "future leadership of the Islamic Republic" was discussed, Montazeri, declaring his "lack of readiness" for the position, submitted his resignation as deputy religious leader. On June 3 the 89-year-old Khomeini died, the Assembly of Experts designating President Khamenei as his successor the following day. On July 28 Iranians overwhelmingly voted their approval of constitutional changes that abolished the office of prime minister and significantly strengthened the powers of the theretofore largely ceremonial presidency. On August 17 Speaker Rafsanjani, who had been elected to succeed Khamenei as chief executive, was sworn in before the *Majlis,* and two days later he submitted a 22-member cabinet list that secured final approval on August 29.

At nationwide elections on October 8, 1990, to the Assembly of Experts, supporters of President Rafsanjani won a majority of seats, thus dealing a major setback to hard-line leaders. Rafsanjani further depleted the hard-liners' influence by, ironically, making assembly membership contingent on successful completion of an Islamic law examination. Furthermore, at parliamentary balloting in April and May 1992 Rafsanjani supporters captured an unexpectedly large majority of the seats, aided in part by the pro-Rafsanjani Council of Guardians' elimination of a number of hard-line *Majlis* candidates in March.

On June 11, 1993, President Rafsanjani was reelected to a second four-year term. However, despite lackluster opposition from three challengers selected by the Council of Guardians from a list of 128 presidential candidates, he won only 63.3 percent of the vote, a severe decline from the 94.5 percent registered in 1989. The president's slippage was also evident when the *Majlis,* while approving the remainder of the reshuffled cabinet on August 16, voted against the reappointment of Mohsen NURBAKHSH as minister of economic affairs and finance. Notwithstanding the obvious legislative dissatisfaction with current policies, Rafsanjani subsequently named Nurbakhsh to the newly created post of vice president for economic affairs, which did not require approval by the *Majlis.*

Cuts in state subsidies and consequent price increases triggered a series of riots in several cities in 1994, the assembly authorizing police to "shoot to kill" in any subsequent outbreaks. Thus, an estimated 30 people died when police opened fire during a disturbance near Teheran in April 1995. Nevertheless, President Rafsanjani vowed to persevere with his free-market reform policies, although it was widely conceded that little progress had been achieved in making the economy more efficient or the government bureaucracy less corrupt.

Elections to a new *Majlis* were held on March 8 and April 19, 1996, the balloting failing to produce a clear-cut victor in the battle between conservatives and moderates for political dominance. The results reflected the continued "quiet power struggle" between President Rafsanjani and Ayatollah Khamenei, whose supporters had accused the administration of having "wandered" from the path set by the 1979 revolution. With political primacy still apparently hanging in the balance, attention subsequently focused on the presidential election scheduled for May 1997, ruling clerics having emphasized that no constitutional amendments would be considered to permit a third term for Rafsanjani.

In what was considered an extraordinarily high voter turnout of 88 percent, Hojatolislam Seyed Mohammad KHATAMI, a moderate cleric, won the May 23, 1997, presidential poll with 20 million votes (69.5 percent) to 9 million combined votes for the three other candidates, including second-place (25 percent) Ali Akbar NATEQ-NURI, the conservative speaker of the *Majlis*, who was supported by Ayatollah Khamenei and the Society of Combatant Clergy, the majority conservative faction of the *Majlis*. Khatami, backed by various leftist groups as well as the moderate Servants of Construction, reportedly did well among women, students, the urban middle class, and other voters who apparently desired an end to Iran's international isolation, an easing of Islamic "vigilantism," and economic reform. The *Majlis* approved Khatami's cabinet recommendations on August 20; meanwhile, outgoing President Rafsanjani was named as president of the newly expanded Council for the Expediency of State Decrees (see Constitution and government, below), which included former cabinet members rejected by Khatami.

The election of President Khatami in May 1997 precipitated an extended tug-of-war for political and economic control between his reformist camp, which enjoyed widespread popular support, and the conservative clerics, who retained broad institutional power, often in alliance with intelligence services and businessmen. For his part, Khatami steadfastly pursued the "rule of law" and a civil society marked by greater nonclerical participation in governing bodies, expanded freedoms for individuals and the media, and tolerance for

divergent religious and political views (including the legalization of parties). He also steadfastly called for warmer ties with the West based on a "dialogue of civilizations" and attempted to convince neighboring states that Iran had no interest in establishing regional dominance. Conservatives tried to block democratization at many levels, including the *Majlis* (which forced the dismissal of several cabinet members) and the judiciary (which banned newspapers and took legal action against a number of reformists). The conservative cause appeared to receive a boost in the October 23, 1998, balloting for the Assembly of Experts, although their success was tainted by a relatively low turnout and the fact that many reform candidates had been barred from running by the conservative Council of Guardians. However, pro-Khatami candidates did very well in the municipal balloting of late February 1999, winning all of the seats on the Teheran Council and some 70 percent of the seats they contested overall. Significantly Ayatollah Khamanei, often associated with the conservative cause, did not support hard-liners in their efforts to ban reform candidates in the local elections.

Reformist candidates reportedly won about 70 percent of the seats in *Majlis* elections of February–May 2000, but the new membership's legislative efforts faced constant resistance from the Council of Guardians and the judiciary. The reformists maintained their electoral momentum in June 2001, when President Khatami was reelected with a reported 78 percent of the vote against nine challengers. The reformists suffered a major defeat in local elections held on February 28, 2003, with conservative candidates winning majorities in most major cities, as former supporters of the reformists chose to stay away from the polls. The conservative Builders of an Islamic Iran Council won 14 of 15 city council seats in Teheran. Turnout in the capital was reported at about 10 percent, with turnout nationwide reported at 39 percent.

In parliamentary elections held on February 20, 2004, conservatives won a sweeping victory after the Council of Guardians disqualified more than a third of the candidates. Some 80 incumbent reformist MPs were among those barred from standing for election. The Builders of an Islamic Iran Council won a majority, securing about 144 of 229 seats. The Interior Ministry reported turnout at 28 percent in Teheran and 50.57 percent nationwide, the lowest since the 1979 revolution. After a second round, held on May 7 to determine remaining seats, the conservatives had secured at least 200 of 290 seats. Within the conservative majority, the Builders of an Islamic Iran Council controlled about 195 of those. Lesser-known reformists without formal ties to established political parties and associations were left with a small bloc of about 40 seats.

In the 2005 presidential elections, conservative candidate Mahmoud AHMADINEJAD, the mayor of Teheran, won a runoff vote against former president Rafsanjani on June 24. Ahmadinejad won 61.64 percent while Rafsanjani received 35.93 percent, a difference of more than 7 million votes. Turnout for the runoff was reported at 59.72 percent compared to 62.66 percent in the first round (in which seven candidates competed). Reformist and former *Majlis* speaker Mehdi KARRUBI, who stood as a candidate in the first round on June 17, alleged rampant voter fraud and irregularities in an open letter to the supreme leader.

Constitution and Government

The constitution of December 1979 established Shi'ite Islam as the official state religion, placed supreme power in the hands of the Muslim clergy, and named Ayatollah Ruhollah Khomeini as the nation's religious leader (*velayat-e faqih*) for life. The *velayat-e faqih* is also supreme commander of the armed forces and the Revolutionary Guard, can declare war, and can dismiss the president following a legislative request or a ruling of the Supreme Court. He is also formally responsible for the "delineation" of national policies in all areas, although some de facto authority was assumed by other officials following Ayatollah Khomeini's death in 1989.

An elected 86-member assembly of Experts appoints the country's spiritual leader and has broad powers of constitutional interpretation. (Members of the Assembly are popularly elected for eight-year terms. Previously, only mullahs were permitted to run; however, revisions approved prior to the 1998 balloting permitted nonclerics to stand for the assembly, although their candidacies were still subject to approval by the Council of Guardians.) The president, the country's chief executive officer, is popularly elected for a maximum of two four-year terms. Members of the unicameral *Majlis,* to which legislative authority is assigned, also serve four-year terms. The post of prime minister was eliminated as part of basic law revisions approved by referendum in July 1989, the president being authorized to appoint members of the Council of Ministers, subject to legislative approval. The *Majlis* was also empowered to impeach the president by a one-third vote of its members and to request his dismissal by a two-thirds vote. In the event of a presidential vacancy, an election to refill the office must be held within 50 days. A Council of Guardians, encompassing six clerics specializing in Islamic law appointed by the *velayat-e faqih* and six nonclerical jurists elected by the legislature from nominees selected by the High Council of the Judiciary, is empowered to veto candidates for the presidency, *Majlis,* and Assembly of Experts and to nullify laws considered contrary to the constitution or the Islamic faith. (No constitutional provision having been made for the vetting by the Council of Guardians of candidates in municipal elections, the *Majlis* established a special committee for that purpose prior to the February 1999 local balloting.) In addition, a Council for the Expediency of State Decrees, composed of six clerics and seven senior governmental officials, was created in February 1988 to mediate differences between the *Majlis* and the more conservative Council of Guardians. (The authority and size of the Expediency Council were expanded in March 1997 by Ayatollah Khamenei, transforming the Council from an arbitrative panel to an "august consultative body," comprising a wider range of members, such as technocrats and faction leaders.) There is also a Supreme Council for National Security, established under the 1989 constitutional amendments to replace the National Defense Council. The new council, which coordinates defense and security policies and oversees all intelligence services, comprises the president, who serves as chairman, two members appointed by the *faqih*, the chief justice of the Supreme Court, the speaker of the *Majlis*, and several military and ministerial representatives. Political parties are technically authorized to the extent that they "do not violate the independence, sovereignty, national unity, and principles of the Islamic Republic."

The civil courts instituted under the monarchy were replaced by Islamic Revolutionary Courts, judges being mandated to reach verdicts on the basis of precedent and/or Islamic law. The legal code subsequently underwent numerous changes, and on several occasions Ayatollah Khomeini called for the purging of judges who were deemed unsuitable or exceeded their authority. In August 1982 it was announced that all laws passed under the former regime would be annulled if contrary to Islam, while on September 23 homosexuality and consumption of alcohol were added to an extensive list of capital offenses. Although individuals are guaranteed a constitutional right to counsel, summary trials and executions were common following the 1979 revolution, many victims being suspected leftists or guerrillas.

Iran is administratively divided into 25 provinces (*ostans*); in addition, there are nearly 500 counties (*shahrestan*) and a similar number of municipalities (*bakhsh*). The first municipal elections ever were conducted in February 1999, reformers hoping that substantial authority would eventually be shifted from the national government to the local councils.

Foreign Relations

Although a charter member of the United Nations, Iran momentarily curtailed its participation in the world body upon the advent of the Islamic Revolution. It boycotted the 1979 Security Council debate on seizure of the US embassy at Teheran but joined in UN condemnation of the Soviet presence in Afghanistan late in the year.

An active member of OPEC, Iran was long in the forefront of those urging aggressive pricing policies, as opposed to the more moderate posture of Saudi Arabia and other conservative members. After 1980, however, a combination of the world oil glut and the need to finance its war effort forced Iran to sell petroleum on the spot market at prices well below those set by OPEC; concurrently, it joined Algeria and Libya in urging a "fair share" strategy aimed at stabilizing prices through drastic production cutbacks.

A major international drama erupted in late 1986 with the revelation that members of the US Reagan administration had participated in a scheme involving the clandestine sale of military equipment to Iran, the proceeds of which were to be used to support anti-Sandinista *contra* forces in Nicaragua. In early 1989 relations with the West, which had recently improved, again plummeted when British authorities refused to enjoin publication of Salman Rushdie's *Satanic Verses,* a work considered deeply offensive to Muslims worldwide, with Khomeini issuing a death decree against the author in February.

Iran and its western neighbor, Iraq, have long been at odds over their borders, principally over control of the Shatt al-'Arab waterway linking the Persian Gulf to the major oil ports of both countries (see Iraq map, p. 547). Although the dispute was ostensibly resolved by a 1975 accord dividing the waterway along the thalweg (median) line, Iraq abrogated the treaty on September 17, 1980, and invaded Iran's Khuzistan Province on September 22. Despite early reversals, Iran succeeded in retaining control of most of the larger towns, including the besieged oil center of Abadan, and by the end of the year the conflict had resulted in a military stalemate. The war had the immediate effect of accentuating disunity within the Islamic world, the more radical regimes of Libya, Syria, and South Yemen supporting Teheran, and the more conservative governments of Jordan, Egypt, and the Gulf states favoring Baghdad.

Despite mediation efforts by the United Nations, the Organization of the Islamic Conference, the Nonaligned Movement, and various individual countries, fighting continued, with Iran advancing into Iraqi territory for the first time in July 1982. Rejecting a cease-fire overture, Teheran demanded $150 billion in reparations, ouster of the Saddam Hussein government, and Iraqi repatriation of expelled Shi'ites. By early 1984 Iranian forces had made marginal gains on the southern front, including capture of the bulk of the Majnoon oil fields north of Basra, with what was essentially a stalemate prevailing for the ensuing three years.

A renewal of Iranian military offensives in late 1987 proved futile, as Iraqi troops drove Iranian troops from Basra and half of the Iranian Navy was reported lost during fighting with US battleships protecting oil tankers in the Gulf. In February 1988 the "war of the cities" recommenced, with Iran and Iraq bombarding each other's capitals and other densely populated centers. Thereafter, the combination of Iraq's increasing use of chemical weapons and major military supply shortages led Iran to agree to a cease-fire on July 18. Ensuing peace talks, mediated by the United Nations, were slowed by friction over the return of prisoners, the Iraqi demand for free passage through the Shatt al-'Arab waterway, and Iranian insistence that Iraq be condemned for initiating the fighting. However, despite allegations by both sides that the other was rearming, the cease-fire continued into 1990, being succeeded by a peace agreement on what were essentially Iranian terms (i.e., a return to the 1975 accord) in the wake of the crisis generated by Iraq's seizure of Kuwait in August 1990. (As of 2002 Iran continued to insist that a final formal peace accord had yet to be negotiated with Iraq regarding the 1980–1988 war, arguing that issues such as reparations and a full accounting of prisoners of war remained unresolved.)

Iran played a somewhat ambivalent role during the Gulf drama of 1990–1991, declaring its "full agreement" with those condemning the Kuwaiti invasion but opposing the deployment of US troops to the region. In September 1990 it denied that it had secretly agreed to help break the UN embargo by importing some 200,000 barrels a day of Iraqi crude oil. Subsequently, it provided "haven" for upwards of 100 Iraqi warplanes upon commencement of Operation Desert Storm in January 1991. Iran retained the planes upon the conclusion of hostilities and a year later confiscated them in what it termed partial satisfaction of reparations stemming from the Iran-Iraq conflict.

As the Gulf crisis subsided, Iran's top two leaders, Ayatollah Khamenei and President Rafsanjani, appeared to have reached an unspoken understanding to cooperate in countering the influence of their more radical colleagues by seeking a reduction in friction with the United States and other Western powers, as well as with regional Arab governments, including Iraq. In the wake of Saddam Hussein's humiliating military defeat, Teheran voiced sympathy for Iraq's Shi'ites, while insisting that it was providing no military support for the southern rebels. In essence, it attempted to position itself midway between two former antagonists: Iraq, which it wished to see weakened but not destroyed, and the United States, whose power it acknowledged, but which it did not welcome as a permanent arbiter of Middle Eastern affairs.

In May 1991 the administration of George Bush announced that it would not welcome improved relations until Teheran used its influence to secure the release of hostages held by pro-Iranian groups in Lebanon. The Iranian foreign ministry indicated in return that the hostage issue might soon become a "non-problem," particularly if some $10 billion of impounded Iranian assets were released by Washington. Shortly thereafter, the United States agreed to resume purchasing Iranian oil with the stipulation that all payments would go into an escrow account established by the ICJ.

For the remainder of 1991 Teheran continued its efforts to emerge from political and economic isolation, hosting an international human rights conference in September and taking an active role in the release of the remaining US and UK hostages in Lebanon. However, despite a US agreement in December to compensate Iran $278 million for undelivered military equipment, further rapprochement was stymied by Teheran's opposition to

US-brokered Middle East talks and President Rafsanjani's condemnation of American efforts to persuade China and India to stop transferring nuclear equipment to Iran.

In April 1991 Iran generated concern among its Persian Gulf neighbors by expelling Arab residents from Abu Musa, a small island in the middle of the waterway that along with two adjacent islands, Large Tunb and Small Tunb, had long been viewed as belonging to the United Arab Emirates, but had been jointly administered since Iranian occupation of Abu Musa in 1971 (see UAE map, p. 1228). The dispute continued into 1997, Iran having rejected the Arab League's call for ICJ arbitration. By that time, Teheran had also been accused by the government of Bahrain of having supported a coup attempt in that island nation (see article on Bahrain).

Complicating matters were a decision in March 1995 by Conoco Inc. under heavy pressure from Washington, to abandon a proposed $1 billion contract with Iran for the development of offshore oil and natural gas fields and the subsequent imposition by US President Bill Clinton of a full embargo on US trade and investment with Iran, effective in mid-June. Describing Iran as an "outlaw state" because of its alleged complicity in international terrorism and its pursuit, according to US officials, of nuclear weapons capability, Washington also called upon Moscow and Beijing to forgo their respective plans to sell nuclear reactors to Iran for the production of electricity.

In January 1996 it was revealed that some $18 million had been approved for the American CIA to support efforts to "change the nature" of the Iranian government. Washington subsequently attempted to intensify pressure on Teheran by authorizing sanctions against foreign companies which invest significantly in Iran's oil and gas industries.

A German court appeared to support American charges that Iran had engaged in "state-sponsored terrorism" when it ruled in April 1997 that senior Iranian officials were involved in the 1992 assassinations of Iranian Kurdish separatists in a German restaurant. Bonn withdrew its ambassador to Teheran following the ruling, with other EU members (except Greece) following suit. The EU's action, however, was temporary (the ambassadors returned in November) and did little to dissuade critics of America's unilateral policy of sanctions against Iran. Former US national security advisors Zbigniew Brzezinski and Brent Scowcroft, for example, said the costly sanctions were not isolating Iran but were instead alienating American allies while driving Teheran and Moscow closer. (Relations were strained, for example, between France and the United States in September 1997 when a French company [part of a multinational consortium] signed a gas deal with Teheran, despite the US announcement that it would target the American assets of any business, domestic or foreign, which made deals larger than $40 million with Iran.) Iran had reportedly been receiving Russian help with a ballistic missile program and, according to the *New York Times*, Moscow agreed to withdraw support of the program under American and Israeli pressure in 1997. Meanwhile, in November the United States bought 21 Soviet-era MIG-29s from Moldova to keep them from being sold to Iran.

Washington seemed more receptive to rapprochement with Teheran following the election of moderate President Khatami in May 1997. At the end of July Secretary of State Madeleine Albright confirmed that the United States would not oppose the construction of a transnational Central Asian gas pipeline that would cross northern Iran, the first major economic concession to Iran since the 1979 revolution. Teheran's relations with Iraq, Syria, and the Gulf states, especially Saudi Arabia, also improved following Khatami's victory.

In a televised interview in January 1998 President Khatami proposed cultural exchanges with the United States. He also expressed a willingness to reconsider Iran's severed relationship with the United States and, in reply, the US State Department suggested direct negotiations. However, Iran's powerful conservative spiritual leader, Ayatollah Ali Khamenei, subsequently lashed out at the United States, reconfirming deep internal divisions in the Iranian leadership.

The most significant regional tension in 1998 involved neighboring Afghanistan, where Taliban forces launched a midyear campaign to gain control of those parts of the country previously held by opposition forces. Teheran, angered at the unexplained killing of a number of its diplomats in Afghanistan and concerned over the fate of the anti-Taliban Shi'ite community in the central area of that country, massed more than 200,000 troops along the border in September, and war seemed imminent. Both sides subsequently showed a degree of restraint, however, moderates in Teheran reportedly expressing the fear that a military adventure would compromise Iran's hope to become the "gateway" for the economic markets opening up in Central Asia. Similar motivation also partially explained Teheran's announcement in September that it had disassociated itself from the *fatwa* against Salman Rushdie, a decision that prompted the reestablishment of full relations with the United Kingdom. President Khatami's "charm offensive" toward Europe subsequently included a visit to the Vatican in March 1999.

Toward the end of the Clinton administration in 1999–2000, trade restrictions against Iran were reduced and Secretary of State Albright announced official "regret" over the US role in the 1953 coup and for supporting Iraq in the 1980–1988 Iraq-Iran War. However, the new Bush administration adopted a much less conciliatory stance in the first half of 2001, based on what it claimed was Iranian support for militant Palestinian groups, such as Islamic Holy War and *Hamas,* as well as *Hezbollah* guerrillas in Lebanon. (The Iranian government contended that it provides only "moral support" and humanitarian aid for such groups and does not belong on the US list of state sponsors of terrorism.) Moderate Iranians had hoped that a new era in relations with Washington would develop following the US-led campaign against *al-Qaeda* and Taliban forces in Afghanistan in late 2001, Iran having reportedly supplied useful intelligence and other assistance to support that effort in light of its different view of Islam than that expressed by *al-Qaeda* and the Taliban. However, expectations of rapprochement with Washington were dashed in

January 2002, when President George W. Bush accused Iran as forming, along with Iraq and North Korea, an "axis of evil" threatening global security. That depiction prompted widespread anti-American demonstrations in February, and President Khatami accused Washington of "bullying" many other countries in the world through its "war on terrorism." Nevertheless, the United States continued its pressure, with Bush in August accusing Iran of seeking to develop weapons of mass destruction and demanding that Russia cease assistance to Iranian nuclear activities. On the other hand, the EU considered Iran's posture in a much less provocative light and launched new talks with Teheran on possible trade liberalization measures.

Iran officially opposed the US-led invasion of neighboring Iraq in 2003 but nevertheless welcomed the ouster of President Saddam Hussein and allowed Iraqi opposition figures to travel freely from Iran to northern Iraq on the eve of the war. While viewing the US military presence in Iraq and Afghanistan (and elsewhere in Central Asia) as a potential threat, the Iranian leadership has moved to assert its influence in a country with a majority Shi'ite population. The US-led campaign in Afghanistan against the Taliban removed another hostile regime on its border. Iran exerts political and economic influence in the Herat region.

In Iraq, Iran enjoys close ties to prominent Shi'ite political figures, especially those from the Supreme Council of Islamic Revolution in Iraq (SCIRI), whose leaders won positions of authority in the new Iraq political system. Iran had provided refuge and assistance to SCIRI during the 1980–1988 Iran-Iraq War, arming the group's military wing, the Badr Brigade. Iran also has long-established ties to Iraqi president, Jalal Talabani, the head of the Patriotic Union of Kurdistan who cooperated with Iran in opposing Hussein. Iran reportedly operates an extensive intelligence network in Iraq and provides support to Shi'ite mosques and influential religious charities. US officials accused Iran of "meddling" in Iraq and failing to police its border with Iraq.

Iran's nuclear program became the focus of international scrutiny following revelations–revealed in satellite photographs provided by the exiled Mujaheddin-e Khalq in August 2002 (see reference to MKO below)–that it had failed to disclose an elaborate underground uranium enrichment facility in Natanz and a heavy-water plant in Arak. Iranian officials obstructed inspectors from the International Atomic Energy Agency (IAEA) and provided contradictory explanations to them when they inquired into the nature of Iran's nuclear program. Facing possible referral to the UN Security Council, in October 2003 Iran negotiated a tentative agreement with Britain, France, and Germany–the E3, acting as representatives of the European Union–to allow more intrusive inspections and to divulge the full history of its program in return for access to civilian nuclear technology. Iran also volunteered to temporarily suspend uranium enrichment activities while negotiations continued with the Europeans. In the meantime, however, additional questions were raised about the nature of Iran's nuclear program and the government's intentions when the IAEA found traces of highly enriched uranium. Iran insisted that its activities were solely for the purpose of producing electricity, but the United States accused Teheran of secretly working to build nuclear weapons.

As of August 2005, talks between Iran and European governments had made little progress, and Iran, dismissing European proposals as "insulting," announced that it would end its voluntary suspension of uranium enrichment activities. The Iranians reopened a uranium conversion plant in Isfahan in August 2005, declaring that it was fully within its rights under the nuclear Non-Proliferation Treaty to pursue uranium enrichment and activities associated with it. Iranian officials have warned that any US or Israeli military action against its nuclear sites would result in retaliation against US and Israeli targets. Support for Iran's nuclear program tends to cut across internal factional and ideological lines, with the establishment viewing the nuclear project as a point of national pride and an assertion of sovereignty. The political and military leadership views the program as a possible deterrent to any possible US military attack.

Current Issues

The success of the "reform tide" in the February 1999 municipal elections triggered a harsh response from the conservative judiciary, which, among other things, suspended the publication of many of the recently established newspapers that had been fueling reformist sentiment. Prodemocracy demonstrations (primarily on the part of students) at midyear were met with violent counterdemonstrations involving what critics described as "Islamic vigilantes," some of them organized in the *Ansar-e Hezbollah* militia. President Khatami played a significant role in quelling what was described as the nation's worst rioting since 1979 by urging his followers to show "restraint." His admonition reportedly cost him a degree of support within the radical reform wing but nevertheless prevented the "extreme polarization" toward which many analysts feared the country was heading. However, tensions intensified substantially following the overwhelming victory of reformist candidates in the 2000 *Majlis* balloting. The Council of Guardians subsequently decreed that the new legislature was not authorized to overturn antireform legislation hastily approved by the outgoing *Majlis* and also barred the reformists from launching investigations into judicial structures and activities. In addition, a number of aides and associates of President Khatami were subsequently arrested or otherwise harassed, as were a number of prominent legislators. For his part, Khatami initially expressed reluctance in early 2001 toward running for another term, saying that prodemocracy activists had paid a "heavy price" and suggesting that expectations for institutional change may have been "too high." Following his landslide reelection, Khatami focused greater attention on economic rather than political reform, the former appearing much less threatening to the conservative power bases. Nevertheless, the "unrelenting" campaign against reformists continued throughout the remainder of 2001 and into 2002. Despite the deep societal cleavages arising from the domestic political deadlock, the Iranian population seemed relatively united regarding foreign affairs. Reformists and conservative hard-liners alike reacted strongly and angrily to President Bush's inclusion of Iran in the "axis of evil" in early 2002. All segments of Iranian society solidly supported the Palestinian cause.

Khatami appeared poised for a collision with the conservative establishment when he submitted two draft laws to the *Majlis* in September 2002 designed to break the conservatives blocking his cabinet and the parliament from implementing their reformist agenda. One bill called for restrictions on the power of the Council of Guardians to vet electoral candidates and the second provided for increased presidential oversight of the judiciary. Khatami's advisers said the president would resign or call a national referendum if the Council of Guardians rejected the bills, but when the bills were vetoed (as expected), Khatami chose to remain in office. His refusal to openly confront the conservatives led to divisions within reformist ranks and growing popular disillusionment. The Council of Guardians' consistent obstruction of parliament and the judiciary's repression of reformist voices and media succeeded in deflating public expectations, intimidating popular opposition, and sowing discord among reformists. After the regime crushed large street demonstrations that erupted in 1999 following the closure of a reformist newspaper, popular protests steadily dwindled. Student activists leading the demonstrations soon broke ranks with the reformist coalition, sharply criticizing Khatami for his cautious stance.

The reformists had once drawn some authority and leverage from their popular mandate, but public support gradually receded as time passed and concrete change failed to materialize. The reformists suffered their first electoral setback in municipal elections in February 2003 amid low voter turnout. The conservatives, having organized their supporters, won in most major cities, including in Isfahan, Kerman, Mahshad, and Shiraz. In Teheran, the newly formed conservative political group Builders of an Islamic Iran Council won 14 of 15 city council seats. The bickering reformist parties failed to agree on a unified candidate list and instead offered voters three rival lists. On May 3, 2003, the new Teheran council selected as mayor Mamoud AHMADINEJAD, an obscure conservative, engineer, and former officer in the Revolutionary Guards.

Prior to the 2004 parliamentary elections, the Council of Guardians had undermined the reformists by banning more than 2,300 of the approximately 8,200 aspiring candidates, including some 80 sitting MPs. The reformist MPs held a sit-in in the parliamentary lobby to protest the ban but failed to rally public support. One-third of the MPs offered their resignations. Following vague calls for compromise by the supreme religious leader, the Council of Guardians reinstated a small number of candidates, though no prominent reformist MPs seeking reelection. The council gave no specific reasons for the disqualifications, but deemed the blacklisted candidates as failing to uphold and respect the principles of the Islamic Republic and the authority of the supreme leader. Calling the ban a "bloodless coup," the largest reformist party, the Islamic Iran Participation Front (IIPF), abstained from participating in the election. The ban meant that reformists had no candidates in more than 70 constituencies. Some reformist candidates allowed to run withdrew in protest. Cabinet ministers hinted that they might refuse to organize the election, but they eventually backed away from their threats.

The elections proceeded as scheduled on February 20, 2004, with the conservative Builders of an Islamic Iran Council winning a large majority, securing some 155 of 229 seats. A second round of voting was held on May 7, 2004, to determine remaining seats (except for certain Teheran constituencies, where voting would be held in conjunction with the 2005 presidential polling). In the second round, the conservatives won a majority, with Builders of an Islamic Iran Council taking an additional 40 seats, bringing their majority in the *Majlis* to at least 195. The overall conservative majority is estimated at 200 to 210 seats. The Interior Ministry reported turnout at 28 percent in Teheran and 50.57 percent nationwide, the lowest since the 1979 revolution. The Council of Guardians disagreed with the ministry, insisting that the turnout was higher. Lesser-known reformists without formal ties to established political parties controlled an insignificant bloc of about 40 seats. The outcome of the dispute over prospective candidates as well as the election results marked a resounding defeat for the reformists. Some voices within the reformists, including leaders of the IIPF, argued that the country's theocratic system was fundamentally undemocratic and required constitutional amendments to enhance the authority of elected representatives.

In the run-up to the 2005 presidential elections, reformists and conservatives were both divided over whom to nominate for office. The Council of Guardians barred hundreds of candidates from running, including all female candidates and Mostafa Moin, who had served as minister of science in Khatami's cabinet. Moin's candidacy, however, was permitted after the supreme leader intervened. In a field of seven candidates, former president Rafsanjani won the most votes in the first round of polling, with 21.01 percent, but failed to secure a majority, forcing an unprecedented run-off. Contrary to forecasts by political commentators, the Teheran mayor, Ahmadinejad, had finished second with 19.48 percent of the vote, beating out more prominent conservative figures. One of the reformist candidates, former *Majlis* speaker Mehdi Karrubi, finished behind Ahmadinejad by a margin of less than 1 percent after leading in earlier tallies. In an open letter to the supreme leader, Karrubi alleged that voting had been rigged and that the son of the supreme leader had been involved in the fraud. Rafsanjani's aides also alleged widespread irregularities and manipulations carried out by paramilitaries and militia.

In the runoff, held on June 24, Ahmadinejad won an overwhelming victory over Rafsanjani, taking 61.64 percent of the vote, or 17,284,782 votes—more than triple the number he had received in the first round. Rafsanjani received 35.93 percent, or 10,046,701 votes. Turnout was reported at 59.6 percent, slightly lower than the 62.66 percent reported in the first round. During the campaign, Ahmadinejad had contrasted his humble background with Rafsanjani's image as a member of the privileged elite and promised to address growing in-

equality between the rich and poor. Reformists had set aside their uneasy relations with Rafsanjani and called on their supporters to vote for him to prevent "fascism."

With Ahmadinejad's election, the conservatives regained control of all the elected institutions; the supreme leader consolidated his power. The reformist project launched by Khatami had scored some successes in foreign relations and fostered a more open atmosphere. It ultimately met with defeat, because in the end the conservative establishment proved unwilling to relinquish authority or to tolerate democratic and social reform. The US military presence in neighboring Iraq and Afghanistan prompted the conservatives to invoke national security concerns, portraying the reformists as traitorous for questioning the premises of the theocracy and reaching out to Western governments. With the reformists in disarray, high oil prices bolstering state revenues, and Shi'ite allies leading the government in Iraq, the supreme leader and the conservative clerical establishment faced no immediate threat to their hold on power.

Political Parties and Groups

Although political parties are permitted under the constitution, none was recognized following the formal dissolution of the government-sponsored Islamic Republican Party in June 1987, despite Teheran's announcement in October 1988 that such groupings would thenceforth be welcomed if they "demonstrated commitment to the Islamic system." A number of new political formations were identifiable during the *Majlis* elections of 1996, although it was carefully noted by the government that they were not official parties. Meanwhile, some former parties appeared to remain informally tolerated. Supporters of President Mohammad Khatami were reported in 1998 to have achieved recognition as the first full-fledged political party since the 1979 revolution (see Islamic Iran Solidarity Party, below), and several others also subsequently achieved legal status. However, the main political formations have continued to be organizations acting in a "pseudo-party" capacity by, among other things, presenting candidate lists for legislative elections without having sought formal party registration. Political parties in Iran tend to operate as small clubs, personal platforms, or loosely defined ideological associations rather than as large organizations with grass roots networks or formal, disciplined structures. Membership in one does not preclude membership in another, and the associations tend to lack detailed policy manifestos. Some appear before an election and quickly fade afterward.

Builders of an Islamic Iran Council (*Etelaf-e Abadgaran-e Iran-e Eslami*). This group, whose name is also translated as Developers of an Islamic Iran Council, first emerged in the local elections of February 2003, presenting largely unknown, younger candidates on the Teheran ballot with strong backing from senior conservatives in the political establishment. The party won control of the Teheran city council, which had been paralyzed by feuds among reformist council members. The council elected Mahmoud Ahmadinejad as mayor, who at one point proposed converting city parks into cemeteries for war dead, a suggestion he later withdrew. The group in some cases operated under alternative names outside of Teheran. Employing vague slogans calling for economic progress and adherence to "Islamic values," the party launched a well-financed campaign for the 2004 parliamentary elections. With more than 2,300 reformist candidates barred from appearing on the ballot, the group secured a large majority of at least 195 seats in the *Majlis*. A significant number of the newly elected MPs included former officers in the Revolutionary Guards. The most powerful figure in the party is Gholam-Ali Haddad-Adel, son-in-law of the supreme leader, who was selected Speaker of the *Majlis*. The group originally endorsed Mohammad Baqer QALIBAF, the former chief of police forces, before the first round of the 2005 presidential elections, but later backed Ahmadinejad in his successful bid. Although encompassing a range of views on economic policy without a clear ideological vision, the group has become the most prominent conservative party, at least in the public arena.

The party has drawn membership from the Society of Islamic Engineers, which has roots in traditional conservative circles and helped publicize the Builders of an Islamic Iran Council. The deputy speaker of the Majlis, Reza BAHONAR, comes from the society, as does Ahmadinejad. Following their election, the party's MPs adopted strident, populist language, impeached Khatami's transport minister, urged an uncompromising stance on the nuclear issue and adopted measures hostile to foreign investment. After successive electoral victories, it may eclipse other older conservative parties, as it has been widely perceived as a vehicle for the supreme leader. Opponents allege that the supreme leader's son, Mojtaba Khamenei, plays an influential role in the party.

Leaders: Gholam-Ali HADDAD-ADEL (Speaker of the *Majlis*), Mehdi KOUCHA-KZADEH (MP), Hossein FADAEI (MP).

Society of Combatant Clergy (*Jam'e Rohaniat Mobarez*–JRM). This hard-line conservative group continues to exert influence within the political establishment although, like other older conservative groups, it has been overshadowed on the public stage by the Builders of an Islamic Iran Council. Along with the Islamic Coalition Society (see below), the group vehemently opposed the reformist agenda and remains committed to perpetuating the country's rigid political and cultural restrictions. With strong ties to the clergy, the party sees Iran as representing the interests of the Islamic world. In the 2005 presidential elections, the group initially backed Ali Larijani, former director of the state television and radio monopoly, prompting criticism from Ahmadinejad's supporters that the group was causing divisions within the conservative camp.

The JRM was formed in late 1970s in support of the then-exiled Ayatollah Khomeini. (The JRM has often been referenced, as it was in recent *Handbooks,* as the Association of Combatant Clergy. The JRM abbreviation and translation of "Jame'e" as "society" has been adopted for this edition of the *Handbook* in order to assist the reader in differentiating between the conservative JRM and its influential moderate offshoot, the Assembly of Combatant Clergy [MRM; see below]. Readers are cautioned to assess news reports carefully, as the two groupings are routinely confused because of the similarity of their names.) The JRM served as the primary vehicle for clerical political representation following the installation of Khomeini as the nation's leader in 1979, with the JRM and Servants of Construction (SC) being seen as breakaway groups. Although the JRM essentially concurred with the SC in the mid-1990s regarding proposed economic reform, it argued that ultimate political authority should remain with the nation's religious leaders, adopting as a result a conservative stance on such issues as proposed expanded press freedoms and reinstitution of a formal party system.

As of late 1995 the society was believed to control about 150 seats in the *Majlis*, giving it significant policy influence under the leadership of Speaker Ali Akbar Nateq-Nuri. Having apparently done poorly in the first round of voting for the new *Majlis* in March 1996, the JRM adopted a hard-line approach for the second round, denouncing "liberals" as a threat to the ideals of the 1979 revolution. According to a number of observers, that campaign was assisted by *Hezbollah* militants, who, among other things, reportedly disrupted meetings of "un-Islamic" groupings.

It was subsequently estimated that society supporters had secured about 110 seats in the new *Majlis* in 1996. Although this represented the loss of its former "overall majority," the JRM was nevertheless able to secure the reelection of Nateq-Nuri as speaker by a reported vote of 146–105. JRM adherents later served as the core of the new *Hezbollah* faction in the *Majlis,* with Nateq-Nuri unsuccessfully carrying the standard of the conservative clerics in the May 1997 presidential election. He received 7.2 million votes to 20 million for the victorious Mohammad Khatami. However, Nateq-Nuri was reelected as *Majlis* speaker in both 1997 and 1998. The JRM was not widely referenced in regard to the 1999 municipal balloting. Many of its 2000 *Majlis* candidates were presented in conjunction with the Islamic Coalition Society. The JRM did not endorse a candidate in the 2001 presidential balloting, thereby diluting the conservatives' chances of mounting an effective challenge to President Khatami.

Leader: Ali Akbar NATEQ-NURI (Former Speaker of the *Majlis*), Mohammad Reza MAHDAVI-KANI (Founder), Assadollah BADA-MCHIAN.

Islamic Coalition Society (*Jameyat-e Motalefe-ye Eslami*). An umbrella organization of hard-line conservative clerics and merchants with links to the late Ayatollah Khomeini, the Islamic Coalition Society is influential in the judiciary as well as the quasi-charitable foundations that having originally been formed to aid war victims and the poor now control much of the non-oil economic sector. Although consensus within the society opposes political liberalization, there is reportedly factionalization concerning economic reform, which is endorsed by some of the business community. In the 2005 presidential elections, the party initially backed Ali Larijani, director of the state television and radio monopoly, but later withdrew its support in favor of Ahmadinejad, reportedly on the orders of the office of the supreme leader.

Leader: Habibollah ASGAROWLADI (Secretary General and Former Commerce Minister).

May 23 Movement. Prior to the reformist victory in the parliamentary elections of 2000, some 20 parties and organizations (including important student organizations) committed to political reform and broadly supportive of President Khatami formed the May 23 Movement. (The coalition was named in honor of Khatami's election victory, which occurred on May 23, 1997; it is also known as the Second Khordad Movement [or Front], the second day of the month of Khordad in the Iranian calendar corresponding to May 23). Once in power, serious divisions within the coalition emerged, as reformists argued over how to respond to the successive vetoes of parliamentary bills and measures stifling dissent and press freedom. The coalition failed to agree on a unified candidate list in Teheran for the 2003 local elections. During the disputed 2004 parliamentary elections, members of the coalition were deeply divided over whether to boycott the vote or to participate in hopes of limiting the size of a conservative victory. Although the coalition leaders continued to hold meetings, they could not reach agreement on a single, reformist candidate for the 2005 presidential elections, splitting reformist votes during the first round.

Islamic Iran Participation Front (*Jebhe-ye Mosharekat-e Iran-e Eslami*–IIPF). Established in December 1998 by pro-Khatami forces, the IIPF presented candidates in the 1999 municipal elections, some in coalition with the SC. For the 2000 *Majlis* balloting, it served as a core component of the May 23 Movement, subsequently reporting that approximately 80 of its members had been elected. The IIPF is led by Mohammad Reza Khatami, the brother of President Khatami. Several senior members of the party had been involved as student activists in the seizure of the US embassy in 1979 but have since evolved into proponents of liberal democratic change. After the 2000 elections, members of the IIPF were the most outspoken advocates for sweeping reforms, arguing as cabinet ministers and MPs for greater media freedom, cultural openness, women's rights, environmental safeguards, and engagement with Western governments. Regarding economic policy, some elements of the IIPF and other reformists remain reluctant to embrace market reform measures.

Some prominent members of the party were targeted and harassed by the conservative judiciary, paramilitaries, and parallel security services. Abbas Abdi was sentenced to four years in prison after publishing a poll in October 2002 showing a majority of Iranians supporting dialogue with the United States. Judges closed newspapers sponsored by the party, including *Sobh-e Emrooz*. Its editor, Saeed Hajarian, was a senior adviser to President Khatami when he was shot and nearly killed in an assassination attempt in 2000. Hardline paramilitaries sometimes broke up IIPF rallies and events. Frustrated with the obstruction of

the Council of Guardians and judicial repression, IIPF members lobbied to confront the conservatives, advocating that Khatami resign or hold a referendum, but the president refused. By the end of Khatami's second term, the IIPF had concluded that reform within the parameters of the current system was unattainable and that the constitutional framework had to be amended to deliver genuine parliamentary democracy. During the crisis preceding the 2004 elections, in which most IIPF candidates were banned from appearing on the ballot, IIPF leaders wrote an unprecedented open letter to the supreme leader questioning the legitimacy of his rule and warning of a betrayal of the revolution. Out of power, some members have turned to promoting new civil society groups and civic education efforts. The party has sought to reach out to liberal activists in the banned but tolerated Liberation Movement of Iran led by Ibrahim YAZDI (see below). The party supported Mostafa Moin, former minister of scientific research in Khatami's cabinet, in the first round of the 2005 presidential elections. In the second round, the party endorsed Rafsanjani largely as a vote against the conservative Ahmadinejad.

Leaders: Mohammad Reza KHATAMI (Secretary General and Former Deputy Speaker of the *Majlis*), Mohsen MIRDAMADI, Saeed HAJARIAN.

Islamic Revolution Mujaheddin Organization (IRMO). Described by some observers as the "third major grouping" (after the JRM and the SC) during the 1996 *Majlis* campaign, the IRMO was supported by a number of leftist organizations and former parties. It was reportedly aligned to a certain degree with the SC in 1996, although its support was considered "feeble" in contrast to *Hezbollah's* efforts on behalf of the SC's main rival, the JRM. The IRMO supported Mohammad Khatami in the 1997 presidential election and served as one of the most liberal components of the May 23 Movement in the 2000 *Majlis* balloting. Although it supported Khatami in his reelection effort in 2001, the IRMO subsequently distanced itself from the government by insisting upon more active resistance to the antireform influence of conservative clerics.

A prominent member of the party, university academic Hashem Aghajari, was convicted of apostasy and sentenced to death in November 2002 for a speech in which he questioned absolute clerical authority and called on Iranians to interpret the Koran for themselves. Following student demonstrations, the supreme leader intervened, ordering the courts to lift the death penalty. Aghajari was later sentenced to a five-year prison term. In the 2005 presidential elections, IRMO supported Mostafa Moin.

Leaders: Behzad NABAVI (former deputy speaker of the *Majlis*), Mohsen ARMIN, Mohammad SACAMATI.

Islamic Iran Solidarity Party. Reportedly recognized in 1998 as Iran's first legal post-1987 party, the Islamic Iran Solidarity Party was launched by a group of Khatami government ministers and other officials. Perhaps more than any other reformist organization, the party has fallen into disarray and possible irrelevance following recent victories by the conservatives in parliament and the presidency.

Leaders: Ebrahim ASGHARZADEH (Secretary General), Reza RAHCHAMANI.

Islamic Labor Party (ILP). An outgrowth of a workers' movement launched in the 1980s in opposition to Marxist groups, the ILP reported that 15 of its members had been elected to the *Majlis* in 2000 as part of the May 23 Movement. ILP leader Ali Reza Mahjoub is also head of the House of Workers, the nation's primary federation of unions. One of the few well-known reformists to return to the *Majlis* in 2005 balloting, Mahjoub managed to win a seat in the new parliament representing a Teheran district (determined in a third round of voting that coincided with the first round of presidential polling on June 17).

Leaders: Ali Reza MAHJOUB, Abolqasem SARHADIZADEH (Secretary General).

Assembly of Combatant Clergy (*Majma' Ruhaniun Mobarez*–MRM). The MRM was launched in 1988 by members of the Society of Combatant Clergy (JRM) who split from the parent group because of their objections over the JRM's unwillingness to support political liberalization. (The MRM was referenced as the Assembly of Militant Clerics in the 1999 *Handbook,* and its name has been routinely translated in news reports as the Association of Militant Clerics [or Clergy], the League of Militant Clerics, and other variations. See the section on the JRM, above, for an explanation of the naming conventions adopted for this edition of the *Handbook* to assist in identifying the two groups.)

Members of the MRM were prominent in the reformists' victory in 1988 *Majlis* balloting, although their influence declined following the 1992 balloting. The MRM returned to center stage on the political front with the surprise presidential victory in 1997 by MRM member Mohammad Khatami, who had been eased out of his position as minister of Islamic culture in 1992 after critics accused him of maintaining too liberal of a stance regarding Western influences. A member of the May 23 Movement in the 2000 *Majlis* balloting, the MRM currently serves as one of the primary moderate groupings within the reform movement.

Within the May 23 Movement, the MRM favored a more gradualist approach to reform, seeking to work solely within the confines of the theocratic system and avoid antagonizing conservative institutions. The MRM opposed boycotting the 2004 elections and supported a rival presidential candidate in the 2005 presidential elections, backing party leader Mehdi Karrubi instead of the IIPF's Mostafa Moin. After losing in the first round of the election and alleging fraud, Karrubi resigned as the organization's secretary general to form his own party (see the National Trust, below). The MRM elected Mohammad Khatami to head its Central Council on August 8, 2005, days after he completed his second and final four-year term as president. Khatami has been associated with the party since the 1980s.

Leader: Mohammad KHATAMI (Secretary General).

Servants of Construction (*Kargozaran-e Sazandegi*–SC). The SC (also sometimes referenced as the Executives of Construction) was launched in January 1996 by 16 top members of the Iranian executive branch, leading to its being informally referenced as the "G-16." Widely viewed as allied with (then) President Rafsanjani, the SC founders called for continued economic reform and moderate political liberalization.

About 90 to 100 SC supporters were believed to have been elected to the *Majlis* in 1996, a strong "antiliberal" campaign on behalf of the JRM/*Hezbollah* having apparently prevented what some observers had expected to be a clear-cut SC victory. The SC supported Interior Minister Abdullah NOURI in his unsuccessful bid to be elected speaker of the new *Majlis.*

The SC supported Mohammad Khatami in the May 1997 presidential election. Although the *Majlis* subsequently approved all of Khatami's cabinet recommendations, some of the harshest debate was over two SC candidates, Nouri and Seyed Ataollah Mohajerani. Early in 1998 the conservative judiciary arrested some Khatami supporters, including the SC's Gholan Hussein Karbaschi, mayor of Teheran, for alleged corruption in an election backlash that was seen by pro-Khatami elements as an escalation of political warfare. The popular mayor, who had been a leading figure in Khatami's surprise presidential victory, was subsequently sentenced to 18 months in prison. By that time, however, the SC had reportedly elected him as its secretary general after the grouping had apparently been officially recognized as a party. After seven months in jail, Karbaschi was pardoned in December 1999 by Ayatollah Ali Khamenei. The SC was subsequently reported to have been fractionalized on the issue of how close to remain aligned with the Khatami administration, some members criticizing the president for failing to take stronger action to challenge the prosecution of SC members by the conservative judiciary.

The SC presented candidates in the 1999 municipal elections, some in alliance with the IIPF. Nouri was the top vote-getter in the local balloting in Teheran, but later in the year he was sentenced to five years in prison for having questioned the powerful role of the religious hierarchy, his case becoming one of the most prominent of the reformist versus conservative battles.

The "centrist, economics-oriented" SC presented joint candidates with other members of the May 23 Movement for many of the seats in the 2000 *Majlis,* although SC candidates competed on an independent SC list for some seats in Teheran. Included in that group was Rafsanjani, who had stated his goal of returning to the speakership of the *Majlis.* Indicative of the ongoing lack of harmony between Rafsanjani and Khatami (as well as their respective supporters), Rafsanjani was also included on the candidate list of the conservative JRM. Although he was elected to the *Majlis,* Rafsanjani ultimately declined his seat in the wake of controversy surrounding electoral decisions in his favor on the part of the Council of Guardians. He, however, remained head of the influential Expediency Council. Meanwhile, the SC claimed representation in the *Majlis* of some 55 members. Following the SC's defeats in the municipal elections of 2003, the parliamentary elections of 2004, and Rafsanjani's crushing loss in the 2005 presidential vote, the group announced plans for a major reorganization and "restructuring" that would result in new leadership. Regardless, it will be difficult to alter the perception of the party as a failed platform for Rafsanjani.

Leader: Gholan Hussein KARBASCHI.

Liberation Movement of Iran (*Nehzat-e Azadi-e Irân*). A liberal Islamic grouping established in 1961 by Mehdi Bazargan, the Liberation Movement, also referenced as the Freedom Movement of Iran, supported the opposition religious leaders during the anti-shah demonstrations of 1978. Named prime minister in February 1979, Bazargan resigned in the wake of the US embassy seizure the following November. Subsequently, he remained one of the most outspoken critics tolerated by the government. In a letter authored in November 1982, he accused the regime of responsibility for an "atmosphere of terror, fear, revenge, and national disintegration." *Nehzat-e Azadi,* which was linked to the Paris-based National Resistance Council, boycotted the legislative balloting in 1984 and in 1988 because of government-imposed electoral restrictions. In May 1988 the publication of a second letter from Bazargan to Ayatollah Khomeini highly critical of the government's war efforts and other "erroneous plans" led to the arrest of leading members of his party and the Association for the Defense and Sovereignty of the Iranian Nation, which had been formed in opposition to continuation of the war with Iraq in March 1986 by Bazargan and others who had participated in the 1979 provisional government. Bazargan charged that the movement was not permitted to participate freely in the 1992 legislative campaign, and supporters were urged to boycott the 1993 presidential balloting.

Bazargan died of heart failure in January 1995, and his longtime assistant, Ibrahim Yazdi, was subsequently named as the movement's new secretary general. Yazdi later called on the government to permit the movement to present candidates in the March 1996 legislative elections. However, the Council of Guardians ruled that movement candidates per se would not be permitted to do so, although four members could run as independents. Those potential candidates subsequently declined to participate in the campaign to protest the council's decision. For his part, Yazdi argued that, while Iranians remained "loyal" to the "ideals" of the revolution, there was growing discontent over the government's "violation" of "rights and liberties." Yazdi was arrested in December 1997 (and later released) after signing a letter with 50 other government critics appealing for protection for Ayatollah Hussein Ali Montazeri, a cleric whose home was attacked by demonstrators after he questioned the authority of Ayatollah Khamenei. Montazeri had once been in line to succeed Ayatollah Khomeini (see Political background,

above, for details). He has been under house arrest for several years for his remarks, prompting mass protests by his supporters in the city of Isfahan.

The Liberation Movement, a strong supporter of the reform tendency since 1997, was not permitted to present candidates in 2000 *Majlis* balloting, and the crackdown on the party by the conservative judiciary resulted in the arrest of some 60 party members in late 2000 and early 2001 on charges of seeking to overthrow the government in relation to, among other things, recent student unrest. The party was formally outlawed in July 2002. It condemned the Council of Guardians' ban on hundreds of reformist candidates in the 2004 parliamentary elections and speaks out frequently on human rights abuses. The most significant case has been that of Akbar Ganji, a journalist jailed for reporting on an alleged conspiracy of assassinations orchestrated against dissidents. He has refused to recant and has engaged in hunger strikes. Eight Nobel laureates have written to Iran demanding his release.

Leader: Ibrahim YAZDI (Secretary General and Former Prime Minister).

Shortly after the 2005 presidential election, former parliamentary speaker and former leader of the MRM, Mehdi KARRUBI, reportedly registered the **National Trust** as a new party. Party founders include Rassoul MONTAJABNIYA, a former prominent member of the Association of Combatant Clergy, and Reza HAJATI, a former student activist.

The **Office for Consolidation of Unity** (*Daftar-e Takhim-e Vahdat*) is a student organization that has served as a platform for outspoken critics of the regime and in 1999 led street demonstrations protesting a crackdown on press freedom. The organization played an important role in the 1979 revolution, supporting the seizure of the US embassy, and many of its leaders participated in the taking of American hostages. The group allied itself with the May 24 Movement (Second of Khordad) but later broke ranks with President Khatami and the reformists, criticizing their refusal to confront the conservatives and arguing that the Islamic Republic is inherently undemocratic. Several leaders have been imprisoned since 1997. Ahmad BATEBI, a student demonstrator with no links to the organization's leadership, was imprisoned in 1999 after his photograph appeared in newspapers and on the cover of *The Economist* holding the bloodied T-shirt of a fellow student. He remains in prison serving a 15-year sentence.

The **Devotees of the Party of God** (*Ansar-e Hezbollah*) is a hard-line paramilitary organization known for breaking up antiregime street demonstrations and attacking those considered to be flaunting social restrictions imposed by the authorities. Its roots date back to the 1979 revolution, when gangs of urban poor organized as "Hezbollah" to support Ayatollah Khomeini. Most members are veterans of the Iran-Iraq War or former members of the Basij militia, which was formed by the revolutionary leadership. The group has been accused of carrying out political assassinations.

The **National Front** (*Jebhe-e Melli*) was established in December 1977 as an essentially secular antiregime coalition of nationalist factions, including followers of former prime minister Mohammad Mossadeq. One of its founders, Shahpur Bakhtiar, was formally expelled upon designation as prime minister by the shah in late 1978; another founder, Karim SANJABI, resigned as foreign minister of the Islamic Republic in April 1979 to protest a lack of authority accorded to Prime Minister Bazargan. Prominent in the front is the longstanding **Iranian Nation Party** (INP), formed by Dariush FORUHAR, a former minister in the postrevolution Bazargan government. The INP (also sometimes referenced as the Iran People's Party) was tolerated by the government, despite remaining technically illegal. The party's newsletter regularly published harsh criticism of the regime, particularly in regard to human rights violations. Foruhar and his wife, Parvaneh ESKANDARI-FORUHAR, were murdered in November 1998, the killings ultimately being attributed to "rogue elements" within government security forces. Several INP members were arrested in July 1999 in connection with

recent student unrest. For the 2000 *Majlis* balloting the INP, now led by Bahran NAMAZI, attempted to present joint candidates with the Liberation Movement of Iran and other groups in a Coalition of National Religious Forces in support of the reformist movement.

The largest guerrilla group–which at one time claimed some 100,000 members but is now considered to have much less support–is the **Mujaheddin-e Khalq** ("People's Warriors," also referenced as the *Mujaheddin Khalq* Organization–MKO or MEK), founded in 1965 in opposition to the shah. Leftist but also Islamic, the *Mujaheddin* confined most of their activities after the revolution to urban areas, frequently engaging in street battles with the Revolutionary Guards and the regular army; many of the political assassinations of 1979–1982 were apparently carried out by its members. The political leader of the *Mujaheddin,* Massoud RAJAVI, accompanied former president Bani-Sadr into exile at Paris in July 1981, but subsequently came under pressure from French authorities and left, with 1,000 of his followers, for Iraq in June 1986; within Iran, guerrilla leader Mussa KHIABANI was killed in February 1982, his successor being Ali ZARKESH. In mid-1988 the *Mujaheddin* captured three Iranian towns before the Iranian army drove them back into Iraq in early August. The 15,000-member guerrilla force reportedly met with stiff resistance from "locals" who considered its attacks on the weakened army treasonous. Subsequently, the *Mujaheddin* claimed that thousands of its adherents had been executed by government forces. In December 1991 many *Mujaheddin* members were arrested during a government crackdown on opposition street protests, while President Rafsanjani ordered air strikes against its bases in Iraq during the run-up to the 1992 balloting.

In late 1993 Teheran strongly criticized Paris's decision to permit Maryam RAJAVI (wife of Massoud Rajavi and recently elected, according to *Middle East International,* as "president of Iran" by the *Mujaheddin* executive committee) to remain, with 200 supporters, in France. Subsequently, in January 1994, some 17 *Mujaheddin* members were arrested as participants in a bombing at the Iranian capital, with leaders of the group denying complicity and accusing the government of routinely linking them to all such disturbances for political purposes. Later in the year the US State Department accused the *Mujaheddin* of engaging in terrorism, Washington's animosity apparently stemming in part from *Mujaheddin* links to the Iraqi regime of Saddam Hussein. The group was reportedly used to assist Hussein's forces in crushing Kurdish and Shi'ite rebellions. In the summer of 1997, apparently as a gesture of goodwill toward the new moderate Khatami government, Israel ordered an end to *Mujaheddin* broadcasts via an Israeli-owned satellite. The *Mujaheddin,* now said to be operating out of Iraq, claimed responsibility for sporadic attacks in Teheran in 2000 and 2001.

In August 2002, the group's political wing, the National Council of Resistance of Iran (NCRI), presented satellite photographs and details of an underground uranium enrichment center in Natanz and a heavy-water nuclear production facility in Arak. The satellite imagery prompted speculation that the group was supplied with intelligence from the United States or Israel, as it would lack sufficient resources to monitor Iran's nuclear activities. The revelations, subsequently confirmed by UN inspectors, indicated that Iran had made substantial progress in its nuclear research and renewed suspicions that the regime was pursuing a clandestine weapons project (possibly involving the purchase of materials and know-how from Pakistani scientists). The group lost its primary sponsor after the fall of Saddam Hussein and was briefly bombarded by US forces. The MKO agreed to a cease-fire and was later disarmed and confined to designated camps under US guard. Some 4,000 MKO members remain under US military supervision or "detention" at Camp Ashraf in Iraq and, after a lengthy review by the US State Department and FBI, none have been charged as suspected terrorists. The political wing, the NCRI, continues to enjoy support from a small number of parliamentary representatives in Europe and in the US Congress.

Of the separatist groups, the largest is the primarily Sunni Muslim **Kurdish Democratic Party of Iran** (KDPI), also referenced as the Democratic Party of Iranian Kurdistan (DPIK), which was outlawed in August 1979. Campaigning under the slogan "Democracy for Iran, Autonomy for the Kurds," the KDPI, like the *Mujaheddin,* has been a principal target of government forces; its guerrilla wing is often referred to as the *Pesh Mergas* (as is a similar Kurdish group in Iraq). Its former secretary general, Abdur Rahman QASSEMLOU was assassinated at Vienna in July 1989, while his successor, Sadeq SHARAFKANDI, and four KDPI colleagues were murdered at Berlin in September 1992. In 1993 German prosecutors charged that the Iranian government had been involved in the latter attack. (Former Iranian prime minister Bani-Sadr testified at a trial in Germany in 1996 that Ayatollah Khamenei had personally signed a death warrant for Sharafkandi.) Late in 1993 it was also reported that KDPI guerrillas had engaged government troops near the Iraqi border. Another KDPI leader, Ghafur HAMZEKI, was reported to have been assassinated in Baghdad in August 1994 while, in what was described as an effort to "crush" the guerrillas, Iranian bombers and missiles attacked KDPI bases in Iraq the following November. In May 1995 it was reported that Abdallah HASSANZADEH had replaced Mustapha HEJRI as KDPI leader and secretary general. The KDPI claimed that its fighters had been attacked by Iranian troops in late 1996 in the wake of the incursion by the Iraqi military into the Kurdish "safe haven" in northern Iraq. In April 1997 a German court ruled that unnamed senior Iranian officials were responsible for the 1992 assassinations in Berlin, a finding that strained Iran's relations with the EU as well as Germany. Perhaps indicating a reduction in tensions between the KDPI and the government, the KDPI was described as openly supporting candidates in Kurdish-populated areas in the 1999 municipal elections. As of 2005, the secretary general of the Iraq-based KDPI was reportedly Mustafa HEJRI.

Legislature

The unicameral **Islamic Consultative Assembly** (*Majlis-e Shoura-e Islami*) currently has 290 members serving four-year terms. Members

Cabinet

As of July 1, 2005

President	Mahmoud Ahmadinejad
First Vice President	Mohammad Reza Aref
Vice President, Chief of the Cultural Heritage and Tourism Organization	Seyed Hoseyn Mar'ashi
Vice President, Chief of the Iran Atomic Energy Organization (IAEO)	Gholamreza Aghazadeh
Vice President, Chief of Iran's Environmental Protection Organization	Massoomeh Ebtekar [f]
Vice President, Chief of the Management and Planning Organization	Hamid Reza Baradaran Shoraka
Vice President, Chief of the Martyrs and Self-Sacrificer's Affairs Foundation	Hoseyn Dehghaan
Vice President, Chief of the Physical Training Organization	Mohsen Mehralizadeh
Vice President, Chief of the President's Office	Seyyed Ali Khatami
Vice President, Legal and Parliamentary Affairs	Majead Ansari

Ministers

Agriculture Jihad	Muhammad Hojjati
Commerce	Mohammad Shariatmadari
Cooperatives	Ali Soofi
Culture and Islamic Guidance	Ahmad Masjed Jamei
Defense and Logistics	Ali Shamkhani
Economic Affairs and Finance	Safdar Hosseini
Education	Morteza Haji
Energy	Habibollah Bitaraf
Foreign Affairs	Kamal Kharrazi
Health	Massoud Pezeshkian
Housing and Urban Development	Ali Abdolalizadeh
Industry and Mines	Eshaq Jahangiri
Intelligence	Ali Younesi
Interior	Abdolvahed Mussavi Lari
Justice	Mohammad Esmail Shushtari
Labor	Naser Khaleghi
Petroleum	Bijan Namdar Zanganeh
Posts, Telegraph, and Telecommunications	Seyed Ahmad Motamedi
Roads and Transport	Seyed Mohammad Rahmati
Scientific Research and Technology	Ja'far Tofigi Darian
Social Affairs	Mohammad Hussein Sharifzadegan

[f] = female

are popularly elected in multiple-member constituencies in which each voter votes for as many candidates as there are seats. (Successful candidates must receive a minimum percentage of the total votes. If some seats remain unfilled after the first round of balloting, a runoff round is held.) Political groups are permitted to present candidate lists, many of the leading groups serving in a quasi-party capacity. All candidates must be approved by the Council of Guardians, which regularly rejects many prospects.

The balloting held on February 20, 2004, was marred by a dispute over the disqualification of more than 2,300 candidates by the Council of Guardians. The conservative Builders of an Islamic Iran Council won a majority, securing about 155 seats in the first round of balloting and another 40 seats in the second round on May 7, giving them a majority of at least 195 in the *Majlis*. The overall conservative majority is estimated at 200 to 210, with the remainder held by independent MPs and a bloc of about 40 reformists without party affiliation.

Speaker: Gholam-Ali Haddad ADEL
Deputy Speaker: Mohammad Reza BAHONAR

Communications

Freedom of the press is provided for in the 1979 constitution, except in regard to violations of public morality and religious belief or impugning the reputation of individuals. Nevertheless, more than 20 newspapers were closed in August 1979, and drastic curbs were imposed on foreign journalists, including a ban on unsupervised interviews with government officials and a requirement that reporters apply for press cards every three months. In August 1980 Ayatollah Khomeini called for increased censorship, and on June 7, 1981, an additional seven publications were banned. Subsequently, on August 25, 1981, the *Majlis* passed a law making it a criminal offense to use "pen and speech" against the government. However, the Rafsanjani government permitted a degree of debate in the press on controversial issues, leading one correspondent to describe the situation as "lively but controlled." Critics of the regime called for an extension of press freedom, noting that newspapers were routinely shut down by the authorities for publishing "antigovernment" articles. The Khatami administration installed in 1997 issued permits to dozens of new publications, apparently hoping through public debate to strengthen independent institutions. The establishment of a more vibrant press was credited with the success of reformists in the February 1999 municipal elections. However, conservatives opposed to the new policy of openness continued to control the "Press Court," which ultimately determines that fate of newspapers. Journalism subsequently became one of the main battlefields in the conflict between reformists and conservatives. New restrictions on the press contributed to large-scale student demonstrations in July 1999.

Shortly after the 2000 legislative elections, the outgoing *Majlis* hurriedly approved a crude press control law, which the conservative Council of Guardians ruled could not be overturned by the new reform-minded *Majlis*. Consequently, some 110 proreform publications were closed over a four-year period, and many journalists were arrested. Journalists and dissident voices sought refuge on the Internet, but the judiciary began cracking down on web-based writers in 2003 and imposing stricter controls on Internet service providers. Nevertheless, some Farsi-language websites based outside the country have managed to circumvent the restrictions. Blogging has also grown rapidly as a form of political and social protest, reducing the regime's ability to control the flow of information. Numerous journalists and editors have been jailed over the past seven years, and about a dozen have languished in prison for several years running. The plight of journalist Akbar Ganji has gained international attention. After writing articles linking conservative authorities to the murders of dissidents, authorities imprisoned Ganji in 2001. Unlike most dissidents under detention, Ganji has refused to recant and has engaged in hunger strikes. Eight Nobel laureates have written to Iran demanding his release.

Press

Iran experienced a rapid increase in the number of daily and weekly newspapers following the election of Khatami to the presidency in 1997, some of them quickly reopening under new names after having been closed by conservative clerics. Newspaper closures and prison sentences since have had a chilling effect on the press, discouraging journalistic inquiry and limiting the range of debate and comment. The breathing space for reformist publications has steadily been reduced since 1999. Prominent newspapers aligned with the conservatives include *Jomhuri Islami*, hard-line conservative; *Kayhan*, hard-line conservative; *Resalat*, considered more "pragamatic"; *Siasat-e Ruz*, hard-line; and *Ettela'at* and *Hamshari*, owned by the Teheran city council. Newspapers backed by reformists include Sharqh, which enjoys the most influence and reach; *Aftab-e Yazd* and *Eqhbal*, associated with the IIPF; and *Entekhab* and *Farhang-e Ashti*. English-language dailies include the moderate *Iran News, Iran Daily*, and the conservative *Teheran Times*.

News Agencies

In December 1981 the domestic Pars News Agency was renamed the Islamic Republic News Agency (IRNA). Following the July 1981 closing of Reuters' Teheran office, Agence France-Presse and Italy's ANSA were the only Western bureaus with operations in Iran. Reuters has subsequently reopened its facility at Teheran, and several other foreign bureaus are now also represented, including the BBC and the New China News Agency (Xinhua). A small number of foreign journalists are allowed to reside in Iran; they must renew their visas every three months. Permission to travel to certain regions, including predominantly Kurdish areas and towns along the border with Iraq and Afghanistan, must be approved by the Ministry of Culture and Islamic Guidance and is often denied.

Broadcasting and Computing

The Islamic Republic of Iran Broadcasting (IRIB), which answers directly to the office of the supreme leader (who appoints the director), operates a comprehensive monopoly on television and radio over two networks and home-service radio broadcasting in a variety of indigenous and foreign languages. IRIB has been frequently criticized by reformists for ignoring reformist voices or manipulating issues to favor conservative viewpoints. The reformist majority in the previous *Majlis* also alleged that the broadcaster had failed to fully account for its expenditures. From the outset of the US-led war in Iraq in 2003, IRIB broadcast an Arabic-language program beamed into Iraq on terrestrial transmitters and throughout the Arab world by satellite. Iranian law prohibits commercial stations. A ban on the use of satellite television is sporadically enforced but widely flouted. Authorities have also attempted to jam satellite reception with mixed success. There were approximately 10.7 million television receivers and 6 million personal computers serving 4.8 million Internet users in 2003.

Intergovernmental Representation

The United States severed diplomatic relations with Iran on April 4, 1980. Iranian diplomatic interests in Washington were handled by an interests section at the Algerian embassy until March 1992, when a successor section was established at the Pakistani embassy. The embassy of Switzerland handles US interests in Iran.

Permanent Representative to the UN
Mohammad Javad ZARIF

IGO Memberships (Non-UN)
CCC, CP, ECO, IDB, Interpol, IOM, IOR-ARC, NAM, OIC, OPEC, PCA

IRAQ

REPUBLIC OF IRAQ

al-Jumhuriyah al-'Iraqiyah

Note: After appointing a Speaker, president, and prime minister, Iraq's new Transitional National Assembly accomplished its principal task—drafting a constitution—in time for an August 2005 referendum on the document. Their constitution won a solid majority, but failed in two Sunni Arab provinces and barely passed in another, narrowly avoiding a veto. Approval of the constitution paved the way for December 2005 parliamentary elections—the country's third nationwide election in a year—in which voter turnout neared 70 percent. Violence was low. Sunni Arabs, who had largely boycotted earlier elections, increased their participation, but preliminary results suggested a victory for the United Iraqi Alliance, a coalition of Shi'ite parties. Optimism over the election's success soon succumbed to accusations of fraud and calls for a new vote. In the ongoing US-led war against Iraqi and foreign insurgents, civilians and coalition forces faced persistent violence; suicide bombings, sniper attacks, and kidnappings continued to be daily occurrences. In December, US President George W. Bush estimated the Iraqi death toll at 30,000; others' estimates were much higher.

The Country

Historically known as Mesopotamia ("land between the rivers") from its geographic position centering in the Tigris-Euphrates Valley, Iraq is an almost landlocked, partly desert country whose population is overwhelmingly Muslim and largely Arabic-speaking but also includes a Kurdish minority of over 4 million in the northeastern region bordering on Syria, Turkey, and Iran. Most Muslims, by a slim majority, are Shi'ite, although the regime had long been Sunni-dominated prior to the 2003 US/UK-led invasion. Women comprised about one-fifth of the paid labor force, nearly one-half of the agricultural work force under Saddam Hussein's government, and one-third of the professionals in education and health care; a moderate interpretation of Islamic law gave women equal rights in divorce, land ownership, and suffrage. Women were given the right to vote and run for office in the interim constitution adopted in 2004, although their ultimate rights regarding civil matters remained a subject of intense focus during the 2005 negotiations regarding a permanent constitution.

Agriculture, which was characterized by highly concentrated land ownership prior to the introduction of land-reform legislation in 1958, occupies about two-fifths of the population but produces less

than one-tenth of the gross national product. The most important crops are dates, barley, wheat, rice, and tobacco. Oil is the leading natural resource and, under normal conditions, accounts for over half of GNP. (Estimated at over 110 billion barrels, Iraq's petroleum reserves are believed to be the second largest in the world, following those of Saudi Arabia.) Other important natural resources include phosphates, sulphur, iron, copper, chromite, lead, limestone, and gypsum. Manufacturing industry is not highly developed, although petrochemical, steel, aluminum, and phosphate plants were among heavy-industrial construction projects undertaken in the 1970s. During most of the 1980s the country experienced severe economic difficulty as the result of depressed oil prices and the heavy cost (including shortfalls in oil output) attributable to war with Iran. However, economic reforms launched in 1987, coupled with postwar optimism, helped propel GDP growth by 10 percent in 1988, the first positive rate since early in the decade.

Serious difficulties were encountered in 1990 in the form of economic sanctions imposed by the United Nations following Iraq's August 2 seizure of Kuwait. Subsequently, the unremitting air campaign launched by US-led coalition forces in early 1991 was described as causing "near apocalyptic results" that relegated Iraq's infrastructure to a "preindustrial" condition. UN sanctions, most importantly an embargo on the export of Iraqi oil, continued into late 1996 because of what Western leaders considered Baghdad's failure to fully implement cease-fire resolutions. As of that time Iraq's economy and social service network remained in near total collapse. Limited oil shipments resumed in December 1996 under the UN's "oil-for-food" plan, which helped to control malnutrition and to permit provisions of basic health services. As of mid-2002 Iraq had earned an estimated $54 billion under the UN plan, producing by that time nearly 2 million barrels per day (4 percent of global production with, ironically, the United States being one of Iraq's leading customers). Nevertheless, conditions for the general population remained dismal in many respects. Child mortality had reportedly doubled since the Gulf war, and an estimated 30 percent of school-age children were no longer enrolled in a country that once boasted one of the highest literacy rates in the Arab world. Many members of the professional class were described as having "fallen into poverty," the Iraqi dinar having collapsed into "near worthlessness" and contributed to rampant unemployment. Meanwhile, serious conflict between Iraq and the UN over weapons inspections effectively barred potential progress toward the complete lifting of sanctions, while the US Bush administration pursued "regime change" in Baghdad by military means if necessary should disarmament efforts be delayed further.

The March 2003 invasion of Iraq by US/UK-led forces further damaged Iraq's infrastructure, although, following the ouster of Saddam Hussein, the US immediately pledged $20 billion for reconstruction; the World Bank, International Monetary Fund, and other international organizations promised an additional $18 billion. Oil exports resumed in August and by March 2004 were estimated at 2.3–2.5 million barrels per day. However, production was regularly disrupted by a determined insurgency on the part of (apparently) disaffected Sunnis, supporters of the Hussein regime, and militant Islamists from other countries. The ongoing conflict also compromised rebuilding efforts, which were described as anemic by Washington's many international critics. A major reconstruction conference at Brussels, Belgium, in June 2005 yielded few new commitments as donors remained wary of the unstable security situation in parts of central Iraq.

Government and Politics

Political Background

Conquered successively by Arabs, Mongols, and Turks, the region now known as Iraq became a British mandate under the League of Nations following World War I. British influence, exerted through the ruling Hashemite dynasty, persisted even after Iraq gained formal independence in 1932; the country continued to follow a generally

Political Status: Independent state since 1932; declared a republic following military coup that overthrew the monarchy in 1958; provisional constitution issued September 22, 1968, and substantially amended thereafter; de facto one-party regime ousted following invasion by US/UK-led forces in March 2003; interim constitution adopted by the US-appointed Iraqi Governing Council on May 8, 2004, providing for popular election of a Transitional National Government. (Negotiations on a permanent new constitution were taking place as of mid-2005.)

Area: 167,924 sq. mi. (434,923 sq. km.).

Population: 22,017,983 (1997C); 25,864,000 (2004E).

Major Urban Centers (2000E): BAGHDAD (4,797,000), Irbil (Arbil, 2,369,000), al-Mawsil (Mosul, 1,034,000).

Official Languages: Arabic, Kurdish.

Monetary Unit: New Dinar (market rate July 1, 2005: 1,469 new dinars = $1US).

President of the Presidential Council: Jalal TALABANI (Patriotic Union of Kurdistan); elected by the Transitional National Assembly on April 5, 2005, and inaugurated on April 7. (Iraq's interim constitution called for drafting of a permanent constitution no later than October 15, 2005, and new presidential balloting no later than December 15.)

Vice Presidents of the Presidential Council: Adil 'Abd al-MAHDI (Supreme Council of the Islamic Revolution in Iraq) and Ghazi Ajil al-YAWAR; elected by the Transitional National Assembly on April 5, 2005, and inaugurated on April 7.

Prime Minister of the Transitional National Government: Ibrahim al-JAAFARI (United Iraqi Alliance); nominated by the Presidential Council on April 7, 2005; formed transitional government on May 3, 2005.

pro-British and pro-Western policy until the overthrow of the monarchy in July 1958 by a military coup that cost the lives of King FAISAL II and his leading statesman, Nuri al-SA'ID. Brig. Gen. 'Abd al-Karim KASSEM (QASIM), leader of the revolt, ruled as head of a left-wing nationalist regime until he too was killed in a coup on February 8, 1963, that brought to power a new military regime led by Lt. Gen. 'Abd al-Salam 'AREF ('ARIF) and, after his accidental death in 1966, by his brother, Gen. 'Abd al-Rahman 'AREF. The 'Aref regime terminated in a third, bloodless coup on July 17, 1968, which established (then) Maj. Gen. Ahmad Hasan al-BAKR, a former premier and leader of the right wing of the Arab Socialist Renaissance Party (*Hizb al-Baath al-Arabi al-Ishtiraki*), as president, prime minister, and chairman of the Revolutionary Command Council (RCC), which was designated as the country's highest authority by the provisional constitution issued on September 22.

Under Bakr a number of alleged plots were used as excuses to move against internal opposi-tion; the most prominent took place in June 1973 when a coup attempt by Col. Nazim KAZZAR, head of national security, led to numerous arrests and executions. Domestic instability was further augmented by struggles within the *Baath* and by relations with the Kurdish minority (see map). The Kurds, under the leadership of Mullah Mustafa al-BARZANI, resisted most Baghdad governments in the two decades after World War II and, with Iranian military support, were intermittently in open rebellion from 1961 to 1975. A 1970 settlement with the Kurds ultimately broke down over distribution of petroleum revenues and exclusion of the oil-producing Kirkuk area from the proposed "Kurdistan." In May 1974 Iraq and Iran agreed to a mutual withdrawal of troops along their common frontier, pending a settlement of outstanding issues, but the Iraqi army subsequently launched a major offensive against the rebels and over 130,000 Kurds fled to Iran to escape the hostilities. Concessions were ultimately made on both sides in an agreement concluded in March 1975 during a meeting of the Organization of Petroleum Exporting Countries (OPEC) at Algiers, with a "reconciliation" treaty being signed at Baghdad the following June. Iraq agreed to abandon a long-standing claim to the Shatt al-'Arab waterway at its southern boundary with Iran and accepted a delimitation of the remaining frontier on the basis of agreements concluded prior to the British presence in Iraq; Iran, in return, agreed to cease all aid to the Kurds, whose resistance momentarily subsided. In mid-1976, however, fighting again erupted between Iraqi forces and the Kurdish *Pesh Merga* guerrillas, ostensibly because of the government's new policy of massive deportation of Kurds to southern Iraq and their replacement by Arabs.

On July 16, 1979, President Bakr announced his resignation from both party and government offices. His successor, Saddam HUSSEIN, had widely been considered the strongman of the regime, and his accession to leadership of the *Baath* and the RCC came as no surprise. Earlier in the year, the Iraqi Communist Party (ICP) had withdrawn from the six-year-old National Progressive Front (see Political Parties and Groups, below) following what Hussein himself had termed a purging of Communists from the government, while reports in late July of a failed "conspiracy" against the new president provided further evidence that he had effectively eliminated opponents from the RCC.

Although former president Bakr was known to be experiencing health problems, his resignation was apparently linked to differences within the RCC in regard to three policies: (1) containment not only of the Kurds but, in the aftermath of the Iranian Revolution, the increasingly restive Shi'ite community, led by Ayatollah Muhammad Bakr al-SADR until his execution in April 1980; (2) an Iraqi-Syrian unification plan (see Foreign relations, below), aspects of which Hussein found objectionable; and (3) suppression of the ICP, including the removal from the cabinet of its two ministers. Although a broad amnesty was proclaimed on August 16, 1979, Kurdish, Shi'ite, and Communist opposition to the Hussein government persisted and appeared to expand following Baghdad's September

17, 1980, abrogation of the 1975 Algiers agreement and the invasion five days later of Iran's Khuzistan Province, which yielded a debilitating conflict that was to preoccupy the regime for the next eight years (see Foreign relations, below).

Iraq also suffered extensive physical destruction from the Western-led "Operation Desert Storm" in early 1991, which had been precipitated by the Iraqi invasion of Kuwait the previous August (for a chronology of relevant events, see the 1991 *Handbook,* Appendix A-II). Upon formal termination of the conflict on March 3, Baghdad faced major rebellions by Kurds in the north and Shi'ites in the south, both of which were largely contained by early April, with many Shi'ite refugees fleeing into southeastern Iran and the Kurds retreating into the mountainous northern region bordering both Iran and Turkey. Late in the month autonomy talks were launched at Baghdad between Kurdish leaders and the Iraqi government. Meanwhile, on March 23 President Hussein announced the formation of a new government, including the appointment of Saadoun HAMMADI to assume the prime ministerial duties theretofore performed by Hussein himself. On May 18 the Kurdish leadership reported that the regime had accepted its demands for a democratic government, separation of the *Baath* from the government, a free press, and elections. Moreover, on July 4 the National Assembly endorsed a bill providing for a limited democracy, wherein political party formations would be legalized but membership in the armed forces and security apparatus would continue to be limited to Baathists.

Although Hussein formally approved the National Assembly bill on September 3, 1991, he subsequently retreated from liberalization measures and moved to consolidate power within a cabinet increasingly dominated by family members. On September 13 the president named Muhammad Hamzah al-ZUBAYDI to replace Hammadi as prime minister after Hammadi, whom analysts had described as the only independent in the regime, had called for a more conciliatory posture in negotiations with UN coalition members and the Kurds. Soon thereafter, Hammadi, who had also been removed from the RCC, was linked to an alleged coup attempt; however, in November, in a further reversal, the former prime minister was named as presidential advisor with cabinet rank.

In January 1992, 80 military officers charged with participating in a coup attempt were executed along with 76 antiregime demonstrators. Four months later, elections were held in the north to an Iraqi Kurdistan National Assembly. However, Baghdad immediately branded the poll as violating a constitutional prohibition of elections by armed groups, the Kurdish leaders defending the action as being in conformity with the 1970 autonomy agreement. On June 4 the new Kurdish Assembly named Fuad MASUM, a member of the political bureau of the Patriotic Union of Kurdistan (PUK), as the first Kurdish prime minister and a Kurdish cabinet was appointed shortly thereafter. Masum resigned on March 18, 1993, amid reported discontent over fuel and food shortages in the north; he was succeeded on April 11 by Kosrat Abdulla RASUL, a popular veteran guerrilla fighter, who announced a new Kurdish cabinet on April 26. (The Kurdish coalition government collapsed in 1994 as renewed fighting broke out between the PUK and its long-standing rival, the Democratic Party of Kurdistan [DPK]. Kurdish territory was subsequently partitioned informally into PUK and DPK spheres of influence until the DPK invited Iraqi troops into the area to participate in an anti-PUK campaign in August 1996. See DPK under Political Parties and Groups, below, for details.) Meanwhile, President Hussein remained firmly in control of the Iraqi government, although growing popular discontent was reported, particularly in regard to the economic and social effects of UN sanctions in place since the Gulf crisis. A number of civilians and army officers (apparently including former supporters of the regime) were executed following the discovery of an alleged coup plot in August 1993, which may also have contributed to a surprise cabinet reshuffle on September 5 in which Prime Minister Zubaydi was replaced by Ahmad Hussein KHUDAYYIR, a longtime *Baath* member and close associate of the president who had served as finance minister since 1991.

Citing the damage inflicted on Iraq by the UN sanctions, President Hussein took formal control of Iraqi administration on May 29, 1994, by assuming the additional post of prime minister in succession to Khudayyir, who retained the finance portfolio. Numerous ministerial changes were reported over the next 15 months as the regime faced continuing economic and political pressures.

In mid-August 1995 two of President Hussein's sons-in-law and their wives (both daughters of the president) fled the country and accepted political asylum in Jordan. The most important of the defectors appeared to be Lt. Gen. Hussein Kamil al-MAJID, who, as head of the Iraqi weapons program, had been one of the most powerful figures in President Hussein's inner circle. Majid, recently reported to have been locked in an intense power struggle with Saddam Hussein's eldest son, Udai HUSSEIN, immediately called for the overthrow of the Hussein regime in order to have the UN sanctions lifted.

Apparently in part to counter perceptions that the defections represented a serious threat to the government's future, the RCC on September 7 amended the constitution to provide for popular confirmation of its chairman as president of the republic. Three days later the National Assembly endorsed the RCC's "nomination" of Saddam Hussein for a seven-year presidential term, while a national referendum on October 13 produced a reported 99.96 percent "yes" vote on the question. Voter turnout was also announced at over 99 percent, a tribute, in the eyes of some observers, to the organizational capabilities of a "revitalized" *Baath*, which also supplied nearly all the candidates for new Assembly elections in March 1996. Meanwhile, any genuine concern the regime may have felt as the result of the much publicized defections of 1995 evaporated in February 1996 when Lt. Gen. Majid accepted a "forgiveness" offer from President Hussein only to be killed in a gunfight shortly after his return to Iraq.

Following the recommendation of the RCC, the National Assembly on August 19, 2002, unanimously nominated President Hussein for another seven-year term. The government reported that

100 percent of those voting in a national referendum on October 15 approved the measure.

After declaring the Iraqi regime to be in violation of UN resolutions relating to inspections designed to determine Iraq's status in regard to weapons of mass destruction, the United States and the United Kingdom launched an invasion in March 2003 that resulted in the ouster of Hussein (see Current issues, below, for additional information). On April 21 US Gen. (Ret.) Jay GARNER arrived to head a US Office for Reconstruction and Humanitarian Assistance (ORHA) that, among other things, was to set up an Iraqi Interim Authority (IIA) as an advisory body to the ORHA. However, the Iraqis slated to participate in the authority (many of whom had just returned from exile) balked at the lack of day-to-day government responsibilities assigned to the proposed IIA. On May 6, L. Paul BREMER, a former ambassador, was named by President Bush as the top civil administration in Iraq and head of the Coalition Provisional Authority (CPA). The UN Security Council endorsed the CPA's legal status as an occupying power in a resolution on May 22 and called upon the CPA (formally launched June 1) to facilitate a quick transition to Iraqi rule.

With a membership determined by the CPA, a new Iraqi Governing Council (IGC) was established on July 13, 2003. The 25 members were carefully divided across religions and ethnic lines (thirteen Shi'ites, five Sunnis, five Kurds, one Assyrian Christian, and one Turkoman). A rotating presidency was instituted for the IGC, which on September 1 announced the formation of a 25-member interim cabinet authorized to assist in drafting an interim constitution and preparing for elections for a transitional government. (The Arab League did not recognize the IGC as Iraq's legitimate government, although OPEC allowed the IGC oil minister to attend OPEC meetings.)

The draft interim constitution was presented on March 1, 2004, and was approved by the US and the IGC (on March 8). On June 28 the IGC was dissolved in favor of the new Iraqi Interim Government (IIG), which accepted the transfer of sovereignty from the CPA (as endorsed by the UN Security Council on June 8). Ayad ALLAWI, a Shi'ite from the Iraqi National Accord, was named prime minister of the interim administration, while Ghazi Ajil al-YAWAR, a Sunni, was named to the largely ceremonial post of interim president.

Elections to a 275-member Transitional National Assembly (TNA) were held on January 30, 2005, with the main Shi'ite coalition (the United Iraqi Alliance) securing 140 seats, followed by the Democratic Patriotic Alliance of Kurdistan with 75, and the multi-ethnic, multi-religious Iraqi List (led by Allawi) with 40. (The main Sunni parties called for a boycott.) Concurrent balloting was held for a new Iraqi Kurdistan National Assembly as well as for various regional councils.

After intense and reportedly often contentious negotiations, the TNA on April 5 elected Jalal TALABANI, a Kurd from the PUK, as president of a new Presidential Council that also included Shi'ite and Sunni vice presidents. On April 7 the Presidential Council appointed Ibrahim al-JAAFARI, a Shi'ite, to head a new cabinet, which was inaugurated (with several key posts still undecided) on May 3.

Constitution and Government

Constitutional processes were largely nonexistent during the two decades after the 1958 coup, despite the issuance of a provisional basic law in 1968, followed in 1971 by a National Action Charter that envisaged the establishment of local governing councils and the reconvening of a legislature. It was not until June and September 1980 that elections were held for a unicameral National Assembly and a Kurdish Legislative Council, respectively. However, the Revolutionary Command Council (RCC), the nation's supreme authority since 1968, was not dissolved, effective power remaining concentrated in its chairman, who continued to serve concurrently as president of the republic and commander in chief of the Armed Forces. (Amendments approved by the RCC in September 1995 directed that its chairman's assumption of the presidency would henceforth be subject to the approval of the National Assembly and a national referendum.) RCC decrees had the force of law and were not automatically subject to any legislative or judicial review, although some bills were passed on to the Assembly for approval. The RCC was also solely responsible for electing and dismissing its own members, who had to come from the leadership of the *Baath*. The judicial system was headed by a Court of Cassation and included five courts of appeal, courts of the first instance, religious courts, and revolutionary courts that deal with crimes involving state security.

As a concession to northern minority sentiment, the Kurds in 1970 were granted "autonomy [as] defined by law," and in 1976 the country's 16 provincial governorates were expanded to 18, 3 of which were designated as Kurdish Autonomous Regions. However, it was not until after the 1991 Gulf war that Baghdad agreed to enter into a dialogue with Kurdish leaders to achieve meaningful implementation of what had been promised more than two decades earlier. After the new talks broke down, Kurdish groups in 1992 established an elected Iraqi Kurdistan National Assembly, which in turn selected a prime minister to oversee a Kurdish government broadly responsible for most services in the region until the collapse of Kurdish cooperation in 1994.

In January 1989 it was announced that the Iraqi constitution would be replaced prior to the National Assembly balloting of April 1; however, a draft of the new basic law did not appear until July 30, 1990, after having secured legislative approval 12 days before. The published version of the document provided, inter alia, for direct election of the president for an eight-year renewable term; replacement of the RCC by a 50-member Consultative Council, composed of an equal number of appointed and directly elected members; and the registration of new political parties, with a proviso that only the *Baath* would be permitted to have branches in the army and security forces. In a speech on March 16, 1991, Saddam Hussein declared that the time had come to "begin building the pillars of the new [constitutional] order" despite the many prob-

lems facing the country. On September 3, 1991, Hussein approved a law technically ending 23 years of one-party rule; however, as of 2002 the other changes had not been submitted to a protected referendum.

The interim constitution adopted in March 2004 following the overthrow of Saddam Hussein in 2003 provided for an appointed Interim Iraqi Government (IIG) to assume sovereignty from the US-led Coalition Provisional Authority for a short time pending the election of transitional government bodies. The 275-member Transitional National Assembly (elected by popular vote on January 20, 2005) was authorized to elect the Presidency Council, dissolve the cabinet, and oversee the drafting of a new permanent constitution. The Presidency Council (elected in April 2005) was empowered to appoint the prime minister, cabinet, and members of the judicial council and veto legislation passed by the assembly. Day-to-day governmental responsibility was given to the prime minister and the cabinet (installed in May 2005). Intense negotiations on a new permanent constitution had not reached agreement as of September 1, 2005.

Foreign Relations

After adhering to a broadly pro-Western posture that included participation in the Baghdad Pact and its successor, the Central Treaty Organization (CENTO), Iraq switched abruptly in 1958 to an Arab nationalist line that was subsequently largely maintained. Relations with the Soviet Union and other Communist-bloc countries became increasingly cordial after 1958, while diplomatic links with the United States (and temporarily with Britain) were severed in 1967. In 1979, however, Baghdad moved against Iraqi Communists, veering somewhat toward the West, particularly France, for military and development aid. The change in direction was reinforced following a June 7, 1981, Israeli air raid against the Osirak nuclear reactor being built outside Baghdad, France indicating that it would assist in reconstructing the facility.

Relations with Arab states have fluctuated, although Iraq has remained committed to an anti-Israel policy. A leading backer of the "rejection front," it bitterly denounced the 1977 peace initiative of Egyptian President Sadat and the Camp David accords of September 1978, after which, on October 26, Syria and Iraq joined in a "National Charter for Joint Action" against Israel. This marked an abrupt reversal in relations between the two neighbors, long led by competing *Baath* factions. The "National Charter" called for "full military union" and talks directed toward its implementation were conducted in January and June 1979. At the latter session, held at Baghdad, presidents Assad of Syria and Bakr of Iraq declared that their two nations constituted "a unified state with one President, one Government and one Party, the *Baath.*" However, the subsequent replacement of Bakr by Saddam Hussein, whom the Syrians had long considered an instigator of subversion in their country, coupled with Hussein's accusations of Syrian involvement in an attempted coup, abruptly terminated the rapprochement.

Relations with Teheran have long been embittered by conflicting interests in the Gulf region, including claims to the Shatt al-'Arab and to three islands (Greater and Lesser Tunb and Abu Musa) occupied by Iran in 1971, as well as by Iranian support for Iraq's Kurdish and Shi'ite communities. Following the advent of the Khomeini regime in Iran in 1979, Iraq bombed a number of Kurdish villages inside Iran, and on September 22, 1980, having repudiated a 1975 reconciliation treaty, Iraq invaded its eastern neighbor. Despite overwhelming Iraqi air superiority and early ground successes, the Iranian military, reinforced by a substantially larger population with religious commitment to martyrdom, waged a bitter campaign against the Western-supplied Iraqi forces, the brief campaign projected by Hussein soon being reduced to a stalemate. In the course of the protracted conflict, numerous Iraqi cease-fire proposals were rebuffed by Teheran, which called for the payment of $150 billion in reparations and Hussein's ouster. It was not until a failed siege of the Iraqi city of Basra, coupled with an increasingly intense political struggle

within Teheran, that Ayatollah Khomeini on July 20, 1988, called for a suspension of hostilities. A cease-fire was subsequently concluded with effect from August 20, although it was not until August 15, 1990, in the midst of the crisis generated by its seizure of Kuwait, that Iraq agreed to a comprehensive settlement based on the 1975 Algiers accord, a rejection of which by Baghdad had precipitated the lengthy conflict. A number of issues, including Iranian demands for reparations, subsequently remained unresolved, however, and a final peace accord had not been signed as of 2002, the status between the two countries being described as "no war, no peace."

The "annexation" of Kuwait in August 1990 had been preceded by Saddam Hussein's delivery of a July 17 Revolution day speech, during which the Iraqi president insisted that Kuwait had not only exceeded OPEC production quotas, but had also stolen oil from Iraqi wells by "slant drilling." Other areas of contention were historic uncertainties regarding the precise demarcation of the Iraq-Kuwait border, plus the status of certain offshore territories (including Bubiyan Island, see map) that had been operationally "loaned" to Iraq as a gesture of Arab solidarity during the Iran-Iraq war (see article on Kuwait). However, there was little international support for Baghdad's position, and the UN Security Council reacted vigorously, demanding an unconditional withdrawal within hours of the Iraqi action on August 2, imposing a trade embargo on August 6, and approving on November 29 the use of any methods needed to force Iraqi compliance as of January 15, 1991. On January 16, following a five-month buildup of US and allied military units, the UN coalition commenced offensive action, which yielded the liberation of Kuwait City on February 26–27 and a suspension of military operations on February 28, followed by Iraqi acceptance of terms for ending the conflict on March 3.

Although most coalition military units withdrew from the Gulf by mid-1991, the UN economic embargo remained in effect, in part because of US displeasure at Saddam Hussein's continuance in office. Nevertheless, while Washington had long demanded that the Iraqi president step down, it was obvious that the Bush administration did not wish to trigger dismemberment of the country. Thus, it stood aside as Iraqi forces crushed a Shi'ite insurrection in the south, while its aid to the northern Kurds was confined largely to humanitarian supplies.

Seemingly encouraged by the coalition's unwillingness to intervene on behalf of either the Kurds or Shi'ites, the Hussein regime subsequently refused to comply with cease-fire provisions requiring its assistance in the location and destruction of Iraq's nonconventional weapons. Nevertheless, by October 1991 the International Atomic Energy Agency (IAEA) had accumulated enough information to charge that an Iraqi atomic weapon had been within 18 months of completion at the outset of the Gulf war and that enough material had survived allied bombing to allow the completion of other such weapons within five years. Consequently, on October 11 the Security Council approved additional restrictions, branded by Baghdad as "colonial," to prevent Iraq from ever again acquiring the means to build weapons of mass destruction.

During 1992 and early 1993 tension continued unabated between Baghdad and UN authorities. On August 27, 1992, US and British warplanes began patrolling a southern "no fly" zone below the 32nd parallel to protect Shi'ite Muslims from Iraqi air attacks. In January 1993 Iraq was obliged to remove surface-to-air missiles that had been moved into the zone, while a series of cross-border raids to retrieve abandoned military equipment from Kuwait were countered by retaliatory allied air strikes. Meanwhile, a northern "no fly" zone, similar to the one in the south, remained in effect to protect the Kurds, although Kurdish secession was effectively blocked by opposition from virtually all interested parties save for the Kurds themselves.

US Tomahawk missiles struck the Iraqi intelligence headquarters at Baghdad on June 26, 1993, Washington claiming it had "compelling evidence" that Iraq had been involved in a plot to kill former President George Bush in Kuwait several months earlier. Moreover, Western powers threatened further military action if the Hussein regime continued to resist measures designed to prevent the development of chemical and nuclear weapons and long-range missiles by the Iraqi military.

An estimated 70,000 Iraqi soldiers massed near the Kuwaiti border in early October 1994, prompting the United States to order "overwhelming" air power and send 40,000 of its troops back to the region in fear of a repetition of the 1990 invasion. In addition, the UN Security Council warned Baghdad against any further "provocative" behavior, while other Arab states (including some, such as Jordan, which had been relatively pro-Iraqi in the previous conflict) strongly condemned the Iraqi buildup. Consequently, the Iraqi forces quickly withdrew, and on November 10, in a major policy shift, the RCC issued a decree, signed by President Hussein and approved by the National Assembly, that accepted Kuwait's sovereignty, political independence, and territorial integrity, based on a recent UN border demarcation.

Despite Iraq's conciliatory measures, the Security Council kept its economic sanctions in place, the United States insisting it would not support their lifting until Baghdad had returned Kuwaiti property seized in 1990–1991, had accounted for numerous missing Kuwaitis (some presumed to still be held in Iraqi prisons), and had established permanent safeguards to protect the rights of the Kurds in the north and the Shi'ite "Marsh Arabs" in the south. Western powers also insisted on full compliance with the demands of the UN weapons monitors, concern focusing on a perceived lack of candor from Baghdad regarding its biological weapons program.

In view of the enormous hardships being endured by the populace as the result of continued UN sanctions, the regime finally agreed in December 1995 to a UN Security Council plan permitting the sale of a limited amount of Iraqi oil to pay for food and medicine. (Baghdad had previously resisted the proposal, saying it represented a compromise of its sovereignty.) The Security Council gave its final approval to the project in May 1996, but implementation was delayed over US concerns that appropriate monitoring mechanisms had not been established. Washington somewhat reluctantly accepted the arrangements for the oil sale in early

August, but action was again suspended later that month when Iraqi troops entered Kurdish territory in the north at the invitation of the DPK.

In early September 1996 the United States launched more than 20 cruise missiles at Iraqi air defense installations in the south as a indirect "punishment" for Iraq's recent military actions in the north. Tension escalated over the next several weeks as Washington dispatched aircraft carriers and additional troops to the Gulf and President Hussein threatened to fire upon Western planes patrolling the "no-fly" zones. Both sides subsequently retreated from the brink of open warfare, however, as Iraqi forces withdrew from the north and the United States discovered a paucity of support from its former coalition allies for renewed hostilities. Consequently, with Iraq facing a potentially "catastrophic" winter, attention again focused on the "oil-for-food" plan, which was finally implemented in mid-December. The plan authorized Iraq to sell $2 billion in oil over the next six months. Some of the revenue was earmarked for victims (primarily Kuwaitis) of Iraq's 1990 aggression, while the Kurds were also scheduled to receive assistance. However, the bulk of the new income was slated for distribution (under UN supervision) throughout Iraq, where it was estimated that nearly 5,000 children had been dying each month from malnutrition or normally treatable diseases.

The UN Special Commission on Iraq (UNSCOM) reported in April 1997 that, although progress was being made in the dismantling of weapons, Iraq was still not cooperating as fully as expected. The issue erupted into a major crisis in October when Baghdad threatened to block all further UN inspections unless the economic sanctions were lifted and US personnel (described as a threat to Iraqi "national sovereignty") were removed from the UN teams. At the same time, new UNSCOM head Richard Butler (former Australian ambassador to the UN) reported that "no remotely credible account" had emanated from the Iraqi government regarding its former biological weapons program. In November the RCC ordered the expulsion of all US inspectors, prompting Washington to send additional forces to the region and to so-

licit support for a possible military response. As in 1996, however, the US found little enthusiasm for its plan among Arab states, many of whom accused the Clinton administration of applying a double standard by taking such a hard line toward Iraq but failing to pressure Israel to proceed with implementation of the peace accord with the Palestinians. Nevertheless, US planes, ships, and soldiers continued to pour into the region in early 1998 in preparation for an attack, despite opposition from fellow Security Council members China, France, and Russia. With time apparently running out, UN Secretary General Kofi Annan met with Hussein at Baghdad in late February, finally securing the Iraqi president's signature on a memorandum of understanding permitting the resumption of inspections at all proposed sites, including the "presidential palaces" previously declared off limits. Tensions having been reduced, at least temporarily, regional leaders subsequently launched a quiet campaign to pursue the "reintegration" of Iraq into the international community, while a number of countries, including France and Russia, continued to promote the lifting of the UN sanctions. (Among other things, many countries were eager to join Iraq in oil and natural gas projects as soon as the sanctions were removed.) Meanwhile, the new phase of the "oil-for-food" program permitted $5.2 billion in oil sales over the next six months.

Encouraged by the apparent moderation in the Iraqi stance on inspections, the United States in the spring of 1998 reduced its forces in the Gulf, and UNSCOM head Butler spoke of a possible breakthrough in negotiations with the Iraqi regime. However, a fresh crisis erupted in August when Baghdad, declaring its disarmament "complete," demanded a reduction in US representation in UNSCOM and suspended cooperation with UNSCOM in some areas. The Security Council adopted a hard line toward the demands, and the Iraqi government subsequently announced it was ending all cooperation with UNSCOM until the UN sanctions were lifted and Butler was replaced as chief of the inspectors. A new US/UK assault on Iraqi sites appeared imminent in mid-November before Hussein, reportedly under heavy pressure from other Arab leaders, agreed to permit UNSCOM to return to work. Significantly, in addition to ordering a continued buildup of US military capabilities in the region, Clinton and other US officials indicated that US policy now sought a regime change in Iraqi, not just "containment." To that end, the US Congress authorized Clinton to allocate $97 million in military and financial assistance to Iraqi opposition groups.

In early December 1998 UNSCOM's Butler reported that the Iraqi government was not living up to its mid-November pledge of cooperation but was in fact refusing inspectors access to some sites and withholding requested documents. Consequently, on December 16 US and UK forces launched Operation Desert Fox, an intensive bombing and missile campaign on military sites throughout Iraq. US and UK officials said the attacks were designed to degrade the weapons capabilities of the Hussein regime and reduce its collateral threat to nearby countries, although China, France, and Russia (the other permanent members of the Security Council) criticized the action. Extensive damage was inflicted by the campaign (which ended on December 20), but Baghdad remained defiant, declaring a permanent cessation in its interactions with UNSCOM and announcing it would no longer respect the no-fly zones. Subsequently, Iraqi pilots routinely challenged the zones, prompting retaliatory strikes by US forces, now operating under expanded rules of engagement and having been authorized to attack a wider array of targets, such as government buildings and communication facilities. US and UK planes continued to pound Iraqi sites into May, as the Security Council remained divided on how to proceed, support for the military action having been further eroded by revelations that some UNSCOM inspectors had conducted intelligence-gathering activities for Washington while engaged in their inspection duties. (For subsequent developments in the dispute with the UN and the US, see Current issues, below.)

As part of Baghdad's efforts to rejoin mainstream Arab activity, a free-trade pact was negotiated with Egypt in January 2001, while economic ties were also promoted with Syria, the final destination for inexpensive Iraqi oil. In addition, Iraq was formally reintegrated into the Arab League at the March 2002 summit at Beirut, Lebanon, during which Baghdad pledged its support for "Kuwaiti sovereignty." Moreover, President Hussein continued to emphasize his regime's support for the Palestinian cause by, among other things, halting oil exports for one month in the spring of 2002 to protest Israeli actions.

Current Issues

In December 1999 the UN Security Council authorized the establishment of the UN Monitoring, Verification, and Inspection Committee (UNMOVIC) to succeed UNSCOM and offered to suspend the sanctions against Iraq if Baghdad were to cooperate with the new disarmament body and the IAEA for 120 days. Although Iraq quickly rejected the proposal, Hans Blix of Sweden, a former IAEA director, was chosen as a compromise candidate in January 2000 to head UNMOVIC, while technical appointments to UNMOVIC in March were designed to produce a broad base of inspectors who would be perceived as less subservient to US and UK influence than the UNSCOM inspectors had been. Nevertheless, Iraq displayed no inclination to let the new inspectors into the country, in part, according to some analyses, because international commitment to the sanctions appeared to be waning. President Hussein subsequently launched a "charm offensive" to reestablish regional ties, particularly through trade accommodations. In addition, he was seen as attempting to deflect attention away from the Iraqi disarmament issue by adopting a vocal pro-Palestinian stance.

The tone of the Iraqi/UN impasse changed significantly with the installation of the Bush administration in Washington in early 2001, the new US president announcing he would give heightened attention to enforcement of the no-fly zones and otherwise intensify the pressure on Baghdad. Lending support to the call for renewed vigilance, UNMOVIC in March 2001 indicated that the Iraqi regime probably still retained the ability to deploy biological and/or chemical weapons.

Following the terrorist attacks in the US in September 2001, President Bush quickly expanded the global US-led "war on terrorism" to include the Iraqi question, arguing that Iraqi weapons of mass destruction could someday end up in the hands of terrorists. Branding Iraq as a member (along with Iran and North Korea) of an "axis of evil," Bush directed the CIA to use "all available tools" to overthrow Hussein and in mid-2002 started planning a US-led invasion of Iraq if complete disarmament was not quickly forthcoming. Although Washington initially indicated it believed previous Security Council resolutions were sufficient to support military action against Iraq, the US administration ultimately responded to domestic and international pressure and decided to seek another "last chance" resolution. Iraq having agreed in September to "unconditional" inspections (while continuing to maintain that it possessed no prohibited weapons or weapon-delivery systems), the Security Council on November 8, 2002, adopted Resolution 1441, which threatened Iraq with "serious consequences" if it failed to comply with the new inspection regime. UNMOVIC inspectors arrived in Iraq later in the month.

The growing possibility of the overthrow of the regime of Saddam Hussein presented a paradox for leaders in the Kurdish north, which in recent years had enjoyed de facto self-rule, the region being divided into separate areas administered by the PUK and the DPK. For some Kurds, a war to remove Hussein actually appeared to represent a risk of relinquishing some of the authority currently exercised, although most of the Kurdish political organizations remained committed to the establishment of a federal Iraq. In addition, the Kurds were leery of Turkey's intentions should hostilities erupt. (Turkey, home to some 20 million Kurds, had battled its own Kurdish separatist movement since the early 1980s [see article on Turkey for details] and was naturally perceived as concerned that a breakup of Iraq could lead to renewed demands for creation of an independent Kurdistan.) Further complicating political and military assessment was the presence of major oil fields near the northern city of Kirkuk, currently controlled by the Hussein regime but deemed by the Kurds to belong rightfully to them.

UN weapons inspectors arrived in Iraq in late November 2002 to resume the search for banned weapons. Meanwhile, Iraq gave the UN a purported list of its current weapons as well as information on its past weapons programs. However, the 12,000-page report was heavily criticized by the US as being misleading and incomplete, and the UN demanded greater cooperation from Iraq, citing numerous incidents of interference. Consequently, on December 19 the US declared that Iraq was in breach of UN resolutions.

In January 2003 the inspectors discovered 12 unreported chemical warheads as well as Iraqi missiles that appeared to violate range limitations. However, Iraq subsequently pledged to be more forthcoming and cooperative, and opposition to the US military build-up grew in France, Germany, and a host of other nations. In February UN inspectors reported that Iraq had agreed to the UN's use of aerial reconnaissance, and the inspectors asked for more time to complete their mission. However, the US and the UK presented a draft UN Security Council resolution on February 24 that would have authorized military action against Iraq if the regime did not meet a deadline of March 17. By this point, the Security Council and NATO seemed locked into pro- and anti-invasion blocs. In response, the Bush administration announced that it would develop a "coalition of the willing" to pursue military action. The pro-war camp withdrew its draft UN resolution on March 17 in light of a threatened French veto. Meanwhile, as the US and the UK deployed more troops to the region and conducted a diplomatic campaign to convince more countries that Iraq was in violation of its UN commitments, Arab leaders tried unsuccessfully to convince Saddam to resign and go into exile.

As the threat of invasion grew larger, the Iraqi regime undertook a number of steps designed to forestall military engagement. On February 4, Iraqi officials made an offer to renegotiate terms with the UN to address any remaining major concerns of the weapons inspectors. The regime also began destroying its stocks of the prohibited missiles in

March. At the same time, the country was divided into four military districts, each led by a relative or close ally of Saddam, and Iraq began defensive deployments of troops around Baghdad.

On March 20, 2003, the US launched a series of missile attacks (the so-called "shock and awe" initiative) in an effort to kill prominent Iraqi leaders. American, British, Australian, and Polish troops began a ground offensive shortly thereafter. The coalition forces drove quickly into Iraq and engaged in both conventional warfare and psychological warfare to convince the Iraqi military to surrender. Both efforts were fairly successful, with the rapid advance to Baghdad being eased by the surrender of major Iraqi commands. Meanwhile, some of the most intense fighting of the war took place between coalition forces and Iraqi special militias known as the *Fedayeen* (martyrs) *Saddam*. (Some of the *Fedayeen* were reportedly non-Iraqis recruited on the eve of the campaign.) Among other things, the US/UK coalition attempted to prompt a Shi'ite uprising in the South, with limited success. However, Kurdish forces in the north operated effectively with US special operations forces and airborne troops and were able to capture the key towns of Mosul and Kirkuk. By April 7, US forces were in Baghdad; the last battle of the campaign took place in Saddam's hometown of Tikrit on April 14.

On May 1 President Bush declared an end to major combat operations, prematurely as it later turned out. Subsequently, the US-led coalition undertook efforts to create a stable interim government and restore security and infrastructure. However, the first attempts to develop a broad-based government failed as Iraqis could not agree on specific terms and opposed US plans to keep the proposed IIA as a mainly advisory body. After the ORHA was deemed to have been a failure (particularly in view of a deteriorating security situation), new chief civilian leader Paul Bremer attempted to "de-Baathify" the government and military by dissolving the security forces, a decision that was later perceived to have had negative consequences.

Security continued to deteriorate as foreign fighters, former regime elements, and Iraqi Sunnis engaged in a bloody insurgency. A truck bomb destroyed the UN compound in Baghdad leading to a UN withdrawal from Iraq, and car bombs and improvised explosives subsequently took a toll on coalition forces and Iraqi leaders. In a major development for the invasion camp, Saddam's two sons were killed in a battle in Mosul in late July 2003. Meanwhile, efforts to identify or discover banned weapons produced no results, even after the deployment of the 1,000-member Iraq Survey Group (composed of US and international weapons experts). (In January 2005 the Bush administration confirmed that no banned weapons or chemical agents had been found.)

The insurgents also began to kidnap foreign workers and Iraqi government and political figures. Over time, the insurgency appeared to become more organized, and many analysts concluded that one of the ringleaders was Jordanian-born Abu Musab al-ZARQAWI, a known terrorist with links to *al-Qaeda* (see section on *al-Qaeda* in article on Afghanistan for additional information).

On December 13, 2003, Saddam was captured near Tikrit, and by January 2004 the coalition had captured or killed 42 of its 55 "most-wanted" former Iraqi leaders. Meanwhile, security improved in the Kurdish north and the Shi'ite South, the ongoing insurgency being concentrated in the central region in an area that came to be known as the Sunni Triangle.

During negotiations on the interim constitution in early 2004, the Shi'ites on the IGC demanded that the document be based on *shari'a* (Islamic law); they also opposed a clause that permitted any three provinces to block a permanent constitution with a two-thirds vote in each of the three provinces. Since there were three Kurdish provinces, that provision gave the Kurds a de facto veto over the future constitution. However, the country's highest Shi'ite leaders eventually agreed to the "Kurdish veto." In return, a plan to use regional bodies to elect representatives to the Transitional National Assembly was revised in favor of direct elections.

In March 2004 Bremer announced the reconstruction of the Iraqi security forces in response to growing unrest in Fallujah on the part of followers of Shi'ite cleric Muqtada al-SADR, the son of a popular cleric killed by the Saddam regime. After two sieges in April and May, a second assault included members of the new Iraqi security forces, and Fallujah was returned to relative calm. Al-Sadr subsequently announced his intention to pursue political participation (including the formation of a political party).

Internal problems continued to plague the IGC and the CPA through 2004. (On May 17, 2004, the chair of the IGC, Izzedin SALIM, was assassinated.) Meanwhile, the credibility of the US was undermined by revelations of a prisoner-abuse scandal at the US military prison at Abu Ghraib in which US troops reportedly mistreated and degraded Iraqi prisoners.

After reportedly contentious negotiations within the Sunni community, Muhsin 'Adb al-HAMID, leader of the Iraqi Islamic Party (the largest mainstream Sunni party) urged Sunnis to boycott the balloting for the Transitional National Assembly on January 30, 2005. Nevertheless, the pictures of Iraqi citizens, including women, voting in a meaningful election for the first time had an undeniably positive emotional impact on democracy supporters throughout the world. The turnout was estimated at approximately 60 percent, and international observers described the balloting as generally free and fair. On the other hand, the lack of significant Sunni representation in the TNA created difficulties in selecting the transitional cabinet that was finally installed in May.

On May 10, 2005, the TNA appointed a 55-member council to draft a new constitution. A deadline of August 15 was set for completion of the draft, which was slated to be presented to a national referendum by October 15 in preparations for new national elections by the end of the year. However, the August 15 deadline was subsequently extended amid disagreement over, among other things, the extent of autonomy to be given to the three main regions. Sunnis in particular were concerned about extensive Shi'ite control of oil-rich areas in the south as well as possible Iranian influence over the southern provinces.

Political Parties and Groups

Following the 1968 coup the dominant force within Iraq was the *Baath,* which under the National Action Charter of 1973 became the core of the regime-supportive National Progressive Front.

Following the onset of the war with Iran in September 1980, various elements announced the formation of antigovernment groupings, all receiving support from abroad. On November 28 the Iraqi Communist Party (ICP), the Democratic Party of Kurdistan (DPK), and the Unified Socialist Party of Kurdistan (USPK) signed a charter establishing a Democratic Iraqi Front (DIF) committed to establishment of a coalition government and Kurdish autonomy, the severance of ties to the "world capitalist market," and solidarity with anti-Zionist and socialist governments. Earlier, on November 12, a National Pan-Arab Democratic Front (NPADF) reportedly encompassing seven different groups, including the Patriotic Union of Kurdistan (PUK) as well as *Baath* and ICP dissidents, was formed at Damascus, Syria.

A more inclusive opposition grouping, the 17-member Iraqi National Joint Action Committee (INJAC) was launched at Damascus on December 27, 1990. The new formation encompassed virtually all members of the DIF, NPADF, and the Supreme Council of the Islamic Revolution of Iraq (SCIRI, below). During an INJAC summit at Damascus in August 1991 the coalition called for efforts to "promote its actions inside Iraq"; however, in December coalition members rejected a plan that called for regional assistance in overthrowing the regime. Coordination of opposition activity passed in June 1992 to the Iraqi National Congress (INC, below).

On September 3, 1991, President Hussein nominally ended 23 years of de facto one-party rule by approving a measure that legalized opposition formations; however, there were no reports of such groups emerging subsequently in areas under government control.

Dissident groups met with top US officials in August 2002 to try to present a coherent, cohesive front in anticipation of possible US-led military action against the regime of Saddam Hussein, but, according to most accounts, the opposition remained fractious. Some 50 groups also met in London in December in pursuit of unified policies. However, success was again limited, although a 75-member follow-up committee was established which proponents hoped would serve as the basis for a "post-Saddam" interim government pending eventual establishment of a parliamentary, democratic, pluralistic, and federal Iraq. Problems reported at the conference included objections by some groups over perceived INC "domination," criticism by smaller Shi'ite organizations over SCIRI's apparent efforts to speak for the entire Shi'ite population, and concerns over the presence of former Iraqi military officers, who may have been involved in human rights abuses while serving in Iraq but were now seeking a role in the next government.

Some 110 electoral lists were reportedly registered for the January 2005 balloting for the Transitional National Assembly.

Parliamentary Parties

United Iraqi Alliance. Formed in December 2004, the United Iraqi Alliance was the brainchild of Grand Ayatollah Ali al-SISTANI, the Shi'ite leader who wanted an umbrella electoral organization for the major Shi'ite parties. By the time of the January 30, 2005, balloting for the Transitional National Assembly, some 22 parties had reportedly joined the Alliance.

Leader: Ibrahim al-JAAFARI (Prime Minister of the Transitional National Government).

Supreme Council of the Islamic Revolution in Iraq (SCIRI). Also referenced as the Supreme Assembly of the Islamic Revolution in Iraq (SAIRI), SCIRI was formed in 1982 as an umbrella for a number of Shi'ite groups, including the **Holy Warriors** (*al-Mujaheddin*), which had been founded in 1979 and was considered to have direct ties to Iranian militants. The **Holy Warriors** had claimed responsibility for a variety of anti-Baghdad terrorist at-

tacks, and in March 1980 the RCC had decreed the death penalty for members of the organization. Other founding members of SCIRI were Islamic Call (*al-Da'wah,* see below); the **Islamic Action Organization,** an *Al-Da'wah* splinter formed in 1980 under the leadership of Skeikh Taqi MODARESSI; the **Islamic Movement in Iraq,** led by Sheikh Muhammad Mahdi al-KALISI; and the **Islamic Scholars Organization,** led by Sheikh al-NASERI.

Each of the SCIRI components was awarded representation on the INJAC in 1990. In late December 1991 the INJAC debated and ultimately rejected a plan formulated by SCIRI leader Hojatolislam Said Muhammad Bakr al-HAKIM (a founder of the Holy Warriors), which called for Syrian, Iranian, and Turkish assistance in overthrowing the Hussein regime.

While SCIRI refused to send delegates to the June 1992 INC meeting in Austria, it participated in subsequent conferences in Iraq and on February 11, 1993, issued a statement denying reports that it had withdrawn from the organization. In early 1994 spokesmen for the Iranian-supported SCIRI called for UN intervention to protect the Shi'ite population in southern Iraq from a government military offensive. The relationship between SCIRI and whatever remained of the INC structure was unclear in 1997. In early 1999 the United States indicated an interest in providing assistance to SCIRI as part of the new US initiative to topple Saddam Hussein. However, SCIRI leaders based in Iran declined the offer and also remained wary over proposed participation in the planned revitalization of the INC. Nevertheless, SCIRI was described as "perhaps the most credible" of the groups in the fragmented Iraqi opposition, based on its ongoing presence in the south and continued support within the Shi'ite population.

SCIRI declined to attend the INC rejuvenation meetings in 1999. It subsequently claimed responsibility for attacks on Iraqi government targets in May 2000 and June 2001. Although SCIRI participated in the 2002 sessions designed to promote a unified opposition front in advance of a potential US-led military campaign against Saddam Hussein, it was clear at that time that SCIRI was not operating as an INC component. Among other things, SCIRI opposed US military intervention, arguing that an overthrow of the Hussein regime should be accomplished by Iraqis themselves. To that end, SCIRI was reported to have an estimated 8,000–12,000 fighters at its command, most in Iran but some already in Iraq.

SCIRI leader Muhammad Bakr al-Hakim was assassinated in August 2003; he was succeeded by his nephew, 'Abd al-Aziz al-Hakim.

Following the overthrow of the regime of Saddam Hussein in 2003, the SCIRI militia (known as the Badr Brigade) reportedly disbanded and reformed as a political entity called the **Badr Organization**, which joined the United Iraqi Alliance.

Leaders: Adil 'Abd al-MAHDI (Vice President of the Republic), 'Abd al-Aziz al-HAKIM (Leader of SCIRI).

Islamic Call (*al-Da'wah al-Islamiyah*). *Al-Da'wah* was established in the 1960s with the support of the Shi'a leader Muhammad Baqir al-Sadr, who was executed by the Hussein regime in April 1980. Also closely affiliated with the Iranian *Mujaheddin,* the Damascus-based *al-Da'wah* claimed responsibility for seven assassination attempts on Hussein and for numerous bombings during the 1980s. Although it was a founding member of the INC, *al-Da'wah* subsequently distanced itself from the Congress because it was unsatisfied with its representation on the group's Executive Council. *Al-Da'wah* reportedly was one of several groups that claimed responsibility for the attempted assassination of Udai Hussein in December 1997. It was subsequently specifically precluded from receiving US aid for its antiregime activities, raising further questions as to its relationship, if any, to SCIRI and/or the INC. In fact, some reports in April 1999 indicated that a "deep political rivalry" had developed between *al-Da'wah* and the SAIRI leadership. By 2002 it was gen-

erally accepted that *al-Da'wah* had broken away from SCIRI, and it was not officially represented at the various Iraqi opposition meetings during 2002, although a moderate wing of the party was reportedly in favor of participating in opposition unity efforts. However, the party (dominated by Shi'ites but said also to have Sunni members) joined the United Iraqi List for the January 2005 legislative balloting.

Leaders: Muhammad Bakr al-NASRI, Sheikh Kazem al-HAERI (Spiritual Leader).

Iraqi National Congress (INC). The INC was launched by a number of largely Kurdish exile groups at Vienna, Austria, on June 16–19, 1992. More than 70 delegates from 33 opposition groups attended the Congress's first conference within Iraq at the northern city of Shaqlawah on September 23–27. During a second such conference at Salahuddin on October 27–31, 170 representatives from virtually all the antiregime formations elected a three-member Presidential Council and a 26-member Executive Council. The participants also committed themselves to the nonviolent overthrow of Saddam Hussein and the establishment of a federal system that would permit a substantial degree of ethnic autonomy without partition of the country. Delegates to a third conference at Salahuddin on February 16–21, 1993, established a constitutional council and approved diplomatic initiatives intended to secure broader international support for their efforts. At that time many groups (including the DPK, PUK, SCIRI, IMIK, and INA) were presenting themselves as components of the INC. However, infighting subsequently disrupted INC cohesion. In late 1993 fighting broke out between the PUK and IMIK, some 200 people being killed before a peace agreement was negotiated at the INC's Salahuddin headquarters in February 1994. Even more serious was ongoing conflict between the DPK and the PUK, the dominant Kurdish groups in the INC. Following the incursion of Iraqi troops into the Kurdish north at the behest of the DPK in the summer of 1996, the INC was described as in complete disarray. Among other things, Iraqi soldiers reportedly ransacked the INC headquarters at Salahuddin and killed a number of Congress members who were believed to have been working with the American Central Intelligence Agency (CIA).

In early 1999 Washington designated the INC as one of the groups eligible to receive US aid in the effort to topple the Iraqi regime. Consequently, in an apparent effort to regroup following the 1996 debacle, the INC held its first general meeting in nearly three years at London in April 1999. The session appointed an "interim collective leadership" to oversee the revitalization effort, although the seat reserved for the SCIRI was not filled.

The United States briefly halted aid to the INC in early 2002 to protest perceived insufficient accounting of the estimated $18 million previously allocated to the INC. However, later in the year the INC's international profile again increased as speculation grew over the role of long-standing Iraqi opposition groups following the potential overthrow of Saddam Hussein. A few observers suggested that INC leader Ahmad Chalabi might serve an important role in a new government. At the same time, however, it appeared that many of its major founding components no longer considered themselves members of the INC. The SCIRI, for example, clearly was maintaining its distance from the INC, while the PUK, DPK, and INA were also regularly being referenced as operating outside of the INC umbrella.

Chalabi and other INC members entered Iraq during the US/UK-led invasion in early 2003. Despite losing the support of the US for alleged improper financial dealings, Chalabi became a deputy prime minister in the Transitional National Government.

Leaders: Ahmad CHALABI (Deputy Prime Minister), Gen. Najib al-SALHI.

Islamic Action Organization. Often referred to as the Islamic Task Organization (ITO), this group was formed in the early 1960s and

takes as its "action" or "task" the establishment of an Islamic government in Iraq. The group coordinates activities with SCIRI and has denounced attacks on US forces.

Leader: Taqi al-MUDARRISI.

Other minor parties in the United Iraqi Alliance included: **Hezbollah**, a "Marsh Arab" Shi'ite grouping; and the **Islamic Union of Iraqi Turkmen**, a grouping of Shi'ite Turkmen formed in 1991 and led by Abbas al-BAYATI.

Democratic Patriotic Alliance of Kurdistan (DPAK). Also referenced simply as the Kurdistan Alliance, the DPAK was formed by the DPK, PUK, and other smaller groups in December 2005 to contest the January 2005 national legislative balloting, at which the DPAK finished second with 40 seats. The PUK, DPK, and most of the other smaller DPAK parties presented a joint Kurdish National Democratic List for the concurrent elections to the Iraqi Kurdistan National Assembly. PUK Secretary General Jalal Talabani was subsequently appointed president of the new national Presidential Council.

Democratic Party of Kurdistan (DPK). The DPK evolved from a KDP offshoot, the Kurdish Democratic Party (Provisional Leadership), that was formed in late 1975 following the Algiers agreement between Iraq and Iran and the collateral termination of aid to the Kurds by Iran and the United States. With Mullah Barzani having withdrawn from the Kurdish insurgency, thereby completing dismemberment of the original KDP, the Provisional Leadership declared itself the legitimate successor to the mullah's party. Having refused to cooperate with the National Front, it undertook renewed guerrilla activity through what had been the military wing of the old party, the *Pesh Mergas* ("Those Who Face Death"). Subsequently, the Provisional Leadership consistently opposed government efforts to "resettle" Kurds in southern Iraq and engaged in clashes with both the Iraqi army and the rival PUK (below). The DPK designation was adopted following the death of Mullah Barzani at Washington, DC, on

March 1, 1979, although differences between so-called "traditionalist" and "intellectual" factions continued.

In mid-July 1979 several hundred party members returned to Iraq from Iran, where they had resided since 1975. In the spring of 1980, however, there were reports that Iraqi Kurds (*Faili*), who had emigrated from Iran in the first half of the century, were being expelled at the rate of 2,000 a day. Collaterally, Massud Barzani, the son of Mullah Barzani and a leader of the DPK Iranian wing, voiced support for the Teheran regime because of collusion between "US imperialism and its [*Baath*] lackeys... [in] relentlessly fighting against... our Shi'a brethren." A subsequent party congress in August 1981 concluded with a denunciation of the "fascist regime" at Baghdad and its "imperialist war."

In 1988 the DPK and the PUK served as the leading components of a new rebel coalition called the Kurdistan Front (KF) that also included the Kurdistan Socialist Party (KSP), the Kurdistan People's Party (a small Marxist grouping), and the IMIK. The DPK controlled the largest rebel force during the 1991 Kurdish uprising following the Gulf War and was represented at the Baghdad peace talks by Nashirwan Barzani, a nephew of Massud Barzani and grandson of the KDP's founder. During the second half of 1991, the gulf between Massud Barzani, who urged immediate negotiations with the Hussein regime, and the PUK's Jalal Talabani, who argued for continued military actions prior to talks, widened, thus hampering action by a coalition that had granted veto power to each of its members. (The revived KF now included the Assyrian Democratic Party [a Kurdish-speaking Assyrian grouping], the Christian Union [another Assyrian formation], and the Kurdish Communist Party [KCP–an offshoot of the ICP, below].)

On May 19, 1992, the KF conducted an inconclusive election for executive leader, neither of the leading contenders (Massud Barzani and Jalal Talabani), with vote shares of 44.6 and 44.3 percent, respectively, being able to secure a majority; concurrently, a 105-seat Iraqi Kurdistan National Assembly was selected (see under Legislatures, below). The DPK and the PUK decided to share power equally in the assembly as well as in a Kurdish "national government" located at Arbil. Moreover, immediately prior to an INC meeting in September 1992, the two groups agreed to place their guerrilla units under a single command. However, the accord was never implemented, and the DPK and PUK retained control of western and eastern "enclaves," respectively. Ongoing tension, fueled by the reported deep animosity between Barzani and Talabani, eventually erupted into open fighting in early 1994, and as many as 2,000 guerrillas were reported killed over the ensuing months. Although an agreement was announced in late November for a cease-fire leading up to new elections in May 1995, PUK forces shortly thereafter seized control of Arbil and expelled DPK representatives from the assembly and cabinet. Yet another cease-fire in the spring of 1995 also proved ineffective, and heavy fighting was reported to have broken out again in July, one correspondent describing the factions as "risking national suicide" at the time when unity was most crucial to Kurdish ambitions. Despite intense US mediation efforts, the DPK/PUK infighting continued throughout the rest of the year and the first half of 1996 as each side retained control of its own territory and no region-wide governance was attempted.

Prompting intense international criticism, the DPK invited the Iraqi military to join it in a "final" offensive against the PUK in late August 1996. (DPK leaders subsequently argued that they had taken that action out of fear that the PUK was planning its own offensive in concert with Iranian forces, who had recently crossed the border to challenge guerrillas from the Kurdish Democratic Party of Iran.) Some 30,000 Iraqi soldiers moved into the north and quickly forced the PUK out of its stronghold at Salahuddin and toward the Iranian border.

On September 26, 1996, DPK leader Barzani announced the formation of a new coalition

Kurdish government, led by Roz Nuri Shawez of the DPK and including representatives from the IMIK and the KCP. Barzani also declared that the "temporary" military alliance with Baghdad had ended (Iraqi troops having already been withdrawn in the face of US retaliatory measures in southern Iraq) and reiterated that he was not pursuing a separate political accord with the Iraqi regime. Subsequently, the PUK launched a counter-offensive and recaptured most of the territory it had recently lost. By late October the DPK and PUK were again reported to be discussing a cease-fire and the possible reactivation of regional authority.

The DPK withdrew from negotiations in March 1997, and KF cohesion was further corroded when new hostilities broke out the following month between the PUK and the IMIK. Kurdish affairs were additionally complicated in May when some 10,000 Turkish troops crossed into northern Iraq to attack camps of the Kurdish Workers' Party (PKK, see article on Turkey). Although Baghdad formally objected to the encroachment on its sovereignty, its protest was apparently not heartfelt enough to stimulate any other action. Despite UN and other international condemnation of its cross-border offensive, Turkey sent even more forces into Iraq in September, claiming, among other things, that it had been invited to do so by the DPK. Subsequently, the PUK launched what it called a "preemptive strike" against DPK strongholds in October; however, the cease-fire was subsequently reinstated (reportedly under heavy US pressure) and the uneasy DPK/PUK territorial and military standoff continued into 1998. At that time, it was estimated that there were approximately 10,000 DPK guerrillas loyal to Barzani, described as a publicity-shy "tribal leader" wary of Western influence in the region. Despite having been branded a "traitor" by other opposition groups for his brief collaboration with the Iraqi regime in 1996 Barzani was invited to Washington to meet with Talabani in the fall of 1998, their subsequent peace agreement reflecting US recognition that the former

remained a significant influence in the Kurdish region and thereby a necessary component of any effective anti-Hussein opposition. Among other things, the two Kurdish leaders agreed to share power in the region and to conduct new assembly elections in the second half of 1999. However, although "relative peace" transpired in the Kurdish-controlled regions, continued friction prevented new assembly balloting. Finally, in October 2002, the assembly reconvened amidst a "display of friendship" between Barzani and Talabani, seemingly prompted by the prospect of the overthrow of Saddam Hussein and the concurrent need for Kurdish unity in discussions regarding a "post-Saddam" Iraq. (It has long been widely accepted that Kurdish sentiment overwhelmingly favors the creation of an independent Kurdish state. However, bowing to opposition to that proposal from regional and Western capitals, the Kurdish groups in Iraq remain formally supportive of a federated Iraq with substantial regional autonomy.) As of late 2002, it was estimated that as many as 25,000 guerrillas were under the command of the DPK, which had governed northwestern Iraq on a de facto basis with an administration based at Arbil. (Most news reports currently reference this group as the Kurdish Democratic Party [KDP] in apparent recognition of its status as the genuine successor to the original KDP.)

Leaders: Massud BARZANI, Jawhar Namiq SALIM, Sami ABDURAHMAN, Hashyar ZUBARI.

Patriotic Union of Kurdistan (PUK). The PUK, which has received support from the Syrian *Baath,* resulted from the 1977 merger of Jalal Talabani's Kurdish National Union (KNU) with the Socialist Movement of Kurdistan and the Association of Marxist-Leninists of Kurdistan. The KNU had been formed in mid-1975 when Talabani, a left-wing member of the original KDP, refused to accept Mullah Barzani's claim that the Kurdish rebellion had come to an end. Supported by *Pesh Merga* units, Talabani subsequently attempted to unify guerrilla activity under his leadership, but the PUK suffered significant losses in June 1978 during skirmishes in northern Iraq with the DPK, which Talabani accused of having links to both the shah of Iran and the US Central Intelligence Agency.

In January 1984 it was reported that an agreement had been concluded between the PUK and government forces that called for a cease-fire, assurances of greater Kurdish autonomy, and the formation of a 40,000-member Kurdish army to counter Iranian incursions into Iraqi Kurdistan. The agreement, if actually undertaken, was never implemented, and Iran's Islamic Republic News Agency asserted in November 1986 that the PUK had entered into an alliance with the DPK to pursue a joint struggle against Baghdad.

PUK forces battled with supporters of the IMIK (below) in late 1993, PUK leaders calling the pro-Iranian fundamentalists "dangerous" and uncommitted to basic Kurdish aspirations. Two years later the PUK was also locked in open conflict with the DPK, Talabani accusing arch rival Barzani, among other things, of "hoarding" revenue generated by trade across the Turkish border. Like the DPK, the PUK was estimated to control about 15,000–25,000 fighters, leading observers to the conclusion that a military resolution of their dispute seemed unlikely. Meanwhile, Talabani, described, in contrast to Barzani, as a "garrulous jet-setter," was considered to have the stronger support among Western powers. The PUK, with which a core of urban intellectuals and leftists could still be identified, also exhibited policy differences with the DPK, its antitribal stance, for example, attracting support from peasant farmers embroiled in land disputes with long-standing tribal leaders. Following attacks by DPK/Iraqi forces in August-September 1996, the PUK was reported to have received military support from Iran, facilitating its subsequent counteroffensive. In September 1998 Talabani reconciled with Barzani during a meeting in Washington in the interest of presenting a united front against the Iraqi regime (see DPK, above, for additional information). Subsequently, the PUK has exer-

cised de facto authority in the eastern half of northern Iraq, designating the city of Sulaimani as its regional "capital."

Leaders: Jalal TALABANI (President of the Republic and leader of the Party), Barham SALIH, Ahmad BAMARMI.

Other minor parties in the DPAK included: the **Assyrian National Party**; the **Kurdistan Communist Party** (KCP) formed in 1993 and led by Kamal SHAKIR; the **Kurdistan Islamic Union**, led by Salah al-Din Baha al-DIN; the **Kurdistan Socialist Democratic Party** (KSDP), led by Muhammad Jahi MAHMUD; and the **Kurdistan Toilers' Party**, formed in 1985 by dissidents from the Kurdistan Socialist Party under the leadership of Qadir AZIZ.

Iraqi List. Formed by Interim Prime Minister Ayad Allawi in December 2004 in advance of the January 2005 legislative balloting, the Iraqi List included tribal leaders and members of several parties and groups, including Allawi's INA, the **Iraqi Democrats Movement**, the **Iraqi Independents Association**, and the **Council of Iraqi Nobles**. The Iraqi List campaigned on promoting national unity by bridging ethnic and religious differences.

Leader: Ayad ALLAWI (Former Interim Prime Minister).

Iraqi National Accord (INA). A predominantly Sunni Muslim grouping formed with support from Saudi Arabia following the Iraqi invasion of Kuwait, the National Accord was the focus of increasing attention in the mid-1990s in light of the disarray within the INC. The American intelligence community in particular reportedly concluded that the accord represented one of the "most promising" of the Iraqi opposition formations, in part because its members included a number of defectors from the Iraqi military. The accord opened an office in 'Amman, Jordan, in February 1996 after King Hussein offered to support anti-Saddam Hussein efforts. An accord office also operated in Kurdish-controlled territory in northern Iraq until operations there were quashed by Iraqi troops in August-September 1996. The group was also one of the seven organizations deemed eligible by Washington in early 1999 to share in $97 million of US aid designed to support antiregime activity. Subsequent reports also regularly referenced the INA, which claimed clandestine support within the current Iraqi military, as a member of the revamped INC. However, although continuing to cooperate (from offices in London and Jordan) with the INC in attempting to establish a unified opposition front in 2002, the INA appeared to be making certain that it was identified as a separate grouping. Meanwhile, former INA members under the leadership of Tawfiq al-YASIRI and other former Iraqi military officers had formed an Iraqi National Coalition to participate in opposition coordination efforts.

Leaders: Dirgham KADHIM, Ayad ALLAWI (Secretary General).

Iraqiyun List. Formed in December 2004 by Interim President Ghazi Ajil al-Yawar, the Iraqiyun List comprised independents and members of small parties from across the political, ethnic, and religious spectrums. It supported a federal system for Iraq based on pluralism. After the Iraqiyun List secured five seats in the Transitional National Assembly in January 2005, al-Yawar was named one of Iraq's two vice presidents.

Leader: Ghazi Ajil al-YAWAR (Vice President of the Republic).

Iraqi Turkmen Front (ITF). A coalition of 26 small Turkmen parties and groups formed in 1995, the ITF advocates greater autonomy for Turkmen ethnic group and recognition of it as one of Iraq's major minority groups. The ITF secured three seats in the 2005 National Assembly elections.

Leader: Faruk Abdullah 'Abd al-RAHMAN.

Independent National Elites and Cadres Party. Formed by radical Shi'ite cleric Muqtada al-Sadr, this party was a political manifestation of Sadr's militia forces, the Mehdi Army. Also known as the Independent National Bloc, the group was designed to provide Sadr a legitimate political role. The Independent National Bloc campaigned for an Islamic government and the withdrawal of foreign

troops. In the 2005 elections, the group gained three seats in the National Assembly.

Leader: Muqtada al-SADR.

Kurdistan Islamic Group (KIG). Formed in 2001 by Muhammad Ali BAPIR, this group is composed mainly of former members of the IMIK. The group is reportedly linked to the *Ansar al-Islam* (see below), an allegation denied by Bapir. However, leadership figures were arrested by US forces in 2003. In the 2005 elections, the KIG secured two seats in the Transitional National Assembly.

Leader: Muhammad Ali BAPIR.

Iraqi Communist Party –ICP (*al-Hizb al-Shuyu'i al-'Iraqi*). Foun-ded in 1934, the Communist Party was legalized upon its entrance into the National Front in 1973. Pro-Moscow in orientation, it occasionally criticized the regime on both domestic and foreign policy grounds, including the latter's pro-Somalian posture in the Ethiopian conflict and its handling of the Kurdish insurgency, with which some elements of the party had been associated. In May 1978 the government executed 21 Communists for engaging in political activities within the armed forces (a right reserved exclusively to *Baath* members), and by March 1979 several hundred ICP members had either fled the country or relocated in Kurdish areas. With the party having withdrawn from the National Front, (then) RCC Vice Chairman Hussein confirmed in April that Communists were in fact being purged.

Following the onset of war with Iran in 1980, First Secretary 'Aziz MUHAMMAD voiced both support for the Kurdish minority and opposition to the Gulf hostilities, which he characterized, at the February-March 1981 Soviet Communist Party Congress, as a "destructive military adventure."

In 1993 an ICP congress rejected a proposal that it transform itself into a more centrist grouping and instead reaffirmed its Marxist identity. The congress also elected Hamid Majid Muza (an Arab) to replace Muhammad (a Kurd) as general secretary, Kurdish members subsequently forming the KCP (above). A 1997 ICP Congress restated its opposition to the Hussein regime and called for establishment of a "united, federal, democratic Iraq."

The ICP was not included on the list of opposition groups approved by Washington to receive US assistance in early 1999, and it did not participate in the 2002 meetings led by the INC, SCIRI, and other groups in the hope of creating a unified opposition front. However, Muza was appointed a member of the Governing Council following the fall of Saddam Hussein, and the ICP campaigned for the January 2005 legislative election under a **People's Union** list that also included non-ICP candidates.

Leader: Hamid Majid MUZA.

Other parties that secured representation in the National Assembly in the 2005 elections, include: the **National Rafidayn List**, a coalition of the **Assyrian Democratic Movement** and the **Chaldean National Council**; the **National Democratic Alliance**; and the **Reconciliation and Liberation Bloc**.

Other Parties and Groups

Iraqi Islamic Party (IIP). Formed in the 1950s, the Sunni IIP was suppressed during the reign of Saddam Hussein, and members of the party conducted an armed struggle against the regime. The IIP resurfaced after the fall of Saddam in 2003, and the party's secretary general, Muhsin 'Abd al-Hamid, was given a seat on the Governing Council. Leaders of the IIP called on followers to boycott the January 2005 legislative elections.

Leader: Muhsin 'Abd al-HAMID (Secretary General).

Free Iraqi Council (FIC). The liberal, generally pro-Western FIC was launched in 1991 under the leadership of Saad Saleh Jabr, theretofore head of the Nation Party (*al-Hizb al-'Umma*), which had been formed in London in 1982 in opposition to the regime of Saddam Hussein. The Nation Party concurrently suspended activity in deference to the "nonpartisan" status of the FIC, which subsequently was described as in "competition" with the INC for Western recognition as the leading external opposition formation.

Leader: Saad Saleh JABIR.

Movement for Constitutional Monarchy. Led by a claimant to the Hashemite throne, which was abolished in 1958, the London-based movement was one of the groups declared eligible for special US aid in early 1999. In 2002 it was described as a component of the INC.

Leaders: Sharif Ali ibn HUSSEIN, Salah al-SHAYKHLY.

Islamic Movement of Iraqi Kurdistan (IMIK). The Sunni Muslim IMIK, also referenced as the Kurdistan Islamic Movement (KIM), long served as the voice of the Islamic fundamentalist movement in northern Iraq. As a member of the Kurdistan Front, the IMIK reportedly won 4 percent of the vote in the May 1992 balloting for the Iraqi Kurdistan National Assembly; however, it subsequently rejected an offer from the DPK and the PUK to fill five seats in the new legislative body. In December 1993 intense fighting broke out between supporters of the IMIK and the PUK, followed by a reported "peace agreement" brokered by representatives of SCIRI in February 1994. Viewed as having Iranian support, the IMIK was subsequently reported to have agreed to participate in the new Kurdish government envisioned by the November 1994 DPK/PUK accord. However, when that plan collapsed, the movement, by then apparently controlling some territory near the Iranian border in its own right, was described as aligned with the DPK in ongoing confrontation with the PUK.

A serious split within the IMIK led to the creation of the more radical *Ansar al-Islam* (see below). Although the IMIK had originally been on the list of groups eligible for US aid under the Iraq Liberation Act, assistance was reportedly denied following the terrorist attacks in the US in September 2001, apparently out of concern in Washington over funding certain Islamist groupings.

Leaders: Sheikh Othman 'Abd al-AZIZ, Ahmad Kakar MAHMOUD, Sheikh Sadiq 'Abd al-AZIZ.

Ansar al-Islam (Supporters of Islam). A Kurdish extremist grouping launched initially as the *Jund al-Islam* (Army of Islam) by IMIK defectors and other fundamentalist militants in mid-2001, *Ansar al-Islam* was subsequently blamed for a number of violent episodes in northern Iraq. One of the group's adversaries—the PUK—alleged that *Ansar al-Islam,* which controlled several villages with a guerrilla force estimated at 400–1,000 fighters, was connected with the *al-Qaeda* terrorist network of Osama bin Laden.

Leaders: Mullah Najm al-Din FARAJ (also known as Mullah KREKAR), Ahson Ali 'Abd al-AZIZ, Abdullah al-SHAFI'I.

Former Government Front

National Progressive and Patriotic Front (NPPF). In 1973 the *Baath* joined the Iraqi Communist Party (ICP, below) in forming what was then styled the National Progressive Front (NPF). The small Kurdish splinter groups (KDP and KRP) were added in 1974. However, the front was significantly weakened when the Communists withdrew in March 1979, serving almost exclusively thereafter as a means of presenting *Baath*-endorsed electoral candidates who were not permitted to campaign under party labels. There was little reference to the NPPF in the 1996 and 2000 National Assembly elections, although the front continued to exist and regularly issued press statements in support of the policies of President Hussein.

Arab Socialist Renaissance Party (*Hizb al-Baath al-Arabi al-Ishtiraki*). The *Baath* was founded in 1947 as an Arab nationalist movement with branches in Syria and other Arab countries. The Iraqi leadership, known as the Regional Command (and recently also referenced as "Iraq's Command"), was headed by President Hussein, who was reconfirmed as regional secretary at an extraordinary National Congress on July 10, 1986. The relevancy of the *Baath's* pan-Arabist orientation was questioned in view of Iraq's growing isolation within the Arab world following the 1990–1991 Gulf war. Although the influence of the *Baath* was believed to have declined in the first half of the 1990s, a rejuvenation was apparent to many observers as the party to a large extent organized the presidential referendum of October 1995 and mobilized a massive voter turnout. In addition, most of the candidates for the 1996 and 2000 assembly elections were *Baath* members. One successful assembly candidate in the 2000 balloting was Saddam Hussein's eldest son, Udai HUSSEIN. However, a younger son, Qusai HUSSEIN, was elevated to important positions in the *Baath* as well as the Regional Command in May 2001, suggesting to some observers that he was being groomed as Saddam Hussein's preferred successor. The *Baath* was disbanded by the CPA following the ouster of Saddam Hussein in 2003.

Leader: Saddam HUSSEIN (Former President of the Republic).

Kurdish Democratic Party–KDP (*al-Hizb al-Dimuqraati al-Kurdi*). The original KDP, founded in 1946 by Mullah Mustafa al-Barzani, experienced a number of cleavages (see above) both before and after the cease-fire of March 1975. The group that joined the National Front in 1974 was a Marxist rump of the original party. In September 1978 it reaffirmed its support of the front and of the *Baath's* "revolutionary struggle." (This grouping, members of which were appointed to the Iraqi National Assembly by President Hussein in 2000, should not be confused with the Democratic Party of Kurdistan [DPK, above], the large anti-Hussein Kurdish faction that is also now widely referenced as the Kurdish Democratic Party.)

Leader: Muhammad Said Ahmad al-ATRUSHI (Secretary General).

Kurdistan Revolutionary Party (KRP). The KRP originated in 1972 as a secessionist offshoot of the original KDP and in 1974 joined the NPF along with the neo-KDP and another offshoot, the Progressive Kurdistan Movement. At a conference in January 1978, KRP members remaining at Baghdad reiterated their support of the National Front, and in August 1981 they reaffirmed their commitment to President Hussein's policies.

Cabinet

As of July 1, 2005

Prime Minister	Ibrahim al-Jaafari
Deputy Prime Ministers	Ahmad Chalabi
	Abid Mutlak al-Jiburi
	Roz Nuri Shawez

Ministers

Agriculture	Ali al-Bahadli
Communication	Juan Massum [f]
Culture	Nuri Farhan al-Rawi
Defense	Sadun al-Dulaimi
Education	'Abd al-Falah Hassan
Electricity	Muhsin Shalash
Environment	Narmin Uthman [f]
Finance	Ali 'Abd al-Amir Allawi
Foreign Affairs	Hushyar Zubari
Health	'Abd al-Mutalib Muhammad Ali
Higher Education	Sami al-Mudhaffar
Housing	Jassim Muhammad Jafar
Human Rights (Acting)	Narmin Uthman
Industry	Usama al-Najaifi
Interior	Bayan Jabr
Justice	'Abd al-Hussayn Shandal
Labor and Social Affairs	Idris Hadi
Migration and Displacement	Suhaila Abid Jaafar [f]
Oil	Ibrahim Bahr al-Ulum
Planning	Barham Salih
Public Works	Nisrin Biwari [f]
Science and Technology	Bassima Yusuf Butrus [f]
Trade	'Abd al-Basit Karim Malud
Transportation	Salaam al-Maliki
Water Resources	'Abd al-Latif Rashid
Youth and Sport	Talib Aziz Zayani

Ministers of State

Civil Society Affairs	Ala Habib Kadhim
Governate Affairs	Saad Naif al-Hardan
National Assembly Affairs	Safaiddin Muhammad Safi
National Security Affairs	'Abd al-Karim al-Anizi
Tourism and Antiquities	Hashim al-Hashimi
Women's Affairs	Azhar al-Shaykh [f]

[f] = female

Members of the KRP were appointed to the Iraq National Assembly by President Hussein in 2000, and the party again confirmed its support for the government in late 2002.

Leader: Ibrahim Tahir SALLAM (Secretary General).

Legislatures

The former bicameral Parliament ceased to exist with the overthrow of the monarchy in 1958, legislative functions subsequently being assumed by the Revolutionary Command Council (RCC). On the basis of a bill approved by the RCC in March 1980, a unicameral National Assembly was established to which elections were first held in June, with subsequent balloting in October 1984, April 1989, March 1996, and March 2000.

Elections were also held in the "autonomous" northern region in September 1980, August 1986, and September 1989 to a 50-member Kurdish Legislative Council, which Baghdad continued to recognize despite balloting for a more inclusive Iraqi Kurdistan National Assembly in May 1992.

Following the ouster of Saddam Hussein in 2003, the interim constitution adopted in 2004 provided for a popularly elected 275-member Transitional National Assembly to serve until a permanent constitution was adopted permitting eventual election of a new assembly.

Transitional National Assembly. In voting on January 30, 2005, the United Iraqi Alliance was credited with 140 seats; the Democratic Patriotic Alliance of Kurdistan, 75; the Iraqi List, 40; the Iraqiyun List, 5; the Iraqi Turkmen Front, 3; the Independent National Elites and Cadres Party, 3; the People's Union, 2; the Kurdistan Islamic Group, 2; the Islamic Action Organization, 2; the National Democratic Alliance, 1; the National Rafidayn List, 1; and the Reconciliation and Liberation Bloc, 1.

Speaker: Hajim M. al-HASSANI.

Iraqi Kurdistan National Assembly. Created after the collapse of a new autonomy agreement with the Iraqi government in late 1991, the unicameral Iraqi Kurdistan National Assembly as then constituted contained 105 seats, five of which were reserved for Christian Assyrians. A minimum vote share of 7 percent was necessary for non-Assyrian representation. Following the balloting of May 19, 1992, the Democratic Party of Kurdistan (DPK) and the Patriotic Union of Kurdistan (PUK) agreed to fill 50 seats each, with four being awarded to the Assyrian Democratic Party and one to the (Assyrian) Christian Union. However, in the wake of renewed Kurdish infighting, the DPK representatives were reportedly expelled in December 1994 after PUK forces had taken control of Arbil, the "capital" of the self-styled Kurdistan Regional Government-Iraq. Although new elections were theoretically due in 1995, ongoing clashes between DPK and PUK precluded them. New elections were envisaged under the DPK/PUK settlement of September 1998 brokered by the US, but infighting continued to be an effective barrier. On October 4, 2002, the assembly reconvened for the first time in eight years as part of a reconciliation initiative launched in anticipation of possible US military action against the Iraqi regime of Saddam Hussein.

Following the ouster of Hussein in 2003, the interim national constitution adopted in 2004 provided for new elections for a 111-member Iraqi Kurdistan National Assembly. At balloting on January 30, 2005, the Kurdistan National Democratic List secured 104 seats; the Kurdistan Islamic Group, 6; and the Kurdistan Toilers' Party, 1.

Speaker: Adnan MUFTI.

Communications

Press

Although the 1968 constitution provided for freedom of the press, all news media were rigidly controlled by the government of Saddam Hussein. Thus a ban against the publication of privately owned newspapers was lifted in 1968 but reimposed in 1969. The following were government-regulated dailies published at Baghdad (prior to the ouster of Hussein in 2003): *al-Thawra* (The Revolution, 250,000), *Baath* organ, in Arabic;

al-Jumhuriyah (The Republic, 150,000), in Arabic; *al-'Iraq* (30,000), Kurdish Democratic Party organ; *Baghdad Observer* (23,000), in English. Another prominent Baghdad daily, *Babil* (Babylon), was owned by Udai Hussein, son of Iraqi President Saddam Hussein.

Following the overthrow of the Hussein regime in 2003, the CPA and the interim and transitional Iraqi governments promoted the establishment of a free press, provided journalists did not incite violence. Several hundred small, and often fleeting, newspapers were reportedly launched under the new policies.

News Agencies

The domestic facility is the Iraqi News Agency (*Wikalat al-Anba al-'Iraqiyah*); several major foreign bureaus maintain offices at Baghdad.

Broadcasting

The government Broadcasting Service of the Republic of Iraq (*Idha'at al-Jumhuriyah al-'Iraqiyah*) transmitted domestically in Arabic, Kurdish, Syriac, and Turkoman during the Hussein regime; foreign broadcasts were in various European languages as well as in Persian, Swahili, Turkish, and Urdu. Baghdad Television (*Mahattat Talafizyun Baghdad*) broadcast daily over two channels, under the control of the Ministry of Information; overall, there were some two dozen stations located throughout the country. There were approximately 5.2 million radio and 1.9 million television receivers in 1999.

Following the ouster of Saddam Hussein in 2003, the CPA reportedly relieved the information ministry of its broadcasting oversight in favor of a new Iraqi Media Network.

Intergovernmental Representation

Ambassador to the US
(Vacant)

US Ambassador to Iraq
Zalmay KHALILZAD

Permanent Representative to the UN
Samir Shakir Mahmud SUMAIDAI

IGO Memberships (Non-UN)
AFESD, AMF, BADEA, CAEU, CCC, IDB, Interpol, LAS, NAM, OAPEC, OIC, OPEC, PCA

ISRAEL

STATE OF ISRAEL

Medinat Yisrael (Hebrew)
Dawlat Isra'il (Arabic)

Note: On November 21, 2005, Prime Minister Ariel Sharon announced his departure from the *Likud* Party to form a new centrist party, *Kadima* (Forward), to stand for parliamentary elections scheduled for March 2006. A number of *Likud* cabinet ministers and *Knesset* members soon joined Sharon in his new party. Benjamin Netanyahu, a former prime minister and a sometime challenger to Sharon within *Likud*, replaced Sharon as party leader. On November 9, 2005, the Labor Party ousted longtime leader Shimon Peres and selected instead trade union leader Amir Peretz as its new chairman. Peres quit the party on November 30, 2005, and endorsed Sharon in the upcoming elections. Sharon suffered a mild stroke on December 18, 2005, and was released from the hospital two days later. A second, massive stroke on January 4, 2006, hospitalized him in grave condition. Vice Premier Ehud Olmert, a Sharon ally, assumed power as acting prime minister.

The Country

The irregularly shaped area constituting the State of Israel is not completely defined by agreed boundaries, its territorial jurisdiction being determined in part by military armistice agreements entered into at the conclusion of Israel's war of independence in 1948–1949. The territory under de facto Israeli control increased substantially as a result of military occupation of Arab territories in the Sinai Peninsula (since returned to Egypt), the Gaza Strip, the West Bank of the Jordan River (including the Old City of Jerusalem), and the Golan Heights following the Arab-Israeli War of 1967. (Most of the Gaza Strip is now under Palestinian control as are sections of the West Bank.) Those currently holding Israeli citizenship encompass a heterogeneous population that is approximately 80 percent Jewish but includes important Arab Christian, Muslim, and Druze minorities. As of 1996, women constituted 36 percent of the paid work force, concentrated in agriculture, teaching, and health care.

Since independence, Israel has emerged as a technologically progressive, highly literate, and largely urbanized nation in the process of rapid development based on scientific exploitation of its agricultural and industrial potentialities. Agriculture has diminished in importance but remains a significant economic sector, its most important products being citrus fruits, field crops, vegetables, and export-oriented nursery items. The industrial sector includes among its major components high-tech manufactures, cut diamonds, textiles, processed foods, chemicals, and military equipment. US financial assistance, tourism, and direct aid from Jews in the United States and elsewhere are also of major economic importance. Defense requirements, however, generated a highly adverse balance of trade and a rate of inflation that escalated to more than 400 percent prior to the imposition of austerity measures in mid-1985 that yielded a dramatic reduction to less than 16 percent in 1988. Israel experienced one of the highest GDP growth rates in the world in the first half of the 1990s while unemployment, which had peaked at more than 11 percent in 1992, dropped to 6.0 percent by the end of 1996. The Netanyahu government (installed in 1996) pursued pro-business policies (most notably extensive privatization of state-run enterprises) and a commitment to budget austerity, which precipitated protests and job actions on behalf of workers and the underprivileged. Nevertheless, growth slowed significantly in subsequent years, GDP increasing by only 2.7 percent in 1997, 3.0 percent in 1998, and 2.6 percent in 1999. Collaterally, unemployment rose to 8.6 percent in 1998; inflation fell from over 8 percent in 1998 to 1.3 percent in 1999. A sharp depreciation of the shekel was registered in late 1998, in part due to turmoil in global financial markets. Israel's economic downturn was also attributed, to a certain degree, to a lack of progress in the Middle East peace process.

The economy rebounded dramatically in 2000, with GDP growth of 7.4 percent being achieved and inflation dropping to nearly zero. However, conditions subsequently reversed just as sharply in the wake of renewed government/Palestinian violence and the "burst of the technology bubble" and the collateral decline in the global economy. Deep recession was marked by declining GDP of 0.9 percent in 2001 and 1.0 percent in 2002. In the face of growing budget deficits, the administration proposed emergency spending cuts in 2002, prompting conflict within the government coalition.

Modest growth (1.3 percent) resumed in 2003, and genuine recovery appeared to be at hand when GDP rose by more than 4 percent in 2004. The International Monetary Fund praised the Sharon government for reforming the pension system and accelerating privatization, although such measures prompted several large-scale strikes on the part of labor groups. In addition, unemployment remained unacceptably high at 10.4 percent. Meanwhile, as of early 2005, more than four years of the "second intifada" had severely damaged economic activity in the Gaza Strip and Palestinian-controlled areas of the West Bank.

Government and Politics

Political Background

Israel's modern history dates from the end of the 19th century with the rise of the world Zionist movement and establishment of Jewish agricultural settlements in territory that was then part of the Ottoman Empire. In the Balfour Declaration of 1917 the British government expressed support for the establishment in Palestine of a national home for the Jewish people, provided that the rights of "existing non-Jewish communities" were not prejudiced. With the abrogation of Turkish rule at the end of World War I, the area was assigned to Great Britain under a League of Nations Mandate that incorporated provisions of the Balfour Declaration. British rule continued until May 1948, despite increasing unrest on the part of local Arabs during the 1920s and 1930s and Jewish elements during and after World War II. In 1947 the UN General Assembly adopted a resolution calling for the division of Palestine into Arab and Jewish states and the internationalization

Political Status: Independent republic established May 14, 1948; under multiparty parliamentary regime.

Land Area: 8,463 sq. mi. (21,920 sq. km.), including inland water (172 sq. mi., 445 sq. km.).

Population: 5,548,523 (1995C); 6,851,000 (2004E). Area and population figures include East Jerusalem (27 sq. mi., 70 sq. km., prior to subsequent unilateral expansion), which Israel occupied in 1967 and formally annexed in 1980 in an action not recognized by the United Nations or the United States (which maintains its embassy at Tel Aviv). Also included is a 444-square-mile (1,150 sq. km.) sector of the Golan Heights to which Israeli forces withdrew under a 1974 disengagement agreement with Syria and which was placed under Israeli law in December 1981. The figures do not include the Gaza Strip (most of which was turned over to Palestinian control in May 1994) and the West Bank (from portions of which Israel began withdrawing in May 1994), which encompassed an area of about 2,320 square miles (6,020 sq. km.) and a combined population of approximately 3,449,000 in mid-2002.

Major Urban Centers (2000E): JERUSALEM (658,000, including East Jerusalem); Tel Aviv/Jaffa (354,000); Haifa (270,000); Holon (166,000); Ramat Gan (127,000).

Official Languages: Hebrew, Arabic. English, which was an official language under the Mandate, is taught in the secondary schools and is widely spoken.

Monetary Unit: New Shekel (market rate July 1, 2005: 4.58 shekels = $1US).

President: Moshe KATSAV (*Likud*); elected by the *Knesset* on July 31, 2000, and sworn in on August 1 for a seven-year term, succeeding Ezer WEIZMAN, who had resigned July 10. (Avraham Burg, Speaker of the *Knesset,* served as acting president between Weizman's resignation and Katsav's inauguration.)

Prime Minister: Ariel SHARON (*Likud*); elected in special balloting for Prime Minister on February 6, 2001, and sworn in on March 7 (following confirmation of his proposed cabinet by the *Knesset* on the same day), succeeding Ehud BARAK (One Israel/Israeli Labor Party); formed new government on February 28, 2003, following *Knesset* elections on January 28; formed new government on January 10, 2005, following collapse of his previous government (which had fallen into minority status) on December 1, 2004.

of Jerusalem and its environs, but the controversial measure could not be implemented because of Arab opposition. Nonetheless, Israel declared its independence coincident with British withdrawal on May 14, 1948. Though immediately attacked by Egypt, Syria, Lebanon, Jordan, and Iraq, the new state was able to maintain itself in the field, and the armistice agreements concluded under UN auspices in 1949 gave it control over nearly one-third more territory than had been assigned to it under the original UN resolution. A second major military encounter between Israel and Egypt in 1956 resulted in Israeli conquest of the Gaza Strip and the Sinai Peninsula, which were subsequently evacuated under US and UN pressure. In

two further Arab-Israeli conflicts, Israel seized territories from Jordan (1967) and from Egypt and Syria (1967 and 1973). Cease-fire disengagements resulted, however, in partial Israeli withdrawal from territory in the Syrian Golan Heights and the Egyptian Sinai. Withdrawal from the remaining Sinai territory, except for Taba (see Occupied and Previously Occupied Territories, below), was completed in April 1982 under a peace treaty with Egypt concluded on March 26, 1979. The Israeli sector of the Golan Heights, on the other hand, was placed under Israeli law on December 14, 1981.

The internal governmental structure of modern Israel emerged from institutions established by the British administration and the Jewish community during the Mandate. For three decades after independence, a series of multiparty coalitions built around the moderate socialist Israel Workers' Party (Mapai)–enlarged in 1968 to become the Israel Labor Party–governed with relatively little change in policy and turnover in personnel. Save for a brief period in 1953–1955, David BEN-GURION was the dominant political figure until his retirement in 1963. He was succeeded by Levi ESHKOL (until his death in 1969), Golda MEIR (until her retirement in 1974), and Yitzhak RABIN, the first native-born Israeli to become prime minister.

Prime Minister Rabin tendered his resignation in December 1976, following his government's defeat on a parliamentary nonconfidence motion, but he remained in office in a caretaker capacity pending a general election. On April 8, 1977, prior to balloting scheduled for May 17, Rabin was forced to resign his party post in the wake of revelations that he and his wife had violated Israeli law concerning overseas bank deposits. His successor as party leader and acting prime minister, Shimon PERES, proved unable to reverse mounting popular dissatisfaction with a deteriorating economy and evidence of official malfeasance. In a stunning electoral upset, a new reform party, the Democratic Movement for Change, captured a significant proportion of Labor's support and the opposition *Likud* party, having obtained a sizable legislative plurality, formed the nucleus of a coalition government under Menachem BEGIN on June 19.

As the result of a fiscal dispute that provoked the resignation of its finance minister, the Begin government was deprived of a committed legislative majority on January 11, 1981, and the *Knesset* approved a bill calling for an election on June 30. Despite predictions of an opposition victory, the *Likud* front emerged with a one-seat advantage, and Begin succeeded in forming a new governing coalition on August 4.

Prime Minister Begin's startling announcement on August 28, 1983, of his intention to resign both his governmental and party positions for "personal reasons" (largely the death of his wife) was believed by many observers also to have been influenced by severe Israeli losses from the 1982 war in Lebanon (see Foreign relations, below). The Central Committee of *Likud's* core party, *Herut,* thereupon elected Yitzhak SHAMIR as its new leader on September 1, and the constituent parties of the ruling coalition agreed to support Shamir, who, after failing in an effort to form a national unity government, was sworn in as prime minister on October 10.

Amid increasing criticism of the Shamir administration, particularly in its handling of economic affairs, five *Likud* coalition deputies voted with the opposition on March 22, 1984, in calling for legislative dissolution and the holding of a general election. At the balloting on July 23, Labor marginally outpolled *Likud,* securing 44 seats to *Likud's* 41. Extensive interparty discussion followed, yielding agreement on August 31 to form a national unity coalition on the basis of a rotating premiership. Thus, Labor's Peres was approved as the new prime minister on September 13 with the understanding that he would exchange positions with Vice Prime Minister and Foreign Affairs Minister Shamir midway through a full parliamentary term of four years; on October 20, 1986, Shamir, in turn, became prime minister, with Peres assuming Shamir's former posts.

The election of November 1, 1988, conducted in the midst of a major Palestinian uprising (*intifada*) that had erupted in the occupied territories 11 months earlier, yielded an even closer balance between the leading parties, with *Likud* winning 40 *Knesset* seats and Labor 39. Conceivably, *Likud* could have assembled a working majority in alliance with a number of right-wing religious parties; most of the latter, however, refused to participate in an administration that did not commit itself to legislation excluding from provisions of the law of return (hence from automatic citizenship) those converted to Judaism under Reform or Conservative (as opposed to Orthodox) auspices. As a result, Shamir concluded a new agreement with the Labor leadership, whereby he would continue as prime minister, with Peres assuming the finance portfolio in a government installed on December 22.

By early 1990 the coalition was under extreme stress because of divergent views on the terms of peace talks with the Palestinians. The principal differences turned on *Likud*'s insistence that no Arabs from East Jerusalem participate in the talks or in future elections and that Israel should be accorded a right of withdrawal should the Palestine Liberation Organization (PLO) become even remotely involved. There were also deep fissures within *Likud* itself, resulting primarily from a group of hard-liners, including Industry and Commerce Minister Ariel SHARON, who were opposed to a Palestinian franchise. Following an angry exchange with Shamir in the *Knesset* on February 12, Sharon resigned from the cabinet. Ten days later the Labor Party issued an ultimatum to the prime minister to accept its peace formula (which called for at least one delegate each from Palestinian deportees and those maintaining partial residence in East Jerusalem) or face dissolution of the government. On March 12 Shamir dismissed Peres from the cabinet, prompting Labor's other ministers to resign. Three days later, in the wake of a successful non-confidence motion (the first in Israeli parliamentary history), Shamir assumed the leadership of a caretaker administration. A lengthy period of intense negotiation followed, with Shamir on June 11 forming a *Likud*-dominated right-wing government whose two-seat majority turned on the support of dissidents from Labor and *Agudat Yisrael,* a periodic Labor ally, respectively. In November 1990 *Agudat Yisrael* formally joined the ruling coalition, increasing the government's *Knesset* majority to six.

In February 1992 former prime minister Rabin gained control of the opposition Labor Party from longtime rival Peres, who had been unable since 1977 to lead Labor to the formation of a government in its own right. Four months later, in what was termed more of a *Likud* debacle than a Labor triumph, Labor won a plurality of 44 *Knesset* seats, and it went on to form a new administration on July 12 in coalition with the recently organized *Meretz* (itself a coalition of three left-of-center parties) and the ultraorthodox Sephardi Torah Guardians (Shas).

On March 24, 1993, Ezer WEIZMAN, a former fighter pilot and *Likud* hard-liner who had subsequently become a Labor Party leader and an outspoken advocate of peace with the Arabs, was elected by the *Knesset* as Israel's seventh president. The following day former deputy foreign minister Benjamin NETANYAHU, who called for "a much tougher line" in addressing the Palestinian issue, was elected in a party contest to succeed Shamir as *Likud* leader. The Labor/*Likud* split on the Palestinian question came into even sharper focus in September when Rabin signed the historic agreement with the PLO that launched the Palestinian self-rule process (see Foreign relations and Occupied and Previously Occupied Territories, below, for details).

In mid-July 1994 two MPs from *Yi'ud,* a breakaway faction of the ultranationalist *Tzomet,* agreed to enter the Labor government; however, they were prevented from doing so until late December because of a High Court ruling that their action would contravene antidefection legislation. Their support gave the Labor coalition 58 of 120 *Knesset* seats. However, on February 3, 1995, the six *Knesset* representatives of Shas, which had withdrawn from the ruling coalition in March 1994, announced that they were formally returning to opposition because of worsening security and the status of Jewish settlers in the West Bank.

Attention subsequently focused on negotiations over the second accord of the Palestinian autonomy process, which was signed on September 28, 1995, and endorsed (in a nonmandatory vote) by the *Knesset* by 61–59 on October 6. However, domestic and regional political affairs were soon thrown into turmoil when Rabin was assassinated on November 4 by a right-wing Israeli opposed to the peace process. (Rabin's assailant, Yigul AMIR, was sentenced to life imprisonment in March 1996.) Foreign Minister Peres assumed the position of acting prime minister upon Rabin's death and was formally nominated by the Labor Party on November 13 to proceed with forming his own cabinet. The leaders of Labor, *Meretz,* and *Yi'ud* signed another government agreement on November 21, and the new cabinet was approved by the *Knesset* the following day, at which time Peres became prime minister.

Peres announced on February 11, 1996, that elections, then scheduled for November, would be moved up, a new date of May 29 subsequently being established following discussion with *Likud* representatives. Running counter to preelection polls, *Likud's* Netanyahu defeated Peres by a vote of 50.5 percent to 49.5 percent in the first-ever direct balloting for prime minister. The election turned primarily on security issues, as Netanyahu adopted a hard-line stance toward any further "concessions" to the Palestinians, categorically ruled out the eventual creation of an independent Palestinian state, and pledged additional support for the Jewish settlers in the West Bank. Although Labor led all parties by winning 34 seats in the *Knesset* elections, Netanyahu was subsequently able to form a coalition government comprising representatives from *Tzomet* and the newly formed *Gesher* (the two parties with whom *Likud* had presented joint *Knesset* candidates), Shas, The Third Way (a new centrist grouping), *Yisrael B'Aliya*, and two ultraorthodox groups (the National Religious Party [NRP] and the United Torah Judaism [UTJ]). Netanyahu formally succeeded Peres as prime minister on June 18 after the *Knesset* approved the new government by a vote of 62–50.

In addition to growing pressure regarding the Palestinian question, Netanyahu also confronted several other significant domestic problems in 1997 and early 1998. Most notable was the controversial demand by the Orthodox Jewish movement that it be formally confirmed as the ultimate authority concerning conversions to Judaism. (The Reform and Conservative movements, strongly represented in the United States, were seeking to have conversions completed under their auspices legally recognized in Israel.) With his coalition government so dependent on backing from orthodox parties, Netanyahu initially announced support for legislation confirming the Orthodox monopoly; however, a special committee was subsequently established to attempt to produce a compromise position. The prime minister also faced dissension within *Likud* and growing restiveness over budget austerity, the latter contributing to the decision by *Gesher* to leave the coalition in January 1998. (The government's legislative majority was reduced to a razor-

thin 61–59 by *Gesher's* withdrawal.) In addition, the administration was buffeted in early 1998 by changes in the leadership of Mossad (brought on by a bungled September 1997 assassination attempt in Jordan and other embarrassments) and the somewhat chaotic and incomplete distribution of gas masks during the most recent US/Iraqi crisis. Regarding that confrontation, the Israeli government had emphasized that, unlike 1991, it had been prepared to respond militarily if fighting had broken out and it had been targeted by Iraqi missiles.

On March 4, 1998, the *Knesset* by a vote of 63–49 reelected President Weizman, who had added a degree of political impact to the previously essentially ceremonial post by criticizing the Netanyahu government's handling of the peace process.

Under heavy international pressure, Prime Minister Netanyahu signed an accord with PLO Chairman 'Arafat in late October 1998 calling for further Israeli withdrawals from West Bank territory (see Foreign relations, below, for details on the so-called Wye agreement). However, implementation of the plan stalled in December as Netanyahu attempted futilely to address the growing popular demand for progress toward a resolution on the Palestinian front while maintaining the allegiance of the religious parties in his coalition, who steadfastly opposed any land-for-peace compromise and, in fact, urged additional construction of Jewish settlements in the occupied territories. The government also exhibited a lack of unity regarding policies to address the deteriorating economic climate. Consequently, in mid-December Netanyahu, facing the threat of a no-confidence motion in the *Knesset,* agreed to early elections.

On May 17, 1999, Ehud BARAK of the Labor-led One Israel coalition was elected prime minister, defeating Netanyahu by 56–44 percent. (Three other minor candidates had withdrawn shortly before the election.) Barak had staked out a more liberal peace posture than Netanyahu, announcing he would, if elected, revitalize the Wye agreement, initiate final status discussions with the Palestinians, withdraw Israeli forces from Lebanon within one year, and relaunch discussions with Syria regarding the Golan Heights. Barak also stressed his economic platform, domestic problems such as burgeoning unemployment, rising inflation, and declining growth appearing to play a greater role in voting decisions that year than in previous elections. In concurrent balloting for the *Knesset,* One Israel secured a plurality of 26 seats, followed by *Likud* (19 seats), Shas (17), Meretz (10), and 11 parties with 6 or less seats. The legislative campaign was noteworthy for a series of "slurs and counterslurs" that underscored the continued intensity of the secular/religious schism within the Israeli population. Meanwhile, in view of his poor showing (as well as *Likud*'s), Netanyahu resigned as chairman of *Likud* and was succeeded by his longtime rival, Ariel Sharon.

After difficult and extended negotiations (during which he ultimately abandoned efforts to form a "national unity" government with *Likud*), Barak on July 6, 1999, received *Knesset* confirmation of a new cabinet including One Israel (Labor, *Gesher,* and *Meimad*), Shas, *Yisrael B'Aliya, Meretz,* the NRP, and the new Center Party. Barak immediately launched into intense diplomatic efforts to resolve the Palestinian conflict (see Current issues, below). However, his coalition proved fractious over the peace initiatives, and Shas, *Yisrael B'Aliya,* and the NRP left the cabinet on July 9, 2000, to protest potential "concessions" to the Palestinians. *Gesher*'s minister also resigned on August 2. Meanwhile, on July 31 the government had suffered another setback when Moshe KATSAV of *Likud* defeated Shimon Peres for the Israeli presidency by a vote of 63–37 percent. (President Weizman had resigned his post, ostensibly because of poor health, although he had recently been subjected to an investigation concerning gifts he had received as a cabinet member a decade earlier.)

Although he narrowly survived several nonconfidence votes, Barak, faced with an apparent lack of support in the *Knesset* for his peace efforts, announced his resignation on December 9 and called for a special prime ministerial election as a national referendum of sorts on the matter. (Barak remained in his post in an acting capacity pending the new balloting.) In view of the outbreak of the "second intifada" (see Current issues, below), the Israeli electorate illustrated its rightward shift on February 6, 2001, by electing the "hawkish" Sharon as

prime minister by a 62.4–37.6 percent margin over Barak, who quickly resigned as Labor's leader.

Somewhat surprisingly, Labor agreed to join the national unity government formed by Sharon on March 7, 2001. *Likud*'s other coalition partners included Shas, *Yisrael B'Aliya,* the new One Nation, the UTJ (represented at the deputy ministerial level), and the new National Union-Yisrael Beiteinu (NU–YB) *Knesset* faction (see National Union under Political Parties, below, for details). On October 15 the NU–YB ministers announced their intention to leave the cabinet, having adopted an even harsher stance toward the Palestinian question than Sharon. However, their resignation was temporarily rescinded following the assassination by Palestinian militants of Tourism Minister Rechavam ZE'EVI, leader of the NU–YB, on October 17. After the NU–YB faction finally departed the cabinet on March 15, 2002, Sharon bolstered his government by appointing new ministers from the NRP and *Gesher.* Sharon dismissed the Shas and UTJ ministers on May 20 when they failed to support his austerity budget proposals, although the Shas ministers were reinstated on June 3 after the package passed on a second vote in the *Knesset. Gesher* leader David Levy resigned his post as minister without portfolio on July 29.

The ministers from the Israel Labor Party resigned from the cabinet on October 30, 2002, because of their opposition to the allocation of funding for Jewish settlements in the West Bank and Gaza Strip. Faced with the collapse of his "national unity" government and the loss of a government majority in the *Knesset,* Prime Minister Ariel Sharon called for new *Knesset* elections to be held on January 28, 2003. On November 19 Maj. Gen. (Ret.) Avraham MITZNA, the mayor of Haifa, was elected as the new Labor leader. He subsequently proposed a markedly "dovish" approach to the Palestinian question, calling for the closure of Jewish settlements in the Gaza Strip, the immediate evacuation of Israeli forces from the region, and the eventual unilateral Israeli withdrawal from portions of the West Bank should a comprehensive peace agreement fail to materialize. Subsequently, Sharon was easily reelected as *Likud* leader on November 28 over arch-rival Benjamin Netanyahu.

Sharon pledged to maintain his hard line regarding negotiations with the Palestinians, announcing that negotiations would not proceed until all violence ceased. Meanwhile, in late December Palestinian officials announced that proposed legislative and presidential elections would be postponed indefinitely in view of continued Israeli "occupation" of areas previously under Palestinian authority.

Likud scored a major victory in the January 28, 2003, *Knesset* election, securing 38 seats (compared to 19 seats for the Labor/*Meimad* coalition). Labor subsequently pulled out of negotiations regarding a new coalition government, and on February 28 Sharon formed a new cabinet comprising *Likud, Shinui,* the NRP, and the National Union. In June 2004 Sharon dismissed two NRP ministers who opposed his plan for unilateral Israeli disengagement from the Gaza Strip (see Current issues, below), placing the government in minority status in the *Knesset*. The coalition finally collapsed on December 1 when the *Knesset* rejected Sharon's proposed 2005 budget. (Sharon dismissed the *Shinui* ministers who voted against the budget.) On January 10, 2005, Sharon secured *Knesset* approval (by a vote of 58–56) for a new cabinet comprising *Likud*, Labor, and the UTJ. Labor leader Peres was named vice premier of the new government.

Constitution and Government

In the absence of a written constitution, the structure of Israeli government is defined by fundamental laws that provide for a president with largely ceremonial functions, a prime minister serving as effective chief executive, and a unicameral parliament (*Knesset*) to which the government is responsible and whose powers include the election of the president. Under legislation passed in March 1992, in what some observers construed as a historic change in the country's electoral system, the *Knesset* approved a law providing for the direct election of the prime minister. However, that legislation was reversed in March 2001, and the prime minister is now once again appointed by the president upon the recommendation of the *Knesset*. The prime minister's term of office corresponds to that of the *Knesset*.

The members of the *Knesset* are elected on a nationwide proportional basis, each voter casting one vote for the party of his or her choice. (The minimum vote percentage for a party to gain representation was raised from 1.0 percent to 1.5 percent in 1992.) Each party must present its platform and a ranked list of its candidates, *Knesset* members being selected in order from those lists. Normally, the term of office of the *Knesset* is four years, although the body can dissolve itself or be dissolved by the prime minister (with the consent of the president).

The role of Judaism in the state has not been formally defined, but the Law of Return of 1950 established a right of immigration for all Jews (with a few exceptions, such as criminals). The judicial system is headed by a Supreme Court. There are five district courts in addition to magistrates' and municipal courts. Specialized courts include labor courts and religious courts with separate benches for the Jewish, Muslim, Druze, and several Christian communities, while military courts are important in the occupied areas.

Israel is divided into six administrative districts (*mehozot*), each of which is headed by a district commissioner appointed by the central government. Regions, municipalities, and rural municipalities are the principal administrative entities within the districts.

Foreign Relations

Israeli foreign relations have been dominated by the requirements of survival in an environment marked by persistent hostility on the part of neighboring Arab states, whose overt measures have ranged from denying Israel use of the Suez Canal (wholly mitigated upon ratification of the 1979 peace treaty) to encouraging terrorist and guerrilla operations on Israeli soil. Once committed to "nonidentification" between East and West, Israel encountered hostility from the Soviet Union and most other Communist governments (Romania and Yugoslavia being the most conspicuous exceptions) and began to rely primarily on Western countries, principally the United States, for political, economic, and military support. A member of the United Nations since 1949, Israel has frequently incurred condemnation by UN bodies because of its reprisals against Arab guerrilla attacks and its refusal both to reabsorb or pay compensation to Arab refugees from the 1948–1949 war and to accept the internationalization of Jerusalem as envisaged in the 1947 UN resolution. Enactment on July 30, 1980, of a law reaffirming a unified Jerusalem as the nation's capital evoked additional condemnation.

In May 1974 a Golan disengagement agreement was concluded with Syria, while Sinai disengagement accords were concluded with Egypt in January 1974 and September 1975. Under the latter, Israel withdrew its forces from the Suez Canal to an irregular line bordered on the east by the Gidi and Mitla passes and evacuated the Abu Rudeis and Ras Sudar oil fields. Both Egypt and the United States agreed to make a "serious effort" to bring about collateral negotiations with Syria for further disengagement on the Golan Heights, although no such negotiations were initiated prior to the launching of US-inspired Middle East peace talks in early 1991.

In what was hailed as a major step toward peace in the region, Egyptian President Anwar Sadat startled the world in November 1977 by accepting an Israeli invitation to visit Jerusalem. While Sadat yielded little during an unprecedented address to the *Knesset* on November 20, his very presence on Israeli soil kindled widespread hope that the lengthy impasse in Arab-Israeli relations might somehow be broken. Subsequent discussions produced potential bases of settlement in regard to the Sinai but no public indication of substantial withdrawal from established positions, on either side, in regard to the West Bank and Gaza. Israel, in responding to Egyptian demands for a meaningful "concession," announced a willingness to grant Palestinians in Gaza and the West Bank "self-rule," coupled with an Israeli right to maintain military installations in the occupied territories. Egypt, on the other hand, rejected the idea of an Israeli military presence and continued to press for Palestinian self-determination.

The prospects for a meaningful accord fluctuated widely during the first eight months of 1978, culminating in a historic summit convened by US President Carter at Camp David, Maryland, on September 5. The unusually lengthy discussions yielded two major agreements, a "Framework for a Peace Treaty between Egypt and Israel" and a "Framework for Peace in the Middle East," which were signed by President Sadat and Prime Minister Begin at the White House on September 17. In the course of subsequent negotiations at Washington, representatives of the two governments agreed on the details of a treaty and related documents, but the signing was deferred beyond the target date of December 17 because of disagreement about linkage to the second of the Camp David accords, which dealt with autonomy for the inhabitants of the West Bank and Gaza and provided for Israeli withdrawal into specified security locations. In addition, Egypt wished to modify an important treaty provision by an "interpretive annex," stating that prior commitments to other Arab states should have precedence over any obligations assumed in regard to Israel. Progress toward resolving the impasse was registered in early March 1979, and the treaty was formally signed at Washington on March 26, followed by an exchange of ratifications on April 25. In a set of minutes accompanying the treaty, the parties agreed that "there is no assertion that this treaty prevails over other treaties or agreements" and that, within a month after the exchange of instruments of ratification, negotiations would be instituted to define "the modalities for establishing the elected self-governing authority" for the Gaza Strip and West Bank. While no significant progress on autonomy for the two regions was immediately forthcoming, the sixth and final phase of withdrawal from the Sinai, save for Taba, was completed on schedule in April 1982.

On June 6, 1982, Israeli forces invaded Lebanon. While the immediate precipitant of the incursion appeared to be the shooting on June 3 of Israel's ambassador to the United Kingdom, the attack was far from unanticipated in view of a substantial buildup of Israeli military strength along the border in May. Code-named "Peace for Galilee," the attack was justified initially as necessary to establish a PLO-free zone extending 40–50 kilometers inside Lebanon. By June 14, however, Israeli forces had completely surrounded Beirut, shortly after US President Reagan had announced that he would approve the dispatch of 800–1,000 US marines to participate in an international force that would oversee the evacuation of Palestinian and Syrian forces from the Lebanese capital. On August 6 US envoy Philip Habib reached agreement, through Lebanese intermediaries, on the PLO withdrawal, which commenced on August 21.

In what was officially described as a "police action" necessitated by the assassination of Lebanese President-elect Bashir Gemayel on September 14, 1982, Israeli contingents entered West Beirut and took up positions around the Chatila and Sabra Palestinian refugee camps, where a substantial number of "terrorists" were alleged to have been left behind by the PLO. On the morning of the 18th it was revealed that a large-scale massacre of civilians had occurred at the hands of right-wing Phalangist militiamen, who had been given access to the camps by Israeli authorities. While the Israeli cabinet expressed its "deep grief and regret" over the atrocities, the affair generated widespread controversy within Israel, with Prime Minister Begin resisting demands for the ouster of Defense Minister Sharon as well as for the establishment of a commission of inquiry into the circumstances of the massacre. Following the largest protest rally in Israeli history at Tel Aviv on September 25, the prime minister reversed himself and asked the chief justice of the Supreme Court to undertake a full investigation. The results of the inquiry (published in February 1983) placed direct responsibility for the slaughter on the Phalangists but also faulted Sharon and several senior officers for permitting the militiamen to enter the camps in disregard of the safety of the inhabitants. In addition, while absolving the prime minister of foreknowledge of the entry, the commission expressed surprise, in view of "the Lebanese situation as it was known to those concerned," that a decision on entry should have been taken without his participation.

Talks between Israeli and Lebanese representatives on military withdrawal commenced in late December 1982 but became deadlocked on a number of issues, including Israeli insistence that it should continue to man early-warning stations in southern Lebanon. Subsequently, a number of attacks by guerrilla groups were mounted against Israeli troops and contingents of the international peacekeeping force, culminating in simultaneous lorry bomb attacks on US and French detachments at Beirut on October 23, 1983, that left over 300 dead. Earlier, on May 17, an agreement had been concluded between Israeli, Lebanese, and US negotiators that provided for Israeli withdrawal, an end to the state of war between Israel and Lebanon, and the establishment of a jointly supervised "security region" in southern Lebanon. Although unable to secure a commitment from Syria to withdraw its forces from northern and eastern Lebanon, Israel redeployed its forces in early September to a highly fortified line south of the Awali river. In March 1984, following departure of the multinational force from Beirut, the Lebanese government, under pressure from Syria, abrogated the troop withdrawal accord, although the Israeli cabinet in January 1985 approved a unilateral three-stage withdrawal that was implemented in several stages over the ensuing six months.

Despite the withdrawal announcement, Shiʻite militants mounted a terror campaign against the departing Israelis, who retaliated with an "iron-fist" policy that included the arrest and transfer to a prison camp in Israel of hundreds of Shiʻites. On June 14, 1985, the militants hijacked an American TWA jetliner, demanding release of the prisoners in exchange for their hostages. After two weeks of negotiations, the Americans were freed and Israel began gradual release of the Lebanese, both Israel and the United States insisting that the two events were unrelated. Meanwhile, negotiations had been renewed with Egypt to resolve the Taba dispute–a move that was condemned by *Likud* and was further jeopardized by the assassination of an Israeli diplomat at Cairo in August, by an Israeli air attack on the PLO's Tunis headquarters (in retaliation for the murder of three Israelis in Cyprus) in September, and by the killing of seven Israeli tourists in Sinai during October.

Throughout 1986 Peres (as prime minister until October 30 and as foreign minister thereafter) continued his efforts on behalf of a comprehensive peace settlement. An unprecedented public meeting in July with King Hassan of Morocco was described as "purely exploratory" but was viewed as enhancing the position of moderate Arab leaders, including Jordan's King Hussein, whose peace discussion with the PLO's Yasir 'Arafat had broken down in January. Late in the year, the government was hard-pressed to defend its role in the US-Iranian arms affair, Peres insisting that Israel had transferred arms to Iran at Washington's request and was unaware that some of the money paid by Teheran had been diverted to Nicaraguan *contras*. The government was also embarrassed by the March 1987 conviction in a Washington court of Jonathan Jay POLLARD on charges of having spied for Israel. Defense Minister Rabin insisted that Pollard was part of a "rogue" spy operation set up without official sanction and that no one else had engaged in such activity since Pollard's arrest in 1985. However, the case aroused deep pro-Pollard feeling within Israel, and it was later reported that "state elements" had paid approximately two-thirds of Pollard's legal expenses. (Pollard, serving a life sentence in the United States, was granted Israeli citizenship in January 1996.)

During 1989 the government drew increasing criticism from international civil rights groups for actions triggered by the continuing Palestinian Arab uprising (*intifada*) in the occupied territories. It also experienced a cooling of relations with Washington because of Prime Minister Shamir's failure to respond positively to the so-called "Baker plan" for Palestinian peace talks, the essentials of which corresponded to proposals advanced by Rabin. By the end of the year the future of the occupied Arab lands had become increasingly critical because of an escalation of immigrants from the Soviet Union, some of whom were settling in the disputed areas.

With the launching of military action against Iraq by UN-backed forces in mid-January 1991, Israel came under attack by Soviet-made Scud missiles. The US Bush administration thereupon dispatched two batteries of Patriot surface-to-air missiles to Israel, while urging Israeli authorities not to retaliate against Baghdad, lest it weaken the Arab-supported coalition. Having obliged with a posture of restraint, the Shamir government on January 22 requested that it be provided with $3 billion in compensation for damages, plus $10 billion in loan guarantees to resettle immigrants from the Soviet Union. Washington responded in late February by approving a $400 million housing loan guarantee, followed, in early March, by a $650 million aid package to help cover increased military and civil defense expenditures. On October 5, 1992, the US Congress approved the $10 billion guarantee program after the new Labor government had announced that it would halt large-scale investment in the Jewish settlements in the occupied territories. On the same date a US foreign aid appropriation bill was approved that included renewal of the annual $3 billion in economic and military aid earmarked for Israel in the wake of the 1978 Camp David accords.

Subsequently, in what was quickly branded a "public relations disaster," Israeli authorities on December 18, 1992, ordered the deportation of more than 400 Palestinians charged with being leaders of the fundamentalist Islamic Resistance Movement (*Hamas*, under Occupied and Previously Occupied Territories, below) that had recently been responsible for a series of attacks on Israeli military personnel and civilians. Since Lebanon refused to accept the deportees, they were confined to a portion of the buffer strip inside the Lebanese border. The action drew almost universal condemnation from abroad, including demands by both the US government and the UN Security Council that the group be returned to the occupied territories. Subsequently, Israel agreed to permit 10 (later 16) of those "wrongly deported" to return and in early February 1993 agreed to the return of 100 of the others, with the remainder to be repatriated by the end of the year. The latter offer was resisted by the deportees, who demanded that all those remaining be released immediately, but was nonetheless implemented by the Israelis.

The Palestinian deportation issue proved particularly disruptive of lengthy Middle East peace talks that had begun in Madrid, Spain, on October 30,

1991, among Israeli, Lebanese, Syrian, and joint Jordanian-Palestinian delegations, with a number of other governmental and intergovernmental representatives present as observers. It was agreed at the meeting that further "two-track" negotiations would be held on Israeli-Palestinian and Israeli-Jordanian matters directed at an interim period of Palestinian self-rule and, eventually, a final settlement with Israel. However, no substantial progress was reported in three rounds of bilateral talks that concluded in mid-January 1992. Subsequently, the 19 participants in a revival of multilateral talks at Moscow on January 28–29 established five working groups dealing with environment, water, disarmament and security, economic development, and refugee issues, although the Palestinians boycotted the meeting because of a dispute over the composition of its delegation, while both Syria and Lebanon refused to participate on the ground that Israel had shown no territorial flexibility in the bilateral discussions. Six inconclusive bilateral rounds followed, with a tenth round from June 15–July 1, 1993, also ending in deadlock, largely because of Israeli refusal to discuss the status of Jerusalem.

In late June 1993, *Hezbollah* began launching rockets against Israeli Defense Force (IDF) and South Lebanese Army (SLA) targets in the South Lebanese "security zone." Within days the IDF began moving more troops into the area, and in mid-July the Israeli cabinet declared that the IDF would respond to any further attacks in the security zone or on its northern settlements. *Hezbollah* nonetheless launched a rocket attack on the Galilee panhandle late in the month. The IDF thereupon commenced bombing raids against reputed terrorist installations north of the security zone that caused widespread civilian casualties prior to a cease-fire on July 21. Further heavy fighting occurred in 1996, and Israeli support for involvement in Lebanon subsequently reportedly declined, particularly after 73 Israeli soldiers were killed in a helicopter crash in February 1997. Consequently, although previous negotiations had always been based on the premise of a comprehensive regional settlement, the Netanyahu government in early 1998 proposed a "Lebanon first" strategy through which Israel would withdraw from Lebanon in return for stringent security guarantees. During the prime ministerial campaign in Israel in early 1999, Labor's Ehud Barak pledged to withdraw Israeli forces from Lebanon if elected, although he hoped it would be as part of a peace agreement with Syria and the Palestinians. Those initiatives having stalled in early 2000, the Israeli *Knesset* in March voted to initiate a unilateral withdrawal, which was completed on May 24 (see article on Lebanon for additional information).

On August 19, 1993, some 14 months of secret talks in Norway between Israeli and PLO representatives yielded a Declaration of Principles on interim self-rule for Palestinians in the Israeli-occupied territories. The declaration provided for a five-year transitional period beginning with Israeli withdrawal from the Gaza Strip and Jericho and culminating in a transfer of authority in most of the rest of the West Bank in all matters save foreign relations, defense, and "other mutually agreed matters" to "authorized Palestinians." Formalized in a historic signing by Israeli Prime Minister Rabin and PLO Chairman 'Arafat at Washington on September 13, the process was targeted for completion by April 13, 1999.

A number of meetings to implement the Israeli/PLO accord were subsequently held in Egypt, but they failed to clear the way for commencement of the Israeli withdrawal from Gaza and Jericho on the agreed date of December 13. An initial dispute turned on Jericho's size, the Israelis proposing 21 square miles, with the PLO insisting on 39 square miles extending south to the Dead Sea. Subsequent disagreement centered on security provisions for settlers in Gaza, in addition to control over the passage of Palestinians from Egypt into Gaza and from Jordan into Jericho. These problems appeared to have been overcome in an agreement initialled by Israeli Prime Minister Peres and PLO Chairman Yasir 'Arafat at Cairo on February 9, 1994; however, the massacre of 29 worshippers at a Muslim mosque in Hebron by a follower of the late extremist, Rabbi Meir KAHANE (see Kahane Lives, under Political Parties, below), brought the peace process to a sudden halt.

It was not until May 4, 1994, that a definitive accord implementing the 1993 declaration was signed at Cairo by Rabin and 'Arafat. Under the settlement, Israel was to withdraw from the Gaza Strip and Jericho within three weeks, legislative and executive powers for the two areas was to be assigned to a "Palestinian authority," and a 9,000-man Palestinian police force was to be established. On the other hand, Israel was to retain authority over Jewish settlements, a military base on the Egyptian border, and external security. The actual degree of Palestinian autonomy was further constrained by annexes to the agreement that provided for an Israeli role at all levels of decision making for the territories. Nonetheless, Palestinian policemen entered the Gaza Strip on May 10, and on May 13 Israeli troops withdrew from Jericho, ending a 27-year occupation.

The declaration was preceded by a January 1994 meeting with President Clinton at Geneva during which Syrian President Assad declared that he was ready for "normal, peaceful relations" with Israel. However, it was noted that such an eventuality would require significant concessions by Israel, including withdrawal from the Golan Heights. Israel appeared to respond on May 17 by offering to withdraw from Golan in three phases over a five-to-eight-year period in return for peace and normalized relations with its longtime adversary. However, observers were quick to point out the sticking point: disagreement as to whether normalization or withdrawal should come first. The issue remained unresolved as of late 2002, despite earlier efforts to pursue a settlement on the part of Israeli Prime Minister Ehud Barak (see Current issues, below).

Israel was more successful in its quest for normalization with Jordan, US-brokered contacts yielding another important White House ceremony on July 25, 1994, when King Hussein and Prime Minister Rabin signed a declaration ending the 46-year-old state of war between their two countries. On October 26 a peace treaty between the two states was signed, and it was ratified shortly thereafter by their respective legislatures. As called for by the treaty, diplomatic relations at the ambas-

sadorial level were established on November 27. (The relationship was severely tested in September 1997 when Israeli intelligence officers attempted to assassinate Khaled MESHAL, a *Hamas* official in 'Amman. The attack on a Jordanian citizen enraged King Hussein, who threatened to break diplomatic relations and put two captured Mossad agents on trial. Prime Minister Netanyahu and other Israeli leaders reportedly made a secret visit to 'Amman in an effort to reduce tension, and the agents were returned to Israel in early October following the release of *Hamas* leader Sheikh Ahmed YASSIN and a large group of Jordanian and Palestinian prisoners from Israeli jails.)

Relations with most other Arab states (Iraq, Libya, and Sudan being conspicuous exceptions) improved measurably as the peace process gained momentum. In mid-1994 first-ever joint naval exercises, involving Israel, Egypt, Tunisia, Qatar, Canada, Italy, and the United States, were held off the Italian coast. In August a senior Israeli foreign ministry official visited Bahrain and Kuwait; in early September agreement was reached with Morocco and Tunisia on the establishment of liaison offices; and on September 30 the Gulf Cooperation Council (GCC) lifted the "secondary" and "tertiary" aspects of its economic boycott of Israel, although retaining the ban on direct trade. In early November Tansu Ciller became the first Turkish prime minister to visit Israel, and on December 26 Rabin became the first Israel prime minister to visit Oman. Turkey and Israel also signed an agreement in August 1996 for the exchange of "technical expertise" on defense matters, a development that was criticized in many Arab capitals, and the two countries conducted a small, yet highly symbolic, joint military exercise in the Mediterranean in January 1998. In addition, Ehud Barak in October 1999 became the first Israeli prime minister to visit Turkey.

Earlier, in a historic ceremony at Jerusalem on December 30, 1993, Israel and the Vatican had agreed to establish diplomatic relations, with representatives from both sides expressing the hope that a 2,000-year rupture between Christians and Jews could thus be overcome.

The funeral of Yitzhak Rabin in November 1995 attracted Israel's largest ever gathering of foreign leaders, including several from prominent Arab states, underscoring, among other things, international concern that the assassinated prime minister might prove nearly irreplaceable in the ongoing Middle East peace process. Despite the shock of his death, the withdrawal of Israeli troops from six more West Bank towns (as authorized in the second Israeli/PLO accord) proceeded smoothly throughout the rest of the year. In addition, Palestinian elections in January 1996 appeared to represent another major milestone toward a final permanent settlement of the long-standing conflict. However, the situation changed dramatically in late February and early March when suicide bombings in Jerusalem and Tel Aviv killed some 60 Israelis.

As was widely expected, Benjamin Netanyahu's election as Israeli prime minister in 1996 slowed progress on the Palestinian front, negotiations on the controversial proposed withdrawal of Israeli troops from most of the West Bank town of Hebron proving fruitless in view of the new government's seemingly intransigent stance. Resentment within the West Bank and Gaza built throughout the summer of 1996 and boiled over in September when the Israeli government, despite foreknown intense religious objections among Arabs, permitted a tunnel in the Old City of Jerusalem to be opened. Subsequent fighting between Palestinians (including some members of the Palestinian police forces) and Israeli soldiers was described as the worst since the *intifada*, prompting US President Clinton to summon Netanyahu, 'Arafat, and Jordan's King Hussein to an emergency summit at Washington in early October. Violence subsequently subsided, and Israeli/Palestinian talks began anew, although each side expressed concern over the other's "sincerity." After a series of face-to-face meetings between Netanyahu and 'Arafat, agreement was finally reached in January 1997 for an immediate resolution to the Hebron impasse and the gradual withdrawal of Israeli troops from more of the West Bank by mid-1998. For the new Israeli prime minister, the accord prompted an immediate backlash from *Likud* hard-liners as well as the smaller religious parties in his government coalition. When

Netanyahu presented the agreement for cabinet endorsement, seven ministers voted no, arguing that it represented a violation of the pledges made in the recent election. Approval was achieved more easily within the *Knesset*, as Labor representatives, claiming vindication of the policies of former prime ministers Rabin and Peres, readily supported the new agreement.

Hope that the January 1997 Hebron settlement would rejuvenate the peace process as a whole was quickly dashed when it became apparent that there was great disagreement between the Israelis and the Palestinians over the extent of the new proposed Israeli withdrawals from West Bank territory. Israel's initial offer for the next phase, which Netanyahu described as covering an additional 9 percent of the West Bank but Palestinians claimed only represented a 2 percent handover, was rejected by 'Arafat and broadly denounced by regional Arab states. Meanwhile, the Israeli cabinet in late February authorized construction of a new Jewish settlement in East Jerusalem, touching off heavy Palestinian protests and bringing negotiations to a halt. Militant Palestinian leaders urged a return to the *intifada*, and three Israelis died in a suicide bomb attack at Tel Aviv in late March, prompting Netanyahu to demand a crackdown by Palestinian security forces on *Hamas* and other groups. In addition, following bombings at Jerusalem in late July and in early September, Israel suspended the transfer of taxes and customs duties to Palestinian authorities and temporarily sealed off the West Bank and Gaza. The United States attempted to revive negotiations in late 1997 and early 1998 by proposing a new 13 percent Israeli withdrawal; however, Netanyahu rejected that figure, and in January 1998 the Israeli cabinet endorsed sweeping new demands (covering areas such as the extradition of suspected militants from Palestinian-controlled areas to Israel) that would have to be met before more land was turned over to Palestinian control. The 'Arafat government rejected the new demands as "unrealistic," an assessment apparently shared by much of the international community, which also widely viewed Israel as being unnecessarily provocative on the settlement front as well. Netanyahu subsequently suggested that final status negotiations should be launched despite the lack of progress regarding troop withdrawals, but that concept was rejected by 'Arafat, who continued to accuse Israel of reneging on its previous promises. By that time it had also become clear that Palestinians were expecting ultimately to gain control of 90 percent of the West Bank, while Israel was considering ceding, at most, 50 percent of the territory. For his part, 'Arafat pledged to declare an independent state of Palestine in May 1999, even if no further progress had been achieved in negotiations with Israel.

In July 1998 Israeli and Palestinian negotiators met for the first time in over a year, and in October Netanyahu travelled to the United States to meet with 'Arafat and Clinton at the Wye Plantation in Maryland. After ten days of reportedly "tortuous" negotiations (capped off by a surprise visit from ailing King Hussein of Jordan), Netanyahu and 'Arafat signed an agreement on October 23 which proposed a three-month timetable for the next withdrawals of Israeli forces from the West Bank. Completion of the new redeployments would have left about 17 percent of the West Bank under full Palestinian control and 23 percent under joint Israeli/Palestinian authority. It was envisaged that negotiations would then begin regarding the third (and last) withdrawal phase and the other outstanding issues.

In addition to the geographic expansion of Palestinian autonomy, Israel also agreed in the Wye accord to release a number of Palestinian prisoners, permit the opening of the Gaza airport, and proceed with the establishment of a transit corridor for Palestinians from the West Bank to Gaza. For their part, Palestinian leaders pledged expanded security measures and additional repudiation of the anti-Israeli sections of the PLO Covenant. The first redeployment (centered around the northern West Bank town of Jenin) occurred on November 20, and later in the month international donors, signalling support for the resumption of progress, pledged some $3 billion in additional aid for development in the autonomous areas. However, Netanyahu faced significant opposition within his cabinet over the accord and appeared to place numerous barriers in the way of further implementation by, among other things, authorizing the expansion of some Jewish settlements in the West Bank and demanding that Palestinian officials adopt a comprehensive weapons collection program, refrain from anti-Israeli "incitement," and drop their plans to unilaterally declare statehood on May 4, 1999, regardless of the status of the peace process. Clinton visited Israel and the self-rule territories on December 12–15 in an effort to reinvigorate the Wye plan, attending the session of the Palestinian National Council at Gaza that endorsed the requested Covenant changes. However, the Netanyahu coalition finally collapsed in the ensuing days, and the cabinet on December 20 voted to suspend further implementation of the Wye provisions pending new national elections later scheduled for May 1999. Meanwhile, 'Arafat defused a potentially explosive situation in late April by announcing that Palestinians would defer their unilateral declaration of statehood.

A number of Arab states closed their offices in Israel following the outbreak of the "second *intifada*" in late 2000 (see Current issues, below), and a March 2001 Arab League summit endorsed the Palestinian "right to resist" Israeli "aggression." In early 2002 Saudi Arabia proposed the full normalization of relations between Israel and Arab states in return for complete Israeli withdrawal from the occupied territories. Arab leaders subsequently urged Washington to propose a specific timetable for creation of a Palestinian state, arguing that the lack of progress in resolving the Palestinian/Israeli conflict was generating widespread anti-US sentiment in the Arab world.

Current Issues

Following his inauguration in July 1999, new Israeli Prime Minister Ehud Barak called for a comprehensive peace settlement with the Palestinians, Syria, and Lebanon within 15 months. On September 4, he and Palestinian leader Yasir 'Arafat signed an agreement at Sharm el-Sheikh in Egypt that provided for the "reactivation" of the 1998 Wye accord via the immediate transfer of additional territory in the West Bank to Palestinian control and the release of some Palestinians under Israeli arrest in

return for the Palestinian leadership's "zero tolerance" of terrorism. So-called "final status" negotiations were subsequently launched on the very difficult issues of Jewish settlements in the occupied
territories, the eventual status of Jerusalem (which
both sides envisioned as their capital), and the future of some 3.6 million Palestinian refugees seeking a return to Israel. Little progress was achieved
by the spring of 2000, however, except for some
redeployment of Israeli forces in the West Bank
(bringing about 43 percent of the West Bank under
complete or partial Palestinian control). In April
Barak appeared to accept the eventual creation of
an independent Palestinian "entity" (he avoided using the word "state") comprising Gaza and 60–70
percent of the West Bank. However, he indicated a
"majority" of the Jewish settlers in the disputed areas would remain under Israeli sovereignty. At the
same time, popular sentiment in Israel appeared to
be turning away from the proposed return of the
Golan Heights to Syria, and the construction of
additional Golan settlements (suspended since the
previous December) resumed in April. Hopes for a
resolution declined further in May when sporadic
violence broke out in Gaza and the West Bank, fueled by Palestinian disenchantment with the lack
of progress in negotiations.

Faced with a collapsing coalition (see Political
background, above), Barak attended a "make-or-
break" summit with 'Arafat and US President Clinton at Camp David in July 2000. Although agreement appeared close on several issues, the summit
ended unsuccessfully when common ground could
not be found regarding the status of Jerusalem
and sovereignty over holy sites there, notably Temple Mount (*Harim-al-Sharif*), a sacred location for
both Jews and Muslims. (Clinton criticized 'Arafat
for being unwilling to make the "difficult decisions" required to conclude a pact.)

Serious rioting on the part of Palestinians
erupted in late September 2000 following a visit
by hard-line *Likud* leader Ariel Sharon to Temple
Mount that was viewed as unnecessarily "provocative" by many observers. Although Barak subsequently indicated a willingness to endorse the establishment of two "separate entities" in Jerusalem,

negotiations collapsed in October in the face of
the "second *intifada*" and heavy reprisals by the
Israeli military that included the use of assault
helicopter and rocket attacks. By the end of December more than 350 people had been killed and
10,000 injured in the violence. In addition, Israel
had banned Palestinian workers from entering Israel and imposed other economic sanctions such as
the withholding of tax payments to the Palestinian
Authority.

At the end of 2000, President Clinton, attempting to cap his eight-year tenure with a "last hurrah"
Middle East breakthrough, proposed a settlement
under which all of Gaza and some 95 percent of the
West Bank would be placed under Palestinian control, although some West Bank settlements would
remain Israeli. The proposed accord also reportedly
called for Palestinian sovereignty over certain areas
of East Jerusalem, the return of a "small number"
of Palestinian refugees, and a mutual "accommodation" regarding Temple Mount. Barak reportedly
approved the compromise, but 'Arafat in early 2001
raised a number of objections, particularly in regard
to the refugee issue.

Barak's defeat by Sharon in the February 2001
special prime ministerial balloting appeared to
doom prospects for any settlement soon, particularly in view of the fact that the new Bush administration in Washington had announced it did
not consider itself in any way bound by the "parameters" endorsed by Clinton. Sharon pledged
that Jerusalem would remain "whole and unified"
under Israeli sovereignty and that no Jewish settlements would be dismantled. Consequently, the
rest of the year was marked by escalating violence that included numerous suicide bombings by
Palestinian militants and massive retaliation by Israel in the form of missile attacks and tank incursions. Late in the year President Bush expressed his
support for the eventual establishment of a Palestinian state and called for the withdrawal of Israeli
forces from the areas previously under Palestinian
control. Peace advocates also saw a glimmer of
hope when 'Arafat, whose compound was besieged
by Israeli troops, subsequently called upon all
Palestinian groups to honor a cease-fire and

indicated "flexibility" on the refugee question. However, suicide bombings continued unabated in early 2002, and Israel in April launched an offensive of unprecedented scale that left it in control of most West Bank towns. When that initiative failed to restrain the suicide bombers, the Sharon government announced at midyear that it would begin to construct a "security fence" around the West Bank. Positions subsequently remained hardened as Sharon called 'Arafat an "enemy" and demanded a change in the Palestinian leadership.

Not surprisingly, security issues dominated the January 2003 *Knesset* balloting. *Likud's* solid victory appeared to indicate a repudiation of the "peace agenda" of Labor's new leader, Avraham Mitzna. At the same time, Sharon warned that "painful concessions" regarding Palestinian statehood would eventually be required.

At the end of April 2003, the so-called Middle East Quartet (the EU, Russia, the UN, and the US) formally unveiled the much-discussed "road map" toward a final comprehensive settlement of the Israeli-Palestinian dispute involving establishment of an "independent, democratic, and viable" Palestinian state. (Attention in this regard had been at least temporarily shunted aside because of the events in Iraq.) The plan called for an immediate "unconditional" cease-fire and a freeze on new Israeli settlements. Completion of a new Palestinian constitution was also envisioned, in the hope that Palestinian elections could be held by the end of the year. The major component of the second phase of the road map was to be the convening of an international conference to, among other things, help determine provisional borders for the new state. Final negotiations were slated for completion by the end of 2005, assuming Palestinian institutions had been "stabilized" and Palestinian security forces had proven adequate in combatting attacks against Israel. Sharon offered "qualified" support for the road map, as did the *Knesset*, although the latter insisted that it be made clear that Palestinian refugees would not be guaranteed the right to return to their former homes in Israel. Meanwhile, Palestinian Prime Minister Mahmoud Abbas (see below) called for an end to the "armed intifada" while

also demanding, unsuccessfully, that construction on the Israeli security wall be stopped.

In the wake of renewed heavy violence, the *Knesset* in September 2003 endorsed the potential expulsion from Israel of 'Arafat, whom Sharon and Bush blamed for the ongoing stalemate. Toward the end of the year, Sharon warned that he might take unilateral action if the road map process failed, and in February 2004 he became more specific, suggesting that Israeli forces might withdraw from Gaza. His disengagement plan also appeared to involve the closure of all 21 Jewish settlements in Gaza (as well as several in the West Bank) and the imposition of new "security lines." Significantly, President Bush in April suggested that the US now believed that it would be appropriate for Israel to keep some of the territory captured in the 1967 war. In June the cabinet endorsed Sharon's plan, while Labor agreed to provide a safety net in the *Knesset* for Sharon in order to allow him to proceed toward disengagement. In October the *Knesset* endorsed the proposal by a vote of 67–47, and in February it approved $900 million in compensation for the settlers who faced displacement. Meanwhile, violence continued on both sides of the dispute, exacerbated by Israel's assassination of prominent leaders of *Hamas* (see below).

For many analysts, the death of 'Arafat in November 2004 offered hope that a negotiated settlement might still be reached. For its part, the Israeli government called upon the new Palestinian leaders to finally come to terms with "terrorism" on the part of Palestinian militants. However, momentum regarding Sharon's unilateral disengagement plan continued to grow, Sharon announcing in the spring of 2005 that the forced evacuation of Jewish settlers in Gaza would begin in mid-August.

Political Parties

Government Parties

Unity–National Liberal Party (*Likud–Liberalim Leumi*). Its name reflecting its contention that Israel was entitled to all land between the

Jordan River and the Mediterranean, *Likud* was formed under the leadership of Menachem Begin in September 1973 in an effort to break the legislative monopoly of the Labor Alignment (see ILP, below). Joining in the grouping were the Herut-Liberal Bloc (*Gush Herut-Liberalim*–Gahal), composed of the *Herut* (Freedom) and Liberal parties; the Integral Land of Israel movement; and the Peace to Zion (*Schlomzion*), Ariel Sharon's small right-wing party that entered *Likud* after the 1977 election. Although often maintaining a common outlook in regard to captured territory, the constituent parties subsequently differed somewhat on domestic policy, though tending theoretically to favor the denationalization of certain industries in the context of a free-enterprise philosophy.

In September 1985 *La'am* (For the Nation), a *Likud* faction that had been launched in 1969 from Rafi (a 1965 offshoot of Mapai, see ILP, below) by former prime minister David Ben-Gurion as the State List, merged with *Herut*. Prior to the 1988 election, two additional groups merged with *Likud:* the Movement for Economic Recovery/Courage (*Ometz*), founded in early 1984 by former Mapai member Yigael HURWITZ, and the Movement for Israel's Tradition (*Tenuat Masoret Yisrael*–Tami), an Oriental orthodox party founded in 1981 as an offshoot of the NRP by Aharon ABU-HAZEIRA.

Relations between *Likud* leader Benjamin Netanyahu and former foreign minister David Levy became tense following the latter's loss to Netanyahu in the March 1993 party election. In early 1995 the situation worsened further, with Levy insisting that the adoption of a primary system to choose party candidates for the next election would marginalize the numerically dominant Sephardi community, of which he was a member. As a result, Levy formed a new party—*Gesher* (below)—although he subsequently supported Netanyahu in the May 1996 prime ministerial balloting. *Likud* also agreed to present joint candidates with *Gesher* and *Tzomet* for the concurrent *Knesset* balloting on a platform that emphasized "security" as the "first condition" in any peace agreement and opposed the establishment of an independent Palestinian state as well as "land-for-peace" negotiations with Syria regarding the Golan Heights.

Surprising many observers, Netanyahu won the 1996 prime ministerial election with 50.5 percent of the vote. At the same time, the *Likud/Gesher/Tzomet* alliance garnered 25.1 percent of the *Knesset* votes, thereby securing 32 seats, 22 of which went to *Likud* under the formula previously established with its electoral partners. Meanwhile, within *Likud* the most contentious issue involved a cabinet post for Sharon, who had reportedly agreed not to challenge Netanyahu for party supremacy in return for a major ministry in the event of a *Likud* victory. Last-minute negotiations finally produced agreement on the creation of a new ministry of national infrastructure for Sharon, who became one of eight *Likud* members to join Netanyahu in the new cabinet. However, friction between Netanyahu and Sharon continued, as evidenced by Sharon's vote against the new Israeli/Palestinian accord when it was presented to the cabinet for approval by Netanyahu in January 1997. Benjamin Begin, Menachem Begin's son and a longtime opponent of territorial negotiations with the Palestinians, also voted against the agreement and resigned as minister of science to protest Netanyahu's decisions in the matter.

In June 1997 Finance Minister Dan Meridor, seen as a rival to Netanyahu within *Likud,* resigned his cabinet post, the fissure representing, in the opinion of many observers, growing disenchantment among some party faithful over a perceived lack of influence upon national policy. Potential factionalization was also apparent at the November party convention when Netanyahu's supporters pushed through a change whereby the former primary system for choosing legislative candidates was replaced by selection by the Central Committee, dominated by Netanyahu loyalists.

In January 1999 Netanyahu was named as *Likud*'s candidate for prime minister, securing 82 percent of the primary vote against Moshe ARENS. (Arens, one of Netanyahu's mentors and a former defense minister, had challenged Netanyahu in order to "stop the hemorrhaging" within the party.)

By that time several prominent *Likud* dissenters had defected to the new Center Party (below), while Benjamin Begin had founded his own party (see New *Herut,* below) and decided to run for prime minister against Netanyahu.

Following his loss to Labor's Ehud Barak in the May 1999 balloting for prime minister, Netanyahu resigned as *Likud*'s leader. He was succeeded on an interim basis by Sharon, who was elected in a permanent capacity on September 3 with 53 percent support of the party membership over two other candidates. Netanyahu declined to challenge Sharon for the party's nomination for prime minister in the February 2001 election. However, in mid-2002 he positioned himself for another run at *Likud* leadership, his supporters sponsoring a resolution that was approved by the Central Committee stating that the party would never support the creation of an independent Palestinian state. However, Sharon easily defeated Netanyahu in the November 28 leadership balloting. Despite their often bitter previous history, Netanyahu was named finance minister in the cabinet appointed in February 2003.

Merger plans with *Yisrael B'Aliya* were under consideration as of early 2005 (see below). By that time Sharon had survived several confrontations with dissident *Likud* members opposed to his plan for unilateral Israeli withdrawal from the Gaza Strip (see Current issues for additional information).

Leaders: Ariel SHARON (Prime Minister and Chairman of the Party), Moshe KATSAV (President of the State of Israel), Benjamin NETANYAHU, Reuven RIVLIN (Speaker of the *Knesset*).

Israel Labor Party–ILP (*Mifleget Ha'avoda Ha'yisra'elit*). The ILP was formed in January 1968 through merger of the Israel Workers' Party (*Mifleget Poalei Eretz Yisrael*–Mapai), a Western-oriented socialist party established in 1929 and represented in the government by prime ministers David Ben-Gurion, Moshe Sharett, Levi Eshkol, Golda Meir, Shimon Peres, and Yitzhak Rabin; the Israel Workers' List (*Reshimat Poalei Yisrael*–

Rafi), founded by Ben-Gurion as a vehicle of opposition to Prime Minister Eshkol; and the Unity of Labor–Workers of Zion (*Achdut Ha'avoda–Poalei Zion*), which advocated a planned economy, agricultural settlement, and an active defense policy.

In January 1969 the ILP joined with Mapam (see *Meretz,* below) in a coalition known initially as the Alignment (*Ma'arakh*) and subsequently as the Labor Alignment (*Ma'arakh Ha'avoda*). The latter was technically dissolved upon Mapam's withdrawal in protest at formation of the national unity government, although the term was subsequently used to reference a linkage between Labor and *Yahad* (Together), a party led by former air force commander and former *Likud* leader Ezer Weizman, who had urged direct talks with Arab leaders until his retirement from partisan politics before the 1992 election.

Following the assassination of Prime Minister Rabin in November 1995, the party's Central Committee endorsed Shimon Peres (who had been serving as foreign minister and the lead Israeli negotiator regarding emerging Palestinian autonomy) to succeed him as party leader and prime minister. Subsequently, in a significant policy change, the Committee in April 1996 eliminated the longstanding section in the party platform that formally opposed the eventual creation of an independent Palestinian state.

Labor retained a slight majority in the May 1996 *Knesset* balloting, (securing 34 seats on the strength of 26.8 percent of the vote); however, Peres was narrowly defeated in the concurrent election for prime minister. Later in the year, amid reported intraparty friction on the question, Peres announced he would not run for prime minister in 2000 or, for that matter, for reelection as party chairman.

In May 1997 the party rejected the proposed creation of a new post of party president for Peres, setting the stage for a subsequent "generational" change of leadership. In early June, Ehud Barak, a hawkish former army chief of staff and foreign minister under Peres, was elected as Labor's new leader with 57 percent of the votes, easily defeating runner-up Yossi BEILIN, the Peres supporter who garnered 29 percent of the vote. Barak subsequently attempted to move the ILP closer to the center of the political spectrum, and, after securing unanimous nominations in January 1999 as the party's candidate for prime minister, he announced in March that Labor would contest the upcoming legislative balloting in a **One Israel** coalition with *Gesher* and *Meimad*.

The ILP secured 23 of the 26 seats won by One Israel (20.2 percent of the vote) in the May 17, 1999, legislative elections, while Barak was elected prime minister with 56 percent of the vote. However, the ILP suffered a major blow when Peres was defeated by *Likud*'s Moshe Katzav for state president in July 2000, and Barak was soundly beaten in the special prime ministerial balloting in February 2001. Barak subsequently resigned as ILP leader, and new elections for that post were held in September 2001. Initial results showed Avraham BURG, the speaker of the *Knesset,* with a small majority over Benjamin BEN-ELIEZER, the current defense minister. However, Ben-Eliezer's supporters challenged the results, and after a partial rerun in December, Ben-Eliezer, a hard-liner regarding the Palestinian question, was declared the winner.

Gen. (Ret.) Avraham MITZNA, the mayor of Haifa, was elected leader of the ILP in November 2002 and subsequently proposed a "radical peace agenda" for the January 2003 *Knesset* balloting (which the ILP contested in a coalition with *Meimad*). Following a poor performance in the elections (only 17 seats on a 14.5 percent vote share), Mitzna resigned the ILP leadership in May. He was succeeded in an acting capacity by Peres.

Leaders: Shimon PERES (Acting Chairman of the Party and Vice Premier of the Republic), Eitan CABEL (General Secretary).

Dimension (*Meimad*). Founded in the late 1980s by former NRP members who believed the parent grouping had become too right-wing, *Meimad* competed unsuccessfully in the 1992 *Knesset* elections. In February 1998 *Meimad* announced its intention to participate in the next legislative balloting as an "Orthodox but open-minded and open-hearted" grouping that could provide a

voice for Zionists who supported the peace process. In early 1999 *Meimad* agreed to join the One Israel electoral coalition with the Labor Party and *Gesher, Meimad. Meimad* secured 1 of the 26 seats won by One Israel in the May *Knesset* balloting, and leader Rabbi Michael Melchior was named to the subsequent Barak cabinet. He also accepted deputy minister positions in subsequent Sharon governments. (*Meimad* ran in coalition with the ILP in the 2003 *Knesset* balloting.)

Leaders: Rabbi Michael MELCHIOR, Rabbi Yehuda AMITAL.

United Torah Judaism (UTJ). Also known as the Orthodox Torah bloc, United Torah Judaism was formed prior to the 1992 balloting as a coalition of the two parties below. It won four *Knesset* seats in both 1992 and 1996, and one of its members was appointed deputy minister for housing and construction in the June 1996 Netanyahu government. The UTJ won five seats in the May 1999 legislative balloting on a vote share of 3.7 percent, and subsequently agreed to support the Barak government in the *Knesset,* albeit without cabinet representation. The UTJ was given several deputy ministerial posts in the Sharon government in March 2001 but lost those positions in May 2002 when the UTJ opposed Sharon's emergency budget cuts. (Rabbi Eliezer SHACH, the longtime spiritual leader of the UTJ as well as its two component groupings, died in November 2001.)

The UTJ won five seats (on a vote share of 4.3 percent) in the 2003 *Knesset* balloting but resisted repeated invitations to join Sharon's subsequent coalition governments because of the presence of *Shinui* in the cabinet. However, after *Shinui* fell out with *Likud* in late 2004, the UTJ agreed to join the cabinet formed in January 2005.

Leaders: Meir PORUSH (*Agudat Yisrael*), Rabbi Avraham RAVITZ (*Degel Hatorah*).

Union of Israel (*Agudat Yisrael*). A formerly anti-Zionist orthodox religious party, *Agudat Yisrael* was allied prior to the May 1977 election with the *Poalei Agudat Yisrael* in the United Torah Front, which called for strict observance of religious law and introduced the no-confidence motion that led to Prime Minister Rabin's resignation in December 1976. Its *Knesset* representation fell from four in 1981 to two in 1984 as a result of the loss of Oriental Jewish votes to the recently organized Shas. After winning five seats in 1988, it declined government representation at full ministerial level but agreed to the appointment of one of its representatives as deputy minister of labor and social affairs. It accepted a Jerusalem Affairs portfolio in November 1990 after Prime Minister Shamir had agreed to endorse a number of its legislative objectives. *Agudat Yisrael* members filled three of the five *Knesset* seats won by the UTJ in 1999.

Leaders: Meir PORUSH, Ya'acov LITZMAN.

Torah Flag (*Degel Hatorah*). Formed in 1988 by a group of *Agudat Yisrael* dissidents, the *Degel Hatorah* is a non-Zionist ultra-Orthodox religious party that captured two *Knesset* seats at the 1988 poll. Its members secured two of the five *Knesset* seats won by the UTJ in 1999.

Leaders: Rabbi Avraham RAVITZ, Moshi GAFNI.

Other Parties in the Knesset

Sephardi Torah Guardians (*Shomrei Torah Sephardiim*–Shas). An offshoot of *Agudat Yisrael* (below), Shas was formed prior to the 1984 balloting, at which it won four seats. It is an orthodox religious party drawing support among Jews of Oriental (Sephardi) descent from North Africa and the Middle East. In December 1984 the group withdrew from the national unity coalition in a dispute with the NRP over the allocation of portfolios, (then) Shas leader Yitzhak Peretz subsequently returning to the interior ministry with a budget enhanced by the transfer of funds from religious affairs. It withdrew again in February 1987 over the registration as Jewish of a US convert but rejoined the coalition after the 1988 election, at which it won six *Knesset* seats. Its representation was unchanged at the 1992 poll, after which it joined the Labor coalition. In September 1993 Shas leader Aryeh Der'i was obliged to resign as interior min-

ister after a lengthy inquiry into alleged corruption had yielded formal charges against him. The result was a six-month withdrawal of Shas from the government coalition, followed by the group's return to opposition status in February 1995. Shas won 8.5 percent of the vote and ten seats in the May 1996 *Knesset* balloting, thereby becoming the third largest legislative party. Its success was in part attributed to the large Shas network of schools and social services, which had won growing grass roots support even among relatively nonobservant Sephardic Jews. In June Shas accepted an invitation to join the new Netanyahu government, in which its two portfolios included, not surprisingly, the ministry of labor and social affairs. In the national campaign of early 1999, Shas was described as "thoroughly domestic" in its political concerns and appeared to be surging in popularity, despite Der'i's conviction in February on bribery and other charges. Shas won 17 seats on a 13 percent vote share in the May 1999 legislative balloting and joined the government subsequently formed by Labor's Ehud Barak.

Der'i resigned as chairman of Shas in June 1999; he was imprisoned in September 2000 after his four-year sentence was upheld by appeal courts.

Leaders: Rabbi Ovadia YOSEF (Spiritual Leader), Eliyahu YISHAI (Chairman).

Movement for Israel and Immigration (*Yisrael B'Aliya*). *Yisrael B'Aliya* was originally launched in 1992 as the National Movement for Democracy and Aliya ("ingathering") as a means of promoting the economic well-being of the ex-Soviet immigrant community that had recently swollen to more than 500,000 persons. Despite the size of its potential constituency, the group failed to secure *Knesset* representation. In mid-1995 its leader declared that the group would not contest the next election "as a Russian ethnic group, but as a social movement." Consequently, the party's 1996 campaign emphasized economic liberalization and human rights in general in addition to support for "newcomers." *Yisrael B'Aliya* won a surprising seven seats in the May 1996 *Knesset* balloting and secured two portfolios in the June cabinet, including, logically, the one for immigrant absorption. Party Chairman Natan Sharansky voted in favor of the recent Israeli/Palestinian agreement when it was presented to the Israeli cabinet in January 1997, although the group's other minister, Yuli Edelstein, voted no.

Yisrael B'Aliya won six seats in the May 1999 legislative balloting on a vote share of 5.1 percent. After joining the subsequent Barak government, it left the cabinet in early August 2000 in opposition to consideration being given to a possible return of the Golan Heights to Syria. The party was awarded cabinet seats in the new Sharon government in early 2001, with Sharansky serving as deputy prime minister. Following the poor showing of *Yisrael B'Aliya* in the January 2003 *Knesset* balloting (two seats on a 2.2 percent vote share), Sharansky resigned his cabinet post with the stated goal of "rebuilding" the party. However, it was quickly announced that the deputies from *Yisrael B'Aliya* would "merge" with the *Likud* faction in the *Knesset*. Sharansky was subsequently named minister for diaspora affairs, but he resigned that post in May 2005 to protest Sharon's disengagement plan. Meanwhile, final arrangements were reportedly being made for the formal merger of *Yisrael B'Aliya* into *Likud*.

Leaders: Natan SHARANSKY (Chairman), Yuli EDELSTEIN.

One Nation (*Am Ehad*). Formed in early 1999 by several dissident members of *Likud* with strong ties to organized labor, One Nation campaigned for the upcoming *Knesset* balloting in support of greater benefits for pensioners and workers. It secured two seats in the May 1999 legislative balloting on a vote share of 1.9 percent and three seats in the January 2003 balloting on a vote share of 2.8 percent. In 2004 Amir PERETZ, the leader of *Am Ehad* and longtime head of Israel's leading labor federation, announced the planned merger of *Am Ehad* with the ILP. However, although Peretz himself had reportedly joined the ILP, the formal merger plans were described as stalled in early 2005.

National Religious Party–NRP (*Mifleget Datit Leumit*–Mafdal). Dedicated to the principles of religious Zionism and evolving, over time, into a militantly nationalist group calling for outright annexation of the West Bank, the NRP was formed in 1956 through the union of two older organizations, *Mizrahi* and the *Mizrahi* Workers (*Hapoel Hamizrahi*). Formerly allied with Labor, the party went into opposition following the 1973 election because of a dispute over religious policy but subsequently reentered the government. In December 1976 Prime Minister Rabin ousted the three NRP cabinet members after nine of the party's ten legislative deputies had abstained on a no-confidence vote, thus precipitating a government crisis that led to a call for the May 1977 election. On the eve of the 1977 balloting the party concluded a coalition with *Likud,* subsequently participating in the Begin government formed on June 20. The arrangement continued after the 1981 election, at which its representation fell from 12 to 6 seats, with a further decline to 4 seats in 1984.

Prior to the 1988 balloting (at which it won five seats) the NRP absorbed Heritage (*Morasha*), a religious grouping formed prior to the 1984 election by merger of the Rally of Religious Zionism (*Mifleget Tzionut Dati*–Matzad) with the Agudat Israel Workers (*Poalei Agudat Yisrael*). The party's legislative strength grew to six in 1992 and nine in 1996, and it secured two seats in the June 1996 government. Underscoring the tenuous nature of the alliance between *Likud* and the ultra-religious parties, the NRP ministers voted against Netanyahu in January 1997 when the recent Israeli/Palestinian agreement was presented to the cabinet. Zevulun HAMMER, longtime chairman of the NRP and deputy prime minister in the Netanyahu cabinet, died in January 1998. He was succeeded as minister of education and culture and party chairman by Yitzhak Levy, the NRP secretary general. The NRP, now considered the primary political voice of the Jewish settlers in the occupied territories, strongly opposed the Wye agreement of October 1998, contributing significantly to the subsequent collapse of the Netanyahu government. The NRP secured five seats in the May 1999 *Knesset* balloting on a vote share of 4.2 percent. It left the new Barak government in mid-2000 in protest over discussion of the possible return of the Golan Heights to Syria. Effi Eitam, a brigadier general in the national reserves, succeeded Levy as NRP chairman in April

2002 as the NRP prepared to join the Sharon government.

In January 2005 plans were reported for the potential merger of the NRP with the National Union.

Leaders: Zevulun ORLEV (Chairman), Effi EITAM, Shalom JERBI (Secretary General).

Power-Democratic Israel (*Meretz–Yisrael Democrati*). *Meretz* was formed prior to the 1992 election as a coalition of the Civil Rights and Peace Movement–CRM (*ha-Tenua le-Zechouot ha-Ezrakh*–Ratz), the United Workers' Party (*Mifleget Hapoalim Hamenchedet*–Mapam), and *Shinui*. The *Meretz* platform called for a phased peace settlement with the Palestinians, Jordan, Lebanon, and Syria, based on withdrawal from the occupied territories and guarantees for the security of Israel through interim agreements, security arrangements, and demilitarization. It also advocated religious pluralism, liberalization of the "law of return," the adoption of a bill of rights, equal status for women, and strict enforcement of anti-pollution legislation. *Meretz* won 12 *Knesset* seats in 1992 and 9 (Ratz, 4; Mapam, 3; and *Shinui*, 2) in 1996, having prior to the latter endorsed the creation of an independent Palestinian state and "land-for-peace" negotiations with Syria.

In February 1996 it was reported that Yossi Sarid, a Ratz member and then environmental minister in the Peres cabinet, had been elected to succeed Shulamit Aloni as *Meretz* chairman. In early 1999 Ratz and Mapam agreed to a formal merger of their groupings, with *Meretz* becoming a political party rather than a coalition. Some *Shinui* members also participated in that initiative, although *Shinui* ultimately retained its own identity and campaigned on its own for the May 1999 *Knesset* elections, at which *Meretz* won ten seats on a vote share of 7.6 percent.

Meretz won six seats in the 2003 *Knesset* balloting on a vote share of 5.2 percent. Subsequently, it was announced that *Meretz* would merge with several other left-wing groups to form a new party, initially known as **Meretz-Yahad**, with the *Meretz* component of the name to be dropped eventually. *Yahad* (Together) opposed Prime Minister Sharon's disengagement plan, calling instead for negotia-

tions with the Palestinians toward a comprehensive settlement. Party leaders hoped to draw support from disaffected ILP members.

Leaders: Yossi BEILIN (Chairman), Yossi SARID (Former Chairman), Michal SHOHAT (General Secretary).

Change (*Shinui*). The original *Shinui* movement under Amnon RUBINSTEIN joined in November 1976 with the Democratic Movement of former army chief of staff Yigael Yadin to form the Democratic Movement for Change (DMC), which, with 15 seats, emerged as the third largest party at the 1977 election, after which it supported the Begin government. Following a split in the DMC in September 1978, the *Shinui* group and supporters of (then) Transport and Communications Minister Meir Amit withdrew to form the opposition Change and Initiative (*Shinui Ve Yozma*–Shai). The DMC was formally dissolved in February 1981, its remnants regrouping with supporters of Shai to contest the June election under the *Shinui* label. A member of the national unity government after the 1984 balloting, *Shinui* withdrew from the coalition in May 1987. A member of the Liberal International, it presented a joint list with the New Liberal Party (below) in 1988. Two *Shinui* members were elected to the *Knesset* in 1996 as part of *Meretz*. However, *Shinui* in early 1999 opted to contest the upcoming *Knesset* balloting on its own under the leadership of Tommy Lapid, a political commentator and television personality who accepted the *Shinui* chairmanship in March. *Shinui*'s subsequent campaign was primarily devoted to opposing the increasing influence of ultraorthodox parties. It secured six seats in the May 1999 *Knesset* balloting on a vote share of 5 percent. It subsequently maintained a position of refusing to join any government that included any ultraorthodox parties.

Leaders: Tommy LAPID (Chairman), Avraham PORAZ.

United Arab List (UAL). The UAL was formed prior to the 1996 *Knesset* elections by Arab groupings hoping to increase the electoral clout of the estimated one million Israeli Arabs by presenting a joint list of candidates. Although reports agreed that one core component of the new grouping was the ADP, there was confusion regarding other participants. Israeli government publications said that, in addition to the Islamic Movement in Israel, the UAL's third component was an **Arab Islamic List.** The UAL won four seats in the 1996 balloting, as several other Arab groupings apparently decided to present their own candidates. The UAL increased its representation in the May 1999 *Knesset* election to five on the strength of 3.4 percent of the vote but fell to two seats in 2003.

Leader: 'Abd al-Malek DAHAMSHA.

Arab Democratic Party (ADP). Formed prior to the 1988 election (at which it won one seat) by a former Arab member of the Labor Party opposed to government policy in the West Bank and Gaza, the ADP is committed to international recognition of the Palestinian people's right to self-determination. The group won two *Knesset* seats in 1992.

Leaders: 'Abd al-Wahab DARAWSHAH, Muhammad KANAN.

Islamic Movement in Israel. This grouping is described by the *Christian Science Monitor* as having "similar goals" to Islamists elsewhere but within the context of "a democratic system and as loyal Israeli citizens."

Leaders: Sheikh Abdullah Nimr DARWISH, Sheikh Raed SALAH.

National Union (*Halchud HaLeumi*). Formed as an electoral alliance in early 1999 by the following two groups and New *Herut* (below), the right-wing National Union won four seats (*Moledet,* 2; *Tequma,* 1; and New *Herut,* 1) in the May *Knesset* elections on the strength of 3 percent of the vote. Shortly thereafter, the National Union formed a joint *Knesset* faction with *Yisrael Beiteinu,* although the New *Herut* legislator objected to that initiative and New *Herut* left the National Union. The National Union–*Yisrael Beiteinu* (NU–YB) faction joined the Sharon government in March 2001 but subsequently found itself to the right even of Sharon regarding the Palestinian question. On October 15 the NU-YB ministers, including Tourism Minister Rechavam Ze'evi of *Moledet,* announced their intention to resign from the cabinet. However, that decision was temporarily rescinded after Ze'evi was assassinated on October 17 by Palestinian militants. In March 2002 the NU–YB finally left the coalition, subsequent efforts by Sharon failing to persuade the ultrarightists to return.

Homeland (*Moledet*). *Moledet* is an ultra-Zionist secular party founded in 1988 by a reserve major general, Rechavam ZE'EVI, who called for annexation of the occupied territories and the ouster of their Arab inhabitants. In a controversial move that was opposed by several senior ministers, Ze'evi was appointed to the Shamir cabinet in February 1991, but the party went into opposition after the 1992 election, at which it increased its representation from two to three seats. In early July 1994 plans were announced for a merger of *Moledet* with the equally right-wing Renaissance party (*Tehiya*). (*Tehiya* had been organized in October 1979 by dissident members of *Likud* opposed to the peace agreements with Egypt and a number of right-wing and nationalist groups that continued to exist outside the party structure. The party advocated formal annexation of the Gaza Strip, the West Bank, and the Golan Heights, without their inhabitants becoming Israeli citizens, in addition to Jewish residency in all quarters of the Old City and Eastern Jerusalem. It joined the Begin coalition in July 1982 after securing exemption from support of government policies calling for Palestinian autonomy in the occupied areas. Its legislative representation fell from five in 1984 to three in 1988 as a result of the defection of *Tzomet;* it failed to win a minimum 1.5 vote percent vote share in 1992.)

Moledet won two seats in the 1996 *Knesset* balloting. Initially it was reported that the party was considering adopting a position of support for the government from outside the cabinet. However, that premise had collapsed by the end of the year, the *Moledet* legislators presenting a token nonconfidence motion in December to protest the government's negotiations regarding further troop withdrawals in the occupied territories.

Leader: Benjamin ELON (Chairman).

Revival (*Tequma*). Launched in late 1998 by spiritual leaders and activists among Jewish settlers in the occupied territories, *Tequma* subsequently joined the National Union electoral coalition with Moledet and New *Herut,* the right-wing parties having concluded they all would face difficulty passing the 1.5 percent vote threshold for *Knesset* representation running individually.

Leaders: Rabbi Menahem FELIBUS, Uri ARIEL, Benny KATZOVER, Zvi HENDEL.

Democratic Front for Peace and Equality– DFPE (*Hazit Democratit le-Shalom ve-Shivayon*– Hadash). The Democratic Front was organized prior to the 1977 election to present candidates drawn from the former New Communist List (*Rashima Kommunistit Hadasha*–Rakah), a section of the "Black Panther" movement of Oriental Jews, and a number of unaffiliated local Arab leaders. (Rakah, a pro-Soviet and largely Arab-supported group, had broken away from Maki [see PLP, below] in 1965 following a dispute over Soviet foreign policy in the Middle East.) The DFPE retained its existing four *Knesset* seats in 1988, lost one in 1992, rebounded to five in 1996 (campaigning on behalf of an independent Palestinian state and "equality" for Israeli Arabs), and fell back to three in 1999 on a 2.6 percent vote share.

Leader: Muhammad BAREKA, Awdah BISHARAT (Secretary General).

National Democratic Alliance (*Balad*). This pro-Arab grouping is led by Azmi Bishara, a former member of Rakah who had been elected to the *Knesset* in 1996 on the Hadash list. In March 1999 Bishara, a Christian, announced his candidacy for prime minister, thereby potentially becoming the first non-Jew to run for that post. *Balad* campaigned primarily in opposition to perceived government discrimination against Israeli Arabs. It was subsequently reported that Ahmed TIBI, a Palestinian leader, had associated his Arab Movement for Change with *Balad*. Formed in early 1996 by Tibi (described as an adviser to Palestinian leader Yasir 'Arafat), the Movement was one the groupings expected to participate in the UAL. However, according to government publications, it

presented its own candidates (unsuccessfully) in the 1996 *Knesset* elections before aligning with *Balad* for the 1999 balloting.

Bishara withdrew from the prime minister's race shortly before the May 17 balloting; he did not specifically endorse Labor's Ehud Barak, but most Bishara supporters were expected to vote for Barak. *Balad* won two seats (filled by Bishara and Tibi) in the concurrent *Knesset* election. The *Knesset* stripped Bishara of his parliamentary immunity in November 2001, and the *Balad* leader went on trial in February 2002 on charges of "incitement to violence" by, among other things, a speech he had given in Syria supporting "popular resistance" on the part of Palestinians.

The Israeli government was unsuccessful in its efforts to have *Balad* disqualified from the 2003 *Knesset* balloting, at which *Balad* secured three seats on a 2.3 percent vote share.

Leader: Azmi BISHARA.

Other Parties Contesting the 2003 Knesset Elections

Love of Israel (*Ahavat Yisrael*). Established in November 2002 by Shas veteran Aryeh Gamliel, Love of Israel called for a return to "traditional Judaism."

Leaders: Rabbi Yitzhak KADOURIE (President and Spiritual Leader), Aryeh GAMLIEL.

Center Party. Formed in mid-1998 by Ronni Milo, a former mayor of Tel Aviv who had recently left *Likud* in opposition to the policies of Prime Minister Netanyahu, the Center Party subsequently attracted the support of other *Likud* dissenters, such as former finance minister Dan Meridor, as well as independents, such as Amnon Lipkin-Sharak, a former chief of the general staff of the Israeli Defense Force. Prior to joining the Center Party, Lipkin-Sharak had announced his intention to run for prime minister against Netanyahu. It initially appeared Sharak would become the Center Party's nominee, but that designation ultimately went to Itzhak MORDECHAI, who joined the party shortly after being dismissed as defense minister by Netanyahu in January 1999. (The four prominent politicians in the Center Party had reportedly agreed to determine the strongest potential nominee among themselves and coalesce behind his candidacy.) Mordechai, arguing that Netanyahu was "incapable" of producing a permanent peace settlement, was attracting the support of about 25 percent of the voters according to preelection public opinion polls. However, he withdrew from the race shortly before the election, throwing his support to Labor's Ehud Barak.

The Center Party won six seats in the May 1999 *Knesset* balloting on a vote share of 5 percent. It joined the original Barak cabinet but withdrew in August 2000. It joined the Sharon government in August 2001. In mid-2002 it was reported that several Center Party legislators were considering a return to *Likud*. Party leader Meridor also subsequently rejoined *Likud*.

Leaders: Ronni MILO (former Mayor of Tel Aviv), Amnon Lipkin SHARAK.

New Freedom (*Herut Hahadasha*). New *Herut* was launched in 1998 by former *Likud* member Benjamin (Benny) BEGIN as a revival of the original *Herut,* which had been formed in the 1970s by his father, Menachem Begin. Benjamin Begin, a steadfast opponent of any "land-for-peace" agreement with the Palestinians, subsequently announced his candidacy for the prime ministerial election of May 1999. He also was a leading figure in the formation of the right-wing National Union electoral coalition with Moledet and *Tequma* for the concurrent *Knesset* balloting. However, Begin, who had withdrawn his prime ministerial candidacy shortly before the balloting, resigned his National Union leadership post following the election and retired from politics. New *Herut* left the National Union when the Union agreed to form a single *Knesset* faction with *Yisrael Beiteinu,* the New *Herut* legislator thereby becoming a single-member faction.

Leader: Michael KLEINER.

Israel is Our Home (*Yisrael Beiteinu*). Recently organized as another party representing the interests of Russian immigrants, *Yisrael Beiteinu* is led by Avigdor Lieberman, a former cabinet secretary in the Netanyahu administration. The party

won four seats in the May 1999 *Knesset* balloting with 2.6 percent of the vote, subsequently forming a single *Knesset* faction with the National Union (see above).

Leaders: Avigdor LIEBERMAN, Yuri STERN.

Crossroads (*Tzomet*). Also known as the Zionist Revival Movement, *Tzomet* was formed by the defection of former army chief of staff Rafael Eitan from *Tehiya* prior to the 1988 balloting, at which it won two *Knesset* seats; *Tzomet* won eight seats in 1992 but split in 1994, when two MPs defected to form a separate faction, which in June took the name *Yi'ud* and subsequently joined the Labor coalition. *Tzomet* joined *Likud* and *Gesher* in an electoral coalition in early 1996, supporting Benjamin Netanyahu for prime minister and presenting joint *Knesset* candidates. *Tzomet* was allocated five of the *Knesset* seats won by the alliance in May, and Eitan was named deputy prime minister and minister of agriculture and rural development in the new cabinet formed in June. As was the case with several other ministers from hard-line groupings, Eitan voted against the accord providing for additional Israeli troop withdrawals from the West Bank when it was presented to the cabinet in January 1997. *Tzomet* contested the 1999 *Knesset* balloting on its own, securing only 0.1 percent of the vote. Former *Tzomet* leader Rafael EITAN drowned in November 2004.

Leader: Moshe GREEN.

Other parties participating without success in the 2003 *Knesset* balloting included: **A Different Israel** (*Yisrael Aheret*), described as founded by "disgruntled twentysomethings"; the **Citizen and State Party**; the **Democratic Action Organization**, a Jewish-Arab grouping led by Asma AG-BARIYA; the **Greens** (*Hayerukim*); **Green Leaf** (*Ale Yarok*), dedicated, among other things, to the legalization of marijuana; **Men's Rights in the Family** (*Ra-ash*), led by Yosef BA-GAD; and the **Progressive National Alliance**, an Arab-Israeli party founded in November 2002.

Other Party

Bridge Party (*Gesher*). Formed in February 1996 by David Levy (who had lost a bid for the chairmanship of *Likud* in 1993), *Gesher* pledged to attempt to build a "social bridge" between the classes and a "political bridge" between the Left and the Right. Levy initially indicated he would run for prime minister but subsequently agreed to support *Likud's* Benjamin Netanyahu for that post and negotiated an electoral alliance with *Likud* and *Tzomet* for *Knesset* balloting as well. *Gesher* was accorded five of the *Knesset* seats won by the alliance, and Levy was named a deputy prime minister and foreign affairs minister in Netanyahu's new government. However, Levy resigned his post (and *Gesher* withdrew its support from the government) in January 1998 to protest the lack of progress in the Palestinian negotiations as well as what was considered to be the failure of the 1998 national budget to adequately address the needs of the country's poor. Levy was reportedly offered another cabinet post in early December 1998 as Netanyahu attempted to salvage his coalition government. However, Levy declined that overture, and in early 1999 he moved *Gesher* into the One Israel grouping with the Labor party for the upcoming *Knesset* balloting, *Gesher* gaining 2 of One Israel's 26 seats. Levy joined the subsequent Barak government as deputy prime minister and foreign minister but resigned those posts in August 2000 to protest what he perceived to be inappropriate "concessions" being considered regarding Palestinian affairs, *Gesher* thereby also becoming disassociated with One Israel. Levy also joined the Sharon government in April 2002 as minister without portfolio but left that position in late July because of his objections to proposed budget cuts. Levy rejoined *Likud* in November 2002, and the status of *Gesher* subsequently remained unclear.

Banned Party

Kahane Lives (*Kahane Chai*). *Kahane Chai* is a derivative of **Thus** (*Kach*), which served as the political vehicle of Rabbi Meir KAHANE, founder of the US-based Jewish Defense League. *Kach* elected its leader to the *Knesset* in 1984, after having competed unsuccessfully in 1977 and 1981. Linked to the activities of the anti-Arab "Jewish underground," the group advocated the forcible expulsion of Palestinians from both Israel and the occupied territories. It was precluded from submitting a *Knesset* list in October 1988, when the High Court of Justice ruled in favor of an Election Commission finding that it was "racist" and "undemocratic." Kahane was assassinated in New York in November 1990, with a number of his followers, including his son, Rabbi Binyamin Zeev KAHANE, subsequently forming *Kahane Chai*.

Baruch GOLDSTEIN, the Jewish settler who killed 29 Muslim worshippers at a Hebron mosque on February 25, 1994, was a Kahane disciple. Three weeks later, on March 13, the Israeli cabinet voted to ban both *Kach* and *Kahane Chai,* although a subsequent official report on the incident found that Goldstein had acted alone.

Binyamin Kahane and his wife were killed in late December 2000 in a drive-by shooting allegedly conducted by Palestinian militants. In late 2001 the United States added *Kahane Chai* to its list of terrorist organizations, despite objections from the Israeli government. *Kahane Chai* was subsequently described as "highly visible" among Jewish settlers in the West Bank.

Legislature

The ***Knesset*** (Assembly or Congregation) is a unicameral legislature of 120 members elected by universal suffrage for four-year terms on the basis of proportional representation (1.5 percent threshold) from national party lists. At the most recent balloting on January 28, 2003, *Likud* secured a plurality of 38 seats followed by: the coalition of the Israel Labor Party and *Meimad*, 19; *Shinui*, 15; Sephardic Torah Guardians (Shas), 11; the National Union, 7; *Meretz*, 6; the National Religious Party, 6; United Torah Judaism, 5; the Democratic Front for Peace and Equality, 3; One Nation, 3; the National Democratic Alliance, 3; *Yisrael B'Aliya*, 2; and the United Arab List, 2.

Speaker: Reuven RIVLIN.

Cabinet

As of September 1, 2005

Prime Minister	Ariel Sharon (*Likud*)
Vice Premier	Shimon Peres (Labor)
Vice Prime Minister	Ehud Olmert (*Likud*)
Deputy Prime Minister	Silvan Shalom (*Likud*)

Ministers

Agriculture and Rural Development	Yisrael Katz (*Likud*)
Communications	Dalia Itzik (Labor) [f]
Defense	Lt. Gen. (Ret.) Shaul Mofaz (*Likud*)
Education, Culture, and Sport	Limor Livnat (*Likud*) [f]
Environment	Shalom Simhon (Labor)
Finance (Acting)	Ehud Olmert (*Likud*)
Foreign Affairs	Silvan Shalom (*Likud*)
Health	Dan Naveh (*Likud*)
Housing and Construction	Isaac Herzog (Labor)
Immigrant Absorption	Tzipi Livni (*Likud*) [f]
Industry, Trade, and Labor	Ehud Olmert (*Likud*)
Interior	Ophir Pines-Paz (Labor)
Justice	Tzipi Livni (*Likud*) [f]
National Infrastructure	Benjamin Ben-Eliezer (Labor)
Prime Minister's Office	Tzachi Hanegbi (*Likud*)
	Martin Vilnai (Labor)
Public Security	Gideon Ezra (*Likud*)
Science and Technology (Acting)	Martin Vilnai (Labor)
Social Welfare	Ariel Sharon (*Likud*)
Tourism	Abraham Hirchson (*Likud*)
Transportation	Meir Sheetrit (*Likud*)
Without Portfolio	Haim Ramon (Labor)

[f] = female

Communications

Israeli newspapers are numerous and diversified, although many of the leading dailies reflect partisan or religious interests. Censorship is largely on national security grounds. Save for numerous cable television outlets, which are technically illegal, radio and television services are government owned and operated.

Press

The following are dailies published in Hebrew at Tel Aviv, unless otherwise noted: *Yedioth Aharonoth* (300,000 daily, 600,000 Friday), independent; *Ma'ariv* (160,000 daily, 270,000 Friday), independent; *Ha'aretz* (65,000 daily, 75,000 Friday), independent liberal; *al-Quds* (Jerusalem, 50,000), in Arabic; *Davar* (39,000 daily, 43,000 Friday),

General Federation of Labor organ; *Jerusalem Post* (Jerusalem, 30,000 daily, 50,000 Friday, not including North American edition published weekly at New York), in English; *Globes* (29,000), business organ; *Hatzofeh* (16,000), National Religious Front organ; *Hamodia* (Jerusalem, 15,000), *Agudat Yisrael* organ. There are also smaller dailies published in Arabic, Bulgarian, French, German, Hungarian, Polish, Romanian, Russian, voweled Hebrew, and Yiddish.

News Agencies

The domestic agency is the News Agency of the Associated Israel Press (*'Itonut Yisrael Me'uchedet*–ITIM); numerous foreign bureaus also maintain offices in Israel, including the Jewish Telegraphic Agency of New York.

Broadcasting and Computing

The commercial, government-controlled Israel Broadcasting Authority (*Reshut Hashidur Hayisra'elit*) provides local and national radio service over six programs, international radio service in 16 languages, and television service in Hebrew and Arabic. *Galei Zahal,* the radio station of the Israeli defense forces, broadcasts from Tel Aviv, as does the Israel Educational Television. There were approximately 2.4 million television receivers and 1.6 million personal computers serving 2.0 million Internet users in 2003.

Intergovernmental Representation

Ambassador to the US
Daniel AYALON

US Ambassador to Israel
Daniel C. KURTZER

Permanent Representative to the UN
Dan GILLERMAN

IGO Memberships (Non-UN)
BIS, CCC, EBRD, IADB, Interpol, IOM, PCA, WTO

Occupied and Previously Occupied Territories

The largely desert Sinai Peninsula, encompassing some 23,000 square miles (59,600 sq. km.), was occupied by Israel during the 1956 war with Egypt but was subsequently evacuated under US and UN pressure. It was reoccupied during the Six-Day War of 1967 and, except for a narrow western band bordering on Suez, was retained after the Yom Kippur War of 1973. The Egyptian-Israeli peace treaty, signed at Washington, DC, on March 26, 1979, provided for a phased withdrawal, two-thirds of which–to beyond a buffer zone running roughly from El Arish in the north to Ras Muhammad in the south–was completed by January 1980. Withdrawal from the remainder of the Sinai, to "the recognized international boundary between Egypt and the former mandated territory of Palestine," was completed on April 25, 1982 (three years from the exchange of treaty ratification instruments), "without prejudice to the issue of the status of the Gaza Strip."

Title to Taba, a small Israeli-occupied area adjoining the southern port of Eilat was long disputed. A 1906 Anglo-Egyptian/Turkish agreement fixed the border as running through Taba itself. However, a 1915 British military survey (admitted to be imperfect) placed the border some three-quarters of a mile to the northeast. A decision to submit the matter to arbitration was made during talks between Egyptian President Mubarak and (then) Prime Minister Peres at Alexandria in September 1986; two years later a five-member tribunal supported the Egyptian claim in regard to a boundary marker 150 yards inland from the shore, and in early 1989 Egypt acquired ownership of a luxury hotel on the beach itself, after agreeing to pay compensation to its owner.

Gaza Strip. The Gaza Strip consists of that part of former Palestine contiguous with Sinai that was still held by Egyptian forces at the time of the February 1949 armistice with Israel. Encompassing some 140 square miles (363 sq. km.), the

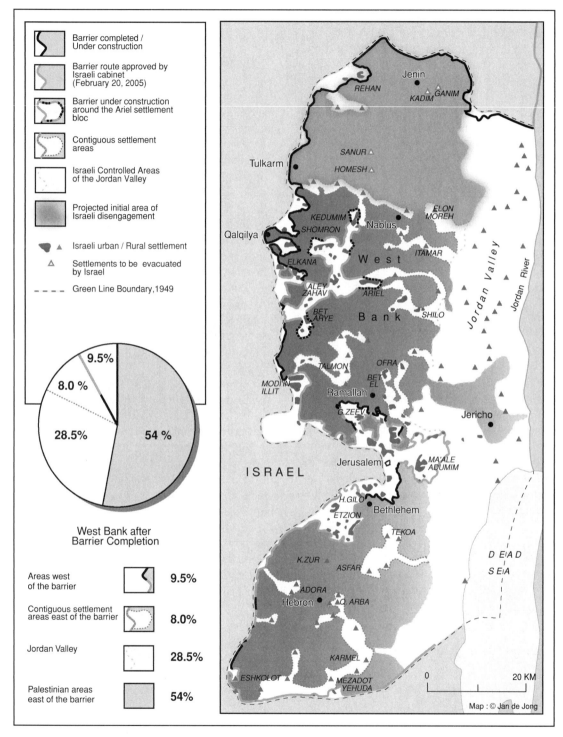

Barrier completed /
Under construction

Barrier route approved by
Israeli cabinet
(February 20, 2005)

Barrier under construction
around the Ariel settlement
bloc

Contiguous settlement
areas

Israeli Controlled Areas
of the Jordan Valley

Projected initial area of
Israeli disengagement

Israeli urban / Rural settlement

Settlements to be evacuated
by Israel

Green Line Boundary, 1949

9.5%

8.0 %

28.5%

54 %

West Bank after
Barrier Completion

Areas west of the barrier	9.5%
Contiguous settlement areas east of the barrier	8.0%
Jordan Valley	28.5%
Palestinian areas east of the barrier	54%

Jenin

REHAN

KADIM △ GANIM

SANUR △

HOMESH △

Tulkarm

ELON
MOREH

KEDUMIM

SHOMRON   Nablus

Qalqilya

ELKANA   West   ITAMAR

ALEY
ZAHAV   ARIEL

BET
ARYE   Bank   SHILO

Jordan Valley   Jordan River

TALMON   OFRA

MODI'IN
ILLIT   BET
EL

Ramallah

G.ZEEV   Jericho

MA'ALE
ADUMIM

Jerusalem

ISRAEL

H.GILO

ETZION   Bethlehem

TEKOA

K.ZUR
ASFAR   D E A D
S E A

ADORA
Hebron   Q. ARBA

KARMEL

ESHKOLOT   MEZADOT
YEHUDA

0   20 KM

Map : © Jan de Jong

Separation and Disengagement, February 2005

territory was never annexed by Egypt and since 1948 has never been legally recognized as part of any state. In the wake of the 1967 war, nearly half of its population of 356,100 (1971E) was living in refugee camps, according to the UN Relief and Works Agency for Palestinian Refugees in the Near East (UNRWA). The population was estimated by Palestinian officials to be 934,000, prior to a census conducted in late 1997, the results of which indicated an increase to about 1,022,000.

Most of Gaza was turned over to Palestinian administration under the Israeli-Palestinian accord of May 4, 1994, with Israel retaining authority over Jewish settlements and responsibility for external defense of the territory.

Judaea and Samaria. Surrounded on three sides by Israel and bounded on the east by the Jordan River and the Dead Sea, Judaea and Samaria encompass the Jordanian (West Bank) portion of former Palestine. It has an area of 2,270 sq. mi. and, according to results of the Palestinian census of late 1997, a Palestinian population of 1,873,000 (including East Jerusalem); earlier figures had also reported over 130,000 Jewish settlers. The West Bank was occupied by Israel following the 1967 war. In July 1988 King Hussein of Jordan announced that his government would abandon its claims to the West Bank and would respect the wishes of Palestinians to establish their own independent state in the territory.

Under the Israeli-Palestinian accord of May 4, 1994, (an extension of the September 13, 1993, agreement) the West Bank enclave of Jericho was turned over to Palestinian administration on May 13. Palestinian control was extended to six more West Bank towns (Bethlehem, Jenin, Nablus, Qalqilya, Ramallah, and Tulkarm) in late 1995 as the result of the second major "self-rule" accord, signed on September 28, 1995. Concurrently, civic authority in more than 450 villages in the West Bank was also turned over to the Palestinians although Israeli forces remained responsible for security in those areas. In January 1997 Israeli troops withdrew from all but about 20 percent of the West Bank town of Hebron. In addition, agreement was

announced for additional redeployment of Israeli troops from other West Bank areas in three stages over the next 18 months. It was generally expected that the withdrawals would occur relatively quickly from most of the villages already under Palestinian civic authority, with as yet ill-defined redeployment from the rural areas in the West Bank to follow. However, none of the withdrawals had occurred by March 1998 as negotiations between Palestinian representatives and the Israeli government collapsed. A new series of withdrawals was authorized by the Wye agreement of October 1998, but only the first of those stages was implemented (see Foreign relations, above). (See map for the status of the occupied and previously occupied territories as of early 1999.) An ambitious timetable for further withdrawals was endorsed by the *Sharm el-Sheikh* agreement of September 1999, but implementation was never achieved (see Current issues, above). The subsequent "effective state of war" between the Palestinians and Israelis precluded further resolution as Israeli forces occupied many of the areas previously turned over to Palestinian control.

Golan Heights. The mountainous Golan Heights, embracing a natural barrier of some 600 square miles (1,550 sq. km.) at the juncture of Israel and Syria southeast of Lebanon, was occupied by Israel during the 1967 war. Its interim status (including demarcation of an eastern strip under UN administration) was set forth in a disengagement agreement concluded with Syria in May 1974. In an action condemned by many foreign governments, including that of the United States, the area under Israeli military control was formally made subject to Israeli "law, jurisdiction, and administration" on December 14, 1981. The latter is largely Druze-populated, with a minority of Jewish settlers; the number of inhabitants in mid-1990 was approximately 25,400.

Palestinian Governmental Structures

Palestinian (National) Authority. The Declaration of Principles signed by Israeli and PLO leaders on September 13, 1993, authorized a

"Palestinian authority" to assume government responsibility (except, significantly, in the areas of foreign affairs and external security) in what was projected to be a gradually expanding area of the occupied territories from which Israeli troops were to withdraw. PLO police forces took control in the West Bank town of Jericho on May 13, 1994, and in most of the Gaza Strip on May 18, and on May 28 PLO Chairman Yasir 'Arafat announced the appointment of a cabinet-like Palestinian National Authority (PNA), with himself as chairman. PNA headquarters were subsequently established at Gaza City. (The PNA name itself was controversial, as was 'Arafat's subsequent reference to himself as "president" of the PNA. In particular, the usages were not sanctioned by the Israeli government because of their implications that agreement had been reached concerning eventual Palestinian statehood, to which Israel remained formally opposed. Meanwhile, the media have been split on the matter, with some referencing the PNA and others the Palestinian Authority [PA], with the latter appearing to predominate recently.)

In their second accord, signed September 28, 1995, Israel and the PLO agreed that Israeli troops would begin immediately to withdraw from six more West Bank towns while negotiations continued on the contentious issue of the town of Hebron, home to a small but highly vocal group of ultra-religious Jewish settlers. The 1995 agreement also envisioned the turning over of authority to Palestinians in more than 450 additional villages in the West Bank, followed by Israeli withdrawal from most other rural areas. Although most details of the latter withdrawal were left unspecified, it was agreed that it would be conducted in three stages—6 months, 12 months, and 18 months after the election of a Palestinian Council (see below), which was designated to succeed the PNA as the primary Palestinian governmental body. It was estimated that the council would be responsible for more than 70 percent of the West Bank following the proposed Israeli withdrawal, with Israel maintaining control of the Jewish settlements there and its numerous military installations. In addition, so-called "final talks" were anticipated to begin in the spring of 1996 on the outstanding issues of the future status of Palestinian refugees throughout the region, the status of East Jerusalem (which Palestinians claim as their "capital"), and the ultimate permanent borders and governmental structures of the Palestinian "entity." An accord on those matters was due no later than May 1999.

Despite concerns that the assassination of Israeli Prime Minister Rabin in November 1995 would interfere with the implementation of the recent agreement, Israeli withdrawals from the six additional towns proceeded even more quickly than expected and were completed by December 30, 1995. Consequently, the elections to the Palestinian Council were held on January 20, 1996, along with a separate election for the head (or "president") of the Council's "executive authority." Only one person (Samihah Yusuf al-Qubbaj KHALIL, an opponent of the Oslo peace agreements) challenged 'Arafat for the latter post, the PLO chairman garnering 87.1 percent of the votes in balloting that was widely construed as confirming strong support for him personally and majority endorsement of his peace policies. 'Arafat was inaugurated in his new position in ceremonies at Gaza City on February 12, 1996, and on May 9 he announced the formation of a new cabinet, technically the "executive authority" of the Palestinian Council but widely referenced as the "new" PNA, which continued the semantic PNA/PA controversy. The government won a vote of confidence in the Palestinian Legislative Council by 50–24 on July 27.

The "final talks" on Palestinian autonomy officially opened on May 5, 1996, but substantive negotiations were postponed until the Israeli election of May 29. Following the surprising *Likud* victory, resulting to some extent from security concerns within the Israeli populace arising from bomb attacks in February and March, progress slowed on the Palestinian front. No agreement was quickly forthcoming regarding Hebron, which became the focus of Israeli right-wing attention, and the planned three-stage withdrawal of Israeli troops from rural areas in the West Bank was not implemented. However, in early January 1997 a new agreement was reached between the PNA and the Netanyahu administration concerning Hebron (some 80 percent of which was slated to be turned over to full Palestinian control) and further Israeli withdrawal from the villages already under Palestinian civic administration as well as various rural areas by mid-1998. However, negotiations collapsed shortly thereafter as agreement could not be reached on the extent of withdrawal, and the Israeli government approved highly controversial Jewish settlement construction in East Jerusalem. Consequently, as of March 1998 there had been no further Israeli withdrawal or transfer of governmental authority and the prospects for launching of final status negotiations remained dim. Meanwhile, the PNA itself had come under heavy domestic and international criticism, one corruption commission suggesting that more than $300 million in aid had been mishandled. The Palestinian Legislative Council demanded in late 1997 that President 'Arafat replace the cabinet with a new government comprising experts in their various fields rather than political appointees. It also called upon him to address allegations that Palestinian police and security forces had been responsible for widespread human rights abuses. The council threatened a noconfidence motion against the PNA in June 1998, which 'Arafat forestalled by indicating a major reshuffle was imminent. However, to the disappointment of the reformists, the new cabinet announced on August 5 contained many incumbents, changes focusing primarily on the addition of new ministers of state. Several incumbent ministers declined reappointment on the grounds that the reorganization failed to address Palestinian problems sufficiently, but the cabinet was approved by a vote of 55–29 in the Legislative Council on August 10. In January 1999 the PNA, reacting to further pressure from the council, released a number of political detainees. A number of council members were also signatories of a leaflet that was distributed in November that charged the PNA with "systematic corruption" and other "abuse of power."

Criticism of 'Arafat's government continued in 2000–2001, although it was muted somewhat by an apparent desire within the Palestinian community to present a unified front in the face of renewed intense Palestinian/Israeli violence. In mid-2002 'Arafat pledged to conduct new presidential and legislative elections when Israeli forces were with-drawn from areas previously under Palestinian control. However, he subsequently came under attack by the Bush administration in Washington, which called for a change in Palestinian leadership on the grounds that the current PNA was "encouraging" rather than combatting terrorism. 'Arafat trimmed his cabinet on June 9, 2002, although he was unable to convince the so-called rejectionist groups such as *Hamas* and *al-Jihad* or certain PLO factions to participate in the new government. Facing a possible nonconfidence vote in the council, 'Arafat again reorganized his cabinet on October 29 in preparation for proposed new elections. 'Arafat also promised reform in social sectors and indicated support for the eventual establishment of the post of prime minister, who would theoretically assume some of the authority heretofore exercised by 'Arafat.

In late 2002 'Arafat declared that new elections would be postponed indefinitely due to Israel's "occupation" of territory formerly under Palestinian control. However, under heavy international pressure, 'Arafat in early 2003 formally endorsed the proposed installation of a Palestinian prime minister. The PLC on March 10 established the new position, although power-sharing arrangements vis-à-vis the president were left vague. ('Arafat retained control over peace negotiations with Israel.) Mahmoud ABBAS was nominated to the premiership, and his new cabinet was installed on April 29. Abbas promised to combat corruption, disarm militants, and pursue additional reform in Palestinian institutions. However, it quickly became clear that Abbas and 'Arafat remained locked in a power struggle, and Abbas resigned on September 6. He was succeeded on September 10 by Ahmad QURAY, the speaker of the PLC.

In July 2004 Prime Minister Quray threatened to resign unless the PLC granted him greater authority, particularly in regard to security. His request was partially granted, and the issue became mostly moot when 'Arafat died of an unknown illness at a hospital near Paris on November 11. Abbas was quickly named to replace 'Arafat as chairman of the PLO executive committee, while PLC speaker Ruhi Fattuh assumed presidential authority on an acting basis.

Municipal elections were held in some 26 West Bank towns and villages in late December 2004, with *Hamas*, Islamic *Jihad*, and the "rejectionist" PLO factions all participating. (Party lists were not permitted, but some candidates were clearly associated with various organizations.) However, those groups boycotted the presidential balloting on January 9, 2005, on the grounds that their involvement would have implied acceptance of the 1993 Oslo accords. In any event, Abbas won the presidency with 62 percent of the vote. (His nearest rival [20 percent of the vote] was Marwan BARGHUTHI, the popular young *Fatah* leader who had recently been sentenced to life in prison by an Israeli court on murder charges in connection with earlier attacks on Israeli forces.) Abbas was sworn in on January 15, and he invited Quray to form a new government. The international community welcomed the installation of a new Palestinian regime, President Bush calling Abbas "a man of courage."

Additional municipal elections were held in Gaza in January 2005 and in Gaza and the West Bank in May. Although *Fatah* maintained majority support in many areas, the vote for *Hamas* (33 percent in May) was considered the most noteworthy development as at least some members of *Hamas* appeared ready to assume a governance role.

Palestinian Legislative Council. The September 1995 Interim Agreement on the West Bank and the Gaza Strip (the second of the Palestinian "self-rule" accords between Israel and the PLO) provided for the election of a Palestinian Council to exercise legislative and executive authority in those areas of the previously occupied territories to which Palestinian autonomy had been or was about to be extended. The agreement initially established the size of the council at 82 members, but that was increased to 88 late in the year by mutual consent of Israeli and Palestinian representatives. Sixteen electoral districts were established in the Gaza Strip, West Bank, and East Jerusalem, and all Palestinians who were at least 18 years of age and had lived in those districts for at least three years were declared eligible to vote.

Nearly 700 candidates, including over 400 independents and some 200 representatives of small parties and political factions, reportedly contested the initial council elections, conducted on January 20, 1996. However, balloting was dominated by Yasir 'Arafat's *Fatah* faction of the PLO, most other major groupings (including *Hamas*, Islamic Holy War, the Democratic Front for the Liberation of Palestine, the Popular Front for the Liberation of Palestine, and other PLO factions opposed to the current peace negotiations) having boycotted the election. According to *Middle East International*, Palestinian officials reported that the successful candidates included 50 of the 70 "official" *Fatah* nominees, 37 independents (including 16 Fatah dissidents), and 1 member of the Palestinian Democratic Union.

The council (by then routinely referenced as the Palestinian Legislative Council) convened for the first time on March 7, 1996, at Gaza City. Ahmad Quray was elected speaker by a vote of 57–31 over Haidar 'Abd al-SHAFI, a critic of 'Arafat and the recent accords with Israel. In addition to serving as leader of the new council, the speaker was also envisioned as the person who would assume the position of head of the council's executive authority in the event of the incapacitation or death of the person in that position. Regarding such matters, the council proposed a Basic Law of Palestine, which would serve as a "constitution" until the completion of the "final talks" with Israel. The council fell into conflict with 'Arafat in 1997 over his failure to sign the Basic Law or to pursue other reforms the council had recommended including the replacement of the current cabinet with a technocrat government better able to deal with the myriad Palestinian economic and development needs. Late in the year the council suspended its sessions to put pressure on the Palestinian leader, who agreed to reorganize the government (see Palestinian National Authority, above).

Following the death of 'Arafat in November 2004 and installation of new Palestinian leadership in early 2005, new PLC elections were scheduled for July 2005. However, they were later postponed as deliberations continued on, among other

Palestinian Authority Cabinet

President	Mahmoud Abbas

As of August 1, 2005

Prime Minister	Ahmad Quray
Deputy Prime Minister	Nabil Sha'ath

Ministers

Agriculture	Walid Abed Rabbo
Civil Affairs	Muhammad Dahlan
Culture	Yehiya Yakhlof
Economy	Mazen Sunukrot
Education and Higher Education	Naim Abu al-Hummus
Finance	Salam Fayyadh
Foreign Affairs	Nassir al-Qidwa
Health	Zihni al-Wiheidi
Information	Nabil Sha'ath
Interior	Nassir Yousef
Justice	Farid al-Jallah
Municipal Affairs	Khalid Qawasmi
Planning	Ghassan al-Khatib
Prisoner Affairs	Sufian 'Abu Zaydeh
Public Works and Housing	Muhammad Ishtayeh
Religious Affairs	Yusef Salame
Social Affairs and Labor	Hassan 'Abu Libdeh
Telecommunications	Sabri Saydun
Tourism	Ziad al-Bandak
Transport	Sa'adeddin Kharma
Women's Affairs	Zuhaira Kamal [f]
Youth and Sports	Sakhir Bessissu
Without Portfolio	Hind Khuri [f]
	Ahmed Majdalani

[f] = female

things, whether a proportional representation system should be established.

Speaker: Ruhi FATTUH.

Political Groups in the Occupied/Previously Occupied Territories

Islamic Resistance Movement (*Hamas*). *Hamas* rose to prominence in 1989 as a voice for the Islamic fundamentalist movement in the occupied territories and as a proponent of heightened conflict with Israeli authorities. It subsequently confronted mainstream PLO elements, particularly *Fatah,* over leadership of the *intifada* as well as Palestinian participation in Middle East peace negotiations. Capitalizing on the initial lack of progress in those talks, *Hamas* scored significant victories in various municipal and professional organization elections in the occupied territories in the first half of 1992. In addition, the movement's military wing, *Izz al-Din al-Qassam* Brigades, was believed to be involved in fighting with *Fatah* supporters and to be responsible for the execution of Palestinians suspected of cooperating with the Israeli authorities. *Hamas* founder Sheikh Ahmed YASSIN, arrested in 1989, was sentenced to life imprisonment by an Israeli court in October 1991 for ordering several such killings of alleged Palestinian "collaborators." Breaking with a long-standing insistence on the annihilation of Israel, Mousa Abu Marzouk, one of the group's leaders (then based in Syria), stated in April 1994 that peace was possible if Israel withdrew from the occupied territories.

On May 14, 1995, Sayid Abu MUSAMEH, a high-ranking *Hamas* official was sentenced by an Israeli court to two years' imprisonment for publishing "seditious" articles in a *Hamas* newspaper, *Al-Watan*. On June 5 Israeli authorities arrested 45 *Hamas* militants on suspicion of plotting attacks on civilian targets, and on August 1 it took steps to secure the extradition of Marzouk, who had been detained as a suspected terrorist upon entering the United States a week earlier. (The United States in 1997 "expelled" Marzouk to Jordan, from which he again relocated to Syria after the Jordanian government ordered the closure of all *Hamas* offices in Jordan in late 1999.)

In 1995 and 1996 *Hamas* was described as deeply divided between those favoring continued violence against Israel and those believing it was time to join the peaceful political process unfolding in the Palestinian self-rule areas. Palestinian leader Yasir 'Arafat met with *Hamas* leaders in late 1995 in what was described as a determined effort to win the movement's participation in upcoming Palestinian elections. After apparently wavering on the proposal, however, *Hamas* announced it would boycott the balloting.

In January 1996 Yahya AYYASH, a *Hamas* militant known as "The Engineer" who had been blamed by Israeli officials for a number of bomb attacks, was assassinated in the Gaza Strip by a bomb

that was widely attributed to Israeli security forces. Subsequently, *Hamas* militants calling themselves the "Yahya Ayyash Units" claimed responsibility for several suicide bombings in Israel in February and March. Following the blasts, Marzouk (in a interview from his US jail) said that the *Hamas* political wing had little direct control over the "militias" in the occupied and previously occupied territories. Meanwhile, 'Arafat outlawed the *al-Qassam* Brigades but continued his political dialogue with *Hamas* moderates, mindful that the grouping retained significant popular support among Palestinians, built, in part, upon its network of schools, health services, and other social programs.

Sheikh Yassin was released from prison on October 1, 1997, apparently as part of the "price" Israel agreed to pay as the result of the bungled assassination attempt of *Hamas* militant Khaled Meshal in Jordan the previous month. Yassin went to Jordan for medical treatment and then to his home at Gaza, where he was welcomed as a hero by ecstatic crowds. He subsequently maintained an apparently deliberately vague position on developments regarding Palestinian autonomy, at times reverting to previous fiery rhetoric exhorting holy war against Israeli forces while at other times appearing conciliatory toward 'Arafat and the PNA, despite the fact that an estimated 80 influential *Hamas* leaders remained in PNA detention.

According to some reports, *Hamas* was approached by 'Arafat about joining the Palestinian cabinet in mid-1998. Although that overture was rejected, Yassin in April 1999 attended a PLO Central Council meeting as an observer, suggesting a growing degree of "accommodation" between the two groups. On the other hand, Palestinian security forces arrested some 90 *Hamas* activists in Gaza in August.

In December 2000 *Hamas* warned of a return of a campaign of suicide bombings in view of renewed Palestinian/Israeli violence, and the grouping subsequently claimed responsibility for a number of car bomb and suicide bomb attacks in Israel, Palestinian leader 'Arafat criticizing *Hamas*'s "aggression." In July 2002 a *Hamas* political leader in Nablus, Jamal MANSUR, was killed in an explosion attributed by *Hamas* to Israeli agents, while an *al-Qassam* leader was also assassinated during that month in Gaza. Yassin promised Israel would "pay a price," and *Hamas* claimed responsibility for several subsequent suicide bombings.

In February 2003 Yassin urged Muslims around the world to attack "Western interests" in the event of a US-led invasion of Iraq. Yassin also rejected the "road map" peace proposal offered by the so-called Middle East Quartet in April and vowed that attacks on Israeli targets would continue.

'Abd al-Aziz RANTISI, a prominent *Hamas* figure, was wounded by an Israeli missile attack in June 2003, but *Hamas* pledged to pursue its "Holy War." International attention focused even more intently on *Hamas* when Yassin was killed by Israeli missiles in March 2004. Israeli Prime Minister Sharon dismissed Yassin as an "arch-terrorist," although the assassination of the blind, wheelchair-bound *Hamas* leader was viewed with dismay in many areas of the world. Such consternation had little effect on Israeli policy, however, and Rantisi, who had succeeded Yassin as the leader of *Hamas*, was himself killed in an Israeli attack in April. No new leadership was announced after Rantisi's death, although *Hamas* officials reportedly continued to negotiate with the PNA over a future political role for *Hamas* in Gaza.

Leaders: Khalil MISH'AL (in Damascus), Mahmud al-ZAHAR (Gaza-based spokesman), Ismail HANIYA.

Islamic National Salvation Party–INSP (*Hizb al-Khalas al-Watani al-Islami*). The formation of the INSP was announced in March 1996 by Islamists, including a number of former *Hamas* activists, who were described by the *New York Times* as sharing the "broad ideology" of *Hamas* while rejecting the use of violence. The new grouping committed itself to a "legal political struggle" aimed at derailing the recent Israeli/Palestinian agreements. In August 2003 INSP leader Ismail Abu SHANAB was killed by an Israeli attack.

Leaders: Fuad NAHDAL, Ahmad BAHA.

Islamic Holy War (*al-Jihad al-Islami*). Islamic Holy War is presumably a Palestinian extension of Egypt's *al-Jihad,* which was originally launched as a splinter of Egypt's Muslim Brotherhood (see Egypt entry). *Al-Jihad* has been linked to a number of bomb attacks against Israeli soldiers both in the occupied territories and within Israel. Fathi SHAQAQI, described as the leader of Islamic Holy War, was assassinated in Malta in October 1995, reportedly by Israeli secret agents. It was subsequently reported that Ramadan Abdullah Shallah, a "Gaza-born militant" who had helped form Islamic Holy War, had assumed leadership of the grouping. Like *Hamas*, the other leading "rejectionist" grouping in the occupied and previously occupied territories, *al-Jihad* boycotted the 1996 Palestinian elections. Following the bomb attacks in Israel in early 1996, the *al-Jihad* military wing was one of the groups formally outlawed by Palestinian leader 'Arafat.

Al-Jihad boycotted the February 1997 "national dialogue" meeting convened by 'Arafat but, in what was seen as a potentially significant shift, attended the August unity conference, which was also chaired by the Palestinian president. Nevertheless, leaders of the group were careful to point out that *al-Jihad* had not renounced the use of violence against Israel, and *al-Jihad* claimed responsibility for some of the attacks on Israeli civilians in 2001–2005.

Leaders: Ramadan Abdullah SHALLAH (in Damascus), 'Abdallah al-SHAMI (Spokesman), Muhammad al-HINDI, Sheikh Bassam SADI.

Muslim Brotherhood (*Ikhwan al-Musilman*). The Muslim Brotherhood was launched in 1946 as an offshoot of Egypt's similarly named formation and was subsequently linked to the Muslim Brotherhood of Jordan. Although a clandestine group, it has tended to avoid the advocacy of violence against Israel.

Note: For information on groups previously or currently affiliated with the PLO, see separate article on the PLO that appears at the end of the country listings.

JORDAN

HASHEMITE KINGDOM OF JORDAN

al-Mamlakah al-Urduniyah al-Hashimiyah

Note: On November 9, 2005, bombs exploded at three hotels in Amman, killing 63 people, including three suicide bombers, and wounding more than a hundred. The organization *al-Qaeda* in Iraq, led by Jordanian-born Abu Musab Zarqawi, claimed responsibility for the deadliest terrorist attack in Jordan's history. After expressions of widespread Jordanian anger at the bombings, the organization felt compelled to defend its actions, claiming that the attacks were aimed at a meeting of US and Israeli intelligence agents, not Jordanians. Six days after the bombings, on November 15, eleven top Jordanian officials resigned, including the national security adviser, Saad Kheir. The shakeup continued on November 24, when King 'Abdallah II appointed Maruf al-Bakhit prime minister, replacing Adnan Badran, who had resigned earlier in the day. Prime Minister Bakhit, former ambassador to Jerusalem, had served as national security adviser since November 15. On November 27, Abdallah swore in a new cabinet comprised of 15 new members and 9 holdovers from the previous cabinet.

The Country

Jordan, a nearly landlocked kingdom in the heart of the Middle East, is located on a largely elevated, rocky plateau that slopes downward to the Jordan Valley, the Dead Sea, and the Gulf of 'Aqaba. Most of the land is desert, providing the barest grazing for the sheep and goats of Bedouin tribesmen, whose traditional nomadic lifestyle has largely been replaced by village settlement. With Israeli occupation in June 1967 of the territory on the West Bank of the Jordan River, the greater part of the country's arable area was lost. The population is mainly Arab, but numerous ethnic groups have intermixed with the indigenous inhabitants. Islam is the state religion, the majority being members of the Sunni sect. Less than 10 percent of Jordanian women are in the work force, mainly in subsistence activities and trading; more than half are illiterate (as compared with 16 percent of men), with the percentage of women enrolled in school dropping dramatically at marriage age. Although enfranchised in 1974, female participation in government has been minimal. Some cabinets have included several female appointees; in addition, a woman was elected to

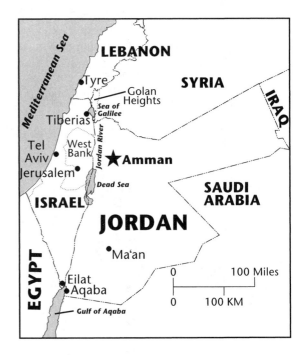

the House of Representatives for the first time in 1993. Although no women won a seat in elections held June 17, 2003, six women were appointed to the House under a February 2003 amended law reserving six seats for them.

Jordan's economy and its political life have been dominated over the past three decades by dislocations and uncertainties stemming from the Arab conflict with Israel. The original East Bank population of some 400,000 was swollen in 1948–1950 by the addition of large numbers of West Bank Palestinian Arabs and refugees from Israel, most of them either settled agriculturalists or townspeople of radically different background and outlook from those of the seminomadic East Bankers. Additional displacements followed the Arab-Israeli War of June 1967. The society has also been strained by a 3.5 percent annual natural increase in population, rapid urbanization, scarce water resources, and the frustrations of the unemployed refugees, many of whom have declined assimilation in the hope of returning to "Palestine." (It has recently been estimated that over 50 percent of the people currently residing in Jordan are of Palestinian origin, about two-thirds of them still formally being considered refugees.)

Agricultural production is insufficient to feed the population and large quantities of foodstuffs (especially grain) have to be imported, while many of the refugees are dependent on rations distributed by the UN Relief and Works Agency for Palestine Refugees in the Near East (UNRWA). Major exports include phosphates, potash, and fertilizers. Manufacturing is dominated by production of import substitutes, mainly cement, some consumer goods, and processed foods.

Although it is not an oil-producing country, Jordan was greatly affected by the oil boom of the 1970s and early 1980s. An estimated 350,000 Jordanians, including many professionals trained in one of the most advanced educational systems in the region, took lucrative jobs in wealthy Gulf states, their remittances contributing significantly to the home economy. Lower-paying jobs in Jordan were filled by foreign laborers, primarily Egyptians. However, the subsequent oil recession led to

Political Status: Independent constitutional monarchy established May 25, 1946; present constitution adopted January 8, 1952.
Area: 34,495 sq. mi. (89,206 sq. km.), excluding West Bank territory of 2,270 sq. mi. (5,879 sq. km.).
Population: 4,095,579 (1994C); 5,557,000 (2004E). Both figures exclude Palestinians in the West Bank, over which Jordan abandoned de jure jurisdiction in 1988.
Major Urban Center (1999E): 'AMMAN (1,430,000).
Official Language: Arabic.
Monetary Unit: Dinar (official rate July 1, 2005: 1 dinar = $1.41US).
Sovereign: King 'ABDALLAH ibn Hussein (King 'Abdallah II); assumed the throne on February 7, 1999, following the death of King HUSSEIN ibn Talal; coronation ceremony held on June 9, 1999.
Heir to the Throne: Undesignated. Prince HAMZEH ibn Hussein, half-brother of the King, had been designated Crown Prince on February 7, 1999, but on November 28, 2004, 'Abdallah stripped him of the crown, making 11-year-old Hussein, his eldest son, heir apparent.
Prime Minister: Adnan BADRAN; appointed by the King on April 5, 2005, to succeed Faisal al-FAYIZ, who had resigned on April 4, 2005; sworn in with new government on April 7, 2005.

the repatriation of many Jordanians in addition to reduced assistance from other Arab countries. Consequently, the government agreed in April 1989 to an austerity program prescribed by the International Monetary Fund (IMF) in return for $100 million in standby funds and partial rescheduling of payments on its $8 billion external debt. Conditions were subsequently strained further as the result of the influx of more than 300,000 Palestinians expelled from Kuwait and Saudi Arabia following the Gulf war of early 1991.

The government promoted its 1994 peace treaty with Israel as a crucial step toward economic development, and, indeed, the accord prompted an immediate influx of aid from the West, which had curtailed assistance because of 'Amman's stance during the 1990–1991 Gulf crisis and war. Although Jordan lost key export markets in Iraq, under UN sanctions, and on the West Bank during the 1990s, its economy benefitted from trade with other Arab states. Exports to the United States have grown since a bilateral free trade agreement took effect in 2001. Jordan hosted the annual World Economic Forum in June 2003, May 2004, and May 2005, raising the kingdom's profile as a leader in global affairs. In 2005, the government put unemployment at 14 percent, while independent sources estimated the actual rate to be more than 20 percent. It asserted that the poverty rate had fallen from 21.3 percent in 1997 to 14.2 percent in 2002. The World Bank reported that GDP growth (3.1 percent in 1999 and 5 percent in 2002) was 3.2 percent in 2003, outpacing population growth for the first time in years. Jordan's external debt, however, approached $8 billion, further discouraging foreign investors, who were already concerned about corruption in the public and private sectors. The new government installed in April 2005 by King 'Abdallah announced that economic reform, including a reinvigorated privatization program and trade liberalization measures, would be its top priority (see Current issues, below).

Government and Politics

Political Background

The territory then known as Transjordan, which only included land east of the Jordan River, was carved out of the Ottoman Empire in the aftermath of World War I, during which Arabs, with the assistance of British forces, had rebelled against Turkish rule. British administration of the region was formalized under a League of Nations Mandate, which also covered the territory between the Jordan River and the Mediterranean (Palestine). Over the next two decades, gradual autonomy was granted to Transjordan under the leadership of 'ABDALLAH ibn Hussein, a member of the region's Hashemite dynasty who had been named emir by the British in 1921. Full independence came when 'Abdallah was proclaimed king and a new constitution was promulgated on May 25, 1946, although special treaty relationships with Britain were continued until 1957. The country adopted its current name in 1949, its boundary having expanded into the West Bank under an armistice concluded with Israel, with which Arab states had been in conflict since Britain relinquished its Palestinian mandate in 1948.

Following the assassination of 'Abdallah in 1951 and the deposition of his son TALAL in 1952, Talal's son HUSSEIN ascended the throne at the age of 16 and was crowned king on May 2, 1953. Hussein's turbulent reign was subsequently marked by the loss of all territory west of the Jordan River in the 1967 Arab-Israeli War (see Israel map, p. 564), assassination and coup attempts by intransigent Arab nationalist elements in Jordan and abroad, and intermittent efforts to achieve a limited *modus vivendi* with Israel. The most serious period of internal tension after the 1967 war involved relations with the Palestinian commando (*fedayeen*) organizations, which began to use Jordanian territory as a base for operations against Israel. In 1970 in what became known as Black September, a virtual civil war ensued between commando and royalist armed forces, with the *fedayeen* ultimately being expelled, primarily to Lebanon, in mid-1971. The expulsion led to the suspension of aid to Jordan by Kuwait and other Arab governments; it was restored following Jordan's nominal participation in the 1973 war against Israel.

In accordance with a decision reached during the October 1974 Arab summit conference at Rabat, Morocco, to recognize the Palestine Liberation Organization (PLO) as the sole legitimate representative of the Palestinians, King Hussein announced that the PLO would thenceforth have responsibility for the West Bank but stopped short of formally relinquishing his kingdom's claim to the territory. The Jordanian government was subsequently reorganized to exclude most Palestinian representatives, and the National Assembly, whose lower house contained 30 West Bank members, entered what was to become a ten-year period of inactivity (see Legislature, below).

In a move toward reconciliation with Palestinian elements, King Hussein met at Cairo in March 1977 with PLO leader Yasir 'ARAFAT, a subsequent meeting occurring in Jordan immediately after the September 1978 Camp David accords. In March 1979 the two met again near 'Amman and agreed to form a joint committee to coordinate opposition to the Egyptian-Israeli peace treaty, while in December the king named Sharif 'Abd al-Hamid SHARAF to replace Mudar BADRAN as head of a new government that also included six West Bank Palestinians. Sharaf's death on July 3, 1980, resulted in the elevation of Deputy Prime Minister Dr. Qasim al-RIMAWI, whose incumbency ended on August 28 by the reappointment of Badran. Following a breakdown of negotiations with 'Arafat in April 1983 over possible peace talks with Israel and a continued deceleration in economic growth, the king reconvened the National Assembly on January 9, 1984, and secured its assent to the replacement of deceased West Bank deputies in the lower house. The next day the king appointed Interior Minister and former intelligence chief Ahmed 'OBEIDAT to succeed Badran as prime minister in a cabinet reshuffle that increased Palestinian representation to 9 members out of 20. 'Obeidat resigned on April 4, 1985, the king naming Zaid al-RIFA'I as his successor.

In mid-1988, after the outbreak of the *intifada* and following an Arab League call for PLO governance of the West Bank, Hussein abruptly severed all "legal and administrative" links to it, discontinued the five-year (1986–1990) aid package for its Palestinian population, and dissolved the House of Representatives. Subsequently, a declared intention to elect a House composed exclusively of East Bank members was suspended pending amendments to the electoral law.

On April 24, 1989, Prime Minister Rifa'i resigned because of widespread rioting in response to price increases imposed as part of the IMF-mandated austerity program. Three days later a new government, headed by Field Marshal Sharif Zaid ibn SHAKER (theretofore Chief of the Royal Court) was announced, with a mandate to prepare for a parliamentary balloting.

On November 8, 1989, following a campaign revealing continued support for the monarchy but intolerance of martial law and government corruption, Jordan held its first national election in 22 years. Urban fundamentalist and leftist candidates won impressive victories, generating concern on the part of a regime whose principal supporters had long been the country's rural conservatives. Nevertheless, following the election, the king lifted a number of martial law restrictions, appointed a new Senate, and reappointed Badran as prime minister. The cabinet that was announced on December 6 included six Palestinians but no members of the Muslim Brotherhood, despite the latter's strong electoral showing.

During the first half of 1990 the regime signalled continued interest in a more inclusive political process, meeting with Palestinian and Communist party leaders and in April appointing a broadly representative group of individuals to a newly formed National Charter Commission. Subsequently, in a move indicative of popular support for Iraq's position in the Gulf crisis and the enhanced status of the Muslim fundamentalists, the king on January 1, 1991, named a prominent Palestinian, Tahir al-MASRI, and five Muslim Brotherhood members to the cabinet.

At a national conference on June 9, 1991, the king and the leaders of all the country's major political groups signed an annex to the constitution that granted parties the right to organize in return for their acceptance of the legitimacy of the Hashemite monarchy. Additional political reform was also expected with the appointment on June 18 of the liberal and (despite his Gulf war stance) generally pro-Western Masri to replace the conservative Badran as prime minister. However, Masri's attempt to form a broad-based coalition government foundered as the Muslim Brotherhood, excluded from his cabinet because of its strident opposition to Middle East peace negotiations, and conservatives, apparently concerned over accelerated democratization as well as their dwindling cabinet influence, joined in October to demand the government's resignation. Their petition, signed by a majority of the members of the (then recessed) House of Representatives being tantamount to a nonconfidence vote, Masri felt obliged to step down on November 16. Signalling a reassertion of monarchical control and an apparent slowdown in the pace of democratization, the king reappointed Shaker to head a new government, which, accommodating the conservatives but not the Brotherhood, survived a nonconfidence motion on December 16 by a vote of 46–27.

On April 1, 1992, King Hussein abolished all that remained of martial law regulations introduced in the wake of the 1967 Arab-Israeli war. Several months later the political party ban was formally lifted, and party registration began in December.

On May 29, 1993, Prime Minister Shaker was replaced by 'Abd al-Salam al-MAJALI, whose initial mission was to oversee the election of a new House. Although the balloting on November 8 was the first to be conducted on a multiparty basis, the effect was minimal, some of the new groups charging that electoral law changes and campaign restrictions had hindered their effectiveness. Only the Muslim Brotherhood's Islamic Action Front (IAF), with 16 seats, secured significant representation while 47 independents, many of them expected to be broadly supportive of the king, were elected.

Majali was reappointed to lead the new government announced on December 1, 1993, his caretaker status being extended pending the outcome of the talks launched between 'Amman and Tel Aviv in the wake of the recent Israeli-PLO accord. On January 5, 1995, following the signing of the Jordanian-Israeli peace treaty (see Foreign relations, below), Majali stepped down as prime minister in favor of Shaker, whose new government was appointed three days later. Included in the 31-member cabinet were 17 House members, although the IAF, leader of the antitreaty opposition, was again unrepresented.

As on three earlier occasions, Shaker, the king's cousin and longtime confidant, assumed the prime ministership in 1995 at a time of some difficulty for the regime. Although the government preferred to emphasize its economic plans, public attention focused primarily on the peace treaty, opposition to normalizing relations with Tel Aviv having been wider, or at least more vocal, than expected. However, the king adopted a relatively hard line toward the accord's opponents, stifling dissent somewhat, even at the expense, in the opinion of some observers, of a slowdown in the democratization process. Consequently, a conference planned by antitreaty Islamic, leftist, and nationalist parties for late May was banned by the government. Perhaps partly as a consequence, the impact of many of the parties was minimal when the first multiparty municipal elections were conducted on July 11–12, entrenched tribal influence dominating the balloting.

On February 4, 1996, King Hussein appointed 'Abd al-Karim KABARITI, another close friend of his and the former foreign affairs minister, to succeed Shaker. Once again the IAF was excluded from the new cabinet, although members of several other fledgling parties were given portfolios. Charged with revitalizing the economy, Kabariti imposed IMF-mandated reforms that led to increases in the price of bread, precipitating Jordan's worst unrest of the decade when riots broke out in mid-August in the northern city of Karak and the poorer sections of 'Amman. While many of the demonstrators were arrested as government forces quashed the disturbances, the king later in the year quietly ordered a rollback in the price of bread and amnestied those involved in the riots.

On March 19, 1997, Hussein dismissed Prime Minister Kabariti and reappointed Majali, whose primary task once again was to oversee the election of a new lower house. Most opposition parties and groups (including the Muslim Brotherhood) boycotted the November 4 balloting, citing new press restrictions and perceived progovernment bias in the electoral law. A number of prominent personalities, including former prime ministers 'Obeidat and Masri, also urged voters to stay away from the polls. Consequently, the balloting was dominated by progovernment, independent tribal candidates. On November 22 Hussein appointed a new 40-member House of Notables, none of whom was a member of the Islamist opposition. Meanwhile Majali remained as prime minister, although the cabinet was extensively reshuffled on February 17, 1998, in the wake of an outbreak of pro-Iraqi demonstrations, which had been quashed by security forces.

In mid-1998 it was confirmed that King Hussein was being treated for cancer, and on August 12 he delegated some authority to his brother, HASSAN ibn Talal, who had been crown prince and heir to the throne since 1965. On August 19 Prime Minister Majali submitted his government's resignation, and the following day Crown Prince Hassan appointed a new cabinet headed by Fayez TARAWNEH, a US-educated economist and former chief of the royal court.

King Hussein, with his health declining rapidly, dismissed Hassan as his appointed successor on January 24, 1999, and replaced him with his eldest son, 'ABDALLAH. King Hussein died on February 7, and 'Abdallah assumed the throne the same day, becoming 'Abdallah II, taking an oath to protect "the constitution and the nation" before the National Assembly. (Formal coronation ceremonies were held on June 9.) On March 4 King 'Abdallah appointed a new 23-member cabinet headed by 'Abd al-Rauf al-RAWABDEH, a prominent proponent of economic reform. However, Rawabdeh, reportedly under pressure from the king, and his government resigned on June 18, 2000. Ali ABU al-RAGHEB, a businessman and former trade minister, was appointed to form a new government, which was sworn in on June 19.

On April 23, 2001, 'Abdallah announced the postponement of legislative elections scheduled for November. On July 22, he approved a new electoral law calling for the redrawing of voting districts, increasing the number of seats in the House of Representatives from 80 to 104 (later raised to 110 to accommodate a six-seat quota for women), and lowering the voting age from 19 to 18.

After elections were held on June 17, 2003, a new 28-member cabinet, headed by al-Ragheb, was announced. Criticized for failing to bring about promised reform, al-Ragheb resigned in October and was replaced on October 25 by Faisal al-FAYIZ, formerly chief of the royal court.

On April 4, 2005, Fayiz resigned amid criticism of his slow pace of reform. The king appointed Adnan BADRAN, a 70-year-old academic, to replace him and reduced the number of cabinet positions as part of his effort to streamline government. The unpopular finance minister, Bassam AWADALLAH, resigned on June 15, forcing Badran to announce a shuffled cabinet on July 3 that included eight new ministers. Fifty-three legislators had threatened a no-confidence vote unless Badran overhauled his economic team and included more ministers from the south. The reshuffled cabinet included four women, and Adel QUDAH replaced Awadallah.

Constitution and Government

Jordan's present constitution, promulgated in 1952, provides for authority jointly exercised by the king and a bicameral National Assembly. Executive power is vested in the monarch, who is also supreme commander of the armed forces. He appoints the prime minister and cabinet; orders general elections; convenes, adjourns, and dissolves the assembly; and approves and promulgates laws. The assembly, in joint session, can override his veto of legislation and must also approve all treaties. The House of Representatives comprises 80 members elected via universal suffrage, while members of the senate-like House of Notables are appointed by the king. The present multiparty system was authorized in a "National Charter" signed by the king and leaders of the country's major political movements in 1991. The judicial system is headed by the High Court of Justice. Lower courts include courts of appeal, courts of first instance, and magistrates' courts. There are also special courts for religious (both Christian and Muslim) and tribal affairs. Martial law, imposed at the time of the 1967 Arab-Israeli war, provided for military tribunals to adjudicate crime against "state security." Although many other martial law elements–such as the ban on large public meetings and restrictions on the press and freedom of speech–were suspended by King Hussein in 1989 and 1991 decrees, the special courts were not abolished until martial law was totally repealed on April 1, 1992.

Local government administration is now based on the five East Bank provinces (liwas) of 'Amman, Irbid, Balqa, Karak, and Ma'n, each headed by a commissioner. The liwas are further subdivided into districts (*aqdiyas*) and subdistricts (*nawahin*). The towns and larger villages are governed by partially elected municipal councils, while the smaller villages are often governed by traditional village headmen (*mukhtars*).

Foreign Relations

Historically reliant on aid from Britain and the United States, Jordan has maintained a generally pro-Western orientation in foreign policy. Its pro-Iraqi tilt during the Gulf crisis and war of 1990–1991 (see below) was a notable exception, prompting the suspension of Western aid and imposition of a partial blockade of the Jordanian port of 'Aqaba to interdict shipments headed for Iraq in violation of UN sanctions. However, relations with the West improved rather quickly thereafter, several meetings between King Hussein and US President Bill Clinton yielding preliminary agreement on external debt rescheduling and the resumption of aid.

Regional affairs have long been dominated by the Arab-Israeli conflict, Jordan's particular concerns being the occupation of the West Bank by Israel since 1967 and the related Palestinian refugee problem, both of which gave rise to policy disputes between King Hussein and PLO Chairman 'Arafat. Jordan tended to be somewhat less intransigent toward Israel than many of its Arab neighbors. After initially criticizing the PLO for conducting secret talks with Israel, Hussein (who over the years had also had secret contacts with Israel) eventually endorsed the Israeli-PLO accord signed in September 1993. Subsequently, Jordanian and Israeli officials began meeting openly for the first time in decades to discuss such matters as water resources, the refugee problem, border delineation, and economic cooperation. Then, on July 25, 1994, King Hussein and Israeli Prime Minister Yitzhak Rabin signed a declaration ending the 46-year-old state of war between their two countries. The agreement was followed by the signing at the Jordanian-Israeli border on October 26 of a formal peace accord in which each nation pledged to respect the other's sovereignty and territorial integrity, based on a recently negotiated demarcation of their mutual border. Cooperation was also pledged in trade, tourism, banking, finance, and numerous other areas. Significantly, US President Clinton attended the treaty ceremony, promising substantial debt relief and increased aid to Jordan in return for its participation in the peace process. PLO Chairman 'Arafat was conspicuously absent from the 5,000 invited guests, many Palestinians having been angered by the agreement's reference to Jordan's "special role" as "guardian" of Islamic holy sites in Jerusalem. However, the concern appeared to lessen somewhat in January 1995 when Jordan and the PLO signed an accord endorsing the Palestinian claim to sovereignty over East Jerusalem while also committing the signatories to wide-ranging cooperation in the financial, trade, and service sectors. In October 1996 King Hussein visited the West Bank for the first time since 1967, the trip apparently having been designed to underscore the king's support for the development of Palestinian autonomy under 'Arafat's direction. The king also played a significant intermediary role in the January 1997 agreement reached by 'Arafat and Israeli Prime Minister Benjamin Netanyahu regarding additional Israeli troop withdrawals from the West Bank.

Diplomatic relations with Egypt, suspended in 1979 upon conclusion of the latter's accord with Israel, were reestablished in September 1984. Prior to the Gulf crisis of the 1990s, relations with Saudi Arabia and other Middle Eastern monarchies were for the most part more cordial than those with such left-wing republics as Libya.

Relations with Syria have been particularly volatile, a period of reconciliation immediately after the 1967 war deteriorating because of differences over guerrilla activity. In September 1970 a Syrian force that came to the aid of the *fedayeen* against the Jordanian army was repulsed, with diplomatic relations being severed the following July but restored in the wake of the 1973 war. Despite numerous efforts to improve ties, relations again deteriorated in the late 1970s and early 1980s, exacerbated by Jordanian support for Iraq in the Gulf war with Iran. A cooperation agreement signed in September 1984 was immediately threatened by Syria's denunciation of the resumption of relations with Egypt; earlier, on February 22, relations with Libya had been broken because of the destruction of the Jordanian embassy at Tripoli, an action termed by 'Amman as a "premeditated act" by the Qadhafi regime. Thereafter, renewed rapprochement with Syria, followed by a resumption of diplomatic relations with Libya in September 1987, paved the way for a minimum of controversy during a November Arab League summit at 'Amman. A Syrian-Jordanian economic summit in February 1989 was preceded in January by a meeting between Hussein and Saudi Arabia's King Fahd to renegotiate an expiring agreement that in 1988 was reported to have provided approximately 90 percent of Jordan's foreign aid receipts.

Jordan's professed goal of maintaining neutrality in the wake of Iraq's occupation of Kuwait in 1990 was challenged by the anti-Iraqi allies who accused the regime of being sympathetic to Baghdad, citing the king's description of Saddam Hussein as an "Arab patriot" and 'Amman's resistance to implementing UN sanctions against Iraq. On September 19 Saudi Arabia, angered by King Hussein's criticism of the buildup of Western forces in the region, suspended oil deliveries to Jordan and three days later expelled approximately 20 Jordanian diplomats. Meanwhile, fearful that Jordan's location between Israel and Iraq made it a likely combat theater, King Hussein intensified his calls for a diplomatic solution, declared an intention to defend his country's airspace, and reinforced Jordanian troops along the Israeli frontier. In January 1991 Jordan temporarily closed its borders, complaining that it had received insufficient international aid for processing over 700,000 refugees from Iraq and Kuwait. Thereafter, in a speech on February 6, 1991, King Hussein made his most explicit expression of support for Iraq to date, assailing the allies' "hegemonic" aims and accusing the United States of attempting to destroy its neighbor. Following the war, the king quickly returned to a more moderate position, calling for "regional reconciliation" based on "forgiveness" among Arabs and a permanent resolution of the Palestinian problem.

In what was perceived as a further effort to rebuild relations with Arab neighbors, who before the war had provided annual aid estimated at $500 million, King Hussein called in late 1992 for the installation of a democratic government in Iraq. In May 1993 the king openly broke with Iraq, charging it with activities inimical to Jordanian interests and declaring his opposition to Saddam Hussein's continued rule. King Hussein also condemned the Iraqi buildup along the Kuwaiti border in October 1994 and, in August 1995, granted asylum to the members of President Hussein's family and governmental inner circle who had recently fled Iraq. In addition, he invited Iraqi opposition groups to open offices in Jordan. The king's unequivocal anti-Iraq stance assisted in the reestablishment of normal relations with all the Gulf states except Kuwait by August 1996, when he was greeted in Saudi Arabia by King Fahd for the first time since the 1990 invasion.

In December 1996 the United Nations implemented its "oil-for-food" deal with Iraq (see chapter on Iraq), which broke Jordan's informal "monopoly" on trade with its neighbor, and precipitated a decline in annual bilateral trade from $400 million in 1996 to just $250 million in 1997. As conflict loomed between the United States and Iraq in the early part of 1998, 'Amman managed to stay in the good graces of both countries by opposing any US military attack while banning demonstrations in support of Iraq and calling on that country to abide by UN resolutions.

Efforts to normalize relations with Israel faced setbacks in early 1997 when Israel announced plans to build another settlement in East Jerusalem. Relations were in part assuaged when, following the shooting death of seven Israeli school girls in Jordan on March 13 by a corporal in the Jordanian army, Hussein immediately responded by visiting the families of the Israeli school children and expressing sympathy for their losses. Nevertheless, relations again took a turn for the worse on September 25 when agents from the Israeli intelligence agency Mossad were caught in 'Amman attempting to poison *Hamas* leader Khaled Meshal. Furious at this attack on Jordanian soil, King Hussein demanded the antidote to the poison and threatened to break off relations with Israel. The Israeli government furnished the antidote and subsequently exchanged a large group of Jordanian and Palestinian prisoners held in Israel for the captured Mossad agents.

Current Issues

The world was first alerted to the seriousness of King Hussein's health problems in August 1998, when he delegated broad powers to Crown Prince Hassan while undergoing extended treatment in the United States. Hassan quickly orchestrated the removal of the Majali government, which had become the focus of popular discontent over a number of issues, including the mishandling of a water crisis in 'Amman and the embarrassing overstatement of economic growth figures. The crown prince also launched a dialogue with the nation's political parties and groups (including the Muslim Brotherhood), which had remained marginalized as Jordan's proposed democratization program stalled under the influence of ongoing regional tensions, and pledged that the administration of Prime Minister Tarawneh would provide a "safety net" to protect the poor from the effects of IMF-mandated fiscal reforms. Moreover, Hassan subsequently attempted to effect changes at the top levels of the military, an initiative that angered Hussein, who returned in the fall to resume full monarchical authority. The perceived "meddling" in army matters was one of the reasons King Hussein cited for the dismissal of his brother as heir apparent in January 1999. Other factors reportedly included the king's long-standing interest in reestablishing a direct father-to-son line of succession and his belief that his eldest son 'Abdallah (married to a Palestinian woman) would ultimately prove a more popular leader than Hassan.

Representatives from some 75 countries (including nearly 50 heads of state) attended the funeral of King Hussein on February 8, 1999, underscoring the widespread respect he had earned for his peacemaking efforts and his skillful management of Jordanian affairs during his 46-year reign. World leaders also wanted to signal their support for King 'Abdallah II, a newcomer to the international stage suddenly forced into the role of a prominent participant in the Mideast peace process. The new king, who had been educated in the West and whose mother was from the United Kingdom, promised a more open government with fewer press restrictions and possible revision of the electoral code to facilitate greater party influence. However, he declared the economy to be his top priority, announcing his support for budget reduction and other reforms recommended by the IMF.

Immediately upon assuming the throne, King 'Abdallah announced that he was "absolutely committed" to peace with Israel, despite the fact that many Jordanians appeared to have become disenchanted with that particular aspect of his father's legacy. Underscoring its antimilitancy posture, the regime in the fall of 1999 ordered the closing of the Jordanian offices of *Hamas* and expelled several leaders of that Islamic fundamentalist movement, which spearheads hard-line anti-Israeli sentiment in the West Bank (and Gaza). In addition, security forces arrested a group of militants with reported ties to the alleged international terrorism organization of Osama bin Laden, charging the detainees with plotting to attack US and Israeli targets. At the same time, 'Abdallah concentrated on improving ties with Syria, Lebanon, Kuwait, and other neighbors, and, in an apparent further attempt to promote Arab solidarity, called for the end of UN sanctions against Iraq.

The change in prime ministers in June 2000 was attributed to the perceived failure of the Rawabdeh government to achieve effective economic change as well as to Rawabdeh's reported "autocratic" style, which had apparently contributed to friction between his administration and the National Assembly. The appointment of Abu al-Ragheb as prime minister was well received in most quarters, the business community in particular endorsing his stated goals of attracting foreign investment and promoting tourism. Investors also welcomed the country's accession to the World Trade Organization in April 2000 and the signing of a rare free trade agreement with the United States later in the year. Meanwhile, political reform remained subordinate to the economic focus, King 'Abdallah reportedly relying even more heavily on secret security and intelligence services than his father had in the later years of his reign.

On June 16, 2001, the king dissolved the National Assembly in anticipation of new balloting for the House of Representatives, expected in November. However, in view of the roiling

Israeli-Palestinian conflict, polling was subsequently postponed until September 2002. The king in August 2002 further delayed new elections until March 2003, citing "difficult regional circumstances" that now included a potential US attack on neighboring Iraq. Analysts suggested that the government feared that "radical elements" might take advantage of surging anti-Israel and anti-US sentiment within the Jordanian population to present a significant electoral challenge to the establishment unless regional tensions were reduced. The elections were finally held on June 17, 2003, two months after the fall of Baghdad to US-led invading forces and the removal of Saddam Hussein from power. Progovernment legislators held a clear majority in the new legislature, but Islamist and tribal members opposed the king's promotion of women's rights. Reforms allowing women to initiate divorce, raising the legal age for marriage to 18, and stiffening penalties for "honor killings" of women were weakened or blocked by legislators arguing that such measures threatened family stability.

Popular opinion presented the government with a difficult act in maintaining strong ties with the United States, with King 'Abdallah calling on Washington to establish a definite timetable for creation of a Palestinian state as a means of tempering Arab frustration over the lack of progress in the Mideast peace process. At the same time, Jordan was a solid supporter of the US-led "war on terrorism" following the al-Qaeda attacks on the United States in September 2001. In addition to contributing troops to peacekeeping forces in Afghanistan following the ouster of the Taliban and al-Qaeda, the government also announced in 2002 that it had thwarted planned attacks against US and Israeli targets through several roundups of Islamic militants. However, critics of the government charged that the crackdown had undercut political liberalization by barring most public demonstrations, dampening legitimate dissent, and tightening restrictions on the media.

On October 28, 2002, Laurence Foley, senior US diplomat, became the first Western official to be assassinated in Jordan. Of the 11 suspects tried for the crime, 8 were sentenced to death. Among them was Abu Musab al-ZARQAWI, who was tried in absentia and subsequently linked to the armed resistance to US forces in Iraq.

King 'Abdallah's effort to maintain Jordan's role as mediator in the Middle East resulted in the June 2003 summit he hosted in the Red Sea port of Aqaba with Bush, Sharon, and Palestinian Authority Prime Minister Mahmud Abbas in attendance to launch the US-backed "road map."

US-Jordanian relations were strained by the 2003 Iraq invasion, which Jordanians strongly opposed. In the run-up to war, 'Abdallah warned the United States and United Kingdom that an attack on Iraq could lead to "regional destabilization." He ultimately adopted an ambivalent stance, accepting the stationing of US forces near the Iraqi border while opposing the invasion. When Iraq's Sunnis boycotted legislative elections held January 30, 2005, the king warned of an impending "Shi'ite crescent" stretching from Iran to Lebanon that might destablize the Sunni-led status quo in the Arab world.

Political Parties and Groups

Parties were outlawed prior to the 1963 election. Subsequently, an "official" political organization, the Arab National Union (initially known as the Jordanian National Union), held sway from 1971 to February 1976, when it was disbanded. On October 17, 1989, King Hussein announced that some party activity could resume but left standing a prohibition against party-affiliated candidacies for the November legislative election. The national charter signed in June 1991 recognized the right of parties to organize, on condition that they acknowledge the legitimacy of the monarchy. Legislation formally lifting the ban on parties was approved by the National Assembly in July 1992 and by King Hussein on August 31. The first groups were recognized the following December.

Legal Parties

National Constitutional Party (NCP). The NCP was officially formed on May 1, 1997, reportedly by nine pro-government parties and the **Jordanian Arab Masses Party** (*Hizb al-Jamahir al-'Arabi al-Urduni*), the **Popular Unity Party**

(*Hizb al-Wahda al-Sha'biyya*), and the **Jordanian Popular Movement.** (Some reports indicated that the component groupings had dissolved themselves in favor of the NCP, although their institutional status, as well as that of the NCP, subsequently remained unclear.) Under the slogan "rejuvenation, democracy, and unity," the NCP ran in the November elections on an agenda of peace with Israel, support for the IMF economic program, and the "Jordanization" of political life. Many observers believe that the NCP was meant by its leaders to serve as a counterweight to the historical dominance of the Islamic, leftist and pan-Arabist movements. The formation of the NCP was one of the reasons that the Islamic and most of the leftist and pan-Arabist parties decided to boycott the elections.

Leader: Ahmad SHUNNAQ (General Secretary).

Jordanian National Alliance Party–JNAP (*Hizb al-Tajammu al-Watani al-Urduni*). At the time of its recognition in December 1992, the JNAP was described as a "coalition of central and southern Bedouin tribes" with, as yet, no stated political or economic platform. It was subsequently viewed as essentially "pro-establishment" and supportive of King Hussein's position on Middle East peace negotiations, Secretary General Mijhim al-Khuraysha having previously served as an adviser to the king. In November 1993 the JNAP announced the formation of a Jordanian National Front (JNF) with *al-Yaqazah, al-Watan,* and the PJP (below). The alliance was seen as primarily a parliamentary bloc (all members but the PJP being represented in the recently elected House of Representatives), and it did not appear to play a role in the 1997 elections.

The JNAP was among the more successful parties in the 1995 municipal elections, primarily because of its continued tribal orientation, and it was represented in the February 1996 cabinet.

Leader: Mijhim al-KHURAYSHA (Secretary General).

Homeland Party (*Hizb al-Watan*). Two members of *al-Watan,* recognized in May 1993, were successful in the 1993 House balloting. Distancing itself from the other JNF components on the issue, *al-Watan* in late 1994 announced its opposition to the recent Jordanian-Israeli peace accord. Nevertheless, it was granted portfolios in the new cabinet announced in February 1996.

Leader: Hakam Khair (Secretary General).

Pledge Party (*Hizb al-'Ahd*). One of the first parties to be recognized, the centrist *al-Ahd* supports a free market economy and development of a strong "national Jordanian identity" in which there would be "a clear distinction" between the Jordanian and Palestinian political entities. The *al-Ahd* secretary general, a former army chief of staff, was one of the party's two members elected to the House in 1993 and became speaker in 2003. He initially called for creation of a common front among centrist parliamentary parties as a counterbalance to the IAF. However, when parliamentary blocs were subsequently announced, *al-Ahd* was aligned not with the other centrist parties in the JNF but rather with a group of 15 independent deputies in a National Action Front (NAF), which was accorded five ministries in the government formed in January 1995. *Al-Ahd* candidates were reported to have achieved significant success in the July 1995 municipal elections, based on the group's strong "tribal" support, and the party was represented in the February 1996 cabinet.

Leader: 'Abd al-Hadi al-MAJALI (Secretary General and Speaker of the House of Representatives).

Awakening Party (*Hizb al-Yaqazah*). Two members of *al-Yaqazah,* including Secretary General 'Abd al-Rauf al-Rawabdeh, were elected to the House of Representatives in 1993. Rawabdeh was also appointed deputy prime minister in the subsequent Majali and Shaker cabinets; he was named prime minister by King 'Abdallah in March 1999.

Leader: 'Abd al-Rauf al-RAWABDEH (Secretary General).

Progress and Justice Party–PJP (*Hizb al-Taqaddumi wa al-'Adl*). The PJP was listed as one of the founding members of the JNF, which was primarily a parliamentary bloc, even though no PJP members were elected to the House in 1993.

Leader: Muhammad Ali Farid al-SA'AD.

Democratic Unionist Arab Party–The Promise (*al-Hizb al-Wahdawi al-'Arabi al-Dimaqrati al-Wa'ad*). The centrist *al-Wa'ad* was formed in early 1993 as a merger of three unrecognized groups (the Democratic Unionist Alliance, the Liberal Unionist Party, and the Arab Unionist Party) with similar platforms regarding greater free market activity and the pursuit of foreign investment. Although *al-Wa'ad* was recognized in February, it was subsequently reported to be in disarray as leaders of the founding groups squabbled over the new party's leadership posts.

Leaders: Anis al-MU'ASHIR (Secretary General), Talal al-UMARI (Assistant Secretary General).

Islamic Action Front–IAF (*Jabhat al-'Amal al-Islami*). The IAF was formed in late 1992 by the influential Muslim Brotherhood (see below) as well as other Islamists, some of the latter subsequently withdrawing because of Brotherhood domination. Like the Brotherhood, the IAF promotes the establishment of a *shari'a*-based Islamic state with retention of the monarchy. Although the IAF is generally perceived as opposing Israeli-PLO and Jordanian-Israeli peace talks, a significant "dovish" minority reportedly exists within the Front.

IAF leaders objected to electoral law changes introduced in mid-1993 and accused the government of interfering in the Front's campaign activities prior to the November House elections. However, after initially threatening to boycott the balloting, the Front presented 36 candidates, 16 of whom were elected.

IAF candidates did not perform as well as anticipated in the July 1995 municipal elections, potential support having apparently gone instead to tribal-based parties. Subsequently, in December, Front/Brotherhood leaders suggested that King Hussein was "trying to restore authoritarian rule." Consequently, it was not surprising that no IAF members were included in the new government announced in February 1996. In view of the re-

cently enacted press restrictions and continued complaints over electoral laws, the IAF boycotted the 1997 legislative balloting. In light of growing public disenchantment with the 1994 peace treaty with Israel, IAF candidates performed well at the July 1999 local balloting, reportedly securing 7 mayoralties, majorities on several local councils in main cities, and 5 of the 20 elected seats on the 40-member 'Amman council. A member of the IAF, 'Abd al-Rahim AKOUR, accepted a post in the new cabinet of June 2000, but he was suspended from the party for that decision. The IAF remained the principal opposition party after the June 17, 2003, parliamentary elections.

Leaders: 'Abd al-Latif ARABIYAT, Ziad Abu GHANIMA, Hamzah MANSUR (Secretary General).

Future Party (*Hizb al-Mustaqbil*). A conservative pan-Arabist grouping described as strongly supportive of the Palestinian *intifada, al-Mustaqbil* was recognized in December 1992. Many of its leaders are businessmen and/or former government officials, including former secretary general Suliman Arrar, who had previously served as a cabinet minister and speaker of the House of Representatives, and former prime ministers 'Obeidat and Masri. The party boycotted the November 1997 elections.

Leaders: Abd al-Salam FREIHAT (Secretary General), Yusuf GHAZAL (Deputy Secretary General).

Communist Party of Jordan–CPJ (*al-Hizb al-Shuyu'i al-Urduni*). Although outlawed in 1957, the small pro-Moscow CPJ subsequently maintained an active organization in support of the establishment of a Palestinian state on the West Bank, where other Communist groups also continued to operate. About 20 of its leaders, including (then) Secretary General Fa'ik (Fa'iq) Warrad, were arrested in May 1986 for "security violations" but were released the following September. Over 100 alleged members were detained for five months in 1989 for leading anti-IMF, antigovernment rioting. One (then) CPJ member, 'Isa Madanat, was elected to the House of Representatives in 1989 and the following spring he and several party associates participated in negotiations on the proposed National Charter, the January repeal of the nation's anti-Communist act having ostensibly put the CPJ on the same footing as other parties preparing for official recognition. After initially being rejected for legal party status in late 1992 on the ground that communism was "incompatible" with the Jordanian constitution, the CPJ was recognized in January 1993. By that time Madanat and his supporters had left the CPJ to form the JSDP (below, under JUDP).

Despite the opposition of its youth wing, the CPJ participated in November 1997 national elections.

Leader: Muni HAMARENEH (General Secretary).

Jordanian Arab Democratic Party–JADP (*al-Hizb al-'Arabi al-Dimaqrati al-Urduni*). The JADP is a leftist group recognized in mid-1993, its supporters including former Baathists and pan-Arabists. The two JADP members who were elected in the 1993 House balloting subsequently joined a parliamentary bloc called the Progressive Democratic Coalition, which also included representatives from the JSDP and *al-Mustaqbil* as well as 18 (mainly liberal) independents. The JADP subsequently announced its opposition to any "normalization" with Israel without full "restoration of Palestinian rights," a stance that aligned the JADP with Palestinian groups opposed to the Israeli-PLO peace accord. The issue appeared to divide the party, some 17 members reportedly resigning in early 1995 in support of the PLO and in protest over a perceived "absence of democracy" within the JADP.

Leaders: Muhammad DAUDIA, Mu'niz RAZZAZ (Secretary General).

Jordanian Baath Arab Socialist Party– JASBP (*Hizb al-Ba'ath al-'Arabi al-Ishtiraki al-Urduni*). The Baathists, who had supported a number of independent candidates in the 1989 House election, were initially denied legal status in December 1992 as the Baath Arab Socialist Party in Jordan because of apparent ties to its Iraqi counterpart. However, the Interior Ministry reversed its

decision in early 1993 after the grouping revised its name and offered "assurances of independence" from Baghdad. An Arab nationalist party that opposes peace talks with Israel as "futile," the JASBP presented three candidates in the 1993 House balloting, one of whom was elected. In late 1996 the government accused the JASBP of having helped to incite "bread riots," and a group of Baathists were arrested in connection with those events. However, some observers questioned the government's assertions, a correspondent for *Middle East International* describing the party as too "splintered and shrunken" to be capable of generating effective action. The newspaper *al-Dustur* reported on May 15, 1997, that the JASBP had formed an alliance with two other pan-Arabist parties–the **National Action Front** (*Haqq*), led by Muhammad al-ZUBI, and the **Arab Land Party,** led by Mohammad Al OURAN. The new grouping was reportedly called the **Nationalist Democratic Front** (NDF), led by Hamad al-FARHAN. The NDF parties did not boycott the November 1997 elections, and the JASBP won one seat in the Lower House.

Leaders: Taysir al-HIMSI (Secretary General), Ahmad NAJDAWI.

Jordan People's Democratic Party (*Hizb al-Sha'ab al-Dimaqrati al-Urduni*–Hashd). The leftist Hashd was formed in July 1989 by the Jordanian wing of the Democratic Front for the Liberation of Palestine (DFLP), a component of the PLO (see separate article). Its initial application for recognition was rejected because of its DFLP ties, but, as an independent "on a friendly basis" with the DFLP, the party was legalized in early 1993. Like the DFLP, the Hashd opposed the Israeli/PLO accord of September 1993 although it supports the peace process in general as a means of resolving the Palestinian problem.

Leader: Salem NAHASS (Secretary General).

Jordanian Unionist Democratic Party–JUDP. Formed in 1995 as a merger of the Jordanian Socialist Democratic Party–JSDP (*al-Hizb al-Dimaqrati al-Ishtiraki al-Urduni*) and the Jordanian Progressive Democratic Party–JPDP (*al-Hizb al-Taqaddumi al-Dimaqrati al-Urduni)*, the

JUDP supports "Arab unity, democracy, and social progress" and opposes the normalization of relations with Israel. The JSDP, whose secretary general ('Isa Madanat) had been a former leader of the CPJ, had been recognized in early 1993 even though it had refused a government request to delete "socialist" from its name and references to "socialism" from its party platform. Meanwhile, the JPDP had been formed in late 1992 by the merger of three leftist groups–the Jordanian Democratic Party, the Palestinian Communist Labor Party Organization, and the Jordanian Party for Progress. (The latter subsequently withdrew from the JPDP, its leader later founding the Freedom Party, subsequently the Progressive Party, below.) The JPDP was recognized in January 1993 after its leaders bowed to government pressure and deleted references to socialist objectives from the party platform. Several leaders of the JPDP were former members of the Palestinian National Council.

The creation of the JUDP was widely attributed to the desire of its leftist components to develop a stronger electoral presence, their impact having been negligible in the 1995 municipal elections. However, in 1997 political differences precipitated the resignation of over 150 members, including former secretary general Mazen al-SAKET. The JUDP fielded four candidates in the November 1997 elections and won one seat.

Leaders: 'Isa MADANAT, Ali 'Abd al-Aziz AMER, Musa al-MA'AYTAH (Secretary General).

Progressive Party .

Formed in 1993 as the Freedom Party (*Hizb al-Huriyya*) by a former official of the CPJ, this grouping is described as "trying to combine Marxist ideology with Islamic tradition and nationalist thinking." The Progressive Party participated in the 1997 lower house election boycott.

Leader: Na'el BARAKAT (Secretary General).

Jordanian Democratic Popular Unity Party– JDPUP (*Hizb al-Wahda al-Sha'biyya al-Dimaqrati al-Urduni*). The leftist JDPUP was formed in 1990 by Jordanian supporters of the Popular Front for the Liberation of Palestine (PFLP, see PLO section). True to its PFLP heritage, the JDPUP opposes

peace negotiations with Israel. The JDPUP joined the boycott of the 1997 lower house elections.

Leader: Sa'eed Thiyab (Secretary General).

Democratic Arab Islamic Movement Party–Propagate (*Hizb al-Haraka al-'Arabiyya al-Islamiyya al-Dimaqrati–Du'a*). A liberal Islamist grouping, *Du'a* is critical of the IAF and the Muslim Brotherhood for their "regressive" interpretation of the Koran. Both women and Christians were included in the party's initial temporary executive committee. *Du'a* boycotted the 1997 lower house elections.

Leader: Yusuf Abu BAKR (Secretary General).

Pan-Arab Action Front Party–PAAFP (*Hizb al-Jabhat al-'Amal al-Qawmi*). Described as having close ties with Syria, the PAAFP was legalized in January 1994, its members reportedly including several prominent Palestinian hard-liners. Ideological differences subsequently led a faction of the PAAFP to form a new grouping, the Nationalist Action Party (above).

Leader: Salim SUWAYS.

Liberal Party (*Hizb al-Ahrar*). Described as a "pro-peace" grouping, the Liberal Party is led by Ahmad al-Zubi, a prominent attorney. In mid-1995 al-Zubi was reportedly disbarred after having met with Israeli leaders, that penalty reflecting a strong bias against the recent peace accord in Jordanian professional groups such as the Bar Association.

Leader: Ahmad al-ZUBI.

Christian Democratic Party. The Christian Democratic Party was reportedly formed in part by a number of dissidents from the Jordan People's Democratic Party (*Hashd*) and the National Action Front (*Haqq*), as well as independents. At its founding in May 1997 the party announced that it would boycott the November elections to the lower house.

Other legal parties include the **Ansar Party,** a moderate grouping recognized in December 1995 and headed by Muhammad MAJALI; the **Arab Land Party,** which was organized in 1996 and contested the 1997 balloting under the leadership of Mohammad al-BATAYNEH, but is now led by Muhammad al-ORAN; the **Jordanian Arab Constitutional Front Party**, led by Milhem al-TALL, who in 1989 election campaign called for Jordanian-Syrian union and participated in the 1997 boycott; the **Jordanian Peace Party,** a strong supporter of the peace process with Israel and headed by Shaher KHREIS; the **Jordanian People's Committees Movement,** launched in 2001 under the leadership of Khalid SHUBAKI; the **Jordanian Welfare Party,** launched in 2001 and led by Mohammad Rijjal SHUMALI; the **Progressive Arab Baath Party** (*Hizb al-Ba'ath al-'Arabi al-Taqaddumi*), led by Mahmud al-MA'AYTA and said to have a political philosophy similar to that of the Syrian Baath Party; and the **Ummah Party** (Community), led by Ahmed HANANDEH and recognized in June 1996 after reportedly having failed to convince other moderate parties to merge with it.

Other Groups

Muslim Brotherhood (*al-Ikhwan al-Muslimin*). An outgrowth of the pan-Arab Islamic fundamentalist group of the same name established in Egypt in 1928, the Brotherhood has played a prominent role in Jordanian political affairs. It promotes the creation of an Islamic state based on strict adherence to Islamic law (*shari'a*) but does not advocate abolition of the monarchy, having generally maintained a cooperative relationship with King Hussein.

Following an impressive showing in the 1989 elections (see Legislature, below), the Brotherhood was given ten seats on the National Charter Commission formed in April 1990. In November one of its leaders, 'Abd al-Latif Arabiyat, was elected speaker of the House of Representatives while five of its members entered the government on January 1, 1991. However, it was unrepresented in the subsequent Masri or Shaker cabinets, underscoring the rift between the Brotherhood and the government regarding Jordan's participation in the US-led Middle East peace negotiations. In December 1992 members of the Brotherhood and other fundamen-

talists established the IAF (above) as their official political party. Primarily because of the Brotherhood's strong opposition to the 1994 peace treaty with Israel, it was not represented in the January 1995 cabinet, reports surfacing that King Hussein and Prime Minister Shaker pointedly had failed even to consult new Brotherhood leader 'Abd al-Majid Thunibat concerning the formation of the government. Indicative of the credibility of the Muslim Brotherhood as an opposition force, it was its decision to boycott the November 1997 elections that led other Islamic as well as non-Islamic opposition parties to also suspend their participation.

Leaders: 'Abd al-Latif ARABIYAT, 'Abd al-Majid al-DHUNAYBAT, Muhammad 'Abd al-Rahman al-KHALIFA, 'Abd al-Munim ABU ZANT, 'Abd al-Majid THUNIBAT.

Other political groups reportedly backing "independent" candidates in the 1989 legislative poll included the Marxist **Arab Nationalist Movement** and the **Union of Democratic Unity** (UDU), a small Christian party led by Jamal SHAIR. In July 1990 a **Jordan Arab Nationalist Democratic Alliance** (JANDA) was reportedly launched by a group of anti-Islamic and pro-democratic pan-Arabists, leftists, and Marxists in the House of Representatives. The objectives of the Alliance included reversal of the IMF-proscribed economic recovery programs, the repeal of martial law, and the legalization of political parties.

In January 1991 Islamic *Jihad* leader Sheikh Asad Bayyud al-TAMINI and **Islamic Liberal Party** leader Atta Abu RUSHTAH called for suicide attacks on Western targets, Rushtah subsequently being arrested by the Jordanian police. In addition, five party members were sentenced to death (two in absentia) in early 1994 for allegedly plotting to assassinate King Hussein. Subsequently, in February 1996, Rushtah was sentenced for three years in prison for "slandering" King Hussein.

Nearly 100 people identified as belonging to the **Prophet Mohammad Army** were arrested in mid-1991 in connection with a series of incidents dating back more than a year. Although many of the detainees were subsequently released, 20 were convicted in November of crimes "against state security."

In 1992 four persons (including two members of the House of Representatives) were convicted by a state security court of belonging to a new illegal organization called the **Vanguard of Islamic Youth** (*Shabab al-Nafir al-Islami*). They were subsequently pardoned by a royal amnesty that also applied to a group of detainees belonging to the **Islamic Resistance Movement** (*Hamas*), the fundamentalist organization based in the occupied territories (see under Israel: Political Groups in Occupied and Previously Territories). A wave of arrests was also reported in mid-1995 of members of a hitherto unknown Islamist grouping called the **Renewal Party** (*Hizb al-Tajdid*.)

Legislature

The bicameral **National Assembly** (*Majlis al-'Umma*) consists of an appointed House of Notables and an elected House of Representatives. The Assembly did not convene between February 1976 and January 1984, a quasi-legislative National Consultative Council, appointed by King Hussein, serving from April 1978 to January 1984.

House of Notables   (*Majlis al-A'yaan*). The upper chamber currently consists of 55 members appointed by the king from designated categories of public figures, including present and past prime ministers, twice-elected former representatives, former senior judges and diplomats, and retired officers of the rank of general and above. The stated term is four years although actual terms, until recently, have been irregular because of various royal decrees directed primarily at the elected House of Representatives, whose suspension requires a cessation of upper house activity. The House of Notables appointed in January 1984 consisted of 30 members, while the body designated in November 1989 was expanded to 40 in keeping with a requirement that the upper house be half the size of its elected counterpart. The king appointed 55 members, including seven women, to the upper

house on November 17, 2003, although activity remained suspended pending new elections to the House of Representatives.

President: Zaid al-RIFA'I.

House of Representatives   (*Majlis al-Nuwaab*). The most recently elected lower chamber consisted of 110 members elected from 45 districts containing one to seven seats each. Twelve seats were reserved for members of the Christian and Circassian minorities and six for women. The constitutionally prescribed term of office is four years, although no full elections were held from 1967 to 1989 as the result of turmoil arising from Israel's occupation of the West Bank.

The House seated in 1967 contained 60 members (30 from West Jordan and 30 from East Jordan) elected in nonparty balloting. After being dissolved by the king in November 1974, its members were called back into session by royal decree in February 1976, at which time the king was authorized to postpone new elections indefinitely and call future special sessions as needed. However, the House did not meet again until January 1984. By-elections were held two months later to fill eight vacant East Bank seats; it being deemed impossible to conduct elections in the West Bank, the six vacant seats from the occupied territory were filled by voting within the House itself. The House continued to meet in special session until its dissolution on July 30, 1988, following which King Hussein announced the severance of all legal and administrative ties with the West Bank. Consequently, the November 8, 1989, election of a new House (expanded to 80 members) excluded the West Bank. Political party activity remained proscribed, although the Muslim Brotherhood (defined as a charitable organization rather than a party) was permitted to present candidates, 20 of whom were elected.

The balloting conducted on November 8, 1993, was the first to be held on a multiparty basis since 1956, though most seats (47) were won by independents, with the largest opposition bloc being the Islamic Action Front (16 seats) and no other party holding more than 4 seats. With the Muslim Brotherhood/IAF and eight other parties boycotting the

Cabinet

As of July 3, 2005

Prime Minister; Defense Minister	Adnan Badran
Deputy Prime Minister	Marwan Muasher
Deputy Prime Minister for Political Development	Hisham al-Tal
Royal Court Chief	Faisal al-Fayiz

Ministers

Agriculture	Muzahim Muhaisin
Awqaf and Islamic Affairs	Abd al-Salam al-Abadi
Culture; Media Affairs	Amin Mahmud
Education; Higher Education and Scientific Research	Khalid Tuqan
Energy and Mineral Resources	Azmi Khrisat
Environment	Khalid al-Irani
Finance	Adel Qudah
Foreign Affairs	Faruq al-Qasrawi
Health	Sa'id Darwazah
Industry and Trade	Sharif al-Zu'bi
Interior	Awni Yarvas
Justice	Abed Shakhanbih
Labor	Bassam al-Salim
Municipal Affairs	Tawfiq Krishan
National Economy	Mohammad Samir Tawil
Planning and International Cooperation	Suhair al-Ali [f]
Public Works and Housing	Yusuf Hyasat
Social Development	Abdullah Uwaydat
Telecommunication and Information Technology	Nadia Said [f]
Tourism and Antiquities	Alia Buran [f]
Transportation	Saud Nsairat
Water and Irrigation	Munther Shara

Ministers of State

Developing Public Sector	Taysir al-Samadi
Government Performance	Ruwaida Maaitah [f]
Legal Affairs	Abed Shakhanbih
Parliamentary Affairs	Abd al-Karim Malahmeh
State	Muhammad al-Najadat

[f] = female

November 4, 1997, elections, only six political parties fielded a total of 22 candidates, with the vast majority of the 524 candidates running as independents and most of these representing progovernment and tribal interests.

King 'Abdallah dissolved the House on June 16, 2001, in anticipation of new elections in the fall. The were postponed repeatedly, however, amid violence in the West Bank and domestic criticism of his policy allowing US troops into Jordan before the US-led invasion of Iraq in 2003. He finally permitted elections to be held on June 17, 2003. A total of 765 candidates competed for 110 seats, raised from 80 by a 2003 decree that also set aside six seats for women. Ending a six-year boycott of the legislature, the IAF fielded 30 candidates, of whom 22, including one woman and two Palestinians, were elected. The IAF charged that the elections were "illegitimate" on the ground that changes to electoral districts had been designed to prevent the country's Palestinian majority from dominating the legislature. Fifty-nine percent of the 2.3 million eligible voters turned out. Progovernment and independent tribal candidates retained their comfortable majority, winning 62 seats (56 percent), while opposition Islamists captured 22 seats (22 percent) (see Current issues, above, for additional information).

Speaker: (Vacant).

Communications

Press

The press has long been subject to censorship, with publication of most papers having been suspended at various times for publishing stories considered objectionable by the government. In early 1989 the government purchased the two largest dailies, *al-Rai* and *al-Dustur,* but concerns that the takeover would result in further press censorship were eased in May when Prime Minister Shaker lifted press restrictions imposed in August 1988. Press freedom expanded somewhat under the National Charter approved in June 1991, and further liberalization was anticipated in conjunction with the legalization of political parties and other democratization measures. However, contrary to that expectation, the House of Representatives in late 1992 approved government-sponsored legislation requiring the licensing of journalists, forbidding criticism of the royal family or the military, and otherwise restricting press activities. The government has reportedly initiated some 40 court cases against journalists or publishers since a new press law was enacted in May 1993. In May 1997

the government announced amendments to the 1993 law that provided for heavy fines for various journalistic transgressions and increased the capital requirements for newspapers 25 fold. However, in January 1998 the Jordanian Supreme Court struck down the May 1997 amendments. The National Assembly in 1998 was considering the reimposition of some of the 1997 provisions, reportedly upon the recommendation of King Hussein; however, following his assumption of the throne in February 1999, King 'Abdallah indicated his intention to ease, rather than tighten, government influence over the press. Nevertheless, additional restrictions were imposed in late 2001 by royal decree, with journalists now facing prison terms for "sowing the needs of hatred." The government defended the new penalties as necessary to maintain stability in light of regional and domestic tensions. The extent of press restrictions became apparent in February 2003, when three journalists for *al-Hilal* (Crescent), a weekly newpaper, received sentences ranging from two- to six-month for libeling and defaming the Prophet Muhammad. The following are Arabic dailies published at 'Amman, unless otherwise noted: *al-Ra'i* (Opinion, 100,000), partially government-owned; *al-Aswag* (Markets, 40,000); *Sawt al-Sha'ab* (Voice of the People, 30,000); *al-Dustur* (The Constitution, 70,000), partially government-owned; al-Akhbar (15,000); *The Jordan Times* (10,000), in English; *al-Arab al-Yawm,* independent; *al-Masaiya,* independent; *al-Mithaq; Arab Daily,* in English.

News Agencies

The domestic facility is the government-owned Jordan News Agency (PETRA). *Agence France-Presse,* AP, Deutsche Presse Agentur (DPA), and Reuters are among the foreign bureaus maintaining offices at 'Amman.

Broadcasting and Computing

Radio and television are controlled by the governmental Jordan Radio and Television Corporation (JRTV), although three private radio stations are permitted to broadcast. There were approximately 627,000 television receivers and 230,000 personal computers serving 457,000 Internet users in 2003.

Intergovernmental Representation

Ambassador to the US
Karim KAWAR

US Ambassador to Jordan
(Vacant)

Permanent Representative to the UN
Zeid Ra'ad Zeid al-HUSSEIN

IGO Memberships (Non-UN)
AFESD, AMF, BADEA, CAEU, CCC, IDB, Interpol, IOM, LAS, NAM, OIC, WTO

KUWAIT

STATE OF KUWAIT

Dawlat al-Kuwayt

The Country

Located near the head of the Persian Gulf, Kuwait is bordered on the north and west by Iraq and on the south by Saudi Arabia. It shared control of a 2,500-square-mile Neutral Zone with the latter until the area was formally partitioned in 1969, with revenues from valuable petroleum deposits in the zone being divided equally by the two states. An extremely arid country, Kuwait suffered from an acute shortage of potable water until the 1950s, when the installation of a number of desalination plants alleviated the problem.

About 95 percent of native Kuwaitis, who constitute less than 35 percent of the country's population, are Muslims; an estimated 70 percent belong to the Sunni sect and the remainder are Shi'ites. The noncitizen population, upon which the sheikhdom has long depended for a labor pool, is composed chiefly of other Arabs, Indians, Pakistanis, and Iranians who settled in Kuwait after World War II. Some 97 percent of native Kuwaitis are employed in the public sector, which accounts for 75 percent of GDP. Women comprise approximately 31 percent of the paid labor force; those who are native Kuwaitis are concentrated in health care and education, with the remainder primarily employed as teachers and domestic servants. The government has recently proposed that women be given the right to vote and to hold elected office, but the National Assembly has so far failed to endorse that initiative (see Current issues, below). The debate on the matter has revealed a deep split, even among women, in the Kuwaiti populace, many of whom still hold to traditional customs. There is also a distinct rift between rural tribal society and what has been described as the "urban oligarchy" dominated by the ruling family.

Kuwait's petroleum reserves, estimated at 100 billion barrels in 1986, are generally ranked as the world's third-largest and comprise about 9 percent of proven global reserves. The oil sector was nationalized in 1975, and Kuwait had become, prior to the events of 1990–91, a highly developed welfare state, providing its citizens with medical, educational, and other services without personal income taxes or related excises. In May 2005 the Kuwaiti government granted a $171 monthly pay raise to

tens of thousands of workers and pensioners to help them meet the rising cost of living.

Economic analysts expected that the systematic destruction of the emirate's oil facilities by retreating Iraqi forces in early 1991 would delay a return to full production for more than five years. However, oil exports resumed in July 1991 and reportedly returned to the pre-invasion production level of 2 million barrels per day by early 1993. Oil production has continued to grow, reaching a record 2.4 million barrels a day by May 2005.

Surging oil prices and the relative political stability in the region since the fall of Iraqi ruler Saddam Hussein in April 2003 have helped bolster Kuwait's booming economy. Yet, non-oil revenues continued to lag, prompting the International Monetary Fund (IMF) in May 2005 to urge a value-added tax, even though the economy shows annual growth (reportedly 10 percent in 2004) and yearly budget surpluses. Free from the threat of invasion by Iraq, analysts say Kuwait has an opportunity to further enhance the role of the private sector and carry out long-overdue structural reforms. The privatization of gas stations is under way, as recommended by the IMF, and the National Assembly has extended its initial approval to privatize Kuwait Airways Corporation.

Government and Politics

Political Background

Kuwait's accession to complete independence in 1961 was preceded by a period of close association with Great Britain that began in the late 19th century when the then-semiautonomous Ottoman province sought British protection against foreign invasion and an extension of Turkish control. By treaty in 1899, Kuwait ceded its external sovereignty to Britain in exchange for financial subsidies and defense support, and in 1914 Britain recognized Kuwait as a self-governing state under its protection. Special treaty relations continued until the sheikhdom was made fully independent by agreement with reigning Emir 'Abdallah al-Salim al-SABAH on June 19, 1961. Iraqi claims

to Kuwaiti territory were rebuffed shortly afterward by the dispatch of British troops at Kuwait's request and were subsequently reduced to a border dispute that appeared to have been substantially resolved in 1975.

On August 29, 1976, the government of Sheikh Jabir al-Ahmad al-SABAH resigned in the wake of alleged "unjust attacks and denunciations against ministers" by members of the National Assembly. Sheikh Sabah al-Salim al-SABAH, who succeeded Emir 'Abdallah in 1965, responded on the same day by dissolving the Assembly, suspending a constitutional provision that would have required a new election within two months, and instituting severe limitations on freedom of the press. On September 6 Sheikh Jabir, who succeeded Emir Sabah in 1977, formed a new government which was virtually identical in membership to the old.

Observers attributed the drastic measures of 1976 to the impact of the Lebanese civil war upon Kuwait, which then counted some 270,000 Palestinians among its nonnative population. The continuing exclusion of immigrant elements from political life accounted in large part for the lack of significant political change during the remainder of the decade, despite growing dissatisfaction among some groups, most noticeably Shi'ite Muslims, upon commencement of the Iranian revolution in early 1979.

Following a return to the earlier constitutional practice, a nonparty poll for a new National Assembly was held on February 23, 1981. Five days later, the heir apparent, Sheikh Saad al-'Abdallah al-Salim al-SABAH, who had first been appointed in 1978, was redesignated as prime minister. He was reappointed on March 3, 1985, after balloting on February 20 for a new Assembly which was itself dissolved on July 3, 1986, in the wake of a series of confrontations between elected and ex officio government members over fiscal and internal security issues. Echoing the events of 1976, the emir postponed new elections and implemented strict press controls.

In early 1989 a group of ex-parliamentarians, led by former speaker Ahmad 'Abd al-Aziz al-SA'DUN, launched a petition drive to revive the

1962 Constitution and restore the National Assembly, reportedly gathering over 30,000 signatures by December. The government's response was that it was pursuing a "new form of popular participation" centered on a National Council of 50 elected and 25 appointed members to serve as a surrogate for the former legislature for the ensuing four years. The opposition nonetheless continued to insist on revival of the earlier body and mounted a largely successful boycott of National Council balloting on June 10, at which all of the contested seats were won by government supporters.

The Iraqi invasion of August 2, 1990, resulted in the flight of virtually all members of the country's ruling elite. In March 1991 they returned, amid massive physical destruction, to face widespread demands for meaningful representative government. Opposition leaders vehemently denounced the composition of a new government formed on April 20 as little more than an extension of its predecessor, in which all major posts were held by members of the royal family. The emir responded with a promise that elections to a new National Assembly would be held in 1992, and on July 9 the interim National Council was reconvened with orders to discuss and organize the elections. Meanwhile, the regime was buffeted by foreign and domestic criticism of its postwar policies, including the perfunctory trials of alleged Iraqi collaborators and the expulsion of tens of thousands of non-Kuwaiti citizens. Subsequently, the government commuted the death sentences of convicted collaborators, promised defendants the right to a fair trial, and on August 14 created criminal appeals courts.

National Assembly balloting was held on October 5, 1992, with candidates considered opponents of the government capturing a majority of the seats. Sheikh Saad resigned as prime minister two days later but was reappointed by the emir on October 12, despite growing demands from the opposition that someone else be named to the post. On the other hand, in a significant concession to the opposition, six members of the Assembly were named to the new cabinet announced on October 17. The cabinet was also extensively reshuffled on April 13,

Political Status: Constitutional hereditary emirate; independent since June 19, 1961, save for occupation by Iraq from August 2, 1990, to February 26, 1991.
Area: 6,880 sq. mi. (17,818 sq. km.).
Population: 1,575,983 (1995C), including 655,820 Kuwaitis and 920,163 non-Kuwaitis; 2,568,000 (2004E). The 1995 figure is not adjusted for underenumeration.
Major Urban Centers (1995C): KUWAIT CITY (28,859), Salmiya (130,215), Hawalli (182,238).
Official Language: Arabic.
Monetary Unit: Dinar (official rate July 1, 2005: 1 dinar = $3.42US).
Sovereign (Emir): Sheikh Jabir al-Ahmad al-Jabir al-SABAH; appointed Prime Minister in 1965 and Heir Apparent in 1966; reappointed Prime Minister in 1971, 1975, and 1976; became Emir upon the death of his cousin, Sheikh Sabah al-Salim al-SABAH, on December 31, 1977.
Prime Minister and Heir Apparent: The emir, Sheikh Jabir al-Ahmad al-Jabir al-SABAH, appointed Sheikh Sabah al-Ahmad al-Jabir al-SABAH, prime minister after the National Assembly elections of July 5, 2003. The cabinet resigned on July 13, 2003; a new cabinet was appointed on July 14. Sheikh Sabah al-Ahmad al-Jabir al-Sabah's appointment to Prime Minister was the first time the post had not been held by the crown prince in the country's history. Crown Prince Sheikh Saad al-'Abdallah al-Salim al-SABAH had held the post of prime minister since February 8, 1978, when the elevation of Sheikh Jabir al-Ahmad al-Jabir al-Sabah to emir created a vacancy.

1994, the new government subsequently announcing it would move ahead with economic reforms, including privatization.

In addition to intensifying Kuwait's "siege mentality" the October 1994 border confrontation with Iraq (see Foreign relations, below) also exacerbated the sheikhdom's budget difficulties, the government in 1995 announcing plans to impose new fees on many public services in an effort to control the deficit. On the political front, attention focused on the conflict between the National Assembly and the government over whether the Assembly had the right to review decrees issued during its 1986–1992 hiatus. Legislators were also pressing for the prosecution of former officials, most of whom are members of the royal family, on corruption charges. In part, the schism reflected the influence of Islamic fundamentalists within the Assembly, 39 of whose 50 elected deputies in 1994 endorsed an appeal, subsequently rejected by the government, to make Islamic religious law (*shari'a*) the sole source of Kuwaiti law. Growing fundamentalist support was also noted within the population as a whole, although many young Kuwaitis were described as having "embraced" Western culture as the outgrowth of a belief that the country's survival hinged on continued strong ties with the United States and Europe.

Following the balloting for a new Assembly on October 7, 1996, it was reported that 17–22 "solidly progovernment" candidates had been elected with the remainder including an estimated 14–18 representatives from the generally antigovernment Islamist camp. The prime minister again entered a pro forma resignation on October 8, but he was reappointed on October 12 and his new, moderately reshuffled, government was sworn in on October 15.

Sheikh Saad and his cabinet resigned on March 15, 1998, as legislators continued to press various ministers on several fronts (see Current issues, below). However, the emir immediately reappointed Sheikh Saad as prime minister, and a new, substantially reshuffled government was announced on March 23.

The cabinet again resigned on January 29, 2001, and substantial debate was reported within the ruling family over the makeup of the next government. On February 17, 2001, the cabinet included eight new members and, significantly, oil and finance ministers who were not members of the ruling family. Although aging Prime Minister Saad remained the titular head of government, many of his responsibilities were turned over to the deputy prime minister, Sheikh Sabah al-Ahmad al-Jabir al-Sabah, the brother of the emir. With age and ill-

ness taking a toll on the ruling family, the question of succession weighed heavily on the state.

On June 1, 2003, four ministers resigned to stand for election. After the Assembly elections on July 5, 2003, Sheikh Sabah was appointed prime minister, replacing the heir apparent, Sheikh Saad al-'Abdallah al-Salim al-Sabah (see Prime Minister and Heir Apparent above), and separating the post from the crown prince for the first time. The move makes the prime minister more accountable to the people. Meanwhile, Islamists and pro-government candidates swept to victory, crushing the pro-Western liberals (see Legislature below) and the full cabinet resigned, in a routine move, the day after the elections. Despite the more conservative trend, the Assembly did grant women the right to vote for the first time in the country's history (see Constitution and government below) in May 2005. Also, this time the responsibility for forming a new government fell to the deputy prime minister and foreign minister, reportedly because Sheikh Saad had been ill for some time. A new cabinet was installed on July 17, 2003. Two ministers resigned in 2005, with only one of the vacancies having been filled as of May 2005.

A group of former Salafists formed what they describe as Kuwait's first political party in January 2005, a move that is somewhat unsettled since political parties are officially illegal in Kuwait (see Political parties below).

Constitution and Government

The constitution promulgated in 1962 vests executive power in an emir selected from the Mubarak line of the ruling Sabah family, whose dynasty dates from 1756. The emir rules through an appointed prime minister and Council of Ministers, while legislative authority is shared by the emir and a National Assembly that is subject to dissolution by decree. The judicial system, since its revision in 1959, is based on the Egyptian model and includes a Constitutional Court, courts of the first degree (criminal assize, magistrates', civil, domestic, and commercial courts), and a Misdemeanors Court of Appeal. The domestic court, which deals with cases involving such personal matters as divorce and inheritance, is divided into separate chambers for members of the Sunni and Shi'ite sects, with a third chamber for non-Muslims. Civil appeal is to a High Court of Appeal and, in limited cases, to a Court of Cassation. Although the 1962 basic law theoretically accorded equal rights to men and women, an election law adopted at the same time precluded women from voting or holding elected office. After decades of controversy over the elimination of these proscriptions, the Assembly amended the country's election law on May 16, 2005, granting women the right to vote in and contest parliamentary and local elections for the first time in the country's history (see Current issues, below).

Foreign Relations

As a member of the Arab League, Kuwait has closely identified itself with Arab causes and through such agencies as the Kuwait Fund for Arab Economic Development and the Organization of Arab Petroleum Exporting Countries has contributed to the economic development of other Arab countries. In 1967 it launched a program of direct aid to countries experiencing hardship as a result of conflict with Israel. In 1981 Kuwait joined five other regional states in forming the Gulf Cooperation Council (GCC).

Dominating external concerns in the 1980s was the Iran-Iraq war, which curtailed oil exports and generated fear of Iranian expansionism in the event of a victory for the Khomeini regime. After a number of attacks on shipping by both participants and a decision by Washington to increase its naval presence in the Gulf, Kuwait, which had previously declined an offer of American tanker escort, proposed in April 1987 that a number of its vessels be transferred to US registry. The reflagging provided enhanced security for oil shipments but was interpreted as solidifying the sheikdom's pro-Iraqi posture. Diplomatic relations between Kuwait and Iran were eventually restored in November 1988, three months after the Iran-Iraq cease-fire.

Despite its support of Iraq during the latter's conflict with Iran, the emirate had experienced periodic strain with Baghdad long before the Gulf crisis of August 1990. For many decades Iraq had laid intermittent claim to all of Kuwait on the basis of its status within the Ottoman province of Basra at the turn of the century. However, the merits of such a case were substantially weakened by an Iraqi agreement in 1963 to respect the independence and sovereignty of its southern neighbor. Unresolved by the 1963 accord was the question of boundary demarcation, in regard to which earlier diplomatic references had been quite vague. Nor was the land boundary the only problem: Iraq had also claimed offshore territory, including, most importantly, Bubiyan Island, which dominated access to the Iraqi port and naval base of Umm Qasr via the Khor Abdallah waterway (see map, p. 547). The boundary uncertainties also lent a degree of credibility to claims that Kuwait was encroaching on Iraqi oil fields, allegedly by "slant drilling," while Baghdad had long complained of the failure of the Gulf emirates, including Kuwait, to hold to OPEC-mandated oil production quotas. Such problems were unaddressed by Security Council Resolution 687, which provided the basis of a formal cease-fire between Iraqi and UN forces. (For a chronology of events associated with the Gulf war, see p. 969 in the *Political Handbook of the World 1991*.)

In June 1991 the Kuwaiti government withdrew its diplomats from Algeria, Jordan, Mauritania, Sudan, Tunisia, and Yemen, saying that it was "reducing" relations with the six countries because of their lack of support during the Gulf crisis. Meanwhile, a ten-year military cooperation agreement signed with the United States on September 19 authorized the US to stockpile military equipment and provided its navy with port access; however, the accord did not sanction the permanent stationing of troops. The agreement came in the immediate aftermath of an Iraqi "invasion" of Bubiyan Island which, although easily repelled by Kuwaiti forces, had heightened Kuwait's anxiety about the Hussein regime.

In February 1992 a UN border commission issued a draft document on delineation of the Kuwait-Iraq border which included division of Umm Qasr. Observers described the commission's recommendations as an attempt to punish Iraq for its invasion. On November 23 the UN commission revised the border even further north, giving

Kuwait complete control of the naval base as well as additional oil fields in the area, effective January 15, 1993. However, Iraq strongly objected to the decision and sent troops into the disputed territory in early January (ostensibly to retrieve weapons), with friction over the issue contributing to a brief resumption of allied air attacks on Iraqi military targets. Subsequently, Kuwait sought and received Western assurance that the 2,000 American troops still in the emirate would be quickly reinforced if Baghdad maintained a confrontational posture.

On April 14, 1993, George H.W. Bush received an enthusiastic reception on his arrival for a three-day visit to the emirate. Subsequently, there were reports of an Iraqi plot to assassinate the former US president, with 14 persons charged in the matter being placed on trial in early June. As the result of what President Clinton termed "compelling evidence" of Iraqi involvement in such a plot, the United States launched a missile attack against Baghdad on June 26. (Subsequent reports suggested that the evidence in question was seriously flawed, although a number of Iraqis were among those ultimately convicted in the case.)

In November 1993 Kuwait signed a ten-year defense cooperation agreement with Russia, similar to post–Gulf war pacts with Britain, France, and the United States. A trade and investment agreement with Russia in November 1994 was considered, in part, an outgrowth of Kuwait's announcement several months earlier that it intended to purchase some $800 million in Russian armaments.

The specter of another Iraqi incursion was raised in early October 1994 when Iraqi troops were once again deployed near the Kuwaiti border. However, Baghdad retreated quickly from its threatening stance in the face of Western military preparations and dropped a long-standing claim to its "19th province" by formally recognizing Kuwait's sovereignty in early November, including acceptance of the UN's recent demarcation of the border between the two countries. The Kuwaiti government called the recognition "a step in the right direction," although tension remained high, with Kuwait charging that more than 600 of its nationals were still being held as "hostages" in Iraqi

jails. Meanwhile, Kuwait agreed to the permanent stationing on its territory of a squadron of US warplanes. Subsequently, additional US planes and troops were deployed in the sheikhdom as a precaution when Iraqi soldiers moved into the Kurdish "safe area" in northern Iraq in August 1996.

Not surprisingly, Kuwait remained uncompromising in its anti-Iraq stance in 1997, even though Gulf neighbors Qatar and the United Arab Emirates were promoting the "rehabilitation" within the Arab world of the regime in Baghdad. Consequently, in early 1998 Kuwait was the only Arab state to unequivocally endorse US plans to take military action against Baghdad in the wake of the recent breakdown of UN inspections there. Additional US troops and warplanes were granted staging rights in Kuwait, with an attack unleashed on Baghdad in December.

In early September 2000, in conjunction with renewed Iraqi complaints of Kuwaiti oil "theft," tensions rose significantly. The UN Security Council agreed that Kuwait ultimately should be awarded $15.9 billion in reparations for the 1990–1991 occupation. However, relations improved significantly following the Arab League Summit in March 2002 at which Iraq reportedly agreed to honor Kuwait's independence and territorial integrity. Tensions continued to escalate between Kuwait and Baghdad until after the US defeated Saddam Hussein, and Kuwait was on board to support creation of a new government in Iraq in 2005. As recently as February 2005 there were reports of a series of gunfights between Islamist groups described as armed extremists and Kuwaiti security forces. These militant groups are reportedly tied to al-Qaeda, suggesting that Kuwait has some security concerns in the war against terrorism. Relations appear to have improved with Jordan and Palestinian officials since the end of the Gulf War, and in May 2005 Kuwait agreed to send 150 soldiers to Sudan as part of the UN peacekeeping mission to help end civil war.

Current Issues

In an unexpected move on May 16, 2005, the National Assembly granted women the right to vote for the first time in the country's history. The prime minister, who had been pushing for the amendment to Kuwait's election law, said women could become cabinet ministers. The 35–23 vote, with one abstention, came after decades of heated debates, demonstrations, and riots, and a 2002 decree by the emir insisting that women be given full political rights by 2003. Finally, in October 2003, despite the objections of Islamists and male politicians, the cabinet approved allowing women to stand for office and vote in municipal elections. Although the cabinet approved a draft law in May 2004 that gave women the right to vote and to run in parliamentary elections, the measure was repeatedly rejected in the Assembly. In early May 2005– with the Assembly deadlocked with 29 members abstaining and only 29 votes in favor and the legislature shy of the necessary 33 votes–it appeared as though women would not be granted voting rights once again. Ultimately, the government invoked a rarely used urgency order to push the measure through in one session, despite heated arguments by Islamists. The Islamists did include a requirement that "females abide by Islamic law," which has been widely interpreted to mean there would be separate polling places for men and women. Women can begin to register in February 2006 to vote in the 2007 parliamentary elections.

The granting of full suffrage to women was hailed throughout the West as a "victory for democracy" and a change that surely will affect the political landscape of the country. Shortly after the positive vote, the speaker of the Assembly called for further, though unspecified, steps toward democracy in Kuwait.

Another significant change was the appointment of Sheikh Sabah as prime minister in 2003, which was the first time the crown prince had not held the post in the country's history. The aging emir and the former prime minister (and official heir apparent) Sheikh Saad reportedly have both been in ill health, resulting in questions about the next generation of Kuwaiti leaders.

Tensions eased to a great extent in Kuwait after US and coalition forces toppled the regime of Iraqi ruler Saddam Hussein in April 2003, greatly relieving security issues for Kuwait. However the government has downplayed the arrests of suspected al-Qaeda terrorists in the intervening years and repeated clashes between government security forces and Islamic militants as the acts of a select few. Kuwait has pledged to help support the new Iraqi government in its efforts to achieve stability. Also, in a meeting with US National Security Adviser Stephen Hadley in Washington on May 18, 2005, the foreign minister, Sheikh Muhammad Sabah al-Salim al-SABAH, reiterated that Kuwait supports the so-called "road map" as the only viable solution to peace between Israelis and Palestinians. The prime minister was expected to make his second visit to Washington since September 2003 to meet with President Bush in July 2005.

Kuwait's oil minister and president of OPEC supported high prices for oil in May 2005, citing increased production costs to meet global demand and pay for exploration in other oil-producing countries. With the price of crude oil high and still climbing, and the economy by all accounts booming, Kuwait is optimistic about the future. Results of a Gallup survey of the Arab world released on May 21, 2004, at the World Economic Forum in Jordan found that seven out of ten people in Kuwait believe 2005 will be better than 2004 in a region the rest of the world sees as troubled.

Political Parties

Although political parties are not legal in Kuwait, a number of political "groupings," many of them loosely organized, have been permitted to function in public without restriction. More candidates in the 2003 National Assembly balloting were identifiable as supported by several of the groupings below. The government in mid-2004 acknowledged that political parties are likely to fully develop at some point, but no specific encouragement appears forthcoming.

Islamic Constitutional Movement (ICM). A moderate Sunni Muslim organization with reported ties to the Muslim Brotherhood in other Arab states such as Egypt and Jordan, the ICM has called for the "adjustment" of all Kuwaiti legislation so as not to "conflict" with *shari'a* (Islamic religious law).

In conjunction with the KDF (below), the ICM led the prodemocracy movement which developed in Kuwait following the expulsion of Iraqi troops in early 1991, with a call for new Assembly elections and formation of a more representative cabinet. However, ICM leaders subsequently stressed that they sought "small steps, not jumps" in liberalization and did not question the authority of the royal family. Several ICM members were victorious in the 1992 and 1996 Assembly balloting, but lost seats in the 2003 election.

Leaders: Ismail al-SHATTI, Sheikh Jasim Muhalhal al-YASIM (Secretary).

Islamic Salafi Alliance. This hard-line Sunni group appears to have replaced the Islamic Popular Group (IPG) among the major Sunni Muslim organizations. The so-called "scientific Salafis" also fall under this umbrella and are known as the Salafi Movement. It advocates social reform and a return to "true Islam." The Salafi gained some seats in the 2003 Assembly balloting.

Leader: Khalid al-ISSA.

Kuwaiti Democratic Forum (KDF). The secularist, center-left KDF was initially described as the best-organized of Kuwait's political groupings, with a membership based primarily in urban areas. Several KDF leaders (including "veteran leftist" Ahmad al-Khatib), who had been instrumental in the growth of the prodemocracy movement following the Gulf crisis, were elected to the Assembly in October 1992, where they aligned with Islamic representatives in a campaign to make the royal family "more accountable." However, Khatib did not run for reelection in 1996.

KDF leader 'Abdallah Nibari, described as a "leading liberal member of the opposition" in the Assembly, was wounded in an apparent assassination attempt in June 1997. Nibari had been critical of the government's handling of recent large military contracts, contending "middlemen" were being exorbitantly enriched by the process. KDF lost its parliamentary representation in the 2003 Assembly balloting when 'Abdallah Nibari lost his seat.

Leaders: Ahmad al-KHATIB, 'Abdallah NIBARI.

Islamic National Alliance (INA). The INA, whose leader was elected to the Assembly in October 1992, represents Kuwaiti Shi'ites. INA reportedly derived from the Cultural Social Society (*Jamiyyat al-Thaqafah al-Ijtimayyah*), established by forces loyal to the Iranian revolution of 1979. However, Shi'ite pressure has been described as less severe on the Kuwaiti government than on other neighboring regimes (such as the one in Bahrain) in part because some Shi'ite leaders in Kuwait are participating in the political process while others remain wealthy supporters of the ruling family.

Leader: Adnan Sayid 'Abd al-Samad Sayid ZAHIR.

Nation Party (Hizb *Al-Ummah*). This group was formed on January 29, 2005, by former Salafists "to promote pluralism and a multi-party system of government" and is described as the first true political party ever formed in Kuwait. The group has called for the removal of foreign troops from Kuwait. Since the constitution and Kuwaiti laws do not provide for the establishment of political parties, the government has not been sure quite how to deal with the group. Members of the group reportedly were called in for questioning by police at the end of January "for violating the Public Gatherings Law," according to a party official. In February, the government imposed a travel ban on all 15 party members.

Leader: Dr. Mohammed al-HADRAN.

National Democratic Movement (NDM). Launched in May 1997 by some 75 founding members (reportedly including national legislators and cabinet ministers), the NDM announced it would pursue broader "personal freedoms" for Kuwaitis as well as new legislation designed to give the Assembly a greater role in overseeing government contracts. A number of NDM members were elected in the 2003 Assembly balloting.

Leader: Khaled al-MUTAIR.

Cabinet

As of May 15, 2005

Prime Minister	Sheikh Sabah al-Ahmad al-Jabir al-Sabah (de facto ruler)
First Deputy Prime Minister, Interior	Sheikh Nawaf al-Ahmad al-Jabir al-Sabah
Deputy Prime Ministers	Sheikh Jabir Mubarak al-Hamad al-Sabah (Defense)
	Muhammad Daifallah Sharar (State Minister of State for National Assembly Affairs and Cabinet Affairs)

Ministers

Awqaf and Islamic Affairs	Abdullah Ma'tuq al-Ma'tuq (var. Abdullah al-Muatuq)
Commerce and Industry	Abdullah al-Rahman al-Tawil
Communications, Planning, and State Minister for Administrative Development Affairs	Sheikh Ahmad al-'Abdallah al-Ahmad al-Sabah
Defense	Sheikh Jabir Mubarak al-Hamad al-Sabah
Education and Higher Education	Dr. Rashid Hamad Muhammad al-Hamad
Energy	Sheikh Ahmad al-Fahad al-Ahmad al-Sabah
Finance	Badir Nasir al-Humaidi
Foreign Affairs	Sheikh Muhammad Sabah al-Salim al-Sabah
Health	Vacant (Muhammad Ahmad al-Jarallah resigned in April 2005)
Information	Anas Muhammad al-Rushaid
Interior	Sheikh Nawaf al-Ahmad al-Jabir al-Sabah
Justice	Ahmad Yaqub Baqir al-'Abdallah
Public Works	Badir Nasir al-Mumaidi
Social Affairs and Labor	Faisal al-Hajji

Ministers of State

Administrative Development Affairs	Sheikh Ahmad al-'Abdallah al-Ahmad al-Sabah
Cabinet Affairs and National Assembly Affairs	Muhammad Daifallah Sharar

Legislature

A National Assembly (*Majlis al-'Umma*) was organized in 1963 to share legislative authority with the emir, although it was dissolved by decree of the ruler from August 1976 to February 1981 and from July 1986 to October 1992. Under the 1962 basic law, the Assembly encompasses 50 representatives (2 each from 25 constituencies) elected for four-year terms, in addition to ministers who, if not elected members, serve ex officio. Only literate, adult, native-born males over 21 years old whose families have resided in Kuwait since 1920 have been allowed to vote, though this will soon change, when women are allowed to vote for the first time in the 2007 Assembly elections.

Balloting for the most recent Assembly was conducted on July 5, 2003. In a field of 246 candidates, 27 Assembly members retained their seats, 18 were elected for the first time, and five new members were elected who had previously held seats. Liberals were reported to have suffered crushing defeat. Although political parties remain proscribed, at least 6 and perhaps as many as 12 Islamist and liberal groupings allegedly contested the elections.

Speaker: Jassim al-KHURAFI.

Communications

Press

The emir suspended constitutional guarantees of freedom of the press on August 29, 1976. Following the National Assembly election of 1981, censorship was relaxed, permitting the reemergence of what the *New York Times* called "some of the most free, and freewheeling, newspapers in the region." However, in conjunction with the dissolution of the Assembly in July 1986 the government imposed new press restrictions, subjecting periodicals to prior censorship and announcing it would suspend any newspapers or magazines printing material "against the national interest." The government also continued its drive to bring more Kuwaitis into the news media and deported an estimated 40 journalists from other Arab countries to open jobs for nationals.

During the 1990–1991 Iraqi occupation a number of clandestine newsletters were issued on an irregular basis, including one that was converted at liberation into a full-fledged tabloid, *26th of February,* with a circulation of 30,000; however, the paper suspended publication in March 1991 because it lacked a government license. In January 1992 the government lifted the 1986 censorship codes in conjunction with an agreement by the major press groups to self-monitor the content of their publications, and the press was subsequently described as having returned to the vitality and relative openness of the early 1980s, with direct criticism of the emir remaining as the only proscription. In November 2002, Kuwait closed the office of Al-Jazeera satellite television station, officially for "security reasons," though it also reportedly accused the station of lacking objectivity. In May 2005 the station was allowed to resume broadcasts.

The following dailies (in Arabic, unless otherwise noted) are published in Kuwait City: *al-Anbaa* ("The News," 107,000); *al-Ra'I al-'Aam* ("Voice of the People," 87,000, published at Shuwaikh); *al-Qabas* ("Firebrand," 80,000); *al-Siyasah* ("Policy," 80,000); *al-Watan* ("Homeland," 60,000); *Kuwait Times* (28,000), in English; *Arab Times* (42,000), in English; and *al-Jamihir* (83,000). A weekly, *ar-Rissalih* ("The Message"), is published at Shuwaikh.

News Agencies

The domestic facility is the Kuwait News Agency–KUNA (*Wakalat al-Anba'al-Kuwayt*); in addition, numerous foreign agencies maintain bureaus at Kuwait City.

Broadcasting and Computing

The Radio of the State of Kuwait and Kuwait Television (*Tilifiziyun al-Kuwayt*) are both controlled by the government. There were approximately 988,000 television receivers and 300,000 personal computers serving 567,000 Internet users in 2003.

Intergovernmental Representation

Ambassador to the US
Sheikh Salim Abdullah al-Jabir al-SABAH

US Ambassador to Kuwait
Richard LeBARON

Permanent Representative to the UN
Nabila Abdallah al-MULLAH

IGO Memberships (Non-UN)
AfDB, AFESD, AMF, BADEA, BDEAC, CAEU, CCC, GCC, IDB, Interpol, LAS, NAM, OAPEC, OIC, OPEC, WTO

LEBANON

REPUBLIC OF LEBANON

al-Jumhuriyah al-Lubnaniyah

Note: On April 7, 2005, UN Security Council Resolution 1595 established an independent commission to investigate the death of former Prime Minister Rafiq Hariri, who was assassinated in a massive car bombing on February 14, 2005, in Beirut. The commission's report strongly implicated Syrian officials and operatives in the operation. As the probe continued, despite alleged interference from Syrian officials, a series of bombings aimed mostly at outspoken critics of Syria rocked Lebanon, killing 23. On December 12, 2005, UN investigators released a second report detailing intimidation efforts and destruction of evidence as well as additional substantiation of Syrian involvement in Hariri's death. The same day, Gebran Tueni, a journalist and an anti-Syrian member of parliament, died in a car bombing. On December 16, 2005, the United Nations passed a resolution to extend the commission's work another six months and to assist investigations into the wave of bombings in Lebanon.

The Country

Lebanon is bounded on the west by the Mediterranean Sea, on the north and east by Syria, and on the south by Israel. A long-standing presumption of roughly equal religious division between Christians and Muslims is no longer valid because of a high birthrate among the latter. (No formal census has been conducted since 1932 for fear that the results might provoke political unrest.) The largest Muslim sects are the Shi'ites and the Sunni, each traditionally encompassing about one-fifth of the permanent population, although recent estimates place the number of Shi'ites at approximately 40 percent of the entire population and 70 percent of the Muslim population. Druses number nearly 200,000, and Christian sects include Maronites, Orthodox Greeks, Greek Catholics, Orthodox Armenians, and Armenian Catholics. An estimated 350,000 Palestinian refugees live in long-standing "camps" in Lebanon. Women comprise approximately 30 percent of the paid labor force, concentrated in lower administrative, commercial, and educational sectors.

Because of a commercial tradition, Lebanon's living standard until the mid-1970s was high in

comparison to most other Middle Eastern countries and developing nations in general. The leading contributor to national income was the service sector, encompassing banking, insurance, tourism, transit trade, income from petroleum pipelines, and shipping. Industrial development, though largely limited to small firms, was also important, the principal components being food processing, textiles, building materials, footwear, glass, and chemical products. However, the civil war that erupted in 1975 and 1976 severely damaged the economy, with 1976 GNP dropping 60 percent compared to 1974. In addition, casualties and dislocations among the civilian population yielded an estimated loss of two-thirds of skilled industrial workers. Although nearly half the plunge in GNP had been recovered by 1978, renewed turmoil contributed to further decline prior to the full-scale Israeli invasion in mid-1982. By 1985 some 70 percent of the country's production had come to a halt, 35 percent of all factories had been destroyed, 80 percent of industrial workers had been laid off, and the national debt had grown by 700 percent in four years to $30.4 billion. The budget deficit grew from $1 billion in 1981 to $10 billion in 1984, absorbing one-third of the gross national product. The agricultural sector declined by 36 percent in 1984 alone, while most government income from customs duties disappeared and the once-stable Lebanese pound lost more than 99 percent of its 1982 value by late 1989.

Although inflation and unemployment continued to run at 100 and 30 percent, respectively, the country's economic future was viewed with cautious optimism following the appointment of multibillionaire Rafiq Hariri as prime minister in October 1992 after the end of the civil war. The United Nations estimated the war's damage at about $25 billion. Lebanon experienced a heavy inflow of foreign investment as it attempted to rebound from the devastation cause by the war. GDP, up about 75 percent since 1990, grew by 4 percent in 1997, with annual inflation running at 8.5 percent. Although described by the World Bank as having made a "remarkable" recovery in the 1990s, the economy remained negatively influenced by high external debt, a growing budget deficit, and severe unemployment.

Consequently, GDP growth began to plummet in 1999, to only 1 percent, and fell to -0.5 percent in 2000 under the continued influence of a plodding bureaucracy, corruption, and resistance by vested interests to reform. Economic growth rebounded from 2 percent in 2001 and 2002 to 3 percent in 2003 and a projected 5 percent in 2004. Lebanon's modest recovery in GDP growth has been due to stronger regional-goods exports. The depreciation of the US dollar, to which the Lebanese pound is pegged, has also strengthened economic competitiveness. Nevertheless, Lebanon's growth remains below potential, and unemployment remains high with job prospects for recent graduates poor. Furthermore, the country continues to suffer from a crippling external debt burden, estimated in 2004 at 164 percent of its GDP.

Government and Politics

Political Background

Home to the Phoenicians in the third millennium B.C., Lebanon was later subjected to invasions by the Romans and the Arabs, with Turkish control being established in the 16th century. During the 19th century Mount Lebanon, the core area of what was to become the Lebanese Republic, acquired a special status as a result of European intervention on behalf of various Christian factions. Following disintegration of the Ottoman Empire after World War I, the country became a French mandate under the League of Nations, France adding to Mount Lebanon areas detached from Syria to enlarge the country's area and its Muslim population. Independence, proclaimed in 1941 and confirmed in an agreement with Free French representatives in 1943, was not fully effective until the withdrawal of French troops in 1946, following a series of national uprisings during the tenure of the Republic's first president, Bishara al-KHURI. The so-called National Pact of 1943, an unwritten understanding reflecting the balance of religious groups within the population at that time, provided for a sharing of executive and legislative functions in the ratio of six Christians to five Muslims. Although this arrangement helped moderate the impact of postwar Arab nationalism, the country was racked by a serious internal crisis in the summer of 1958 that led to the temporary landing of US Marines at the request of President Camille CHAMOUN. The crisis was alleviated in July 1958 by the election of a compromise president, Gen. Fu'ad CHEHAB, who was acceptable to the dissident leadership. Internal stability was further consolidated by the peaceful election of Charles HELOU as president in 1964.

Although Lebanon was an active participant in only the first Arab-Israeli war, Palestinian guerrilla groups based in southern Lebanon began launching attacks on Israel in the mid-1960s. In November 1969 Yasir 'ARAFAT, who had emerged as chairman of the Palestine Liberation Organization (PLO) the previous February, met with representatives of the Lebanese Army at Cairo, Egypt, to conclude a secret pact under which Lebanon recognized the right of Palestinians to engage in action against the Jewish state, with the military agreeing to facilitate movement of commandos through border zones. Although the so-called Cairo Agreement was subsequently amended to restrict Palestinian activity, a sharp increase in the number of cross-border raids, particularly after the expulsion of the Palestinian guerrilla groups from Jordan in 1970 and 1971, generated Israeli reprisals and, in turn, demands from the Christian Right that the Lebanese government restrain the commandos.

Serious fighting between the Maronite right-wing Phalangist Party and Palestinian guerrilla groups erupted at Beirut in April 1975, exacerbated by growing tensions between status quo and anti-status quo factions. The status quo forces, mainly Maronite, opposed demands by nationalists, most of whom were Muslim, who wanted the government to identify more closely with the Palestinians and other pan-Arab causes, and also demanded revisions in Lebanon's political system to reflect Muslim population gains.

The conflict escalated further in 1976, causing widespread destruction and the virtual collapse of

Political Status: Independent parliamentary republic proclaimed November 26, 1941, with acquisition of de facto autonomy completed upon withdrawal of French troops in December 1946.

Area: 4,036 sq. mi. (10,452 sq. km.).

Population: 3,717,000 (2004E). Estimates vary widely; the most recent official figure (2,126,325 in 1970), which excluded Palestinian refugees, was based on a population sample and was much lower than UN estimates of the period. In recent years the UN appears to have accepted the 1970 figure, discarding most of its previous estimates for the late 1970s and early 1980s.

Major Urban Centers (1975E): BEIRUT (1,500,000), Tripoli (160,000), Zahlé (45,000), Saida (Sidon, 38,000), Tyre (14,000).

Official Language: Arabic (French is widely used).

Monetary Unit: Lebanese Pound (market rate July 1, 2005: 1,507 pounds = $1US).

President: Gen. (Ret.) Emile LAHOUD (Maronite Christian); elected for a six-year term by the National Assembly on October 15, 1998, and inaugurated on November 24 to succeed Ilyas HRAWI (Maronite Christian). Although the president's tenure is limited to one six-year term, the National Assembly voted on September 4, 2004, to extend Lahoud's term for an additional three years by amending the constitution.

Prime Minister: Fouad SINIORA (Sunni Muslim); appointed by the President on June 30, 2005, to succeed Najib MIKATI. Siniora formed a cabinet on July 19, 2005.

the economy. In March a group of Muslim army officers, calling for the resignation of President Sulayman FRANJIYAH, mounted an abortive coup, and on April 9 regular Syrian army units intervened in support of the Lebanese leadership following its break with the leftists headed by Kamal Jumblatt. The Syrian intervention permitted the election by the Lebanese parliament on May 8 of Ilyas SARKIS to succeed President Franjiyah.

During a meeting at Riyadh, Saudi Arabia, on October 17 and 18, 1976, Syrian president Assad and Egyptian president Sadat agreed on the establishment of a definitive cease-fire, commencing October 21, to be maintained by a 30,000-man Arab Deterrent Force (ADF) theoretically directed by President Sarkis but actually under Syrian control. Despite appeals from Iraq and Libya for a limit on Syrian participation, the plan was approved during an Arab League summit meeting at Cairo on October 25 and 26. By late November, hostilities had largely ceased, and on December 9 President Sarkis designated Salim Ahmad al-HUSS to form a new government (Prime Minister Karami having tendered his resignation on September 25).

Notwithstanding the assassination of Muslim Druse leader Jumblatt on March 16, which negated efforts by President Sarkis and Prime Minister Huss to secure agreement on constitutional reform, an uneasy truce prevailed throughout much of the country during 1977. The principal exception was the southern region, where fear of Israeli intervention prevented deployment of Syrian-led peacekeeping units. Thus insulated, rightist forces made a strenuous effort to bring the entire border area under their control, but they were rebuffed in the coastal sector, which remained in Palestinian hands.

The formation of a new Israeli government under Likud's Menachem Begin in June 1977 resulted in an escalation of support for the Phalange-led Maronite militia, which now called for withdrawal of the Syrian-led ADF from Lebanese territory. As a result, the political situation during 1978 became more complex, and the level of conflict intensified. On March 15 Israeli forces invaded southern Lebanon in an attempt to "root out terrorist bases" that had supported a guerrilla raid four days earlier on the highway between Haifa and Tel Aviv. Less than a month later, the UN Security Council authorized the dispatch of an Interim Force in Lebanon (UNIFIL) to assist in restoring peace to the area.

On April 18, 1979, Maj. Saad HADDAD, commander of some 2,000 Christian militiamen loyal to the rightist Lebanese Front, proclaimed an "independent free Lebanese state" consisting of an eight-mile-wide strip of southern Lebanon along the Israeli border. The move was prompted by the deployment of units of the Lebanese Army, which Haddad had accused of complicity with both Syria and Palestinian guerrillas, alongside UNIFIL forces in the south. A week later, the Israeli government, which was providing matériel to Haddad's troops, announced that it would initiate preemptive strikes against terrorists in response to continuing infiltration from Lebanon. On June 6, in the context of increased Israeli shelling, "search-and-destroy" missions, and air strikes, the PLO and the National Movement stated that they would remove their forces from the port city of Tyre as well as villages throughout the south in order to protect the civilian population. In both June and September, Israeli and Syrian jet fighters dueled south of the Litani River (below the so-called red line, beyond which Israel refused to accept a Syrian presence), while UNIFIL forces were, at various times throughout the year, attacked by all sides, despite a series of UN-sponsored cease-fires. The situation was no better at Beirut and farther north. On the Right, Phalangist, National Liberal Party (NLP), Armenian, and Franjiyah loyalists clashed; on the Left, intrafactional fighting involved Nasserites, members of the Arab Socialist Union, 'Arafat's al-Fatah and other Palestinian groups, and forces of the Syrian Socialist Nationalist Party. Meanwhile, Syrian troops found themselves fighting elements of the Right, the Left, and increasingly militant pro-Iranian Shi'ites.

By mid-1981, in addition to the largely emasculated Lebanese military, the Syrian presence, and the sporadic incursion of Israeli units, it was estimated that more than 40 private armies were operating throughout the country, including al-Amal, a military wing of the Shi'ite community, which had grown to a force of some 30,000 men engaged largely in operations against the Palestinians and Lebanese leftist groups sympathetic to Iraq. The most important engagements during the first half of the year, however, occurred between Syrian forces and Phalangist militiamen at Beirut and at the strategically important town of Zahlé in the central part of the country. In the course of the fighting at Zahlé, the Israeli air force intervened to assist Phalangist forces against

Syrian air attacks. As Israeli attacks in Lebanon intensified and PLO guerrilla actions increased in Israel, US presidential envoy Philip Habib arranged a cease-fire between Israeli and PLO forces. The uneasy peace ended on June 6, 1982, when Israel again attacked PLO forces in Lebanon, supposedly in retaliation for an unsuccessful assassination attempt by a Palestinian gunman on the Israeli ambassador to Britain. In little more than a week, the Israeli army succeeded in encircling PLO forces in West Beirut while driving the Syrians back into the eastern Bekaa Valley. Subsequently, on August 6, US envoy Habib announced that agreement had been reached on withdrawal of the PLO from Lebanon, the actual evacuation commencing on August 21 and concluding on September 1.

On August 23, 1982, Maronite leader Bashir GEMAYEL was designated by the Lebanese Assembly to succeed President Sarkis; however, the president-elect was assassinated in a bombing of the Phalangist Party headquarters on September 14. His brother, Amin Pierre GEMAYEL, was named on September 21 as his replacement and was sworn in two days later. The new president promptly reappointed Prime Minister Wazzan, whose new government was announced on October 7.

The assassination of Bashir Gemayel was followed, September 16–18, 1982, by the massacre of numerous inhabitants of the Sabra and Shatila Palestinian refugee camps at Beirut, where a group of fighters had allegedly been left behind by the PLO. While the perpetrators of the massacre were right-wing Phalangist militiamen, they had been given access to the camps by Israeli authorities, whose de facto complicity generated intense controversy within Israel and widespread condemnation from abroad.

During late 1982 and early 1983 the presence of a multinational peacekeeping force of US, French, Italian, and British units helped stabilize the situation in the vicinity of Beirut, while direct negotiations between Israeli and Lebanese representatives yielded, with US participation, a troop withdrawal agreement on May 17, 1983, that included provision for the establishment of a "security region" in southern Lebanon. The agreement was strongly opposed by Lebanese Arab nationalists and by Syria,

which refused to discuss the withdrawal of its own forces from northern and eastern Lebanon, and Israel began construction in August of a defense line along the Awali River, to which it redeployed its troops in early September. The action was followed by a resurgence of militia activity in West Beirut, clashes between pro- and anti-Syrian groups in the northern city of Tripoli, and fighting between Druse and Phalangist forces in the Chouf Mountains and elsewhere.

A series of "national reconciliation" talks, involving all the leading factions, commenced at Geneva, Switzerland, in late September 1983, but they were adjourned six weeks later, following simultaneous bomb attacks on the headquarters of the US and French peacekeeping contingents at Beirut. Subsequently, the Western peacekeeping forces were withdrawn, and on March 5 Lebanon, under strong pressure from Syria, abrogated the unratified withdrawal accord concluded ten months earlier.

In March 1985 a rebellion broke out within the Lebanese Forces against the political leadership of the Phalange and its ostensible leader, Amin Gemayel. Deeply opposed to the president's close ties to Syria, the anti-Gemayel forces seized much of the Maronite-held sector of Beirut, the area around the port of Junieh, and the mountains north of the capital. The rebellion was led by Samir GEAGEA, a young Phalangist commander who had led the raid in which Tony Franjiyah had been slain in 1978. Geagea's forces, styled the "Independent Christian Decision Movement," called for a confederation of sectarian-based mini-states and rejected an appeal in April by 50 of Lebanon's senior Christian leaders for intercommunal talks to achieve national reconciliation. In May, reportedly under pressure from Syria, Phalangist officials removed Geagea as head of their executive committee; his successor, Elie HOBEIKA, who reportedly had commanded the forces that perpetrated the Sabra and Shatila massacres in 1982, immediately affirmed the "essential" Syrian role in Lebanon and Lebanon's place in the Arab world.

Within Muslim-controlled West Beirut, the Shi'ite *al-Amal* militia fought several battles against the Nasserite *al-Murabitun,* the

Palestinians, and its former ally, the Druse-led Progressive Socialist Party (PSP); it also continued the struggle against government forces across the Green Line in East Beirut. In April a coalition of *al-Amal* and PSP forces defeated *al-Murabitun* and seized control of West Beirut. Subsequently, *al-Amal* opened a campaign against Palestinian forces in Beirut and laid siege to two Palestinian refugee camps. The renewed "war of the camps" precipitated an emergency session of the Arab League Council in June, which called for a cease-fire, and, under pressure from Syria, *al-Amal* agreed to withdraw its forces.

While the siege of the camps was momentarily lifted, *al-Amal* and the PSP repeatedly clashed during the ensuing three months for control of Beirut. Damascus attempted to end the fighting between its Lebanese allies with a security plan drawn up under the auspices of Syrian vice president Khaddam in September. According to the plan, the Lebanese army and police would end the rule of sectarian militias in Beirut under supervision of Syrian observers. Earlier, although the various militias continued their struggle for control of the city, PSP leader Walid JUMBLATT and *al-Amal* chief Nabih BERRI had launched a National Unity Front that included the Lebanese Communist Party, the *Baath,* the PSNS, and 50 independent political leaders, several of them Christian. Formed under Syrian auspices, the Front called for a political program rejecting partition, confessionalism, or other division of the country.

In mid-September 1985 the northern city of Tripoli became the scene of some of the most violent clashes in the civil war. The chief protagonists were the Islamic Unification Movement, allied with pro-Arafat Palestinians against the pro-Syrian Arab Democratic Party. Although surrounded by Syrian forces, Tripoli had become the base of an anti-Syrian coalition that Damascus wished to destroy. As a result of the fighting, 80 percent of the city's 400,000 inhabitants fled.

Events in southern Lebanon were dominated by the redeployment of Israeli troops and its consequences. During the phased departure, militant Shi'ites stepped up guerrilla activity against the Israelis. In retaliation, as part of its "iron fist" policy, Israel seized several hundred men from Shi'ite villages and imprisoned them in Israel. To obtain their release, a fundamentalist Shi'ite faction hijacked an American TWA airliner en route from Athens to Rome, forced the plane to land at Beirut, and removed the passengers to various locations throughout the city. After 17 days the hostages were released through the intercession of *al-Amal* leader Berri. Concurrently, Israel began a gradual release of the Shi'ites, both the United States and Israel denying that there was any link between the two actions.

The departure of the Israelis precipitated bloody clashes among Shi'ites, PSP, Palestinian, and Maronite forces seeking to gain control of the evacuated areas. However, most Maronite and Palestinian forces were defeated, the southern part of the country falling largely under Shi'ites control, with PSP forces confined to traditionally Druse enclaves.

Although the Israeli occupation of Lebanon officially ended on June 6, 1985, numerous Israeli security advisors remained with the South Lebanese Army (SLA), which retained control of a narrow border strip, with Israel continuing its policy of hot pursuit of forces that continued their attacks on the SLA.

During 1986 the military alignments within Lebanon underwent substantial (in some cases remarkable) change. In January, following the conclusion of a December 28 "peace agreement" at Damascus between Druse leader Jumblatt, Shi'ite leader Berri, and Phalangist leader Hobeika, Lebanese Forces units commanded by Hobeika were decisively defeated in heavy fighting north and east of Beirut by hard-line Phalangists loyal to his predecessor, Samir Geagea. After Hobeika had fled to Paris (although returning within days to Damascus), both Jumblatt and Berri called for the removal of President Gemayel, who declared that he was "not the problem" and would refer the accord to the National Assembly, which contained a Christian majority. In the south, numerous clashes occurred in ensuing months between Palestinian and Lebanese groups, on the one hand, and opponents of the Israeli-backed SLA on the other, with increased anti-Israeli guerrilla activity by an "Islamic Resistance Front" that included the pro-Iranian *Hezbollah,* a radical Shi'ite group that had refused to endorse the December agreement. By the end of the year, it was apparent that the more moderate *al-Amal* had lost many of its militiamen to *Hezbollah.* Of greater consequence, however, was the reappearance of numerous PLO guerrillas, many of whom had returned via the Phalangist-controlled port of Junieh, north of Beirut. In November the Palestinians surged from refugee camps near Sidon and, in heavy fighting, forced *al-Amal* units to withdraw from hillside positions around the adjacent town of Maghdousheh. Druse leader Jumblatt, who had previously supported the Palestinians, immediately announced that his forces would join with other pro-Syrian leftist groups to "confront jointly any attempt by the Palestinians to expand outside their camps." By early 1987 the "war of the camps" had returned in the north, while fighting broke out at Beirut between Shi'ites and their intermittent Druse allies, prompting a renewed intervention by Syrian army forces to restore a semblance of order to the battle-scarred capital.

The assassination, in a helicopter bombing on June 1, 1987, of Prime Minister Karami reportedly shocked a country already traumatized by seemingly endless bloodshed. Although Karami had earlier declared his wish to resign because of an inability to resolve the nation's political and economic crises, he had been one of Lebanon's most durable and widely respected Muslim leaders.

The most important development during the latter half of 1987 was the increased influence of *Hezbollah,* which had supplanted *al-Amal* in many of the poorer Shi'ite areas, particularly in the south. During early 1988 the group also moved to augment its strength in the suburbs of West Beirut, provoking violent clashes with *al-Amal* that were contained in May by the second deployment of Syrian army units to the area in 15 months. Further conflict between the two Shi'ite groups broke out in southern Lebanon in October and at Beirut in early January 1989, after *al-Amal* had entered into a peace agreement with the PLO. However, on January 30,

during a meeting convened at Damascus by high-level Syrian and Iranian representatives, a cease-fire was concluded, under which *Hezbollah* agreed to accept *al-Amal*'s primacy in the south.

Meanwhile, the political process in Lebanon had come to a virtual standstill. The National Assembly failed to secure a quorum to elect a successor to President Gemayel, despite a compromise agreement at Damascus on September 21, 1988, in support of a Christian deputy, Michel DAHER. Maronite leaders immediately denounced Syrian "imposition" of the candidate, and, bowing to pressure before leaving office on September 22, Gemayel appointed an interim military government headed by Gen. Michel AOUN, the commander-in-chief of the Lebanese Army. Pro-Syrian Muslim groups responded by branding the action a military coup and pledged their continued support of the Huss administration, which, following the resignation of its Christian members, continued to function on a caretaker basis in Muslim West Beirut.

Bitter fighting resumed between Lebanese Army and Muslim forces at Beirut in March 1989 in the wake of an attempted Christian naval blockade of ports controlled by Druse and Muslim militias, with General Aoun declaring a "war of liberation" against Syria. Fighting subsequently broke out between units of the Lebanese Army reporting to Aoun and Geagea's Lebanese Forces, placing Lebanese civil war for the first time squarely within the Christian community.

In late September 1989, 62 of the 70 survivors of the 99-member Assembly elected in 1972 met at Taif, Saudi Arabia, to discuss a peace plan put forward by the Arab League that called for transfer of most executive powers of the traditionally Maronite Christian president to the Sunni Muslim prime minister, an end of sectarianism in the civil and military services, and an increase in legislative seats to permit more accurate representation of the country's varied socio-religious groupings. Aoun rejected the plan in late October because it did not call for an immediate Syrian troop withdrawal. Nevertheless, the assembly members convened at the northern town of Qlaiaat on November 5 to ratify the Taif accord and elect René MOUAWAD as the new president. Less than three weeks later, on November 17, President Mouawad was assassinated, with the legislators assembling again on November 24 to elect Ilyas HRAWI as his successor. On the following day Prime Minister Huss formed a new government that was carefully balanced between Muslim and Christian officeholders.

Despite Aoun's objection, President Hrawi on September 21, 1990, approved a series of constitutional amendments implementing the Taif accord, and in mid-October Lebanese and Syrian forces ousted the renegade general from his stronghold in East Beirut. Subsequently, most other militia units withdrew from the vicinity of the capital, and on December 20 Hrawi asked 'Umar KARAMI, the brother of the former prime minister, to form a "government of the second republic," the composition of which was announced on December 24 and accorded a parliamentary vote of confidence on January 9, 1991.

In early 1992 a severe decline in the value of the Lebanese pound yielded an escalation in prices that triggered mass protests by consumers. With no relief forthcoming, the Confederation of Trade Unions (CTU) launched a general strike on May 6 (the fourth in two months), in response to which Prime Minister Karami submitted his government's resignation. On May 7 the CTU suspended the strike, and on May 16 Rashid al-Sulh, who had served as prime minister 17 years earlier, formed a new government that won a vote of confidence from the National Assembly on May 29. On October 31, following the country's first general election in 21 years, Rafiq HARIRI, a wealthy businessman who held dual Lebanese-Saudi citizenship, formed a predominantly "technocratic" administration that contained representatives of most of the former militias with the conspicuous exception of *Hezbollah* and the (Maronite) Lebanese Forces.

In mid-July 1993 Israel launched an extensive bombing campaign of both military and civilian targets in and north of its self-proclaimed security zone in response to a series of attacks by Palestinian and *Hezbollah* forces opposed to the Middle East peace talks. In early August regular Lebanese army units, with apparent backing by both the US and Syrian governments, were deployed to the south in an effort to maintain a cease-fire that had taken somewhat tenuous effect on July 31. However, additional clashes in late August included two *Hezbollah* ambushes that yielded a number of Israeli deaths and renewed Israeli air strikes against *Hezbollah* installations. In mid-November the guerrillas launched a major offensive against SLA positions.

On October 17, 1995, the Assembly approved a "one-time" amendment to the constitutional provision limiting presidents to a single six-year term, President's Hrawi's stay in office thereby being extended for three years (until November 24, 1998). Legislative elections were held in August and September 1996, with progovernment (and by implication, Syrian-backed) candidates dominating. However, the balloting generated much more controversy than expected by those promoting the country's new "democratic" orientation. Among other things, the government was accused of intimidating and/or bribing voters, unconstitutionally restructuring the sensitive Mount Lebanon voting district, and harassing opponents, who pointed to the presence of some 35,000 Syrian soldiers as evidence of how limited Lebanese autonomy really was. Following the election, Hrawi invited Hariri on October 24 to form a new government. However, the cabinet was not announced until November 7, Syrian intervention having reportedly been required to settle differences among Hrawi, Hariri, and Berri regarding ministerial seats. Although some new cabinet members were appointed, the changes did not appear to reflect any significant revision of government philosophy. Following Hrawi's policy statement to the Assembly, in which he emphasized continued "economic recovery" and support for the "liberation" of the Israeli-occupied area of southern Lebanon, the government received a 102–19 vote of confidence from the legislators.

Labor unrest in March 1996 prompted the government to impose, rather heavy-handedly, a state of emergency banning public demonstrations of any sort. Also during the first part of the year the self-perpetuating cycle of attacks and retaliatory strikes between *Hezbollah* guerrillas and Israeli forces intensified, and on April 11 the Israel government launched the Grapes of Wrath campaign against suspected *Hezbollah* locations throughout southern Lebanon and even on the outskirts of Beirut. More than two weeks of Israeli air raids and shelling displaced some 400,000 people, caused widespread damage, and left more than 200 Lebanese civilians dead. Many of the casualties occurred when Israeli rockets hit a UN Palestinian refugee camp at Qana; although Israel (facing severe international criticism) claimed the incident had been a mistake arising from "technical errors," UN personnel assigned to review the matter concluded that the Israeli interpretation was difficult to accept. In any event, a five-nation monitoring group (France, Israel, Lebanon, Syria, and the United States) was established to oversee a "cease-fire" against civilian targets brokered as of April 26.

Heavy fighting resumed in 1997 in southern Lebanon, as it became apparent that *Hezbollah*'s military capacity had increased to the point of making an indefinite standoff possible. At the same time, Israeli public opinion turned against their military's involvement in Lebanon, the death of 73 soldiers in a February helicopter crash helping convince many Israelis that they had become mired in their own "Vietnam."

Domestic political attention in the first half of 1998 focused on the first municipal balloting in 35 years, scheduled for May and June and including the Christian parties, many of which had boycotted the 1992 and 1996 elections. Observers described the voting as "fairly clean," an important assessment for the nation's fledgling democratic system in view of the controversy surrounding the 1996 national poll. On October 15 the National Assembly unanimously elected Gen. Emile LAHOUD, the army chief of staff, as the next head of state. (Lahoud had been made eligible for the post the day before, when the Assembly eliminated the constitutional provision that required state officials to resign their positions six months prior to running for office.) Following his inauguration on November 24, Lahoud asked Hariri to stay on as head of a new cabinet, but the prime

minister ultimately declined over what he described as Lahoud's "inappropriate" involvement in the selection of ministers. Lahoud therefore on December 2 appointed former prime minister Huss to the post for the fourth time; the new "technocratic" cabinet (containing only two incumbents) was announced on December 4 and received the required legislative vote of confidence on December 17, following several days of intense debate on Huss's economic proposals.

In May 2000, Israeli forces unilaterally withdrew from southern Lebanon. (Earlier in the year at Shepherdstown, West Virginia, Israel and Syria had held unsuccessful meetings.) Within weeks, the United Nations demarcated a "line of withdrawal" between Lebanese territory on the one side and Israel and the Golan Heights on the other and declared Israel's withdrawal complete. *Hezbollah* claimed, however, that the "Shab'a farms," a 25-square-kilometer patch of land on the Israeli-occupied Golan Heights, was actually part of Lebanon and that continued "resistance" to "Israeli occupation" was therefore justified. Under pressure from *Hezbollah* and Syria, the Lebanese government officially voiced claims to Shab'a farms, thus endorsing the "resistance," and declined to post Lebanese army troops to the border with Israel and the Golan Heights.

Later in 2000 national elections brought *Hezbollah* into parliament and Rafiq Hariri back to the premiership. Over the next three years, Syria would gradually reduce the public profile of its military presence in Lebanon by moving forces from Beirut to the Biqa' Valley and by reducing the overall size of its Lebanese contingent, all the while strengthening its political and economic domination of the country. Meanwhile, *Hezbollah* fighters harassed Israeli forces in the Shab'a farms area and responded to Israeli military overflights by sending unpiloted drones into Israeli airspace and firing antiaircraft guns at angles that permitted debris to rain down on Israeli border towns.

In March 2002 Syrian president Bashar al-Assad made an official visit to Lebanon, calling on his close ally President Lahoud. Relations between Lahoud and Prime Minister Hariri, never good,

deteriorated steadily during their joint incumben-
cies, with neither man inclined to demonstrate ci-
vility toward the other. Hariri had employed part
of his vast personal fortune in spearheading the reconstruction of downtown Beirut, increasing the
country's national debt and bruising many egos in
the process. Lahoud (and Syria) tolerated Hariri's
premiership out of grudging respect for his ties to
France, Saudi Arabia, and the United States and his
ability to prime the pump of economic reconstruction.

By mid-2004 speculation ran rife concerning
who would succeed Lahoud. By August Syria had
made the decision: Emile Lahoud would remain in
office three years beyond his legal mandate (thus
requiring amendment of the constitution). Hariri
bitterly opposed the extension, but was ordered by
Assad to comply. He did so but subsequently resigned, setting in motion a dramatic series of events
leading ultimately to his assassination (see Current
issues below).

Constitution and Government

Lebanon's constitution, promulgated May 23,
1926, and often amended, established a unitary republic with an indirectly elected president, a unicameral legislature elected by universal suffrage,
and an independent judiciary. Under the National
Pact of 1943, the principal offices of state were
divided among members of the different religious communities. The president, traditionally a
Maronite Christian, is elected by a two-thirds majority of the legislature, while the prime minister is
a Sunni Muslim formally nominated by the president following endorsement by a legislative majority. The Taif Accord provides for an equal number
of Christian and Muslim parliamentary deputies.
The National Assembly is composed of 128 seats.

Lebanon is administratively divided into six
provinces (*muhafazat*), each with a presidentially
appointed governor who rules through a Provincial
Council. The judicial system is headed by 4 courts
of cassation and includes 11 courts of appeal and
numerous courts of the first instance. Specialized
bodies deal with administrative matters (Council

of State) and with the security of the state (Court
of Justice) and also include religious courts and a
press tribunal.

Foreign Relations

A member of the United Nations and the Arab
League, Lebanon has traditionally pursued a foreign policy reflecting its self-image as a democratic Arab state with a significant Christian population, a country serving as a "bridge" between
the West and the balance of the Arab world. From
1948 until 1975 the salient characteristics of this
approach were good relations with the West (particularly the United States and France), a correct but
arm's-length relationship with Arab nationalists
and the Palestinian resistance, a cordial (if wary)
relationship with Syria, and conflict avoidance with
Israel.

During the first three decades of its existence,
Lebanon's foreign policy aimed squarely at preserving domestic tranquility. In 1948 the country
participated in the first Arab–Israeli war but did
the absolute minimum in terms of combat. Its 1949
armistice with Israel restored the 1922 Palestine–
Lebanon border as an armistice demarcation line.
Although Lebanon and Israel remained techni-
cally at war, the Israel-Lebanon Mixed Armistice
Commission under UN auspices was a model of
Arab–Israeli cooperation. For nearly 20 years the
Lebanese–Israeli frontier was unfenced and quite
peaceful. Lebanon avoided involvement in the
Arab–Israeli wars of 1956, 1967, and 1973.

The catastrophic defeat of Arab armies in the
June 1967 war and the rise of an independent Palestinian resistance movement posed a new and ultimately mortal challenge to Lebanon's foreign policy. In 1948 some 100,000 Palestinian refugees
had made their way into Lebanon to be housed in
UN-run camps. In the late 1960s and early 1970s
Palestinian fighters from these camps and from Jordan and Syria began to establish a "state within
a state" in southern Lebanon, a largely Shi'ite
area of subsistence farms and poor villages all
but neglected by Lebanon's Christian, Sunni, and
Druse political elite. The Lebanese government

tried simultaneously to appease Palestinian fighters intent upon raiding and firing into Israel while persuading Israel (through the West) that it harbored no aggressive intent and was itself a victim.

Growing Palestinian–Israeli violence exposed deep fissures in Lebanon's body politic, as Muslims and Druse generally sympathized with Palestinian fighters while Christians (especially Maronites) generally resented the Palestinian presence. Lebanon's descent into civil war in 1975 reflected the failure of foreign policy to preserve domestic tranquility in a country lacking consensus on the vital issue of national identity.

Lebanon's reputation for moderation and its tradition of effective participation in the United Nations made it the object of international interest, sympathy, and occasional intervention during its 15-year civil war. UN observers were deployed to the southern part of the country before, during, and after Israel's 1982 invasion. Multinational forces consisting mainly of American and French troops tried to stabilize the country in 1982 and 1983. The UN Secretariat exerted considerable effort in 2000 to confirm the full withdrawal of Israeli forces from Lebanon by actually drawing a "line of withdrawal."

In the end, however, Syrian intervention and influence proved decisive. From 1990 to 2005 Syria was Lebanon's suzerain, and Lebanese foreign policy reflected Syria's vital interests. Lebanon's traditional inclination toward warm relations with the West manifested itself clearly whenever Syria's normally frigid relationship with the West thawed. Yet when Syrian interests dictated that the Lebanese government endorse *Hezbollah*'s "resistance" to Israeli occupation–even after the occupation ended in May 2000–the government complied without objection. Israel's unilateral withdrawal from Lebanon had seemingly robbed Syria of a convenient way to remind Israel–through violence along the Lebanon–Israel frontier–that there could be no peace without the return of the Golan Heights. When *Hezbollah* and Syria claimed that the Shab'a farms, a small piece of the Golan Heights, was actually part of Lebanon and therefore an appropriate object of continued

"resistance," the Lebanese government supinely complied, although a map of Lebanon on the country's currency clearly showed the Shab'a farms to be part of the Israeli-occupied Golan Heights–that is, part of Syria.

The adoption of UN Security Council Resolution 1559 in September 2004 also placed the Lebanese government in an awkward position with the international community. The government objected to the UN demand for the removal of Syrian forces until Syria itself decided to end its military presence there. Even after elections in June 2005 produced a majority opposed to Syrian suzerainty, the resolution's call for the disarmament of militias presented a potentially explosive dilemma. *Hezbollah*'s electoral success among Lebanon's Shi'ite community and its decision to join a cabinet headed by Fouad Siniora seemed to dictate that the incoming government would continue to define the party's armed wing as the "Lebanese resistance" rather than a "militia," thereby raising the possibility of increasing tensions between Lebanon's freely elected, post-"Syrian occupation" government and the West–particularly the United States, which considers *Hezbollah* a terrorist organization.

Three decades after the outbreak of bloody and destructive civil war, it was not at all clear that Lebanese foreign policy would return to the pro-Western, bridge-building approach of the republic's first three decades. National identity remains Lebanon's fundamental crisis and a weak, shifting foundation on which to build a steady, consistent foreign policy.

Current Issues

National legislative elections in June 2005 and the announcement of a new cabinet on July 19 under Prime Minister Fouad Siniora completed a turbulent cycle of events launched in August 2004, when Syria dictated the extension of President Emile Lahoud's term in office. Syrian heavy-handedness produced UN Security Council Resolution 1559, calling for the withdrawal of foreign forces, free elections, and the disarmament of the militias. Lebanon's parliament nonetheless approved Lahoud's extension, and Prime Minister Hariri resigned and began organizing opposition to Syria. Lahoud immediately appointed veteran politician Omar Karami as prime minister.

On February 14, 2005, Hariri was killed by a massive explosion that tore through his motorcade in Beirut. Suspicion, both within Lebanon and internationally, focused immediately on the Syrian and Lebanese intelligence services, bringing massive crowds of Lebanese protesters into the streets of Beirut and increasing pressure on Syria to withdraw its military forces and intelligence operatives. Two weeks after the Hariri assassination, Karami resigned and was ultimately replaced on April 19 by Najib Mikati, who formed a caretaker government to oversee national elections.

International pressure and Lebanese protesters obliged Syria to withdraw the last of its forces on April 26. A UN team verified the withdrawal on May 23. Meanwhile, retired general Michel Aoun, an arch foe of Syria, returned to a hero's welcome after 14 years in exile and announced his intention to compete in the forthcoming elections. Soon thereafter, Saad Hariri, the son of the assassinated former prime minister, unveiled his own list of candidates in alliance with Walid Jumblatt. Unable to agree with Hariri and Jumblatt on terms for a unified list of anti-Syrian candidates, Aoun formed his own list in alliance with pro-Syrian Christian politicians from the north of Lebanon.

National elections produced mixed results. The Hariri list won 72 of parliament's 128 seats. Yet Aoun emerged as Lebanon's leading Maronite political figure, Hezbollah increased its parliamentary strength in alliance with *al-Amal*, and Lebanon's Maronite community (led by its patriarch) seemed to be insisting that the widely reviled Lahoud be kept in office as a symbol of Christian political status, notwithstanding his close relationship with Syria. Confusion over Lebanon's political direction was punctuated by car bombings that killed journalist Samir Qaseer and former Communist Party leader George Hawi (both critics of Syria) and injured caretaker defense minister Elias Murr, an erstwhile ally of Syria who had backed Aoun in the election.

For the first time in nearly 35 years Lebanese territory was essentially free of foreign–that is, Israeli, Palestinian, and Syrian–forces, except for UN contingents in the country's south. Although it seemed unlikely that the civil war of 1975–1990 would reignite, it seemed equally clear that the fundamental conditions that nearly destroyed Lebanon–ongoing Arab–Israeli violence and a lack of national unity–had not been rectified.

In Lebanon's recent past, Palestinians and Syrians had used Lebanese territory to press their respective claims against Israel. With the withdrawal of Syrian forces in the spring of 2005, anti-Israeli activity revolved more intensely around *Hezbollah,* a Lebanese political movement rooted in the country's Shi'ite community but linked closely to Iran and Syria. *Hezbollah* seemed intent on maintaining its status as a Muslim, Shi'ite, Arab, and Lebanese organization in the forefront of "resistance" to Israeli "occupation," resisting international pressure to disarm while insisting that it was not a "militia" in the context of Resolution 1559. Although the focus of *Hezbollah*'s "resistance" rested on the Shab'a farms, a small sector of the Israeli-occupied Golan Heights, the organization also characterized itself as a leading actor in efforts to "liberate" Jerusalem, defeat Israel's occupation of Palestinian (and Syrian) lands, and facilitate the return of Palestinian refugees. By increasing its representation in Lebanon's parliament and agreeing to take a cabinet position (minister of electricity and water) in the Siniora government, *Hezbollah* seemed to be adopting the tactic of "burrowing" into Lebanon's political system in order to resist and deflect pressure to disarm. This raised the possibility that Lebanon–normally the subject of sympathetic, anti-Syrian resolutions raised in the US Congress–might eventually become a target of US economic sanctions if it "failed" to disarm *Hezbollah* or simply did not try hard to do so.

Regardless, any autonomous Lebanese effort to disarm *Hezbollah* seemed out of the question. It enjoyed widespread support among Lebanon's largest sect and commanded grudging respect from the others. Although the elections of June 2005 had produced a parliamentary majority formally in opposition to Syrian suzerainty and a Maronite leader who had plagued Syria in exile, it did not produce the one key ingredient that has eluded Lebanon for its entire existence: national unity. While opposition to Syrian excesses had produced a kind of unity among most Christian, Sunni, and Druse Lebanese, Lebanon's Shi'ites overwhelmingly supported the pro-Syrian positions of *Hezbollah* and *al-Amal*. Moreover, the ground rules and conduct of the election itself drove a wedge deep within the anti-Syrian opposition, pulling Maronites away from their erstwhile allies among the Sunni, Druse, and other Christian sects. Clearly, the Siniora government will have its hands full maintaining a modicum of national consensus in the face of an embittered Syria and an uneasy Israel. To try to forcibly disarm a military-capable *Hezbollah* represented a nonstarter. To achieve disarmament through negotiation seemed equally unlikely.

Indeed, the salient majority in Lebanon's newly elected parliament was not a dedicated band of anti-Syrian nationalists, but a wide array of sect-based politicians belonging to or representing the traditional political families, most of whom had worked closely with Syria in the past to maintain their long-held privileges. While opposition to Syria had brought the Lebanese flag out into the streets, including in the hands of pro-Syrian *Hezbollah* demonstrators, there seemed to be no positive theme emerging on which to build a sense of Lebanese national identity of citizenship superseding the primordial identities of sect, clan, and locality.

Even in the wake of elections that seemed to have been conducted honestly and openly, Lebanon remained a loose mosaic of sects and political chieftains instead of a nation. Lebanon's greatest challenges will be to surmount chronic disunity and mediocre political "leadership" and to maintain domestic tranquility, implement economic reform, and steer clear of its more powerful neighbors. For the talented young professionals who spearheaded the opposition to Syrian suzerainty, building a civil society (including real political parties) across sectarian lines would be the key to living in a viable

nation or leaving, in large numbers, a dying fragment of the Ottoman Empire to pursue productive lives elsewhere.

Political Parties and Groups

Lebanese parties have traditionally been ethnic and denominational groupings, rather than parties in the Western sense, with seats in the National Assembly distributed primarily on a religious, rather than on a party, basis.

Phalangist Party (*al-Kata'ib al-Lubnaniyah/ Phalanges Libanaises*). Founded in 1936 by Pierre Gemayel, the Phalangist Party, a militant Maronite organization and the largest member of the Lebanese Front, was deeply involved in provoking the 1975 civil war. Phalangist leader Amin Gemayel became president of Lebanon in 1982, following the assassination of his brother, Bashir Gemayel. Amin Gemayel went into exile in 1988 at the end of his term, after which the Phalangist movement lost direction and broke into different factions, thus losing its predominant role in the Lebanese political landscape.

Amin Gemayel returned to Lebanon in mid-2000 and subsequently accused other leaders of the Phalangist Party of being "too cooperative" with Syria. The party today has effectively split into two groups—one that supports Karim Paqraduni and one that backs Amin Gemayel's Kata'ib Corrective Movement, which takes a strong anti-Syrian stance.

Lebanese Forces Party. Organized as a Maronite militia by Bashir Gemayel in 1976 and subsequently commanded by Samir Geagea, the Lebanese Forces was licensed as a political party in 1991. In March 1994 the party was banned, and a number of members (including Geagea's deputy, Fouad MALIK) were arrested because of alleged involvement in the February bombing of a Maronite church north of Beirut. On April 21 Geagea was arrested and charged with complicity in the November 1990 assassination of Maronite rival Dany Chamoun. In June 1995 Geagea and a codefendant, Karim KARAM, were found guilty and sentenced to death for the 1990 killing, but the sentences were immediately commuted to life imprisonment at hard labor. Subsequently, in 1996, Geagea was also charged with the assassination of Prime Minister Karami in 1987. In the 2005 elections the Lebanese Forces Party was part of the anti-Syrian coalition led by the son of assassinated prime minister Rafiq Hariri. Following the election, the Lebanese parliament passed legislation to release Geagea from prison.

Al-Wa'ad Party. The al-Wa'ad Party was formed in 1991 by members of the Lebanese Forces loyal to Elie HOBEIKA, the pro-Syrian former chairman of the militia's Executive Committee. Hobeika was assassinated in a bomb attack in Beirut in January 2002, while another party leader, Jean GHANEM, died the same month in a car crash considered suspicious by his supporters.

Leader: Jina HOBEIKA.

Free Patriotic Movement (*Tayyar al-Watani al-Horr*). This party is led by Michel Aoun, former general in the Lebanese Army who served as the provisional prime minister of one of two governments that contended for power in the final years of the civil war. Most of its leadership and support comes from Lebanon's Christian community. Aoun led the FPM from abroad while he was exiled in Paris. He returned to Lebanon in May 2005 to run in the legislative elections held in May and June. The Free Patriotic Movement and its allies won 21 seats in the 128-member National Assembly.

National Liberal Party (*Hizb al-Ahrar al-Watani/Parti National Libéral*–NLP). The NLP, a largely Maronite right-wing grouping founded in 1958, rejected any coalition with Muslim groups with Palestinian involvement. It repeatedly called for the withdrawal of Syrian and other Arab troops from Lebanon and argued that only a federal system could preserve the country's unity. Periodic clashes between NLP and Phalangist militias culminated in early July 1980 in a major defeat for National Liberal forces.

The NLP has lost considerable influence over the last decade, despite the return from exile of its leader Dory Chamoun in 1998, the older brother of former leader Dany Chamoun, who was assassinated in October 1990. In 2005 Dory Chamoun became a prominent figure in demands for the withdrawal of Syrian forces from Lebanon, and the NLP participated in that year's parliamentary elections.

National Bloc (*al-Kutla al-Wataniyah/Bloc National*). The National Bloc, a Maronite party formed in 1943, has been opposed to military involvement in politics. In 2005 parliamentary elections, the bloc became part of the anti-Syrian coalition.

Leaders: Carlos EDDE, Antoine KLIMOS (General Secretary).

Future Movement (*Tayyar al Mustaqbal*). Formed by the late Rafiq Hariri after he resigned from the post of prime minister(to protest the extension of President Lahoud's tenure, this movement became the largest bloc in the anti-Syrian coalition that successfully competed in the 2005 National Assembly elections. It is now led by Saad Hariri, the former prime minister's son.

Progressive Socialist Party (*al-Hizb al-Taqaddumi al-Ishtiraki/Parti Socialiste Progressif*–PSP). Founded in 1948, the PSP is a largely Druse group that advocates a socialist program with nationalist and anti-Western overtones. Relations between former party president Kamal Jumblatt and President Assad of Syria soured in the 1970s, before the Syrian intervention of April 1976. Jumblatt was assassinated in March 1977, and the party leadership shifted to his son, Walid, who subsequently became a Syrian ally and during the Israeli occupation established close ties with the Shi'ite *al-Amal* organization (see below). The alliance ended in early 1987, when the PSP intervened on the side of the PLO in the war of the camps in Beirut. The PSP became steadily more vocal in its opposition to the Syrian presence in Lebanon and opposed the three-year extension given by the National Assembly for President Lahoud's term. The PSP became part of the broad anti-Syrian coalition in the 2005 parliamentary elections.

Syrian Socialist Nationalist Party (*Parti Socialiste Nationaliste Syrien*–PSNS). Organized as the Syrian Nationalist Party in 1932 in support of a "Greater Syria" embracing Iraq, Jordan, Lebanon, Syria, and Palestine, the PSNS was considered a rightist group until 1970. Also known as the Syrian People's Party, it was banned from 1962 to 1969 after participating in an attempted coup in December 1961. The party split into two factions in 1974; one group, led by 'Abdallah SAADA, subsequently joined the National Movement, and the other, led by George KENIZEH and Issam MAHAYRI, participated in the pro-Syrian Nationalist Front. In November 1978 its leadership announced that the party had been reunited.

Arab Socialist Renaissance Party (*Hizb al-Baath al-Arabi al-Ishtiraki*). *Al-Baath*, a pan-Arab secular party, split into competing factions as a result of the Syrian intervention in 1976. Pro-Iraqi leader Musa SHA'IB was assassinated in July 1980, apparently by pro-Iranian Shi'ites.

Lebanese Communist Party (*al-Hizb al-Shuyui al-Lubnani/Parti Communiste Libanais*–LCP). The LCP was founded in 1924 as the Lebanese People's Party, banned in 1939 by the French Mandate Authority, but legalized in 1970. Although primarily Christian in the first half-century of its existence, the party became predominantly Muslim in the wake of the civil war. Its long-time secretary general, George Hawi, also served as a vice president of the National Movement. In January 1999, at its eighth congress, the LCP re-elected Faruq Dahruj as secretary general, while Hawi was named president of the party's National Congress. In June 2005 Hawi was assassinated, making him the third highly visible anti-Syrian identity in Lebanon to be killed in that year.

Movement of the Deprived (*al-Amal*). Most familiarly known by the name of its militia, *al-Amal*, an acronym for *Afwaj al-Muqawa al-Lubnaniyya* (Groups of the Lebanese Resistance), which also means "hope," the movement was founded by Imam Musa SADR, an Iranian who disappeared in August 1978 while in Libya. Although allied with the Palestinian Left during the civil war, *al-Amal* subsequently became increasingly

militant on behalf of Lebanon's Shi'ites, many of whom had been forced from their homes in the south, and in support of the Iranian revolution of 1979.

After the 1982 Israeli invasion, several pro-Iranian offshoots of *al-Amal* emerged as well-organized guerrilla movements, among of them *Hezbollah,* which operated against US, French, and Israeli forces with great effectiveness.

A "war of words" developed between *al-Amal* and *Hezbollah* prior to the 1996 legislative balloting, and it initially appeared that they would present competing candidates (unlike in 1992). However, reportedly under pressure from Syrian leaders, the two groups finally agreed (a week before the balloting) on a joint Accord and National List, which secured nearly all the seats in southern Lebanon. *Al-Amal* leader Nabih Berri was subsequently re-elected Speaker of the National Assembly. *Al-Amal* has been largely disarmed in recent years, as *Hezbollah* presented the primary military opposition to Israeli forces in southern Lebanon. Following the parliamentary elections of 2005, Berri was reelected speaker on the National Assembly. Most of *al-Amal*'s support today comes from coastal cities in Lebanon's south.

Leaders: Nabih BERRI (President of the Party and Speaker of the National Assembly).

Party of God (*Hizb Allah,* commonly rendered as *Hezbollah*). *Hezbollah* rose to prominence in the mid-1980s, when it engaged in a bitter power struggle with its parent, *al-Amal,* and subsequently became involved in the kidnapping of numerous Westerners. The group participated for the first time as an electoral party in the balloting of August–September 1993.

Hezbollah subsequently assumed the major role in the "war of liberation" against Israeli forces in southern Lebanon. It was widely believed to be financed by Syria and Iran. By 1996, however, *Hezbollah* was thought to have earned significant grassroots support within the Shi'ite populace because of its network of health and other social services and might therefore be less "subservient" to Syria. At the time, *Hezbollah* bowed to pressure from Damascus in agreeing, at the last minute, to present joint candidates with *al-Amal* for the 1996 legislative balloting.

Although *Hezbollah* formally endorsed the "liberation" of Jerusalem through *jihad* (holy war) and condemned Western culture and political influence, its primary goal was the withdrawal of Israeli troops from southern Lebanon. Following the unilateral withdrawal of Israeli forces from southern Lebanon in 2000, *Hezbollah* was widely viewed in the Middle East as having engineered the first Arab "victory" in the long-standing conflict with Israel.

In late 2001 the United States, having included *Hezbollah* on its list of terrorist organizations, called on countries to freeze *Hezbollah*'s financial assets. Washington cited continuing, albeit significantly reduced, conflict between *Hezbollah* and Israeli forces and reports of the transfer of missiles to *Hezbollah* from Iran and Syria. However, as expected, the Lebanese government rejected the US demand, calling *Hezbollah*'s anti-Israeli stance legitimate "resistance" and praising the organization for its social programs. The European Union also declined to include *Hezbollah* on the list of organizations that it considers supportive of terrorism.

The adoption of UNSC Resolution 1559, which calls for "the disbanding and disarmament of all Lebanese and non-Lebanese militias," put pressure on *Hezbollah,* particularly after the assassination of Rafiq Hariri. However, *Hezbollah* performed well in the 2005 parliamentary elections, winning 35 seats as part of a coalition with *al-Amal.* In July 2005 *Hezbollah* agreed to join a government, heading a ministry for the first time.

Leaders: Sheikh Mohammad Hossein FADLALLAH (Spiritual Leader), Ibrahim MUSSAWI, Sheikh Nabil QAOUK (Military Commander), Sheikh Naim QASSEM, Sheikh Hassan NASRALLAH (Secretary General).

Among the more important smaller leftist parties are Mustafa SAAD's **Popular Nasserite Organization;** the predominately Sunni Muslim **Lebanese People's Congress,** led by Kamal SHATILA; the **Movement for Democratic Renewal** (MDR), launched in April 2001 by legislator Nassib LAHOUD as a nonsectarian party devoted to abolition of the confessional system and to development of "more balanced" ties with Syria; and the **People's Movement,** a secular party led by former Nasserite Najah WAKIM. Sunni Muslim groups include the **Islamic Unification Movement,** whose *Tawheed* militia has coordinated activity with *Hezbollah* in southern Lebanon.

Other Groups

Armenian Revolutionary Federation (*Parti Dashnak*–ARF). The federation, a socialist Armenian party with a past history of anti-Soviet activity, was allied with Maronite groups in 1958 but, along with a number of leftist Armenian organizations, remained politically neutral during the civil war. The Armenian population is also currently represented by the **Hunchak Party,** a social-democratic grouping led by Vahrij JERIJIAN.

Leader: Sebouh HOVNANIAN (General Secretary).

Note: For a discussion of Palestinian groups formerly headquartered in Lebanon, see article on the PLO at the end of the National Governments section.

Legislature

The former Chamber of Deputies, which in March 1979 changed its name to the **National Assembly** (*Majlis al-'Umma/Assemblée Nationale*), is a unicameral body elected by universal suffrage for a four-year term (subject to dissolution) through a proportional system based on religious groupings. The National Pact of 1943 specified that the presiding officer of the body be a Shi'ite Muslim. The distribution of seats was on the basis of a 6:5 Christian:Muslim ratio until 1990 when, in implementation of a provision of the Taif accord, the total number of seats was raised from 99 to 108, with half being assigned to each group. That ratio was maintained in 1996, when the number of seats was increased to 128.

Candidates are not presented as nominees of political parties, but rather on lists supportive of

Cabinet

Prime Minister	Fouad Siniora (Sunni, Future Movement)
Vice-Prime Minister	Elias Murr (Greek Orthodox, Lahoud ally)

Ministers

Agriculture	Talal al-Sahili (Shi'ite, *al-Amal* ally)
Culture	Tarek Mitri (Greek Orthodox, independent)
Defense	Elias Murr (Greek Orthodox, Lahoud ally)
Displaced	Nehmé Tohmé (Greek Catholic, Progressive Socialist Party)
Economy and Trade	Sami Haddad (Maronite, independent)
Education and Higher Education	Khaled Kabbani (Sunni, Future Movement ally)
Energy and Water	Mohamed Fneich (Shi'ite, *Hezbollah*)
Environment	Yacoub Sarraf (Greek Orthodox, Lahoud ally)
Finance	Jihad Azour (Maronite, independent)
Foreign Affairs and Emigrants	Fawzi Salloukh (Shi'ite, independent)
Industry	Pierre Gemayel (Maronite, Kataìb Corrective Movement)
Information	Ghazi Aridi (Druse, Progressive Socialist Party)
Interior	Hassan Sabaa (Sunni, Future Movement ally)
Justice	Charles Rizk (Maronite, Lahoud ally)
Labor	Trad Kenj Hamadé (Shi'ite, *Hezbollah* ally)
Public Health	Mohamed Jawad Khalifé (Shi'ite, *al-Amal* ally)
Public Works and Transportation	Mohamed Safadi (Sunni, Future Movementally)
Social Affairs	Nayla Mouawad (Maronite, Qornet Chehouane) [f]
Telecommunications	Marwan Hamadé (Druse, Progressive Socialist Party)
Tourism	Joseph Sarkis (Maronite, Lebanese Forces)
Youth and Sports	Ahmad Fatfat (Sunni, Future Movement)

Ministers of State

Administrative Development	Jean Ogassabian (Armenian Orthodox, Future Movement)
Parliamentary Affairs	Michel Pharaon (Greek Catholic, Future Movement)
[f] = female	

prominent politicians or alliances of political organizations. An anti-Syrian coalition polled successfully in the 2005 elections, winning 72 of 128 seats. Hezbollah, *al-Amal,* and their allies won 35 seats while 21 seats went to Michel Aoun's Free Patriotic Movement. *Al-Amal*'s Nabih Berri was subsequently reelected as speaker by the new assembly.

Speaker: Nabih BERRI.

Communications

For a time, relative to other Middle Eastern countries, in Lebanon the press was traditionally free from external controls, but Syrian troops forced suspension of a number of newspapers in December 1976. Following the imposition of formal censorship on January 1, 1977, most suspended newspapers were permitted to resume publication;

a number of newspapers and periodicals decided to publish from abroad. Between March and July 1994 the government also banned political broadcasting by private stations.

Press

The following are published daily in Beirut in Arabic, unless otherwise noted: *al-Nahar* (78,000), independent; *al-Anwar* (The Light, 59,000), independent; *al-Safir* (The Envoy, 50,000), independent; *al-Amal* (Hope, 35,000), Phalangist; *al-Hayat* (Life, 32,000), independent; *al-Dunia* (The World, 25,000); *al-Liwa'* (The Standard, 15,000); *al-Mustaqbal* (The Future), founded by Rafiq Hariri; *al-Sharq* (The East, 36,000); *al-Nida* (The Appeal, 10,000), communist; *al-Jarida* (The News, 22,000), independent; *Daily Star,* independent (in English); *L'Orient–Le Jour* (in French, 23,000), independent; *Le Soir* (in French, 17,000).

News Agencies

The principal domestic facility is the National News Agency (*Wakalat al-Anba'al-Wataniyah*). In addition, most foreign bureaus maintain offices at Beirut.

Broadcasting and Computing

The government-controlled Radio Lebanon (*Idha'ah Lubnan/Radio Liban*) broadcasts nationally in Arabic, Armenian, English, and French and internationally to three continents. Television Lebanon (*Tilifiziyun Lubnan/Tele Liban*) broadcasts over three channels. In addition, the chaotic conditions of the lengthy civil war prompted the unlicensed launching of some 100 radio and 20 television stations that the government, since early 1992, has been attempting to shut down. In 1994 a law was enacted that revoked the monopoly held by Television Lebanon and Radio Lebanon over licensed broadcasting and laid the legal groundwork for the operation of privately owned television and radio stations. In 1996 the government approved new licensing regulations that were expected to result in the closing of about two-thirds of television and radio stations. However, the enterprises in jeopardy continued to operate, pending a government review of the new code, which had prompted domestic and international complaints regarding attempted "press muzzling."

Today there are several legal private television and satellite channels. Some, such as Manar TV (operated by *Hezbollah*) and Future TV (operated by the Future Movement), were founded by political organizations. Others include the Lebanese Broadcasting Corporation, New TV, and the National Broadcasting Network. There were approximately 1.3 million television receivers and 300,000 personal computers serving 400,000 Internet users in 2003.

Intergovernmental Representation

Ambassador to the US
Farid ABBOUD

US Ambassador to Lebanon
Jeffrey FELTMAN

Permanent Representative to the UN
Ibrahim ASSAF (Charges d'Affaires)

IGO Memberships (Non-UN)
AFESD, AMF, BADEA, CCC, IDB, Interpol, LAS, NAM, OIC, OIF, PCA

LIBYA

GREAT SOCIALIST PEOPLE'S LIBYAN ARAB JAMAHIRIYA

al-Jamahiriyah al-'Arabiyah al-Libiyah al-Sha'biyah al-Ishtirakiyah al-Uzma

The Country

Extending for 910 miles along Africa's northern coast, Libya embraces the former Turkish and Italian provinces of Tripolitania, Cyrenaica, and Fezzan. Some 95 percent of its territory is desert and barren rockland, and cultivation and settlement are largely confined to a narrow coastal strip. Tribal influences remain strong within a population that is predominantly Arab (with a Berber minority) and almost wholly Sunni Muslim in religion. Arabic is the official language, but Italian, English, and French are also spoken. The government has made efforts in recent years to increase the education of females (about 50 percent of whom are reportedly illiterate), and women comprised 21 percent of the official labor force in 1996, up from less than 9 percent in the 1980s. Female representation in government continues to be minimal.

Libya's reputation as a country largely devoid of natural resources was rendered obsolete by the discovery of oil in the late 1950s; the ensuing development of export capacity resulted in its achieving the highest per capita GNP in Africa (more than $8,600 in 1980). However, world market conditions subsequently reduced the country's oil revenue from a high of $22 billion in 1980 to $5 billion in 1988, with per capita GNP declining to less than $5,500 through the same period. Oil production (about 1.4 million barrels per day) currently accounts for more than 95 percent of export income, the primary market being Western Europe. Other industry has been limited by the weakness of the domestic market, uneven distribution of the population, and a shortage of skilled manpower. Recent large-scale development has focused on building chemical and steel complexes, in addition to the controversial Great Man-Made River Project, a $30 billion plan to pipe water from aquifers deep below the Sahara Desert to coastal areas. The government hopes that the project, the first phase of which was inaugurated in mid-1991 and the second in 1996, will eventually permit dramatic agricultural expansion as well as provide bountiful drinking water to major cities. Due to limited rainfall and an insufficient labor pool resulting from migration to the cities, agriculture currently contributes only minimally to domestic

output. Barley, wheat, tomatoes, olives, citrus, and dates are the primary crops.

After decades of rigid state control of the economy, liberalization measures, including the promotion of limited private enterprise, were introduced in 1988. Results were initially viewed as encouraging, but domestic opposition was kindled by concurrent government efforts to eliminate food subsidies, reduce state employment, and trim financing for medical, educational, and other social programs. Consequently, about 70 percent of the economy remains under government control, and much of the populace still relies heavily on various subsidies. Falling oil prices in 1998 contributed to a devaluation of the dinar in November and cutbacks in the proposed 1999 budget before economic pressures were eased by the return of high oil prices in the second half of 1999 and 2000. Early in the 21st century, Libyan leader Mu'ammar al-Qadhafi called for promotion of the agricultural, manufacturing, and tourism sectors in the name of economic diversification; however, his perceived resistance to even modest free-market reforms constrained foreign investment, despite significant interest on the part of Western companies in tapping into the Libyan consumer market as well as participating in the potentially lucrative upgrading of the oilfield infrastructure.

Economic affairs, particularly in regard to the West, changed dramatically in September 2004 when the United States lifted most of its long-standing unilateral sanctions against Libya. (UN sanctions, imposed in 1992, had been suspended in 2000 and formally lifted in September 2003.) Western companies immediately began to negotiate substantial oil contracts with Tripoli in conjunction with pledges from the Qadhafi regime to enact broad economic policy changes (see Foreign relations and Current issues, below).

Government and Politics

Political Background

Successively ruled by the Phoenicians, Greeks, Romans, Arabs, Spaniards, and others, Libya was under Ottoman Turkish control from the middle of the 16th century to the beginning of the 20th century. It was conquered by Italy in 1911 and 1912 and was ruled as an Italian colony until its occupation by British and French military forces during World War II. In conformity with British wartime pledges and a 1949 decision of the UN General Assembly, Libya became an independent monarchy under Emir Muhammad IDRIS al-Sanussi (King IDRIS I) on December 24, 1951. A constitution promulgated two months earlier prescribed a federal form of government with autonomous rule in the three historic provinces, but provincial autonomy was wiped out and a centralized regime instituted under a constitutional amendment adopted in 1963.

The 1960s witnessed a growing independence in foreign affairs resulting from the financial autonomy generated by rapidly increasing petroleum revenues. This period marked the beginnings of Libyan radicalism in Third World politics and in its posture regarding Arab–Israeli relations. Increasingly, anti-Western sentiments were voiced, especially in regard to externally controlled petroleum companies and the presence of foreign military bases on Libyan soil. The period following the June 1967 Arab–Israeli conflict saw a succession of prime ministers, including the progressive 'Abd al-Hamid al-BAKKUSH, who took office in October 1967. His reforms alienated conservative leaders, however, and he was replaced in September 1968 by Wanis al-QADHAFI. The following September, while the king was in Turkey for medical treatment, a group of military officers led by Col. Mu'ammar al-QADHAFI seized control of the government and established a revolutionary regime under a military-controlled Revolutionary Command Council (RCC).

After consolidating his control of the RCC, Colonel Qadhafi moved to implement the goals of his regime, which reflected a blend of Islamic behavioral codes, socialism, and radical Arab nationalism. By June 1970 both the British and US military installations had been evacuated, and in July the Italian and Jewish communities were dispossessed and their members forced from the country.

Political Status: Independent state since December 24, 1951; revolutionary republic declared September 1, 1969; name changed from Libyan Arab Republic to Libyan Arab People's Republic in 1976; present name adopted March 2, 1977.

Area: 679,358 sq. mi. (1,759,540 sq. km.).

Population: 4,811,902 (1995C); 5,661,000 (2004E). Both figures include nonnationals (approximately 8.6 percent).

Major Urban Centers (1984C): TRIPOLI (990,697), Benghazi (485,386), Azzawiya (220,075), Misurata (178,295). (Many secretariats have reportedly been relocated recently to Sirte–about 400 miles east of Tripoli–and other cities.)

Official Language: Arabic.

Monetary Unit: Dinar (official rate July 1, 2005: 1.37 dinar = $1US).

Revolutionary Leader: (De Facto Head of State): Col. Mu'ammar Abu Minyar al-QADHAFI (Col. Moammar GADDAFY); assumed power as Chairman of Revolutionary Command Council (RCC) following coup d'état of September 1, 1969; became prime minister in January 1970, relinquishing the office in July 1972; designated General Secretary of General People's Congress concurrent with abolition of the RCC on March 2, 1977, relinquishing the position March 1–2, 1979.

Secretary General of General People's Congress: Muhammad al-ZANATI; appointed by the General People's Congress on November 18, 1992, to succeed 'Abd al-Raziq al-SAWSA; most recently reappointed on March 1, 2000.

Secretary General of General People's Committee: (Prime Minister): Shukri Muhammad GHANIM; appointed by the General People's Congress on June 13, 2003, to succeed Mubarak Abdullah al-SHAMIKH.

In June 1971 an official party, the Arab Socialist Union (ASU), was organized, and in September the Federation of Arab Republics (a union of Egypt, Libya, and Syria) was approved by separate referenda in each country. The federation, while formally constituted at the legislative level in March 1972, became moribund shortly thereafter. Meanwhile, the regime had begun acquiring shares in the country's petroleum industry, resorting to outright nationalization of foreign interests in numerous cases; by March 1976 the government controlled about two-thirds of oil production.

Periodically threatening to resign because of conflicts within the RCC, Colonel Qadhafi turned over his prime-ministerial duties to Maj. 'Abd al-Salam JALLUD in July 1972 and was in seclusion during the greater part of 1974. In August 1975 Qadhafi's rule was seriously threatened by a coup attempt involving army officers–some two dozen of whom were ultimately executed; a number of drastic antisubversion laws were promptly enacted. In November a quasi-legislative General National Congress (renamed the General People's Congress a year later) was created, while in March 1977 the RCC and the cabinet were abolished in accordance with "the installation of the people's power" under a new structure of government headed by Colonel Qadhafi and the four remaining members of the RCC. The political changes were accompanied by a series of sweeping economic measures, including limitations on savings and consolidation of private shops ("nests of exploitation") into large state supermarkets, which generated middle-class discontent and fueled exile-based opposition activity. The government was further reorganized at a meeting of the General People's Congress in March 1979, Colonel Qadhafi resigning as secretary general (but retaining his designation as revolutionary leader and supreme commander of the armed forces) in favor of 'Abd al-'Ati 'UBAYDI, who was in turn replaced as secretary general of the General People's Committee (prime minister) by Jadallah 'Azzuz al-TALHI.

At a Congress session in January 1981, Secretary General 'Ubaydi was succeeded by Muhammad al-Zarruq RAJAB, who, in February 1984, was replaced by Miftah al-Usta 'UMAR and named to succeed Talhi as secretary general of the General People's Committee. Talhi was returned to the position of nominal head of government in a major ministerial reshuffle announced on March 3, 1986; in a further reshuffle on March 1, 1987, Talhi was replaced by 'Umar Mustafa al-MUNTASIR.

In October 1990 a government shakeup was undertaken that included the appointment of 'Abd al-Raziq al-SAWSA to succeed 'Umar as secretary general of the General People's Congress and Abu Zaid 'Umar DURDA to succeed Muntasir as head of the General People's Committee. Durda was reappointed in November 1992 while Sawsa was replaced by Muhammad al-ZANATI. The 1992 reorganization was otherwise most noteworthy for the designation of Muntasir, a moderate who had earlier cultivated a good working relationship with the West, as the equivalent of foreign secretary.

The sanctions imposed by the United Nations in 1992 (see Foreign relations, below) subsequently contributed to what was widely believed to be growing domestic discontent with the regime. Internal difficulties were most sharply illustrated by an apparent coup attempt in early October 1993, reportedly involving thousands of troops at several military locations. Although loyalist forces quashed the revolt in about three days, the government was described as "severely shaken" by the events.

In a cabinet reshuffle on January 29, 1994, 'Abd al-Majid al-QA'UD was named to succeed Durda as secretary general of the General People's Committee. Qa'ud was succeeded on December 29, 1997, by Muhammad Ahmad al-MANQUSH, who was reappointed, along with most other senior ministers, in a cabinet reshuffle on December 15, 1998. On March 1, 2000, Manqush was succeeded by Mubarak Abdullah al-SHAMIKH, Colonel Qadhafi concurrently ordering a sharp reduction in the number of ministries in the name of further devolution of power to local "people's" bodies. SHAMIKH remained in his post during a reshuffle on October 1, 2000, but was replaced in a subsequent reorganization on June 13, 2003, by

Shukri Muhammad GHANIM, theretofore the secretary for economy and trade.

Constitution and Government

Guided by the ideology of Colonel Qadhafi's *Green Book,* which combines elements of nationalism, Islamic theology, socialism, and populism, Libya was restyled the Socialist People's Libyan Arab Jamahiriya in March 1977. The *Jamahiriyah* is conceived as a system of direct government through popular organs interspersed throughout Libyan society. A General People's Congress is assisted by a General Secretariat, whose secretary general serves as titular head of state, although effective power has remained in Colonel Qadhafi's hands since the 1969 coup. Executive functions are assigned to a cabinet-like General People's Committee, whose secretary general serves as the equivalent of prime minister. The judicial system includes a Supreme Court, courts of appeal, courts of the first instance, and summary courts. In 1988 the government also established a People's Court and a People's Prosecution Bureau to replace the unofficial but powerful "revolutionary courts" that had reportedly assumed responsibility for nearly 90 percent of prosecutions. In what was seen as an effort to placate the expanding Islamic fundamentalist movement, Colonel Qadhafi in April 1993 called for more widespread implementation of *shari'a* (Islamic religious law), and in February 1994 the General People's Congress granted new powers to the country's religious leaders, including (for the first time under Colonel Qadhafi) the right to issue religious decrees (*fatwas*).

Libya's three provinces are subdivided into ten governorates, with administration based on "Direct People's Authority" as represented in local People's Congresses, People's Committees, Trade Unions, and Vocational Syndicates.

Foreign Relations

Under the monarchy, Libya tended to adhere to a generally pro-Western posture. Since the 1969 coup its foreign policy has been characterized by the advocacy of total war against Israel, a willingness to use petroleum as a political weapon, and (until 1998–see Current issues, below) a strong commitment to Arab unity that has given rise to numerous failed merger attempts with sister states (Libya, Egypt, Sudan, and Syria in 1969; Libya, Egypt, and Syria in 1971; Libya and Egypt in 1972; Libya and Tunisia in 1974; Libya and Syria in 1980; Libya and Chad in 1981; Libya and Morocco in 1984).

Libya's position within the Arab world has been marked by an improbable combination of ideological extremism and pragmatic compromise. Following the 1978 Camp David accords, relations were severed with Egypt, both sides fortifying their common border. Thereafter, Tripoli strove to block Cairo's reentry into the Arab fold (extending its condemnation to Jordan following the warming of ties between Jordan and Egypt) and provided support to Syrian-based elements of the Palestinian Liberation Organization (PLO) opposed to Yasir 'Arafat. Relations with the Mubarak government began to warm, however, during an Arab League meeting at Casablanca, Morocco, in May 1989 and, stimulated by a "reconciliation" summit at Mersa Metruh, Egypt, in October, continued to improve with a series of cooperation agreements in 1990 and the opening of the border between the two countries in 1991. By mid-decade, Egypt had become what one correspondent described as Libya's most important potential "bridge to the West," Cairo's supportive stance reflecting the importance of Libya as a provider of jobs for Egyptian workers and the value attached by the Mubarak regime to Colonel Qadhafi's pronounced antifundamentalist posture.

Relations with conservative Morocco, broken following Tripoli's 1980 recognition of the Polisario-backed government-in-exile of the Western Sahara, resumed in 1981. Ties with neighboring Tunisia, severely strained during much of the 1980s, advanced dramatically in 1988, the opening of the border between the two countries precipitating a flood of option-starved Libyan consumers to Tunis. Regional relations stabilized even further with the February 1989 formation of the Arab Maghreb Union (AMU), although Colonel

Qadhafi remained a source of controversy within the ineffective and largely inactive grouping.

A widespread expression of international concern in the 1980s and 1990s centered on Libyan involvement in Chad. Libya's annexation of the Aozou Strip (see map, p. 217) in the mid-1970s was followed by active participation in the Chadian civil war, largely in opposition to the forces of Hissein Habré, who in 1982 emerged as president of the strife-torn country. By 1983 Libya's active support of the "National Peace Government" loyal to former Chadian president Goukhouni Oueddei (based in the northern Tibesti region) included the deployment of between 3,000 and 5,000 Libyan troops and the provision of air support for Oueddei's attacks on the northern capital of Faya-Largeau. Although consistently denying direct involvement and condemning the use of French troops in 1983 and 1984 as "unjustified intervention," Qadhafi agreed in September 1984 to recall "Libyan support elements" in exchange for a French troop withdrawal. The agreement was hailed as a diplomatic breakthrough for Paris but was greeted with dismay by Habré and ultimately proved to be an embarrassment to the Mitterrand government because of the limited number of Libyan troops actually withdrawn. Two and a half years later, in March 1987, the militarily superior Qadhafi regime suffered the unexpected humiliation of being decisively defeated by Chadian government forces, which, after capturing the air facility at Quadi Doum, 100 miles northeast of Faya-Largeau, forced the Libyans to withdraw from all but the Aozou Strip, leaving behind an estimated $1 billion worth of sophisticated weaponry.

In early August 1987, Chadian forces, in a surprise move, captured Aozou, administrative capital of the contested border area, although the town was subsequently retaken by Libya. Despite a September cease-fire, skirmishes continued as the Islamic Legion, composed largely of Lebanese mercenaries, attacked Chadian posts from bases inside Sudan, with Libyan jets supporting counteroffensives in the Aozou Strip. A year later, the warring neighbors had resumed intermittent peace negotiations, Libya having reportedly lost

10 percent of its military capability, although retaining most of the disputed territory.

In July 1989 the Organization of African Unity (OAU) sponsored negotiations between President Habré and Colonel Qadhafi, which set the stage for the signing of a peace treaty by the countries' foreign ministers on August 31. The treaty called for immediate troop withdrawal from the disputed territory, exchange of prisoners of war, mutual "noninterference," and continued efforts to reach a permanent settlement. Relations subsequently deteriorated, however, with Habré accusing Libya of supporting Chadian rebels operating from Sudan. A year of talks having achieved little progress, the dispute was referred to the International Court of Justice (ICJ) several months before the ouster of the Habré regime in December 1990.

New Chadian president Idriss Déby announced in early 1991 that a "new era" had begun in relations between Chad and Libya, the belief being widespread that Libya had supplied arms and logistical support (but not personnel) to the victorious Chadian rebels. However, Déby subsequently described the Aozou issue as still a "bone of contention" requiring resolution by the ICJ. Consequently, hearings in the case began in June 1993 at The Hague, Netherlands, and in February 1994 the ICJ ruled by a vote of 16–1 that Libya had no rightful claim to the Aozou Strip or any other territory beyond the boundary established in a 1955 treaty between Libya and France. On May 30 the lengthy dispute ended with Libya's withdrawal and a symbolic raising of the Chadian flag. Shortly thereafter, Colonel Qadhafi received President Déby at Tripoli for the signing of a friendship and cooperation treaty, which, among other things, provided for a Libyan–Chadian Higher Joint Committee to discuss mutual concerns. Following the inaugural meeting of the Committee in July, (then) Chadian prime minister Kassiré Koumakoyé reportedly described the Aozou issue as "settled for good," while announcing his country's support for Libyan efforts to have UN economic sanctions lifted.

Relations with the West have been problematic since the 1969 coup and the expulsion, a year later, of British and US military forces. Libya's subsequent involvement in negotiations between Malta and the United Kingdom over British naval facilities on the Mediterranean island contributed to a further strain in relations with London. In December 1979 the United States closed its embassy at Tripoli after portions of the building were stormed and set afire by pro-Iranian demonstrators, while in May 1981 the Reagan administration ordered Tripoli to shut down its Washington "people's bureau" in response to what it considered escalating international terrorism sponsored by Colonel Qadhafi. Subsequent US–Libyan relations have been characterized as "mutual paranoia," with each side accusing the other of assassination plots amid hostility generated by US naval maneuvers in the Gulf of Sirte, which Libya has claimed as an internal sea since 1973.

Simultaneous attacks by Palestinian gunmen on the Rome and Vienna airports on December 27, 1985, brought US accusations of Libyan involvement, which Colonel Qadhafi vehemently denied. In January 1986 President Reagan announced the freezing of all Libyan government assets in US banks, urged Americans working in Libya to depart, banned all US trade with Libya, and ordered a new series of air and sea maneuvers in the Gulf of Sirte. (US officials charged that Libya was harboring members of the Revolutionary Council of Fatah, the radical Palestinian grouping led by Abu Nidal and allegedly behind the 1985 attacks. See PLO article for further details.) Three months later, during the night of April 14, eighteen F-111 bombers based in Britain, assisted by carrier-based attack fighters, struck Libyan military targets at Tripoli and Benghazi. The action was prompted by what Washington termed "conclusive evidence," in the form of intercepted cables, that Libya had ordered the bombing of a Berlin discotheque nine days before, in the course of which an off-duty US soldier had been killed. The US administration also claimed to have aborted a planned grenade and machine-gun attack on the American visa office at Paris, for which French authorities ordered the expulsion of two Libyan diplomats.

Tripoli's adoption of a more conciliatory posture during 1988 did not yield relaxation of tension with

Washington, which mounted a diplomatic campaign against European chemical companies that were reported to be supplying materials for a chemical weapons plant in Libya. Despite Libyan denial of the charges, reports of US readiness to attack the site were believed to be the catalyst for a military encounter between two US F-14s and two Libyan MiG-23 jets over the Mediterranean Sea on January 4, 1989, which resulted in downing of the Libyan planes. Concern subsequently continued in some Western capitals over the alleged chemical plant (the site of a much-publicized fire in March 1990), as well as Libya's ongoing efforts to develop nuclear weapons. Suspicion also arose over possible Libyan involvement in the bombing of Pan Am Flight 103, which blew up over Lockerbie, Scotland, in December 1988, and the crash of a French DC-10 in Niger near the Chad border in September 1989.

Colonel Qadhafi was described as maintaining an "uncharacteristically low profile" following the August 1990 Iraqi invasion of Kuwait (which he publicly criticized) and the US-led Desert Storm campaign against Iraqi forces in early 1991. However, the respite from the international spotlight proved short-lived as the investigations into the Lockerbie and Niger plane explosions once again focused Western condemnation on Libya.

In October 1991 the French government issued warrants for six Libyans (one of them a brother-in-law of Colonel Qadhafi) in connection with the Niger crash, while American and British authorities announced in mid-November that they had filed charges against two Libyan nationals in connection with the Pan Am bombing. In early December the Arab League Council expressed its "solidarity" with Libya in the Lockerbie matter and called for an inquiry by a joint Arab League–UN committee. Two days later a Libyan judge declared that the two suspects were under house arrest and that Tripoli would be willing to send judicial representatives to Washington, London, and Paris to discuss the alleged acts of terrorism.

On January 21, 1992, the UN Security Council unanimously demanded extradition of the Lockerbie detainees to either Britain or the United States and insisted that Libya aid the French investigation into the Niger crash. Although Libya announced its willingness to cooperate with the latter demand, which involved no extradition request, it refused to turn over the Lockerbie suspects, declaring it would try the men itself. Consequently, the Security Council ordered the imposition of selective sanctions, including restrictions on air traffic and an embargo of shipments of military equipment as of April 15.

On May 14, 1992, in partial compliance with the Security Council, Libya announced that it would sever all links with organizations involved in "international terrorism," admit UN representatives to verify that there were no terrorist training facilities on its soil, and take action to preclude the use of its territory or citizens for terrorist acts. In addition, a special session of the General People's Congress in June agreed that the Lockerbie suspects could be tried in a "fair and just" court in a neutral country as suggested by the Arab League. However, the Security Council reiterated its demand for extradition to the United States or United Kingdom, ordered that the sanctions be continued, and warned that stiffer measures were being considered. After mediation efforts by UN Secretary General Boutros Boutros-Ghali failed to resolve the impasse, the Security Council voted on November 11, 1993, to expand the sanctions by freezing Libya's overseas assets and banning the sales to Libya of certain oil-refining and pipeline equipment. The sanctions were subsequently regularly extended, although the Security Council rejected a US proposal for a total oil embargo.

Libya continued to face heavy pressure from the United States in 1996. In April, US defense secretary William Perry warned that force would be used if necessary to prevent Libya from completing an alleged underground chemical weapons plant. In addition, in August the US Congress authorized the president to impose sanctions against foreign companies that invest heavily in Libya, although the plan subsequently remained largely unimplemented.

Attention in 1998 and 1999 remained focused on efforts to negotiate a resolution of the Lockerbie impasse, the Libyan government having previously argued (with the support of the OAU and the Arab League) that the suspects should be tried in a neutral country. Finally, Libya agreed in late March 1999 to send the two men ('Abd al-Basset al-MEGRAHI and Lamin Khalifah FHIMAH) to the Netherlands in early April to face a trial under Scottish law before three Scottish judges. Colonel Qadhafi's acceptance of the plan apparently was predicated on assurances that the trial would not be used to attempt to "undermine" his regime. For their part, Washington and London appeared to compromise on the issue of the trial's location, in part at least, out of recognition that international support for continued sanctions was diminishing. The Security Council announced that the UN sanctions had been suspended as soon as the suspects arrived in the Netherlands on April 5. However, unilateral US sanctions were expected to remain in place as long as Libya stayed on Washington's official list of countries perceived to be "state sponsors of terrorism."

An antiterrorism court in Paris convicted, in absentia, six suspects in the Niger plane crash case, including Abdallah SENOUSSI, Qadhafi's brother-in-law, in March 1999 and issued warrants for their arrest, which could be enforced only if they left Libya. Meanwhile, Colonel Qadhafi had also permitted German investigators to question Libyan intelligence officers concerning the 1986 Berlin disco bombing, although prosecution of the case had been thrown into disarray in 1997 when the main witness apparently recanted his previously incriminating testimony against alleged Libyan operatives. (Four defendants were convicted of the Berlin bombing in October 2001, the court also accepting the prosecution's argument that the Libyan secret service had been involved in planning the attack.)

In July 1999 full diplomatic relations were reestablished with the United Kingdom, which had severed ties after a British policewoman was killed during an anti-Qadhafi demonstration outside the Libyan mission at London. (It had been argued that the policewoman was killed by gunfire directed from the mission at the demonstrators.) Resolution of the dispute included Libya's agreement to cooperate in the investigation and to pay compensation to the victim's family.

The Lockerbie trial opened in May 2000, and on January 31, 2001, Megrahi was convicted of murder in connection with the bombing, the judges having accepted the admittedly circumstantial evidence that he had been at the airport when the bomb was allegedly planted and was working for Libyan intelligence at the time. Megrahi was sentenced to life in prison, but Fhimah returned to Libya after the judges did not convict him of any charges. (For subsequent developments see Current issues, below.)

Current Issues

Colonel Qadhafi announced in the late 1990s that he was turning his focus away from pan-Arabism and toward pan-Africanism, having described most other Arab states as "defeatist" in dealing with the West and Israel. The quixotic Libyan leader attended his first OAU summit in 20 years in July 1999 to promote his new vision and hosted a special summit in September to address proposed changes in the charter that would permit creation of OAU peacekeeping forces. Subsequently, Qadhafi participated prominently in efforts to resolve the conflicts in Sudan and Democratic Republic of the Congo and served as a mediator in the war between Eritrea and Ethiopia. However, Libya's image as a potential continental unifier suffered a severe blow in late September 2000 when scores of Black African workers died in a series of attacks by Libyans on nonnational workers in a suburb of Tripoli. (Underscoring the continued deterioration of the African initiative, in 2003 Libya recalled its troops from the Central African Republic, a trade agreement with Zimbabwe collapsed, and Qadhafi abolished the ministry for African unity.)

In early 2001 Colonel Qadhafi criticized the conviction of one of the defendants in the Lockerbie trial (see Foreign relations, above) as politically motivated. However, by that time it was widely accepted that the Libyan government had not supported any terrorist activities or groups in several years and was genuinely interested in reintegration into the global community. Qadhafi had also improved his international image by cooperating extensively with the US-led "war on terrorism," by freeing a number of political prisoners and by reportedly indicating a willingness to discuss the proposed payment of compensation to the families of the victims of the Lockerbie bombing.

Qadhafi subsequently continued his drive to improve Libya's international standing, and the initiative appeared to reach critical mass with an August 2003 announcement of final resolution of the Lockerbie affair. Under the carefully crafted language of the settlement, Libya accepted "responsibility for the actions of its officials" and agreed to pay an estimated $10 million (in three installments) to each of the families of the 270 killed in the attack. The UN Security Council formally lifted UN sanctions against Libya in September, permitting payment of the Lockerbie settlements to begin. In January 2004 Libya also agreed to pay a total of $170 million to the families of those killed in the 1989 Niger plane crash. The final piece of the puzzle appeared to be put in place in September 2004 when Libya agreed to pay $35 million to the non-US victims of the 1986 bombing in Berlin.

Meanwhile, dramatic progress was also achieved regarding the other long-standing area of intense Western concern, that is, Libya's perceived pursuit of weapons of mass destruction (WMD). In December 2003 the US and UK announced that after nine months of secret negotiations Qadhafi had agreed to abandon all WMD programs and to permit international inspectors to verify compliance. (Some analysts suggested that the process had been accelerated by the aggressive stance taken by the US Bush administration against Iraq.) Washington announced in February 2004 that it would permit flights to Libya and allow US oil companies to launch talks with Tripoli aimed at further exploitation of oil fields. Many US commercial sanctions were lifted the following April, and in October the EU removed its embargo on arms sales to Libya, and other economic sanctions. Underscoring the dramatic transformation of the West's perception of Qadhafi, he was visited in 2004 by the British, French, and German heads of

state, and a number of US companies were awarded permits in 2005 for oil exploration. Collaterally, the Libyan regime, which celebrated its 35th year in power in 2004, pledged sweeping economic reforms to broaden trade and expand investment opportunities. Although Libya officially remained on the US list of terrorist-sponsoring states (possibly in part to permit investigation of charges by Saudi Arabia that Crown Prince Abdallah had been the target of an assassination plot), by April 2005 US officials were discussing the potential for joint military activity with Libyan forces in the war on terrorism.

Political Parties

Under the monarchy, all political parties were banned. In 1971 an official government party, the Arab Socialist Union (ASU), was founded with the Egyptian ASU as its model. The formation was designed primarily to serve as a "transmission belt," helping implement government decisions at local levels and serving to channel local concerns upward to the central government; however, there was no public reference to it after 1975. At present all parties are proscribed, Colonel Qadhafi arguing that their legalization would only lead to disorder.

Opposition Groups

National Front for the Salvation of Libya (NFSL). Formation of the NFSL was announced at Khartoum, Sudan, on October 7, 1981, under the banner "Finding the democratic alternative." In September 1986 the Front published a list of 76 regime opponents that it claimed had been assassinated in exile, and in January 1987 it joined with a number of other exile formations in establishing a joint working group during a meeting at Cairo, Egypt. The NFSL also participated in the formation of the LNLA (below), which, however, announced its independent status in early 1994.

Operating out of Egypt and the United States, the NFSL was in the forefront of efforts to coordinate anti-Qadhafi activity in the first half of the 1990s, including a conference in Washington in late 1993 attended by most of the regime's leading opponents. However, a "statement of principles" of a proposed front was not negotiated.

In early 1994 it was reported that the NFSL had begun to transmit its antiregime radio program, the *Voice of the Libyan People,* via European Satellite. The program had previously been intermittently broadcast by shortwave radio from neighboring countries. In 1997 the NFSL issued a report alleging that more than 300 Qadhafi opponents had been killed by government operatives abroad or by domestic security forces between 1977 and 1994. In mid-2004 NFSL leaders warned Western leaders that the Qadhafi regime continued to hold political prisoners despite the country's improved international reputation.

Leaders: Ibrahim SAHAD, Mahmud DAKHIL, Muhammad Fayiz JIBRIL, Muhammad MAGARIAF (Secretary General). (Jabal MATAR, described as leader of the NFSL's "military wing," has been missing since 1990.)

Libyan National Liberation Army (LNLA). The LNLA, a paramilitary unit organized with covert US backing to destabilize the Libyan government, was formed in Chad in 1988. The existence of the Army, comprising an estimated 600–700 Libyan soldiers taken prisoner by Chadian forces and subsequently molded into an anti-Qadhafi force, became known following the overthrow of the Habré regime in late 1990. Washington quickly airlifted the Libyan *"contras"* out of Chad after the fall of N'Djamena, US embarrassment over the affair increasing as the LNLA participants entered a "floating exile." About 250 eventually returned to Libya, the rest reportedly finding temporary asylum in Zaire and, subsequently, Kenya. In late 1991 some of the guerrillas were reported to have been moved to a Central Intelligence Agency (CIA) training base in the United States, and in April 1992 LNLA members participated in an NFSL congress at Dallas, Texas. Two years later, as the apparent result of a policy dispute, the LNLA severed its links to the NFSL. There has been little subsequent information regarding any LNLA activity.

Leaders: Col. Khalifa HIFTER, Braek SWESSI.

The **Libyan Alliance,** an anti-Qadhafi front, was announced in the late 1980s. Although *Middle East International* reported in late 1993 that most of its constituent groups had "drifted away," Mansur KIKHIA, a former Libyan foreign minister and UN representative, remained the group's titular secretary general. Kikhia, a human rights activist and one of Libya's most prominent dissidents, disappeared during a visit to Cairo in December 1993, his supporters subsequently charging he had been kidnapped by Qadhafi agents. In June 1994 the Libyan leader announced that Kikhia was alive, but he insisted that Tripoli had nothing to do with his disappearance and had no knowledge as to his whereabouts. In 1997 US intelligence reports indicated that Kikhia had apparently been executed in Libya in early 1994. In 1998 an Egyptian court ordered the Egyptian government to pay Kikhia's wife $30,000 as the result of the apparent involvement of its security agents in turning Kikhia over to Libya.

Another anti-Qadhafi umbrella organization, the **Cooperation Bureau for Democratic and National Forces,** has been chaired by former foreign minister 'Abd al-Munim al-HUNI, who has been an exile in Egypt since breaking with the regime in the mid-1980s. (Other prominent members of the Bureau have included Izzidin GHADANSI, Bashir RABTI, and Abdullah SHARAFFEDIN.) Huni, who reportedly declined an invitation from Colonel Qadhafi in mid-1992 to return to Libya, subsequently participated in meetings with the NFSL and Libyan Alliance representatives to develop a common program. Like-minded overtures were reportedly made to former Libyan prime minister 'Abd al-Hamid al-BAKKUSH, who founded the Cairo-based **Libyan Liberation Organization** in 1982. (As of early 1999 there was little evidence that the Alliance, the Bureau, or the Organization remained active.)

In May 1996 a number of opposition groups reportedly issued a statement condemning the "despotic practices" of the Qadhafi regime, according to the *Africa Research Bulletin,* which said

Cabinet

As of April 1, 2005

Secretary General, General People's Committee	Shukri Muhammad Ghanim
Assistant Secretary General	Al-Baghdadi Ali al-Mahmudi

Secretaries

Culture	Al-Mahdi Miftah Mubarij
Economy and Trade	'Abd al-Qadir Umar Bilkhayr
Energy	Fathi Umar Bin Shitwan
Finance	Muhammad Ali al-Houeiz
Foreign Liaison and International Cooperation	Abdurrahman Muhammad Shalgam
Higher Education	'Abd al-Salam Abdallah al-Qallali
Justice	Ali Umar abu-Bakr
Planning	Ali Tahir al-Juhaimi
Public Security	Nasr al-Mabruk Abdallah
Tourism	Ammar Mabruk al-Lutayyif
Workforce, Training, and Employment	Ma'tuq Muhammad Ma'tuq
Youth and Sports	Ali Mursi Sha'iri

signatories included the **Libyan Constitutional Union,** the **Libyan Nationalist Organization,** and the **Libyan Democratic Nationalist Grouping.** Also listed were a **Movement for Change and Reform** (a nationalist grouping) and the **Libyan Islamic Group,** an underground but nonviolent organization that has been compared to groups such as the Muslim Brotherhood in Egypt. A number of supporters of the Libyan Islamic Group (including professors and other professionals) were reportedly arrested at Benghazi and other northeastern cities in mid-1998. Libyan security forces also reportedly clashed at that time with members of the **Libyan Islamic Fighting Group** (LIFG, also referenced as the Libyan Militant Islamic Group–LMIG), an Islamic fundamentalist grouping that had earlier been linked to the antigovernment disturbances in northeastern Libya in March 1996 and had claimed that it had planned an assassination of Colonel Qadhafi. The Libyan leader subsequently criticized the United Kingdom for permitting the Group to maintain operations in London in view of its avowed goal of overthrowing the Libyan government. In 1998 leaders of the LIFG denied that

UK intelligence forces had been involved in the earlier assassination plot, which was aborted when Qadhafi changed travel plans suddenly. (A "rogue" UK agent had reportedly alleged that the LIFG had been given money to assist in the plot, a charge that London vehemently denied.) The LIFG has been accused of having connections to the *al-Qaeda* terrorist network, and in 2001 it was included on the US list of terrorist organizations whose assets were to be frozen. Meanwhile, a number of LIFG members remained in prison in Libya in 2002.

Another group reportedly involved in recent clashes with security forces is the **Islamic Martyrs Movement,** whose reputed leader Muhammad al-HAMI, was believed to have been killed by government security forces in July 1996. (Abdullah AHMAD has subsequently been identified as a spokesman for the Movement.) The grouping, described as operating out of the mountains near Benghazi, claimed that it had wounded Qadhafi in an attack on his motorcade on the night of May 31–June 1, 1998. (The government denied that such an attack had taken place.) Meanwhile, the formation of the **Libyan Patriots Movement** had been announced at London in January 1997, founders calling for the ouster of Colonel Qadhafi and creation of a "free Libya" based on free-market economic principles.

In August 2000 the formation of a new external opposition grouping–the **National Reform Congress**–was reported as a vehicle for promoting a multiparty system in Libya.

Legislature

The Senate and House of Representatives were dissolved as a result of the 1969 coup, Colonel Qadhafi asserting that all such institutions are basically undemocratic, "as democracy means the authority of the people and not the authority of a body acting on the people's behalf."

A government decree of November 13, 1975, provided for the establishment of a 618-member General National Congress of the ASU to consist of the members of the Revolutionary Command Council and leaders of existing "people's congresses," trade unions, and professional groups. Subsequent to its first session held January 5–18, 1976, the body was identified as the **General People's Congress** (GPC).

Secretary General: Muhammad al-ZANATI.

Communications

Press

In October 1973 all private newspapers were nationalized, and censorship remains heavy. The country's major daily, *al-Fajr al-Jadid* (The New Dawn, 40,000), is published at Tripoli in Arabic,

by JANA. Also published daily in Arabic at Tripoli is the "ideological journal" *Al-Zahf al-Akhdar* (The Green March).

News Agencies

The official facility is the Jamahiriya News Agency (JANA). Italy's ANSA and Russia's ITAR-TASS maintain offices at Tripoli.

Broadcasting and Computing

Radio and television transmission in both Arabic and English is under the administration of the Great Socialist People's Libyan Arab Jamahiriya Broadcasting Corporation. There were approximately 988,000 television receivers and 140,000 personal computers serving 160,000 Internet users in 2003.

Intergovernmental Representation

There were no diplomatic relations between Libya and the United States until June 2004, when, in the wake of perceived progress toward the resolution of several long-standing areas of severe contention (see Foreign relations and Current issues, above) Washington announced it would open a liaison office in Tripoli.

Permanent Representative to the UN
(Vacant)

IGO Memberships (Non-UN)
AfDB, AFESD, AMF, AMU, AU, BADEA, CAEU, IDB, Interpol, IOM, LAS, NAM, OAPEC, OIC, OPEC, PCA

MOROCCO

KINGDOM OF MOROCCO

al-Mamlakah al-Maghribiyah

The Country

Located at the northwest corner of Africa, Morocco combines a long Atlantic coastline and Mediterranean frontage facing Gibraltar and southern Spain. Bounded by Algeria on the northeast and (following annexation of the former Spanish Sahara) by Mauritania on the south, the country is topographically divided into a rich agricultural plain in the northwest and an infertile mountain and plateau region in the east that gradually falls into the Sahara Desert in the south and southwest. The population is approximately two-thirds Arab and one-third Berber, with small French and Spanish minorities. Islam is the state religion, most of the population adhering to the Sunni sect. Arabic is the language of the majority, most others speaking one or more dialects of Berber; Spanish is common in the northern regions and French among the educated elite. Women comprise 35 percent of the paid labor force, concentrated mainly in textile manufacture and domestic service; overall, one-third of the female population is engaged in unpaid family labor on agricultural estates. While an increasing number of women from upper-income brackets have participated in local and national elections, they have thus far obtained only minimal representation.

The agricultural sector employs approximately 40 percent of the population; important crops include cereals and grains, oilseeds, nuts, and citrus fruits. One of world's leading exporters of phosphates, Morocco also has important deposits of lead, iron, cobalt, zinc, manganese, and silver; overall, mining accounts for about 45 percent of export receipts. The industrial sector emphasizes import substitution (textiles, chemicals, cement, plastics, machinery), while tourism and fishing are also major sources of income. Trade is strongly oriented towards France, whose economic influence has remained substantial. Since the early 1980s the economy has suffered from periodic droughts, declining world demand for phosphate, rapid urbanization, and high population growth. Unemployment remains a problem, with youth and talent seeking opportunity in Europe. Economic growth has been disappointing according to a report by the

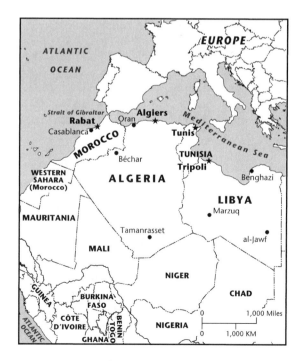

country's Higher Planning Authority. Morocco has failed to meet targets in growth, investment, and exports during the past five years. One piece of good news has been the improved performance of agriculture, which has benefited because of better rainfall, but it also points to Morocco's continued dependence on that sector of the economy. Remittances from workers abroad and steady tourist receipts have also helped the economic picture. Trade liberalization continues with the European Union, and in 2004 Morocco and the United States signed a free trade agreement. While these measures were expected to strengthen foreign business and investment, they also represent competition to Moroccan farmers and textile industries.

Living conditions remain low by regional standards, and wealth is poorly distributed. However, with its low inflation rate, cheap labor pool, and reputation as an "oasis of stability" in an otherwise turbulent region, Morocco is considered by some as a potential target for substantial Western (particularly European) investment. To encourage such interest, the government continues to privatize many state-run enterprises, address the high (52 percent) illiteracy rate; and reform the stock market, tax system, and banking sector. Recent political liberalization has also reportedly been aimed, at least in part, at securing additional Western support.

Government and Politics

Political Background

Originally inhabited by Berbers, Morocco was successively conquered by the Phoenicians, Carthaginians, Romans, Byzantines, and Arabs. From 1912 to 1956 the country was subjected to de facto French and Spanish control, but the internal authority of the sultan was nominally respected. Under pressure by Moroccan nationalists, the French and Spanish relinquished their protectorates, and the country was reunified under Sultan MOHAMED V in 1956. Tangier, which had been under international administration since 1923, was ceded by Spain in 1969.

King Mohamed V tried to convert the hereditary sultanate into a modern constitutional monarchy but died before the process was complete. It remained for his son, King HASSAN II, to implement his father's goal in a constitution adopted in December 1962. However, dissatisfaction with economic conditions and the social policy of the regime led to rioting at Casablanca in March 1965, and three months later the king assumed legislative and executive powers.

In June 1967 the king relinquished the post of prime minister, but the continued hostility of student and other elements led to frequent governmental changes. A new constitution, approved in July 1970, provided for a partial resumption of parliamentary government, a strengthening of royal powers, and a limited role for political parties. Despite the opposition of major political groups, trade unions, and student organizations, an election for a new unicameral House of Representatives was held in August 1970, yielding a pro-government majority. However, the king's failure to unify the country behind his programs was dramatically illustrated by abortive military revolts in 1971 and 1972.

A new constitution was overwhelmingly approved by popular referendum in March 1972, but the parties refused to enter the government because of the monarch's reluctance to schedule legislative elections. After numerous delays, elections to communal and municipal councils were finally held in November 1976, to provincial and prefectural assemblies in January 1977, and to a reconstituted national House of Representatives in June 1977. On October 10 the leading parties agreed to participate in a "National Unity" cabinet headed by Ahmed OSMAN as prime minister.

Osman resigned on March 21, 1979, ostensibly to oversee reorganization of the proroyalist National Assembly of Independents (RNI), although the move was reported to have been precipitated by his handling of the lengthy dispute over the Western Sahara (see below). He was succeeded on March 22 by Maati BOUABID, a respected Casablanca attorney.

On May 30, 1980, a constitutional amendment extending the term of the House of Representatives from four to six years was approved by referendum, thus postponing new elections until 1983. The king indicated in June 1983 that the legislative poll, scheduled for early September, would be further postponed pending the results of a referendum in the Western Sahara to be sponsored by the Organization of African Unity (OAU). On November 30 a new "unity" cabinet headed by Mohamed Karim LAMRANI was announced, with Bouabid, who had organized a new moderate party eight months earlier, joining other party leaders in accepting appointment as ministers of state without portfolio.

The long-awaited legislative poll was finally held on September 14 and October 2, 1984, with Bouabid's Constitutional Union (UC) winning a plurality of both direct and indirectly elected seats, while four centrist parties collectively obtained a better than two-to-one majority. Following lengthy negotiations, a new coalition government, headed by Lamrani, was formed on April 11, 1985.

Although King Hassan appeared to remain popular with most of his subjects, domestic opposition leaders and Amnesty International continued to charge the government with human rights abuses and repression of dissent, including the alleged illegal detention and mistreatment of numerous leftists and Islamic fundamentalists arrested in 1985 and 1986. On September 30, 1986, the king appointed Dr. Azzedine LARAKI, former national education minister, as prime minister, following Lamrani's resignation for health reasons.

Attributed in large measure to improvements in the economy, calm subsequently ensued, with domestic and international attention focusing primarily on the Western Sahara. Thus, a national referendum on December 1, 1989, overwhelmingly approved the king's proposal to postpone legislative elections due in 1990, ostensibly to permit participation by Western Saharans following a self-determination vote in the disputed territory.

In mid-1992, amid indications that the referendum might be delayed indefinitely or even abandoned, the government announced that forthcoming local and national elections would include the residents of Western Sahara as participants. On

Political Status: Independent since March 2, 1956; constitutional monarchy established in 1962; present constitution approved March 1, 1972.

Area: 274,461 sq. mi. (710,850 sq. km.), including approximately 97,343 sq. mi. (252,120 sq. km.) of Western Sahara, two-thirds of which was annexed in February 1976 and the remaining one-third claimed upon Mauritanian withdrawal in August 1979.

Population: 29,891,708 (2004C); 32,725,847 (2005E), including Western Saharans (273,008 in 2005E).

Major Urban Centers (2004C): RABAT (1,622,860), Casablanca (3,111,977), Fez (946,815), Marrakesh (823,154), Oujda (400,738).

Official Language: Arabic.

Monetary Unit: Dirham (official rate July 1, 2005: 9.09 dirhams = $1US).

Sovereign: King MOHAMED VI, became King on July 23, 1999, following the death of his father, HASSAN II.

Heir to the Throne: Crown Prince HASSAN, born May 8, 2003.

Prime Minister: Driss JETTOU (nonparty), appointed by King Mohamed in October 2002, replacing Abderrahmane YOUSSOUFI (Socialist Union of Popular Forces); reappointed on June 8, 2004.

August 11 King Hassan reappointed Lamrani as prime minister and announced a "transitional cabinet" to serve until a postelection cabinet could be established under new constitutional provisions (see Constitution and government, below).

The basic law revisions were approved on September 4, 1992, by a national referendum, which the government hailed as a significant step in its ongoing democratization program. Widespread disbelief greeted the government's claim that 97.5 percent of the electorate had participated and that a 99.9 percent "yes" vote had been registered.

In balloting for directly elective House seats, delayed until June 25, 1993, the newly established

Democratic Bloc (*Koutla*), a coalition of center-left opposition groups led by the old-guard *Istiqlal* party and the Socialist Union of Popular Forces (USFP), secured 99 seats. They won only 15 more in the September 17 voting in electoral colleges made up of local officials, trade unionists, and representatives of professional associations. Meanwhile, the National Entente (*Wifaq*), a group of center-right royalist parties, increased its representation from 116 at the first round of balloting to 195 after the second. The Democratic Bloc subsequently charged that the indirect election encompassed widespread fraud, an allegation that received some support from international observers.

Although King Hassan rejected the Democratic Bloc's demand that the results of the indirect poll be overturned, he did propose that the bloc participate in the formation of a new cabinet, the first of what the king envisioned as a series of alternating left–right governments. The offer was declined because of the monarch's insistence that he retain the right to appoint the prime minister and maintain de facto control of the foreign, justice, and interior portfolios. Consequently, Lamrini formed a new nonparty government on November 11.

With his poor health again cited as the official reason for the change, Lamrini was succeeded on May 25, 1994, by former foreign minister Abdellatif FILALI, a longtime close advisor to the king. On June 7 Filali presented the monarch with a ministerial list unchanged from that of his predecessor, while King Hassan continued to seek Democratic Bloc leadership of a new coalition government. The negotiations eventually collapsed in early 1995, in part, because of the king's wish that Driss BASRI, long-term minister of state for interior and information, remain in the cabinet. The opposition parties had objected to Basri's influence for many years, charging that he had sanctioned human rights abuses and tolerated electoral fraud. Nonetheless, Basri retained the interior post on February 28 when Filali's new government, including 20 members of the National Entente, was announced.

Despite his failure to draw the leftist parties into the government, the king continued to pursue additional democratization, particularly regarding the proposed creation of an upper house of the legislature that, theoretically, would redistribute authority away from the monarchy to a certain degree. The king's proposal was affirmed by a reported 99.56 percent "yes" vote in a national referendum on September 13, 1996, most opposition parties having endorsed the amendment (see Constitution and government, below, for details).

Local elections were held on June 13, 1997, with seats being distributed along a wide spectrum of parties and no particular political dominance being apparent. Such was also the case with the November 14 balloting for a new House of Representatives as the *Koutla, Wifaq,* and a bloc of centrist parties each won about one-third of the seats. On the other hand, the indirect elections to the new House of Councillors revealed a decided tilt toward the *Wifaq,* not a surprising result considering its long-standing progovernment stance.

Continuing to pursue an alternating left–right series of governments, King Hassan was subsequently able to finally convince the Democratic Bloc to assume cabinet control, and on February 4, 1998, he appointed Abderrahmane YOUSSOUFI of the USFP (which had won the most seats in the House of Representatives) as the next prime minister. As formed on March 14, the new cabinet included representatives from seven parties, although the King's supporters (most notably Basri) remained in several key posts.

King Hassan, whose health had been a concern since 1995, died of a heart attack on July 23, 1999; Crown Prince SIDI MOHAMED succeeded his father immediately, the official ceremony marking his enthronement as King MOHAMED VI being held on July 30. Shortly thereafter, the long-suspect Driss Basri was dismissed as minister of the interior and moved to Paris. The new king confirmed his support for Prime Minister Youssoufi and his government. The cabinet was reshuffled on September 6, 2000, with Youssoufi retaining the top post, but the new king replaced him with an independent,

Driss JETTOU, in 2002. In 2004 the cabinet was again reshuffled, with many new cabinet appointments and Jettou remaining as prime minister.

Constitution and Government

Morocco is a constitutional monarchy, the Crown being hereditary and normally transmitted to the king's eldest son, who acts on the advice of a Regency Council if he accedes before age 20. Political power is highly centralized in the hands of the king, who serves as commander in chief and appoints the prime minister; in addition, he can declare a state of emergency, dissolve the legislature, veto legislation, and initiate constitutional amendments. Constitutional revisions approved in 1992 empowered the prime minister, instead of the king, to appoint and preside over the cabinet (albeit still subject to the king's approval); broadened the authority of the House of Representatives to include, inter alia, the initiation of confidence motions and the launching of investigations; and established new Constitutional and Economic/Social Councils. The preamble of the basic law was also altered to declare "the kingdom's attachment to human rights as they are universally recognized."

Until recently, legislative power had been nominally vested in a unicameral House of Representatives, one-third of whose members were indirectly designated by an electoral college. The new upper house (House of Councillors), provided for in the 1996 referendum, is elected indirectly from various local government bodies, professional associations, and employer and worker organizations. All members of the House of Representatives are now elected directly. Included in the new legislature's expanded authority is the power to censure the government and to dismiss cabinet members, although such decisions can still be overridden by the king.

The judicial system is headed by a Supreme Court (*Majlis al-Aala*) and includes courts of appeal, regional tribunals, magistrates' courts, labor tribunals, and a special court to deal with corruption. All judges are appointed by the king on the advice of the Supreme Council of the Judiciary.

The country is currently divided into 49 provinces and prefectures (including four provinces in Western Sahara), with further division into municipalities, autonomous centers, and rural communes. The king appoints all provincial governors, who are responsible to him. In addition, the basic law changes of September 1996 provided for 16 regional councils, with some members elected directly and others representing various professional organizations.

Foreign Relations

A member of the UN and the Arab League, Morocco has been chosen on many occasions as a site for Arab and African Islamic conferences at all levels. It has generally adhered to a nonaligned policy, combining good relations with the West with support for African and especially Arab nationalism. Morocco has long courted economic ties with the European Community (EC, now the European Union–EU), although its request for EC membership was politely rebuffed in 1987 on geographic grounds. An association agreement was negotiated in 1995 with the EU, which reportedly had begun to perceive the kingdom as the linchpin of a European campaign to expand trade with North Africa.

Relations with the United States have been friendly, US administrations viewing Morocco as a conservative counter to northern Africa's more radical regimes. An agreement was signed in mid-1982 that sanctioned, subject to veto, the use of Moroccan air bases by US forces in emergency situations. Periodic joint military exercises have since been conducted, with Washington serving as a prime supplier of equipment for Rabat's campaign in the Western Sahara.

During early 1991 Rabat faced a delicate situation in regard to the Iraqi invasion of Kuwait the previous August. Many Arab capitals were critical of King Hassan for contributing 1,700 Moroccan troops to the US-led Desert Shield deployment in Saudi Arabia and other Gulf states; domestic sentiment also appeared to be strongly tilted against Washington. However, the king defused the issue by permitting a huge pro-Iraq demonstration in the capital in early February and by expressing his personal sympathy for the Iraqi people during the Gulf war. His middle-of-the-road approach was widely applauded both at home and abroad.

Morocco's role in regional affairs has been complicated by a variety of issues. Relations with Algeria and Mauritania have been marred by territorial disputes (until 1970, Morocco claimed all of Mauritania's territory). The early 1970s brought cooperation with the two neighboring states in an effort to present a unified front against the retention by Spain of phosphate-rich Spanish Sahara, but by 1975 Morocco and Mauritania were ranged against Algeria on the issue. In an agreement reached at Madrid on November 14, 1975, Spain agreed to withdraw in favor of Morocco and Mauritania, who proceeded to occupy their assigned sectors (see map) on February 28, 1976, despite resistance from the Polisario Front, an Algerian-backed group that had proclaimed the establishment of an independent Saharan Arab Democratic Republic (SADR). Following Mauritanian renunciation of all claims to the territory in a peace accord with Polisario on August 5, 1979, Moroccan forces entered the southern sector, claiming it, too, as a Moroccan province.

Relations with Algeria were formally resumed in May 1988 prior to an Arab summit at Algiers on the uprising in the Israeli-occupied territories. The stage was thus set for diplomatic activity that in the wake of first-ever talks between King Hassan and Polisario representatives in early 1989 appeared to offer the strongest possibility in more than a decade for settlement of the Western Sahara problem. Although little progress was achieved over the next seven years on a proposed UN-sponsored self-determination vote, a new UN mediation effort in 1997 rekindled hopes for a settlement (see Disputed territory, below). Relations with Algeria improved further following the 1999 election of the new Algerian President, Abdelaziz Bouteflika, who suggested that bilateral affairs be handled independently of the conflict in the Western Sahara.

Long strained ties with Libya (which had been accused of complicity in several plots to overthrow the monarchy) began to improve with a state visit by Mu'ammar Qadhafi to Rabat in mid-1983. The process of rapprochement culminated in a treaty of projected union signed by the two leaders at Oujda on August 13, 1984. An inaugural meeting of a joint parliamentary assembly was held at Rabat in July 1985, and commissions were set up to discuss political, military, economic, cultural, and technical cooperation. By February 1989 cordial relations paved the way for a summit at Marrakesh, during which Qadhafi joined other North African leaders in proclaiming the Arab Maghreb Union.

Morocco's attitude toward Israel has been markedly more moderate than that of many Arab states, in part because more than 500,000 Jews of Moroccan ancestry live in Israel. King Hassan was known to relish his conciliatory potential in the Middle East peace process and was believed to have assisted in the negotiations leading up to the Israeli/PLO agreement of September 1993. Israeli Prime Minister Yitzhak Rabin made a surprise visit to Rabat on his return from the historic signing in Washington, his talks with King Hassan being heralded as an important step toward the establishment of formal diplomatic relations between the two countries.

In late 2001 relations between Morocco and Spain were strained by disagreements over illegal immigration, fishing rights, and smuggling. In July 2002, the countries were involved in a brief military standoff over an uninhabited islet (called Perejil by Spain, Leila by Morocco, and claimed by both) off the coast of Ceuta. With US, EU, and Egyptian mediation, the two sides agreed to withdraw their troops from the islet and to begin cooperating on various issues. Tensions eased dramatically when Spain's conservative government was replaced by the Spanish Socialist Workers Party in March 2004. In January 2005, Spain's King Juan Carlos paid an official visit to Morocco, a further sign of improved relations.

Current Issues

Western capitals appeared to be generally satisfied with King Mohamed's efforts at democratization. His coalition government works efficiently, and the approval of young ministers indicates his commitment to moving Morocco forward. Past abuses of human rights, including the disappearance of dissenters, seem to have diminished. The status of women in Moroccan society has been officially reformed, with the legal age for marriage raised from 15 to 18 and polygamy virtually outlawed.

The rise of radical Islamists–spurred on by the suicide attacks and the war in Iraq–has been of concern to the palace. Several blasts on one day in early 2003 in Casablanca killed more than 40 people. Some 2,000 Moroccans were convicted for the bombings, with several given death sentences and others long prison terms. A new anti-terrorism law was swiftly passed amid concerns in the media that increased powers of detention and surveillance would erode the gains in human rights. Although a survey by the US-based Pew Research Center indicated that 45 percent of Moroccans had a favorable view of Osama Bin Laden (compared with 65 percent in Pakistan and 55 percent in Jordan), Moroccans seemed to support the government's efforts to crack down on perpetrators of political violence. Also encouraging was the government's initiation of a new housing program and renewed efforts to industrialize the northern coast in recognition that poverty and joblessness in the slums create potential breeding grounds for radicalism.

The unresolved conflict over Western Sahara continues to hang like a shadow over the nation. Settling the thorny question of Western Saharan sovereignty versus Moroccan control could ease tensions and open doors in the region. In the meantime, Morocco continues to privatize, democratize, and modernize while trying to placate those who cling to more traditional ways.

Political Parties

Government Parties

Democratic Bloc (*Bloc Démocratique*). Launched in May 1992 to promote the establishment of a "healthy democracy within the framework of a constitutional monarchy," the Democratic Bloc or *Koutla* ("coalition"), currently includes the following four groups. (The UNFP was reportedly an initial member of the Bloc, but recent references have not listed it as a component.) All of the Bloc's founding members except the PPS (under PRP, below) urged voters to abstain from the September 1992 constitutional referendum, while in February 1993 all except the UNFP withdrew from participation in the national commission created to supervise upcoming legislative elections. The protesters charged that the commission was failing to pursue electoral law revision necessary to ensure "free and fair elections." However, all of the Bloc's components participated in the 1993 balloting, securing 114 seats overall, with affiliated labor organizations winning 6 more. Most of the Bloc's success (99 seats) came in the direct election, leading to its contention that the results of the indirect election had been "falsified." After protracted debate, the Bloc in November rejected King Hassan's invitation to name most of the ministers in a new government, insisting that it should be given a right of veto over all appointments. However, after its components secured 102 seats in the 1997 balloting for the House of Representatives, the *Koutla* agreed to lead a new coalition government, which was appointed in March 1998 under the leadership of the USFP's Abderrahmane Youssoufi. In October 2002, Youssoufi was replaced by the independent Driss Jettou, who was renominated in 2004.

Independence Party (*Parti de l'Istiqal*, or *Istiqlal*–PI). Founded in 1943, *Istiqlal* provided most of the nation's leadership before independence. It split in 1959, and its members were relieved of governmental responsibilities in 1963. Once a firm supporter of the throne, the party now displays a reformist attitude and supports the king only on selected issues. Stressing the need for better standards of living and equal rights for all Moroccans, it has challenged the government regarding alleged human rights abuses. In July 1970 *Istiqlal* formed a National Front with the UNFP (below) but ran alone in the election of June 1977, when it emerged as the (then) leading party. It suffered heavy losses in both the 1983 municipal elections and the 1984 legislative balloting.

In May 1990 *Istiqlal* joined the USFP (below), the PPS (under PRP, below), and the OADP (below) in supporting an unsuccessful censure motion that charged the government with "economic incompetence" and the pursuit of "antipopular" and "antisocial" policies. In November 1991 *Istiqlal* announced the formation of a "common front" with the USFP to work toward "establishment of true democracy," and the two parties presented a joint list in 1993, *Istiqlal's* 118 candidates securing 43 seats in the direct *Majlis* poll. As with many other long-standing parties, *Istiqlal* has recently been described as suffering conflict between its aging leaders and younger members. *Istiqlal* was the leading party in the June 1997 local elections but fell to fifth spot in the November House balloting. In the 2002 direct elections, the party won 48 seats, and its Secretary General, Abbas El Fassi, was named minister of state.

Leaders: Mohamed DOURI, Abbas EL FASSI (Secretary General).

Socialist Union of Popular Forces (*Union Socialiste des Forces Populaires*–USFP). The USFP was organized in September 1974 by the UNFP-Rabat Section (see UNFP, below), which had disassociated itself from the Casablanca Section in July 1972 and was accused by the government of involvement in a Libyan-aided plot to overthrow King Hassan in March 1973. The USFP subsequently called for political democratization, nationalization of major industries, thorough reform of the nation's social and administrative structures, and the cessation of what it believed to be human rights abuses by the government. It secured the third-largest number of legislative seats at the election of June 1977 but withdrew from the Chamber in October 1981 in protest at the extension of the parliamentary term. A year later it announced that it would return for the duration of the session ending in May 1983 so that it could participate in the forthcoming electoral campaigns. The majority of nearly 100 political prisoners released during July–August 1980 were USFP members, most of whom had been incarcerated for alleged antigovernment activities in 1973–1977.

After 52 of its 104 candidates (the USFP also supported 118 *Istiqlal* candidates) won seats in the June 1993 *Majlis* balloting, the Union was reportedly divided on whether to accept King Hassan's offer to participate in a coalition government, the dispute ultimately being resolved in favor of the rejectionists. Subsequently, the USFP was awarded only 4 additional House seats in the September indirect elections, First Secretary Abderrahmane Youssoufi resigning his post and departing for France in protest over "irregularities" surrounding the process. The party also continued to denounce the "harassment" of prominent USFP member Noubir el-Amaoui, secretary general of the Democratic Confederation of Labor (*Confédération Démocratique du Travail*), who had recently served 14 months in prison for "insulting and slandering" the government in a magazine interview.

Youssoufi returned from his self-imposed exile in April 1995, apparently in response to overtures from King Hassan, who was again attempting to convince leftist parties to join a coalition government. Although observers suggested that the USFP would soon "redefine" the party platform and possibly select new leaders, a July 1996 congress simply reconfirmed the current political bureau. Meanwhile, one USFP faction was reportedly attempting to "re-radicalize" the party under the direction of Mohamed BASRI, a longtime influential opposition leader known as *"Fiqh"* ("Learned One"). In June 1995 Basri had returned from 28 years in exile, during which he had been sentenced (in absentia) to death three times.

The USFP was the leading party in the November 1997 House balloting, securing 57 seats and distancing itself somewhat from its *Koutla* partner *Istiqlal* (32), with which it had previously been considered to be at comparable strength. Subsequently, the 74-year-old Youssoufi (once again being referenced as the USFP first secretary) was named by King Hassan to lead a new coalition government, although many younger USFP members reportedly opposed the party's participation. Internal dissent continued, as some radical members charged Youssoufi and the party administration with acting timidly in government and failing to push for further reforms in state institutions. Demands for a leadership change were reportedly voiced in the party congress in March 2001, especially by younger members and those associated with labor unions. However, Youssoufi managed to retain his post, prompting some members to leave the party to form the National Ittihadi Congress (CNI, below). USFP was the leading party in the 2002 elections, winning 50 seats.

Leaders: Abderrahmane YOUSSOUFI (First Secretary of the Party), Noubir el-AMAOUI, Mohamed El YAZGHI, Abdelwahed RADI, Fathallah OUALALOU.

Party of Renewal and Progress (*Parti du Renouveau et du Progrès*–PRP). The PRP is the successor to the Moroccan Communist Party (*Parti Communiste Marocain*), which was banned in 1952; the Party of Liberation and Socialism (*Parti de la Libération et du Socialisme*), which was banned in 1969; and the Party of Progress and Socialism (*Parti du Progrès et du Socialisme*–PPS), which obtained legal status in 1974. The single PPS representative in the 1977 chamber, 'Ali Yata, was the first Communist to win election to a Moroccan legislature. The fourth national congress, held in July 1987 at Casablanca, although strongly supportive of the government's position on the Western Sahara, criticized the administration's recent decisions to privatize some state enterprises and implement other economic liberalization measures required by the International Monetary Fund (IMF). However, by mid-1991 the PPS was reported to be fully converted to *perestroika,* a stance that had apparently earned the party additional support within the Moroccan middle class. In late 1993 Yata un-

successfully urged his Democratic Bloc partners to compromise with King Hassan in formation of a new government.

The party's current name was adopted in 1994 in conjunction with its "repositioning" as a social democratic grouping under the growing influence of 'Ali Yata's son, Nadir. However, subsequent news reports have often still referenced the group under the PPS rubric. 'Ali Yata, who had been reelected to his post of PRP secretary general in mid-1995, died in August 1997 after being struck by a car. In March 2002 the PRP and the PSD (below) announced that they had launched the Socialist Alliance (*Alliance Socialiste*) and that they were planning to cooperate in the legislative poll in September. In that election the PRP collected only 11 seats.

Leaders: Nadir YATA, Khalid NACIRI, Ismail ALAOUI (Secretary General).

National Assembly of Independents (*Rassemblement National des Indépendants*–RNI). The RNI was launched at a Constitutive Congress held October 6–9, 1978. Although branded by left-wing spokesmen as a "King's party," it claimed to hold the allegiance of 141 of 264 deputies in the 1977 Chamber. Subsequent defections and other disagreements, both internal and with the king, resulted in the party's designation as the "official" opposition in late 1981. It won 61 House seats in 1984, thereafter returning to a posture of solid support for the king and the government. RNI leader Ahmed Osman, a former prime minister and former president of the House of Representatives, is one of the country's best-known politicians. Previously affiliated with the National Entente, the RNI participated (as did the MNP) in the November 1997 elections as an unaligned "centrist" party (winning 46 seats) and subsequently agreed to join the *Koutla*-led coalition government named in early 1998. In 2002 RNI won 41 seats.

Leaders: Ahmed OSMAN (President), Moulay Mustafa Ben Larbi ALAIOU.

Popular National Movement (*Mouvement National Populaire*–MNP). The MNP was organized in October 1991 by longtime Berber leader

Mahjoubi Aherdane, who was ousted as secretary general of the MP in 1986. The new party won 25 House seats in 1993. A number of MNP members left the party in mid-1996 to form the MDS (below). The MNP won 19 seats in the 1997 balloting for House of Representatives, having shed its National Entente orientation. Ahmed Moussaoui, the minister of youth and sports, was expelled from the MNP in April 2001 and was subsequently reported to have joined the new Democratic Union. MNP won 18 seats in 2002.

Leaders: Mahjoubi AHERDANE (Secretary General), Hassan MAAOUNI.

Socialist Democratic Party (*Parti Socialiste et Démocratique*–PSD). The PSD was established in October 1996 by OADP members who disagreed with that group's rejection of King Hassan's proposed constitutional changes. The party won six seats in 2002 balloting.

Leaders: Abdessamad BELKEBIR, Mohamed Habib TALEB, Aissa QUARDIGHI (Secretary General).

Democratic Forces Front (*Front des Forces Démocratiques*–FFD). Launched in 1997 by PRP dissidents, the FFD won 9 seats in the November House balloting, and its leader was named to the March 1998 cabinet. In 2002 the party won 12 seats.

Leader: Thami KHYARI (National Secretary).

Opposition Parties

National Entente (*Entente Nationale*). The National Entente, also known as the *Wifaq* (Agreement) Bloc, initially comprised five center-right parties, the three listed below and the MNP and RNI (above). The UC, MP, PND, and RNI had served as leading government parties from April 1985 to August 1992. In November 1993 King Hassan announced that the Entente, whose members held 195 of 333 seats in the recently elected House of Representatives, had decided not to enter the new government in order to permit component parties to concentrate on internal matters. However, after the failure of a protracted effort to convince leftist parties to participate, 20 Entente members (9 from the UC, 8 from the MP, and 3 from the PND) were named to the cabinet formed in February 1995. Although the MNP and the RNI declined cabinet representation, they announced they would provide the government with legislative support. Those two parties were subsequently listed as operating outside the *Wifaq* umbrella for the 1997 elections, at which the UC, MP, and PND secured 100 House seats. In 2002 the three parties dropped to 55 seats.

Constitutional Union (*Union Constitutionelle*–UC). Founded in 1983 by Maati Bouabid, the UC is a moderate party that emphasizes economic self-sufficiency. Said to have royal support, the party won 83 House seats in 1984. The UC's representation fell to 54 seats in 1993, although it retained a slim plurality and one of its members was elected president of the new House. Bouabid died in November 1996, exacerbating problems within a party described as already in disarray. The UC was the second leading party in the November 1997 House balloting, winning 50 seats, but dropped to 16 in 2002.

Leader: Mohamed Jalal ESSAID (former Speaker of the House of Councillors).

Popular Movement (*Mouvement Populaire*–MP). Organized in 1958 as a monarchist party of Berber mountaineers, the MP was a major participant in government coalitions of the early 1960s. It secured the second-largest number of legislative seats at the election of June 1977 and was third-ranked after the 1984 and 1993 elections.

In October 1986 an extraordinary party congress voted to remove the MP's founder, Mahjoubi Aherdane, from the post of secretary general, replacing him the Mohand Laenser. Aherdane subsequently formed a new Berber party (see MNP, above). In the 2002 elections the MP won 27 seats and Laenser was named minister of agriculture.

Leader: Mohand LAENSER (Secretary General).

National Democratic Party (*Parti National Démocrate*–PND). The PND was founded as the

Democratic Independents (*Indépendants Démocrates*–ID) in April 1981 by 59 former RNI deputies in the House of Representatives. At the party's first congress on June 11–13, 1982, its secretary general, Mohamed Arsalane al-Jadidi, affirmed the PND's loyalty to the monarchy while castigating the RNI for not providing an effective counterweight to the "old" parties.

Leader: Abdallah KADIRI.

Justice and Development Party (*Parti de la Justice et du Développement*–PJD). The PJD was formerly known as the Popular Constitutional and Democratic Movement (*Mouvement Populaire Constitutionnel et Démocratique*–MPCD). The MPCD was a splinter from the Popular Movement. It won 3 legislative seats in 1977 and none in 1984 or 1993.

In June 1996 the moribund MPCD was rejuvenated by its merger with an unrecognized Islamist grouping known as Reform and Renewal (*Al Islah wa Attajid*), led by Abdelillah Benkirane. The Islamists were allocated 3 of the MPCD's secretariat seats, and Benkirane was generally acknowledged as the party's primary leader. He announced that his supporters had relinquished their "revolutionary ideas" and were now committed to "Islam, the constitutional monarchy, and nonviolence." The party won 9 seats in the House of Representatives in 1997, while Benkirane was successful in a by-election on April 30, 1999. The PJD has gained popularity. In local elections in 2003, it scaled back the candidates it presented, with leader Eldine OTHMANI explaining that the party did not want to scare off foreign investors with high-profile wins.

Leader: Eldine Othmani (Secretary General).

Action Party (*Parti de l'Action*–PA). The PA was organized in December 1974 by a group of Berber intellectuals dedicated to the "construction of a new society through a new elite." It won two legislative seats in 1977, none in 1984, and 2 in 1993 and 1997.

Leader: Mohammed EL IDRISSI.

Democratic Party for Independence (*Parti Démocratique pour l'Indépendance*–PDI). The PDI, a small but long-standing grouping (also referenced as the *Parti de la Choura et de l'Istiqlal,* or *Choura*), won 3 seats in the 1993 direct House election and a surprising 6 seats in the indirect election.

Leaders: Thami el-OUAZZANI, Said BOUACHRINE.

Democratic and Social Movement (*Mouvement Démocratique et Social*–MDS). Launched in June 1996 (as the National Democratic and Social Movement) by MNP dissidents, the Berber MDS is led by a former official of the interior ministry.

Leader: Mahmoud ARCHANE (Secretary General).

Other Parties and Groups

United Socialist Left (*Gauche Socialiste Unifiée*–GSU). The GSU is a left-wing formation that was launched at a constitutive congress in July 2002 when the OADP merged with three minor radical groupings, namely the Movement of Independent Democrats, the Movement for Democracy, and the Independent Left Potentials.

Leader: Mohamed BENSAID (Secretary General).

Organization of Democratic and Popular Action (*Organisation de l'Action Démocratique et Populaire*–OADP). Claiming a following of former members of the USFP and PPS, the OADP was organized in May 1983. It obtained 1 seat in 1984 balloting and 2 seats in 1993. A new 74-member Central Committee was elected at the third OADP congress, held November 5–6, 1994, at Casablanca.

The OADP was one of the few major parties to oppose the king's constitutional initiatives of 1996, some of its members subsequently splitting off to form the PSD (above) because of the issue. The OADP won 4 seats in the November 1997 *Majlis* elections. Although the OADP was a member of the ruling Democratic Bloc, it was not listed as having any members in the March 1998 cabinet. The

OADP sources defined the group's stance as one of "critical" support of the coalition government.

Leader: Mohamed BENSAID (Secretary General).

National Union of Popular Forces (*Union Nationale des Forces Populaires*–UNFP). Formed in 1959 by former *Istiqlal* adherents, the UNFP subsequently became a coalition of left-wing nationalists, trade unionists, resistance fighters, and dissident members of minor parties. Weakened by internal factionalism, government repression, the disappearance of its leader Mehdi Ben Barka (while visiting France in 1965), and the neutrality of the Moroccan Labor Union (UMT), the party subsequently split into personal factions. In 1972 the National Administrative Committee replaced the ten-man Secretariat General and three-man Political Bureau with a group of five permanent committees. The Political Bureau thereupon formed its own organization, UNFP–Rabat Section, which was banned for several months in 1973 for activities against the state and subsequently reorganized as the USFP (above). The UNFP formally boycotted the legislative elections of 1977 and 1984, as well as the municipal balloting of June 1983; it won no seats in 1993. Recent references to the Democratic Bloc have not listed the UNFP among its components, despite its previous inclusion in that umbrella group.

Leader: Moulay Abdallah IBRAHIM (Secretary General).

Party of the Democratic and Social Vanguard (*Parti de l'Avant-Garde Démocratique et Social*–PAGDS). Formed by USFD dissidents in 1991, the PAGDS boycotted the 1997 elections on the ground that its members had been harassed by the government.

Leader: Ahmed BENJELLAIME.

Other parties, a number of which won seats in 2002, include the **Alliance of Freedoms** (*Alliance des Libertés*–ADL), led by ali BEL HAJ; the **Citizens' Initiatives for Development** (*Initiatives Citoyennes pour le Développement*–ICD), led by Mohammed BENHAMOU; the **Democratic Union** (*Union Démocratique*–UD), led by Bouazza IKKEN; the **Moroccan Liberal Party** (*Parti Marocain Libéral*–PML), led by Mohammed ZIANE; the **National Ittihadi Congress** (*Congrès National Ittihadi*–CNI), a breakaway group from the USFP led by Abdelmajid BOUZOUBAA; the **National Party for Unity and Solidarity** (*Parti National pour l'Unité et la Solidarité*–PNUS), led by Muhammad ASMAR; the **Party of Citizens' Forces** (*Parti des Forces Citoyennes*–PFC), led by Abderrahim LAHJOUJI; the **Party of Environment and Development** (*Parti de l'Environnement et du Développement*–PED), led by Ahmed AL ALAMI; the **Party of Promise** (*Parti Al Ahd*), led by Najib EL OUAZZANI; the **Party of Reform and Development** (*Parti de la Réforme et du Développement*–PRD), led by former RNI member Abderrahmane EL KOHEN; the **Party of Renewal and Equity** (*Parti du Renouveau et de l'Equitie*–PRE), led by Chakir ACHEHBAR; and the **Social Center Party** (*Parti du Centre Social*–PCS), led by Lachen MADIH.

Clandestine Groups

Justice and Welfare (*Adl wal Ihsan*). The country's leading radical Islamist organization, *Adl wal Ihsan* was formed in 1980. Although denied legal party status in 1981, it was informally tolerated until a mid-1989 crackdown, during which its founder, Sheikh Abd Assalam Yasine, was placed under house arrest and other members were imprisoned. The government formally outlawed the group in January 1990; two months later, five of its most prominent members were given two-year prison terms, and Yasine's house detention was extended, touching off large-scale street disturbances at Rabat. Although the other detainees were released in early 1992, Yasine remained under house arrest, King Hassan describing fundamentalism as a threat to Moroccan stability. An estimated 100 members of *Adl wal Ihsan* were reportedly among the prisoners pardoned in mid-1994, Yasine pointedly not among them. The Islamist leader was finally released from house arrest in December 1995 but was soon thereafter placed under "police protection" for apparently having criticized the government too strenuously. (Among Yasine's transgressions, in the eyes of the government, was his failure to acknowledge King Hassan as the nation's supreme religious leader.) His house arrest prompted protest demonstrations in 1998 by his supporters, whom the government also charged with responsibility for recent among university students and a mass demonstration in late December 1998 protesting US–UK air strikes against Iraq. Although the group remained proscribed, Yasine was released from house arrest in May 2000. He reportedly continued to be critical of the royal family and the government, but based on Yasine's rejection of violence, the government tolerated the group's activities.

Leader: Sheikh Abd Assalam YASINE.

In 1985 and 1986 there were a number of arrests of persons appearing to be members of two left-wing groups: *Il al-Amam* (To the Future), formed in the 1960s by a number of PPS Maoist dissidents, and *Qa'idiyyin* (The Base), an outgrowth of a *23 Mars* group of the 1970s, most of whose supporters entered the OADP. Many of the detainees were released in mid-1989 under a royal amnesty. *Il al-Amam's* former leader, Abraham SERFATY, was allowed to return to Morocco in late 1999. Members of another banned organization, *Shabiba al-Islamiya* (Islamic Youth), have also been sentenced to prison terms, often in absentia, for antiregime activity. The group was founded by Abdelkarim MOUTIA, a former nationalist.

Legislature

The constitutional amendments of September 1996 provided for a bicameral **Parliament** (*Barlaman*) comprising an indirectly elected House of Councillors and a directly elected House of Representatives. Previously, the legislature had consisted of a unicameral House of Representatives, two-thirds of whose members were directly elected with the remainder being selected by an electoral college of government, professional, and labor representatives.

House of Councillors (*Majlis al-Mustacharin*). The upper house consists of 270 members indirectly elected for nine-year terms (one-third of the house is renewed every three years) by local councils, regional councils, and professional organizations. At the first election on December 5, 1997, the National Assembly of Independents won 42 seats; the Democratic and Social Movement, 33; the Constitutional Union, 28, the Popular Movement, 27; the National Democratic Party, 21; the Independence Party, 21; the Socialist Union of Popular Forces, 16; the Popular National Movement, 15; the Action Party, 13; the Democratic Forces Front, 12; the Party of Renewal and Progress, 7; the Socialist Democratic Party, 4; the Democratic Party for Independence, 4; and various labor organizations, 27. In the election to renew one-third of the house on September 15, 2000, the National Assembly of Independents won 14 seats; the Popular National Movement, 12; the National Democratic Party, 10; the Popular Movement, 9; the Constitutional Union, 8; the Independence Party, 7; the Democratic and Social Movement, 6; the Democratic Forces Front, 5; the Socialist Union of Popular Forces, 3; the Party of Renewal and Progress, 2; the Action Party, 2; the Socialist Democratic Party, 2; the Democratic Party for Independence, 1; and various labor organizations, 3.

Speaker: Mustapha OUKACHA.

House of Representatives (*Majlis al-Nawab*). The lower house has 325 members directly elected on a proportional basis for five-year terms. (Under electoral law revision of May 2002, 30 seats were set aside for women; those seats were to be contested on a proportional basis from national lists for the September 2002 balloting, while the other 295 seats were to be elected on a proportional basis from 92 multi-member constituencies.) Following the election of September 27, 2002, the distribution of seats was as follows: Socialist Union of Popular Forces, 50; Independence Party (*Istiqlal*), 48; Justice and Development, 42; National Assembly of Independents, 41; Popular Movement, 18; Constitutional Union, 16; National Democratic Party, 12; Democratic Forces Front, 12; Party of Renewal and

Cabinet

As of June 1, 2005

Prime Minister	Driss Jettou (ind.)
Minister of State	Abbas El Fassi (*Istiqlal*)

Ministers

Agricultural, Rural Development, and Marine Fisheries	Mohand Laenser (MNP)
Communication, Spokesman of the Government	Mohamed Nabil Benabdallah (ind.)
Culture	Mohamed Achaari (USFP)
Energy and Mining	Mohammed Boutaleb (ind.)
Employment and Vocational Training	Mustapha Mansouri (*Istiqlal*)
Environment, Territory Development	Mohamed El-Yazghi (USFP)
Equipment and Transport	Karim Gellab (ind.)
Finance and Privatization	Fathallah Oualalou (USFP)
Foreign Affairs and Cooperation	Mohamed Benaissa (RNI)
Foreign Trade	Mustapha Mechahouri (ind.)
General Secretary of the Government	Abdessadek Rabiaa (ind.)
Habous (Religious Endowments) and Islamic Affairs	Ahmed Toufig (ind.)
Health	Mohammed Chaik Biadillah (ind.)
Industry, Trade, and Upgrading the Economy	Salaheddine Mezouar (ind.)
Interior	Al Mustapha Sahel (ind.)
Justice	Mohamed Bouzoubaa (ind.)
Modernization of the Public Sector	Mohamed Boussaid (ind.)
National Education, Higher Education, Staff Training, and Scientific Research	Habib El Malki (ind.)
Relations with Parliament	Mohammed Saad El Alami (*Istiqlal*)
Social Development, The Family, and Solidarity	Abderrahman Harouchi (ind.)
Tourism, Handicraft, and Social Economy	Adil Douiri (*Istiqlal*)

Ministers Delegate (*Ministries*)

Foreign Affairs and Cooperation	Tayeb Fassi Fihri
Foreign Affairs, Moroccans Living Abroad	Nouzha Chekrouni [f]
Interior	Fouad Ali El-Himma

Secretaries of State

Agriculture, Rural Development, and Sea Fisheries	Mohamed Mohattane
Employment and Vocational Training	Said Oulbacha
National Education, Higher Education, Staff Training, and Scientific	Research Anis Birou
Social Development, Family, and Solidarity	Yasmina Baddou [f]
Youth	Mohammed El Gahs

[f] = female

Progress, 11; Democratic Union, 10; Democratic and Social Movement, 7; Socialist Democratic Party, 6; Party of Promise, 5; Alliance of Freedom, 4; Party of Reform and Development, 3; United Socialist Left, 3; Moroccan Liberal Party, 3; Party of Citizens' Forces, 2; Party of Environment and Development, 2; National Ittihadi Congress, 1.

Speaker: Abdelwahed RADI.

Communications

Press

Moroccan newspapers have a reputation for being highly partisan and outspoken, although those incurring the displeasure of the state face reprisal, such as forced suspension, and government control has at times been highly restrictive. The following are published daily at Casablanca in French, unless otherwise noted: *Le Matin du Sahara* (100,000), replaced *Le Petit Marocain* following government shutdown in 1971; *al-Alam* (Rabat, 100,000), *Istiqlal* organ, in Arabic; *L'Opinion* (Rabat, 60,000), *Istiqlal* organ; *Maroc Soir* (50,000), replaced *La Vigie Marocaine* in 1971; *al-Maghrib* (Rabat, 15,000), RNI organ; *al-Mithaq al-Watani* (Rabat, 25,000), RNI organ, in Arabic; *al-Anba'a* (Rabat, 15,000), Ministry of Information, in Arabic; *al-Bayane* (5,000), PRP organ, in French and Arabic; *Libération,* USFP organ; *al-Ittihad al-Ichtiraki,* USFP organ, in Arabic; *Rissalat al-Umma,* UC organ, in Arabic; *Anoual* (Rabat), OADP weekly, in Arabic; *Al Mounaddama*, in Arabic. A*l-Mouharir,* a USFP organ, and *al-Bayane* were suspended in the wake of the June 1981 riots at Casablanca. The latter was permitted to resume publication in mid-July but, having had a number of its issues confiscated in early 1984 because of its reporting of further Casablanca disturbances, it was suspended again from October 1986 until January 1987. Two months later, the government seized an issue of *Anoual,* apparently in response to its coverage of prison conditions, and took similar action against *al-Bayane* in January 1988 because of its stories on problems in the educational system and recent demonstrations at Fez University. The USFP's *al-Ittihad al-Ichtiraki* was also informed that it would be censored because of its coverage of the student disturbances. In mid-1991 the government banned distribution of the first issue of *Le Citoyen,* a weekly established by political dissidents to promote government reform. Following the enthronement of the reform-minded King MOHAMED VI in 1999, the government somewhat relaxed its grip on the print media. However, from 2000 through mid-2002 various issues of *Le Journal,* the independent weekly *L'Economiste, Maroc-Hebdo,* the Islamist weekly *Risahat al-Foutawah, Le Reporter al-Moustaquil, Le Quoditien du Maroc, Chamal, Demain,* and *Assahifa* were banned. Domestic and international journalists' organizations criticized a libel law adopted in April 2002, accusing the government of eroding civil and press liberties by making it easier to file libel suits.

News Agencies

The Moroccan Arab News Agency (*Wikalat al-Maghreb al-'Arabi*–WMA), successor to the former *Maghreb Arabe Presse,* is an official, government-owned agency. Most major foreign agencies maintain offices at Rabat.

Broadcasting and Computing

Broadcasting is under the supervision of the Broadcasting Service of the Kingdom of Morocco (*Idha'at al-Mamlakat al-Maghribiyah*). The government-controlled *Radiodiffusion-Télévision Marocaine* provides radio service over three networks (national, international, and Berber) as well as commercial television service; transmission by a private TV company was launched in 1989. In addition, the Voice of America operates a radio station at Tangier. There were approximately 7.1 million television receivers and 600,000 personal computers serving 800,000 Internet users in 2003.

Intergovernmental Representation

Ambassador to the US
Aziz MEKOUAR

US Ambassador to Morocco
Thomas RILEY

Permanent Representative to the UN
Mohamed BENNOUNA

IGO Memberships (Non-UN)
AfDB, AFESD, AMF, AMU, BADEA, CCC, EBRD, IDB, Interpol, IOM, LAS, NAM, OIC, OIF, PCA, WTO

Disputed Territory

Western Sahara

The region known since 1976 as Western Sahara was annexed by Spain in two stages: the coastal area in 1884 and the interior in 1934. In 1957, the year after Morocco attained full independence, Rabat renewed a claim to the territory, sending irregulars to attack inland positions. In 1958, however, French and Spanish troops succeeded in quelling the attacks, with Madrid formally uniting Saguia el Hamra and Rio de Oro, the two historical components of the territory, as the province of Spanish Sahara. Mauritanian independence in 1960 led to territorial claims by Nouakchott, with the situation being further complicated in 1963 by the discovery of one of the world's richest phosphate deposits at Bu Craa. During the next dozen years, Morocco attempted to pressure Spain into relinquishing its claim through a combination of diplomatic initiatives (the UN first called for a referendum on self-determination for the Sahrawi people in 1966), direct support for guerrilla groups, and a legal challenge in the International Court of Justice (ICJ).

Increasing insurgency led Spain in May 1975 to announce that it intended to withdraw from Spanish Sahara, while an ICJ ruling the following October stated that Moroccan and Mauritanian legal claims to the region were limited and had little bearing on the question of self-determination. Nevertheless, in November King Hassan ordered some 300,000 unarmed Moroccans, in what became known as the Green March, to enter the territory. Although Spain strongly objected to the action, a tripartite agreement with Morocco and Mauritania was concluded at Madrid on November 14. As a result, Spanish Sahara ceased to be a province of Spain at the end of the year; Spanish troops withdrew shortly thereafter, and Morocco and Mauritania assumed responsibility for Western Sahara on February 28, 1976. On April 14 Rabat and Nouakchott reached an agreement under which Morocco claimed the northern two-thirds of the region and Mauritania claimed the southern one-third.

The strongest opposition to the partition was voiced by the Popular Front for the Liberation of Saguia el Hamra and Rio de Oro (Polisario, see below), which in February 1976 formally proclaimed a government-in-exile of the Sahrawi Arab Democratic Republic (SADR), headed by Mohamed Lamine OULD AHMED as prime minister. Whereas Polisario had originally been based in Mauritania, its political leadership was subsequently relocated to Algeria, with its guerrilla units, recruited largely from nomadic tribes indigenous to the region, also establishing secure bases there. Neither Rabat nor Nouakchott wished to precipitate a wider conflict by operating on Algerian soil, which permitted Polisario to concentrate militarily against the weaker of the two occupying regimes and thus to aid in the overthrow of Mauritania's Moktar Ould Daddah in July 1978. On August 5, 1979, Mauritania concluded a peace agreement with Polisario at Algiers, but Morocco responded by annexing the southern third of Western Sahara. Meanwhile, Polisario launched its first raids into Morocco while continuing a diplomatic offensive that by the end of 1980 had resulted in some 45 countries according recognition to the SADR.

During a summit meeting of the Organization of African Unity (OAU) at Nairobi, Kenya, in June 1981, King Hassan called for a referendum on the future of the disputed territory, but an OAU special implementation committee was unable to move on the proposal because of Rabat's refusal to engage in direct negotiations or to meet a variety of other conditions advanced by Polisario as necessary to effect a cease-fire. As a result, conflict in the region intensified in the second half of the year.

At an OAU Council of Ministers meeting at Addis Ababa, Ethiopia, on February 22, 1982, a SADR delegation was, for the first time, seated, following a controversial ruling by the organization's secretary general that provoked a walkout by 18 member states, including Morocco. For the same reason, a quorum could not be declared for the next scheduled Council of Ministers meeting at Tripoli, Libya, on July 26, or for the 19th OAU summit, which was to have convened at Tripoli on August 5. An attempt to reconvene both meetings in November, following the "voluntary and temporary" withdrawal of the SADR, also failed because of the Western Sahara impasse, coupled with disagreement over the composition of a delegation from Chad. Another "temporary" withdrawal of the SADR allowed the OAU to convene the long-delayed summit at Addis Ababa in May 1983 at which it was decided to oversee a referendum in the region by the end of the year. Morocco's refusal to meet directly with Polisario representatives forced postponement of the poll, while the 1984 Treaty of Oujda with Libya effectively reduced support for the front's military forces. Subsequently, Moroccan soldiers crossed briefly into Algerian soil in "pursuit" of guerrillas, while extending the area under Moroccan control by 4,000 square miles. The seating of an SADR delegation at the 20th OAU summit in November 1985 and the election of Polisario Secretary General Mohamed 'Abd al-Azziz as an OAU vice president prompted Morocco's withdrawal from the organization.

At the sixth triennial Polisario congress, held in "liberated territory" in December 1985, 'Abd al-Azziz was reelected secretary general; he subsequently appointed a new 13-member SADR government that included himself as president, with Ould Ahmed continuing as prime minister. The following May a series of "proximity talks" involving Moroccan and Polisario representatives concluded at UN headquarters in New York, with no discernible change in the territorial impasse. Subsequently, Rabat began construction of more than 1,200 miles of fortified sand walls that forced the rebels back toward the Algerian and Mauritanian borders. Polisario, while conceding little likelihood of victory by its 30,000 fighters over an estimated 120,000 to 140,000 Moroccan soldiers, nonetheless continued its attacks, hoping that the economic strain of a "war of attrition" would induce King Hassan to enter into direct negotiations–a position endorsed by a 98–0 vote of the 41st UN General Assembly. The UN also offered to administer the Western Sahara on an interim basis pending a popular referendum, but Rabat insisted that its forces remain in place. In 1987 the SADR reported an assassination attempt against 'Abd al-Azziz, alleging Moroccan complicity. Rabat denied the allegation and suggested that SADR dissidents may have been responsible.

Following the resumption of relations between Rabat and Algiers in May 1988, which some observers attributed in part to diminishing Algerian support for Polisario, progress appeared to be developing toward a negotiated settlement of the militarily stalemated conflict. On August 30, shortly after a new SADR government had been announced with Mahfoud Ali BEIBA taking over as prime minister, both sides announced their "conditional" endorsement of a UN-sponsored peace plan that called for a cease-fire and introduction of a UN peacekeeping force to oversee the long-discussed self-determination referendum. However, agreement was lacking on the qualifications of those who would be permitted to participate in the referendum and whether Moroccan troops would remain in the area prior to the vote. Underlining the fragility of the negotiations, Polisario launched one of its largest attacks in September before calling a cease-fire on December 30 pending face-to-face talks with King Hassan in January 1989. Although the talks eventually broke down, the cease-fire continued throughout most of the year as UN Secretary General Javier Pérez de Cuéllar attempted to mediate an agreement on referendum details. However, Polisario, accusing Rabat of delaying tactics, initiated a series of attacks in October, subsequent fighting being described as some of the most intense to date in the conflict. Another temporary truce was implemented in March 1990, and in June the UN Security Council formally authorized creation of a Western Saharan mission to supervise the proposed referendum. However, it was not until April 29, 1991, that the Security Council endorsed direct UN sponsorship of the poll, with the General Assembly approving a budget of $180 million, plus $34 million in voluntary contributions, for a UN Mission for the Referendum in Western Sahara (referenced by its French acronym, MINURSO). The mission's charge included the identification of bona fide inhabitants of the territory, the assembly of a voting list, the establishment of polling stations, and supervision of the balloting itself. The plan appeared to be in jeopardy when fierce fighting broke out in August between Moroccan and Polisario forces prior to the proposed deployment of MINURSO peacekeeping troops; however, both sides honored the UN's formal cease-fire date of September 6.

By early 1992 the broader dimensions of the Western Sahara conflict had significantly changed. The collapse of the Soviet Union and heightened internal problems for Polisario's principal backers, Algeria and Libya, created financial and supply problems for the rebels. At midyear it was estimated that more than 1,000 rank and file had joined a number of dissident leaders in defecting to Morocco. Meanwhile, Morocco had moved tens of thousands of settlers into the disputed territory, thereby diluting potential electoral support for Polisario. In addition, the proposed self-determination referendum, which the UN had planned to conduct in February, had been postponed indefinitely over the issue of voter eligibility, Polisario leaders charging that UN representatives had compromised their impartiality through secret dealings with Rabat. An unprecedented meeting, brokered by the UN at El Aaiún between Moroccan and Polisario representatives, ended on July 19, 1993, without substantial progress. The main difficulty lay in a dispute about voting lists, Polisario insisting they should be based on a census taken in 1974, and Morocco arguing that they should be enlarged to include the names of some 100,000 individuals subsequently settling in the territory.

A second round of face-to-face talks, scheduled for October 1993, was cancelled at the last moment when Polisario objected to the presence of recent defectors from the Front on the Moroccan negotiating team. Although the prospects for agreement on electoral eligibility were regarded as slight, MINURSO began identifying voters in June 1994 with the hope that balloting could be conducted in October 1995. Registration proceeded slowly, however, and UN officials in early 1995 protested that the Moroccan government was interfering in their operations. In April UN Secretary General Boutros Boutros-Ghali reluctantly postponed the referendum again, sentiment reportedly growing within the UN Security Council to withdraw MINURSO if genuine progress was not achieved shortly.

In May 1996 the Security Council ordered a reduction in MINURSO personnel, UN officials declaring an impasse in the voter identification dispute and observers suggesting that hostilities could easily breakout once again. However, face-to-face contacts between Polisario and Moroccan officials resumed in September, but no genuine progress ensued. It was reported that only 60,000 potential voters had been approved with the cases of some 150,000 other "applicants" remaining unresolved at the end of the year.

New UN Secretary General Kofi Annan made the relaunching of the UN initiative in Morocco one of his priorities in early 1997 and in the spring appointed former US secretary of state James Baker as his personal envoy on the matter. Baker's mediation led to face-to-face talks between Polisario and representatives of the Moroccan government in the summer, culminating in the announcement of a "breakthrough" in September. Essentially, the two sides agreed to revive the 1991 plan with the goal of conducting the self-determination referendum in December 1998. They also accepted UN "supervision" in the region pending the referendum and agreed to the repatriation of refugees under the auspices of the UN High Commissioner for Refugees. MINURSO resumed the identification of voters in December 1997; however, the process subsequently again bogged down, with most observers concluding that the Moroccan government bore primary responsibility for the foot-dragging. Annan launched what he said would be his final push for a resolution in early 1999, calling for the resumption of voter registration at midyear leading up to a referendum by the end of July 2000.

In September 1999 several pro-independence riots in Western Sahara were suppressed by what some saw as an overreaction by the police, who beat and arrested scores. The heavy-handedness of the security forces reportedly strengthened the resolve of King Mohamed VI to oust the "old guard" of the Moroccan regime, especially Interior Minister Driss Basri. Although the new king subsequently espoused a more flexible stance toward the Western Sahara issue, UN special envoy Baker noted in April 2000 that he remained pessimistic about the prospects of a resolution of the conflict, citing Morocco's insistence that Moroccan settlers in Western Sahara be eligible in the proposed referendum. In September 2001 Polisario rejected Baker's proposal to grant the Western Sahara political autonomy rather than holding an independence referendum. Recent interest in oil drilling in the region reportedly further complicated the matter. In November 2002 King Mohamed described the notion of a self-determination referendum as "obsolete." In mid-2004 the UN Security Council adopted a resolution urging Morocco and Polisario to accept the UN plan to grant Western Sahara self-government. Morocco rejected the proposal and continued to insist that the area be granted autonomy within the framework of Moroccan sovereignty. In August 2005 Polisario released 404 Moroccan prisoners, the last of the soldiers it had captured in fighting. The front said it hoped that the gesture would lead to Moroccan reciprocity and help toward a peace settlement.

Moroccan administration of the annexed territory is based on its division into four provinces: three established in 1976 (Boujdour, Es-Smara, El-Aaiún) and one added in 1979 (Oued ed-Dahab). The SADR administers four Algerian camps that house some 165,000 Sahrawis, while claiming to represent some 70,000 others that remain in the Western Sahara.

Sahrawi Front

Popular Front for the Liberation of Saguia el Hamra and Rio de Oro (*Frente Popular para la Liberación de Saguia el Hamra y Rio de Oro*–Polisario). Established in 1973 to win independence for Spanish (subsequently Western) Sahara, the Polisario Front was initially based in Mauritania, but since the mid-1970s its political leadership has operated from Algeria. In consonance with recent developments throughout the world, the once strongly socialist Polisario currently promises to institute a market economy in "the future Sahrawi state," except in regard to mineral reserves (which would remain state property). The Front also supports "eventual" multipartyism, its 1991 Congress, held at Tindouf, Algeria, pledging to draft a "democratic and pluralistic" constitution to present for a national referendum should the proposed self-determination vote in the Western Sahara go in Polisario's favor. In other activity, the Congress reelected longtime leader Mohamed 'Abd al-Azziz as secretary general of the Front and thereby president of the SADR. However, in August 1992 the defection to Morocco of the SADR foreign minister, Brahim HAKIM, served to point up the increasingly tenuous position of the rebel movement. Subsequently, a new SADR government-in-exile announced in September 1993 was most noteworthy for the appointment of hard-liner Brahim GHALI as defense minister.

In 1995 Polisario reportedly was still threatening to resume hostilities if the UN plan collapsed. However, it was widely believed that the Front's military capacity had by then diminished to about 6,000 soldiers.

The Ninth Polisario Congress, held August 20–27, 1995, reelected 'Abd al-Azziz as secretary general and urged the international community to pressure the Moroccan government regarding its perceived stonewalling. In September a new SADR government was announced under the leadership of Mahfoud Ali Larous Beiba, a former SADR health minister. On October 12 the first session of an SADR National Assembly was convened at Tindouf, its 101 members having been elected via secret ballot at local and regional "conferences." A new SADR government was named on January 21, 1998, although Beiba remained as prime minister and a number of incumbents were reappointed. Beiba was succeeded on February 10, 1999, by Bouchraya Hamoudi BAYOUN.

Secretary General: Mohamed 'Abd al-AZZIZ (President of the SADR).

Prime Minister of the SADR: Bouchraya Hamoudi BAYOUN.

OMAN

SULTANATE OF OMAN

Sultanat 'Uman

The Country

The Sultanate of Oman (known prior to August 1970 as Muscat and Oman), which occupies the southeast portion of the Arabian Peninsula and a number of offshore islands, is bounded by the United Arab Emirates on the northwest, Saudi Arabia on the west, and Yemen on the extreme southwest. A small, noncontiguous area at the tip of the Musandam Peninsula extends northward into the Strait of Hormuz, through which much of the world's ocean-shipped oil passes. Although the Omani population is predominantly Arab (divided into an estimated 200 tribes), small communities of Iranians, Baluchis, Indians, East Africans, and Pakistanis are also found. Ibadhi Muslims constitute up to 75 percent of the population; most of the remainder are Wahhabis of the Sunni branch, although there is a small Shi'ite population. In addition to Arabic, English, Farsi, and Urdu, several Indian dialects are spoken.

Prior to 1970 the Sultanate was an isolated, essentially medieval state without roads, electricity, or significant educational and health facilities; social behavior was dictated by a repressive and reclusive sultan. However, following his overthrow in 1970, the country underwent rapid modernization, fueled by soaring oil revenue. Oman currently provides free medical facilities, housing assistance for most of its citizens, and schools for more than 550,000 students. Economic growth has been concentrated in the coastal cities with an accompanying construction boom relying on a large foreign work force. However, under a government program designed to reduce migration to urban areas, services have in the last several years been extended to most of the vast rural interior. It has been estimated that about half of the population still engages in farming, herding, or fishing, with a large percentage of the country's women working as unpaid agricultural laborers on family landholdings. Growing access to education (more than 40 percent of Omani students are female) has reduced the once high illiteracy rate among women. Women have visible roles in both private and public sectors in part because of the relatively moderate (in regional terms) stance of the sultan.

Although much of the work force works in agriculture, most food must be imported; dates, nuts,

limes, and fish are exported. Cattle are bred extensively in the southern province of Dhofar, and Omani camels are prized throughout Arabia. Since petroleum production began in 1967, the Sultanate has become heavily dependent on oil revenue, which, at a production rate of more than 900,000 barrels per day, accounts for more than 70 percent of foreign export earnings, 90 percent of government revenue, and 40 percent of GDP. However, significant natural gas fields accounted for about $1.2B in exports in 2002, and liquefied natural gas continues to be a rapidly growing segment of the economy. In a further effort to offset the nation's dependence on oil, the government has launched a program of economic diversification, intended to encourage foreign investment, promote small-scale private industry, and enhance the fledgling tourism sector. Recent initiatives include changes in investment law to permit Omani companies to be owned by non-nationals. The government of Oman solicited for a number of large infrastructure projects, including the construction of the giant maritime trans-shipment terminal at the port of Mina Raysut, and development of gas exports.

Real GDP growth was 3.3 percent in 2004 and expected to be 3.5 per- cent in 2005. Exports increased some 38 percent in 2003, and the International Monetary Fund (IMF) has taken note in recent years of Oman's sound policies. These policies, in combination with high crude oil prices, rising government consumption and investment, and an improved business climate, have contributed to the positive economic forecast. Inflation remained negligible.

The IMF has recommended that a luxury tax or property tax be instituted, as well as further privatization, though it notes that "robust growth" continues in the nonoil sector and that the government has reduced its debt considerably.

Government and Politics

Political Background

Conquered by the Portuguese in 1508, the Omanis successfully revolted in 1650 and subsequently extended their domain as far south as Zanzibar. A brief period of Iranian intrusion (1741–1743) was followed in 1798 by the establishment of a treaty of friendship with Great Britain; thereafter, the British played a protective role, although formally recognizing the Sultanate's independence in 1951.

Oman is home of the Ibadhi sect, centered at Nazwa, which evolved from the egalitarianist Kharijite movement of early Islam. During much of the twentieth century, Omani politics centered on an intrasect rivalry between imams, who controlled the interior, and sultans of the Sa'id dynasty, who ruled over the coastal cities of Muscat and Muttrah, although the Treaty of Sib, concluded in 1920, acknowledged the nation's indivisibility. On the death of the incumbent imam in 1954, Sultan Sa'id ibn Taymur Al SA'ID attempted, without success, to secure election as his successor. However, revolts against the sultan by the new imam's followers were ended with British help in 1959, thus cementing the sultan's authority over the entire country. The foreign presence having become the subject of a number of UN debates, the remaining British bases were closed in 1977, although a number of British officers remained attached to the Omani armed forces.

The conservative and isolationist Sultan Sa'id was ousted on July 23, 1970 by his son, Qabus ibn Sa'id Al SA'ID. The former sultan fled to London, where he died in 1972. Qabus, whose takeover was supported by the British, soon began efforts to modernize the country, but his request for cooperation from rebel groups who had opposed his father evoked little positive response. In 1971–1972 two left-wing guerrilla groups merged to form the Popular Front for the Liberation of Oman and the Arabian Gulf (renamed in July 1974 as the Popular Front for the Liberation of Oman—PFLO), which continued resistance to the sultan's regime, primarily from bases in the (then) People's Democratic Republic of Yemen. Qabus maintained his superiority with military assistance from Saudi Arabia, Jordan, Iran, and Pakistan, and in December 1975 he asserted that the rebellion had been crushed, with a formal cease-fire being announced in March 1976.

Although the sultan subsequently stated his desire to introduce democratic reforms, a Consultative Assembly established in 1981 consisted entirely of appointed members, and Oman remained for all practical purposes an absolute monarchy. In November 1990 the sultan announced plans for a Consultative Council of regional representatives in an effort to provide for more citizen participation.

By the mid-1990s the Consultative Council had become the forum for rigorous questioning of government ministers, as well as sporadic grumbling over alleged corruption on the part of members of the ruling elite.

On November 6, 1996, Sultan Qabus issued "The Basic Law of the Sultanate of Oman," the nation's first quasi-constitutional document. Although it confirmed the final authority of the sultan in all government matters, it also codified the responsibilities of the Council of Ministers and provided for a second consultative body, the Council of State (see Legislature, below). Subsequently, following preliminary balloting for a new Consultative Council on October 16, 1997, Sultan Qabus reshuffled his cabinet on December 16, designating several "young technocrats" as new ministers.

New elections to the Consultative Council were held on September 14, 2000, successful candidates for the first time not being subject to approval by the sultan. Elections were next held on October 4, 2003, with women continuing to hold two seats. Members were elected to four-year terms in the first balloting open to all citizens (See Current issues and Legislature, below).

Constitution and Government

Lagging behind most other Arab states in this regard, Oman until recently had no constitution or other fundamental law, absolute power resting with the sultan, who ruled by decree. However, on November 6, 1996, Sultan Qabus issued "The Basic Law of the Sultanate of Oman," formally confirming the government's status as a hereditary Sultanate, which is an "independent, Arab, Islamic, fully sovereign state" and for which *shari'a*

Political Status: Independent sultanate recognized December 20, 1951; present regime instituted July 23, 1970; new "basic law" decreed on November 6, 1996.
Area: 119,500 sq. mi. (309,500 sq. km.).
Population: 2,018,074 (1993C); 2,662,000 (2004E). The 1993 census (the country's first) included 534,848 non-Omanis.
Major Urban Centers (2005E): MUSCAT (urban area, 880,000).
Official Language: Arabic.
Monetary Unit: Oman Rial (official rate July 1, 2005: 1 rial = $2.60US).
Head of State and Government: Sultan Qabus ibn Sa'id Al SA'ID; assumed power July 23, 1970, in a coup d'état that deposed his father, Sultan Sa'id ibn Taymur Al SA'ID.

(Islamic religious law) is the "basis for legislation." Total authority for the issuance of legislation remains with the sultan, designated as head of state and commander in chief of the armed forces. The "ruling family council" is authorized to appoint a successor should the position of sultan become vacant. The sultan rules with the assistance of a Council of Ministers, whose members he appoints. The first woman was appointed to the cabinet in 2004. The sultan may appoint a prime minister but is not so required. Consultation is also provided by the Oman Council, comprising a new Council of State and the Consultative Council. (See Legislature, below.) Among other things, the basic law provides for freedom of opinion, expression, and association "within the limits of the law." The basic law can be revised only by decree of the sultan.

The judicial system is also based on *shari'a* and is administered by judges (*qadis*) appointed by the minister of justice. Appeals are heard at Muscat. In remote areas the law is based on tribal custom. Administratively, the country is divided into nine regions in the north and one province in the south (Dhofar). Governors (*walis*) posted in the country's 59 *wilayats* (administrative districts) work largely through tribal authorities and are responsible for maintaining local security, settling minor disputes, and collecting taxes. Municipal councils are presently being established in the larger towns as instruments of local government.

Foreign Relations

Reversing the isolationist policy of his father, Sultan Qabus has fostered diplomatic relations with most Arab and industrialized countries. Britain has been deeply involved in Omani affairs since 1798, while the United States and the Sultanate signed their first treaty of friendship and navigation in 1833. In recent years Japan has also become a major trading partner. Diplomatic relations were established with the People's Republic of China in 1978 and with the Soviet Union in September 1985. In June 1989 the Sultanate signed a military cooperation agreement with France.

Relations with the more radical Arab states, already cool, were not improved by Sultan Qabus's endorsement of the Egyptian-Israeli peace treaty of March 1979. However, Oman broke off relations with Israel in the wake of the Intifada. Long-standing tension with the (then) People's Democratic Republic of Yemen, occasioned largely by that country's support of the sultan's opponents in Dhofar, moderated substantially at an October 1982 "reconciliation" summit, which was followed by an exchange of ambassadors in late 1983. In October 1988 the steady improvement in relations yielded a cooperation pact between the two regimes, and in 1997 Oman concluded a formal border agreement with the recently established Republic of Yemen.

In June 1980, after statements by Sultan Qabus opposing what he viewed as Soviet efforts to destabilize the Middle East, Washington and Muscat concluded an agreement granting the US access to Omani air and naval facilities in return for economic and security assistance. Since that time, and despite a May 1988 rebuff in regard to the purchase of Stinger missiles, Oman has become a base for US activities in the Persian Gulf.

Sultan Qabus strongly supported the Saudi decision to invite US forces to defend the Gulf in the wake of Iraq's invasion of Kuwait in August 1990, and Oman subsequently contributed troops to Operation Desert Storm. Following the end of the war, Sultan Qabus proposed that a 100,000-member regional army be established to combat future security threats; however, the plan was eventually rejected by Oman's partners in the Gulf Cooperation Council (GCC). Oman's already warm relations with the US further improved after the September 11, 2001, terrorist attacks in the US. Oman and Saudi Arabia issued a joint statement calling for greater cooperation in combating terrorism, and Oman was subsequently described as highly cooperative in the US-led "war on terrorism." The sultan also favors stronger ties with Iran as a means of promoting long-term stability in the region. For a similar reason, Oman has held to the moderate Arab position concerning a possible peace settlement with Israel. In 2005, Oman was reinforcing bilateral cooperation in meetings with Jordan and Iran. Oman considers Iran's nuclear power an asset to the region inasmuch as there is a peaceful application of the technology.

Despite its importance as an oil-producing state, Oman is not a member of either the Organization of Petroleum Exporting Countries (OPEC) or the Organization of Arab Petroleum Exporting Countries (OAPEC). However, since the late 1980s it has cooperated with OPEC regarding production quotas.

Current Issues

The balloting for the Consultative Council in September 2000 attracted significant international attention because only one other GCC member (Kuwait) had conducted such a nationwide poll and because no other member had extended the franchise in national elections to women. (Qatar in 1999 permitted women to participate in municipal elections.) The Omani government continued to pursue "quiet progress" toward political liberalization by mandating that 30 percent of the electors in the electoral college be women. As it turned out, only two women candidates were successful then

Cabinet

As of June 20, 2005

Prime Minister	Sultan Qabus ibn Sa'id al-Sa'id
Deputy Prime Minister	Sa'id Fahd ibn Mahmud al-Sa'id
Secretary General of the Cabinet	Hamud ibn Fasal ibn Sa'id al-Busaidi

Ministers

Personal Representative of the Sultan	Sa'id ibn Tariq ibn Taimur al-Sa'id
Agriculture and Fisheries	Sheikh Salim ibn Hilal al-Khalili
Civil Service	Sheikh Hilal ibn Khalid ibn Nassir al-Ma'wali
Commerce and Industry	Maqbul ibn 'Ali Sultan
Defense	Sa'id Badr ibn Saud ibn Hareb al-Busaidi
Diwan of Royal Court	Sa'id Ali ibn Hamad al-Busaidi
Education	Yahya ibn Sa'ud al-Sulaimi
Finance	Sultan Qabus ibn Sa'id al-Sa'id
Foreign Affairs	Yusuf ibn Alawi ibn 'Abdallah
Health	Dr. 'Ali ibn Muhammad ibn Musa
Higher Education	Rawya bint Saud al-Busaidi [f]
Housing, Electricity, and Water	Khamis ibn Mubarak Isa al-Alawi
Information	Hamid ibn Muhammad al-Rashdi
Interior	Sa'id Sa'ud ibn Ibrahim al-Busaidi
Justice	Sheikh Muhammad ibn 'Abdallah ibn Zahir al-Hinai
Legal Affairs	Muhammad ibn Ali ibn Nasir al-Alawi
Manpower	Juma ibn ali ibn Juma
National Economy and Finance	Ahmed ibn 'Abd al-Nabi al-Makki
National Heritage and Culture	Sa'id Haitham ibn Tariq al-Sa'id
Palace Office Affairs	Lt. Gen. 'Ali ibn Majid Ma'mari
Petroleum and Gas	Muhammad ibn Saif al-Ramhi
Regional Municipalities and Environmental Affairs	Sheihk 'Abdallah ibn Salim al-Ruwas
Religious Trusts (*Awqaf*) and Islamic Affairs	Sheikh 'Aballah ibn Muhammad al-Salami
Social Development	Amir ibn Shuwayn al-Husni
Transportation and Telecommunications	Sheikh Muhammad ibn 'Abdallah ibn Isa al-Harthi
Tourism	Rajihah bint 'Abdallah Amir [f]
President of the Public Authority for Craft Industries	Sheika A'isha bint Khalfan al-Siyabiah [f]

Ministers of State

Adviser at the Diwan of the Royal Court	Sa'id Ali ibn Ali al-Busaidi
Governor of the Capital	Sa'id al-Mutasim ibn Hamud al-Busaidi
Governor of Dhofar	Sheikh Muhammad ibn Ali al-Qatabi
Special Adviser to the Sultan	Salim ibn 'Abdallah al-Ghazali
Special Adviser to the Sultan for Culture	'Abd al-Aziz ibn Muhammad al-Ruwas
Special Adviser to the Sultan for Economic Planning Affairs	Muhammad al-Zubayr
Special Adviser to the Sultan for Environmental Affairs	Shabib ibn Taimur al-Sa'id
Special Adviser to the Sultan for External Liaison	'Umar ibn 'Abd al-Munim al-Zawawi

[f] = female

and in the October 4, 2003, elections, the first time that all citizens could participate. Voters appeared to favor fellow tribesmen, as in the previous election, making it less likely that women would be elected.

Significantly, of the hundreds arrested in early 2005 for allegedly attempting "to form an organization to tamper with national security," those convicted were neither jihadists linked to *al-Qaeda* nor Shi'ites loyal to Iran or Iraq. The thirty people convicted by a state security court were members of an Ibani sect that seeks to restore the Imamate, or leadership by an imam. Their arrests may be a sign of growing dissension in a historically pro-Western country.

Political Parties

There are no political parties in Oman. Most opposition elements previously were represented by the Popular Front for the Liberation of Oman (PFLO), although there has been no reference to PFLO activity for many years. (See the 1999 edition of the *Handbook* for a history of the PFLO.)

Legislature

The basic law decreed by the sultan in November 1996 provided for a consultative **Oman Council,** consisting of a new, appointed Council of State and the existing Consultative Council.

Council of State (*Majlis al-Dawlah*). Considered roughly the equivalent of an upper house in a bicameral legislature, the Council of State was expected to debate policy issues at the request of the sultan, although the ultimate extent of its authority and its relationship to the Consultative Council remained unclear. On December 16, 1997, Sultan Qabus appointed 41 members (including four women) from among prominent regional figures to the first Council of State.

President: Sheikh Yaqoub ibn Hamad al-HARTHY.

Consultative Council (*Majlis al-Shura*). The former Consultative Assembly, established in

1981, was replaced on December 21, 1991, by the Consultative Council, an advisory body appointed by the sultan (or his designee) from candidates presented by local "dignitaries" and "people of valued opinion and experience." The council is authorized to propose legislation to the government but has no formal lawmaking role. The initial council consisted of 59 regular members (one from each *wilayat*) and a speaker who served three-year terms. In 1994 the council was expanded to 80 regular members (two from each *wilayat* with a population over 30,000 and one from each of the other *wilayats*) and a president. For the first time women were allowed to stand as candidates (albeit only from six constituencies at or around Muscat), and two women were among those seated at the new council's inaugural session on December 26, 1994. The council was expanded to 82 members in 1997, and women from all of Oman were allowed to stand as candidates and participate in the preliminary balloting for the new council on October 16. An "electoral college" of 51,000 people (all approved by the government, primarily based on literacy requirements) elected 164 potential council members from among 736 candidates (also all approved by the government). Final selections were made in December by the sultan, who had essentially been presented with two candidates from which to choose for each seat.

Elections were most recently held on October 4, 2003, for an expanded council of 83 elected members to serve a four-year term. This was the first ballot open to all citizens. The president of the council, appointed by the sultan, serves as the 84th member.

President: Sheikh 'Abdullah ibn 'Ali al-QATABI.

Communications

Press

Strict press censorship is maintained. The following are published at Muscat: *al-Watan* (32,500), Arabic daily; *'Uman* (15,000), daily government publication, in Arabic; *Times of Oman* (15,000),

English weekly; *Oman Daily Observer* (22,000), in English.

News Agency

There is an official Oman News Agency (*Wikalat al-Anba' al-'Umaniyal*) located at the capital.

Broadcasting and Computing

Radio Oman transmits from Muscat in Arabic and English, and Radio Salalah from Salalah in Arabic and Dhofari; both are government controlled. The BBC Eastern Relay on Masirah Island transmits Arabic, Hindi, Persian, and Urdu programming. Color television was initiated at Muscat in 1974 and at Salalah in 1975. There were approximately 1.4 million television receivers and 105,000 personal computers serving 180,000 Internet users in 2003.

Intergovernmental Representation

Ambassador to the US
Mohamed Ali al-KHUSAIBY

US Ambassador to Oman
Richard Lewis BALTIMORE III

Permanent Representative to the UN
Zawan bint Ahmad al-Akhzami [f]

IGO Memberships (Non-UN)
AFESD, AMF, BADEA, CCC, GCC, IDB, Interpol, IOR-ARC, LAS, NAM, OIC, WTO

PAKISTAN

ISLAMIC REPUBLIC OF PAKISTAN

Islami Jamhuria-e-Pakistan

Note: On October 8, 2005, a 7.6-magnitude earthquake devastated northwestern Pakistan, killing more than 74,000 people and displacing more than 3 million. The epicenter was in the Muzaffarabad area of the disputed territory of Kashmir. By December, the international community had pledged more than the $5 billion in aid that Pakistani President Pervez Musharraf had requested for help in rebuilding ravaged areas. Some two-thirds of the funds, however, were in the form of loans to the already impoverished nation. As winter approached, Pakistani officials and various aid groups warned that thousands of quake survivors—especially those inhabiting the harsh Himalayan region—could die of hunger, exposure, and disease unless relief soon arrived. While acknowledging the despair created by the situation, Musharraf also noted that the disaster had provided an opportunity for Pakistan and India to overcome long-standing disputes, as the two countries agreed to open border crossings in Kashmir to facilitate the flow of relief supplies and allow separated families to reunite.

The Country

Located in the northwest of the Indian subcontinent, Pakistan extends from the Arabian Sea a thousand miles northward across eastern plains to the Hindu Kush and the foothills of the Himalayas. The racial stock is primarily Aryan, with traces of Dravidian. The dominant language is Punjabi (50 percent), followed by Pushtu, Sindhi, Saraiki, Urdu, Gujarati, and Baluchi. In addition, English is widely spoken in business and government. Islam, the state religion, is professed by over 95 percent of the people; Christians and Hindus constitute most of the balance. Women make up only 29 percent of the labor force, but many others participate in unpaid agricultural work. In addition, women are often engaged in home-based or cottage industry. Female participation in government has been constrained by Islamic precepts, although Benazir BHUTTO was the Muslim world's first woman prime minister (1988–1990, 1993–1996).

Much of the country consists of mountains and deserts, but some of the most fertile and best-irrigated land in the subcontinent is provided by the Indus River system. Agriculture continues to employ just under half of the population, the principal crops being cotton, wheat, rice, sugarcane, and maize. In addition, the western province of Baluchistan supplies a rich crop of fruits and dates. The agricultural sector contributes about

Political Status: Formally became independent August 15, 1947; republic established March 23, 1956; national territory confined to former West Pakistan with de facto independence of Bangladesh (former East Pakistan) on December 16, 1971; independence of Bangladesh formally recognized on February 22, 1974; martial law regime instituted following military coup of July 5, 1977; modified version of 1973 constitution introduced on March 2, 1985; martial law officially lifted December 30, 1985; constitution suspended and state of emergency imposed on October 14, 1999, following military coup of October 12; constitution restored on November 16, 2002, as amended by Legal Framework Order (LFO) promulgated by the President on August 21; 17th constitutional amendment, containing many of the LFO provisions, approved by Parliament on December 29–30, 2003, and signed by the President on December 31.

Area: 310,402 sq. mi. (803,943 sq. km.), excluding Jammu and Kashmir, of which approximately 32,200 sq. mi. (83,400 sq. km.) are presently administered by Pakistan.

Population: 130,579,571 (1998C), excluding population of Pakistani-controlled portion of Jammu and Kashmir (see Related Territories); 152,165,000 (2004E).

Major Urban Centers (1998C): ISLAMABAD (529,180), Karachi (9,339,093), Lahore (5,143,495), Faisalabad (2,008,861), Rawalpindi (1,409,768), Multan (1,197,384), Hyderabad (1,166,894), Gujranwala (1,132,509), Peshawar (982,816). Opponents of the census, claiming widespread urban underenumeration, have estimated the population of Karachi at 15 million.

National Language: Urdu.

Monetary Unit: Rupee (market rate July 1, 2005: 59.72 rupees = $1US).

President and Chairman of the National Security Council: Gen. Pervez MUSHARRAF; deposed Prime Minister Mohammad Nawaz SHARIF (Pakistan Muslim League-Nawaz) on October 12, 1999, and assumed title of Chief Executive two days later; assumed, ex officio, chairmanship of National Security Council, the civilian members of which were sworn in on November 6; assumed the presidency on June 20, 2001, upon his dismissal of President Rafiq TARAR (Pakistan Muslim League-Nawaz); confirmed in office for an additional five years by disputed referendum of April 30, 2002; took the oath of office as President again on November 16, 2002, upon restoration of the amended constitution; transferred Chief Executive authority to the newly installed Prime Minister on November 23, 2002.

Prime Minister: Shaukat AZIZ (Pakistan Muslim League); named by the President on June 26, 2004, upon the resignation of Zafarullah Khan JAMALI (Pakistan Muslim League); confirmed by the National Assembly on August 27 and sworn in on August 28, succeeding interim Prime Minister Chaudhry Shujaat HUSSAIN (Pakistan Muslim League).

---

one-quarter of the gross domestic product, as does industry, which employs less than one-fifth of the labor force. Though not heavily endowed in mineral resources, the country extracts petroleum, natural gas, iron, limestone, rock salt, gypsum, and coal. Manufacturing includes production of cotton and other textile yarns and fabrics, which account for half of merchandise export earnings; other leading manufactures are clothing and accessories, cement, petroleum products, sugar and other foodstuffs, and fertilizer. Pakistan's exports also include fruits, seafood, carpets, and handicrafts. Major trading partners are the United States, the United Arab Emirates, Saudi Arabia, the United Kingdom, and Germany.

Overall, the economy registered an average growth rate of 6–7 percent during the 1980s, with remittances from Pakistanis employed in the Arabian Gulf largely offsetting a substantial trade imbalance. GDP growth averaged over 4 percent in

1990–1996, but inflation exceeded 11 percent annually during the same period. Although growth slowed to 1.3 percent in the 1996–1997 fiscal year, it rebounded to 5.4 percent in the following year, in part due to ongoing economic reforms, which included liberalizing trade and promoting privatization in banking, utilities, and industry. However, the government's decision to conduct nuclear weapons tests in late May 1998 had immediate economic repercussions, including the imposition of sanctions by other countries, capital flight, and a drop in remittances and foreign-exchange reserves. Thus in the 1998–1999 fiscal year GDP growth missed the target of 6 percent by 1.8 percent. In the first quarter of 2000 the newly installed government moved forward on privatizing nonstrategic state-owned enterprises, improving tax collection, and cutting nonessential spending as components of an economic program partly designed to secure additional assistance from the International Monetary Fund (IMF). Growth for fiscal year 1999–2000 declined to 3.9 percent, which was nevertheless considerably better than the 2.5 percent rate obtained in 2000–2001. By 2002–2003 the growth rate had risen to 5.1 percent, with projections for the following fiscal year exceeding 6 percent.

In the long term, the most serious impediment to sustained progress is one of Asia, highest population growth rates, currently about 2.4 percent annually, and a fertility rate of 4.5 children per woman. About one-third of Pakistanis live below the national poverty line, two-fifths do not have access to safe drinking water, and three-fifths of adults remain illiterate.

Government and Politics

Political Background

Subjected to strong Islamic influences from the seventh century onward, the area that comprises the present state of Pakistan, together with former East Pakistan (now Bangladesh), became part of British India during the 18th and 19th centuries and contained the bulk of India's Muslim population in prepartition days. First articulated in the

early 1930s, the idea of a separate Muslim state was endorsed in 1940 by the All-India Muslim League, the major Muslim political party. After the league swept the 1946–1947 election, the British accepted partition and Parliament passed the Indian Independence Act, which incorporated the principle of a separate Pakistan. Transfer of power occurred on August 14, 1947, with the new state formally coming into existence at the stroke of midnight, August 15.

India's Muslim-majority provinces and princely states were given the option of remaining in India or joining Pakistan. Sindh, the North-West Frontier, Baluchistan, and three-fifths of the Punjab accordingly combined to form what became West Pakistan, while a part of Assam and two-thirds of Bengal became East Pakistan. The Hindu maharaja of the predominantly Muslim state of Jammu and Kashmir subsequently acceded to India, but Pakistan challenged the action by sending troops into the territory; resultant fighting between Indian and Pakistani forces was halted by a UN cease-fire on January 1, 1949, leaving Pakistan in control of territory west and north of the cease-fire line (see map, p. 890). However, communal rioting and population movements stemming from partition caused further embitterment between the two countries.

Mohammad Ali JINNAH, head of the All-India Muslim League and independent Pakistan's first governor general, died in 1948. The assassination in 1951 of LIAQUAT Ali Khan, the country's first prime minister, was a second serious blow to Pakistan's political development. By 1954 the influence of the Muslim League had dwindled, particularly in East Pakistan, and Governor General Ghulam MOHAMMAD declared a state of emergency. The installation of President Iskander MIRZA in August 1955 and the belated implementation of a republican constitution in March 1956 contributed little to political stability, and in October 1958 Mirza abrogated the constitution, declared martial law, dismissed the national and provincial governments, and dissolved all political parties. Field Marshal Mohammad Ayub KHAN, appointed supreme commander of the armed forces and chief martial law administrator, took over the presidency from Mirza later in October and was confirmed in office by a national referendum of so-called "basic democrats" in February 1960.

Constitutional government, under a presidential system based on indirect election, was restored in June 1962, and Ayub Khan was designated president for a five-year term in January 1965. Despite a second war with India in late 1965, Pakistan experienced considerable economic progress during most of Ayub Khan's tenure, but growing political and economic discontent, particularly in East Pakistan, led the president to announce in early 1969 that he would not seek reelection but would permit a return to decentralized parliamentary government. The announcement failed to quell the disorders and, acknowledging that his government had lost control, Ayub Khan resigned in March. Gen. Agha Mohammad Yahya KHAN, army commander in chief, thereupon assumed authority as chief martial law administrator, suspended the constitution, dismissed the national and provincial assemblies, and took office as president.

January 1970 marked a return to normal political activity, the major unresolved issue being East Pakistani complaints of underrepresentation in the central government and an inadequate share of central revenues. In preparing for the nation's first direct election on the basis of universal suffrage (ultimately held in December 1970 and January 1971), efforts were made to assuage the long-standing political discontent in the more populous East Pakistan by allotting it majority representation in the new assembly, rather than, as in the previous legislature, mere parity with West Pakistan. Of the 300 seats up for direct election (162 from East Pakistan, 138 from West Pakistan), Sheikh Mujibur RAHMAN's East Pakistani Awami League won 160 and the Pakistan People's Party (PPP), 82.

After repeated postponements of the assembly opening, originally scheduled to take place at Dacca (East Pakistan) in March 1971, the government banned the Awami League and announced in August the disqualification of 79 of its representatives. By-elections to the vacated seats, scheduled for December, were prevented by the outbreak of war between Pakistan and India in late November and the occupation of East Pakistan by Bengali guerrilla and Indian military forces. Following the surrender of some 90,000 of its troops, Pakistan on December 17 agreed to a cease-fire on the western front. Yahya Khan stepped down as president three days later and was replaced by Zulfikar Ali BHUTTO as president and chief martial law administrator. In July 1972 President Bhutto and Indian Prime Minister Indira Gandhi met at Simla, India, and agreed to negotiate outstanding differences. As a result, all occupied areas along the western border were exchanged, except in Kashmir, where a new "line of control" was drawn. In July 1973 the National Assembly granted Bhutto the authority to recognize Bangladesh, and in August a new constitution was adopted. The speaker of the assembly, Fazal Elahi CHAUDHRY, was elected president of Pakistan, and Bhutto was designated prime minister.

A general election held in March 1977 resulted in an overwhelming victory for the ruling PPP; however, the opposition Pakistan National Alliance (PNA) denounced the returns as fraudulent and initiated a series of strikes and demonstrations that led to outbreaks of violence throughout the country. Faced with impending civil war, the army mounted a coup on July 5 that resulted in the arrest of many leading politicians, including Prime Minister Bhutto, and the imposition of martial law under Gen. Mohammad ZIA ul-Haq. Later in the year, General Zia announced a search for a "new political system" that would reflect purely Islamic values. Shortly after President Chaudhry's term expired in August 1978, General Zia assumed the presidency, announcing that he would yield to a regularly elected successor following legislative balloting in 1979.

On April 4, 1979, despite worldwide appeals for clemency, former prime minister Bhutto was hanged. Riots immediately erupted in most of the country's urban areas, and on April 15 PNA representatives withdrew from the government. Later in the year Zia postponed elections, banned all forms of party activity, and imposed strict censorship on the communications media.

An interim constitution promulgated in March 1981 provided for the eventual restoration of representative institutions "in conformity with Islam," while the formation the same year of the PPP-led Movement for the Restoration of Democracy (MRD) created a force against both the regime and right-wing Islamic parties. In late 1984 the president announced a December referendum on an "Islamization" program, endorsement of which would also grant him an additional five-year presidential term. In the wake of an MRD call for a boycott of the balloting, the size of the turnout was hotly disputed, estimates ranging from as low as 15 percent to as high as 65 percent; an overwhelming margin of approval, however, led Zia to schedule parliamentary elections on a nonparty basis for February 1985. Despite another opposition call for a boycott, five incumbent ministers and a number of others associated with the martial law regime lost their bids for parliamentary seats. As a result, the president dissolved the cabinet and designated Mohammad Khan JUNEJO, of the center-right Pakistan Muslim League (PML), as the country's first prime minister in eight years. In the absence of legal parties, the assembly divided into two camps—a government-supportive Official Parliamentary Group (OPG) and an opposition Independent Parliamentary Group (IPG).

The first serious disruption in the "peaceful transition" came in July 1985, following the death in Paris under mysterious circumstances of the former prime minister's son, Shahnawaz BHUTTO. After his funeral his sister, PPP leader Benazir BHUTTO, who had arrived from London, was placed under house arrest for "inciting public unrest," and she returned shortly thereafter to Britain. In August Prime Minister Junejo announced the impending end of martial law.

In October 1985 the assembly approved a political parties law, despite objection by President Zia, who continued to view a multiparty system as "un-Islamic." Dissent immediately ensued within the MRD, some components (including the PML and the moderate *Jamaat-e-Islami,* which controlled the OPG and IPG, respectively) announcing their intention to register, while others termed the entire

exercise "fraudulent" and continued to press for fresh elections under a fully restored 1973 constitution. Without responding to the pressure, Zia proceeded with the scheduled termination of martial law on December 30.

In what was dubbed a "constitutional coup" on May 29, 1988, President Zia abruptly dismissed the Junejo government because of alleged corruption. He also dissolved the National Assembly, the provincial assemblies, and local governments. On June 9 he appointed a PML-dominated caretaker administration headed by himself and on July 20 announced that "free, fair and independent" elections to the national and provincial assemblies would be held on November 16 and 19, respectively.

On August 17, 1988, General Zia, the US ambassador, and a number of senior military officers were killed in a plane crash in southeastern Punjab. Immediately afterwards the Senate chairman, Ghulam Ishaq KHAN, was sworn in as acting president and announced the formation of a caretaker Emergency National Council to rule the country pending the November balloting, which was to proceed on schedule. Intense political maneuvering followed, with the PPP securing a substantial plurality in the National Assembly poll but achieving only second place in three of the four provincial elections. Nonetheless, in what some viewed as a political "deal," on December 1 Ishaq Khan formally appointed as prime minister Benazir Bhutto, who had returned to Pakistan in 1986, and was himself elected to a five-year term as president on December 12. Thereafter, relations between the two became increasingly strained.

Accusing her government of corruption, abuse of power, and various other unconstitutional and illegal acts, President Khan dismissed Bhutto on August 6, 1990, appointing as her interim successor Ghulam Mustafa JATOI, leader of the Islamic Democratic Alliance (IDA), a somewhat disparate coalition of conservative anti-Bhutto groups that had been organized two years earlier. Two months later the PPP was decisively defeated in balloting for national and provincial assemblies, including a loss in its traditional stronghold of Sindh. On

November 6 the IDA's Mian Mohammad Nawaz SHARIF was sworn in as Pakistan's first Punjabi prime minister.

On April 18, 1993, in the wake of a failed effort by Nawaz Sharif to curtail the president's constitutional power, Ishaq Khan dismissed the Sharif government, naming Balkh Sher MAZARI, a dissident member of Sharif's PML, as acting prime minister. However, on May 26 the Supreme Court reinstated Sharif, thereby canceling a general election that had been scheduled for July 14. The action failed to resolve the widening split within the PML, and on July 18, following intervention by the recently appointed army chief of staff, Gen. Abdul WAHEED, both the president and prime minister stepped down. The former was succeeded, on an acting basis, by Senate chairman Wasim SAJ-JAD, and the latter by a relatively unknown former World Bank vice president, Moeenuddin Ahmad QURESHI.

Nawaz Sharif attempted to regain power as leader of the PML's largest faction. Although the PML-Nawaz outpolled the PPP 41–38 percent at the National Assembly election of October 9, 1993, the latter gained a plurality of seats (86, as opposed to 72 for Sharif supporters) and Bhutto was returned to office on October 19. In electoral college balloting for president on November 13, the PPP's Sardar Farooq Ahmad Khan LEGHARI defeated the acting incumbent, and he was inaugurated the following day.

On July 24, 1996, in the wake of increased tension with India over Kashmir and heightened domestic unrest on the part of Islamic fundamentalists and activists of the *Muhajir* National Movement (MQM), 13 opposition parties announced an alliance to topple Bhutto, and on July 31 the prime minister greatly enlarged her cabinet. Among 14 new appointees was her controversial husband, Asif Ali ZARDARI, who, in his first ministerial assignment, was named to head an investment portfolio. Shortly thereafter, on September 20, the prime minister's estranged brother, Murtaza BHUTTO, was one of seven breakaway PPP faction members killed in a gunfight outside his Karachi home.

Citing evidence of corruption, intimidation of the judiciary, misdirection of the economy, and failure to maintain law and order, President Leghari on November 5, 1996, dismissed Prime Minister Bhutto, naming Malek Meraj KHALID, a former legislative speaker and long-estranged Bhutto confidant, as her successor in a caretaker capacity pending balloting for a new National Assembly in February 1997. In the interim, President Leghari announced in January 1997 the formation of a Council for Defense and National Security (CDNS) comprising himself, the prime minister, several cabinet ministers, and the heads of the branches of the armed forces.

Voter turnout was low for the February 3, 1997, legislative balloting, in which the PML-Nawaz swept to power by securing 134 of the 207 seats, compared to 19 seats for Bhutto's PPP. The PML subsequently invited a number of smaller parties to join the governing coalition, giving it more than the two-thirds majority required for constitutional amendment. Following the installation of a new cabinet on February 26, Prime Minister Sharif quickly oversaw the abolition of the CDNS and directed constitutional revision that, among other things, removed the president's authority to dismiss the prime minister and assembly at will and to appoint military leaders.

In the wake of renewed violence at Karachi (much of it perpetrated by rival MQM factions) as well as conflict between minority Shi'ite and majority Sunni Muslim militants in Punjab, a new antiterrorism bill was adopted in August 1997, granting sweeping new powers to security forces and establishing special courts to try terrorism cases. The collateral usurpation of power from traditional courts served to exacerbate tension between the government and the judiciary, already at loggerheads over the proposed expansion of the Supreme Court and challenges from certain judges to the earlier constitutional amendments. Chief Justice Sajjad Ali SHAH in November established several special courts to hear a number of constitutional and political challenges, including contempt citations against Sharif for alleged antijudiciary public statements. On December 2, calling Sharif an "elected dictator," President Leghari resigned rather than comply with the prime minister's order to swear in a new acting chief justice, Shah having been suspended from office when a majority of the deeply divided Supreme Court asserted that he had been improperly promoted to the post in 1995. On December 31 a Sharif ally, Mohammad Rafiq TARAR, was elected president by an overwhelming majority of electors.

Throughout 1998 the upsurge in religious, ethnic, and political violence resisted resolution. In August the Sharif administration's failure to contain the violence led the principal MQM faction to withdraw its support for the government, which in February had already lost a principal ally when the Awami National Party (AWP) left the cabinet because of the prime minister's reluctance to endorse renaming the North-West Frontier Province as Pakhtoonkhwa ("Land of the Pakhtoon").

Demands for greater provincial autonomy also continued to gather momentum in 1998, and in early October the AWP was a leading force behind the announcement of a new opposition alliance, the Pakistan Oppressed Nations' Movement (PONM), its principal focus being a greater assertion of provincial and minority rights. By then the PML-Nawaz was, in effect, governing on its own.

A deeply divided society came together briefly in late May 1998 when Pakistan exploded six nuclear weapons beneath the Chagai Hills of the Baluchistan desert. The tests on May 28 and 30 came in response to similar explosions conducted earlier in the month by India. Pakistan's Muslim fundamentalists were particularly jubilant, welcoming the tests as confirmation that Islamabad had developed the first "Islamic bomb."

To the surprise of many observers, on October 7, 1998, Gen. Jehangir KARAMAT, chairman of the joint chiefs of staff, resigned, two days after calling for greater military participation in the government and criticizing the prime minister for his administration's economic shortcomings and its inability to stem domestic disorder. On April 9, 1999, Prime Minister Sharif named Karamat's replacement as army chief of staff, Gen. Pervez MUSHARRAF,

to the chairmanship of the Joint Chiefs of Staff Committee.

Although relations with India had improved following the May 1998 nuclear weapons tests, culminating in a meeting between Prime Ministers Sharif and Vajpayee at Lahore on February 20–21, 1999 (see Foreign relations, below), renewed conflict in Kashmir once again disrupted diplomatic progress. In early May 1999 India discovered that militant Islamic separatists, backed by Pakistani forces, had crossed the Line of Control into the mountainous Kargil area. For two months heavy shellings and clashes ensued, with India gradually gaining the upper hand. Military commanders from both sides met on July 11 and agreed to a timetable for withdrawal, which was completed late in the month, but sporadic fighting continued as the government's actions were widely denounced within Pakistan, particularly by Islamic groups.

On October 12, 1999, while attending a conference in Sri Lanka, General Musharraf was alerted by supporters within the army that Prime Minister Sharif was replacing him. Musharraf immediately flew back to Pakistan on a commercial flight, but, on the prime minister's order, his plane was denied permission to land at Karachi, whereupon the military moved in and secured the airport. At the same time, Prime Minister Sharif and his cabinet were arrested. On October 14 Musharraf proclaimed a state of emergency (but not martial law), suspended the constitution, and named himself "chief executive" of Pakistan. President Tarar continued in office. Addressing the nation on October 17, Musharraf identified his priorities as preventing economic collapse, pursuing corruption, and paving the way for "true democracy." He also announced that he had ordered troop reductions along the Indian border, but not the Line of Control. On October 25 the chief executive named the initial civilian members of a governing National Security Council (NSC), which also included, ex officio, the naval and air force chiefs. The civilian members of the NSC and a nonparty cabinet were sworn in by President Tarar on November 6.

On April 6, 2000, an antiterrorism court sentenced Nawaz Sharif to life imprisonment following his conviction for hijacking and terrorism in connection with his refusal to let General Musharraf's plane land. The terrorism conviction was ultimately overturned on appeal, and on December 10, 2000, Musharraf granted a pardon to Nawaz Sharif, who flew to exile in Saudi Arabia with members of his family. In a national address, General Musharraf justified the pardon as a step toward ending the country's "feudal political culture" and the rivalry with Benazir Bhutto, which had corrupted Pakistan's governmental institutions.

Ruling unanimously on May 12, 2000, the Supreme Court legitimized the October 1999 coup as justified and necessary to end political corruption and lawlessness, despite being "extra-constitutional." It also ruled that democratic national and provincial assembly elections should be held no later than October 2002, a timetable that General Musharraf publicly accepted on May 25. On August 15 the NSC was reconstituted to include four civilian ministers, and the cabinet was expanded.

On June 20, 2001, General Musharraf dismissed President Tarar, assumed the presidency himself, dissolved both houses of Parliament, and also disbanded all provincial legislatures. In an apparent effort to legitimize his standing, General Musharraf called an April 30, 2002, referendum in which voters were asked to extend his presidency for another five years, support a crackdown against Islamic extremists, and support economic reforms. Although 97.7 percent of those casting ballots reportedly voted "yes," the referendum was replete with irregularities, and the outcome was rejected by the boycotting Alliance for the Restoration of Democracy (ARD), an umbrella grouping of more than a dozen opposition parties, including the PPP and the PML-N.

In August–December 2001, searching for domestic stability as well as increased international legitimacy, Musharraf had begun freezing assets and detaining the leaders of some militant Islamic groups. On January 12, 2002, in what was widely regarded as a landmark speech, Musharraf rejected the "intolerance and hatred" of extreme sectarianism, banned a number of militant Islamic political parties and groups (see "Banned Organizations," below), stated that all fundamentalist Islamic schools (madrasses) would be brought under government supervision to ensure that they adopted adequate educational goals, and called for creation of a modern, progressive Islamic society based on the "true teachings of Islam."

On August 21, 2002, President Musharraf promulgated a controversial Legal Framework Order (LFO) that incorporated 29 constitutional amendments, including the creation of a permanent National Security Council (NSC) to institutionalize a governmental role for the military leadership. The LFO also enlarged both houses of Parliament and gave the president sweeping powers, including the right to dismiss the cabinet, dissolve the National Assembly, appoint provincial governors if he saw fit, name Supreme Court judges, and unilaterally increase his term of office.

Balloting for the 272 directly elective seats in Pakistan's reconfigured, 342-seat National Assembly took place on October 10, 2002, with the Musharraf-supportive *Qaid-i-Azam* faction of the PML (PML-Q) finishing ahead of the newly registered PPP Parliamentarians (PPPP) and the *Muttahida Majlis-e-Amal* (MMA), an Islamic coalition. (Most international observers regarded the electoral process as seriously deficient in meeting democratic standards.) When the 60 seats reserved for women and 10 seats reserved for religious minorities were distributed at the end of the month, the PML-Q held a plurality of 118 seats, followed by the PPPP with 81 and the MMA with 60.

In simultaneous provincial assembly elections, the PML-Q won in Punjab and the MMA assumed control in the North-West Frontier Province (NWFP), with the two parties forming coalition administrations in Baluchistan and, in conjunction with smaller parties, in Sindh. Immediately upon assuming power in the NWFP, the MMA government announced that it would impose Islamic law in the province. The MMA's success in the NWFP was also viewed as a setback for efforts by Musharraf and the United States to track down members of the *al-Qaeda* terrorist network and the deposed Taliban regime in neighboring Afghanistan, given the MMA's opposition to Islamabad's participation in the US-led "war on terrorism" and the consequent presence of US forces on Pakistani soil.

At the central level, over the next several weeks the PML-Q and PPPP jockeyed for MMA support in an effort to establish a governing coalition, but neither succeeded. The process culminated on November 21, 2002, when the National Assembly confirmed Zafarullah Khan JAMALI of the PML-Q as prime minister after he had secured the backing of several small parties and of ten dissenters within the PPPP, who organized as the PPPP-Patriots. Runner-up in the voting was the MMA's Fazlur RAHMAN, followed by the PPPP's Shah Mahmood QURESHI.

During the following year the National Assembly was unable to overcome the obstructive tactics of LFO opponents, including the PPPP and MMA, who also demanded that President Musharraf should resign as chief of the army staff. Indirect elections to the Senate were held on February 25 and 27, 2003, with the PML-Q again attaining a plurality, but the opposition parties extended their LFO protest into a Senate boycott. The stalemate over the LFO was not resolved until late December, when Musharraf announced an agreement with the MMA under which he agreed to step down as army chief by December 2004, to submit to a vote of confidence by Parliament, and to permit review by the Supreme Court of any presidential decision to dissolve the National Assembly. In addition, it was agreed that the NSC would be established by legislative act, not by constitutional amendment. With the deadlock broken, on December 29 the National Assembly voted, 248–0, to incorporate most LFO provisions as the 17th amendment to the constitution, although the PPPP and the PML-N walked out of the session. The Senate, 72–0, approved the amendment the following day. On January 1, 2004, Musharraf received a vote of confidence from both houses, 191–0 in the assembly (the MMA abstaining and the ARD boycotting), and 56–1 in the Senate, as well as from the provincial assemblies. A bill establishing a 13-member NSC, to include the chiefs of the army, navy, and air force, was signed into law by the president on April 19.

On June 26, 2004, Prime Minister Jamali resigned under pressure from President Musharraf. Chaudhry Shujaat HUSSAIN, leader of the largely reunited PML (minus the PML-N), was confirmed as an interim successor on June 29 and sworn in on June 30. He was expected to serve until Finance Minister Shaukat AZIZ won a National Assembly seat, thereby making him eligible for designation as prime minister. Following a by-election victory on August 18, Aziz won assembly approval as prime minister on August 28 and assumed office on August 29. Most members of a substantially reconfigured cabinet were sworn in three days later.

On November 30, 2004, Mohammad Mian SOOMRO, chairman of the Senate and acting president during a trip abroad by General Musharraf, signed into law a bill permitting Musharraf to continue as both army chief of staff and president. The new law, which proponents justified as necessary to maintain stability in the face of terrorism and subversion, was attacked by the MMA as a betrayal of its December 2003 agreement with Musharraf.

Constitution and Government

On October 14, 1999, General Musharraf proclaimed a state of emergency under which he suspended the constitution; assumed the title of chief executive; suspended both houses of the Parliament and the provincial assemblies; dismissed the federal cabinet, provincial governors, and provincial governments; and placed the country under the control of the armed forces. The next day he issued "Provisional Constitution Order No. 1 of 1999," which specified that Pakistan would continue to be governed, "as nearly as may be," in accordance with the constitution. The order also mandated the continued functioning of the existing court system, with the proviso that no court could act against the chief executive, his orders, or his appointees; restricted the president to acting on the "advice" of the chief executive; and left intact all fundamental constitutional rights, including freedom of the press, not in conflict with the state of emergency.

Between 1947 and 1973 Pakistan had adopted three permanent and four interim constitutions. In

August 1973 a presidential system introduced by Ayub Khan was replaced by a parliamentary form of government. Following General Zia's assumption of power in 1977, a series of martial law decrees and an interim constitution promulgated in March 1981 progressively increased the powers of the president, as did various "revisions" accompanying official restoration of the 1973 document in March 1985. Constitutional revisions introduced in April 1997 revoked major provisions of the 1985 changes, reducing the president to little more than a figurehead.

The Legal Framework Order (LFO) instituted by General Musharraf in August 2002, with effect from October 12, incorporated 29 constitutional changes, enhancing presidential power, enlarging both houses of Parliament, and creating as a permanent body a civilian-military National Security Council (NSC) that would include the president, the prime minister, the speaker of the National Assembly, the chairman of the Senate, the leader of the parliamentary opposition, the four provincial governors, the chairman of the joint chiefs of staff, and the chiefs of staff of the army, navy, and air force. The LFO also disqualified convicted criminals from running for the legislature, thereby ensuring that neither Benazir Bhutto nor Nawaz Sharif could stand in the October 2002 election. Opposition to promulgation of the LFO remained strong even after the October balloting, which ultimately led to a December 2003 compromise under which most of the LFO provisions were enacted as the 17th amendment to the constitution. The NSC provision was removed, however, and enacted by law in April 2004.

The president, who serves a five-year term, is chosen by vote of the Parliament and the four provincial assemblies sitting jointly as an electoral college. The bicameral Parliament features an indirectly elected Senate and a popularly elected National Assembly; the latter includes reserved seats for women and religious minorities, and it has sole jurisdiction over money bills. Sitting in joint session, the Parliament may by a simple majority enact bills that have been returned to it by the president. The prime minister, who must be a member of the

National Assembly, may be removed by a majority vote of the house's total membership; the president may be removed by a two-thirds vote of the full Parliament.

The judicial system includes a Supreme Court, a Federal Shariat Court to examine the conformity of laws with Islam, high courts in each of the four provinces (Baluchistan, North-West Frontier, Punjab, and Sindh), and a number of antiterrorism courts authorized by legislation in 1997. The assembly approved a measure in May 1991 that called for formal appeal to the Koran as the country's supreme law, and in August mandated the death penalty for blasphemy.

Provincial administration is headed by centrally appointed governors. Each province also has an elected Provincial Assembly and a Council of Ministers led by a prime minister, the latter named by the governor. The Federally Administered Tribal Areas, located between the North-West Frontier Province and Afghanistan, and the Federal Capital Territory are governed by central appointees.

A Federal Legislative List defines the exclusive authority of the center; there also is a Concurrent Legislative List, with residual authority assigned to the provinces. To safeguard provincial rights, a Council of Common Interests is mandated, comprising the chief ministers of the four provinces plus four federal ministers.

Foreign Relations

Relations between India and Pakistan reflect a centuries-old rivalry based on mutual suspicion between Hindus and Muslims. The British withdrawal in 1947 was accompanied by widespread communal rioting and competing claims to Jammu and Kashmir. A start toward improved relations was made in 1960 with an agreement on joint use of the waters of the Indus River basin, but continuing conflict over Kashmir and the Rann of Kutch on the Indian Ocean involved the countries in armed hostilities in 1965, followed by a withdrawal to previous positions, in conformity with the Tashkent Agreement negotiated with Soviet assistance in January

1966. After another period of somewhat improved relations, the internal crisis in East Pakistan, accompanied by India's open support of the Bengali cause, led to further hostilities in 1971. Following recognition by Pakistan of the independent nation of Bangladesh, bilateral negotiations were renewed and a number of major issues were resolved by the return of prisoners of war, a mutual withdrawal from occupied territory, and the demarcation of a new Line of Control in Kashmir. Further steps toward normalization were partially offset by Pakistani concern over India's explosion of a nuclear device in May 1974, and formal diplomatic ties were not resumed until July 1976.

Following General Zia's death in August 1988, Rajiv Gandhi and Benazir Bhutto held a number of private discussions during a meeting of the South Asian Association for Regional Cooperation (SAARC) at Islamabad in late December. The two signed a treaty not to attack each other's nuclear facilities and concluded a number of economic and cultural agreements, without, however, addressing the Kashmir issue. The rapprochement abruptly ceased in early 1990 as Kashmir became the scene of escalating violence on the part of Muslim separatists. By April thousands of residents had fled to Pakistan from the Indian-controlled Kashmir valley.

Despite a resumption of talks in 1997—the first since 1994—bilateral tensions remained high because of continuing skirmishes, both military and diplomatic, over Kashmir. On April 6, 1998, Pakistan test fired its first domestically produced medium-range surface-to-surface missile, the Ghauri, which provoked immediate criticism from India's recently installed Vajpayee administration. Then on May 11 and 13 India exploded five nuclear weapons in underground testing, prompting Pakistan to respond on May 28 and 30 with six nuclear tests of its own. The international community quickly condemned the tests, with a number of countries imposing economic sanctions against both governments. Shortly after, however, Prime Ministers Sharif and Vajpayee adopted less belligerent stances, meeting during the July 29–31

SAARC session at Colombo, Sri Lanka, and again on September 23 in New York, where they announced that renewed talks on Kashmir and other matters would begin in October. Addressing the UN General Assembly separately, both heads of government also stated their intentions to sign the Comprehensive Test Ban Treaty (CTBT) within a year if the recently imposed economic sanctions were lifted, but neither has done so.

Although the Kashmir talks produced no tangible results, the prime ministers met again on February 20–21, 1999, at Lahore. The resulting "Lahore Declaration" included pledges by both administrations to reduce the possibility of accidental nuclear war. Pakistan, however, continued to reject India's proposed "no first use" policy, citing India's superiority in conventional weapons.

Diplomatic moves, both public and behind the scenes, stalled in May 1999 because of the renewed fighting in Kashmir. In October India reacted cautiously to Prime Minister Sharif's overthrow but found little substance in Chief Executive Musharraf's announcement that he was immediately pulling some troops back from the Pakistan-India border. The Vajpayee government dismissed Musharraf's subsequent announcement that he was prepared to continue the Lahore dialogue as long as India recognized the "centrality" of the Kashmir issue.

Responding to a May 2001 invitation, General Musharraf met for the first time with Indian Prime Minister Vajpayee at Agra, India, on July 15–16. Although the two sides agreed to further meetings, they remained far apart, with Pakistan insisting on the primacy of Kashmir and with India unsuccessfully attempting to broaden the discussion to such other concerns as trade and cultural relations. On October 1 militants carried out an assault on the state assembly building at Srinagar, the summer capital of Jammu and Kashmir, resulting in nearly 40 deaths. Charging that Pakistan had failed to stop terrorist infiltrators, India ordered additional troops to Kashmir, with Pakistan responding in kind. On December 13 terrorists attacked India's Parliament, leaving 14 dead, including the terrorists, and by May 2002, when three gunmen stormed a Kashmiri army base and left nearly three dozen dead, India and Pakistan had a combined million troops or more stationed along the Line of Control. Diplomatic intervention, led by the United States, ultimately helped to diffuse the immediate situation.

When Prime Minister Vajpayee called on April 18, 2003, for "open dialogue" with Pakistan, Islamabad announced its willingness to cooperate, which led to a mutual upgrading of diplomatic relations. On November 26 the two governments instituted a cease-fire, the first in 14 years, between Pakistani and Indian forces in the disputed border region. The cease-fire was followed by an announcement at the January 4–6, 2004, SAARC session that the two governments would undertake "composite talks" on bilateral issues, and in late June 2005 Prime Minister Aziz described the peace process as "irreversible."

Relations with Bangladesh have improved considerably in recent years, although no formula has yet been found for relocating some 230,000 Biharis stranded in the former East Pakistan since the 1972 breakup. An agreement in August 1992 led to the airlifting of an initial contingent to Lahore in early 1993, but the Bhutto government suspended the program later in the year. Although Pakistan recommitted itself in early 1998 to resettling the Biharis, no substantive move toward that goal had been achieved by 2004. In May 2003 the Bangladeshi High Court opened the way for Baharis to be counted as Bangladeshi citizens.

Although Pakistan and Afghanistan had long been at odds over the latter's commitment to the creation of an independent "Pushtunistan" out of a major part of Pakistan's North-West Frontier Province, Islamabad reacted strongly to the Soviet invasion of its neighbor in late 1979, providing Muslim rebel groups (*mujaheddin*) with weapons and supplies for continued operations against the Soviet-backed regime at Kabul. Support for the rebels occasionally provoked bombing raids in the Peshawar area, and the presence of over 3.5 million Afghan refugees proved economically burdensome.

Following the Soviet departure, which was completed in early 1989, Pakistan supported the installation of an interim coalition government at Kabul, and by late 1992 some 1.5 million of the displaced Afghans were reported to have returned home. Kabul later accused Islamabad of supporting the fundamentalist Taliban militia, which Pakistan in fact recognized as Afghanistan's government shortly after it took power in September 1996. Subsequent relations were complicated by the fact that Islamic fundamentalists, having been permitted to establish education and training camps in the Peshawar area during the Afghan revolution, became increasingly active within Pakistan itself, particularly in the Federally Administered Tribal Areas and the North-West Frontier Province, and in the divided Kashmir.

From the mid-1990s US-Pakistani relations were dominated by concerns over terrorism. In February 1995 the government permitted American agents to join in the apprehension of Ramzi Ahmed YOUSEF, the suspected mastermind of the 1993 World Trade Center bombing, and then approved his prompt extradition to New York. In the wake of the March killing by Pakistani gunmen of two US consular officials, Prime Minister Bhutto appealed for foreign assistance in closing down Muslim schools and other facilities used as fronts for international terrorism. In 1997 agents of the US Federal Bureau of Investigation (FBI) apprehended in Pakistan Mir Aimal KASI, who in January 1993 had shot five people, killing two of them, outside the Virginia headquarters of the US Central Intelligence Agency. Kasi, who described his assault as a protest against American involvement in Islamic countries, was sentenced to death in January 1998 by a Virginia court. (The sentence was carried out in November 2002.) In addition, in August 1997 Pakistan arrested three suspects in the bombing of US embassies in Kenya and Tanzania.

Although a planned visit to Pakistan by US President Bill Clinton had been cancelled soon after the October 1999 coup, a brief stopover was rescheduled for March 25, 2000, during a trip to the Indian subcontinent. The United States used the occasion to urge that Pakistan set a timetable for a return to democratic rule, exert greater control over separatist infiltration into Indian-held Kashmir, and help combat regional terrorism. Following the September 11, 2001, terrorist assaults on the United States, relations with the new US George W. Bush administration were significantly strengthened by Pakistan's assistance against the *al-Qaeda* terrorist network and, ultimately, the Taliban (see Current issues, below).

In early 2002 the Musharraf regime reacted swiftly to the murder of American journalist Daniel Pearl, who had been abducted by members of a group calling itself the National Movement for Restoration of Pakistan's Sovereignty. The principal suspect, Ahmad Omar Sayed SHAIKH, a UK national, was captured in February and, on July 15, sentenced to death. Three codefendants received life in prison. As of August 2005 the appeals process was ongoing. Another leading suspect, Amjad Hussain FAROOQI, allegedly a member of the outlawed militant group *Lashkar-i-Jhangvi,* was killed in a shootout with police in September 2004. Washington received less support for its 2003 invasion of Iraq, with Pakistan consistently declining to supply troops in the aftermath.

Current Issues

Following the September 11, 2001, attacks on the US World Trade Center and Pentagon, President Musharraf faced the stiffest test of his tenure as he sought to balance competing forces: on the one hand, external pressure from Washington and its allies, which demanded Pakistan's aid in an assault on Osama bin Laden's *al-Qaeda* terrorist network and Afghanistan's Taliban, and, on the other hand, internal pressure from pro-Taliban, anti-American Islamic fundamentalists. On September 19, in a nationwide address, the president explained why he had granted the United States use of Pakistani airspace and had pledged cooperation in intelligence gathering, a decision that intensified a wave of anti-American street protests. The situation was further exacerbated when he derecognized the Taliban and ordered his security forces to prevent

the flight into Pakistan of Taliban officials and army personnel and of *al-Qaeda* operatives.

The border has nevertheless remained porous. As of mid-2005 Pakistan had reportedly handed over to the United States some 700 *al-Qaeda* suspects, including key operatives, but opposition to the government's actions remain strong in the NWFP and especially in the Federally Administered Tribal Areas (FATA), where Islamabad has never had firm control. Resistance has been particularly fierce in Waziristan, bordering Afghanistan, where in 2004 Pakistan's armed forces launched a major offensive against *al-Qaeda.*

Objections to central authority have also flared up in Baluchistan Province. In January 2005 the alleged rape of a woman doctor by one or more military personnel triggered a spate of unrest by Bugti tribesmen, who centered their attacks on the vital Sui natural gas facility, temporarily shutting it down. By the end of March several dozen individuals had died in the fighting, amid continuing demands from tribal leaders that the military withdraw from the province.

The United States continues to praise and support Musharraf, largely because Washington's war on terrorism depends on Pakistani assistance. Not even a February 4, 2004, public admission by Abdul Qadeer KHAN, the former head of Pakistan's nuclear weapons program, that he had passed nuclear secrets to Iran, Libya, and North Korea damaged the US-Pakistani relationship. Musharraf, knowing full well the destabilizing consequences if he turned Khan, a national hero, over to the justice system, instead pardoned him on February 6, without protest from Washington. (The International Atomic Energy Agency [IAEA] subsequently speculated that Khan's revelations were merely the "tip of the iceberg" in an operation that also involved the sale of nuclear components in a number of countries.) On March 17–18, US Secretary of State Colin Powell, making his fourth visit to Pakistan, announced that Pakistan was regarded as a "major non-NATO ally," and a week later US President Bush lifted the few remaining sanctions imposed after the 1998 nuclear tests and the 1999 coup. Musharraf's recent steps toward democracy were also rewarded in May when the Commonwealth lifted Pakistan's four-and-a-half year suspension.

Speaking to a joint session of Parliament on January 17, 2004 (amid heckling from some members of the ARD), Musharraf called for a "sustainable democratic system," which was generally regarded as an indirect reference to instituting a permanent governmental role for the military. In that capacity the controversial NSC, by providing the military leadership with a means of influencing the government on questions of security and sovereignty, will, at least in theory, forestall future coups. In the January speech Musharraf also advocated economic development to alleviate poverty, supported a negotiated resolution of the Kashmir issue, and called for a "jihad" to be waged against "myopic" extremism, terrorism, and sectarianism.

Sectarian violence, particularly between Sunni and Shi'ite groups in Karachi, has been a persistent problem, and it escalated once again in April 2004, when a new wave of assassinations and bombings began. Allegedly involved in the violence was a group identified as "313," apparently an alliance of three pro-*al-Qaeda*, pro-Taliban Sunni groups bent on destabilizing the government.

The June 2004 decision to replace Prime Minister Jamali with Finance Minister Aziz was not a surprise to most observers. Aziz was credited with stabilizing the Pakistani economy, whereas Jamali had apparently failed to speed governmental and economic reforms advocated by Musharraf. On July 30 Aziz, who was in the midst of campaigning for a National Assembly seat, escaped an assassination attempt, allegedly by *al-Qaeda* members in retaliation for the government's having handed over to the United States a suspect in the 1998 US embassy bombings in East Africa. Musharraf himself has been targeted for assassination several times, including twice in December 2003—first when a remote-controlled bomb missed his motorcade and then when suicide bombers struck another motorcade, killing at least 17 and injuring another 50. The president was unscathed. Speculation about the perpetrators centered on members

of banned Islamic organizations, which have denounced Musharraf's recent cooperation with India on the Kashmiri issue, although in May 2004 Musharraf himself also implicated junior members of the army and air force.

Prime Minister Aziz's election by the National Assembly on August 27, 2004, was largely pro forma, although it did provide an opportunity for the opposition ARD and MMA to boycott the voting when assembly Speaker Chaudhry Amir HUSSAIN refused to issue a production order for the opposition's candidate, Makhdoom Javed HASHMI of the PML-N. Hashmi remained in custody pending appeal of his April conviction on treason, forgery, and other charges related to distribution of a letter in which senior military officers had allegedly criticized President Musharraf and the army leadership.

Political Parties and Groups

Political parties have functioned only intermittently since Pakistan became independent. Banned in 1958, they were permitted to resume activity in 1962, and the Pakistan Muslim League (PML), successor to Mohammad Ali Jinnah's All-India Muslim League, continued its dominance during Ayub Khan's tenure. Opposition parties, though numerous, were essentially regional in character and largely ineffectual.

Though the military government of Yahya Khan did not ban political formations as such, the lack of opportunity for overt activity restricted their growth. The election of December 1970, however, provided a major impetus to the reemergence of parties. The PML's supremacy ended with the rise of Zulfikar Ali Bhutto's Pakistan People's Party (PPP) in West Pakistan and the Awami League in East Pakistan (now Bangladesh). At the election of March 1977, the PPP faced a coalition of opposition parties organized as the Pakistan National Alliance (PNA). Although formal party activity was suspended following the coup of July 5, the ban was subsequently relaxed, and the PNA, with but minor defection from its ranks, became a de facto government party until withdrawing in 1979. In

October all formal party activity was again proscribed.

In February 1981 nine parties agreed to form a joint Movement for the Restoration of Democracy (MRD), of which the most important component was the PPP under the leadership of Begum Nusrat Bhutto and her daughter, Benazir Bhutto. The composition of the alliance changed several times thereafter, although it remained the largest opposition grouping for the balance of the Zia era. Despite the president's denunciation of parties as "non-Islamic" and the fact that the 1985 assembly balloting was on a nonparty basis, some political leaders subsequently organized informal legislative coalitions and immediately prior to the lifting of martial law supported legislation permitting legalization of parties under highly controlled circumstances. While most MRD participants declined to register under the new law, the PML, led by Prime Minister Mohammad Khan Junejo, did so in February 1986, thus becoming the de facto ruling party.

Following the legislative dissolution of May 1988, all of the leading parties agreed to participate in the upcoming national and provincial elections. As the result of disagreement with the PPP over electoral strategy, the other MRD parties decided in October to campaign separately in a loose coalition of their own, the MRD becoming, for all practical purposes, moribund. Concurrently, two factions within the PML, which had split after Zia's death in August, reunited and joined a number of other groups, including the *Muhajir Qaumi* Movement (MQM), the National People's Party (NPP), and the *Jamaat-e-Islami-e-Pakistan* (JIP), to form the Islamic Democratic Alliance–IDA (*Islam-e-Jamhoori Ittehad*). The IDA routed the PPP at the balloting of October 1990 but fell into disarray thereafter, the PPP recovering to defeat the PML's Nawaz Group (PML-N) in a basically two-party contest on October 6, 1993.

On February 3, 1997, the PML-N scored a smashing victory over Benazir Bhutto's PPP. Although initially governing with the support of several smaller parties, including the principal faction of the MQM and the Awami National Party (ANP), by late 1998 the PML-N was essentially

governing on its own. Meanwhile, as in the past, various groups were attempting to coordinate their policies through loose multiparty alliances, the principal ones being the Islamic *Milli Yakjehti* Council–MYC (National Unity Council), spearheaded by the *Jamaat-e-Islami;* the largely secular Pakistan National Conference (PNC), formed in June 1997 by 12 opposition parties; and the Pakistan *Awami Ittehad* (PAI), an amalgam of 15 secular, religious, and regional opposition groups, including the PPP and two anti-Nawaz PML factions. In early 1999 some 16 mostly regional parties, some of them with concurrent connections to the PAI, were still in the process of formally establishing another alliance, the **Pakistan Oppressed Nations' Movement** (PONM), which had been announced in October 1998 at a conference called to advance the cause of autonomy for Sindhis, Pushtoons, Baluchs, and Seraikis within a federal system. Some party leaders had already raised the possibility that the PAI-PONM interconnections might lead to formation of a "grand alliance," but the PONM remained aloof from the anti-Nawaz Grand Democratic Alliance (GDA) formed on September 14, 1999, by the PAI, the MQM, the ANP, and the *Tehrik-e-Insaaf.* Of these alliances, all are defunct except the PONM, which reportedly encompasses some 30 parties.

In mid-April 2000 the GDA and the PML-N began discussions on forming a "political front" devoted to restoring democracy. Despite the objections of some party leaders, the PML-N allied with the PPP and over a dozen other parties in November 2000. Subsequently named the **Alliance for the Restoration of Democracy** (ARD), the grouping selected veteran politician Nawabzada Nasrullah Khan of the Pakistan Democratic Party (PDP) as its president. (Khan died in September 2003 and was succeeded in October by Javed Hashmi of the PML-N.)

A total of 73 parties and alliances contested the October 2002 election. In addition to the ARD, whose constituent parties ran independently, the principal alliances were the newly formed Islamic **Muttahida Majlis-e-Amal** (MMA) and the government-supportive **National Alliance** (NA) of the Millat Party (MP), National Awami Party (NAP), NPP, Sindh Democratic Alliance (SDA), and Sindh National Front (SNF). A looser **Grand National Alliance** encompassed the PML's dominant *Qaid-i-Azam* faction and the NA plus the ANP, the MQM, the PPP (Sherpao), and a number of other progovernment, predominately regional groups, all running independently. In May 2004 the NA parties agreed in principle to merge with the substantially reunited PML (excluding the separate PML-N).

Leading Party

Pakistan Muslim League (PML). The PML was launched in 1962 as successor to the preindependence All-India Muslim League. Long ridden by essentially personalist factions, it split over participation in the February 1985 election. A so-called "Chatta Group," led by Kawaja KHAIRUDDIN, joined the MRD's boycott call, while the mainstream, led by Pir Sahib PAGARO, announced that it would participate "under protest." Pagaro was subsequently reported to have invited President Zia to join the league, 27 of whose members were elected to the assembly, and to have urged the selection of Mohammad Khan JUNEJO, a long-time party member, as prime minister. In the absence of a party-based legislature, the PML served as the core of the government-backed Official Parliamentary Group (OPG) and was the first to register as a legal party following the lifting of martial law in early 1986. Later in the year a cleavage emerged between grassroots party loyalists, led by Pagaro, and office holders (many of no previous party affiliation), led by Junejo. The PML split again in August 1988, an army-supported faction of Zia loyalists (the PML-Fida) emerging under Fida Mohammad KHAN. The party reunited as a component of the IDA prior to the November balloting, at which the IDA routed the PPP, Mohammad Nawaz SHARIF of the PML thereupon being named prime minister.

Pagaro formed the PML-Functional (PML-F), in mid-1992, while Junejo died in March 1993. In May 1993 the Junejo group split into a majority (Nawaz, or PML-N) faction headed by Nawaz Sharif and a rump (Junejo, or PML-J) faction led by Hamid Nasir CHATTHA. The latter joined the Bhutto government following the October 1993 election, while the PML-N became the core of the parliamentary opposition.

Following the elections of February 3, 1997, at which it won a majority of the assembly seats, the PML-N took power. The party remained prone to factionalism, however, with the PML-J and a Qasim Group (PML-Qasim) joining the opposition PAI alliance upon its formation in 1998. Following the October 1999 coup another faction, the PML-*Qaid-i-Azam* ("Father of the Nation," a reference to Mohammad Ali Jinnah), or the PML-Q, was formed with the tacit support of the military.

Entering the 2002 election, the PML-Q was allied with the National Alliance in the Grand National Alliance. The separate PML-N (see below) ran independently as part of the ARD. The PML-J, although running independently, appeared to be drawing closer to the PML-Q. Also running independently were the PML-F; the PML-Zia ul-Haq (PML-Z), which had been formed by the son of the late president in August 2002; and the PML-Jinnah, which had been established in 1998 following a factional dispute within the PML-J. Electoral results gave the PML-Q 118 seats; the PML-F, 5; the PML-J, 3, and the PML-Z, 1.

With the PML-Q in the ascendancy, holding a plurality of seats in both houses of Parliament and dominating the government, efforts to unite the PML factions gathered strength in 2003, leading to the announcement in May 2004 of a "united PML," excluding only the PML-N. In August, however, objecting in particular to the leadership of Chaudhry Shujaat Hussain, Pir Sahib Pagaro declared that he intended to restore the PML-F's separate standing, which raised the question of whether dissatisfied members of other factions would also opt for independence.

Days after the formation of the "united PML," the five National Alliance parties, which had won 16 seats at the October 2002 election, announced that they were merging with the PML. There was, however, some opposition within a number of the parties, with the attendant possibility that those objecting to the merger might seek to retain their party designations. The five NA parties were the following:

The **Millat Party** (MP), launched in August 1998 by former president Sardar Farooq Ahmad Khan LEGHARI, advocated creation of an egalitarian society based on Islamic principles, respect for human rights, clean government, and "true federalism."

The **National People's Party** (NPP) had been formed in 1986 by a group of PPP moderates led by former Sindh chief minister Ghulam Mustafa JATOI, who accused Benazir Bhutto of "authoritarian tendencies" prior to being removed as provincial PPP president. Jatoi served as interim prime minister following the dismissal of Bhutto in 1990. The NPP entered the first Sharif government coalition but was expelled in 1992 because of alleged collusion with the PPP. The NPP turned to the PPP (Shaheed Bhutto) for an electoral alliance in 1997, winning one seat under the leadership of former communications minister Ghulam Murtaza Jatoi. Following the merger announcement, NPP founder Ghulam Mustafa Jatoi stated that while the party's parliamentary group may have decided to join the PML, he had not.

The **National Awami Party** (NAP) was formed in 2000 by defectors from the Awami National Party (ANP, below) led by Ajmal Khan KHATTAK. They were joined by a faction of the Pakistan National Party (PNP) under Raziq BUGTI.

The **Sindh Democratic Alliance** (SDA), led by Ghulam Murtaza JATOI and Arbab Ghulam RAHIM, was launched in September–October 2001 and quickly established a working relationship at the provincial level with the PML-Q. In June 2004 Rahim, now a PML vice president, was elected chief minister of Sindh by the provincial assembly.

The **Sindh National Front** (SNF) was launched by Mumtaz Ali BHUTTO, an uncle of the former prime minister, following the dissolution in 1989 of the Sindh-Baluch-Pushtoon Front (SBPF), of which Bhutto had been a leader. Like the SBPF, the SNF called for a confederation of Pakistan's four provinces, with each free to establish its own domestic and foreign policies.

In mid-June 2004 the Election Commission approved the merger of the PML-F, PML-J, PML-Jinnah, PML-Z, and SDA into the PML-Q and the redesignation of the latter as, simply, the Pakistan Muslim League (PML). Earlier, the Baluchistan National Party (Awami) had indicated that it, too, would consider joining the PML.

Leaders: Chaudhry Shujaat HUSSAIN (President), Shaukat AZIZ (Prime Minister), Zafarullah Khan JAMALI (former Prime Minister), Chaudhry Hamid Nasir CHATTA (PML-J), Muhammad Ijaz ul-HAQ (PML-Z), Manzoor Ahmad WATTOO (PML-Jinnah), Abdul Razzaq THAHEEN (PML-F), Mushahid HUSSAIN (Secretary General).

Other Parliamentary Parties

Pakistan People's Party (PPP). An avowedly Islamic socialist party founded in 1967 by Zulfikar Ali Bhutto, the PPP held a majority of seats in the National Assembly truncated by the independence of Bangladesh in 1971. Officially credited with winning 155 of 200 assembly seats in the election of March 1977, it was the primary target of a postcoup decree of October 16 that banned all groups whose ideology could be construed as prejudicial to national security. Bhutto was executed in April 1979, the party leadership being assumed by his widow and daughter, both of whom, after being under house arrest for several years, went into exile at London. After having briefly returned to Pakistan in July 1985 to preside over the burial of her brother, Shahnawaz, Benazir Bhutto again returned in April 1986. The PPP won a sizeable plurality (92 of 205 contested seats) at the National Assembly balloting of November 1988, Bhutto being designated prime minister. The party lost ministerial control with Bhutto's dismissal on August 6, 1990; its legislative strength was subsequently cut by more than half at the election of October 24 and 27 (for which it joined with a number of smaller groups to campaign as the People's Democratic Alliance–PDA). It regained its plurality at the 1993 legislative poll, with Ms. Bhutto being reinstalled as prime minister.

In December 1993 the PPP's Executive Council ousted Prime Minister Bhutto's mother, Begum Nusrat BHUTTO, as party cochair. The action was the product of estrangement between the two over the political role of Benazir's brother, Murtaza Bhutto, who had returned from exile in November to take up a seat in the Sindh provincial legislature and who in March 1995 announced the formation of a breakaway faction of the PPP. Murtaza died in a firefight with gunmen on September 20, 1996. Following the ouster of Prime Minister Bhutto in November, her husband, Asif Ali ZARDARI, was charged with complicity in the killing. The new PML-led government formed an "accountability" department to investigate the allegations and corruption in general, a principal target being the PPP leadership. Meanwhile, Benazir Bhutto was meeting with leaders of smaller opposition parties, which ultimately led to the formation of the PAI alliance in late February 1998, with Bhutto as the most prominent leader.

Earlier, at the end of 1996, allegations about the death of Murtaza Bhutto had led his widow, Ghinwa BHUTTO, to form the **Pakistan People's Party (Shaheed Bhutto)**, or PPP-SB, to challenge Benazir Bhutto's hold on the party. The subsequent national legislative campaign in early 1997 contained an added element of personal hostility between the two women, although both suffered disastrous defeats in the election.

During 1998–1999 new corruption allegations or charges were repeatedly brought against Benazir Bhutto and her husband: kickbacks involving gold transactions, commissions from foreign defense manufacturers, abuse of power in making political appointments, use of Swiss bank accounts to launder money. Her political viability suffered a major blow on April 15, 1999, when a two-person Lahore court sentenced her and her husband to five years in prison, disqualified them from public office for five years, and fined them $8.6 million for corruption and abuse of power. Bhutto asserted from England that she would appeal the conviction to the Supreme Court, which on April 6, 2001, threw out the decision and ordered a retrial because of apparent government involvement in the verdict.

In early 1999 Benazir Bhutto dismissed the party's senior vice president, Aftab Ahmad Khan SHERPAO, for breaking party discipline over political developments involving the North-West Frontier Province government. He went on to form the Pakistan People's Party (Sherpao), or PPP-S. In March the party leadership elected the former prime minister chairperson for life, a decision reiterated by a party convention on September 11, 2000, in defiance of the government's August announcement that convicted criminals could not hold party offices. She remained in self-imposed exile, the Musharraf regime having refused to lift outstanding arrest warrants. In July 2002 she was again convicted, in absentia, of corruption, as was her husband in September. He had been imprisoned since 1986. Other cases against the two were pending in Switzerland, the United States, and the United Kingdom as well as Pakistan. In September 2004 Zardari's corruption conviction was overturned, and on November 22, he was released on bail.

To get around a proscription against the electoral participation of any party having a convicted criminal as an officeholder, the PPP organized the legally separate **Pakistan People's Party Parliamentarians** (PPPP) in August 2002. Two months later the PPPP won 81 National Assembly seats, but in November it suffered the defection of ten representatives who supported the installation of the Jamali government. (The move was possible because the antidefection clause of the constitution remained suspended.) Six of the ten were offered cabinet posts, and the group organized under Rao Sikander Iqbal as the **Pakistan People's Party Parliamentarians (Patriots)** (PPPP-P). To further complicate matters, in June 2004 the PPPP-P and the PPP (Sherpao), the latter of which had won two seats at the 2002 election, merged, with the new party being registered by the Election Commission as the official **Pakistan People's Party** (PPP).

Leaders: Benazir BHUTTO (former Prime Minister and Chairperson for Life of the deregistered PPP), Makhdoom Amin FAHIM (PPPP President and Senate Leader), Chawdhry Aitzaz AHSAN (PPPP National Assembly Leader), Rao Sikander IQBAL (Leader of the officially recognized PPP).

Muttahida Majlis-e-Amal (MMA). The MMA ("United Council for Action") was organized in June 2001 by the Islamist parties discussed below plus the *Jamiat-e-Ahle Hadith* (JAH), which withdrew before the 2002 election campaign. The MMA campaigned on a platform that included restoration of the constitution, creation of an Islamic state, and resolution of the Kashmir issue through negotiation. Only the two JUI factions supported the Taliban regime in Afghanistan, but all of the constituent parties opposed Musharraf's subsequent decision to join the US-led "war on terrorism" and to permit US forces to operate from Pakistani soil.

Having won 60 seats in the National Assembly, the MMA was courted by both the PML-Q and the PPPP (with which it had little in common ideologically) to form a coalition government, but it rejected both. Its firm opposition to the 2002 Legal Framework Order was largely responsible for the year-long stalemate in the National Assembly, until an agreement was reached with President Musharraf in December 2003. Although chaired from its inception by the moderate Maulana Shah Ahmad NOORANI Siddiqui of the JUP, until his death in December 2003, the JUI's Fazlur Rahman and the JI's Qazi Hussain Ahmad have exerted more influence.

Leaders: Qazi Hussain AHMAD (President), Fazlur RAHMAN.

Jamiat-ul-Ulema-e-Islam–JUI (Assembly of Islamic Clergy). Founded in 1950, the *Jamiat-ul-Ulema-e-Islam* is a progressive formation committed to constitutional government guided by Sunni Islamic principles. In December 1988 the JUI's Darkhwasty Group withdrew from the IDA to reunite with the parent formation,

although a faction headed by Maulana Sami ul-Haq remained within the government coalition until November 1991. Factionalization subsequently remained a problem, with Sami ul-Haq heading one group, (JUI-S, or JUI-Haq) and Fazlur Rahman heading another (JUI-F, or JUI-Fazlur). The latter, which won two National Assembly seats from Baluchistan in 1997, emerged as the dominant faction, although ul-Haq was a prominent leader of the MYC alliance. Rahman supported Afghanistan's Taliban and, following the 1999 coup, condemned ousted prime minister Sharif's "lust for unlimited powers." Rahman was placed under house arrest in October 2001, at the opening of the US-led military campaign in Afghanistan. At the 2002 National Assembly election the JUI-F claimed the most MMA seats, while the JUI-S finished third.

Leaders: Maulana Fazlur RAHMAN (Leader of JUI-F), Maulana Sami ul-HAQ (Leader of JUI-S).

Jamaat-e-Islami-e-Pakistan–JIP (Pakistan Islamic Assembly). Organized in 1941, the *Jamaat-e-Islami* is a right-wing fundamentalist group that has called for an Islamic state based on a national rather than a purely communalistic consensus. Members of the party ran as individuals in the 1985 assembly election, and ten were elected; subsequently, although party leaders agreed to legislative coordination with the PML, the *Jamaat* dominated the anti-martial law Independent Parliamentary Group (IPG) and, despite its unregistered status, functioned as the largest legislative opposition party.

The group participated in formation of the IDA in 1988 but withdrew in May 1992, in part because the coalition had failed to implement a promised Islamization program. In 1993 it was instrumental in launching a Pakistan Islamic Front (PIF), which won only three seats at the October legislative poll. Although the JIP held no national legislative seats following the 1997 election, it remained politically influential. It welcomed the October 1999 coup but called for setting up a caretaker civilian government.

Officially a branch of the *Jamiat-e-Islami* in Pakistan but so independent that it might well be considered a separate movement, the **Jammu and Kashmir Jamiat-e-Islami** was active in electoral politics by 1970 and even participated to a limited degree in Indian *Lok Sabha* and provincial elections. In 1997 the party denied that it was the political wing of the militant *Hizb-ul-Mujaheddin,* and in October 40 of its members challenged the militant campaign as not contributing to the goal of an independent Kashmir.

Leaders: Amir Qazi Hussain AHMAD (Chairman), Syed Munawwar HASAN (Secretary General).

Jamiat-ul-Ulema-e-Pakistan–JUP (Assembly of Pakistani Clergy). Founded in 1968, the *Jamiat-ul-Ulema-e-Pakistan* is a popular Islamic group that withdrew from the PNA in 1978. It joined the MRD in February 1981, severed its membership the following March, then rejoined in August 1983 at the commencement of the civil disobedience campaign. Its president, Ahmed Noorani, was among those failing to secure an assembly slot in 1988; its secretary general, Maulana Abdul Sattar Khan Niazi, quit the Sharif cabinet in March 1991 after being criticized by the prime minister for not supporting government policies on the Gulf war. The party subsequently split into Noorani and Niazi factions, the latter emphasizing religious issues. Niazi died in May 2001 and Noorani, in December 2003. At the 2002 election the JUP won no National Assembly seats.

Leaders: Shah Farid al-HAQ (President, Noorani Group), Pir Syed Anis HAIDER (President, Niazi Group).

Islami Tehrik-i-Pakistan (TiP). Also identified as the *Tehrik Millat-e-Islami Pakistan,* the TiP is the successor to the banned *Tehrik-e-Jafariya-e-Pakistan*–TJP (Pakistan Jafari Movement). The TJP was an outgrowth of the Movement for the Implementation of Shi'a Jurisprudence (*Tehrik-e-Nifaz Fiqh Jafariya*–TNFJ), an activist group representing Pakistan's Shi'a minority. The TNFJ launched a campaign in 1980 against the government's Islamization campaign, insisting that it was entirely Sunni-based. In July 1987 it decided to reorganize as a political party committed to the principles of Iran's Ayotollah Khomeini. An electoral ally of the PPP in 1990, it was frequently a target of Sunni violence. The TJP was closely associated with the extremist Shi'ite **Sipah-i-Muhammad,** which has been a major participant in Pakistan's ongoing sectarian warfare. The latter group was banned in August 2001, as was the TJP in January 2002. In an effort to get around the ban, the organization assumed the TiP designation, but the TiP was itself banned in November 2003. Its leader, Sajid Naqvi, was arrested in the same month in connection with the assassination of Maulana Azam Tariq of the Sunni *Sipah-i-Sahaba* (below).

Leader: Allama Sajid Ali NAQVI.

Pakistan Muslim League (Nawaz) (PML-N). Under the leadership of former Punjab chief minister and then Prime Minister Mohammad Nawaz SHARIF, the PML-N emerged from the PML-Junejo Group in 1993 and quickly established itself as the dominant PML grouping. In 1997 the PML-N won a parliamentary majority under Nawaz Sharif. Following the October 199 coup the PML-N established a 15-member Coordination Committee to consider party reorganization. It did not, however, call for the immediate restoration of the Sharif government, having concluded that directly confronting the military would be inadvisable.

As of October 2000, efforts by Sharif's wife, Kulsoom SHARIF, to exert greater control over the party had succeeded primarily in preventing her husband's removal as party president. As a condition of his release from prison two months later, Sharif agreed to abandon politics for at least two decades, although he continues to exert considerable influence from exile. In May 2004 his brother, Shabaz, having received a favorable ruling from the Supreme Court on his right to return, attempted to end his four-year exile but was immediately ushered back out of the country by officials.

At the October 2002 National Assembly election the PML-N ran as part of the ARD, winning 19 seats. A year later the party's acting president, Javed Hashmi, was arrested for distributing a letter, allegedly written by army officers, that was critical of President Musharraf. Despite widespread expressions of outrage from the ARD and other elements of the opposition, Hashmi was convicted in April 2004 of treason, mutiny, and forgery but immediately launched an appeal.

Leaders: Mian Shabaz SHARIF (President of the Party and former chief minister of Punjab), Makhdoom Javed HASHMI (Acting President and Parliamentary Leader of the PML-N, and President of the ARD), Raja Zafar ul-Haq (Chairman), Ishaq DAR (Senate Leader), Saranjam KHAN (Secretary General).

Muttahida Qaumi Movement–MQM (Nationalist People's Movement). Organized in 1981 as the *Muhajir* National Movement, the MQM was primarily concerned with the rights of postpartition migrants to Pakistan, whom it wanted to see recognized as constituting a "fifth nationality." Originally backed by Zia ul-Haq as a counter to Zulfikar Bhutto's Sindh-based PPP, the party became the third-largest National Assembly grouping, with 13 seats, after the 1988 election. It was subsequently allied, at different times, with both the PPP and the PML.

The assassination of party chairman Azim Ahmad TARIQ on May 1, 1993, exacerbated a violent cleavage that had emerged within the group the year before, the principal leaders being Altaf Hussain (MQM-Altaf), currently resident in London, and Afaq AHMED (MQM-Haqiqi). The party boycotted the National Assembly balloting in 1993, although participating in the Sindh provincial poll, where it was runner-up to the PPP. In June 1994 Altaf Hussain and two of his senior associates were each sentenced in absentia to 27-year prison terms for terrorism, but in January 1997 the convictions were quashed.

In February 1997 balloting the MQM-Altaf, under the banner of the Haq Parast Group, won 12 National Assembly seats, all from Sindh, and thereafter entered a governing alliance with the PML-N at both provincial and national levels. Also in 1997, the party changed its named from "*Muhajir*" to "*Muttahida*" to indicate that its interests had broadened to encompass Pakistanis in general rather than only the Muslim migrants from India.

In August 1998 the MQM announced its intention to withdraw from the governing coalitions, in part because the Nawaz Sharif administration had not done enough to stem increasingly violent clashes in Karachi between the MQM-Altaf and the MQM-Haqiqi, the latter of which was functioning primarily as a collection of urban street fighters. However, when Islamabad responded to the violence by dismissing the Sindh provincial government and imposing federal rule, Altaf Hussain loyalists accused the Nawaz Sharif government of trying to take away the party's power base. In 1999 a number of party leaders broke with Hussain and threatened to form a separate party unless he adopted a stronger stance toward autonomy for Sindh.

At the 2002 National Assembly election the MQM won 17 seats, after which it joined the Jamali government.

Leaders: Altaf HUSSAIN (President, MQM-Altaf), Farooq SATTAR (MQM-Altaf, Parliamentary Leader).

Awami National Party (ANP). The Awami (People's) National Party was formed in July 1986 by four left-of-center groups: the National Democratic Party (NDP), a group of Pakistan National Party (PNP) dissidents led by Latif AFRIDI, and elements of the *Awami Tehrik* (PAT, below) and the *Mazdoor Kissan* Party (MKP, below). As originally constituted, the ANP was unusual in that each of its constituent groups drew its primary support from a different province.

The NDP had been organized in 1975 upon proscription of the National Awami Party, a remnant of the National Awami Party of Bangladesh that, under the leadership of Abdul Wali Khan, was allegedly involved in terrorist activity aimed at secession of Baluchistan and North-West Frontier provinces. A founding component of the PNA, the NDP withdrew in 1978, and in 1979 a group of dissidents left to form the PNP (below).

The ANP won three assembly seats in October 1993 and ten seats—all from the North-West Frontier Province—in February 1997. A year later the ANP terminated its alliance with the governing PML-N because of the latter's refusal to support the redesignation of the North-West Frontier Province as Pakhtoonkhwa, the area's precolonial name. Later in 1998 the ANP was a prime mover in formation of the PONM opposition alliance, but it parted ways in 1999 with what it considered the PONM's unrealistic goals for national reconfiguration.

The ANP failed to win representation at the National Assembly election of 2002 but won two Senate seats in February 2003.

Leaders: Asfandyar WALI Khan (President), Begum Nasim WALI Khan.

Baluchistan National Party (BNP). One of several rival political formations in Baluchistan, the BNP evolved from the Baluchistan National Movement (Mengal Group) to win three National Assembly seats in February 1997. It initially backed the Nawaz Sharif government but later withdrew its support. In October 1998 it participated in the founding conference of the PONM opposition alliance. At the 2002 National Assembly election the BNP-Mengal won one seat; at the 2003 Senate election the BNP-Mengal and the BNP-Awami each won one.

Leaders: Sardar Ataullah MENGAL, Mohim Khan BALOCH (Senator, BNP-Awami), Tahir BIZENJO (BNP-Awami).

Jamhoori Watan Party (JWP). A successor to the Baluchistan National Alliance (BNA), the JWP is active at both provincial and national levels. Its leader is a tribal chief of the Bugti. The JWP won two seats from Baluchistan at the February 1997 National Assembly election and as of early 1999 held five Senate seats. Although initially extending support to the Nawaz Sharif government, the JWP later moved into opposition, but without joining either the PNC or the PAI alliance. As a participant in the ARD, the JWP won one lower house seat in 2002 and one Senate seat in 2003.

Leader: Nawab Akbar BUGTI (President).

Muhajir Qaumi Movement Pakistan (MQM Pakistan). The MQM Pakistan, like the MQM (above), was organized to represent the interests of immigrant Muhajirs, who mostly reside in the urban centers of Sindh. Although the MQM Pakistan advocates "peaceful struggle," many of its leaders remain under arrest. At the October 2002 national election it won one seat.

Leaders: Afaq AHMED (Chairman), Amir KHAN (Secretary).

National Party (NP). The NP was formed in 2003 by merger of the Baluchistan National Movement (BNM) and the Baluchistan National Democratic Party (BNDP). Competing primarily against supporters of the BNP's Sardar Ataullah Mengal, the BNM had failed to win any National Assembly seats in February 1997 but remained a significant force in Baluchistan. The BNM participated in the formation of the PNC opposition alliance in 1997 and won one Senate seat in the 2003 election.

Leaders: Abdul HAYEE Baluch, Muhammad Aslam BULEDI (Senator).

Pakistan Tehrik-e-Insaaf–PTI (Pakistan Justice Movement). The *Tehrik-e-Insaaf* was launched in 1996 by former national cricket captain Imran Khan, who announced that the new group's objective was to work for change in a country "on the brink of disaster" by "demanding justice, honesty, decency and self-respect." Despite high expectations, Khan failed to attract voter support in the February 1997 national election, and the party won no assembly seats. In 1998 Khan confirmed that he and Asghar Khan of the *Tehrik-e-Istiqlal* had broached the subject of a merger, but none appeared imminent. In August 2000 Imran Khan was expelled from the GDA for "undemocratic" comments. The party won one assembly seat in October 2002.

Leaders: Imran KHAN (Chairman), Miraj Mohammad KHAN (Secretary General).

Pakistan Awami Tehrik–PAT (Pakistan People's Movement). The *Awami Tehrik* originally served as a Sindh-based Maoist youth group. Its leader, Rasul Bakhsk PALEJO, was released from prison in 1986, having been held without trial since 1979, and later served as secretary general of the ANP. Party leader Tahir ul-Qadri left the leadership of the PAI alliance in February 1999, apparently because of policy differences with the PPP and the ANP, but the PAT subsequently joined the GDA. In August 2000, however, the GDA expelled Qadri.

In May 2002 the PAT was a founding member of the National Alliance (see PML, above), but it withdrew a month later and contested the October 2002 National Assembly election independently, winning one seat.

Leader: Tahir ul-QADRI.

Pakhtoonkhwa Milli Awami Party (PkMAP). Drawing its support mainly from the Pakhtoon ethnic group in the North-West Frontier Province, the PkMAP has campaigned for greater regional autonomy. It elected three National Assembly members in 1993 but none in 1997. In 1998 it participated in formation of the PONM opposition alliance.

At the 2002 National Assembly election the PkMAP won one seat; in 2003 it won two Senate seats.

Leader: Mahmood Khan ACHAKZAI (Chairman).

Other Parties

Awami Qiadat Party–AQP (People's Leadership Party). Formed in 1995, the AQP serves primarily as a personal vehicle for Aslam Beg, a retired general. Linked to Pakhtoon issues, the party also supports the military. Although committed to democratic procedures, General Beg has argued for a stronger response to civil disorder and sectarian violence. Prior to the 2002 National Assembly election he chastized the secular opposition parties for failing to unite.

Leader: Gen. (Ret.) Mirza Aslam BEG (Chairman).

Jamiat-e-Ahle Hadith (JAH). A militant Sunni group, the JAH had close ties to former prime minister Nawaz Sharif. Originally a component of the MMA, it withdrew when the latter decided to function as an electoral alliance for the 2002 National Assembly election.

Leader: Sajid MIR.

Khaksar Tehrik (Service Movement). A right-wing Islamic organization advocating universal military training, the *Khaksar Tehrik* is also known as *Bailcha Bardar* (Shovel Carriers) because the group's founder, Inayatullah Khan MASHRIQI, adopted the spade as a symbol of self-reliance. Following the 1999 coup, which the party leader termed a "blessing," the party called for an anticorruption drive. It subsequently opposed the Musharraf government, however, supporting restoration of the constitution and democracy.

Leader: Hameeduddin al-MASHRIQI.

Pakistan Democratic Party (PDP). A former component of the PNA and the MRD, the PDP is a strongly Islamic party organized in 1969. Its president, Nawabzada Nasrullah KHAN, joined with the PPP and a number of smaller parties to launch the PAI opposition alliance in early 1998 and the GDA in September 1999. Khan later assumed the leadership of the postcoup ARD. He died in September 2003 and was succeeded as PDP leader by his son.

Leader: Nawabzada Mansoor Ali KHAN (President).

Tehrik-e-Istiqlal (Solidarity Movement). The *Tehrik-e-Istiqlal* is a democratic Islamic group that was a founding member of the PNA, from which it withdrew in November 1977. One of its leaders, Air Mar. (Ret.) Mohammad Asghar Khan, was a leading proponent of election boycotts, stating "there can be no compromise" under martial law; however, following the lifting of martial law, the party broke ranks with its coalition partners by announcing its intention to register as a legal party. It was a leading component of the MRD until September 1986, when most of its leadership withdrew in opposition to Benazir Bhutto's domination of the alliance. In October 1988 *Tehrik-e-Istiqlal* formed an electoral alliance with the JUP (immediately below) for the November legislative balloting, although agreeing not to contest seats for which the IDA was presenting candidates. Asghar Khan resigned from the presidency of *Tehrik-e-Istiqlal* in December in the wake of poor results in the November poll. The party was subsequently a member of the PPP-led PDA in 1990. Following the 1997 national elections, which the *Tehrik-e-Istiqlal* boycotted, Asghar Khan returned to the head of the party and became a major figure in the development of the PNC opposition alliance.

Leaders: Qaiser Ahmed SHAIKH (Chairman), Rehmat Khan WARDAG (President), Air Mar. (Ret.) Mohammad Asghar KHAN.

Pakistan has many other relatively small legal parties, most with a provincial or religious focus. Parties on the Left include the **Mazdoor Kissan Party** (Workers' and Peasants' Party, MKP), which was known from 1994, when it merged with the Communist Party of Pakistan, until 2003 as the Communist Mazdoor Kissan Party (CMKP). A revived **Communist Party of Pakistan** (CPP), currently split into two factions, separated from the CMKP in 1999, as did a new **Communist Mazdoor Kissan Party** from the MKP in 2003. Other leftist groups include the **National Workers' Party,** the **Labor Party of Pakistan,** and the **Social Democratic Party of Pakistan.**

Banned Organizations

Jaish-e-Muhammad Mujaheddin-e-Tanzeem (JMMT or JeM). Formation of the *Jaish-e-Muhammad* ("Movement of the Army of the Holy Warriors of Muhammad") was announced on February 4, 2000, by Masood Azhar. A founding member of the *Harkat-ul-Ansar* (subsequently renamed the **Harkat-ul-Mujaheddin**), he had been detained by India from 1994 until late December 1999, when the hijackers of an Indian Airlines jet demanded his release before freeing their hostages. Azhar has called for a holy war against India as part of the effort to establish an independent, Islamic Kashmir. He was detained in December 2001 but released three months later. The JeM has been linked to many recent terrorist incidents in India, including a December 2001 attack on the Parliament.

Having been banned in January 2002, the JeM restyled itself as the **Khudam-ul-Islam,** which was then banned in November 2003 along with the **Jamaat-al-Ansar,** the new designation of the *Harkat-ul-Mujaheddin.* In 2002 a JeM splinter, the **Jamaat-ul-Furqan** (JuF) had been established by Abdul JABBAR; the JuF was also banned in November 2003. The JeM and the *Harkat-ul-Mujaheddin* are both regarded by the United States as terrorist organizations.

In August 2003 the Indian Border Security Force killed the JeM field commander, Shahnawaz KHAN (also known as Ghazi BABA), alleged mastermind of the 2001 attack on Parliament. In April 2004 Qari Mohammed ASIF, a JeM military operations chief, was also killed.

Leader: Maulana Masood AZHAR.

Lashkar-i-Taiba (LiT). The LiT ("Army of the Pure") was established in 1993 as the military wing of an above-ground religious group, the **Markaz ad-Dawa Wal Irshad,** which was formed in 1986 to organize Pakistani Sunni militants participating in the Afghan revolution. The *Markaz* was officially dissolved in December 2001 and all its assets transferred to the "new" **Jamaat-ud-Dawa** in an effort to avoid proscription. The LiT, which the United States has labeled a terrorist group, was banned by Pakistan in January 2002. Since then it has often been referenced as the *Jamaat-ud-Dawa*, which was placed on a "watch list," but not banned, by the Pakistani government in November 2003. The LiT, which may be the largest Pakistan-based militant group seeking separation of Jammu and Kashmir from India, has claimed responsibility for and been implicated in innumerable attacks within Kashmir and elsewhere. Many of its members have been jailed in India and Pakistan. An LiT commander, Bashir Ahmad KHAN, was killed by Indian forces in April 2004.

Leader: Hafiz Mohammed SAYEED.

Sipah-i-Sahaba (SiS). The *Sipah-i-Sahaba* (Guardians of the Friends of the Prophet) is a militant Sunni group founded in 1982 as a JUI breakaway by Maulana Haq Nawaz JHANGVI, who was later murdered. It has close connections to the extremist **Lashkar-i-Jhangvi** (LiJ) and the equally militant TNSM (below) both of which have been involved in sectarian bloodshed.

In February 2000 the SSP announced that it was prepared to give nearly 100,000 workers to Maulana Masood AZHAR's newly organized JMMT (below) to aid in holy war (*jihad*). Both were banned in January 2002, as the LiJ had been in August 2001. The LiJ's leader, Riaz BASRA, was killed by Indian police on May 14, 2002. Another leader, Asif RAMZI, who had been linked to the kidnapping and murder of American journalist Daniel Pearl, was killed in a bomb explosion in December 2002. ATTAULLAH, an alleged LiJ leader, was sentenced to death in September 2003.

In October 2003 SiS leader Muhammad Azam TARIQ, who had won election to the National Assembly a year earlier as an independent while still in prison, was assassinated, allegedly by members of the Shi'ite TJP (see TiP, above). Earlier, the SiS had been renamed the **Millat-i-Islamia Pakistan** (MIP) to circumvent a government ban, but the MIP was then proscribed in November 2003. The United States has placed both the SiS and the LiJ on its list of terrorist organizations.

Leader: Maulana Muhammad Ahmad LUDHIANVI.

Tehrik-e-Nifaz-e-Shariat-e-Mohammadi–TNSM (Mohammadan Movement for the Enforcement of Islamic Law). The TNSM is a fundamentalist group that was blamed by the government for the deaths of 11 persons in May 1994 and of ten more the following November as the result of tribal demands in the northern areas of Malakand and Swat for the introduction of Islamic law. The TNSM responded to the August 1998 US missile attack against terrorist camps in Afghanistan by organizing a rally in Peshawar at which it threatened to lay siege to US property and kidnap Americans. It was banned in January 2002.

Leaders: Maulana Sufi MUHAMMAD, Maulana Muhammad ALAM.

Harkat-ul-Mujaheddin al-Alami (HMA). A splinter from the **Hizb-ul-Mujaheddin** (HuM; see the article on India), the HMA was implicated in an April 2002 assassination attempt against President Musharraf and a June 2002 bombing at the US consulate at Karachi. Some of its members were previously associated with the banned **Harkat-ul-Jihad-i-Islami.** The two groups and the LiJ are believed to be linked through the **313** alliance.

Hizb-ut-Tahrir. Based in London, England, the Islamist *Hizb-ut-Tahrir* was banned by the Pakistani government in November 2003. It has ostensibly disavowed terrorism but is believed to have links to many jehadist groups around the world.

Legislature

The **Parliament** (*Majlis-e-Shoora*), also known as the Federal Legislature, is a bicameral body consisting of the President, an indirectly elected Senate, and a directly elected National Assembly. The 87-member Senate and the 217-member National Assembly were "suspended" by proclamation of Chief Executive Musharraf on October 15, 1999, and dissolved by him on June 20, 2001. Elections to expanded lower and upper houses were held in October 2002 and February 2003, respectively.

Senate

The current upper house comprises 100 members: 22 elected by each of the four provincial legislatures (16 general seats, 4 reserved for women, and 4 reserved for technocrats/*ulema*), plus 8 from the Federally Administered Tribal Areas (FATA) and 4 from the Federal Capital (2 general, 1 woman, 1 technocrat/*'aalim*). In 2003 the FATA and Islamabad senators were chosen by the National Assembly members of their respective jurisdictions. Senatorial terms are six years, with one-half of the body retiring every three years, although the election of February 24 and 27, 2003, was for the full, reconfigured house. Immediately

Cabinet

As of July 15, 2005

Prime Minister	Shaukat Aziz (PML)
Senior Minister of Defense	Rao Sikander Iqbal (PPP)

Ministers

Commerce	Hamayoon Akhtar Khan (PML)
Communication	Muhammad Shamim Siddiqui (MQM)
Culture, Sports, and Youth Affairs	Muhammad Ajmal Khan (ind.)
Defense Production	Habibullah Khan Warraich (PML)
Education	Javed Ashraf Qazi (PML)
Food, Agriculture, and Livestock	Sikandar Hayat Bosan (PML)
Environment	Tahir Iqbal (PML)
Finance	Shaukil Aziz (PML)
Foreign Affairs	Mian Khursheed Mehmood Kasuri (PML)
Frontier Affairs	Sardar Yar Muhammad Rind (PML)
Health	Muhammad Nasir Khan (PML)
Housing and Works	Syed Safwanullah (MQM)
Industries and Production and Special Initiatives	Jehangir Khan Tareen (PML)
Information and Broadcasting	Sheikh Rasheed Ahmad (PML)
Information Technology and Telecommunication	Awais Ahmed Khan Leghari (PML)
Interior	Aftab Ahmed Khan Sherpao (PPP)
Kashmir Affairs and Northern Areas	Makhdoom Syed Faisal Saleh Hayat (PPP)
Labor, Manpower, and Overseas Pakistanis	Ghulam Sarwar Khan (PML)
Law, Justice, and Human Rights	Muhammad Wasi Zafar (PML)
Local Government and Rural Development	Abdul Razzaq Thahim (PML)
Narcotics Control	Ghaus Bakhsh Khan Mahar (PML)
Parliamentary Affairs	Sher Afghan Khan Niazi (PPP)
Petroleum and Natural Resources	Amamullah Khan Jadoon (PML)
Population and Welfare	Chaudhry Shahbaz Hussain (PML)
Ports and Shipping	Babar Khan Ghauri (MQM)
Privatization and Investment	Abdul Hafeez Shaikh (PML)
Railways	Mian Shahmin Haider (PML)
Religious Affairs, *Zakat*, and *Ushr*	Muhammad Ijaz ul Haq (PML)
Science and Technology	Nouraiz Shakoor Khan (PPP)
Social Welfare and Special Education	Zubaida Jalal (PML) [f]
Textile Industry	Mushtaq Ali Cheema (PML)
Tourism	Ghazi Gulab Jamal Syiad (ind.)
Water and Power	Liaqat Ali Jatoi (PML)

[f] = female

Note: The PPP designation refers to the former Pakistan People's Party Parliamentarians (Patriots) group, which was officially registered as the PPP in June 2004. This PPP should not be confused with the now deregistered PPP of former prime minister Benazir Bhutto.

following the balloting the Pakistan Muslim League-*Qaid-i-Azam* held 34 seats; the *Muttahida Majlis-i-Amal* (MMA), 19; the Pakistan People's Party-Parliamentarians, 11; the *Muttahida Qaumi* Movement, 6; the Pakistan Muslim League-Nawaz, 4; the National Alliance, 3; the Awami National Party, 2; the Pakistan People's Party-Sherpao, 2; the *Pakhtoonkhwa Milli Awami* Party, 2; the Baluchistan National Movement, Baluchistan National Party-Awami, Baluchistan National Party-Mengal, *Jamhoori Watan* Party, and Pakistan Muslim League-Functional, 1 each; independents 12. The eight FATA senators are all considered to be independents, but the majority were reported to support the MMA.

Chairman: Mohammad Mian SOOMRO.

National Assembly

Serving a five-year term, subject to premature dissolution, the current National Assembly has 342 seats: 272 directly elected in single-member constituencies, 60 seats reserved for women and distributed on a proportional basis, and 10 proportional seats designated for members of religious minorities (4 Christian; 4 Hindu; 1 Sikh, Buddhist, or Parsi; 1 Qadiani). The most recent balloting for the directly elected seats took place on October 10, 2002, after which the Election Commission ordered reballoting in two constituencies that was held on November 2 and 18. Seats reserved for women were allocated on October 31; religious minority representatives were announced on November 1.

Some 29 independent candidates were elected on October 10, but by early November 2002 most had declared party allegiances. The following totals represent the standing of the parties when the final seat was filled on November 18, 2002: Pakistan Muslim League-*Qaid-i-Azam,* 118 seats; the Pakistan People's Party Parliamentarians, 81; the *Muttahida Majlis-i-Amal* (MMA), 60; the Pakistan Muslim League-Nawaz, 19; the *Mutahida Qaumi* Movement, 17; the National Alliance, 16; the Pakistan Muslim League-Functional, 5; the Pakistan Muslim League-Junejo, 3; the Pakistan

People's Party-Sherpao, 2; the Baluchistan National Party-Mengal, *Jamhoori Watan* Party, *Muhajir Qaumi Movement* Pakistan, Pakistan *Awami Tehreek,* Pakistan Muslim League-Zia, Pakistan *Tehrik-e-Insaaf, Pakhtoonkhwa Milli Awami* Party, 1 each; independents, 14. Although all 12 representatives elected from the Federally Administered Tribal Areas are regarded as independents, the majority support the MMA.

Speaker: Chaudhry Amir HUSSAIN.

Communications

Formal censorship was imposed in late 1978 and reimposed in October 1979. Prior censorship of political news was lifted in January 1982 but was reimposed in July, remaining in effect until the termination of martial law in December 1985. The constitution guarantees press freedom, but in the late 1990s journalists asserted that the Nawaz Sharif government was engaged in a "systematic pattern of harassment and victimization." In July 2003 a court in the North-West Frontier Province, where Islamic law was imposed in 2002, sentenced an editor of the *Frontier Post* to life in prison for blasphemy.

Press

The following are among the more than 400 daily Pakistani newspapers: *Daily Jang* (Karachi, Lahore, Quetta, and Rawalpindi, 750,000), in Urdu, independent; *Nawa-i-Waqt* (Voice of the Time, Karachi, Lahore, Multan, and Islamabad, 560,000), in Urdu and English, conservative; *Dawn* (Karachi, Islamabad, and Lahore, 110,000 daily; 125,000 Sunday), in English and Gujarati; *Jasarat* (Karachi, 50,000), in Urdu, conservative; *The Nation* (Lahore, 50,000), in English; *Frontier Post* (Peshawar and Lahore), in English, leftist.

News Agencies

There are three principal domestic news agencies: the government-owned Associated Press of

Pakistan (APP) and the privately owned Pakistan Press International (PPI) and News Network International (NNI); a number of foreign agencies also maintain offices in leading cities.

Broadcasting and Computing

The government-owned Pakistan Broadcasting Corporation (PBC) offers regional, national, and international programming in a variety of languages. Additional service is provided by Azad Kashmir Radio. The public Pakistan Television Corporation (PTC) and the public-private Shalimar Television Network are based in Islamabad. There were approximately 28.6 million television receivers and 800,000 personal computers serving 1.5 million Internet users in 2003.

Intergovernmental Representation

Ambassador to the US
Jehangir KARAMAT

US Ambassador to Pakistan
Ryan C. CROCKER

Permanent Representative to the UN
Munir AKRAM

IGO Memberships (Non-UN)
ADB, CCC, CP, CWTH, ECO, IDB, Interpol, IOM, NAM, OIC, PCA, SAARC, WTO

Related Territories

The precise status of predominantly Muslim Jammu and Kashmir has remained unresolved since the 1949 cease-fire, which divided the territory into Indian- and Pakistani-administered sectors. While India has claimed the entire area as a state of the Indian Union, Pakistan has never regarded the portion under its control as an integral part of Pakistan. Rather, it has administered "Azad Kashmir" and the "Northern Areas" (see map) as de facto dependencies for whose defense and foreign affairs it is responsible.

Azad Kashmir

Formally styled Azad ("Free") Jammu and Kashmir, the smaller (4,200 sq. mi.) but more populous (2,973,000 in 1998C) of the Jammu and Kashmir regions administered by Pakistan is a narrow strip of territory lying along the northeastern border adjacent to Rawalpindi and Islamabad. It is divided into two divisions (Muzaffarabad and Mirpur) and seven districts (Bagh, Bhimber, Kotli, Mirpur, Muzaffarabad, Poonch, and Sudhnuti). Muzaffarabad City serves as the territory's capital. An Interim Constitution Act of 1974 provided for a Legislative Assembly, now comprising 48 members-40 directly elected plus 5 women and single representatives for technocrats, overseas Kashmiris, and *mashaikh* (Muslim spiritual leaders), all named by those directly elected. In addition, an Azad Kashmir Council consists of the president of Pakistan (chairman), the president of Azad Kashmir (vice chairman), the prime minister of Azad Kashmir, members designated by the Legislative Assembly of Azad Kashmir, and others.

In April 1985, 13 parties, most of them affiliated with pro-Pakistani groups in Indian Kashmir, began campaigning for the first assembly election in ten years; however, the military government in March had established a cutoff of 12 percent of the overall vote and 5 percent of the vote in each district for a party to remain legal, thus ensuring that the Islamabad-supported **All-Pakistan Jammu and Kashmir Conference** (also known simply as the *Muslim Conference*–MC), led by former president Sardar Abdul QAYYUM Khan, would remain politically dominant. Qayyum was reelected president in August 1990.

In April 1991 the prime minister, Mumtaz Hussain RATHORE of the Azad Kashmir affiliate of the Pakistan People's Party (PPP), annulled the results of a state election, claiming they had been rigged by the central government, only to be subsequently dismissed for the action by Qayyum. On July 5 Islamabad announced Rathore's arrest to "prevent him from committing further illegal and unconstitutional acts"; six days later Qayyum was named prime minister after resigning as president and being elected to an assembly seat reserved for Muslim scholars.

In late June 1996 the governing MC suffered an unprecedented drubbing by PPP candidates in the Azad Kashmir Legislative Assembly election, and on July 30 Sultan Mahmood CHAUDHRY, president of the Azad Kashmir PPP, was sworn in as prime minister, replacing the MC's Qayyum. Except for a brief period in 1990, the MC had been in power for 13 years. On August 12 President Sikander Hayat Khan, also of the MC, lost a no-confidence motion in the assembly, in which the PPP now controlled more than three-fourths of the 48 seats. On August 25 Mohammad IBRAHIM Khan was sworn in as his successor. The transition marked the fourth time the octogenarian Ibrahim had assumed the presidency.

The existing Azad Kashmir government remained in place following the October 1999 coup at Islamabad. Ibrahim ultimately retired in August 2001, and he died in July 2003. Sikander Hayat returned as prime minister in July 2001, defeating the incumbent by a vote of 30–17 in the wake of an MC victory at the polls on July 5. The *Jamiat-i-Islami* and the **Kashmir Freedom Movement,** led by Afsar SHAHID, also competed in the election, but the **Jammu and Kashmir Liberation Front** of Yasin MALIK (JKLF-Y) and Amanullah KHAN (JKLF-A) boycotted the vote after its candidates' nomination papers were rejected.

Following Islamabad's crackdown on militant Islamic groups in 2001, several reportedly moved their headquarters from Lahore to Azad Kashmir.

President: Sardar Muhammad ANWAR Khan.
Prime Minister: Sardar Sikander HAYAT Khan.

Northern Areas

The Northern Areas of Baltistan, Diamir, Ganche, Ghizar, and Gilgit encompass approximately 28,000 square miles, with a population (2001E) of 870,000. The Northern Areas have served as the principal conduit for supplying troops and matériel to the Line of Control. Pakistan's overland route to China, the Karakoram Highway, also traverses the region. Approximately half the population is Shi'ite, with the other half divided between Sunnis and Ismailis.

A Northern Areas Council, now of 29 members (24 elected seats plus 5 reserved for women, who are chosen by the elected members), originally served in an advisory capacity. On October 4, 1993, Pakistan's caretaker government announced that some provincial powers would be delegated to the region, with the minister for Kashmir and the Northern Areas serving as chief executive and chairman of the Northern Areas Legislative Council. In practice, however, authority has continued to reside in Islamabad, in the person of the minister, a deputy chief executive chosen from the Legislative Council, and an advisory panel drawn from the council.

In May 1999 Pakistan's Supreme Court ruled that residents of the Northern Areas were entitled to full constitutional rights, including an elected legislature and an independent judiciary, and gave the government six months to institute the changes. In early October the Sharif administration announced that party-based elections would be held on November 3 for a 33-member Northern Areas Legislative Council having the same powers as provincial assemblies. The announcement marked a significant departure in that the government had previously argued that no permanent institutions could be established until the fate of the entire Jammu and Kashmir was determined through a UN-sponsored plebiscite.

Although the October military coup at Islamabad intervened, the November 1999 balloting took place as scheduled, but only for the existing 24 elective Northern Areas Council seats. Of the leading parties, the Pakistan Muslim League (PML) won six seats (five more than it had previously held); the Pakistan People's Party (PPP), six; and the *Tehrik-e-Jafariya-e-Pakistan* (TJP), six. Voter turnout was very low, which analysts attributed in part to the council's severely limited role. After the reserved seats for women were finally filled nearly nine months later, a PML-TJP alliance controlled 19 of the 29 seats. As a result, the PML's Sahib

KHAN was elected Council speaker and the TJP's Fida Muhammad NASHAD won election as deputy chief executive.

At the Northern Area Legislative Council election of October 12, 2004, the PML and PPP Parliamentarians each won six seats and the PML-N won two, the balance being claimed by independents, eight of whom then aligned with the PML. Reforms anticipated under a new PML administration included creation of a new district, Astore, and devolution of greater financial and administrative authority from Islamabad.

Chief Executive of the Northern Areas: Makhdoom Syed Faisal Salah HAYAT.

QATAR

STATE OF QATAR

Dawlat Qatar

The Country

A flat, barren, peninsular projection into the Persian Gulf from the Saudi Arabian mainland, Qatar consists largely of sand and rock. The climate is quite warm with very little rainfall, and the lack of fresh water has led to a reliance on desalination techniques. The population is almost entirely Arab, but indigenous Qataris (mainly Sunni Muslims of the conservative Wahhabi sect) comprise substantially less than a majority, as thousands have flocked from abroad to cash in on Qatar's booming economy; the nonindigigenous groups include Pakistanis, Iranians, Indians, and Palestinians. The percentage of women in the work force grew substantially in the 1990s, and religious and governmental strictures upon women are less severe than in most other Gulf states. However, most women continue to wear veils in public, accept arranged marriages, and generally defer to the wishes of the male members of their families. Qatari culture as a whole continues to reflect the long history of "feudal tribal autocracy" and the "puritanical" (in the eyes of many Western observers) nature of Wahhabism, which is also practiced in Saudi Arabia, Qatar's influential neighbor.

The economy remains largely dependent upon revenue from oil, which has been produced for export since 1949 and under local production and marketing control since 1977. During the oil boom years of the 1970s, Qatar became one of the world's wealthiest nations, its annual GNP per capita peaking at more than $26,000 by the end of the decade. The sheikhdom was therefore able to develop a modern infrastructure, emphasizing schools, hospitals, roads, communication facilities, and water and electric plants. In contrast, per capita GNP dropped to below $10,000 in the mid-1980s as the result of declining oil prices; government investment also plummeted, leaving some projects unimplemented or incomplete. However, new discoveries such as oil recovery techniques and soaring oil prices have since revitalized the sector and propelled the economy–though it only produces a fraction of OPEC's oil output.

Qatar is also home to the world's third-largest reserves of liquid natural gas (LNG). As other industrialized countries see their domestic supplies dwindling, they are poised to invest in Qatar's developing natural gas sector. By the end of the decade, Qatar is expected to produce 250 tons a year, double the amount of LNG it produced

in 2003. The government has invested heavily in projects designed to exploit that resource.

Policymakers' attention has also been given to the development of new small- and medium-scale industries under joint public/private ownership. The government recently established a Qatari stock exchange partly to facilitate that process, and rewrote investment laws to encourage foreign investment. In early 2005, Qatar was named the most competitive Arab economy by the World Economic Forum. Investments in new projects totaling more than $60 billion (as of April 2005) are indicators of growing confidence in the economy. The GDP of $28.5 billion in 2004 reflects the tremendous reliance (61 percent) on oil and gas revenues, and marks rapid growth—35 percent—over the previous year's GDP.

Recognizing that oil and gas reserves are finite, the Qatari government continues to put great emphasis on diversifying into health and education, marked in part by plans for a $900 million specialty research and teaching hospital. It will be the centerpiece of Doha's "Education City," featuring professors from top colleges in the US and other countries. The government states it is spending two-thirds of its total budget in these areas and is also looking to develop a high-end tourist market. In addition to his efforts to advance and diversify the economy, Sheikh Hamad has introduced a modest degree of political liberalization (see Political background and Current issues, below).

Government and Politics

Political Background

Qatar was dominated by Bahrain until 1868 and by the Ottoman Turks from 1878 through World War I, until it entered into treaty relations with Great Britain in 1916. Under the treaty, Qatar stipulated that it would not conclude agreements with other foreign governments without British consent; in return, Britain agreed to provide for the defense of the sheikhdom. When the British government announced in 1968 that it intended to withdraw from the Persian Gulf by 1971, Qatar

Political Status: Traditional sheikhdom; proclaimed fully independent September 1, 1971. The country's first permanent constitution was approved by voters on April 29, 2003 (see Current Issues, below) and officially went into effect on June 9, 2005.

Area: 4,247 sq. mi. (11,000 sq. km.).

Population: 579,200 (2000C, provisional); 660,000 (2004E), including nonnationals, who constitute more than two-thirds of the resident population.

Major Urban Centers (1999E): DOHA (al-Dawhah, 509,000), Rayyan (214,000).

Official Language: Arabic.

Monetary Unit: Qatar Riyal (official rate July 1, 2005: 3.64 riyals =$1US).

Sovereign: (Emir): Sheikh Hamad ibn Khalifa Al THANI; assumed supreme power June 27, 1995, deposing his father Sheikh Khalifa ibn Hamad Al THANI; also served as Prime Minister July 11, 1995–October 28, 1996.

Heir to the Throne: Crown Prince Sheikh Tamin ibn Hamad Al THANI, fourth son of the emir, replacing his older brother, Sheikh Jassim ibn Hamad Al THANI; designated August 5, 2003.

Prime Minister: Sheikh 'Abdallah ibn Khalifa Al THANI; appointed by the emir on October 28, 1996.

attempted to associate itself with Bahrain and the Trucial Sheikhdoms in a Federation of Arab Emirates. Qatar declared independence when it became apparent that agreement on the structure of the proposed federation could not be obtained; its independence was realized in 1971.

The new state was governed initially by Sheikh Ahmad ibn 'Ali ibn 'Abdallah Al THANI, who proved to be an inattentive sovereign. In February 1972 his cousin the prime minister, Sheikh Khalifa ibn Hamad Al THANI, deposed Sheikh Ahmad in a bloodless coup approved by the royal family. Although modernist elements subsequently emerged, the sheikhdom remained a virtually absolute monarch with close relatives of the emir occupying senior government posts.

In May 1989 Sheikh Hamad ibn Khalifa Al THANI, the emir's heir apparent, was named head of the newly formed Supreme Council for Planning, which was commissioned to oversee Qatar's resource development projects. The government's economic efforts gained additional momentum on July 18 when the first cabinet reshuffling since 1978 resulted in the replacement of seven elderly ministers.

Like its Arab neighbors, Qatar faced international and domestic pressure for political reform following the 1990–1991 Gulf crisis, which focused Western attention on the dearth of democratic institutions in the region. The issue came to a head in early 1992 when 50 prominent Qataris expressed "concern and disappointment" over the ruling family's "abuse of power" and called for economic and educational reform, ultimately demanding the abolition of the Consultative Council in favor of a true legislative body. However, the government responded harshly to the criticism and briefly detained some of the petitioners, effectively muting the debate over democratization. On the other hand, reformists considered it a hopeful sign that the new cabinet, announced September 1, 1992, included men who were not members of the royal family in several key ministerial positions.

Though Qataris liked Sheikh Khalifa on a personal level, they reportedly believed he was allowing Qatar to slip behind other Gulf countries in economic and political progress. They expressed little dissent when Sheikh Hamad deposed his father on June 27, 1995, while the emir was on a private visit to Switzerland. Sheikh Hamad consolidated his authority and reorganized the cabinet on July 11, naming himself as prime minister and defense minister. (Sheikh Khalifa, who now resides in Europe, returned to Qatar on October 14, 2004, to attend his wife's funeral. It was his first visit to Qatar since he was deposed in the 1995 palace coup.)

In February 1996 the government announced that it had uncovered a coup plot, and those arrested reportedly included army and police officers. Although Sheikh Khalifa strongly denied any involvement in the alleged plot, he argued that it

indicated popular support for his reinstatement. The government concluded an out-of-court financial settlement with Sheikh Khalifa in October 1996, which permitted Sheikh Hamad to establish a sense of permanence to his reign and facilitated an at least partial reconciliation between father and son. In November 1997 some 110 people, including many military officers, were tried for alleged participation in the February 1996 coup attempt. While 85 of the defendants were acquitted in February 2000, about 30 were convicted and received sentences of either life in prison or death. An appeals court upheld their sentences in May 2001. Meanwhile, Sheikh Hamad had gained broader support from the populace and continued to promote his liberalized administration as a potential model for other countries in the region where long-standing regimes have resisted political and economic reform.

On October 22, 1996, Sheikh Hamad appointed his third son, Sheikh Jassim ibn Hamad Al THANI, as crown prince and his heir apparent. Six days later the emir appointed his younger brother, Sheikh 'Abdallah ibn Khalifa AL THANI, as prime minister to the government named on October 20, which included a number of younger ministers. The crown prince relinquished his position on August 5, 2003, to his younger brother, Sheikh Tamin ibn Hamad Al THANI. In September the emir conferred the title of deputy prime minister upon two of his ministers: Sheikh Hamad ibn Jasim ibn Jabir Al THANI and 'Abdallah ibn Hamad al-ATTIYAH. The new crown prince also was named commander-in-chief of the armed forces. Sheikh Hamad also appointed the first woman to the Qatari cabinet, Sheikha Ahmad AL MAHMUD, in 2003 (see Cabinet, below). In April 2005 the emir fired two ministers and his chief of staff without explanation.

The nation's first elections (for a Consultative Central Municipal Council) were held on March 8, 1999 (see Current issues, below). In July of that year, a committee newly appointed by the emir held its first meeting to draft a constitution that would ultimately provide for a popularly elected legislature. The new constitution was overwhelmingly approved by voters (96.6 percent) in a national referendum on April 29, 2003, and officially in-stituted June 9, 2005 (see Constitution, below).

Constitution and Government

Qatar employs traditional patterns of authority, onto which a limited number of modern govern-mental institutions have been grafted. The provi-sional constitution of 1970 provided for a Council of Ministers, headed by an appointed prime minis-ter, and an Advisory Council (Consultative Coun-cil) of 20 (subsequently 35) members. Three of the Advisory Council members were to be appointed and the rest elected, although national elections have yet to be held. The judicial system embraces five secular courts (two criminal as well as civil, la-bor, and appeal) and religious courts, which apply Muslim law (*shari'a*).

In November 1998 Sheikh Hamad announced that a constitutional committee would draft a new permanent basic law, one that should provide for a directly elected National Assembly to replace the Consultative Council. The emir announced that all Qataris over 18, including women, would be per-mitted to vote, while those over 25, also including women, would be allowed to run for the new leg-islative body. The new constitution, which went into effect June 9, 2005, after gaining approval in a national referendum in 2003, sanctions Islam as the state religion. However, officials say Muslim law only "inspires" the new charter and is not the only source for its content. Under the new charter, 30 of 45 members of the National Assembly will be elected, the remainder appointed by the emir.

Foreign Relations

Until 1971 Qatar's foreign relations were admin-istered by Britain. Since reaching independence it has pursued a policy of nonalignment in foreign af-fairs as a member of the United Nations (UN), the Arab League, and the Organization of Petroleum Exporting Countries (OPEC).

In 1981 Qatar joined with five other Gulf states (Bahrain, Kuwait, Oman, Saudi Arabia, and the United Arab Emirates) in establishing the Gulf Cooperation Council (GCC) and has since partici-pated in joint military maneuvers and the formation of economic cooperation agreements. However, territorial disputes between Qatar and its neighbors have sporadically threatened GCC unity. In April 1986 fighting nearly erupted between Qatari and Bahraini troops over a small, uninhabited island, Fasht al-Dibal, that Bahrain had reclaimed from an underlying coral reef. Although Qatar subse-quently acquiesced to temporary Bahraini control of the island, sovereignty remained in question. In mid-1991 Qatar asked the International Court of Justice (ICJ) to rule on Fasht al-Dibal as well as several other Bahraini-controlled islands of con-tested ownership (for details and map, see Bahrain: Foreign relations). The Court ruled in early 1995 that it had jurisdiction in the case, despite Bahrain's argument to the contrary and insistence that the dispute be resolved through negotiations under the GCC's aegis. GCC mediation produced an apparent truce in the spring of 1997 under which Qatar and Bahrain agreed to open embassies in each other's capitals and await the ICJ ruling. The ICJ finally issued its ruling in March 2001, awarding the dis-puted islands to Bahrain while reaffirming Qatar's sovereignty over the town of Zubara and its sur-rounding territory (which Bahrain had claimed as part of the case). The two countries have since ded-icated themselves to "building bridges," both figu-ratively and literally–a causeway connecting them is being planned).

Another simmering dispute erupted in violence in late September 1992 when two Qatari border guards were killed in a confrontation along the border with Saudi Arabia. Saudi leaders dismissed the incident as an inconsequential clash among Bedouin tribes, but Qatar reacted with surprising hostility, boycotting several GCC ministerial ses-sions over the issue and reportedly threatening to quit the organization altogether. After three-and-a-half years of negotiations, Qatar accepted Saudi Arabia's demands and a final agreement on land and sea border demarcation was announced in June 1990.

The sheikhdom denounced the August 1990 Iraqi invasion of Kuwait and responded further by offering its territory as a base for allied forces, expelling PLO representatives, and taking part in joint military exercises. At the GCC's December summit Qatar supported the "Doha Declaration," which called for a plan to prevent a repetition of Iraqi aggression, the departure of "friendly" forces upon the resolution of the crisis, and an Iranian role in security arrangements. In early 1991, Qatari forces (composed primarily of foreigners) participated in allied air and ground actions. Qatar remained closely aligned with the other GCC states on most security issues following the war and signed a defense agreement with the United States in June 1992 in the wake of similar US pacts with Bahrain and Kuwait.

At the same time, Qatar distanced itself from the GCC majority by calling for improved relations with Iran as a means of promoting regional stability. In May 1992 Doha signed a number of agreements with Teheran (covering such matters as air traffic, customs procedure, and the possibility of supplying the sheikhdom with fresh water via a trans-Gulf pipeline); Qatar's good relations with Iran continue to this day.

Qatar has also adopted a more lenient posture than most of its GCC partners regarding Iraq. In early 1995 it called for the lifting of UN sanctions against Iraq, for humanitarian reasons. However, in the wake of the brief crisis generated by the massing of Iraqi troops near the Kuwaiti border in October 1994, Doha agreed to let the US permanently store its armor in Qatar.

Qatar has also continued "to bring Israel into the Gulf" as a contribution to the Middle East peace process, despite contrary sentiments in the region. For example, Arab neighbors "forced" Qatar to close an Israeli trade office in 2000, but reports persist that the office is still staffed. In May 2005, Israel agreed to Qatar's unprecedented request for support of Doha's candidacy for a rotating seat in the UN Security Council. The request marked the first time an Arab state had sought Israel's help in such a matter, and signals increasingly positive relations between the two countries.

Qatar has recently become an important American ally in the Middle East. In mid-2000 the US

financed and built a massive staging area for its ground troops in eastern Qatar, which later became the US Central Command site in the 2003 invasion of Iraq.

On another front, Qatar faces troubled relations with Russia, dating back to 1999, when Qatar harbored an exiled Chechen rebel leader. Two members of the Russian secret service were sentenced to life in prison in Qatar in 2004 for assassinating the Chechen exile. Russia denied any involvement but later detained two Qatari sports officials passing through the country. Qatar then retaliated by expelling a Russian diplomat.

On the second anniversary of the US-Iraqi invasion in March 2005, a car bomb exploded in a Qatari theater frequented by Westerners. It was the first incident of its kind in Qatar; an Egyptian expatriate, allegedly linked to *al-Qaeda*, was later blamed in the attack.

Current Issues

In April 2003, elections were held for the Central Municipal Council, which the government established to introduce representative popular elections in Qatar. While voter turnout was low, it did yield the first appointment of a woman to the Council.

Sheikh Hamad recently ordered a new constitutional committee to provide a draft basic law that would include a directly elected national legislature, thereby improving his reputation as an iconoclast in a region where political reform has generally proceeded at a snail's pace. As mandated, the constitutional committee presented the new proposed constitution to the emir in July 2002 and it was put into effect June 9, 2005 (see Government and Politics, above). Equal rights for women are now codified, as are general rights of freedom of association, expression, and worship. The constitution endorses a free press and independent judiciary, but does not provide for the formation of political parties. National elections are scheduled to take place between June 2005 and June 2006.

Qatar is now internationally viewed as a country moving quickly ahead with major reforms, as well as an attractive and lucrative place for global

Cabinet

As of June 13, 2005

Prime Minister	Sheikh 'Abdallah ibn Khalifa Al Thani
First Deputy Prime Minister	Sheikh Hamad ibn Jasim ibn Jabir Al Thani
Second Deputy Prime Minister	'Abdallah ibn Hamad al-Attiyah
Deputy Commander-in-Chief of the Armed Forces	Sheikh Tamin ibn Hamad Al Thani

Ministers

Civil Service Affairs and Housing	Sheikh Falah ibn Jasim ibn Jabir Al Thani
Communications and Transport	Sheikh Ahmad ibn Nasir Al Thani
Defense	Sheikh Hamad ibn Khalifa Al Thani
Education and Culture and Higher Education	Sheikha Ahmad al-Mahmud [f]
Endowments and Islamic Affairs	Faisal ibn 'Abdallah al-Mahmud
Energy, Industry, Water, and Electricity	'Abdallah ibn Hamad al-Attiyah
Economy and Commerce	Sheikh Muhammad ibn Ahmad ibn Jasim Al Thani
Finance	Yusuf Hussein al-Kamal
Foreign Affairs	Sheikh Hamad ibn Jasim ibn Jabir Al Thani
Justice	Hassan ibn 'Abdallah al-Ghanim
Municipal Affairs and Agriculture	Sultan Hassan al-Dhabit al-Dousari
Public Health	Dr. Hajar ibn Ahmad al-Hajar

Ministers of State

Foreign Affairs	Ahmad 'Abdallah al-Mahmud
Interior Affairs	'Abdallah ibin Nasir ibin Khalifa Al Thani
Without Portfolio	Sheikh Muhammad ibn Khalid Al Thani

[f] = female

investment. It is intently focused on becoming a modern regional hub, especially in the area of energy technology. Many modernization projects are underway, as well as efforts to enhance education and medical research, the arts, and tourism.

Political Parties

There are no political parties in Qatar.

Legislature

The **Consultative Council** (*Majlis al-Shura*), created in 1972, was increased from 20 members to 30 in 1975 and to 35 in 1988. Although the provisional constitution of 1970 stipulated that members would serve three-year terms and that all but three are to be elected, the present Council consists exclusively of the emir's appointees, most of them named in 1972 and subsequently reappointed. Arrangements for a partially elected National Assembly are included in the new constitution that was officially adopted June 9, 2005. See Current issues, above, for details.

Speaker: Muhammad ibn Mubarak al-KHALIFI.

Communications

Press

Sheikh Hamad relaxed censorship of the press following his assumption of power in 1995, so

Qatari newspapers generally operate in a less restricted fashion than their counterparts in other Gulf states. The following are published at Doha: *Al Watan* (The Nation, 25,000, daily), in Arabic; *al-Rayah* (The Banner, 25,000), Arabic political daily; *al-'Arab* (The Arab, 25,000), Arabic daily; *al-Sharq* (The Orient, 45,000), Arabic daily; *Gulf Times* (15,000 daily), in English; *Daily News Bulletin*, in English and Arabic.

News Agency

The domestic facility is the Qatar News Agency (*Wikalat al-Anba' al-Qatariya*).

Broadcasting

Radio programming is provided by the government-operated Qatar Broadcasting Service (QBS) and television by Qatar Television Service (QTS). In addition, the government in 1997 launched a satellite television station (*al-Jazeera*), which has become well-known in the Gulf and elsewhere for offering "differing" and allegedly inaccurate, at times, views (particularly on the Iraqi conflict) in a region where most such transmissions seldom stray from official government positions.

In 2004, it was reported that the Bush administration was pressuring Qatar to restrain the al-Jazeera cable TV network.

Intergovernmental Representation

Ambassador to the US
Badir Umar al-DAFA

US Ambassador to Qatar
Charles Graves UNTERMEYER

Permanent Representative to the UN
Nasir 'Abd al-Aziz al-NASIR

IGO Memberships (Non-UN)
AFESD, AMF, BADEA, CCC, GCC, IDB, Interpol, LAS, NAM, OAPEC, OIC, OPEC, WTO

SAUDI ARABIA

KINGDOM OF SAUDI ARABIA

al-Mamlakah al-ʿArabiyah al-Suʿudiyah

The Country

A vast, largely desert country occupying the greater part of the Arabian Peninsula, the Kingdom of Saudi Arabia exhibits both traditional and contemporary lifestyles. Frontiers were poorly defined for many years, and no census was undertaken prior to 1974. Some 85 percent of the indigenous inhabitants, who have traditionally adhered to patriarchal forms of social organization, are Sunni Muslim of the conservative Wahhabi sect. The Shiʿite population (15 percent) is located primarily in the east. A strict interpretation of Islam has limited female participation in the paid labor force to about 5 percent. Mecca and Medina, the two most holy cities of Islam and the goals of an annual pilgrimage by Muslims from all over the world, lie within the western region known as the Hijaz, where the commercial and administrative center of Jiddah is also located.

Saudi Arabia is the leading exporter of oil and possesses the largest known petroleum reserves (estimated at upwards of 300 billion barrels), which have made it one of the world's richest nations. The government acquired a 60 percent interest in the Arabian-American Oil Company (Aramco) in 1974 and completed payment for the remaining 40 percent in 1980. Dramatic surges in oil revenue permitted heightened expenditure after 1973 that focused on the development of airports, seaports, and roads as well as the modernization of medical, educational, and telecommunications systems. In addition, large-scale irrigation projects and heavy price subsidies yielded agricultural self-sufficiency in a country that once produced only 10 percent of its food needs. Vast sums were also committed to armaments, particularly modern fighter planes, missiles, and air defense systems.

Because of a reversal in oil prices and substantial support to Iraq in its eight-year war with Iran, the Saudis experienced the onset of a major recession in the early 1980s. An economic revival was, however, sparked in the early 1990s by increased oil production as an offshoot of Iraq's invasion of Kuwait in 1991. Subsequently, concern over falling cash reserves and growing external debt prompted substantial budgetary retrenchment, including reductions in the traditionally high subsidies upon which Saudis had come to rely. The government also introduced programs designed to help move Saudis into private-sector jobs, which are held primarily by foreign workers.

Generally higher oil prices in 1996 and 1997 permitted a return to moderately expansive budgets, with emphasis being placed on infrastructure designed to promote private-sector development. However, financial difficulties returned in 1998 as the result of a sharp drop in oil prices and the effects of the Asian economic crisis. In July 2003, the government bolstered its "Saudization" effort to help reduce unemployment, most significantly by replacing 17,800 foreign white-collar workers with Saudis. Unemployment is at nearly 30 percent and is a problem particularly among those under the age of 20, a group that constitutes more than half the population.

As a result of the 2003 US-led invasion and war in Iraq, Saudi oil prices and production increased, bringing in an estimated extra billion dollars a week. The Organization of the Petroleum Exporting Countries (OPEC) allowed pumping capacity to increase to 9 million barrels per day (bpd) (up from 7 million bpd), with Saudi Arabia compensating for losses in Iraqi production during the war. In September 2003, Russia and Saudi Arabia agreed to a landmark deal paving the way toward a multibillion-dollar Saudi investment in the Russian oil industry, thus ensuring long-term capacity. In early 2005, Saudi oil capacity increased to 9.5 million bpd as the price per barrel soared to a historic high of nearly $60. OPEC continued to raise output limits even as prices climbed. As a result, Saudi Arabia's 2005 GDP was expected to surpass the 2004 figure by 17 percent. The kingdom has taken advantage of the surge in revenue to improve roads, schools, and hospitals. It also continued to move ahead with privatization efforts, and as of mid-2005 the government continued to pursue full membership in the WTO.

Government and Politics

Political Background

Founded in 1932, the Kingdom of Saudi Arabia was largely the creation of King 'Abd al-'Aziz Al SA'UD (Ibn Sa'ud), who devoted 30 years to reestablishing the power his ancestors had held in the 18th and 19th centuries. Oil concessions were granted in the 1930s to what later became Aramco, but large-scale production did not begin until the late 1940s.

Ibn Sa'ud was succeeded in 1953 by an ineffectual son, Sa'ud ibn 'Abd al-'Aziz Al SA'UD, who was persuaded by family influence in 1958 to delegate control to his younger brother, Crown Prince Faysal (Faisal) ibn 'Abd al-'Aziz Al SA'UD. Faysal began a modernization program, abolished slavery, curbed royal extravagance, adopted sound fiscal policies, and personally assumed the functions of prime minister prior to the formal deposition of King Sa'ud on November 2, 1964. Faysal was assassinated by one of his nephews, Prince Faysal ibn Musa'id ibn 'Abd al-Aziz Al SA'UD, while holding court at Riyadh on March 25, 1975, and was immediately succeeded by his brother, Crown Prince Khalid ibn 'Abd al-'Aziz Al SA'UD.

Despite a number of coup attempts, the most important occurring in mid-1969 following the discovery of a widespread conspiracy involving civilian and military elements, internal stability has tended to prevail under the monarchy. The regime was visibly shaken, however, in late 1979 when several hundred Muslim extremists seized the Grand Mosque at Mecca on November 20, during the annual pilgrimage to the city. Under the leadership of a *mahdi* (messiah), the men involved in the takeover called for an end to corruption and monarchical rule, and for a return to strict Islamic precepts. They held parts of the complex for two weeks; several hundred casualties resulted among the insurgents, hostages, and government forces. Citizens of several other predominantly Muslim countries, including Egypt and South Yemen, were among the 63 participants publicly beheaded on January 9, 1980, for their role in the seizure. Collaterally, the Shi'ite minority initiated antigovernment demonstrations in eastern areas of the kingdom following the event.

King Khalid died on June 13, 1982, and was immediately succeeded, as monarch and prime minister, by his half-brother and heir, Crown Prince Fahd ibn 'Abd al-'Aziz Al SA'UD. On the same day, Prince 'Abdallah ibn 'Abd al-'Aziz Al SA'UD was designated heir to the throne and first deputy prime minister. King Fahd's rule subsequently encountered potential instability, with declining oil revenues threatening social programs, and a radical Islamic movement, supported by Iran, attempting to undermine the regime diplomatically and militarily.

King Fahd's decision in August 1990 to request Western, as well as regional, assistance in defending Saudi Arabia's border against the possibility of an Iraqi invasion was widely supported within the kingdom. However, the presence of Western forces and media resulted in intense scrutiny of Saudi government and society, raising questions about the nation's inability to defend itself despite massive defense expenditures; generating calls for modernization of the political system, which the king answered by promising reforms; and eliciting signs of dissent, including a quickly suppressed, but highly publicized protest by Saudi women for greater personal liberties. The government also faced growing pressure from Islamists, even though the regime was already considered one of the most conservative in the Arab world because of its active enforcement of Islamic interdictions. In May 1991 Islamist leaders sent a highly publicized letter to King Fahd demanding 12 reforms, including extended implementation of *shari'a* and creation of an independent consultative council that would be responsible for domestic and foreign policy.

In a partial response to Islamists as well as to "liberals," King Fahd issued royal decrees on March 1, 1992, creating Saudi Arabia's first written rules of governance and providing for the formation of a national Consultative Council. At the same time, he rejected the notion that "the prevailing democratic system in the world" was suitable for Saudi Arabia and insisted that no elections would be in the offing.

In September 1992 Islamist leaders again formally challenged government policy, this time in a "memorandum" to religious leaders that was viewed as "more defiant and bolder" than the 1991 document. The action was followed in May 1993 with establishment of a Committee for the Defense of Legitimate Rights (CDLR; see Political Groups, below). However, the government quickly declared

---

Political Status: Unified kingdom established September 23, 1932; under absolute monarchical system; Basic Law of Government based on Islamic law promulgated by royal decree on March 1, 1992.

Area: 829,995 sq. mi. (2,149,690 sq. km.).

Population: 16,948,388 (1992C); 24,792,000 (2004E). The 1992 figure includes 4,624,459 foreign nationals.

Major Urban Centers (1992C): RIYADH (royal capital, 2,776,100), Jiddah (administrative capital, 2,046,300), Makhah (Mecca, 965,700), al-Madinah (Medina, 608,300), Dammam (482,300), al-Ta'if (416,100).

Official Language: Arabic.

Monetary Unit: Riyal (official rate July 1, 2005: 3.75 riyals = $1US).

Ruler and Prime Minister: King 'Abdallah ibn 'Abd al-'Aziz Al SA'UD; confirmed on August 1, 2005, by the royal court upon the death of King Fahd ibn 'Abd al-'Aziz Al SA'UD.

Heir Apparent: Crown Prince Sultan ibn 'Abd al-'Aziz Al SA'UD; appointed Crown Prince and Heir to the throne on August 1, 2005.

---

the organization illegal, with King Fahd warning the Islamists to cease distributing antigovernment material and using mosques as "political pulpits."

The most conspicuous result of a July 1993 cabinet reshuffle was the creation of a new Ministry of Islamic Guidance, which was seen as an attempt to buttress the kingdom's "religious establishment" against Islamist pressure within the Shi'ite and Sunni populations. The following month the king appointed the members of the national Consultative Council.

The Council consisted entirely of men, none drawn from the royal family, representing a broad social spectrum. Although the government heralded the inauguration of the Council in December 1993 as a major advance, some observers derided it as a "public relations exercise," noting that Council sessions would not be open to the public and that topics for debate required advance approval by the king.

Questions also surrounded the king's October 1994 appointment of the new Supreme Council on Islamic Affairs, which was dominated by members of the royal family and technocrats owing their livelihood to the government. The new body was viewed as a further effort by the monarchy to undercut the appeal of the Islamists, who had been pressing for further Islamization of government policy and a curtailment of Western ties since the 1990–1991 Gulf crisis and war.

On August 2, 1995, in the most sweeping ministerial shakeup in two decades, no less than 13 portfolios, including those of finance, industry, and petroleum, changed hands, with many political veterans being succeeded by younger, Western-educated technocrats. While members of the royal family were left in charge of several key ministries (notably defense, interior, and foreign affairs) the obvious intent was to improve efficiency by bringing in a new generation of officials.

King Fahd was hospitalized in early November 1995, suffering from what was widely reported but never officially confirmed to be a stroke. On January 1, 1996, he formally transferred responsibility for "affairs of state" to Crown Prince 'Abdallah. Although that decision had been expected by many observers to lead to a permanent succession, King Fahd formally reassumed full authority on February 22.

An explosion near a US Air Force building at Dhahran in June 1996 killed 19 US servicemen, prompting the subsequent transfer of American forces to more secure desert bases. Meanwhile, in what was seen as a possibly related development, the Saudi government launched a crackdown on Shi'ite dissidents in the east, where antimonarchical and anti-Western sentiment appeared to be the strongest.

A cabinet reshuffle was announced on June 6, 1999, with members of the ruling family retaining six key posts. A Supreme Economic Council was established in August to oversee proposed reform in non-oil sectors, and a Supreme Council for Petroleum and Mineral Affairs was created in January 2000. By 2003, major reforms had begun to take shape. In an unprecedented move in January

of that year, Crown Prince 'Abdallah met with reformists, some of whom the government had jailed in the 1990s for advocating reforms. Government representatives also met for the first time on Saudi soil with a UN human rights group, and in October, for the first time a woman was named dean at a major university. The most stunning news, however, came on October 13, 2003, when the government announced that it would hold nationwide elections for municipal councils in 2004 (postponed to 2005) to be followed by elections for city councilors and members of the Consultative Council. The announcement coincided with the country's first human rights conference, held in Riyadh, October 13–15.

Further, King Fahd granted greater legislative powers to the Consultative Council in November 2003, effectively shifting some influence from the cabinet to the legislative body. The reforms followed in the wake of increasing pressure from "liberals," but more significantly after an attack in May 2003 on a luxury residential compound that killed 35 and wounding hundreds (see Foreign relations, below). The government had been under increasing pressure from the United States since the September 11, 2001, attacks to undertake social and political reforms. With *al-Qaeda*-linked organizations targeting Westerners with increasing frequency and ferocity, the government launched a major crackdown on members of such groups and on Islamic religious leaders preaching violence (see Current issues, below).

King Fahd died on August 1, 2005, at the age of 82 after extended illness and a 23-year reign. He was immediately succeeded by Crown Prince 'Abdallah, his half-brother, who is believed to be 82 years old. Sultan ibn 'Abd al-'Aziz Al SA'UD, the long-time defense minister, replaced 'Abdallah as crown prince (while continuing to hold the defense portfolio and several other positions).

Constitution and Government

Saudi Arabia is a traditional monarchy with all power ultimately vested in the king, who is also the country's supreme religious leader. The kingdom held its first national elections (for men) in some 30 years on February 10, 2005. (Women continued to be disenfranchised.) There are no political parties in Saudi Arabia, and legislation is by royal decree, though in 2003 King Fahd granted a greater legislative role to the Consultative Council, shifting some influence from the cabinet. In recent years an attempt was made to modernize the machinery of government by creating ministries to manage affairs of state. However, the king serves additionally as prime minister, and many sensitive cabinet posts are held by members of the royal family, often for long periods of time. The judicial system, encompassing summary and general courts, a Court of Cassation, and a Supreme Council of Justice, is largely based on Islamic religious law (*shari'a*), but tribal and customary law are also applied. Sweeping judicial reforms were announced on April 3, 2005, including establishment of a supreme court and appeals courts in the 13 provinces.

For administrative purposes Saudi Arabia is currently divided into 13 provinces or regions, each headed by a governor appointed by the king. In April 1994 the provinces were subdivided into 103 governorates. The principal urban areas have half-elected, half-appointed municipal councils, while villages and tribes are governed by sheikhs in conjunction with legal advisers and other community leaders.

On March 1, 1992, King Fahd had authorized the creation of a 60-member national Consultative Council (*Majlis al-Shura*) headed by a chairman (Speaker) appointed by the king to four-year terms. The *Majlis* (inaugurated on December 29, 1993) was empowered to initiate laws, review domestic and foreign policies, and scrutinize budgets "in the tradition of Islamic consultation." Council membership was raised to 90 in 1997 and to 120 in 2001. In late 1993 the king also issued a decree authorizing the formation of Consultative Councils in each province, encompassing the provincial governor and at least ten appointed individuals. Another decree codified a "basic system of government" based on Islamic law. The 83-article document is widely described as the country's first written constitution, which went beyond previous unwritten

conventions by guaranteeing individual rights. It also formally delineated the rules of succession, institutionalizing the king's unilateral authority to designate (and dismiss) his heir, a son or grandson of King 'Abd al-'Aziz Al Sa'ud, who died in 1953.

In October 1994 King Fahd appointed a Supreme Council on Islamic Affairs to review educational, economic, and foreign policies to ensure that they are conducted in appropriate concert with Islamic precepts. Three other councils recently established are the Supreme Economic Council (1999), the Supreme Council for Petroleum and Mineral Affairs (2000), and the Royal Family Council (2000).

As expected during municipal elections held in February, March, and April 2005, Islamists dominated in Riyadh, Mecca, and Medina after three rounds of voting. In the eastern provinces, a number of Shi'ites were elected, as they comprise most of the populace there. Turnout was low in the major cities, and there were accusations that in violation of election laws some Islamists had formed coalitions to garner votes. The first Consultative Council elections are still under consideration by the ruling family, while the government in the meantime continues to arrest reformists calling for a constitutional monarchy.

Foreign Relations

Since the late 1950s Saudi Arabia has stood as the leading conservative power in the Arab world. The early 1960s were marked by hostility toward Egypt over North Yemen, with Riyadh supporting the royalists and Cairo backing the ultimately victorious republicans during the civil war that broke out in 1962. By 1969, however, Saudi Arabia had become a prime mover behind the pan-Islamic movement and subsequently sought to mediate such disputes as the Lebanese conflict in 1976 and the Iran-Iraq war. An influential member of OPEC, the kingdom was long a restraining influence on oil price increases. Since the US-led invasion of Iraq in 2003, Saudi Arabia, a swing producer, has been authorized by OPEC to continue to boost production to meet global demand.

The Saudis provided financial support for other Arab countries involved in the 1967 and 1973 Arab-Israeli conflicts and broke diplomatic relations with Cairo in April 1979 to oppose the Egyptian-Israeli peace treaty. Otherwise, the kingdom has been generally allied with the United States. The outbreak of war between Iraq and Iran in September 1980 prompted the Carter administration, which earlier in the year had rejected a Saudi request for assistance in upgrading its military capability, to announce the "temporary deployment" of four Airborne Warning and Control Systems (AWAC aircraft). An additional factor was the strong support given by Riyadh to Washington's plan, introduced following the Soviet intervention in Afghanistan in 1979, to increase the US military presence throughout the Gulf region. Subsequently, despite vehement Israeli objections, the Reagan administration secured Senate approval in October 1981 of a major package of arms sales to Saudi Arabia that included five of the surveillance aircraft, although delivery did not commence until mid-1986 because of controversy over US supervisory rights. Earlier, in an effort to win congressional support for their arms purchases, the Saudis had indicated a willingness to allow American use of bases in the kingdom in the event of Soviet military action in the Gulf. As the US Iran-*contra* scandal unfolded in late 1986 and 1987, it was alleged that the Saudis had agreed to aid anti-Communist resistance groups around the world as part of the AWAC purchase deal, ultimately making some $32 million available to the Nicaraguan rebels between July 1984 and March 1985 after US funding for the *contra* cause had been suspended by Congress. Subsequently, plans announced by the White House in May 1987 to sell more than a billion dollars' worth of planes and missiles to Saudi Arabia were delayed by congressional hearings into the Iran-contra affair. In July 1988 relations were further strained when Riyadh, citing congressional delays and other "embarrassments" caused by Washington's criticism of Chinese missile imports, purchased $25 billion of British armaments, thus undercutting reliance on the United States as its leading military supplier.

In December 1981 Saudi Arabia concluded a treaty with Iraq confirming an unratified 1975 agreement to partition the diamond-shaped Neutral Zone that had been established in 1922 to accord nomads unimpeded access to traditional pasture and watering areas. In March 1989 Iraqi and Saudi officials signed a mutual noninterference pact.

During 1987 and 1988 the Iran-Iraq war yielded continued political tension between revolutionary Teheran and pro-Western Riyadh. In July 1987 the seizure of Mecca's Grand Mosque by Muslim extremists resulted in the death of an estimated 400 Iranian pilgrims; subsequently, Iranian officials called for the immediate "uprooting" of the Saudi royal family, while King Fahd, supported by most of the Arab states, vowed to continue as "custodian" of Islam's holy shrines. In April 1988, citing the Mecca riot and increasing Iranian attacks on its shipping vessels, Saudi Arabia became the first member of the Gulf Cooperation Council (GCC) to sever diplomatic relations with Teheran. The Khomeini regime's subsequent decision to forbid its citizens to participate in the 1988 pilgrimage was seen as an attempt to discredit Saudi's administration of the holy cities. However, the subsequent rise of a more moderate leadership in Iran paved the way for a restoration of diplomatic relations in March 1991.

In late 1982 Foreign Minister Sa'ud al-Faisal became the first representative of the monarchy known to have traveled to the (then) Soviet Union in several decades. Remarks by the prince that Moscow could play a role in Mideast negotiations gave rise to speculation that relations between the two countries might improve. In 1985 there were indications that the kingdom was moving closer to establishing formal diplomatic relations (suspended since 1938), but not until Moscow's 1988 announcement that it would withdraw from Afghanistan (Riyadh long having been a highly vocal supporter of the rebel president-in-exile, Sibgahatullah Mojaddidi) did the 50-year-old impasse appear capable of resolution. Diplomatic relations were restored in 1990, and in return for the Soviet Union's support during the Gulf crisis, Saudi

Arabia provided some \$2 billion in previously pledged emergency economic aid to Moscow. In 1992 the kingdom moved quickly to establish ties with the Commonwealth of Independent States (CIS), offering economic aid and pursuing private-sector ties. Particular attention was given to the Central Asian republics, where the Saudis were expected to vie with Turkey and Iran for influence.

In the wake of Iraq's invasion of Kuwait on August 2, 1990, and amid reports that Iraqi troops were massing on the Saudi border, the Saudi government shed its traditional role as regional consensus builder, criticized the invasion as "vile aggression," and called for international assistance to prevent further Iraqi gains. The ensuing buildup of Western and regional forces along the Saudi border with Kuwait caused a rupture in relations with pro-Iraqi leaders of Yemen, Jordan, and the Palestine Liberation Organization (PLO). On September 19 Riyadh rescinded special privileges for Yemeni and PLO workers, prompting repatriation of more than half of the 1.5 million Yemeni citizens in the kingdom. Shortly thereafter oil deliveries to Jordan were suspended, Jordanian diplomats were expelled, and the Saudi ambassador to 'Amman recalled. Meanwhile, the Saudi government moved to reimburse and reward its allies, particularly Egypt and Syria. The kingdom's most dramatic Gulf crisis decision was, however, to acknowledge its effective alliance with the United States, which responded by promising to sell the Saudis \$20 billion in armaments. Saudi Arabia's pivotal role in the US-led, anti-Iraqi coalition included, during the 1991 war phase of the conflict, participation in 6,500 air sorties, the eviction of Iraqi forces from Khafji, and the liberation of Kuwait City.

The stationing of US forces in Saudi Arabia became a sensitive matter after the 1991 Gulf war. The Saudi government allowed US troops to remain in the kingdom—the birthplace of Islam and home to its most sacred places—angering many people, including Osama bin Laden and his followers and supporters. During the buildup to the 2003 US-led invasion of Iraq, King Fahd announced that the kingdom would not participate in a war against

Iraq, and he proposed that Iraqi leader Saddam Hussein go into exile to avert a war. US forces were, however, eventually allowed to deploy to Saudi Arabia prior to the war. After the May 12, 2003, suicide bombings of a compound in Riyadh that killed 35 and wounded hundreds, Riyadh became more attuned to the US "war on terror," with the government declaring its own such war in August 2003. As the number of attacks on Western and Arab targets grew, the government began a crackdown on Islamic extremists and Muslim clergy, aggressively rounding up terror suspects and fighting battles with extremists. This shift in policy shaped the country's relations with other nations to a greater extent than any other issue.

The kingdom strengthened its relationship with the United States in 2004 when the two countries joined in asking the United Nations to crack down on one of the kingdom's largest charities, which allegedly helps fund *al-Qaeda*. In June 2005, some 57 Islamic nations–Saudi Arabia among them–met in Yemen and agreed to fight terrorism, which is now as much a defining issue in the Middle East as any other political or social factor.

In early 1993 the Saudis had responded favorably to a US request for resumption of aid to the PLO as an inducement to the Palestinians to rejoin stalled peace talks with Israel. Riyadh also underscored its backing for the regional peace process the following September, when it convinced the GCC countries to end their long-standing boycott of companies doing business with Israel (see Arab League article for details). In 2003 Crown Prince 'Abdallah presented the Arab League an initiative for peace with Israel in return for its withdrawal from occupied territories. The following day, however, Israel launched a massive invasion to reoccupy the West Bank.

Saudi Arabia's relations with North Yemen and South Yemen and, since 1990, the unified Republic of Yemen have often been strained, particularly regarding border demarcations (see Yemen map, p. 1307). Tensions escalated when Riyadh supported the unsuccessful southern secessionists in the 1994 Yemeni civil war. In early 1995 the two countries announced the formation of a joint committee to negotiate a resolution to their border dispute and agreed not to harbor each other's opponents. In June 2000 San'a and Riyadh signed an accord that defined most of the border and reaffirmed commitments not to interfere in one another's internal affairs. Battles at the border continued, however, and at various times the kingdom set up barriers and security barricades along it. On March 17, 2005, the two countries signed a border agreement, influenced heavily by their increasing desire to halt the flow of weapons and drug smuggling and an increasing number of terrorist suspects. In April 2005, Yemen and Saudi Arabia held their first joint military exercise.

Current Issues

Crown Prince 'Abdallah became for many years the de facto ruler in Saudi Arabia in light of King Fahd's poor health, adopting a clearly "pro-Arab" stance designed to enhance regional ties. That inclination was apparent in the kingdom's decision in late 1998 not to permit US warplanes stationed in Saudi Arabia to participate in US-British bombing campaigns against Iraqi targets, with Riyadh criticizing the attacks as inappropriately "punitive." In addition, 'Abdallah was considered the primary architect of March 1999 OPEC production cutbacks that triggered a dramatic surge in oil prices to the benefit, among others, of the GCC states. Although Riyadh responded to pressure from Washington and other Western capitals in 2000 by supporting production increases to dampen prices, the Saudi government again underscored its growing outspokenness on the international stage by criticizing European governments for contributing to high energy prices through taxation.

In 2000 and 2001 Crown Prince 'Abdallah continued to emphasize the economic reform program he launched in 1998, courting foreign investment with tax reductions and easing of land ownership restrictions while the kingdom pursued membership in the World Trade Organization. The government also invited Western companies to help develop largely untapped natural gas resources and participate in related applications of the gas sector within Saudi Arabia. Domestic political reform proceeded at a slower pace, however, in view of the heavy influence of religious conservatives as well as other "vested interests" in government. Meanwhile, the international community intensified its criticism of alleged human rights violations and discrimination against women in Saudi Arabia. Responding to external pressure and perhaps to criticism by reformists, the kingdom on March 9, 2004, established the National Human Rights Association, composed of 41 members, including 10 women.

The *al-Qaeda* attacks on the United States in September 2001 put an unwelcome spotlight on Saudi Arabia because 15 of the 19 hijackers were Saudi citizens, while Osama bin Laden, the presumed mastermind behind the plot, is a member of one of the wealthiest Saudi families. (For complete information on bin Laden, who was stripped of his Saudi citizenship in 1995, and *al-Qaeda,* see the article on Afghanistan.) (See Foreign relations, above). After the US invasion of Iraq in 2003, Riyadh instituted a dedicated crackdown on militant insurgents and clerics. It also overcame criticism of previous years for its support of Islamic extremists by implementing laws to combat the financing of terrorism. These moves resulted from increasing attacks against Westerners and Arabs, such as the May 2003 bombings in Riyadh.

With Saudi Arabia's heightened focus on the fight against terrorism and extremists inside its own borders came renewed efforts by reformists to push the royal family toward more democratic elections and allowing women to vote. Social and political reforms are becoming apparent, with changes to the judicial system (see Constitution and government, above), and in April 2005 the grand mufti, Sheikh 'Abd al-'Aziz al-Asheikh, issued an edict opposing the practice of forcing women to marry against their will. Meanwhile, thousands of alleged terror suspects have been arrested or killed by security forces within the country and along the border, particularly the border with Yemen, while the high oil prices fill government coffers, increasing GDP and the government's efforts to employ more Saudis.

Crown Prince 'Abdallah ascended the throne on August 1, 2005, after the death of King Fahd.

Political Groups

There are no political parties, as such, in Saudi Arabia.

Committee for the Defense of Legitimate Rights (CDLR). The CDLR was formed in early May 1993 by several prominent Islamists who described the grouping as the kingdom's first human rights organization. However, the government charged that the CDLR was in reality a vehicle for extending fundamentalist criticism of the monarchy, which had been on the rise since the Gulf crisis. Consequently, the CDLR was ordered to disband only two weeks after its creation; in addition, CDLR leader Muhammad al-Mas'ari and some 1,000 followers were arrested, and a number of CDLR supporters were fired from their government positions. After his release the following November, al-Mas'ari moved to London, where the CDLR was reestablished in April 1994 as an exile organization. The Committee subsequently issued numerous communiqués criticizing the Saudi regime's human rights and economic policies. Although accused by Riyadh of attempting to promote "destabilization" so as to facilitate elimination of the monarchy in favor of a fundamentalist regime, CDLR leaders took no official antimonarchical stance and steadfastly avowed a policy of nonviolence. However, the CDLR remained critical of what it alleged to be widespread corruption within the ruling family and direct in its call for imposition of strict Islamic rule in the kingdom.

In 1996 a conflict was reported between CDLR leaders Muhammad al-Mas'ari and Sa'ad al-FAQIH, with the latter reportedly forming a breakaway grouping called the **Movement for Islamic Reform in Arabia** (MIRA). Subsequent activity has been minimal on the part of both groups, although in 2003 MIRA led an unprecedented demonstration in Riyadh, coinciding with the opening of the kingdom's first human rights conference.

MIRA maintains a strongly antigovernment Web site that in March 2005 posted an audiotape purporting to represent the new *al-Qaeda* leader in Saudi Arabia. According to MIRA, he was killed in April 2005.

Leader: Muhammad al-MAS'ARI.

Reform Movement. A loosely organized Shi'ite grouping, the Reform Movement (also referenced as the Islamic Revolutionary Organization in the Arabian Peninsula) originally operated out of London and Damascus, its activities including publication of the *Arabian Peninsula,* a newsletter critical of, among other things, the Saudi government's human rights record. In late 1993 the Movement's leaders agreed to discontinue its attacks on the government in return for the release of Shi'ite dissidents from prison and permission for Shi'ite expatriates to return to Saudi Arabia. However, some Movement members reportedly remained in "revolutionary" mode and opposed to the proposed reconciliation pact. A number of Shi'ites were arrested in the government crackdown that followed the 1996 bombing at Dhahran, prompting observers to suggest that the agreement with the Reform Movement had collapsed. However, little formal activity was subsequently reported on behalf of the Movement, though it continues to press for change and its members are routinely arrested, convicted, and jailed.

Leaders: Sheikh Hassan al-SAFAR.

In January 1992 a number of fundamentalist groups reportedly coalesced under the banner of the **Islamic Awakening** with the intention of leading a demonstration against government policies. However, the rally was cancelled after the group was warned that the government had ordered security forces to arrest protestors. In October 1996 the government reportedly arrested "scores" of alleged adherents of a Shi'ite dissident group known as **Saudi Hezbollah,** operating in eastern Saudi Arabia under the leadership of Sheikh Jafar al-MUBARAK. (For information on former Saudi citizen Osama bin Laden and *al-Qaeda,* see article on Afghanistan.)

Cabinet

As of August 1, 2005

Prime Minister	King 'Abdallah ibn 'Abd al-'Aziz Al Sa'ud
Deputy Prime Minister, Defense and Aviation Minister, and Inspector General	Prince Sultan ibn 'Abd al-'Aziz Al Sa'ud

Ministers

Agriculture	Fahd ibn 'Abd al-Rahman ibn Sulayman Balqhanaim
Civil Service	Muhammad ibn Ali al-Fayiz
Commerce and Industry	Hashim ibn 'Abdallah ibn Hashim al-Yamani
Communications and Information Technology	Muhammad ibn Jamil ibn Ahmad Mulla
Culture and Information	Iyad ibn Amin Madani
Economy and Planning	Khalid ibn Muhammad al-Qusaibi
Education	'Abdallah ibn Salih Ubayd
Finance	Ibrahim ibn 'Abd al-'Aziz al-Assaf
Foreign Affairs	Prince Sa'ud al-Faisal ibn 'Abd al-Aziz Al Sa'ud
Health	Hamad ibn 'Abdallah al-Mani
Higher Education	Khalid ibn Muhammad al-'Angari
Interior	Prince Nayif ibn 'Abd al-'Aziz Al Sa'ud
Islamic Affairs, Endowments, Call, and Guidance	Salih ibn 'Abd al-'Aziz al-Ashaikh
Justice	'Abdallah ibn Muhammad ibn Ibrahim al-Ashaikh
Labor	Ghazi ibn 'Abd al-Rahman al-Qusaibi
Municipal and Rural Affairs	Mit'ib ibn 'Abd al-Aziz Al Sa'ud
National Economy and Planning	Khalid ibn Muhammad al-Qusaibi
Petroleum and Mineral Resources	'Ali ibn Ibrahim al-Naimi
Social Affairs	'Abd al-Muhsin ibn 'Abd al-'Aziz al-Akkas
Pilgrimage	Fuad ibn 'Abd al-Salaam ibn Muhammad al-Farsi
Transport	Jubarah ibn Ayd al-Suraysiri
Water and Electricity	'Abdallah ibn 'Abd al-Rahman al-Husayn
Ministers of State	Musaid ibn Muhammad al-Ayban
	'Abd al-Aziz ibn 'Abdallah al-Khuwaytir
	Nizar Ubayd Madani
	Saud ibn Said al-Mat'hami
	Mutlaab ibn 'Abdallah al-Nafissa
	Prince 'Abd al-Aziz ibn Fahd ibn 'Abd al-'Aziz Al Sa'ud
	Abdallah ibn Ahmad ibn Yusuf Zaynal

Legislature

On March 1, 1992, King Fahd decreed that a **Consultative Council** (*Majlis al-Shura*) of 60 members (plus a speaker) would be appointed within six months. In accordance with the decree, a speaker was named the following September. Other members were not appointed until August 20, 1993, and the council convened in December 29. Upon the expiration of the first term of the council in July 1997, King Fahd increased its membership to 90 for the subsequent four-year term. Membership increased to 120 for the new council appointed on May 24, 2001. Elections to the Consultative

Council were still under consideration by the ruling family in 2005.

Chairman: Salih ibn HUMAYD.

Communications

Most newspapers and periodicals are published by privately (but not individually) owned national press institutions. The government also publishes a number of periodicals. Although censorship was formally abolished in 1961, criticism of the king and government policy is frowned upon, and a genuinely free flow of ideas from the outside world is discouraged. In May 2003, the editor of the liberal daily *al-Watan* was removed after criticizing Wahhabi Islam as extremism. However, earlier in 2003 the government allowed journalists to organize and form their own association.

Press

The following papers are Arabic dailies published at Jiddah, unless otherwise noted: *al-Asharq al-Awsat* (224,992); *Okaz* (107,614); Urdu News (30,000); *Riyadh Daily* (Riyadh, 50,000) in English; *al-Hayat*; *al-Massaiyah*; *al-Riyadh* (Riyadh, 150,000); *'Ukaz* (110,200); *al-Jazirah* (Riyadh, 94,000); *al-Bilad* (66,200); *Arab News* (110,000), in English; *al-Yaum* (Dammam, 50,000); *Saudi Gazette* (50,000), in English; *al-Madina* (46,370); *al-Nadwah* (Mecca, 35,000); *al-Watan* (Abha); *al-Sharq al-Awsat*.

News Agency

The Saudi Press Agency (*Wakalat al-Anba' al-Sa'udiyah*–SPA) is located at Riyadh.

Broadcasting and Computing

The Broadcasting Service of the Kingdom of Saudi Arabia (*Idha'at al-Mamlakat al-'Arabiyat al-Sa'udiyah*), a government facility, operates a number of radio stations broadcasting in both Arabic and English, while Aramco Radio broadcasts from Dhahran in English. Television is transmitted from a dozen locations, including Riyadh, Jiddah, and Medina. On January 11, 2004, a state-owned all-news satellite TV channel was launched, with the country's first female news presenter. Also, al-Jazeera began airing TV broadcasts from its base in Qatar. Founded at Riyadh in September 1991, the Middle East Broadcasting Center (MBC) transmits Western-style news and entertainment shows throughout the region. The MBC operates with the king's tacit approval. There were approximately 6.4 million television receivers and 3.5 million personal computers serving 1.5 million Internet users in 2003.

Intergovernmental Representation

Ambassador to the US
Prince Turki al-FAISAL

US Ambassador to Saudi Arabia
James OBERWETTER

Permanent Representative to the UN
Fawzi A. SHOBOKSHI

IGO Memberships (Non-UN)
AfDB, AFESD, AMF, BADEA, CCC, GCC, IDB, Interpol, LAS, NAM, OAPEC, OIC, OPEC, PCA

SYRIA

SYRIAN ARAB REPUBLIC

al-Jumhuriyah al-'Arabiyah al-Suriyah

Note: The UN commission investigating the car bombing that killed former Lebanese Prime Minister Rafiq Hariri in February in Beirut issued its report on October 19, 2005. It strongly implicated Syria in the assassination. President Bashar al-Assad pledged cooperation with the investigation while at the same time defying UN efforts to question key Syrian officials. A second report issued by the commission on December 12, 2005, provided fresh evidence of Syrian complicity in Hariri's death as well as widespread Syrian interference with the commission's work. The United Nations passed a resolution on December 16, 2005, authorizing the commission to continue its work for at least another six months. An earlier, October 26, UN report had concluded that although Syria had fully withdrawn its troops from Lebanon and free parliamentary elections had been held there, important issues remained on the two countries' agenda, including normalization of relations and clear demarcation of their mutual border.

The Country

The Syrian Arab Republic is flanked by Turkey on the north; the Mediterranean Sea, Lebanon, and Israel on the west; Jordan on the south; and Iraq on the east. Its terrain is distinguished by the Anti-Lebanon and Alawite mountains running parallel to the Mediterranean, the Jabal al-Druze Mountains in the south, and a semidesert plateau in the southeast, while the economically important Euphrates River Valley traverses the country from north to southeast. Ninety percent of the population is Arab; the most important minorities are Kurds, Armenians, and Turks. Islam is professed by 87 percent of the people, most of whom belong to the Sunni sect, which dominated the region for some 1,400 years prior to the assumption of power in 1970 by Hafiz al-Assad, an Alawite. (About 12 percent of the population is Alawite, a Shi'ite offshoot that also draws on some Christian traditions and is viewed as "non-Muslim" by many Sunnis. Alawites have dominated governmental affairs under the regimes of Hafiz al-Assad and, more recently, his son, Bashar al-Assad, which also have afforded greater latitude to the Christian community, about 10 percent of the population, than many other Arab governments.) Arabic is the official language, but French and English are spoken in government and business circles.

Syria is one of the few Arab countries with adequate arable land. One-third of the work force is engaged in agriculture (more than half of the

women as unpaid family workers on rural estates). However, a lack of proper irrigation facilities makes agricultural production dependent on variations in rainfall. An agrarian reform law, promulgated in 1958 and modified in 1963, limits the size of individual holdings. Wheat, barley, and cotton are the principal crops, while Syria is one of the world's leading producers of olive oil. Major industries have been nationalized, the most important of which are food processing, tobacco, and textiles. Industrial growth has been rapid since the 1950s, with petroleum, Syria's most valuable natural resource, providing an investment base. Increased agricultural production and oil transit revenues contributed to a sharp increase in the GNP, which expanded by an average annual rate of 10 percent in the early 1980s. Subsequently, the economy deteriorated because of the cost of maintaining troops in Lebanon, increased arms purchases, closure of the Iraqi pipeline at the outset of the Iran–Iraq war, a drop in oil prices, and a growing debt burden.

The economy rebounded in the early 1990s as the result of increased oil exports and aid payments from Gulf Arab states grateful for Syrian support against Iraq in the 1990–1991 Gulf crisis and war. Subsequent efforts to increase capital investment included liberal benefits for expatriate and regional investors, a new tax law, and an easing of foreign exchange restrictions. On the other hand, inefficient centralized planning remained a barrier to progress in the non-oil sectors. Consequently, in late 1994 the government announced that state-owned enterprises would be afforded greater autonomy and promised additional reforms concerning banking and exchange rate mechanisms. However, progress on those fronts was slow, with observers suggesting that the regime of President Hafiz al-Assad was reluctant to relinquish the extensive political control inherent in an extensive public sector. Pressure for liberalization has continued, particularly from the European Union (EU), which receives 65 percent of all Syrian exports.

In 1998 further liberalization efforts allowed foreign investors to own or rent land and permitted foreign banks to open branches. In 2003 six

Political Status: Republic proclaimed in 1941; became independent April 17, 1946; under military regime since March 8, 1963.
Area: 71,586 sq. mi. (185,408 sq. km.).
Population: 13,782,315 (1994C); 17,980,000 (2004E). Both figures include Palestinian refugees, numbering approximately 400,000.
Major Urban Centers (1994C): DAMASCUS (1,494,322), Aleppo (1,582,930), Homs (540,133), Latakia (311,784), Hama (264,348).
Official Language: Arabic.
Monetary Unit: Syrian Pound (principal rate July 1, 2005: 51.98 pounds = $1US; market rate September 1, 2002, 48.85 pounds = $1US).
President: Lt. Gen. Bashar al-ASSAD (*Baath* Party); sworn in for a seven-year term on July 17, 2000, following endorsement by the People's Assembly on June 27 and by a national referendum on July 10 of a successor to Lt. Gen. Hafiz al-ASSAD, who had died on June 10.
Vice Presidents: 'Abd al-Halim ibn Sa'id KHADDAM and Muhammad Zuhayr MASHARQA; appointed by President Hafiz al-ASSAD on March 11, 1984.
Prime Minister: Muhammad Naji al-UTRI; appointed by the president on September 10, 2003, following the resignation of Muhammad Mustafa MIRO.

foreign banks were granted licenses to operate, and the government announced the establishment of a stock exchange. Negotiations with the EU over the signing of an association agreement are ongoing and were complicated by the fallout from the assassination of Rafiq Hariri, the former Lebanese prime minister. Syria's recent record in economic growth has been mixed, with negative growth of 0.9 percent in 1999 followed by 3.2 percent growth in 2002 and 2.5 percent in 2003.

Government and Politics

Political Background

Seat of the brilliant Omayyad Empire in early Islamic times before being conquered by the

Mongols in 1400, Syria was absorbed by the Ottoman Turks in 1517 and became a French-mandated territory under the League of Nations in 1920. A republican government, formed under wartime conditions in 1941, secured the evacuation of French forces in April 1945 and declared the country fully independent on April 17, 1946. Political development was subsequently marked by an alternation of weak parliamentary governments and unstable military regimes. Syria merged with Egypt on February 1, 1958, to form the United Arab Republic but seceded on September 29, 1961, to reestablish itself as the independent Syrian Arab Republic.

On March 8, 1963, the *Baath* Arab Socialist Party assumed power through a military-backed coup, Gen. Amin al-HAFIZ becoming the dominant figure until February 1966 when a second coup led by Maj. Gen. Salah al-JADID resulted in the flight of Hafiz and the installation of Nur al-Din al-ATASSI as president. With Jadid's backing, the Atassi government survived the war with Israel and the loss of the Golan Heights in 1967, but governmental cohesion was weakened by crises within the *Baath* that were precipitated by conflicts between the civilian and doctrinaire Marxist "progressive" faction, led by Jadid and Atassi, and the more pragmatic and military "nationalist" faction under Lt. Gen. Hafiz al-ASSAD. In November 1970 the struggle culminated in a coup by nationalist elements, General Assad becoming president and subsequently being elected to the post of secretary general of the party. The new regime established a legislature (the first since 1966) and, following a national referendum in September 1971, joined with Egypt and Libya in a short-lived Federation of Arab Republics. The first national election in 11 years was held in 1973, with the National Progressive Front (NPF), consisting of the *Baath* and its allies, winning an overwhelming majority of seats in the People's Assembly. In 1977 the Front won 159 of 195 seats, with 36 awarded to independents, while all of the seats were distributed among Front members in 1981.

General Assad's assumption of the presidency marked the growing political and economic prominence of the Alawite Muslim sect of north-western Syria, which constitutes about 12 percent of the country's population. The Alawite background of Assad and some of his top associates triggered opposition among the country's predominantly urban Sunni majority, which had experienced economic adversity as a result of the regime's socialist policies. This opposition turned into a rebellion led by the Muslim Brotherhood (see Political Parties, below) after Syria's 1976 intervention on the Maronite side in the Lebanese civil war. The incidents perpetrated by the fundamentalists included the murder of 63 Alawite military cadets at Aleppo in June 1979, another 40 deaths at Latakia in August of the same year, a series of bombings that resulted in several hundred casualties at Damascus in 1981, and numerous clashes between the dissidents and the regime's special forces led by the president's brother, Col. Rif'at al-ASSAD. The struggle reached its climax in a three-week uprising at the northern city of Hama in February 1982, which was suppressed with great bloodshed (estimates of the number killed range as high as 10,000). By 1983 the seven-year insurgency had been decisively crushed, along with the Muslim Brotherhood's stated aim of establishing an Islamic state.

In late 1983 President Assad suffered a serious illness (widely rumored to have been a heart attack), and a committee that included 'Abd al-Halim KHADDAM and Muhammad Zuhayr MASHARQA was established within the *Baath* national command to coordinate government policy. In March 1984 Khaddam and Mashariqa were named vice presidents, as was Rif'at al-Assad, a move that was interpreted as an attempt to curb the latter's ambitions as successor to the president by assigning him more carefully circumscribed responsibilities than he had theretofore exercised as commander of the Damascus-based Defense Forces. In addition, Rif'at was temporarily exiled, along with two adversaries, as apparent punishment for employing confrontationist tactics in the power struggle during his brother's illness. He returned in November to reassume responsibility for military and national security affairs. However, soon after the president's reelection to a third term in February

1985, Rif'at al-Assad again went into exile and in April 1988 was reported to have relinquished all official responsibilities. Economic recovery in 1988 was attributed to the policies of Prime Minister Mahmud al-ZUBI, who had been appointed in November 1987 to replace 'Abd al-Ra'uf al-KASM.

President Assad was the sole presidential nominee in November 1991 and at a referendum on December 2 secured his fourth term with the reported support of 99.98 percent of the voters. In early 1992 Assad announced plans to adopt an economic liberalization program and hold a conference to discuss political reform and the formation of new national parties. However, the president rejected the possibility of a immediate transition to a democratic government, saying that a democracy would be appropriate only when the "income of the individual in Syria reaches that of the Western states." Collaterally, the regime announced that 600 political prisoners were being released.

The Zubi government resigned en masse on June 24, 1992, but the prime minister was requested by the president to form a new cabinet which, when announced on June 29, contained many former ministers in their old posts. Later in the year Rif'at al-Assad returned to Syria from exile, once again prompting speculation regarding a successor to the president, about whom rumors of ill health had recently resurfaced. The succession question became the focus of even greater attention in early 1994 following the death in an automobile accident of President Assad's oldest son, Maj. Basel al-ASSAD, who had been assigned a growing number of official responsibilities in recent years. President Assad's next oldest son, Bashar al-ASSAD, was subsequently viewed as having assumed a role similar to that of his late brother.

More than 7,000 candidates reportedly contested the Assembly balloting on August 24, 1994, some 158 new members being elected. However, the *Baath* and its NPF partners retained solid control, securing 167 seats to 83 for independent candidates.

In December 1996 President Assad reportedly exiled his younger brother, Jamil al-ASSAD, to France in the wake of allegations concerning Jamil's business dealings. The delicate nature of the Assad family relationships (and their significance regarding succession) was further illustrated in February 1998 when the president formally dismissed Rif'at al-Assad from his vice presidential post. Although no official reason was given for the decision, some observers suggested that Rif'at's moderate advocacy of political pluralism and opposition to Syrian involvement in Lebanon had upset his brother.

The NPF remained in control of 167 legislative seats (all that it contested) in balloting on November 30–December 1, 1998, while President Assad, as the only candidate, was reelected to a seven-year term in a national referendum on February 10, 1999.

Reportedly under heavy pressure from President Assad and Bashar al-Assad, who had launched a highly publicized anticorruption campaign, Prime Minister Zubi and his cabinet resigned on March 7, 2000. President Assad invited Muhammad Mustafa MIRO, the governor of the city of Aleppo with a reputation for honesty, to form a new government which, as sworn in on March 14, contained 22 newcomers among its 36 members. Shortly thereafter, Zubi reportedly committed suicide as security forces prepared to arrest him on corruption charges.

After nearly 30 years in power, President Assad died on June 10, 2000. Vice President Khaddam assumed the position of acting president, although it was immediately apparent that careful plans had been laid for the swift succession of Bashar al-Assad to the presidency. Khaddam promoted Bashar from colonel to lieutenant general and named him commander-in-chief of the armed forces, while also signing a constitutional amendment quickly approved by the Assembly reducing the minimum age of the president from 40 to 34 (Bashar's age). Shortly thereafter the *Baath* Regional Command confirmed Bashar as its presidential nominee, endorsement by a full *Baath* congress ensuing within days. The Assembly nominated Bashar for the presidency by acclaim on June 27, and a "yes or no" national referendum on the question on July 10 yielded a reported 97.3 percent yes vote.

Prime Minister Miro and his cabinet resigned on December 10, 2001; after which President Assad reappointed Miro to head a new government, which was formed on December 13. This move was widely attributed to the new president's pursuit of economic liberalization, as a number of independent and reform-minded new ministers were appointed. The retention of the prime minister and the defense and foreign ministers, however, implied the continued influence of the "old guard." As reform efforts seemed to founder and relations with the US worsened, on September 10, 2003, President Assad appointed Muhammad Naji al-Utri as the new prime minister and tasked him with picking up the pace of reform. Utri's government remained, however, effectively hamstrung on the reform front, as Syria's national security challenges multiplied with insurrection in Iraq, anti-Syrian ferment in Lebanon, and worsening relations with the US. The *Baath* Party Regional Congress in June 2005 appeared to accord the government more freedom of action in designing and implementing economic reform measures, but it also seemed to fall far short of expectations in terms of political liberalization. (See Current issues, below.)

Constitution and Government

According to the 1973 constitution, which succeeded provisional constitutions of 1964 and 1969, Syria is a "socialist popular democracy." Nominated by the legislature upon proposal by the Regional Command of the *Baath* Party, the president, who must be a Muslim, is elected by popular referendum for a seven-year term. The chief executive wields substantial power, appointing the prime minister and other cabinet members, military personnel, and civil servants; he also serves as military commander-in-chief. Legislative authority is vested in a People's Assembly, which is directly elected for a four-year term. The judicial system, based on a blend of French, Ottoman, and Islamic legal traditions, is headed by a Court of Cassation and includes courts of appeal, summary courts, courts of first instance, and specialized courts for military and religious issues. Constitutional amendments may be proposed by the president but must secure the approval of two-thirds of the Assembly.

For administrative purposes Syria is divided into 13 provinces and the city of Damascus, which is treated as a separate entity. Each of the provinces is headed by a centrally appointed governor who acts in conjunction with a partially elected Provincial Council.

Foreign Relations

Syrian foreign policy priorities are rooted in the fundamental objective of regime survival and center on four issues: Lebanon, the Arab–Israeli conflict, Syria's place in the Arab world, and relations with the United States.

Lebanon has been a problem and an opportunity for Syria since the emergence of the two independent states in the mid-1940s. France carved Lebanon out of Ottoman Syria, adding coastal cities, the Biqa Valley, the Akkar region of the north, and the Jabal Amal region of the south to Mount Lebanon to create a state containing a small Christian majority. Syrians have never accepted the legitimacy of this action, even if the existence of an independent Lebanon is grudgingly accepted. From the standpoint of successive Syrian governments dating back some 50 years, a real "red line" is the specter of Lebanon falling altogether out of Syria's orbit and becoming a national security threat to the Damascus regime.

This possibility became manifest in two ways during Lebanon's 1975–1990 civil war and reemerged in a new incarnation in 2005. In 1975 a rambunctious alliance of non-Christian Lebanese organizations and the Lebanon-based Palestinian resistance movement threatened to overthrow Lebanon's system of political "confessionalism" (involving set-asides for various religious groups) and plunge Syria into an unwanted war with an alarmed Israel. With tacit US and Israeli blessing, Syrian forces entered Lebanon in 1976, under the official auspices of the Arab League, to neutralize the Lebanese Muslim/Druse-Palestinian alliance to preserve the system (buttressing Christian primacy) and dampen the prospects of armed confrontation with Israel. Syria succeeded, but it then found itself faced with Christian militias resentful of its presence and influence and eager to make common cause with Israel against it, the Palestinians, and Lebanese Muslims/Druse.

This volatile situation boiled over in June 1982, when Israel invaded Lebanon, and Israeli and Syrian forces clashed. It appeared at first that Lebanon might be detached from Syria's orbit–with Israeli forces in control–but Damascus took action, supporting the rise of the anti-Israeli, anti-US *Hezbollah* and arming its erstwhile Lebanese Druse and Muslim foes. The resistance resulted in the withdrawal from Lebanon of American and French "peacekeeping" forces, the redeployment of Israeli forces to the south of Lebanon, and the abrogation of a Lebanese–Israeli security pact. In 1990 Syrian suzerainty over Lebanon (except for the Israeli-occupied south) was solidified when Syrian forces ousted and exiled Michel Aoun, the Christian general who headed a rival government in East Beirut. Syrian suzerainty spread to the entire country in May 2000, with the evacuation of the Israeli forces from southern Lebanon.

Syria aimed further to strengthen its position in Lebanon in the summer of 2004 by compelling the Lebanese parliament to adopt a constitutional amendment extending the term of President Emile Lahoud. By doing so, however, it fueled Lebanese resentment and drew international condemnation. The UN Security Council passed Resolution 1559, calling for (among other things) the withdrawal of Syrian military and intelligence personnel from Lebanon and the holding of free elections. Rafiq Hariri, the former prime minister, emerged as the focal point of opposition to Syria and was assassinated on February 14, 2005. International pressure and massive Lebanese protests against Syria ensued, as Damascus topped the list of suspects. Syrian military forces withdrew from Lebanon in April 2005, and Lebanese elections in June produced a majority in parliament supportive of ending Syrian suzerainty.

Through the upheaval of Lebanon stretching back three decades, one thing remained constant: Syria's determination to keep Lebanon devoid of threats to Syrian national security, that is, threats to regime survival. Short of a militarily powerful outsider–for example, Israel, Turkey, or the United States–threatening invasion of Syria, there is no greater foreign policy priority for Damascus and no greater foreign policy test for President Bashar al-Assad than keeping Lebanon within Syria's orbit.

Syria's hard-line policy toward Israel dates back to the first Arab-Israeli war in 1948. At the war's end, Syria alone among the Arab participants was in possession of land allotted to the Jewish state in the UN partition plan. Successive Syrian governments have employed anti-Zionist policies–including wars in 1967, 1973, and 1982–as an essential element of legitimacy within the country. Syrians have traditionally found the dispossession of the Palestinians, the occupation of the Golan Heights, and the willingness of other Arab states to make formal peace with Israel unacceptable and unjust. Yet Syrian policy has not been one of unremitting hostility toward Israel. Since 1974 Damascus has ensured that the cease-fire line on the Golan Heights has remained quiet, even as it supported attacks by others from Lebanese territory to remind Israel of unresolved grievances. More important, however, since the mid-1990s–after the Palestinians embarked on their own peace process with Israel–Syria indicated its desire for a "strategic decision" for peace with Israel provided that Israel agree to withdraw from the Golan Heights to the "line of June 4, 1967"–the line in the Jordan River valley separating Syrian and Israeli forces on the eve of war in 1967. Syria under President Hafiz al-Assad and Israel under Prime Minister Yitzhak Rabin had reportedly agreed to a full Israeli withdrawal in return for peace. Rabin, however, was assassinated before a deal could be formalized.

Just prior to Israel's withdrawal from Lebanon in May 2000 there was reason to believe that Syria and Israel–with US assistance–might agree on terms for peace, but Israeli Prime Minister Ehud Barak effectively scuttled peace talks being held in Shepherdstown, West Virginia, in January 2000 by leaking the substance of negotiations to the press. Later, he provided to President Bill Clinton "talking points" to deliver in Geneva to the dying President Hafiz al-Assad that clearly indicated Israel's refusal to withdraw to the line of June 4, 1967. Assad, having consistently expressed that the only deal would require a full Israeli withdrawal, dismissed Clinton's overture.

Although President Bashar al-Assad has publicly stated a willingness to resume negotiations, Israel and the US have expressed doubts about his seriousness and his ability to take such action given domestic political dynamics. In addition, since the death of Hafiz al-Assad, Israel has focused instead on its relations with Palestinians. Ongoing Syrian attempts to put pressure on Israel—by supporting Palestinian groups engaging in violence and *Hezbollah* attacks along the line separating Lebanon from the Golan Heights—remain a source of tension and potential armed conflict. In the end, Syria wishes to avoid a war with Israel that it cannot win and to recover all occupied territory as defined by its late president, in return for which it is prepared to enter into a formal treaty of peace with Israel.

Syria's search for a leadership role in the Arab world has likewise been an important tool for successive regimes seeking to capture the elusive quality of governing legitimacy in a "nation-state" artificially created by France. The *Baath* Party—which has ruled Syria since 1963 and which has been (along with the military) the vehicle for the rise of minority Alawites in Syrian politics—was founded on the notion of an Arab nation, which would transcend states with boundaries established by colonial masters. Achieving the image and reality of an Arab nationalist leadership role has traditionally been a Syrian foreign policy objective with important domestic political implications, albeit a goal modified (but not abandoned) considerably in recent years.

Syria's striving and pretensions in the Arab leadership sphere have taken on many manifestations over the years. A combined fear of an internal communist takeover and devotion to Arab nationalism

caused Syria's leaders to subordinate the country to Egypt in 1958 by joining in the United Arab Republic; three years later the republic would be split by Syria's secession. Syria's pre-1967 rhetorical recklessness toward Israel—punctuated occasionally by military clashes in the Jordan Valley—egged Egypt into making catastrophic provocations in the spring of 1967. In the wake of the June 1967 war, Syria steadfastly opposed the Egyptian–Israeli peace process and treaty and became a leader among the so-called rejectionist states of the Arab world. Its rivalry with the Hashemite Kingdom of Jordan culminated in a botched invasion in 1970 that encouraged Hafiz al-Assad to seize power in a coup. The desire by Damascus to dominate the Palestinian resistance movement led to a three-decade feud with Yasser Arafat that was played out in part during Syria's intervention in the Lebanese civil war and through its support for Palestinian groups opposed to Arafat.

By the late 1970s, Syria had begun to perceive that the Arab nationalist movement characterized by Nasserism and even Baathism was running its course and that its call for a collective Arab approach toward Israel would not be heeded. Indeed, Syria's decision to support Iran during the Iran–Iraq war placed it at odds with the entire Arab world. President Hafiz al-Assad's intense dislike of Iraqi leader Saddam Hussein, the rivalry between the Syrian and Iraqi branches of the *Baath* Party, and fear of an emerging regional hegemon in Baghdad combined to dictate a national interests–driven break with the Arab world. This schism was eventually mended by Iraq's 1990 invasion of Kuwait. Although Syrian–Iranian relations remain cordial, Iraq is no longer the factor that brings them together. Indeed, Iran takes a dim view of the role played by Syria in the growth of the Sunni Arab insurgency in Iraq after the overthrow of Hussein. A tactical reconciliation had emerged between Syria and Iraq in the years preceding the US-led invasion that conferred significant economic benefits on Syria.

Syria's decisions to participate in the coalition that ousted Iraq from Kuwait and join in the

Arab–Israeli peace process launched at the 1991 Madrid Conference helped reconcile Damascus with Cairo and strengthened an already cordial relationship with Saudi Arabia, whose financial assistance was essential. At the same time, the PLO's closeness to Iraq under Hussein and its decision to seek a separate peace with Israel only hardened the Assad–Arafat enmity and convinced Assad to pursue a peace process of his own.

In 1998 Turkey threatened to counter Syrian support of Kurdish nationalists with an invasion. Syria capitulated completely and eventually found common ground with Turkey over the issue of Kurdish separatism, a concern that overcame differences between the two countries over Euphrates River water and Syria's claim to the Turkish province of Hatay.

With US forces fighting an insurgency in Iraq and jihadists entering the country across the largely unfortified Syria–Iraq border, US–Syrian relations took on a new and dangerous salience in 2004–2005. Although the cold war had permitted Syria to oppose US Middle East policies under the umbrella of a close security relationship with the Soviet Union, the fall of communism changed matters drastically, contributing to President Hafiz al-Assad's decisions concerning the Gulf war and the US-sponsored peace process. Assad apparently calculated that only the US could help bring about a complete Israeli withdrawal from the Golan, a calculation that led to a fundamental shift in Syrian policy toward the US in the early 1990s.

Although Syria's alleged links to international terrorism (including ongoing support for rejectionist Palestinian groups and Lebanon's *Hezbollah*) made cordial relations with Washington impossible and landed the country on the State Department's list of countries supporting terrorism, Syrian–US relations during the Clinton administration rose to the level of "correctness" and featured sporadic US efforts to broker a Syrian–Israeli treaty of peace. Yet these efforts failed in 2000, and the advent of the George W. Bush administration, the *al-Qaeda* attacks of September 11, 2001, the US-led invasion of Iraq in March 2003, and the Lebanese crisis of 2004–2005 plunged US–Syrian relations to a new nadir.

Syria's immediate reaction to the September 11 attacks was to cooperate with US intelligence in neutralizing *al-Qaeda* operations and personnel. Its cooperation, however, was not enough to sustain a correct, working relationship. The Bush administration saw the threat posed by terrorism as broader than *al-Qaeda* and viewed Syria, with its support of radical Palestinian groups and *Hezbollah*, as a problem in this regard. Syria, in turn, saw the invasion of Iraq as a national security threat and reportedly permitted insurgents to cross into Iraq from Syria. The US applied economic sanctions and called its ambassador home for extended "consultations" in February 2005. Although a combination of US military difficulties in Iraq and ramped-up Syrian efforts to restrict the passage of insurgents into Iraq seemed to dampen speculation about an imminent US attempt at "regime change," Damascus and Washington seemed as far apart than ever from establishing a relationship of cordiality. Indeed, US-led international pressure to terminate Syrian suzerainty in Lebanon and disarm *Hezbollah* opened another line of confrontation between the two states in 2004–2005.

Current Issues

Syria's decision during the summer of 2004 to compel Lebanon's parliament to extend the term of the country's pro-Syrian president, Emile Lahoud, set in motion a turbulent chain of events leading to the February 2005 assassination of former Prime Minister Rafiq Hariri, who had opposed the Lahoud extension, and the withdrawal of Syrian military forces by the end of April 2005. Apparently by crudely overplaying its hand, Syria empowered its critics in Lebanon, worsened already bad relations with the United States, inspired France to associate itself with anti-Syrian US policies, and brought about UN Security Council Resolution 1559, which presented a significant challenge to Syria's national security interests in Lebanon and the region. The UN's investigation into Hariri's murder raised the possibility of the Assad regime being labeled a criminal enterprise.

Lebanon may have been the spark that ignited a Syrian–US crisis, but other issues would have kept the relationship in a deep trough regardless. As the insurgency in Iraq grew in scope and violence, the US focused attention on Syria as a major transit route for foreign jihadists and more generally on its perception of Syrian support for Iraqi insurgents. The possibility that US frustration with Damascus might boil over into violence was the topic of much speculation, although decreasing public support for the Iraq War in the US seemed to increasingly militate against such action.

The issues confronting the Assad regime are daunting, although it appears likely that it will survive its self-imposed challenges. Keeping Lebanon firmly in Syria's orbit, even by means short of suzerainty, is an obvious national security issue of extraordinary importance, requiring a carefully mixed blend of coercion and soft persuasion. Avoiding US military strikes goes directly to the transcendent issue of regime survival. At the same, despite external national security challenges, efforts must continue to modernize Syria and make its economy more than a relic of failed socialism with a thin veneer of "crony capitalism." In this regard, the *Baath* Party Regional Conference of June 2005 produced mixed results. On the one hand, there appeared to be some progress in terms of liberating government ministers from *Baath* Party interference and directives in the arena of economic liberalization. On the other hand, however, major steps toward political liberalization were not approved. Growing unemployment, dwindling domestic oil and gas exports, the continued dead hand of bureaucracy, and the drying up of external cash sources (from Iraq, Saudi Arabia, and possibly Lebanon) point in the direction of economic deterioration and increasing public frustration. While debates continue about the reformist intentions and credentials of President Bashar al-Assad, it seems clear that the regime faces a serious dilemma: how to bring Syria within political and economic shouting distance of the 21st century without yielding power entirely to Syrians sufficiently talented and motivated to make the required changes.

Political Parties

The *Baath* Party has enjoyed de facto dominance of the Syrian political system since 1963, its long tenure being partly attributable to its influence among the military. In 1972 President Hafiz al-Assad formed the NPF, a coalition of parties that has always been heavily dominated by the Syrian Baathists.

Following the death of Hafiz al-Assad in 2000, the other NPF components joined the *Baath* in endorsing his son, Bashar, as his presidential successor. Some observers suggested at that time that the future might hold a more significant role for the NPF, whose influence, never substantial, had become trifling during the elder Assad's later years. Meanwhile, reformists hoped that Bashar al-Assad's pledge to promote greater openness would translate into permission for new parties to form. Currently the *Baath*-dominated NPF (now comprising six parties) holds the vast majority of seats in the Syrian legislature.

National Progressive Front

Baath Party. Formally known as the *Baath* (Renaissance) Arab Socialist Party (*Hizb al-Baath al-'Arabi al-Ishtiraki*), the *Baath* is the Syrian branch of an international political movement that began in 1940. The contemporary party dates from a 1953 merger of the Arab Resurrectionist Party, founded in 1947 by Michel Aflak and Salah al-Din Bitar, and the Syrian Socialist Party, founded in 1950 by Akram al-Hawrani. The *Baath* philosophy stresses socialist ownership of the principal means of production, redistribution of agricultural land, secular political unity of the Arab world, and opposition to imperialism.

At the *Baath* Party's 2005 Congress younger members were elected to key committee positions, reflecting efforts by President Bashar al-Assad to give the party a more youthful look. Nevertheless, in terms of policy direction there was little substantive change from the party's core principles.

Leaders: Bashar al-ASSAD (President of the Republic, Secretary General of the Party, and Chairman of the NPF), 'Abdallah al-AHMAR (Assistant Secretary General), Suleiman al-QADDAH (Regional Assistant Secretary General).

Minor parties that make up the remainder of the NPF are the **Arab Socialist Union Party** (*Hizb al-Ittihad al-Ishtiraki al-'Arabi*), **Socialist Unionist Party** (*Hizb at-Tawhidiyah al-Ishtirakiyah*), **Arab Socialist Movement** *(al-Haraka al-Ishtiraki al-'Arabi)*, **Syrian Communist Party** *(al-Hizb al-Shuyu'I al-Suriyah),* and **Democratic Socialist Unionist Party**(*Hizb al-Dimuqrati al-Tawhidiyah al-Ishtiraki).*

Other Groups

Syrian Social Nationalist Party (SSNP). Formally banned in the 1970s, the SSNP supports creation of a "Greater Syria" (see SSNP under Political Parties and Groups in article on Lebanon for further details).

Opposition Groups

Reform Party of Syria. The Reform Party of Syria (RPF), led by Farid Ghadry, is a US-based opposition party formed in 2001. It is opposed to the Baathist (and what it calls "pan-Arabist") ideology of the Syrian government and advocates widespread political, economic, social, and judicial reforms based on Western, secular principles.

Muslim Brotherhood. The Brotherhood is a Sunni Islamist movement that long maintained an active underground campaign against the *Baath* and its leadership, being charged, inter alia, with the massacres at Aleppo and Latakia in 1979 as well as the killing of a number of Soviet technicians and military advisers in 1980. In February 1982 it instigated an open insurrection at Hama that government troops quelled after three weeks of intense fighting that resulted in the devastation of one-fourth of the city and deaths of thousands. The Brotherhood was subsequently viewed as a spent force in Syria, although it nominally participated in several domestic and expatriate opposition groupings. Brotherhood members were among political prisoners released in 2000, the new government of Bashar al-Assad lending the impression of being more accommodating toward the Islamists and anxious to downplay any ongoing Sunni-Shi'ite friction. At the same time "antipathy" remained within the government toward any formal activity on the part of the Brotherhood, whose leadership, including Ali Sadr al-Din al-BAYANUNI, remained in exile.

More recently, the Brotherhood has stopped insisting on the right to use violence, no longer calls for the introduction of *shari'a*, and claims to support a democratic system of government. At the same time, it has not accepted responsibility for violence in the 1970s and early 1980s and has not made it clear whether it will seek retribution for past human rights abuses.

Islamic Liberation Party (ILP). Hundreds of ILP members were reportedly detained by security forces in late 1999 and early 2000 in connection with a crackdown that coincided with fighting between Islamists militants and the Lebanese army in northern Lebanon. The ILP also had strongly criticized the resumption of peace talks between Syria and Israel. Many of the ILP detainees were reportedly released in November 2000 under an amnesty issued by the new president, Bashar al-Assad. In 2003 five ILP members were sentenced to prison terms ranging from eight to ten years.

Arab People's Democratic Party. Led by Sumer al-Assad, the son of Rif'at al-Assad, exiled brother of Hafiz al-Assad and a former vice president of Syria, this grouping positioned itself as a prodemocracy party following the death of Assad in 2000. Rif'at al-Assad, living in Spain, initially laid claim to a constitutional right of succession to his brother, although that assertion received little support within the *Baath* or the Syrian populace. In May 2005 Rif'at al-Assad announced that he would return to Syria and resume political activities.

Cabinet

As of October 2004

Prime Minister	Muhammad Naji al-Utri
Agriculture	Adel Safar
Communications and Technology	Muhammad Bashir al-Munajid
Construction and Building	Muhammad Nihad Mushantat
Culture	Mahmud al-Sayyed
Defense	Hasan Turkmani
Economy and Trade	Amer Husni Lutfi
Education	Ali Saad
Electricity	Munib Saim al-Dahr
Environment	Hilal al-Atrash
Expatriates	Buthaina Shaaban [f]
Finance	Muhammad al-Hussein
Foreign Affairs	Faruq al-Shara'
Health	Maher Hussami
Higher Education	Hani Murtada
Industry	Ghassan Tayyara
Information	Mahdi Dakhlallah
Interior	Ghazi Kanaan
Irrigation	Nader al-Buni
Religious Trusts	Muhammad Ziyad al-Ayubi
Justice	Muhammad al-Ghafri
Local Administration and Environment	Hilal al-Atrash
Oil and Mineral Resources	Ibrahim Haddad
Presidential Affairs	Ghassan al-Lahham
Social Affairs and Labor	Dialla al-Haj Aref [f]
Tourism	Sa'dalla Agha al-Kall'a
Transport	Makram Ubayd

Ministers of State

Chair of Contracts Committee	Hussam al-Aswad
Administrative Development	Yussef Sulayman al-Ahmad
Red Crescent Affairs; Chair of Maritime Legal committee	Bashar al-Shaar
People's Council Affairs	Muhammad Yahya Kharrat
Population Affairs	Ghiyath Jaraatli

[f] = female

Communist Party Politburo. Previously referenced as the Communist Workers Party, the Communist Party Politburo is an antigovernment splinter of the Syrian Communist Party. A number of members, including Secretary General Riad Turk, were arrested in the 1980s after campaigning for "free elections," the government charging them with belonging to an illegal organization. Turk was released in mid-1998, and many of the remaining detainees were amnestied in 2000. However, Turk was again detained in mid-2001 along with several other opposition figures. He was released in

November 2002 on "humanitarian grounds," reportedly due to his deteriorating health.

Leader: Riad TURK (Secretary General).

Other small parties include the **Communist Action Party,** the **Nasserite Popular Organization,** and the **Islamic Movement for Change,** which claimed responsibility for a December 31, 1996, attack in central Damascus as a protest against the US presence in Saudi Arabia.

Legislature

The **People's Assembly** (*Majlis al-Sha'ab*) is a directly elected, unicameral body presently consisting of 250 members serving four-year terms. In elections held in March 2003 the NPF (which comprises the Syrian *Baath* Party and six small parties) won 167 seats, and independents won 83 seats.

Speaker: 'Abd al-Qadir QADDURAH.

Communications

Press

The press is strictly controlled, with most publications being issued by government agencies or under government license by political, religious, labor, and professional organizations. The following are Arabic dailies published at Damascus, unless otherwise noted: *Tishrin* ("October," 75,000); *al-Thawra* ("Revolution," 40,000); *al-Baath* ("Renaissance," 40,000), organ of the *Baath Party; Syria Times* (15,000), in English; *al-Jamahir al-'Arabiyah* ("The Arab People," 10,000); *al-Shabab* ("Youth," Aleppo, 9,000); *Barq al-Shimal*

("The Syrian Telegraph," Aleppo, 6,500); *al-Fida* ("Redemption," Hama, 4,200). Other publications include the pro-Communist Party, *al-Nour;* the satirical newspaper, *al-Damari;* and the SNNP paper, *al-Cham.*

News Agencies

The Syrian Arab News Agency (*Wikilat al-Anba' al-Arabiyat al-Suriyah*–SANA) issues Syrian news summaries to foreign news agencies; several foreign bureaus also maintain offices at Damascus.

Broadcasting and Computing

Broadcasting is a government monopoly and operates under the supervision of the Syrian Arab Republic Broadcasting Service (*Idha'at al-Jumhuriyah al-'Arabiyah al-Suriyah*). There were approximately 1.1 million television receivers and 360,000 personal computers serving 250,000 Internet users in 2003.

Intergovernmental Representation

Ambassador to the US
Imad MOUSTAPHA

US Ambassador to Syria
Margaret SCOBEY

Permanent Representative to the UN
Faysal MEKDAD

IGO Memberships (Non-UN)
AFESD, AMF, CAEU, CCC, IDB, Interpol, LAS, NAM, OAPEC, OIC

TUNISIA

REPUBLIC OF TUNISIA

al-Jumhuriyah al-Tunisiyah

The Country

Situated midway along the North African littoral between Algeria and Libya, Tunisia looks north and eastward into the Mediterranean and southward toward the Sahara Desert. Along with Algeria and Morocco, it forms the Berber-influenced part of North Africa known as the "Maghreb" (West) to distinguish it from other Middle Eastern countries, which are sometimes referred to as the "Mashreq" (East). Tunisia's terrain, well wooded and fertile in the north, gradually flattens into a coastal plain adapted to stock-raising and olive culture and becomes semidesert in the south. The ethnically homogeneous population is almost exclusively of Arab-Berber stock, Arabic in speech (save for a small Berber-speaking minority), and Sunni Muslim in religion. Although most members of the former French community departed after Tunisia gained independence in 1956, French continues as a second language, and small French, Italian, Jewish, and Maltese minorities remain. Women, who constitute approximately 31 percent of the paid labor force, are the focus of relatively progressive national policies on equal rights, educational access for girls, and family planning. In addition, by presidential decree 20 women were elected to the national legislature in 1999 and 43 in 2004. Moreover, the current government includes several female ministers and secretaries of state.

About one quarter of the working population is engaged in agriculture, which is responsible for about 13 percent of GNP; the main products are wheat, barley, olive oil, wine, and fruits. Petroleum has been a leading export, although there is also some mining of phosphates, iron ore, lead, and zinc. Industry has expanded to more than 30 percent of GDP, with steel, textiles, and chemicals firmly established. Most development is concentrated in coastal areas, where tourism is the largest source of income; however, poverty is widespread in the subsistence farming and mining towns of the south. Rising oil exports underpinned rapid economic growth in the 1970s, but declining prices and reserves precipitated a tailspin in the early 1980s. Consequently, high unemployment, a large external debt, and growing budget and trade deficits led

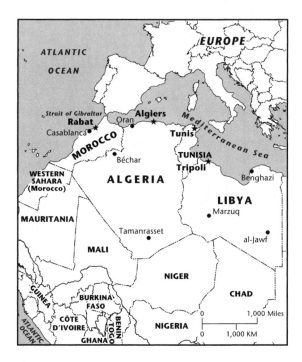

the government, with encouragement by the International Monetary Fund (IMF) and World Bank, to abandon much of its former socialist orientation in favor of economic liberalization in the second half of the decade. Led by growth in the agriculture and food processing sectors, the economy rebounded strongly in the 1990s as the government endorsed further privatization and measures designed to attract foreign investment. As a result, the IMF has touted Tunisia as an example of how effective adjustment programs can be in developing nations if pursued faithfully. At the same time economic advances have not been accompanied by significant democratization measures, and government at all levels remains totally dominated by the ruling party.

GDP grew at an annual average of 5.7 percent from 1996–2000, with inflation running at 3 percent in 2000. The most worrisome economic indicator involved unemployment, estimated at 15 percent (higher among young workers). Although the IMF in early 2001 continued to praise the government for "prudent" economic policies, the fund called for intensification of the privatization program (the government still controls 40 percent of economic production). Real GDP growth was 5 percent for 2001, with inflation stabilized at around 2.5 percent for the year. GDP continued to grow at an average rate of more than 5 percent a year in 2003–2004, although no progress was achieved in reducing unemployment.

Government and Politics

Political Background

Seat of the Carthaginian empire destroyed by Rome in 146 BC, Tunisia was successively conquered by Romans, Arabs, and Turks before being occupied by France in 1881 and becoming a French protectorate under a line of native rulers (beys) in 1883. Pressure for political reforms began after World War I and in 1934 resulted in establishment of the nationalist Neo-Destour (New Constitution) Party, which spearheaded the drive for independence under the leadership of Habib

Political Status: Independent state since 1956; republic proclaimed July 25, 1957; under one-party dominant, presidential regime.
Area: 63,170 sq. mi. (163,610 sq. km.).
Population: 8,785,364 (1994C); 9,998,000 (2004E).
Major Urban Centers (1994C): TUNIS (674,100), Sfax (Safaqis, 230,900), Ariana (152,700), Ettadhamen (149,200).
Official Language: Arabic; French is widely spoken as a second language.
Monetary Unit: Dinar (market rate July 1, 2005: 1.32 dinars = $1US).
President: Gen. Zine El-Abidine BEN ALI (Democratic Constitutional Assembly); appointed Prime Minister on October 2, 1987; acceded to the presidency upon the deposition of Habib BOURGUIBA on November 7; returned to office, unopposed, at elections of April 2, 1989, and March 20, 1994; reelected in multicandidate balloting on October 24, 1999, and on October 24, 2004.
Prime Minister: Mohamed GHANNOUCHI (Democratic Constitutional Assembly); appointed by the President on November 17, 1999, to succeed Hamed KAROUI (Democratic Constitutional Assembly), who had resigned the same day.

BOURGUIBA. Nationalist aspirations were further stimulated by World War II, and an initial breakdown in independence negotiations led to the outbreak of guerrilla warfare against the French in 1952. Internal autonomy was conceded by France on June 3, 1955, and on March 20, 1956, the protectorate was terminated, with the country gaining full independence.

A national constituent assembly controlled by the Neo-Destour Party voted on July 25, 1957, to abolish the monarchy and establish a republic with Bourguiba as president. A new constitution was adopted on June 1, 1959, while Bourguiba's leadership and that of the party were overwhelmingly confirmed in presidential and legislative elections in 1959 and 1964.

Bourguiba was reelected in 1969, but his failing health precipitated a struggle for succession to the presidency. One-time front-runner Bahi LADGHAM, prime minister and secretary general of the party, was apparently too successful: the attention he received as chairman of the Arab Superior Commission on Jordan and as effective executive during the president's absences led to a falling-out with an eventually rejuvenated Bourguiba; he was dismissed in 1970 and replaced by Hedi NOUIRA. President Bourguiba encountered an additional challenge from Ahmed MESTIRI, interior minister and leader of the liberal wing of the party. The liberals succeeded in forcing democratization of the party structure during the Eighth Party Congress in October 1971, but Bourguiba subsequently reasserted his control over the party apparatus. Mestiri was expelled from the party in January 1972 and from his seat in the National Assembly in May 1973, while Bourguiba was named president for life on November 2, 1974.

In February 1980 Prime Minister Nouira suffered a stroke, and on April 24 Mohamed MZALI, the acting prime minister, was asked to form a new government. Mzali was reappointed following a general election on November 1, 1981, in which three additional parties were allowed to participate, although none secured legislative representation. Bourguiba dismissed Mzali on July 8, 1986, replacing him with Rachid SFAR, theretofore finance minister.

Gen. Zine El-Abidine BEN ALI was named to succeed Sfar on October 2, 1987, reportedly because of presidential displeasure at recent personnel decisions. Five weeks later, after a panel of doctors had declared the aged president medically unfit, Bourguiba was forced to step down in favor of Ben Ali, who designated Hedi BACCOUCHE as his prime ministerial successor.

Although widely termed a "bloodless coup," the ouster of Bourguiba and succession of Ben Ali were in accord with relevant provisions of the Tunisian constitution. Moreover, the takeover was generally welcomed by Tunisians, who had become increasingly disturbed by Bourguiba's erratic behavior and mounting government repression of the press, trade unions, legal opposition parties, and other sources of dissent, including the growing Islamic fundamentalist movement. (Following his deposition, Bourguiba retired from public view. He died in April 2000.)

Upon assuming office the Ben Ali government announced its commitment to domestic pluralism and launched a series of wide-ranging political and economic liberalization measures, which included the legalization of some political parties, the loosening of media restrictions, and the pardoning of more than 8,000 detainees, many of them fundamentalists. Additionally, in late 1988, the new regime negotiated a "national pact" regarding the country's political, economic, and social future with a number of political and labor groups. However, the Islamic Tendency Movement (*Mouvement de la Tendance Islamique*–MTI) refused to sign the accord, foreshadowing a steady deterioration in relations between the fundamentalists and the government.

Presidential and legislative elections, originally scheduled for 1991, were moved up to April 2, 1989, Ben Ali declaring they would serve as an indication of the public's satisfaction with the recent changes. No one challenged the popular Ben Ali in the presidential poll, but the legal opposition parties and fundamentalist independent candidates contested the House of Representatives balloting, albeit without success.

On September 27, 1989, Ben Ali dismissed Baccouche and named former Justice Minister Hamed KAROUI as prime minister. The change was reportedly precipitated by disagreement over economic policy, Baccouche having voiced concern over the "social effects" of the government's austerity program. Shortly thereafter, the government announced the formation of a "higher council" to oversee implementation of the national pact, although several opposition parties and MTI followers, now operating as the Renaissance Party (*Hizb al-Nahda*—generally referenced as *Nahda*) boycotted the council's meetings. Charging that the democratic process was in reality being "blocked" by the government, the opposition also refused to contest municipal elections in June 1990 or national by-elections in October 1991. Apparently in response to criticism that the government's enthusiasm for democratization had waned as its antifundamentalist fervor had surged, electoral law changes were adopted in late 1993 to assure opposition parties of some legislative representation in the upcoming general election (see Legislature, below). Nevertheless, the RCD, officially credited with nearly 98 percent of the vote, won all 144 seats for which it was eligible in the balloting for a 163-member House on March 20, 1994. On the same date, Ben Ali was reelected without challenge, two potential independent candidates being stricken from the ballot by their failure to receive the required endorsement of at least 30 national legislators or municipal council presidents.

The RCD won control of all 257 municipal councils in local elections on May 21, 1995. While opposition candidates (standing in 47 municipalities) won only 6 of 4,090 seats, it was the first time since independence that the opposition had gained any such representation at all.

Ben Ali was reelected to a third full presidential term (then the constitutional limit) in balloting on October 24, 1999, securing more than 99 percent of the vote against two candidates presented by small opposition parties. Meanwhile, the RCD again secured all the seats for which it was eligible (148) in the concurrent legislative poll. Two days after being sworn in for his new term, President Ben Ali appointed Mohamed GHANNOUCHI, theretofore the minister for international cooperation and foreign investment, as the new prime minister.

Constitutional revision in 2002 removed the limit on the number of presidential terms, thereby permitting Ben Ali on October 24, 2004, to seek a fourth term, which he won with 95 percent of the vote against three other minor candidates. On the same date the RCD won all 152 seats contested on a district basis for an expanded assembly.

Constitution and Government

The constitution of June 1, 1959, endowed the Tunisian Republic with a presidential system backed by the dominant position of the (then) Neo-Destour Party. The president was given exceptionally broad powers, including the right to designate the prime minister and to rule by decree during legislative adjournments. In addition, the incumbent was granted life tenure under a 1975 amendment to the basic law. In the wake of President Bourguiba's ouster in 1987, the life presidency was abolished, the chief executive being limited to no more than three five-year terms. (See Current issues, below, for details of constitutional revision in 2002 affecting the presidency.) The succession procedure was also altered, the president of the House of Representatives being designated to serve as head of state for 45–60 days, pending a new election, at which he could not present himself as a candidate. Other changes included reduction of the role of prime minister from leader of the government to "coordinator" of ministerial activities.

The unicameral House of Representatives (styled the National Assembly until 1981 and also referenced as the Chamber of Deputies) is elected by universal suffrage for a five-year term. Under Bourguiba it had limited authority and in practice was wholly dominated by the ruling party, whose highly developed, all-pervasive organization served to buttress presidential policies both nationally and locally. Constitutional changes approved in July 1988 contained measures designed to expand the house's control and influence, although their impact has been minimal to date. Consultative bodies at the national level include a Social and Economic Council and a Higher Islamic Council. The judicial system is headed by a Court of Cassation and includes three courts of appeal, 13 courts of first instance, and 51 cantonal courts. Judges are appointed by the president. A new constitution that was approved in a referendum on May 26, 2002, and signed into law by the president on June 2, 2002, introduced a second legislative body, an upper house (House of Advisors, also see below, under Legislature), removed presidential term limits, and raised the age limit for a presidential candidate to 75 (from 70), among other things.

Tunisia is administratively divided into 23 provinces, each headed by a governor appointed by the president. The governors are assisted by appointed government councils and 257 elected municipal councils.

Foreign Relations

Tunisia assumed a nonaligned posture at independence, establishing relations with both Eastern and Western countries, although placing particular emphasis on its relations with the West and with Arab governments. It became a member of the United Nations in 1956 and is active in all the UN-related agencies. It joined the Arab League in 1958 but boycotted its meetings from 1958 to 1961 and again in 1966 as a result of disagreements with the more "revolutionary" Arab states. As a signal of its support for peace negotiations (particularly the 1993 accord between Israel and the Palestine Liberation Organization), Tunisia exchanged low-level economic representatives with Israel in October 1994 in what was considered a possible precursor to eventual establishment of full diplomatic relations. However, Tunisia recalled those representatives from Israel in 1997 as part of the broad Arab protest over a perceived intransigence on the part of the Netanyahu administration in Israel.

Beginning in 1979 a series of agreements were signed with Algeria, culminating in a March 1983 "Maghreb Fraternity and Co-Operation Treaty," to which Mauritania acceded the following December. Relations with Libya, though reestablished in 1982 after a 1980 rupture over seizure of a southern town by alleged Libyan-trained insurgents, continued to be difficult. President Bourguiba's visit to Washington in June 1985 led to a mass expulsion of Tunisian workers from Libya as well as reported Libyan incursions into Tunisia and efforts to destabilize its government. The Libyan threat brought pledges of military support from Algeria, Egypt, France, and the United States, with Tunis suspending relations with Tripoli in September 1986. Relations were resumed a year later, following a pledge by Libya to reimburse the expelled workers. Further economic and social agreements, including provisions for the free movement of people and goods between the two countries, were announced in 1988 as Tunisia stepped up its call for regional cooperation and unity, the latter bearing fruit with the formation of the Arab Maghreb Union in February 1989 (see article under Intergovernmental Organizations). Earlier, in January 1988, relations had also been reestablished with Egypt, after an eight-year lapse.

The Iraqi invasion of Kuwait in August 1990 appeared to precipitate a change in Tunisia's theretofore unwavering pro-Western orientation. Although critical of the Iraqi occupation, Tunis strongly condemned the subsequent deployment of US troops in Saudi Arabia and the allied bombing of Iraq in early 1991. However, security forces clamped down on large-scale pro-Iraqi demonstrations which broke out during the Gulf war, apparently out of concern that the situation might be exploited by Islamic fundamentalists.

President Ben Ali welcomed the antifundamentalist stance adopted by the Algerian military in early 1992, and Tunis was subsequently in the forefront of efforts among North African capitals to coordinate an "antiterrorist" campaign against Muslim militants. Earlier, in October 1991, Tunisia had recalled its ambassador from Sudan, charging Khartoum with fomenting fundamentalist unrest and providing sanctuary and financial support for groups intent on overthrowing the Tunisian government.

Tunisia is prominent among those nations hoping to develop economic cooperation, and possibly a free trade area, in the Mediterranean region. "Partnership" discussions have been emphasized with the European Union (EU), the focus of an estimated 75 percent of Tunisia's trade, and Tunis signed an association agreement with the EU in 1995 which provided for the progressive reduction of tariffs (and elimination of many by 2008).

Current Issues

Government/fundamentalist conflict dominated domestic affairs in the early and mid-1990s, the Ben Ali regime denouncing *Nahda* adherents as "terrorists" intent on seizing power. However, the government's own hard-line tactics were the subject of increasing domestic and international condemnation, human rights organizations accusing security forces of arbitrary detention and widespread mistreatment of prisoners. Government critics also alleged that the antifundamentalist campaign was being used to deflect attention from the RCD's continuing status as "virtually a state party" and the retention of as many as 2,000 political prisoners. The situation was seen as creating a problem for Western capitals: on the one hand, the administration's economic policies had generated widespread success while, on the other, its human rights record was difficult to condone. In 1998 the US State Department describing the Ben Ali administration as "intolerant of dissent" and Amnesty International charging that human rights activists in Tunisia had themselves become the targets of intimidation and imprisonment.

Once again adopting a seemingly unnecessarily restrictive stance, the administration announced that candidates in the 1999 presidential election would be allowed to run only if they had served five years as the leader of a party currently represented in the legislature. Only two challengers qualified and, although the administration heralded the multicandidate nature of the balloting as an important democratization step, critics dismissed the poll as a "parody," citing the fact that each opposition candidate won less than 0.5 percent of the vote. The RCD's total domination of the concurrent legislative poll and the municipal elections in May 2000 further supported the argument that the legal opposition parties remained "subservient or marginalized."

Perhaps in response to growing criticism in the West over human rights issues and the lack of genuine political liberalization, the government released some political prisoners in late 1999 and appeared to accept a more vocal dissent in 2000. However, this modest "Tunisian spring" was the focus of a crackdown in early 2001 as the administration faced intensifying attacks from domestic human rights organizations and challenges in the form of several high-profile petitions and manifestos.

In November 2001 the government introduced controversial proposed constitutional amendments that, among other things, called for the revocation of presidential term limits and the raising of the maximum age of presidential candidates from 70 to 75. Critics described the changes as being designed to permit Ben Ali, currently 65, to govern for many more years. A national referendum on May 26, 2002, approved the basic law revisions by more than 99 percent, according to official reports.

Another focus of attention in 2002 was a reported increase in activity on the part of radical Islamic militants. In April an Islamic Army for the Liberation of Holy Places claimed responsibility for a bomb attack on a synagogue on the island of Djerba that killed more than 20 people. Several months later it was reported that a senior *al-Qaeda* leader had suggested that *al-Qaeda* had also been involved in the bombing.

Despite continued criticism from human rights groups, there appeared to be little subsequent improvement in the treatment of political prisoners. Collaterally, in the wake of the September 11, 2001, terrorist attacks in the United States, Washington concentrated less on the issue of human rights and more on Tunisia's antiterror efforts. (In December 2003 the Ben Ali administration adopted broad new antiterrorism legislation that critics claimed could be used to apply harsh penalties to nearly any crime.) During a visit in February 2004, US Secretary of State Colin Powell gently urged the Ben Ali administration to permit greater freedom of the press and pursue other reform. Prior to the October 2004 presidential and legislative balloting, Ben Ali pledged to "deepen the democratic exercise," but opposition parties characterized those elections as a "charade" that was simply propelling Ben Ali toward a "life presidency." Among other things, the opposition candidates claimed they were victims of intense harassment by the government prior to the balloting. Underscoring its undiluted control of the levers of governmental power, the RCD won an estimated 94 percent of the seats in the May 2005 municipal elections.

Political Parties

Although not constitutionally mandated, Tunisia was effectively a one-party state from the time the

Communist Party (PCT) was banned in January 1963 until its return to legal status in July 1981. In June 1981 the government had announced that recognition would be extended to all parties obtaining at least 5 percent of the valid votes in legislative balloting on November 1. On September 9 the PCT indicated that it would participate in the election after receiving official assurances that the 5 percent requirement would not be imposed in its case, and in 1983 recognition was extended to two additional opposition parties, the PUP and the MDS (below). All three boycotted the 1986 election because of the rejection of many of their candidate lists and administrative suspension of their publications. In November 1987 the Ben Ali government endorsed the legalization of any party that would consent to certain conditions, one (advanced by the House of Representatives in April 1988) being that "no party has the right to refer, in its principles, its objectives, its activities or its programs, to religion, language, race or a regime," a stipulation which served as a barrier to the legalization of militant Islamic groups. Prior to the 1989 balloting, the government party (RCD, below) offered to head an electoral front which would have guaranteed at least minimal opposition representation in the house. However, the proposal was rejected, ultimately to the dismay of the legal opposition parties, none of which succeeded in winning more than three percent of the popular vote. In April 1991 the Ben Ali government agreed to provide the six legal opposition parties with moderate state financial support and limited access to government-controlled television and radio broadcasting facilities. Subsequently, in what the administration described as a further effort to strengthen the role of the opposition parties, the RCD also offered not to present candidates for the house by-elections in October. However, the opposition boycotted the balloting as a protest against the government's unwillingness to revise the electoral law or reduce the RCD's "stranglehold" on the civil service. Electoral law changes guaranteed the opposition a minimal number of seats in the March 1994 national elections, but non-RCD candidates still secured less than three percent of the votes even though all the legal parties

participated. The government announced in 1997 that the house would be expanded for the 1999 balloting and that electoral revision would attempt to promote opposition representation of up to 20 percent. The house was expanded to 182 members for the 1999 balloting, electoral revision in 1998 having guaranteed opposition representation of at least 34 members.

Government Party

Democratic Constitutional Assembly (*Rassemblement Constitutionnel Démocratique*–RCD). Founded in 1934 as the Neo-Destour Party, a splinter from the old Destour (Constitution) Party, and known from October 1964 as the Destourian Socialist Party (*Parti Socialiste Destourien*–PSD), Tunisia's ruling party was given its present name in February 1988 to provide new impetus to "the practice of democracy" within its ranks. Its moderately left-wing tendency was of less political significance than its organizational strength, derived in large part from affiliated syndicates representing labor, agriculture, artisans and merchants, students, women, and youth. Party members have filled most major government positions since independence.

At the 12th party congress in June 1986 President Bourguiba personally selected a new 90-member Central Committee and 20-member Political Bureau, ignoring party statutes calling for election by delegates. By the end of the year the PSD had ended a 1985 rift in returning to close alignment with the General Union of Tunisian Workers (*Union Générale des Travailleurs Tunisiens*–UGTT). A special "Congress of Salvation," held at Tunis July 29–31, 1988, endorsed the political liberalization policies of new President Ben Ali (who was reelected party chairman), included a number of young party members in a new 150-member Central Committee, and named a new 12-member Political Bureau.

At a congress held July 29–31, 1993, Ben Ali was unanimously reelected party chairman and designated as the RCD presidential candidate in the elections scheduled for March 1994. A new Central Committee was selected, more than half of its 200 members serving for the first time in a reflection of the RCD's "revitalization" campaign which also included enlargement of the Political Bureau to include several young cabinet ministers and the first female member. In addition, the congress reconfirmed its commitment to free-market economic policies and stated its strong opposition to Islamic fundamentalist "militancy."

The third RCD congress, held July 30–August 22, 1998, reelected Ben Ali as chairman and nominated him as the party's candidate for the 1999 presidential election, which he won with more than 99 percent of the vote. In the 1999 legislative balloting, the RCD secured 92 percent of the vote; municipal elections in May 2000 produced similar support for the RCD, which reportedly won all but about 240 of nearly 4,150 seats.

Political Bureau: Gen. Zine El-Abidine BEN ALI (President of the Republic and President of the Party), Mohamed GHANNOUCHI (Prime Minister and Second Vice President of the Party), Hamed KAROUI (First Vice President of the Party and Former Prime Minister), Abdelaziz BEN DHIA, Abderrahim ZOUARI, Chedli NEFFATI, Dali JAZI, Fouad M'BAZAA (President of the House of Representatives), Habib BEN YAHIA, Abdallah KALLEL, Neziha ZARROUK, Ali CHAOUCH (General Secretary).

Other Legal Parties

Democratic Socialist Movement (*Mouvement des Démocrates Socialistes*–MDS). Organized as the Democratic Socialist Group in October 1977 by a number of former PSD cabinet ministers who sought liberalization of the nation's political life, the MDS was refused formal recognition in 1978, although its leader, Ahmed Mestiri, had served as an intermediary between the government and the trade union leadership in attempting to resolve labor unrest. The new grouping was runner-up at the 1981 election but obtained only 3.28 percent of the vote, thus failing to secure either legislative representation or legal status. However, recognition was granted by President Bourguiba in November 1983.

Mestiri was arrested in April 1986 and sentenced to four months in prison for leading demonstrations against the US bombing of Libya. The conviction automatically disqualified him from running for legislative office, the MDS thereupon becoming an early advocate of the November electoral boycott. (Under the amnesty program initiated by the Ben Ali government in late 1987, Mestiri was pardoned for the conviction.) The MDS fared poorly in the 1989 balloting, and Mestiri was criticized for rejecting the RCD's preelection offer of an electoral front with the MDS and other parties. Subsequently, Mestiri resigned as MDS secretary general, assistant secretary general Dali Jazi having earlier quit the party to join the government. Mestiri was reported to have left the party altogether in early 1992, as criticism grew of the "authoritarian" approach of its new leader, Mohamed Mouada. Factionalization also contributed to the "suspension" by the MDS of another of its prominent leaders, Mustafa BEN Jaafar.

The MDS supported President Ben Ali for reelection in 1994 but challenged the RCD in the national legislative balloting. Although no MDS candidates were successful on their own, ten were subsequently seated in the house under the proportional arrangement enacted to guarantee a multiparty legislature.

In early October 1995 Mouada published a letter criticizing the "lack of political freedom" in Tunisia. Within days he was arrested on charges of having had illegal contacts with representatives of the Libyan government, and in February 1996 he was sentenced to 11 years in prison. Mouada dismissed the charges as "obviously politically motivated," and his conviction was widely condemned by international observers. Khemais CHAMMARI, a member of the MDS as well as the House of Representatives, was also given a five-year sentence in July for "attacking state security." Both men were released in December, although Mouada was briefly detained again one year later. Meanwhile, an MDS congress in May 1997 had elected Ismaïl Boulahia to the new leadership post of secretary general, his discussion of the future of the "new MDS" apparently reflecting a diminution of Mouada's authority. However, Boulahia was not eligible to contest the 1999 presidential election, since he had not held his MDS post the requisite five years, and he subsequently announced that the MDS was supporting President Ben Ali for reelection. Meanwhile, the party secured 13 seats in the legislative balloting of 1999, again thanks solely to electoral law guarantees regarding opposition representation.

Mouada was held under house arrest for one month in late 1999 on a charge of defaming the government, and in early 2001 he issued a joint declaration with *Nahda* leader Rachid Ghanouchi calling for creation of a joint antigovernment front. However, apparently underscoring continued disagreement within the MDS regarding the extent of cooperation with the regime, Boulahia met with President Ben Ali in early 2001 and praised his commitment to "democratic values." Meanwhile, Ben Jafaar continued his heavy criticism of the administration through an unrecognized grouping called the Democratic Forum for Labor and Liberties (*Forum Démocratique pour le Travail et les Libertés*–FDTL), of which he was described as the secretary general, and the CNLT (see below), of which he was a founding member.

Leaders: Mohamed MOUADA, Ismaïl BOULAHIA (Secretary General).

Renewal Movement (*Harakat Ettajdid/ Mouvement de la Rénovation*–MR). The Renewal Movement is heir to the Tunisian Communist Party (*Parti Communiste Tunisien*–PCT), which was founded in 1934 as an entity distinct from the French Communist Party. The PCT was outlawed in 1963 and regained legality in July 1981. Historically of quite limited membership, the party secured only 0.78 percent of the vote at the 1981 legislative balloting. Prior to the opposition boycott, the PCT had intended to participate in the 1986 election in alliance with the RSP (below). Delegates to the party's 1987 congress denounced IMF-supported changes in the government's economic policies, particularly the emphasis on the private sector and free-market activity. Subsequently, the PCT supported the political

reforms instituted by the Ben Ali government, before joining the MDS and MUP in boycotting the municipal elections in 1990 to protest the "failure" of democratization efforts.

The party's new name was adopted at an April 1993 congress, leaders announcing that Marxism had been dropped as official doctrine in favor of a "progressive" platform favoring "democratic pluralism." None of the MR's 93 candidates was successful in the 1994 national legislative balloting, although four MR members were subsequently seated in the House under the proportional arrangement established for opposition parties. Party leaders complained of widespread fraud in the legislative balloting and described Tunisia's slow pace of political liberalization as a national "scandal."

The MR secretary general, Mohamed Harmel, was constitutionally prohibited from contesting the 1999 presidential election due to his age (70). The MR was accorded five seats in the legislature elected in 1999.

MR Chairman Mohamed Ali el-Halouani was one of three candidates to oppose President Ben Ali in the 2004 elections. In a rare occurrence, MR supporters demonstrated in Tunis after el-Halouani complained that the party had been blocked from distributing its manifesto. El-Halouani received about 1 percent of the vote and denounced the poll as a "sham."

Leaders: Mohamed Ali el-HALOUANI (Chairman), Boujamma RMILI, Mohamed HARMEL (Secretary General).

Unionist Democratic Union (*Union Démocratique Unioniste*–UDU). Legalized in November 1988, the UDU was led by Abderrahmane TLILI, a former member of the RCD who had resigned from the ruling party to devote himself to the unification of various Arab nationalist tendencies in Tunisia. Tlili garnered 0.23 percent of the vote in the 1999 presidential balloting, the UDU securing seven of the seats distributed to the opposition following the concurrent legislative poll.

Tlili was sentenced to nine years in prison in 2004 on embezzlement charges relating to his former government tenure. The UDU supported President Ben Ali in the 2004 presidential election.

Popular Union Party (*Parti de l'Unité Populaire*–PUP). The PUP is an outgrowth of an "internal faction" that developed within the Popular Unity Movement (MUP, below) over the issue of participation in the 1981 legislative election. Although garnering only 0.81 percent of the vote in 1981, it was officially recognized in 1983 as a legal party, subsequently operating under its current name. The PUP attempted to offer candidates for the 1986 balloting, but most were declared ineligible by the government. The party therefore withdrew three days before the election, citing the same harassment that had led to the boycott by other opposition groups. It participated in "national pact" discussions with the government in 1988, thus asserting an identity separate from that of its parent. PUP Secretary General Mohamed Belhadj Amor won 0.31 percent of the vote in the 1999 presidential campaign, during which he expressed deep dismay over the failure of the so-called "opposition parties" to mount any effective challenge to the RCD. He subsequently resigned PUP leadership post. His successor, Mohamed Bouchiha, received 3.8 percent of the vote in the 2004 election.

Leaders: Jalloud AZZOUNA, Mohamed Belhadj AMOR (1999 presidential candidate), Mohamed BOUCHIHA (Secretary General).

Progressive Democratic Assembly (*Rassemblement Démocratique Progressiste*–RDP). The RDP had been established as the Progressive Socialist Assembly (*Rassemblement Socialiste Progressiste*–RSP) by a number of Marxist groups in 1983. The pan-Arabist RSP was tolerated by the Bourguiba government until mid-1986. It formed a "Democratic Alliance" with the PCT and planned to field candidates for the 1986 balloting. However, the coalition boycotted the election after the government disqualified some of its candidates and sentenced 14 of its members to six-month jail terms for belonging to an illegal organization. The party was officially recognized in September 1988. The RSP did not secure any of the legislative seats reserved for opposition parties in 1994 or 1999, and

it called for a boycott of the municipal elections of May 2000. The RSP changed its name to the RDP in July 2001 in an effort to "broaden its ideological base." The RDP reportedly included many Marxists as well as moderate Islamists and liberals.

RDP Secretary General Ahmed Chebbi was blocked from contesting the 2004 presidential election because of a recent decree by President Ben Ali that candidates could only be presented by parties with legislative representation. The RDP consequently called for a boycott of the presidential balloting and withdrew its candidates from the legislative poll.

Leader: Ahmed Néjib CHEBBI (Secretary General).

Liberal Social Party (*Parti Social Liberal*–PSL). Formed to advocate liberal social and political policies and economic reforms, including the privatization of state-run enterprises, the PSL was officially recognized in September 1988 under the name of the Social Party for Progress (*Parti Social pour le Progrès*–PSP). The current name was adopted at the first party congress, held at Tunis on October 29–30, 1994. The PSL secured 2 of the 34 seats reserved for opposition parties in the 1999 legislative balloting. PSL Secretary General Mounir Beji won less than 1 percent of the vote in the 2004 presidential poll.

Leaders: Hosni HAMMANI, Mounir BEJI (Secretary General).

Democratic Forum for Labor and Liberties (*Le Forum Démocratique pour le Travail et les Libertés*–FDTL). Legalized in 2002, the FDTL called for a boycott of the 2004 elections and urged opposition parties to work toward cohesion.

Leader: Mustafa BEN JAFAAR.

Other Groups

Popular Unity Movement (*Mouvement de l'Unité Populaire*–MUP). The MUP was formed in 1973 by Ahmed Ben Salah, a former "superminister" who directed the economic policies of the Bourguiba cabinet from 1962 to 1969. Ben Salah was sentenced to ten years' imprisonment in 1969 for "high treason," although the action was generally attributed to his having fallen out of favor with Bourguiba. After his escape from prison in 1973, Ben Salah directed the MUP from exile, urging the government to return to the socialist policies of the 1960s. The Movement reorganized itself as a political party in June 1978 but was unable to gain legal recognition. In early 1981 friction developed within the MUP leadership after the government granted amnesty to all members theretofore subject to legal restriction, the sole exception being Ben Salah. Ben Salah subsequently declared his opposition to the group's participation in the November 1 balloting, causing a split between his supporters and an "internal" faction (see PUP, above). After maintaining a high international profile throughout his exile, Ben Salah returned to Tunisia in 1988 in the wake of Bourguiba's ouster. However, the MUP did not sign the "national pact" of late 1988, primarily to protest the government's refusal to restore Ben Salah's civil rights, a requirement for his participation in national elections. The MUP joined two legal parties (the MDS and the PCT, above) in an antigovernment coalition in 1990.

Ben Salah was one of several opposition leaders who issued a joint communiqué at London in November 1995 attacking the Tunisian government as repressive. In 1996 the MUP leader was described by *Africa Confidential* as no longer commanding a significant popular base, and he returned to Tunisia from ten years of voluntary exile in Europe in September 2000.

Leader: Ahmed BEN SALAH (General Secretary).

Renaissance Party (*Hizb al-Nahda/Parti de la Renaissance*–PR). Also known as the Renaissance Movement (*Harakat al-Nahda/Mouvement de la Renaissance*), *Nahda* was formed as the Islamic Tendency Movement (*Mouvement de la Tendance Islamique*–MTI) in early 1981 by a group of Islamic fundamentalists inspired by the 1979 Iranian revolution. Charged with fomenting disturbances, many MTI adherents were jailed during a series of subsequent crackdowns by the Bourguiba government. However, the MTI insisted that

it opposed violence or other "revolutionary activity," and the Ben Ali government pardoned most of those incarcerated, including the movement's leader, Rachid Ghanouchi, shortly after assuming power. The new regime also initiated talks which it said were designed to provide moderate MTI forces with a legitimate means of political expression in order to undercut support for the movement's radical elements. As an outgrowth of that process, the MTI adopted its new name in early 1989; however, the government subsequently denied legal status to *Nahda,* ostensibly on the grounds that it remained religion-based. Undaunted, the group quickly established itself as the government's primary opposition, its "independent" candidates collecting about 13 percent of the total popular vote (including as much as 30 percent of the vote in some urban areas) in 1989 legislative balloting.

Nahda boycotted "higher council" negotiations and municipal elections in 1990, Ghanouchi remaining in exile to protest the lack of legal recognition for the formation and the continued "harassment" of its sympathizers. Friction intensified late in the year following the arrest of three groups of what security forces described as armed extremists plotting to overthrow the government. Although the government alleged that some of those arrested had *Nahda* links, the party leadership strongly denied the charge, accusing the regime of conducting a propaganda campaign aimed at discrediting the fundamentalist movement in order to prevent it from assuming its rightful political role.

On October 15, 1991, the government announced that it had uncovered a fundamentalist plot to assassinate President Ben Ali and other government officials in order to "create a constitutional vacuum." However, *Nahda* leaders again denied any connection to violent antigovernment activity, reiterating their commitment to "peaceful methods" of protest and stressing that their vision for the "Islamization" of Tunisia was "compatible" with democracy and a pluralistic society. The disclaimers notwithstanding, the government flatly labeled *Nahda* "a terrorist organization" and intensified the campaign to "silence" it. Thousands of suspected *Nahda* sympathizers were detained, many later claiming that they had been tortured or otherwise abused in prison (a charge supported by Amnesty International). At a widely publicized trial in mid-1992 about 170 *Nahda* adherents were convicted of sedition. A number were sentenced to life imprisonment, including Ghanouchi and several other leaders who were tried *in absentia*. The government subsequently issued an international arrest warrant for Ghanouchi, who was living in London, but in mid-1993 the United Kingdom granted him political asylum. In 1994 Ghanouchi dismissed the recent Tunisian presidential and legislative elections as "a joke." Despite the "banned and fragmented" status of *Nahda,* Ghanouchi was described in 1996 as still the only possible "serious challenger" to Ben Ali. A number of *Nahda* adherents were released in November 1999 from long prison terms. In March 2001 Ghanouchi, in conjunction with MDS leader Mohamed Mouada, proposed establishment by *Nahda* and the legal opposition parties of a National Democratic Front to challenge the RCD, suggesting to some observers that *Nahda* hoped to return to mainstream political activity. However, *Nahda* remained relatively quiescent during the 2004 election campaign.

Leaders: Rachid GHANOUCHI (President, in exile), Habib ELLOUZE, Sahah KARKAR (in exile), Sheikh Abdelfatah MOURROU (Secretary General).

Commandos of Sacrifice (*Commandos du Sacrifice*–CS). Although the government insisted that the CS was the "military wing" of *Nahda,* the group's leader, Habib Laasoued, described it as independent and, in fact, a rival to *Nahda* for support among fundamentalists. About 100 members of the commandos were convicted in mid-1992 of planning terrorist acts, although the trials were surrounded by allegations of human rights abuses and other governmental misconduct. Laasoued, who was sentenced to life imprisonment, reportedly acknowledged that the commandos had engaged in theoretical discussions of *jihad* (Islamic holy war) but denied that any antigovernment military action had actually been endorsed.

Leader: Habib LAASOUED (imprisoned).

Party of Tunisian Communist Workers (*Parti des Ouvriers Communistes Tunisiens*– POCT). An unrecognized splinter of the former PCT, the POCT is led by Hamma Hammani, who had been the director of the banned newspaper *El Badil* (The Alternative). Hammani was sentenced to eight years in prison in early 1994 on several charges, including membership in an illegal organization, his case being prominently cited in criticism leveled at the government by human rights organizations. Hammani and another POCT member who had been imprisoned with him were pardoned by President Ben Ali in November 1995. A number of POCT members were convicted in July 1999 of belonging to an illegal association, but most were released later in the year. Hammani and several associates were charged again in absentia in 1999 for having been members of an unrecognized group. In February 2002 they were retried and committed to various prison sentences. In September, however, Hammani and some of the others were released following a hunger strike that had attracted increasing international scrutiny to their case. Hammani called for a boycott of the 2004 elections.

Leader: Hamma HAMMANI.

Several human rights groups have been prominent in the increasingly vocal opposition movement in recent years. They include the unrecognized National Council for Tunisian Freedoms (*Conseil National pour les Libertés Tunisiennes*–CNLT), founded in 1998 by, among others, Moncef MARZOUKI, who had unsuccessfully attempted to run for president in 1994. In a case that attracted wide international attention, Marzouki was sentenced in December 2000 to one year in prison for belonging to an illegal organization. Meanwhile, as of early 2001 the status of the officially sanctioned Tunisian Human Rights League (*Ligue Tunisienne des Droits de l'Homme*–LTDH) remained unclear, a Tunisian court having ordered new elections for LTDH leadership posts. The leaders elected in October 2000, including LTDH President Mokhtar TRIFI, had sharply condemned the Ben Ali government after wresting control of the organization

Cabinet

As of July 1, 2005

Prime Minister	Mohamed Ghannouchi
Secretary General of the Government in charge of Relations with the House of Representatives and the House of Advisors	Mounir Jaidane

Ministers

Agriculture and Water Resources	Mohamed Habib Haddad
Communication Technologies	Montassar Ouaïli
Culture and Heritage Preservation	Mohamed El Aziz Ben Achour
Development and International Cooperation	Mohamed Nouri Jouini
Director of Presidential Cabinet	Tadh Ouderni
Education and Training	Mohammad Raouf Najjar
Employment and Professional Integration of Youth	Chadli Laroussi
Equipment, Housing, and Territorial Management	Samira Khayach Belhadj [f]
Finance	Mohamed Rachid Kechiche
Foreign Affairs	Abdelaki Hermassi
Higher Education	Lazhar Bou Ouni
Industry, Energy, and Small Medium Enterprises	Afif Chelbi
Interior and Local Development	Rafik Belhaj Kacem
Justice and Human Rights	Béchir Tekkari
Minister of State (Special Advisor to the President)	Abdelaziz Ben Dhia
National Defense Prime Minister's Office	Hedi Mhenni Zouhair Mdhaffer
Public Health	Ridha Kechrid
Religious Affairs	Boubaker El Akhzouri
Scientific Research, Technology, and Competence Development	Sadok Korbi
Social Affairs, Solidarity, and Tunisians Abroad	Rafaa Dekhil
State Property and Land Affairs	Ridha Grira
Tourism	Tijani Haddad
Trade and Handcrafts	Mondher Zenaïdi
Transport	Abderrahim Zouari
Women, Family, Children, and Elderly Affairs	Salova Ayachi Labben [f]

[f] = female

from RCD adherents. Trifi was arrested in March 2001.

In mid-1994 it was reported that a militant Islamic group had been organized among Tunisian exiles under the leadership of Mohamed Ali el-HORANI to support armed struggle against the Ben Ali government. The group, which reportedly adopted the name of Algeria's outlawed **Islamic Salvation Front** (*Front Islamique du Salut*–FIS), was described as critical of *Nahda's* official rejection of violence. References have also been made to a **Tunisian Islamic Front** (*Front Islamique Tunisien*–FIT), which reportedly has committed itself to armed struggle against the Ben Ali regime. In addition, some 14 members of a fundamentalist group called *Ansar* were sentenced in December

2000 to jail terms for belonging to an illegal organization, which the government described as having Iranian ties.

Legislature

House of Representatives

(*Majlis al-Nuwab/Chambre des Députés*). The Tunisian legislature is a unicameral body presently consisting of 189 members serving five-year terms. (A national referendum on May 26, 2002, approved constitutional changes that, among other things, provided for the creation of an upper house, the House of Advisers, slated to comprise 120 members elected for a six-year term. Initial balloting [by an electoral college of local officials] for the new upper house was scheduled for July 2005.) Under a new system adopted for the 1994 election, most representatives (148 in 1999 and 152 in 2004) are elected on a "winner-takes-all" basis in which the party whose list gains the most votes in a district secures all the seats for that district. (There are 25 districts comprising two to ten seats each.) The remaining seats (19 in 1994, 34 in 1999, and 37 in 2004) are allocated to parties which failed to win in any districts, in proportion to the parties' national vote totals.

From the establishment of the house in 1959 until 1994, members of the ruling party (RCD) occupied all seats. Although six opposition parties were permitted to offer candidates at the 1989 balloting and a number of independent candidates sponsored by the unsanctioned Renaissance Party also ran, the RCD won all seats with a reported 80 percent of the vote. RCD candidates also won all 9 seats contested in October 1991 by-elections, which were boycotted by the opposition parties. The house was enlarged from 141 members to 163 for the 1994 election and to 182 for the 1999 balloting. The membership was expanded to 189 seats for the most recent election on October 24, 2004, President Ben Ali decreeing that 43 of the seats be filled by women. The RCD won all 152 seats that were contested on a district basis. However, under the proportional system for distributing 37

additional seats, five other parties were allocated seats as follows: The Democratic Socialist Movement, 14; the Popular Union Party, 11; the Unionist Democratic Union, 7; the Renewal Movement, 3; and the Liberal Social Party, 2.

President: Fouad M'BAZAA.

Communications

The media during most of the Bourguiba era were subject to pervasive party influence and increasingly repressive government interference. The Ben Ali government initially relaxed some of the restrictions, although the fundamentalist press remained heavily censored and mainstream publications continued to practice what was widely viewed as self-censorship, bordering on what one foreign correspondent described as "regime worship." In addition, several foreign journalists were subsequently expelled and some international publications were prevented from entering the country for printing articles critical of the government. (The French dailies *Le Monde* and *Libération* were banned from March 1994 until March 1995 because of their coverage of events prior to the national elections.) In recent years international journalists' groups have called for Western nations to apply pressure upon the Tunisian government to reduce what has been widely perceived as pervasive restraints on freedom of the press, including the arrests of journalists.

Press

The following, unless otherwise noted, are published daily at Tunis: *As-Sabah* (The Morning, 50,000), government-influenced, in Arabic; *al-Amal* (Action, 50,000), RCD organ, in Arabic; *L'Action* (50,000), RCD organ, in French; *Le Temps* (42,000), weekly in French; *La Presse de Tunisie* (40,000), government organ, in French; *Le Quotidien* (The Daily, 30,000), independent, in French; *Le Renouveau* (23,000), RCD organ, in French; *La Presse-Soir,* evening; *as-Sahafa,* in Arabic; *al-Huriyya,* in Arabic; *as-Shourouq* (Sunise), independent, in Arabic.

News Agencies

The domestic facility is *Tunis Afrique Presse–TAP* (*Wakalah Tunis Afriqiyah al-Anba'*); in addition, a number of foreign bureaus maintain offices at Tunis.

Broadcasting and Computing

The *Etablissement de la Radiodiffusion-Télévision Tunisienne* (ERTT) operates a radio network broadcasting in Arabic, French, and Italian. It also operates three television channels, one of which links the country with European transmissions. The first privately owned radio station was launched in 2003, and the first private television station began broadcasting in early 2005. (Although President Ben Ali portrayed these developments as expansion of freedom of the press, thus far programming on the new stations has lacked political commentary.) There were approximately 3.9 million television receivers and 400,000 personal computers serving 630,000 Internet users in 2003.

Intergovernmental Representation

Ambassador to the US
Mohamed Nejib HACHANA

US Ambassador to Tunisia
William J. HUDSON

Permanent Representative to the UN
Ali HACHANI

IGO Memberships (Non-UN)
AfDB, AFESD, AMF, AMU, AU, BADEA, CCC, IDB, Interpol, IOM, LAS, NAM, OIC, OIF, WTO

TURKEY

REPUBLIC OF TURKEY

Türkiye Cumhuriyeti

The Country

Guardian of the narrow straits between the Mediterranean and Black seas, present-day Turkey occupies the compact land mass of the Anatolian Peninsula together with the partially European city of İstanbul and its Thracian hinterland. The country, which borders on Greece, Bulgaria, Georgia, Armenia, the Nakhichevan Autonomous Republic of Azerbaijan, Iran, Iraq, and Syria, has a varied topography and is subject to extreme variation in climate. It supports a largely Turkish population (more than 80 percent, in terms of language) but has a substantial Kurdish minority of approximately 12 million, plus such smaller groups as Arabs, Circassians, Greeks, Armenians, Georgians, Lazes, and Jews. Some 98 percent of the populace, including both Turks and Kurds, adheres to the Islamic faith, which maintains a strong position despite the secular emphasis of government policy since the 1920s. Sunni Muslims constitute a substantial majority, but between 10 and 20 percent of the population belong to the Alevi (Alawi) sect of Islam.

Women constitute approximately 36 percent of the official labor force, with large numbers serving as unpaid workers on family farms. While only 10 percent of the urban labor force is female, there is extensive participation by upper-income women in such professions as medicine, law, banking, and education, with the government being headed by a female prime minister during 1993–1995.

Turkey traditionally has been an agricultural country, with about 50 percent of the population still engaged in agricultural pursuits; yet the contribution of industry to GDP now exceeds that of agriculture (24.9 and 11.8 percent, respectively, in 2004). Grain (most importantly wheat), tobacco, cotton, nuts, fruits, and olive oil are the chief agricultural products; sheep and cattle are raised on the Anatolian plateau, and the country ranks among the leading producers of mohair. Natural resources include chrome, copper, iron ore, manganese, bauxite, borax, and petroleum. The most important industries are textiles, iron and steel, sugar, food processing, cement, paper, and fertilizer. State economic enterprises (SEEs) account for more than 60 percent of fixed investment, although substantial privatization has recently been decreed.

Economic growth during the 1960s was substantial but not enough to overcome severe balance-of-payments and inflation problems, which intensified

following the oil price increases of 1973–1974. By 1975 the cost of petroleum imports had more than quadrupled and was absorbing nearly two-thirds of export earnings. A major devaluation of the lira in mid-1979 failed to resolve the country's economic difficulties, and in early 1980, with inflation exceeding 100 percent, a $1.16 billion loan package was negotiated with the Organization for Economic Cooperation and Development (OECD), followed in June by $1.65 billion in credits from the International Monetary Fund (IMF). Subsequently, aided by improving export performance and a tight curb on foreign currency transactions, the economy registered substantial recovery, with inflation being reduced to a still unsatisfactory level of 39 percent in 1987, before returning to 70 percent in 1989. High inflation rates plagued Turkey throughout the 1990s, reaching 99 percent by 1997. An economic stabilization program introduced in 1997 brought the rate down to 55 percent in 1998.

Although annual inflation had been lowered to about 35 percent in 2000 and solid GNP growth (estimated at over 6 percent) had been reestablished, a financial crisis erupted in late February 2001, forcing a currency devaluation and other intervention measures. In April 2001 the government announced it anticipated 3 percent economic contraction for the year. Among other things, resolution of the economic problems was considered a prerequisite to Turkey's long-standing goal of accession to the European Union (EU) (see Foreign relations, below for details). The IMF approved a $15.7 billion "rescue package" in May 2001 and endorsed up to $10 billion in additional aid in November after the government pledged to intensify its efforts to reorganize the banking sector, improve tax collection, combat corruption, promote foreign investment, and accelerate the privatization program. Consequently, the government narrowly avoided defaulting on its debt repayments, much to the relief of Western capitals for whom Turkey represents a geographic, political, and military linchpin amid the turbulence of the Middle East.

Turkey has weathered the financial crises of 2000–2001 and, thanks in part to conditions imposed by an agreement with the IMF, the economy is stabilizing. Indeed, inflation was down to 12 percent during 2004, and some analysts say the real inflation rate was below 10 percent. The government set a target of 8 percent inflation for 2005. At the same time, the country's real gross domestic product grew by 8 percent in 2002, 6 percent in 2003 and was projected to grow 5 percent in 2004.

Observers give much of the credit for Turkey's improved economic performance to tighter fiscal policies as well as to reform of the financial sector, including especially the creation of an independent Banking Regulation and Supervision Agency, recapitalization of the state banks, and tighter auditing procedures. After its 2004 consultations with Turkey, however, the IMF has cautioned that Turkey's economy is still vulnerable. In particular, the IMF has frowned upon recent government-backed increases in wages, which it feared would fuel inflation. And the IMF has called specifically for reform of the social security system, which has large deficits, and called on the government to refrain from large increases in public spending. Foreign direct investment has also remained relatively low—averaging less than $1 billion annually—though it is expected that such investment will increase as Turkey implements reforms aimed at eventual membership in the EU. On April 12, 2005, Turkey and the IMF reached agreement on a $10 billion loan conditioned upon recent and continuing economic reforms.

Government and Politics

Political Background

The present-day Turkish Republic is the surviving core of a vast empire created by Ottoman rule in late medieval and early modern times. After a period of expansion during the 15th and 16th centuries in which Ottoman domination was extended over much of central Europe, the Balkans, the Middle East, and North Africa, the empire underwent a lengthy period of contraction and fragmentation, finally dissolving in the aftermath of a disastrous alliance with Germany in World War I.

A secular nationalist republic was proclaimed in October 1923 by Mustafa Kemal ATATÜRK, who launched a reform program under which

Turkey abandoned much of its Ottoman and Islamic heritage. Its major components included secularization (separation of religion and state), establishment of state control of the economy, and creation of a new Turkish consciousness. Following his death in 1938, Atatürk's Republican People's Party (*Cumhuriyet Halk Partisi*–CHP) continued as the only legally recognized party under his close associate, İsmet İNÖNÜ. One-party domination was not seriously contested until after World War II, when the opposition Democratic Party (*Demokrat Parti*–DP) was established by Celal BAYAR, Adnan MENDERES, and others.

Winning the country's first free election in 1950, the DP ruled Turkey for the next decade, only to be ousted in 1960 by a military coup led by Gen. Cemal GÜRSEL. The coup was a response to alleged corruption within the DP and the growing authoritarian attitudes of its leaders. Many of those so charged, including President Bayar and Prime Minister Menderes, were tried and found guilty of violating the constitution, as a result of which Bayar was imprisoned and Menderes executed.

Civilian government was restored under a new constitution in 1961, with Gürsel remaining as president until his incapacitation and replacement by Gen. Cevdet SUNAY in 1966. The 1961 basic law established a series of checks and balances to offset a concentration of power in the executive and prompted a diffusion of parliamentary seats among several parties. A series of coalition governments, most of them led by İnönü, functioned until 1965, when a partial reincarnation of the DP, Süleyman DEMİREL's Justice Party (*Adalet Partisi*–AP), won a sweeping legislative mandate.

Despite its victory in 1965, the Demirel regime soon became the target of popular discontent and demands for basic reform. Although surviving the election of 1969, it was subsequently caught between left-wing agitation and military insistence on the maintenance of public order (a critical issue because of mounting economic and social unrest and the growth of political terrorism). The crisis came to a head in 1971 with an ultimatum from the military that resulted in Demirel's resignation and the formation of a "nonparty" government by Nihat ERİM, amendment of the 1961 constitution,

Political Status: Independent republic established in 1923; parliamentary democracy since 1946, save for military interregna from May 1960 to October 1961 and September 1980 to November 1983; present constitution approved by referendum of November 7, 1982.
Area: 300,948 sq. mi. (779,452 sq. km.).
Population: 67,803,927 (2000C); 70,420,000 (2004E).
Major Urban Centers (2000C): ANKARA (3,203,362), İstanbul (8,803,460), İzmir (2,232,265), Bursa (1,194,687), Adana (1,130,710).
Official Language: Turkish. A 1982 law banning the use of the Kurdish language was rescinded in early 1991.
Monetary Unit: Turkey New Lira (market rate July 1, 2005: 1.33 Turkey New Liras = $1US).
President of the Republic: Ahmet Necdet SEZER (nonparty); elected by the Grand National Assembly on May 5, 2000, and sworn in for a seven-year term on May 16 to succeed Süleyman DEMİREL (True Path Party).
Prime Minister: Recep Tayyip ERDOGAN (Justice and Development Party–AKP) invited by the president on March 11, 2003, to form a new government, following general elections on November 3, 2002.

the declaration of martial law in eleven provinces, the arrest of dissident elements, and the outlawing of the left-wing Turkish Labor Party (*Türkiye İşçi Partisi*–TİP) and moderate Islamist National Order Party (*Millî Nizam Partisi*–MNP). The period immediately after the fall of the Erim government in 1972 witnessed another "nonparty" administration under Ferit MELEN and the selection of a new president, Adm. (Ret.) Fahri KORUTÜRK. Political instability was heightened further by an inconclusive election in 1973 and by both foreign and domestic policy problems stemming from a rapidly deteriorating economy, substantial urban population growth, and renewed conflict on Cyprus that yielded Turkish intervention in the summer of 1974.

Bülent ECEVİT was appointed prime minister in January 1974, heading a coalition of his own moderately progressive CHP and the smaller, religiously oriented National Salvation Party (*Millî Selâmet Partisi*–MSP). Although securing widespread domestic acclaim for the Cyprus action and for his insistence that the island be formally divided into Greek and Turkish federal regions, Ecevit was opposed by Deputy Prime Minister Necmettin ERBAKAN, who called for outright annexation of the Turkish sector and, along with his MSP colleagues, resigned, precipitating Ecevit's own resignation in September. Both Ecevit and former prime minister Demirel having failed to form new governments, Sadi IRMAK, an independent, was designated prime minister on November 17, heading an essentially nonparliamentary cabinet. Following a defeat in the National Assembly only twelve days later, Irmak also was forced to resign, although he remained in office in a caretaker capacity until Demirel succeeded in forming a Nationalist Front coalition government on April 12, 1975.

At an early general election on June 5, 1977, no party succeeded in gaining a lower house majority, and the Demirel government fell on July 13. Following Ecevit's inability to organize a majority coalition, Demirel returned as head of a tripartite administration that failed to survive a nonconfidence vote on December 31. Ecevit thereupon formed a minority government.

Widespread civil and political unrest throughout 1978 prompted a declaration of martial law in 13 provinces on December 25. The security situation deteriorated further during 1979, and, faced with a number of ministerial defections, Prime Minister Ecevit was on October 16 again obliged to step down, with Demirel returning as head of an AP minority government on November 12.

Divided by rising foreign debt and increasing domestic terrorism, the National Assembly failed in over 100 ballots to elect a successor to Fahri Korutürk as president of the Republic. Senate President İhsan Sabri ÇAĞLAYANGİL assumed the office on an acting basis at the expiration of Korutürk's seven-year term on April 6. On August 29 Gen. Kenan EVREN, chief of the General Staff, publicly criticized the assembly for its failure both

to elect a new president and to promulgate more drastic security legislation, and on September 12 he mounted a coup on behalf of a five-man National Security Council (NSC) that suspended the constitution, dissolved the assembly, proclaimed martial law in all of the country's 67 provinces, and on September 21 designated a military-civilian cabinet under Adm. (Ret.) Bülent ULUSU. The junta banned all existing political parties; detained many of their leaders, including Ecevit and Demirel; imposed strict censorship; and arrested upwards of 40,000 persons on political charges.

In a national referendum on November 7, 1982, Turkish voters overwhelmingly approved a new constitution, under which General Evren was formally designated as president of the Republic for a seven-year term. One year later, on November 6, 1983, the recently established Motherland Party (*Anavatan Partisi*–ANAP) of former deputy prime minister Turgut ÖZAL won a majority of seats in a newly constituted, unicameral Grand National Assembly. Following the election, General Evren's four colleagues on the NSC resigned their military commands, continuing as members of a Presidential Council upon dissolution of the NSC on December 6. On December 7 Özal was asked to form a government and assumed office as prime minister on December 13.

Confronted with a governing style that was viewed as increasingly arrogant and ineffective in combating inflation, Turkish voters dealt Prime Minister Özal a stinging rebuke at local elections on March 26, 1989. ANAP candidates ran a poor third overall, securing only 22 percent of the vote and losing control of the three largest cities. Özal refused, however, to call for new legislative balloting and, despite a plunge in personal popularity to 28 percent, utilized his assembly majority on October 31 to secure the presidency in succession to Evren. Following his inauguration at a parliamentary ceremony on November 9 that was boycotted by opposition members, Özal announced his choice of Assembly Speaker Yıldırım AKBULUT as the new prime minister.

Motherland's standing in the opinion polls slipped to a minuscule 14 percent in the wake of a political crisis that erupted in April 1991 over the somewhat heavy-handed installation of the president's wife, Semra ÖZAL, as chair of the ruling party's İstanbul branch. Both Özals declared their neutrality in a leadership contest at a party congress in mid-June, but they were viewed as the principal architects of an unprecedented rebuke to Prime Minister Akbulut, who was defeated for reelection as chairman by former foreign minister Mesut YILMAZ.

Yılmaz called for an early election on October 20, 1991, "to refresh the people's confidence" in his government. The outcome, however, was a defeat for the ruling party, with former prime minister Demirel, now leader of the right-of-center True Path Party (*Doğru Yol Partisi*–DYP), negotiating a coalition with the left-of-center Social Democratic People's Party (*Sosyal Demokrat Halkçı Parti*–SHP) and returning to office for the seventh time on November 21, with the SHP's Erdal İNÖNÜ as his deputy.

Demirel's broad-based administration, which brought together the heirs of Turkey's two oldest and most prominent political traditions (the CHP and the DP), claimed greater popularity—50 percent voter support and more than 60 percent backing in the polls—than any government in recent decades. Thus encouraged, Demirel and İnönü launched an ambitious program to counter the problems of rampant inflation, Kurdish insurgency, and obstacles to full democratization.

On April 17, 1993, President Özal died of a heart attack, and on May 16 the Grand National Assembly elected Prime Minister Demirel head of state. The DYP's search for a new chairperson ended on June 13, when Tansu ÇİLLER, an economics professor, defeated two other candidates at an extraordinary party congress. On July 5 a new DYP–SHP coalition government, committed to a program of further democratization, secularism, and privatization, was accorded a vote of confidence by the assembly, and Çiller became Turkey's first female prime minister.

A major offensive against guerrillas of the Kurdistan Workers' Party (*Partîya Karkerén Kurdistan*–PKK) in northern Iraq was launched on

March 20, 1995. Six weeks later the government announced that the operation had been a success and that all of its units had returned to Turkey. The popularity of the action was demonstrated at local elections on June 4, when the ruling DYP took 22 of 36 mayoralties on a 39 percent share of the vote. However, on September 20 a revived CHP, which had become the DYP's junior coalition partner after absorbing the SHP in February, withdrew its support, forcing the resignation of the Çiller government.

On October 2, 1995, Çiller announced the formation of a DYP minority administration that drew unlikely backing from the far-right Nationalist Action Party (*Milliyetçi Hareket Partisi*–MHP) and the center-left Democratic Left Party (*Demokratik Sol Parti*–DSP). However, the prime minister was opposed within the DYP by former National Assembly speaker Hüsamettin CİNDORUK, who resigned on October 1 and was one of ten deputies expelled from the party on October 16, one day after Çiller's defeat on a confidence motion. On October 31 President Demirel appointed Çiller to head a DYP–CHP interim government pending a premature election in December.

At the December 24, 1995, balloting the pro-Islamic Welfare Party (*Refah Partisi*–RP) emerged as the legislative leader, although its 158 seats fell far short of the 276 needed for an overall majority. Eventually, on February 28, 1996, agreement was reached on a center-right coalition that would permit the ANAP's Yılmaz to serve as prime minister until January 1, 1997, with Çiller occupying the post for the ensuing two years and Yılmaz returning for the balance of the parliamentary term, assuming no dissolution.

Formally launched on March 12, 1996, the ANAP–DYP coalition collapsed at the end of May amid renewed personal animosity between Yılmaz and Çiller over the former's unwillingness to back the DYP leader against corruption charges related to her recent premiership. The DYP then opted to become the junior partner in an alternative coalition headed by RP leader Necmettin ERBAKAN, who on June 28 became Turkey's first avowedly Islamist prime minister since the creation of the secular republic in 1923. Under the coalition agreement, Çiller was slated to take over as head of government in January 1998. However, the military reportedly feared that Erbakan's tolerance for rising religious activism would seriously threaten the country's secular tradition, and, after months of pressure from the military, Erbakan resigned on June 18, 1997, with the hope that a new government under the leadership of his coalition partner, Çiller, would bring the paralyzed government back to life. However, on June 20 President Demirel bypassed Çiller, whose DYP had been weakened by steady defections, and selected the ANAP's Yılmaz to return as next prime minister. A new coalition composed of the ANAP, the DSP, and the new center-right Democratic Turkey Party (*Demokrat Türkiye Partisi*–DTP) was approved by Demirel on June 30, and Yılmaz and his cabinet were sworn in the following day.

The new coalition government tried to reverse the Islamic influence of its predecessor and in July 1997 proposed an eight-year compulsory education plan that included the closure of Islamic secondary schools, prompting weeks of right-wing and militant Islamic demonstrations.

The Yılmaz government collapsed on November 25, 1998, when he lost a vote of confidence in the Grand National Assembly following accusations of corruption against members of his cabinet. President Demirel asked Bülent Ecevit to form a new government on December 2, thereby abandoning the long-standing tradition of designating the leader of the largest party in the legislature as prime minister. (Such action would have put Recai KUTAN's moderate Islamist Virtue Party [*Fazilet Partisi*–FP] in power, an option opposed by the military.) When Ecevit proved unable to form a government, Demirel turned to an independent, Yalım EREZ, who also failed when former prime minister Çiller rejected his proposal that her DYP be part of a new coalition. After Erez abandoned his initiative on January 6, 1999, President Demirel reinvited Ecevit to form the government. This time Ecevit succeeded in forming a minority cabinet made up of the DSP and independents; the DYP and ANAP agreed to provide external support.

Ecevit's cabinet survived a crisis that erupted in mid-March 1999, when the FP threatened to topple the government and joined forces with disgruntled members of parliament from various political parties who were not nominated for reelection. At balloting on April 18, 1999, Ecevit's DSP received 22 percent of the votes and became the largest party in the assembly with 136 seats. On May 28 Ecevit announced the formation of a coalition cabinet comprising the DSP, MHP, and ANAP. Meanwhile, on May 16 Ahmet Necdet SEZER, chief justice of the Constitutional Court, had been sworn in as the new president following the legislature's rejection of President Demirel's request for constitutional revision that would have permitted him a second term.

In October 2001, the Grand National Assembly approved several constitutional amendments aimed at easing Turkey's path into the EU. The changes provided greater protection for political freedom and civil leaders, including protection for the Kurdish minority. Also, the number of civilians on the National Security Council was increased from five to nine, with the military continuing to hold five seats.

In January 2002, the Constitutional Court banned AKP leader Recep Tayyip ERDOGAN from running for the legislature because of alleged seditious activities. The court also ordered the party to remove Erdogan from party leadership.

In July 2002, Prime Minister Ecevit was forced to call early elections to the Grand National Assembly as a result of resignations causing the DSP-led coalition to lose its majority in the legislature. The general election on November 3, 2002, was a disaster for the ruling DSP. The largest winner was the AKP, which attracted 34.3 percent of the vote and 363 seats in the Grand National Assembly. The only other party to exceed 10 percent of the vote and win seats in the legislature was the CHP, which won 19.4 percent of the vote and 178 seats. The DSP won only 1.2 percent of the vote.

Because Erdogan was prohibited from holding a seat in the Grand National Assembly, AKP deputy leader Abdullah GÜL was appointed prime minister, though Erdogan reportedly acted as de facto prime minister. With its strong numbers in the Grand National Assembly, the AKP was able to enact constitutional reforms allowing Erdogan to become prime minister. Erdogan was elected to the Grand National Assembly on March 9 and was appointed prime minister on March 11. Under AKP leadership, the Grand National Assembly adopted further reforms aimed at eventual accession to the EU, including legislation allowing broadcasting and education in Kurdish. Another piece of legislation would have allowed peaceful advocacy of an independent Kurdish state. This measure was vetoed by President Sezur only to be made law when the Grand National Assembly overrode the veto.

In March 2003, Turkey's Constitutional Court banned the People's Democracy Party (HADEP) from politics as a result of its alleged support for the PKK. In addition, 46 party members were individually banned from politics for five years.

In August 2003, for the first time, a civilian assumed control of the National Security Council. This event followed amendments to the constitution earlier in the year that reduced the number of seats reserved for the military in the council. Another sign of the waning power of the military in Turkey was the fact that, for the first time since the republic was founded in 1923, public spending on education ($6.7 billion) exceeded that spent on defense ($5.6 billion) in 2004.

The AKP further solidified its position with a strong showing in local elections on March 28, 2004, winning 42 percent of the vote. The CHP had the second-best showing, but won only 18 percent of the vote.

Constitution and Government

The 1982 constitution provided for a unicameral, 400-member Grand National Assembly elected for a five-year term (the membership being increased to 450 in 1987 and 550 in 1995). The president, elected by the assembly for a nonrenewable seven-year term is empowered to appoint and dismiss the prime minister and other cabinet members; to dissolve the assembly and call for a new election, assuming the concurrence of two-thirds

of the deputies or if faced with a government crisis of more than 30 days' duration; to declare a state of emergency, during which the government may rule by decree; and to appoint a variety of leading government officials, including senior judges and the governor of the Central Bank. Political parties may be formed if they are not ethnic- or class-based, linked to trade unions, or committed to communism, fascism, or religious fundamentalism. Strikes that exceed 60 days' duration are subject to compulsory arbitration.

The Turkish judicial system is headed by a Court of Cassation, which is the court of final appeal. Other judicial bodies include an administrative tribunal styled the Council of State, a Constitutional Court, a Court of Accounts, various military courts, and twelve state security courts.

The country is presently divided into 80 provinces, which are further divided into subprovinces and districts. Mayors and municipal councils have long been popularly elected, save during the period 1980–1984.

Foreign Relations

Neutral until the closing months of World War II, Turkey entered that conflict in time to become a founding member of the United Nations and has since joined all of the latter's affiliated agencies. Concern for the protection of its independence, primarily against possible Soviet threats, made Turkey a firm ally of the Western powers with one of the largest standing armies in the non-Communist world. Largely on US initiative, Turkey was admitted to the North Atlantic Treaty Organization (NATO) in 1952 and in 1955 became a founding member of the Baghdad Treaty Organization, later the Central Treaty Organization (CENTO), which was officially disbanded in September 1979 following Iranian and Pakistani withdrawal.

Relations with a number of Western governments cooled in the 1960s, partly because of a lack of support for Turkey's position on the question of Cyprus. The dispute, with the fate of the Turkish Cypriot community at its center, became critical upon the island's attaining independence in 1960 and nearly led to war with Greece in 1967. The situation assumed major international importance in 1974 following the Greek officers' coup that resulted in the temporary ouster of Cypriot President Makarios, and the subsequent Turkish military intervention on July 20 that yielded Turkish occupation of the northern third of the island (for details see articles on Cyprus and Cyprus: Turkish Sector).

Relations with the United States, severely strained by a congressional ban on military aid following the Cyprus incursion, were further exacerbated by a Turkish decision in July 1975 to repudiate a 1969 defense cooperation agreement and force the closure of 25 US military installations. However, a new accord was concluded in March 1976 that called for reopening of the bases under Turkish rather than dual control, coupled with substantially increased US military assistance. The US arms embargo was finally lifted in September 1978, with the stipulation that Turkey continue to seek a negotiated resolution of the Cyprus issue.

While the Turkish government under Evren and Özal consistently affirmed its support of NATO and its desire to gain full entry to the EC (having been an associate member of the European Economic Community since 1964), relations with Western Europe deteriorated in the wake of the 1980 coup because of alleged human rights violations. The credentials of Turkish delegates to the Parliamentary Assembly of the Council of Europe were suspended from 1981 until May 1984, when the assembly noted that progress had been made toward the restoration of democracy while urging greater consideration for human rights and full freedom of action for political parties.

Ankara submitted a formal membership request to the EC, and in December 1989 the EC Commission laid down a number of stringent conditions for admission to the community, including an enhanced human rights record, progress toward improved relations with Greece, and less dependence on agricultural employment. Because of these concerns, Turkey remained outside the EU upon the latter's inception in November 1993, although, in an action viewed as linked to its EC bid, it had become an associate member of the Western European Union in 1992.

On March 6, 1995, Turkey and the EU agreed to a customs union, which entered into force January 1, 1996. However, in July 1997 the EU Commission included five East European states but excluded Turkey from among those invited to join first-round enlargement negotiations scheduled for early 1998. Moreover, the commission recommended Cyprus for full membership, a decision that was controversial given the lack of a settlement between Turkey and Greece over the Cyprus question. The United States and the EU subsequently assured both sides that Cyprus would not be accepted into the EU until a settlement is reached. In light of improving Turkish/Greek relations, a December 1999 EU summit finally accepted Turkey as an official candidate for membership.

Apart from Cyprus, the principal dispute between Greece and Turkey has centered on territorial rights in the Aegean. In late 1984 Ankara vetoed a proposal by Greek Prime Minister Papandreou to assign Greek forces on Lemnos to NATO, invoking a long-standing contention that militarization of the island was forbidden under the 1923 Treaty of Lausanne. The controversy revived in early 1989 with Turkey refusing to recognize insular sea and airspace limits greater than six miles on the premise that to do otherwise would convert the area into a "Greek lake." The dispute intensified in September 1994, with Greece declaring that it would formally extend its jurisdiction to twelve nautical miles upon entry into force of the UN Convention on the Law of the Sea on November 16. Turkey immediately warned that the move would be considered an "act of aggression," and on October 30 Athens announced that it would defer the introduction of what it continued to view as a "sovereign right."

Another dispute between the Aegean neighbors flared in January 1996 with a mutual deployment of warships to an islet off the Turkish coast known to the Greeks as Imia and to the Turks as Kardak (see map, p. 451). Turkey had long insisted that the islet and adjacent rocks were not part of Italy's 1947 conveyance of the main Dodecanese Islands to Greece because an Italian-Turkish convention of 1932 had specified that all such territory within 18 kilometers (11.2 miles) of the coast belonged to the nearest country. On January 30, US President Clinton succeeded in defusing the crisis by persuading Greece to withdraw a unit that had been dispatched to halt the flying of a Turkish flag over the islet.

In October 1984 an agreement was concluded with Iraq that permitted security forces of each government to pursue "subversive groups" (interpreted primarily as Kurdish rebels) up to a distance of five kilometers on either side of the border and to engage in follow-up operations for five days without prior notification. The hot pursuit agreement notwithstanding, the Turkish government strongly supported UN-endorsed sanctions against Iraq in the wake of its invasion of Kuwait in August 1990. Despite considerable revenue loss, Turkey moved quickly to shut down Iraqi oil pipelines by banning ships from loading crude at offshore terminals. In September, despite opposition criticism, the legislature granted the administration special authority to dispatch troops to the Gulf and to allow foreign forces to be stationed on Turkish soil for non-NATO purposes (most importantly, the stationing of F-111 fighter bombers at İncirlik air base to monitor the UN-sanctioned Iraqi no-fly zone north of the 36th parallel).

In 1994 Ankara angered Moscow by seeking to impose restrictions on shipping through the Bosphorus. The issue was highly charged because of the 1936 Montreaux treaty, which provided complete freedom of transit through both the Bosphorus and Dardanelles during peacetime. Turkey insisted that the new regulations (including the prohibition of automatic pilots for navigation and limitations on dangerous cargo) were prompted only by technical considerations that had not existed at the time of the treaty's adoption.

During 1992 Turkey faced a dilemma in regard to the conflict in Bosnia and Herzegovina. Both the Bosnians and Turkish citizens of Bosnian descent appealed for action to oppose Serbian advances in Muslim areas; however, Atatürk's secularist heirs were reluctant to move in a manner that might be seen as religiously inspired. Deeply opposed to unilateral action, Turkey launched a pro-Bosnian campaign in various international venues, including the UN, the Conference on (subsequently the Organization for) Security and Cooperation in Europe (CSCE/OSCE), NATO, the Council of Europe, and the OIC. Throughout, it urged limited military intervention by the UN and the lifting of the arms embargo for Bosnia should existing sanctions and diplomatic efforts prove ineffective.

The military action launched by Turkey against the Kurds in northern Iraq on March 20, 1995, was condemned by most West European governments. On April 10 the EU foreign ministers, while acknowledging Turkey's "terrorism problems," called on Ankara to withdraw its troops "without delay," and on April 26 the Parliamentary Assembly of the Council of Europe approved a resolution calling for suspension of Turkey's membership if it did not leave Iraq by late June. For its part, the Turkish government reacted angrily to an announcement on April 12 that political exiles had established a Kurdish "parliament in exile" in the Netherlands, and a renewed cross-border offensive was launched by some 30,000 troops on July 5–10. In any event, no action was taken to suspend Turkey's Council of Europe membership, despite further vigorous Turkish action against the Kurdish insurgency. In July 1997 Turkey and the Democratic Party of Kurdistan (DPK) reached a preliminary agreement to boost security in northern Iraq. However, in August Turkish warplanes crossed the Iraqi border to bomb PKK rebel bases, drawing the condemnation of Baghdad.

A major diplomatic dispute erupted in 1998 over Syria's alleged sheltering of PKK rebels, Ankara warning Damascus in October of possible military action unless Syrian policy changed. The crisis was also colored by Syria's concern over the recent rapprochement between Turkey and Israel, which had produced a defense agreement and a recent visit by Prime Minister Yılmaz to Israel. Following intense mediation by several Arab leaders from the region, Syria subsequently agreed that it would not allow the PKK to set up "military, logistical, or financial bases" on Syrian territory. Collaterally, PKK leader

Abdullah ÖCALAN was forced to leave Syrian-controlled territory in Lebanon. Öcalan moved to Russia, which, under intense Turkish pressure, also refused him asylum. He then entered Italy, prompting a row between Rome and Ankara. Italy rejected Turkey's extradition request on the grounds that it could not send a detainee to a country that permitted the death penalty. Italy therefore attempted to negotiate Öcalan's transfer to Germany, where he also faced terrorism charges. However, Bonn, apparently fearing violence between its own Turkish and Kurdish minorities, declined to file an extradition request. Consequently, Öcalan was released from detention in Italy in mid-December and reportedly left that country in January 1999 for an unknown destination.

In mid-February 1999 Öcalan was arrested by Turkish security forces shortly after he had left the home of the Greek ambassador at Nairobi, Kenya. The incident proved to be highly embarrassing for the government in Athens. Despite the renewed animosity surrounding Öcalan's arrest, Turkish/Greek relations thawed noticeably in late 1999 when Greece lifted its veto on EU financial aid earmarked to Turkey and accepted a carefully worded agreement that permitted the EU to accept Turkey as a candidate for membership. In early 2000 the two countries agreed to establish a joint commission to "reduce military tensions" in the Aegean and to pursue cooperation in several other areas.

In 2003, Turkey's relationship with the United States faced a major challenge with Turkey's refusal to allow US troops to use Turkish territory as a staging area for the invasion of Iraq in March 2003. Some observers attributed this refusal, which was an embarrassment to the Turkish government and military, to a political power struggle taking place within Turkey. While the governing Justice and Development Party (AKP) was in favor of such cooperation, many nationalistic members of the Grand National Assembly, including some AKP members, were not. Relations with the United States have also been strained over what the Turkish government has seen as a lack of concern with Kurdish terrorist activity in Turkey and

northern Iraq. Indeed, in November 2004, Turkish newspapers published unconfirmed reports that the Turkish government had formulated a plan to move 20,000 Turkish troops into northern Iraq to prevent Kurds from taking complete control of Kirkuk. On January 26, 2005, a senior Turkish army general said bluntly that the Turkish military was prepared to intervene if clashes erupted in northern Iraq or if Iraqi Kurds attempted to form an independent state.

Iran and Turkey signed a security agreement on July 30, 2004, to place rebels opposed to either government on each government's list of terrorist organizations.

Relations with Russia have also been strained by Turkey's efforts to control the passage of oil tankers through the Bosphorus straits. Turkey says that the increased number of oil tankers represents an environmental threat to Turkey's coastline and waterways. Turkey has imposed tighter regulations on passage, which Russia claims have added greatly to transit time and, accordingly, to costs. In August 2004, Turkey also proposed, and offered to help fund, construction of pipelines to reduce waterborne traffic. Apart from the issue of the Bosphorus strait, however, Turkish relations with Russia have been generally good. Tourism between the two countries has jumped to around $1 billion a year and bilateral commerce has grown to about $6.5 billion.

Current Issues

Three intertwined issues have dominated politics in Turkey over the past several years: accession to the EU, a significant rise in nationalist and Islamist sentiments among the populace, and the continuing Kurdish insurgency in the southeast part of the country.

While the Turkish government, along with the majority of Turks, is in favor of joining the EU, the reforms required before Turkey would be allowed to join are seen by some as interference in Turkish affairs. Nevertheless, since 2001 the Grand National Assembly has enacted a number of reforms aimed at easing the path to joining the

EU. In October 2001, the legislature approved constitutional amendments aimed at broadening civil liberties and human rights. In November, legislation granting equal status to women in certain areas was passed. In February 2002, the legislature revoked a law allowing schoolgirls to be forced to undergo "virginity tests." In August 2002, the Grand National Assembly abolished the death penalty in peacetime. And on September 26, 2004, the Turkish parliament approved major revisions to the penal code, specifically aimed at bringing the code in line with those prevalent in the EU. A further reform of the penal code in June 2005 provided greater protections for women and children and imposed harsher penalties for torture and "honor" killings.

At the same time, the EU has repeatedly criticized Turkey for backsliding on reforms. The government was embarrassed in November 2000 when hundreds of political prisoners joined a hunger strike in protest of plans to move them to high-security prisons. In December, security forces raided 20 of the prisons. Thirty prisoners and two soldiers were killed. By January 2003, 104 people had died as a result of the hunger strikes. In August 2002, the government was further embarrassed by an Amnesty International report that accused Turkey of extensive and regular use of torture by police. And in April 2004, after a Turkish military court affirmed a 15-year sentence for Leyla ZANA, a human rights activist, the EU's enlargement commissioner, Günther Verheugen, said that he "strongly deplores" the verdict. "It gives rise to serious concern in the light of the [EU's] political criteria and casts a negative shadow on the implementation of political reforms in Turkey," he added. In 2001, the European Court of Human Rights ruled that the Zana's previous trial had been unfair.

The EU has continued to warn Turkey about the slow pace of its reforms. Most recently, at a meeting in Luxembourg on April 26, 2005, EU officials told Turkey's foreign minister of their concerns about recent police beatings of women demonstrators and mob attacks on prison reform campaigners. The European Court of Human Rights (ECHR)

also issued a ruling in May 2005 that the trial of Abdullah Öcalan, leader of the PKK Kurdish separatist movement, was unfair. Turkey indicated immediately that it would retry Öcalan, though the ruling by the ECHR raised hackles among some Turkish nationalists in parliament and the military.

When the EU in October 2004 agreed to move forward with negotiations leading to Turkey's accession to the union, it also placed two unusual conditions on the talks. First, the commission stressed that the talks would be open ended and with no guarantee of eventual membership. Secondly, the commission recommended that the negotiations, which could take up to ten years in any case, should be suspended if Turkey is seen to backtrack on reforms. Some observers saw these conditions as providing an opportunity for member countries— some of which are already nervous about Islamic extremism in their own countries—to back out of the arrangement. Nevertheless, on December 17, 2004, Prime Minister Erdogan formally accepted the offer of the EU to proceed with accession talks.

The EU Commission has also indicated that a resolution of the situation in Cyprus may be a requirement for Turkey's accession to the EU. While Greece has recently backed Turkey's accession, Greek and Turkish voters on Cyprus have not managed to find common ground. The Greek part of the island joined the EU in 2004, but negotiations to bring the Turkish section in fell apart. And when Turkey signed a protocol on July 29, 2005, extending a customs union with the EU to include ten new member states, including Cyprus, it immediately followed up with a declaration that its signing of the accord did not constitute official recognition of Cyprus. This declaration, in turn, angered Greek Cypriots and Greece. At the same time, Erdogan's move angered nationalists in Turkey who charged that his move did, in fact, amount to recognition.

While the Erdogan government has been trying to reassure Europe that it is a secular country intent on reform, some domestic moves by the government have generated concern within Turkey—and particularly within the military—that

Prime Minister Erdogan, a devout Muslim, is intent on bringing Islamic values into government. The AKP's greatest support is seen by most observers as coming from middle-class, conservative Muslims. Prime Minister Erdogan generated controversy with his proposal in May 2004 to give Islamic schools equal standing with the public schools with respect to gaining admission to secular universities. The proposal—which critics described as a thinly disguised effort to promote religious schools and Islamic law–caused some university rectors to threaten to resign and opposition members of parliament to walk out on hearings in protest.

Recent years have also seen a resurgence of domestic unrest. In November 2003 a suicide bombing outside of two of Istanbul's largest synagogues killed 25 people and injured 300 people. Later in the month, suicide bombers attacked the Hong Kong and Shanghai Banking Corporation and the British Embassy, killing 31 people and injuring more than 450. These attacks were attributed to domestic Islamic extremists with possible ties to *al Qaeda*. Violence from the Kurdish insurgency has also been increasing over the past several years. In September 2003, the Kurdish rebel group PKK announced that it was ending its cease-fire, adopted five years previously, with the Turkish government. In a September 2004 offensive, the largest in five years, government troops killed 11 Kurdish rebels in the southeast province of Hakkari. The government blamed Kurdish rebels for a series of bombings—including two hotel bombings and the bombing of a pop concert—in August and September. The numbers of roadside bombings in the southeastern part of the country have also increased. While the Kurdish population remains generally loyal to the PKK, many Kurds have started to question the rebels' tactics, particularly since government reforms aimed at EU membership have resulted in a steady improvement in rights and protections for Kurds.

Political Parties

Turkey's multiparty system developed gradually out of the monopoly originally exercised by the historic Republican People's Party (*Cumhuriyet Halk Partisi*–CHP), which ruled the country without serious competition until 1950 and which, under Bülent Ecevit, was most recently in power from January 1978 to October 1979. The Democratic Party (*Demokrat Parti*–DP) of Celal Bayar and Adnan Menderes, founded by CHP dissidents in 1946, came to power in 1950, maintained control for the next decade, but was outlawed in consequence of the military coup of 1960, many of its members subsequently entering the conservative Justice Party (*Adalet Partisi*–AP). Other formations included an Islamic group, the National Salvation Party (*Millî Selâmet Partisi*–MSP); the ultra-rightist Nationalist Action Party (*Milliyetçi Hareket Partisi*–MHP); and the leftist Turkish Labor Party (*Türkiye İşçi Partisi*–TİP). All party activity was banned by the National Security Council on September 12, 1980, while the parties themselves were formally dissolved and their assets liquidated on October 16, 1981.

Approval of the 1982 constitution ruled out any immediate likelihood that anything resembling the earlier party system would reappear. In order to qualify for the 1983 parliamentary election, new parties were required to obtain the signatures of at least 30 founding members, subject to veto by the National Security Council (NSC). Most such lists were rejected by the NSC, with only three groups (the Motherland, Populist, and Nationalist Democracy parties) being formally registered for the balloting on November 6 in an apparent effort to promote the emergence of a two-party system. Of the three, only the ruling Motherland Party remained by mid-1986: the Populist Party merged with the Social Democratic Party in November 1985 to form the Social Democratic People's Party (see under CHP, below), while the center-right Nationalist Democracy Party (*Milliyetçi Demokrasi Partisi*–MDP) dissolved itself in May 1986.

In July 1992 the government lifted bans on all of the parties closed during the military interregnum and by mid-1996 their number had risen to over 30, distributed almost equally to the right and left of the political spectrum.

Government Party

Justice and Development Party (*Adalet ve Kalkinma Partisi*–AKP). The AKP was launched in August 2001 by the reformist wing of the FP (see below) as a moderate religious, center-right formation. Out of the former parliamentarians from the FP and other parties, 53 later joined the AKP, making it the second-largest opposition party in the assembly (after the DYP). Some analysts noted that the AKP might prove to be a strong challenger to the coalition parties in the next legislative elections.

In January 2002 the Constitutional Court ruled that AKP President Recep Tayyip Erdogan was ineligible to run for office due to his imprisonment in 1999 on charges of having "incited hatred on religious grounds." In November 2002 elections, the AKP won 34.2 percent of the vote and 363 legislative seats. Abdullah Gül formed his government on November 18, 2002. Erdogan's ineligibility for office was removed when the Turkish Grand National Assembly changed select articles of the Constitution. Erdogan was elected an MP at by-elections on March 9, 2003, and formed his government on March 14, 2003. (AKP's legislative seats went down to 355 by July 2005.)

The party revealed some cracks in its solidarity in February 2005 with the resignation from the government and the party of Erkan MUMCU, the minister for tourism and culture. Mumcu, a liberal and secular member considered a rising star in the party, indicated he was resigning because he felt he could no longer influence government decisions.

Leaders: Recep Tayyip ERDOGAN (President), Idris Naim ŞAHIN (Secretary-General).

Opposition Parties

Republican People's Party (*Cumhuriyet Halk Partisi*–CHP). The CHP is a left-of-center party founded in 1923 by Kemal Atatürk. It was dissolved in 1981 and reactivated in 1992 by 21 MPs who resigned from the Social Democratic People's Party (*Sosyal Demokrat Halkçı Parti*–SHP) to reclaim the group's historic legacy. The CRP absorbed the SHP on February 18, 1995.

A member of the Socialist International, the SHP had been formed in November 1985 by merger of the Populist Party (*Halkçı Parti*–HP), a center-left formation that secured 117 seats in the 1983 Grand National Assembly election, and the Social Democratic Party (*Sosyal Demokrat Parti*–SODEP), which was not permitted to offer candidates for the 1983 balloting. A left-of-center grouping that drew much of its support from former members of the CHP, SODEP had participated in the 1984 local elections, winning 10 provincial capitals. The SHP was runner-up to ANAP in November 1987, winning 99 assembly seats despite the defection in December 1986 of 20 of its deputies, most of whom joined the DSP. Its parliamentary representation was reduced to 82 upon formation of the People's Labor Party, whose candidates were, however, entered on SHP lists for the 1991 campaign. Subsequently, 18 of those so elected withdrew from the SHP, reducing its representation to 70.

On September 20, 1995, former CHP chairman Deniz BAYKAL, who had been succeeded by the SHP's Hikmet CETIN at the time of the February merger, was reelected to his earlier post. Immediately thereafter he withdrew the party from the government coalition, thereby forcing Tansu Çiller's resignation as prime minister. In the resultant December election the CHP fell back to 49 seats on a 10.7 percent vote share. Baykal's CHP gave outside support to the Yilmaz-led ANAP–DSP–DTP coalition government of June 1998. However, amid accusations of corruption against various ministers, the CRP's call for a vote of no confidence against the Yilmaz cabinet brought the coalition down in November 1998. The CHP failed to surpass the 10 percent threshold in the April 18, 1999 elections, securing only 8.5 percent of the vote, and was therefore left out of the assembly. Baykal resigned from his chairman's post on April 22. The CHP elected famous journalist and former tourism minister Altan ÖYMEN as its new leader on May 23; however, Baykal regained the post at an extraordinary congress in October 2000, defeating Öymen and two other minor candidates. The CRP's ranks were strengthened in 2002 by defections from the DSP.

In the November 2002 elections the CHP won 19.3 percent of the vote and 178 legislative seats, thus becoming the main opposition party. In October 2004 the New Turkey Party (*Yeni Türkiye Partisi*–YTP) merged with the CHP. YTP had been launched in July 2002 by former DSP cabinet ministers, legislators and members including Ismail Cem, former cabinet minister. TP had scored poorly (1.1 percent) in the November 2002 elections. In January 2005, Baykal's presidency was challenged at a highly explosive CHP Party Congress by Mustafa Sarigül, the highly popular mayor of the İstanbul district of Şişli, who eventually lost his bid but vowed to continue his opposition. A few pro-Sarigül legislators left the party following the congress to join the SHP (see below). By mid-2005, CHP was ridden with internal turmoil, with numerous dissidents (including legislators) resigning from the party and charging Baykal with "single-person authoritarian rule." CHP's legislative seats were down to 158 by mid-2005.

Leaders: Deniz BAYKAL (President), Onder SAV (Secretary-General).

Motherland Party (*Anavatan Partisi*–ANAP). The right-of-center ANAP supports the growth of private enterprise and closer links to the Islamic world as well as the EU. It won an absolute majority of assembly seats in 1983 and at the local elections of March 1984 obtained control of municipal councils in 55 of the country's 67 provincial capitals. Its ranks having been augmented by most former deputies of the Free Democratic Party (*Hür Demokrat Parti*–HDP), which was formed by a number of independents in May 1986 but dissolved the following December, ANAP won a commanding majority of 292 seats at the election of November 1987. Following the poll, Prime Minister Özal announced that he would seek a merger of ANAP and the DYP to ensure a right-wing majority of sufficient magnitude to secure constitutional amendments without resort to referenda. However, the overture was rebuffed, with DYP leader Demirel describing Özal in September 1988 as an "incompetent man" who represented "a calamity for the nation."

Following Özal's inauguration to the technically nonpartisan post of president of the Republic in November 1989, Yıldırım AKBULUT was named prime minister and party president. Upon his ouster in June 1991 he was succeeded by former foreign minister Mesut Yılmaz. At the early legislative balloting of October 20 ANAP trailed the DYP by only 3 percentage points (24 to 27), but its representation plummeted to 115, leading to the collapse of the Yılmaz administration.

ANAP was runner-up to the RP with a 19.7 vote share at the legislative poll of December 24, 1995, although placing third in representation with a seat total of 132. After considerable delay, it entered into a coalition with the DYP whereby Yılmaz would serve as prime minister for the remainder of 1996, with former prime minister Çiller slated to succeed him for a two-year period on January 1, 1997 Yılmaz had less than three months as head of government, being forced to resign in early June after the DYP had withdrawn from the coalition. ANAP then went into opposition to an RP–DYP coalition, amid much acrimony with its erstwhile government partner. Yılmaz was appointed to form a new cabinet on June 20, 1997, following RP Prime Minister Erbakan's resignation under military pressure two days earlier. Yılmaz's ANAP–DSP–DTP coalition government lasted only five months, however; after which ANAP gave parliamentary support to the Ecevit-led DSP government.

At the elections of April 18,1999, ANAP fared poorly, securing only 13 percent of the votes and 86 seats. Although the party became a junior partner in the subsequent Ecevit-led government, ANAP's image was subsequently tarnished by press allegations of corruption among some of its members.

ANAP suffered a major electoral defeat in November 2002 and received 5.1 percent of the vote and no legislative seats. Mesut Yılmaz resigned on November 4, 2002, and the party underwent a prolonged and deep crisis. Following the short-lived presidencies of Ali Talip Özdemir and Nesrin Nas, former AKP legislator and minister of Culture and Tourism, Erkan Mumcu became the party's president in April 2005. After being joined by legislators defecting from AKP and

CHP, the party had, by mid-2005, 14 legislative seats.

Leaders: Erkan MUMCU (President), Muharrem DOĞAN (Secretary-General).

True Path Party (*Doğru Yol Partisi*–DYP). The center-right DYP was organized as a successor to the Grand Turkey Party (*Büyük Türkiye Partisi*–BTP), which was banned shortly after its formation in May 1983 because of links to the former Justice Party of Süleyman Demirel. The new group was permitted to participate in the local elections of March 1984 but won control in none of the provincial capitals. By early 1987, augmented by assemblymen of the recently dissolved Citizen Party (*Vatandaş Partisi*–VP), it had become the third-ranked party in the Grand National Assembly. The DYP remained in third place by winning 59 seats at the November 1987 balloting and became the plurality party, with 178 seats, in October 1991. In November it formed a coalition government under Demirel with the SHP (see under CHP). A second DYP–SHP government was formed by the new DYP leader, Tansu Çiller, following Demirel's assumption of the presidency in May 1993. A new coalition was formed with the CHP in March 1995, following the latter's absorption of the SHP. However, a CHP leadership change in September led to the party's withdrawal and the collapse of the Çiller government.

The DYP placed second in the December 1995 election (with 19.2 percent of the vote), eventually forming a coalition government with ANAP on March 12, 1996, that featured a "rotating" leadership under which the ANAP's Mesut Yılmaz became prime minister and Çiller was to return to the top post in January 1997. However, animosity between the DYP and ANAP leaders quickly resurfaced, with Çiller calling the prime minister a "sleazeball" (for allegedly expediting press exposés of her questionable use of official funds as prime minister) and withdrawing the DYP's support for the coalition in late May. Overcoming its previous antipathy toward the RP, the DYP the following month entered a new coalition as junior partner of the Islamist party, with Çiller becoming deputy premier and foreign minister, pending a scheduled resumption of the premiership at the beginning of 1998. By mid-January 1997 a parliamentary inquiry had cleared the DYP leader of all corruption charges relating to her tenure as premier. After the DYP–RP coalition collapsed under intense pressure from the military and the secular political establishment in June 1997, the DYP remained in the opposition during the Yılmaz-led ANAP–DSP–DTP coalition. By backing CHP leader Deniz Baykal's proposal for a vote of no-confidence against the Yılmaz government, the DYP facilitated its collapse in November 1998. The DYP then gave outside support to Bülent Ecevit's minority government. The DYP fared badly in the April 1999 elections, securing only 12 percent of the votes and 85 seats.

The DYP experienced a major electoral defeat in November 2002, and received 9.5 percent of the vote and no legislative seats. This defeat prompted Tansu Çiller to resign following the election. Independent legislator and a former hard-line and controversial director of security (national police) Mehmet Ağar was elected president of the party in December 2004. With defections from other parties, the party had, by mid-2005, four legislative seats.

Leaders: Mehmet AĞAR (President), Kamil TURAN (Secretary-General).

Social-Democrat People's Party (*Sosyaldemokrat Halk Partisi*–SHP). Launched by former Deputy Prime Minister Murat Karayalçin in hopes of reclaiming the historical legacy of an earlier formation of a similar name, SHP did not contest the November 2002 elections. SHP was later joined by former CHP legislators who had left the party in protest of Deniz Baykal's reelection as the president over challenger Mustafa Sarigül (see above, under CHP). With these additions, by mid-2005, SHP had four legislative seats.

Leaders: Murat KARAYALÇIN (President), Ahmet Giiryüz KETENCİ (Secretary-General).

Party of the People's Rise (*Halkin Yiikselişi Partisi*–HYP). The centrist HYP was established in February 2005 by Yaşar Nuri ÖZTÜRK, a former scholar of Islamic theology who became popular with his "reformist" and modernist interpretations of religion, and a former CHP legislator who had left his party in April 2004 to protest Deniz Baykal's leadership style. Currently Öztürk is the only legislator of the HYP.

Other Parties

Democratic Left Party (*Demokratik Sol Parti*–DSP). Formation of the DSP, a center-left populist formation, was announced in March 1984 by Rahşan Ecevit, the wife of former prime minister Bülent Ecevit, who was barred from political activity prior to the constitutional referendum of September 1987. At the October 1991 election the party attracted sufficient social democratic support to weaken the SHP (see under CHP, below), although winning only seven seats. It recovered in the December 1995-balloting, winning 76 legislative seats with 14.6 percent of the vote. The DSP became a junior partner in a Mesut-Yılmaz-led coalition government that also included the DTP (below), on June 30, 1998. After the Yilmaz-led coalition government collapsed in November 1998, Ecevit formed a minority government on January 12, 1999, that ruled the country until the early elections of April 18. The DSP became the largest party at that balloting with 22 percent of the votes and 136 seats, and Ecevit subsequently formed a DSP–MHP–ANAP coalition cabinet.

In 2002 the DSP reportedly was riddled with internal dissent, some prominent members resigning to form the TDP in January and the YTP in July. The DSP suffered a major electoral defeat in November 2002, receiving only 1.2 percent of the vote and no legislative seats. Bülent Ecevit resigned leadership of the party and nominated Zeki Sezer, a former cabinet minister, to replace him. Sezer was elected to the position at the party's congress in July 2004.

Leaders: Zeki SEZER (President), Tayfun İÇLI (Secretary-General).

Nationalist Action Party (*Milliyetçi Hareket Partisi*–MHP). Until 1969 the ultranationalist MHP was known as the Republican Peasant Nation Party (*Cumhuriyetçi Köylü Millet Partisi*–CKMP), formed in 1948 by conservative dissidents from the old Democratic Party. Dissolved in 1953, the grouping reformed in 1954, merging with the Turkish Villager Party in 1961 and sustaining the secession of the Nation Party (below) in 1962.

The MHP dissolved following the 1980 military coup; in 1983 its sympathizers regrouped as the Conservative Party (*Muhafazakar Parti*–MP), which then was renamed the Nationalist Labor Party (*Milliyetçi Çalişma Partisi*–MCP) in 1985. (The MHP rubric was reassumed in 1992.) The MHP's extremist youth wing, members of which were known as the Grey Wolves (*Bozkurtlar*), remained proscribed, although similar activities were reportedly carried out under semi-official youth clubs. Holding 17 legislative scats as of September 1995, the MHP's 8.18 percent vote share on December 24 was short of the 10 percent required for continued representation. However, it subsequently acquired two seats from defections.

Historic MHP leader Alparslan TÜRKES died in 1998; following the election of Devlet Bahçeli as the new MHP president, members close to Türkeş's son and wife left the party to form the ATP and UBP.

The MHP won surprising support in the election of April 1999, gathering 18 percent of the votes and gaining 129 assembly seats. Some analysts noted that the party's popular support faded during its years in the coalition government between 1999–2002. Indeed, MHP suffered a major electoral blow in November 2002 when it received only 8.3 percent of the vote and no legislative seats. Although following the election, Devlet Bahçeli initially announced he would step down from his leadership position, he ran for and won the party's presidency again in October 2003.

Leaders: Devlet BAHÇELI (President), M. Cihan PAÇACI (Secretary-General).

Felicity Party (*Saadet Partisi*–SP). The SP was formed in July 2001 by the traditionalist core of the

Virtue Party (*Fazilet Partisi*–FP), which had been shut down by the constitutional court in June. The Virtue Party had been launched in February 1998 days before a constitutional court decision banned the Islamic-oriented Welfare Party (which was in the coalition government until June 18, 1997) on charges of undermining the secular foundations of the Turkish Republic.

The Welfare Party (*Refah Partisi*–RP) had been organized in 1983 by former members of the Islamic fundamentalist MSP. It participated in the 1984 local elections, winning one provincial capital. It failed to secure assembly representation in 1987.

Having absorbed Aydin MENDERES' faction of the Democrat Party (DP), the RP attained a plurality in the December 1995 election with 21.4 percent of the vote but at that stage was unable to recruit allies for a government. However, the speedy collapse of an alternative administration brought the RP to office for the first time in June 1996, heading a coalition with the DYP. Under intense pressure from the military and secular political establishment, Prime Minister Necmettin ERBAKAN resigned on June 18, 1997, and the RP–DYP coalition failed. On February 22,1998, the Constitutional Court banned the RP and barred some of its founders, including Erbakan, from political activity for five years.

Some 135 parliamentarians of the proscribed Welfare Party joined the FP, making it the main opposition party in the parliament. Although FP leaders denied their party was a successor to the RP, Turkey's secularists did not find the denial credible. The FP assumed the role of the main opposition party to both the Yılmaz-led ANAP–DSP–DTP coalition government that ended in November 1998 and to the Ecevit-led minority DSP government that was installed in January 1999. Although some analysts initially saw the FP as a likely winner of the general elections in April, the party secured only 15 percent of the votes and 111 seats. Recai Kutan was narrowly reelected as FP chairman at the party congress in May 2000, fending off a challenge from a "reformist" wing led by Recep

Tayyip ERDOGAN (former mayor of Istanbul) and Abdullah GÜL, which then broke away to launch its own formation, the Justice and Development Party (*Adalet ve Kalkinma Partisi*–AKP) in August 2001 following the banning of the FP in June.

Further weakened by legislative defections and a marked shift of popular support to AKP (see above), FP received an electoral setback in November 2002, winning only 2.5 percent of the vote and no legislative seats.

Leaders: Recai KUTAN (President), Suat PAMUKÇU (Secretary-General).

Communal Democratic Party (*Toplumcu Demokratik Parti*–TDP). The left-wing TDP was launched in January 2002 by Sema Pişkinsüt, a member of the assembly and former DSP dissident. During her post as the head of the parliamentary human rights commission, she had antagonized the prime minister as well as DSP Chairman Bülent Ecevit, against whom she unsuccessfully ran at the DSP's congress in April 2001. After charging the DSP leadership with conducting "anti-democratic practices," Pişkinsüt resigned from the DSP in September. The TDP currently has three seats in the assembly, all defectors from the DSP.

In September 2002, TDP merged with ÖDP.

Leader: Sema PIŞKINSÜT (President).

Party of Liberty and Change (*Hürriyet ve Değişim Partisi*–HÜRPARTI). In May 2005, the Democratic Turkey Party (*Demokrat Tükiye Partisi*–DTP) decided to change its name to the Party of Liberty and Change.

The DTP was launched in January 1997 by a group of prominent members of the DYP opposed to the leadership of Tansu Çiller. They included former interior minister İsmet SEZGIN, who had been a close supporter of former DYP leader Suleyman Demirel. The DTP entered the ANAP-led coalition government on June 30, 1998, having secured representation in the assembly in 1997 through defections from the DYP. The DTP assumed an opposition party role after the Yılmaz-led ANAP–DSP–DTP government collapsed in November 1998. The party fared poorly in the April 18, 1999, elections securing less than 1 percent of the votes. In June 2002 a former diplomat, Mehmet Ali BAYAR, was elected to the presidency of the DTP.

In June 2005, Yaşar Okuyan was elected the president of HÜRPARTI.

Leader: Yaşar OKUYAN (President)

Great Unity Party (*Büyük Birlik Partisi*–BP). A nationalist Islamic grouping, the BBP was launched in 1993 by a member of dissident MCP parliamentarians prior to the reactivation of the MHP in 1992. The party, whose members are known as "Turkish-Islamic Idealists" (*Türk-Islam Ülkücüleri*), returned 13 deputies on the ANAP ticket in the 1995 election but subsequently opted for separate parliamentary status. The BBP won only 1.5 percent of the votes in the general election of April 1999. In November 2002, the party received 1.1 percent of the vole and no legislative seats.

Leader: Muhsin YAZICIOĞLU (President).

Democratic People's Party (*Demokratik Halk Partisi*–DEHAP). The Kurdish-based DEHAP was launched in January 1999 by former members of HADEP (People's Democracy Party–*Halkin Demokrasi Partisi*). Fearing that the Constitutional Court would ban HADEP, numerous leaders and members joined DEHAP. (Indeed HADEP was banned in March 2003.) In November 2002, the party won 6.2 percent of the vote and no legislative seats.

Leader: Tuncer BAKIRHAN.

Party of Nation (*Millet Partisi*–MP). Descended from the original MP, the present party is a more immediate outgrowth of the Reformist Democratic Party (*Islahatçi Demokrasi Partisi*–IDP), a relatively ineffectual right-wing formation that displayed ideological affinities with both the RP and MÇP. Its parliamentary deputies, technically sitting as independents after the 1991 election, readopted the MP name in 1992. It won no seats in 1995 or in 1999. In November 2002, the party won 0.22 percent of the vote and no legislative seats.

Leader: Aykut EDİBALİ (President).

Party of Liberty and Solidarity (*Özgurhik ve Dayantsma Partisi*–ÖDP). Backed by many leftist intellectuals, feminists and human rights activists, the ODP was launched after the December 1995 election as a broad alliance of various socialist factions together with elements of the once powerful Dev-Yol movement (see Extremist Groups, below). Some of the socialist groups, notably the United Socialist Party (*Birleşik Sosyalist Parti*–BSP), had contested the balloting as part of the HADEP bloc. The BSP had been formed as a merger of various socialist factions, including the Socialist Unity Party (*Sosyalist Birlik Partisi*–SBP), itself founded in February 1991 (and represented in the 1991–1995 assembly) as in large part successor to the United Communist Party of Turkey (*Türkiye Birlesik Komünist Partisi*–TBKP), led by Haydar KUTLU and Nihat SARGIN.

The TBKP had been formed in 1988 by merger of the Turkish Communist Party (*Türkiye Komünist Partisi*–TKP) and the Turkish Labor Party (*Türkiye Işçi Partisi*–TİP). Proscribed since 1925, the pro-Soviet TKP had long maintained its headquarters in Eastern Europe, staffed largely by exiles and refugees who left Turkey in the 1930s and 1940s. Although remaining illegal, its activities within Turkey revived in 1983, including the reported convening of its first congress in more than 50 years. The TİP, whose longtime leader, Behice BORAN, died in October 1987, had been formally dissolved in 1971 and again in 1980, but had endorsed the merger at a congress held on the first anniversary of Boran's death. Prior to the November 1987 election the TKP and TİP general secretaries, Kutlu and Sargin, respectively, had returned to Turkey for the prospective merger but had been promptly arrested and imprisoned.

Until early 1990, with the Constitutional Court subsequently confirming a ban on the TBKP. Former TBKP elements were prominent in the new ÖDP. The ÖDP fared poorly in the April 1999 elections, gaining less than 1 percent of the votes. Several constituent groups reportedly left the ÖDP in 2002. In November 2002, the party won 0.34 percent of the vote and no legislative seats.

Leader: Hayri KOZANOGLU (President).

Democracy and Peace Party (*Demokrasi ve Bariş Partisi*–DBP). The leftist, pro-Kurdish DBP is the successor to the Democracy and Change Party (*Demokrasi ve Değişim Partisi*–DDP), which was shut down by the Constitutional Court in 1996. The DDP had been founded by elements of the Democracy Party following the latter's banning in June 1994. As part of the broader Bloc of Labor, Peace, and Liberty, the DDP contested the December 1995 election on the unsuccessful list of HADEP.

The DBP fared poorly in the April 1999 legislative elections, gaining less than 1 percent of the vote. The party did not contest November 2002 elections. In February 2003, DBP decided to merge with the newly formed HAK-PAR (the Party of Rights and Liberties–*Hak ve Özgürlükler Partisi*), led by Abdülmerik FIRAT.

Leader: Refik KARAKOC (President).

Communist Party of Turkey (*Türkiye Komünist Partisi*–TICP). The TKP was launched in November 2001 as a merger of the Party for Socialist Power (*Sosyalist Iktidar Partisi*–SIP), and the Communist Party (*Komünist Partisi*–KP). The SIP was a continuation of the banned Party of Socialist Turkey (*Sosyalist Türkiye Partisi*–STP). The hard-line Marxist-Leninist SIP contested the 1995 election under the HADEP rubric. It secured less than 1 percent of the vote in 1999. The KP was formed in July 2000 by former SIP members. In November 2002, the party won 0.2 percent of the vote and no legislative seats.

Leaders: Aydemir GÜLER (President), Kemal OKUYAN (Vice President).

Workers' Party (*İşçi Partisi*–IP). The Maoist-inspired IP, founded in 1992, is the successor of the Socialist Party (*Sosyalist Parti*–SP), which was launched in February 1988 as the first overtly socialist formation since the 1980 coup. The party called for Turkey's withdrawal from NATO and nationalization of the economy. The SP was deregistered by order of the Constitutional Court in June 1992, the IP securing less than 0.5 percent of the vote in 1995. Since 2000 the IP, self-described as

"national leftist," has garnered public attention due to its staunchly anti-EU stance.

In November 2002, the party received 0.5 percent of the vote and no legislative seats.

Leader: Doğu PERİNÇEK (President).

Other nonparliamentary centrist and rightist groups include the **Liberal Democrat Party** (*Liberal Demokrat Parti*–LDP), a free-market grouping led by Besim TİBÜK; the **Young Party** (*Genç Parti*–GP) led by controversial media magnate Cem UZAN; the **Renaissance Party** (*Yeniden Doğuş Partisi*–YDP), led by Ahmet Rüştü ÇELEBİ; the **Party for Independent Turkey** (*Bağımsız Türkiye Partisi*–BTP), led by Haydar BAŞ; the **Main Path Party** (*Anayol Partisi*–Anayol), which has sought to convince the leaders of two main center-right parties (ANAP and DYP) to unify under a single powerful center-right party structure; and the **Justice Party** (*Adalet Partisi*–AP), which claims to be the legitimate heir of the historic AP. The extreme-right-wing **Party of Luminous Turkey** (*Aydınlık Türkiye Partisi*–ATP), led by Tuğrul TÜRKEŞ, and the **National Unity Party** (*Ulusal Birlik Partisi*–UBP), led by Fehmi KURAL, reportedly compete to attract former MHP dissidents. Among other parties are **My Turkey Party** (*Türkiyem Partisi*), led by Durmuş Ali EKER; **Our Existence Party** (*Varlığımız Partisi*), led by Köksal SATIR; the **Turkey is Happy with Her Handicapped Party** (*Türkiye Özürlüsüyle Mutludur Partisi*), organized to defend the rights of the disabled; and the **Party of Land** (*Yurt Partisi*–YP), an ANAP breakaway formation led by former minister Sadettin TANTAN.

The **Revolutionary Workers' Party** (*Devrimci İşçi Partisi*–DİP); the **Revolutionary Socialist Workers 'Party** (*Devrimci Sosyalist İşçi Partisi*–DSİP), led by Doğan TARKAN and Ahmet YILDIRIM; the **Turkish Socialist Workers 'Party** (*Türkiye Sosyalist İşçi Partisi*–TSİP), led by Mehmet SÜMBÜL; and the **Socialist Democracy Party** (*Sosyalist Demokrasi Partisi*–SDP), a breakaway formation from ÖDP (above), led by Filiz Koçali, are all minor Marxist formations. In January 1999 a group of former HADEP members launched the

Democratic People's Party (*Demokratik Halk Partisi*–DHP) as a new pro-Kurdish grouping. In late 2001 another pro-Kurdish formation, the **Party of Rights and Liberties** (*Hakve Özgürlükler Partisi*–HAK-PAR) was launched by Abdülmerik FIRAT. Other minor center-left formations include the **Equality Party** (*Eşitlik Partisi*); the **Party for Independent Republic** (*Bağımsız Cumhuriyet Partisi*), led by former Foreign Minister Mümtaz SOYSAL; the **Social Democrat Party** (*Sosyal Demokrat Parti*); the **Party of Turkey in Change** (*Değişen Türkiye Partisi*–DEPAR), led by a former DSP deputy Gökhan ÇAPOĞLU; the **Republican Democracy Party** (*Cumhuriyetçi Demokrasi Partisi*–CDP), led by Yekta Güngör ÖZDEN; and the **Social-Democrat People's Party** (*Sosyaldemokrat Halk Partisi*–SHP), launched by former Deputy Prime Minister Murat KARAYALÇIN in the hopes of reclaiming the historical legacy of an earlier formation of a similar name (see SHP, above).

Extremist Groups

Pre-1980 extremist and terrorist groups included the leftist **Revolutionary Path** (*Devrimci Yol*–Dev-Yol) and its more radical offshoot, the **Revolutionary Left** (Dev-Sol, below), both derived from the **Revolutionary Youth** (*Dev Genç*), which operated in the late 1960s and early 1970s; some of its members also joined the far leftist **Turkish People's Salvation Army** (*Türkiye Halk Kurtuluş Ordusu*–THKO). The **Turkish People's Liberation Party Front** (*Türkiye Halk Kurtuluş Partisi-Cephesi*–THKP-C), the **Turkish Workers' and Peasants' Liberation Army** (*Türkiye İşçi Köylü Kurtuluş Ordusu*–TİKKO, below), and the **Kurdistan Workers' Party** (PKK, below) all experienced numerous arrests–often leading to executions-of members. In addition, Armenian guerrilla units, composed almost entirely of non-nationals, variously operated as the Secret Army for the Liberation of Armenia (Asala), including a so-called Orly Group; the Justice Commandos for the Armenian Genocide; the Pierre Gulmian Commando; the Levon Ekmekçiyan Suicide Commando; and the Armenian Revolutionary Army. The activities of many of these groups have subsided, notable exceptions being Dev-Sol and the PKK.

Revolutionary Left (*Devrimci Sol*–Dev-Sol). Organized in 1978, Dev-Sol appeared to have retained its organizational vitality after the 1980 crackdown, although many of its subsequent activities took the form of interfactional struggle. Its founder, Dursun KARATAŞ, who had been given a death sentence in absentia that was later commuted to life imprisonment, was arrested by French authorities on September 9, 1994; subsequently, the group claimed responsibility for the murder on September 29 of a hard-line former justice minister, Mehmet TOPAÇ.

In 1993 or earlier Dev-Sol apparently split into two factions, the "Karataş" and the "Yağan" wings, with the former emerging in March 1994 as the **Revolutionary People's Liberation Party-Front** (*Devrimci Halk Kurtuluş Partisi-Cephesi*–DHKP-C). Violent clashes between the two factions have been reported in a number of European countries, and in August 1998 Germany banned both. DHKP-C militants were active in organizing the hunger strikes and prison riots since December 2000.

Kurdistan Workers' Party (*Partîya Karkerén Kurdistan*–PKK). Founded in 1978, the PKK, under the leadership of Abdullah (Apo) Öcalan, was for a long time based principally in Lebanon's Bekaa Valley and northern Iraq. In southeast Anatolia, where it continues to maintain a presence, the party's 1992 call for a general uprising on March 21, the Kurdish New Year (Nevruz), was generally unheeded. Subsequently, a unilateral cease-fire declared by Öcalan under pressure from northern Iraq Kurdish leaders proved short-lived, and PKK terrorism reescalated. In late July 1994 Turkish warplanes reportedly completely destroyed a PKK base in northern Iraq, and in mid-August a London court convicted three separatists of a number of attacks on Turkish property in the United Kingdom. Öcalan thereupon reiterated his call for a cease-fire as a prelude to the adoption of constitutional reforms that would acknowledge the "Kurdish identity." The government again failed to respond and in September charged the PKK with responsibility for the killing of a number of Turkish teachers in the southeastern province of Tunceli. Government military offensives against the Kurdish insurgents in 1995–1996 were combined with efforts to eradicate the PKK party organization.

Through 1997 and 1998 extensive Turkish military operations seriously undermined the PKK's ground forces. On April 13, 1998, the PKK's second-highest ranking commander, Şemdin SAKIK, who had left the organization a month earlier, was captured in northern Iraq by Turkish security forces. But the major blow to the organization was without doubt Party Chairman Öcalan's arrest by Turkish commandos in Nairobi, Kenya (see under Foreign relations, and Current issues, above), in February 1999. The commander of the PKK's armed wing, People's Liberation Army of Kurdistan (ARGK), Ceril BAYIK, had reportedly threatened Turkish authorities and foreign tourists on March 15, claiming that the whole of Anatolia "is now a battlefield." Some sources also reported a leadership struggle between Bayik and Abdullah Öcalan's brother, Osman ÖCALAN.

From February to July 1999 Kurdish militants engaged in various attacks, including suicide bombings, in response to their leader's arrest. A State Security Court accused Öcalan of being responsible for 30,000 deaths between 1984–1999. He was found guilty of treason and sentenced to death on June 29. During his defense, Öcalan argued that he could "stop the war" if the Turkish state would let him "work for peace" and spare his life. He apologized for the "sufferings PKK's actions may have caused," claiming that the "armed struggle had fulfilled its aims" and that the PKK would now "work for a democratic Turkey, where Kurds will enjoy cultural and linguistic rights." On August 2, Öcalan called on his organization to stop fighting and leave Turkish territory starting September 1. The PKK's "Presidential Council" quickly announced that it would follow their leader's

commands, and during the PKK's congress in February 2000, it was announced that the party's political and armed wings would merge into a front organization called the People's Democratic Union of Kurdistan. Some analysts argued that the decision was in line with the PKK's decision to stop its armed struggle and seek Kurdish political and cultural rights within the framework of Turkey's integration with the European Union. In 2001 a small group of renegade PKK members launched the Kurdistan Workers' Party-Revolutionary Line Fighters (*Partîya Karkerén Kurdistan-Devrimci Çizgi Savaşçıları*–PKK-DÇS) with the expressed aim to continue the armed struggle. In April 2002 the PKK decided to dissolve itself (announcing it had fulfilled its "historical mission") to launch a new organization called the Kurdistan Freedom and Democracy Congress (*Kongreya Azadî û Demokrasiya Kurdistan*–KADEK). The KADEK claimed to be against armed struggle, to have rejected fighting for an independent Kurdish homeland, and to have espoused a "political" line to press for cultural and linguistic rights for Turkey's Kurds as "full and equal members under a democratic and united Turkey." However, in May the EU announced it still considered the PKK a "terrorist organization." The Turkish government continued to claim that the PKK's transformation into KADEK was a "tactical ploy."

In September 2003, KADEK was restyled as the Peoples' Congress of Kurdistan (*Kongra Gelê Kurdistan*–Kongra-Gel). Several high-level defections occurred in the ranks, including that of Osman ÖCALAN, who reportedly joined a splinter group, the Democratic Solution Party of Kurdistan (*Partiya Welatparézén Demokratén Kurdistan*–PWDK) that was established in April 2004. In June 2004, Kongra-Gel announced that the cease-fire declared by Abdullah Öcalan in September 1999 was not respected by the Republic of Turkey and that they would return to "legitimate armed defense" to counter military operations against their "units." In April 2005 it was announced that PKK was reconstituted and the new formation was styled as the PKK–Kongra-Gel. Since the announcements, numerous sporadic clashes have been reported between the Turkish security forces and PKK–Kongra-Gel's armed wing, People's Defense Forces (*Hezen Parastina Gel*–HPG).

Since March 2005, a hitherto unknown group called "Kurdistan Freedom Falcons" (*Teyrêbazên Azadiya Kurdistan* –TAK) has taken responsibility for numerous car bomb explosions and other urban terrorist acts. Although some press reports argued TAK was one among many out-of-control wings of PKK–Kongra-Gel, the organization quickly denounced any links with the group.

Leaders:Abdullah ÖCALAN (Honorary President), Zübeyir AYDAR (President), Murat KARAYILAN (Chair of the Executive Council).

Other extreme left groupings include the **Communist Party of Turkey-Marxist Leninist** (*Türkiye Komünist Partisi-Marksist-Leninist*–TKP-ML) and its armed wing, the **Turkish Workers' and Peasants' Liberation Army** (*Türkiye İşçi Köylü Kurtuluş Ordusu*–TİKKO), which claimed responsibility for an attack on a police bus at İstanbul in December 2000 in retaliation for government action to break the prison hunger strikes; and the **Communist Labor Party of Turkey-Leninist** (*Türkiye Komünist Emek Partisi-Leninist*–TKEP-L).

On January 17, 2000, Hüseyin VELİOĞLU, reportedly a leader of the **Party of God** (*Hizbullah,* a militant Islamist Sunni group unrelated to the Lebanon-based Shi'ite *Hezbollah*) was killed and two of his associates were arrested in a shootout with police in İstanbul. The event brought attention to the group, which was believed to have been particularly active in southeast Anatolia in the early 1990s, when *Hizbullah* had reportedly launched a campaign of violence against PKK militants and pro-Kurdish lawyers, intellectuals, and human rights activists. Some unconfirmed press reports claimed that the group members were tolerated if not encouraged by the state security forces, which allegedly explained the fact that none of its members were caught until the shoot-out. During the months of January and February 2000, police

arrested over 400 alleged members of *Hizbullah,* some reportedly civil servants. State security forces also found several safe-houses of the group where they reportedly recovered mutilated bodies of dozens of victims, including famous moderate Islamic feminist Konca KURİŞ, who was kidnapped in July 1998.

On February 10, 2000, the **Great Eastern Islamic Raiders-Front** (*İslami Büyük Doğu Akıncıları-Cephesi*–BDA-C) claimed responsibility for four bomb attacks in İstanbul. The militant Islamist group had previously been accused of masterminding the mob attack on a hotel that left 36 people dead, including many famous leftist and secularist intellectuals and musicians, during a cultural festival in a central Anatolian town, Sivas, on July 2, 1992.

On May 7, 2000, Turkish authorities announced that they had apprehended those responsible for the murder of the former foreign minister and secularist professor, Ahmet Taner Kışlalı, killed on October 21, 1999. Turkish police claimed that those arrested were members of a hitherto unknown militant Islamist group, **Unity** (*Tevhid*), and were also responsible for the murders several years ago of famous leftist newspaper columnist Uğur Mumcu and academician Bahriye Üçok.

Following the arrest of PKK leader Abdullah Öcalan in February 1999, a shadowy far-right group, **Turkish Avenger Brigade** (*Türk İntikam Tugayı*–TİT), issued death threats against pro-Kurdish activists and politicians, and claimed responsibility for attacks on various HADEP buildings. Some unconfirmed reports suggest that the group is merely a facade for occasional "agent-provocateur" activities allegedly linked to factions within the Turkish security forces.

Legislature

The 1982 constitution replaced the former bicameral legislature with a unicameral **Turkish Grand National Assembly** (*Türkiye Büyük Millet Meclisi*) elected for a five-year term on a proportional basis (10 percent threshold).

Cabinet

As of July, 29 2005

Prime Minister	Recep Tayyip Erdogan
Deputy Prime Minister and Minister of Foreign Affairs	Abdulla Gül
Deputy Prime Minister and State Minister	Abdüllatif Şener
Deputy Prime Minister and State Minister	Mehmet Ali Şahin
State Minister	Beşir Atalay
State Minister	Mehmet Aydin
State Minister	Ali Babacan
State Minister	Kürşad Tüzmen
State Minister	Nimet Çubukçu [f]

Ministers

Agriculture and Village Affairs	Mehmet Mehdi Eker
Culture and Tourism	Atilla Koç
Energy and Natural Resources	Mehmet Hilmi Güler
Environment and Forestry	Osman Pepe
Finance	Kemal Unakitan
Health	Recep Akdağ
Industry and Trade	Ali Coşkun
Interior	Abdülkadir Aksu
Justice	Cemil Çiçek
Labor and Social Security	Murat Başesgioğlu
National Defense	Mehmet Vecdi Gönül
National Education	Hüseyin Çelik
Public Works and Housing	Faruk Nafiz Özak
Transport	Binali Yıldırım

All ministers are members of the Justice and Development Party (AKP)

[f] = female

After the general election of November 2002, the seat distribution was: Justice and Development Party, 363; Republican People's Party, 178.

Speaker: Bülent ARINÇ.

Communications

Formal censorship of the media in regard to security matters was imposed in late 1979 and was expanded under the military regime installed in September 1980. A new press law promulgated in November 1982 gave public prosecutors the right to confiscate any publication prior to sale, permitted the government to ban foreign publications deemed to be "a danger to the unity of the country," and made journalists and publishers liable for the issuance of "subversive" material. However, freedom of the press was largely restored in the first half of the 1990s. On July 21, 1997, the Council of Ministers accepted a draft granting amnesty to imprisoned journalists. Under current law, however, journalists still face prosecution and imprisonment for reporting on issues deemed sensitive by the government.

Press

The following are dailies published at İstanbul: *Posta* (680,000), populist; *Hürriyet* (540,000), centrist; *Sabah* (465,000), centrist; *Zaman* (444,000), conservative; *Fanatik* (330,000), sports; *Takvim* (294,000), populist; *Pas Fotomac* (280,000), sports; *Milliyet* (240,000), centrist; *Vatan* (230,000), centrist; *Türkiye* (215,000), conservative; *Akşam* (210,000), conservative; *Güneş* (130,000), populist; *Gözcü* (125,000), sensationalist; *Star* (105,000), populist; *Yeni Şafak* (100,000), moderate religious, pro-AKP; *Dünden Bugüne Tercüman* (98,000), conservative; *Şok* (75,000), sensationalist; *Andolu'da Vakit* (69,000), radical-religious; *Cumhuriyet* (58,000), center left, secularist; *Yeniçağ* (56,000), far-right; *Milli Gazete* (50,000), conservative-religious pro-SP); *Radikal* (41,000), liberal; *Bulvar* (36,000 , sensationalist; *Halka ve Olaylara Tercüman* (29,000), conservative Birgün (14,000), left-wing; *Ülkede Özgür Gündem* (12,000), pro-Kurdish, pro-DEHA *Ortadoğu* (10,000), far-right, pro-MHP; *Referans* (10,000), finance and economics; *Yeni Asya* (7,500), conservative-religious; *Önce Vatan* (6,500), nationalist; *Günluk Evrensel* (5,500), far-left, pro-EMEP; *Yeni Mesaj* (3,500), far-right, pro-MHP; *Dünya* (2,500), finance and economics; *Hürses* (1,500), finance and economics.

Non-Turkish-language publications include *Jamanak* (daily) and *Nor Marmara* (daily) in Armenian; *Agos* (weekly) in Turkish and Armenian; *Turkish Daily News* (daily) and *The New Anatolian* (daily) in English, *Apoyevmatini* (bi-weekly) in Greek; *Azadiya Welat* (bimonthly), and *Zend* (monthly) in Kurdish; an *Şalom* (weekly) Sephardic Jewish/ Ladino and Turkish.

News Agencies

The leading news source is the government-owned Anatolian News Agency (*Anadolu Ajansı–AA*). Virtually all of the leading international agencies maintain Ankara bureaus.

Broadcasting and Computing

The state-controlled Turkish Radio Television Corporation (*Türkiye Radyo Televizyon Kurumu–TRT*) currently offers domestic service over several radio networks and television channels. In April 1992 a TRT International Channel (Avrasya) began broadcasting via satellite to an area from Germany to Central Asia, earning third place in international transmission after CNN International and BBC International. In July 1993 a constitutional amendment formally abolished the state broadcast monopoly. In 1994 a Higher Council of Radio and Television (*Radyo Televizyon Üst Kurulu–RTÜK*) was established to oversee all radio and television emissions and programming. The appointed body reports to the prime minister and has the authority to license and shut down radio and television stations for up to a year on the grounds of such offenses as libel and the transmission of "offensive" or "hate-inciting" programs. The council has closed down numerous radio and television stations since its inception and has been widely criticized for using vague criteria that reportedly amount to censorship. There were approximately 26.7 million television receivers and 3.5 million personal computers serving 5.5 million Internet users in 2003.

Intergovernmental Representation

Ambassador to the US
Osman Faruk LOGOGLU

US Ambassador to Turkey
Eric S. EDELMAN

Permanent Representative to the UN
Baki İLKIN

IGO Memberships (Non-UN)
ADB, BIS, BSEC, CCC, CEUR, ECO, EBRD, Eurocontrol, IDB, IEA, Interpol, IOM, NATO, OECD, OIC, OSCE, PCA, *WEU,* WTO

UNITED ARAB EMIRATES

AL-IMARAT AL-'ARABIYAH AL-MUTTAHIDA

The Country

Formerly known as the Trucial States because of truces concluded with Britain in the 19th century, the United Arab Emirates extends some 400 miles along the Persian Gulf from the southeastern end of the Qatar peninsula to a point just short of Ras Musandam. It encompasses a barren, relatively flat territory characterized by extreme temperatures and sparse rainfall. The majority of the indigenous population is Arab and adheres to the Sunni sect of Islam; there are also significant numbers of Iranians, Indians, Pakistanis, Baluchis, and descendants of former African slaves among the noncitizen population. It was estimated in 2003 that non-national workers, numbering about 1.7 million, represented 90 percent of the workforce. Although Arabic is the official language, English, Persian, and Hindi are also spoken.

Traditionally, the area was dependent upon trading, fishing, and pearling; however, the discovery in 1958 of major oil reserves in Abu Dhabi and subsequently of smaller deposits in Dubai and Sharjah dramatically altered the economy. Oil wealth led to rapid infrastructural modernization, advances in education and health services, and a construction boom requiring a massive inflow of foreign labor. New industrial cities established at Jebel Ali in Dubai and Ruwais in Abu Dhabi gave rise to shipyards, cement factories, and other manufacturing sites. During the 1980s, on the other hand, the UAE experienced a slowdown in economic growth. At the beginning of the decade it had the world's highest gross national product (GNP) per capita, nearly $28,000; by 1988 the figure had dropped to less than $15,000 because of declining export revenue. As a result, the government moved to streamline

the petroleum industry, which continued to account for 70 percent of government income, and began developing downstream (marketing, refining, and petrochemical) aspects of the oil trade. Partly because of these efforts, per capita GNP has recovered to more than $22,000.

In addition to its vast oil capacity—reserves are estimated at more than 97.8 billion barrels, approximately 8 percent of the world's total—the UAE possesses one of the largest reservoirs of natural gas in the world. The government controls 60 percent of the energy sector, although, unlike several Gulf neighbors, it has permitted partial foreign ownership, thereby maintaining links with Western companies that have provided important ongoing infrastructure support. Moreover, the nation has firmly established itself as the region's leading trading center, partly on the strength of the Jebel Ali

Free Trade Zone, where more than 350 companies operate. Dubai, in particular, has been effectively promoted in recent years as the region's trading and financial "hub." Successful diversification efforts have also contributed to rapid economic growth. On a less positive note, pervasive aspects of Western culture have been criticized by conservative elements, who have attempted to "preserve" Islamic traditions through stricter imposition of Islamic law (*shari'a*) and policies designed to reduce dependence on foreign workers. GDP rose by 15 percent in 2004 over the previous year, and projected growth for 2005 was expected to be 5.7 percent. Increasing oil revenues and investments in the building and manufacturing sectors are major reasons behind the booming economy. The Emirates also boasted in 2005 of having 52,800 millionaires.

Government and Politics

Political Background

Originally controlling an area known in the West as a refuge for pirates, some sheikhs of the eastern Persian Gulf entered into agreements with the British in the early 19th century. After the failure of the initial treaty agreements of 1820 and 1835, a Perpetual Maritime Truce was signed in 1853. Relations with Britain were further strengthened by an Exclusive Agreement of 1892, whereby the sheikhs agreed not to enter into diplomatic or other foreign relations with countries other than Britain. In return, Britain guaranteed defense of the sheikhdoms against aggression by sea.

The treaty arrangements with Britain lasted until 1968, when the British announced their intention to withdraw from the Persian Gulf by 1971. An early attempt at unification, the Federation of Arab Emirates, was initiated in 1968 with British encouragement but collapsed when Bahrain and Qatar declared separate independence in 1971. Subsequently, the leaders of the Trucial States organized a new grouping, the United Arab Emirates, which was formally constituted as an independent state on December 2, 1971, with Sheikh Zayed ibn Sultan Al NUHAYYAN as president; Ras

al-Khaima, which initially rejected membership, acceded to the UAE two months later.

Apart from the death of Sheikh Khalid ibn Muhammad al-QASIMI (ruler of Sharjah) following an attempted coup in 1972, few major political developments occurred until the spring of 1979, when a series of disputes, principally between Abu Dhabi and Dubai over the extent of federal powers, led to the April 25 resignation of Prime Minister Sheikh Maktum ibn Rashid Al MAKTUM and his replacement five days later by his father, Sheikh Rashid ibn Sa'id Al MAKTUM, ruler of Dubai, who retained his position as vice president. In 1981 the emirs of 'Ajman, Sheikh Rashid ibn Humayd al-NU'AYMI, and of Umm al-Qaiwain, Sheikh Ahmad ibn Rashid al-MU'ALLA, both of whom had ruled for more than 50 years, died and were succeeded by their sons, Sheikh Humayd ibn Rashid al-NU'AYMI and Sheikh Rashid ibn Ahmad al-MU'ALLA, respectively.

On June 17, 1987, Sheikh 'Abd al-Aziz al-QASIMI seized power in Sharjah, accusing his brother Sheikh Sultan ibn Muhammad al-QASIMI of fiscal mismanagement. On July 20 Sheikh Muhammad was reinstated by the Supreme Council, which decreed that Sheikh 'Abd al-Aziz should thenceforth hold the title of crown prince and deputy ruler; however, he was stripped of the title on February 4, 1990.

Following the death of Sheikh Rashid ibn Sa'id Al Maktum on October 7, 1990, his son Sheikh Maktum ibn Rashid was named vice president and returned to his former position as prime minister.

In 1991 the UAE suffered a major blow to its international prestige by the collapse at mid year of the Luxembourg-chartered Bank of Credit and Commerce International (BCCI), 77 percent of whose shares were owned by President Zayed and a group of financial associates. The bank, originally founded in 1972 by Agha Hassan ABEDI, a Pakistani entrepreneur, had previously acknowledged the loss of more than $500 million in the wake of money-laundering charges by US authorities. It was seized in a coordinated action by bank regulators in seven countries on July 5, after the Bank of England had released evidence of

Political Status: Federation of six former Trucial States (Abu Dhabi, Dubai, Sharjah, Fujaira, 'Ajman, and Umm al-Qaiwain) established December 2, 1971; the seventh, Ras al-Khaima, joined in 1972.

Area: 32,278 sq. mi. (83,600 sq. km.).

Population: 2,377,453 (1995C), embracing Abu Dhabi (928,360), Dubai (674,100), Sharjah (400,400), Ras al-Khaima (164,930), 'Ajman (89,962), Fujaira (78,716), and Umm al-Qaiwain (41,232); 4,317,000 (2004E). Figures include noncitizens, who in 1995 represented approximately three-quarters of the population.

Major Urban Center (2002E): ABU DHABI (527,000). (The "interim" constitution of 1971 had designated Abu Dhabi as the "provisional" capital, plans being approved concurrently for construction of a permanent capital at Karama on the border of Abu Dhabi and Dubai, the two largest emirates. No action was ever taken regarding the Karama site, however, and constitutional amendments approved in 1996 formally declared Abu Dhabi to be the permanent capital.)

Official Language: Arabic.

Monetary Unit: Dirham (official rate July 1, 2005: 3.67 dirhams = $1US).

Supreme Council: Composed of the rulers of the seven emirates (with dates of accession): Sheikh Khalifa ibn Zayed Al NUHAYYAN (Abu Dhabi, 2004), Sheikh Maktum ibn Rashid Al MAKTUM (Dubai, 1990), Sheikh Sultan ibn Muhammad al-QASIMI (Sharjah, 1972), Sheikh Saqr ibn Muhammad al-QASIMI (Ras al-Khaima, 1948), Sheikh Hamad ibn Muhammad al-SHARQI (Fujaira, 1974), Sheikh Humayd ibn Rashid al-NU'AYMI ('Ajman, 1981), and Sheikh Rashid ibn Ahmad al-MU'ALLA (Umm al-Qaiwain, 1981).

President: Sheikh Khalifa ibn Zayed Al NUHAYYAN (Ruler of Abu Dhabi); succeeding his father, the first president of the union, Sheikh Zayed ibn Sultan Al NUHAYYAN, who died in office on November 2, 2004. Sheikh Zayed was elected by the six original emirs to a five-year term on December 2, 1971; reelected to five-year terms in 1976, 1981, 1986, 1991, 1996, and on December 2, 2001.

Vice President and Prime Minister: Sheikh Maktum ibn Rashid Al MAKTUM (Ruler of Dubai); named vice president and prime minister by the Supreme Council on November 20, 1990, succeeding his father, Sheikh Rashid ibn Sa'id Al MAKTUM, who died on October 7; reappointed on March 25, 1997, and December 2, 2001.

widespread fraud over a period of several years. Subsequently, it was revealed that Sheikh Zayed had provided at least $1 billion to shore up the troubled institution since 1989. In early 1994 it was reported that a $1.5-billion lawsuit against Zayed had been dropped in the United States after the UAE agreed to give US investigators access to Mohammed Swaleh NAQVI, Abedi's "deputy" at BCCI. Naqvi was extradited to the United States later in the year, shortly before he and Abedi, residing in Pakistan and reportedly suffering from a stroke, were sentenced in absentia to prison terms by a UAE court. A plan was approved in December 1995 under which BCCI creditors would be reimbursed a total of $1.8 billion by the bank's major shareholders, observers estimating the paybacks would cover 20 to 40 percent of most deposits. BCCI was formally liquidated by the UAE Central Bank in February 1996. Negotiations continued with the Abu Dhabi government, and as of 2003 $5.7 billion had been authorized in paybacks to BCCI creditors, total claims having been estimated at $9 billion among some 80,000 depositors. The case went to court in London in January 2004.

The UAE cabinet submitted its resignation on March 17, 1997, and Sheikh Maktum was asked to form a new government, which was announced on March 25. The president and vice president were reelected to their posts by the Supreme Council on December 2, 2001. The first cabinet shuffle since 1997 took place on November 1, 2004, as decreed by President Zayed one day before he died. Among the new cabinet members was the first woman minister, a move in line with a policy to involve more women in decision making.

Constitution and Government

The institutions of the UAE were superimposed upon the existing political structures of the member states, which generally maintain their monarchical character. (Effective power within the federation remains in the hands of senior members of the ruling families of the seven emirates, led by Abu Dhabi, by far the most oil-rich emirate, and, to a lesser extent, Dubai, a major business center.) Under the federal constitution adopted in 1971 (designated an "interim" basic law until 1996), the rulers of the constituent states are members of the Supreme Council, which elects a president and vice president for five-year terms. Supreme Council decrees require the approval of the rulers of Abu Dhabi and Dubai and at least three other emirates. The president appoints a prime minister and a cabinet, and the consultative Federal National Council consists of delegates appointed by the various rulers. In July 1976 the Federal National Council, following a failure to reach agreement on a new constitutional draft, voted to extend the life of the existing constitution for another five years beyond December 2. Further extensions were voted at five-year intervals thereafter until 1996, when the Supreme Council (May 20) and the Federal National Council (June 18) approved an amendment removing "interim" from the language in the constitution, thereby effectively making it a permanent document.

Judicial functions have traditionally been performed by local courts applying Islamic law (*shari'a*) and by individual decisions rendered by the ruling families. In June 1978 the president signed a law establishing four Primary Federal Tribunals (in Abu Dhabi, 'Ajman, Fujaira, and Sharjah) to handle disputes between individuals and the federation, with appeal to the federal Supreme Court. However, a later decree of February 1994 specified that a variety of crimes (including murder, theft, adultery, and juvenile and drug-related offenses) would be tried in Islamic, rather than civil, courts. The basic administrative divisions are the constituent states, each of which retains local control over mineral rights, taxation, and police protection. Abu Dhabi effectively controls the UAE's 65,000-member federal army. Dubai has maintained its own force of some 15,000 soldiers since federation, although it announced plans in 1997 to merge its central military command with the UAE forces.

Foreign Relations

The United Arab Emirates is a member of the United Nations, the Arab League, OPEC, and various regional groupings. Relations have been cordial with most countries, including the United States, although there have been territorial disputes with Iran, Oman, Qatar, and Saudi Arabia.

In 1971 Iran occupied Abu Musa, a small island in the Persian Gulf, and laid claim to the Greater and Lesser Tunbs, two uninhabited but potentially strategically important islands (see map). Soon after, an agreement was reached between Teheran and the emir of Sharjah that provided for joint administration of Abu Musa and the sharing of revenue from offshore oil wells. However, no accord was reached regarding the Tunbs (claimed by Ras al-Khaima). Following the establishment of diplomatic relations between Iran and the UAE in 1972, the issue remained relatively dormant with an occasional flare up.

A dispute with Saudi Arabia and Oman concerned portions of Abu Dhabi, including the potentially oil-rich Buraimi Oasis, located at the juncture of the three states. Under the terms of an agreement reached in 1974, six villages of the oasis were awarded to Abu Dhabi and two to Oman; Saudi Arabia, in return for renouncing its claim, was granted a land corridor coterminous with the existing Abu Dhabi–Qatar border to the Persian Gulf port of Khor al-Adad. The border demarcation issue resurfaced in September 1992 in the form of a clash between Saudi Arabian and Qatari forces (see Qatar: Foreign relations). In June 2002 Oman and the UAE implemented an agreement to demarcate their border.

In early 1981 the UAE joined with five neighbors—Bahrain, Kuwait, Oman, Qatar, and Saudi Arabia—in establishing the Cooperative Council of the Arab Gulf States (more commonly known as the Gulf Cooperation Council–GCC) as a means of coordinating members' policies bearing on security and stability in the area. Concern over the Iran–Iraq war led the UAE to participate in the GCC's annual Peninsula Shield joint military maneuvers. Although the hazards of the regional conflict did not preclude an increase in trade with Teheran, the UAE and the other GCC states became increasingly aware of their vulnerability to possible Iranian aggression and to the potentially destabilizing effects of an Iranian-inspired Islamic revolution; thus, during a December 1987 GCC summit at Riyadh, Saudi Arabia, discussion centered on negotiations with Egypt for military aid and support. Meanwhile, in the wake of oilfield bombings by the Gulf combatants, including one by unidentified aircraft that killed eight people and destroyed two of five platforms in Abu Dhabi, the UAE took steps to purchase advance-warning systems from Britain, France, and the United States.

The UAE reacted nervously to Iraq's occupation of Kuwait on August 2, 1990, because it, like Kuwait, had been charged by Baghdad with overproduction of oil. On August 19, having joined with other GCC governments in calling for Iraq's withdrawal, the UAE agreed to the deployment of foreign military units on its soil; it also cooperated with coalition forces during the confrontation that concluded with Iraq's defeat in February 1991. In April it was reported that the UAE had contributed nearly $3 billion to US Gulf War costs.

With Iraqi belligerence still appearing to present a challenge to regional security, the Gulf states attempted to improve relations with Iran, the UAE in July 1991 naming its first ambassador to Teheran since the latter's 1979 revolution. However, in early 1992 Iran reignited the long-dormant Gulf dispute between the two nations by expelling some 700 UAE nationals from Abu Musa and seizing complete control of the island. After the GCC demanded in September that Iran repudiate its "annexation" of Abu Musa, Teheran reasserted its claim of sovereignty over the island as well as over the Greater and Lesser Tunbs, vowing that UAE forces would have to cross a "sea of blood" to retake the territory. Although the UAE subsequently sought international mediation of the dispute, Iran rejected the proposal, and tension between the countries continued. The UAE at the same time continued to lead efforts to "rehabilitate" the regime of Saddam Hussein, in part with an eye on future economic ties with Baghdad, and in April 2000 the UAE's embassy at Baghdad was reopened. In March 2003, the president offered a vague plan for Hussein's permanent exile, defying the Arab League stance on noninterference in the internal affairs of a neighboring country. After the US invasion and occupation of Iraq, the UAE was among the first countries to send relief shipments, and it continues to provide humanitarian aid, including building a desalination plant and equipping Iraqi hospitals.

In July 1994 the UAE became the fourth GCC country to conclude a military cooperation pact with the United States. The agreement, which provides for joint military exercises and the stationing of a US naval task force on UAE territory, was reportedly entered into because of the Emirates' vulnerability to attack by both Iran and Iraq. In November 2004 the commander of US Central Command called US–UAE military cooperation among the strongest in the region. France's defense minister expressed similar sentiments in April 2004. The United Kingdom in 2005 announced its commitment to developing military and industrial cooperation with the Emirates as well.

As did its GCC neighbors, the UAE expressed concern in the 1990s over the security implications of growing Islamist militancy in North Africa and the Middle East. Following years of political violence in the region, the cabinet decided in June 2005 to formally fight against terrorism. The move calls for specific punishments for people who organize, commit, finance, or contribute to terrorist acts.

Money laundering and smuggling have long been troublesome issues in the Emirates (see Current issues, below) and were among the topics addressed by GCC members in June 2005. At least two senior *al-Qaeda* operatives have been arrested since 2002.

The UAE historically has objected to the slow pace of progress in the Middle East peace process, joining a number of other Arab countries in boycotting a regional economic development conference in November 1997 to protest what it perceived as an inappropriate US tilt toward Israel at the expense of the Palestinian cause. The UAE has also adopted a strongly pro-Palestinian, pro-Arab stance regarding the future status of Jerusalem, a major sticking point in the Israeli–Palestinian impasse. The late President Zayed was a major supporter of the Palestinian people and contributed heavily to housing projects in Gaza. In May 2005 reports surfaced from Jerusalem that Israel planned to soon open an "economic interest section" in Dubai, but UAE officials denied any such possibility. The two countries have never had an official relationship.

Current Issues

Attention in the late 1990s focused on the allocation of what was expected to be up to $10 billion in new weapons and military supplies. The United States, France, and the United Kingdom—all of whom had negotiated defense pacts with the UAE (as required by the UAE government for countries to be considered as potential arms suppliers)—were particularly anxious about the upcoming deals. In March 2000 the UAE, as part of its ambitious defense program, signed a contract with the US-based Lockheed Martin Corporation worth $6.4 billion for 80 F-16 fighters, having previously concluded a deal in 1998 for $3.5 billion of French planes. Washington had initially objected to the inclusion of certain components that had previously only been shared with members of the North Atlantic Treaty Organization [NATO]. The first delivery of the US planes was to have been in 2004, with the remainder delivered by 2007.

In March 2000 the UAE announced plans to spearhead an $8-billion regional gas network in conjunction with other GCC members as well as Western energy companies, including US-based Enron and the French–Belgian firm Total Fina Elf. As a first stage of the 25-year project, Abu Dhabi negotiated a $3.5-billion agreement to develop gas fields in Qatar and ship gas from there initially to the other emirates and Gulf states such as Oman and eventually to India and Pakistan. The project, the first such cross-border arrangement in GCC history, was considered an important element in establishing the UAE as the hub of a regional "energy security" network. At the same time, however, it brought increasing pressure from the international community on the UAE to establish procedures to ensure greater transparency and accountability in its financial sector. Critics have charged that long-standing secrecy has contributed to UAE banks being used for money laundering, while lack of oversight of business dealings has permitted unnoticed transshipment of drugs and illegal weapons through UAE ports. The UAE's banking system and financial practices were further criticized after the September 2001 attacks in the United States when it became evident that close associates of Osama bin LADEN had used the country's banks to transfer and receive money from several of the hijackers. Promising reform, the UAE in January 2002 adopted a series of policy changes to monitor banking practices and financial transactions more closely and instituted new penalties to combat money laundering. In June 2005 the UAE joined the UN Convention Against Transnational Organized Crime, it being especially concerned about money laundering, terrorism, and drug trafficking. As of April 1, 2003, the UAE Central Bank has required *hawala* (informal money transfer) operators to register and provide details of transactions.

Following the attacks on the United States in September 2001, the UAE agreed to cooperate closely with the Bush administration's "war on terrorism." Among other measures, the UAE severed diplomatic relations with the Taliban administration in Afghanistan after it refused to hand over Osama bin Laden. (The UAE had been one

Cabinet

As of July 12, 2005

Prime Minister and Vice President	Sheikh Maktum ibn Rashid Al Maktum
Deputy Prime Minister	Sultan ibn Zayed Al Nuhayyan
Deputy Prime Minister	Sheikh Hamdan ibn Zayed Al Nuhayyan

Ministers

Agriculture and Fisheries	Sa'id Muhammad al-Raqabani
Communications	Sultan ibn Sa'id al-Mansouri
Defense	Gen. Sheikh Muhammad ibn Rashid ibn Sa'id al-Maktum
Economy and Planning	Shaikha Lubna al-Qasimi [f]
Education	Sheikh Nuhayyan ibn Mubarak Al Nuhayyan
Energy	Muhammad ibn Zaen al-Hamili
Finance and Industry	Sheikh Hamdan ibn Rashid ibn Sa'id Al Maktum
Foreign Affairs	Rashid ibn 'Abdallah al-Nu'aymi
Health	Hamad ibn 'Abd al-Rahman al-Madfa
Information and Culture	Sheikh 'Abdallah ibn Zayed Al Nuhayyan
Interior	Lt. Gen. Sheikh Saif ibn Zayed Al Nuhayyan
Justice, Islamic Affairs, and Religious Endowments	Muhammad Nakhira al-Dhahiri
Labor and Social Affairs	Ali ibn 'Abdallah al-Ka'abi
Presidential Affairs	Sheikh Mansur ibn Zayed Al Nuhayyan
Public Works	Sheikh Hamdan ibn Mubarak Al Nuhayyan
Supreme Council and Gulf Cooperation Council Affairs	Sheikh Fahim ibn Sultan al-Qasimi

Ministers of State

Cabinet Affairs	Sa'id ibn Khalfan al-Ghayth
Foreign Affairs	Sheikh Hamdan ibn Zayed Al Nuhayyan

[f] = female

of the three countries that recognized the Taliban government.) Since the US occupation of Iraq following the 2003 invasion, the UAE has been a major supplier of humanitarian aid.

The continued surge in world oil prices has contributed to a real-estate boom in Dubai, as well as a boom in commerce. Plans are under way for the world's tallest building, the world's largest shopping mall, and a Disneyland-like park, all in Dubai, which is on the path to becoming a tourism hub.

Political Parties

There are no political parties in the United Arab Emirates.

Legislature

Federal National Council

(*Majlis al-Watani al-Itihad*). The UAE's consultative body consists of 40 delegates appointed by the rulers of the constituent states for two-year terms. There are eight delegates each from Abu Dhabi and Dubai, six each from Sharjah and Ras al-Khaima, and four each from the other emirates.

Speaker: Sa'id Muhammad Sa'id al-Ghandi.

Communications

Press

The following are published daily in Arabic, unless otherwise noted: *Khalij Times* (Dubai and Abu Dhabi, 72,000), English daily; *al-Ittihad* (Abu Dhabi, Dubai, and Sharjah, 58,000), designated as the official daily of the UAE; *Gulf News* (Dubai and Abu Dhabi, 91,000), English daily; *al-Khalij* (Sharjah, 85,000), independent daily; *Emirates News* (Abu Dhabi, 2,000), English daily; *al-Wahdah* (Abu Dhabi, 20,000), independent daily; *al-Bayan*, (32,000); *al-Fajr* (Abu Dhabi and Dubai, 28,000); Mathrubhumi (Malayalam).

News Agencies

The official Emirates News Agency (*Wikalat al-Anba' al-Imarat.*–WAM) was founded in 1977. Reuters maintains an office at Dubai.

Broadcasting and Computing

The United Arab Emirates Broadcasting Service (*Idha'at al-Imarat al-'Arabiyat al-Muttahidah*) operates radio stations in five of the seven emirates; in addition, most of the individual emirates engage in radio and/or television programming. There were approximately 940,000 television receivers and 500,000 personal computers serving 1.1 million Internet users in 2003.

Intergovernmental Representation

Ambassador to the US
Alasri Saeed al-DHAHRI

US Ambassador to the United Arab Emirates
Michele J. SISON

Permanent Representative to the UN
Abdulaziz Nasser al-SHAMSI

IGO Memberships (Non-UN)
AFESD, AMF, BADEA, CCC, GCC, IDB, Interpol, IOR-ARC, LAS, NAM, OAPEC, OIC, OPEC, WTO

YEMEN

REPUBLIC OF YEMEN

al-Jumhuriyah al-Yamaniyah

The Country

Located at the southern corner of the Arabian peninsula, where the Red Sea meets the Gulf of Aden, the Republic of Yemen shares a lengthy but (until recently) largely undefined northern border with Saudi Arabia and a narrow eastern border with Oman (formally demarcated in 1992). Hot, semidesert terrain separates both the Red Sea and Gulf coasts from a mountainous interior. The people are predominantly Arab and are divided into two Muslim religious communities: the Zaidi of the Shi'a sect in the north and east, and the Shaffi'i community of the Sunni sect in the south and southwest. Tribal influences remain strong, often taking priority over formal governmental activity outside of urban areas. The population growth rate has been estimated recently at about 3.7 percent per year, among the highest rates in the world.

At the time of the Iraqi invasion of Kuwait in August 1990, more than a million Yemeni men were employed outside the country, primarily in Saudi Arabia and other oil-rich Arab states. Their exodus (partially reversed by Saudi action following the onset of the Gulf crisis) had created an internal labor shortage and increased female responsibility for the bulk of subsistence agricultural production. In the former Yemen Arab Republic the requirements of purdah precluded any substantial female participation outside the household; by contrast, the Marxist government of the former People's Democratic Republic emphasized women's rights, as contrasted with an earlier feudal attitude of total female subservience. Unification brought mixed results. On the one hand women were granted suffrage in the new republic's constitution, on the other observers cited a "turn to the Islamic right" in Yemeni society which led, *inter alia,* to the legalization of polygamy and the adoption of conservative Muslim dress, already widespread in the north, by many women in the south.

As a result of topographical extremes, a variety of crops are produced, including cotton (the leading export), grains, fruits, coffee, tobacco, and *qat* (a mild narcotic leaf which is chewed daily by an estimated 90 percent of the northern population and is estimated to account for nearly 50 percent of GDP). Significant water discoveries have been made recently in connection with oil exploration, raising the possibility of major agricultural expansion in the near future.

While Yemen is currently one of the poorest Arab countries and one of the 20 poorest nations

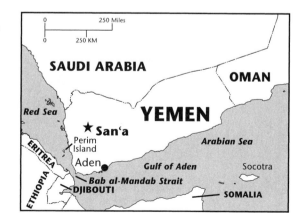

in the world, significant (and potentially dramatic) economic improvement is expected with the exploitation of extensive oil reserves (see map), first discovered in 1984. (Yemen currently produces nearly 450,000 barrels of oil per day, with proven reserves of at least 4 billion barrels. Oil revenue accounts for an estimated 70 percent of government income.) Significant gas reserves have also been discovered, and the Yemen Liquid Natural Gas Company in 2005 signed a contract with French, Swiss, and South Korean firms. In addition, the port of Aden, one of the world's leading oil bunkering and entrepôt centers prior to being crippled by the 1967–1975 closure of the Suez Canal, has been rehabilitated and now thrives as part of the Aden Free Trade Zone.

In 1995 the government adopted a structural adjustment program recommended by the International Monetary Fund (IMF), priorities including promotion of the private sector, trade liberalization, civil service and judicial reform, subsidy reductions, support for the non-oil sector, and tax changes. In view of encouraging developments, the Paris Club of creditor nations rescheduled repayments of much of Yemen's external debt in 1997.

GDP grew only by 3.4 percent in 2003 and 2.7 percent in 2004. However, non-oil GDP growth was estimated to be 4.1 percent in 2004, based on progress in construction, transportation, and trade.

The International Monetary Fund (IMF) reported in early 2005 that while progress had been made in structural reforms the previous year, the country was still at a "crossroads" over the prospect of declining oil production in years to come. The IMF applauded Yemeni authorities' plans to diversify and to drum up public support for reforms. Privatization laws and a bank reform plan are already in place. Other measures proposed by the IMF included the implementation of a general sales tax. However, the government's decision to impose a 10 percent sales tax beginning in July 2005 prompted violent protests in San'a. Meanwhile, little foreign investment was reported beyond the Aden area.

Government and Politics

Political Background

Yemen Arab Republic (YAR). Former site of the Kingdom of Sheba and an early center of Near Eastern civilization, the territory subsequently known as North Yemen fell under the rule of the Ottoman Turks in the 16th century. The withdrawal of Turkish forces in 1918 made it possible for Imam YAHYA, the traditional ruler of the Zaidi religious community, to gain political supremacy. Yahya remained as theocratic ruler until 1948, when he was murdered in an attempted coup and succeeded by his son, Sa'if al-ISLAM Ahmad. The new leader instituted a more outward-looking policy: diplomatic relations were established with the Soviet Union in 1956, and in 1958 the monarchy joined with the United Arab Republic (Egypt and Syria) in a federation styled the United Arab States that was dissolved three years later.

A series of unsuccessful uprisings against the absolute and antiquated regime of the imams culminated on September 26, 1962, in the ouster of the newly installed Iman Muhammad al-BADR by a group of army officers under Col. (later Field Marshal) Abdallah al-SALAL, who established a republic with close UAR ties. Although the new regime was recognized by the United States and many other governments, resistance by followers of the imam precipitated a civil war that continued intermittently until early 1969.

The external forces, including those of Saudi Arabia (which supported the royalists) and Egypt (which supported the republicans), were withdrawn in late 1967 following the UAR's defeat in the June war with Israel and the conclusion of an agreement with Saudi Arabia at an Arab summit at Khartoum, Sudan. President Salal was subsequently ousted in favor of a three-man Presidential Council headed by 'Abd al-Rahman al-IRYANI. Internal factional rivalry continued, but in May 1970 an informal compromise was reached whereby royalist elements were assimilated into the regime. The rudiments of modern governmental institutions were established with the adoption of a new constitution

Political Status: Independent Islamic Arab republic established by merger of former Yemen Arab Republic and People's Democratic Republic of Yemen on May 22, 1990.

Area: 205,355 sq. mi. (531,869 sq. km.), encompassing 75,290 sq. mi. (130,065 sq. km.) of the former Yemen Arab Republic and 195,000 sq. mi. (336,869 sq. km.) of the former People's Democratic Republic of Yemen.

Population: 14,587,807 (1994C); 20,715,000 (2004E).

Major Urban Centers (1994C): SAN'A (954,448), Aden (398,294), Ta'iz (317,571), Hodeida (Hudayda, 298,452).

Official Language: Arabic.

Monetary Unit: YAR Rial (market rate July 1, 2005: 183.20 rials = $1US).

President: Fld. Mar. 'Ali Abdallah SALIH (General People's Congress); former president of the Yemen Arab Republic; assumed office upon merger of North and South Yemen on May 22, 1990; elected for an anticipated five-year term by the Presidential Council on October 16, 1993; elected for a new five-year term by the House of Representatives on October 1, 1994, in accordance with constitutional amendments approved September 28; directly elected for an anticipated five-year term on September 23, 1999; current term extended from five to seven years by national referendum of February 20, 2001.

Vice President: Gen. 'Abdurabu Mansur HADI (General People's Congress); appointed by the President on October 2, 1994.

Prime Minister: 'Abd al-Qadir 'Abd al-Rahman BAJAMMAL (General People's Congress); appointed by the President on March 31, 2001, to succeed 'Abd al-Karim 'Ali al-IRYANI (General People's Congress).

in late 1970 and the election of a Consultative Council in early 1971, although political stability continued to depend on the personal success of such leaders as prime ministers Hassan al-'AMRI and Muhsin Ahmad al-'AYNI. On June 13, 1974, in another, apparently bloodless, coup, the Iryani regime was superseded by a seven-man Military Command Council (MCC) led by Lt. Col. Ibrahim Muhammad al-HAMADI. In January 1975, Prime Minister 'Ayni, who had been appointed only seven months earlier, was replaced by 'Abd al-'Aziz 'Abd al-GHANI.

On October 11, 1977, Colonel Hamadi was assassinated at San'a by unknown assailants, and the MCC immediately established a Presidential Council headed by Lt. Col. Ahmad Husayn al-GHASHMI, with Prime Minister Ghani and Maj. Abdallah 'Abd al-'ALIM, commander of the paratroop forces, as the other members. Ghashmi was assassinated on June 24, 1978, by a bomb-bearing "special emissary" of the South Yemeni government. A new four-member provisional Presidential Council was thereupon organized, including Prime Minister Ghani, Constituent Assembly Speaker 'Abd al-Karim al-ARASHI, Armed Forces Commander 'Ali al-SHIBA, and Maj. 'Ali Abdallah SALIH. The Assembly elected Salih president of the Republic on July 17 and three days later named Arashi to the newly created office of vice president, Ghani being continued as prime minister.

Attempts to overthrow Salih were reported in July and October 1978, while a prolonged delay in reaching agreement on constitutional issues was attributed to continuing conflict between republican and traditionalist groups. The situation was further complicated in early 1979 when South Yemeni forces crossed into North Yemen and were joined by rebels of the leftist National Democratic Front (NDF), led by Sultan Ahmad 'UMAR. Following mediation by the Arab League, a cease-fire was implemented on March 16, the southern troops being withdrawn. On March 30 talks in Kuwait between President Salih and Council Chairman Isma'il of the People's Democratic Republic concluded with a mutual pledge to reopen discussions on eventual unification of the two Yemens. Toward that end, a number of high-level meetings between San'a and Aden took place during the next 18 months, while on October 15, 1980, in a significant internal reorganization, Prime Minister Ghani was replaced by 'Abd al-Karim 'Ali al-IRYANI and named covice president. On May 22, 1983, the Assembly reelected Salih for a second five-year term, while on November 12 Vice President Ghani was reappointed prime minister, with Iryani being assigned to direct the reconstruction of earthquake-damaged areas.

Balloting for 128 members of a new 159-seat Consultative Council (*Majlis al-Shura*) to replace the Constituent Assembly took place on July 5, 1988, the remaining 31 seats being filled by presidential appointment. On July 17 the Council reelected Salih to a third five-year term as head of state, with Vice President Arashi being designated Council speaker. On July 31 Salih reappointed Major Ghani to head a partially reorganized administration. (See Republic of Yemen, below, for information on negotiations leading to unification with the People's Democratic Republic of Yemen (PDRY) and political developments from 1990 to the present.)

People's Democratic Republic of Yemen. British control of South Yemen began with the occupation of Aden in 1839 and, through treaties with numerous local rulers, was gradually extended north and eastward to include what came to be known as the Western and Eastern Protectorates. Aden was ruled as part of British India until 1937, when it became a separate Crown Colony. In preparation for eventual independence, the British established the Federation of South Arabia, in which the colony of Aden was associated with 16 dependent states that had previously belonged to the Protectorates. Plans for a transfer of power to the rulers of the Federation were frustrated, however, by increasing nationalist agitation and terrorist activity on the part of radical elements. By 1967 a power struggle among rival nationalist groups had resulted in the emergence of the left-wing National Liberation Front (NLF) as the area's strongest political organization. Control of the territory was

accordingly handed over by Britain to representatives of the NLF (restyled as the National Front–NF) on November 30, 1967.

Qahtan al-SHAABI, the principal NF leader, became president and prime minister of the new People's Republic of Southern Yemen, which, though beset by grave internal problems and revolts, rapidly emerged as a center of left-wing revolutionary nationalist agitation in South Arabia. The position of the comparatively moderate Shaabi became progressively weaker, and, as the result of a continuing power struggle between the moderate and radical wings of the NF, he was forced from office in June 1969, the country's name being changed in December 1970 to the People's Democratic Republic of Yemen. In August 1971 another change of government brought into power Salim Rubay'i 'ALI and 'Abd al-Fattah ISMA'IL, heads of the NF's pro-Chinese and pro-Soviet factions, respectively; both participated in a three-member Presidential Council, chaired by 'Ali as head of state.

In the course of a leadership struggle that erupted into street fighting at the capital on June 26, 1978, 'Ali was removed from office and executed after allegations (largely discounted by foreign observers) that he had been involved in the assassination two days earlier of President Ghashmi of North Yemen. Following 'Ali's ouster, Prime Minister 'Ali Nasir MUHAMMAD al-Hasani was designated chair of the Presidential Council, with Isma'il and Defense Minister 'Ali Ahmad Nasir ANTAR al-Bishi as the other members. Although expanded to five members on July 1, the presidential collegium was superseded on December 27 by an 11-member Presidium of a recently elected Supreme People's Council (SPC), Isma'il serving as chair. Earlier, in mid-October, the Yemeni Socialist Party (YSP) had been organized, in succession to the NF, as the country's controlling political organization.

On March 30, 1979, Council Chairman Isma'il and President Salih of North Yemen concluded a three-day meeting in Kuwait that had been called in the wake of renewed hostilities between their two countries. Despite obvious ideological differences between the conservative North and the

Marxist-Leninist South, the leaders pledged that they would renew efforts first broached in 1972, but suspended in 1975, to unify the two Yemens.

On April 21, 1980, Council Chairman Isma'il, ostensibly for reasons of ill health, resigned his government and party posts, with Prime Minister Muhammad being named by the YSP Central Committee as his successor in both capacities. Five days later, the SPC confirmed Muhammad (who retained the prime ministership) as head of state. His position was further consolidated at an extraordinary party congress held October 12–14, when a Politburo and a Secretariat dominated by his supporters were named, and at an extraordinary session of the SPC on October 16, when a revamped cabinet was approved.

At the conclusion of an SPC session on February 14, 1985, Muhammad resigned as chair of the Council of Ministers, while retaining his position as head of state. Concurrently, a new cabinet was approved, headed by former construction minister Haydar Abu Bakr al-ATTAS. In October Muhammad was reelected secretary general of the YSP, albeit as part of a political compromise that necessitated enlargement of the Central Committee from 47 to 77 members and the Politburo from 13 to 16. In particular, the reinstatement of former chair Isma'il to the Politburo indicated that there would be increased opposition to the policies of the incumbent state and party leader.

On January 13, 1986, SPC Chair Muhammad mounted a "gangland style massacre" of YSP opponents, in the course of which Isma'il and a number of others, including Defense Minister Salih Muslih QASIM, were killed. However, the chair's opponents regrouped and, after more than a week of bitter fighting at the capital, succeeded in defeating "the 'Ali Nasir clique," with Muhammad gaining asylum in North Yemen. On January 24 ministerial chair al-Attas, who had been in India at the time of the attempted purge, was designated interim head of state. On February 6 the YSP Central Committee named 'Ali Salim al-BIEDH to succeed Muhammad as its secretary general, while the SPC on February 8 confirmed al-Attas as Presidium chair and appointed a new government headed by

Dr. Yasin Sa'id NU'MAN; both were reconfirmed on November 6, 1986, by a new Council elected October 28–30.

Republic of Yemen. In the fall of 1981 unification talks between North Yemen's President 'Ali Abdallah Salih and his South Yemen counterpart, 'Ali Nasir Muhammad, culminated in an agreement signed at Aden on December 2 to establish a Yemen Council, embracing the two chief executives, and a Joint Ministerial Council to promote integration in the political, economic, and social spheres. On December 30 the Aden News Agency reported that a draft constitution of a unified Yemeni Republic would be submitted to referenda in the two states at an unspecified date. Progress toward unification slowed, however, in the wake of domestic turmoil in the south in early 1986 that resulted in Muhammad's ouster and flight to the north.

Strongly influenced by the impact of Mikhail Gorbachev's policy of restructuring (*perestroika*) on the PDRY's Marxist-oriented leadership, the Yemen and Joint Ministerial councils were revived in May 1988, while on December 1, 1989, a draft joint constitution was published that called for an integrated multiparty state headed by a five-member Presidential Council. The new basic law was implemented on May 22, 1990, after having been ratified the previous day by the constituent states' respective parliaments. On the same day, as agreed upon earlier by both parliaments, newly promoted General Salih assumed the presidency of the Republic of Yemen for what was initially proclaimed as a 30-month transitional term. The PDRY's 'Ali Salim al-Biedh was named vice president for a projected term of the same duration. On May 26 former South Yemen President al-Attas was named prime minister by the transitional House of Representatives, with a joint administration being installed on May 27.

The first general elections were postponed by Salih from the original date of November 1992 (the end of the proposed 30-month transitional period) because of domestic unrest. When the voting for a new House of Representatives was finally conducted on April 27, 1993, Salih's General

People's Congress (GPC) outpolled the more than 40 participating parties, followed by the conservative Yemeni Congregation for Reform (*Islah*) and the YSP. On May 30 the three leading parties announced the formation of a coalition government, again led by al-Attas and initially encompassing 15 GPC, 9 YSP, and 4 *Islah* members. However, *Islah* subsequently demanded greater representation on the basis of its electoral showing and was awarded two newly created additional cabinet posts on June 10.

On October 11, 1993, the House of Representatives elected Salih and al-Biedh to a new Presidential Council, along with former YAR Prime Minister Ghani of the GPC, the YSP's Salim Salih MUHAMMAD, and *Islah*'s 'Abd al-Maguid al-ZINDANI. Five days later the Council elected Salih as its chairman and thereby president of the Republic, al-Biedh being renamed vice president. However, al-Biedh, who had refused to leave Aden since August because of security concerns, did not attend the induction or take the oath of office.

In February 1994 Salih and al-Biedh signed a Document of Pledge and Agreement that had been brokered by a multiparty Committee for National Dialogue formed in November 1993 to resolve the political stalemate between the two leaders. The accord provided for many of the so-called "18-points" al-Biedh had recently issued as requirements for continued southern support for the union. They included the withdrawal of army units from the former north/south border, establishment of a new national intelligence organization, investigation into the numerous assassinations of YSP members since unification, decentralization of government authority, and a review of national economic policy.

Despite widespread internal and external relief over the signing of the "peace agreement" in early 1994, it quickly became apparent that no true reconciliation had been achieved, al-Biedh and Muhammad refusing to attend a March Presidential Council session at San'a. Intense international mediation notwithstanding, sporadic fighting between northern and southern military units (never unified under the 1990 arrangements) broke out in late April 1994.

As hostilities escalated into full-fledged war, Salih declared a state of emergency on May 5, 1994, and dismissed al-Biedh and Muhammad from the Presidential Council and Prime Minister al-Attas and several other YSP members from the government. Industry Minister Muhammad Sa'id al-'ATTAR, a member of the GPC, was named acting prime minister.

Heavy fighting over the next two weeks appeared to favor northern forces, which had launched a sustained offensive toward Aden. Consequently, in an apparent attempt to garner international support for his cause, al-Biedh on May 21, 1994, announced the south's secession from the union and the formation of an independent Democratic Republic of Yemen. A Presidential Council, with al-Biedh as its president, was established for the new state along with a provisional National Salvation Council, while al-Attas was named prime minister of a YSP-dominated government announced on June 2. However, no international recognition was forthcoming for the new republic, and the south's military position became increasingly precarious, several cease-fires quickly collapsing. Following a week of heavy shelling, during which most separatist leaders (including al-Biedh) fled the country, northern forces secured control of Aden on July 7, effectively ending the civil war and the short-lived secession.

On September 28, 1994, the House of Representatives approved several constitutional amendments, the most important of which eliminated the Presidential Council, whose unwieldiness had contributed to prewar friction. Three days later, acting as an "electoral college" on a onetime basis as provided for in the basic law revision, the House by a nearly unanimous vote elected Salih to a new five-year presidential term. On October 2 Salih appointed Maj. Gen. 'Abdurabu Mansur HADI as vice president, and on October 6 he named former YAR co-vice president al-Ghani to head the first postwar government. A new cabinet, announced the day of al-Ghani's appointment as prime minister, included 16 ministers from the GPC, nine from *Islah*, and one independent, the rump YSP having gone into opposition.

President Salih subsequently adopted a conciliatory stance, issuing a general amnesty for all southerners except former Vice President al-Biedh and 15 other separatist leaders. (However, Salih and al-Biedh reconciled at a May 2003 meeting in Abu Dhabi, and Salih reportedly promised that all exiled socialist officials could return). Salih also placed the nation's military forces under a unified command and announced similar plans for the police and intelligence organizations. In addition, the government pledged to place restrictions on civilian weapons, some reports suggesting that there were as many as 50 million guns in the country (an average of more than three per person). On the political front, the constitutional changes approved in September 1994 served to consolidate power in the hands of Salih, who was declared eligible for two five-year terms in the newly strengthened presidency.

The first new legislative poll since the civil war was conducted on April 27, 1997, with the GPC securing 187 seats, followed by *Islah* with 53. (The YSP, deemed unlikely to recover from the secessionist debacle for many years, if ever, boycotted the balloting, as did several small parties.) On March 14 the president named Faraj Said ibn GHANIM, a nonparty economist from the south who had once been a member of the YSP, as the new prime minister. The cabinet appointed the following day included a relatively even mix of old and new faces but, most notably, no representatives from *Islah,* which moved into a position of formal opposition.

Despite the YSP boycott, the peaceful legislative balloting of April 1997 was broadly viewed as an important step toward cementing Yemen's image as a stable country genuinely committed to democracy. International observers described the balloting as generally free and fair, while the participation of women both as candidates and voters earned Western praise. However, the explosion of several bombs at Aden in late July underscored the ongoing fragility of the social fabric, while the subsequent arrest of over 100 opposition figures reminded observers of the government's continued penchant for heavy-handed action.

Amid reports of growing friction between him and the president over economic issues, Prime Minister Ghanim offered his resignation in mid-April 1998. Salih formally accepted the resignation on April 29 and asked Deputy Prime Minister 'Abd al-Karim 'Ali al-Iryani (former prime minister of the Yemen Arab Republic) to take over the government on a caretaker basis. Salih formally appointed Iryani as prime minister on May 14, and a new (only slightly changed) government was sworn in on May 17. All ministers were affiliated with the GPC except for one independent and one member of the small Truth Party; the latter resigned four months later.

In the country's first direct presidential election on September 23, 1999, Salih was credited with 96.3 percent of the vote, only one challenger having been sanctioned under controversial electoral regulations (see Current issues, below). Subsequently, in another development that was strongly criticized by the government's opponents, Salih and the GPC proposed constitutional amendments extending the presidential term from five to seven years and the legislature's term from four to six years. The amendments received a reported 73 percent "yes" vote in a national referendum on February 20, 2001.

On March 31, 2001, President Salih named 'Abd al-Qadir 'Abd al-Rahman BAJAMMAL, theretofore the deputy prime minister, to replace Prime Minister Iryani. (Reports variously said that Iryani had resigned for health reasons or had been dismissed by the president in order to inject "new blood" into the government.) Bajammal on April 4 announced a new cabinet, which was inaugurated on April 7.

In the legislative elections on April 27, 2003, the GPC significantly increased its majority, winning 238 seats, with some 8 million Yemenis reportedly going to the polls. In the wake of the US invasion of Iraq in March, Yemeni authorities wanted to show the strength of their determined steps toward democracy. Significantly, the YSP, which had boycotted the 1997 elections, yielded some 100 candidates and negotiated with *Islah* and other constituencies to avoid splitting the antigovernment vote. However, YSP won only 7 seats, and *Islah,* 46. In a conciliatory move, President Salih appointed a prominent socialist, Salim Salih MUHAMMAD, as his special adviser. Some accusations of vote fraud surfaced, and three people died and 15 were injured in polling-day violence. A cabinet reshuffle followed the election, with half of the 35 members being replaced. A new ministry of human rights was established a few months later, headed by a woman.

Constitution and Government

The 1990 constitution of the Republic of Yemen provided for a five-member Presidential Council, chosen by a popularly elected House of Representatives. The Council was empowered to select its own chairman and vice chairman, who served effectively as the Republic's president and vice president. The term of office was set at five years for the Presidential Council and four years for the House of Representatives. However, in the aftermath of the recent civil war, the House on September 28, 1994, revised the basic law, abolishing the Presidential Council and providing for an elected chief executive with broadened powers, including the right to name the vice president and prime minister. In view of the turmoil remaining from the secessionist conflict, the House empowered itself to select the next president for a five-year term, after which chief executives were to be chosen by direct popular election. In addition, future presidents were limited to two five-year terms. (The presidential term of office was extended to seven years in 2001). Following the legislative balloting of April 1997, President Salih announced the creation of a new Consultative Council, an advisory body of 59 presidentially appointed members. The Council was expanded to 111 members in 2001.

In a move of widespread political implications, the transitional government in 1990 appointed a commission to redraw the boundaries of local governorates, some of which had traditionally been ruled as virtual fiefdoms by tribal chiefs.

The 1990 basic law stipulated that the Islamic legal code (*shari'a*) was to be utilized as "one source"

of Yemeni law but the wording was changed to "the source" in 1994.

Foreign Relations

North Yemen broke out of its age-long, largely self-imposed isolation in the mid-1950s, when the imam's government accepted economic and military aid from the Soviet Union, the People's Republic of China, the United Arab Republic, and the United States. Diplomatic relations with Washington were broken off in June 1967 during the Arab-Israeli war, but a reconciliation was effected in July 1972. Subsequent foreign concerns turned primarily on relations with the country's two immediate neighbors, conservative Saudi Arabia and Marxist South Yemen. Despite the former's previous record of support for Yemen's defeated royalists, Saudi money and arms were instrumental during intermittent border warfare with South Yemen in 1971–1972 and again in February–March 1979. However, subsequent reaffirmation of the two Yemens' intention to merge (originally announced in 1972) was coolly received by Riyadh, which withheld several hundred million dollars in military supplies. In turn, North Yemen renewed its military dealings with the Soviet Union, and in October 1979 the Saudis were reported to have ended their annual budgetary supplement of $250 million. In May 1988 an unimplemented 1985 accord between the two Yemens to create an 850-square-mile "joint economic zone" straddling the poorly demarcated border between the YAR's Marib region and the PDRY's Shabwa area (see map, p. 1307) was reactivated. However, Saudi Arabia had previously entered a claim for much of the disputed territory on the basis of recently published maps that extended its border with North Yemen many miles to the west of the previously assumed location.

The People's Democratic Republic of Yemen professed a policy of nonalignment in foreign affairs, but its relations with other Arab countries were mixed because of its long-standing opposition to all conservative regimes and its record of close association with the Soviet Union. It voted against admission of the Persian Gulf sheikhdoms to the Arab League, while numerous border clashes resulted from tensions with Saudi Arabia and the Yemen Arab Republic. Elsewhere, as a member of the hard-line Arab "steadfastness front," Aden rejected any partial settlement of the Middle East question, particularly the 1979 Egyptian-Israeli peace treaty.

Iraq's incursion into Kuwait dominated the Republic of Yemen's foreign policy agenda throughout the second half of 1990 and early 1991. Having initially deplored the invasion, San'a was criticized for maintaining a pro-Iraqi stance by abstaining in early August from both a UN Security Council vote for sanctions against Baghdad and an Arab League vote to condemn the occupation. Subsequently, the government withdrew its threat to ignore international sanctions, but its unremitting criticism of the presence of Western troops in Saudi Arabia led Riyadh on September 19 to withdraw special privileges granted to Yemeni citizens. By late November upwards of 700,000 Yemeni nationals had been repatriated, with San'a claiming that Yemen should be compensated $1.7 billion for losses caused by the crisis. On November 29 Yemen (the sole Arab UN Security Council member) voted against the Council's resolution to use "all necessary means to uphold and implement" its earlier resolutions concerning Iraq, calling instead for a peaceful, Arab-negotiated settlement. Consequently, in January 1991 the United States announced it would withhold $18 million of aid promised to Yemen, with the Gulf states subsequently following suit. Tension between Yemen and Saudi Arabia was described as being at an all-time high in mid-1992, their border conflict having taken on greater significance in view of recent oil discoveries in the region. Meanwhile, the antipathy generated in the West by Yemen's pro-Iraqi tilt during the Gulf crisis had also largely dissipated, Western attention again focusing on oil exploration licenses being issued by San'a.

After some initial uncertainty, the United States strongly endorsed unity and thereby the northern cause during the 1994 civil war. In addition, Washington reportedly pressured Saudi Arabia (which apparently preferred a divided Yemen) and several other Arab countries into forgoing plans to recognize the DRY, thereby hastening the secessionist regime's collapse.

Riyadh's "quiet" financial and military support for the southern forces exacerbated tension with San'a, and sporadic clashes were reported in late 1994 between Saudi and Yemeni troops in the contested border region. Under heavy international pressure to avoid further hostilities, however, the two countries agreed in February 1995 to negotiate, and the result was a preliminary accord that called for joint committees to demarcate the border and monitor future troop movements in the region. On June 3 Yemen and Oman completed demarcation of their frontier in accordance with the 1992 agreement.

In late 1995 a major foreign relations problem arose when Eritrean forces invaded Greater Hanish, one of nine islands in the archipelago between the two countries near the mouth of the Red Sea (see map, p. 365). Although sovereignty over the islands had never been formally established by international convention, Yemeni fisherman had operated from Greater Hanish for many years, and some 200 Yemeni soldiers had been garrisoned there recently to provide "security" for a new hotel construction site. Eritrea, which based its claim on a 1938 agreement between Britain and Ethiopia, assumed control of Greater Hanish in December after three days of fighting which took some 12 lives. Yemen, which supports its sovereignty stance by reference to Britain having turned over control of two lighthouses on the islands to South Yemen in 1967, subsequently agreed to submit the dispute to binding arbitration by a panel of five judges. Tension stayed high over the issue into early 1999, however, as Eritrea's war with Ethiopia complicated regional affairs. However, Eritrea returned control of Greater Hanish to Yemen shortly after the international tribunal ruled in the latter's favor in December regarding sovereignty over it and nearby islands. The tribunal also demarcated the maritime border between the two countries, whose relationship was subsequently described as "normalized." Relations with Saudi Arabia, strained by significant border clashes in 1997, 1998, and early

2000, also improved substantially after a border agreement was announced in June 2000. Finally, in May 2004 both sides accepted the border demarcation plans drawn up by a German firm. In March 2005 officials from both countries, in a small sign of warming relations, discussed bilateral cooperation. However, with arms smuggling a major problem along the porous border, Saudi Arabia in 2004 installed a ten-foot-high "pipeline" barrier, "much to the annoyance of some Yemenis." Meanwhile, Yemeni officials said the barrier violated the treaty signed in 2000 to end the 65-year border dispute.

In mid-2004 Yemen was invited to take part in a G-8 Summit in Georgia meant to promote democracy in the region. Yemen's presence was seen as a mark of its value to the US, a result of the government's contributions to the US-led war on terror. Yemen claimed to have arrested or jailed a large number of terror suspects linked to *al-Qaeda*, thus inducing the US to resume arms sales to Yemen as of 2004.

Current Issues

Upon its installation in the spring of 1998, the Iryani government quickly enacted a 40 percent increase in the price of oil and basic foods, prompting disturbances in June in which as many as 100 people may have died. Several bombings throughout the rest of the year also contributed to the nation's image problem, as did sporadic abductions on the part of tribesmen seeking ransom or government concessions. However, the most serious incident was the politically motivated kidnapping in December of 16 westerners by Islamic militants; four hostages died in the rescue effort by Yemeni security forces, whose tactics were criticized by UK officials, touching off a diplomatic row. (See Aden-Abyan Islamic Army, under Political Parties and Groups, below, for further information.)

During his 1999 reelection campaign President Salih urged his countrymen to withdraw from "the culture of drugs and guns," and the government issued new regulations regarding the use of *qat* by officials and the public display of weapons. However, observers questioned whether such policy

directives would be of much influence outside the major cities, effective authority in rural areas still resting for the most part in the hands of tribal leaders.

Yemen became the focus of intense international attention when 17 US sailors died following a suicide bombing attack against the destroyer *Cole* while it was refueling in Aden harbor on October 12, 2000. (The refueling arrangement had been implemented in 1999 as part of Washington's "engagement" policy which also included mine-clearing assistance by US soldiers in Yemen and a White House audience in the spring of 2000 for President Salih.) Almost four years later, a Yemeni court sentenced two men to death and jailed four others for their role in the bombing, now considered by the US an *al-Qaeda* attack. A year earlier, ten suspects in the Cole attack escaped from a Yemeni jail, aided by some two dozen others during a time of heightened violence in the country by Islamic militants. Many were suspected of being linked to Osama bin Laden, who, the US warned, might be trying to regroup in his ancestral home.

Relations with Washington improved following the *al-Qaeda* attacks in the US in September 2001, Salih announcing that Yemen would cooperate with the subsequent US-led global "war on terrorism." Among other things, the Yemeni government shut down a number of religious and educational institutions suspected of serving as recruiting grounds for Islamic militants, an initiative which intensified friction with the opposition *Islah* party, which had established some of the schools. However, terrorist attacks continued to plague Yemen, with high-profile episodes such as the killing of three American missionaries at a Baptist hospital in December 2002. A member of the opposition *Islah* party was sentenced to death for that crime in September 2003. Earlier in 2003 "scores" of Muslim militants with suspected terror links were arrested, and another *Islah* official who claimed to be bin Laden's "spiritual leader" was captured in Germany. Government forces also attacked the Islamic Army of Aden-Abyan, said to be linked to *al-Qaeda,* with the leader of the Army being executed in 2003. In an effort to deal with the growing terrorist arrests, authorities in 2003 began experimenting with a "re-education" program in response to complaints about the large number of detainees being held without trial. The detainees were given religious instruction about "the true meaning of *jihad*" and those who signed consenting documents were released to their families.

Adding to Yemen's difficulties was the uprising in 2004 led by popular cleric Husayn al-HUTHI and his Organization of Believing Youth (*Shabab al-Mu'min*). Hundreds of followers were killed, and more continued to die in violent clashes even after Yemeni army officials announced in September 2004 that al-Huthi himself had been killed. Confrontations in the mountainous northwest province of Saada were sustained through April 2005.

With several hundred suspected *al-Qaeda* members jailed as of March 2005, the US praised Yemen's crackdown on terrorists. At the same time, analysts suggested that Salih faced a difficult job in balancing cooperation with the US with growing sentiment within the populace against Israel and the US. To enhance its standing, Yemen created a new ministry of human rights, and Salih continued to publicly endorse democracy, although skeptics reportedly viewed that stance as "window dressing" in response to President Bush's pressure for more democracy in the Middle East. Most recently, in June 2005, heated debate erupted over women's representation in politics with a group of women having formed a coalition to support women's participation in elections–which they say all parties have failed to do.

Political Parties and Groups

Under the imams, parties in North Yemen were banned, political alignments being determined largely by tribal and religious loyalties. Prior to independence, the National Liberation Front (NLF) and the Front for the Liberation of Occupied South Yemen (FLOSY) fought for control of South Yemen, with adherents of the latter subsequently going into exile. In October 1975 the NLF's successor, the National Front (NF), joined with the Popular Vanguard Party (a *Baath* group)

and a Marxist formation, the Popular Democratic Union (PDU), to form the United Political Organization of the National Front (UPONF). In 1978 the UPONF was supplanted by the Yemeni Socialist Party (YSP, below).

Under the liberalized constitutional provisions of the successor Republic of Yemen, some 70 groups were reportedly legalized, with about 40 presenting candidates in the April 1993 legislative balloting. In February 1995 a Democratic Opposition Coalition (DOC) was formed by 13 groups, including the YSP, the Arab Socialist *Baath* Party, the League of the Sons of Yemen, the National Democratic Front, and a number of small parties. Coordination within the DOC appeared to collapse, however, with some members choosing to participate in the April 1997 legislative elections and others supporting a boycott. Ongoing involvement of a YSP-led Opposition Coordination Council was subsequently reported, the Council unsuccessfully attempting to present a candidate in the 1999 presidential balloting and opposing the constitutional amendments ratified in early 2001.

Government Party

General People's Congress–GPC (*al-Mu'tamar al-Sha'bi al-'Am*). Encompassing 700 elected and 300 appointed members, the GPC was founded in 1982 in the YAR with the widespread expectation that it would assume the quasi-legislative duties of the nonelected Constituent People's Assembly. However, the latter body continued to function until replaced in 1988 by a predominately elected Consultative Assembly, the GPC essentially taking on the role of an unofficial ruling party, with delegates to its biennial sessions being selected by local congresses. Longtime YAR president 'Ali Abdallah Salih relinquished his position as secretary general of the GPC upon assuming the presidency of the Republic of Yemen in May 1990; however, the group continued as one of the parties (along with the YSP, below) responsible for guiding the new republic through the transitional period culminating in the 1993 legislative election.

The GPC won a plurality (123 seats) in the April 1993 House of Representatives balloting, its support coming primarily from northern tribal areas. Although a coalition government with the YSP was announced on May 30, the two leading parties grew increasingly estranged prior to the onset of the 1994 civil war. Following that conflict, the GPC announced the formation of a new government in coalition with *Islah* (below). At its fifth congress, held June 25, 1995, the GPC reelected all incumbent party leaders, including Salih as chair.

The GPC, aided by a YSP boycott, won a majority of 187 seats in the April 1997 House balloting and, following *Islah*'s decision to join the opposition, GPC members filled all but three posts in the new government named the following month. GPC Secretary General 'Abd al-Karim 'Ali al-Iryani was named prime minister in May 1998 following the resignation of Faraj Said ibn Ghanim, who was not a GPC member. Salih was reelected to another term as president of the Republic in September 1999 in the nation's first direct balloting for that post.

In the balloting of April 27, 2003, the GPC won 238 seats. The opposition *Islah* negotiated, though ultimately unsuccessfully, to avoid splitting the antigovernment vote.

Leaders: 'Ali Abdallah SALIH (President of the Republic and Chair of the Party), 'Abd al-Qadir 'Abd al-Rahman BAJAMMAL (Prime Minister), Abdurabu Mansur HADI (Vice President of the Republic and Vice Chair of the Party), 'Abd al-'Aziz 'Abd al-GHANI (Former Prime Minister), 'Abd al-Karim 'Ali al-IRYANI (Former Prime Minister and Secretary General of the Party).

Opposition Parties

Yemeni Congregation for Reform (*al-Tajmu al-Yamani li al-Islah*). Also referenced as the Yemeni *Islah* Party (YIP), *Islah* was launched in September 1990 under the leadership of influential northern tribal leader Sheikh Abdallah ibn Husayn al-Ahmar, formerly a consistent opponent of unification. The party subsequently campaigned against the 1990 constitution in alliance with several other groups advocating strict adherence to *shari'a*.

Somewhat surprisingly, *Islah* finished second in the April 1993 House balloting by winning 62 seats, its success due primarily to strong support from the conservative pro-Saudi population in northern tribal areas. Its principal leader, Sheikh al-Ahmar, was elected speaker of the new House, while its initial allocation of four cabinet posts in May was increased to six in June, with one *Islah* representative being named to the five-member Presidential Council in October. The party's influence grew further during the 1994 civil war because of its strong support for President Salih and the northern unity forces, and it was given nine portfolios in the postwar coalition government with the GPC. Four of the ministerial posts were filled by members of the Muslim Brotherhood, the influential charitable and quasi-political organization with branches in many Arab nations. Observers suggested that the appointments reflected the growing strength of the Islamist tendency within the YIP at the possible expense of conservative, tribal-based elements. For the moment, a balance was seemingly maintained during the *Islah*'s September 1994 congress at San'a, with Sheikh al-Ahmar being reelected party leader and "fundamentalist ideologue" 'Abd al-Maguid al-Zindani being elected chair of the party's 100-member governing council.

Islah's subsequent relationship with the GPC remained tenuous, the minority government partner continuing to question the GPC's handling of economic and administrative reform. At one point prior to the 1997 legislative balloting *Islah* was reportedly considering not participating in the elections. However, an arrangement was apparently concluded under which the GPC agreed not to challenge *Islah* candidates in a number of constituencies. After securing 53 seats in the new House, *Islah* declined to join the new cabinet, although Sheikh al-Ahmar was reelected as House speaker. Among other things, by exiting the cabinet *Islah* lost control of the education portfolio, which had accorded it authority over the religious component of the nation's schools. Despite remaining outside the government, *Islah* continued to support some major proposals of the Salih administration, including the constitutional amendments approved in early 2001. However, the relations between *Islah* and the government soured in early 2001 due to the government's continued efforts to take over religious schools organized by *Islah*. The party also criticized the government for its close cooperation with the United States following September 2001. In the elections of April 27, 2003, *Islah* garnered 46 seats, and al-Ahmar was subsequently reelected as speaker of the House of Representatives.

Leaders: Sheikh Abdallah ibn Husayn al-AHMAR (Speaker of the House of Representatives), 'Abd al-Maguid al-ZINDANI (Chair of *Islah* Governing Council), Muhammad Ali al-YADUMI (Secretary General), Sheikh 'Abd al-Wahab Ali al-UNSI (Deputy Secretary General).

Yemeni Socialist Party–YSP (*al-Hizb al-Ishtirakiya al-Yamaniya*). Modeled after the Communist Party of the Soviet Union, the YSP was formed in 1978 as a Marxist-Leninist "vanguard party" for the PDRY, subsequently maintaining strict one-party control of South Yemen's political affairs despite several serious leadership battles (see Political background, above). In February 1990 the YSP Central Committee announced the separation of state and party functions under a multiparty system as a means of promoting Yemeni unity. Upon unification, YSP secretary general 'Ali Salim al-Biedh was named vice president of the new republic.

The YSP won 56 seats in the April 1993 House of Representatives election, party leaders subsequently announcing a potential merger with the GPC. However, with substantial opposition to the plan having reportedly been voiced within the YSP's 33-member Politburo, no progress toward the union ensued, and the YSP on its own was allocated nine cabinet seats in the government formed in May.

Personal animosity between al-Biedh and Yemeni President Salih was considered an important element in the subsequent north/south confrontation which culminated in the 1994 civil war. However, al-Biedh and his supporters attributed the friction to the inability (or, possibly, the disinclination) of security forces to protect YSP members.

(An estimated 150 YSP members had been assassinated between May 1990 and early 1994.)

Following the collapse of the YSP-led Democratic Republic of Yemen in July 1994, the party appeared to be in disarray. Al-Biedh announced from exile that he was "retiring from politics," although some of the other secessionist leaders who had fled the country pledged to pursue their goal of an independent south. Meanwhile, the YSP rump in Yemen elected a new Politburo (comprising 13 southerners and 10 northerners) in September. Aware that a significant portion of the YSP had opposed the ill-fated independence movement, President Salih announced that the reorganized party would be allowed to keep its legal status. However, he declared al-Biedh and 15 other separatist leaders to be beyond reconciliation and subject to arrest for treason should they return to Yemen. Subsequently, when the GPC/YIP coalition government was formed in October, the YSP announced it was assuming the role of "leading opposition party." A bitter dispute was reported within the party in 1997 concerning the decision not to participate in the April House balloting, boycott supporters claiming government fraud during voter registration. Meanwhile, al-Biedh, former PDRY prime minister Haydar Abu Bakr al-Attas, and three others were sentenced to death in absentia at the conclusion of a trial in March 1998.

YSP Secretary General Ali Saleh Obad attempted to run for president of the Republic in 1999 but, as was the case with nearly all of the other potential challengers, failed to achieve the required support in the legislature. The party subsequently continued to challenge the GPC's stranglehold on power, and, in what was described as a "provocative" decision, al-Biedh and al-Attas were included in the next Central Committee elected at the YSP General Congress in August 2000 at San'a. Not surprisingly, the YSP strongly opposed the constitutional amendments approved in early 2001 that extended the presidential and legislative terms of office.

In late 2002 the Secretary General of the YSP, Jarallah UMAR, was assassinated by an Islamic extremist. His assassin was believed to be an associate of the man who killed the American missionaries days later (see Current issues, above).

In 2003 Salih reconciled with al-Biedh and pardoned the YSP members who had been sentenced to death. The party secured seven seats in the 2003 elections.

Leader: Ali Salih MUQBIL.

Arab Socialist Baath Party. Seven *Baath* Party candidates were successful in the April 1993 legislative election and party member Mujahid ABU SHAWARIB was subsequently named a deputy prime minister in the cabinet announced in May. However, *Baath* leaders announced that the party would sit in opposition, with Abu Shawarib serving essentially as an independent rather than a *Baath* representative. The grouping secured two seats in the 1997 House elections and two seats in the 2003 elections.

Leader: Dr. Qasim SALAM.

Nasserite Unionist People's Party –NUPP (*al-Tantheem al- Wahdawi al-Sha'bi al-Nasseri*). Formed in 1989 and reportedly the largest of the nation's Nasserite groupings, the NUPP won one seat in the 1993 legislative balloting, three in 1997, and three in 2003.

Leader: Abdul Malik al-MAKHLAFI.

Other Parties and Groups

Truth Party (*al-Haq*). Founded by Islamic religious scholars in late 1991, *al-Haq* won two seats in the 1993 parliamentary balloting. Although *al-Haq* had no successful candidates in the 1997 elections, party leader Ibrahim al-Wazir was named minister of justice in the new GPC-led cabinet formed in May. He was replaced after the 2003 reshuffle. Sheikh Ahmad ibn Ali Shami, the secretary general of *al-Haq*, was named minister of religious guidance in the May 1998 reshuffle, although he left the post in September because of what he described as "interference" from other officials in carrying out his duties. In October 2004 a party official was beaten in what could well have been a politically motivated attack. The government has accused the group of backing the rebellion of cleric

and former Truth leader Husayn al-Huthi (see Current issues, above).

Leaders: Ibrahim al-WAZIR, Sheikh Ahmad ibn Ali SHAMI (Secretary General).

Yemeni Unionist Alliance (*Tajammu*). *Tajammu* was formed in 1990 by human rights proponents from both north and south, party leaders subsequently criticizing the national government for its pro-Iraqi stance during the Gulf crisis. In late 1991 it was reported that a mainstream Islamic party, *Nahdah* (Renaissance), had merged with *Tajammu,* partly in response to government efforts to get smaller parties to coalesce; however, in 1995 *Nahdah* was reported to have entered the DOC as a discrete entity.

Leaders: Omar al-JAWI, Muhammed 'Abd ar-RAHMAN.

League of the Sons of Yemen (*Rabibat Abna al-Yaman*). Founded in 1990 to represent tribal interests in the south, the League campaigned against the proposed constitution for the new republic because it did not stipulate *shari'a* as the only source of Yemeni law. The party offered 92 candidates in the 1993 general elections, none of whom were successful. League leader 'Abd al-Rahman al-Jifri, born in Yemen but now a citizen of Saudi Arabia, was named vice president of the breakaway Democratic Republic of Yemen in 1994. Following the separatists' defeat, al-Jifri moved to London, from where he subsequently served as chair of the Yemeni National Opposition Front (normally referenced as MOWJ, an abbreviation derived from the transliteration of its Arabic name). Al-Jifri maintained that he was also still the leader of the League of the Sons of Yemen, but it was also reported that League members remaining in Yemen had voted to dismiss him from his post. A small League rump participated in the 1997 elections without success.

In March 1998 al-Jifri was sentenced in absentia to ten years in prison for his role in the 1994 conflict. However, the sentence was immediately suspended, separating the MOWJ leader from the YSP separatists who had been tried at the same time. Although critical of government policies that had contributed to the "deterioration in living conditions," the MOWJ Executive Committee in March 2000 called for national reconciliation through "dialogue with the Salih administration," and, following the accord between Saudi Arabia and Yemen at midyear, the MOWJ announced that it was suspending its antigovernment activities.

Leaders: 'Abd al-Rahman al-JIFRI, Mohsen FARID.

National Democratic Front (NDF). Formed in 1976 by an assortment of *Baathists,* Marxists, Nasserites, and disaffected Yemenis, the leftist NDF subsequently conducted a sporadic guerrilla campaign against the government of North Yemen and supported the South Yemen army in the 1979 invasion. However, although the Front remained an opponent of the YAR regime, its antigovernment activities were relatively muted during the 1980s. Four of the new members appointed to the House of Representatives upon the creation of the Republic of Yemen were identified as NDF members. No NDF candidates were successful in the 1997 legislative balloting. There was no record of this party in the 2003 elections.

Two other parties gained seats in the April 2003 elections: the **Nasserite Unionist Popular Organization**, led by Secretary General Abdul Malik al-MEKHLAFI; and the **Arab Socialist Baath Party**.

The **Liberation Party** (*Hizb al-Tahrir*) organized in 2003 with the aim of creating an orthodox Islamic state but did not participate in the elections. Its leaders remained anonymous.

A previously unknown group, the **Aden-Abyan Islamic Army,** claimed responsibility for the December 1998 kidnapping of 16 westerners in southern Yemen. Zein al-Abidine al-MIHDAR, described as one of the leaders of the group, reportedly called for strikes against US installations and an end to US "aggression" against Iraq. Mihdar and several others went on trial in April 1999. Meanwhile, US and UK officials were reportedly investigating possible links between the Aden-Abyan Islamic Army, which reportedly comprised so-called "Arab Afghans" who moved to Yemen in the early 1990s after fighting Soviet forces in Afghanistan, and the terrorist network of Osama bin Laden. (Several of those accused in the bombings of US embassies in Kenya and Tanzania in mid-1998 had carried Yemeni passports.) Mihdar was executed in October 1999 after being found guilty of terrorism in August. The reported new head of the Aden-Abyan Islamic Army, Hatim Muhsin ibn FARID, was sentenced to seven years in prison in October 2000. In October 2002 the group claimed responsibility for an explosion in a French tanker off the Yemeni coast, and Yemeni officials subsequently arrested others in the attack who were suspected of having ties to *al-Qaeda.* The government continued its attacks on the Aden-Abyan Islamic Army, widely believed in recent years to be linked to *al-Qaeda.*

Legislature

The transitional **House of Representatives** (*Majlis al-Nuwab*) installed in 1990 was a 301-member body encompassing the 159 members of the former YAR Consultative Assembly, the 111 members of the former PDRY Supreme People's Council, and 31 persons named by the government (in part to represent opposition groups). A new 301-member House was directly elected by universal suffrage on April 17, 1993. Following the most recent elections on April 27, 2003, the seats were distributed as follows: the General People's Congress (GPC), 238; the Yemeni *Islah* Party, 46; the Yemeni Socialist Party, 8; the Nasserite Unionist People's Party, 3; the Arab Socialist *Baath* Party, 2; independents, 4.

A national referendum on February 20, 2001, approved a constitutional amendment increasing the legislative term of office from four to six years.

Speaker: Sheikh Abdallah ibn Husayn al-AHMAR.

Communications

Press

Although government control of the press was strict in both North and South Yemen, unification yielded considerable liberalization. By late

Cabinet

As of July 1, 2005

Prime Ministers	'Abd al-Qadir 'Abd al-Rahman Bajammal
Deputy Prime Ministers	Alawi Salah al-Salami Ahmad Muhammad
	Abdallah al-Sufan

Ministers

Agriculture and Irrigation	Hassan Umar Suwaid
Communications	'Abd al-Malik al-Mu'alimi
Culture and Tourism	Khalid al-Rowishan
Defense	Maj. Gen. Abdallah Ali Ulaywah
Education	'Abd al-Salam al Jawfi
Electricity	'Abd al-Rahman Muhammad Tarmoom
Finance	Alawi Salah al-Salami
Fisheries	Muhammad Mujwar
Foreign Affairs	Abu-Bakr 'Abdallah al-Qirbi
Higher Education and Scientific Research	'Abd al-Wahhab al-Rawhani
Human Rights	Amat al-Alim al-Suswah [f]
Immigrant Affairs	Abduh Ali al-Qubati
Industry and Trade	Khalid Rajih Shaikh
Information	Husayn Dhaifallah al-Awadhi
Interior	Rashad al-Alimi
Justice	Adnan Umar al-Gafri
Labor and Social Affairs	'Abd al-Karim al-Arhabi
Legal Affairs	Rashad Ahmed al-Rassas
Local Administration	Sadiq Amin Husayn Abu Ras
Oil and Mineral Resources	Rachid Ba Raba'a
Planning and Development	Ahmad Muhammad Abdallah al-Sufan
Public Health and Population	Muhammad al-Noami
Public Works and Urban Development	Abdallah Husayn al-Dafai
Religious Guidance	Hamud Ubad
Social Security and Civil Service	Hamud Khalid al-Sufi
Technical Education and Vocational Training	Ali Mansur Muhammad Safa
Transportation	Umar Muhsen Amud
Water and Environment	Muhammad Lutf al-Iryani
Youth and Sport	'Abd al-Rahman Muhammad al-Akwa

Ministers of State

Consultative Council and Parliamentary Affairs	Muhammad Yahya al-Sharafi
Secretary General to the Presidency	Maj. Gen. Abdallah Husayn al-Bashiri
Without Portfolio	Qasim Ahmad al-Aajam
	Muhammad Ali Yasir
	Kassim al-Ajam

[f] = female

1991 it was reported that Yemen boasted over 100 newspapers and other periodicals, many of them critical of the government. However, extensive censorship was reimposed at the outbreak of the 1994 civil war, ongoing restrictions prompting a demonstration in support of freedom of expression at San'a in February 1995 which was broken up by government forces. Harassment (including prosecution) of journalists by the government has subsequently been reported on a regular basis. In April 2005 the Ministry of Information drafted amendments to expand freedom of the press and free speech, and the following month President Salih asked for legislation that would not include prison or detention for journalists. However, press freedoms remained uneven, with some 11 journalists sentenced to prison for two years in early 2005 for "criminal acts" in Yemen and abroad, allegedly related to terrorism. Except as noted, the following are published at San'a in Arabic: *al-Thawra* (The Revolution, 110,000), government-owned daily; *al-Jumhuriya* (100,000), government-controlled daily published at Ta'iz; *Yemen Times* (30,000), independent weekly in English; *26th September* (25,000), armed forces weekly; *al-Rabi Ashar Min Uktubar* (14th October, 20,000), government-controlled daily published at Aden; *al-Shoura* (15,000), weekly; *Ash-Sharara* (The Spark, 6,000), government-controlled daily published at Aden; *al-Sahwa* (Awakening), Islamic fundamentalist weekly; *al-Mithaq* (The Charter), GPC weekly; *al-Wahdawi,* NUPP weekly; *Yemen Observer,* independent weekly in English; *al-Bilad* (The Country), rightist weekly; *San'a,* leftist monthly. In recent reports *Al-Ayyan,* published at Aden, has been described as the biggest-selling independent newspaper.

News Agency

The Saba News Agency is located at the capital; there is also an Aden News Agency.

Broadcasting and Computing

At unification the northern and southern state broadcast organizations were combined to form the Broadcasting Service of the Republic of Yemen (*Idha'at al-Jumhuriyat al-Yamaniyah*), which operates radio stations at San'a, Ta'iz, Hodeida, and Aden, and television services at San'a and Aden. There were approximately 580,000 television receivers and 150,000 personal computers serving 110,000 Internet users in 2003.

Intergovernmental Representation

Ambassador to the US
Abdulwahab A. al-HAJJRI

US Ambassador to Yemen
Thomas KRAJESKI

Permanent Representative to the UN: 'Abdallah M. al-SAIDI

IGO Memberships (Non-UN)
AFESD, AMF, CAEU, CCC, IDB, Interpol, IOM, IOR-ARC, LAS, NAM, OIC

PALESTINE LIBERATION ORGANIZATION

MUNATHAMAT AL-TAHRIR AL-FALISTINIYYA

Note: In November 2005, *Fatah* shut down its primary for upcoming parliamentary elections in the Gaza Strip when gunmen disrupted polling places. In December, *Hamas* (Islamic Resistance Movement) candidates swept municipal elections in Nablus and won control in Jenin and El Bireh. *Hamas* candidates also won three seats in the key West Bank city of Ramallah. The results represented a serious blow to the political power of Fatah, whose declining fortunes eventually led rival factions within the organization to agree to a united front in parliamentary elections scheduled for January 25, 2006; one group, headed by Marwan Barghuthi, had previously drafted and submitted a separate list of candidates to run as members of the *Mustaqbal* (Future) Party. In the parliamentary elections, Hamas scored a decisive victory, winning 74 of the 132 seats; Fatah secured 45 seats; the Popular Front for the Liberation of Palestine won 3 seats; *al Badeel* (Alternative)–a coalition of the Democratic Front for the Liberation of Palestine, the Palestinian Democratic Union, and Palestine Peoples Party–won 2 seats, as did Independent Palestine and the Third Way; the remaining 4 seats went to independent candidates.

Establishment of the Palestine Liberation Organization (PLO) was authorized on January 17, 1964, during an Arab summit held at Cairo, Egypt. Largely through the efforts of Ahmad SHUQAIRI, the Palestinian representative to the Arab League, an assembly of Palestinians met at (East) Jerusalem the following May 28–June 2 to draft a National Covenant and General Principles of a Fundamental Law, the latter subsequently serving as the constitutional basis of a government-in-exile. Under the Fundamental Law, the assembly became a 315-member Palestinian National Council (PNC) comprised primarily of representatives of the leading *fedayeen* (guerrilla) groups, various Palestinian mass movements and trade unions, and Palestinian communities throughout the Arab world. An Executive Committee was established as the PLO's administrative organ, while an intermediate Central Council (initially of 21 but eventually 100 members) was created in 1973 to exercise legislative-executive responsibilities on behalf of the PNC between PNC sessions.

In its original form, the PLO was a quasi-governmental entity designed to act independently of the various Arab states in support of Palestinian

interests. Its subordinate organs encompassed a variety of political, cultural, and fiscal activities as well as a Military Department, under which a Palestine Liberation Army (PLA) was established as a conventional military force of recruits stationed in Egypt, Iraq, and Syria.

In the wake of the 1967 Arab-Israeli war, the direction of the PLO underwent a significant transformation. Shuqairi resigned as chairman of the Executive Committee and was replaced in December 1967 by Yahia HAMMUDA, who was in turn succeeded in February 1969 by Yasir 'ARAFAT, leader of *Fatah* (below). At that time the PNC adopted a posture more favorable to guerrilla activities against Israel, insisted upon greater independence from Arab governments, and for the first time called for the establishment of a Palestinian state in which Muslims, Christians, and Jews would have equal rights. In effect, the PLO thus tacitly accepted a Jewish presence in Palestine, although it remained committed to the eradication of any Zionist state in the area.

In 1970–1971 the PLO and the *fedayeen* groups were expelled from Jordan, and Lebanon became their principal base of operations. The Israeli victory in the October 1973 war, and the fear that Jordan might negotiate on behalf of Palestinians from the occupied territories, resulted in another change in the PLO's strategy: in June 1974 it formally adopted a proposal that called for the creation of a "national authority" in the West Bank and Gaza as a first step toward the "liberation" of historical Palestine. This tacit recognition of Israel precipitated a major split among the PLO's already ideologically diverse components, and on July 29 a leftist "rejection front" was formed in opposition to any partial settlement in the Middle East. In December 1976 the PLO Central Council voiced support for establishment of an "independent state" in the West Bank and Gaza, which was widely interpreted as implying acceptance of Israel's permanent existence. Shortly thereafter, contacts were established between the PLO and the Israeli Left.

On September 1, 1982, immediately after the PLO withdrawal from West Beirut (see Lebanon article), US President Reagan proposed the cre-

ation of a Palestinian "entity" in the West Bank and Gaza, to be linked with Jordan under King Hussein. The idea was bitterly attacked by pro-Syrian radicals during a PNC meeting at Algiers in February 1983, with the council ultimately calling for a "confederation" between Jordan and an independent Palestinian state, thus endorsing an Arab League resolution of five months earlier that implicitly entailed recognition of Israel. Over radical objections, the Algiers meeting also sanctioned a dialogue with "progressive and democratic" elements within Israel, i.e., those favoring peace with the PLO. This position, however, was also unacceptable to the group's best-known moderate, Dr. Issam SARTAWI, who resigned from the council after being denied an opportunity to deliver a speech calling for formal discussions with Israeli leaders on the possibility of a clear-cut "two-state" solution. Subsequently, in an apparent trial balloon, *Fatah*'s (then) deputy chairman, Salah KHALAF, declared that the group would support the Reagan peace initiative if the United States were to endorse the principle of Palestinian self-determination. The meeting's final communiqué, on the other hand, dismissed the Reagan proposal as not providing "a sound basis for a just and lasting resolution of the Palestinian problem."

PLO chairman 'Arafat met for three days in early April 1983 with King Hussein without reaching agreement on a number of key issues, including the structure of a possible confederation, representation of Palestinians in peace negotiations with Israel, and removal of PLO headquarters to 'Amman. As the discussions concluded, Dr. Sartawi was assassinated at Albufeira, Portugal, by a member of an extremist *Fatah* splinter, headed by the Damascus-based Sabry Khalil al-BANNA (also known as Abu NIDAL). A week later, amid evidence of growing restiveness among Palestinian guerrillas in eastern Lebanon, the PLO Executive Committee met at Tunis to consider means of "surmounting the obstacles" that had emerged in the discussions with Hussein.

In mid-May 1983 'Arafat returned to Lebanon for the first time since the Beirut exodus to counter what had escalated into a dissident rebellion led by

Musa AWAD (also known as Abu AKRAM) of the Libyan-backed Popular Front for the Liberation of Palestine–General Command (PFLP-GC), a splinter of the larger PFLP. In late June 'Arafat convened a *Fatah* meeting at Damascus to deal with the mutineers' insistence that he abandon his flirtation with the Reagan peace plan and give greater priority to military confrontation with Israel.

On June 24, 1983, President Assad ordered 'Arafat's expulsion from Syria after the PLO leader had accused him of fomenting the PFLP-GC rebellion, and a month later 'Arafat ousted two senior commanders whose promotions had precipitated tension within the ranks of the guerrillas in Lebanon's Bekaa Valley. The fighting nonetheless continued, and in early November one of 'Arafat's two remaining Lebanese strongholds north of Tripoli fell to the insurgents. Late in the month the PLO leader agreed to withdraw from an increasingly untenable position within the city itself, exiting from Lebanon for the second time on December 20 in a Greek ferry escorted by French naval vessels.

In early 1985 'Arafat strengthened and formalized his ties with Jordan's King Hussein in an accord signed by both leaders on February 11. The agreement, described as "a framework for common action towards reaching a peaceful and just settlement to the Palestine question," called for: total withdrawal by Israel from the territories it had occupied in 1967 in exchange for comprehensive peace; the right of self-determination for the Palestinians within the context of a West Bank-Gaza/Jordan confederation; resolution of the Palestinian refugee problem in accordance with UN resolutions; and peace negotiations under the auspices of an international conference that would include the five permanent members of the UN Security Council and representatives of the PLO, the latter being part of a joint Jordanian-Palestinian delegation.

'Arafat's peace overtures deepened divisions within the ranks of the Palestine national movement. In reaction to the February 1985 pact with Jordan, six PLO-affiliated organizations formed a Palestine National Salvation Front (PNSF) at Damascus to oppose 'Arafat's policies. Differences over peace initiatives also erupted during a November meeting at Baghdad of the PNC's Central Council. Disagreement turned mainly on whether to accept UN Security Council Resolutions 242 and 338, which called for withdrawal from the occupied territories and peaceful settlement of the Palestine dispute in a manner that would imply recognition of Israel. Shortly thereafter, 'Arafat attempted to reinforce his image as "peacemaker" with a declaration denouncing terrorism. The "Cairo Declaration" was issued after lengthy discussions with Egyptian President Husni Mubarak on ways to speed up peace negotiations. 'Arafat cited a 1974 PLO decision "to condemn all outside operations and all forms of terrorism." He promised to take "all punitive measures against violators" and stated that "the PLO denounces and condemns all terrorist acts, whether those involving countries or by persons or groups, against unarmed innocent civilians in any place."

Meanwhile, relations between 'Arafat and Hussein had again been strained by a number of incidents that displeased the king. In October 1985 guerrillas allegedly linked to the Palestine Liberation Front (PLF) hijacked the Italian cruise ship, *Achille Lauro,* which resulted in the murder of an American tourist, while talks were broken off between the British government and a joint Palestinian-Jordanian delegation because of PLO refusal to sign a statement recognizing Israel and renouncing the use of terrorism.

The PLO sustained a major setback at the hands of Shi'ite *al-Amal* forces that besieged two Palestinian refugee camps in Lebanon during May and June 1985. From Tunis an extraordinary session of the Arab League Council called on all parties to end the siege, which was accomplished by Syrian mediation in mid-June. One effect of the action was to temporarily heal the rift between pro- and anti-'Arafat Palestinian factions.

By early 1986 it had become apparent that the Jordanian-PLO accord had stalled over 'Arafat's refusal, despite strong pressure from King Hussein and other Arab moderates, to endorse UN Resolutions 242 and 338 as the basis of a solution to the Palestinian issue. Among the PLO's objections were references to Palestinians as refugees and a failure to grant them the right of self-determination.

On the latter ground, 'Arafat rejected a secret US tender of seats for the PLO at a proposed international Middle East peace conference. In February Hussein announced that the peace effort had collapsed and encouraged West Bank and Gaza Strip Palestinians to select new leaders. He underscored the attack on 'Arafat during ensuing months by proposing an internationally financed, $1.3 billion development plan for the West Bank, which he hoped would win the approval of its "silent majority." The PLO denounced the plan, while describing Israeli efforts to appoint Arab mayors in the West Bank as attempts to perpetuate Israeli occupation. The rupture culminated in Hussein's ordering the closure of *Fatah*'s Jordanian offices in July.

Hussein's overture elicited little support from the West Bank Palestinians, and by late 1986 it was evident that 'Arafat still commanded the support of his most important constituency. Rather than undercutting 'Arafat's position, Hussein's challenge paved the way for unification talks between *Fatah* and other PLO factions that had opposed the accord from the outset. Following initial opposition from the PNSF in August, the reunification drive gained momentum in early 1987 with indications that Georges HABASH of the PFLP (the PNSF's largest component) might join leaders of the Democratic Front for the Liberation of Palestine (DFLP) and other groups in trying to rescue the PLO from its debilitating fractionalization. Support was also received from PLO factions in Lebanon that had recently coalesced under *Fatah* leadership to withstand renewed attacks by *al-Amal* forces. Indeed, Syria's inability to stem the mass return of heavily armed *Fatah* guerrillas to Lebanon was viewed as a major contribution to 'Arafat's resurgence within the PLO. Meanwhile, King Hussein also attempted to mend relations with the PLO by announcing that the Jordanian-PLO fund for West Bank and Gaza Strip Palestinians, suspended at the time of the February 1986 breach, would be reactivated. Subsequently, the fund was bolstered by new pledges totalling $14.5 million from Saudi Arabia and Kuwait.

Although hard-line factions continued to call for 'Arafat's ouster, the PLO leader's more militant posture opened the way for convening the long-delayed 18th session of the PNC (its membership reportedly having been expanded to 426) at Algiers on April 20–26, 1987. Confounding critics who had long predicted his political demise, 'Arafat emerged from the meeting with his PLO chairmanship intact, thanks in part to a declared willingness to share the leadership with representatives of non-*Fatah* factions. Thus, although several Syrian-based formations boycotted the Algiers meeting, 'Arafat's appearance at its conclusion arm-in-arm with former rivals Habash of the PFLP and Nayif HAWATMEH of the DFLP symbolized the success of the unity campaign.

During the last half of 1987 there were reports of secret meetings between the PLO and left-wing Israeli politicians to forge an agreement based on a cessation of hostilities, a halt to Israeli settlement in the Gaza Strip and West Bank, and mutual recognition by the PLO and Israel. However, nothing of substance was achieved, and by November it appeared that interest in the issue had waned, as evidenced by the far greater attention given to the Iran-Iraq war at an Arab League summit in November.

The Palestinian question returned to the forefront of Arab concern in December 1987 with the outbreak of violence in the occupied territories. Although the disturbances were believed to have started spontaneously, the PLO, by mobilizing grassroots structures it had nurtured throughout the 1980s, helped to fuel their transformation into an ongoing *intifada* (uprising).

In an apparent effort to heighten PLO visibility, 'Arafat demanded in March 1988 that the organization be accorded full representation (rather than participation in a joint Jordanian-Palestinian delegation) at any Middle Eastern peace conference. However, the prospects for such a conference dimmed in April when the PLO's military leader, Khalil al-WAZIR (also known as Abu JIHAD), was killed, apparently by an Israeli assassination team. Whatever the motive for the killing, its most immediate impact was to enhance PLO solidarity and provide the impetus for a dramatic "reconciliation" between 'Arafat and Syrian President Assad. However, that rapprochement soon disintegrated, as bloody clashes broke out between

Fatah and Syrian-backed *Fatah* dissidents (see Fatah Uprising, below) for control of the Beirut refugee camps in May. Elsewhere in the Arab world, the position of the PLO continued to improve. A special Arab League summit in June 1988 strongly endorsed the *intifada* and reaffirmed the PLO's role as the sole legitimate representative of the Palestinian people. In addition, a number of countries at the summit reportedly pledged financial aid to the PLO to support continuance of the uprising.

On July 31, 1988, in a move that surprised PLO leaders, King Hussein announced that Jordan would discontinue its administrative functions in the West Bank on the presumption that Palestinians in the occupied territories wished to proceed toward independence under PLO stewardship. Although Jordan subsequently agreed to partial interim provision of municipal services, the announcement triggered extensive debate within the PLO on appropriate policies for promoting a peace settlement that would yield creation of a true Palestinian government.

Upon convocation of the 19th PNC session at Algiers in mid-November 1988 it appeared that a majority within the PLO and among Palestinians in the occupied territories favored "land for peace" negotiations with Israel. On November 15 'Arafat, with the endorsement of the PNC, declared the establishment of an independent Palestinian state encompassing the West Bank and Gaza Strip with the Arab sector of Jerusalem as its capital, based on the UN "two-state" proposal that had been rejected by the Arab world in 1947. The PLO Executive Committee was authorized to direct the affairs of the new state pending the establishment of a provisional government.

In conjunction with the independence declaration, the PNC adopted a new political program that included endorsement of the UN resolutions that implicitly acknowledged Israel's right to exist. The PNC also called for UN supervision of the occupied territories pending final resolution of the conflict through a UN-sponsored international conference. Although Israel had rejected the statehood declaration and the new PLO peace initiative in advance, many countries (over 110 as of April 1989)

subsequently recognized the newly proclaimed entity. The onrush of diplomatic activity following the PNC session included a speech by 'Arafat in December to the UN General Assembly, which convened at Geneva for the occasion because of US refusal to grant the PLO chairman a visa to speak in New York. A short time later, after a 13-year lapse, the United States agreed to direct talks with the PLO, Washington announcing it was satisfied that 'Arafat had "without ambiguity" renounced terrorism and recognized Israel's right to exist.

On April 2, 1989, the PLO's Central Council unanimously elected 'Arafat president of the self-proclaimed Palestinian state and designated Faruk QADDUMI as foreign minister of the still essentially symbolic government. Israel remained adamantly opposed to direct contact with the PLO, however, proposing instead that Palestinians end the *intifada* in return for the opportunity to elect non-PLO representatives to peace talks. Nevertheless, hope subsequently grew that a compromise was possible under the influence of continued US-PLO discussions and intensified Egyptian mediation efforts.

During the rest of 1989 and early 1990 the PLO appeared to make several significant concessions, despite growing frustration among Palestinians and the Arab world generally over a perceived lack of Israeli reciprocity. Of particular note was 'Arafat's "conditional" acceptance in February 1990 of a US plan for direct Palestinian-Israeli peace talks, theretofore opposed by the PLO in favor of the long-discussed international peace conference. However, the Israeli government, unwilling to accept even indirect PLO involvement, rejected the US proposal, thus further undercutting the PLO moderates. By June the impasse had worsened, in part because of PLO protests over the growing immigration to Israel of Soviet Jews. Moreover, Washington decided to discontinue its talks with the PLO because of a lack of disciplinary action against those claiming responsibility for an attempted commando attack in Tel Aviv (see PLF, below).

Subsequently, the PLO leadership and a growing proportion of its constituency gravitated to the hard-line, anti-Western position being advocated by Iraqi President Saddam Hussein, a stance that created serious problems for the PLO following Iraq's invasion and occupation of Kuwait in August 1990. Despite anti-Iraq resolutions approved by the majority of Arab League members, 'Arafat and other prominent PLO leaders openly supported President Hussein throughout the Gulf crisis. As a result, Saudi Arabia and the other Gulf states suspended their financial aid to the PLO (estimated at about $100 million annually), while Western sympathy for the Palestinian cause eroded. Following the defeat of Iraqi forces by the US-led coalition in March 1991, the PLO was left, in the words of a *Christian Science Monitor* correspondent, "hamstrung by political isolation and empty coffers." Consequently, the PLO's leverage in Middle East negotiations initiated by the United States at midyear was reduced, and the 20th PNC session at Algiers in late September agreed to a joint Palestinian-Jordanian negotiating team with no official link to the PLO for the multilateral peace talks inaugurated at Madrid, Spain, in October. However, it was generally conceded that the Palestinian negotiators were handpicked by 'Arafat and represented a direct extension of PLO strategy.

As the peace talks moved into early 1992, 'Arafat and *Fatah* faced growing criticism that concessions had yielded little in return, fundamentalist groups such as the Islamic Resistance Movement (*Hamas,* see under Israel: Political Groups in Occupied and Previously Occupied Territories) in particular benefitting from mainstream PLO defections in the West Bank and Gaza. Consequently, it was widely believed that 'Arafat would face yet another strong challenge at the Central Council meeting scheduled for April. However, circumstances changed after the PLO leader's plane crashed in a sandstorm in the Libyan desert on April 7, with 'Arafat unaccounted for, and widely presumed dead, for 15 hours. Panic reportedly overcame many of his associates as they faced the possible disintegration of a leaderless organization. Thus, when 'Arafat was found to be alive, a tumultuous celebration spread throughout the Palestinian population, reconfirming his preeminence. As a result, even though the succession issue remained a deep concern, 'Arafat's policies, including contin-

ued participation in the peace talks, were endorsed with little opposition when the Central Council finally convened in May. Negotiations were put on hold, however, until the Israeli election in June, after which PLO leaders cautiously welcomed the victory of the Israel Labor Party as enhancing the peace process.

Although peace talks resumed in August 1992, they failed to generate any immediate progress, and criticism of 'Arafat's approach again intensified. In September the DFLP, the PFLP, *Hamas,* and a number of other non-PLO groups established a coalition in Damascus to oppose any further negotiations with Israel. In addition, it was subsequently reported that 'Arafat's support had dwindled at the October session of the PLO's Central Council.

Israel's expulsion of some 400 Palestinians from the occupied territories to Lebanon in late December 1992 further clouded the situation, the PLO condemning the deportations and ordering the Palestinian representatives to suspend their participation in the peace negotiations. Even after the talks resumed in mid-1993, they quickly appeared deadlocked, and rancorous debate was reported within the PLO leadership on how to proceed. By that time, with *Hamas*'s influence in the occupied territories continuing to grow, some onlookers were describing the PLO and its aging chairman as "fading into oblivion" and "collapsing." However, those writing off 'Arafat were unaware that PLO and Israeli representatives had been meeting secretly for nearly eight months at Oslo, Norway, and other European capitals to discuss mutual recognition and the beginning of Palestinian self-rule in the occupied territories. Although initial reports of the discussions in late August were met with widespread incredulity, an exchange of letters on September 9 between 'Arafat and Israeli Prime Minister Yitzhak Rabin confirmed that the peace process had indeed taken a hopeful turn. For his part, 'Arafat wrote that the PLO recognized "the right of the State of Israel to exist in peace and security" and described PLO Charter statements to the contrary to be "inoperative and no longer valid." The chairman also declared that the PLO "renounces the use of terrorism and other acts of violence." In return, Rabin's short letter confirmed that Israel had "decided to recognize the PLO as the representative of the Palestinian people and commence negotiations with the PLO within the Middle East peace process."

For all practical purposes the initial round of direct PLO-Israeli negotiations had already been completed, and the mutual recognition letters were quickly followed by unofficial but extensive reports of a draft Declaration of Principles regarding Palestinian autonomy. The PLO Executive Committee endorsed the draft document on September 10, 1993, although several members resigned in protest over 'Arafat's "sell-out," and the stage was set for a dramatic ceremony on September 13 at Washington, D.C., that concluded with signing of the Declaration by 'Arafat and Rabin.

The peace accord proposed the establishment of an interim Palestinian government in the Gaza Strip and the West Bank town of Jericho and committed Israel and the PLO to negotiating a permanent settlement on all of the occupied territories within five years. However, mention of the agreement was rarely made without immediate reference to the many obstacles in its path, including strong opposition from Israel's *Likud* Party and, on the Palestinian side, from *Hamas,* the DFLP, and the PFLP. There was also widespread concern that militant activity could sabotage the peace agreement. In addition, many details remained to be resolved before the Declaration of Principles could be transformed into a genuine self-rule agreement. Finally, there still appeared to be a wide, and possibly unbridgeable, gulf between the Israeli and PLO positions on several issues, such as the future of Jerusalem and whether a completely independent Palestinian state would ultimately be created. Nevertheless, the remarkable image, flashed via television to a transfixed world, of 'Arafat and Rabin shaking hands at the Washington ceremony seemed to persuade even the most skeptical observers that a historic corner had been turned. For the PLO chairman the agreement represented an extraordinary personal triumph, his surging status being reflected by a private session with US President Bill Clinton after the signing ceremony and by a meeting the next day with UN Secretary General Boutros Boutros-Ghali.

International donors quickly expressed their enthusiasm for the agreement by pledging $2.4 billion to promote economic development in Gaza/Jericho over the next five years. Shortly thereafter, the PLO's Central Committee approved the accord by a reported vote of 63–8. However, the declaration's projection that Israeli troops would begin their withdrawal by mid-December proved unrealistic, and extended negotiations were required on issues such as the size of the Jericho enclave and the control of border crossings.

Amid growing international concern that the peace plan could unravel, negotiations resumed in April 1994, and at a May 4 ceremony at Cairo, Egypt, 'Arafat and Rabin signed a final agreement formally launching Israeli troop withdrawal and Palestinian self-rule. The Israeli pullout, and concurrent assumption of police authority by PLO forces, was completed in Jericho on May 13 and Gaza on May 18. (Israeli troops remained stationed in buffer zones around 19 Jewish settlements in Gaza.)

The accord provided for all government responsibilities in Gaza/Jericho (except, significantly, for external security and foreign affairs) to be turned over to the "Palestinian authority" for a five-year interim period. Negotiations were to begin immediately on the second stage of Israeli redeployment, under which additional West Bank territory was to be turned over to Palestinian control, while a final accord on the permanent status of the occupied territories was to be completed no later than May 1999.

On May 28, 1994, 'Arafat announced the first appointments to the Palestinian National Authority (PNA), with himself as chairman of the cabinet-like body. (The PLO leader subsequently routinely referred to himself as "president" of the PNA. However, the title, and indeed the Palestinian insistence on including "National" in the PNA's name, was not sanctioned by the Israeli government, which remained officially opposed to the eventual creation of a Palestinian state.) With most PLO offices in Tunis having been closed, 'Arafat entered Gaza on

July 1, setting foot on "Palestinian soil" for the first time in 25 years. It was initially assumed that the PNA's headquarters would be in Jericho, where the PNA, which had already held several preliminary sessions, was formally sworn in before 'Arafat on July 5. However, 'Arafat and most government officials subsequently settled in Gaza City.

Internal security initially proved to be less of a concern than anticipated within the autonomous areas, and the PNA focused primarily on efforts to revive the region's severe economic distress. The World Bank, designated to manage the disbursement of the aid pledged by international donors the previous fall, announced plans to distribute about $1.2 billion over the next three years, primarily for infrastructure projects. On the Palestinian side, coordination of such assistance fell to a recently established Palestinian Economic Council for Development and Reconstruction (PECDAR).

In late August 1994, Israeli officials announced they were turning educational responsibilities for all of the West Bank over to the PNA as the beginning of an "early empowerment" program. The PNA was scheduled to assume authority throughout the West Bank soon in four additional areas—health, social welfare, taxation, and tourism. On the political front, the PNA proposed that elections to a Palestinian Council be held in December. However, no consensus had been reached by September either between the PLO and Israel or among Palestinians themselves on the type, size, constituency, or mandate of the new body.

Pessimism over the future of the self-rule plan deepened in ensuing months as security matters distracted attention from political and economic discussions. Under heavy pressure from Israel, the PNA authorized the detention of several hundred members of *Hamas* after that grouping had claimed responsibility for a gun and grenade attack in Jerusalem on October 9. Ten days later a *Hamas* suicide bomber blew up a bus in Tel Aviv, killing 22 people and prompting Israel to close its borders with the West Bank and Gaza and implement other new security measures. In addition, Palestinian police arrested nearly 200 members of the militant group Islamic Holy War (*al-Jihad*

al-Islami) after it claimed responsibility for a bombing in Gaza in early November that left three Israeli soldiers dead. The tension culminated on November 18 in the killing of 13 people as police exchanged gunfire with *Hamas* and *al-Jihad* demonstrators in Gaza, some observers suggesting that the Palestinians were on the brink of a civil war. Further complicating matters for the PLO/PNA, a meeting of the PLO Executive Committee called by 'Arafat in November failed to achieve a quorum when dissidents refused to attend. Among other things, the PLO chairman had hoped that the committee would formally rescind the sections in the organization's National Covenant that called for the destruction of Israel.

Another *al-Jihad* suicide bombing on January 22, 1995, killed more than 20 people in the Israeli town of Netanya, Israel responding by suspending negotiations with the PNA until stronger measures were taken to prevent such attacks from the West Bank and Gaza. Consequently, 'Arafat authorized the creation of special military courts in February to deal with issues of "state security" and thereby permit a crackdown on militants. While the action appeared to appease Israel, it was criticized by human rights leaders and non-PLO Palestinian organizations. As a result, facing what was described as yet another test of his leadership, 'Arafat called for a PLO Executive Committee meeting, the absence of the proposed covenant change from the agenda apparently facilitating the achievement of a quorum.

Although reportedly facing intense scrutiny from the Executive Committee, which was seen as attempting to recover some of the influence it had lost to the PNA, the PLO chairman nevertheless emerged with a mandate to pursue negotiations with Israel. Following a further intensification in April of the PNA campaign against "terrorists," peace talks regained momentum, 100-member negotiating teams from each side sequestering themselves at the Egyptian resort of Taba for several months. Finally, after six consecutive days of direct negotiations between 'Arafat and Israeli Foreign Affairs Minister Shimon Peres, agreement was reached on September 24 on the next phase of Israeli troop redeployment and the extension of Palestinian self-rule to much of the West Bank.

Israeli troops were to start withdrawing immediately from six towns and some 450 villages in the West Bank, with the PNA assuming control therein. Temporary joint responsibility was arranged for rural areas, while Israeli troops would continue to guard the numerous Jewish settlements in the West Bank and Gaza. Upon completion of the Israeli redeployment, elections were to be held, under international supervision, to a new Palestinian Council. Provision was also made for a 25-member "executive authority," whose head would be elected in separate balloting. It was this post for which 'Arafat was expected to be a candidate, public opinion polls indicating he would be the likely winner.

It was estimated that self-rule would initially be extended to about 30 percent of the West Bank, with additional territory (up to a 70 percent total) to be ceded following the elections. In support of the accord, Israel pledged a three-stage release of thousands of Palestinian prisoners, while the PLO agreed to revoke the anti-Israeli articles in its covenant within two years.

The Israeli-Palestinian Interim Agreement on the West Bank and Gaza (informally referred to as "Oslo II") was signed by 'Arafat and Prime Minister Rabin at another White House ceremony on September 28, 1995, the attendees including King Hussein of Jordan and President Mubarak of Egypt. Although "less mesmerizing" than its 1993 predecessor, the signing was considered no less consequential since the 400-page accord delineated "in intricate detail" most of the substantive aspects of the Israeli-Palestinian "divorce." On the other hand, very contentious issues remained to be resolved, including the rights of several million Palestinian refugees in countries such as Jordan, Lebanon, and Syria, many of whom hoped to return "home" to the West Bank and Israel. Talks were scheduled to begin in May 1996 on that question as well as the future status of Jerusalem, the eastern portion of which Palestinians claimed as their "capital." Difficult negotiations were also forecast regarding the estimated 140,000 Jewish settlers, who vowed never to leave the region to which, in their opinion, "Greater Israel" has a biblically ordained right. A final agreement on these and all other outstanding issues was due no later than May 1999, at which point the Palestinian Council was scheduled to turn over authority to whatever new governmental organs had been established. It was by no means clear what the final borders of the Palestinian "entity" would be or, for that matter, what official form of government it would assume. Although Israeli officials maintained their formal opposition to an independent Palestine, 'Arafat described the 1995 agreement as leading to "an era in which the Palestinian people will live free and sovereign in their country." However, in a decision that was to have major repercussions later, the Israeli and PLO negotiators postponed further discussions of the contentious issue of the proposed withdrawal of Israeli troops from the West Bank town of Hebron, home to a militant group of ultraconservative Jewish settlers. The peace process was also shaken, at least indirectly, by Rabin's assassination on November 5 by an Israeli opposed to recent developments.

With the formal encouragement of the PLO Executive Committee (which met at Cairo on November 12–13, 1995, to discuss the matter), 'Arafat subsequently attempted to convince *Hamas* and theretofore "rejectionist" PLO factions to participate in the upcoming Palestinian elections. Although those discussions initially appeared promising, *Hamas* and a number of major PLO components (most notably the DFLP and the PFLP) ultimately urged their supporters to boycott the balloting on the ground that electoral regulations were skewed in favor of 'Arafat's *Fatah* at the expense of smaller formations. Nevertheless, the elections of January 20, 1996, were still viewed as a major milestone in the self-rule process, 'Arafat's "presidential" victory and *Fatah*'s success in the legislative voting being widely construed as a significant popular endorsement of the current peace plans. (For details on the elections see Palestinian Governmental Structures under Occupied and Previously Occupied Territories in Israeli article.)

Militant opposition to the Oslo accords moved even further to the forefront of concerns in late February and early March 1996 when bomb attacks left some 60 Israelis dead at Jerusalem and Tel Aviv. Temporary closure of the borders of the self-rule areas by Israeli forces created pressure upon 'Arafat from within the Palestinian population, while added concerns about security were seen as a substantial political problem for Israeli Prime Minister Shimon Peres, facing an early election in May. For his part, 'Arafat implemented several measures apparently designed to help Peres, including the arrest of a number of militants from *Hamas* and other groups and the banning of some six Palestinian "militias." In addition, the PLO chairman convened the 21st session of the PNC (now reported as comprising 669 members) at Gaza City on April 22–24, to consider formal revision of the National Covenant to reflect recent understanding of the issue. The PNC session, the first to be held on "Palestinian" soil since 1966, agreed by a vote of 504–54 that all clauses in the covenant that contradict recent PLO pledges were to be annulled. In general, the changes would recognize Israel's right to exist and renounce "terrorism and other acts of violence" on the part of the PLO. Final language on the revisions was to be included in a new charter, which the PNC directed the Central Council to draft.

Despite the PLO's efforts to allay the fears of Israeli voters, the security question dominated the May 29, 1996, Israeli election in which *Likud* leader Benjamin Netanyahu eked out a victory over Peres. As expected, those results cast an immediate pall over the peace process, Netanyahu's hard line throwing even previously negotiated compromises into question, let alone future deliberations. Israeli-PLO talks resumed in late July, but no progress ensued, even after the much sought after "face-to-face" discussions between 'Arafat and Netanyahu in early September. International concern that the autonomy plan was unraveling and growing criticism from moderate Arab states also seemingly failed to move the Netanyahu government (a tenuous coalition that included several ultraconservative groupings). Rising pressure finally erupted in fighting between Palestinians and Israelis in late September. US President Bill Clinton quickly summoned 'Arafat, Netanyahu, and Jordan's King Hussein to a "crisis summit" at Washington, which appeared to reduce tensions, albeit without any apparent resolution of the underlying issues, particularly the status of Hebron, described as a "powder keg" that seemingly had assumed a psychological importance well out of proportion to its intrinsic significance.

As Netanyahu continued to resist redeployment of Israeli troops from Hebron throughout the rest of the year, 'Arafat warned of the risk of the spontaneous resumption of the *intifada*. Finally, under apparent heavy US pressure, Netanyahu accepted an agreement in early January 1997 that essentially reaffirmed the provisions of Oslo II. Among other things, the new accord (approved by the PLO Executive Committee on January 15) provided for Palestinian control to be extended to about 80 percent of Hebron, with Israeli withdrawal from additional rural West Bank areas to occur in stages from March 1997 through mid-1998. Assuming satisfactory progress on that front (not a certainty considering differing Israeli and Palestinian views on how much territory would ultimately be ceded to Palestinian rule), final talks were to be conducted on the still highly charged issues of the status of Palestinian refugees throughout the region, the nature of permanent governmental structures for the Palestinian "entity," and disposition of sovereignty claims to East Jerusalem.

Chairman 'Arafat convened a "national dialogue" meeting in February 1997 in an effort to involve the formerly dissident PLO factions as well as non-PLO Palestinian groups in adopting a consensus on Palestinian proposals should final status talks be launched with Israel. However, with Israeli-Palestinian negotiations having collapsed, 'Arafat's "national unity" conference in August appeared primarily aimed not at negotiations but rather at portraying solidarity in the face of perceived Israeli intransigence, the presence of *Hamas* and *al-Jihad* at the session lending weight to his assertions that military resistance (including resumption of the *intifada*) was becoming a growing possibility.

In February 1998 the PLO Executive Committee deferred a final decision on the proposed new PLO charter, eliciting Israeli concern that the 1996 action by the PNC remained insufficient as far as guaranteeing Israel's security was concerned. Meanwhile, a degree of attention within the PLO focused on the question of a successor to 'Arafat, whose health was believed to be in decline. No dominant candidate had emerged, once again spotlighting the difficulties that would be faced if 'Arafat were unable to continue as the champion of the Palestinian cause.

The peace process appeared to have been relaunched by the Wye accords of October 1998 (see article on Israel for details), and, as part of that agreement, the PLO Central Council met on December 10 to consider Israeli requests regarding the PLO covenant. 'Arafat and other Palestinian representatives had argued that no further action was required, claiming that the PLO chairman's earlier letter to President Clinton had delineated which articles in the covenant had been voided by the PNC in 1996. However, the Central Council endorsed the particulars in 'Arafat's letter, and on December 14 the PNC reaffirmed the covenant changes by a nearly unanimous show of hands. Although that action finally appeared to put Israeli concerns on the issue to rest, instability in the Israeli government subsequently led to the suspension of additional implementation of the Wye accords and postponement of further negotiations until the new Israeli elections scheduled for May 1999. In that context, under heavy international pressure, the Central Council in late April 1999 endorsed 'Arafat's recent decision to postpone the unilateral declaration of Palestinian statehood, which had been planned for May 4, 1999.

In September 1999 'Arafat and new Israeli Prime Minister Ehud Barak signed the Sharm el-Sheikh agreement for the resumption of negotiations (see the article on Israel for details on that accord as well as for additional information on a number of points referenced below). In view of rising hopes for progress on that front, the PLO Central Council extended the deadline for statehood declaration until September 30. Meanwhile, by early 2000 the PFLP and the DFLP had resumed participation in the council's deliberations. For Palestinians, at least, another positive development was a meeting in February 2000 between 'Arafat and Pope John Paul II at which the Vatican reportedly recognized the PLO as the legitimate voice of Palestinian sentiment and endorsed eventual "international status" for Jerusalem.

Prior to the "make or break" summit between 'Arafat and Barak (who faced growing opposition to his peace efforts within Israel) in the United States in July 2000, the Central Council indicated its solid support for 'Arafat and authorized him to declare statehood on September 13. However, when the summit collapsed, the Central Council, under intense international pressure, agreed at a meeting on September 9–10 to postpone the declaration once again. ('Arafat had travelled to some 40 countries to solicit support for the declaration. The US, EU, and many others resisted the idea, however, in part because of the prevailing sentiment in many capitals that 'Arafat had missed a significant opportunity at the US summit. The PLO chairman had reportedly been offered substantial concessions by Barak but had ultimately rejected terms regarding the status of holy sites in Jerusalem as well as the return of Palestinian refugees and their descendants to Israel.)

In light of the outbreak of the "second intifada" in Gaza and the West Bank in late September 2000, US President Clinton proposed a "last ditch" settlement in December under which 95 percent of Gaza and the West Bank would be turned over to Palestinian control while substantial authority would also be extended to the Palestinians over the disputed holy sites in Jerusalem. Although 'Arafat accepted portions of the proposal, he objected to provisions regarding refugees. (The Palestinian position—that all refugees and their descendants be permitted to return to Israel—had been rejected as an impossibility by most Western capitals and, of course, Israel, on the grounds that the Jewish Israeli electorate would be overwhelmed politically by the returnees.) Subsequently, the election of hard-liner Ariel Sharon as the new Israeli prime minister in February 2001 effectively ended negotiations, and

Israeli/Palestinian violence escalated to unprecedented levels. Further complicating matters for the Palestinian leaders was the fact that the new Bush administration in Washington appeared to support Sharon's posture and questioned 'Arafat's ability to control "terrorist" attacks on Israeli citizens or to lead his constituency to a negotiated settlement. In the spring of 2002 'Arafat, whose compound in Ramallah had been under siege by Israeli forces for months as part of a broad Israeli incursion into areas previously under Palestinian control, reportedly admitted "errors" in peace negotiations as well as in the administration of the PNA, and he promised significant reform efforts. However, concerned over the number of suicide bombings and other attacks on Israeli citizens, US President Bush called for the "removal" of 'Arafat, calling him an obstacle to successful completion of Bush's new "road map" for peace. (Many analysts had concluded by that time that 'Arafat had little control over the attacks being claimed by *Hamas* and Islamic Jihad, who, along with the PFLP and DFLP, had refused to join 'Arafat's new "reform" cabinet.) 'Arafat initially announced that new presidential and legislative elections would be held in January 2003 to assess the thinking of the Palestinian electorate, but in December the elections were postponed indefinitely due to Palestinian objections over the continued Israeli military presence in "self-rule" areas.

Although the PLO was not one of the groups demanding the creation of the post of prime minister to share PNA responsibilities with 'Arafat, *Fatah* dutifully approved the cabinet installed under new Prime Minister Mahmoud ABBAS (the secretary general of the PLO executive committee) in April 2003. Subsequently, differences within *Fatah* and the PLO seemed to mirror those in the PLC and PNA over the power struggles between 'Arafat and Abbas (see section on the PNA in article on Israel for details) and between 'Arafat and Abbas's successor, Ahmad QURAY. PLO reformists pressed for significant power-sharing and implementation of genuine anticorruption measures, while 'Arafat's long-standing backers in the organization supported his demand for retention of the responsibility for peace negotiation and control of Palestinian security forces.

Apparently in response to the growing reform tide, 'Arafat in mid-2004 once again acknowledged that he had "made mistakes," indicating that he was prepared to lead a renewed negotiation initiative. However, by that time it was clear that his health had failed to a point of unlikely recovery, and attention mostly focused on ensuring a smooth transition to the new PNA and PLO leaderships. Consequently, Abbas was elevated to the chairmanship of the PLO executive committee only hours after 'Arafat's death on November 11, and Faruk Qaddumi was named chairman of the Fatah Central Council with no apparent tumult.

Following a funeral at Cairo (his birthplace), 'Arafat was buried in Ramallah, where he had lived under virtual Israeli siege for three years. (Israel refused 'Arafat's request to be buried in Jerusalem.) The Cairo ceremony was attended by many Arab leaders and dignitaries from around the world, while public demonstrations in Ramallah and elsewhere clearly illustrated the deep grief felt by the Palestinian population at the loss of the only leader the PLO had known for 35 years. At the same time, the occasion appeared even sadder to many observers because of their belief that 'Arafat had missed several opportunities in the past decade to see much of his Palestinian dream accomplished prior to his death. For their part, the United States and Israel focused on the transition to new Palestinian leaders as an opportunity to revive the peace process.

Following Abbas's election as president in January 2005 and Prime Minister Quray's formation of a new cabinet, the two leaders indicated a desire to establish a clear "separation" between the "political" PLO and the "governmental" PNA. Plans were also announced to expand, restructure, and revitalize the PNC. In addition, at midyear Abbas called for negotiations with *Hamas* and Islamic Jihad toward their possible membership in the PLO. Moreover, Abbas launched talks with the hitherto "rejectionist" PLO factions with the goal of having them participate in a new PNA following the anticipated unilateral withdrawal of Israeli forces from Gaza in August.

Executive Committee: Mahmoud ABBAS (Chairman), Zakaria al-AGHA, Yasir AMR, Samir GHOSHEH, Ali IS'HAQ, Mahmoud ISMAIL, Emile JARJOUI, Taysir KHALID, Riyad al-KHUDARY, 'Abd al-Rahim MALLOUGH, Sulayman al-NAJJIB, Muhammad Zudi al-NASHASHIBI, Mahmoud ODEH, Yasir Abed RABBO, Dr. Assad 'Abd al-RAHMAN, Ghassen al-SHARAA, Faruk QADDUMI (Secretary General).

Factions Represented in the Executive Committee of April 1996

Fatah. The term *Fatah* is a reverse acronym of *Harakat Tahrir Filastin* (Palestine Liberation Movement), established mainly by Gulf-based Palestinian exiles in the late 1950s. The group initially adopted a strongly nationalist but ideologically neutral posture, although violent disputes subsequently occurred between traditional (rightist) and leftist factions. While launching its first commando operations against Israel in January 1965, it remained aloof from the PLO until the late 1960s, when divisiveness within the PLO, plus *Fatah*'s staunch (though unsuccessful) defense in March 1968 of the refugee camp at Karameh, Jordan, contributed to the emergence of Yasir 'Arafat as a leading Palestinian spokesman. Since 'Arafat's election as PLO chairman in 1969, *Fatah* has been the PLO's core component.

Commando operations in the early 1970s were a primary responsibility of *al-'Asifa,* then the formation's military wing. Following expulsion of the *fedayeen* from Jordan, a wave of "external" (i.e., non-Middle Eastern) operations were conducted by "Black September" terrorists, although *Fatah* has never acknowledged any association with such extremist acts as the September 1972 attack against Israeli athletes at the Munich Olympics. By early 1973 the number of "external" incidents had begun to diminish, and during the Lebanese civil war of 1975–1976 *Fatah,* unlike most other Palestinian organizations, attempted to play a mediatory role.

As the result of a *Fatah* leadership decision in October 1973 to support the formation of a "national authority" in any part of the West Bank it managed to "liberate," a hard-line faction supported by Syria broke from *Fatah* under the leadership of Sabry Khalil al-Banna (see Revolutionary Council of *Fatah,* below). Smaller groups defected after the defeat at Beirut in 1982.

Internal debate in 1985–1986 as to the value of diplomatic compromise was resolved in early 1987 by the adoption of an essentially hard-line posture, a decision apparently considered necessary to ensure continuance of *Fatah*'s preeminence within the PLO. However, *Fatah*'s negotiating posture softened progressively in 1988 as 'Arafat attempted to implement the PNC's new political program. Thus, *Fatah*'s Fifth Congress, held August 3–9, 1989, at Tunis, Tunisia, strongly supported 'Arafat's peace efforts, despite growing disappointment over the lack of success in that regard to date. The Congress, the first since 1980, also reelected nine of ten previous members to an expanded 18-member Central Committee and elected 'Arafat to the new post of Central Committee Chairman.

Salah KHALAF (alias Abu IYAD), generally considered the "number two" leader within Fatah, was assassinated at Tunis in January 1991, the motivation for the attack subsequently remaining unclear. Several other prominent *Fatah* leaders were also assassinated in 1992, some of the killing being attributed to *Fatah*'s continuing confrontation with hard-line PLO splinters as well as with the Islamic fundamentalist movement.

It was reported that prior to the September 1993 signing of the PLO-Israel peace settlement, the Central Committee had endorsed its content by a vote of 12–6. As implementation of the accord proceeded in 1994, some friction was reported between formerly exiled leaders returning to Gaza/Jericho and *Fatah* representatives who had remained in those regions during Israeli occupation. In part to resolve such conflict, new by-laws were proposed under which *Fatah* "would operate more like a normal party" with numerous local branches and national committees led by elected chairmen. Meanwhile, as would be expected, many of those named to the new Palestinian National Authority (PNA) and other governmental bodies were staunch *Fatah* supporters. Some discord was reported within *Fatah* during late 1994 and the first half of 1995 as progress in the gradual self-rule accord for Gaza/Jericho stalled. However, several public opinion polls showed *Fatah's* support within the occupied territories to be about 50 percent of the population, a figure that was significantly higher than some observers had estimated.

Fatah presented 70 candidates (reportedly handpicked by 'Arafat) in the January 1996 Palestinian legislative elections; about 50 of these "official" *Fatah* candidates were successful. However, a number of *Fatah* dissidents ran as independents and secured seats. In concurrent balloting for president of the Palestinian National Authority, 'Arafat was elected with 87.1 percent of the vote, further underpinning *Fatah's* dominance regarding Palestinian affairs. However, 'Arafat and *Fatah* were subsequently subjected to intense legislative scrutiny (surprisingly rigorous in the opinion of many observers) over perceived governmental inefficiency, or worse (see Palestinian Governmental Structures in Israel article).

Following the outbreak of the "second *intifada*" (or the al-Aqsa *intifida*, a reference to a mosque on Temple Mount in Jerusalem) in 2000 and the collapse of Israeli/Palestinian peace negotiations, "deep dialogue" was reported within *Fatah* regarding the military and political future for Palestinians. A new guerrilla formation, the al-Aqsa Martyrs' Brigade, was reportedly organized as an offshoot of *Tanzim,* the grassroots *Fatah* "militia" in the West Bank. Al-Aqsa claimed responsibility for a number of attacks against targets within Israel in the first few months of 2002, and the United States placed the group on its list of terrorist organizations. Marwan Barghuthi, the reported leader of *Tanzim* and generally considered as the second most popular Palestinian leader after 'Arafat, was arrested by Israeli security forces in April 2002 and charged with terrorism. At about the same time, al-Aqsa announced it would not carry out any attacks on civilians in Israel but reserved the right to attack military targets and Jewish settlements in Gaza and the West Bank.

On the political front, a number of *Fatah* members were among reformists who pressured 'Arafat in 2002 to combat perceived corruption and mismanagement within the PNA and to appoint a prime minister to share executive authority. *Fatah* subsequently endorsed the appointments of Mahmoud Abbas and Ahmad Quray to the new prime ministership in March 2003 and September 2003, respectively. Meanwhile al-Aqsa claimed responsibility for a number of attacks on Israeli soldiers and suicide bombings in 2002–2004. (To some observers *Fatah* appeared schizophrenic, or at best dysfunctional, at that point because some of its members were regularly perpetrating attacks while others in the government and police forces were attempting to establish "security.") Following 'Arafat's death in November 2004, Faruk Qaddumi was named to succeed 'Afarat as chairman of *Fatah's* Central Council. Subsequently, *Fatah* successfully presented Abbas as its presidential candidate in the January 2005 balloting. (Barghuthi, sentenced to life in prison in mid-2004 on the terrorism charges, had initially expressed an interest in running for president from jail, observers suggesting he would have had a good chance of success. However, his supporters apparently chose unity over confrontation, and Barghuthi withdrew from contention.)

In February 2005 reformist elements in *Fatah* reportedly blocked efforts by *Fatah's* old guard to retain dominance in the new Palestinian cabinet. Among other things, the reformists argued that *Fatah* was losing popular support to *Hamas* because of perceived ties of many 'Arafat loyalists to longstanding corruption.

Leaders: Faruk QADDUMI (Chairman), Mahmoud ABBAS, Ahmad QURAY (Speaker of the Palestinian Legislative Council), Marwan BARGHUTHI, Mohammad DAHLAN, Ahmad HILLIS, Nabil SHA'ATH.

Palestine People's Party (PPP). A Soviet-backed Palestine Communist Party (PCP) was formed in 1982 to encompass Palestinian

Communists in the West Bank, Gaza Strip, Lebanon, and Jordan with the approval of parent communist organizations in those areas. Although it had no formal PLO affiliation, the PCP in 1984 joined the Democratic Alliance's campaign to negotiate a settlement among sparring PLO factions. As part of the reunification program approved in April 1987, the PNC officially embraced the PCP, granting it representation on PLO leadership bodies. The PCP, which was technically illegal but generally tolerated in the occupied territories, endorsed the creation of a Palestinian state adjacent to Israel following withdrawal of Israeli troops from occupied territories. In late 1991 the PCP changed its name to the PPP.

In September 1993 the PPP endorsed the PLO-Israeli accord on the condition that substantial "democratic reform" be implemented within the PLO. Although it was subsequently not represented in the Palestine National Authority formed in 1994, the PPP was described as an "effective ally" of *Fatah* and PLO chairman 'Arafat in the fledgling Palestinian self-rule process.

The PPP contested the January 1996 Palestinian legislative elections, albeit without success. However, PPP General Secretary Bashir al-Barghuthi was named minister of industry in the Palestinian cabinet named in May. The PPP's presidential candidate, Basan al-SALHI, secured 2.7 percent of the vote in the January 2005 presidential balloting.

Leaders: Sulayman al-NAJJIB, Bashir al-BARGHUTHI (General Secretary).

Arab Liberation Front (ALF). The ALF has long been closely associated with the Iraqi branch of the *Baath*. Its history of terrorist activity included an April 1980 attack on an Israeli kibbutz. Subsequently, there were reports of fighting at Beirut between the ALF and pro-Iranian Shi'ites. ALF leader Ahmed Abderrahim died in June 1991, and the status of the front's leadership subsequently remained unclear. Although the ALF was reported to have considered withdrawing from the PLO following the September 1993 agreement with Israel, it was apparently persuaded to remain as part of the "loyal opposition." In 1995, however, the front

was reported to have split into two factions over the question.

Leader: Mahmoud ISMAIL.

Democratic Front for the Liberation of Palestine (DFLP). Established in February 1969 as a splinter from the PFLP (below), the DFLP was known as the Popular Democratic Front for the Liberation of Palestine (PDFLP) until adopting its present name in 1974. A year earlier the front had become the first Palestinian group to call for the establishment of a democratic state—one encompassing both banks of the Jordan—as an intermediate step toward founding a national entity that would include all of historic Palestine. Its ultimate goal, therefore, was the elimination of Hashemite Jordan as well as Zionist Israel. The DFLP advocated a form of secular nationalism rooted in Marxist-Leninist doctrine, whereas *Fatah* initially envisaged a state organized on the basis of coexistent religious communities. Despite their political differences, the DFLP and *Fatah* tended to agree on most issues after their expulsion from Jordan in 1971. The DFLP did, however, support the Muslim Left in the Lebanese civil war of 1975–1976.

The front, which since 1984 had taken a middle position between pro-and anti-'Arafat factions, played a major role in the 1987 PLO reunification. In addition, its close ties with the PFLP, reduced in 1985 when the DFLP opted not to join the PFLP-led Palestine National Salvation Front (PNSF), were reestablished during the unity campaign. The DFLP endorsed the declaration of an independent Palestinian state by the PNC in November 1988, although its leaders interpreted the new PLO political position with less moderation than PLO chairman 'Arafat, declaring they had no intention of halting "armed struggle against the enemy." Subsequently, differences were reported between supporters of longtime DPLF leader Nayif Hawatmeh, who opposed granting any "concessions" to facilitate peace negotiations, and supporters of Yasir Abed Rabbo, a DFLP representative on the PLO Executive Committee, who called for a more "realistic" approach and became one of the leading PLO negotiators attempting to implement the PNC's proposed "two-state" settlement. In early 1990 the DFLP Political Bureau reported it was unable to resolve the internal dispute, which was symptomatic of disagreement among Palestinians as a whole. After his supporters had failed to unseat Hawatmeh at a party congress late in the year, Rabbo formed a breakaway faction in early 1991. Both factions were represented on the new PLO executive committee late in the year, although Hawatmeh continued to criticize 'Arafat's endorsement of the US-led Middle East peace talks. He also called for formation of a "collective" PLO leadership to reduce dependence on 'Arafat.

Rabbo's wing subsequently continued to support 'Arafat, but the main DFLP faction remained dedicated to a "no negotiations" stance. Not surprisingly, Hawatmeh and his followers rejected the September 1993 peace accord with Israel, the DFLP leader describing the May 1994 Cairo Agreement as "not binding on the people of Palestine." Meanwhile, Rabbo was given the culture and arts portfolio in the new Palestine National Authority and he was subsequently described as a leader of the recently formed PDU (see below).

In January 1994 the DFLP joined with five PLO groupings (the PFLP, the PLF, the PPSF, the RPCP, and the PNSF), plus the Islamic Resistance Movement (*Hamas*), and Islamic Holy War (*al-Jihad al-Islami*) to form a loosely knit coalition known as the Alliance of Palestinian Forces. (For details on *Hamas* and *al-Jihad,* which have never been affiliated with the PLO, see Political Groups in Occupied and Previously Occupied Territories in the article on Israel.) Earlier, in October 1993, the same groups had reportedly formed a National Islamic Front, the subsequent name change appearing to reflect concern among secularist PLO factions over participation in an "Islamic" organization. In any event, the Alliance of Palestinian Forces was based on the opposition of its constituent groups to the accord negotiated by PLO Chairman 'Arafat with Israel in September 1993. The alliance pledged to "confront and resist" the Gaza/Jericho agreement and to pursue an independent Palestinian state and the return of Palestinian refugees to Israel. A ten-member Executive Committee was announced and

20 members of what was expected eventually to be a larger Central Council were appointed. Although policy coordination was envisioned, it was reportedly agreed that each component of the alliance would determine how to proceed with its own "resistance" activities. However, the alliance subsequently collapsed, apparently due to the "incompatibility" of its leftist and Islamic elements.

Meanwhile, several DFLP "lieutenants" were reported in mid-1995 to have relocated from Damascus to Gaza, prompting speculation that the grouping might participate in the proposed election of a Palestinian Council. Although the DFLP ultimately boycotted that balloting, it encouraged its supporters to register as voters in anticipation of municipal elections that were expected to be held following the completion of the proposed Israeli withdrawal from the West Bank. The DFLP attended Palestinian conferences chaired by 'Arafat in February and August 1997, indicating that it was hoping to have a say in the proposed negotiations with Israel concerning the final status of Palestinian autonomy. However, in early 1998 it was reported that a plenary session of the DFLP at Damascus had agreed to draw up new strategies, apparently out of conviction that the current peace process was moribund.

In August 1999 DFLP leaders met with 'Arafat for the first time since 1993, and the DFLP resumed participation in the PLO's Central Council later in the year. In October the United States dropped the DFLP from the US list of terrorist organizations. However, the DFLP claimed responsibility for an attack in mid-2001 in Gaza that left three Israeli soldiers dead. The DFLP later blamed Israel for a car bombing in Gaza in February 2002 that killed several DFLP members.

The DFLP joined the PFLP in mid-2004 in denouncing the fledgling unilateral disengagement plan being considered by Israeli Prime Minister Sharon, and the groups announced that the "armed struggle" would continue. The DFLP participated in the January 2005 presidential elections (its candidate, Taysir Khalid, won 3.4 percent of the vote), but as of midyear the DFLP had not yet agreed to participate in the PNA following the scheduled unilateral withdrawal of Israeli forces from Gaza in August.

Leaders: Nayif HAWATMEH (Secretary General), Taysir KHALID.

Popular Front for the Liberation of Palestine (PFLP). The leftist PFLP was established in 1967 by merger of three main groups: an early Palestine Liberation Front, led by Ahmad Jabril; and two small offshoots of the Arab Nationalist Movement—the Youth for Revenge and Georges Habash's Heroes of the Return. However, Jabril and some of his followers quickly split from the PFLP (see PFLP-GC, below). The PFLP favored a comprehensive settlement in the Middle East and resisted the establishment of a West Bank state as an intermediate strategy. Its ultimate goal was the formation of a Palestinian nation founded on scientific socialism, accompanied by its own evolution into a revolutionary proletarian party.

After the failure of efforts to achieve PLO unity in 1984, the PFLP played a key role in formation of the anti-'Arafat PNSF. However, despite initial hesitation, it endorsed the 1987 reunification in light of *Fatah*'s increased militancy. PFLP delegates to the 1988 PNC session voted against the new PLO political program, with Habash announcing that his group, the second largest PLO faction, would accept the will of the majority "for the sake of unity." He added that he expected the peace initiatives to fail and vowed continued attacks by PFLP fighters against Israeli targets. In early 1990 Habash was described as in "open opposition" to 'Arafat's acceptance of a US plan for direct talks between Palestinian representatives and Israel, calling instead for increased military confrontation. Habash subsequently continued to criticize 'Arafat's policies, particularly the PLO leader's concessions in the new Middle East peace talks. The PFLP reportedly suspended its membership in the PLO executive committee in late 1991 to protest the negotiations and was apparently considering the possible establishment of an anti-'Arafat coalition with other hard-line groups. On the other hand, as of mid-1992 the PFLP continued to be viewed as part of the "loyal opposition" within the PLO, a

clear break with 'Arafat seeming unlikely because, in part, of Habash's poor health. (The PFLP leader had been the center of an international furor earlier in the year when he went to France for emergency medical treatment, French police detaining him because of alleged PFLP terrorist involvement in the late 1970s, then permitting him to leave the country in the wake of widespread outcries from Arab leaders.)

During its Fifth Congress, held December 12–14, 1992, at Damascus, Syria, the PFLP vowed to return to "radical action" in order to "regain credibility" among Palestinians. Consequently, Habash condemned the peace accord of September 1993, urging an "intensification" of the struggle for "an independent state with Jerusalem as its capital." However, the PFLP remained represented in the new PLO executive committee named in April 1996, although several subsequent shootings of Israeli settlers (which prompted the arrest by Palestinian police of some 30 PFLP members) apparently indicated continued resistance to the current peace process on the part of at least some of the PFLP faithful. By 1997 the PFLP was described in general as interested in participating with 'Arafat's *Fatah* and other PLO factions in establishing a consensus position to present in proposed "final status talks" with Israel should the peace process develop that far. Meanwhile, in November 1997 a breakaway group reportedly formed as the **Palestinian Popular Forces Party** (PPFP) under the leadership of Adnan Abu NAJILAH.

The PFLP subsequently suspended its activity in the PLO's Central Council to protest the lack of progress in negotiations with Israel, although it resumed its role in that body in February 2000. In late April 2000 Habash announced his retirement; he was succeeded by his longtime deputy, Mustafa al-ZIBRI (Abu Ali Mustafa), who had returned to the West Bank in 1999 after 32 years in exile. Mustafa was killed by rockets fired at his Ramallah office by an Israeli helicopter in August 2001, thereby becoming the highest ranking Palestinian leader to die in such an attack. The PFLP subsequently claimed responsibility for four bomb explosions in Jerusalem in September 2001 and the assassination of Israeli Tourism Minister Rechavam Ze'evi in October. A number of PFLP adherents, including Secretary General Ahmed Saadat, were subsequently arrested by Palestinian security forces, and the PFLP military wing was reportedly "banned" from Palestinian self-rule areas.

The PFLP claimed joint responsibility with *Fatah* for an attack on Israeli soldiers in February 2003. Several PFLP members were killed in subsequent Israeli reprisals. Although PFLP leaders joined other dissident PLO factions in meeting with Palestinian President Abbas in mid-2005, they reported that "no real coalition" had been formed and complained of ongoing *Fatah* domination of PLO affairs.

Leaders: Ahmed SAADAT (Secretary General), Jamil MAJDALAWI, Nasser IZZAT, Mahir al-TAHER, Abdel Rahim MALOUH.

Palestine Liberation Front (PLF). The PLF emerged in 1976 as an Iraqi-backed splinter from the PFLP-GC. In the early 1980s the group itself split into two factions—a Damascus-based group led by Talaat Yacoub, which opposed PLO Chairman Yasir 'Arafat, and a Baghdad- and Tunis-based group led by Muhammad ABBAS (Abdul ABBAS), who was sentenced in absentia to life imprisonment by Italian courts for his alleged role in masterminding the hijacking of the cruise ship *Achille Lauro* in 1985. Although 'Arafat had vowed that Abbas would be removed from his seat on the PLO Executive Committee because of the conviction, Abbas was granted "provisional" retention of the position at the 1987 PNC unity meeting, which was supported by both PLF factions. Reconciliation within the PLF was subsequently achieved, at least nominally: Yacoub was named general secretary, while Abbas accepted a position as his deputy. However, Yacoub died in 1988, leaving control largely in Abbas's hands. In May 1990 the PLF accepted responsibility for a failed attack on Tel Aviv beaches by Palestinian commandos in speedboats, an event that precipitated a breakdown in the US-PLO dialogue because of a lack of subsequent disciplinary action against Abbas. Apparently by mutual agreement, Abbas was not included in the new PLO Executive Committee selected in September 1991. In March 2004 it was reported that Abbas had died of "natural causes" while in "unexplained US custody in Iraq." New PLF Secretary General Umar Shibli said he hoped to reintegrate the PLF into PNA activity.

Leader: Umar SHIBLI (Secretary General).

Palestinian Democratic Union (PDU). The PDU (also referenced as FIDA ["sacrifice" in Arabic], which is also a reverse acronym for the group's Arabic name, *Al-Democrati al-Itihad al-Falestini*) was launched in early 1993, not as a challenge to the PLO (then headquartered at Tunis, Tunisia) but, in the words of a spokesman, as a means of "moving the center of gravity" of the Palestinian opposition to "the occupied territories." Although some of the group's organizers were described as members of the DFLP, the PDU identified itself as nonideological and committed to the Mideast peace process. Operating under the reported leadership of Yasir Abed Rabbo (a longstanding 'Arafat loyalist), the PDU was one of the few non-*Fatah* groupings to contest the January 1996 elections to the Palestinian Legislative Council, securing one seat.

Leaders: Yasir Abed RABBO, Zuheira KAMAL, Jamil SALHUT, Saleh RA'FAT (Secretary General).

Palestine Popular Struggle Front (PPSF). The PPSF broke from the PFLP while participating in the Lebanese civil war on behalf of the Muslim Left. Although the PPSF was represented at the 1988 and 1991 PNC sessions, it denounced the council's political initiatives on both occasions and was not subsequently represented on the PLO Executive Committee. In 1995 it was reported that the PPSF had split into several factions, one of which had expressed support for PLO Chairman 'Arafat and the Palestinian National Authority.

Leader: Samir GHOSHEH.

Popular Front for the Liberation of Palestine–General Command (PFLP-GC). Although the General Command broke from the parent front in late 1967, both organizations fought on the side of the Muslim Left in the Lebanese civil war. The PFLP-GC was one of the founding members (along with the PFLP, PLF, PPSF, *al-Sa'iqa,* and *Fatah* Uprising) of the Palestine National Salvation Front (PNSF), launched in February 1985 at Damascus in opposition to the policies of PLO chairman 'Arafat. Following the reconciliation of the PFLP and the PLF with other major PLO factions at the 1987 PNC meeting, PFLP leader Georges Habash declared that the PNSF had been dissolved; the remaining "rejectionist" groups continued to allude to the PNSF umbrella, however. The PFLP-GC, headquartered at Damascus, was reported to have influenced the uprisings in the West Bank and Gaza Strip in late 1987 and 1988, having established a clandestine radio station, the Voice of Jerusalem, that attracted numerous listeners throughout the occupied territories. In addition to refusing to participate in the 1988 PNC session, the PFLP-GC pledged to step up its guerrilla attacks against Israel. US and other Western officials reportedly suspected the PFLP-GC of complicity in the December 1988 bombing of a Pan American airliner over Lockerbie, Scotland, although PFLP-GC officials vehemently denied that the group was involved. In early 1990 PFLP-GC leader Ahmad Jabril called upon 'Arafat to step down as PLO chairman on the ground that "concessions to Israel have achieved nothing."

In May 1991 the PNSF, by then representing only the PFLP-GC, *al-Sa'iqa,* and *Fatah* Uprising (the PPSF having attended the 1988 PNC meeting), negotiated a preliminary "unity" agreement of its own with the mainstream PLO under which each PNSF component was to be given representation in the PNC. The proposed settlement was generally perceived as an outgrowth of a desire by Syria, the primary source of support for the PNSF, to normalize relations with the PLO and thereby enhance its influence in projected Middle East peace talks. However, negotiations with *Fatah* ultimately proved unproductive, yielding a PNSF boycott of the 1991 session.

In September 1993 PFLP-GC leader Jabril warned that 'Arafat had become an appropriate target for assassination because of the peace settlement with Israel. In mid-1996 the PFLP-GC was described as the primary conduit for the transfer of Syrian weapons to *Hezbollah* guerrillas in southern Lebanon, where Jabril's son, Jihad JABRIL, was reportedly in charge of a PFLP-GC "training center."

The PFLP-GC declined to join the PFLP in resuming activity in the PLO's Central Council in early 2000. In April 2002 the PFLP-GC claimed responsibility for rocket attacks from Lebanon into the Golan Heights and Israel, and Jihad Jabril was killed in a car bomb attack in Beirut the following month. (His father attributed the attack to Israeli agents.) In mid-2005 Ahmad Jabril announced that the PFLP-GC was not yet ready to commit to participation in the Palestinian government following the planned withdrawal of Israeli forces from Gaza, although he agreed to join negotiations on the matter.

Leaders: Talal NAJI, Musa AWAD, Ahmad JABRIL (Secretary General).

Al-Sa'iqa. Established in 1968 under the influence of the Syrian *Baath* Party, *al-Sa'iqa* ("Thunderbolt") came into conflict with *Fatah* as a result of its active support for Syrian intervention during the Lebanese civil war. The group's longtime leader, Zuheir Mohsen, who served as the PLO's chief of military operations, was assassinated at Paris in July 1979, his successor being a former Syrian air force general. Denouncing the decisions of the November 1988 PNC session, *al-Sa'iqa* leaders said they would attempt to get the PLO "back on its original revolutionary course of struggle."

Leaders: Issam al-KADE, Mohamed KHALI-FAH.

Other Groups

Revolutionary Palestinian Communist Party (RPCP). The existence of the RPCP was first reported in 1988, the party having apparently been formed by former PCP members who wished to support the *intifada* in the occupied territories but objected to the PCP's endorsement of the "two-state" peace proposal being pursued by the PNC.

Leader: Abdullah AWWAD (General Secretary).

Fatah Uprising. An outgrowth of the 1983 internal PLO fighting in Lebanon, the Uprising is a *Fatah* splinter group that draws its membership from PLO dissidents who remained in Beirut following the departure of Yasir 'Arafat. One of the most steadfast of the anti-'Arafat formations, it waged a bitter (and largely successful) struggle with mainstream adherents for control of Beirut's refugee camps in May–July 1988. It condemned the PNC declaration of November 1988 as a "catastrophe" and in early 1990 called for attacks on US interests worldwide "because America is completely biased towards the Zionist enemy." The Uprising also called for the assassination of 'Arafat in the wake of the PLO's September 1993 agreement with Israel.

Leader: Saed MUSA (Abu MUSA).

Revolutionary Council of Fatah. The Revolutionary Council (also known as the Abu Nidal Group) was held responsible for more than 100 terrorist incidents in over 20 countries after it broke away from its parent group in 1974. Targets included Palestinian moderates as well as Israelis and other Jews, and the group's predilection for attacks in public places in Europe and Asia led to allegations of its involvement in the assaults on the Vienna and Rome airports in December 1985. The shadowy organization, which operated under numerous names, was formed by Sabry Khalil al-BANNA, better known as Abu Nidal, one of the first PLO guerrillas to challenge the leadership of Yasir 'Arafat. Nidal reportedly plotted to have 'Arafat killed soon after their split, prompting his trial in absentia by the PLO, which issued a death sentence. Somewhat surprisingly, the Revolutionary Council of *Fatah* sent representatives to the preparatory meeting for the April 1987 PNC session, although they walked out during the first day of the regular session. After its Syrian offices were closed by President Assad in 1987, the council transferred the bulk of its military operations to Lebanon's Bekaa Valley and Muslin West Beirut, with Abu Nidal and other leaders reportedly moving to Libya. Fierce personal rivalries and disagreements over policy were subsequently reported within the group, apparently prompting Abu Nidal to order the killing of about 150 dissidents in Libya in October 1989. Consequently, several former senior commanders of the organization fled to Algiers and Tunis, where they established an "emergency leadership" faction opposed to the "blind terrorism" still espoused by Abu Nidal's supporters. The internecine fighting subsequently spread to Lebanon where in June 1990 the dissidents were reported to have routed Nidal's supporters with the aid of fighters from 'Arafat's *Fatah.*

In July 1992 Walid Khalid, described as Abu Nidal's top aide, was assassinated in Lebanon, apparently as part of a series of "score settling" killings by rival guerrilla groups. In November 1995 Palestinian police arrested a group of reported council members in connection with an alleged plot against 'Arafat's life.

In mid-1998 it was reported that an ailing Abu Nidal was being detained in Egypt after having crossed the border from Libya, possibly as the result of a falling out with Libyan leader Mu'ammar al-Qadhafi. However, Egyptian officials denied that report, and US officials subsequently suggested Abu Nidal may have relocated to Iraq. In August 2002 the Iraqi security forces reported that Abu Nidal had committed suicide during their attempt to arrest him in connection with an alleged plot to overthrow the regime of Saddam Hussein. Although uncertain of the circumstances, Western analysts accepted the fact of Abu Nidal's death, noting that it presumably meant the end of the Revolutionary Council, for which no activity had been reported since 1996.

PART THREE

INTERGOVERNMENTAL ORGANIZATIONS

ARAB LEAGUE

AL-JAMI'A AL-'ARABIYAH

Official Name: League of Arab States.

Established: By treaty signed March 22, 1945, at Cairo, Egypt.

Purpose: To strengthen relations among member states by coordinating policies in political, cultural, economic, social, and related affairs; to mediate disputes between members, or between members and third parties.

Headquarters: Cairo, Egypt. (In 1979 the League transferred its headquarters from Cairo to Tunis, Tunisia, because of Egypt's peace treaty with Israel. In early 1990 the members agreed unanimously to return the headquarters to Cairo, although some offices were scheduled to remain in Tunis. Extensive debate on the issue was reported later in the year as an outgrowth of the schism arising from the Iraqi invasion of Kuwait, but the relocation was formally completed on January 1, 1991.)

Principal Organs: Council of the League of Arab States (all members), Economic and Social Council (all adherents to the 1950 Collective Security Treaty), Joint Defense Council (all adherents to the 1950 Collective Security Treaty), Permanent Committees (all members), Arab Summit Conferences, General Secretariat.

Secretary General: Amr Mahmoud Moussa (Egypt).

Membership (22): Algeria, Bahrain, Comoro Islands, Djibouti, Egypt, Iraq, Jordan, Kuwait, Lebanon, Libya, Mauritania, Morocco, Oman, Palestine, Qatar, Saudi Arabia, Somalia, Sudan, Syria, Tunisia, United Arab Emirates, Yemen.

Official Language: Arabic.

Origin and development. A long-standing project that reached fruition late in World War II, the League was founded primarily on Egyptian initiative following a promise of British support for any Arab organization that commanded general endorsement. In its earlier years the organization focused mainly on economic, cultural, and social cooperation, but in 1950 a Convention on Joint Defense and Economic Cooperation was concluded that obligated the members in case of attack "immediately to take, individually and collectively, all steps available, including the use of armed force, to repel the aggression and restore security and peace." In 1976 the Palestine Liberation Organization (PLO), which had participated as an observer at all League conferences since September 1964, was admitted to full membership. Egypt's participation was suspended from April 1979 to May 1989 because of its peace agreement with Israel.

Structure. The principal political organ of the League is the Council, which meets in regular session twice a year, normally at the foreign ministers level. Each member has one vote in the Council; decisions usually bind only those states that accept them, although a two-thirds majority vote on financial and administrative matters binds all members. The Council's main functions are to supervise the execution of agreements between members, to mediate disputes, and to coordinate defense in the event of attack. There are numerous committees and other bodies attached to the Council, including permanent committees dealing with finance and administration, legal affairs, and information.

The Council has also established an Administrative Court, an Investment Arbitration Board, and a Higher Auditing Board. Additional Ministerial Councils, attended by relevant ministers or their representatives, are held in a dozen areas, including transport, justice, health, telecommunications, and environmental affairs.

Three additional bodies were established by the 1950 Convention: a Joint Defense Council to function in matters of collective security and to coordinate military resources; a Permanent Military Commission, composed of representatives of the general staffs, to draw up plans for joint defense; and an Economic Council, composed of the ministers of economic affairs, to coordinate Arab economic development. The last was restructured as an Economic and Social Council in 1977. An Arab Unified Military Command, charged with the integration of strategy for the liberation of Palestine, was formed in 1964.

The General Secretariat is responsible for internal administration and the execution of Council decisions. It also administers several agencies, including the Bureau for Boycotting Israel (headquartered at Damascus, Syria).

Membership in the League generally carries with it membership in an array of Specialized Agencies, including the Arab Bank for Economic Development in Africa (BADEA) and the Arab Monetary Fund (AMF), as well as a variety of other bodies dealing with economic, social, and technical matters.

Nearly three dozen ordinary and extraordinary Arab Summit Conferences have been held since the first one met in 1964. Summit resolutions give direction to the work of the Council and other League organs, although the organization's Charter did not provide a framework for convening summits.

Activities. After many years of preoccupation with Arab-Israeli issues, the League's attention in 1987 turned to the Iraq-Iran conflict as Arab moderates sought a united front against Iran and the potential spread of militant Islamic fundamentalism. An extraordinary summit conference held November 8–11 at 'Amman, Jordan, condemned "the Iranian regime's intransigence, provocations, and threats to the Arab Gulf States" and called for international "pressure" to encourage Iran to accept a UN-sponsored cease-fire. Although Syrian and Libyan opposition blocked a proposed restoration of membership privileges to Egypt, the summit declared that members could establish relations with Cairo individually. A number of countries, including the Gulf states, quickly did so.

Palestinian issues quickly returned to the forefront of the League's agenda in early 1988 because of the uprising (*intifada*) in the Gaza Strip and West Bank. A June summit affirmed "moral, political, and diplomatic" support for the *intifada* while most of the members made individual financial pledges to the PLO. The major development at the May summit at Casablanca, Morocco, was the readmission of Egypt, whose president, Husni Mubarak, urged the other attendees to stop "wasting time and opportunities" for formulating a "vision" for peace in the Middle East.

A special summit at Baghdad, Iraq, in late May 1990, although convened at the PLO's urging to discuss the mass immigration of Soviet Jews to Israel, focused primarily on US policy. In condemning Washington as bearing a "fundamental responsibility" for Israel's "aggression, terrorism, and expansionism," the League reflected growing frustration among Arabs over the lack of progress in peace negotiations as well as an increased militancy, most forcefully expressed by Iraqi President Saddam Hussein. In an apparent effort to reinforce Arab political unity, the leaders agreed to hold regular annual summits at Cairo, beginning in November.

The prospect for effective cooperation was severely compromised by Iraq's takeover of Kuwait on August 2, 1990, which split the League into two deeply divided blocs. The majority (comprising Bahrain, Djibouti, Egypt, Kuwait, Lebanon, Morocco, Oman, Qatar, Somalia, Syria, Saudi Arabia, and the United Arab Emirates) on August 10 voted to send a pan-Arab force to guard Saudi Arabia against possible Iraqi attack, several members (most notably Egypt and Syria) ultimately contributing troops to the US-led liberation of Kuwait in early 1991. The minority included members overtly sympathetic to Baghdad (such as Jordan, the PLO, and Sudan) and those which, while critical of the Iraqi invasion, were adamantly opposed to US military involvement.

Although both sides continued to promote an "Arab solution" throughout the Gulf crisis, the schism precluded the League from playing any meaningful negotiating role. Symptomatic of the disarray in the Arab world, longtime League Secretary General Chedli Klibi of Tunisia resigned in September 1990 after a blistering attack upon him by Saudi Arabian officials. The League observer at the United Nations also resigned soon after, citing his inability to cope with Arab fragmentation.

Following the coalition victory over Iraqi forces and the restoration of the Kuwaiti government in early 1991, it appeared that Egypt, the leading Arab coalition member, had regained League dominance, although "intense animosities" reportedly remained from the Gulf crisis. Evidence of Cairo's standing included the May appointment by the Arab League Council of Egypt's retiring foreign minister, Ahmad Ismat 'Abd al-Magid, as the next secretary general.

In September 1993 the League's foreign ministers gave quick approval to the recently negotiated peace accord between Israel and the PLO. However, the League subsequently announced it would not lift the Arab economic boycott against Israel until Israeli troops were withdrawn from all the occupied territories. The ban, adopted at the creation of the Jewish state in 1948, precluded any direct commercial contact between Arab countries and Israel. In 1951 a "secondary" boycott had been declared against any companies in the world that conducted business with Israel, followed by a "tertiary" boycott against any companies dealing with those companies already blacklisted. However, the secondary and tertiary boycotts have been widely ignored recently, and in September 1994 the members of the Gulf Cooperation Council (Bahrain, Kuwait, Oman, Qatar, Saudi Arabia and United Arab Emirates) announced their formal abandonment.

Nevertheless, for the League as a whole the boycotts subsequently remained formally in place. In addition, League officials remained skeptical of the proposed formation of a regional economic cooperation union that would include Israel, as had been proposed by the Middle East and North Africa Summit, held at Casablanca, Morocco, on October 30–November 1, 1994. The League argued that its members should establish an Arab Free Trade Association, which would exclude Israel.

In the wake of the victory of the right-wing *Likud* party of Benjamin Netanyahu in the May 1996 Israeli elections, the League held its first full summit since 1990 at Cairo on June 21–23 to address, among other things, Netanyahu's perceived retreat from previous Israeli positions regarding the Palestinian self-rule process. The summit reaffirmed its positions supporting full Israeli withdrawal from the occupied territories, Palestinian self-determination, and an end to settlement building in the West Bank. However, divisions among members on the issue were readily apparent, moderate states such as Jordan and Egypt leading successful efforts to dilute stronger language proposed by Syria. In other activity, the summit again criticized Iraq (which was not invited to the session) for its lack of cooperation with the United Nations and issued a statement of support for Bahrain and the United Arab Emirates in their disputes with Iran.

The summit's final communiqué also called for greater Arab solidarity and a strengthening of the organization's institutions, although skeptics noted a "hollow ring" to the language. The prospects for institutional reform were also constrained by financial difficulties: only four members (Egypt, Jordan, Saudi Arabia, and Syria) had paid their full dues, while the remaining members were a combined $80 million in arrears. As a consequence, the League was forced to close several foreign offices and reportedly had difficulty in meeting its payroll at times.

Despite the League's financial troubles, in November 1997 17 members agreed to proceed with the establishment of the Arab Free Trade Zone in 1998, with the goal of cutting customs duties by 10 percent a year until their elimination at the end of 2007. In other activity during the year, the Arab League foreign ministers, meeting at Cairo in March, recommended that members reactivate the economic boycott of Israel and cease all activity geared toward normalizing relations with that country, given the stalled peace process. For the same reason, the League also urged a boycott of the fourth Middle East and North Africa economic conference held at Qatar in November.

In late 1997 and early 1998 the League expressed concern over rising tension between Iraq and Western capitals. It reportedly encouraged Baghdad to adopt a more conciliatory posture while at the same time warning against "unilateral" action on the part of the United States. An emergency summit convened in early January 1999 to address Iraq's request that the League condemn the recent US/UK air assaults. However, the final statement from the summit was mild in tone, expressing "uneasiness and concern" over the attacks while at the same time criticizing Baghdad for its "provocative" rhetoric. Similarly, an Arab League Council session in March declined to label (as Baghdad had demanded) the "no-fly zones" in Iraq as illegal.

Another recent focus of attention has been antiterrorism. An accord was signed in April 1998 by the interior and justice ministers of the League's members, who pledged to exchange evidence in terrorist investigations and extradite suspects. The Arab states also agreed not to harbor or assist groups responsible for terrorist acts against Arab nations, although an exemption was granted regarding "national liberation" groups.

In March 2000 the Council addressed Israel's announcement of a pending pullout from its "security zone" in southern Lebanon by warning that renewed Palestinian attacks could result unless Israel provided for the repatriation of Palestinians from refugee camps in the region. The League basically adopted what had been the Syrian position on the matter, rejecting the pullout in the absence of a comprehensive peace agreement–clearly, an effort by Syria to interweave the issue of an Israeli pullout from the occupied Golan Heights.

Although the League subsequently cosponsored peace talks at Djibouti on the Somali conflict, from late September 2000 League concerns were largely dominated by the renewal of the Palestinian *intifada,* which quickly led to the first emergency summit in four years, at Cairo on October 20–21. As in the past, however, League reaction was far

from unified. Libya's Colonel Qadhafi pointedly avoided the session altogether, anticipating, from his hard-line perspective, an inadequate response to the renewed hostilities. Iraq's representative called for holy war (*jihad*), while the majority endorsed a halt to further diplomatic normalization with Israel. (At the time, Mauritania, Morocco, Oman, Qatar, and Tunisia had representative offices in Israel.) The summit communiqué continued to call for a renewal of the peace process, while the participants agreed to set up a $1 billion fund to aid Palestinians affected by the uprising and Israeli counteractions.

The 'Amman summit of March 27–28, 2001, marked the first regular summit since 1990, with Iraq in attendance as a full participant. The *intifada* remained a principal subject, although no significant new initiatives resulted. Presummit speculation had largely centered on efforts to repair the rift between Iraq and Kuwait, but only marginal progress toward that end occurred. The League ended up calling, once again, for an end to the sanctions against Iraq, but also for Baghdad to work out its differences with the United Nations over inspections and related issues. In other matters, the summit advocated accelerating the movement toward free trade as well as forming a customs union and promoting cooperative development in such areas an transport, telecommunications, and information technology. Two months later, on May 16, Amr Mahmoud Moussa, theretofore Egypt's foreign minister, began his tenure as the League's new secretary general.

At the 14th League summit, held at Beirut, Lebanon, on March 27–28, 2002, attention focused on Iraqi-Kuwaiti relations and on a "land-for-peace" plan offered by Saudi Arabia's Crown Prince Abdullah to settle the Arab-Israeli conflict. Although Iraq and Kuwait appeared ready to resolve their differences, with Baghdad stating that it would henceforth respect Kuwait's territorial integrity and sovereignty, positive international expectations for the Saudi plan were undercut even before the summit got under way. In the context of continuing Israeli-Palestinian violence, PLO leader Yasir 'Arafat initially rejected Israeli conditions for his departure from Ramallah and ultimately decided not to attend the summit for fear that the government of Prime Minister Sharon would not permit his return. Egypt's President Mubarak and Jordan's King Abdullah also chose not to attend, while several of the smaller Gulf states sent less senior delegations. In addition, on the summit's opening day the Palestinian delegation withdrew over Lebanon's refusal to permit a satellite address by 'Arafat. As a consequence of these developments, Crown Prince Abdullah's plan failed to register as great an impact as had been anticipated, although it was endorsed by the attendees.

The Saudi plan called for normalization of relations with Israel and affirmed that state's right to security. In return, Israel was expected to withdraw from all occupied territories and recognize a Palestinian state having East Jerusalem as its capital. The summit's concluding Beirut Declaration both called for a "just solution" to the Palestinian refugee problem and rejected "all forms of Palestinian repatriation which conflict with the special circumstances of the Arab host countries."

In October 2002 Libya's Qadhafi announced that he would pull his country from the organization because of its demonstrated inability to deal effectively not only with the Palestinian situation, but also the looming crisis involving Iraq and the United States. A summit at Sharm el Sheikh, Egypt, on March 1, 2003, to discuss the Iraq crisis left the League divided after a heated exchange between Qadhafi, who attacked Saudi Arabia for permitting US forces on its soil, and Crown Prince Abdullah. The summit concluded with condemnation of any "aggression" against Iraq but also called for Baghdad's compliance with UN weapons inspections. As late as April 2003 Libya maintained its intention to withdraw from the League, but in May, apparently at the urging of the Egyptian president, Qadhafi reversed himself.

With regard to the "road map" for peace in the Middle East that was formally introduced on April 30, 2003, by the "quartet" of the European Union, the United Nations, Russia, and the United States, the Arab League expressed its cautious support. The League welcomed the June decision of militant Palestinian groups to introduce a three-month cease-fire, but a League spokesman cautioned that Israel had yet to "implement its obligations" and cease assassinations, incursions, demolitions, and seizures. He further urged the United States, in particular, to ensure Israeli compliance with the terms of the peace initiative. On February 25, 2004, in the course of oral presentations before the International Court of Justice at the Hague, the League argued that the separation barrier being erected on Palestinian land by Israel was illegal and "an affront to international law."

In December 2003, the League sent its first official delegation to Iraq, signaling a change in attitude from its earlier criticism of the US invasion in March.

A League summit scheduled for March 29, 2004, in Tunis was abruptly called off two days in advance of the opening because of divisions over peace overtures to Israel, with tensions heightened following Israel's assassination of the leader of the radical Palestinian group *Hamas* just days prior to the summit. The resulting outrage in the Arab world inflamed League ministers and complicated plans to relaunch the Saudi-backed peace initiative adopted at the 2002 Beirut summit. The collapse of the Tunis summit was widely reported as reflective of the turmoil in Arab ranks.

The rescheduled Tunis summit of May 22, 2004, was marred the first day by the walkout of Libya's Qadhafi, who again threatened to withdraw from the League. Qadhafi said he was "disgusted" by the treatment of Saddam Hussein and Yasir 'Arafat and wholly dissatisfied with the summit agenda. Meanwhile, 10 of the 22 League members did not attend the two-day summit, which ultimately issued a strongly worded denunciation of abuse inflicted on Iraqi prisoners by US forces, pledged further reforms to be launched in League countries, and called for an international security force for the Palestinians. The League also called for an extensive UN role in rebuilding Iraq.

An emergency session of the League was called on August 8, 2004, to address ways to help Sudan resolve the humanitarian crisis in Darfur, but little was reported from that event. The issue was again addressed at a meeting specific to that purpose on

May 16, 2005, producing a resolution promoting resumption of negotiations between Khartoum and Darfur rebels.

On March 22–23, 2005, only 13 of 22 leaders attended the League summit in Algiers, and the resolutions adopted "were of comparatively little significance," according to the *New York Times*. However, plans were unveiled for an Arab common market by 2015 and a regional security system.

ARAB MAGHREB UNION (AMU)

Established: By the Arab Maghreb Treaty, signed by the heads of state of the member countries on February 17, 1989, at Marrakesh, Morocco, with effect from July 1, 1989.

Purpose: "To strengthen the bonds of brotherhood which bind the member states and their peoples to each other...to work gradually towards the realization of the freedom of movement of [the member states'] people, goods, services, and capital...to safeguard the independence of every member state...to realize the industrial, agricultural, commercial, and social development of the member states...by setting up joint ventures and preparing general and specialized programs...to initiate cooperation with a view to developing education at various levels, to preserving the spiritual and moral values derived from the tolerant teachings of Islam, to safeguarding the Arab national identity...."

Headquarters: Casablanca, Morocco.

Principal organs: Presidential Council (heads of member states), Council of Prime Ministers, Council of Foreign Ministers, Consultative Council, Judicial Body, Follow-up Committee, Specialized Ministerial Commissions, General Secretariat.

Secretary General: Mohamed Habib Boularès (Tunisia).

Membership (5): Algeria, Libya, Mauritania, Morocco, Tunisia.

Official Language: Arabic.

Origin and development. The idea of a unified northern Africa was first voiced by Arab nationalists in the 1920s and subsequently received widespread support throughout the turbulence of World War II and the independence movements of the 1950s and early 1960s. By contrast, the postindependence era yielded a variety of territorial disputes, political rivalries, and ideological differences that blunted meaningful integration efforts. However, the Maghrebian movement regained momentum following the 1987 rapprochement between Algeria and Morocco (see articles on those countries). Meeting together for the first time in June 1988 at Algiers, Algeria, the leaders of the five Maghrebian countries appointed a commission and five subcommittees to draft a treaty that would encompass the "Greater Arab Maghreb." After intensive negotiations, the treaty was signed on February 17, 1989, following a two-day summit at Marrakesh, Morocco, with formal ratification following shortly thereafter.

Although the five heads of state appeared arm-in-arm after the summit, reports indicated that volatile Libyan leader Mu'ammar al-Qadhafi, upset at the rejection of his proposal that Chad, Mali, Niger, and Sudan be brought into the Union, had attended only at the last minute. After the summit Qadhafi continued to push for "one invincible Arab nation" from the Atlantic to the Persian Gulf, and, apparently at his insistence, the Arab Maghreb Treaty left AMU membership open to other countries "belonging to the Arab nation or the African group."

Structure. The supreme political organ of the AMU is the Presidential Council, comprising the heads of state of the member nations; the chairmanship of the Council rotates among the heads of state, who are assisted by a Council of Prime Ministers. The Council of Foreign Ministers is empowered to attend sessions of the Presidential Council and is responsible for preparing summit agendas. Reporting to the Council of Foreign Ministers is a Follow-up Committee, comprising the members' secretaries of state for Maghreb affairs, who are mandated to oversee the implementation of integrationist measures. In addition, Specialized Ministerial Commissions have been established in five areas (with each commission empowered to create subsidiary committees): interior, human resources (judicial affairs, youth and sports, culture and information, labor and social affairs, higher education and scientific research, health), infrastructure (transport, public works, housing and urban development, posts and communications), economy and finance (financial and monetary affairs, commerce, energy and mines, industry, tourism and crafts), and food security.

The original treaty provided for a Consultative Council of ten representatives from each member state; in 1994 the size of each delegation was increased to 30. The Consultative Council meets in ordinary session once a year and in emergency session at the request of the Presidential Council, to which it submits recommendations and draft resolutions. The treaty also calls for a "judicial body," consisting of two judges appointed by each member state, to "deal with disputes concerning the implementation of the treaty and the accords concluded within the framework of the Union. . . ." A small General Secretariat operates from Morocco, the participants having pledged to keep the Union's bureaucracy to a bare minimum.

Activities. Despite economic and political differences among its members, the AMU was perceived at its formation as having the capacity to provide a significant regional response to the single internal market then being planned by the European Community (EC, later the European Union–EU). In subsequent months preliminary agreement was reported on the establishment of a regional airline and unification of postal and telecommunications services. In addition, several joint industrial projects were approved and a campaign was launched to vaccinate children against an array of diseases. However, by early 1990 AMU proponents acknowledged that progress had been slower than they had anticipated in reducing trade barriers, facilitating the movement of people across national borders, and otherwise moving toward economic integration. Consequently, the AMU heads of state, during a January summit at Tunis, Tunisia, agreed to appoint a secretary general, establish a permanent headquarters, and implement other changes to strengthen AMU authority and effectiveness. It was also announced that the AMU defense and foreign ministers had been asked to study ways of achieving "cooperation and coordination" in security matters. Nevertheless, several difficult political issues continued to work against regional unity, including Mauritania's displeasure over lack of support from Morocco in its border dispute with Senegal (see articles on Mauritania and Senegal), irritation among several members over positions taken by Libya's Colonel Qadhafi, and failure to resolve the Western Sahara dispute (see Morocco article).

A lack of cohesion was also evident during a July 1990 summit at Algiers, the heads of state being unable to agree upon a location for the permanent AMU headquarters or to select a secretary general. Moreover, as was the case in many Arab organizations, activity within the AMU was subsequently constrained by events associated with the Iraqi invasion of Kuwait in August. Although Morocco adopted a solidly anti-Iraq stance and contributed troops to the US-led Desert Shield operation, the other AMU members opposed the presence of US troops in the Gulf. In addition, strong pro-Iraqi sentiment surfaced within all of the AMU states, creating concern among some officials over a possible backlash against those North African countries perceived by the EC and other Western nations to have been on the "wrong side" of the Gulf crisis. As a result, the AMU summit at Ras Lanuf, Libya, in March 1991 called upon the Arab League to work quickly to heal the divisions created by the war so that a pan-Arab consensus could be reached on economic, political, and security issues.

During the 1991 summit the AMU heads of state (with the exception of Libya's Colonel Qadhafi, whose absence was unexplained) agreed to establish the organization's General Secretariat at Casablanca, the Maghreb Consultative Council in Algeria, the Maghreb University and Science Academy in Libya, the Maghreb Court in Mauritania, and a Maghreb Bank for Investment and External Trade (*Banque Maghrébine d'Investissement et de Commerce Extérieur*–BMICE) in Tunisia. In October Mohammed Amamou of Tunisia was selected as the AMU's first secretary general. However, most of the AMU's planned initiatives subsequently remained unimplemented as conflict among the members left the impression, in the words of the *Middle East International*, that the Union was "dead, if not quite buried."

One major stumbling block to effective regional action was the imposition of limited sanctions by the United Nations against Libya in the spring of 1992 because of Tripoli's refusal to turn over two suspects in the bombing of an airliner over Lockerbie, Scotland, in the late 1980s. Despite strong protests from Colonel Qadhafi, Libya's AMU partners honored the sanctions, although the AMU summit held November 10–11 at Nouakchott, Mauritania, urged that the UN reconsider its position. The summit also issued a declaration condemning the "terrorism" stemming from militant Islamic fundamentalism in the region and called for "concerted effort" to keep it in check.

Some rhetorical commitment to Union aims returned at the sixth AMU summit, held, after several postponements, on April 2–3, 1994, at Tunis. In addition to urging faster implementation of previous agreements, the AMU leaders called for intensified trade and security negotiations with the EU. However, the Libyan regime, which prior to the summit had bluntly labeled the AMU a "failure," reportedly remained "bitter" that the AMU members were still upholding the UN sanctions. For their part, the AMU leaders expressed "concern" over the effects of the sanctions on the Libyan people and called for a "just, honorable, and swift settlement" based on "international laws, resolutions, and charters."

The next AMU summit was postponed indefinitely after Libya announced that it would not assume its scheduled chairmanship because of the Lockerbie impasse. Following the apparent resolution of the sanctions issue in early 1999, observers suggested that a revival of AMU progress was at hand, but the AMU remained essentially moribund because of differences between Morocco and Algeria over the latter's support for the Polisario insurgents in the Western Sahara. The 35th session of the Follow-up Committee convened at Algiers in mid-May, ostensibly to relaunch the Union, but little came of the meeting. In August newly crowned King Mohamed of Morocco proposed to Algerian President Bouteflika that the AMU be reinvigorated, and a month later a Moroccan spokesman described the Union as "still a fundamental project in our view." Nevertheless, a summit anticipated for November never occurred, and in February 2000 Tunisian President Ben Ali, marking the Union's 11th anniversary, once again urged that the AMU be revived, calling it "a strategic choice and an historical aspiration."

A March 2001 meeting of the Council of Foreign Ministers at Algiers was partly undercut by Morocco's unenthusiastic participation. Later in the year, however, it appeared that the Moroccan and Algerian leaders were attempting to work around the Western Sahara issue. The fourth session of the Consultative Council met at Rabat, Morocco, in September after a lapse of nine years. In October 2001 the AMU trade ministers announced agreement on a draft free-trade area and customs union, while a foreign ministers meeting in January 2002 was viewed as a prelude to a seventh summit in mid-2002, eight years after the sixth. At the January session the ministers appointed Habib Boularès of Tunisia as successor to Secretary General Amamou.

The anticipated June 2002 summit ultimately fell victim to continuing differences over the Western Sahara. Earlier, Colonel Qadhafi had offered to mediate the dispute between Algiers and Rabat, with the Polisario Front expressing conditional support for the proposal. Morocco, however, termed the offer unrealistic, and in early June King

Mohamed indicated that he would not attend the summit. As a consequence, the meeting was postponed indefinitely.

The Council of Foreign Ministers convened on January 3–4, 2003, at Algiers, where one of the concerns was the need for the AMU to adapt to the challenges posed by increasing globalization. The concluding communiqué again denounced Israeli aggression against Palestinians, called for the lifting of sanctions against Iraq as well as remaining sanctions against Libya, and condemned terrorism (while noting the right of resistance against foreign occupation). The foreign ministers also supported continuation of the "5 + 5 dialogue" on Mediterranean issues, begun in 1991 with France, Italy, Spain, Portugal, and Malta.

On December 22, 2003, a day before the much-discussed AMU summit was to have been held, the AMU foreign ministers, meeting at Algiers, indefinitely postponed the meeting. The cancellation followed announcements that the king of Morocco, the president of Mauritania, and the Libyan leader had all declined to attend. Shortly before, Mauritania had accused Libya of financing a plot to overthrow Mauritania's government. After the cancellation Colonel Qadhafi indicated that the summit might be rescheduled following Algeria's 2004 presidential election.

ARAB MONETARY FUND (AMF)

Established: By Articles of Agreement signed April 27, 1976, at Rabat, Morocco, with effect from February 2, 1977.

Purpose: To correct disequilibria in the balance of payments of member states; to promote the stability of exchange rates among Arab currencies, rendering them mutually convertible; to promote Arab economic integration and development; to encourage the creation of a unified Arab currency; and to coordinate policies in other international monetary and economic forums.

Headquarters: Abu Dhabi, United Arab Emirates.

Principal Organs: Board of Governors (all members), Board of Executive Directors (9 members), Loan and Investments Committees.

Director General: Jassim al-Mannai (Bahrain).

Membership (21): Algeria, Bahrain, Djibouti, Egypt, Iraq, Jordan, Kuwait, Lebanon, Libya, Mauritania, Morocco, Oman, Palestine, Qatar, Saudi Arabia, Somalia, Sudan, Syria, Tunisia, United Arab Emirates, Yemen. (The memberships of Iraq, Somalia, and Sudan were suspended in February 1993 because of payments arrears. Sudan reached a repayment agreement and its membership was reactivated in April 2000.)

Official Language: Arabic.

Origin and development. Although a proposal to form an Arab Payments Union was made by the Arab Economic Council in the 1960s and a meeting was subsequently held for that purpose, the idea was discarded as attention was drawn to more pressing political issues. With the quadrupling of oil prices in 1974, however, concern once again focused on the issue of monetary problems. The objective was now more ambitious: an organization to deal with recycling, or investing, Arab "petrodollars" in order to decrease dependence upon foreign handling of surplus funds. This goal is clearly implicit in the Articles of Agreement signed in April 1976. Since then, the AMF has gradually expanded its mission to promote economic integration and development, to aid Arab financial institutions, to encourage intra-Arab trade, and to assist member countries in structural financial reforms.

Structure. The Board of Governors, comprising one governor and one alternate governor from each member state, serves as the Fund's general assembly and holds all administrative powers. Meeting at least once a year, it is responsible for capitalization, income distribution, the admission and suspension of members, and the appointment of the Fund's director general. The Board of Executive Directors, consisting of the director general and eight experts elected for three-year terms from the member states, performs tasks assigned it by the Board of Governors. Subsidiary departments include the Economic and Technical Department, the Economic Policy Institute, and the Treasury and Investments Department.

One of the AMF's principal aims has been to foster the economic integration of member states. Thus the Fund has guaranteed loans to Arab countries to correct payment imbalances resulting from unilateral or pan-Arab development projects. It has also used its capital as a catalyst to advance Arab financial instruments and has promoted creation of a unified Arab currency. It provides technical assistance to the monetary and banking agencies of member countries, largely through training seminars in such areas as branch banking and accounting, bank supervision and internal auditing, and documentary credit. It also cooperates with other Arab and international organizations to discuss and promote areas of common interest.

In late 1987 the AMF launched a restructuring program apparently with widespread support from Arab bankers; its "fresh priorities" included the creation of a regional securities market and the strengthening of securities markets in member states to provide long-term financing for development. In September 1988 the Fund endorsed further changes, such as an emphasis on "productive projects" leading directly to economic growth, rather than on the infrastructural programs of earlier years. Although not yet willing to say it would attach conditions to AMF loans, the Board of Executive Directors announced its intention to take a more active interest in how loans were used. The Board also approved the creation of an Economic Policy Institute to assist member states in formulating national policies as well as to promote the development of financial strategies for the Arab countries as a group.

Attention subsequently shifted to the Arab Trade Financing Program (ATFP), established by the AMF and other pan-Arab financial institutions to promote trade among Arab countries. The AMF agreed to provide $250 million of the initial $500 million of authorized capital and was accorded control of five of the nine seats on the Program's board of directors. Approved in 1989, the ATFP was scheduled to become operational in 1990 but its launching was delayed by the Gulf crisis. The first ATFP loan agreement (with Morocco) was signed in January 1992.

As was the case with most Arab financial institutions, AMF activity was severely curtailed by the 1990–1991 Gulf War, although it began to rebound in the mid-1990s. Cumulative approvals reached 718.8 million Arab Accounting Dinars (AAD) ($2.9 billion) for 103 projects as of January 1, 1998. Since then, a majority of loans have involved a new Structural Adjustment Facility (SAF), which was set up to support reforms in the financial sector. Through 2002, the AMF had approved 124 loans totaling AAD 932 million ($3.8 billion at the year-end exchange rate).

For 2002 the AMF saw its assets grow to AAD 1.08 billion ($4.40 billion), up marginally from the previous year. Three loans (to Egypt, Djibouti, and Lebanon) totaling AAD 35.0 million ($143 million) were approved, all but the last (AAD 3.7 million) through the SAF. In the previous year, the AMU had authorized six loans totaling AAD 69.3 million ($261 million at the 2001 year-end exchange rate), although, in a marked departure from the post-1997 trend, the SAF accounted for only 38 percent of the approved funding.

With the addition of its 2002 loan of AAD 30.9 million, Egypt moved ahead of Iraq as the member with the largest outstanding balance. However, Iraq, which has been unable to meet its obligations since the Gulf War, remained the biggest problem: its arrears of AAD 158 million ($644 million), about half in interest, equaled nearly half of the Fund's paid-up capital of AAD 324 million. Sudan and Somalia also were in serious arrears.

COUNCIL OF ARAB ECONOMIC UNITY (CAEU)

Established: By resolution of the Arab Economic Council of the League of Arab States at Cairo, Egypt, June 3, 1957, effective at its first meeting May 30, 1964.

Purpose: To provide a flexible framework for achieving economic integration of Arab states.

Headquarters: 'Amman, Jordan.

Principal Organs: Council, General Secretariat.

Secretary General: Ahmed Guweili (Egypt).

Membership (11): Egypt, Iraq, Jordan, Kuwait, Libya, Mauritania, Palestine, Somalia, Sudan, Syria, Yemen. (Egypt's membership was suspended from 1979 to 1988. Although not a de jure state, Palestine succeeded the Palestine Liberation Organization as a member following formation of the Palestinian Authority in 1994.)

Official Language: Arabic.

Origin and development. In January 1956 the Arab League agreed on the necessity for an organization that would deal specifically with the economic problems of Arab countries. As a result, on June 3, 1957, a resolution was passed creating the Council of Arab Economic Unity. The organization officially came into existence on May 30, 1964.

In December 1988 the CAEU announced that it was lifting a nine-year suspension of Egypt's membership that had been occasioned by Cairo's conclusion of a peace agreement with Israel.

In March 1990 Kuwait announced its intention to withdraw over the Council's "poor performance" and the fact that CAEU objectives overlapped those of other Arab organizations. Continuing disputes over budget assessments and shortfalls, including Kuwait's back dues, also played a part in the decision. The CAEU lost its only other Gulf member when the United Arab Emirates withdrew in late November 1999, immediately after a summit of the Gulf Cooperation Council.

Structure. The Council, consisting of the economic, finance, and trade ministers of member states, meets twice a year to discuss and vote on the organization's agenda. The Secretariat oversees implementation; it also has responsibility for drawing up work plans, which are presented to the Council.

Activities. Since its inception, activities have focused on furthering economic development and encouraging economic cooperation among Arab countries. To promote these ends, an Arab Common Market was established by the Council in 1964. Seven years later the Market achieved its initial aim of abolishing all taxes and other duties levied on items of trade between Arab countries. The second part of the plan, a customs union of all members, has not yet been fully implemented. Emphasis has also been given to forming joint Arab companies and federations, to coordinating agricultural and industrial programs, and to improving road and railway networks. Industries in which joint ventures and federations or unions have been formed include textiles, processed foods, pharmaceuticals, fertilizers, building materials, iron and steel, shipping, petrochemicals, and information technology. The CAEU has also promoted harmonization of statistics and data collection.

The CAEU was thrown into disarray by the Persian Gulf crisis in August 1990. Several prominent CAEU members participated in the US-led coalition that succeeded in driving Iraqi forces from Kuwait in early 1991. Subsequently, in part to restore a sense of normalcy to Arab affairs, as well as for humanitarian reasons, the CAEU repeatedly called upon the UN Security Council to discontinue its sanctions against Iraq.

The CAEU continues to encounter considerable difficulty in achieving its economic goals. The planned introduction in 1998 of an Arab Free Trade Zone, which had the support of the majority of Arab League members as well as the overlapping CAEU membership, was undermined by requests for exceptions involving nearly 3,000 commodities.

The CAEU Council session held June 6–7, 2001, was notable primarily because it constituted the first such meeting at Baghdad, Iraq, since the 1991 Gulf war. At the session Egypt, Iraq, Libya, and Syria announced that they were establishing their own free-trade zone, which once again called into question the CAEU's long-term prospects.

The December 2002 CAEU Council session heard Arab League Secretary General Amr Mussa warn of the political, economic, and social consequences posed by threats to the Arab world, principally US antagonism toward the Iraqi government as well as the ongoing Israeli confrontation with Palestinian militants. Also in 2002 the CAEU established a committee to encourage inter-Arab investment by redirecting some of the estimated $1 trillion in Arab funds that have been invested elsewhere. More recently, a CAEU-sponsored economic conference at Cairo also called for the repatriation of investment capital, particularly in view of rapid Arab population growth and an unemployment rate that was already approaching 20 percent.

GULF COOPERATION COUNCIL (GCC)

Formal Name: Cooperation Council for the Arab States of the Gulf.

Established: Initial agreement endorsed February 4–5, 1981, in Riyadh, Saudi Arabia; constitution formally adopted in Abu Dhabi, United Arab Emirates, on May 25–26, 1981.

Purpose: "(i) To achieve coordination, integration, and cooperation among the member states in all fields in order to bring about their unity; (ii) to deepen and strengthen the bonds of cooperation existing among their peoples in all fields; (iii) to draw up similar systems in all fields . . . ; and (iv) to promote scientific and technical progress in the fields of industry, minerals, agriculture, sea wealth, and animal wealth . . . for the good of the peoples of the member states."

Headquarters: Riyadh, Saudi Arabia.

Principal Organs: Supreme Council; Ministerial Council; General Secretariat; various economic, social, industrial and trade, and political committees.

Secretary General: Abdul Rahman bin Hamad al-Attiya (Qatar).

Membership (6): Bahrain, Kuwait, Oman, Qatar, Saudi Arabia, United Arab Emirates.

Official Language: Arabic.

Origin and development. The formal proposal for an organization designed to link the six Arabian Gulf states on the basis of their cultural and historical ties emerged from a set of plans formulated by the Kuwaiti government. At a meeting February 4–5, 1981, the Gulf foreign ministers codified the Kuwaiti proposals and issued the Riyadh Agreement, which proposed cooperative efforts in cultural, social, economic, and financial affairs. On March 10, after settling on legal and administrative provisions, the ministers initialed a constitution for the GCC in Muscat, Oman; the Council came into formal existence with the signing of the constitution by the Gulf heads of state during the first Supreme Council meeting on May 25–26, 1981, in Abu Dhabi, United Arab Emirates. Two years later the Gulf Investment Corporation was established to finance joint venture projects.

Although members had earlier denied that the GCC was intended as a military grouping, events in the Middle East prompted Gulf leaders to consider joint security measures, leading to the first GCC joint military exercises in late 1983 and the formation of a defense force called the "Peninsula Shield." However, the GCC's failure to mount a coordinated diplomatic or military response to Iraq's occupation of Kuwait on August 2, 1990, threatened to erode the alliance's credibility. The organization was described as slow in condemning the invasion and then proved unable to deploy its defense force for three weeks (its troops then being absorbed into the US-led international force being assembled in Saudi Arabia).

Shortly after the initiation of military action to liberate Kuwait in early 1991, the GCC began to discuss the creation of a new regional defense organization with Egypt and Syria, the two other major Arab members of the anti-Iraq coalition. The so-called "six plus two" defense arrangement was further delineated by a declaration signed in Damascus, Syria, in early March in the wake of the successful conclusion of Operation Desert Storm but, initial enthusiasm for reliance on an Arab force to preserve Gulf security subsequently waned. An exclusively GCC military committee was established in 1994, and another step toward military coordination was taken in December 2001, when the Supreme Council authorized formation of a Supreme Defense Council of defense ministers to oversee a previously adopted joint defense pact.

Structure. The Supreme Council, composed of the six members' heads of state, convenes annually and is the highest authority of the GCC, directing the general course and policies of the organization. Since 1998 a consultative session has been held between these summits. Extraordinary Council sessions also may be convened when requested by two member states. Substantive decisions require consensus. On an ad hoc basis, the Supreme Council may establish a Commission for the Settlement of Disputes. Advising the Supreme Council is a 30-member, citizen's Consultative Commission, formation of which was authorized December 1997.

The foreign ministers of the member states, or other ministers representing them, comprise the Ministerial Council, which meets in regular session four times per year to formulate policy, make recommendations to the Supreme Council, initiate studies, and authorize projects. The Secretariat, headquartered in Riyadh, Saudi Arabia, is the GCC's principal administrative body. The secretary general, who is chosen by the Supreme Council, serves a once-renewable, three-year term and is assisted by three assistant secretaries for economic, military, and political affairs. Following a flap over election of a new secretary general in December 1995, the Ministerial Council agreed that the office would be rotated among the member countries in the future.

In addition to the Office of the Secretary General, divisions within the Secretariat include the following: Economic Affairs, Finance and Administrative Affairs, Human and Environment Affairs, Legal Affairs, Military Affairs, and Political Affairs. Each is headed by a director general. The Secretariat also encompasses Administrative Development and Internal Auditing units, a Patent Bureau, an Information Center, and a Telecommunications Bureau, the last located in Bahrain. The GCC Delegation in Brussels, Belgium, also is included in the Secretariat.

Activities. In its early years the GCC emphasized economic integration, signing, for example, a Unified Economic Agreement in 1981 to provide coordination in commerce, industry, and finance and to prepare the way for an eventual common market. Further harmonization of investment and trade regulations was reached later the same year, while in 1983 the Gulf Investment Corporation opened.

During much of the 1980s, however, the protracted Iran–Iraq war generated concern over the resultant disruption of oil transport through the Gulf. With a cease-fire having been concluded in mid-1988, the December Supreme Council session called on GCC members for a renewed focus on regional economic integration and industrial diversification. The 1990 Iraqi invasion of Kuwait and its destructive consequences once again diverted attention from the GCC's economic mission.

At the conclusion of their 15th summit, held December 19–21, 1994, in Manama, Bahrain, the GCC heads of state called for a "redoubling" of efforts to resolve border disputes between members. (A dispute involving Qatar and Saudi Arabia had nearly sidetracked the December 1992 summit.) The summit's final declaration also noted concern over "extremism and excesses" associated with the Islamic fundamentalist movement in the region. Earlier in the year, a slump in oil prices had put most members in the unfamiliar position of adopting austerity budgets, which may have influenced a subsequent decision by the GCC to end its boycott of foreign companies trading with Israel.

Despite the call for greater cohesion at the 1994 summit, tensions among members continued throughout 1995. At the 16th summit, held in Muscat on December 4–6, 1995, the Qatari delegation boycotted the closing ceremonies to protest of the appointment of new GCC Secretary General

Jamil al-Hujaylan of Saudi Arabia. Qatar had presented its own candidate and objected to what it perceived as Saudi maneuvering that had led to the violation of the long-standing "rule of unanimity" on such matters. A reported coup attempt in Qatar on February 20, 1996, further exacerbated the tension. Qatar's new emir, Sheikh Hamad (who had deposed his father in June), suggested possible involvement in the coup plot on the part of the UAE, Bahrain, and Saudi Arabia.

At the ministerial meetings March 17, 1996, Oman crafted an initiative designed to mend relations among the GCC partners. Among other things, Qatar agreed to recognize the new secretary general in return for structural changes in regard to future selections (see above). However, other issues continued to separate the GCC members, Bahrain, for one thing, accusing Qatar (and by extension, Iran, with whom Qatar's Sheikh Hamad had sought expanded relations) of meddling in its internal affairs. As a consequence of these claims and its territorial dispute with Qatar, Bahrain boycotted the 17th GCC summit held in Doha, Qatar, on December 1, 1996. Although the summit's official communiqué attempted to downplay the rift, observers suggested that "serious cracks" were apparent in the GCC structure.

In January 1997 the GCC initiated talks to try to mediate the Qatar-Bahrain dispute. Later in the year, the GCC took steps to improve relations with Iran. In contrast, Iraq was severely criticized at the GCC summit for its failure to comply with all UN Security Council resolutions. The Council also declared the European Parliament's disapproval of the judicial systems in the Gulf to be unwanted "interference in internal affairs."

The November 27–29, 1999, Supreme Council session in Riyadh was highlighted by an agreement to establish a GCC Customs Union in March 2005 (four years later than initially proposed). The accord was achieved despite continuing political differences among members, particularly between Saudi Arabia and the United Arab Emirates. A recent warming of relations between the Saudi and Iranian governments had been greeted with consternation by the UAE because of its long-standing insular dispute with Teheran over Persian Gulf islands (see the UAE article).

The concluding communiqué of the 21st Supreme Council summit, held in Manama on December 30–31, 2000, included what had become routine criticism of Iraqi and Israeli policies. A more substantive development was the signing of a Joint Defense Treaty pledging mutual aid in the event of attack. Talks on economic and trade issues also moved forward. The heads of state urged continued work toward the anticipated customs union and toward coordinating financial, fiscal, and banking policies. Except for a few "reserved" areas, the summit participants also concurred that the nationals of all member states should be permitted to "engage in all economic activities and occupations" in any of the six GCC countries.

Meeting in Muscat on December 30–31, 2001, the Supreme Council called for an international summit on counterterrorism. Three months earlier, in the wake of the September 11 terrorist attacks in the United States, the GCC foreign ministers had voiced support for US efforts to form a coalition that would undertake a "war on terror," but at the same time they had reiterated their call for an end to Israeli actions against Palestinians. On the economic front, the December summit advanced the date for introducing the GCC Customs Union to January 2003 and also indicated that the GCC would seek a uniform currency by January 2010. Although the leaders had rejected Council membership for Yemen in the mid-1990s, they now agreed to permit its ministerial-level participation in matters of health, education, and labor and social affairs. Also at the summit, Qatar saw its minister of energy, minerals, water, and electricity, Abdul Rahman al-Attiya, named as successor to Secretary General Jamil al-Hujaylan.

As scheduled, the Customs Union was introduced on January 1, 2003. The union established a uniform 5 percent external tariff while permitting duty-free trade within the six GCC members. Introduction of the union had the added benefit of meeting a principal condition for achieving an anticipated free trade agreement with the European Union (EU).

In March 2003, responding to the US/UK-led invasion of Iraq, the GCC urged a return to negotiation but also noted Saddam Hussein's failure to meet all the terms of UN Security Council resolutions. The 24th summit, held December 21–22, 2003, in Kuwait City, saw the leaders support efforts to return power to the Iraqi people by mid-2004 and reaffirmed their own noninterference in Iraqi affairs–a somewhat disingenuous statement given that the land assault against Iraq had been initiated and directed from GCC territory. They also broached the possibility of eventually allowing a new Iraqi government to join Yemen as an external participant in certain GCC functions. In other business, the summit passed resolutions on education, economic reform, and social affairs; agreed to take a joint stand on debt forgiveness for Iraq; and announced plans to draft an antiterrorism pact. On December 29, meeting in emergency session, the GCC finance and economy ministers authorized $400 million in aid to assist Iran in recovering from its recent devastating earthquake.

A rift surfaced in December 2004 after Bahrain signed a free-trade agreement with the United States. Saudi leaders said the unilateral pact violated the GCC rules, but perhaps more significantly, the pact was seen as undermining the economic power of Saudi Arabia in the region. At a GCC meeting in Manama, Bahrain, in December, the Saudi Crown Prince was replaced in attendance by the second deputy premier, the Crown Prince refusing to attend because of the breach. Simmering below the surface was the reported "competition" between Saudi Arabia and the United States for greater control in the region.

Economic issues took a back seat to political and security issues, however, during the GCC summit of May 28, 2005, in Riyadh. Council leaders focused on stability and security in Lebanon, calling for a united Lebanese front and promoting peace efforts in the Middle East in nonspecific ways. The scope of the leaders' conference covered environmental, humanitarian, and military matters as well.

ORGANIZATION OF ARAB PETROLEUM EXPORTING COUNTRIES (OAPEC)

Established: By agreement concluded at Beirut, Lebanon, on January 9, 1968.

Purpose: To help coordinate members' petroleum policies, to adopt measures for harmonizing their legal systems to the extent needed for the group to fulfill its mission, to assist in the exchange of information and expertise, to provide training and employment opportunities for their citizens, and to utilize members' "resources and common potentialities" in establishing joint projects in the petroleum and petroleum-related industries.

Headquarters: Kuwait City, Kuwait.

Principal Organs: Ministerial Council, Executive Bureau, Judicial Tribunal, General Secretariat.

Secretary General: Abdul Aziz A. Al-Turki (Saudi Arabia).

Membership (10): Algeria, Bahrain, Egypt, Iraq, Kuwait, Libya, Qatar, Saudi Arabia, Syria, United Arab Emirates. (Egyptian membership was suspended 1979–1989.)

Official Language: Arabic.

Origin and development. Established by Kuwait, Libya, and Saudi Arabia in early 1968 in recognition of the need for further cooperation among Arab countries that relied on oil as their principal source of income, OAPEC was expanded in May 1970 by the accession of Algeria, Bahrain, Qatar, and Abu Dhabi and Dubai. In May 1972

the last two combined their membership as part of the United Arab Emirates. In December 1971 the founding Agreement was liberalized to permit membership by any Arab country having oil as a significant–but not necessarily the major–source of income, with the result that Syria and Egypt joined in 1972 and 1973, respectively. Also in 1972, Iraq became a member. A Tunisian bid for membership failed at the December 1981 ministerial meeting because of Libyan opposition stemming from a dispute with Tunis over conflicting claims to offshore oil deposits. Tunisia was admitted in 1982 but four years later withdrew from active membership because it had become a net importer of energy and could not make its OAPEC contributions.

OAPEC joint ventures and projects include the Arab Maritime Petroleum Transport Company (AMPTC), founded in 1973 with headquarters at Kuwait; the Arab Shipbuilding and Repair Yard Company (ASRY), established in Bahrain in 1974; the Arab Petroleum Investments Corporation (Apicorp), set up in 1975 at Damman, Saudi Arabia; and the Arab Petroleum Services Company (APSC), founded in 1977 and operating from Tripoli, Libya. The Arab Engineering Company (Arec), established in 1981 in Abu Dhabi, was dissolved in 1989. Shareholders in these ventures are typically either the member governments themselves or state-owned petroleum enterprises.

Subsidiary companies are the Arab Drilling and Workover Company (ADWOC), based at Tripoli since its formation in 1980; the Arab Well Logging Company (AWLCO), established at Baghdad in 1983; and the Arab Geophysical Exploration

Services Company (AGESCO), formed at Tripoli in 1984. The APSC is the sole shareholder in AWLCO and the principal shareholder in the other two. The Arab Company for Detergent Chemicals (Aradet), founded at Baghdad in 1981, is an Apicorp subsidiary.

Structure. The Ministerial Council, OAPEC's supreme authority, is composed of the members' petroleum ministers, who convene at least twice a year to draw up policy guidelines and direct ongoing activities. An Executive Bureau, which meets at least three times a year, assists the Council in management of the Organization. A Judicial Tribunal, established in 1980, serves as an arbitration council between OAPEC members or between a member and a petroleum company operating in that country, with all decisions final and binding. The Secretariat, headed by a secretary general and no more than three assistant secretaries general, encompasses the secretary's office and four Departments: Finance and Administrative Affairs, Information and Library, Economics, and Technical Affairs. The last two comprise the Arab Center for Energy Studies.

Activities. Although OAPEC's activities are directly affected by the world oil market, it plays no institutional role in determining either output quotas or prices, deferring in both cases to the more encompassing Organization of Petroleum Exporting Countries (OPEC). Instead, OAPEC focuses on coordinating related policies within the Arab community. Over the years, it has also invested billions of dollars in its associated ventures and affiliates. Apicorp, for example, has helped finance petroleum and petrochemical projects around the world, including gas liquefaction plants, refineries, pipelines and other means of transport, and facilities for making fertilizers and detergents. In addition to its administrative tasks, the OAPEC Secretariat has compiled and continually updates a comprehensive database of information on oil and energy markets, reserves, production, refining, consumption, and downstream industries, such as petrochemicals. OAPEC also conducts related research projects, sponsors seminars, and produces technical papers and studies.

The December 1990 Ministerial Council meeting was held at Cairo, Egypt, that city having been chosen as OAPEC's temporary headquarters following the Iraqi invasion of Kuwait the previous August. In mid-1992 a report co-authored by OAPEC estimated that the Gulf crisis had cost Arab countries as much as $620 billion and had contributed to rising inflation and a decline of 7 percent in the gross national product of 21 Arab nations in 1991. The destruction of oil wells, pipelines, and other infrastructure alone cost Iraq an estimated $190 billion and Kuwait $160 billion, the report said.

Arab oil affairs remained turbulent into 1994 as several OAPEC members continued to quarrel over OPEC production quotas. There was ongoing disagreement over how and when Iraq would resume oil exports, while OAPEC officials described recent wide fluctuations in oil prices as making it difficult for member states to effectively plan development programs. The Organization hoped, however, to return to a degree of normal activity following return to its permanent headquarters in Kuwait at midyear.

Low oil prices remained a major OAPEC concern throughout 1998, a December session of the Ministerial Council urging all oil-producing countries to exercise restraint regarding production levels. In 1999 OAPEC officials also suggested that some members might be well served to encourage private investment in their oil sectors as a means of accelerating economic advancement.

Oil output and the condition of world oil markets, which experienced a dramatic increase in prices in 2000, remained a major focus of the four Ministerial Council sessions held at Cairo in 2000–2001. In mid-2000 an OAPEC report indicated that Arab countries were contributing about 26 percent of world oil production and that, as of 1999, Arab reserves amounted to 63 percent of the world total.

In recent years OAPEC has also been giving increasing attention to environmental concerns, in part to ensure that the economic standing of its members are not adversely affected by international initiatives intended to reduce greenhouse gases and other pollutants. The Eighth Coordinating Meeting of Environmental Experts was held at Cairo on September 29–30, 2001, its principal focus being coordination of member countries' positions regarding, for example, the UN Framework Convention on Climate Change and the associated Kyoto Protocol. At the same time, OAPEC was preparing for the Seventh Arab Energy Conference, held May 11–12, 2002, at Cairo, where the focus was again directed toward "Energy and Arab Cooperation." Other organizations sponsoring the conference were the Arab Fund for Economic and Social Development (AFESD), the Arab League, and the Arab Industrial Development and Mining Organization (AIDMO).

During 2001–2003 oil prices and resultant income remained somewhat volatile despite improving communication between oil suppliers and consuming nations. At the same time, OAPEC reported, Arab petroleum-refining capacity was increasing, as was regional consumption of natural gas. Known Arab reserves of the latter commodity, about one-fourth of the world total, nevertheless continued to increase as new discoveries outpaced consumption. OAPEC also projected that global oil consumption would rise by about 1.6 percent annually, from 76 billion barrels per day in 2000 to nearly 90 billion barrels per day in 2010.

In March–May 2003 the invasion of Iraq by US-led forces had a minimal impact on oil supplies. It was unclear, however, given the dilapidated state of Iraq's petroleum infrastructure, when or if Iraqi oil production would regain the levels that predated the 1991 Gulf War. A representative of the US-sponsored interim Iraqi Governing Council was expected to attend the OAPEC Ministerial Council session held at Cairo on December 13, 2003, but he withdrew because of an unspecified "emergency."

ORGANIZATION OF THE ISLAMIC CONFERENCE (OIC)

Established: By agreement of participants at the Conference of the Kings and Heads of State and Government held at Rabat, Morocco, September 22–25, 1969; Charter signed at the Third Islamic Conference of Foreign Ministers, held at Jiddah, Saudi Arabia, February 29–March 4, 1972.

Purpose: To promote Islamic solidarity and further cooperation among member states in the economic, social, cultural, scientific, and political fields.

Headquarters: Jiddah, Saudi Arabia.

Principal Organs: Conference of Kings and Heads of State and Government (Summit Conference), Conference of Foreign Ministers, General Secretariat.

Secretary General: Ekmeleddin İhsanoğlu (Turkey).

Membership (57): Afghanistan, Albania, Algeria, Azerbaijan, Bahrain, Bangladesh, Benin, Brunei, Burkina Faso, Cameroon, Chad, Comoro Islands, Côte d'Ivoire, Djibouti, Egypt, Gabon, Gambia, Guinea, Guinea-Bissau, Guyana, Indonesia, Iran, Iraq, Jordan, Kazakhstan, Kuwait, Kyrgyzstan, Lebanon, Libya, Malaysia, Maldives, Mali, Mauritania, Morocco, Mozambique, Niger, Nigeria, Oman, Pakistan, Palestine, Qatar, Saudi Arabia, Senegal, Sierra Leone, Somalia, Sudan, Suriname, Syria, Tajikistan, Togo, Tunisia, Turkey, Turkmenistan, Uganda, United Arab Emirates, Uzbekistan, Yemen. Afghanistan's membership was suspended in January 1980, following the Soviet invasion, but the seat was given in March 1989 to the government-in-exile announced by Afghan guerrillas and subsequently to the Afghan government formed after the guerrilla victory. The advent of the Taliban regime at Kabul in September 1996 yielded competition for OIC recognition between it and the overthrown government, with both being refused formal admittance to the OIC foreign ministers' conference at Jakarta in December, although Afghanistan as such continued to be regarded as a member. Egypt's membership, suspended in May 1979, was restored in April 1984. Nigeria's government approved that nation's admission into the OIC in 1986, but the membership was formally repudiated in 1991 in the wake of intense Christian opposition; the OIC has not recognized the latter decision. There has also been uncertainty about the status of Zanzibar, whose membership request had been approved in December 1992; eight months later it was announced that Zanzibar's application, which had precipitated contentious legislative debate in Tanzania, had been withdrawn pending the possible forwarding of a Tanzanian membership request.

Observers (10): Bosnia and Herzegovina, Central African Republic, Economic Cooperation Organization, League of Arab States, Moro National Liberation Front, Nonaligned Movement, Organization of African Unity, Thailand, Turkish Republic of Northern Cyprus, United Nations.

Official Languages: Arabic, English, French.

Origin and development. Although the idea of an organization for coordinating and consolidating the interests of Islamic states originated in 1969 and meetings of the Conference were held throughout the 1970s, the Islamic Conference only began to achieve worldwide attention in the early 1980s. From a base of 30 members in 1969, the OIC has doubled in size, with the most recent member, Côte d'Ivoire, being admitted in 2001.

Structure. The body's main institution is the Conference of Foreign Ministers, although a summit of members' heads of state and government is held every three years. Sectoral ministerial conferences have also convened in such areas as information, tourism, health, and youth and sports.

Over the years an array of committees and departments have evolved to provide input for policy decisions and to carry out the OIC's executive and administrative functions. The Organization's general secretary, who serves a four-year, once-renewable term, heads the General Secretariat and is aided by four assistant secretaries general–for Science and Technology; Cultural, Social, and Information Affairs; Political Affairs; and Economic Affairs–and a director of the cabinet, who helps administer various departments. The Secretariat also maintains permanent observer missions to the United Nations at New York, United States, and Geneva, Switzerland, and an Office for Afghanistan was recently established at Islamabad, Pakistan. Other OIC organs include the Al-Quds (Jerusalem) Committee, the Six-Member Committee on Palestine, the Standing Committee for Information and Cultural Affairs (COMIAC), the Standing Committee for Economic and Trade Cooperation (COMCEC), the Standing Committee for Scientific and Technological Cooperation (COMSTECH), and various additional permanent and specialized committees. Recent ad hoc committees and groups have included an Ad Hoc Committee on Afghanistan and Contact Groups for Jammu and Kashmir, Sierra Leone, and Bosnia and Herzegovina and Kosovo.

To date, the OIC has established four "specialized institutions and organs": the International Islamic News Agency (IINA, founded in 1972); the Islamic Development Bank (IDB,1974), the Islamic States Broadcasting Organization (ISBO, 1975), and the Islamic Educational, Scientific, and Cultural Organization (ISESCO, 1982). Of the Organization's eight "subsidiary organs," one of the more prominent is the Islamic Solidarity Fund (ISF, 1977). The founding conference of a Parliamentary Union of the OIC Member States was held in June 1999.

Activities. During the 1980s the OIC's agenda was dominated by three lengthy conflicts: the Soviet occupation of Afghanistan, which began in December 1979 and concluded with the final withdrawal of Soviet troops in February 1989; the Iran–Iraq war, which began in September 1980 and ended with the cease-fire of August 1988; and the ongoing Arab–Israeli conflict. At their August 1990 meeting the foreign ministers described the Palestinian problem as the primary concern for the Islamic world. However, much of the planned agenda was disrupted by emergency private sessions concerning the Iraqi invasion of Kuwait on August 2. A substantial majority of those attending the meeting approved a resolution condemning the incursion and demanding the withdrawal of Iraqi troops. In addition to other ongoing conflicts among conference members (such as the dispute between Mauritania and Senegal), the Gulf crisis contributed to the postponement of the heads of state summit that normally would have been held in 1990.

When the sixth summit was finally held on December 9–11, 1991, at Dakar, Senegal, more than half of the members' heads of state failed to attend. Substantial lingering rancor concerning the Gulf crisis was reported at the meeting, while Black African representatives asserted that Arab nations were not giving sufficient attention to the problems of sub-Saharan Muslims. On the whole, the summit was perceived as unproductive, *Middle East International* going so far as to wonder if the Conference would "fade from the international political scene" because of its failure to generate genuine "Islamic solidarity."

In the following three years much of the Conference's attention focused on the plight of the

Muslim community in Bosnia and Herzegovina. The group's foreign ministers repeatedly called upon the United Nations to use force, if necessary, to stop Serbian attacks against Bosnian Muslims, but the Conference stopped well short of approving creation of an Islamic force to intervene on its own in Bosnia and Herzegovina, as reportedly proposed by Iran and several other members.

The seventh OIC summit, held December 13–15, 1994, at Casablanca, Morocco, reached consensus on a code of conduct regarding terrorism and religious extremism in the hope of improving the "global image" of Islam. Among other things, the OIC nations agreed that their territories would not be used for terrorist activities nor would any of them support, "morally or financially," any Muslim "terrorists" opposed to member governments. However, with states such as Iran and Sudan (both charged with supporting extremist fundamentalists in other nations) signing the OIC statement, some observers described the document as a "face-saving" measure that masked ongoing deep divisions on the issue.

OIC efforts to improve the international image of Islam continued in 1995, notably in conjunction with ceremonies marking the Organization's 25th anniversary. US Vice President Gore had talks with OIC Secretary General Hamid Algabid at Jiddah, Saudi Arabia, in March, receiving assurances of the OIC's "unwavering" support for international stability and offering in return a US commitment to dialogue with the Islamic world in the interests of peace and mutual understanding. The desire for a greater Islamic role in resolving international disputes, expressed in an anniversary declaration issued in September, was also apparent in enhanced OIC participation in UN and other mediatory frameworks.

The 24th OIC foreign ministers' conference, held at Jakarta, Indonesia, on December 9–13, 1996, reiterated familiar positions, including the demand for an independent Palestinian state and Israel's withdrawal from all territory "captured in war." With regard to Afghanistan, neither the new Taliban regime nor the government ousted in September was accorded official status, it being resolved that Afghanistan's OIC seat should remain vacant pro tem "without prejudice to the question of recognition of the government of Afghanistan." A Taliban delegation was also sent to an extraordinary summit of heads of government held at Islamabad on March 23, 1997, to celebrate 50 years of Pakistani independence. While it was again denied official recognition, the delegation was allowed to attend.

The renewed Palestinian *intifada* and the Israeli response to it provided a principal focus for OIC meetings in 2000. These included the June 27–30 Conference of Foreign Ministers at Kuala Lumpur, Malaysia, and the ninth summit at Doha, Qatar, on November 12–13, which devoted its first day to discussing "the serious situation prevailing in the Palestinian occupied territories following the savage actions perpetrated by the Israeli forces." Representatives of Iraq, Sudan, and Syria insisted that waging *jihad* against Israel was required, while others urged political and economic retaliation.

An eighth extraordinary session of the foreign ministers met on May 26, 2001, in the context of the continuing hostilities. Meeting at Bamako, Mali, on June 25–29, the regular 28th Conference of Foreign Ministers reiterated a call for member countries to halt political contacts with the Israeli government, sever economic relations, and end "all forms of normalization." The concluding declaration of the session also urged resolution of a familiar list of other conflicts involving, among others, Afghanistan, Armenia and Azerbaijan, Cyprus, Jammu and Kashmir, Iraq, Kosovo, and Somalia. In other areas, the Conference urged member states to ratify the Statute of the International Islamic Court of Justice, called for formation of an expert group that would begin drafting an Islamic Convention on Human Rights, condemned international terrorism, noted the progress made toward instituting an Islamic Program for the Development of Information and Communication (PIDIC), and cautioned that care must be taken to ensure that the economic benefits of globalization are shared and the adverse effects minimized.

Immediately after the September 11, 2001, *al-Qaeda* attacks on the United States, the OIC secretary general, Abdelouahed Belkeziz, condemned the terrorist acts, as did an extraordinary Conference of Foreign Ministers session at Doha on October 10. The Doha session did not directly oppose the ongoing US-led military campaign against *al-Qaeda* and the Taliban regime in Afghanistan, although it did argue that no state should be targeted under the pretext of attacking terrorism. The foreign ministers session also rejected as counter to Islamic teachings and values any attempt to justify terrorism on religious grounds. Four months later, as part of an effort to foster intercultural dialogue, the OIC foreign ministers met at Istanbul with counterparts from the European Union.

On April 1–3, 2002, a special OIC session on terrorism convened at the Malaysian capital. In addition to establishing a 13-member committee to implement a plan of action against terrorism, the session issued a declaration that, among other things, condemned efforts to link terrorism and Islam and called for a global conference to define terrorism and establish internationally accepted procedures for combating it. Notably, however, the conference did not voice consensual support for a speech by Malaysian Prime Minister Mahathir bin Mohamad in which he described all attacks on civilians, including those by Palestinians and Sri Lanka's Tamil Tigers, as terrorist acts. The call for a UN-sponsored conference on terrorism was repeated by the Council of Foreign Ministers at their June session at Khartoum.

The impending US-led war against the Saddam Hussein regime in Iraq generated a Second Extraordinary Session of the Islamic Summit Conference at Doha on March 5, 2003. The meeting included an exchange of personal insults by the Iraqi and Kuwaiti representatives and a warning from the secretary general that a US military campaign would lead to occupation and foreign rule. Concern was also expressed that the Israeli government was taking advantage of the world's preoccupation with the Iraqi crisis to intensify its campaign against Palestinians. The session concluded with a call for the elimination of all weapons of mass destruction (WMDs) from the Middle East.

The tenth OIC Summit Conference, which met at Putrajaya, Malaysia, on October 16–18, 2003, featured an address by Prime Minister Mahathir that many Western countries condemned as anti-Semitic because of its stereotypical description of Jewish and Israeli intentions and tactics. The comments came in the context of Mahathir's argument that the Islamic world should focus on winning "hearts and minds" by abjuring violence and adopting new political and economic strategies. The summit concluded with issuance of the Putrajaya Declaration, which noted the "need to restructure and strengthen the Organisation on the basis of an objective review and evaluation of its role, structure, methodology, and decision-making processes, as well as its global partnerships." Included in the closing declaration's Plan of Action were provisions that called for drafting strategies to strengthen unity, especially at international forums; engaging in further dialogue with the West and international organizations; completing a review of the structure, methods, and needs of the Secretariat; promoting the advancement of science and technology (particularly information and communication technology) among member states; and taking steps to encourage the expansion of trade and investment.

In response to subsequent international developments, the secretary general praised improved cooperation between Iran and the International Atomic Energy Agency; condemned the November 2003 terrorist attacks against synagogues at Istanbul as well as those against a housing complex at Riyadh, Saudi Arabia; and welcomed Libya's decision to end the development of WMDs. On February 25, 2004, appeared before the International Court of Justice at The Hague, the OIC argued that the security wall being constructed by Israel on Palestinian land was illegal.

The OIC subsequently continued to condemn acts of terrorism around the world, including the bombings at Madrid, Spain, in March 2004; the attacks against London's transit system in July 2005; and the explosions at the Egyptian resorts of Sharm El-Shiekh and Naama Bay later the same month. With regard to developments in Iraq, in August

2005 the OIC urged "prudence and consensus" during deliberations on the draft Iraqi constitution. In particular, the OIC advocated a policy of inclusion, cautioning that the "exclusion of any component of the population" (implicitly, the Sunni minority) would ill serve "the creation of commonly desired conditions of democracy, stability, peace, and welfare in this important member of the OIC."

ORGANIZATION OF THE PETROLEUM EXPORTING COUNTRIES (OPEC)

Established: By resolutions adopted at Baghdad, Iraq, on September 14, 1960, and codified in a Statute approved by the Eighth (Extraordinary) OPEC Conference, held April 5–10, 1965, at Geneva, Switzerland.

Purpose: To coordinate and unify petroleum policies of member countries; to devise ways to ensure stabilization of international oil prices to eliminate "harmful and unnecessary" price and supply fluctuations.

Headquarters: Vienna, Austria.

Principal Organs: Conference, Board of Governors, Economic Commission, Secretariat.

Secretary General: (Acting) Adnan Shihab-Eldin.

Membership: (11, with years of entry): Algeria (1969), Indonesia (1962), Iran (1960), Iraq (1960), Kuwait (1960), Libya (1962), Nigeria (1971), Qatar (1961), Saudi Arabia (1960), United Arab Emirates (Abu Dhabi in 1967, with the membership being transferred to the UAE in 1974), Venezuela (1960). Ecuador and Gabon, who had joined OPEC in 1973, withdrew on January 1, 1993, and January 1, 1997, respectively. Iraq currently does not participate in OPEC production quotas.

Official Language: English.

Origin and development. A need for concerted action by petroleum exporters was first broached in 1946 by Dr. Juan Pablo Pérez Alfonso of Venezuela. His initiative led to a series of contacts in the late 1940s between oil-producing countries, but it was not until 1959 that the first Arab Petroleum Conference was held. At that meeting Dr. Pérez Alfonso convinced the Arabs, in addition to Iranian and Venezuelan observers, to form a union of producing states, with OPEC being formally created by Iran, Iraq, Kuwait, Saudi Arabia, and Venezuela on September 14, 1960, during a conference at Baghdad, Iraq.

The rapid growth of energy needs in the advanced industrialized states throughout the 1960s and early 1970s provided OPEC with the basis for extracting ever-increasing oil prices. However, OPEC demands were not limited to favorable prices; members also sought the establishment of an infrastructure for future industrialization including petrochemical plants, steel mills, aluminum plants, and other high-energy industries as a hedge against the anticipated exhaustion of their oil reserves in the 21st century.

The addition of new members and negotiations with petroleum companies on prices, production levels, and tax revenues dominated OPEC's early years, prices remaining low and relatively stable. On the other hand, largely because of increases mandated by OPEC, prices soared dramatically from about $3 for a 42-gallon barrel in the early 1970s to a peak of nearly $40 per barrel by the end of the decade. Thereafter, a world glut of petroleum, brought on by overproduction, global recession, and the implementation of at least rudimentary energy conservation programs by many industrialized nations, subsequently reversed that trend. The influence of formal price setting by OPEC waned as the Organization began to depend more and more on negotiated production quotas to stabilize prices (see Activities, below).

Structure. The OPEC Conference, which normally meets twice a year, is the supreme authority of the Organization. Comprising the oil ministers of the member states, the Conference formulates policy, considers recommendations from the Board of Governors, and approves the budget. The Board consists of governors nominated by the various member states and approved by the Conference for two-year terms. In addition to submitting the annual budget, various reports, and recommendations to the Conference, the Board directs the Organization's management, while the Secretariat performs executive functions. Operating within the Secretariat are a Division of Research, and departments for Administration and Human Resources, Data Services, Energy Studies, Petroleum Market Analysis, and Public Relations and Information. In addition, an Economic Commission, established as a specialized body in 1964, works within the Secretariat framework to promote equitable and stable international oil prices. A Ministerial Monitoring Committee was established in 1982 to evaluate oil market conditions and to make recommendations to the Conference.

The OPEC Fund for International Development has made significant contributions to developing countries, mostly Arabian and African, in the form of balance-of-payments support; direct financing of imports; and project loans in such areas as energy, transportation, and food production. All current OPEC members plus Gabon are members of the Fund. As of 2002 more than $5 billion in loans had been approved for nearly 1,000 operations in the public sector and about $200 million for private sector operations. In addition, grants totaling $300 million had been approved for more than 600 operations.

Activities. In December 1985, as spot market prices dropped to $24 a barrel and production dipped to as low as 16 million barrels per day, OPEC abandoned its formal price structure to secure a larger share of the world's oil market. By mid-1986, however, oil prices had dropped by 50 percent or more to their lowest level since 1978, generating intense concern among OPEC members with limited oil reserves, large populations, extensive international debts, and severe shortages of foreign exchange. As a result, Saudi Arabia increased its output by 2 million barrels per day in January 1986 to force non-OPEC producers to cooperate with the cartel in stabilizing the world oil market.

The acceptance of production ceilings in June 1986 appeared to signify a reduction of conflict within OPEC. Iran, which had previously insisted that any increase in Iraq's quota be matched by an increase in its own allocation, reversed its position. Saudi Arabia, while maintaining that the ceilings did not preclude OPEC's attainment of a fair market share, relaxed its insistence that quotas be completely overhauled and appeared to have realigned itself with Algeria, Iran, and Libya, all of whom had long supported an end to the price war. In response to the renewed cohesiveness of the Organization, oil prices increased slightly.

Relative calm prevailed within the Organization during the first half of 1987, with prices ranging from $18 to $21 per barrel. By midyear, however, overproduction by most members and a weakening of world oil demand began to push prices downward. At the end of June, OPEC had adjusted its quota down to 16.6 million barrels per day, but individual quotas were largely ignored. Production subsequently approached 20 million barrels per day later in the year. Consequently, Saudi Arabia warned its partners that if the "cheating" continued, it would no longer serve as the oil market's stabilizer by reducing its own production to support higher prices.

During their December meeting at Vienna, OPEC oil ministers attempted to reimpose discipline, but the talks became embroiled in political considerations stemming from the Iran–Iraq war. Iraq again refused to accept quotas lower than those of Iran, while Teheran accused Gulf Arab states of conspiring with Baghdad against Iranian interests. For their part, non-Arab states protested that war issues were inhibiting the adoption of sound economic policies. The meeting concluded with 12 members endorsing the $18 per barrel fixed-price concept and agreeing to a 15 million barrel per day production quota, Iraq's non-participation leaving it free to produce at will. However, widespread discounting quickly forced prices down to about $15 per barrel. Subsequently, in the wake of a report that OPEC's share of the oil market (66 percent in 1979) had fallen below 30 percent, an appeal was issued to nonmember states to assume a greater role in stabilizing prices and production.

A sharp drop in oil prices to between $13 and $14 per barrel in early 1988 prompted OPEC to meet with non-OPEC oil-exporting countries for the first time to formulate joint strategies for control of the oil market. Although six non-OPEC countries agreed to a 5 percent cut in exports, OPEC was unable to reach consensus on a reciprocal 5 percent decrease; as a result, the agreement collapsed.

Disarray continued at the June 1988 OPEC meeting at which ministers, unable to reach a new accord, formally extended the December 1987 agreement despite the widespread assessment that it had become virtually meaningless. Led by the United Arab Emirates (UAE), quota-breaking countries subsequently pushed members' production to an estimated high of 22–23 million barrels per day, with prices dropping below $12 per barrel. In the wake of the Gulf cease-fire, however, OPEC cohesion seemed to return. In their first unanimous action in two years, the members agreed in late November to limit production to 18.5 million barrels per day as of January 1, 1989, while maintaining a "target price" of $18 per barrel. Responding to the Organization's apparent renewal of self-control, oil prices rose to nearly $20 per barrel by March 1989. However, contention broke out again at the June OPEC session, with Saudi Arabia resisting demands for sizable quota increases. Although a compromise agreement was concluded, Kuwait and the UAE immediately declared that they would continue to exceed their quotas.

In November 1989 OPEC raised its official production ceiling from 20.5 to 22 million barrels per day, allowing Kuwait a quota increase from 1.2 to 1.5 million barrels per day. However, the UAE,

whose official quota remained at 1.1 million barrels per day, did not participate in the accord and continued, as did Kuwait, to produce close to 2 million barrels per day. Pledges for restraint were again issued at an emergency meeting in May 1990, but adherence proved negligible. Consequently, in July Iraq's President Saddam Hussein, in what was perceived as a challenge to Saudi leadership within OPEC as well as part of a campaign to achieve dominance in the Arab world, threatened to use military intervention to enforce the national quotas. While the pronouncement drew criticism from the West, a number of OPEC leaders quietly voiced support for Hussein's "enforcer" stance and, mollified by the Iraqi leader's promise not to use military force to settle a border dispute with Kuwait, OPEC agreed on July 27 to Iraqi-led demands for new quotas. However, on August 29, in a dramatic reversal prompted by Iraq's invasion of Kuwait on August 2 and the ensuing embargo on oil exports from the two countries, the Organization authorized producers to disregard quotas to avert possible shortages. OPEC's action legitimized a 2 million barrels per day increase already implemented by Saudi Arabia and dampened Iraq's hope that oil shortages and skyrocketing prices would weaken the resolve of the coalition embargo. In December production reached its highest level in a decade, while prices fluctuated between $25 and $40 in response to the continuing crisis.

In early March 1991, following Iraq's defeat, OPEC agreed to cut production from 23.4 to 22.3 million barrels per day for the second quarter of the year. The decision to maintain production at a level that would keep prices below the July 1990 goal was opposed by Algeria and Iran, who called for larger cuts. Observers attributed the agreement to Saudi Arabia's desire to assert its postwar "muscle" and to continue producing 2.5 million barrels per day over its prewar quota. In June OPEC rejected Iraq's request to intercede with the UN to lift the Iraqi oil embargo.

In September 1991 OPEC agreed to raise its collective production ceiling to 23.6 million barrels per day in preparation for normal seasonal increases in demand. However, Iran and Saudi Arabia remained in what analysts described as a "trial of strength" for OPEC dominance, the former lobbying for lowered production ceilings and higher prices and the latter resisting production curbs or any challenge to its market share. Thereafter, between October and January 1992 prices fell to $16.50 per barrel, $4.50 below the new OPEC target, as production rose to over 24 million barrels per day and projected demand levels failed to materialize. Consequently, on February 15, 1992, OPEC members agreed to their first individual production quotas since August 1990, with the Saudis grudgingly accepting a 7.8 million barrels per day quota. In April and May the Organization extended the February quotas despite reports of overproduction, citing the firm, albeit lower than desired, price of $17 per barrel.

Prices remained low for the rest of 1992 as the global recession undercut demand and overproduction continued to plague OPEC; meanwhile, Kuwait attempted to recover from the economic catastrophe inflicted by the Gulf crisis by pumping oil "at will." With a relatively mild winter in the northern hemisphere having further reduced demand, a February 1993 emergency OPEC meeting sought to reestablish some sense of constraint by endorsing a 23.5 million barrels per day limit on its members.

Actual levels continued at more than 25 million barrels per day, however, and a more realistic quota of 24.5 million barrels per day was negotiated in September 1993. The new arrangements permitted Kuwait's quota to rise from 1.6 million to 2.0 million barrels per day while Iran's quota grew from 3.3 million to 3.6 million. Meanwhile, Saudi Arabia agreed to keep its production at 8 million.

With prices still depressed, some OPEC members, particularly Iran, argued for substantial quota cuts in 1994, but once again resistance from Saudi Arabia precluded such action. Those favoring current levels appeared to be expecting that increased demand, and therefore higher prices, would result soon from economic recovery in much of the industrialized world.

The term of office of the OPEC Director General, Dr. Subroto of Indonesia, expired on June 30, 1994, but agreement was not reached immediately on a successor. It was reported that many members supported Alirio Parra of Venezuela for the position, but Iran held out for its own candidate. Since unanimity was required, Libyan Energy Minister Abdullah Salem al-Badri, at that time the president of the OPEC conference, was named acting secretary general. Subsequently, at their November session, the OPEC oil ministers appointed Rilwanu Lukman, the oil minister from Nigeria, as the permanent secretary general. Although OPEC announced that the selection was "unanimous," it was reported that Iran remained critical of the decision.

The November 1994 Conference also agreed to maintain the current quota of 24.5 million barrels per day for at least one more year. However, pressure for change grew in 1995, particularly as non-OPEC production continued to expand. Secretary General Lukman and oil ministers from several OPEC countries argued that failure on the part of the non-OPEC nations to curb production could lead to serious problems for all oil producers. Among the options which at least some OPEC members were expected to pursue was the temporary lifting of quotas, which would permit the Organization to use its vast oil reserves to "recapture" a greater market share. (It was estimated that OPEC countries controlled over 75 percent of the world's reserves while being responsible for only 40 percent of total oil production at that time.)

The announcement of Gabon's impending withdrawal from OPEC was made at the ministerial meeting on June 5–7, 1996. Among the reasons cited for the decision were the high membership fee and constraints imposed by OPEC production quotas. Meanwhile, the OPEC ministers agreed to raise the production ceiling to 25 million barrels per day, despite the anticipated return of Iraqi crude into the market soon. The Iraqi pipelines were partially reopened in December 1996 under the UN's "oil for food" plan (see article on Iraq).

In late 1997 OPEC decided to increase production by 10 percent to 27.5 million barrels per day for the first half of 1998. However, the organization reversed course sharply when the price fell to

$12.80 per barrel, a nine-year low, in March 1998. Saudi Arabia and Venezuela (joined by nonmember Mexico) immediately announced a reduction of 2 million barrels per day in their output. When prices failed to rebound, OPEC announced a further reduction of 1.3 million barrels per day in July. Additional cuts were considered in November, but consensus on the question could not be reached. Overall, OPEC's revenues in 1998 fell some 35 percent from the previous year, raising questions about the Organization's ability to control prices on its own. Among other things, Saudi Arabia proposed creating a larger, albeit less formal, group of oil-producing countries (comprising OPEC and non-OPEC members) to address price stability.

Oil prices fell to under $10 per barrel in February 1999, prompting an agreement in March under which OPEC cut production by 1.7 million barrels per day while Mexico, Norway, Oman, and Russia accepted a collective reduction of 400,000 barrels per day. Prices subsequently rebounded to more than $26 per barrel late in the year and more than $30 per barrel in early 2000. Consequently, from March to October 2000 OPEC increased production four times by a total of 3.4 million barrels per day before prices, which reached a high of $37.80 per barrel in September, fell in December to $26 per barrel, safely within the OPEC target range of $25–$28 per barrel.

The heads of state of the OPEC countries met for only their second summit in history (the first had been in 1975) in Venezuela in September 2000 amid intensified concern over the impact of high oil prices on the global economy. Among other things, the OPEC leaders criticized a number of European countries for imposing high taxes on oil products, thereby driving up consumer energy costs. The summit also reportedly agreed to extend OPEC's political profile, and in November Ali Rodríguez Araque, the energy and mines minister from Venezuela (considered one of the more "activist" OPEC members), was elected to succeed Secretary General Lukman effective January 2001.

Declining economic conditions in the first eight months in 2001 sharply reduced the demand for oil, and OPEC responded with production cuts in February, April, and September totaling 3.5 million barrels per day. Prices for the most part remained within the target range for that period. However, the terrorist attacks in the United States in September 2001 severely undercut demand, in part due to plummeting air travel, and prices fell below $17 per barrel by November. OPEC demanded that non-OPEC producers again assist in reducing production, and Russia reluctantly agreed to cut its production by 150,000 barrels per day beginning in January 2002 in conjunction with an additional OPEC cut of 1.5 million barrels per day.

Prices rose to nearly $30 per barrel in the autumn of 2002, despite evidence that many OPEC countries were producing above the quotas established in late 2001. Among other things, OPEC leaders argued that prices were being artificially inflated because of fears over a possible US invasion of Iraq and concern emanating from other Mideast tensions. In December OPEC established a quota of 23 million barrels per day, formally an increase over 2001 levels but in reality a decrease considering the year-long "cheating" on the part of some members.

In other activity in 2002, Alvaro Silva Calderón of Venezuela was elected to serve out the remainder of the term of OPEC Secretary General Rodríguez Araque, who was recalled to Venezuela in April during the coup attempt against the government of President Hugo Chávez. OPEC also during the year opposed a proposal from Iraqi President Saddam Hussein that the oil "spigot" be manipulated to pressure the West and Israel regarding Palestinian affairs.

To address the potential for disturbances in the global oil market from the strikes by oil workers in Venezuela, OPEC agreed in January 2003 to raise quotas to 24.5 million barrels per day. However, by April discussion had turned to what was viewed as an "unavoidable" production cut. Complicating factors included the potential for the full return of Iraqi oil to world markets following the toppling of the regime of Saddam Hussein. In that regard, Iraq sent a delegation to OPEC's September session, at which quotas were cut by 900,000 barrels per day.

Despite rising prices, OPEC declined to increase production in January 2004 and, citing the upcoming seasonal dip in demand, reduced quotas again in February. Consequently, the United States warned OPEC that the cuts might harm an already fragile global economy. By March oil prices peaked at $37.45 per barrel, and some non-OPEC countries (such as Mexico) snubbed OPEC's request for production constraint.

Terror attacks on the oil infrastructures in Iraq and Saudi Arabia contributed to continued price increases in mid-2004, finally prompting OPEC to expand its production quotas. Nevertheless, "spare" oil capacity remained at its thinnest in decades. The Group of Eight issued a stern warning about the effects of rising oil prices, which reached a 21-year high in July of more than $43 per barrel. By October the price had topped out at more than $55 per barrel; it then declined by 23 percent by the end of the year.

In December 2004 OPEC announced a production cut to stem the slide in oil prices. Meanwhile, it was estimated that OPEC members were enjoying their highest oil revenue ever in nominal terms. OPEC informally relaxed quota compliance in March 2005, and prices hovered at about $50 per barrel. However, the International Monetary Fund and the United States called for significant additional OPEC production increases to, among other things, provide a more substantial cushion against unforeseen oil shocks. OPEC agreed to that request in June, but the per barrel price subsequently grew to almost $60.

In other recent OPEC activity, Indonesia announced in early 2005 that it had established a panel to assess that country's possible exit from OPEC. Falling oil production in Indonesia has forced it at times to import oil.

REGIONAL AND SUBREGIONAL DEVELOPMENT BANKS

Regional development banks are intended to accelerate economic and social development of member states by promoting public and private investment. The banks are not meant, however, to be mere financial institutions in the narrow sense of the term. Required by their charters to take an active interest in improving their members' capacities to make profitable use of local and external capital, they engage in such technical assistance activities as feasibility studies, evaluation and design of projects, and preparation of development programs. The banks also seek to coordinate their activities with the work of other national and international agencies engaged in financing international economic development. Subregional banks have historically concentrated more on integration projects than have regional development banks.

Arab Bank for Economic Development in Africa

Banque Arabe de Développement
Economique en Afrique (BADEA)

The idea of an Arab bank to assist in the economic and social development of all non-Arab African states was first discussed by the Arab heads of state during the Sixth Arab Summit at Algiers, Algeria, in November 1973. The BADEA, with headquarters at Khartoum, Sudan, began operations in March 1975. Its main functions include financing development projects, promoting and stimulating private Arab investment in Africa, and supplying technical assistance. BADEA financing, which cannot exceed $15 million, is limited to 80 percent of projects with total costs up to $12 million and 50 percent of those above that level. Technical assistance is provided in grant form. All member states of the Organization of African Unity, except Arab League participants, are eligible for funding. To date the preponderance of aid has been devoted to infrastructural improvements although the Board of Directors has also accorded additional priority to projects promoting increased food production. The Bank has traditionally favored the least-developed countries in its disbursements.

The Bank's highest authority is the Board of Governors (one governor for each member), with day-to-day administration assigned to a Board of Directors, one of whose eleven members serves as board chairman. The Board of Governors appoints the Bank's director general from among the countries not represented on the Board of Directors. The subscribing members of the Bank, listed in descending order of contribution, are: Saudi Arabia, Libya, Kuwait, Iraq, United Arab Emirates, Qatar, Algeria, Morocco, Oman, Tunisia, Lebanon, Jordan, Bahrain, Sudan, Palestine, Egypt, Mauritania, and Syria. Egypt's membership was suspended from 1979 to 1988.

In a review of its first 25 years of activity, the BADEA reported that infrastructure had received more than 50 percent of total commitments, followed by agriculture (30 percent), energy (8 percent), banking (4 percent), and industry (2 percent). In addition to maintaining support for "traditional fields of intervention," beginning with its 1990–1994 five-year plan the Bank has placed greater emphasis on projects having a "direct impact on the life of African citizens," such as water supply and food security projects.

In 2000 the BADEA approved $119 million (for 16 projects) in new loans and $5.0 million in technical assistance (for 21 projects), for a total of $124 million. This marked a significant increase over the 1996 total of $90 million. Lending concentrated on potable water supplies, irrigation, and transportation (roads and rail) but also included projects involving fisheries development, a shipyard, an industrial training center, and a hospital.

In 2000 cumulative commitments reached $2.08 billion for 284 development projects, 15 lines of credit, 14 special emergency aid operations, and 239 technical assistance operations. Cumulative disbursements reached $1.17 billion, while cancellations reached $444 million. The BADEA has also administered 37 "soft" loans totalling $214 million that were extended through the Special Arab Fund for Africa (SAAFA) from its commencement of operations in 1974 until 1977, at which time the SAFAA capital was incorporated into that of the BADEA. The Bank's subscribed capital is currently $1.5 billion.

The Fourth Five-Year Plan (2000-2004) projected $675 million in new commitments—a 35 percent increase over its predecessor—including $125 million in its first year. In general, loans were to carry an interest rate of 1–4 percent over an amortization period of 18–30 years, with a grace period of 4–10 years. The plan included continued financing of Arab exports to African countries, which the Bank has handled as a revolving fund.

The BADEA approved $129 million in new loans in 2001, $134 million in 2002, $140 million in 2003, and $139 million (for 21 projects) and $5.7 million in technical assistance (for 24 projects) in 2004. Lending in 2004 centered on infrastructure projects and agriculture. Cumulative disbursements reached $1.4 billion at the end of 2004. In December 2004 the Board of Directors approved the Fifth Five-Year Plan, which projected new lending of $900 million in 2005–2009.

Arab Fund for Economic and Social Development (AFESD)

The Arab Fund for Economic and Social Development, which originated in an accord reached on May 16, 1968, and began functioning in December 1971, is headquartered at Safat, Kuwait. Its aim is to assist in the financing of economic and social development projects in Arab states by offering loans on concessional terms to governments, particularly for joint ventures, and by providing technical expertise. The chief policymaking organ of the fund is the Board of Governors (one representative from each participating country), which elects an eight-member Board of Directors chaired by a director general. Members are Algeria, Bahrain, Djibouti, Egypt (suspended from 1979 to 1988), Iraq, Jordan, Kuwait, Lebanon, Libya, Mauritania, Morocco, Oman, Palestine, Qatar, Saudi Arabia, Somalia, Sudan, Syria, Tunisia, United Arab Emirates, and Yemen. (The memberships of Iraq and Somalia have been suspended since 1993 because of their failure to make loan repayments.)

The AFESD serves as the secretariat for the Coordination Group of the Arab and Regional Development Institutions, which also includes the Abu Dhabi Fund for Development, the Arab Bank for Economic Development in Africa (BADEA), the Islamic Development Bank (IDB), the Kuwait Fund for Arab Economic Development, the OPEC Fund for International Development, and the Saudi Fund for Development. The annual *Unified Arab Economic Report,* covering current economic issues and prospects, is prepared by the fund in cooperation with the Arab Monetary Fund (AMF), the Arab League, and the Organization of Arab Petroleum Exporting Countries (OAPEC).

The AFESD has been in the forefront of efforts to boost inter-Arab trade, which culminated in an early 1990 agreement to establish the $500 million Arab Trade Financing Program (see the article on the AMF). The AFESD agreed to provide $100 million, making it the new program's second leading contributor after the AMF.

In 1990 the fund approved 15 loans for a total of $656 million, up from $540 million in 1989 and $396 million in 1988. However, disbursements during the second half of 1990 and much of 1991 were inhibited by the Gulf crisis, which also forced the temporary relocation of the AFESD's headquarters to Bahrain. In early 1992 it was reported that disbursements of previous commitments had, for the most part, resumed on a normal schedule. Approvals for 1993 totalled about $618 million for 12 projects in six countries.

In 2001–2003 AFESD-backed projects continued to emphasize infrastructure, while technical assistance grants concentrated on improving government efficiency and manpower skills. Lending approvals in 2003 totaled 308.5 million Kuwaiti dinars ($1.05 billion) for 14 projects. Energy projects accounted for 63 percent of that lending. Cumulative loan disbursements since 1974 reached 4.4 billion KD.

The AFESD authorized capital remains at KD 800 million (80,000 shares). At the end of 2001 paid-up capital stood at KD 663 million, unchanged since 1989, although reserves have grown over the same period from KD 513 million to KD 1.32 billion ($4.30 billion), for a total of KD 1.98 billion ($6.45 billion) in resources. Together, Kuwait and Saudi Arabia account for nearly half of the paid up capital, followed by Algeria and Libya.

Islamic Development Bank (IDB)

The IDB originated in a Declaration of Intent issued by the Conference of Finance Ministers of Islamic Countries during their December 15, 1973, meeting at Jiddah, Saudi Arabia. The Bank's Articles of Agreement were approved and adopted by the Second Conference of Finance Ministers on August 10, 1974, with the Bank commencing activities in October 1975.

The purpose of the IDB, which is headquartered at Jiddah, is to "foster the economic development and social progress of member countries and Muslim communities individually as well as jointly," guided by the tenets of *shari'a* (Islamic law). In addition to providing assistance for feasibility studies, infrastructural projects, development

of industry and agriculture, import financing, and technology transfers, the IDB operates several special funds, including one to aid Muslim populations in nonmember countries. Since *shari'a* proscriptions include the collection of interest, various alternative financing methods, such as leasing and profit-sharing, are pursued, with service charges for loans being based on the expected administrative costs of the loan operations. The IDB also attempts to promote cooperation with Islamic banks as well as with national development institutions and other international agencies.

The Bank uses as its unit of account the Islamic dinar (ID), which is at par with the special drawing rights (SDR) of the International Monetary Fund. In July 1992 the Board of Governors, acting upon a recommendation of the Organization of the Islamic Conference (OIC), agreed to raise the authorized capital from ID 2 billion to ID 6 billion (about $8.5 billion) and subscribed capital to ID 4 billion (about $5.7 billion).

The Bank's primary decisionmaking and administrative organs are a Board of Governors and a Board of Executive Directors, the former comprised of the member countries' ministers of finance or their designees. Of the 14 executive directors, 7 are appointed by the 7 largest subscribers to the Bank's capital (Saudi Arabia, 24 percent; Kuwait, 12 percent; Libya, 10 percent; Iran, 9 percent; Egypt, 9 percent; Turkey, 8 percent; and the United Arab Emirates, 7 percent), while 7 are elected by the governors of the other member states.

A prerequisite to joining the Bank is membership in the Organization of the Islamic Conference (OIC), 55 of whose members now belong to the IDB. The Bank governors voted to suspend Afghanistan's membership at their 1981 annual meeting in conjunction with a similar suspension by the OIC. In early 1989 the OIC gave the vacant IDB seat to the government-in-exile announced by Afghan guerrilla groups, with the membership returning to normal status after the fall of the Najibullah government in April 1992.

In 1986 the Board of Governors approved the establishment of a Longer-term Trade Financing Scheme (LTTFS, subsequently renamed the Export

Financing Scheme—EFS) as a strategy to increase member countries' exports; contributions for the scheme, in operation since 1988, are made to a trust fund within the IDB. An Import Trade Financing Operation (ITFO) also exists to help fund the import of capital, rather than consumer, goods.

The Bank launched a $100 million IDB Unit Investment Fund (UIF) in 1990 to serve as a secondary market for mobilizing additional financial resources by pooling the savings of investors and directing them to projects that would achieve a "reasonable level of investment return" while accelerating social and economic development. The Fund's authorized resources were later increased to $500 million, although the full amount has not yet been achieved.

In March 1987 the IDB was selected to manage the new Islamic Banks' Portfolio (IBP), a fund established by 21 Islamic banks primarily to finance private sector trade and investment between Islamic countries. The portfolio currently boasts paid-up capital equivalent to $3.2 billion. The IDB also launched an Islamic Corporation for the Insurance of Investment and Export Credit (ICIEC) in mid-1995 to support trade and investment between Muslim states.

The UIF, the IBP, the ICIEC, and the IDB itself are core components of the "IDB Group." Other participating institutions include the Islamic Research and Training Institute (IRTI), which began operations in 1983; the International Center for Biosaline Agriculture (ICBA), which the IDB, the Arab Fund for Economic and Social Development (AFESD, above), the OPEC Fund for International Development, and the United Arab Emirates founded in 1996 as a research and development facility; the $1.5 billion IDB Infrastructure Fund, which was formed in October 1998 to finance infrastructural projects; and the Islamic Corporation

for the Development of the Private Sector, which was created by the Board of Governors in September 1999.

Recently the Bank has given lending priority to projects designed to promote food security (particularly through increased agricultural productivity), improve health and educational services, alleviate poverty in rural areas, and modernize members' infrastructures. Special consideration has also been given to Muslim communities in the states that emerged from the breakup of the Soviet Union and former Yugoslavia.

Activity in 1994–1995 included the dedication of the Bank's new headquarters building at Jiddah and the opening of regional offices at Rabat, Morocco, and Kuala Lumpur, Malaysia. The IDB subsequently emphasized cooperation with the OIC designed to enhance foreign trade among members, although the Bank acknowledged that tariffs and nontariff barriers continued to hamper effectiveness. Remedies proposed by the IDB included greater private sector development in member states. In September 1998 Bank Chairman Ahmad Mohammad Ali asserted that one of the IDB's goals was a 13 percent increase in trade among its members.

In October 2002 the IDB pledged $2 billion in loans to poor African countries. The aid was earmarked for, among other things, education, health services, and provision of safe drinking water. In 2004 the Bank approved $500 million for reconstruction in Iraq. Other loans were approved for earthquake relief in Algeria and Iran and for reconstruction in southern Lebanon. Lending approvals for 2004 totaled $4.0 billion for 98 projects and 24 technical assistance programs. The Bank reported that approvals had risen at an average annual rate of 8 percent over the past five years. Cumulative net approvals reached $34.2 billion.

UNITED NATIONS (UN)

Established: By charter signed in San Francisco, United States, June 26, 1945, effective October 24, 1945.

Purpose: To maintain international peace and security; to develop friendly relations among states based on respect for the principle of equal rights and self-determination of peoples; to achieve international cooperation in solving problems of an economic, social, cultural, or humanitarian character; and to harmonize the actions of states in the attainment of these common ends.

Headquarters: New York, United States.

Principal Organs: General Assembly (all members), Security Council (15 members), Economic and Social Council (54 members), Trusteeship Council (five members), International Court of Justice (15 judges), Secretariat.

Secretary General: Kofi Annan (Ghana).

Membership: (191): See Appendix C.

Official Languages: Arabic, Chinese, English, French, Russian, Spanish. All are also working languages.

Origin and development. The idea of creating a new intergovernmental organization to replace the League of Nations was born early in World War II and first found public expression in an Inter-Allied Declaration signed in London, England, on June 12, 1941, by representatives of five Commonwealth states and eight European governments-in-exile. Formal use of the term United Nations first occurred in the Declaration by United Nations, signed in Washington, DC, on January 1, 1942, on behalf of 26 states that subscribed to the principles of the Atlantic Charter (August 14, 1941) and pledged their full cooperation for the defeat of the Axis powers. At the Moscow Conference on October 30, 1943, representatives of China, the Union of Soviet Socialist Republics, the United Kingdom, and the United States proclaimed that they "recognized the necessity of establishing at the earliest practicable date a general international organization, based on the principle of the sovereign equality of all peace-loving states, and open to membership by all such states, large and small, for the maintenance of international peace and security." In meetings at Dumbarton Oaks, Washington, DC, between August 21 and October 7, 1944, the four powers reached agreement on preliminary proposals and determined to prepare more complete suggestions for discussion at a subsequent conference of all the United Nations.

Meeting in San Francisco, California, from April 25 to June 25, 1945, representatives of 50 states participated in drafting the United Nations Charter, which was formally signed June 26. Poland was not represented at the San Francisco Conference but later signed the charter and is counted among the 51 "original" UN members. Following ratification by the five permanent members of the Security Council and most other signatories, the charter entered into force October 24, 1945. The General Assembly, convened in its first regular session January 10, 1946, accepted an invitation to establish the permanent home of the organization in the United States; privileges and immunities of the UN headquarters were defined in a Headquarters Agreement with the United States government signed June 26, 1947.

The membership of the UN, which increased from 51 to 60 during the period 1945–1950, remained frozen at that level for the next five years as a result of US-Soviet disagreements over admission. The deadlock was broken in 1955 when the superpowers agreed on a "package" of 16 new members: four Soviet-bloc states, four Western states, and eight "uncommitted" states. Since then, states have normally been admitted with little delay. The exceptions are worth noting. The admission of the two Germanies in 1973 led to proposals for admission of the two Koreas and of the two Vietnams. Neither occurred prior to the formal unification of Vietnam in 1976, while action in regard to the two Koreas was delayed for another 15 years. On November 16, 1976, the United States used its 18th veto in the Security Council to prevent the admission of the Socialist Republic of Vietnam, having earlier in the same session, on June 23, 1976, employed its 15th veto to prevent Angola from joining. Later in the session, however, the United States relented, and Angola gained admission. In July 1977 Washington dropped its objection to Vietnamese membership as well.

With the admission of Brunei, the total membership during the 39th session of the General Assembly in 1984 stood at 159. The figure rose to 160 with the admission of Namibia in April 1990, fell back to 159 after the merger of North and South Yemen in May, advanced again to 160 via the September admission of Liechtenstein, and returned to 159 when East and West Germany merged in October. Seven new members (Estonia, Democratic People's Republic of Korea, Republic of Korea, Latvia, Lithuania, Marshall Islands, and Federated States of Micronesia) were admitted September 17, 1991, at the opening of the 46th General Assembly. Eight of the new states resulting from the collapse of the Soviet Union (Armenia, Azerbaijan, Kazakhstan, Kyrgyzstan, Moldova, Tajikistan, Turkmenistan, and Uzbekistan) were admitted March 2, 1992, along with San Marino. Russia announced the previous December that it was assuming the former USSR seat. Three of the breakaway Yugoslavian republics (Bosnia and Herzegovina, Croatia, and Slovenia) were admitted May 22. Capping an unprecedented period of expansion, Georgia became the 179th member on July 31.

The total dropped back to 178 with the dissolution of Czechoslovakia on January 1, 1993, then moved up to 180 when the Czech Republic and Slovakia joined separately January 19. On April 8 the General Assembly approved the admission of "The former Yugoslav Republic of Macedonia," the name being carefully fashioned because of the terminological dispute between the new nation and Greece (see Macedonia article). Monaco and newly independent Eritrea were admitted May 28, followed by Andorra on July 28. Palau, which had finally achieved independence following protracted difficulty in concluding its US trusteeship status (see section on Trusteeship Council), became the 185th member December 15, 1994. Kiribati, Nauru, and Tonga were admitted September 14, 1999, and Tuvalu joined September 5, 2000.

A change of government in October 2000 led to the November 1, 2000, admission of the Federal Republic of Yugoslavia. On September 22, 1992, the General Assembly, acting on the recommendation of the Security Council, decided the Federal Republic could not automatically assume the UN membership of the former Socialist Federal Republic of Yugoslavia. The Assembly informed the Federal Republic that it would have to apply on its own for UN membership, and such an application was submitted the following day. However, no action on the request was taken by the Assembly because of concern over the Federal Republic's role in the conflict in Bosnia and Herzegovina and, later, its actions regarding the ethnic Albanian population in the Yugoslavian province of Kosovo. As a consequence, the rump Yugoslavia was excluded from participation in the work of the General Assembly and its subsidiary bodies. Throughout this period, however, the UN membership of the Socialist Federal Republic technically remained in effect. A certain ambiguity, apparently deliberate, surrounded the issue, permitting the Federal Republic and others to claim that it was still a member, albeit excluded from active participation, while some nations argued that the membership referred only to the antecedent Yugoslavian state. In any event, the flag of the Socialist Federal Republic, which was also the flag of the Federal Republic, continued to fly outside UN headquarters with the flags of all other UN members, and the old nameplate remained positioned in front of an empty chair during Assembly proceedings. In October 2000 the Security Council, in a resolution recommending admission of the Federal Republic, acknowledged "that the State formerly known as the Socialist Federal Republic of Yugoslavia has ceased to exist." A representative of the Federal Republic took up the empty seat, and a new Federal Republic flag replaced that of the Socialist Federal Republic.

On September 10, 2002, the UN admitted Switzerland, which had long maintained a permanent observer mission at UN headquarters and had actively participated as a full member of the various UN Specialized and Related Agencies. The Swiss government, having concluded that UN membership in the post-Cold War era would not jeopardize its long-standing international neutrality, sought admission after winning majority support from Swiss voters at a March 2002 referendum. On September 27 the world's newest independent state, Timor-Leste (East Timor), was also admitted, becoming the UN's 191st member.

The Holy See (Vatican City State) has formal observer status in the General Assembly and maintains a permanent observer mission at UN headquarters.

Structure. The UN system can be viewed as comprising (1) the principal organs, (2) subsidiary organs established to deal with particular aspects of the organization's responsibilities, (3) a number of specialized and related agencies, and (4) a series of ad hoc global conferences to examine particularly pressing issues.

The institutional structure of the principal organs resulted from complex negotiations that attempted to balance both the conflicting claims of national sovereignty and international responsibility, and the rights of large and small states. The principle of sovereign equality of all member states is exemplified in the General Assembly; that of the special responsibility of the major powers, in the composition and procedure of the Security Council. The other principal organs included in the Charter are the Economic and Social Council (ECOSOC), the Trusteeship Council (whose activity was suspended in 1994), the International Court of Justice (ICJ), and the Secretariat.

The bulk of intergovernmental bodies related to the UN consists of a network of Specialized Agencies established by intergovernmental agreement as legal and autonomous international entities with their own memberships and organs and which, for the purpose of "coordination," are brought "into relationship" with the UN. While sharing many of their characteristics, the International Atomic Energy Agency (IAEA) remains legally distinct from the Specialized Agencies; the World Trade Organization, which emerged from the UN-sponsored General Agreement on Tariff and Trade (GATT), has no formal association with the UN.

The proliferation of subsidiary organs can be attributed to many complex factors, including new demands and needs as more states attained independence; the effects of the Cold War; a subsequent diminution of East-West bipolarity; a greater concern with promoting economic and social development through technical assistance programs (almost entirely financed by voluntary contributions); and a resistance to any radical change in international trade patterns. For many years, the largest and most politically significant of the subordinate organs were the United Nations Conference on Trade and Development (UNCTAD) and the United Nations Industrial Development Organization (UNIDO), both of which were initial venues for debates, for conducting studies and presenting reports, for convening conferences and specialized meetings, and for mobilizing the opinions of nongovernmental organizations. They also provided a way for less-developed states to formulate positions vis-à-vis the industrialized states. During the 1970s both became intimately involved in activities related to program implementation and on January 1, 1986, UNIDO became the UN's 16th Specialized Agency.

One of the most important developments in the UN system has been the use of ad hoc conferences to deal with major international problems. For a listing of such conferences and a brief description of their activities, see Appendix B. Some conferences are also discussed under General Assembly: Origin and Development, below, or within entries for various General Assembly Special Bodies or UN Specialized Agencies.

Economic and Social Council: Regional Commissions

The primary aim of the five Regional Commissions, which report annually to ECOSOC, is to assist in raising the level of economic activity in their respective regions and to maintain and strengthen the economic relations of the states in each region, both among themselves and with others. The commissions adopt their own procedural rules, including how they select officers. Each commission is headed by an executive secretary, who holds the rank of under secretary of the UN, while their Secretariats are integral parts of the overall United Nations Secretariat.

The commissions are empowered to make recommendations directly to member governments and to Specialized Agencies of the United Nations, but no action can be taken in respect to any state without the agreement of that state.

Economic and Social Commission for Western Asia (ESCWA)

Established: August 9, 1973, as the Economic Commission for Western Asia; current name adopted in 1985.

Purpose: To "initiate and participate in measures for facilitating concerted action for the economic reconstruction and development of Western Asia, for raising the level of economic activity in Western Asia, and for maintaining and strengthening the economic relations of the countries of that area, both among themselves and with other countries of the world."

Temporary Headquarters: Beirut, Lebanon.

Principal Subsidiary Organs: Preparatory Committee; Advisory Committee; six specialized committees: Energy, Liberalization of Foreign Trade and Economic Globalization, Social Development, Statistics, Transport, Water Resources; Secretariat. The Secretariat includes seven divisions: Administrative Services; Programme Planning and Technical Cooperation; Economic Analysis, Information and Communication Technology; Globalization and Regional Integration; Social Development; and Sustainable Development and Productivity. There is also a ESCWA Center for Women.

Executive Secretary: Mervat M. Tallawy (Egypt).

Membership (13): Bahrain, Egypt, Iraq, Jordan, Kuwait, Lebanon, Oman, Palestine, Qatar, Saudi Arabia, Syria, United Arab Emirates, Yemen.

Recent activities. The most important procedural event in the commission's history was the 1977 decision to grant full membership to the Palestine Liberation Organization (PLO)—the first nonstate organization to achieve such standing in a UN agency—despite a fear on the part of some UN members that the PLO would use its status in the commission as a precedent for launching an effort to gain full membership in the General Assembly. Israeli-Palestinian agreements beginning with the 1993 Declaration of Principles led to the redesignation of the PLO membership as, simply, Palestine, even though no de jure Palestinian state currently exists.

In view of growing regional economic cooperation throughout the world, the commission at the 1992 Ministerial Session urged members to adopt policies designed to promote inter-Arab trade and the eventual creation of an Arab common market. In other activity at the meeting, a decision was postponed on the designation of a new permanent headquarters for the commission, which had moved to 'Amman, Jordan, from Baghdad, Iraq, during the Gulf crisis. It was subsequently decided that the headquarters would be moved to Beirut, Lebanon, and the relocation was completed in early 1998.

During the mid-1990s the ESCWA reorganized its work agenda, reducing the number of operational programs from 15 to 5: Natural Resources and Environmental Management; Improvement of the Quality of Life; Economic Development and Global Changes; Coordination of Policies and Harmonization of Norms and Regulations for Sectoral Development; Coordination and Harmonization of Statistics and Information Development.

In 1997 ECOSOC established the Technical Committee on Liberalization of Foreign Trade and Globalization in Countries of the ESCWA Region in order to observe movement towards free trade in other parts of the world and advise members on how they can benefit from it.

At its 19th session, held at Beirut on May 5–8, 1997, ESCWA discussed a proposed 1998–2001 medium-term plan that stressed sustainable development and cooperation within the region, reported on the development of data bases on population and gender issues, and followed up on actions taken at the previous session regarding new committees on energy and water resources. The 1999 biennial session coincided with the commission's 25th anniversary, while the May 8–11, 2000, ministerial meeting focused on the topic of "Regional Integration and Globalization." In November 2000 Marvat M. Tallawy of Egypt had succeeded Hazem El Beblawi, also of Egypt, as executive secretary.

In 2003 Tallaway lamented the fact that UN negotiations had failed to prevent the US/UK-led invasion of Iraq and called for the UN to take on a greater role than initially envisioned in regard to reconstruction in Iraq following the war. For its part, ESCWA pledged to concentrate on reviving civil society in Iraq, noting that "turmoil and anxiety" in the region had diverted resources away from development. The 2005 ESCWA session further addressed the question of "peace and security," noting that too much money was being spent on armaments at the expense of programs to combat unemployment (16 percent regionally) and support other social improvements. Among other things, ESCWA announced plans for its own restructuring to provide additional emphasis on local community development and cooperation with the private sector. The commission also continued to express deep concern over the repercussions of Israeli "occupation" on the living conditions of Palestinians.

General Assembly: Special Bodies

United Nations Relief and Works Agency for Palestine Refugees in the Near East (UNRWA)

Established: By General Assembly resolution of December 8, 1949; mandate most recently extended through June 30, 2005.

Purpose: To provide relief, education, and health and social services to Palestinian refugees (i.e., persons or the descendants of persons whose normal residence was Palestine for a minimum of two years preceding the Arab-Israeli conflict in 1948 and who, as a result of that conflict, lost both their homes and their means of livelihood).

Headquarters: Gaza Strip and 'Amman, Jordan. (Most of the operations of the UNRWA which were previously located at Vienna, Austria, were moved to the Gaza Strip in July 1996. The remainder were relocated at the agency's other long-standing headquarters at 'Amman.)

Commissioner General: (Acting): Karen Koning Abu Zayd (United States).

Advisory Commission: Comprised of representatives of the governments of Belgium, Egypt, France, Japan, Jordan, Lebanon, Syria, Turkey, United Kingdom, United States. The Palestine Liberation Organization (PLO) is an observer.

Recent activities. Of the persons who fell under the established definition of Palestinian refugee at the end of 2003, about 4.14 million were registered with the agency. About 1.32 million of that number lived in 59 refugee "camps," many of which have in effect become permanent towns, while the remainder lived in previously established towns and villages in the area served by the UNRWA— Jordan, Lebanon, Syria, and the West Bank and Gaza Strip. The UNRWA's original priority was to provide direct humanitarian relief to refugees uprooted by fighting that followed the creation of Israel. In the absence of a peaceful settlement to the Palestinian question as initially envisioned by the United Nations, the UNRWA's attention shifted to education (it runs about 660 schools attended by approximately 490,000 students) and the provision of public health services (it operates about 120 health centers) to a basically self-supporting population. The UNRWA employs some 25,000 people, including 15,800 educators and 3,600 medical personnel.

In the late 1980s the UNRWA budget came under severe pressure from the demands of population growth, an increase in the number of refugees qualifying for "special hardship" assistance as the result of economic decline in the Middle East, and emergency relief needs stemming from the *intifada* in the occupied territories. Also constricted was a separate Project Fund for specific projects, and a Capital Construction Fund for UNRWA facilities.

In 1988 the UNRWA found itself "back in the relief business" in three of the five geographic areas it served. In Lebanon, where 33 UNRWA employees had been killed since 1982, deteriorating conditions in and around Beirut prompted the agency to offer its services to the non-Palestinian population in addition to its traditional clientele. In the West Bank and Gaza Strip, the UNRWA was forced to divert some of its resources to emergency medical treatment, food relief, and physical rehabilitation services, while many schools were closed for much of the year because of the *intifada*. Several special emergency funds were established for the occupied territories, where an estimated 55 percent of the population consisted of Palestinian refugees.

In mid-1990 UNRWA officials reported that Palestinian "frustration" was increasing as peace prospects appeared to recede and emergency conditions persisted in Lebanon, the West Bank, and Gaza Strip. The agency's difficulties intensified still further during the subsequent Gulf crisis as hundreds of thousands of Palestinians fled the conflict (many returning to UNRWA camps) while others, particularly those working in Kuwait, lost their sources of income and thereby the ability to remit funds to family members in UNRWA's service area.

Repercussions from the Gulf war subsequently continued to exacerbate refugee problems, particularly when several hundred thousand Palestinians were expelled from Kuwait following the allied liberation of that country from Iraqi control. In contrast, in early 1992 Commissioner General İlter Türkmen welcomed an improved security situation in Lebanon, which permitted some stabilization of UNRWA activity in that conflict-wracked country.

Shortly after the September 1993 accord between Israel and the Palestine Liberation Organization (PLO), UNRWA established an internal task force to determine how best to support the peace process. Its first action was to establish a Peace Implementation Program (PIP) designed to rehabilitate long-neglected infrastructure and create jobs for Palestinians. Donors pledged more than $100 million for the first phase of the operation (PIP 1), most of whose projects were located in the Gaza Strip and West Bank, sites of the beginning stages of Palestinian self-rule. PIP 2 envisioned about $250 million of additional projects in all five geographical areas served by UNRWA; the largest proposed project was the construction of a hospital in Gaza, to be financed by the European Union.

Meanwhile, as negotiations between Israel and the PLO inched forward, discussions were initiated regarding the possible consequences for Palestinian refugees of a definitive peace settlement. Commissioner General Türkmen called upon donors to underwrite a five-year plan for the agency beyond which, if all went well, it would be appropriate to consider a reduction of services. However, Türkmen cautioned that refugees, particularly those outside the West Bank and Gaza, felt "a great sense of concern and apprehension about their future."

In December 1995 the General Assembly extended the UNRWA's mandate to June 30, 1999, hopeful that Palestinians would at that point be fully responsible for their own affairs under whatever final agreement was concluded with Israel. The following month Türkmen retired from the post of UNRWA commissioner general and was succeeded by Peter Hansen of Denmark, theretofore UN undersecretary general for humanitarian affairs.

The outlook for the agency was relatively bright in many ways as 1996 began, the September 1995 "Interim Agreement" between Israel and the PLO having prompted a further withdrawal of Israeli troops from the West Bank. In addition, the UNRWA welcomed the January 1996 Palestinian elections as an important step toward a permanent Mideast peace. However, the UNRWA lamented the lack of progress throughout the remainder of the year in implementing further Israeli withdrawals and further extending responsibility to the new Palestinian (National) Authority, with which, as directed by the General Assembly, the UNRWA had recently established a full working relationship. Commissioner General Hansen also reported that the agency was in the midst of a financial crisis that threatened its ability to fulfill its mandate. In the face of an $8.4 million deficit for 1995 the UNRWA imposed austerity measures while calling for a special meeting of the agency's donors to resolve the ongoing financial difficulties.

Continuing financial straits brought the agency to near breakdown in 1998, and the Palestinian staff held a one-day strike on September 15, protesting poor pay and work conditions. Subsequently, the *Middle East International* reported in October and November 1998 that serious allegations of corruption and misuse of funds had been leveled at several agency staff and that UN Secretary General Kofi Annan had sent a team to the region to look into the allegations and to check the agency's accounts.

Beginning in September 2000, UNRWA efforts to contain expenditures without jeopardizing its programs were set back as open hostilities between Israel and the Palestinians resumed. The so-called second *intifada* led the UNRWA to launch in October a "flash" appeal for additional funds. This was followed in November by an emergency appeal targeted primarily at job creation in an effort to offset the unemployment caused by Israel's closure of its border. From November 2000 into the first half of 2004, the UNRWA issued seven emergency appeals for sums totaling over $650 million. Compounding an increased need for basic food and medical supplies were efforts to repair local infrastructure, to provide temporary shelter for those whose homes had been damaged or destroyed during Israeli incursions into the West Bank and Gaza camps, and to find additional employment for Palestinians whose movements had been restricted. Commissioner General Hansen has stated that two-thirds of the Palestinians were without work and one-half were living in absolute poverty. Meanwhile, a recent study conducted by Johns Hopkins University indicated that one-third of Palestinian children were either chronically or acutely malnourished.

At the same time, the agency has faced charges from some Israelis and some US congressmen, among others, of UNRWA complicity in the use of refugee camps for terrorist training and activities. The UNRWA has responded that it has "no police force, no intelligence service and no mandate to report on political and military activities" in the camps. Its role is to provide health, education, and humanitarian services, with security being the responsibility of host countries or the Palestinian Authority, the UNRWA said. A recent audit by the US General Accounting Office concluded that no money provided by the United States—the source of some 30 percent of UNRWA funds—could be linked to terrorist activities in the refugee camps.

Security Council: Peacekeeping Forces

United Nations Disengagement Observer Force (UNDOF)

Established: By Security Council resolution of May 31, 1974.

Purpose: To observe the cease-fire between Israel and Syria following the 1973 Arab-Israeli War.

Headquarters: Camp Faouar (Syrian Golan Heights). (A UNDOF office is located at Damascus, Syria.)

Force Commander: Maj. Gen. Bala Nanda Sharma (Nepal).

Composition: As of September 1, 2005, 1, 036 troops from the Austrian, Canadian, Japanese, Nepalese, Polish, and Slovakian armed forces.

United Nations Force in Cyprus (UNFICYP)

Established: By Security Council resolution of March 4, 1964, after consultation with the governments of Cyprus, Greece, Turkey, and the United Kingdom.

Purpose: To serve as a peacekeeping force between Greek and Turkish Cypriots.

Headquarters: Nicosia, Cyprus.

Force Commander: Maj. Gen. Herbert Joaquin Figoli Almandos (Uruguay).

Composition: As of September 1, 2005, 863 troops and 51 civilian police from Argentina (including soldiers from six other South American countries), Austria, Canada, Croatia, Finland, Hungary, Slovakia, United Kingdom, and Uruguay.

United Nations Interim Force in Lebanon (UNIFIL)

Established: By Security Council resolution of March 19, 1978.

Purpose: To confirm the withdrawal of Israeli troops from Lebanon and to restore peace and help ensure the return of Lebanese authority to southern Lebanon.

Headquarters: Naqoura, Lebanon.

Force Commander: Maj. Gen. Alain Pellegrini (France).

Composition: As of September 1, 2005, 1,198 troops from France, Ghana, India, Ireland, Italy, Poland, and Ukraine.

United Nations Military Observer Group in India and Pakistan (UNMOGIP)

Established: By resolutions adopted by the United Nations Commission for India and Pakistan on August 13, 1948, and January 5, 1949; augmented and brought under the jurisdiction of the Security Council by resolution of September 6, 1965, in view of a worsening situation in Kashmir.

Purpose: To assist in implementing the cease-fire agreement of January 1, 1949.

Headquarters: Rawalpindi, Pakistan (November–April), Srinagar, India (May–October).

Chief Military Observer: Maj. Gen. Guido Palmieri (Italy).

Composition: As of September 1, 2005, 42 military observers from Belgium, Chile, Croatia, Denmark, Finland, Italy, Republic of Korea, Sweden, and Uruguay.

United Nations Mission for the Referendum in Western Sahara

Mission des Nations Unies pour le Référendum dans le Sahara Ouest (MINURSO)

Established: By Security Council resolution of April 29, 1991.

Purpose: To enforce a cease-fire in the Western Sahara between Morocco and the Polisario Front, to identify those eligible to vote in the proposed self-determination referendum there, and to supervise the referendum and settlement plan.

Headquarters: Laayoune, Western Sahara.

Force Commander: Brig. Gen. Kurt Mosgaard (Denmark).

Composition: As of September 1, 2005, 198 military observers, 6 civilian police, and 25 troops from Argentina, Austria, Bangladesh, China, Croatia, Egypt, El Salvador, France, Ghana, Greece, Guinea, Honduras, Hungary, Ireland, Italy, Kenya, Republic of Korea, Malaysia, Mongolia, Nigeria, Pakistan, Poland, Russia, Sri Lanka, and Uruguay. An additional 2,200 troops and observers had been authorized but not deployed because of the lack of progress in referendum negotiations.

United Nations Truce Supervision Organization (UNTSO)

Established: By Security Council resolution of May 29, 1948.

Purpose: To supervise the cease-fire arranged by the Security Council following the 1948 Arab-Israeli War. Its mandate was subsequently extended to embrace the armistice agreements concluded in 1949, the Egyptian-Israeli peace treaty of 1979, and assistance to other UN forces in the Middle East, specifically the UNDOF and UNIFIL.

Headquarters: Jerusalem, Israel.

Chief of Staff: Brig. Gen. Clive Lilley (New Zealand).

Composition: As of September 1, 2005, 148 military observers from Argentina, Australia, Austria, Belgium, Canada, Chile, China, Denmark, Estonia, Finland, France, Ireland, Italy, Nepal, Netherlands, New Zealand, Norway, Russia, Slovakia, Slovenia, Sweden, Switzerland, and United States.

PART FOUR

APPENDIX

CHRONOLOGY OF MAJOR MIDDLE EASTERN EVENTS, 2005

The following chronology is adapted from *The Middle East,* 10th ed. (Washington, D.C.: CQ Press, 2005, pp. 552–553) and has been updated through 2005. That volume uses a narrower definition of the Middle East and, therefore, does not cover some of the countries that appear in *Political Handbook of the Middle East.*

AFGHANISTAN

September 18. Voters Cast Ballots for Parliamentary Elections. More than six million Afghan voters cast ballots in the first free parliamentary elections in 33 years.

September–November. Taliban Fighters Step Up Attacks. Attacks by Taliban and *al-Qaeda* fighters on US forces, Afghan security and law enforcement officials, religious leaders, and reconstruction workers increase after parliamentary elections. The increasing use of suicide bombings and remote-controlled explosive devices, especially in urban areas, signals a shift in tactics, mimicking those used by insurgents in Iraq.

November 12. Parliamentary Election Results Certified. The final results of the September 18 legislative elections are certified by the Afghan–United Nations Joint Electoral Management Body.

December 19. Parliament Convenes. The Afghan National Assembly, or *Wolesi Jirga,* convenes in Kabul with 249 directly elected representatives in the lower house and 102 members in the upper house, 34 of whom are appointed by President Hamid Karzai.

ARAB-ISRAELI CONFLICT

January 16. Sharon Orders Military Operations. After a Palestinian suicide attack kills six Israelis at a Gaza crossing, Israeli Prime Minister Ariel Sharon cuts ties with Palestinian leader Mahmoud Abbas.

January 21. Palestinians Begin Policing Gaza. About 3,000 armed Palestinian police begin patrolling the northern Gaza Strip to prevent rocket fire on Israeli communities. Abbas continues negotiations with Palestinian groups to win their commitment to a cease-fire.

January 26. Israel Says It Will Halt Assassinations. Israeli officials say the military will halt the practice of targeting Palestinians for assassination.

February 8. Israeli and Palestinian Leaders Declare Cease-Fire. At a summit in Sharm el-Sheikh, Israeli and Palestinian leaders announce an informal cease-fire, ending more than four years of fighting.

February 20. Jordanian Ambassador Returns to Israel. Maruf al-Bakhit, the Jordanian ambassador, returns to Israel after a four-year downgrade in relations.

February 20. Israeli Cabinet Approves New Barrier Route, Gaza Pullout. The Israeli cabinet gives final approval to Prime Minister Sharon's plans to withdrawal from the Gaza Strip and for a revised route for the West Bank separation barrier more in line with Israel's frontier.

February 21. Israel Releases Prisoners. Israel releases 500 Palestinian prisoners in accordance with the agreement signed February 8 in Sharm el-Sheikh.

February 25. Suicide Attack Kills Four Israelis. Sharon halts talks with Palestinian authorities after a suicide bombing kills four Israelis in Tel Aviv.

February 27. Sharon Halts West Bank Redeployment. Israel delays plans to hand over five West Bank towns to the Palestinian Authority and free 400 more prisoners as agreed at the February 8 summit.

March 16. Israel Hands Reins to Palestinians in Jericho. Israel turns over Jericho to Palestinian authorities.

March 17. Egyptian Ambassador Returns to Israel. Egypt returns its ambassador, Assem Ibrahim, to Israel after a four-year downgrade in relations.

March 22. Tulkarm Comes under Palestinian Control. Israel completes the handover of the West Bank town of Tulkarm to the Palestinians.

March 28. Gaza Pullout Plan Survives. The Israeli parliament rejects efforts to block a Sharon plan to withdraw from the Gaza Strip.

July 12. Suicide Bomber Kills Five. A suicide bomber kills five Israelis in an attack outside the Hasharon Mall in Netanya.

July 13. Israel Reoccupies Tulkarm. Israeli forces sealed off the Gaza Strip and the West Bank and reoccupied Tulkarm.

August–September. Israel Evacuates Settlements and Withdraws Forces from Gaza and Parts of the West Bank. In mid-August, Israeli forces evacuate Jewish settlers from 21 settlements in Gaza and 4 in the West Bank. They then demolish the emptied settlements before withdrawing from Gaza in September. Approximately 120 settlements remain in the West Bank.

November 15. US Secretary of State Brokers Deal to Open Gaza Crossings. Secretary of State Condoleezza Rice brokers a deal to open the Gaza Strip border crossing between Palestinian-controlled Gaza and Egypt, allow for construction of a Gaza seaport, and permit the flow of trucks and buses from Gaza into Israel.

December 5. Suicide Bomber Attacks Shopping Mall. A suicide bomber from Islamic Jihad kills at least five Israelis outside a shopping mall in Netanya. The group claims it is in retaliation for the assassination of two of its leaders. Israeli Defense Minister Shaul Mofaz approves orders for the assassination of senior leaders of the organization.

December 8. Israeli Air Force Strikes Northern Gaza. Israeli aircraft fire missiles at suspected al-Aqsa Martyrs' Brigades fighters near Jabalya, killing two and wounding six others.

EGYPT

January 29. Opposition Leader Detained. Authorities arrest Ayman Nur, a legislator and founder of the Tomorrow Party, on charges of forging election documents. Nur denies the accusations.

February 26. Mubarak Orders Election Law Review. President Husni Mubarak orders a review and amendment of the country's presidential election law, potentially laying the groundwork for multiple candidates to run in elections scheduled for September.

March 9. Parliament Agrees to Election Reform. The legislature agrees to amend the constitution to allow multicandidate presidential elections. The amendment requires nominees to be endorsed by members of parliament and local councils.

March 16. Opposition Candidate Plans to Run. Ayman Nur, released from prison on March 12, announces his candidacy for the presidency.

May 26. Voters Approve Electoral Reform. Egyptian voters approved a constitutional referendum to allow multicandidate presidential elections. Voter turnout is estimated at 54 percent, and the referendum passes with 83 percent approval. Opposition groups boycott the vote, and police reportedly intimidate and beat opposition protesters.

June 28. Nur Trial Begins. The forgery trial of the Tomorrow Party's Nur begins. It is then postponed until after the presidential elections scheduled for September.

September 7. Mubarak Reelected. In Egypt's first multicandidate presidential election, Mubarak wins reelection to a fifth six-year term, officially securing 88.6 percent of the vote.

November 9. Parliamentary Balloting Begins. Balloting begins in the first of three rounds of elections for the 444-member *Majlis al-Sha'ab*, or People's Assembly. Tomorrow Party leader Nur loses his seat in the first round.

December 7. Judge Orders Nur Detained. A judge orders the detention of Tomorrow Party leader Nur on forgery charges in anticipation of a guilty verdict.

December 12. Mubarak Calls for a Review in the Wake of Election Violence. Mubarak appoints 10 members to parliament and calls for a review of violent clashes between police and protesters during the legislative elections completed December 1. Preliminary results have the ruling National Democratic Party (NDP) and it allies capturing as many as 335 seats (311 seats for the NDP), independent candidates affiliated with the Muslim Brotherhood winning 88 seats, and other opposition parties taking 9 seats (New Wafd Party, 6; National Progressive Unionist Party, 2; Tomorrow Party, 1).

IRAN

January 9. Parliament Rejects Reformist Appointee. The *Majlis* rejects President Mohammad Khatami's reformist nominee to head the Transportation Ministry.

February 27. Russia and Iran Sign Nuclear Pact. Iran and Russia sign a deal to exchange nuclear fuel, announcing mid-2006 as the deadline for bringing Iran's first reactor online.

March 23. Nuclear Talks with Europeans Falter. Iranian negotiations with England, France, and German, representing the European Union, reach an impasse, with Iran refusing to scrap its uranium enrichment program.

May 10. Government Confirms Processing of Uranium Ore. Iran acknowledges its conversion of 37 tons of uranium into gas, an initial step toward producing enriched uranium.

May 18. Representative Visits Iraq. Foreign Minister Kamal Kharrazi travels to Iraq for talks with the new Shi'ite-majority government.

June 24. Ahmadinejad Wins Presidency. In a presidential run-off election, Mahmoud Ahmadinejad, the conservative mayor of Teheran, wins a landslide victory over former president Ali Akbar Hashemi Rafsanjani.

August 1. Iran to Resume Uranium Enrichment. Iran says it will break UN seals and resume activities at one of its nuclear facilities but will maintain its freeze on a more advanced process needed to make fuel or weapons.

September 24. IAEA Votes to Report Iran to the Security Council. The board of the International Atomic Energy Agency (IAEA) declares Iran guilty of not meeting its obligations under the nuclear Non-Proliferation Treaty.

October 26. Ahmadinejad Calls for Defeat of Israel. President Ahmadinejad tells an audience that Israel "must be wiped off the map."

December 12. Parliament Approves Oil Minister. The parliament accepts Ahmadinejad's nomination of Kazem Vaziri-Hamaneh as oil minister, ending a three-month-old dispute over the post. The legislature had rejected three previous nominees.

December 14. Ahmadinejad Questions the Holocaust. Ahmadinejad asserts that the Holocaust is a myth created by Europe to justify the establishment of a Jewish state in the heart of the Islamic world.

IRAQ

January 4. Baghdad Governor Shot Dead. Iraqi provincial governor Ali al-Haidari, whose jurisdiction included Baghdad, is assassinated.

January 6. Government Extends State of Emergency. Iraqi officials extend a state of emergency by thirty days in an attempt to quell attacks aimed at derailing upcoming elections. US military commanders admit that security is poor in four of eighteen provinces.

January 17. Expatriates Begin Voter Registration. Exiled Iraqis in fourteen countries begin registering for January 30 legislative elections.

January 30. Legislative Voting Begins. In the first free elections in more than 50 years, Iraqis vote to fill 275 seats in the National Assembly, defying threats of violence from insurgents.

February 13. Election Results Announced. Election officials report that the majority-Shi'ite United Iraqi Alliance won 48 percent of the vote in legislative elections. The Kurdish Alliance won 26 percent.

February 28. Car Bombing Kills 110. A car bomb kills 110 people and wounds 133 among a crowd of police and national guard recruits in Hillah, south of Baghdad.

April 6. Talabani Elected President. The National Assembly selects Kurdish leader Jalal Talabani as president and Ibrahim al-Jaafari, a Shi'ite, as prime minister.

May 4. New Cabinet Sworn In. The new cabinet is sworn in with at least six positions still undecided.

June 12. Barzani Chosen President of the Kurdish Region. Massud Barzani is selected as the first president of Iraqi Kurdistan.

August 28. Draft Constitution Endorsed. The ruling Shi'ite and Kurdish coalition approves the draft of a new constitution over the objections of Sunni Arabs.

August 31. Pilgrims Die in Stampede. More than 1,000 Shi'ite pilgrims die crossing a Baghdad bridge when fears of a suicide bombing set off a stampede.

September 14. Attacks Kill More Than 150. Al-Qaeda in Iraq claims responsibility for multiple bombings and shootings targeting Shi'ites in an around Baghdad.

October 15. Voters Approve New Constitution. The constitution wins a solid majority but narrowly avoids a veto as it fails in two Sunni Arab provinces and barely passes in another.

October 19. Trial of Saddam Hussein Opens. Former president Saddam Hussein appears in court for the first day of his trial for the 1982 killing of 142 Shi'ites.

December 15. Iraqis Vote in National Elections. Iraqis go to the polls to choose the first, full-term government and parliament since the US-led invasion. Early results point to a victory for the governing alliance of Shi'ite parties.

ISRAEL

November 9. Labor Party Ousts Peres, Chooses New Leader. The Labor Party replaces longtime leader Shimon Peres with trade union leader Amir Peretz.

November 21. Sharon Leaves Likud, Forms New Party. Prime Minister Ariel Sharon announces his departure from the *Likud* to form *Kadima* (Forward), billed as a centrist party, to stand for parliamentary elections in March 2006.

November 30. Peres Quits Labor, Endorses Sharon. Former Labor leader Peres quits the party and endorses Sharon for the upcoming elections.

December 18. Sharon Suffers Stroke. Sharon suffers a mild stroke.

JORDAN

January 27. 'Abdallah Announces Democratic Reforms. King 'Abdallah II says he will institute limited democratic reforms, including the creation of elected councils to oversee reform.

November 9. Suicide Bombings Kill 63. Al-Qaida in Iraq, led by Jordanian-born Abu Musab Zarqawi, claims responsibility for suicide bombings at three hotels in Amman.

November 15. Government Shakeup. Eleven top officials, including the national security adviser, Saad Kheir, resign.

November 24. Bakhit Appointed Prime Minister. 'Abdallah appoints Maruf al-Bakhit to replace Prime Minister Adnan Badran, who resigned.

November 27. New Cabinet Sworn In. Abdallah swears in a new cabinet.

LEBANON

February 14. Hariri Assassinated. Former Prime Minister Rafiq Hariri is killed in a massive car bombing, along with 16 other people. The assassination sparks anti-Syrian demonstrations.

February 24. Syria Commits to Withdraw from Lebanon. Facing increasing international pressure, Syrian authorities say they are committed to withdrawing their 15,000 troops, in accordance with the 1989 Taif agreement.

February 28. Thousands Protest Syrian Involvement in Lebanon. In Beirut, some 10,000 people demonstrate against Syrian control in Lebanon.

March 9. Hezbollah Organizes Pro-Syrian Rally. Hezbollah stages a rally in Beirut attended by hundreds of thousands of people in praise of Syria and its president, Bashar al-Assad.

March 10. Karami Reappointed. Ten days after resigning under local and international pressure, pro-Syrian Prime Minister Omar Karami is asked by President Emile Lahoud to form another government.

March 11. Syrian Troops Begin Pullout. Syria begins redeploying some 15,000 troops from northern Lebanon.

March 14. Anti-Syrian Demonstrations Demand Pullout. Hundreds of thousands of Lebanese gather in Beirut to demonstrate against the Syrian presence and influence.

April 7. UN Commission to Investigate Hariri Assassination. The UN Security Council establishes an independent commission to investigate the assassination of Hariri.

April 26. Last Syrian Troops Leave Lebanon. The Syrian military completes its withdrawal from Lebanon, ending a 29-year deployment.

June 19. Election Results Announced. Opposition leader Saad Hariri, son of Rafiq Hariri, and his anti-Syrian alliance win the fourth and final round of parliamentary elections. His Future Movement garners 72 of 128 seats in the country's first elections free of foreign interference in three decades.

July 1. Siniora Designated Prime Minister. Lahoud designates Fouad Siniora, a former finance minister under Hariri, as the new prime minister.

December 12. Car Bomb Kills Anti-Syrian Journalist. Gebran Tueni, an anti-Syrian member of parliament and journalist, is killed in what appears to be attacks against critics of Syria. UN investigators release a second report further implicating Syria in the Hariri assassination.

December 16. UN Extends Commission. The United Nations extends the commission investigating the Hariri assassination for another six months and grants it authority to investigate the series of attacks against outspoken critics of Syria.

PAKISTAN

February 24. Musharraf Declares al-Qaeda Broken in Pakistan. President Pervez Musharraf says that Pakistani forces have destroyed *al-Qaeda*'s infrastructure along the Afghan border but adds that Osama bin Laden's whereabouts remain unknown.

April 7. Pakistan and India Begin Bus Service in Kashmir. In a sign of improving relations between Pakistan and India, bus service across the Line of Control begins in Kashmir.

October 8. Earthquake Hits Northwestern Pakistan. A 7.6 earthquake, with its epicenter in the Muzaffarabad area of the disputed Kashmir, kills more than 74,000 people and displaces more than 3 million.

PALESTINIAN AFFAIRS

January 9. Abbas Elected to Succeed Arafat. Palestinians elect Mahmoud Abbas to succeed Yasir Arafat as president of the Palestinian Authority.

June 4. Abbas Postpones Parliamentary Elections. Abbas issues a presidential decree postponing elections for the Palestinian Legislative Council (PLC) originally scheduled for July 17. He had been negotiating with the council about procedures for electing its 132 members.

November 18. Fatah Cancels Gaza Primary. After gunmen disrupt polling and steal ballot boxes, Fatah shuts down it legislative primary elections in Gaza.

November 25. Border Crossing Opens between Gaza and Egypt. The Palestinian Authority assumes control from Israel over the Rafah border crossing between Egypt and the Gaza Strip in keeping with an agreement brokered November 15 by Secretary of State Condoleezza Rice. The event represents the Palestinian government's first international point of access not controlled by Israel.

December 15. Hamas Wins in West Bank Municipal Elections. Hamas (Islamic Resistance Movement) candidates sweep municipal elections in the West Bank town of Nablus, win control in Jenin and El Bireh, and take three seats in Ramallah.

PERSIAN GULF STATES

January 15. Bahraini Cabinet Sworn In. Emir Hamad bin 'Isa al-Khalifa appoints a new cabinet. Several members are supporters of his economic and political reform efforts. Several hardliners are dismissed.

February 9. Islamic Parties Successful in Saudi Elections. In the first round of Saudi city council elections, seven Islamist candidates win seats from Riyadh.

February 27. Qatar Announces New Energy Deal. Qatar's state-run petroleum company and two major international oil companies sign deals worth some $19 billion to develop liquefied natural gas for European and US markets.

August 1. King Fahd Dies. King Fahd dies and is succeeded by Crown Prince 'Abdallah.

SYRIA

October 12. Interior Minister Dies. Interior Minister Ghazi Kanaan, formerly Syria's head of intelligence in Lebanon, reportedly commits suicide.

October 19. UN Report Implicates Syria. A UN commission investigating the assassination of former Lebanese Prime Minister Rafiq Hariri issues a report pointing toward Syrian involvement.

INDEX

Entries of only a single page number, and the first number in a multiple-page entry, indicate the first or primary reference to that individual. Additional page numbers typically indicate first references in a different section of a profile or in a closely related profile.

AAL, Mohammad Abdul, 128
al-AASAR, Abdul Moneim, 128
ABBAS, Abdul, 451
ABBAS, Mahmoud, 219, 445–447
ABBAS, Muhammad, 451
ABBOUD, Farid, 270
Abd al-'ALIM, Abdallah, 419
'ABDALLAH II, 225, 226
ABDEL RAHMAN, Omar, 130
ABDELAZIZ, Maged Abdelfattah, 134
ABDELGHANI, Mohamed Ben Ahmed, 61
ABDESSELAM, Belaid, 63
ABDUR RAHMAN Khan, 37
ABDURAHMAN, Sami, 179
ABEDI, Agha Hassan, 410
ABU-HAZEIRA, Aharon, 204
ABU al-RAGHEB, Ali, 229
ABU SHAWARIB, Mujahid, 430
ABU ZANT, Abd al-Munim, 238
ACHAKZAI, Mahmood Khan, 332
ACHEHBAR, Chakir, 294
ADAMI, Lahbib, 73
ADDA, Abdelkrim Ould, 77
AFRIDI, Latif, 330
AĞAR, Mehmet, 399
AGBARIYA, Asma, 212
al-AGHA, Zakaria, 446
AHADI, Anwar al-Haq, 53
AHERDANE, Mahjoubi, 292
AHMAD, Abdullah, 281
AHMAD, Amir Qazi Hussain, 329
AHMAD, Qari, 51
AHMAD, Qazi Hussain, 328
AHMADINEJAD, Mahmoud, 137, 142
AHMADZAY, Ahmad Shah, 49
AHMADZAY, Shahpur, 42
al-AHMAR, 'Abdallah, 367
al-AHMAR, Abdallah ibn Husayn, 429, 431
AHMED, Afaq, 330, 331
AHSAN, Chawdhry Aitzaz, 328
AÏT-AHMED, Hocine, 74
AKBULUT, Yıldırım, 388

AKEF, Muhammad Mahdi, 129
AKHUND, Mohammed Hassan, 43
AKIF, Abderrahman, 75
AKINCI, Mustafa, 111
AKOUR, Abd al-Rahim, 235
AKRAM, Abu, 436
AKRAM, Munir, 337
ALAIOU, Moulay Mustafa Ben Larbi, 291
ALAM, Muhammad, 334
AL ALAMI, Ahmed, 294
ALAOUI, Ismail, 291
ALI, Kamal Hasan, 118
ALI, Salim Rubay'i, 420
ALLAWI, Ayad, 166, 180, 181
ALMANSUR, Tawfiq Ahmad, 91
el-AMAOUI, Noubir, 291
AMER, Ali 'Abd al-Aziz, 237
AMERIKANOS, Stelios, 103
AMIN, Hafizullah, 38
AMIR, Yigul, 191
AMITAL, Yehuda, 206
AMOR, Mohamed Belhadj, 379
AMOUZEGAR, Jamshid, 138
AMR, Yasir, 446
al-'AMRI, Hassan, 419
ANASTASIADES, Nicos, 102
ANGOLEMLİ, Hüseyin, 112
ANTAR al-Bishi, Ali Ahmad Nasir, 420
ANWAR Khan, Sardar Muhammad, 338
ANWARI, Hosayn, 53
AOUN, Michel, 259
ARABACIOĞLU, Mustafa, 110
ARABIYAT, Abd al-Latif, 235, 238
ARAFAT, Yasir, 227, 255, 435
al-ARASHI, Abd al-Karim, 419
ARCHANE, Mahmoud, 293
ARDEBILI, Abdolkarim Musavi, 139
AREF, Mohamed Reza, 137
ARENS, Moshe, 204
ARIEL, Uri, 211
ARINÇ, Bülent, 407
ARMIN, Mohsen, 153
ARYAN, Abdul Rashid, 53
ASGAROWLADI, Habibollah, 151

ASGHARZADEH, Ebrahim, 153
ASIF, Qari Mohammed, 333
ASMAR, Muhammad, 294
al-ASSAD, Basel, 361
al-ASSAD, Bashar, 359, 361, 367
al-ASSAD, Hafiz, 359, 360
al-ASSAD, Jamil, 361
al-ASSAD, Rif'at, 360
ASSAF, Ibrahim, 270
al-ATASSI, Nur al-Din, 360
ATATÜRK, Mustafa Kemal, 386
ATEF, Mohammed, 55
al-ATRUSHI, Muhammad Said Ahmad, 183
al-'ATTAR, Muhammad Sa'id, 422
al-ATTAS, Haydar Abu Bakr, 421
ATTAULLAH, 334
al-ATTIYAH, 'Abdallah ibn Hamad, 342
ATUN, Hakki, 107, 110
AWAD, Musa, 436, 452
AWADALLAH, Bassam, 229
al-AWALI, Majid, 89
AWWAD, Abdullah, 453
al-AYADI, Abdel-Haq, 79
AYALON, Daniel, 215
AYDAR, Zübeyir, 406
AYEB, Aly, 72
al-'AYNI, Muhsin Ahmad, 419
AYYASH, Yahya, 222
AZHAR, Masood, 333, 334
AZHARI, Gholam Reza, 138
al-AZIZ, Ahson Ali 'Abd, 183
al-AZIZ, Othman 'Abd, 182
AZIZ, Qadir, 180
al-AZIZ, Sadiq 'Abd, 182
AZIZ, Shaukat, 311, 318, 326
al-AZZIZ, Mohamed 'Abd, 302
AZZOUNA, Jalloud, 379

BAALI, Abdallah, 82
BABA, Ghazi, 333
BACCOUCHE, Hedi, 372
BADAMCHIAN, Assadollah, 151
BADAWI, El Sayed, 127
al-BADR, Iman Muhammad, 418

BADRAN, Adnan, 225, 229
BADRAN, Mudar, 227
BA-GAD, Yosef, 212
BAHA, Ahmad, 223
BAHÇELI, Devlet, 400
BAHONAR, Mohammad Javad, 139
BAHONAR, Mohammad Reza, 159
BAHONAR, Reza, 150
BAJAMMAL, 'Abd al-Qadir 'Abd
   al-Rahman, 419, 423, 428
BAKHTIAR, Shahpur, 138
BAKIRHAN, Tuncer, 402
al-BAKKUSH, Abd al-Hamid, 272, 280
al-BAKR, Ahmad Hasan, 163
BAKR, Yusuf Abu, 237
BALOCH, Mohim Khan, 331
BALTIMORE III, Richard Lewis, 309
BAMARMI, Ahmad, 180
BANI-SADR, Abol Hasan, 139
al-BANNA, Sabry Khalil, 435, 453
BAPIR, Muhammad Ali, 181
BARAK, Ehud, 189, 192
BARAKAT, Na'el, 237
BAREKA, Muhammad, 211
al-BARGHUTHI, Bashir, 448
BARGHUTHI, Marwan, 220, 447
BARZANI, Massud, 179
al-BARZANI, Mustafa, 163
BAŞ, Haydar, 403
BASRA, Riaz, 334
BASRI, Driss, 286
BASRI, Mohamed, 290
al-BATAYNEH, Mohammad, 238
BATEBI, Ahmad, 156
al-BAYANUNI, Ali Sadr al-Din, 367
BAYAR, Celal, 387
BAYAR, Mehmet Ali, 402
al-BAYATI, Abbas, 177
BAYIK, Ceril, 405
BAYKAL, Deniz, 397, 398
BAYOUN, Bouchraya Hamoudi, 302
BAZARGAN, Mehdi, 138
BEG, Mirza Aslam, 332
BEGIN, Benjamin, 212
BEGIN, Menachem, 190
BEHESHTI, Mohammad Hossein, 139
BEIBA, Mahfoud Ali, 299
BEILIN, Yossi, 205, 209
BEJI, Mounir, 379
BEL HAJ, Ali, 294
BELGRAVE, Sir Charles, 84
BELHADJ, Ali, 77
BELKEBIR, Abdessamad, 292
BELKHADEM, Abdelaziz, 71
BEN ALI, Zine El-Abidine, 371, 372, 377
BEN BELLA, Ahmed, 60
BEN DHIA, Abdelaziz, 377
BEN-ELIEZER, Benjamin, 206
BEN JAFAAR, Mustafa, 379
BEN SALAH, Ahmed, 380
BEN YAHIA, Habib, 377

BENBAIBECHE, Tahar, 71
BENBITOUR, Ahmed, 65
BENDJEDID, Chadli, 60
BENFLIS, Ali, 61, 65, 71
BEN-GURION, David, 190
BENHAMOU, Mohammed, 294
BENHAMOUDA, Boualem, 71
BENJELLAIME, Ahmed, 294
BENNOUNA, Mohamed, 298
BENSAID, Mohamed, 293, 294
BENSALAH, Abdelkader, 72, 81
BENSLIM, Mohammed, 79
BERBEROĞLU, Ahmet Mithat, 106
BERRI, Nabih, 258, 267, 269
BHUTTO, Begum Nusrat, 327
BHUTTO, Benazir, 310, 314, 328
BHUTTO, Ghinwa, 327
BHUTTO, Mumtaz Ali, 326
BHUTTO, Murtaza, 315
BHUTTO, Shahnawaz, 314
BHUTTO, Zulfikar Ali, 313
al-BIEDH, Ali Salim, 421
BIN LADEN, Osama, 42, 56
BISHARA, Azmi, 211
BISHARAT, Awdah, 211
BITAT, Rabah, 60
BIZENJO, Tahir, 331
BOLAYIR, Kemal, 113
BORAN, Behice, 402
BOUABID, Maati, 284
BOUACHA, Omar, 75
BOUA-CHRINE, Said, 293
BOUAKOUIR, Samir, 74
BOUCHIHA, Mohamed, 379
BOUDIAF, Mohamed, 63
BOUDIAFI, Nourredine, 79
BOUKHAMKHAM, Abdelkader, 77
BOUKHAZNA, Ali, 73
BOUKROUH, Noureddine, 64, 73
BOULAHIA, Ismaïl, 378
BOUMEDIENNE, Houari, 60
BOURGUIBA, Habib, 371
BOUSLIMANI, Mohamed, 72
BOUTEFLIKA, Abdelaziz, 61, 65, 71
BOUTROS-GHALI, Boutros, 123
BOUTROS-GHALI, Yussef, 116
BOUZOUBAA, Abdelmajid, 294
BRAHIMI, Abdelhamid, 61
BREMER, L. Paul, 166
BUGTI, Nawab Akbar, 331
BUGTI, Raziq, 326
BULEDI, Muhammad Aslam, 331
BURG, Avraham, 206

CABEL, Eitan, 206
ÇAPOĞLU, Gökhan, 404
ÇELEBİ, Ahmet Rüştü, 403
CETIN, Hikmet, 397
CHAABANE, Younes, 79
CHALABI, Ahmad, 177
CHAMKANI, Haji Mohammad, 38

CHAMMARI, Khemais, 377
CHAMOUN, Camille, 255
CHAOUCH, Ali, 377
CHATTA, Chaudhry Hamid Nasir, 326
CHATTHA, Hamid Nasir, 325
CHAUDHRY, Fazal Elahi, 313
CHAUDHRY, Mahmood, 338
CHEBBI, Ahmed Néjib, 379
CHEHAB, Fu'ad, 255
CHELLAL, Toufik, 74
CHERIF, Hachemi, 76
CHRISTOFIAS, Dimitris, 101, 103
CHRISTOU, Andreas, 101
ÇİLLER, Tansu, 389
CİNDORUK, Hüsamettin, 389
CLERIDES, Glafcos, 93, 94, 102
COSAR, Salih, 113
CROCKER, Ryan C., 337

DAHAMSHA, Abd al-Malek, 210
DAHER, Michel, 259
DAHLAN, Mohammad, 447
DAKHIL, Mahmud, 280
DAOUD, Abdel Salam, 128
DAOUD, Diaeddin, 128
DAOUD, Sardar Mohammad, 38
DAR, Ishaq, 330
DARAWSHAH, Abd al-Wahab, 210
DARWISH, Abdullah Nimr, 210
DAUDIA, Muhammad, 236
DEMİREL, Süleyman, 387
DENKTAŞ, Rauf R., 93, 95, 106, 107
DENKTAŞ, Serdar, 110
al-DHAHRANI, Khalifa, 91
al-DHAHRI, Alasri Saeed, 416
al-DHUNAYBAT, Abd al-Majid, 238
DICHOU, Abdelmadjid, 79
al-DIN, Salah al-Din Baha, 180
DJABALLAH, Abdallah, 73
DJEDDAI, Ahmed, 74
DOĞAN, Muharrem, 399
DOSTAM, Abdul Rashid, 40, 50
DOURI, Mohamed, 290
DURANI, Ahmad Shah, 36
DURDA, Abu Zaid 'Umar, 274
DURDURAN, Alpay, 112
DÜSENKALKAR, Eşref, 113

EDDE, Carlos, 266
EDELMAN, Eric S., 408
EDELSTEIN, Yuli, 208
EDİBALİ, Aykut, 402
EITAM, Effi, 209
EITAN, Rafael, 212
EKENOĞLU, Fatma, 113
EKER, Durmuş Ali, 403
ELAMAADI, Abul, 128
ELLOUZE, Habib, 381
ELON, Benjamin, 210
EMİN, Enver, 112
ERBAKAN, Necmettin, 388, 389, 401

ERBİLEN, Mustafa, 112
ERDMAN, Richard W., 82
ERDOGAN, Recep Tayyip, 387, 390, 397, 401
EREL, Ali, 112
EREZ, Yalım, 390
EROĞLU, Derviş, 108, 110, 111
ESHKOL, Levi, 190
ESKANDARI-FORUHAR, Parvaneh, 156
ESSAID, Mohamed Jalal, 292
EVREN, Kenan, 388
EVRIVIADES, Euripides L., 105

FADAEI, Hossein, 150
FADLALLAH, Mohammad Hossein, 268
FAHIM, Makhdoom Amin, 328
FAHIM, Mohammad Qasim, 48, 50
FAHMY, Nabil, 134
al-FAISAL, Turki, 357
FAISAL II, 163
FARAJ, Najm al-Din, 183
FARHADI, Ravan A.G., 58
al-FARHAN, Hamad, 236
FARID, Hatim Muhsin ibn, 431
FARID, Mohsen, 431
FARID, Ustad, 40
FAROOQI, Amjad Hussain, 322
FAROUK I, 116
EL FASSI, Abbas, 290
FATTUH, Ruhi, 221
al-FAYIZ, Faisal, 225, 229
FAZL, 51
FELIBUS, Menahem, 211
FELTMAN, Jeffrey, 270
FHIMAH, Lamin Khalifah, 278
FILALI, Abdellatif, 286
FIRAT, Abdülmerik, 403, 404
FORUHAR, Dariush, 156
FRANJIYAH, Sulayman, 255
FREIHAT, Abd al-Salam, 235
FU'AD I, 116

GAFNI, Moshi, 207
GAILANI, Ishaq, 53
GAILANI, Sayed Ahmad, 51
GALANOS, Alexis, 97, 101
al-GALIL, Ahmad Hassan 'Abd, 131
GAMLIEL, Aryeh, 211
al-GANZOURI, Kamal Ahmed, 119
GARNER, Jay, 166
GEAGEA, Samir, 257
GEMAYEL, Amin Pierre, 257
GEMAYEL, Bashir, 257
GHADANSI, Izzidin, 280
GHALI, Brahim, 301
GHANEM, Jean, 266
al-GHANI, 'Abd al-'Aziz 'Abd, 419, 428
al-GHANI, Safwat 'Abd, 131
GHANIM, Faraj Said ibn, 423
GHANIM, Shukri Muhammad, 273, 274
GHANIMA, Ziad Abu, 235

GHANNOUCHI, Mohamed, 371, 373, 377
GHANOUCHI, Rachid, 381
al-GHASHMI, Ahmad Husayn, 419
GHAZAL, Yusuf, 235
GHAZI, Mahmud, 53
GHOSHEH, Samir, 446, 451
GHOZALI, Sid Ahmed, 62, 76
GILLERMAN, Dan, 215
GOLDSTEIN, Baruch, 213
GOMAA, Numan, 127
GORGUN, Ali Riza, 112
GREEN, Moshe, 212
GRIVAS, George, 94
GÜL, Abdullah, 401
GÜLER, Aydemir, 403
GÜNKAN, Güngör, 112
GÜRSEL, Cemal, 387

HABASH, Georges, 437
HABIBI, Hasan Ebrahim, 137
HACHANA, Mohamed Nejib, 384
HACHANI, Abdelkader, 76
HACHANI, Ali, 384
HADDAD, Saad, 256
HADDAD-ADEL, Gholam-Ali, 150, 159
HADDAM, Anwar, 77
HADEF, Mohamed, 75
HADI, Abdurabu Mansur, 419, 422, 428
HADJIDEMETRIOU, Takis, 102
al-HADRAN, Mohammed, 250
al-HAERI, Kazem, 176
al-HAFIZ, Amin, 360
HAIDER, Syed Anis, 329
HAJARIAN, Saeed, 152
HAJATI, Reza, 155
al-HAJJRI, Abdulwahab A., 433
al-HAKIM, Abd al-Aziz, 176
HAKIM, Brahim, 301
al-HAKIM, Said Muhammad Bakr, 175
HAKIMI, Laftullah, 54
el-HALOUANI, Mohamed Ali, 378
al-HAMADI, Ibrahim Muhammad, 419
HAMARENEH, Muni, 236
HAMDANI, Ismail, 65
al-HAMI, Muhammad, 281
al-HAMID, Muhsin 'Abd, 174, 182
HAMMADI, Saadoun, 164
HAMMAN, Talaat Yassin, 131
HAMMANI, Hamma, 381
HAMMANI, Hosni, 379
HAMMER, Zevulun, 208
HAMMOUMA, Mohamed, 75
HAMMUDA, Yahia, 435
HAMROUCHE, Mouloud, 62
HAMZA, Mustapha, 131
HAMZEH ibn Hussein, 225
HAMZEKI, Ghafur, 157
HANANDEH, Ahmed, 238
HANIYA, Ismail, 223
HANNOUN, Louisa, 73
al-HAQ, Farid, 329

ul-HAQ, Sami, 328
ul-HAQ, Muhammad Ijaz, 326
al-HARIRI, Qabbari 'ABDALLAH, Abu al-'Izz, 128
HARIRI, Rafiq, 260
HARMEL, Mohamed, 378
HAROUN, Ali, 75
al-HARTHY, Yaqoub ibn Hamad, 308
HASAN, Munawar, 50
HASAN, Syed Munawwar, 329
HASHEM, Salah, 131
HASHMI, Makhdoom Javed, 323, 330
HASIPOĞLU, Ertuğrul, 112
HASSAN ibn Talal (of Jordan), 229
HASSAN II (of Morocco), 284, 285
HASSAN (of Morocco), 285
al-HASSANI, Hajim M., 185
HASSANZADEH, Abdallah, 157
HATAB, Hassan, 79
HAWATMEH, Nayif, 437, 450
HAYAT Khan, Sardar Sikander, 338
HAYAT, Makhdoom Syed Faisal Salah, 339
HAYEE Baluch, Abdul, 331
HEJRI, Mustafa, 157
HEKMATYAR, Gulbuddin, 39, 52
HELOU, Charles, 255
HENDEL, Zvi, 211
HIFTER, Khalifa, 280
HILLIS, Ahmad, 447
al-HIMSI, Taysir, 236
al-HINDI, Muhammad, 223
HOBEIKA, Elie, 257, 266
HOBEIKA, Jina, 266
al-HODAIBI, Mamoun, 129
el-HORANI, Mohamed Ali, 382
HOVEYDA, Emir Abbas, 138
HOVNANIAN, Sebouh, 268
HRAWI, Ilyas, 255, 260
HUDSON, William J., 384
HUMAYD, Salih ibn, 357
al-HUNI, Abd al-Munim, 280
HURWITZ, Yigael, 204
al-HUSS, Salim Ahmad, 256
HUSSAIN, Altaf, 330
HUSSAIN, Amir, 323
HUSSAIN, Chaudhry Amir, 336
HUSSAIN, Chaudhry Shujaat, 311, 318, 326
HUSSAIN, Mushahid, 326
HUSSEIN ibn Talal (of Jordan), 225, 226
HUSSEIN, Qusai, 183
HUSSEIN, Saddam, 164, 183
HUSSEIN, Sharif Ali ibn, 182
HUSSEIN, Udai, 165, 183
al-HUSSEIN, Zeid Ra'ad Zeid, 242
al-HUTHI, Husayn, 427

IACOVOU, George, 97
IBRAHIM Khan, Mohammad, 338
IBRAHIM, Moulay Abdallah, 294

IBRAHIM, Saad Eddin, 125
IBRAHIMI, Ahmed, 65
IBRAHIMI, Ahmed Taleb, 76
İÇLI, Tayfun, 400
IDRIS I, 272
EL IDRISSI, Mohammed, 293
IKKEN, Bouazza, 294
İLKIN, Baki, 408
IQBAL, Rao Sikander, 328
IRMAK, Sadi, 388
al-IRYANI, 'Abd al-Karim 'Ali, 419, 420, 428
al-IRYANI, Abd al-Rahman, 418
IS'HAQ, Ali, 446
al-ISLAM, Sa'if, 418
al-ISLAMBOULI, Essam, 128
ISMA'IL, Abd al-Fattah, 420
ISMAIL, Mahmoud, 446, 448
al-ISSA, Khalid, 250
IYAD, Abu, 446
IZZAT, Nasser, 451

al-JAAFARI, Ibrahim, 163, 166, 175
JABBAR, Abdul, 333
JABIR, Saad Saleh, 182
JABRIL, Ahmad, 452
JABRIL, Jihad, 452
al-JADID, Salah, 360
JALLUD, Abd al-Salam, 273
JAMALI, Zafarullah Khan, 311, 318, 326
al-JAMRI, 'Abd al-Amir, 85
al-JAMRI, Mansur, 89
JARJOUI, Emile, 446
JATOI, Ghulam Murtaza, 326
JATOI, Ghulam Mustafa, 314, 326
JAWAD, Said Tayeb, 58
al-JAWI, Omar, 430
JAWID, Mohammad Ali, 49
JAZI, Dali, 377
JERBI, Shalom, 209
JERIJIAN, Vahrij, 268
JETTOU, Driss, 285, 287
JHANGVI, Haq Nawaz, 334
JIBRIL, Muhammad Fayiz, 280
al-JIFRI, Abd al-Rahman, 431
JIHAD, Abu, 437
JINNAH, Mohammad Ali, 312
JUMBLATT, Walid, 258
JUNEJO, Mohammad Khan, 314, 325

KABARITI, Abd al-Karim, 228
KABRI, Tayeb, 74
al-KADE, Issam, 452
KADHIM, Dirgham, 181
KADIRI, Abdallah, 293
KADOURIE, Yitzhak, 211
KAFI, Ali, 63
KAHANE, Binyamin Zeev, 213
KAHANE, Meir, 198, 213

al-KALISI, Muhammad Mahdi, 175
KALLEL, Abdallah, 377
KAMAL, Zuheira, 451
KAMEL, Michel, 131
KANAN, Muhammad, 210
KARAKOC, Refik, 403
KARAM, Karim, 265
KARAMAT, Jehangir, 316, 337
KARAMI, Umar, 260
KARATAŞ, Dursun, 404
KARAYALÇIN, Murat, 399, 404
KARAYILAN, Murat, 406
KARBASCHI, Gholan Hussein, 154
KARKAR, Sahah, 381
KARMAL, Babrak, 38
KAROUI, Hamed, 371, 372, 377
KARQAR, Azizullah, 50
KARRUBI, Mehdi, 142, 155
KARZAI, Hamid, 37, 44
KASI, Mir Aimal, 321
al-KASM, 'Abd al-Ra'uf, 361
KASSEM, Abd al-Karim, 163
KATSAV, Moshe, 189, 193, 205
KATZOVER, Benny, 211
KAWAR, Karim, 242
KAZZAR, Nazim, 163
KEBIR, Rabeh, 77
KENIZEH, George, 267
KESHTMAND, Soltan Ali, 39
KETENCİ, Ahmet Giiryüz, 399
KHADDAM, 'Abd al-Halim, 359, 360
KHADIR, Abdul, 38
KHADIR, Idriss, 75
KHAIRUDDIN, Kawaja, 325
KHALAF, Salah, 435, 446
KHALES, Mohammad Yunos, 52
KHALID, Malek Meraj, 315
KHALID, Taysir, 446, 450
al-KHALIFA, Abd al-Rahman, 238
KHALIFA, Hamad ibn 'Isa Al, 85, 86
KHALIFA, 'Isa ibn Salman Al, 85, 86
KHALIFA, Khalifa ibn Salman Al, 86
KHALIFA, Salman ibn Hamad Al, 85
KHALIFAH, Mohamed, 452
al-KHALIFI, Muhammad ibn Mubarak, 345
KHALIL, Mustafa, 118
KHALIL, Samihah Yusuf al-Qubbaj, 218
KHALILI, Karim, 37, 51
KHALILZAD, Zalmay, 58, 186
KHALIQYAR, Fazil Haq, 39
KHAMENEI, Ali, 137, 140
KHAN, Abdul Qadeer, 322
KHAN, Agha Mohammad Yahya, 313
KHAN, Amanullah, 338
KHAN, Amir, 331
KHAN, Bashir Ahmad, 333
KHAN, Fida Mohammad, 325
KHAN, Ghulam Ishaq, 314
KHAN, Imran, 332

KHAN, Miraj Mohammad, 332
KHAN, Mohammad Asghar, 333
KHAN, Mohammad Ayub, 312
KHAN, Nawabzada Mansoor Ali, 332
KHAN, Nawabzada Nasrullah, 332
KHAN, Sahib, 339
KHAN, Saranjam, 330
KHAN, Shahnawaz, 333
KHATAMI, Mohammad, 137, 141, 154
KHATAMI, Mohammad Reza, 152
al-KHATIB, Ahmad, 250
KHATTAK, Ajmal Khan, 326
al-KHAWAJA, Abd al-Hadi, 88
KHERBI, Amine, 82
KHIABANI, Mussa, 156
KHOMEINI, Ruhollah Musavi, 137, 138
KHREIS, Shaher, 238
al-KHUDARY, Riyad, 446
KHUDAYYIR, Ahmad Hussein, 165
al-KHURAFI, Jassim, 251
al-KHURAYSHA, Mijhim, 234
al-KHURI, Bishara, 254
al-KHUSAIBY, Mohamed Ali, 309
KHYARI, Thami, 292
KIKHIA, Mansur, 280
KIRDAĞ, Arif Salih, 112
KLEINER, Michael, 212
KLIMOS, Antoine, 266
KLOSSON, Michael, 105
EL KOHEN, Abderrahmane, 294
KORUTÜRK, Fahri, 387
KOTAK, İsmet, 110
KOUCHAKZADEH, Mehdi, 150
KOUTSOU, Nicholaos, 97
KOUTSOU, Nicos, 103
KOZANOGLU, Hayri, 402
KRAJESKI, Thomas, 433
KREKAR, Mullah, 183
KURAL, Fehmi, 403
KURİŞ, Konca, 406
KURTZER, Daniel C., 215
KUTAN, Recai, 390, 401
KUTLU, Haydar, 402
KYPRIANOU, Spyros, 95

LAASOUED, Habib, 381
LADEN, Osama bin, 414
LADGHAM, Bahi, 372
LAENSER, Mohand, 292
LAHJOUJI, Abderrahim, 294
LAHOUD, Emile, 255, 261
LAHOUD, Nassib, 268
LAMRANI, Mohamed Karim, 285
LAPID, Tommy, 209
LARAKI, Azzedine, 285
LASSOUED, Amar, 73
LeBARON, Richard, 252
LEGHARI, Sardar Farooq Ahmad Khan, 315, 326
LEKHAL, Yacine, 75
LERARRI, Rashid, 76

LIAQUAT Ali Khan, 312
LIEBERMAN, Avigdor, 212
LITZMAN, Ya'acov, 207
LOGOGLU, Osman Faruk, 408
LUDHIANVI, Maulana Muhammad Ahmad, 334
LUTFI, 'Ali Mahmud, 119
LYSSARIDES, Vassos, 95, 97, 102

M'BAZAA, Fouad, 377, 383
al-MA'AYTA, Mahmud, 238
al-MA'AYTAH, Musa, 237
MAAOUNI, Hassan, 292
MABROUK, Sassi, 75
MADANAT, Isa, 237
MADANI, Abassi, 77
MADANI, Hassan, 89
MADIH, Lachen, 294
MAGARIAF, Muhammad, 280
MAHAYRI, Issam, 267
MAHDAVI-KANI, Mohammad Reza, 140, 151
al-MAHDI, Abd, 163
al-MAHDI, Adil 'Abd, 176
al-MAHDI, Sadiq, 128
MAHERZI, Slimane, 78
MAHFOUZ, Naguig, 131
MAHFUZ, Muhammad Ali, 89
al-MAHGOUB, Rifa'at, 119
MAHJOUB, Ali Reza, 153
MAHMOUD, Ahmad Kakar, 182
MAHMUD, Muhammad Jahi, 180
MAHMUD, Ahmad Al, 342
al-MAJALI, Abd al-Hadi, 234
al-MAJALI, Abd al-Salam, 228
MAJALI, Muhammad, 237
MAJDALAWI, Jamil, 451
al-MAJID, Hussein Kamil, 165
MAKARIOS, 94
al-MAKHLAFI, Abdul Malik, 430
MAKTUM, Maktum ibn Rashid Al, 410, 411
MAKTUM, Rashid ibn Sa'id Al, 410, 411
MALEK, Abdul, 53
MALEK, Redha, 63, 75
MALIK, Fouad, 265
MALIK, Yasin, 338
MALLOUGH, Abd al-Rahim, 446
MALOUH, Abdel Rahim, 451
al-MANQUSH, Muhammad Ahmad, 274
MANSUR, Hamzah, 235
MANSUR, Jamal, 223
MARZOUKI, Moncef, 381
al-MAS'ARI, Muhammad, 355
MASHARQA, Muhammad Zuhayr, 359, 360
al-MASHRIQI, Hameeduddin, 332
MASHRIQI, Khan, 332
MASOUD, Ahmad Wali, 53
MASOUD, Ahmad Zia, 37, 53
MASOUD, Ahmed Shah, 40

al-MASRI, Tahir, 227
MASUM, Fuad, 165
MATAR, Jabal, 280
MAVROYIANNIS, Andreas D., 105
MAZARI, Abdul Ali, 51
MAZARI, Balkh Sher, 315
al-MEGRAHI, Abd al-Basset, 278
MEHRI, Abdelhamid, 70
MEIR, Golda, 190
MEKDAD, Faysal, 369
al-MEKHLAFI, Abdul Malik, 431
MEKOUAR, Aziz, 297
MELCHIOR, Michael, 206
MELEN, Ferit, 387
MENDERES, Adnan, 387
MENDERES, Aydin, 401
MENGAL, Sardar Ataullah, 331
MERBAH, Abd al-Kader, 74
MERBAH, Kasdi, 62
MESHAL, Khaled, 199
MESSAADIA, Mohamed Cherif, 70
MESTIRI, Ahmed, 372
MEZRAG, Madani, 78
MICHAILADES, Dinos, 103
MIHAILIDES, Alekos, 102
al-MIHDAR, Zein al-Abidine, 431
MIKATI, Najib, 255
MILO, Ronni, 212
MIR, Sajid, 332
MIRDAMADI, Mohsen, 152
MIRO, Muhammad Mustafa, 359, 361
MIRZA, Iskander, 312
MISH'AL, Khalil, 223
MITZNA, Avraham, 193, 206
MODARESSI, Taqi, 175
MOHAMED V, 284
MOHAMED VI, 285, 286, 297
MOHAMMAD, Ghulam, 312
MOHAMMAD, Khalid Shaikh, 56
MOHAMMAD, Maulawi Mohammad Nabi, 41
MOHAQEQ, Mohammad, 49, 53
MOHAZZIZI, Zaidi, 51
MOHSENI, Aseh, 51
MOJADEDI, Hashimatullah, 52
MOJADEDI, Sibghatullah, 39, 52
MONROE, William T., 91
MONTAJABNIYA, Rassoul, 155
MONTAZERI, Hussein Ali, 140
MORDECHAI, Itzhak, 211
MOSSADEQ, Mohammad, 137
MOTAHARI, Morteza, 138
MOUADA, Mohamed, 378
MOUAWAD, René, 260
MOURROU, Abdelfatah, 381
MOUSTAPHA, Imad, 369
MOUTIA, Abdelkarim, 295
al-MU'ALLA, Rashid ibn Ahmad, 410, 411
al-MU'ALLA, Ahmad ibn Rashid, 410
al-MU'ASHIR, Anis, 235

al-MUBARAK, Jafar, 355
MUBARAK, Gamal, 127
MUBARAK, Muhammad Husni, 117, 118, 127
al-MUDARRISI, Taqi, 177
MUFTI, Adnan, 185
MUHAMMAD, Ali Nasir, 420
MUHAMMAD, Aziz, 181
MUHAMMAD, Sufi, 334
MUHAMMAD, Salim Salih, 422, 424
MUHI al-DIN, Ahmad Fu'ad, 118
al-MULLAH, Nabila Abdallah, 252
MUMCU, Erkan, 397, 399
al-MUNTASIR, Umar Mustafa, 274
MUQBIL, Ali Salih, 430
al-MUQRIN, Abdelaziz Issa Abdul-Mohson, 56
MUSA, Abu, 453
MUSA, Saed, 453
MUSAMEH, Sayid Abu, 222
MUSAVI, Mir Hosein, 140
al-MUSAWI, Faisal Radhi, 91
MUSHARRAF, Pervez, 311, 316
MUSHAYMA, Husayn, 89
MUSSAWI, Ibrahim, 268
al-MUTAIR, Khaled, 250
MUZA, Hamid Majid, 182
MZALI, Mohamed, 372

NABAVI, Behzad, 153
NABI, Ahmad, 49
NACIRI, Khalid, 291
NAGIB, Muhammad, 116
NAHASS, Salem, 236
NAHDAL, Fuad, 223
NAHNAH, Mahfoud, 64
NAJDAWI, Ahmad, 236
NAJI, Talal, 452
NAJIBULLAH, Mohammad, 38
NAJILAH, Adnan Abu, 450
al-NAJJIB, Sulayman, 446, 448
NAMAZI, Bahran, 156
NAQVI, Allama Sajid Ali, 329
NAQVI, Mohammed Swaleh, 411
al-NASERI, 175
NASHAD, Fida Muhammad, 339
al-NASHASHIBI, Muhammad Zudi, 446
al-NASIR, Jamal 'Abd, 116
NASRALLAH, Hassan, 268
al-NASRI, Muhammad Bakr, 176
NASSER, Gamal Abdel, 116
NATEQ-NURI, Ali Akbar, 141, 151
NAZIF, Ahmed, 116, 117
NEFFATI, Chedli, 377
NEJRABI, Ghulam Faruq, 53
NETANYAHU, Benjamin, 191, 205
NIBARI, Abdallah, 250
NIDAL, Abu, 435
NOORANI Siddiqui, Shah Ahmad, 328
NOUIRA, Hedi, 372

NOURI, Abdullah, 154
al-NU'AYMI, Humayd ibn Rashid, 410, 411
al-NU'AYMI, Rashid ibn Humayd, 410
NU'MAN, Yasin Sa'id, 421
al-NUAIMI, Abdul Rahman, 89
NUHAYYAN, Khalifa ibn Zayed Al, 411
NUHAYYAN, Zayed ibn Sultan Al, 410, 411
NUR, Ayman, 125, 128
NURBAKHSH, Mohsen, 140
NUROLLAH, Sayyed, 50

OBAIDULLAH, Mullah, 54
OBEID, Atef Muhammad, 117, 120
OBEIDAT, Ahmed, 227
OBERWETTER, James, 357
ÖCALAN, Abdullah, 394, 406
ÖCALAN, Osman, 405
ODEH, Mahmoud, 446
OJABER, Nasir, 53
OKUYAN, Kemal, 403
OKUYAN, Yaşar, 402
OMAR, Abdelkader, 77
OMAR, Mohammad, 42, 54
OMIROU, Yiannakis, 102
al-ORAN, Muhammad, 238
ORLEV, Zevulun, 209
OSMAN, Ahmed, 284, 291
OTHMANI, Eldine, 293
OUALALOU, Fathallah, 291
EL OUAZZANI, Najib, 294
el-OUAZZANI, Thami, 293
OUKACHA, Mustapha, 295
OULD AHMED, Mohamed Lamine, 298
OURAN, Mohammad Al, 236
OUYAHIA, Ahmed, 61, 64, 72
ÖYMEN, Altan, 397
ÖZAL, Semra, 389
ÖZAL, Turgut, 388
ÖZDEN, Yekta Güngör, 404
ÖZGÜR, Ösker, 108, 112
ÖZTÜRK, Yaşar Nuri, 400

PAÇACI, M. Cihan, 400
PAGARO, Sahib, 325
PAHLAVI, Mohammad Reza, 137
PAHLAWAN, Abdul Malik, 42
PALEJO, Rasul Bakhsk, 332
PALMAS, Vassilis, 101
PAMUKÇU, Suat, 401
PAPADOPOULIS, Yiannis, 103
PAPADOPOULOS, Tassos, 93, 97, 101
PAPAPETROU, Mikhalis, 103
PEDRAM, Abdul Latif, 53
PERDIKIS, George, 103
PERES, Shimon, 190, 206
PERETZ, Amir, 208
PERİNÇEK, Doğu, 403
PHILIPPOU, Savvas, 103

PIŞKINSÜT, Sema, 401
POLLARD, Jonathan Jay, 197
PORAZ, Avraham, 209
PORUSH, Meir, 206, 207

al-QA'UD, Abd al-Majid, 274
al-QADDAH, Suleiman, 367
QADDUMI, Faruk, 438, 446, 447
QADDURAH, 'Abd al-Qadir, 369
al-QADHAFI, Mu'ammar, 272, 273
al-QADHAFI, Wanis, 272
ul-QADRI, Tahir, 332
QALIBAF, Mohammad Baqer, 150
QANUNI, Mohammad Yunos, 48, 49
QAOUK, Nabil, 268
QASIM, Salih Muslih, 421
QASIM, Talaat Fuad, 131
al-QASIMI, 'Abd al-Aziz, 410
al-QASIMI, Khalid ibn Muhammad, 410
al-QASIMI, Saqr ibn Muhammad, 411
al-QASIMI, Sultan ibn Muhammad, 410, 411
QASSEM, Naim, 268
QASSEMLOU, Abdur Rahman, 157
al-QATABI, 'Abdullah ibn 'Ali, 308
QAYYUM Khan, Sardar Abdul, 337
QUARDIGHI, Aissa, 292
QUDAH, Adel, 229
QURAY, Ahmad, 219, 445, 447
QURESHI, Mahmood, 318
QURESHI, Moeenuddin Ahmad, 315

RA'FAT, Saleh, 451
RABBANI, Burhanuddin, 40, 50
RABBANI, Mohammad, 42
RABBO, Yasir Abed, 446, 451
RABI, Ali Qasem, 89
RABIE Youssef, Gamal Eldin, 128
RABIN, Yitzhak, 190
RABTI, Bashir, 280
RADI, Abdelwahed, 291, 297
RAFSANJANI, Ali Akbar Hashemi, 135
RAHCHAMANI, Reza, 153
RAHIM, Arbab Ghulam, 326
al-RAHMAN, Assad 'Abd, 446
al-RAHMAN, Faruk Abdullah 'Abd, 181
RAHMAN, Fazlur, 318, 328
RAHMAN, Fazlur, 41
ar-RAHMAN, Muhammed 'Abd, 430
RAHMAN, Mujibur, 313
RAJAB, Muhammad al-Zarruq, 273
RAJAI, Mohammad Ali, 137, 139
RAJAVI, Maryam, 156
RAJAVI, Massoud, 139, 156
RAMZI, Asif, 334
RANTISI, Abd al-Aziz, 223
RASUL, Kosrat Abdulla, 165
RATHORE, Mumtaz Hussain, 337
RAVITZ, Avraham, 206, 207
al-RAWABDEH, Abd al-Rauf, 229, 234

RAZZAZ, Mu'niz, 236
REBAINE, Ali Fawzi, 74
REZA Khan, 137
al-RIFA'I, Zaid, 227, 239
RILEY, Thomas, 298
al-RIMAWI, Qasim, 227
RIVLIN, Reuven, 205, 213
RMILI, Boujamma, 378
ROLANDIS, Nikos, 97, 102
ROZI, Abdul Majid, 50
RUBINSTEIN, Amnon, 209
RUSHTAH, Atta Abu, 238

al-SA'AD, Muhammad Ali Farid, 235
al-SA'ID, Rif'at, 127
SAAD, Mustafa, 268
SAADA, Abdallah, 267
SAADAT, Ahmed, 451
SAADI, Saïd, 75
al-SA'DUN, Ahmad 'Abd al-Aziz, 244
al-SABAH, Abdallah al-Salim, 244
al-SABAH, Jabir al-Ahmad, 244, 245
al-SABAH, Muhammad Sabah al-Salim, 249
al-SABAH, Saad al-'Abdallah al-Salim, 244, 245
al-SABAH, Sabah al-Ahmad al-Jabir, 245
al-SABAH, Sabah al-Salim, 244, 245
al-SABAH, Salim Abdullah al-Jabir, 252
al-SABAHI Awadallah, Ahmad, 128
SABRI, Ali, 117
SACAMATI, Mohammad, 153
al-SADAT, Anwar, 117
SADI, Bassam, 223
SADIKOĞLU, Okyay, 112
SADIQI, Golam-Hossein, 138
al-SADR, Muhammad Bakr, 164
al-SADR, Muqtada, 174, 181
SADR, Musa, 267
al-SAFAR, Hassan, 355
SAHAD, Ibrahim, 280
ŞAHIN, Idris Naim, 397
SAHRAOUI, Nabil, 79
SAID, Mohammed, 76, 79
SAIDANI, Amar, 81
al-SAIDI, Abdallah M., 433
SAIFI, Amari, 79
SAJJAD, Wasim, 315
al-SAKET, Mazen, 237
SAKIK, Şemdin, 405
SALAH, Raed, 210
al-SALAL, Abdallah, 418
SALAM, Qasim, 430
al-SALHI, Basan, 448
SALHI, Chawki, 76
al-SALHI, Najib, 177
SALHUT, Jamil, 451
SALIH, Ali Abdallah, 419, 428
SALIH, Barham, 180

SALIM, Hilmi, 127
SALIM, Izzedin, 174
SALIM, Jawhar Namiq, 179
SALLAM, Ibrahim Tahir, 185
SALMAN, Ali, 85, 89
SAMPSON, Nikos Giorgiades, 94
SANJABI, Karim, 138, 156
SANJAR, Sebghatullah, 53
SARGIN, Nihat, 402
SARHADIZADEH, Abolqasem, 153
SARID, Yossi, 209
SARKIS, Ilyas, 255
SARTAWI, Issam, 435
SATIR, Köksal, 403
SATTAR, Farooq, 330
SAV, Onder, 398
al-SAWSA, Abd al-Raziq, 273, 274
SAYAF, Abdul Rasul, 39, 52
SAYEED, Hafiz Mohammed, 333
SCOBEY, Margaret, 369
SENOUSSI, Abdallah, 278
SERAGEDDIN, Fuad, 127
SERFATY, Abraham, 295
SERTER, Vehbi Zeki, 111
SEZER, Ahmet Necdet, 387, 390
SEZER, Zeki, 400
SFAR, Rachid, 372
SHA'ATH, Nabil, 447
SHA'IB, Musa, 267
al-SHAABI, Qahtan, 420
SHACH, Eliezer, 206
al-SHAFI, Haidar 'Abd, 220
al-SHAFI'I, Abdullah, 183
SHAH, Sajjad Ali, 315
al-SHAHABI, Naji, 128
SHAHID, Afsar, 338
SHAIKH, Ahmad Omar Sayed, 322
SHAIKH, Qaiser Ahmed, 333
SHAIR, Jamal, 238
SHAKER, Marshal Sharif Zaid ibn, 227
SHAKIR, Kamal, 180
SHALLAH, Ramadan Abdullah, 223
SHALTOUT, Usama Mohammad, 128
al-SHAMI, Abdallah, 223
SHAMI, Ahmad ibn Ali, 430
al-SHAMIKH, Mubarak Abdullah, 273, 274
SHAMIR, Yitzhak, 190
al-SHAMSI, Abdulaziz Nasser, 416
SHANAB, Ismail Abu, 223
SHAQAQI, Fathi, 223
al-SHARAA, Ghassen, 446
SHARAF, Sharif 'Abd al-Hamid, 227
SHARAFFEDIN Huni, Abdullah, 280
SHARAFKANDI, Sadeq, 157
SHARAK, Amnon Lipkin, 212
SHARANSKY, Natan, 208
SHARIATMADARI, Seyed Kazem, 138
SHARIF, Kulsoom, 329
SHARIF, Mian Mohammad Nawaz, 315
SHARIF, Mian Shabaz, 330

SHARIF, Mohammad Nawaz, 311, 325, 329
SHARIF-EMAMI, Ja'afar, 138
SHARON, Ariel, 189, 191, 205
SHARQ, Mohammad Hasan, 39
al-SHARQI, Hamad ibn Muhammad, 411
SHATILA, Kamal, 268
al-SHATTI, Ismail, 250
al-SHAYKHLY, Salah, 182
al-SHAZLY, Kamal, 127
al-SHERIF, Muhammad Safwat, 127
SHERPAO, Aftab Ahmad Khan, 327
al-SHIBA, Ali, 419
SHIBLI, Umar, 451
al-SHIRAZI, Muhammad Mahdi, 89
SHOBOKSHI, Fawzi A., 357
SHOHAT, Michal, 209
SHUBAKI, Khalid, 238
SHUMALI, Mohammad Rijjal, 238
SHUNNAQ, Ahmad, 234
SHUQAIRI, Ahmad, 434
SIDI MOHAMED, 286
SIDQI, Atif Muhammad, 119
SIFI, Mokdad, 64
SINIORA, Fouad, 255
al-SIRRI, Yasser, 130
SISON, Michele J., 416
al-SISTANI, Ali, 175
SOLTANI, Abou Djerra, 72
SOOMRO, Mohammad Mian, 318, 336
SOYER, Ferdi Sabit, 107, 108, 110
SOYSAL, Mümtaz, 404
STERN, Yuri, 212
SÜLEYMANOĞLU, Mehmet, 113
SULTAN, Gamal, 131
SUMAIDAI, Samir Shakir Mahmud, 186
SÜMBÜL, Mehmet, 403
SUNAY, Cevdet, 387
SURUR, Ahmad Fathi, 119, 133
SUWAYS, Salim, 237
SWESSI, Braek, 280

TAHA, Rifai, 131
al-TAHER, Mahir, 451
TAHSIN, Arif Hasan, 112
TAHSİN, Özel, 110
TALABANI, Jalal, 163, 166, 180
TALAL, 226
TALAT, Mehmet Ali, 107, 108, 110
TALEB, Mohamed Cherif, 74
TALEB, Mohamed Habib, 292
al-TALHI, Jadallah 'Azzuz, 273
al-TALL, Milhem, 238
al-TAMINI, Asad Bayyud, 238
TANAY, Shahnawaz, 39, 53
TANTAN, Sadettin, 403
TARAKI, Nur Mohammad, 38
TARAR, Mohammad Rafiq, 316
TARAR, Rafiq, 311
TARAWNEH, Fayez, 229
TARIQ, Azim Ahmad, 330

TARIQ, Muhammad Azam, 334
TARKAN, Doğan, 403
THAHEEN, Abdul Razzaq, 326
THANI, 'Abdallah ibn Khalifa Al, 341, 342
THANI, Ahmad ibn 'Ali ibn 'Abdallah Al, 341
THANI, Hamad ibn Jasim ibn Jabir Al, 342
THANI, Hamad ibn Khalifa Al, 341, 342
THANI, Jassim ibn Hamad Al, 341, 342
THANI, Khalifa ibn Hamad Al, 341
THANI, Tamin ibn Hamad Al, 341, 342
al-THAWADI, Ahmad, 89
THEMISTOCLEUS, Kostas, 103
THUNIBAT, Abd al-Majid, 238
TIBI, Ahmed, 211
TIGZIRI, Mohamed Ouramadane, 75
TLILI, Abderrahmane, 378
TOPAÇ, Mehmet, 404
TÖRE, Zorlu, 112
TORKMANE, Yacine, 73
TOUATI, Moussa, 73
TOURAB, Rachid Abou, 79
TRIFI, Mokhtar, 381
TURAN, Kamil, 399
TURK, Muhammad Abd al-Munim, 128
TURK, Riad, 369
TÜRKES, Alparslan, 400

UBAYD, Muna Makram, 128
ULUSU, Bülent, 388
UMAR, Ahmad, 419
UMAR, Jarallah, 429
UMAR, Miftah al-Usta, 274
al-UMARI, Talal, 235
al-UNSI, Abd al-Wahab Ali, 429
al-UTRI, Muhammad Naji, 359
UZAN, Cem, 403

VASSILIOU, George, 96, 103
VRAHIMI, Eleni, 102

WAHEED, Abdul, 315
WAKIM, Nasserite Najah, 268
WALI Khan, Asfandyar, 331
WALI Khan, Begum Nasim, 331
WARDAG, Rehmat Khan, 333
WATTOO, Manzoor Ahmad, 326
al-WAZIR, Ibrahim, 430
al-WAZIR, Khalil, 437
WEIZMAN, Ezer, 189, 191

al-YADUMI, Muhammad Ali, 429
YAHYA, Imam, 418
al-YASIM, Jasim Muhalhal, 250
YASINE, Abd Assalam, 295
al-YASIRI, Tawfiq, 181
YASSIN, Ahmed, 199, 222
YATA, Nadir, 291
al-YAWAR, Ghazi Ajil, 163, 166, 181
YAZDI, Ibrahim, 152, 155

YAZGHI, Mohamed El, 291
YAZICIOĞLU, Muhsin, 402
YILDIRIM, Ahmet, 403
YILMAZ, Mesut, 389
YISHAI, Eliyahu, 207
YOSEF, Ovadia, 207
YOUSEF, Ramzi Ahmed, 321
YOUSSOUFI, Abderrahmane, 285, 286, 291

al-ZAHAR, Mahmud, 223
ZAHIR, Adnan Sayid 'Abd al-Samad Sayid, 250
ZAHIR SHAH, Mohammad, 38

ZAKI, Faysollah, 50
ZANA, Leyla, 395
al-ZANATI, Muhammad, 273, 274, 282
ZAOUI, Ahmed, 79
ZARDARI, Asif Ali, 315, 327
ZARIF, Mohammad Javad, 160
ZARKESH, Ali, 156
al-ZARQAWI, Abu Musab, 56, 173, 233
ZARROUK, Neziha, 377
al-ZAWAHIRI, Ayman, 56, 130
al-ZAWAHIRI, Mohammad, 130
ZBIRI, Tahir, 60
ZE'EVI, Rechavam, 193, 210
ZEROUAL, Liamine, 61, 63

ZHARA, Najia, 49
ZIA ul-Haq, Mohammad, 313
ZIANE, Mohammed, 294
al-ZIBRI, Mustafa, 450
al-ZINDANI, Abd al-Maguid, 422, 429
ZITOUNI, Dhamel, 78
ZOUABI, Antar, 78
ZOUARI, Abderrahim, 377
ZUBARI, Hashyar, 179
ZUBAYDAH, Abu, 55
al-ZUBAYDI, Muhammad Hamzah, 164
al-ZUBI, Ahmad, 237
al-ZUBI, Mahmud, 361
al-ZUBI, Muhammad, 236

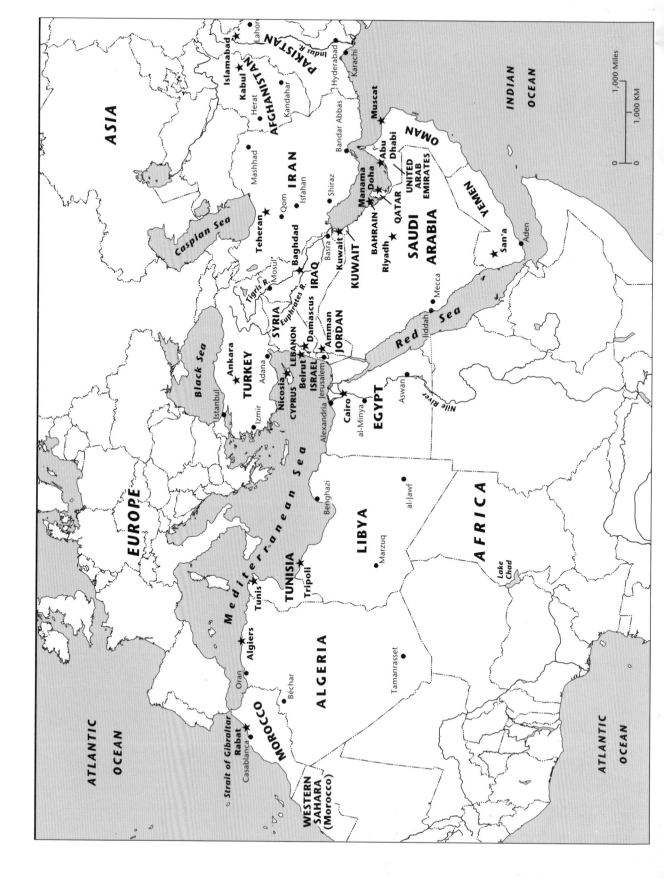